The Chartered Management Institute

DICTIONARY OF BUSINESS AND MANAGEMENT

The Chartered Management Institute
DICTIONARY OF BUSINESS AND MANAGEMENT

BLOOMSBURY

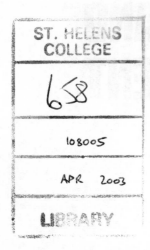
A BLOOMSBURY REFERENCE BOOK
Created from the Bloomsbury Business Database
www.ultimatebusinessresource.com

© Bloomsbury Publishing Plc 2003
Management terms © Chartered Management Institute 2002

First published in 2003 by
Bloomsbury Publishing Plc
38 Soho Square
London W1D 3HB

British Library Cataloguing in Publication Data
A CIP record for this book is available from the British Library.

ISBN 0 7475 6236-9

Design by Fiona Pike, Pike Design, Winchester
Typeset by RefineCatch Limited, Bungay, Suffolk
Printed in the United Kingdom

Contents

Publishing, Editorial, and Production Staff   vi

User's Guide   vii

The Chartered Management Institute Dictionary of
   Business and Management   1

Multilingual Glossary   377

Facts and Figures   641

Publishing, Editorial, and Production Staff

Editor-in-Chief
Dr Kathy Rooney

Publisher
Nigel Newton

Product Director
Jonathan Glasspool

Database Manager
Edmund Wright

Managing Editor
Lisa Carden

Project Manager
Katy McAdam

Assistant Editor
Helen Szirtes

Production Director
Penny Edwards

Marketing Manager
Gordon Kerr

Editors, Translators, and Proofreaders

Marion Alexander-Gruschka
Sandra Anderson
Aradco VSI Ltd
John Andrew
David Barnett
Miguel Balbás
Enrique Bonail
Pat Bulhosen
Alison Crann
Santiago de Domingo
Barbara Docherty
Akiko Eddis
Corey Egge
Luisa Fernandez Sierra
Kate Gaylor
José Galvez
Gloria George
Isabel González Montes
Sarah M. Hall
David Hallworth
Kate Hardcastle
Isabelle Helaine
Ruth Hillmore
Corinne Hornby-Sauvage
Sheelagh Hughes
Ben Jones
Martin Lee
Catherine Roux
Isabel Sanchez Gallego
Silke Schoenbuchner
Yi-Hong Shi
Pamela Skipwith
Karen Stern
Thomas Tsang
Jill Williams
Yang Jing

Advisors
Dictionary Unit of South Africa
Margery Fee,
    University of British Columbia
Lise Winer,
    McGill University
Matt Haig
John Paxton

User's Guide

The Chartered Management Institute *Dictionary of Business and Management* provides clear, jargon-free definitions to more than 6,000 international business and management terms. Updated and expanded from the flagship edition of *BUSINESS: The Ultimate Resource*, the Dictionary has been compiled by an international team of expert researchers and business information specialists. It is an up-to-date, practical resource that will help the user understand both basic and complex terms business terms from around the world. Easy-to-use and full of helpful information, it aims to define the world of business.

TOPIC AREAS

The terms have been drawn from eight key topic areas, and each term labelled accordingly. The topic areas have been abbreviated for ease of use, and they appear in the Dictionary as follows:

E-commerce	*E-com*
Economics	*Econ*
Finance, Banking, and Accounting	*Fin*
General Management	*Gen Mgt*
HR & Personnel	*HR*
Marketing	*Mkting*
Operations and Production	*Ops*
Statistics	*Stats*

The topic areas help to give extra context to each term, especially when it can have more than one meaning depending on the situation in which it is used. For example:

churn rate 1. *Fin* a measure of the frequency and volume of trading of stocks and bonds in a brokerage account **2.** *Gen Mgt* the rate at which new customers try a product or service and then stop using it

ORDER OF TERMS

All terms are listed in strict alphabetical order, apart from when a term is part of a phrase. In these cases, the definition is shown at the most valid element of the phrase. For example:

ball
take the ball and run with it *Gen Mgt* to take an idea and implement it (*slang*)

STANDARD AND EXTENDED DEFINITIONS

Each term in the Dictionary has been given a clear, jargon-free definition. For example:

keyword *E-com* a word used by a search engine to help locate and register a website. Companies need to think very carefully about the keywords they place in their **meta-tags** and in web pages in order to attract relevant search-engine traffic.

However, mini-essays are used at more complex terms to help explain a concept in greater depth:

Boston Box *Gen Mgt* a model used for analysing a company's potential by plotting **market share** against growth rate. The Boston Box was conceived by the Boston Consulting Group in the 1970s to help in the process of assessing in which businesses a company should invest and of which it should divest itself. A business with a high market share and high growth rate is a **star**, and one with a low market share and low growth rate is a **dog**. A high market share with low growth rate is characteristic of a **cash cow**, which could yield significant but short-term gain, and a low market share coupled with high growth rate produces a **question mark company**, which offers a doubtful return on investment. To be useful, this model requires accurate assessment of a business's strengths and weaknesses, which may be difficult to obtain.

WORKED EXAMPLES

In addition to the mini-essays, at terms which explain financial ratios, we show a fully worked example of how the ratio functions. These examples are indicated by the ⎍EXAMPLE⎍ icon:

bond yield *Fin* the annual return on a bond (the rate of interest) expressed as a percentage of the current market price of the bond. Bonds can tie up investors' money for periods of up to 30 years, so knowing their yield is a critical investment consideration.
⎍EXAMPLE⎍ Bond yield is calculated by multiplying the face value of the bond by its stated annual rate of interest, expressed as a decimal. For example, buying a new ten-year £1,000 bond that pays 6% interest will produce an annual yield amount of £60:

$$1,000 \times 0.060 = 60$$

The £60 will be paid as £30 every six months. At the end of ten years, the purchaser will have earned £600, and will also be repaid the original £1,000. Because the bond was purchased when it was first issued, the 6% is also called the 'yield to maturity'.

This basic formula is complicated by other factors. First is the 'time-value of money' theory: money paid in the future is worth less than money paid today. A more detailed computation of total bond yield requires the calculation of the present value of the interest earned each year. Second, changing interest rates have a marked impact on bond trading and, ultimately, on yield. Changes in interest rates cannot affect the interest paid by bonds already issued, but they do affect the prices of new bonds.

CROSS-REFERENCES

Cross-reference are used in the Dictionary to link terms that are closely related, or which expand on information given in another entry. For example, at this entry:

accountability *Gen Mgt* the allocation or acceptance of *responsibility* for actions

the concept of 'responsibility' is referred to, and highlighted in bold italics to show that it has an entry in its own right:

responsibility *Gen Mgt* the duty to carry out certain activities and be accountable for them to others

Terms that are defined at another word (as part of an associated concept), or which are less preferred versions of a standard term, are cross-referred to the term whose definition contains the information you need. For example:

pull strategy *Mkting see* **push and pull strategies**

BIOGRAPHICAL ENTRIES

The Dictionary also includes many biographical entries, which detail the lives, careers, and influence of international business writers, educators, and practitioners. These entries are found at the surname of the person profiled. For example:

Kotler, Philip (*b.* 1931) *Gen Mgt* US academic. Acknowledged as an expert in **marketing** theory, which he has made a major business function and academic discipline, and which he explained in *Marketing Management* (first published 1980).

Mini-essays have been included for the world's most influential business thinkers. For example:

Drucker, Peter (*b.* 1909) *Gen Mgt* US academic. Recognised as the father of management thinking. His earlier works studied management practice, while later he tackled the complexities and the management implications of the post-industrial world. *The Practice of Management* (1954), best known perhaps for the introduction of **management by objectives**, remains a classic. He also anticipated other management themes such as the importance of marketing (see **marketing management**) and the rise of the **knowledge worker**.

ABBREVIATIONS

Business English is full of abbreviations and acronyms, and the Dictionary features many of these. Where the abbreviation is the most commonly used version of a term or phrase, the abbreviation's full form is given at that entry:

B2B *abbr E-com* business-to-business: relating to an advertising or marketing programme aimed at businesses doing business with other businesses as opposed to consumers. The term is most commonly used in reference to commerce or business that is conducted over the Internet between commercial enterprises.

In cases where the full form of an abbreviation is the most commonly known form of the concept, the expanded form is shown at the entry for the abbreviation:

EDC *abbr E-com* electronic data capture

Variant names of a word or phrase are also shown in the Dictionary:

points plan *HR* a method of *job evaluation* that uses a points scale for rating different criteria. *Also known as* **point-factor system**

MULTILINGUAL GLOSSARY

Immediately after the main Dictionary, there is a Multilingual Glossary which translates all the Dictionary terms with definitions into the five key business languages of Chinese, French, German, Spanish, and Japanese. For example:

management
管理
gestion; management
Management
gestión; administración
マネジメント

FACTS AND FIGURES

Expanding on the wealth of knowledge in the Dictionary, this section contains a variety of helpful information, including:

- fascinating data on the world economy
- practical examples of key business documents
- comprehensive listings of world currencies and stock exchanges

For more information about BUSINESS: The Ultimate Resource™ and other related titles, please visit: www.ultimatebusinessresource.com

To register for free electronic upgrades, please go to **www.ultimatebusinessresource.com/register**, type in your e-mail address, and key in your password: **Drucker**

The Chartered Management Institute

DICTIONARY OF BUSINESS AND MANAGEMENT

AAA¹ *abbr* **1.** *E-com* authentication, authorisation, and accounting: the software security verification procedures that acknowledge or validate an e-commerce user or message **2.** *Fin* American Accounting Association

AAA² *Fin* the prime maximum safety rating given by Standard & Poor's, one of the two best known bond-rating agencies

AAMOF *abbr Gen Mgt* as a matter of fact (*slang*)

AARF *abbr Fin* Australian Accounting Research Foundation

AAS *abbr Fin* Australian Accounting Standard

AASB *abbr Fin* Australian Accounting Standards Board

AAT *abbr Fin* Association of Accounting Technicians

abandonment option *Fin* the option of terminating an investment before the time that it is scheduled to end

abandonment value *Fin* the value that an investment has if it is terminated at a particular time before it is scheduled to end

ABB *abbr Fin* activity-based budgeting

ABC *abbr Fin* activity-based costing

Abilene paradox *Gen Mgt* a theory stating that some decisions that seem to be based on consensus are in fact based on misperception and lead to courses of action that defeat original intentions. The Abilene paradox was proposed by Jerry Harvey in 1974 following a trip made by his family to the town of Abilene. One person suggested the visit as he felt the others needed entertainment, and the others agreed as they all believed that everyone else wanted to go. On their return, everyone admitted that they would rather have stayed at home. Harvey used this experience to illustrate the mismanagement of agreement, and of *decision-making* in organisations when apparent consensus is actually founded on poor communication. The Abilene paradox shows similarities to the *attribution theory of leadership*.

ABN *abbr Fin* Australian Business Number: a numeric code that identifies an Australian business for the purpose of dealing with the Australian Tax Office and other government departments. ABNs are part of the new tax system that came into operation in Australia in 1998.

abnormal loss *Fin* any losses which exceed the normal loss allowance. Abnormal losses are generally costed as though they were completed products.

abnormal spoilage *Fin* the unexpectedly high level of shrinkage that has contributed to an *abnormal loss*

above-the-line **1.** *Fin* used to describe entries in a company's profit and loss accounts that appear above the line separating those entries that show the origin of the funds that have contributed to the profit or loss from those that relate to its distribution. Exceptional and extraordinary items appear above the line. *See also* ***below-the-line*** *(sense 2)* **2.** *Fin* in macroeconomics, used to describe a country's revenue transactions. *See also* ***below-the-line*** *(sense 3)* **3.** *Mkting* relating to marketing expenditure on advertising in media such as press, radio, television, cinema, and the World Wide Web, on which a commission is usually paid to an agency

ABS *abbr Fin* Australian Bureau of Statistics

absenteeism *HR* the problem of employees taking short-term, unauthorised ***leave*** from work, resulting in lost ***productivity*** and increased costs. Absenteeism is usually sickness-related. Other causes may include a lack of ***motivation***, domestic difficulties, or poor management.

absorbed account *Fin* an account that has lost its separate identity by being combined with related accounts in the preparation of a financial statement

absorbed business *Gen Mgt* a company that has been merged into another company

absorbed costs *Fin* the indirect costs associated with manufacturing, for example, insurance or property taxes

absorbed overhead *Fin* overhead attached to products or services by means of **absorption rates**

absorption costing *Fin* an accounting practice in which fixed and variable costs of production are absorbed by different cost centres. Providing all the products or services can be sold at a price that covers the allocated costs, this method ensures that both fixed and variable costs are recovered in full. However, should sales be lost because the resultant

---

price is too high, the organisation may lose revenue that would contribute to its over-heads. *See also* **marginal costing**

absorption rate *Fin see* **overhead absorption rate**

abusive tax shelter *Fin* a tax shelter that somebody claims illegally to avoid or min-imise tax

ACA *abbr Fin* Australian Communications Authority

ACCA *abbr Fin* **1.** Association of Chartered Certified Accountants **2.** associate of the Association of Chartered Certified Account-ants

ACCC *abbr Fin* Australian Competition and Consumer Commission: an independent statutory body responsible for monitoring trade practices in Australia. It was set up in November 1995 as a result of the merger of the Trade Practices Commission and the Prices Surveillance Authority.

accelerated cost recovery system *Fin* a system used in the United States for comput-ing the depreciation of some assets acquired before 1986 in a way that reduces taxes. *Abbr* **ACRS**

accelerated depreciation *Econ, Fin* a sys-tem used for computing the depreciation of some assets in a way that assumes that they depreciate faster in the early years of their acquisition. *Also known as* **declining balance method**

acceptable quality level *Ops* the level at which an output of manufactured com-ponents is considered to be of satisfactory quality. Acceptable quality level is usually expressed with the number of defective items shown as a proportion of the total output. Today, owing to a general increase in competi-tive pressure, the only acceptable quality level is **zero defects**, so the term is rarely used.

acceptance *Fin* the signature on a bill of exchange, indicating that the drawee (the per-son to whom it is addressed) will pay the face amount of the bill on the due date

acceptance bonus (*US*) *HR* a **bonus** paid to a new **employee** on acceptance of the job. An acceptance bonus can be a feature of a **golden hello** and is designed both to attract and to retain staff.

acceptance credit *Fin* a line of credit granted by a bank to an importer against which an exporter can draw a bill of exchange. After acceptance by the bank, the bill can

either be sold in the market or held until maturity.

acceptance house *Econ, Fin* an institution that accepts financial instruments and agrees to honour them should the borrower default

acceptance region *Stats* the set of values in a test statistic for which the null hypothesis can be accepted

acceptance sampling *Ops* a **quality control** decision-making technique used in a manu-facturing environment, in which acceptance or rejection of a batch of parts is decided by testing a sample of the batch. The sample is checked against established standards and, if it meets those standards, the whole batch is deemed acceptable.

accepting bank *Fin* the bank that accepts a bill of exchange drawn under a **documentary credit**

acceptor *Fin* the person to whom a signed bill of exchange is addressed

access bond (*S Africa*) *Fin* a type of mortgage that permits borrowers to take out loans against extra capital paid into the account, home-loan interest rates being lower than interest rates on other forms of credit

ACCI *abbr Fin* Australian Chamber of Com-merce and Industry

account 1. *Fin* a business arrangement involving the exchange of money or credit in which payment is deferred, or a record main-tained by a financial institution itemising its dealings with a particular customer **2.** *Mkting* a client of an advertising or PR agency

accountability *Gen Mgt* the allocation or acceptance of **responsibility** for actions

accountability concept *Fin* management accounting presents information measuring the achievement of the objectives of an organ-isation and appraising the conduct of its internal affairs in that process. In order that further action can be taken, based on this information, it is necessary at all times to identify the responsibilities and key results of individuals within the organisation.

accountancy *Fin* the practice of accounting

accountancy bodies *Fin* professional institutions and associations for accountants

accountancy profession *Fin* professional bodies of accountants that establish and regu-late training entry standards, professional examinations, and ethical and technical rules

---

and guidelines. These bodies are organised on national and international levels.

accountant *Fin* a professional person who maintains and checks the business records of a person or organisation and prepares forms and reports for financial purposes

accountant's letter *Fin* a written statement by an independent accountant that precedes a financial report, describing the scope of the report and giving an opinion on its validity

account day *Fin* the day on which an executed order is settled by the delivery of securities, payment to the seller, and payment by the buyer. This is the final day of the *accounting period*.

account debtor *Fin* a person or organisation responsible for paying for a product or service

account director *Mkting* a senior person within an advertising agency responsible for overall policy on a client's advertising account

account executive *Mkting* an employee of an organisation such as a bank, public relations firm, or advertising agency who is responsible for the business of a particular client

accounting cost *Fin* the cost of maintaining and checking the business records of a person or organisation and the preparation of forms and reports for financial purposes

accounting cycle *Fin* the regular process of formally updating a firm's financial position by recording, analysing, and reporting its transactions during the accounting period

accounting equation *Fin* a formula in which a firm's assets must be equal to the sum of its liabilities and the owners' equity. *Also known as* **balance sheet equation**

accounting exposure *Econ, Fin* the risk that foreign currency held by a company may lose value because of exchange rate changes when it conducts overseas business

accounting insolvency *Econ, Fin* the condition that a company is in when its liabilities to its creditors exceed its assets

accounting period *Fin* an amount of time in which businesses may prepare internal accounts so as to monitor progress on a weekly, monthly, or quarterly basis. Accounts are generally prepared for external purposes on an annual basis.

accounting principles *Fin* the rules that apply to accounting practices and provide guidelines for dealing appropriately with complex transactions

accounting profit *Fin* the difference between total revenue and explicit costs

accounting rate of return *Fin* the ratio of profit before interest and taxation to the percentage of capital employed at the end of a period. Variations include using profit after interest and taxation, equity capital employed, and average capital for the period.

accounting ratio *Fin* an expression of accounting results as a ratio or percentage, for example, the ratio of *current assets* to *current liabilities*

accounting reference date *Fin* the last day of a company's *accounting reference period*

accounting reference period *Fin* the period for which a company makes up its accounts. This period is normally, although not necessarily, 12 months. Also used for taxation where it represents the period for which corporation tax is calculated.

accounting system *Fin* the means, including staff and equipment, by which an organisation produces its accounting information

accounting year *Fin* the annual *accounting period*

account reconciliation *Fin* **1.** a procedure for ensuring the reliability of accounting records by comparing balances of transactions **2.** a procedure for comparing the register of a chequebook with an associated bank statement

account sales *Fin* a statement rendered to a consignor of merchandise by the consignee, giving particulars of sales, the quantity remaining unsold, gross proceeds, expenses incurred, consignee's commission, and net amount due to the consignor

accounts payable *Fin* the amount that a company owes for goods or services obtained on credit

accounts receivable *Fin* the money that is owed to a company by those who have bought its goods or services and have not yet paid for them

accounts receivable ageing *Fin* a periodic report that classifies outstanding receivable balances according to customer and month of the original billing date

accounts receivable factoring (*US*) *Fin* the buying of accounts receivable at a discount with the aim of making a profit from collecting them

accounts receivable financing *Econ, Fin* a form of borrowing in which a company uses money that it is owed as collateral for a loan it needs for business operations

accounts receivable turnover *Econ, Fin* a ratio that shows how long the customers of a business wait before paying what they owe. This can cause cash-flow problems for small businesses.

EXAMPLE The formula for accounts receivable turnover is straightforward. Simply divide the average amount of receivables into annual credit sales:

Sales / Receivables = Receivables turnover

If, for example, a company's sales are £4.5 million and its average receivables are £375,000, its receivables turnover is:

4,500,000 / 375,000 = 12

A high turnover figure is desirable, because it indicates that a company collects revenues effectively, and that its customers pay bills promptly. A high figure also suggests that a firm's credit and collection policies are sound. In addition, the measurement is a reasonably good indicator of cash flow, and of overall operating efficiency.

accreditation of prior learning *HR* a process through which formal recognition for the achievements of past learning and experiences may be obtained. Accreditation of prior learning may be used to support the award of a vocational qualification.

accredited investor *Fin* an investor whose wealth or income is above a particular amount. It is illegal for an accredited investor to be a member of a private limited partnership.

accreted value *Fin* the value of a bond if interest rates do not change

accretion *Fin* the growth of a company through additions or purchases of plant or value-adding services

accrual *Fin* a charge that has not been paid by the end of an accounting period but must be included in the accounting results for the period. If no invoice has been received for the charge, an estimate must be included in the accounting results.

accrual basis *Fin see accrual method*

accrual bond *Fin see zero coupon bond*

accrual concept *Fin* the idea that income and expense items must be included in financial statements as they are earned or incurred. *See also cash accounting*

accrual method *Fin* an accounting method that includes income and expense items as they are earned or incurred irrespective of when money is received or paid out. *Also known as accrual basis*

accrual of discount *Fin* the annual gain in value of a bond owing to its having been bought originally for less than its par value

accrue *Fin* to include an income or expense item in the transaction records at the time it is earned or incurred

accrued expense *Fin* an expense that has been incurred within a given accounting period but not yet paid

accrued income *Fin* income that has been earned but not yet received

accrued interest *Fin* the amount of interest earned by a bond or similar investment since the previous interest payment

accruing *Fin* added as a periodic gain, for example, as interest on an amount of money

accumulated depreciation *Fin* the cumulative annual depreciation of an asset that has been claimed as an expense since the asset was acquired. *Also known as aggregate depreciation*

accumulated dividend *Fin* the amount of money in dividends earned by a stock or similar investment since the previous dividend payment

accumulated earnings tax *or* **accumulated profits tax** *Fin* the tax that a company must pay because it chose not to pay dividends that would subject its owners to higher taxes

accumulating shares *Fin* ordinary shares issued by a company equivalent to and in place of the net dividend payable to ordinary shareholders

accumulation unit *Fin* a unit of a unit trust that retains dividend income instead of distributing it to individual investors

accuracy *Stats* the degree to which data conforms to a recognised standard value

ACH *abbr E-com* automated clearing house

achievement test *HR* a type of *psychometric test* which measures what a person already knows and can do at the time of testing. The two most common types of achievement tests measure verbal reasoning and mathematical ability. There are many test preparation books available. As well as explaining how the questions are structured, they offer test strategies and sample tests. As with other psychometric tests, it has been proven that people perform better at these tests when they are well-rested, in good physical shape, and slightly hungry.

acid-test ratio *Fin* an accounting ratio used to measure an organisation's liquidity. The most common expression of the ratio is:

(Current assets – Inventory) / Current liabilities = Acid-test ratio

If, for example, current assets total £7,700, inventory amounts to £1,200 and current liabilities total £4,500, then:

(7,700 – 1,200) / 4,500 = 1.44

A variation of this formula ignores inventories altogether, distinguishes assets as cash, receivables, and short-term investments, then divides the sum of the three by the total current liabilities, or:

Cash + Accounts receivable + Short-term investments / Current liabilities = Acid-test ratio

If, for example, cash totals £2,000, receivables total £3,000, short-term investments total £1,000, and liabilities total £4,800, then:

(2,000 + 3,000 + 1,000) / 4,800 = 1.25

In general, the ratio should be 1:1 or better. It means a company has a unit's worth of easily convertible assets for each unit of its current liabilities.

Ackoff, Russell Lincoln (*b.* 1919) *Gen Mgt* US academic. Pioneer of operations research and systems thinking, whose publications include *Ackoff's Fables: Irreverent Reflections on Business and Bureaucracy* (1991).

ACM *abbr Gen Mgt* Australian Chamber of Manufactures

acquiescence bias *Stats* the bias produced when respondents in a survey give positive answers to two mutually conflicting questions

acquirer *or* **acquiring bank** *E-com* a financial institution, commonly a bank, that processes a merchant's credit card authorisations and payments, forwarding the data to a credit card association, which in turn communicates with the issuer. *Also known as* **clearing house**, **processor**

acquisition *Gen Mgt see* **merger**

acquisition accounting *Fin* the standard accounting procedures that must be followed when one company merges with another

acquisition rate *Gen Mgt* a measure of the ability of marketing programmes to win new business

ACRS *abbr Fin* accelerated cost recovery system

action-centred leadership *Gen Mgt* a **leadership** model developed by *John Adair* that focuses on what leaders actually have to do in order to be effective. The action-centred leadership model is illustrated by three overlapping circles representing the three key activities undertaken by leaders: achieving the task, building and maintaining the team, and developing the individual.

action learning *HR* learning by sharing real problems with others, as opposed to theoretical classroom learning. Action learning was introduced in the mid-1940s by *Reg Revans*, who expressed it as: Learning = Programmed knowledge + the ability to ask insightful Questions, or L = P + Q. The technique works best when people in small groups tackle real work-based problems with a view to solving them. Action learning differs from *experiential learning*, which can apply to an individual alone.

action research *Gen Mgt* research in which the researcher takes an involved role as a participant in planning and implementing change. Action research was originated by *Kurt Lewin*, and it involves conducting experiments by making changes while simultaneously observing the results.

active asset *Fin* an asset that is used in the daily operations of a business

active fund management *Fin* the managing of a unit trust by making judgments about market movements instead of relying on automatic adjustments such as indexation. *See also* **passive investment management**

active listening *HR* a technique for improving understanding of what is being said by taking into account how something is said and the non-verbal signs and **body language** that accompany it. This technique requires receptive awareness and response on the part of the listener. Six principles form the core of active listening: encourage people to express opinions; clarify perceptions of what is said; restate essential points and ideas; reflect the speaker's feeling and opinions; summarise the content of the message to check validity; acknowledge the opinion and contribution of the speaker. It is used particularly in counselling.

active portfolio strategy *Fin* the managing of an investment portfolio by making judgments about market movements instead of relying on automatic adjustments

---

activist fiscal policy *Fin* the policy of a government or national bank that tries to affect the value of its country's money by such measures as changing interest rates for loans to banks and buying or selling foreign currencies

activity-based budgeting *Fin* the allocation of resources to individual activities. Activity-based budgeting involves determining which activities incur costs within an organisation, establishing the relationships between them, and then deciding how much of the total *budget* should be allocated to each activity. *Abbr* **ABB**

activity-based costing *Fin, Gen Mgt* a method of calculating the cost of a business by focusing on the actual cost of activities, thereby producing an estimate of the cost of individual products or services.

An ABC cost-accounting system requires three preliminary steps: converting to an *accrual method* of accounting; defining cost centres and cost allocation; and determining process and procedure costs.

Businesses have traditionally relied on the cash basis of accounting, which recognises income when received and expenses when paid. ABC's foundation is the accrual-basis income statement. The numbers this statement presents are assigned to the various procedures performed during a given period. Cost centres are a company's identifiable products and services, but also include specific and detailed tasks within these broader activities. Defining cost centres will of course vary by business and method of operation. What is critical to ABC is the inclusion of all activities and all resources.

Once cost centres are identified, management teams can begin studying the activities each one engages in and allocating the expenses each one incurs, including the cost of employee services.

The most appropriate method is developed from time studies and direct expense allocation. Management teams who choose this method will need to devote several months to data collection in order to generate sufficient information to establish the personnel components of each activity's total cost.

Time studies establish the average amount of time required to complete each task, plus best- and worst-case performances. Only those resources actually used are factored into the cost computation; unused resources are reported separately. These studies can also advise management teams how best to monitor and allocate expenses which might otherwise be expressed as part of general overheads, or go undetected altogether. *Abbr* **ABC**

activity-based management *Gen Mgt* a management control technique that focuses on the resource costs of organisational activities and processes, and the improvement of quality, profitability, and customer value. This technique uses *activity-based costing* information to identify strategies for removing resource waste from operating activities. Main tools employed include: *strategic analysis*, *value analysis*, cost analysis, *life-cycle costing*, and *activity-based budgeting*.

activity driver *Gen Mgt see cost driver*

activity indicator *Econ* a statistic used to measure labour productivity or manufacturing output in an economy

activity sampling *Ops* a *work measurement* technique used to analyse the activities of employees, machines, or business operations. Activity sampling requires random observations of the amount of time spent on a given activity to be recorded over a fixed period. The results are used to predict the total time spent on each activity and to highlight areas in need of quality, efficiency, or effectiveness improvement. *Also known as* **work sampling**, *ratio-delay study*, *random observation method*

ACTU *abbr Gen Mgt* Australian Council of Trade Unions

actuals *Fin* earnings and expenses that have occurred rather than being only projected, or commodities that can be bought and used, as contrasted with commodities traded on a futures contract

actual to date *Fin* the cumulative value realised by something between an earlier date and the present

actual turnover *Fin* the number of times during a particular period that somebody spends the average amount of money that he or she has available to spend during that period

actuarial age *Fin* the statistically derived life expectancy for any given chronological age, used, for example, to calculate the periodic payments from an annuity

actuarial analysis *Fin* a life expectancy or risk calculation carried out by an actuary

actuarial science *Fin, Stats* the branch of statistics used in calculating risk and life expectancy for the administration of pension funds and life assurance policies

actuary *Fin, Stats* a statistician who calculates probable lengths of life so that the insurance premiums to be charged for various risks can be accurately determined

ACU *abbr Fin* Asian Currency Unit

ad *E-com* a banner, button, pop-up screen, or other on-screen device calling attention to an e-commerce product or business

Adair, John Eric (*b*. 1934) *Gen Mgt* British academic. Best known for his three-circle model of **leadership**, which is based on overlapping circles representing the task, the team, and the individual. Adair's model, otherwise known as **action-centred leadership**, is described in the book of the same name (1973). Like **Warren Bennis**, Adair, who has a military background, believes that leadership can be taught.

Adams, Scott (*b*. 1957) *Gen Mgt* US humorist. Creator of the **Dilbert principle**, he satirises the many absurdities of business life through his cartoons.

adaptive control *Ops* a system of automatic monitoring and adjustment, usually by computer, of an industrial process. Adaptive control allows operating parameters to be changed continuously in response to a changing environment in order to achieve optimum performance.

adaptive measure *Stats* a means of choosing the most appropriate method for a statistical analysis

ad banner *E-com see* **banner**

ad click *E-com see* **click-through**

ad click rate *E-com see* **click-through rate**

ADDACS *abbr Fin* Automated Direct Debit Amendments and Cancellation Service

added value 1. *Gen Mgt see* **value added 2.** *Mkting* an increase in the attractiveness to customers of a product or a service achieved by adding something to it

address book *E-com* an e-mail software facility enabling people and businesses to store and manage e-mail addresses and contact information

address verification *E-com* a procedure used by the processor of a credit card to verify that a customer's ordering address matches the address in the customer's record

ADF *abbr Fin* Approved Deposit Fund

ad hoc research *Mkting* a single, one-off piece of research designed for a particular purpose, as opposed to continuous, regularly repeated, or syndicated research

ad impression *E-com see* **ad view**

adjusted book value *Fin* the value of a company in terms of the current market values of its assets and liabilities. *Also known as* **modified book value**

adjusted futures price *Fin* the current value of a futures contract to buy a commodity at a fixed future date

adjusted gross income *Fin* the amount of annual income that a person or company has after various adjustments for income or corporation tax purposes

adjusted present value *Fin* the value of a commodity when costs and advantages associated with taxes and borrowing are taken into consideration in addition to its market value

adminisphere *Gen Mgt* the part of an organisation that deals with administrative matters, often perceived negatively by employees because of the apparently unnecessary nature of decisions taken by its members (*slang*)

administration *Gen Mgt* the management of the affairs of a business, especially the planning and control of its operations

administration school *Gen Mgt see* **business administration**

administrative expenses *Fin* the cost of management, secretarial, accounting, and other services which cannot be related to the separate production, marketing, or research and development functions

administrivia *E-com* the often tedious tasks associated with maintaining a website, mailing list, or any other form of Internet resource (*slang*)

admissibility *Stats* the property of a procedure if, and only if, no other of its class exists that performs as well as it and better than it in at least one case

ADR *abbr Fin* American depository receipt: a document that indicates a US investor's ownership of stock in a foreign corporation

Adshel™ *Mkting* a type of bus shelter, specifically designed to carry advertising posters

ADSL *abbr E-com* asymmetrical digital subscriber line: a system that provides high-speed, high-bandwidth connections to the

Internet. ADSL is asymmetric because it has more capacity for data received by a computer than for data to be sent from it. This uneven upload/download balance means that downloaded text and graphics appear quickly and that audio-visual elements are of better quality than when sent via a normal telephone line. ADSL was initially developed by Bellcore Labs in New Jersey in 1993 as a means of bringing bandwidth to homes and small businesses.

adspend *Mkting see* **advertising expenditure**

ad transfer *E-com see* **click-through**

ad valorem *Fin* a tax or commission, for example, Value Added Tax, that is calculated on the value of the goods or services provided, rather than on their number or size

Advance Corporation Tax *Fin* formerly, in the United Kingdom, a tax paid by a company equal to a percentage of its dividends or other distributions of profit to its shareholders. It was abolished in 1999.

advanced manufacturing technology *Gen Mgt, Ops* a high-technology development in computing and microelectronics, designed to enhance manufacturing capabilities. Advanced manufacturing technology is used in all areas of manufacturing, including design, control, fabrication, and assembly. This family of technologies includes *robotics*, *computer-aided design* (CAD), *computer-aided engineering* (CAE), *MRP II*, automated *materials handling* systems, *electronic data interchange* (EDI), computer-integrated manufacturing (CIM) systems, *flexible manufacturing systems*, and *group technology*. *Abbr* **AMT**

advance payment *Fin* an amount paid before it is earned or incurred, for example, a prepayment by an importer to an exporter before goods are shipped, or a cash advance for travel expenses

advance payment guarantee *or* **advance payment bond** *Fin* a guarantee that enables a buyer to recover an advance payment made under a contract or order if the supplier fails to fulfil its contractual obligations

adventure training *HR* activities undertaken out of doors and away from the everyday work environment with a view to developing the skills and abilities of participants. Adventure training often takes place at a residential outdoor activity centre and may include physically challenging activities such as climbing and abseiling or group exercises and games. The activities are designed to promote *experiential learning* in areas such as *interpersonal communication*, *problem-solving*, *decision-making*, and *teamwork*, and to develop self-confidence and *leadership* skills. Adventure training has its origins in the work of Kurt Hahn, the founder of Gordonstoun School, who developed the Outward Bound programme of outdoor activities during the second world war. Adventure training programmes for organisational personnel became popular during the late 1970s and 1980s, although some have doubted their value and effectiveness. *Also known as* **outdoor training**, **outward bound training**

adverse balance *Fin* the deficit on an account, especially a nation's balance of payments account

adverse opinion *Fin* a statement in the auditor's report of a company's annual accounts indicating a fundamental disagreement with the company to such an extent that the auditor considers the accounts misleading

advertisement *Mkting* a public announcement by a company in a newspaper, on television or radio, or over the Internet, intended to attract buyers for a product or service

advertising *Mkting* the promotion of goods, services, or ideas, through paid announcements. Advertising aims to persuade or inform the general public and can be used to induce purchase, increase *brand awareness*, or enhance *product differentiation*. An advertisement has two main components: the message and the medium by which it is transmitted. Advertising forms just one part of an organisation's total marketing strategy.

advertising agency *Mkting* an organisation that, on behalf of clients, drafts and produces advertisements, places advertisements in the media, and plans *advertising campaigns*. Advertising agencies may also perform other marketing functions, including *market research* and consultancy.

advertising campaign *Mkting* a planned programme using *advertising* aimed at a particular target market or audience over a defined period of time for the purpose of increasing sales or raising awareness of a product or service

advertising department *Mkting* the department within an organisation that is responsible for advertising its products or services. The advertising department is also the name given to the section of a publishing house that co-ordinates the placing of advertisements in its magazines, newspapers, or other publications. It is involved in the sale of advertising space to clients.

advertising expenditure *Mkting* the amount spent by an organisation on advertising, usually per year. Advertising expenditure is analysed by breaking it down into the main advertising channels used by companies, such as newspapers, magazines, television, radio, cinema, and outdoor advertising. Expenditure can show the total spend nationally, by sector, by type and size of company, or may relate to one company's spend on advertising, including the proportion spent on its specific brands. *Also known as* **adspend**

advertising manager *Mkting* an employee of a business who is responsible for planning and controlling its advertising activities and budgets

advertising media *Mkting* the communication channels used for advertising, including television, radio, the printed press, and outdoor advertising

advertising research *Mkting* research carried out before or after advertising to ensure or test its effectiveness

advertorial *Mkting* a combination of an *advertisement* and an article. The content of an advertorial is significantly influenced, and may even be entirely written, by the advertisers. Examples of advertorials include travel or leisure supplements in newspapers or magazines that are designed to attract advertisements from suppliers of relevant goods or services. A criticism of advertorials is that it is sometimes difficult to distinguish between an advertising article and ordinary journalistic articles, particularly when they appear in the same typeface as the other contents of the newspaper or magazine. To overcome this, some advertorials are headed 'Advertisement'. (*slang*)

advice note *Fin see* **delivery note**

advice of fate *Fin* immediate notification from a drawer's bank as to whether a cheque is to be honoured or not. This special presentation of a cheque bypasses the normal clearing system and so saves time.

advid *Mkting* a video used to promote a product or service (*slang*)

ad view *E-com* the number of times a banner or other ad is downloaded and presumably seen on a web page. *Also known as* **ad impression**, **exposure**

AFAIK *abbr Gen Mgt* as far as I know (*slang*)

affiliate *Gen Mgt* a company that is controlled by another or is a member of a group, or either of two companies that owns a minority of the voting shares of the other

affiliate directory *E-com* a directory that indexes sites belonging to affiliate schemes. Affiliate directories offer information for companies seeking to subscribe to a scheme, as well as for those wanting to set up affiliate schemes of their own.

affiliate marketing *E-com* the use of *affiliate programmes*

affiliate partner *Mkting* a company that markets a product or service on the Internet for another company

affiliate programme *E-com* an advertising programme in which one merchant induces others to place his or her banners and buttons on their websites in return for a commission on purchases made by their customers. *Also known as* **associate programme**

affinity card *Fin* a credit card issued to members of a particular group, for example, past students of a college, owners of a particular make of car, or supporters of a particular charity. The organisation may benefit from a donation upon issue or first use, and a small percentage of the card's subsequent turnover. Other cards give benefits such as air miles.

affluent society *Fin* a community in which material wealth is widely distributed

affluenza *Gen Mgt* feelings of unhappiness, stress, and guilt induced by the pursuit and possession of wealth (*slang*)

AFTA *abbr Fin* ASEAN Free Trade Area

after-acquired collateral *Fin* collateral for a loan that a borrower obtains after making the contract for the loan

after date *Fin see* **bill of exchange**

after-sales service *Mkting* customer support following the purchase of a product or service. In some cases, after-sales service can be almost as important as the initial purchase. The manufacturer, retailer, or service provider determines what is included in any warranty (or guarantee) package. This will include the duration of the warranty—traditionally one year from the date of purchase, but increasingly two or more years—maintenance and/or replacement policy, items included/excluded, labour costs, and speed of response. In the case of a service provider, after-sales service might include additional top-up training or helpdesk availability. Of equal importance is the customer's perception of the degree of willingness with which a supplier deals with a query or complaint, speed of response, and action taken. Underpinning any warranty is the additional statutory protection afforded to consumers by the Sale of Goods Acts and related legislation that require that all goods must be of merchantable quality.

after-tax *Fin* relating to earnings or income from which tax has already been deducted

AG *abbr Fin* Aktiengesellschaft: the German, Austrian, or Swiss equivalent of PLC

against actuals *Fin* relating to a trade between owners of futures contracts that allows both to reduce their positions to cash instead of commodities

age analysis of debtors *Fin* the amount owed by debtors, classified by age of debt

aged debt *Fin* a debt that is overdue by one or more given periods, usually increments of 30 days

aged debtor *Fin* a person or organisation responsible for an overdue debt

age discrimination *or* **ageism** *HR* unfavourable treatment in employment based on prejudice in relation to a person's age. While age discrimination affects people at all stages of their working lives, difficulties experienced in selection, development, and promotion can be particularly acute at the two extremes of the age spectrum. Countries such as Australia and the United States have passed legislation to make it unlawful to discriminate on grounds of age.

agency *Gen Mgt* a relationship between two people or organisations in which one is empowered to act on behalf of the other in dealings with a third party

agency commission *Mkting* a percentage of advertising expenditure rebated to an advertising agency, media buyer, or client organisation by a media owner

agency mark-up *Mkting* a management fee charged by an advertising agency in addition to the cost of external services that it buys on behalf of a client

agency theory *Fin* a hypothesis that attempts to explain elements of organisational behaviour through an understanding of the relationships between principals (such as shareholders) and agents (such as company managers and accountants). A conflict may exist between the actions undertaken by agents in furtherance of their own self-interest, and those required to promote the interests of the principals. Within the hierarchy of firms, the same goal incongruence may arise when divisional managers promote their own self-interest over those of other divisions and of the company generally.

agenda *Gen Mgt* a list of topics to be discussed or business to be transacted during the course of a meeting, usually sent prior to the meeting to those invited to attend

agent *Gen Mgt* **1.** a person or organisation empowered to act on behalf of another when dealing with a third party **2.** *see* **executive**

agent bank (*ANZ*) *Fin* a bank that acts on behalf of a foreign bank, or a bank that participates in another bank's credit card programme, acting as a depository for merchants

age pension (*ANZ*) *Fin* a sum of money paid regularly by the government to people who have reached the age of retirement, currently 65 for men and 60 for women

aggregate demand *Econ* the sum of all expenditures in an economy that makes up its **GDP**, for example, consumers' expenditure on goods and services, investment in **capital stocks**, and government spending

aggregate depreciation *Fin* see **accumulated depreciation**

aggregate income *Fin* the total of all incomes in an economy without adjustments for inflation, taxation, or types of double counting

aggregate output *Econ* the total value of all goods and services produced in an economy

aggregate planning *Ops* medium-range **capacity planning**, typically covering a period of 3 to 18 months. Aggregate planning is used in a manufacturing environment and determines not only the overall output levels planned but the appropriate resource input mix to be used for related groups of products. Generally, planners focus on overall or aggregate capacity rather than on individual products or services. Aggregate planning can be used to influence demand as well as supply, in which case variables such as price, advertising, and the product mix are taken into account.

aggregate supply *Econ* the total of all goods and services produced in an economy

aggregator (*US*) *E-com, Mkting* an organisation that acts as an intermediary between producers and customers in an Internet business web. The aggregator selects products, sets prices, and ensures fulfilment of orders.

aggressive *Gen Mgt* relating to an investment strategy marked by willingness to accept high risk while trying to realise higher than average gains. Such a strategy involves investing in rapidly growing companies that promise capital appreciation but produce little or no income from dividends and de-emphasises income-producing instruments such as bonds.

aggressive growth fund *Fin* a unit trust that takes considerable risks in the hope of making large profits

agile manufacturing *Ops* a manufacturing philosophy that focuses on meeting the demands of customers by adopting flexible manufacturing practices. Agile manufacturing emerged as a reaction to *lean production*. It differs by focusing on meeting the demands of customers without sacrificing quality or incurring added costs. Based on the idea of *virtual organisation*, agile manufacturing aims to develop flexible, often short-term, relationships with suppliers, as market opportunities arise. Stock control is considered less important than satisfying the customer, and so *customer satisfaction* measures become more important than output measures. Agile manufacturing requires an adaptable, innovative, and empowered workforce.

agility *Gen Mgt* the organisational capability to be flexible, responsive, adaptive, and show initiative in times of change and uncertainty. Agility has origins in manufacturing and has been cited as a source of *competitive advantage* by many management gurus, including *Rosabeth Moss Kanter* and *Tom Peters*. One writer who has explored the concept of agility in greater depth is *Richard Pascale*, for whom the key to agility lies in what the organisation is, as opposed to what it does. Agility grew as a reaction against the slowness of bureaucratic organisations to respond to changing market conditions. The *virtual organisation* has been quoted as one extreme example of an agile organisation.

AGM *abbr Gen Mgt* annual general meeting, a yearly meeting at which a company's management reports the year's results and shareholders have the opportunity to vote on company business, for example, the appointment of directors and auditors. Other business, for example, voting on dividend payments and board- and shareholder-sponsored

resolutions, may also be transacted. *US term* **annual meeting**

agora *E-com* a marketplace on the Internet. The term comes from an ancient Greek word for 'market'.

agreement of sale *Gen Mgt* a written contract specifying the terms under which the buyer agrees to buy a property and the seller agrees to sell it

agricultural produce *Fin see* **biological assets**

AHI (*S Africa*) *Gen Mgt* Afrikaanse Handelsinstituut, the national chamber of commerce for Afrikaans businesses

aim *Gen Mgt see* **objective**

AIM *abbr Fin* Alternative Investment Market: the London market trading in shares of emerging or small companies not eligible for listing on the London Stock Exchange. It replaced the Unlisted Securities Market (USM) in 1995.

air bill *Fin* a US term for the documentation accompanying a package sent using an express mail service

AIRC *abbr HR* Australian Industrial Relations Commission

airtime *Mkting* the amount of time given to an advertisement on television, radio, or in cinemas

air waybill *Fin* a UK term for a receipt issued by an airline for goods to be freighted

AITC *abbr Fin* Association of Investment Trust Companies

Aktb *abbr Fin* Aktiebolaget, the Swedish equivalent of PLC

alignment *Gen Mgt* the process of building a corporate culture to achieve strategic goals

all equity rate *Fin* the interest rate that a lender charges because of the apparent risks of a project that are independent of the normal market risks of financing it

All Industrials Index *Fin* a subindex of the Australian All Ordinaries Index that includes all the companies from that index that are not involved in resources or mining

All Mining Index *Fin* a subindex of the Australian All Ordinaries Index that includes all the companies from that index that are involved in the mining industry

---

True creativity often starts where language ends. *Arthur Koestler*

All Ordinaries Accumulation Index *Fin* a measure of the change in share prices on the Australian Stock Exchange, based on the All Ordinaries Index, but assuming that all dividends are reinvested

All Ordinaries Index *Fin* the major index of Australian share prices, comprising more than 300 of the most active Australian companies listed on the Australian Stock Exchange. *Abbr* **All Ords**

all-or-none underwriting (*ANZ*) *Fin* the option of cancelling a public offering of shares if the underwriting is not fully subscribed

All Resources Index *Fin* a subindex of the Australian All Ordinaries Index that includes all the companies from that index that are involved in the resources industry

alphabet theories of management *Gen Mgt* management theories named along the lines of **Douglas McGregor**'s **Theory X** and **Theory Y**. Alphabet theories of management include **Theory E, Theory J, Theory O, Theory W**, and **Theory Z**.

alpha geek *Gen Mgt* the person who knows most about computer technology in a company or department (*slang*)

alpha rating *Fin* the return a security or a portfolio would be expected to earn if the market's rate of return were zero. Alpha expresses the difference between the return expected from a stock or unit trust, given its **beta rating**, and the return actually produced. A stock or trust that returns more than its beta would predict has a positive alpha, while one that returns less than the amount predicted by beta has a negative alpha. A large positive alpha indicates a strong performance, while a large negative alpha indicates a dismal performance.

To begin with, the market itself is assigned a beta of 1.0. If a stock or trust has a beta of 1.2, this means its price is likely to rise or fall by 12% when the overall market rises or falls by 10%; a beta of 7.0 means the stock or trust price is likely to move up or down at 70% of the level of the market change.

In practice, an alpha of 0.4 means the stock or trust in question outperformed the market-based return estimate by 0.4%. An alpha of –0.6 means the return was 0.6% less than would have been predicted from the change in the market alone.

Both alpha and beta should be readily available upon request from investment firms, because the figures appear in standard performance reports. It is always best to ask for them, because calculating a stock's alpha rating requires first knowing a stock's beta rating, and beta calculations can involve mathematical complexities. *See also* **beta rating**

alpha test *Gen Mgt* a test of a new or upgraded piece of computer software or hardware carried out by the manufacturer before it is released to the public

alpha value *Fin* a sum paid to an employee when he or she leaves a company that can be transferred to a concessionally taxed investment account such as an **Approved Deposit Fund**

alternate director *Fin* a person who is allowed to act for an absent named director of a company at a board meeting

alternative investment *Fin* an investment other than in bonds or shares of a large company or one listed on a stock exchange

Alternative Investment Market *Fin see* **AIM**

alternative mortgage instrument *Fin* any form of mortgage other than a fixed-term amortising loan

amalgamation *Gen Mgt* the process of two or more organisations joining together for mutual benefit, either through a **merger** or **consolidation**

Amazon *E-com* to claim a significant portion of the market from a traditional retail business that failed to develop an effective e-business strategy. The term stems from the seemingly overnight success of online bookseller Amazon.com™. (*slang*)

ambit claim (*ANZ*) *Gen Mgt* a claim made to an arbitration authority for higher pay or improved conditions that is deliberately exaggerated because the claimants know that they will subsequently have to compromise

American depository receipt *Fin see* **ADR**

American option *Fin* an option contract that can be exercised at any time up to and including the expiry date. Most exchange-traded options are of this style. *See also* **European option**. *Also known as* **American-style option**

American Stock Exchange *Fin see* **AMEX**

American-style option *Fin see* **American option**

AMEX *abbr Fin* American Stock Exchange: a New York stock exchange listing smaller and less mature companies that those listed on the larger New York Stock Exchange (NYSE)

amortisation *Fin* **1.** a method of recovering (deducting or writing off) the capital costs of intangible assets over a fixed period of time.

EXAMPLE For tax purposes, the distinction is not always made between amortisation and depreciation, yet amortisation remains a viable financial accounting concept in its own right.

It is computed using the straight-line method of depreciation: divide the initial cost of the intangible asset by the estimated useful life of that asset. For example, if it costs £10,000 to acquire a patent and it has an estimated useful life of 10 years, the amortised amount per year is £1,000.

Initial cost / useful life = amortisation per year
£10,000 / 10 = £1,000 per year

The amount of amortisation accumulated since the asset was acquired appears on the organisation's balance sheet as a deduction under the amortised asset.

While that formula is straightforward, amortisation can also incorporate a variety of non-cash charges to net earnings and/or asset values, such as depletion, write-offs, prepaid expenses, and deferred charges. Accordingly, there are many rules to regulate how these charges appear on financial statements. The rules are different in each country, and are occasionally changed, so it is necessary to stay abreast of them and rely on expert advice.

For financial reporting purposes, an intangible asset is amortised over a period of years. The amortisable life—'useful life'—of an intangible asset is the period over which it gives economic benefit.

Intangibles that can be amortised can include:

Copyrights, based on the amount paid either to purchase them or to develop them internally, plus the costs incurred in producing the work (wages or materials, for example). At present, a copyright is granted to a corporation for 75 years, and to an individual for the life of the author plus 50 years. However, the estimated useful life of a copyright is usually far less than its legal life, and it is generally amortised over a fairly short period.

Cost of a *franchise*, including any fees paid to the franchiser, as well legal costs or expenses incurred in the acquisition. A franchise granted for a limited period should be amortised over its life. If the franchise has an indefinite life, it should be amortised over a reasonable period not to exceed 40 years.

Covenants not to compete: an agreement by the seller of a business not to engage in a competing business in a certain area for a specific period of time. The cost of the not-to-compete covenant should be amortised over the period covered by the covenant unless its estimated economic life is expected to be less. Easement costs that grant a right of way may be amortised if there is a limited and specified life.

Organisation costs incurred when forming a corporation or a partnership, including legal fees, accounting services, incorporation fees, and other related services. Organisation costs are usually amortised over 60 months.

Patents, both those developed internally and those purchased. If developed internally, a patent's 'amortisable basis' includes legal fees incurred during the application process. A patent should be amortised over its legal life or its economic life, whichever is the shorter.

Trademarks, brands, and trade names, which should be written off over a period not to exceed 40 years.

Other types of property that may be amortised include certain intangible drilling costs, circulation costs, mine development costs, pollution control facilities, and reforestation expenditures.

Certain intangibles cannot be amortised, but may be depreciated using a straight-line approach if they have 'determinable' useful life. Because the rules are different in each country and are subject to change, it is essential to rely on specialist advice. **2.** the repayment of the principal and interest on a loan in equal amounts over a period of time

amortise *Fin* to gradually reduce the value of an asset by systematically writing off its cost over a period of time, or to repay a debt in a series of regular instalments or transfers

amortised value *Fin* the value at a particular time of a financial instrument that is being amortised

AMPS *abbr Fin* auction market preferred stock

AMT *abbr Ops* advanced manufacturing technology

analysis of variance *Stats* the process of separating the statistical variance caused by a particular factor from that caused by other factors

analysis of variance table *Stats* a table that shows the total variation in the observations in a statistical data set

analytical review *Fin* the examination of ratios, trends, and changes in balances from one period to the next, to obtain a broad understanding of the financial position and results of operations and to identify any items requiring further investigation

angel investor *E-com* an individual or group of individuals willing to invest in an unproven but well-researched e-business idea. Angel investors are typically the first port of call for Internet start-ups looking for financial backing, because they are more inclined to provide early funding than *venture capital* firms are. After investing in a company, angel investors take an advisory role without making demands.

angry fruit salad *E-com* a garish and unattractive visual interface on a computer (*slang*)

angular histogram *Stats* a histogram that represents data in a circular form

announcement *Fin* a statement that a company makes to provide information on its trading prospects that will be of interest to its existing and potential investors

annoyware *E-com* a shareware program that repeatedly interrupts normal functioning to remind users they are using an unregistered copy and will have to pay in order to continue (*slang*)

annual general meeting *Gen Mgt see* **AGM**

annual hours *HR* a *flexible working hours* practice in which working hours are averaged over a year. Employees are contracted to work a given number of hours per year rather than the traditional number of hours per week. Earnings are determined on a similar basis, but usually a fixed weekly or monthly salary is paid regardless of the number of hours worked. Hours are worked when demand dictates and therefore the need for *overtime* diminishes. Annual hours systems usually cover manual *shiftworkers*, rather than other parts of the workforce.

annual meeting (*US*) = **AGM**

annual percentage rate *or* **annualised percentage rate** *Fin see* **APR**

annual percentage yield *Fin* the effective or true annual rate of return on an investment, taking into account the effect of *compounding*. For example, an annual percentage rate of 6% compounded monthly translates into an annual percentage yield of 6.17%.

annual report *Fin* a document prepared each year to give a true and fair view of a company's state of affairs.
Annual reports are issued to shareholders and filed at Companies House in accordance with the provisions of company legislation. Contents include a profit and loss account and *balance sheet*, a *cash-flow statement*, directors' report, *auditor's report*, and, where a company has subsidiaries, the company's group accounts.
The financial statements are the main purpose of the annual report, and usually include notes to the accounts. These amplify numerous points contained in the figures and are critical for anyone wishing to study the accounts in detail.

annuity *Fin* a contract in which a person pays a lump-sum premium to an insurance company and in return receives periodic payments, usually yearly, often beginning on retirement.
There are several types of annuity. They vary both in the ways they accumulate funds and in the ways they disperse earnings. A fixed annuity guarantees fixed payments to the individual receiving it for the term of the contract, usually until death; a variable annuity offers no guarantee but has potential for a greater return, usually based on the performance of a stock or unit trust; a deferred annuity delays payments until the individual chooses to receive them; a hybrid annuity, also called a combination annuity, combines features of both the fixed and variable annuity.

annuity in arrears *Fin* an annuity whose first payment is due at least one payment period after the start date of the annuity's contract

anorexic organisation *Gen Mgt* an organisation that has become so small that it has lost the strength and depth to compete effectively. An anorexic organisation may have been through the process of extreme *downsizing* or *delayering*, probably with accompanying *redundancies*. (*slang*)

ANSI X.12 standard *E-com* an American National Standards Institute-supported protocol for the electronic interchange of business transactions. *Also known as X.12*

Ansoff, H. Igor (1918–2002) *Gen Mgt* Russian-born manager and academic. Established *strategic planning* as a management activity, developing a framework of tools and techniques by which strategic planning decisions could be made. He explained his approach in *Corporate Strategy* (1965). One of his most well known models is the *three Ss*. He later introduced the concept of *strategic management*.

Contract: an agreement that is binding on the weaker party.　　　　　　　*Frederick Sawyer (attrib.)*

anticipation note *Fin* a bond that a borrower intends to pay off with money from taxes due or money to be borrowed in a later and larger transaction

anticipatory hedging *Fin* hedging carried out before the transaction to which the hedge applies occurs

anticipointment *Gen Mgt* high public expectations of a new product, entertainment, or service that are subsequently disappointed (*slang*)

anti-dumping *Econ* intended to prevent the sale of goods on a foreign market at a price below their **marginal cost**

anti-site *E-com* a website devoted to attacking a company or organisation. Typically, an anti-site is set up by an aggrieved customer who has been unable to contribute his or her opinion to the company's website. Anti-sites are often intended to parody or replicate the site they are targeting. In some instances, an anti-site can beat the official site in the search engine rankings by generating more site visits. *Also known as* **hate site**

antitrust *Gen Mgt* relating to US legislative initiatives aimed at protecting trade and commerce from monopolistic business practices that restrict or eliminate competition. Antitrust laws also attempt to curb trusts and cartels and to keep them from employing monopolistic practices to make unfair profits.

ANZCERTA *abbr Fin* Australia and New Zealand Closer Economic Relations Trade Agreement

APEC *Fin* Asia-Pacific Economic Co-operation, a forum designed to promote trade and economic co-operation among countries bordering the Pacific Ocean. It was set up in 1989. Members include Australia, Indonesia, Thailand, the Philippines, Singapore, Brunei, and Japan.

applet *E-com* a small application, usually written in **Java**. Owing to their miniature size, applets can be set to download automatically when an Internet user visits a web page.

application form *HR* a form used in the **recruitment** process to enable a job candidate to supply information about his or her qualifications, skills, and experience. Employers may ask a candidate to complete an application form instead of, or as well as, providing a **curriculum vitae**. Application forms should be reviewed regularly to ensure that questions asked take account of current legislation, accepted good practice, and internal organisa-

tional developments. These questions should be job-related and avoid unjustifiable intrusion into a candidate's personal life.

application program interface *Gen Mgt* a computer program or piece of software designed to perform a function directly for a user, for example, a word processor, spell-checker, or spreadsheet

application server *E-com* an advanced type of server used to run programming languages that help websites to deliver dynamic information such as the latest news headlines, stock quotes, personalised information, or shopping baskets

application service provider *E-com see* **ASP**

applied economics *Econ* the practical application of theoretical economic principles, especially in formulating national and international economic policies

appointment **1.** *Gen Mgt* an engagement to meet at a particular place and time for a particular purpose **2.** *HR* the selection of somebody for a position or job

apportion *Fin* to spread revenues or costs over two or more cost units, centres, accounts, or time periods

appraisal *HR see* **performance appraisal**

appreciation *Fin* **1.** the value that certain assets, particularly land and buildings, accrue over time. Directors of companies are obliged to reflect this in their accounts. **2.** the increase in value of one currency relative to another

appropriation *Fin* a sum of money that has been allocated for a particular purpose

appropriation account *Fin* in trading and non-profit entities, a record of how the profit/loss or surplus/deficit has been allocated to distributions, reserves, or funds

Approved Deposit Fund (*ANZ*) *Fin* a concessionally taxed fund managed by a financial institution into which **Eligible Termination Payments** can be transferred from a superannuation fund. *Abbr* **ADF**

APR *abbr Fin* Annual or Annualised Percentage Rate of interest: the interest rate that would exist if it were calculated as simple rather than compound interest.
EXAMPLE Different investments typically offer different compounding periods, usually quarterly or monthly. The APR allows them to be compared over a common period of time: one year. This enables an investor or borrower to compare like with like, providing an excellent

basis for comparing mortgage or other loan rates. In the United Kingdom, lenders are required to disclose it.

APR is calculated by applying the formula:

$$APR = [1 + i/m]m - 1.0$$

In the formula, **i** is the interest rate quoted, expressed as decimal, and **m** is the number of compounding periods per year.

The APR is usually slightly higher than the quoted rate, and should be expressed as a decimal, that is, 6% becomes 0.06. When expressed as the cost of credit, other costs should be included in addition to interest, such as loan closing costs and financial fees. *Also known as **annual percentage rate, effective annual rate, nominal annual rate***

APRA *abbr Fin* Australian Prudential Regulation Authority

aptitude test *HR* a measure of a person's natural ability or potential to learn a skill or set of skills. Abilities that are typically measured by aptitude tests include abstract, verbal, and numerical reasoning, because these give a rounded view of a person's general ability in relation to the workplace. Aptitude tests are a form of ***psychometric test*** and are administered by trained users.

arb *Gen Mgt* an ***arbitrageur*** (*slang*)

arbitrage *Fin* the buying and selling of foreign currencies, products, or financial securities between two or more markets in order to make an immediate profit by exploiting differences in market prices quoted

arbitrage pricing theory *Fin* a model of financial instrument and portfolio behaviour that provides a benchmark of return and risk for capital budgeting and securities analysis. It can be used to create portfolios that track a market index, estimate the risk of an asset allocation strategy, or estimate the response of a portfolio to economic developments.

arbitrageur *Fin* a firm or individual who purchases shares or financial securities to make a windfall profit

arbitration *Gen Mgt, HR* the settlement of a dispute by an independent third person, rather than by a court of law. Arbitration allows for claims or grievances to be settled quickly, cost-effectively, privately, and by somebody who is suitably qualified. A contract may include an arbitration clause to be invoked in the case of a dispute. ***Mediation*** is a related term.

arbitrator *Gen Mgt* an impartial person accepted by both parties in a dispute to hear both sides and make a judgment

area sampling *Stats* a form of sampling in which a region is subdivided and some of the divisions are then selected at random for a complete survey

area under a curve *Stats* a means of summarising the information from a series of statistical measurements made over a period of time such as a month

Argyris, Christopher (*b.* 1923) *Gen Mgt* US academic and consultant. Known for his work on ***training*** and ***organisational learning***, specifically T-Groups (see ***sensitivity training***), and single-loop and double-loop learning. Argyris's research is set out in *Organizational Learning* (1978), co-written with **Donald Schön**. Their work also produced the idea of a ***learning organisation***, later developed by **Peter Senge**.

Argyris argues that organisations depend fundamentally on people, but too often stand in the way of people fulfilling their potential. The main thrust of his work has been to explore the relations between personality and the organisation and to suggest how these relations can best be made mutually beneficial.

arithmetic mean *Fin* a simple average calculated by dividing the sum of two or more items by the number of items

Arizmendietta, Jose Maria (1915–77) *Gen Mgt* Basque priest, more commonly known as Father Arizmendi. Co-founder of the **Mondragon co-operative** movement.

armchair economics *Gen Mgt* economic forecasting or theorising based on insufficient data or knowledge of a subject (*slang*)

arm's-length price *Fin* a price at which an unrelated seller and buyer agree to transact on an asset or a product

ARPAnet *E-com* the precursor to the Internet, an experimental network that linked scientists engaged in military research. It was developed by the US Defence Department in the late 1960s, and was originally intended to link together different computers spread out throughout the world.

arrow shooter *Gen Mgt* a person within an organisation who produces visionary new ideas (*slang*)

art director *Mkting* a person who is responsible for planning and designing the creative element for advertisements and other communications material

articles of association *Gen Mgt* an official document governing the running of a company, that is placed with the **Registrar of Companies**. The articles of association constitute a contract between the company and its members, set out the voting rights of shareholders and the conduct of shareholders' and directors' meetings, and detail the powers of management of the company. A **memorandum of association** is a related document.

articles of incorporation *Fin* in the United States, a legal document that creates a privately held company whose powers are governed by the general corporation laws of the state in which it was founded

articles of partnership *Fin see* **partnership agreement**

artificial intelligence *Gen Mgt* a branch of computer science concerned with the development of computer systems capable of performing functions that normally require human intelligence, for example, reasoning, problem-solving, learning from experience, and speech recognition. Artificial intelligence research combines elements of computer science and cognitive psychology. It is a controversial field because of the difficulty of defining its goals and disagreement over whether these goals are attainable. Much research has been done since the second world war, beginning with the theoretical work of Alan Turing during the 1940s. The term became known with the publication in 1961 of the paper *Steps towards Artificial Intelligence* by Marvin Minsky, co-founder with John McCarthy of the Artificial Intelligence Laboratory at Massachusetts Institute of Technology. Branches of artificial intelligence with applications in business and management include **expert systems** and **robotics**.

ASAP *abbr Gen Mgt* as soon as possible (*slang*)

ASEAN Free Trade Area *Fin* a conceptual regional free trade agreement supported by Singapore to foster trade within the region. *Abbr* **AFTA**

A share *Fin* **1.** a non-voting share in a company issued to raise additional capital without diluting control of the company **2.** in the United States, a type of mutual fund share that has a sales charge associated with it

A shares (*US*) *Fin* = **non-voting shares**

Asian Currency Unit *Fin* a book-keeping unit used for recording transactions made by approved financial institutions operating in the Asian Dollar market. *Abbr* **ACU**

ASIC *abbr Fin* Australian Securities and Investments Commission

ask *Fin* **1.** the bid price at which a dealer in stocks and shares, commodities, or financial securities is prepared to buy the stocks and shares, commodities, or securities **2.** (*US*) the price that a security is offered for sale, or the net asset value of a mutual fund plus any sales charges. *Also known as* **asked price**, **offering price**

asked price *Fin see* **ask** (*sense 2*)

asking price *Fin* the price that a seller puts on something before any negotiation

ASP *abbr E-com* application service provider: a hosting service that will operate, support, manage, and maintain a company's software applications for a fee.

The advantages to an organisation of using an ASP are several. It can save time and money: rented applications can be cost-effective and (in theory) can be up and running more quickly than buying an application. It gives them access to the best and latest software without worrying about upgrades and costly installations. It can fill any IT skills shortage.

However, there are disadvantages too, including considerable risk: the ASP industry is still young, and many ASPs have gone out of business. Problems may also arise because many applications are simply not designed to be accessed over a network, especially the Internet, and speed of access is often slow.

assembly *Ops* the joining together of components to make a complete product

assembly line *Ops* a line of production in which a number of assembly operations are performed in a set sequence. The speed of movement of an assembly line has to be matched with the skills and abilities of the **workforce** and the complexity of the assembly process to be performed. The assembly line emerged from the ideas of **scientific management** and was popularised by a number of entrepreneurs, including **Henry Ford** in the car production industry.

assembly plant *Ops* the building in which an **assembly line** is housed

assessed loss *Fin* the excess of tax-deductible expenses over taxable income as confirmed by the South African Revenue Service. It may be carried forward and deducted in determining the taxpayer's taxable income in subsequent years of assessment.

assessed value *Fin* a value for something that is calculated by a person such as an investment advisor

assessment centre *HR* a process whereby a group of participants undertake a series of job-related exercises under observation, so that skills, competencies, and character traits can be assessed. Specially trained assessors evaluate each participant against predetermined criteria. Various methods of assessment may be used, including interviews, *psychometric tests*, group discussions, group problem-solving exercises, individual job-simulated tasks, and role plays. Assessment centres are used in selection for recruitment and promotion, and in training and development, and aim to provide an organisation with an assessment process that is consistent, free of prejudice, and fair.

assessment of competence *HR* the measurement of an employee's performance against an agreed set of standards for work-based activities. In the United Kingdom, assessment of competence is generally made against indicators of the successful achievement of a particular job function. There are four dimensions to assessment: the knowledge and understanding required to carry out a task; the *performance indicators* to be looked for; the scope or range of situations across which an employee is expected to perform; and any particular evidence requirements. *Vocational qualifications* for a wide range of jobs in the United Kingdom are based on a set of occupational standards that contain these elements. A wide variety of techniques or instruments exists to assess *competence*. These include specific work-based ability and *aptitude tests*, as well as traditional methods of *performance appraisal* and evaluation. Recent years have seen a dramatic rise in the use of direct observation at work by trained assessors, the collection of personal portfolios, and peer assessment techniques such as *360 degree appraisal*. All require the careful review of work behaviour against a set of indicators that have been clearly shown to be associated with successful performance.

asset *Fin, Gen Mgt* any tangible or intangible item to which a value can be assigned. Assets can be physical, such as machinery and consumer durables, or financial, such as cash and accounts receivable.

Assets are typically broken down into five different categories. Current assets include cash, cash equivalents, marketable securities, inventories, and prepaid expenses that are expected to be used within one year or a normal operating cycle. All cash items and inventories are reported at historical value. Securities are reported at market value.

Non-current assets, or long-term investments, are resources that are expected to be held for more than one year. They are reported at the lower of cost and current market value, which means that their values will vary. Fixed assets include property, plants and facilities, and equipment used to conduct business. These items are reported at their original value, even though current values might well be much higher. Intangible assets include legal claims, patents, franchise rights, and accounts receivable. These values can be more difficult to determine. FR10, published by the Accounting Standards Board of the Institute of Chartered Accountants for England and Wales is essential reading for dealing with this issue. Deferred charges include prepaid costs and other expenditures that will produce future revenue or benefits.

asset allocation *(ANZ) Fin* an investment strategy that distributes investments in a portfolio so as to achieve the highest investment return while minimising risk. Such a strategy usually apportions investments among cash equivalents, shares in domestic and foreign companies, fixed-income investments, and property.

asset-backed security *Econ, Fin* a security for which the collateral is neither land nor land-based financial instruments

asset-based lending *Fin* the lending of money with the expectation that the proceeds from an asset or assets will allow the borrower to repay the loan

asset conversion loan *Fin* a loan that the borrower will repay with money raised by selling an asset

asset coverage *Fin* the ratio measuring a company's solvency and consisting of its net assets divided by its debt

asset demand *Econ* the amount of assets held as money, which will be low when interest rates are high and high when interest rates are low

asset financing *Fin* the borrowing of money by a company using its assets as collateral

asset for asset swap *Fin* an exchange of one bankrupt debtor's debt for that of another

asset management *Fin* an investment service offered by some financial institutions that combines banking and brokerage services

asset play *Fin* a purchase of a company's stock in the belief that it has assets that are not

---

Miracles can be made, but only by sweating. *Giovanni Agnelli*

properly documented and therefore unknown to others

asset pricing model *Fin* a model used to determine the profit that an asset will yield

asset protection trust *Fin* a trust, often set up in a foreign country, used to make the trust's principal inaccessible to creditors

asset restructuring *Fin* the purchase or sale of assets worth more than 50% of a listed company's total or net assets

asset side *Fin* the side of a balance sheet that shows the economic resources a firm owns, for example, cash on hand or in bank deposits, products, or buildings and fixtures

assets requirements *Fin* the assets needed for a business to continue trading

asset-stripper *Fin* a company that acquires another company and sells its assets to make a profit without regard for the acquired company's future business success

asset-stripping *Fin* the purchase of a company whose market value is below its asset value, usually so that the buyer may sell the assets for immediate gain. The buyer usually has little or no concern for the purchased company's employees or other *stakeholders*, so the practice is generally frowned upon.

asset substitution *Fin* the purchase of assets that involve more risk than those a lender expected the borrower to buy

asset swap *Fin* an exchange of assets between companies so that they may divest parts no longer required and enter another product area

asset turnover *Fin* the ratio of a firm's sales revenue to its total assets, used as a measure of the firm's business efficiency.
EXAMPLE Asset turnover's basic formula is simply sales divided by assets:
Sales revenue / Total assets
Most experts recommend using average total assets in this formula. To determine this figure, total assets at the beginning of the year are added to total assets at the end of the year and divided by two. If, for instance, annual sales totalled £4.5 million, and total assets were £1.84 million at the beginning of the year and £1.78 million at the year end, the average total assets would be £1.81 million, and the asset turnover ratio would be:
4,500,000 / 1,810,000 = 2.49
A variation of the formula is:
Sales revenue / Fixed assets

If average fixed assets were £900,000, then asset turnover would be:
4,500,000 / 900,000 = 5
Asset turnover numbers are useful for comparing competitors within industries, and for growth companies to gauge whether or not they are growing revenue, for example, turnover, in healthy proportion to assets. Too high a ratio may suggest overtrading: too much sales revenue with too little investment. Conversely, too low a ratio may suggest undertrading and inefficient management of resources. A declining ratio may be indicative of a company that overinvested in plant, equipment, or other fixed assets, or is not using existing assets effectively.

asset valuation *Fin* the aggregated value of the assets of a firm, usually the capital assets, as entered on its balance sheet

asset value per share *Fin* a way of measuring the value of assets per share, to assist with investment and disinvestment decisions, usually for the benefit of equity shareholders. It is calculated as follows:
Total assets less liabilities / Number of issued equity shares

assign *Fin* to transfer ownership of an asset to another person or organisation

assignable cause of variation *Ops* an evident reason for deviation from the norm. An assignable cause exists when variation within a process can be attributed to a particular cause that is a fundamental part of the process. Once identified, the assignable cause of the errors must be investigated and the process adjusted before other possible causes of variation are examined. Using the technique of *statistical process control*, control charts can be used to distinguish causes that are assignable from those that are random.

assigned risk *Fin* a poor insurance risk that a company is required by law to insure against

associate (*ANZ*) *Fin* a member of a stock exchange who does not have a seat on it

associate programme *E-com see affiliate programme*

Association of British Insurers *Fin* an association that represents over 400 UK insurance companies to the government, the regulators, and other agencies as well as providing a wide range of services to its members

assumable mortgage *Fin* a mortgage that the buyer of a property can take over from the seller

---

assumed bond *Fin* a bond for which a company other than the issuer takes over responsibility

assumption *Stats* the conditions under which valid results can be obtained from a statistical technique

assured shorthold tenancy *Gen Mgt* a tenancy for a fixed period of at least six months during which the tenant cannot be evicted other than by court order. Any new tenancy without a written agreement is an assured shorthold tenancy.

assured tenancy *Fin* a tenancy for an indefinite period in which the tenant cannot be evicted other than by court order

ASX *abbr Fin* Australian Stock Exchange

ASX 100 *Fin* a measure of the change in share prices on the *Australian Stock Exchange* based on changes in the stocks of the top 100 companies. Similar indexes include the ASX 20, ASX 50, ASX 200, and ASX 300.

asymmetrical digital subscriber line *E-com see ADSL*

asymmetrical distribution *Stats* a frequency or probability distribution of statistical data that is not symmetrical about a central value in the data

asymmetric taxation *Fin* a difference in tax status between parties to a transaction, typically making the transaction attractive to both parties because of taxes that one or both can avoid

asynchronous transmission *E-com* the transmission of data in which the end of the transmission of one unit denotes the start of the next, rather than transmission at fixed intervals

at best *Fin* an instruction to a stockbroker to buy or sell securities immediately at the best possible current price in the market, regardless of adverse price movements. It is equally applicable to the commodity or currency markets. *See also at limit*

at call *Fin* used to describe a short term loan that is repayable immediately upon demand

Athos, Anthony *Gen Mgt* US academic. *See Pascale, Richard Tanner*

at limit *Fin* an instruction to a stockbroker to buy or sell a security within certain limits, usually not to sell below or to buy above a set price. A time limit is stipulated by the investor and if there has been no transaction within that period, the instruction lapses. It is

equally applicable to the commodity or currency markets. *See also at best*

ATM *Gen Mgt* an electronic machine from which bank customers can withdraw paper money using an encoded plastic card

ATO *abbr Fin* Australian Taxation Office

atom *Mkting* any traditional non-digital means of delivering information such as a newspaper, book, or magazine

atomise *Gen Mgt* to split a large organisation into smaller operating units

at sight *Fin see bill of exchange*

attachment 1. *E-com* a file that is attached to a standard text e-mail message **2.** *Fin* a process that enables a judgment creditor to secure dues from a debtor. A debtor's earnings and/or funds held at his or her bankers may be attached.

attendance *HR* presence at work, normally noted in an attendance register. The phenomenon of irregular attendance is referred to as *absenteeism*. One method of improving attendance is by paying an *attendance bonus*.

attendance bonus *(US) HR* a financial or non-financial incentive offered to employees by an employer to arrive for work on time

attention management *Gen Mgt* a method of ensuring that employees are focused on their work and on organisational goals. Attention management is similar to *time management*, as inattentiveness results in wasted time. An important factor in winning and sustaining attention is tapping into people's emotions.

at-the-money *Fin* used to describe an option with a strike price roughly equivalent to the price of the underlying shares

attitude *Gen Mgt* a mental position consisting of a feeling, emotion, or opinion evolved in response to an external situation. An attitude can be momentary or can develop into a habitual position that has a long-term influence on an individual's behaviour. Attempts can be made to modify attitudes that have a negative effect in the workplace, for example, through education and training. The *employee attitude survey* is one tool used to assess prevalent attitudes in the workforce.

attitude research *Gen Mgt* an investigation into people's beliefs regarding an organisation, its products or services, or its activities. Attitude research is used in marketing to ascertain opinions among consumers and the

---

The finest eloquence is that which gets things done; the worst is that which delays them.
David Lloyd-George

public in general. It is also used within organisations when *employee attitude surveys* are conducted.

attitude survey *Mkting* a piece of research carried out to assess the feelings of a target audience towards a product, brand, or organisation

attribute sampling *Ops* a random testing method for determining the quality of a finished product by inspecting a sample number of the items in each batch. The items selected are examined for a particular attribute, which is usually an abnormal or negative characteristic—for example, a sample of cars from one production run might be inspected for poor paintwork, and the number of sampled cars found with this attribute used to calculate the number of defective items in the whole batch.

attribution theory of leadership *Gen Mgt* the theory that leaders observe their followers' behaviour, attribute it to particular causes, and as a result respond in a particular way

auction *E-com, Fin* a sale of goods or property by competitive bidding on the spot, by mail, by telecommunications, or over the Internet

auction market preferred stock *Fin* stock in a company owned in the United Kingdom that pays dividends whose amounts track a money-market index. *Abbr* **AMPS**

AUD *abbr Fin* Australian dollar

audience *Mkting* the total number of readers, viewers, or listeners who are exposed to an advertisement

audience research *Mkting* research carried out to measure the size or composition of the target audience for a piece of advertising

audit *Fin* an accountant's formal examination and verification of the accuracy and completeness of financial records, especially those of a business. An *internal audit* is conducted by an employee of the business, and an *external audit* is performed by an independent outsider.

audit committee *Fin* a committee of a company's board of directors, from which the company's executives are excluded, that monitors the company's finances

Auditing Practices Board *Fin* a body formed in 1991 by an agreement between the six members of the Consultative Committee of Accountancy Bodies, to be responsible for developing and issuing professional auditing standards in the United Kingdom and the Republic of Ireland

Auditor-General *Fin* an officer of an Australian state or territory government who is responsible for ensuring that government expenditure is made in accordance with legislation

auditor's report *Fin* a certification by an auditor that a firm's financial records give a true and fair view of its profit and loss for the period

audit trail *Gen Mgt* the records of all the sequential stages of a transaction. An audit trail may trace the process of a purchase, a sale, a customer complaint, or the supply of goods. Tracing what happened at each stage through the records can be a useful method of *problem-solving*. In financial markets, audit trails may be used to ensure fairness and accuracy on the part of the dealers.

aural signature *Mkting* a musical theme that is part of a company or product's brand identity

Aussie Mac *Fin* an informal name for a mortgage-backed certificate issued in Australia by the National Mortgage Market Corporation. The corporation has been issuing such certificates since 1985.

Austrade *Fin* Australian Trade Commission, a federal government body responsible for promoting Australian products abroad and attracting business to Australia. It currently has 108 offices in 63 countries.

Australia and New Zealand Closer Economic Relations Trade Agreement *Fin* an accord between Australia and New Zealand designed to facilitate the exchange of goods between the two countries. It was signed on 1 January 1983. *Abbr* **ANZCERTA**

Australian Accounting Standards Board *Fin* a body that is responsible for setting and monitoring accounting standards in Australia. It was established under Corporations Law in 1988, replacing the Accounting Standards Review Board. *Abbr* **AASB**

Australian Bureau of Statistics *Stats* an Australian federal government body responsible for compiling national statistics and conducting regular censuses. It was set up in 1906. *Abbr* **ABS**

Australian Chamber of Commerce and Industry *Fin* a national council of business organisations in Australia. It represents around 350,000 businesses and its members include state chambers of commerce as well as major national employer and industry associations. *Abbr* **ACCI**

Australian Chamber of Manufactures *Gen Mgt* a body representing Australian manufacturers, established in 1878. *Abbr* **ACM**

Australian Communications Authority *Fin* a government body responsible for regulating practices in the communications industries. It was set up in 1997 as a result of the merger of the Australian Telecommunications Authority and the Spectrum Management Agency. *Abbr* **ACA**

Australian Council of Trade *Gen Mgt* Australia's national trade union organisation. It was founded in 1927 and is based in Melbourne. *Abbr* **ACTU**

Australian Industrial Relations Commission *HR* an administrative tribunal responsible for settling industrial disputes by conciliation and for setting and modifying industrial awards. It was established in 1988 to replace the Arbitration Commission and other specialist tribunals. *Abbr* **AIRC**

Australian Prudential Regulation Authority *Fin* a federal government body responsible for ensuring that financial institutions are able to meet their commitments

Australian Securities and Investments Commission *Fin* an Australian federal government body responsible for regulating Australian businesses and the provision of financial products and services to consumers. It was established in 1989, replacing the Australian Securities Commission. *Abbr* **ASIC**

Australian Stock Exchange *Fin* the principal market for trading shares and other securities in Australia. It was formed in 1987 as a result of the amalgamation of six state stock exchanges and has offices in most state capitals. *Abbr* **ASX**

Australian Taxation Office *Fin* a statutory body responsible for the administration of the Australian federal government's taxation system. It is based in Canberra and is also responsible for the country's superannuation system. *Abbr* **ATO**

authentication *E-com* a software security verification procedure to acknowledge or validate the source, uniqueness, and integrity of an e-commerce message to make sure data is not being tampered with. The verification is typically achieved through the use of an electronic signature in the form of a key or algorithm that is shared by the trading partners.

authorisation *Fin* the process of assessing a financial transaction, confirming that it does not raise the account's debt above its limit, and allowing the transaction to proceed. This would be undertaken, for example, by a credit card issuer. A positive authorisation results in an authorisation code being generated and the relevant funds being set aside. The available credit limit is reduced by the amount authorised.

authorised capital *Fin* the money made by a company from the sale of authorised ordinary and preference shares. It is measured by multiplying the number of authorised shares by their par value.

authorised share *Fin* a share that a company is authorised to issue

authorised share capital *Fin* the type, class, number, and amount of the shares which a company may issue, as empowered by its memorandum of association. *Also known as nominal share capital, registered share capital*

authorised signatory *Fin* the most senior issuer of authorisation certificates in an organisation, recognised by a signatory authority and designated in a signatory certificate

authority *Gen Mgt* the right to act or command. People willingly obey a person in authority, because they believe he or she has a legitimate entitlement to exercise power. *Max Weber* distinguishes three types of legitimate authority: rational-legal, derived from the office held; traditional, from custom, an ancient tradition of obedience; and charismatic, exerted by those whose exceptional abilities confer the right to lead. The third form is the basis for the *charismatic authority* leadership theory.

authority chart *Gen Mgt* a diagram showing the hierarchical lines of *authority* and reporting within an organisation. *Organisation charts* are similar.

authority-compliance management *Gen Mgt see Managerial Grid™*

automated clearing house *E-com* a payment network available to *POS* or *ATM* systems for interbank clearing and settlement of financial transactions. The network is also used for electronic fund transfers from a current or savings account.

Automated Direct Debit Amendments and Cancellation Service *Fin* in the United Kingdom, a *BACS* service that allows paying banks to inform direct debit payees of a change of instruction, for example, an amendment to the customer's account details or a request to cancel the instructions. *Abbr* **ADDACS**

automated handling *Ops* the use of computers to control the moving and positioning of materials in a warehouse or factory. Automated handling may involve the use of robots.

Automated Order Entry System *Fin* in the United States, a system that allows small orders to bypass the floor brokers and go straight to the specialists on the exchange floor

automated screen trading *Fin* an electronic trading system for the sale and purchase of securities. Customers' orders are entered via a keyboard, a computer system matches and executes the deals, and prices and deals are shown on monitors, thus dispensing with the need for face-to-face contact on a trading floor.

automated storage and retrieval systems *Ops* the use of computerised vehicles to store, select, and move pallets around a large warehouse

automated teller machine *Fin see* ATM

automatic assembly *Ops* a computerised *production control* technique used in the production of manufactured goods to balance output of production with demand. All factors affecting production performance are input when setting the operating parameters of an automatic assembly system, including sales information and production *capacity*.

automatic debit *(US) Fin* = **standing order**

automatic guided vehicle system *Ops* a transportation system consisting of driverless electric vehicles that follow a predetermined track, used for the distribution of materials around a plant

automatic rollover *Fin* on the London Money Market, the automatic reinvestment of a maturing fixed term deposit for a further identical fixed term, an arrangement that can be cancelled at any time

automation *Ops* the self-controlling operation of machinery that reduces or dispenses with human communication or control when used in normal conditions. Automation was first introduced in the late 1940s by the Ford Motor Company. *Also known as* **mechanisation**

autonomation *Ops* a production system in which workers are allowed, and machines are equipped with a mechanism, to stop production if a defect in a product is detected during the production process. Autonomation became known through the *Toyota production system*. The concept evolved from braking devices on machines that automatically stop if a problem occurs. Within Toyota, the concept has been carried forward so that all machines are equipped with various safety devices to prevent defective products, and production workers are allowed to stop the production line if a problem occurs. The problem is then properly explored in order to find a solution and to ensure that everyone understands the underlying reasons for the problem. In the long term, this creates a more efficient production line.

autonomous work group *HR* a small group of people who are empowered to manage themselves and the work they do on a day-to-day basis. The members of an autonomous work group are usually responsible for a whole process, product, or service, and not only carry out the work but also design and manage it. *Also known as* **self-directed team**, **self-managed team**, **self-managed work team**, **self-managing team**

Auto Pact *Fin* the informal name for the Agreement Concerning Automotive Products between Canada and the United States, by which duties were reduced on imported cars for US car makers assembling vehicles in Canada. Subsequent provisions of the North American Free Trade Agreement reduced its effect.

autoresponder *E-com* an e-mail software application that enables Internet users to send automated e-mails when they are not able to respond to incoming e-mail. Some autoresponse software enables a degree of personalisation, for example, by incorporating the recipient's name in the responding message.

availability float *Fin* money that is available to a company because cheques that it has written have not yet been charged against its accounts

available hours *Fin* the number of hours for which a worker or machine is available to work.
EXAMPLE In a simple case for a worker this could be as follows for a four-week period:

The sad truth is that excellence makes people nervous. *Shana Alexander*

	Hours
Number of contractual hours	40
Overtime hours	20
Absence:	
Public holidays	7
Annual holidays	28
Certified sickness	14
Other absence	1 (50)
Available hours	110

average *Stats* the arithmetic mean of a sample of observations

average accounting return *Fin* the percentage return realised on an asset, as measured by its book value, after taxes and depreciation

average collection period *Fin* the mean time required for a firm to liquidate its accounts receivable, measured from the date each receivable is posted until the last payment is received.
Its formula is:

Accounts receivable / Average daily sales = Average collection period

For example, if accounts receivable are £280,000, and average daily sales are 7,000, then:

280,000 / 7,000 = 40

average cost of capital *Fin* the average of what a company is paying for the money it borrows or raises by selling stock

average deviation *Stats* the spread of a sample of observations

average nominal maturity *Fin* the average length of time until a unit trust's financial instruments mature

average option *Fin* an option whose value depends on the average price of a commodity during a particular period of time

Average Weekly Earnings *Stats* a measure of wage levels in the Australian workforce that is calculated regularly by the *Australian Bureau of Statistics*. The measure is considered one of Australia's key economic indicators. *Abbr* **AWE**

Average Weekly Ordinary Time Earnings *Stats* a measure of wage levels in the Australian workforce that excludes overtime payments, published by the *Australian Bureau of Statistics*

avoidable costs *Fin* the specific costs of an activity or sector of a business which would be avoided if that activity or sector did not exist

award *HR* **1.** the terms of employment set by an industrial court or tribunal for a particular occupation **2.** (*ANZ*) a decision handed down by a court of arbitration

award wage (*ANZ*) *HR* a rate of pay set by an industrial court or tribunal for a particular occupation

AWE *abbr Stats* Average Weekly Earnings

axis *Stats* a reference line used in geometry to locate a point in space or in a plane

B2B *abbr* *E-com* business-to-business: relating to an advertising or marketing programme aimed at businesses doing business with other businesses as opposed to consumers. The term is most commonly used in reference to commerce or business that is conducted over the Internet between commercial enterprises.

B2B advertising *Mkting* advertising that is aimed at buyers for organisations rather than domestic consumers

B2B agency *Mkting* an advertising agency that specialises in planning, creating, and buying advertising aimed at buyers for organisations rather than domestic consumers

B2B auction *E-com* a Web marketplace that provides a mechanism for negotiating prices and bidding for services. Web-based B2B auctions reverse the traditional auction formula in which the aim is to help the seller get the best price. B2B Web auctions involve suppliers competing with one another by bidding down the price of their service. This inevitably benefits the buyer, as instead of having to bid higher for a particular service or product he or she can wait till the suppliers have bid themselves down to a reasonable price. Typically, online auctions require companies to follow a registration process in order to take part. During this process, users have to provide their credit-card information and shipping preferences as well as agree to the site's code of conduct. Some sites also manage secure auctions, which restrict potential bidders to specific firms or individuals (www.businessauctions.com is one example).

B2B commerce *E-com* the business conducted between companies, rather than between a company and individual consumers

B2B exchange *Gen Mgt see* **exchange**

B2B marketing *E-com* the planning, promotion, and distribution of goods or services for use by businesses rather than individual consumers

B2B Web exchange *E-com see* **exchange**

B2C *abbr* *E-com* business-to-consumer: relating to an advertising or marketing programme aimed at businesses doing business directly with consumers as opposed to other businesses. The term is most commonly used in reference to commerce or business that is

conducted over the Internet between a commercial enterprise and a consumer.

B4N *abbr* *Gen Mgt* bye for now (*slang*)

BAA *abbr* *Fin* British Accounting Association

back duty *Fin* tax relating to a past period that has not been paid due to the taxpayer's failure to disclose relevant information through negligence or fraud. If back duty is found to be payable, the relevant authorities may instigate an investigation and penalties or interest may be charged on the amount.

back-end loading *Fin* the practice of charging a redemption fee or deferred sales charge if the holder of an investment decides to sell it. This is used as a discouragement to selling. *See also* **front-end loading**

backflush costing *Fin* a method of costing, associated with a *JIT* production system, which applies cost to the output of a process. Costs do not mirror the flow of products through the production process, but are attached to output produced (finished goods stock and cost of sales), on the assumption that such backflushed costs are a realistic measure of the actual costs incurred.

backlink checking *E-com* a means of finding out which web pages are linking to a specific website. Many **search engines** enable users to conduct backlink searches by entering the name of a website into the search box preceded by a special command (for example, 'link':). AltaVista and HotBot are two of the most popular search engines to offer this facility. The backlink checking process can be automated by using a service such as Link-Popularity.com, which enables users to search for linking sites at various search engines at once. Backlink checking enables e-business and website managers to keep track of their own and their competitors' online popularity.

backlog *Ops* the build-up of unfulfilled orders for a product or process that is behind schedule. A backlog can result from bad scheduling, production delays, an unanticipated demand for a product or process, or where the capacity of the process is not able to keep up with demand. Some large products, for example, aircraft and ships, have to be built to a backlog of orders as it is not feasible to supply them on demand.

backlog depreciation *Fin* the additional depreciation required when an asset is revalued to make up for the fact that previous depreciation had been calculated on a now out-of-date valuation

back office *Fin, Gen Mgt* the administrative staff of a company who do not have face-to-face contact with the company's customers

back pay *HR* pay that is owed to an employee for work carried out before the current payment period and is either overdue or results from a backdated pay increase

back-to-back loan *Fin* an arrangement in which two companies in different countries borrow offsetting amounts in each other's currency and each repays it at a specified future date in its domestic currency. Such a loan, often between a company and its foreign subsidiary, eliminates the risk of loss from exchange rate fluctuations.

back-to-school sale *(US) Gen Mgt* a shop sale that is timed to coincide with the return of children to school after the summer holidays *(slang)*

back-up *Fin* a period in which bond yields rise and prices fall, or a sudden reversal in a stock market trend

back-up facility *Gen Mgt* a secondary system, record, or contract intended to take the place of another that fails

back-up withholding *Fin* withholding tax that a payer sends to the Internal Revenue Service in the United States so that somebody receiving income cannot avoid all taxes on that income

backward integration *Ops* the building of relationships with *suppliers* in order to secure the supply of *raw materials*. Backward integration can involve taking control of supply companies and is a feature of Japanese *keiretsu*. It is the opposite of *forward integration*.

backward scheduling *Ops* a *production scheduling* technique for planning work on the basis of when the completed work is due. By using backward scheduling, managers are able to assign work to particular workstations so that the overall task is completed exactly when it is due. The technique allows potential bottlenecks and idle time for particular workstations to be identified in advance.

BACS *Fin* an electronic bulk clearing system generally used by banks and building societies for low-value and/or repetitive items such as standing orders, direct debits, and automated

credits such as salary payments. It was formerly known as the Bankers Automated Clearing Services.

BADC *abbr Fin* Business Accounting Deliberation Council of Japan

bad debt *Fin* a debt that is unlikely to be repaid because a company or customer has become insolvent

bad debt reserve *Fin* an amount of money that a company sets aside to cover bad debts

bad debts ratio *Fin* a way of calculating the significance of bad debts as a proportion of credit sales:

Bad debts × 100 / Turnover on credit

To calculate the significance of bad debts as a proportion of debtors, however:

Bad debts × 100 / Total debtors at a point in time

bad debts recovered *Fin* money formerly classified as *bad debts* and therefore written off that has since been recovered either wholly or in part

badwill *Fin* negative goodwill *(slang)*

bailment *Fin* the delivery of goods from the owner to another person on the condition that they will eventually be returned

bait and switch *Mkting* a marketing practice whereby customers are encouraged to enter a shop by an advertisement for one product and are then persuaded to buy another more expensive product *(slang)*

balance *Fin* **1.** the state of an account, for example, a debit or a credit balance, indicating whether money is owed or owing **2.** in double-entry bookkeeping, the amount required to make the debit and credit figures in the books equal

balance billing *Fin* the practice of requesting payment from a receiver of a service such as medical treatment for the part of the cost not covered by the person's insurance

balanced budget *Econ* a budget in which planned expenditure on goods and services and debt income can be met by current income from taxation and other central government receipts

balanced design *Stats* an experimental design in which the same number of observations is used for each combination of the experimental factors

balanced fund *Fin* a unit trust that invests in a variety of types of companies and financial instruments to reduce the risk of loss through poor performance of any one type

balanced investment strategy *Fin* a strategy of investing in a variety of types of companies and financial instruments to reduce the risk of loss through poor performance of any one type

balanced line *Ops* an *assembly line* in which the cycle time for all the workstations is equal. A balanced line is achieved by allocating the right amount of work and the correct amount of operators and machinery to produce a given flow of product over a set period, taking into account the fact that each workstation will have a different capacity and that each process involved has a different cycle time.

balanced quantity *Ops* an *inventory* measure of the quantity of materials and parts required by a workstation to achieve a planned level of output

balanced scorecard *Gen Mgt* a system that measures and manages an organisation's progress towards strategic objectives. Introduced by *Robert Kaplan* and *David Norton* in 1992, the balanced scorecard incorporates not only financial indicators but also three other perspectives: customer, internal business, and learning/innovation. The scorecard shows how these measures are interlinked and affect each other, enabling an organisation's past, present, and potential performance to be tracked and managed.

balance off *Fin* to add up and enter the totals for both sides of an account at the end of an accounting period in order to determine the balance

balance of payments *Econ* a list of a country's credit and debit transactions with international financial institutions and foreign countries in a specific period

balance of payments on capital account *Fin* a system of recording a country's investment transactions with the rest of the world during a given period, usually one year. Among the included transactions are the purchase of physical and financial assets, intergovernmental transfers, and the provision of economic aid to developing nations.

balance of payments on current account *Fin* a system of recording a country's imports and exports of goods and services during a period, usually one year

balance of trade *Econ* the difference between a country's exports and imports of goods and services

balance sheet *Fin* a financial report stating the total assets, liabilities, and owner's equity of an organisation at a given date, usually the last day of the accounting period. The format of a company's balance sheet is strictly defined by the 1985 Companies Act. The debit side of the balance sheet states assets, while the credit side states liability and equity, and the two sides must be equal, or balance.

EXAMPLE Assets include cash in hand and cash anticipated (receivables), inventories of supplies and materials, properties, facilities, equipment, and whatever else the company uses to conduct business. Assets also need to reflect depreciation in the value of equipment such as machinery that has a limited expected useful life.

Liabilities include pending payments to suppliers and creditors, outstanding current and long-term debts, taxes, interest payments, and other unpaid expenses that the company has incurred.

Subtracting the value of aggregate liabilities from the value of aggregate assets reveals the value of owners' equity. Ideally, it should be positive. Owners' equity consists of capital invested by owners over the years and profits (net income) or internally generated capital, which is referred to as 'retained earnings'; these are funds to be used in future operations.

As an example:

ASSETS	£
Current:	
Cash	8,200
Securities	5,000
Receivables	4,500
Inventory & supplies	6,300
Fixed:	
Land	10,000
Structures	90,000
Equipment (less depreciation)	5,000
Intangibles/other	
TOTAL ASSETS	129,000

LIABILITIES	£
Payables	7,000
Taxes	4,000
Misc.	3,000
Bonds & notes	25,000
TOTAL LIABILITIES	39,000
SHAREHOLDERS' EQUITY (stock, par value × shares outstanding)	80,000
RETAINED EARNINGS	10,000
TOTAL LIABILITIES AND SHAREHOLDERS' EQUITY	129,000

A lawyer with his briefcase can steal more than a hundred men with guns. ***Mario Puzo***

balance sheet audit *Fin* a limited audit of the items on a company's balance sheet in order to confirm that it complies with the relevant standards and requirements. Such an audit involves checking the value, ownership, and existence of assets and liabilities and ensuring that they are correctly recorded.

balance sheet equation *Fin see* **accounting equation**

balance sheet total *Fin* in the United Kingdom, the total of assets shown at the bottom of a balance sheet and used to classify a company according to size

balancing figure *Fin* a number added to a series of numbers to make the total the same as another total. For example, if a debit total is higher than the credit total in the accounts, the balancing figure is the amount of extra credit required to make the two totals equal.

ball
carry the ball *Gen Mgt* to have responsibility for a project (*slang*)
drop the ball *Gen Mgt* to avoid your responsibilities (*slang*)
take the ball and run with it *Gen Mgt* to take an idea and implement it (*slang*)

balloon loan *Fin* a loan repaid in regular instalments with a single larger final payment

balloon payment *Fin* the final larger payment on a balloon loan

ballpark *Gen Mgt* an informal term for a rough, estimated figure. The term was derived from the approximate assessment of the number of spectators that might be made on the basis of a glance around at a sporting event.

BALO *Fin* Bulletin des annonces légales obligatoires: a French government publication that includes financial statements of public companies

banded pack *Mkting* a product pack that has an additional product or promotional offer attached to it

bandwidth *E-com* the capacity of fibre-optic cables that carry information to and from the Internet. The higher the bandwidth, the faster information will pass through a cable, and therefore the faster information can be downloaded or uploaded via the Internet.

bang for the buck (*US*) *Gen Mgt* a return on investment (*slang*)

bangtail *Mkting* an order form for a new product that is attached by a perforated join to an envelope flap (*slang*)

bank *Fin* a commercial institution that keeps money in accounts for individuals or organisations, makes loans, exchanges currencies, provides credit to businesses, and offers other financial services

bank bill *Fin* **1.** a bill of exchange issued or accepted by a bank **2.** (*US*) a banknote

bank card *Fin* a plastic card issued by a bank and accepted by merchants in payment for transactions. The most common types are **credit cards** and **debit cards**. Bank cards are governed by an internationally recognised set of rules for the authorisation of their use and the clearing and settlement of transactions.

bank certificate *Fin* a document, often requested during an audit, that is signed by a bank official and confirms the balances due or from a company on a specific date

bank charge *Fin* an amount charged by a bank to its customers for services provided, for example, for servicing customer accounts or arranging foreign currency transactions or letters of credit, but excluding interest

bank confirmation *Fin* verification of a company's balances requested by an auditor from a bank

bank credit *Fin* the maximum credit available to an individual from a particular bank

bank discount *Fin* the charge made by a bank to a company or customer who pays a note before it is due

bank discount basis *Fin* the expression of yield that is used for US treasury bills, based on a 360-day year

bank draft *Fin see* **banker's draft**

bank-eligible issue *Fin* US Treasury obligations that commercial banks may buy

banker *Fin* somebody who owns or is a senior executive of a bank

banker's acceptance *Fin see* **banker's credit**

banker's cheque *Fin see* **banker's draft**

banker's credit *Fin* a financial instrument, typically issued by an exporter or importer for a short term, that a bank guarantees. *Also known as* **banker's acceptance**

banker's draft *Fin* a bill of exchange payable on demand and drawn by one bank on another. Regarded as being equivalent to cash, the draft cannot be returned unpaid. *Also known as* **bank draft**, **banker's cheque**

bankers' hours *Fin* short hours of work. The term refers to the relatively short time that a bank is open in some countries. (*slang*)

banker's order *Fin* an instruction by a customer to a bank to pay a specific amount at regular intervals, usually monthly or annually, until the order is cancelled

banker's reference *Fin* a written report issued by a bank regarding a particular customer's creditworthiness

bank fee *Fin* a charge included in most lease transactions that is either paid in advance or is included in the gross capitalised cost. The fee usually covers administrative costs such as the costs of obtaining a credit report, verifying insurance coverage, and checking the lease documentation.

Bank for International Settlements *Fin* see *BIS*

bank giro *Fin* see *giro* (sense 1)

bank guarantee *Fin* a commitment made by a bank to a foreign buyer that the bank will pay an exporter for goods shipped if the buyer defaults

bank holding company *Fin* a company that owns one or more banks as part of its assets

banking insurance fund *Fin* in the United States, a fund maintained by the Federal Deposit Insurance Corporation to provide deposit insurance for banks other than savings and savings and loan banks

Banking Ombudsman *Fin* an official of the Australian or New Zealand government responsible for dealing with complaints relating to banking practices

banking passport *Fin* a document used to provide somebody with a false identity for banking transactions in another country

banking syndicate *Fin* a group of investment banks that jointly underwrite and distribute a new security offering

banking system *Fin* a network of commercial, savings, and specialised banks that provide financial services including accepting deposits, loans and credit, and providing money transmission and investment facilities

bank investment contract *Fin* a contract that specifies what a bank will pay its investors

bankmail *Fin* an agreement by a bank not to finance any rival's attempt to take over the same company that a particular customer is trying to buy

Bank of England *Fin* the central bank of the United Kingdom, established in 1694. Originally a private bank, it became public in 1946 and increased its independence from government in 1997 when it was granted sole responsibility for setting base interest rates.

bank overdraft *Fin* borrowings from a bank on a current account, repayable on demand. The maximum permissible overdraft is normally agreed with the bank prior to the facility being made available, and interest, calculated on a daily basis, is charged on the amount borrowed, and not on the agreed maximum borrowing facility.

bank reconciliation *Fin* a detailed statement reconciling, at a given date, the cash balance in an entity's cash book with that reported in a bank statement.

EXAMPLE

Bank Reconciliation Statement
Cash book balance

	£	£
Cash book balance o/d		(1,205)
Bank charges not in cash book	(110)	
Dividends collected by the bank, not in cash book	113	3
Updated cash book balance		**(1,202)**
Cheques drawn, not presented to bank	4,363	
Cheques received, not yet credited by bank	(1,061)	3,302
Bank statement balance		**2,100**

bank reserve ratio *Fin* a standard established by a central bank governing the relationship between the amount of money that other banks must keep on hand and the amount that they can lend. By raising and lowering the ratio, the central bank can decrease or increase the money supply.

bank reserves *Fin* the money that a bank has available to meet the demands of its depositors

bankroll *Fin* the money used as finance for a project

bankrupt *Fin* a person who has been declared by a court of law as unable to meet his or her financial obligations

bankruptcy *Fin* the condition of being unable to pay debts, with liabilities greater than assets. There are two types of bankruptcy: involuntary bankruptcy, where one or more creditors bring a petition against the debtor; and voluntary bankruptcy, where the debtor files a petition claiming inability to meet debts.

bank statement *Fin* a record, sent by a bank to its customer, listing transactions since the date of the previous statement

bank term loan *Fin* a loan from a bank that has a term of at least one year

banner *or* **banner ad** *E-com* an online interactive ad, often using graphic images and sound as well as text, placed on a web page that is linked to an external advertiser's website. The banner typically is sized so as to appear at the top or bottom of the web page. *Also known as* **ad banner**

banner advertising *Mkting* the use of rectangular advertisements or logos across the width of a page on a website. Organisations frequently place such ads on a third party's website in order to attract users to visit their own.

Debate still continues on whether banner advertising is an efficient and cost-effective way of promoting a website. However, prices for banner advertising have dropped significantly in recent years, and it can be effective if the website is visited by people whose profile accurately matches the advertiser's target market. Banner ads are particularly useful for raising awareness when a new website, product, or service is being launched.

banner exchange *E-com* an advertising programme in which one merchant induces others to place his or her banners and buttons on their websites in return for similarly displaying theirs

bar *or* **outside the bar** *Fin* one million pounds sterling (*slang*)

bar chart *Gen Mgt* the presentation of data in the form of a graph, using blocks or bars of colour or shading. A bar chart is especially useful for showing the impact of one factor against another, for example, income over time, or customer calls against sales.

bar coding *Ops* the process of attaching a machine-readable code to a product, package, container, or sub-assembly, and using a scanner to relate its location to the product characteristics. Bar codes have uses in **stock control** and order picking and are used to validate every single transaction from packaging through to customer delivery.

barefoot pilgrim (*US*) *Fin* an unsophisticated investor who has lost everything trading in securities (*slang*)

bargain *Fin* a transaction on a stock market (*slang*)

bargaining chip *Fin* something that can be used as a concession or inducement in negotiation

bargain tax date *Fin* the date of a transaction on a stock market

Barnard, Chester (1886–1961) *Gen Mgt* US business executive. President of the New Jersey Bell Telephone Company, whose book, *The Functions of the Executive* (1938), looked at the relationship of the individual to the organisation and at **organisation structure**. Barnard's observations also covered the topics of **communication**, **authority**, and organisational **core values**.

Barnevik, Percy (*b.* 1941) *Gen Mgt* Swedish business executive. Formerly chief executive, and now chairman, of Asea Brown Boveri, where he reduced **bureaucracy**, decentralised resources and **authority**, introduced a **matrix management** structure, and ran a global expansion strategy.

barometer stock *Fin* a widely held security such as a blue chip that is regarded as an indicator of the state of the market

barren money *Fin* money that is unproductive because it is not invested

barrier option *Fin* an option that includes automatic trading in other options when a commodity reaches a specified price

barrier to entry *Gen Mgt* a factor preventing a company from entering a market. A barrier to entry may be created, for example, by the fact that current companies in that market have patents so that goods cannot be copied, or by the high cost of advertising needed to gain any **market share**. There may be strong **brand loyalty** to an existing product, or a large company may be able to produce goods very cheaply, whereas a small newcomer would have to charge higher prices. If too many barriers to entry exist, then competition within that market will be limited.

barrier to exit *Gen Mgt* a factor preventing a company from leaving a market in which it is currently doing business. A barrier to exit makes it difficult for a company to abandon an unprofitable product or service because of factors such as possession of specialist equipment only suited to the manufacture of one product, high costs of retraining the workforce in different skills, or the detrimental effect of withdrawing one product from a range on the rest of the product family. There may also be legal considerations or trade union agreements that prevent closure of a factory or redundancies.

barter *Fin* the direct exchange of goods between two parties without the use of money as a medium

Bartlett, Christopher (*b.* 1943) *Gen Mgt* Australian-born academic. Professor at Harvard Business School, and co-author with *Sumantra Ghoshal* of *Managing Across Borders* (1989).

BAS *abbr Gen Mgt* Business Activity Statement

base
touch base *Gen Mgt* to make contact with a person or group after a time of absence. To touch base is important for *teleworkers*, *homeworkers*, or *sales representatives* who work away from a main office. They may touch base by taking part in a *team briefing* or other real or virtual meeting, which enables them to renew contact and establish meaningful communication. (*slang*)

base currency *Fin* the currency used for measuring the return on an investment

base date *Econ* the reference date from which an index number such as the *retail price index* is calculated

base interest rate *Fin* in the United States, the minimum interest rate that investors will expect for investing in a non-Treasury security

base pay (*US*) *HR* = *basic pay*

base rate *Fin* the interest rate at which the Bank of England lends to other banks and which they in turn charge their customers

base rate tracker mortgage *Fin* a mortgage whose interest rate varies periodically, usually annually, so as to remain a specified amount above a particular standard rate

base year *Econ* the year from which an index is calculated

basic pay *HR* a guaranteed sum of money given to an employee in payment for work, disregarding any fringe benefits, allowances, or extra rewards from an *incentive scheme*. US term *base pay*

basic wage *HR* the minimum rate of pay set by an industrial court or tribunal for a particular occupation

basic wage rate *Fin* the wages paid for a specific number of hours work per week, excluding overtime payments and any other incentives

basis of apportionment *Fin* a physical or financial unit used to apportion costs equitably to cost centres

basis point *Fin* one hundredth of 1%, used in relation to changes in bond interest rates. Thus a change from 7.5% to 7.4% is 10 basis points.

basis risk *Fin* the risk that price variations in the cash or futures market will diminish revenue when a futures contract is liquidated, or the risk that changes in interest rates will affect re-pricing interest-bearing liabilities

basket case *Fin* a company or individual considered to be in such dire circumstances as to be beyond help (*slang*)

basket of currencies *Fin* a group of selected currencies used in establishing a standard of value for another unit of currency

batch *Fin* a group of similar articles which maintains its identity throughout one or more stages of production and is treated as a cost unit

batch costing *Fin* a form of specific order costing in which costs are attributed to batches of products

batch-level activities *Fin* activities which vary directly with the number of batches of output produced, and which are independent of the number of units within a batch. Set up costs are batch-level activities. *See also hierarchy of activities*

batch production *Ops* a production system in which a process is broken down into distinct operations that are completed on a batch or group of products before moving to the next production stage. As batch sizes can vary from very small to extremely large quantities, batch production offers greater flexibility than other production systems.

bath
take a bath (*US*) *Fin* to suffer a serious financial loss (*slang*)

baud *Fin* a unit used to measure speed of data transmission, equal to one data unit per second

Bayesian theory *Stats* a statistical theory and method for drawing conclusions about the future occurrence of a given parameter of a statistical distribution by calculating from prior data on its frequency of occurrence. The theory is useful in the solution of theoretical and applied problems in science, industry, and government, for example, in econometrics and finance.

College professors are suspect because whenever emotion is in control, anti-intellectualism prevails.
Gordon Allport

Bayes' theorem *Stats* a probability theorem that allows statisticians continually to revise the probability of an event according to new evidence

BBS *abbr E-com* bulletin board system: a system enabling Internet users to read and post messages in newsgroups. *See also* **discussion board**

BCA *abbr Gen Mgt* Business Council of Australia

bcc *abbr E-com* blind carbon copy: a function that enables a user to send an e-mail message to any number of e-mail addresses while concealing each recipient's e-mail address. The bcc box is widely used for distributing press releases, newsletters, and other mass mailings via e-mail. If there is no desire to conceal names, the *cc* address line can be used.

BCCS *abbr Fin* Board of Currency Commissioners

BCNU *abbr Gen Mgt* be seeing you (*slang*)

bean counter (*slang*) **1.** *Gen Mgt* a person of low rank within an organisation who has no real influence on the decision-making process **2.** *Fin* a derogatory term for an accountant, especially one who works in a large organisation

bear *Fin* somebody who anticipates unfavourable business conditions, especially somebody who sells stocks or commodities expecting their prices to fall, often with the intention of buying them back cheaply later. *See also* **bull**

bearer bond *Fin* a bond that is not registered on the books of the issuer and is therefore payable only to the party that presents it for payment

bearer instrument *Fin* a financial instrument such as a cheque or bill of exchange that entitles the person who presents it to receive payment

bearer security *Fin* a share or bond that is owned by the person who possesses it. For example, a eurobond can change hands without registration and so protect the owner's anonymity.

bear hug *Gen Mgt* an attempt to get the board of a company that is a target acquisition to recommend an offer to its shareholders. A bear hug may include the acquiring company offering to buy shares in the target at a premium. In a **reverse bear hug**, the board of the company to be acquired demonstrates its willingness to recommend an offer, usually on particular conditions. (*slang*)

bearish *Fin* relating to unfavourable business conditions or selling activity in anticipation of falling prices. *See also* **bullish**

bear market *Fin* a market in which prices are falling and in which a dealer is more likely to sell securities than to buy them. *See also* **bull market**

bear raid *Fin see* **raid**

bear spread *Fin* a combination of purchases and sales of options for the same commodity or stock with the intention of making a profit when the price falls. *See also* **bull spread**

bear tack *Fin* a downward movement in the value of a stock, part of the market, or the market as a whole

bed
get into bed with somebody *HR* to begin a business association with an individual or organisation (*slang*)
put something to bed *Gen Mgt* to dismiss an idea or put an end to a project (*slang*)

bed and breakfast deal *Fin* a transaction in which somebody sells shares at the end of one trading day and repurchases them at the beginning of the next. This is usually done to formally establish the profit or loss accrued to these shares for tax or reporting purposes.

beepilepsy *Gen Mgt* the sudden jerk of surprise given by a person when his or her beeper goes off (*slang*)

Beer, Stafford (*b.* 1926) *Gen Mgt* British industrialist. Organisation systems thinker associated with cybernetics. Also a writer, his approach was first laid out in *Cybernetics and Management* (1959).

before-tax profit margin *Fin* the amount by which net income before tax exceeds expenditure

beginning inventory (*US*) *Fin* = **opening stock**

behavioural accounting *Fin* an approach to the study of accounting that emphasises the psychological and social aspects of the profession in addition to the more technical areas

behavioural implications *Fin* the ways in which humans affect, and are affected by, the creation, existence, and use of accounting information

behavioural interview *HR see* **interviewing**

behavioural modelling *HR* **1.** a process of capturing and encoding unconscious human expertise to make it transferable to others

It does seem the more you get the more you spend. It is rather like being on a golden treadmill.

Charles Allsop

2. a skills training technique that seeks to imitate models and maintain learned behaviours

behavioural science *HR* academic disciplines such as sociology and psychology that relate to the study of the way in which humans conduct themselves. In the field of management, the behavioural sciences are used to study *organisation behaviour*.

behaviourist theories of leadership *Gen Mgt* a school of thought that defines *leadership* by leaders' actions, rather than by their personality characteristics or their sources of *power*. Behaviourist theories were developed in the 1970s as disillusionment with situational theory grew. There are many different behaviourist theories. One of the most prominent—the *Managerial Grid*™—was developed by *Robert Blake* and *Jane Mouton* as a tool to enable leaders to understand their own behaviour patterns. *Rensis Likert* also conducted research in this area, focusing on how behaviour adapts to take account of people and situations.

Behn, Hernand (1880–1933) *Gen Mgt* US industrialist. Founder, with his brother *Sosthenes Behn*, of the conglomerate International Telephone and Telegraph (ITT) in 1920.

Behn, Sosthenes (1882–1957) *Gen Mgt* US industrialist. Founder, with his brother *Hernand Behn*, of the conglomerate International Telephone and Telegraph (ITT) in 1920. Under Behn's leadership, ITT expanded from the United States into Europe and South America. When Behn retired from ITT in 1956, most of its turnover came from its overseas interests. Under the leadership of *Harold Geneen*, ITT then developed into a massive diverse multinational incorporating hotels, car hire, frozen foods, potato crisps, and confectionery. The history of ITT is detailed in *Sovereign State—The Secret History of ITT* (1973).

Belbin, R. Meredith (*b.* 1926) *Gen Mgt* British academic and consultant. Acknowledged as the father of team-role theory, which identifies nine useful roles necessary for a successful team of managers. Belbin's approach to *team building* and *teamwork* was described in *Management Teams: Why They Succeed or Fail* (1981). Other models of team relationships include the Team Management System, developed by *Charles Margerison* and *Dick McCann*.

bell cow *Fin* a product that sells well and makes a reasonable profit (*slang*)

bells and whistles (*slang*) **1.** *Fin* special features attached to a derivatives instrument or securities issue that are intended to attract investors or reduce issue costs **2.** *Mkting* unnecessary but desirable peripheral features of a product

bellwether *Fin* a security whose price is viewed by investors as an indicator of future developments or trends

belly
go belly up (*US*) *Fin* to fail financially or go bankrupt (*slang*)

below-the-line 1. *Fin* used to describe entries in a company's profit and loss account that show how the profit is distributed, or where the funds to finance the loss originate. *See also **above-the-line** (sense 2)* **2.** *Fin* in macroeconomics, used to describe a country's capital transactions. *See also **above-the-line** (sense 3)* **3.** *Mkting* relating to the proportion of marketing expenditure allocated to non-advertising activities such as public relations, sales promotion, printing, presentations, sponsorship, and salesforce support

benchmark *Gen Mgt* a point of reference or standard against which to measure performance. Originally used for a set of computer programs to measure the performance of a computer against similar models, benchmark is now used more generally to describe a measure identified in the context of a *benchmarking* programme against which to evaluate an organisation's performance in a specific area.

benchmark accounting policy *Fin* one of a choice of two possible policies within an International Accounting Standard. The other policy is marked as an 'allowed alternative', although there is no indication of preference.

benchmarking *Mkting* a systematic process of comparing the activities and work processes of an organisation or department with those of outstanding organisations or departments in order to identify ways to improve performance. Benchmarking was first developed by the Xerox Corporation in the late 1970s in order to learn from the achievements of Japanese competitors and was described by a Xerox manager, Robert C. Camp, in his book *Benchmarking: The Search for Industry Best Practices That Lead to Superior Performance* (1989). The use of benchmarking has become widespread and individual organisations have developed distinct approaches towards it. Benchmarking programmes commonly include the following stages: identifying the area requiring benchmarking and the process to use, collecting and analysing the data, implementing changes, and monitoring and reviewing improvements. Benchmarking is used in business appraisal, often as part of a *total quality management* or *business process re-engineering* programme.

Types of benchmarking include: internal benchmarking, a method of comparing one operating unit or function with another within the same industry; functional benchmarking, in which internal functions are compared with those of the best external practitioners of those functions, regardless of the industry they are in; competitive benchmarking, in which information is gathered about direct competitors, through techniques such as reverse engineering; and strategic benchmarking, a type of competitive benchmarking aimed at strategic action and organisational change.

benchmark interest rate *Fin* the lowest interest rate that US investors will accept on securities other than Treasury bills

beneficial owner *Fin* somebody who receives all the benefits of a stock such as dividends, rights, and proceeds of any sale but is not the registered owner of the stock

beneficiary bank *Fin* a bank that handles a gift such as a bequest

benefit *Fin* something that improves the profitability or efficiency of an organisation or reduces its risk, or any non-monetary reward given to employees, for example, paid holidays or employer contributions to pensions

benefit in kind *HR* a *benefit* other than cash received by employees as part of their total *compensation package*

benefits plan *HR* a Canadian government programme for the employment of Canadian citizens and for providing Canadian manufacturers, consultants, contractors, and service companies with opportunities to compete for projects

Bennis, Warren (*b.* 1925) *Gen Mgt* US academic. Guru of *leadership* theory, who has also carried out work in the areas of small *group dynamics*, change in social systems, and T-Groups (see *sensitivity training*). Bennis wrote his first article on leadership in 1959, and subsequently carried out extensive research in the United States into common leadership factors. His findings are reported in *Leaders: The Strategies for Taking Charge* (1985). He was influenced by the theories of *Douglas McGregor*.

bequest *Fin* a gift that has been left to somebody in a will

Berhad *Fin* a Malay term for 'private'. Companies can use 'sendiran berhad' or 'Sdn Bhd' in their name instead of 'plc'. *Abbr* **Bhd**

Berners-Lee, Tim (*b.* 1955) *Gen Mgt* British computer scientist. Creator of the World Wide Web and director of the World Wide Web Consortium, the world co-ordinating body for developing the Web. Berners-Lee is concerned that the growth of the Web should benefit all, rather than make money for the few. His experiences and thoughts are recorded in *Weaving the Web: The Original Design and Ultimate Destiny of the World Wide Web* (1999).

Berne Union *Fin see International Union of Credit and Investment Insurers*

best-in-class *Gen Mgt* leading a market or industrial sector in efficiency. A best-in-class organisation exhibits exemplary *best practice*. Such an organisation is clearly singled out from the pack and is recognised as a leader for its procedures for dealing with the acquisition and processing of materials, and the delivery of end products or services to its customers. The concept of best in class is closely allied with *total quality management*, and one tool that can help in achieving this status is *benchmarking*.

best practice *Gen Mgt* the most effective and efficient method of achieving any objective or task. What constitutes best practice can be determined through a process of *benchmarking*. An organisation can move towards achieving best practice, either across the whole organisation or in a specific area, through *continuous improvement*. In production-based organisations, *world class manufacturing* is a related concept. More generally, a market or sector leader may be described as *best-in-class*.

best value *Gen Mgt* a UK government initiative intended to ensure cost efficiency and effectiveness in the delivery of public services by local authorities. The best value initiative was announced in early 1997 to replace compulsory competitive tendering (CCT), and pilot schemes in selected local authorities began in April 1998. The Local Government Act 1999 requires councils, as part of the best value process, to review all services over a five-year period, setting standards and performance indicators for each service, comparing performance with that of other bodies, and undertaking consultation with local taxpayers and service users.

beta *Fin* a numerical measure of the change in value of something such as a stock

---

Dr __ well remembered that he had a salary to receive, and only forgot that he had a duty to perform.
Edward Gibbon

beta coefficient *Fin* an indication of the level of risk attached to a share. A high beta coefficient indicates that a share is likely to be more sensitive to market movements.

beta factor *Fin* The measure of the volatility of the return on a share relative to the market. If a share price were to rise or fall at double the market rate, it would have a beta factor of 2.0. Conversely, if the share price moved at half the market rate, the beta factor would be 0.5. The beta factor is defined mathematically as a share's covariance with the market portfolio divided by the variance of the market portfolio.

beta rating *Fin* a means of measuring the volatility (or risk) of a stock or fund in comparison with the market as a whole.

The beta of a stock or fund can be of any value, positive or negative, but usually is between +0.25 and +1.75. Stocks of many utilities have a beta of less than 1. Conversely, most high-tech NASDAQ-based stocks have a beta greater than 1; they offer a higher rate of return but are also risky.

Both alpha and beta ratings should be readily available upon request from investment firms, because the figures appear in standard performance reports. It is always best to ask for them, because beta calculations can involve mathematical complexities. *See also* ***alpha rating***

beta software *E-com* a version of a software product that is almost ready for release but needs more testing. It is possible to download beta software on the Internet free, as software companies like to test their products on members of the public before they are put on the market.

beta test *E-com* a test of a new or upgraded piece of computer software or hardware carried out by a few chosen customers before it is released to the public

BFH *Fin* Bundesfinanzhof: in Germany, the supreme court for issues concerning taxation

Bhd *abbr Fin* Berhad

BHP *abbr Gen Mgt* Broken Hill Proprietary Company Ltd: Australia's largest manufacturing company. Also known as ***Big Australian***.

bias *Stats* inaccuracy or deviation in inferences, results, or a statistical method

bid *Fin* an offer to buy all or a majority of the capital shares of a company in an attempted takeover, or the highest price a prospective bidder is prepared to pay

bid-ask quote *Fin* a statement of the prices that are being offered and asked for a security or option contract

bid-ask spread *Fin* the difference between the buying and the selling prices of a traded commodity or a financial instrument

bid bond *Fin* a guarantee by a financial institution of the fulfilment of an international tender offer

bidding war *Fin* a competition between prospective buyers who successively offer more than each other for the same stock or security

bid form *Fin* in the United States, a form containing details of an offer to underwrite municipal bonds

bid-offer spread *Fin* the difference between the highest price that a buyer is prepared to offer and the lowest price that a seller is prepared to accept

bid price *Fin* the price a stock exchange dealer will pay for a security or option contract

bid-to-cover ratio *Fin* a number that shows how many more people wanted to buy US Treasury bills than actually did buy them

bid up *Fin* to bid for something merely to increase its price, or to make successive increases to the bid price for a security so that unopened orders do not remain unexecuted

Big Australian (*ANZ*) *Gen Mgt see* ***BHP***

Big Bang *Fin* radical changes to practices on the London Stock Exchange implemented in October 1986. Fixed commission charges were abolished, leading to an alteration in the structure of the market, and the right of member firms to act as market makers as well as agents was also abolished. (*slang*)

big bath *Fin* the practice of making a particular year's poor income statement look even worse by increasing expenses and selling assets. Subsequent years will then appear much better in comparison. (*slang*)

Big Board *Fin* the New York Stock Exchange (*slang*). *See also* ***Little Board***

big business *Gen Mgt* powerful business interests or companies in general. The term is particularly used when referring to ***large-sized businesses*** or ***multinational businesses***.

Big Four (*ANZ*) *Fin* Australia's four largest banks: the Commonwealth Bank of Australia, Westpac Banking Corporation, National Australia Bank, and ANZ Bank

Big GAAP *Fin* the *Generally Accepted Accounting Principles* that apply to large companies (*slang*)

big picture *Gen Mgt* an informal term for a broad perspective on an issue that encompasses its surrounding context and long-term implications

big swinging dick *Fin* a very successful financial trader (*slang*)

bilateral facility *Fin* a loan by one bank to one borrower

bilateral monopoly *Econ* a market in which there is a single seller and a single buyer

bilateral trade *Econ* trade between two countries who give each other specific privileges such as favourable import quotas that are denied to other trading partners

bill *Fin* **1.** an invoice **2.** to send an invoice

bill broker *Fin* somebody who buys and sells promissory notes and bills of exchange

bill discount *Fin* the interest rate that the Bank of England charges banks for short-term loans. This establishes a de facto floor for the interest rate that banks charge their customers, usually a fraction above the discount rate.

bill discounting rate *Fin* the amount by which the price of a US Treasury bill is reduced to reflect expected changes in interest rates

billing cycle *Fin* a period of time, often one month, between successive requests for payment

bill of entry *Fin* a statement of the nature and value of goods to be imported or exported, prepared by the shipper and presented to a customs house

bill of exchange *Fin* an unconditional order in writing from one person (the drawer) to another (the drawee and signatory), requiring the drawee to pay on demand a sum to a specified person (the payee) or bearer. It is now usually used in overseas trade and the drawee may be a bank as opposed to an importer.

The supplier or drawer usually submits the bill with the relative shipping documents. It is then anticipated by the drawee either as the agreed or implied method of payment. On receipt, the drawee either makes the required payment, or if payment is to be made at a future date, indicates acceptance by signing it. Wording on the bill will state when payment

has to be made, for example, '60 days after date, we promise to pay. . .' means 60 days after the date of the bill; '60 days after sight, we promise to pay. . .' means 60 days after acceptance; and **at sight** means the bill is payable upon presentation.

Once accepted, a bill of exchange is a negotiable instrument. The drawer can therefore obtain the money it represents by selling it to a financial institution at a discount. In the United Kingdom, the complex statutory law relating to these instruments is found in the Bills of Exchange Act (1882).

bill of goods *Fin* a consignment of goods, or a statement of their nature and value

bill of lading *Fin* a statement of the nature and value of goods being transported, especially by ship, along with the conditions applying to their transport. Drawn up by the carrier, this document serves as a contract between the owner of the goods and the carrier.

bill of materials *Fin* a specification of the materials and parts required to make a product

bill of sale *Fin* a document confirming the transfer of goods or services from a seller to a buyer

bill payable *Fin* a bill of exchange or promissory note payable

bill receivable *Fin* a bill of exchange or promissory note receivable

binary thinker *Gen Mgt* somebody who thinks only in absolute, black-and-white terms (*slang*)

bin card *Fin* a record of receipts, issues, and balances of the quantity of an item of stock handled by a store

bingo card *Mkting* a postcard advertisement for a product that is bound into a publication and can be returned to the manufacturer for additional information on the product (*slang*)

biodata *HR* **1.** information taken from an *application form, curriculum vitae*, or questionnaire concerning an employee's or potential employee's background and experience that is objectively scored by recruiters to predict job performance **2.** a potted biography placed in a periodical article or conference paper

biological assets *Fin* farm animals and plants classified as assets. International Accounting Standards require that they are recorded on balance sheets at market value.

Once they have been slaughtered or harvested, the assets become **agricultural produce**.

biometrics *E-com* the study of measurable biological characteristics, or in computer security, authentication techniques that use characteristics such as speech, fingerprints, or scans of the human eye

biomimicry *Gen Mgt* the use in business of processes that imitate natural ones to reduce waste and limit impact on the environment

biorhythm *HR* any recurring biological cycle thought to affect the physical or mental state of a person, particularly patterns of digestion, sleep, and fatigue

BiRiLiG *Fin* Bilanzrichtlinieniengesetz: the 1985 German accounting directives law

birth-death ratio *Stats* the ratio of the number of births to the number of deaths in a population over a period of time such as 10 years

BIS *abbr Fin* Bank for International Settlements: a bank that promotes co-operation between central banks, provides facilities for international financial operations, and acts as agent or trustee in international financial settlements. The 17-member board of directors consists of the governors of the central banks of Belgium, Canada, France, Germany, Italy, Japan, the Netherlands, Sweden, Switzerland, the United Kingdom, and the United States.

bit *E-com* **1.** a binary digit number (0 or 1), the smallest unit of computerised data **2.** an item of information or knowledge

bivariate data *Stats* data in which two variables are involved in each subject

bivariate distribution *Stats* a form of distribution involving two random variables

black
in the black *Fin* making profit, or having more assets than debt (*slang*)

black-box engineering *Ops* the manufacturing of a component in which the supplier has total control over the design and content of the component and the purchaser knows only its external and physical specifications. The term black-box engineering is derived from the fact that the component in question appears as a black box on the design drawings for the purchaser.

black chip (*S Africa*) *Gen Mgt* a company that is owned or managed by black people, or is controlled by black shareholders

black economic empowerment (*S Africa*) *Gen Mgt* the promotion of black ownership and control of South Africa's economic assets

black economy *Econ* economic activity that is not declared for tax purposes and is usually carried out in exchange for cash

black hole *Gen Mgt* a project that consumes unlimited amounts of resources without yielding any profit (*slang*)

black knight *Gen Mgt see* **knight**

black market *Gen Mgt* an illegal *market*, usually for goods that are in short supply. Black market trading breaks government regulations or legislation and is particularly prevalent during times of shortage, such as rationing, or in industries that are very highly regulated, such as pharmaceuticals or armaments. *Also known as* **shadow market**

black market economy *Fin* a system of illegal trading in officially controlled goods, or an illicit secondary currency market that has rates markedly different from those in the official market

Black Monday *Fin* either of two Mondays, 29 October 1929 or 19 October 1987, that were marked by the largest stock market declines of the 20th century. Although both market crashes originated in the United States, they were immediately followed by similar market crashes around the world.

black money *Econ* money circulating in the *black economy* in payment for goods and services

Black Tuesday *Fin* 29 October 1929, when values of stocks fell precipitously

Blake, Robert (*b*. 1918) *Gen Mgt* US psychologist. Collaborated with *Jane Mouton* on the development of *The Managerial Grid*™ (1964), a framework for understanding managerial behaviour.

blamestorming *Gen Mgt* group discussion as to the reasons why a project has failed or is late and who is to blame for it. The term is modelled on 'brainstorming'. (*slang*)

blame-time *Gen Mgt* the moment in an organisation when blame for the failure of a project or task is publicly allocated (*slang*)

Blanchard, Kenneth (*b*. 1939) *Gen Mgt* US academic. Best known for his concept of one-minute management. *The One Minute Manager* (1982), co-written with *Spencer Johnson*, became a bestseller in the tradition of management self-help books alongside those by **Dale Carnegie** and **Stephen Covey**.

blanket bond *Fin* an insurance policy that covers a financial institution for losses caused by the actions of its employees

bleed *Mkting* an area of a piece of printed material that extends beyond given margins or its edges

blended rate *Fin* an interest rate charged by a lender that is between an old rate and a new one

blind carbon copy *Gen Mgt see* **bcc**

blind certificate *E-com* a **cookie** from which the user's name is omitted so as to protect his or her privacy while making collected data available for marketing studies

blind entry *Fin* **1.** (*ANZ*) a document issued by a supplier that stipulates the amount charged for goods or services as well as the amount of GST payable **2.** a bookkeeping entry that records a debit or credit but fails to show other essential information

blind offer *Mkting* an inconspicuous offer buried in the body copy of a print advertisement, often used to determine the degree of reader attention to the advertisement

blind pool *Fin* a limited partnership in which the investment opportunities the general partner plans to pursue are not specified

blindside *Mkting* to attack somebody in a way that he or she cannot anticipate (*slang*)

blind trust *Fin* a trust that manages somebody's business interests, with contents that are unknown to the beneficiary. People assuming public office use such trusts to avoid conflicts of interest.

block diagram *Stats* a diagram that represents statistical data by rectangular blocks

blocked account *Fin* a bank account from which funds cannot be withdrawn for any of a number of reasons, for example, bankruptcy proceedings, liquidation of a company, or government order when freezing foreign assets

blocked currency *Fin* a currency that people cannot easily trade for other currencies because of foreign exchange control

blocked funds *Fin* money that cannot be transferred from one place to another, usually because of **exchange controls** imposed by the government of the country in which the funds are held

block grant *Fin* money that the government gives to local authorities to fund local services

blockholder *Fin* an individual or institutional investor who holds a large number of shares of stock or a large monetary value of bonds in a given company

block investment (*ANZ*) *Fin* the purchase or holding of a large number of shares of stock or a large monetary value of bonds in a given company

block release *HR* an arrangement whereby an employer permits an employee to be away from work to attend an educational institution for a period of time, usually several weeks

block trade *Fin* a sale of a large round number of stocks or amount of bonds

blow-in *Mkting* advertising in the form of cards bound inside magazines or newspapers (*slang*)

blow-off top *Fin* a rapid increase in the price of a financial stock followed by an equally rapid drop in price (*slang*)

bludge (*ANZ*) *Gen Mgt* to shirk work or responsibility, or live off the earnings of others

blue chip *Gen Mgt* relating to the highest-quality and lowest-risk ordinary equity shares or to high-quality established stable companies. The term is derived from the game of poker, in which blue is the highest value chip.

blue-chip stocks *Fin* ordinary shares of stock in a company that is considered to be well established, highly successful, and reliable, and is traded on a stock market

blue-collar job *HR* a position that involves mainly physical labour. With the decline in manufacturing and an increase in harmonisation agreements, the term blue-collar is now rarely used. Blue-collar refers to the blue overalls traditionally worn in factories in contrast to the white shirt and tie supposedly worn by an office worker, known as a **white-collar worker**.

blue-collar worker *HR* somebody whose job involves mainly physical labour

blue hair (*US*) *Mkting* used in advertising and marketing to refer to elderly women customers (*slang*)

blueshirt (*US*) *Gen Mgt* an employee of the computer company IBM (*slang*)

blue-sky ideas *Gen Mgt* extremely ambitious, idealistic, or unrealistic proposals, apparently unconfined by conventional thinking (*slang*)

blue-sky law *Fin* a US state law that regulates investments to prevent investors from being defrauded

blue-sky securities *Fin* stocks and bonds that have no value, being worth the same as a piece of 'blue sky' (*slang*)

blur *Gen Mgt* a period of transition for a business in which changes occur at great speed and on a large scale

board *Gen Mgt see* **board of directors**

board dismissal *Gen Mgt* the dismissal and removal from power of an entire **board** or **board of directors**

Board of Currency Commissioners *Fin* the sole currency issuing authority in Singapore, established in 1967. *Abbr* **BCCS**

Board of Customs and Excise *Fin* in the United Kingdom, the government department responsible for administering and collecting indirect taxes, such as customs and excise duties and Value Added Tax. It also prepares UK overseas trade statistics.

board of directors *Gen Mgt* the people selected to sit on an authoritative standing committee or governing body, taking responsibility for the management of an organisation. Members of the board of directors are officially chosen by shareholders, but in practice they are usually selected on the basis of the current board's recommendations. The board usually includes major shareholders as well as directors of the company. *Also known as* **board**

Board of Inland Revenue *Fin* in the United Kingdom, the government department responsible for the administration and collection of the main direct taxes, such as income tax. Its duties include appointing tax inspectors, advising on new legislation, and providing statistical information. *Also known as* ***Inland Revenue***

board of trustees *Gen Mgt* a committee or governing body that takes responsibility for managing, and holds in trust, funds, assets, or property belonging to others, for example, charitable or pension funds or assets

boardroom *Gen Mgt* a room in which board meetings are held. A boardroom may be a room used only for board meetings or can be a multi-use room that becomes a boardroom for the duration of a board meeting.

boardroom battle *Gen Mgt* a conflict or power struggle between individual board members or between groups of board members

board seat *Gen Mgt* a position of membership of a board, especially a ***board of directors***

board secretary *Gen Mgt see* ***company secretary***

body corporate *Fin* an association, such as a company or institution, that is legally authorised to act as if it were one person

body language *HR* the combination of often subconscious gestures, postures, and facial expressions that send out messages about a person's feelings and emotions. Body language is an important aspect of ***non-verbal communication***.

body of creditors *Fin* the creditors of a company or individual treated as a single creditor in dealing with the debtor

body of shareholders *Fin* the shareholders of a company treated as a single shareholder in dealing with the company

BOGOF *Mkting* buy one get one free, a sales promotion technique in which consumers are offered two products for the price of one

bogus degree *HR* a qualification awarded by an organisation of questionable or unrecognised standing, usually capitalising on the naivety of overseas students and the reputation of the education system of the host country. A bogus degree is normally offered by an organisation that has adopted a similar sounding name to a university of good standing.

boilerplate (*US*) *Gen Mgt* a standard version of a contract that can be used interchangeably from contract to contract (*slang*)

bona fide *Fin* used to describe a sale or purchase that has been carried out in good faith, without collusion or fraud

bona vacantia *Fin* the goods of a person who has died intestate and has no traceable living relatives. In the United Kingdom, these goods become the property of the state.

bond *Fin* **1.** a promise to repay with interest on specified dates money that an investor lends a company or government **2.** a certificate issued by a company or government that promises repayment of borrowed money at a set rate of interest on a particular date.
  Short-term bonds mature in up to three years, intermediate-term bonds in three to ten

---

*We cannot hide behind our boundaries, or hold onto the belief that we can survive alone. Meg **Wheatley***

years, and long-term bonds in more than ten years, with 30 years generally being the upper limit. Longer-term bonds are considered a higher risk because interest rates are certain to change during their lifetime. They tend to pay higher interest rates to attract investors and reward them for the additional risk.

Bonds are traded on the open market, just like stocks. They are reliable economic indicators, but perform in the reverse direction to interest rates: if bond prices are rising, interest rates and stock markets are likely to be falling, while if interest rates have gone up since a bond was first issued, prices of new bonds will fall. **3.** (*ANZ*) a sum of money paid as a deposit, especially on rented premises **4.** (*S Africa*) a mortgage bond

bond anticipation note *Fin* a loan that a government agency receives to provide capital that will be repaid from the proceeds of bonds that the agency will issue later

bond covenant *Fin* part of a bond contract whereby the lender promises not to do certain things, for example, borrow beyond a particular limit

bonded warehouse *Fin* a warehouse that holds goods awaiting duty or tax to be paid on them

bond equivalent yield *Fin* the interest rate that an investor would have to receive on a bond to profit as much as from investment in another type of security. *Also known as equivalent bond yield*

bond fund *Fin* a unit trust that invests in bonds

bondholder *Fin* an individual or institution owning bonds issued by a government or company and entitled to payments of the interest as due and return of the principal when the bond matures

bond indenture *Fin* a document that specifies the terms of a bond

bond indexing *Fin* the practice of investing in bonds in such a way as to match the yield of a designated index

bond issue *Fin* additional shares of stock in a company given by the company to existing shareholders in proportion to their prior holding

bond quote *Fin* a statement of the current market price of a bond

bond swap *Fin* an exchange of some bonds for others, usually to gain tax advantage or to diversify a portfolio

bond value *Fin* the value of an asset or liability recorded in the accounts of an entity

bond-washing *Fin* the practice of selling a bond before its dividend is due and buying it back later in order to avoid paying tax

bond yield *Fin* the annual return on a bond (the rate of interest) expressed as a percentage of the current market price of the bond. Bonds can tie up investors' money for periods of up to 30 years, so knowing their yield is a critical investment consideration.

EXAMPLE Bond yield is calculated by multiplying the face value of the bond by its stated annual rate of interest, expressed as a decimal. For example, buying a new ten-year £1,000 bond that pays 6% interest will produce an annual yield amount of £60:

$$1{,}000 \times 0.060 = 60$$

The £60 will be paid as £30 every six months. At the end of ten years, the purchaser will have earned £600, and will also be repaid the original £1,000. Because the bond was purchased when it was first issued, the 6% is also called the 'yield to maturity'.

This basic formula is complicated by other factors. First is the 'time-value of money' theory: money paid in the future is worth less than money paid today. A more detailed computation of total bond yield requires the calculation of the present value of the interest earned each year. Second, changing interest rates have a marked impact on bond trading and, ultimately, on yield. Changes in interest rates cannot affect the interest paid by bonds already issued, but they do affect the prices of new bonds.

bonus *HR* a financial incentive given to employees in addition to their *basic pay* in the form of a one-off payment or as part of a *bonus scheme*

bonus dividend *Fin* a one-off extra dividend in addition to the usual twice-yearly payment

bonus issue *Fin* additional shares of stock in a company given by the company to existing shareholders in proportion to their prior holding

bonus offer *Mkting* a sales promotion technique offering consumers an additional amount of product for the basic price

bonus scheme *HR* a form of *incentive scheme* under which a *bonus* is paid to employees in accordance with rules concerning eligibility, performance targets, time period, and size and form of payments. A bonus scheme may apply to some or all employees and may be determined on organisation, business unit, or individual performance, or on a combination of these. A bonus payment may be expressed as a percentage of salary or as a flat-rate sum.

bonus shares *Fin* **1.** *see* **scrip issue 2.** in the United Kingdom, extra shares paid by the government as a reward to founding shareholders who did not sell their initial holding within a certain number of years

book-building *Fin* the research done among potential institutional investors to determine the optimum offering price for a new issue of stock

book cost *Fin* the price paid for a stock, including any commissions

book-entry *Fin* an accounting entry indicated in a record somewhere but not represented by any document

book inventory *Fin* the number of items in stock according to accounting records. This number can be validated only by a physical count of the items.

bookkeeper *Fin* a person who is responsible for maintaining the financial records of a business

bookkeeping *Fin* the activity or profession of recording the money received and spent by an individual, business, or organisation

bookkeeping barter *Fin* the direct exchange of goods between two parties without the use of money as a medium, but using monetary measures to record the transaction

bookmark[1] *E-com* a web-browser software tool that enables users to select and store pages they are likely to return to, so that they can be accessed quickly and conveniently. On Microsoft Internet Explorer (the most popular web browser) this function is referred to as 'Favorites'.

bookmark[2] *Gen Mgt* to make a mental note to remember somebody or something for future reference (*slang*)

book of account *Fin* the ledgers and journals used in the preparation of financial statements

book of prime/original entry *Fin* a chronological record of a business's transactions arranged according to type, for example, cash or sales. The books are then used to generate entries in a double-entry bookkeeping system.

books of prime entry *Fin* a first record of transactions, such as sales or purchases, from which either detail or totals, as appropriate, are transferred to the ledgers

book-to-bill ratio *Fin* a ratio of the value of orders that a company has received to the amount for which it has billed its customers

book transfer *Fin* a transfer of ownership of a security without physical transfer of any document that represents the instrument

book value *Fin* the value of a company's stock according to the company itself, which may differ considerably from the market value. *Also known as* **carrying amount**, **carrying value**

EXAMPLE It is calculated by subtracting a company's liabilities and the value of its debt and preference shares from its total assets. All of these figures appear on a company's balance sheet. For example:

	£
Total assets	1,300
Current liabilities	−400
Long-term liabilities, preference shares	−250
Book value	**= 650**

Book value per share is calculated by dividing the book value by the number of shares in issue. If our example is expressed in millions of pounds and the company has 35 million shares outstanding, book value per share would be £650 million divided by 35 million:

650 / 35 = £18.57 book value per share

Book value represents a company's net worth to its shareholders. When compared with its market value, book value helps reveal how a company is regarded by the investment community. A market value that is notably higher than book value indicates that investors have a high regard for the company. A market value that is, for example, a multiple of book value suggests that investors' regard may be unreasonably high.

book value per share *Fin* the value of one share of a stock according to the company itself, which may differ considerably from the market value

Boolean search *E-com* a search allowing the inclusion or exclusion of documents containing certain words through the use of operators such as AND, NOT, and OR

boomerang worker *HR* an employee who returns to work for a previous employer (*slang*)

boot camp (*US*) *HR* an **induction** or orientation programme for new employees, designed to push recruits to their limits. Boot camps are modelled on the basic training of the US Marine Corps and aim to immerse new employees in the *corporate culture* of the employer, as well as transferring knowledge about technical skills.

bootstrapping *Gen Mgt* the early stages of setting up a new business, when a lot of effort is required (*slang*)

border crosser *HR* a multiskilled employee who is able to move from job to job within a company (*slang*)

borderless world *E-com* the global economy considered as having had barriers to international trade removed by use of the Internet

border tax adjustment *Fin* the application of a domestic tax on imported goods while exempting exported goods from the tax in an effort to make the exported goods' price competitive both nationally and internationally

borrowing costs *Fin* expenses, for example, interest payments, incurred from taking out a loan or any other form of borrowing. In the United States, such costs are included in the total cost of the asset whereas in the United Kingdom, and in International Accounting Standards, this is optional.

bosberaad (*S Africa*) *Gen Mgt* **1.** a *think tank*, *strategy*, or long-term planning meeting. *Also known as* **lekgotla 2.** a meeting of leaders at a remote place to avoid distractions. The word means literally 'bush summit'.

boss *Gen Mgt* the person in charge of a job, process, department, or organisation, more formally known as a *manager* or *supervisor*

Boston Box *Gen Mgt* a model used for analysing a company's potential by plotting *market share* against growth rate. The Boston Box was conceived by the Boston Consulting Group in the 1970s to help in the process of assessing in which businesses a company should invest and of which it should divest itself. A business with a high market share and high growth rate is a *star*, and one with a low market share and low growth rate is a *dog*. A high market share with low growth rate is characteristic of a *cash cow*, which could yield significant but short-term gain, and a low market share coupled with high growth rate produces a **question mark company**, which offers a doubtful return on investment. To be useful, this model requires accurate assessment of a business's strengths and weaknesses, which may be difficult to obtain.

Boston Consulting Group matrix *Fin* a representation of an organisation's product or service offerings which shows the value of product sales (depicted by the area of a circle) expressed in relation to the growth rate of the market served and the market share held. The objective of the matrix is to assist in the allocation of funds to projects.

bottleneck *Ops* a limiting factor on the rate of an operation. A workstation operating at its maximum *capacity* becomes a bottleneck if the rate of production elsewhere in the plant increases, but throughput at that workstation cannot be increased to meet demand. An understanding of bottlenecks is important if the efficiency and capacity of an *assembly line* are to be increased. The techniques of *fishbone charts*, **Pareto charts**, and *flow charts* can be used to identify where and why bottlenecks occur.

bottom fisher *Fin* an investor who searches for bargains among stocks that have recently dropped in price (*slang*)

bottom line 1. *Fin* the net profit or loss that a company makes at the end of a given period of time, used in the calculation of the earnings-per-share business ratio **2.** *Gen Mgt* work that produces net gain for an organisation

bottom-of-the-harbour scheme (*ANZ*) *Fin* a tax avoidance strategy that involves stripping a company of assets then selling it a number of times so that it is hard to trace

bottom out *Fin* to reach the lowest level in the downward trend of the market price of securities or commodities before the price begins an upward trend again

bottom-up *Fin* relating to an approach to investing that seeks to identify individual companies that are fundamentally sound and whose shares will perform well regardless of general economic or industry-group trends

bottom-up approach *Gen Mgt* a consultative *leadership* style that promotes *employee participation* at all levels in *decision-making* and *problem-solving*. A bottom-up approach to leadership is associated with *flat organisations* and the *empowerment* of employees. It can encourage *creativity* and flexibility and is the opposite of a *top-down approach*.

bottom-up budgeting *Fin see participative budgeting*

bought-in goods *Ops* components and sub-assemblies that are purchased from an outside supplier instead of being made within the organisation

bounce *Fin* to refuse payment of a cheque because the account for which it is written holds insufficient money (*slang*) *Also known as* **dishonour**

bounced cheque *Fin* a draft on an account that a bank will not honour, usually because there are insufficient funds in the account

bourse *Fin* a European stock exchange, especially the one in Paris

boutique investment house *Fin see* **niche player**

box
think outside the box *Gen Mgt* to think imaginatively about a problem (*slang*)

box spread *Fin* an arbitrage strategy that eliminates risk by buying and selling the same thing

Boyatzis, Richard Eleftherios (*b.* 1946) *Gen Mgt* US academic. One of the key movers of the *competence* movement. His book, *The Competent Manager* (1982), acknowledged *David McClelland*'s earlier work.

BPR *abbr Gen Mgt* business process re-engineering

bracket creep (*US*) *Fin* the way in which a gradual increase in income moves somebody into a higher tax bracket

Brady bond *Fin* a bond issued by an emerging nation that has US Treasury bonds as collateral

braindrain *Gen Mgt* the overseas migration of specialists, usually highly qualified scientists, engineers, or technical experts, in pursuit of higher salaries, better research funding, and a perceived higher quality of working life

brainiac *HR* a highly intelligent and creative employee who is also unpredictable and eccentric (*slang*)

brainstorming *Gen Mgt* a technique for generating ideas, developing *creativity*, or *problem-solving* in small groups, through the free-flowing contributions of participants. The concept of brainstorming was originated by A. F. Osborn and described in his book *Applied Imagination: Principles and Practices of Creative Thinking* (1957). To encourage the free flow of ideas, brainstorming sessions operate according to a set of guidelines, and the production and evaluation of ideas are kept separate. Several variations of brainstorming and related techniques have emerged such as **brainwriting**, where ideas are written down by individuals, and *buzz groups*.

brainwriting *Gen Mgt see* **brainstorming**

branch accounts *Fin* the *books of account* or *financial statements* for the component parts of a business, especially those that are located in a different region or country than the main enterprise

branch office *Fin* a bank or other financial institution that is part of a larger group and is located in a different part of a geographical area from the parent organisation

branch tax *Fin* a South African tax imposed on non-resident companies that register a branch rather than a separate company

brand *Mkting* the distinguishing proprietary name, symbol, or *trademark* that differentiates a particular product, or service, from others of a similar nature

brand awareness *Mkting* the level of *brand recognition* that consumers have of a particular brand and its specific product category. Brand awareness examines three levels of recognition: whether the brand name is the first to come to mind when a consumer is questioned about a particular product category; whether the brand name is one of several that come to mind when a consumer is questioned about a particular product category; and whether or not a consumer has heard of a particular brand name.

brand building *Mkting* the establishment and improvement of a brand's identity, including giving the brand a set of values that the consumer wants, recognises, identifies with, and trusts. Values developed in the process of brand building include psychological, physical, and functional properties that consumers desire and should always identify a property that is unique to that brand.

brand champion *Mkting* an employee of an organisation who is responsible for the development, performance, and communication of a particular brand

brand equity *Mkting* the estimated value of a *brand*

brand extension *Mkting* the exploitation, diversification, or stretching of a brand to revive or reinvigorate it in the marketplace. Products developed in the brand extension process may be directly recognisable derivatives or may look and feel completely different.

brand image *Mkting* the perception that consumers have of a brand. Brand image is usually carefully developed by the brand owner through marketing campaigns or product positioning. Occasionally, the image of a brand may develop spontaneously through customer responses to a product. The image of a brand can be seriously tarnished through inappropriate advertising or association with somebody or something that has fallen from public favour.

branding *Mkting* a means of distinguishing one firm's products or services from another's and of creating and maintaining an image that encourages confidence in the quality and performance of that firm's products or services

brand leader *Mkting* the brand with the largest *market share*

brand life cycle *Mkting* the three phases through which brands pass as they are introduced, grow, and then decline. The three stages of the brand life cycle are: the introductory period, during which the brand is developed and is introduced to the market; the growth period, when the brand faces competition from other products of a similar nature; and, finally, the maturity period in which the brand either extends to other products or its image is constantly updated. Without careful *brand management*, the maturity period can lead to decline and result in the brand being withdrawn. Similar stages can be observed in the *product life cycle*.

brand loyalty *Mkting* a long-term customer preference for a particular product or service. Brand loyalty can be produced by factors such as customer satisfaction with the performance or price of a specific product or service, or through identifying with a *brand image*. It can be encouraged by *advertising*.

brand management *Mkting* the marketing of one or more proprietary products. Brand managers (see *product management*) have responsibility for the promotion and marketing of one or more commercial brands. This includes setting targets, advertising, and retailing, and co-ordinating all related activities to achieve those targets. In the case of multiple brand management, consideration needs be given to questions relating to the treatment of the brands as equal or as having some differentiating value. This may affect the amount of resources committed to each brand.

brand manager *Mkting* see *brand management*

brand positioning *Mkting* the development of a brand's position in the market by heightening customer perception of the brand's superiority over other brands of a similar nature. Brand positioning relies on the identification of a real strength or value that has a clear advantage over the nearest competitor and is easily communicated to the consumer.

brand recognition *Mkting* a measurement of the ability of consumers to recall their experience or knowledge of a particular brand. Brand recognition forms part of *brand awareness*.

brand value *Mkting* the amount that a brand is worth in terms of income, potential income, reputation, prestige, and market value. Brands with a high value are regarded as considerable assets to a company, so that when a company is sold, a brand with high value may be worth more than any other consideration.

brand wagon *Mkting* the trend towards using branding in marketing concepts and techniques (*slang*)

brandwidth *Mkting* the degree to which a brand of product or service is recognised (*slang*)

Branson, Sir Richard (*b.* 1950) *Gen Mgt* British entrepreneur. Chairman of the Virgin Group, whose dominant *corporate strategy* has been to enter a variety of industries and challenge the existing leaders, using his flair for publicity. This *diversification* strategy is balanced by that of limiting *risk*. Branson's approach is explained in *Losing My Virginity: The Autobiography* (1998).

BRB *abbr Gen Mgt* be right back (*slang*)

breach of contract *Gen Mgt* a refusal or failure to carry out an obligation imposed by a *contract*

breadth-of-market theory *Fin* the theory that the health of a market is measured by the relative volume of items traded that are going up or down in price

breakeven *Mkting* the point at which revenue equals costs

breakeven analysis *Gen Mgt* a method for determining the point at which fixed and variable production costs are equalled by sales revenue and where neither a profit nor a loss is made. Usually illustrated graphically through the use of a *breakeven chart*, breakeven analysis can be used to aid *decision-making*, set product prices, and determine the effects of changes in production or sales volume on costs and profits.

breakeven chart *Gen Mgt* a management aid used in conjunction with *breakeven analysis* to calculate the point at which fixed and variable production costs are met by incoming revenue. Lines are plotted to indicate expected sales revenue and production costs. The point at which lines intersect marks the **breakeven point** where no profit or loss is made.

breakeven point *Fin* the point or level of financial activity at which expenditure equals income, or the value of an investment equals its cost so that the result is neither a profit nor a loss

breaking-down time *Fin* the period required to return a workstation to a standard condition after completion of an operation

breakout 1. *Fin* a rise in a security's price above its previous highest price, or a drop below its former lowest price, taken by technical analysts to signal a continuing move in that direction **2.** *Gen Mgt* a summary or breakdown of data that has been collected

breakthrough strategy *Gen Mgt* a strategy that achieves significant new results

break-up value *Fin* the combined market value of a firm's assets if each were sold separately as contrasted with selling the firm as an ongoing business. Analysts look for companies with a large break-up value relative to their market value to identify potential takeover targets.

Brech, Edward Francis Leopold (*b.* 1909) *Gen Mgt* British manager, writer, and historian. A publiciser and developer of the theories of **Henri Fayol** and **Frederick Winslow Taylor**, in common with **Lyndall Urwick**. Brech's *Principles and Practice of Management* (1953), sets down a structural and functional approach to management. In the 1990s, Brech completed a history of British management.

Bretton Woods *Econ* an agreement signed at a conference at Bretton Woods in the United States in July 1944 that set up the **IMF** and the **IBRD**

bribery *HR* the act of persuading somebody to exercise his or her business judgment in your favour by offering cash or a gift and thereby gaining an unfair advantage. Many organisations have **codes of conduct** that expressly forbid the soliciting or payment of bribes.

brick
hit the bricks (*US*) *Gen Mgt* to go out on strike (*slang*)

bricks-and-mortar *E-com* relating to a traditional business not involved in e-commerce

and incurring the cost of physical structures such as warehouses

bricolage *E-com* the opportunist way in which the Web is put together, with Web designers being able to take **GIFs**, formats, and links from elsewhere on the Web to create new pages

bridge financing *Fin* borrowing that the borrower expects to repay with the proceeds of later larger loans. *See also* **takeout financing**

bridge loan (*US*) *Fin* = **bridging loan**

bridging *Fin* the obtaining of a short-term loan to provide a continuing source of financing in anticipation of receiving an intermediate- or long-term loan. Bridging is routinely employed to finance the purchase or construction of a new building or property until an old one is sold.

bridging loan *Fin* a temporary loan providing funds until further money is received, for example, for buying one property while trying to sell another. *US term* **bridge loan**

brief *Mkting* a document or set of instructions issued to somebody as guidance in developing a marketing or advertising proposal. A brief should be as comprehensive as possible, covering all aspects of the project: background, objectives, research, media, competitors, product information, and the target audience at which it is aimed. If possible, the objectives should be measurable, so the success or otherwise of the project can be assessed.

briefing group *HR see* **team briefing**

Briggs, Katherine Cook (1875–1968) *Gen Mgt* US researcher. Inventor, together with her daughter, *Isabel Briggs-Myers*, of the **Myers-Briggs type indicator**.

Briggs-Myers, Isabel (1897–1980) *Gen Mgt* US researcher. Inventor, together with her mother, *Katherine Cook Briggs*, of the **Myers-Briggs type indicator**.

brightsizing *HR* the reduction of staff numbers within a company by making the mostly recently recruited employees redundant, an unintentional byproduct of which being that often the most highly capable or qualified employees are lost (*slang*)

bring forward *Fin* to carry a sum from one column or page to the next

Brisch system *Ops* a coding system developed principally for the engineering industry by E. G. Brisch and Partners in which a code is assigned to every item of resources, including materials, labour, and equipment.

British Accounting Association *Fin* in the United Kingdom, the main professional accounting body, founded in 1947. As well as promoting accounting education and research, it also organises conferences and publishes *The British Accounting Review*.

broadband *E-com* a class of transmission system that allows large amounts of data to be transferred at high speed

broadbanding *HR* the reworking of the pay hierarchy into fewer, wider *pay scales*. Broadbanding provides a more flexible reward structure that is more in tune with the *flat organisation*. Pioneered by GEC in the United States, the introduction of broadbanding can provide a method for pay increases and *career development*, even without a formal career ladder, and consequently can help improve *motivation*.

brochure *Fin* a booklet or pamphlet that contains descriptive information or advertising, for example, in relation to a product or property for sale, or an available service

brochureware *E-com* a website that is the on-line equivalent of a printed brochure providing information about products and services. The term is most often used in a derogatory way to refer to electronic advertising for planned but nonexistent products.

broker[1] *Gen Mgt* to act as an agent in arranging a deal, sale, or contract

broker[2] *Fin* a person who acts as a financial agent in arranging a deal, sale, or contract

brokerage *Fin* 1. a company whose business is buying and selling stocks and bonds for its clients 2. the business of being a broker 3. a fee paid to somebody who acts as a financial agent for somebody else

brokered market *Fin* a market in which brokers bring buyers and sellers together

broker loan rate *Fin* the interest rate that banks charge brokers on money that they lend for purchases on margin

Brown, Wilfred (1908–85) *Gen Mgt* British business executive. Chairman and managing director of the Glacier Metal Company who introduced *works councils* as an attempt at *industrial democracy*. During Brown's leadership, the Glacier Metal Company was used as the basis for the *Glacier studies*, carried out

by *Elliot Jaques* of the Tavistock Institute of Human Relations.

brownfield site *Gen Mgt* an industrial site, usually located in an urban area, that is abandoned, inactive, or underutilised because of real or perceived environmental contamination

brown goods *Mkting* electrical consumer goods used primarily for home entertainment, for example, televisions, radios, and hi-fis

browser *E-com* a piece of software that allows people to access the Internet and World Wide Web. Internet Explorer and Netscape Navigator are the most commonly used browsers.

B share *(ANZ) Fin* a share in a unit trust that has no front-end sales charge but carries a redemption fee, or back-end load, payable only if the share is redeemed. This load, called a CDSC, or contingent deferred sales charge, declines every year until it disappears, usually after six years.

BTI *abbr Fin* Business Times Industrial index

BTW *abbr Gen Mgt* by the way (*slang*)

bubble economy *Econ* an unstable boom based on speculation in shares, often followed by a financial crash. This happened, for example, in the 1630s in the Netherlands and in the 1720s in England.

bucket shop *Fin* a firm of brokers or dealers that sells shares of questionable value

bucket trading *Fin* an illegal practice in which a stockbroker accepts a customer's order but does not execute the transaction until it is financially advantageous to the broker but at the customer's expense

budget *Fin* a plan specifying how a company's or department's resources will be spent or allocated during a particular period

budget account *Fin* a bank account set up to control a person's regular expenditures, for example, the payment of insurance premiums, mortgage, utilities, or telephone bills. The annual expenditure for each item is paid into the account in equal monthly instalments, bills being paid from the budget account as they become due.

budgetary *Fin* relating to a detailed plan of financial operations, with estimates of both revenue and expenditures for a specific future period

---

Economics and ethics are not mutually exclusive. *Lionel Tiger*

budgetary control *Fin* the establishment of budgets relating the responsibilities of executives to the requirements of a policy, and the continuous comparison of actual with budgeted results, either to secure by individual action the objectives of that policy or to provide a basis for its revision

budget centre *Fin* a section of an entity for which control may be exercised and budgets prepared

budget committee *Fin* the group within an organisation responsible for drawing up budgets that meet departmental requirements, ensuring they comply with policy, and then submitting them to the board of directors

budget cost allowance *Fin* the budgeted cost ascribed to the level of activity achieved in a budget centre in a control period. It comprises variable costs in direct proportion to volume achieved and fixed costs as a proportion of the annual budget. *Also known as flexed budget*

budget deficit *Fin* the extent by which expenditure exceeds revenue. *Also known as deficit*

budget director *Fin* the person in an organisation who is responsible for running the budget system

budgeted capacity *Fin* an organisation's available output level for a budget period according to the budget. It may be expressed in different ways, for example, in machine hours or standard hours.

budgeted revenue *Fin* the income that an organisation expects to receive in a budget period according to the budget

budget lapsing *Fin* withdrawal of unspent budget allowance due to the expiry of the budget period

budget management *Fin* the comparison of actual financial results with the estimated expenditures and revenues for the given time period of a budget and the taking of corrective action as necessary

budget manual *Fin* a detailed set of documents providing guidelines and information about the budget process. A budget manual may include: a calendar of budgetary events; specimen budget forms; a statement of budgetary objective and desired results; a listing of budgetary activities; original, revised, and approved budgets; and budget assumptions regarding inflation, interest rates etc.

budget period *Fin* the period for which a budget is prepared and used, which may then be subdivided into control periods

budget slack *Fin* the intentional overestimation of expenses and/or underestimation of revenues in the budgeting process

budget surplus *Fin* the extent by which revenue exceeds expenditure. *Also known as surplus*

buffer inventory *Ops* the products or supplies of an organisation maintained on hand or in transit to stabilise variations in supply, demand, production, or lead time

buffer stock *Fin* a stock of materials, or of work in progress, maintained in order to protect user departments from the effect of possible interruptions to supply

Buffett, Warren (*b*. 1930) *Gen Mgt* US investment banker. Chairman and CEO of Berkshire Hathaway, a vehicle for investing his vast wealth realised from a unique and successful share-purchase strategy. Buffett, dubbed the 'sage of Omaha', is much admired by *Bill Gates*.

building society *Fin* a financial institution that offers interest-bearing savings accounts, the deposits being reinvested by the society in long-term loans, primarily mortgage loans for the purchase of property

bull *Fin* somebody who anticipates favourable business conditions, especially somebody who buys particular stocks or commodities in anticipation that their prices will rise, often with the expectation of selling them at a large profit at a later time. *See also bear*

bulldog (*US, Canada*) *Gen Mgt* to attack a problem relentlessly (*slang*)

bulletin board *E-com* a computer-based forum used by an interest group to allow members to exchange e-mails, chat online, and access software. *Also known as newsgroup*

bulletin board system *E-com see* **BBS**

bullet loan *Fin* a loan that involves specified payments of interest until maturity, when the principal is repaid

bullish *Fin* conducive to or characterised by buying stocks or commodities in anticipation of rising prices. *See also bearish*

bull market *Fin* a market in which prices are rising and in which a dealer is more likely to be a buyer than a seller. *See also bear market*

bullshit bingo *Gen Mgt* a game that involves counting how frequently words of incomprehensible jargon are used (*slang*)

If you tell the truth you don't have to remember anything.   *Mark Twain*

bull spread *Fin* a combination of purchases and sales of options for the same commodity or stock intended to produce a profit when the price rises. *See also* ***bear spread***

bullying *HR see* ***workplace bullying***

bump up *Gen Mgt* to upgrade somebody to a higher class of service than has been paid for, for example in an aeroplane or hotel (*slang*)

bundle *Mkting* to group together two or more products or services into a single package that is then offered to the consumer at one price, for example, by providing software with a personal computer

bundling *Mkting* the practice of grouping together two or more products or services into a single package that is then offered to the consumer at one price

Bundy (*ANZ*) *HR* a timing system that records the arrival and departure of employees at their place of work

Bundy off (*ANZ*) *HR* to clock off from work

Bundy on (*ANZ*) *HR* to clock on for work

bureaucracy *Gen Mgt* an ***organisation structure*** with a rigid hierarchy of ***personnel***, regulated by set rules and procedures. ***Max Weber*** believed that a bureaucracy was technically the most efficient form of organisation. He described a bureaucracy as an organisation structured around official functions that are bound by rules, each function having its own specified competence. The functions are structured into offices, which are organised into a hierarchy that follows technical rules and norms. Managers in a bureaucracy possess a rational-legal type of ***authority*** derived from the office they hold. Bureaucracies have been criticised for eradicating inspiration and ***creativity*** in favour of impersonality and the mundaneness and regularity of corporate life. This was best described in ***William Whyte***'s *The Organization Man*, published in 1956, in which the individual was taken over by the bureaucratic machine in the name of efficiency. A more recent and humorous interpretation of life in a bureaucracy has been depicted by ***Scott Adams*** in *The Dilbert Principle* (1996). The term bureaucracy has gradually become a pejorative synonym for excessive and time-consuming paperwork and administration. Bureaucracies fell subject to ***delayering*** and ***downsizing*** from the 1980s onwards, as the flatter organisation became the target structure to ensure swifter market response and organisational flexibility.

Burns, James MacGregor (*b*. 1918) *Gen Mgt* US political scientist. Noted in the business sphere for identifying two approaches to leadership, the ***transactional theory of leadership*** and the ***transformational theory of leadership***, described in his book *Leadership* (1978), which has an historical, social, and political perspective.

bush telegraph *Gen Mgt* a method of communicating information or rumours swiftly and unofficially by word of mouth or other means

Business Accounting Deliberation Council *Fin* in Japan, a committee controlled by the Ministry of Finance that is responsible for drawing up regulations regarding the consolidated financial statements of listed companies

Business Activity Statement *Fin* a standard document used in Australia to report the amount of ***GST*** and other taxes paid and collected by a business. *Abbr* **BAS**

business administration *Gen Mgt* **1.** a form of ***management***. Business administration is used as a synonym for management, notably in government or the public sector. This use has developed from the **administration school** of thought established by ***Henri Fayol***, which defines management activities as a set of processes. He argued that to manage was to plan, organise, co-ordinate, command, and control. These principles were put into exemplary practice by ***Alfred Sloan Jr*** at General Motors and are often seen as characteristic of large ***bureaucracies***. **2.** the establishment and maintenance of ***procedures***, records, and regulations in the pursuit of a commercial activity. Business administration involves the conduct of activities leading to, and resulting from, the delivery of a product or service to the customer. Administration is often seen as paperwork and form-filling, but it reaches wider than that to encompass the co-ordination of all the procedures that enable a product or service to be delivered, together with the keeping of records that can be checked to identify errors or opportunities for improvement.

business card *Fin* a small card printed with somebody's name, job title, business address, and contact numbers or e-mail address

business case *Gen Mgt* the essential value to the organisation of a proposal. A business case is made through the preparation and presentation of a business plan and is used to prevent ***blue-sky ideas*** taking root without justifiable or provable value to an organisation.

business cluster *Gen Mgt* a group of small firms from similar industries that team up and act as one body. Creating a business cluster enables firms to enjoy economies of scale usually only available to bigger competitors. Marketing costs can be shared and goods can be bought more cheaply. There are also networking advantages, in which small firms can share experiences and discuss business strategies.

business combinations *(US) Fin* acquisitions or mergers involving two or more enterprises

business continuity *Gen Mgt* the uninterrupted maintenance of business activities. Ensuring business continuity requires a proactive process of identifying essential business functions within an organisation and threats to those functions. Plans and procedures may then be put in place to ensure that key functions can continue whatever the circumstances. Plans may be drawn up, for example, for *contingency*, *disaster*, and *risk management*, or for *total loss control*.

Business Council of Australia *Gen Mgt* a national association of chief executives, designed as a forum for the discussion of matters pertaining to business leadership in Australia. *Abbr* **BCA**

business cycle *Econ* a regular pattern of fluctuation in national income, moving from upturn to downturn in about five years

business efficiency *Gen Mgt* a situation in which an organisation maximises benefit and profit, while minimising effort and expenditure. Maximisation of business efficiency is a balance between two extremes. Managed correctly, it results in reduced costs, waste, and duplication. *Max Weber*, who developed the concept of the *bureaucracy*, believed that efficiency was the goal of all bureaucratic organisations, which were designed to run like smooth machines. The greater the efficiency, the more impersonal, rational, and emotionally detached a bureaucracy becomes. The flatter organisations more prevalent today attempt to be more customer-responsive than efficient in this sense, and the notion of such an ordered and impersonal efficiency has lost favour in an era when *creativity* and *innovation* are valued as a *competitive advantage*.

business entity concept *Fin* the concept that financial accounting information relates only to the activities of the business entity and not to the activities of its owner(s)

business ethics *Gen Mgt* a system of moral principles applied in the commercial world.

Business ethics provide guidelines for acceptable behaviour by organisations in both their strategy formulation and day-to-day operations. An ethical approach is becoming necessary both for corporate success and a positive *corporate image*. Issues that have raised the profile of business ethics include the Guinness, Maxwell, Polly Peck, and Barings scandals in the United Kingdom, high profits and high executive salaries, and the reports by Sir Anthony Nolan on disclosure of information and standards in public life and *Sir Adrian Cadbury* on *corporate governance*. Following the publication of these reports and pressure from consumers for more ethical and responsible business practices, many organisations are choosing to make a public commitment to ethical business by formulating *codes of conduct* and operating principles. In doing so, they must translate into action the concepts of personal and corporate accountability, *corporate giving*, corporate governance, and *whistleblowing*. *Also known as* **morality in business**

business excellence *Gen Mgt see* **excellence**

business excellence model *Gen Mgt see* **EFQM Excellence Model**

business failure *Gen Mgt* an organisation that has gone bankrupt. A business that is at risk of failure may be saved by *turnaround management*, which identifies and deals with the reasons for decline. *Also known as* **failure**

business game *Gen Mgt* a type of *simulation game* in which a model of a business situation is explored competitively for the purpose of learning

business gift *Mkting* a present, usually from a supplier to a customer, often used to maintain good relations. Business gifts may range from a pen to a hamper and are often a form of *merchandising*. The acceptance of a business gift is often governed by an organisation's *code of conduct* and is often forbidden on the grounds that business gifts, particularly high-value ones, may be seen as an attempt to bribe.

business intelligence *Gen Mgt* any information that can be of strategic use to a business

business interruption insurance *Fin* a policy indemnifying an organisation for loss of profits and continuing fixed expenses when some insurable disaster, for example, a fire, causes the organisation to stop or reduce its activities. *Also known as* **consequential loss policy**

Labour is the superior of capital and deserves much the higher consideration.   *Abraham Lincoln*

business name *Fin* in the United Kingdom, the legal term for the name under which an organisation operates

business objective *Gen Mgt* a goal that an organisation sets for itself, for example, profitability, sales growth, or return on investment. These goals are the foundation upon which the strategic and operational policies adopted by the organisation are based.

business plan *Gen Mgt* a document describing the current activities of a business, setting out its aims and objectives and how they are to be achieved over a set period of time. A business plan may cover the activities of an organisation or a group of companies, or it may deal with a single department within the organisation. In the former case, it is sometimes referred to as a corporate plan. The sections of a business plan usually include a market analysis describing the target market, customers, and competitors, an operations plan describing how products and services will be developed and produced, and a financial section providing profit, budget, and cash flow forecasts, annual accounts, and financial requirements. Businesses may use a business plan internally as a framework for implementing strategy and improving performance or externally to attract investment or raise capital for development plans. A business plan may form part of the overall planning process, or *corporate planning*, within an organisation and be used for the implementation of corporate strategy.

business process re-engineering *Gen Mgt, Ops* the initiation and control of the change of *processes* within an organisation, in order to derive *competitive advantage* from improvement in the quality of products. Business process re-engineering was popularised by *Michael Hammer*. It requires a review and imaginative analysis of the processes currently used by the organisation. BPR, therefore, has similarities to *benchmarking*, as this review of processes can reveal critical points where significant improvements in *quality* can be made. Business process re-engineering was at the height of its popularity in the early-to mid-1990s. It has been criticised as one of the root causes of the bouts of *downsizing* and *delayering* that have affected many parts of industry. It has also received a negative press because few BPR projects have delivered the benefits expected of them. *Abbr* **BPR**

business property relief *Fin* in the United Kingdom, a reduction in the amount liable to inheritance tax on certain types of business property

business rates *Fin* in the United Kingdom, a tax on businesses calculated on the value of the property occupied. Although the rate of tax is set by central government, the tax is collected the local authority.

business risk *Fin* the uncertainty associated with the unique circumstances of a particular company, for example, the introduction of a superior technology, as they might affect the price of that company's securities

business school *Gen Mgt* a higher education institution that offers undergraduate and postgraduate courses in business-related subjects. Business schools provide courses of varying length and level, up to the *Master of Business Administration*. They cater for full-time students, but also offer part-time and *distance learning* to those already in employment. Subject coverage is broad, and courses cover all areas of business administration, management, technology, finance, and interpersonal skills.

business segment *Fin* a distinguishable part of a business or enterprise that is subject to a different set of risks and returns than any other part. Listed companies are required to declare in their annual reports certain information, for example, sales, profits, and assets, for each segment of an enterprise.

business strategy *Fin* a long-term approach to implementing a firm's business plans to achieve its business objectives

Business Times Industrial index *Fin* an index of 40 Singapore and Malaysian shares. *Abbr* **BTI**

business-to-business *E-com see* **B2B**

business-to-consumer *E-com see* **B2C**

business transfer relief *Fin* the tax advantage gained when selling a business for shares in stock of the company that buys it

business unit *Gen Mgt* a part of an organisation that operates as a distinct function, department, division, or stand-alone business. Business units are usually treated as a separate *profit centre* within the overall, owning business.

business web *E-com see* **b-web**

bust-up proxy proposal *Fin* an overture to a company's shareholders for a *leveraged buyout* in which the acquirer sells some of the company's assets in order to repay the debt used to finance the takeover

---

There is no end to what you can accomplish if you don't care who gets the credit.   *Florence Luscomb*

busymeet *Gen Mgt* a business meeting (*slang*)

butterfly spread *Fin* a complex option strategy based on simultaneously purchasing and selling calls at different exercise prices and maturity dates, the profit being the premium collected when the options are sold. Such a strategy is most profitable when the price of the underlying security is relatively stable.

button *E-com* an online interactive ad, smaller than the traditional **banner**, placed on a web page and linked to an external advertiser's site. Buttons are usually square in shape, represented to look like a push button, and located down the left or right edge of the page.

buy and hold *Fin* an investment strategy based on retaining securities for a long time

buy and write *Fin* an investment strategy involving buying stock and selling options to eliminate the possibility of loss if the value of the stock goes down

buy-back *Fin* the repurchase of bonds or shares, as agreed by contract

buy-down *Fin* the payment of principal amounts that reduce the monthly payments due on a mortgage

buyer *Fin* **1.** somebody who is in the process of buying something or who intends to buy something **2.** somebody whose job is to choose and buy goods, merchandise, services, or media time or space for a company, factory, shop, or advertiser

buyer expectation *Gen Mgt see* **customer expectation**

buyer's guide *Mkting* a document that offers information on a range of related products, usually from a number of different organisations

buyer's market *Fin* a situation in which supply exceeds demand, prices are relatively low, and buyers therefore have an advantage

buy in *Fin* to buy stock in a company so as to have a controlling interest. This is often done by or for executives from outside the company.

buying economies of scale *Fin* a reduction in the cost of purchasing raw materials and components or of borrowing money due to the increased size of the purchase

buying manager *Ops see* **purchasing manager**

buy on close *Fin* a purchase at the end of the trading day

buy one get one free *Mkting see* **BOGOF**

buy on opening *Fin* a purchase at the beginning of the trading day

buy or make *Ops see* **purchasing versus production**

buy out *Gen Mgt* **1.** to purchase the entire stock of, or controlling financial interest in, a company **2.** to pay somebody to relinquish his or her interest in a property or other enterprise

buy-out 1. *Gen Mgt* the purchase and **takeover** of an ongoing business. It is more formally known as an acquisition (see **merger**). If a business is purchased by managers or staff, it is known as a **management buy-out**. **2.** *Gen Mgt* the purchase of somebody else's entire stock ownership in a firm. It is more formally known as an acquisition (see **merger**). **3.** *HR* an option to transfer benefits of an occupational pension scheme on leaving a company

buy stop order *Fin* an order to buy stock when its price reaches a specified level

Buzan, Tony (*b.* 1942) *Gen Mgt* British writer. Originator of the **Mind Map**™, a technique he explained in *Use Your Head* (1974).

buzz group *Gen Mgt* a small discussion group formed for a specific task such as generating ideas, solving problems, or reaching a common viewpoint on a topic within a specific period of time. The use of buzz groups was first associated with J.D. Phillips and is sometimes known as the Phillips 66 technique. Large groups may be divided into buzz groups after an initial presentation in order to cover different aspects of a topic or maximise participation. Each group appoints a spokesperson to report the results of the discussion to the larger group. Buzz groups are a form of **brainstorming**.

buzzword-compliant *E-com* familiar with the latest Internet jargon (*slang*)

BV *abbr Fin* the Dutch term for a limited liability company

b-web *E-com* a business web, a group of complementary businesses that come together over the Internet. While each company retains its autonomous identity, the businesses work in unison to generate more income than they could do individually. Characteristics of b-webs include **extranets**, **viral marketing**, online marketplaces, and affiliate schemes. The term was originally used by Don Tapscott, David Ticoll, and Alex

Lowry in an article published by *eCompany Now* magazine.

by-bidder *Fin* somebody who bids at an auction solely to raise the price for the seller

Byham, William *Gen Mgt* US consultant and writer. Co-author of *Zapp! The Lightning of Empowerment* (1987), a modern fable in an industrial setting that popularised the benefits that *empowerment* can bring to the workplace.

bylaws *Fin* the rules that govern the oper-ation of an enterprise. In the United kingdom, they are known as the *articles of association*.

bypass trust *Fin* a trust that leaves money in a will in trust to people other than the prime beneficiary in order to gain tax advantage

by-product *Fin* output of some value that is produced incidentally in manufacturing something else. *See also joint products*

byte *E-com* a unit of computer memory equal to that needed to store a single character, now commonly a group of eight adjacent *bits*

CA *abbr Fin* chartered accountant

cache *E-com* a small memory bank inside a computer that stores all the images and text from every website visited. This speeds up the download time when an Internet user revisits a site.

CAD *abbr Ops* computer-aided design

Cadbury, Sir George Adrian Hayhurst (*b.* 1929) *Gen Mgt* British business executive. Former chairman of Cadbury Schweppes and, in the 1990s, chairman of the Committee on the Financial Aspects of *Corporate Governance*.

Cadbury, Sir Nicholas Dominic (*b.* 1940) *Gen Mgt* British industrialist. Chair of the Wellcome Trust, and past chair of Cadbury Schweppes. Sir Dominic Cadbury is celebrated for his oft-quoted dictum 'There is no such thing as a career path; it is crazy-paving and you have to lay it yourself'.

Cadbury Report *Fin* the report of the Cadbury Committee (conducted in December 1992) on the Financial Aspects of Corporate Governance. It was established to consider the following issues in relation to financial reporting and accountability, and to make recommendations on good practice: the responsibilities of executive and non-executive directors for reviewing and reporting performance to shareholders and other financially interested parties; and the frequency, clarity and form in which information should be provided; the case for audit committees of the board, including their composition and role; the principal responsibilities of the auditors and the extent and value of the audit; the links between shareholders, boards and auditors; and any other relevant matters. The report established a Code of Best Practice, and has been influential in the United Kingdom and overseas. *See also Corporate Governance Combined Code*

CAD/CAM *Gen Mgt* the integration of data and technologies from *computer-aided design* and *computer-aided manufacturing* into the entire design-to-manufacture cycle. Data from a combined CAD/CAM database can be used for the control of a totally automated computer-integrated manufacturing system.

CAE *abbr Ops* computer-aided engineering

call *Fin* an option to buy stock. *Also known as call option*

callable *Fin* a financial instrument with a call provision in its indenture

call centre *Gen Mgt* a department or business wholly focused on telephone enquiries. Call centres usually provide a centralised point of contact for an organisation and support *telephone selling*, *after-sales service*, telephone helplines, or information services either for a parent organisation or on a contract basis for other businesses.

called-up share capital *Fin* the amount which a company has required shareholders to pay on shares issued

calling line identification *Gen Mgt see computer telephony integration*

call money *Fin* money that brokers use for their own purchases or to help their customers buy on margin

call off *Fin* a system whereby inventory is held at the customer's premises, to be invoiced only on use

call option *Fin see call*

call payment *Fin* an amount that a company demands in partial payment for stock such as a rights issue that is not paid for at one time

call provision *Fin* a clause in an indenture that lets the issuer of a bond redeem it before the date of its maturity

CAM *abbr Ops* computer-aided manufacturing

campaign *Mkting* a programme of advertising and marketing activities with a specific objective

camp on the line *Gen Mgt* to wait on hold for a long time on the telephone (*slang*)

can (*US*) *HR* to dismiss somebody from employment (*slang*)

Canadian Institute of Chartered Accountants *Fin* in Canada, the principal professional accountancy body that is responsible for setting accounting standards. *Abbr* **CICA**

cap *Fin* an upper limit such as on a rate of interest for a loan

CAPA *abbr Fin* Confederation of Asian and Pacific Accountants: an umbrella organisation

---

Research is always incomplete.

for a number of Asia-Pacific accountancy bodies

capacity *Ops* the measure of the capability of a workstation or a plant to produce output. Capacity measures can focus on a variety of factors, which typically include: quantity, for example, the number of items produced over a given period; and scope, for example, the range of items produced by type or size.

capacity planning *Ops* the process of measuring the amount of work that can be completed within a given time and determining the necessary physical and human resources needed to accomplish it. Capacity planning uses *capacity utilisation* to ensure that the maximum amount of product is made and sold. The planning process involves a regulation process that identifies deviations from the plan, allowing corrective action to be taken. A *capacity requirements planning* program can aid in the process of capacity planning.

capacity ratios *Fin* measures of performance in the use of capacity.

EXAMPLE The more commonly used capacity levels are: full capacity—output (expressed in standard hours) that could be achieved if sales orders, supplies and workforce were available for all installed workplaces; practical capacity—full capacity less an allowance for known unavoidable volume losses; budgeted capacity—standard hours planned for the period, taking into account budgeted sales, supplies, workforce availability, and efficiency expected; and normal capacity.

On the following given data, the related ratios are set out below:

Full capacity standard hours	100
Practical capacity standard hours	95
Budgeted capacity (budgeted input hours, 90 at 90 per cent efficiency)	81
Actual input hours	85
Standard hours produced	68

Idle capacity ratio:
(**Practical capacity – budgeted capacity**) $\times$ **100/Practical capacity = (95 – 81)** $\times$ **100/95 = 15%**

This figure indicates the budgeted shortfall in capacity as a proportion of practical capacity.

capacity requirements planning *Gen Mgt, Ops* a computerised tracking process that translates production requirements into practical implications for manufacturing resources. Capacity requirements planning is part of manufacturing resource planning and is carried out after a manufacturing resource planning program has been run. This pro-

duces an **infinite capacity plan**, as it does not take account of the capacity constraints of each workstation. Where the process is extended to cover capacity requirements, a **finite capacity plan** is produced. This enables *loading* at each workstation to be smoothed and determines the need for additional resources.

capacity usage variance *Fin* the difference in gain or loss in a given period compared to budgeted expectations, caused because the hours worked were longer or shorter than planned

capacity utilisation 1. *Econ* the output of an economy, firm, or plant divided by its output when working at full capacity **2.** *Gen Mgt, Ops* a measure of the plant and equipment of a company or industry that is actually being used to produce goods or services. Capacity utilisation usually is the measure of output over a specific period, for example, the average output for a month, or at a given point in time, for example, on a given date. It can be expressed as a ratio, where utilisation = actual output/design capacity. This measure is used in both *capacity planning* and *capacity requirements planning* processes.

Caparo case *Fin* in England, a court decision taken by the House of Lords in 1990 that auditors owe a duty of care to present (and not prospective) shareholders as a body but not as individuals

capital *Fin* money that can be invested by an individual or organisation in order to make a profit

capital account *Fin* the sum of a company's capital at a particular time

capital allowances *Fin* in the United Kingdom and Ireland, an allowance against income or corporation tax available to businesses or sole traders who have purchased plant and machinery for business use. The rates are set annually and vary according to the type of fixed asset purchased, for example, whether it is machinery or buildings. This system effectively removes subjectivity from the calculation of depreciation for tax purposes.

capital appreciation *Fin* the increase in a company's or individual's wealth

capital appreciation fund *Fin* a unit trust that aims to increase the value of its holdings without regard to the provision of income to its owners

capital asset *Fin* an asset that is difficult to sell quickly, for example, land

capital asset pricing model *Econ* a model of the market used to assess the cost of capital for a company based on the rate of return on its assets.

EXAMPLE The capital asset pricing model (CAPM) holds that the expected return of a security or a portfolio equals the rate on a risk-free security plus a risk premium. If this expected return does not meet or beat a theoretical required return, the investment should not be undertaken. The formula used to create CAPM is:

Risk-free rate + (Market return – Risk-free rate) x Beta value = Expected return

The risk-free rate is the quoted rate on an asset that has virtually no risk. The market return is the percentage return expected of the overall market, typically a published index such as Standard & Poor's. The beta value is a figure that measures the volatility of a security or portfolio of securities, compared with the market as a whole. A beta of 1, for example, indicates that a security's price will move with the market. A beta greater than 1 indicates higher volatility, while a beta less than 1 indicates less volatility.

Say, for instance, that the current risk-free rate is 4%, and the S&P 500 index is expected to return 11% next year. An investment club is interested in determining next year's return for XYZ Software Ltd, a prospective investment. The club has determined that the company's beta value is 1.8. The overall stock market always has a beta of 1, so XYZ Software's beta of 1.8 signals that it is a more risky investment than the overall market represents. This added risk means that the club should expect a higher rate of return than the 11% for the S&P 500. The CAPM calculation, then, would be:

4% + (11% – 4%) x 1.8 = 16.6% Expected Return

What the results tell the club is that given the risk, XYZ Software Ltd has a required rate of return of 16.6%, or the minimum return that an investment in XYZ should generate. If the investment club does not think that XYZ will produce that kind of return, it should probably consider investing in a different company. *Abbr* **CAPM**

capital budget *Fin* a subsection of a company's master budget that deals with expected capital expenditure within a defined period. *Also known as* **capital expenditure budget**, **capital investment budget**

capital budgeting *Fin* the selection, appraisal, and monitoring of a business's fixed assets

capital commitment *Fin* the estimated amount of capital expenditure that is contracted for but not yet provided for and authorised by the directors of a company but not yet contracted for

capital consumption *Fin* in a given period, the total depreciation of a national economy's fixed assets based on replacement costs

capital controls *Econ* regulations placed by a government on the amount of capital residents may hold

capital cost allowance *Fin* a tax advantage in Canada for the depreciation in value of capital assets

capital costs *Fin* expenses on the purchase of fixed assets

capital deepening *Econ* more capital-intensive production that results when a country's **capital stock** increases but the numbers employed fall or remain constant

capital employed *Fin* the funds used by an entity for its operations. This can be expressed in various ways depending upon the purpose of the computation. For example, for operations evaluation, capital employed may be defined as the total value of non-current assets plus working capital, whereas for investor evaluation, owners' capital plus reserves may be used.

capital expenditure *Fin* an outlay of money, especially on fixed assets. *Also known as* **capital investment**

capital expenditure budget *Fin see* **capital budget**

capital flight *Fin* the transfer of large sums of money between countries to seek higher rates of return or to escape a political or economic disturbance

capital formation *Econ* addition to the stock of a country's **real capital** by investment in fixed assets

capital funding planning *Fin* the process of selecting suitable funds to finance long-term assets and working capital

capital gain *Fin* the financial gain made upon the disposal of an asset. The gain is the difference between the cost of its acquisition and net proceeds upon its sale.

capital gains distribution *Fin* a sum of money that, for example, a unit trust pays to its owners in proportion to the owners' share of the organisation's capital gains for the year

capital gains reserve *Fin* a tax advantage in Canada for money not yet received in payment for something that has been sold

capital gains tax *Fin* a tax on the difference between the gross acquisition cost and the net proceeds when an asset is sold. In the United Kingdom, this tax also applies when assets are given or exchanged, although each individual has an annual capital gains tax allowance that exempts gains within that tax year below a stated level. In addition, certain assets may be exempt, for example, a person's principal private residence and transfers of assets between spouses, and the tax may not be levied on the absolute gain. An adjustment is made for inflation and the length of time that the asset has been held. There are also concessions on the sale of a business at retirement. *Abbr* **CGT**

capital gearing *Fin* the amount of fixed-cost debt that a company has for each of its ordinary shares

capital goods *Econ* stocks of physical or financial assets that are capable of generating income

capital inflow *Econ* the amount of capital that flows into an economy from services rendered abroad

capital instruments *Fin* the means that an organisation uses to raise finance, for example, the issue of shares or debentures

capital-intensive *Fin* using a greater proportion of capital as opposed to labour

capital investment *Fin* see *capital expenditure*

capital investment appraisal *Fin* the application of a set of methodologies (generally based on the discounting of projected cash flows) whose purpose is to give guidance to managers with respect to decisions as to how best to commit long-term investment funds. *See also* **discounted cash flow**

capital investment budget *Fin* see *capital budget*

capitalisation *Fin* **1.** the amount of money invested in a company or the worth of the bonds and stocks of a company **2.** the conversion of a company's reserves into capital through a scrip issue

capitalisation issue *Fin* a proportional issue of free shares to existing shareholders. *US term* **stock split**

capitalisation rate *Fin* the rate at which a company's *reserves* are converted into capital by way of a *capitalisation issue*

capitalisation ratio *Fin* the proportion of a company's value represented by debt, stock, assets, and other items.

EXAMPLE By comparing debt to total capitalisation, these ratios provide a glimpse of a company's long-term stability and ability to withstand losses and business downturns.

A company's capitalisation ratio can be expressed in two ways:

= Long-Term Debt / Long-Term Debt + Owners' Equity

and

= Total Debt / Total Debt + Preferred + Common Equity

For example, a company whose long-term debt totals £5,000 and whose owners hold equity worth £3,000 would have a capitalisation ratio of:

5,000 / (5,000 + 3,000) = 5,000 /8,000 = 0.625 capitalisation ratio

Both expressions of the ratio are also referred to as 'component percentages', since they compare a firm's debt with either its total capital (debt plus equity) or its equity capital. They readily indicate how reliant a firm is on debt financing.

Capitalisation ratios need to be evaluated over time, and compared with other data and standards. Care should be taken when comparing companies in different industries or sectors. The same figures that appear to be low in one industry can be very high in another.

capitalise *Fin* **1.** to finance the vehicles, plant, etc. of a business. **2.** to include money spent on the purchase of an asset as an element in a balance sheet

capitalism *Econ* an economic and social system in which individuals can maximise profits because they own the means of production

capitalist *Fin* an investor of capital in a business

capital lease (*US*) *Gen Mgt* = *finance lease*

capital levy *Fin* a tax on fixed assets or property

capital loss *Fin* a loss made through selling an asset for less than its cost

capital maintenance concept *Fin* a concept used to determine the definition of profit, that provide the basis for different systems of inflation accounting

---

capital market *Fin* a financial market dealing with securities that have a life of more than one year

capital project *Ops* see *capital project management*

capital project management *Gen Mgt* control of a *project* that involves expenditure of an organisation's monetary resources for the purpose of creating *capacity* for *production*. Capital project management often involves the organisation of major construction or engineering work. **Capital projects** are usually large scale, complex, need to be completed quickly, and involve capital investment. Different techniques have evolved for capital project management from those used for normal *project management*, including methods for managing the complexity of such projects, and for analysing return on investment afterwards.

capital property *Fin* under Canadian tax law, assets that can depreciate in value or be sold for a capital gain or loss

capital ratio *Fin* a company's income expressed as a fraction of its tangible assets

capital rationing *Fin* the restriction of new investment by a company

capital redemption reserve *Fin* an account required to prevent a reduction in capital, where a company purchases or redeems its own shares out of distributable profits

capital reserves *Fin* a former name for *undistributable reserves*

capital resource planning *Fin* the process of evaluating and selecting long-term assets to meet strategies

capital stock *Fin* the stock authorised by a company's charter, representing no ownership rights

capital structure *Fin* the proportions of a company's assets and liabilities of various sorts, especially long-term debt

capital sum *Fin* a lump sum of money that an insurer pays, for example, on the death of the insured person

capital surplus *Fin* the value of all of the stock in a company that exceeds the par value of the stock

capital transactions *Fin* transactions affecting non-current items such as fixed assets, long-term debt, or share capital, rather than revenue transactions

capital transfer tax *Fin* in the United Kingdom, a tax on the transfer of assets that was replaced in 1986 by inheritance tax

capital turnover *Fin* the value of annual sales as a multiple of the value of the company's stock

capital widening *Econ* less capital-intensive production that results when both a country's *capital stock* and the numbers employed increase

CAPM *abbr* **1.** *Fin* capital asset pricing model **2.** *Ops* computer-aided production management

captive finance company *Fin* an organisation that provides credit and is owned or controlled by a commercial or manufacturing company, for example, a retailer that owns its store card operation or a car manufacturer that owns a company for financing the vehicles it produces

captive insurance company *Fin* an insurance company that has been established by a parent company to underwrite all its insurance risks and those of its subsidiaries. The benefit is that the premiums paid do not leave the organisation. Many captive insurance companies are established offshore for tax purposes.

capture *E-com* the submission of a credit card transaction for processing and settlement. Capture initiates the process of moving funds from the *issuer* to the *acquirer*.

carbon copy *E-com* see *cc*

cardholder *E-com* an individual or company that has an active credit card account with an *issuer* with which transactions can be initiated

card-issuing bank *E-com* see *issuer*

card-not-present merchant account *E-com* an account that permits e-merchants to process credit card transactions without the purchaser being physically present for the transaction

career anchor *HR* a guiding force that influences people's career choices, based on self-perception of their own skills, *motivation*, and values. The term was coined by *Edgar Schein* in *Career Anchors: Discovering Your Real Values*, published in 1985. He believed that people develop one underlying anchor, perhaps subconsciously, that they are unwilling to give up when faced with different pressures. Schein distinguishes several career anchor groups such as technical/functional competence, managerial *competence*, *creativity*, security or stability, and autonomy.

career break *HR* a planned interruption to working life, usually for a predetermined period of time. A career break is usually designed either to aid *career development* or to enable somebody to balance work and family life. It may take the form of parental leave, or a *sabbatical* for study, research, or exploring alternative activities. A career break may be sanctioned by an employer or taken without the support of an employer.

career change *HR* a switch in profession or in type of job, often to a different employer. Career change may be planned as part of the *CPD* or *career development* processes, or it may be forced on an employee by *redundancy*, ill-health, or a change in personal circumstance.

career development *HR* progression through a sequence of jobs, involving continually more advanced or diverse activities and resulting in wider or improved skills, greater responsibility and prestige, and higher income. Formerly, career development was seen as the responsibility of the employer, and many organisations had formal career development programmes that marked an employee's advancement through the levels of management. It is now more usually held to be the responsibility of the employees, sometimes as part of the *CPD* process.

career ladder *HR* a sequence of posts from most junior to most senior within an organisation or department. A career ladder provides a structured path for an employee to climb up through an organisation. It is most typical of *bureaucracies*, as *flat organisation* structures tend not to be hierarchical to the same extent.

career-limiting move *HR see* **CLM**

career path *HR* a planned, logical progression of jobs within one or more professions throughout working life. A career path can be planned with greater assurance in market conditions of stability and little change. In times of great change and uncertainty, some people, such as *Dominic Cadbury*, have argued that there is no longer such a thing as a planned career path and instead place greater emphasis on the importance of *CPD* in order to maintain *employability*.

career pattern *HR* the sequence of jobs undertaken by somebody during his or her working life. A career pattern can be structured in advance as part of *career development* planning, and may allow for *career breaks* or *career changes*. Career patterns can also be discerned more generally as trends in employee development within particular sectors of the *labour force*.

careline *Mkting* a telephone service allowing customers to obtain information, advice, or assistance from retailers

caring economy *Econ* an economy based on amicable and helpful relationships between businesses and people

Carnegie, Dale Breckinridge (1888–1955) *Gen Mgt* US writer and trainer. Best known for his advice on self-improvement, which focused on *interpersonal communication* and effective *communication skills*, including public speaking. Carnegie's best-seller, *How to Win Friends and Influence People* (1936), included guidance on never criticising, complaining about, or condemning another person, giving sincere appreciation to others, and stimulating in others a specific desire in order to motivate them.

carriage inwards *Fin* delivery expenses incurred through the purchase of goods

carriage outwards *Fin* delivery expenses incurred through the sale of goods

carrier *Gen Mgt* a telecommunications company that provides network infrastructure services and charges customers for carrying their communications over the network. Carriers do not necessarily own their own network, but may rent time on a number of networks.

carrier's note *Fin see* **delivery note**

carrying amount *Fin see* **book value**

carrying cost *Fin* expenses associated with holding stock for a given period, for example, from the time of delivery to the time of despatch. These will include storage and insurance.

carrying value *Fin see* **book value**

cartel *Fin* an alliance of business companies formed to control production, competition, and prices

cartogram *Stats* a diagrammatic map on which statistical information is represented by shading and symbols

cash *Fin* money in the form of banknotes and coins that are legal tender

---

The test for whether or not you can hold a job should not be the arrangement of your chromosomes.
Bella Abzug

cash account *Fin* a brokerage account that permits no buying on margin

cash accounting *Fin* **1.** an accounting method in which receipts and expenses are recorded in the accounting books in the period when they actually occur. *See also accrual concept* **2.** in the United Kingdom, a system for Value Added Tax that enables the tax payer to account for tax paid and received during a given period, thus allowing automatic relief for bad debts

cash advance *Fin* a loan on a credit card account

cash and carry *Gen Mgt see wholesaler*

cash at bank *Fin* the total amount of money held at the bank by an individual or company

cash available to invest *Fin* the amount, including cash on account and balances due soon for outstanding transactions, that a client has available for investment with a broker

cashback *Mkting* a sales promotion technique offering customers a cash refund after they buy a product

cash basis *Fin* the bookkeeping practice of accounting for money only when it is actually received or spent

cash bonus *Fin* an unscheduled dividend that a company declares because of unexpected income

cashbook *Fin* a book in which all cash payments and receipts are recorded. In a double-entry bookkeeping system, the balance at the end of a given period is included in the trial balance and then transferred to the balance sheet itself.

cash budget *Fin* a detailed budget of estimated cash inflows and outflows incorporating both revenue and capital items

cash contract *Fin* a contract for actual delivery of a commodity

cash conversion cycle *Fin* the time between the acquisition of a raw material and the receipt of payment for the finished product. *Also known as* **cash cycle**

cash cow 1. *Fin* a subsidiary enterprise that performs well and consistently makes a substantial profit (*slang*) **2.** *Gen Mgt see* **Boston Box 3.** *Mkting* a product that sells well and makes a substantial profit without requiring much advertising or investment (*slang*)

cash crop *Econ* a crop, for example, tobacco, that can be sold for cash, usually by a developing country

cash cycle *Fin see* **cash conversion cycle**

cash deficiency agreement *Fin* a commitment to supply whatever additional cash is needed to complete the financing of a project

cash discount *Fin* a discount offered to a customer who pays for goods or services with cash, or who pays an invoice within a particular period

cash dividend *Fin* a share of a company's current earnings or accumulated profits distributed to shareholders

cash equivalents *Fin* short-term investments that can be converted into cash immediately and that are subject to only a limited risk. There is usually a limit on their duration, for example, three months.

cash float *Fin* notes and coins held by a retailer for the purpose of supplying customers with change

cash flow *Fin* the movement of money through an organisation that is generated by its own operations as opposed to borrowing. It is the money that a business actually receives from sales (the cash inflow) and the money that it pays out (the cash outflow).

cash-flow coverage ratio *Fin* the ratio of income to cash obligations

cash-flow life *HR* a lifestyle characterised by working for individual project fees rather than a regular salary

cash flow per common share *Fin* the amount of cash that a company has for each of its ordinary shares

cash-flow risk *Fin* the risk that a company's available cash will not be sufficient to meet its financial obligations

cash-flow statement *Fin* a record of a company's cash inflows and cash outflows over a specific period of time, typically a year. EXAMPLE It reports funds on hand at the beginning of the period, funds received, funds spent, and funds remaining at the end of the period. Cash flows are divided into three categories: cash from operations; cash-investment activities; and cash-financing activities. Companies with holdings in foreign currencies use a fourth classification: effects of changes in currency rates on cash.

A standard direct cash-flow statement looks like this:

CRD Ltd
Statement of Cash Flows
For year ended 31 December 20__

CASH FLOWS FROM OPERATIONS

	£
Operating Profit	82,000
Adjustments to net earnings	
Depreciation	17,000
Accounts receivable	(20,000)
Accounts payable	12,000
Inventory	(8,000)
Other adjustments to earnings	4,000
Net cash flow from operations	**87,000**

CASH FLOWS FROM INVESTMENT ACTIVITIES

Purchases of marketable securities	(58,000)
Receipts from sales of marketable securities	45,000
Loans made to borrowers	(16,000)
Collections on loans	11,000
Purchases of plant and land and property assets	(150,000)
Receipts from sales of plant and land and property assets	47,000
Net cash flow from investment activities:	**(–121,000)**

CASH FLOWS FROM FINANCING ACTIVITIES

Proceeds from short-term borrowings	51,000
Payments to settle short-term debts	(61,000)
Proceeds from issuing bonds payable	100,000
Proceeds from issuing capital stock	80,000
Dividends paid	(64,000)
Net cash flow from financing activities	**106,000**
Net change in cash during period	**72,000**
Cash and cash equivalents, beginning of year	27,000
Cash and cash equivalents, end of year	99,000

cash-generating unit *Fin* the smallest identifiable group of assets that generates cash inflows and outflows that can be measured

cashless pay *HR* the payment of a weekly or monthly wage through the electronic transfer of funds directly into the bank account of an *employee*

cashless society *Econ* a society in which all bills and debits are paid by electronic money

media, for example, bank and credit cards, direct debits, and online payments

cash loan company (*S Africa*) *Fin* a micro-lending business that provides short-term loans without collateral, usually at high interest rates

cash management models *Fin* sophisticated cash-flow forecasting models which assist management in determining how to balance the cash needs of an organisation. Cash management models might help in areas such as optimising cash balances, in the management of customer, supplier, investor, and company investment needs, in the decision as to invest or buy back shares, or in the decision as to the optimum method of financing working capital.

cash offer *Fin* an offer to buy a company for cash rather than for stock

cash payments journal *Fin* a chronological record of all the payments that have been made from a company's bank account

cash ratio *Fin* the ratio of a company's liquid assets such as cash and securities divided by total liabilities. *Also known as* **liquidity ratio**

cash receipts journal *Fin* a chronological record of all the receipts that have been paid into a company's bank account

cash sale *Fin* a sale in which payment is made immediately in cash rather than put on credit

cash settlement *Fin* **1.** an immediate payment on an options contract without waiting for expiry of the normal, usually five-day, settlement period **2.** the completion of a transaction by paying for securities

cash surrender value *Fin* the amount of money that an insurance company will pay to terminate a policy at a particular time if the policy does not continue until its normal expiry date

casual worker *HR* somebody who provides labour or services under an irregular or informal working arrangement. A casual worker is usually considered as an independent contractor rather than an *employee*. Consequently, there is no obligation on the part of an employer to provide work, and there is no obligation on the part of the casual worker to accept all offers of work made by an employer.

category management *Mkting* the process of manufacturers and retailers working together to maximise profits and enhance customer value in any given product category. Category management has developed from **brand management** and the techniques of efficient consumer response, and is most prevalent in the fast-moving consumer goods sector. It is founded on the assumption that consumer purchase decisions are made from a range of products within a category and not merely by **brand** and has gained in prominence, as it is believed to meet customer needs better than standard brand management. *Abbr* **CM**

causality *Stats* the relation of events to the effects they produce

cause and effect diagram *Gen Mgt see fishbone chart*

CBD *abbr Gen Mgt* central business district: the area of a city where most company offices are located

cc *abbr E-com* carbon copy: a function included on most e-mail programs that enables Internet users to send a copy of the same message to as many people as they choose. All they need to do is place the e-mail addresses of intended recipients in the cc address line. Recipients see all other names. To conceal names, the **bcc** address line can be used.

CC *abbr (S Africa) Fin* close corporation

CCA *abbr Fin* current-cost accounting

CCAB *abbr Fin* Consultative Committee of Accountancy Bodies

ccc *abbr Fin* cwmni cyfyngedig cyhoeddus: the Welsh term for a public limited company

ceiling effect *Stats* the occurrence of clusters of scores near the upper limit of the data in a statistical study

cellular manufacturing *Ops see group technology*

cellular organisation *Ops* a form of organisation consisting of a collection of self-managing firms or cells held together by mutual interest. A cellular organisation is built on the principles of self-organisation, member ownership, and entrepreneurship. Each cell within the organisation shares common features and purposes with its sister cells but is also able to function independently. The idea is an extension of the principles of **group technology**, or cellular manufacturing.

cellular production *Ops see* **group technology**

census *Stats* a study in which every member of a population is observed

central bank *Econ* the bank of a country that controls its credit system and its money supply

central business district *Gen Mgt see* **CBD**

centralisation *Gen Mgt* the gathering together, at a corporate headquarters, of specialist functions such as finance, personnel, and information technology. Centralisation is usually undertaken in order to effect economies of scale and to standardise operating procedures throughout the organisation. Centralised management can become cumbersome and inefficient and may produce communication problems. Some organisations have shifted towards **decentralisation** to try to avoid this.

centralised purchasing *Ops* the control by a central department of all the purchasing undertaken within an organisation. In a large organisation centralised purchasing is often located within the headquarters. Centralisation has the advantages of reducing duplication of effort, pooling volume purchases for discounts, enabling more effective inventory control, consolidating transport loads to achieve lower costs, increasing skills development in purchasing personnel, and enhancing relationships with **suppliers**.

Central Provident Fund *HR* in Singapore, a retirement benefit scheme. All employees and employers make compulsory contributions each month. *Abbr* **CPF**

Centrelink *Gen Mgt* an Australian government authority responsible for providing access to government services, including social security allowances and employment schemes. Established in 1997, it maintains a network of around 1,000 outlets.

CEO *abbr Gen Mgt* chief executive officer

CEO churning *Gen Mgt* the rapid rate at which chief executive officers are often removed from their posts (*slang*)

certainty equivalent method *Fin* an approach to dealing with risk in a capital budgeting context. It involves expressing risky future cash flows in terms of the certain cash flow which would be considered, by the decision-maker, as their equivalent.

certificate *Fin* a document representing partial ownership of a company that states the

---

number of shares that the document is worth and the names of the company and the owner of the shares

certificate authority *E-com* an independent organisation that verifies the identity of a purchaser or merchant and issues a *digital certificate* attesting to this for use in e-commerce transactions

certificate of deposit *Fin* a negotiable instrument which provides evidence of a fixed-term deposit with a bank. Maturity is normally within 90 days, but can be longer.

certificate of incorporation *Fin* in the United Kingdom, a written statement by the Registrar of Companies confirming that a new company has fulfilled the necessary legal requirements for incorporation and is now legally constituted

certificate to commence business *Fin* in the United Kingdom, a written statement issued by the Registrar of Companies confirming that a public limited company has fulfilled the necessary legal requirements regarding its authorised minimum share capital

certified accountant *Fin* an accountant trained in industry, the public service, or in the offices of practising accountants, who is a member of the Association of Chartered Certified Accountants. Although they are not chartered accountants, they fulfil much the same role and they are qualified to audit company records.

certified public accountant (*US*) *Fin* an accountant trained in industry, the public service, or in the offices of practising accountants, who is a member of the American Institute of Certified Public Accountants. Although they are not chartered accountants, they fulfil much the same role and they are qualified to audit company records.

cessation *Fin* the discontinuation of a business for tax purposes or its trading on the stock market

CFO *abbr Gen Mgt* chief financial officer

CFR *abbr E-com* cost and freight

CGI Joe *HR* a computer programmer who lacks social skills and charisma. The term is modelled on 'GI Joe', a word for a US soldier that dates from the second world war; its first part is an abbreviation of 'computer generated imagery'. (*slang*)

CGT *abbr Fin* capital gains tax

chaebol *Gen Mgt see* **keiretsu**

chain of command *HR* the line of authority in a hierarchical organisation through which instructions pass. The chain of command usually runs from the most senior personnel, through all reporting links in an organisation's or department's structure, to a targeted person or to front-line employees. *Line management* relies on the chain of command in order for instructions to pass throughout an organisation.

chainsaw consultant *HR* an outside expert brought into a company to reduce staff levels (*slang*)

chair *Gen Mgt* the most senior executive in an organisation. The chair of an organisation is responsible for running the *AGM*, and meetings of the *board of directors*. He or she may be a figurehead, appointed for prestige or power, and may have no role in the day-to-day running of the organisation. Sometimes the roles of chair and *chief executive* are combined, and the chair then has more control over daily operations; sometimes the chair is a retired chief executive. In the United States, the person who performs this function is often called a **president**. Historically, the term **chairman** was more common. The terms **chairwoman** or **chairperson** are later developments, although chair is now the most generally acceptable. Chairman, however, remains in common use, especially in the corporate sector.

chairman *Gen Mgt see* **chair**

chairman's report *or* **chairman's statement** *Fin* a statement included in the annual report of most large companies in which the chair of the board of directors gives an often favourable overview of the company's performance and prospects

chairperson *Gen Mgt see* **chair**

chairwoman *Gen Mgt see* **chair**

Champy, James (*b.* 1942) *Gen Mgt* US consultant. *See also* **Hammer, Michael**

Chandler, Alfred (*b.* 1918) *Gen Mgt* US academic. Pioneer of business history who established a framework and rationale for the subject and suggested that the main function of an organisation is to implement *strategy*. In *Strategy and Structure* (1962), he argued that the optimum use of resources stemmed not merely from the way they were organised but, more importantly, from the organisation's strategic goals. He concluded that organisational structures are driven by the changing demands and pressures of the marketplace, and that market-driven organisations favour a loosely coupled divisional structure.

change agent *Gen Mgt see change management*

change management *Gen Mgt* the co-ordination of a structured period of transition from situation A to situation B in order to achieve lasting change within an organisation. Change management can be of varying scope, from *continuous improvement*, which involves small ongoing changes to existing processes, to radical and substantial change involving organisational strategy. Change management can be reactive or proactive. It can be instigated in reaction to something in an organisation's external environment, for example, in the realms of economics, politics, legislation, or competition, or in reaction to something within the processes, structures, people, and events of the organisation's internal environment. It may also be instigated as a proactive measure, for example, in anticipation of unfavourable economic conditions in the future. Change management usually follows five steps: recognition of a trigger indicating that change is needed; clarification of the end point, or 'where we want to be'; planning how to achieve the change; accomplishment of the transition; and maintenance to ensure the change is lasting. Effective change management involves alterations on a personal level, for example, a shift in attitudes or work routines, and thus personnel management skills such as *motivation* are vital to successful change. Other important influences on the success of change management include leadership style, communication, and a unified positive attitude to the change among the workforce. *Business process re-engineering* is one type of change management, involving the redesign of processes within an organisation to raise performance. **Change agents** are those people within an organisation who are leaders and champions of the change process. With the accelerating pace of change in the business environment in the 1990s and 2000s, change has become accepted as a fact of business life and is the subject of books on management.

changeover time *Fin* the period required to change a workstation from a state of readiness for one operation to a state of readiness for another

channel *Mkting* a method of selling and distributing products to customers, directly or through intermediaries. Channels include direct sales, retail outlets, the Internet, and wholesalers.

channel communications *Mkting* communications aimed at organisations that sell and distribute products to customers, for example, retailers, sales teams, or wholesalers

channel management *Mkting* the organisation of the ways in which companies reach and satisfy their customers. Channel management involves more than just distribution and has been described as management of how and where a product is used and of how the customer and the product interact. Channel management covers processes for identifying key customers, communicating with them, and continuing to create value after the first contact.

channel strategy *Mkting* a management technique for determining the most effective method of selling and distributing products to customers

channel stuffing *Fin* the artificial boosting of sales at the end of a financial year by offering distributors and dealers incentives to buy a greater quantity of goods than they actually need (*slang*)

channel support *Mkting* marketing or financial support aimed at improving the performance of organisations that sell and distribute products to customers, for example, retailers, sales teams, or wholesalers

chaos 1. *Gen Mgt* a situation of unpredictability and rapid change. **Chaos theory** emerged in the 1970s as a mathematical concept that defied the theory of cause and effect to assert that behaviour is essentially random. Such writers as *Tom Peters*, who wrote *Thriving on Chaos* in 1987, have applied the theory to management, arguing that attempts to plan and control management processes are fundamentally doomed to failure and that, instead, managers should embrace change and flexibility in order to cope with an environment that is altering at an ever-increasing rate. **2.** *Stats* a situation in which a deterministic model displays behaviour that appears to be random

chaos theory *Gen Mgt see chaos*

CHAPS *abbr Fin* Clearing House Automated Payment System: a method for the rapid electronic transfer of funds between participating banks on behalf of large commercial customers, where transfers tend to be of significant value

Chapter 11 *Fin* the US Bankruptcy Reform Act (1978) that entitles enterprises experi-

---

When I saw something that needed doing, I did it. *Nellie Cashman*

encing financial difficulties to apply for protection from creditors and thus have an opportunity to avoid bankruptcy

charge *Fin* a legal interest in land or property created in favour of a creditor to ensure that the amount owing is paid off

chargeable assets *Fin* in the United Kingdom, assets that are subject to *capital gains tax*. Exempt assets include an individual's principal private residence, investments held within a PEP or ISA, and gilts and individual chattels worth no more than a certain sum.

chargeable gain *Fin* in the United Kingdom, a profit from the sale of an asset that is subject to *capital gains tax*

chargeable transfer *Fin* in the United Kingdom, gifts that are liable to inheritance tax. Under UK legislation, individuals may gift assets to a certain value during their lifetime without incurring any liability to inheritance tax. These are regular transfers out of income that do not affect the donor's standard of living. Additionally, individuals may transfer up to £3,000 a year out of capital. If this exemption is not used in one year, or is only partially used, then the unused allowance may be carried forward to the next year providing the full exemption is then used. Each person may also make small annual gifts of up to £250 per donee. Additionally a parent may give up to £5,000 on the occasion of an offspring's marriage, while a grandparent or more remote ancestor may give up to £2,500, and any other person up to £1,000. Other outright gifts during a lifetime to an individual, and certain types of trust, are known as **potentially exempt transfers**: there is no inheritance tax to be paid on these at the time of the gift, but a liability arises if the donor dies within seven years, with that liability decreasing the longer the donor survives. If the donor dies within seven years of the gift, then potentially exempt transfers become chargeable transfers for inheritance tax purposes.

charge account *Fin* a facility with a retailer that enables the customer to buy goods or services on credit rather than pay in cash. The customer may be required to settle the account within a month to avoid incurring interest on the credit. *Also known as* **credit account**

charge and discharge accounting *Fin* formerly, a bookkeeping system in which a person charges himself or herself with receipts and credits himself or herself with payments. This system was used extensively in medieval times before the advent of double-entry bookkeeping.

charismatic authority *Gen Mgt* a style of *leadership* based on the leader's exceptional personal qualities. Charismatic authority is one of *Max Weber*'s three types of legitimate *authority*. A charismatic leader is set apart from others by special qualities that inspire employees to follow and obey of their own free will. This is similar to the *great man theory* of leadership.

charitable contribution *Fin* a donation by a company to a charity

charity accounts *Fin* the accounting records of a charitable institution, that include a statement of financial activities rather than a profit and loss account. In the United Kingdom, the accounts should conform to the requirements stipulated in the Charities Act (1993).

chartered accountant *Fin* in the United Kingdom, a qualified professional accountant who is a member of an Institute of Chartered Accountants. Chartered accountants are qualified to audit company accounts and some hold management positions in companies. *Abbr* **CA**

Chartered Association of Certified Accountants *Fin* former name for the Association of Chartered Certified Accountants

chartered company *or* **chartered entity** *Fin* in the United Kingdom, an organisation formed by the grant of a royal charter. The charter authorises the entity to operate and states the powers specifically granted.

Chartered Institute of Management Accountants *Fin see* **CIMA**

Chartered Institute of Public Finance and Accountancy *Fin see* **CIPFA**

Chartered Institute of Taxation *Fin* in the United Kingdom, an organisation for professionals in the field of taxation, formerly Institute of Taxation

chartist *Fin* an analyst who studies past stock market trends, the movement of share prices, and changes in the accounting ratios of individual companies. The chartist's philosophy is that history repeats itself: using charts and graphs, he or she uses past trends and repetitive patterns to forecast the future. Although the chartist approach is considered narrower than that of a traditional analyst, it nevertheless has a good following.

Power like a desolating pestilence/Pollutes whate'er it touches. *Percy Bysshe Shelley*

chart of accounts *Fin* a comprehensive and systematically arranged list of the named and numbered accounts applicable to an enterprise. Originally devised in Germany, it provides a standard list of account codes for assets, liabilities, capital, revenue, and expenses. It is still used in Germany on a voluntary basis and was adopted as part of the French general accounting plan after the second world war.

chase demand plan *Ops* a *production control* plan that attempts to match *capacity* to the varying levels of forecast demand. Chase demand plans require *flexible working* practices and place varying demands on equipment requirements. Pure chase demand plans are difficult to achieve and are most commonly found in operations where output cannot be stored or where the organisation is seeking to eliminate stores of finished goods.

chat system *E-com* a system that enables Internet users to engage in text-based communication in real time. Messages posted via a chat system will be seen by every member of the participating group. It is a useful means for an organisation to take the pulse of consumers to find out what they are thinking, and to generate unique content.

Online chat can be particularly effective when there is a specific event occurring that is of interest to people, or when an expert can be made available to talk about a subject or product. To be productive, online chat needs to be well moderated, and is really only suited to small groups of people (2 to 20) at any one time.

cheap money *Fin* low interest rates, used as a government strategy to stimulate an economy either at the initial signs of, or during, a recession

check *(US) Fin* = *cheque*

checking account *(US) Fin* = *current account*

cheque *Fin* an order in writing requiring the banker to pay on demand a certain sum in money to a specified person or bearer. Although a cheque can theoretically be written on anything—in a P.G. Wodehouse story, one was written on the side of a cow—banks issue preprinted, customised forms for completion by an account holder who inserts the date, the name of the person to be paid (the payee), the amount in both words and figures, and his or her signature. The customer is the drawer. *US term* **check**

cherry picking *Gen Mgt* the selection of what

is perceived to be the best or most valuable from a series of ideas or options

CHESS *Gen Mgt* Clearing House Electronic Subregister System, a centralised electronic share transfer and settlement system operated by the Australian Stock Exchange. It issues shareholders with regular holding statements.

chief executive *Gen Mgt* the person with overall responsibility for ensuring that the daily operations of an organisation run efficiently and for carrying out strategic plans. The chief executive of an organisation normally sits on the *board of directors*. In a limited company, the chief executive is usually known as a *managing director*.

chief executive officer *Gen Mgt* the highest ranking executive officer within a company or corporation, who has responsibility for overall management of its day-to-day affairs under the supervision of the board of directors. *Abbr* **CEO**

chief financial officer *Gen Mgt* the officer in an organisation responsible for handling funds, signing cheques, the keeping of financial records, and financial planning for the company. *Abbr* **CFO**

chief information officer *Gen Mgt* the officer in an organisation responsible for its internal information systems and sometimes for its e-business infrastructure. *Abbr* **CIO**

chief operating officer *Gen Mgt* the officer in a corporation responsible for its day-to-day management and usually reporting to the chief executive officer. *Abbr* **COO**

chief technology officer *or* **chief technical officer** *Gen Mgt* the officer in an organisation responsible for research and development and possibly for new product plans. *Abbr* **CTO**

childcare provision *HR* a *personnel policy* to supply or to help towards the cost of care for the children of employees during working hours. The aim of childcare provision is to enable primary carers to return to work despite childcare responsibilities. It may apply to children of all ages and can be implemented in a single scheme or as a combination of options, for example, by setting up a workplace nursery or giving childcare vouchers or allowances. To comply with *equal opportunities* legislation, childcare provision has to be made available to both male and female employees.

Chinese wall *Gen Mgt* the procedures enforced within a securities firm to prevent the exchange of confidential information between the firm's departments so as to avoid the illegal use of inside information

chit
call in chits *Gen Mgt* to ask favours from people indebted to you (*slang*)

churn 1. *Fin* to encourage an investor to change stock frequently because the broker is paid every time there is a change in the investor's portfolio (*slang*) **2.** *Gen Mgt* to suffer a high labour turnover rate, especially in areas such as call centres or at chief executive level in large companies **3.** *Gen Mgt* to purchase a quick succession of products or services without displaying loyalty to any of them, often as a result of competitive marketing strategies that continually undercut rival prices, thus encouraging customers to switch brands constantly in order to take advantage of the cheapest or most attractive offers

churn rate 1. *Fin* a measure of the frequency and volume of trading of stocks and bonds in a brokerage account **2.** *Gen Mgt* the rate at which new customers try a product or service and then stop using it

chute
right out of the chute (*US*) *HR* extremely inexperienced (*slang*)

CICA *abbr Fin* Canadian Institute of Chartered Accountants

CIF *abbr E-com* cost, insurance, and freight

cigar
close, but no cigar *Gen Mgt* almost correct, but not quite. The term refers to the fact that cigar-smoking is seen by many businesspeople as a symbol of the celebration of a success. (*slang*)

CIMA *Fin* Chartered Institute of Management Accountants: an organisation that is internationally recognised as offering a financial qualification for business, focusing on strategic business management. Founded in 1919 as the Institute of Cost and Works Accountants, it has offices worldwide, supporting over 128,000 members and students in 156 countries.

CIO *abbr Gen Mgt* chief information officer

CIPFA *abbr Fin* Chartered Institute of Public Finance and Accountancy: in the United Kingdom, one of the leading professional accountancy bodies and the only one that specialises in the public services, for example, local government, public service bodies, and national audit agencies, as well as major

accountancy firms. It is responsible for the education and training of professional accountants and for their regulation through the setting and monitoring of professional standards. CIPFA also provides a range of advisory, information, and consultancy services to public service organisations. As such, it is the leading independent commentator on managing accounting for public money.

circle the drain *Gen Mgt* to be on the brink of complete failure (*slang*)

circuit breaker *Fin* a rule created by the major US stock exchanges and the *Securities and Exchange Commission* by which trading is halted during times of extreme price fluctuations (*slang*)

circular file *Gen Mgt* a wastepaper basket in an office (*slang*)

circular flow of income *Econ* a model of a country's economy showing the flow of resources when consumers' wages and salaries are used to buy goods and so generate income for manufacturing firms

circularisation of debtors *Fin* the sending of letters by a company's auditors to debtors in order to verify the existence and extent of the company's assets

circular merger *Gen Mgt* see **merger**

circulation *Mkting* the number of copies sold or distributed of a single issue of a newspaper or magazine

City Code on Takeovers and Mergers *Fin* in the United Kingdom, a code issued on behalf of the Panel on Takeovers and Mergers that is designed principally to ensure fair and equal treatment of all shareholders in relation to takeovers. The Code also provides an orderly framework within which takeovers are conducted. It is not concerned with the financial or commercial advantages or disadvantages of a takeover nor with those issues, such as competition policy, which are the responsibility of government. The Code represents the collective opinion of those professionally involved in the field of takeovers on how fairness to shareholders can be achieved in practice.

claims adjuster (*US*) *Fin* = **loss adjuster**

class action *Fin* a civil law action taken by a group of individuals who have a common grievance against an individual, organisation, or legal entity

class of assets *Fin* the grouping of similar assets into categories. This is done because under International Accounting Standards Committee rules, tangible assets and intangible assets cannot be revalued on an individual basis, only for a class of assets.

classical economics *Econ* a theory focusing on the functioning of a market economy and providing a rudimentary explanation of consumer and producer behaviour in particular markets. The theory postulates that, over time, the economy would tend to operate at full employment because increases in supply would create corresponding increases in demand.

classical system of corporation tax *Fin* a system in which companies and their owners are liable for corporation tax as separate entities. A company's taxed income is therefore paid out to shareholders who are in turn taxed again. This system operates in the United States and the Netherlands. It was replaced in the United Kingdom in 1973 by an *imputation system*.

classification *Fin* the arrangement of items in logical groups having regard to their nature (subjective classification) or purpose (objective classification). *See also code*

classified advertising *Mkting* advertising placed in newspapers or magazines under specific categories, for example, motoring or property

classified stock (*US*) *Fin* a company's common stock divided into classes such as Class A and Class B

class interval *Stats* any of the intervals of the frequency distribution in a set of statistical observations

clean float *Econ* a floating exchange rate that is allowed to vary without any intervention from the country's monetary authorities

clean opinion *or* **clean report** *Fin* an auditor's report that is not qualified

clean surplus concept *Fin* the idea that a company's income statement should show the totality of gains and losses, without any of them being taken directly to equity

clearing bank *Fin* a bank that deals with other banks through a clearing house

clearing house 1. *E-com see* **acquirer 2.** *Fin* an institution that settles accounts between banks

Clearing House Automated Payment System *Fin see* **CHAPS**

clearing system *Fin* the system of settling accounts among banks

clear title *Fin see* **good title**

clerical work improvement programme *Gen Mgt* a **clerical work measurement** technique that applies **standard time** data to clerical and administrative jobs, the aim of which is to ensure higher productivity and greater efficiency

clerical work measurement *Gen Mgt* an umbrella term for a collection of methods for measuring administrative and clerical work activities. Clerical work measurement is a variation on conventional **work measurement** practices. The main clerical work measurement techniques include **clerical work improvement programmes** and **group capacity assessment**.

CLI *abbr Gen Mgt* calling line identification

clickable corporation *E-com* a company that operates on the Internet

click rate *E-com see* **click-through rate**

clicks-and-mortar *or* **clicks-and-bricks** *E-com* combining a traditional bricks-and-mortar organisation with the click technology of the Internet. A clicks-and-mortar organisation has both a virtual and a physical presence. Examples include retailers with physical shops on the high street and also websites where their goods can be bought online.

clickstream *E-com* the virtual trail that a user leaves behind while surfing the Internet. A clickstream is a record of a user's activity on the Internet, including every web page visited, how long each page is visited for, and the order in which the pages are visited. Both **ISPs** and individual websites are able to track an Internet user's clickstream.

click-through *E-com* the selection of an ad by clicking on the banner or other on-screen device to take the user to the advertiser's website. The number of times users click on an ad can be counted, the total number of click-throughs being a measure of the success of the ad. *Also known as* **ad click**, **ad transfer**

click-through rate *E-com* the percentage of ad views that result in a click-through, a measure of the success of the ad in enticing users to the advertiser's website. *Also known as* **ad click rate**, **click rate**

click wrap agreement *or* **click wrap licence** *E-com* a contract presented entirely over the Internet, the purchaser indicating assent to be bound by the terms of the contract by clicking on an 'I agree' button. The

---

term stems from 'shrink wrap' agreements, licences that become enforceable when the user removes designated packaging containing a copy of the agreement. *Also known as* **point and click agreement**

client 1. *Mkting* a person or organisation that employs the services of a professional person or organisation 2. *E-com see* **server**

client base *Mkting* the regular *clients* of an organisation or professional person

clientele effect *Fin* the preference of an investor or group of investors for buying a particular type of security

clinical trial *Stats* a statistical study of human subjects to determine the effectiveness of a medical treatment

Clintonomics *Econ* the policy of former US President Clinton's Council of Economic Advisors to intervene in the economy to correct market failures and redistribute income

CLM *abbr HR* career-limiting move: an action that could endanger your career prospects, for example, criticising your boss publicly (*slang*)

CLOB International *Fin* in Singapore, a mechanism for buying and selling foreign shares, especially Malaysian shares

clock card *Fin* A document on which is recorded the starting and finishing time of an employee, e.g. by insertion into a time-recording device, for ascertaining total actual attendance time.

Where an employee also clocks on and off different jobs within total attendance time, such cards are referred to as job cards.

clock in 1. *Gen Mgt* to register arrival at work without actually inserting a card into a time clock (*slang*) 2. *HR* to register your arrival for work by inserting a card into a machine to record the time. Clocking in is a method of officially monitoring employees' *time keeping*.

close company *or* **closed company** *Gen Mgt* a company in which five or fewer people control more than half the voting shares, or in which such control is exercised by any number of people who are also directors

close corporation *or* **closed corporation** 1. (*US*) *Gen Mgt* a public corporation in which all of the voting stock is held by a few shareholders, for example, management or family members. Although it is a public company, shares would not normally be available for trading because of a lack of liquidity. 2. (*S Africa*) *Fin* a business registered in terms of

the Close Corporations Act of 1984, consisting of not more than 10 members who share its ownership and management. *Abbr* **CC**

closed-door policy *Gen Mgt see* **open-door policy**

closed economy *Econ* an economic system in which little or no external trade takes place

closed-end credit *Gen Mgt* a loan, plus any interest and finance charges, that is to be repaid in full by a specified future date. Loans that have property or motor vehicles as collateral are usually closed-end. *See also* **open-ended credit**

closed-end fund *or* **closed-end investment company** *Fin* a unit trust that has a fixed number of shares. *See also* **open-ended fund**

closed-end mortgage *Fin* a mortgage in which no prepayment is allowed. *See also* **open-ended mortgage**. *Also known as* **closed mortgage**

closed-loop production system *Ops* an environmentally friendly production system in which any industrial output is capable of being recycled to create another product

closed loop system *Fin* a management control system which includes a provision for corrective action, taken on either a feedforward or a feedback basis

closed mortgage *Fin see* **closed-end mortgage**

closed shop *HR* an agreement requiring members of a particular group of employees to be or to become members of a specified *trade union*. In the United Kingdom, the effect of trade-union and employment-law reforms have made closed shop agreements legally unenforceable.

closely-held corporation *Fin* a company whose shares are publicly traded but held by very few people

closely-held shares *Fin* shares that are publicly traded but held by very few people

Closer Economic Relations agreement *Fin see* **Australia and New Zealand Closer Economic Relations Trade Agreement**

closing balance *Fin* 1. the amount in credit or debit in a bank account at the end of a business day 2. the difference between credits and debits in a ledger at the end of one accounting period that is carried forward to the next

closing bell (*US*) *Fin* the end of a trading session at a stock or commodities exchange

closing entries *Fin* in a double-entry bookkeeping system, entries made at the very end of an accounting period to balance the expense and revenue ledgers

closing price *Fin* the price of the last transaction for a particular security or commodity at the end of a trading session

closing quote *Fin* the last bid and offer prices recorded at the close of a trading session

closing rate *Fin* the exchange rate of two or more currencies at the close of business of a balance sheet date, for example at the end of the financial year

closing-rate method *Fin* a technique for translating the figures from a set of financial statements into a different currency using the *closing rate*. This method is often used for the accounts of a foreign subsidiary of a parent company.

closing sale *Fin* a sale that reduces the risk that the seller has through holding a greater number of shares or a longer term contract

closing stock *Fin* a business's remaining stock at the end of an accounting period. It includes finished products, raw materials, or work in progress and is deducted from the period's costs in the balance sheets.

club culture *Gen Mgt* a *corporate culture* in which all lines of communication lead formally or informally to the leader. Club culture was identified by *Charles Handy*.

cluster analysis *Gen Mgt* a statistical method used to analyse complex data and identify groupings that share common features. Cluster analysis is a form of *multivariate analysis* that attempts to explain variability in a set of data. It involves finding unifying elements that enable identification of groups or clusters displaying common characteristics. It could be used, for example, to analyse results of *attitude research* and delineate groups of respondents that share certain attitudes.

clustered data *Stats* data in which sampling units in a study are grouped into clusters sharing a common feature, or longitudinal data in which clusters are defined by repeated measures on the unit

cluster sampling *Ops see random sampling*

Clutterbuck, David (*b.* 1947) *Gen Mgt* British academic. Best known for his work on *mentoring*, and his research, with Walter Gold-

smith, on consistently high-performing companies. Their findings were published in *The Winning Streak* (1984), which was viewed as the British equivalent of *Tom Peters*'s and *Robert Waterman*'s *In Search of Excellence* (1982).

CM *abbr Gen Mgt* category management

CNCC *abbr Fin* Compagnie Nationale des Commissaires aux Comptes

coaching *HR* the development of somebody's skills and knowledge through one-to-one *training*. Coaching is usually conducted by a more senior and experienced colleague. It involves planned training activities that have measurable outcomes and is designed to facilitate learning by providing guidance and support as well as tutoring. *Executive coaching* is a form of coaching used with senior managers.

COAG *abbr Gen Mgt* Council of Australian Governments

COB *abbr Fin* Commission des Opérations de Bourse

co-browsing *E-com* a facility that enables two or more Web users to synchronise their *browsers*, so that they can see the same web pages at the same time.
Frequently employed by customer support services, co-browsing means that a customer service representative, using *live chat* or the telephone, can take a customer through a process, changing the customer's web page as they change their own. It is a particularly valuable feature if complex processes and information have to be delivered. *Also known as page pushing*

cobweb site *E-com* an Internet site that has not been updated for a long time (*slang*)

code *Fin* a system of symbols designed to be applied to a classified set of items to give a brief, accurate reference, facilitating entry, collation and analysis. For example, in costing systems, composite symbols are commonly used. In the composite symbol 211.392 the first three digits might indicate the nature of the expenditure (subjective classification), and the last three digits might indicate the cost centre or cost unit to be charged (objective classification).

codec *E-com* either a hardware or a software component, used in *videoconferencing*, that compresses and decompresses the audio and video signals. Hardware codecs are generally faster.

---

*Loyalty saves the wear and tear of making daily decisions as to what is best to do. **Thomas J. Watson, Sr***

code of conduct *Gen Mgt* a statement and description of required behaviours, responsibilities, and actions expected of employees of an organisation or of members of a professional body. A code of conduct usually focuses on ethical and socially responsible issues and applies to individuals, providing guidance on how to act in cases of doubt or confusion.

code of practice *Gen Mgt* a policy statement and description of preferred methods for organisational *procedures*.

Codes of practice may govern procedures for industrial relations, health and safety, and, more recently, customer service and professional development. An agreed code of practice enables activities to be carried out to a required organisational standard and provides a basis for dispute resolution.

coefficient of variation *Stats* a measure of the spread of a set of statistical data, calculated as the mean or standard deviation of the data multiplied by 100

co-financing *Fin* the joint provision of money for a project by two or more parties

coherence *Stats* a measure of the strength of association between two time series

cohesion fund *Gen Mgt* the main financial instrument for reducing economic and social disparities within the European Union by providing financial help for projects in the fields of the environment and transport infrastructure

cohort *Stats* a group of individuals in a statistical study that have a common characteristic

cohort study *Stats* a study in which a group of individuals such as children with the same birth date are observed over several years

coin analysis *Fin* the quantities and denominations of banknotes and coins required to pay employees on a payroll

coincidence *Stats* the occurrence of events that are related but have no apparent common cause

cold calling *Mkting* the practice of making unsolicited calls to customers or consumers in an attempt to sell products or services. Cold calling is disliked, particularly by individual consumers, and is an inefficient way of selling as the take-up rate is very low.

cold transfer *Gen Mgt* an incoming phone call that is transferred by an operator without giving any notice or explanation to the caller or to the recipient of the call (*slang*)

collaborative working *HR* a method of working in which people at different locations or from different organisations work together electronically using videoconferencing, e-mail, networks, and other communication tools

collar *Fin* a contractually imposed lower limit on a financial instrument

collateral *Fin* property or goods used as security against a loan and forfeited to the lender if the borrower defaults

collateral trust certificate *Fin* a bond for which shares in another company, usually a subsidiary, are used as collateral

collection ratio *Fin* the average number of days it takes a firm to convert its accounts receivable into cash.

  EXAMPLE   Ideally, this period should be decreasing or constant. A low figure means the company collects its outstanding receivables quickly. Collection ratios are usually reviewed quarterly or yearly.

Calculating the collection ratio requires three figures: total accounts receivable, total credit sales for the period analysed, and the number of days in the period (annual, 365; six months, 182; quarter, 91). The formula is:

Accounts receivable / total credit sales for the period × number of days in the period

For example: if total receivables are £4,500,000, total credit sales in a quarter are £9,000,000, and number of days is 91, then:

4,500,000 / 9,000,000 × 91 = 45.5

Thus, it takes an average 45.5 days to collect receivables.

Properly evaluating a collection ratio requires a standard for comparison. A traditional rule of thumb is that it should not exceed a third to a half of selling terms. For instance, if terms are 30 days, an acceptable collection ratio would be 40 to 45 days.

Companies use collection ratio information with an *accounts receivable ageing* report. This lists four categories of receivables: 0–30 days, 30–60 days, 60–90 days, and over 90 days. The report also shows the percentage of total accounts receivable that each group represents, allowing for an analysis of delinquencies and potential bad debts. *Also known as days' sales outstanding*

collective agreement *HR* a contract between a *trade union* and an employer, resulting from *collective bargaining* and covering **conditions of employment** and procedural arrangements for resolving disputes. In the United Kingdom, a collective agreement is not legally binding unless it is in writing and specifically states the parties' intention to be bound. An agreement can become legally binding by being incorporated into an employee's personal **contract of employment**. Agreements may be concluded at organisation or industry level.

collective bargaining *HR* negotiations about **conditions of employment** between an employer, a group of employers or their representatives, and employees' representatives such as **trade unions** with a view to reaching a **collective agreement**

collocation hosting *E-com* a **hosting option** which involves a customer placing their own servers with a hosting vendor. The customer manages everything that happens on their servers: content, software, and the hardware itself. The hosting provider supplies an agreed speed of access to the Internet and amount of **data transfer**, and usually some minimum service, such as ensuring that the customer's server is up and running, and rebooting it if necessary.

colour supplement *Mkting* a magazine printed in colour and distributed with a newspaper

combination bond *Fin* a government bond for which the collateral is both revenue from the financed project and the government's credit

combined financial statement *Fin* a written record covering the assets, liabilities, net worth, and operating statement of two or more related or affiliated companies

COMEX *abbr Fin* commodity exchange

comfort letter *Fin* **1.** in the United States, a statement from an accounting firm provided to a company preparing for a public offering, that confirms that the unaudited financial information in the prospectus follows **Generally Accepted Accounting Principles 2.** a letter from the parent company of a subsidiary that is applying for a loan, stating the intention that the subsidiary should remain in business

command and control approach *Gen Mgt* a style of leadership that uses standards, **procedures**, and output statistics to regulate the organisation. A command and control approach to leadership is authoritative in nature and uses a **top-down approach**, which

fits well in bureaucratic organisations in which privilege and power are vested in **senior management**. It is founded on, and emphasises a distinction between, executives on the one hand and workers on the other. It stems from the principles of **Frederick Winslow Taylor**, and the applications of **Henry Ford** and **Alfred Sloan, Jr**. As more empowered, **flat organisations** have come to the fore, command and control leaders have been increasingly criticised for stifling creativity and limiting flexibility.

command economy *Econ* an economy in which all economic activity is regulated by the government, as in the former Soviet Union or China

commerce *Fin* the large-scale buying and selling of goods and services, usually applied to trading between different countries

commerce integration *Fin* the blending of Internet-based commerce capabilities with the **legacy systems** of a traditional business to create a seamless transparent process

commerce server *E-com* **1.** a computer in a network that maintains all transactional and backend data for an e-commerce website **2.** a networked computer that contains the programs required to process transactions via the Internet, including dynamic inventory databases, shopping cart software, and online payment systems

commerce service provider *E-com* an organisation or company that provides a service to a company to facilitate some aspect of electronic commerce, for example, by functioning as an Internet **payment gateway**. *Abbr* **CSP**

commercial¹ *Fin* relating to the buying and selling of goods and services

commercial² *Mkting* an advertising message that is broadcast on television or radio

commercial bank *Fin* a bank that primarily provides financial services to businesses. *See also* **merchant bank**

commercial exposure potential *(US) Mkting* the estimated number of possible recipients of a commercial message

commercial hedger *Fin* a company that holds options in the commodities it produces

commercialisation *Fin* the application of business principles to something in order to run it as a business

---

commercial law *Gen Mgt* the body of law that deals with the rules and institutions of commercial transactions, including banking, commerce, contracts, copyrights, insolvency, insurance, patents, trademarks, shipping, storage, transportation, and warehousing

commercial loan *Fin* a short-term renewable loan or line of credit used to finance the seasonal or cyclical working capital needs of a company

commercial paper *Fin* uncollateralised loans obtained by companies, usually on a short-term basis. *Also known as* **mercantile paper**

commercial report *Fin* an investigative report made by an organisation such as a credit bureau that specialises in obtaining information regarding a person or organisation applying for something such as credit or employment

commercial substance *Fin* the economic reality that underlies a transaction or arrangement, regardless of its legal or technical denomination. For example, a company may sell an office block and then immediately lease it back: the commercial substance may be that it has not been sold.

commercial time *Mkting* an interval of time, usually measured in multiples of 15 seconds, during a radio or television broadcast available for purchase by an advertiser to broadcast its commercial message

commercial version *Gen Mgt* a version of a software program that is released for sale to customers. Earlier versions, called test versions or beta versions, are used to develop and test the software.

commercial year *Fin* an artificial year treated as having 12 months of 30 days each, used for calculating such things as monthly sales data and inventory levels

commission *HR* a payment made to an intermediary, often calculated as a percentage of the value of goods or services provided. Commission is most often paid to sales staff, brokers, or agents.

Commission des Opérations de Bourse *Fin* the body, established by the French government in 1968, that is responsible for supervising France's stock exchanges. *Abbr* **COB**

Commissioners of the Inland Revenue *Fin* in the United Kingdom, officials responsible for hearing appeals by taxpayers against their tax assessment

commitment accounting *Fin* a method of accounting which recognises expenditure as soon as it is contracted

commitment document *Fin* a contract, change order, purchase order, or letter of intent pertaining to the supply of goods and services that commits an organisation to legal, financial, and other obligations

commitment fee *Fin* a fee that a lender charges to guarantee a rate of interest on a loan a borrower is soon to make. *Also known as* **establishment fee**

commitment letter *(US) Fin* an official notice from a lender to a borrower that the borrower's application has been approved and confirming the terms and conditions of the loan

commitments basis *Fin* the method of recording the expenditure of a public sector organisation at the time when it commits itself to it rather than when it actually pays for it

commitments for capital expenditure *Fin* the amount a company has committed to spend on fixed assets in the future. In the United Kingdom, companies are legally obliged to disclose this amount, and any additional commitments, in their **annual report**.

committed costs *Fin* costs arising from prior decisions, which cannot, in the short run, be changed. Committed cost incurrence often stems from strategic decisions concerning capacity, with resulting expenditure on plant and facilities. Initial control of committed costs at the decision point is through investment appraisal techniques. *See also* **commitment accounting**

committee *Gen Mgt* a group of people appointed and authorised to study, investigate, or make recommendations on a particular matter

Committee on Accounting Procedure *Fin* in the United States, a committee of the American Institute of Certified Public Accountants that was responsible between 1939 and 1959 for issuing accounting principles, some of which are still part of the Generally Accepted Accounting Principles

commodities exchange *Fin* a market in which raw materials are bought and sold in large quantities as **actuals** or **futures**

commodity *Econ* a good or service, for example, cotton, wool, or a laptop computer, resulting from the process of **production**

Take care to sell your horse before he dies. The art of life is passing losses on.   *Robert Frost*

commodity-backed bond *Fin* a bond tied to the price of an underlying commodity, for example, gold or silver, often used as a hedge against inflation

commodity contract *Fin* a legal document for the delivery or receipt of a commodity

commodity exchange *Fin* an exchange where futures are traded, for example, the commodity exchange for metals in the United States. *Abbr* **COMEX**

commodity future *Fin* a contract to buy or sell a commodity at a predetermined price and on a particular delivery date

commodity paper *Fin* loans for which commodities are collateral

commodity pool *Fin* a group of people who join together to trade in options

commodity pricing *Fin* pricing a product or service on the basis that it is undifferentiated from all competitive offerings, and cannot therefore command any price premium above the base market price

commodity-product spread *Fin* co-ordinated trades in both a commodity and a product made from it

common cost *Fin* cost relating to more than one product or service

common market *Econ* an economic association, typically between nations, with the goal of removing or reducing trade barriers

common seal *Fin* the impression of a company's official signature on paper or wax. Certain documents, such as share certificates, have to bear this seal. *Also known as* **company seal**

common-size financial statements *Fin* statements in which all the elements are expressed as percentages of the total. Such statements are often used for making performance comparisons between companies.

common stock *Fin* a stock that pays a dividend after dividends for preferred stock have been paid

common stock ratio *Fin* a measure of the interest each stockholder has in the company's capital

Commonwealth of Australia *Gen Mgt* the full, official name of the country of Australia

Commonwealth of Australia Gazette *Gen Mgt* a journal that reports the actions and decisions of the Australian federal government. It has been published since 1901.

Commonwealth Scientific and Industrial Research Organisation *abbr (ANZ) Gen Mgt* CSIRO

commorientes *Fin* the legal term for two or more people who die at the same time. For the purposes of inheritance law, in the event of two dying at the same time, it is assumed that the older person died first.

communication *Gen Mgt* the exchange of messages conveying information, ideas, attitudes, emotions, opinions, or instructions between individuals or groups with the aim of creating, understanding, or co-ordinating activities. Communication is essential to the effective operation of an organisation. It may be conducted informally through a *grapevine* or formally by means of letters, reports, briefings, and *meetings*. Communication may be verbal or *non-verbal communication* and include spoken, written, and visual elements.

communications *Gen Mgt* **1.** systems or technologies used for the communication of messages, such as postal and telephone networks, or for communicating within an organisation **2.** messages exchanged in the process of *communication*

communications channel *Gen Mgt* a medium through which a message is passed in the process of *communication*. Communications channels include the spoken, written, and printed word, and electronic or computer-based media such as radio and television, telephones, video-conferencing, and electronic mail. The most effective channel for a specific message depends on the nature of the message and the audience to be reached, as well as the context in which the message is to be transmitted.

communications envelope *E-com see electronic envelope*

communication skills *HR* skills that enable people to communicate effectively with one another. Effective communication involves the choice of the best *communications channel* for a specific purpose, the technical knowledge to use the channel appropriately, the presentation of information in an appropriate manner for the target audience, and the ability to understand messages and responses received from others. The ability to establish and develop mutual understanding, trust, and co-operation is also important. More specifically, communication skills include the ability to speak in public, make presentations, write letters and reports, chair committees and meetings, and conduct negotiations.

Give me fruitful error any time, full of seeds, bursting with its own corrections. Vilfredo Pareto

communications management *Mkting* the management, measurement, and control activities undertaken to ensure the effectiveness of communications

communications strategy *Mkting* a management technique for determining the most effective method of communicating with the marketplace

communication technology *Gen Mgt* electronic systems used for communication between individuals or groups. Communication technology facilitates communication between individuals or groups who are not physically present at the same location. Systems such as telephones, telex, fax, radio, television, and video are included, as well as more recent computer-based technologies, including *electronic data interchange* and *e-mail*.

Communism *Econ* a classless society where private ownership of goods is abolished and the means of production belong to the community

community *E-com* a group of Internet users with a shared interest or concept who interact with each other in newsgroups, mailing-list discussion groups, and other online interactive forums

community initiative *Gen Mgt see community involvement*

community involvement *Gen Mgt* programmes through which organisations aim to make a positive contribution to the local community by identifying problems and initiating practical action in order to address them in partnership with local people. Community involvement programmes developed through the growing emphasis on the social responsibility of business in the 1960s and 1970s. Such **community initiatives** often seek to promote economic and social regeneration in urban or rural areas and include activities such as the *secondment* of employees with appropriate skills, educational and training initiatives, *sponsorship* of arts and sports programmes, and *corporate giving* programmes.

Compagnie Nationale des Commissaires aux Comptes *Fin* in France, an organisation that regulates external audit. *Abbr* **CNCC**

companion bond *Fin* a class of a collateralised mortgage obligation that is paid off first when interest rates fall leading to the underlying mortgages being prepaid. Conversely, the principal on these bonds will be repaid more slowly when interest rates rise and fewer mortgages are prepaid.

company *Gen Mgt* an association of people formed into a legal entity for the purpose of doing business. The most common form of company in the United Kingdom is the *registered company*. This is established by registering Articles and a Memorandum of Association with the *Registrar of Companies* at Companies House in accordance with *company law*. The most common forms of registered company are the *public limited company* and the *private company*.

company law *Gen Mgt* the body of legislation that relates to the formation, status, conduct, and *corporate governance* of companies as legal entities

company limited by guarantee *Fin* a type of organisation normally formed for non-profit purposes in which each member of the company agrees to be liable for a specific sum in the event of liquidation

company limited by shares *Fin* a type of organisation in which each member of the company is liable only for the fully paid value of the shares they own. This is the most common form of company in the United Kingdom.

company pension scheme *HR see occupational pension scheme*

company policy *Gen Mgt* a statement of desired standards of behaviour or procedure applicable across an organisation. Company policy defines ways of acting for staff in areas where there appears to be latitude in deciding how best to operate. This may concern areas such as time off for special circumstances, drug or alcohol abuse, *workplace bullying*, personal use of *Internet* facilities, or business travel. Company policy may also apply to customers, for example, policy on *complaints*, *customer retention*, or *disclosure of information*. Sometimes a company policy may develop into a *code of practice*.

company report *Gen Mgt* a document giving details of the activities and performance of a company. Companies are legally required to produce particular reports and submit them to the competent authorities in the country of their registration. These include *annual reports* and financial reports. Other reports may cover specific aspects of an organisation's activities, for example, environmental or social impact.

company seal *Fin see common seal*

company secretary *HR* a senior employee in an organisation with director status and administrative and legal authority. The appointment of a company secretary is a legal requirement for all limited companies. A company secretary can also be a **board secretary** with appropriate qualifications. In the United Kingdom, many company secretaries are members of the Institute of Chartered Secretaries and Administrators.

comparative advantage *Gen Mgt* an instance of higher, more efficient production in a particular area. A country that produces far more cars than another, for example, is said to have the comparative advantage in car production. *David Ricardo* originally argued that specialisation in activities in which individuals or groups have a comparative advantage will result in gains in trade.

comparative advertising *Mkting* a form of advertising that gives carefully selected details of competitor products for comparison with a company's own product, usually to the detriment of competitors. Comparative advertising is frequently used to advertise cars, where the availability of features such as a sun roof, air conditioning, advanced braking systems, fuel efficiency, safety features, and warranty terms in similarly priced cars are given.

comparative balance sheet *Fin* one of two or more financial statements prepared on different dates that lend themselves to a comparative analysis of the financial condition of an organisation

comparative credit analysis *Fin* an analysis of the risk associated with lending to different companies

comparative management *Gen Mgt* the simultaneous study of management or business practice in two or more different cultures, countries, companies, or departments

compassionate leave *HR* exceptional leave that may be granted to an employee on the death or serious illness of a close relative

compensating balance *Fin* **1.** the amount of money a bank requires a customer to maintain in a non-interest-bearing account, in exchange for which the bank provides free services **2.** the amount of money a bank requires a customer to maintain in an account in return for holding credit available, thereby increasing the true rate of interest on the loan

compensation *HR* **1.** *pay* given in recompense for work performed **2.** money paid by an employer on the order of an employment tribunal to an employee who has been

unfairly dismissed. In the case of **unfair dismissal**, compensation comprises a basic award calculated by reference to length of **continuous service** and a compensatory award representing the employee's financial losses incurred as a result of the **dismissal**, including loss of future earnings, benefits, and pension. Additional compensation may be made if the employer fails to comply with an order to reinstate the employee. If the employee refuses an offer of reinstatement, or if the employee's conduct has contributed to the dismissal, the tribunal may reduce the amount of compensation awarded.

compensation package (*US*) *HR* a bundle of rewards including *pay*, financial incentives, and fringe benefits offered to, or negotiated by, an employee

competence *Gen Mgt, HR* an acquired personal skill that is demonstrated in an employee's ability to provide a consistently adequate or high level of performance in a specific job function. Competence should be distinguished from *competency*, although in general usage the terms are used interchangeably. Early attempts to define the qualities of effective managers were based on lists of the personality traits and skills of the ideal manager. This is an input model approach, focusing on the skills that are needed to do the job. These skills are competencies and reflect potential ability to do something. With the advent of scientific management, people turned their attention more to the behaviour of effective managers and to the outcomes of successful management. This approach is an output model, in which a manager's effectiveness is defined in terms of actual achievement. This achievement manifests itself in competences, which demonstrate that somebody has learned to do something well. There tends to be a focus in the United Kingdom on competence, whereas in the United States, the concept of competency is more popular. Competences are used in the workplace in a variety of ways. Training is often competence-based, and the UK **National Vocational Qualification** system is based on competence standards. Competences also are used in reward management, for example, in competence-based pay. The **assessment of competence** is a necessary process for underpinning these initiatives by determining what competences an employee shows. At an organisational level, the idea of **core competence** is gaining popularity.

competency *Gen Mgt, HR* an innate personal skill or ability. *See also* **competence**

competition *Gen Mgt* rivalry between companies to achieve greater *market share*. Competition between companies for customers will lead to product *innovation* and improvement, and ultimately lower prices. The opposite of market competition is either a *monopoly* or a **controlled economy**, where production is governed by quotas. A company that is leading the market is said to have achieved *competitive advantage*.

competitive advantage *Gen Mgt* a factor giving an advantage to a nation, company, group, or individual in competitive terms. Used by **Michael Porter** for the title of his classic text on international corporate strategy, *The Competitive Advantage of Nations* (1990), the concept of competitive advantage derives from the ideas on *comparative advantage* of the 19th-century economist **David Ricardo**.

competitive analysis *Gen Mgt* analysis carried out for marketing purposes that can include industry, customer, and *competitor analysis*. A thorough competitive analysis done within a strategic framework can provide in-depth evaluation of the capabilities of key competitors.

competitive equilibrium price *Econ* the price at which the number of buyers willing to buy a good equals the number of sellers prepared to sell it

competitive forces *Gen Mgt* the external business and economic factors that compel an organisation to improve its competitiveness

competitive intelligence *Gen Mgt* data gathered to improve an organisation's competitive capacity. Competitive intelligence may include, for example, information about competitors' plans, activities, or products, and may sometimes be gained through *industrial espionage*. Such information can have a significant impact on a company's own plans: it could limit the effectiveness of a new product launch, or identify growing threats to important accounts, for example. Unless organisations monitor competitor activity and take appropriate action, their business faces risk.

competitiveness index *Gen Mgt* an international ranking of states using economic and other information to list countries in order of their competitive performance. A competitiveness index can show which countries have overall or industry-sector *competitive advantage*.

competitive pricing *Fin* setting a price by reference to the prices of competitive products

competitive saw *Fin* illustration of the principle that every investment in a product, while initially improving the reported performance in relation to competitors, eventually degrades and has to be succeeded by further investment(s) to maintain the competitive position

competitor analysis *or* **competitor profiling** *Gen Mgt* the gathering and analysis of information about competitors, especially in a corporate context, for *competitive intelligence* purposes

complaint *Gen Mgt* an expression of dissatisfaction with a product or service, either orally or in writing, from an internal or external customer. A customer may have a genuine cause for complaint, although some complaints may be made as a result of a misunderstanding or an unreasonable expectation of a product or service. How a complaint is handled will affect the overall level of *customer satisfaction* and may affect long-term customer loyalty. It is important for providers to have clear procedures for dealing rapidly with any complaints, to come to a fair conclusion, and to explain the reasons for what may be perceived by the customer as a negative response. *Also known as* **customer complaint**

complaints management *Mkting* a management technique for assessing, analysing, and responding to customer complaints

complementary goods *Mkting* goods sold separately, but dependent on each other for sales. Examples of complementary goods include toothbrushes and toothpaste or computers and computer desks.

complementor *Gen Mgt* a company that supplies a product that complements a product supplied by another company, for example, computers and software

complex adaptive system *Gen Mgt* a system that overrides conventional human controls because those controls will subdue inevitable change and development within that system. Complex adaptive systems are a product of the application of chaos theory (see *chaos*) and *complexity theory* to the world of organisations. According to writers such as **Richard Pascale**, organisations that are subject to too much control are at risk of failure. The *bureaucracy* has been cited as an example of extreme control and the *top-down approach* to management. However, if a bureaucracy is left to adapt naturally, it could become capable of self-organisation and of creating new methods of operating.

A committee is an animal with four back legs.   *John Le Carré*

complexity theory *Gen Mgt* the theory that random events, if left to happen without interference, will settle into a complicated pattern rather than a simple one. Complexity theory is a development of chaos theory (see *chaos*). In a business context, it suggests that events within organisations and in the wider economic and social spheres cannot be predicted by simple models but will develop in a seemingly random and complex manner.

compliance audit *Fin* an audit of specific activities in order to determine whether performance is in conformity with a predetermined contractual, regulatory, or statutory requirement

compliance documentation *Fin* documents that a share-issuing company publishes in line with regulations on share issues

compliance officer *Fin* an employee of a financial organisation who ensures that regulations governing its business are observed

compounding *Fin* the calculation, payment, or receipt of *compound interest*

compound interest *Fin* interest calculated on the sum of the original borrowed amount and the accrued interest. *See also* **simple interest**

comprehensive auditing *Fin* see *value for money audit*

compressed workweek (*US*) *HR* a standard number of working hours squeezed into fewer than five days. Common models of the compressed working week include four ten-hour days or three twelve-hour days each week. An alternative variation is to lengthen the normal working day to a lesser extent, for example, by 45 minutes, to allow an extra day off every two or three weeks. The minimum modification is to work a slightly longer day for four days in return for a shorter Friday. A compressed workweek is often introduced as an employee benefit to provide an extended weekend through shorter Friday working.

compulsory acquisition *Fin* the purchase, by right, of the last 10% of shares in an issue by a bidder at the offer price

computer-aided design *Ops* the use of a computer to assist with the design of a product. Computer graphics, modelling, and simulation are used to represent a product on screen, so that designers can produce more accurate drawings than is possible on paper alone and to perform calculations easily, thereby optimising designs for production.

Abbr **CAD**. *Also known as* **computer-assisted design**

computer-aided diagnosis *Stats* the use of a computer program that presents a patient with a series of diagnostic questions designed to produce a diagnosis of a health problem

computer-aided engineering *Ops* the application of computers to the generation of the engineering specifications of a product. Computer-aided engineering fits into the production process between **computer-aided design** and **computer-aided manufacturing**. It is similar to **CAD/CAM** software, but with a focus on the engineering processes required for converting a design to a manufacturable product. The software package can include aspects of design, analysis, process planning, numerical control, mould and tool design, and **quality control**. *Abbr* **CAE**

computer-aided manufacturing *Ops* a system in which the manufacture and assembly of a product are directed by a computer. Computer-aided manufacturing can be integrated with **computer-aided design** to create a **CAD/CAM** system. *Abbr* **CAM**. *Also known as* **computer-assisted manufacturing**

computer-aided production management *Ops* a system that enables all functions within an organisation that are associated with production management to be directed by computer. **MRP II** is a well-known form of computer-aided production management. *Abbr* **CAPM**

computer-assisted design *Ops* see *computer-aided design*

computer-assisted interview *Stats* an interview in which the interviewee keys in answers to questions displayed on screen by a computer program

computer-assisted manufacturing *Ops* see *computer-aided manufacturing*

computer-based training *HR* training carried out via a stand-alone or networked computer. Programs are usually interactive, so that students can select from multiple-choice options or key in their own answers. A popular medium for computer-based training is CD-ROM, although there is a growing trend towards **online training**, where computer-based training is delivered over the Internet or through company intranets. Computer-based training is a form of *e-learning*.

computer telephony integration *Gen Mgt* the combining of computer and telephone technology to allow a computer to dial telephone numbers, route calls, and send and

---

I learned then what a bunch of gangsters the banks are. They really are gangsters.   Alan Sugar

receive messages. One product of computer telephony integration is the process of **calling line identification**, or CLI. CLI identifies the telephone number a customer is calling from, searches the customer database to identify the caller, and pops up the customer account on the receiver's computer screen, using the facility known as **screen popping**, before the call is answered. *Abbr* **CTI**

computer worm *E-com* a computer *virus* that does not try to damage the files it infects. Its objective is instead to replicate itself as quickly and as often as possible. Computer worms are a major drain on the Internet because they clog up *bandwidth*.

concentration services *Fin* the placing of money from various accounts into a single account

concept board *Mkting* a board used for presenting creative advertising ideas

concept search *E-com* an online search for documents related conceptually to a word, rather than specifically containing the word itself

concept testing *Mkting* research carried out to test the effectiveness of a creative advertising idea

concession *Gen Mgt* **1.** a compromise in opinion or action by a party to a dispute **2.** a reduction in price for a particular group of people **3.** the right of a retail outlet to set up and sell goods within another establishment **4.** an agreement to ignore the failure of a product or service to conform to its specification, with a possible resultant deterioration in the quality of the product or service

conciliation *HR* action taken by an independent negotiator to bring disputing sides together with the aim of restoring trust or goodwill and reaching an agreement or bringing about a reconciliation

concurrent engineering *Ops* a team-based co-operative approach to product design and development, in which all parties are involved in *new product development* work in parallel. Concurrent engineering reduces or removes the time-lag between the different stages of a product's development, and earlier entry into a market is therefore possible. Product quality is improved, development and product costs are minimised, and competitiveness is increased. *Also known as* **parallel engineering, simultaneous engineering**

conditional distribution *Stats* the probability distribution of a random variable while the values of one or more random variables are fixed

conditions of employment *Gen Mgt, HR* terms agreed between an employer and employee that are legally enforceable through a **contract of employment**. Conditions of employment include conditions that may be unique to the individual, for example, *notice periods*, remuneration, fringe benefits, and *hours of work*, as well as those that form organisation-wide policies, for example, discipline and *grievance procedures*, and those dictated by legislation.

conference *Gen Mgt* a type of *meeting* held between members of often disparate organisations to discuss matters of mutual interest. Conferences are held for a variety of reasons, including resolving problems, taking decisions, developing co-operation, and publicising ideas, products, and services. They may take place within an organisation but often draw people together regionally, nationally, or internationally, and involve a large number of speakers and delegates. Many conferences are organised for commercial profit.

conference call *Gen Mgt* a telephone call that connects three or more lines so that people in different locations can communicate and exchange information by voice. Conference calls reduce the cost of *meetings* by eliminating travel time and expenditure. Public switched telephone networks or dedicated private networks and a centrally located device called a bridge are used to connect the participants. Microphones and loudspeakers may also be used to make group-to-group communication possible. Conference calls are a type of *teleconferencing*.

confidence indicator *Fin* a number that gives an indication of how well a market or an economy will fare

confidence interval *Stats* the range of values of sample observations in a statistical study that contain the true parameter value within a given probability

confidentiality agreement *Gen Mgt* an agreement whereby an organisation that has access to information about the affairs of another organisation makes an undertaking to treat the information as private and confidential. A potential buyer of a company who requires further information in the process of due diligence may be asked to sign a confidentiality agreement stating that the information will only be used for the purpose of deciding whether to go ahead with the deal and will only be disclosed to employees involved in the negotiations. Such agreements are also used where information is shared in the context of a partnership or **benchmarking** programme.

conflict management *Gen Mgt, HR* the identification and control of conflict within an organisation. There are three main philosophies of conflict management: all conflict is bad and potentially destructive; conflict is inevitable and managers should attempt to harness it positively; conflict is essential to the survival of an organisation and should be encouraged.

conflict of interests *Gen Mgt* a situation in which a person or institution is caught between opposing concerns, loyalties, or objectives that prejudice impartiality. A conflict of interests may be between self-advantage and the benefit of an organisation for which somebody works, or it could arise when somebody is connected with two or more companies that are competing. The correct course of action in such cases is for the person concerned to declare any interests, to make known the way in which those interests conflict, and to abstain from participating in the **decision-making** process involving those interests. A conflict of interests may also arise when an institution acts for parties on both sides of a transaction and could derive an advantage from a particular outcome.

confusion matrix *Gen Mgt see* **discriminant analysis**

conglomerate *Fin* an entity comprising a number of dissimilar businesses

conglomerate company *Gen Mgt* an organisation that owns a diverse range of companies in different industries. Conglomerates are usually **holding companies** with subsidiaries in wide-ranging business areas, often built up through mergers and takeovers and operating on an international scale.

conglomerate diversification *Gen Mgt* the **diversification** of a **conglomerate company** through the setting up of **subsidiary companies** with activities in various areas

conjoint analysis *Gen Mgt* a research method aimed at discovering the most attractive combination of attributes, including price, package style, and size, for a product or service. In conjoint analysis, respondents express their preferences by filling in a questionnaire and ranking a number of contrasting combinations of attributes from the most to the least preferred. This enables values to be

assigned to the range of features that customers consider when making a decision to purchase. *Also known as* **trade-off analysis**

connectivity *Gen Mgt* the ability of electronic products to connect with others, or of individuals, companies, and countries to be connected with one another electronically

connexity *Gen Mgt* the condition of being closely and intricately connected by worldwide communications networks

consequential loss policy *Fin see* **business interruption insurance**

consignment note *Fin see* **delivery note**

consol *Fin* irredeemable UK government stocks carrying fixed coupons. Sometimes used as a general term for an undated or irredeemable bond.

consolidated accounts *Fin see* **consolidated financial statement**

consolidated balance sheet *Fin* a listing of the most significant details of a company's finances

consolidated debt *Fin* the use of a large loan to eliminate smaller ones

consolidated financial statement *Fin* a listing of the most significant details of a company and of all its subsidiaries. *Also known as* **consolidated accounts**

consolidated fund *Fin* a fund of public money, especially from taxes, used by the government to make interest payments on the national debt and other regular payments

consolidated invoice *Fin* an invoice that covers all items shipped by one seller to one buyer during a particular period

consolidated loan *Fin* a large loan, the proceeds of which are used to eliminate smaller ones

consolidated tape *Fin* a ticker tape that lists all transactions of the New York and other US stock exchanges

consolidated tax return *Fin* a tax return that covers several companies, typically a parent company and all of its subsidiaries

consolidation *Fin* **1.** the uniting of two or more businesses into one company **2.** the combination of several lower-priced shares into one higher-priced one

consortium *Gen Mgt* a group of independent organisations that join forces to achieve a particular goal, for example, to bid for a project or

---

If I have seen further, it is by standing on the shoulders of giants.   *Isaac Newton*

to carry out co-operative purchasing. A consortium goes on to complete the project if its bid is successful and is often dissolved on completion. This form of temporary alliance allows diverse skills, capabilities, and knowledge to be brought together.

Constable, John (*b.* 1936) *Gen Mgt* British educator and consultant. Best known for the report *The Making of British Managers* (1987), with **Roger McCormick**, which led to major changes in the structure of *management development* in the United Kingdom. The publication of the report coincided with the equally influential *The Making of Managers: A Report on Management Education, Training, and Development in the USA, West Germany, France, Japan, and the UK* (1987) by **Charles Handy** and others.

constitutional strike (*US*) *HR* a form of *industrial action* that takes place after all dispute procedures or other provisions for the avoidance of strikes agreed between trade-union and employer representatives have been exhausted. A *no-strike agreement* effectively precludes constitutional strikes because it generally provides for automatic *arbitration*.

constraint *Fin* an activity, resource or policy that limits the ability to achieve objectives. Constraints are commonly used in mathematical programming to describe a restriction which forms part of the boundary for the range of solutions to a problem, and which define the area within which the solution must lie.

constructive dismissal *HR* a form of *unfair dismissal* that occurs when an employee leaves a job and his or her claim of *breach of contract* or overbearing conduct by the employer is proven

consultant *Gen Mgt* an expert in a specialised field brought in to provide independent professional advice to an organisation on some aspect of its activities. A consultant may advise on the overall management of an organisation or on a specific project such as the introduction of a new computer system. Consultants are usually retained by a client for a set period of time during which they will investigate the matter in hand and produce a report detailing their recommendations. Consultants may set up in business independently or be employed by a large consulting firm. Specific types of consultants include *management consultants* and *internal consultants*.

consultative committee *HR* a meeting of representatives of management and staff, convened for the purposes of joint consultation

consultative management *Gen Mgt* a style of management that takes employees' views into account for decision-making purposes

consumer *Mkting* somebody who uses a product or service. A consumer may not be the purchaser of a product or service and should be distinguished from a *customer*, who is the person or organisation that purchased the product or service. *Also known as end consumer*

consumer advertising *Mkting* advertising aimed at individuals and the domestic and family market as opposed to *industrial advertising*, which is aimed at businesses

consumer behaviour *Mkting* see *consumer demand*

consumer demand *Mkting* the patterns of **consumer behaviour** that affect their buying decisions. Consumer demand is influenced in various ways. Psychologists and marketers have identified three important factors affecting buying decisions: needs, which are things we must have, such as food; wants, which are nice to have but not essential, such as a new car; and motives, such as keeping up appearances. These factors form part of a profile that includes motivations, personality, perceptions, cognition, attitudes, and values. Other factors that influence demand include gender, age, social grouping, education, location, income, culture, and the seasons. Consumers can therefore be divided into discrete segments, each of which has a particular pattern of buying behaviour. Products and services can then be targeted at specific segments of the market.

consumer goods marketing *Mkting* the promotion of products to members of the public. Consumer goods marketing is aimed at individuals rather than organisations and promotes products directly to the end user rather than to intermediaries. Marketing strategies will be different from those used in *industrial goods marketing*.

consumerism *Mkting* the influence of the general public, as end users of products and services, on the way companies manufacture and sell their goods. Consumers exert considerable power over companies as organisations become more customer-focused. Demand is rising for products that are high quality, ethically produced, well priced, and

---

Run with your head the first two-thirds of a race and with your heart the final one third. **Jack Daniels**

safe, and consumerism pressurises companies to operate and produce goods and services in accordance with the public's wishes. In fact, the aims of consumerism are not at odds with those of marketing (see **marketing management**), as both have the end goal of pleasing the consumer. In practice, however, marketing does not always succeed, and there is still a need for legislation to back up the right of consumers to demand products that are of good quality and for consumer protection bodies that influence the commercial world on consumers' behalf. A particular form of consumer pressure, motivated by environmental concerns, is **green consumerism**, which campaigns for environmentally friendly goods, services, and means of production.

consumer market research *Mkting market research* that focuses on gathering and analysing data on individual or domestic consumers, as opposed to industrial or business customers. *Also known as* **consumer research**

consumer panel *Mkting* a carefully selected group of people whose purchasing habits are regularly monitored. A consumer panel usually consists of a large cross-section of the population so as to provide meaningful data. There are two types of panel: **diary panels**, where members fill in a regular detailed diary of purchases, and, less commonly, **home audit panels**, where visits are made to the homes of members to check purchases, packaging, and used cartons. These panels run over a period of time to gain a broad overview of purchasing habits. A *focus group* is similar to a consumer panel, but is usually used to determine customers' views of a specific product or range of products. Members of a group meet together under the guidance of a facilitator to discuss their opinions on a face-to-face basis.

consumer price index *Econ* an index of the prices of goods and services that consumers purchase, used to measure the cost of living or the rate of inflation in an economy. *Abbr* **CPI**

consumer profile *Mkting* a detailed analysis of a group of like *consumers*, covering influences on their purchasing habits such as age, gender, education, occupation, income, and personal and psychological characteristics. Consumer profiles are built up from extensive *market research* and are used for market segmentation purposes.

consumer protection *Mkting* the safeguarding of *consumer* interests in terms of quality, price, and safety, usually within a statutory framework. In the United Kingdom, the Sale of Goods Acts and related legislation require that goods sold must be of a merchantable quality. The growing purchasing power of consumers and the rise in *consumerism* from the late 1950s onwards led to increased demands for protection against unsafe goods and services and unscrupulous trading practices. As a result, the Office of Fair Trading was set up in 1973 with the main aim of promoting and safeguarding the economic interests of consumers at a national level. Regulators have been set up for all the utility companies—telecommunications, gas, electricity, water, railways—and local authorities have their own Trading Standards Offices. The National Consumer Council was set up in 1975 to represent the views of consumers to local and central government, and a number of smaller consumer councils represent consumers on a sectoral basis, for example, the Gas Consumer Council. Citizens' Advice Bureaux provide legal advice on a very wide range of consumer and other issues.

consumer research *Mkting see* **consumer market research**

consumer services marketing *Mkting* the marketing of services to domestic consumers. Consumer services marketing may promote such services as banking, insurance, travel and tourism, leisure, telecommunications, and services provided by local authorities. Strategies to market these services to business constitute *industrial services marketing*.

consumer spending *Mkting* the total value of household and personal expenditure measured at macro and micro levels. At the macro level, consumer confidence can be measured by the overall levels of consumer spending as published in, for example, *Social Trends* (Stationery Office), the *Family Expenditure Survey*, and other official publications, and from a demonstration that earnings have increased at a faster rate than prices, which indicates that spending power, or disposable income, has increased. At a micro level, there are innumerable market reports on the value of actual and predicted spend on a vast range of consumer goods, including food, pharmaceuticals, clothing, cars, and holidays. *Consumer demand* is a related concept.

consumer-to-consumer commerce *E-com* e-business transactions conducted between two individuals

consumption *Econ* the quantity of resources that consumers use to satisfy their current needs and wants, measured by the sum of the current expenditure of the government and individual consumers

contact card *E-com* a *smart card* in which the microprocessor chip is visible and can make physical contact with the reading device

contactless card *E-com* a *smart card* in which the microprocessor chip is not visible and is accessed by the reading device by radio signals rather than by physical contact. An increasingly common use of this technology is in such applications as toll collection where the card is accessed as the motorist displays it to the reading device in passing.

contact list *HR* a list of people created for the purpose of networking, job searching, and marketing and selling products and services.

Someone wanting to expand and develop their contact list should seek to do so both inside and outside the organisation they work for. Joining professional associations and volunteering for committees are good ways of doing this. Building relationships can take time, and it's better to do this before going to someone for help. It's also important that the relationships are reciprocal; someone building a contact list should think about what they can offer to their contacts, as well as what their contacts can do for them.

A contact list should cover three basic types of network: the personal (friends, family, church, local community), the professional (current and former colleagues, supervisors, teachers, customers, consultants, members of professional organisations), and the work life network (executive recruiters, college placement officers, career counsellors). A good system is needed for keeping track of these contacts, their details (including personal information), and any correspondence with them. Keeping in regular contact with them is vital, and finding ways to thank them for their help will ensure good future relations.

content *E-com* the textual, graphical, and multimedia material that constitutes a web page or website

content management *E-com* the means and methods of managing the textual and graphical content of a website. For large sites with thousands of pages and many interchangeable words and images, it pays to invest in a content management application system that facilitates the creation and organisation of web content. Some content management systems also offer caching (where a server stores frequently requested information) and analysis of site traffic.

Recent years have seen a vast growth in the quantity of content produced by organisations, particularly in digital form. In 2001, it was estimated that there were over 550 billion documents on Internet, intranet, and extranet websites—making professional content management vital. Without it, it becomes almost impossible for a user to find the information they are looking for.

However, excellent content management is expensive, and organisations need to establish a solid business case in order to justify it. The initial point for consideration is that content is not a low-level commodity that merely needs to be stored—it is a critical resource, and its value lies in it being read. So an understanding of who will read it is essential. Decisions need to be taken over what languages the material needs to be published in, and in what media (Web or e-mail, for example). The form of the content—text, audio, video—is also important, as is the sensitivity of the material and the consequent security required.

Simply storing content is data management, but content management should have publication as its main focus, with the intention of informing or entertaining readers. There is a big difference in approach between the two.

contestable market *Econ* a market in which there are no barriers to entry, as in *perfect competition*

context *E-com* information about a product made available on an Internet site that is seen as adding value for the consumer, for example, book reviews on a book site

contingency allowance *Gen Mgt see standard time*

contingency management *Gen Mgt* the capacity for flexibility in varying responses and attitudes to meet the needs of different situations. Contingency management may be practised by both individuals and organisations. Within the latter, it may be formalised through a *contingency plan* linked to *risk* or *crisis management* strategies, or be derived from the results of *scenario planning*.

contingency plan *Gen Mgt* a plan, drawn up in advance, to ensure a positive and rapid response to a changing situation. A contingency plan often results from *scenario planning* and may form part of an organisation's *disaster management* strategy.

contingency table *Stats* a table in which observations on several categorical variables are cross-classified

---

Work keeps us from three great evils: boredom, vice, and poverty.   *Voltaire*

contingency tax *Econ* a one-off tax levied by a government to deal with a particular economic problem, for example, too high a level of imports coming into the country

contingency theory *Fin* the hypothesis that there can be no universally applicable best practice in the design of organisational units or of control systems such as management accounting systems. The efficient design and functioning of such systems is dependent on an awareness by the system designer of the specific environmental factors which influence their operation, such as the organisational structure, technology base, and market situation.

continuing professional development *HR see* **CPD**

continuous budget *Fin see* **rolling budget**

continuous disclosure *Fin* in Canada, the practice of ensuring that complete, timely, accurate, and balanced information about a public company is made available to shareholders

continuous improvement *Gen Mgt, Ops* the seeking of small improvements in processes and products, with the aim of increasing quality and reducing waste. Continuous improvement is one of the tools that underpin the philosophies of *total quality management* and *lean production*. Through constant study and revision of processes, a better product can result at reduced cost. *Kaizen* has become a foundation for many continuous improvement strategies, and for many employees it is synonymous with continuous improvement.

continuous operation costing *or* **continuous process costing** *Fin* the costing method applicable where goods or services result from a sequence of continuous or repetitive operations or processes. Costs are averaged over the units produced during the period, being initially charged to the operation or process.

continuous service *HR* a period of employment with one *employer*, which begins with the day on which the *employee* starts work and ends with the date of *resignation* or *dismissal*. All service, regardless of hours worked, counts towards calculating continuous service. The length of continuous service may affect the length of *notice period* and is taken into account when calculating redundancy pay.

continuous shiftwork *HR* a pattern of work designed to provide cover seven days a week, 24 hours a day, comprising three eight-hour or two twelve-hour *shifts*, or a mix of the two. Continuous shiftwork may be necessary to make full use of expensive capital equipment or to provide round-the-clock customer service. It may be confined to one group of employees, such as computer or security staff, while other parts of the organisation use different shift patterns.

contour plot *Stats* a graphical representation of data in which three variables are plotted on a topographical map

contra *Fin* a bookkeeping term meaning against, or on the opposite side. It is used where debits are matched with related credits, in the same or a different account.

contract *Gen Mgt* a legally binding agreement between two or more parties. A contract is made as a result of an offer by one party and acceptance on the part of the other. It normally involves an undertaking made by one party in consideration of an undertaking made by the other party or parties. Contracts are generally written but may be oral. Contract law may lay down additional conditions for the creation of valid contracts in some cases. Types of contract include contracts for the supply of goods or services and *contracts of employment*.

contract broker *Fin* a broker who fills an order placed by somebody else

contract cost *Fin* aggregated costs of a single contract; usually applies to major long-term contracts rather than short-term jobs

contract costing *Fin* a form of specific order costing in which costs are attributed to individual contracts

contract distribution *Gen Mgt* the *outsourcing* of a company's distribution requirement to a third party under contract. Contract distribution can help a company drive down costs, reduce stockholdings, and achieve increased flexibility of delivery.

contract hire *Gen Mgt* an arrangement whereby an organisation enters into a *contract* for the use of assets owned by another organisation, as an alternative to purchasing the assets itself. Contract hire agreements normally cover a period shorter that the useful economic life of the assets concerned and often include arrangements for maintenance and replacement. Organisations frequently use contract hire arrangements for the provision of company cars or office equipment.

Man is born perfect. It is the capitalist system which corrupts him. *Arthur Scargill*

contracting *Gen Mgt* the process of making an agreement governed by a *contract* for the provision of goods or services to an organisation

contracting out 1. *HR* the withdrawal of employees by an employer from the State Earnings-Related Pension Scheme and their enrolment in an occupational pension scheme that meets specified standards **2.** *HR* the withdrawal by an employee from the State Earnings-Related Pension Scheme and the purchase by the employee of an appropriate *personal pension* **3.** *Gen Mgt see* **outsourcing**

contract manufacturing *Ops* the *outsourcing* of a requirement to manufacture a particular product or component to a third-party company. Contract manufacturing enables companies to reduce the level of investment in their own capabilities to manufacture, while retaining a product produced to a high quality, at a reasonable price, and delivered to a flexible schedule.

contract month *Fin* the month in which an option expires and goods covered by it must be delivered. *Also known as* **delivery month**

contract note *Fin* a document with the complete description of a stock transaction

contract of employment *Gen Mgt, HR* a legally enforceable agreement, either oral or written, between an employer and employee that defines terms and *conditions of employment* to which both parties must adhere. Express terms of the contract are agreed between the two parties and include the organisation's normal terms and conditions in addition to those that relate specifically to the individual. These terms can only be changed by employee agreement, if the contract itself allows for variation, or by terminating the contract. Terms are also implied in the contract by custom and practice or by common law.

contract purchasing *Ops* a mechanism for buying leased goods. In contract purchasing, a purchaser agrees to buy goods or equipment to be paid for in a series of instalments, each comprising a proportion of the capital and an interest element. After a final payment, legal ownership passes to the user. This mechanism is sometimes used in the United Kingdom to finance the purchase of company cars so that the organisation can get the full writing-down allowance.

contractual obligation *HR* the legal duty to take a stated course of action, as imposed by a commercial *contract* or a *contract of employment*

contributed content website *E-com* a website which allows visitors to contribute content, such as information about their identity, or postings on message boards. A good example is Amazon.com, which encourages users to publish reviews of the books they have read.

contributed surplus *Fin* the portion of shareholders' equity that comes from sources other than earnings, for example, from the initial sale of stock above its par value

contribution *Fin* sales value less variable cost of sales. Contribution may be expressed as total contribution, contribution per unit, or as a percentage of sales.

contribution centre *Fin* a profit centre in which marginal or direct costs are matched against revenue

contribution margin *Fin* a way of showing how much individual products or services contribute to net profit.
| EXAMPLE | Its calculation is straightforward:

Sales price – variable cost = contribution margin
Or, for providers of services:

Total revenue – total variable cost = contribution margin
For example, if the sales price of a good is £500 and variable cost is £350, the contribution margin is £150, or 30% of sales. This means that 30 pence of every sales pound remain to contribute to fixed costs and to profit, after the costs directly related to the sales are subtracted.

Contribution margin is especially useful to a company comparing different products or services. For example:

	Product A £	*Product B £*	*Product C £*
Sales	260	220	140
Variable costs	178	148	65
Contribution margin	82	72	75
Contribution margin (%)	31.5	32.7	53.6

Corporate courage is usually no greater than personal courage. *Edward Teller*

Obviously, Product C has the highest contribution percentage, even though Product A generates more total profit. The analysis suggests that the company might do well to aim to achieve a sales mix with a higher proportion of Product C. It further suggests that prices for Products A and B may be too low, or that their cost structures need attention. Notably, none of this information appears on a standard income statement.

Contribution margin can be tracked over a long period of time, using data from several years of income statements. It can also be invaluable in calculating volume discounts for preferred customers, and break-even sales or volume levels.

contribution per unit of limiting factor ratio *Fin* a ratio used in marginal costing to measure the contribution to fixed overhead and profit generated by the use of each unit of limiting factor. It is calculated by dividing the product or service contribution by the product or service usage of units of limiting factor. The ratio is used to rank alternative uses of the limiting factor.

contributions holiday *Fin* a period during which a company stops making contributions to its pension plan because the plan is sufficiently well funded

contribution to sales ratio *Fin* a ratio used in product profit planning and as a means of ranking alternative products. It is calculated as follows:
Revenue minus all variable costs × 100 /Revenue

control *Gen Mgt* the effective monitoring, regulation, and direction of operations and budgets by senior managers. Control is often considered to be the primary task of management and has traditionally been strongly linked to accounting, **stock control**, **production** or **operations management**, and **quality control**. It is usually linked to **management control systems** such as performance measurement and **performance indicators**, procedures, and inspections.

control account *Fin* a ledger account which collects the sum of the postings into the individual accounts which it controls. The balance on the control account should equal the sum of the balances on the individual accounts, which are maintained as subsidiary records.

controllability concept *Fin* the principle that management accounting identifies the elements or activities which management can or cannot influence, and seeks to assess risk and sensitivity factors. This facilitates the

proper monitoring, analysis, comparison, and interpretation of information which can be used constructively in the control, evaluation, and corrective functions of management.

controllable cost *Fin* a cost which can be influenced by its budget holder

controlled circulation *Mkting* the number of copies of a newspaper or magazine distributed, usually free of charge, to an approved target audience

controlled disbursement *Fin* the presentation of cheques only once each day

controlled economy *Gen Mgt see* **competition**

control limits *Fin* quantities or values outside which managerial action is triggered. *See also* **management by exception**

conversion *Fin* **1.** a trade of one convertible financial instrument for another, for example, a bond for shares **2.** a trade of shares of one unit trust for shares of another in the same family

conversion price *Fin* the price per share at which the holder of convertible bonds, or debentures, or preference shares, can convert them into ordinary shares.

EXAMPLE Depending on specific terms, the conversion price may be set when the convertible asset is issued. If the conversion price is set, it will appear in the indenture, a legal agreement between the issuer of a convertible asset and the holder, that states specific terms. If the conversion price does not appear in the agreement, a conversion ratio is used to calculate the conversion price.

A conversion ratio of 25:1, for example, means that 25 shares of stock can be obtained in exchange for each £1,000 convertible asset held. In turn, the conversion price can be determined simply by dividing £1,000 by 25:
£1,000 / 25 = £40 per share
Comparison of a stock's conversion price to its prevailing market price can help decide the best course of action. If the shares of the company in question are trading at £52 per share, converting makes sense, because it increases the value of £1,000 convertible to £1,300 (£52 × 25 shares). But if the shares are trading at £32 per share, then conversion value is only £800 (£32 × 25) and it is clearly better to defer conversion.

conversion rate *Mkting* the percentage of potential customers who actually make a purchase

---

Three failures denote uncommon strength. A weakling has not enough grit to fail thrice. **Minna Antrim**

conversion ratio *Fin* an expression of the quantity of one security that can be obtained for another, for example, shares for a convertible bond.

EXAMPLE The conversion ratio may be established when the convertible is issued. If that is the case, the ratio will appear in the indenture, the binding agreement that details the convertible's terms.

If the conversion ratio is not set, it can be calculated quickly: divide the par value of the convertible security (typically £1,000) by its conversion price.

£1,000 / £40 per share = 25

In this example, the conversion ratio is 25:1, which means that every bond held with a £1,000 par value can be exchanged for 25 ordinary shares.

Knowing the conversion ratio enables an investor to decide whether convertibles (or group of them) are more valuable than the ordinary shares they represent. If the stock is currently trading at 30, the conversion value is £750, or £250 less than the par value of the convertible. It would therefore be unwise to convert.

A convertible's indenture can sometimes contain a provision stating that the conversion ratio will change over the years.

Conversion ratio also describes the number of ordinary shares of one type to be issued for each outstanding ordinary share of a different type when a merger takes place.

conversion value *Fin* the value a security would have if converted into shares

convertible ARM *Fin* an adjustable-rate mortgage that the borrower can convert into a fixed-rate mortgage under specified terms

convertible bond *Fin* a bond that the owner can convert into another asset, especially ordinary shares

convertible loan stock *Fin* a loan which gives the holder the right to convert to other securities, normally ordinary shares, at a predetermined price/rate and time

convertible preference shares *Fin* shares that give the holder the right to exchange them at a fixed price for another security, usually ordinary shares.

EXAMPLE Preference shares and other convertible securities offer investors a hedge: fixed-interest income without sacrificing the chance to participate in a company's capital appreciation.

When a company does well, investors can convert their holdings into ordinary shares that are more valuable. When a company is less successful, they can still receive interest and principal payments, and also recover their investment and preserve their capital if a more favourable investment appears.

Conversion ratios and prices are key facts to know about preference shares. This information is found on the indenture statement that accompanies all issues. Occasionally the indenture will state that the conversion ratio will change over time. For example, the conversion price might be £50 for the first five years, £55 for the next five years, and so forth. Stock splits can affect conversion considerations.

In theory, convertible preference shares (and convertible exchangeable preference shares) are usually perpetual in time. However, issuers tend to force conversion or induce voluntary conversion for convertible preference shares within ten years. Steadily increasing ordinary share dividends is one inducement tactic used. As a result, the conversion feature for preference shares often resembles that of debt securities. Call protection for the investor is usually about three years, and a 30– to 60-day call notice is typical.

About 50% of convertible equity issues also have a 'soft call provision'. If the ordinary share price reaches a specified ratio, the issuer is permitted to force conversion before the end of the normal protection period.

convertible security *Fin* a convertible bond, warrant, or preference share

convertible share *Fin* non-equity share such as a preference share, carrying rights to convert into equity shares on predetermined terms

convertible term insurance *Fin* term insurance that the policyholder can convert to fixed life assurance under particular conditions

COO *abbr Gen Mgt* chief operating officer

cookie *E-com* a file written to a computer's hard disk by an Internet application to store small amounts of information that can be accessed to identify users and customise interactions with them. Cookies contain such data as registration or logon information, user preferences, shopping basket items, and credit-card numbers and expiry dates. The name is derived from UNIX objects called 'magic cookies'.

cooling-off period *HR* an agreed pause in a dispute, especially a labour dispute, to allow the tempers of the negotiating parties to cool before the resumption of negotiations

---

The only thing experience teaches us is that experience teaches us nothing. **André Maurois (attrib.)**

Cooper, Cary (*b.* 1940) *Gen Mgt* US-born academic. Based at the School of Management, University of Manchester Institute of Science & Technology, United Kingdom, Cooper focuses on *occupational psychology*, particularly *stress* management issues. His biggest-selling book is *Living with Stress* (1988, co-author).

co-operative *Mkting* a business that is jointly owned by the people who operate it, with all profits shared equally

co-operative advertising *Mkting* a joint advertising campaign between groups with a shared objective, for example, retailer groups, or manufacturer and retailer

co-operative movement *Gen Mgt* a movement that aims to share profits and benefits from jointly owned commercial enterprises among members. The movement was begun in Rochdale, Lancashire in 1844 by 28 weavers and developed to include manufacturing and wholesale businesses as well as insurance and financial services. The Co-op in the United Kingdom and the *Mondragon co-operative* in Spain are two of the best known examples.

co-opetition *Gen Mgt* co-operation between competing companies (*slang*)

copyright *Mkting* the legal protection for creative ideas, trademarks, and other brand-related material

copy testing *Mkting* research carried out to test the effectiveness of creative advertising copy

copywriter *Mkting* somebody who devises the wording of an advertisement or promotional material. A copywriter may be employed by an advertising agency or, in scientific or technical areas, directly by a manufacturing or distribution company. Many copywriters also work *freelance*.

core business *Gen Mgt* the central, and usually the original, focus of an organisation's activities that differentiates it from others and makes a vital contribution to its success. The concept of core business became prominent in the 1980s when *diversification* by large companies failed to generate the anticipated degree of commercial success. In 1982, *Tom Peters*'s and *Robert Waterman*'s book *In Search of Excellence* suggested that organisations should *stick to the knitting* and avoid diversifying into areas beyond their field of expertise. An organisation's core business should be defined by the *core competences* of the organisation.

core capability *Gen Mgt see* **core competence**

core competence *Gen Mgt, HR* a key ability or strength that an organisation has acquired that differentiates it from others, gives it *competitive advantage*, and contributes to its long-term success. The concept of core competence is most closely associated with the work of *Gary Hamel* and *C.K. Prahalad*, notably in their book *Competing for the Future* (1994). They describe core competences as bundles of skills and technologies resulting from *organisational learning*. These provide access to markets, contribute to customer value, and are difficult for competitors to imitate. Core competence is a resource-based approach to *corporate strategy*. The terms core competence and **core capability** are often used interchangeably, but some writers make varying distinctions between the two concepts.

core values 1. *Gen Mgt* the guiding principles of an organisation, espoused by senior management, and accepted by employees, often reflected in the *mission statement* of the organisation. Core values often influence the culture of an organisation and are normally long-standing beliefs. As **shared values**, they are included in the *McKinsey 7-S framework*, and are reported in *Richard Pascale*'s and *Anthony Athos*'s *The Art of Japanese Management* in their analysis of the rise of *Konosuke Matsushita*. **2.** *HR* a small set of key concepts and ideals that guide a person's life and help him or her to make important decisions

corpocracy *Gen Mgt* excessive or unwieldy corporate management resulting from the merger of several companies (*slang*)

corporate action *Fin* a measure that a company takes that has an effect on the number of shares outstanding or the rights that apply to shares

corporate amnesia *Gen Mgt* loss of organisational history and memory. Corporate amnesia occurs when senior or long-standing members of staff leave and their personal knowledge, built up from years of experience in the company, goes with them. This is occurring more frequently with the rise in *downsizing* and *delayering*, and the phenomenon goes hand in hand with the *anorexic organisation*. Amnesia can be a significant disadvantage to an organisation, causing it to forget the lessons it has learned and to waste time and effort in doing things again.

corporate appraisal *Fin* a critical assessment of strengths and weaknesses, opportunities and threats (**SWOT analysis**) in relation to the internal and environmental factors affecting an entity in order to establish its condition prior to the preparation of the long-term plan

corporate bond *Fin* a long-term bond with fixed interest issued by a corporation

corporate brand *Gen Mgt* the coherent outward expression projected by an organisation. A corporate brand is a product of an organisation's *corporate strategy*, mission, image, and activities. Corporate brands distinguish organisations from their competitors, orient the organisation in the minds of customers and employees, and create a perception of what an organisation stands for. There is much debate about the precise nature of corporate brands, and about their depth. Corporate branding has been seen as a superficial quick fix to restore a company's tarnished image or revitalise an ailing company. It requires board level co-ordination, however, and rather than being arbitrarily imposed on an organisation, it is actually a product of the sum of its activities. Changing a corporate brand, or re-branding a company, can only be accomplished by changing strategy and activity within the company.

corporate climate *Gen Mgt* the environment created by the managerial style and attitudes that pervade an organisation. Corporate climate is strongly linked to *corporate culture* in creating the general feeling and atmosphere of an organisation. The climate within an organisation can affect aspects such as *productivity*, *creativity*, and *customer focus*, and each organisation needs to create a climate that will facilitate organisational success.

corporate communication *Gen Mgt* the activities undertaken by an organisation to communicate both internally with employees and externally with existing and prospective customers and the wider public. Corporate communication is sometimes used to refer principally to external communication and sometimes to internal communication, but strictly speaking covers both. The term implies an emphasis on promoting a sense of *corporate identity* and presenting a consistent and coherent *corporate image*.

corporate concierge (*US*) *Gen Mgt* an employee whose job involves doing personal tasks such as booking hotels or collecting shopping on behalf of other employees who have little time for these tasks (*slang*)

corporate culture *Gen Mgt* the combined beliefs, values, ethics, procedures, and atmos-phere of an organisation. The culture of an organisation is often expressed as 'the way we do things around here' and consists of largely unspoken values, norms, and behaviours that become the natural way of doing things. An organisation's culture may be more apparent to an external observer than an internal practitioner. The first person to attempt a definition of corporate culture was *Edgar Schein*, who said that it consisted of rules, procedures, and processes that governed how things were done, as well as the philosophy that guides the attitude of senior management towards staff and customers. The difficulty in identifying the traits of culture and changing them is borne out by the fact that culture is not merely climate, power, and politics, but all those things and more. There can be several subcultures within an organisation, for example, defined by hierarchy—shopfloor or executive—or by function—sales, design, or production. Changing or renewing corporate culture in order to achieve the organisation's strategy is considered one of the major tasks of organisation *leadership*, as it is recognised that such a change is hard to achieve without the will of the leader. *Also known as* **organisational culture**

corporate evolution *Gen Mgt* the way in which organisations are transformed through the use of information technology

corporate giving *Gen Mgt* monetary or in-kind donations by organisations as part of the process of *community involvement*

corporate governance *Gen Mgt* the managerial and directorial control of an incorporated organisation, which, when well-practised, can reduce the risk of fraud, improve company performance and leadership, and demonstrate *social responsibility*. The structure of the legislation surrounding corporate governance varies from country to country. In the United Kingdom, the importance of good corporate governance was brought to public attention after a series of corporate collapses and scandals in the 1980s and 1990s. The effectiveness of the *board of directors* of the organisations involved was questioned, and the importance of independent, impartial *non-executive directors* was highlighted. To address the issues raised, the 'Committee on the Financial Aspects of Corporate Governance' was set up, chaired by *Sir Adrian Cadbury*. Following the publication of this committee's report in 1992, a code of best practice was established. Although it is voluntary, all listed companies are expected to comply. Since the Cadbury report, a number of other

---

If we see light at the end of the tunnel, it's the light of the oncoming train.　　　　　*Robert Lowell*

committees have established best practice in specific areas such as directors' pay. These culminated in the Hampel committee, which established a 'Combined Code' incorporating the Cadbury guidelines, 'Principles of Good Governance', and a 'Code of Best Practice'.

Corporate Governance Combined Code *Fin* the successor to the Cadbury Code, established by the Hampel Committee. The code consists of a set of principles of corporate governance and detailed code provisions embracing the work of the Cadbury, Greenbury, and Hampel Committees. Section 1 of the code contains the principles and provisions applicable to UK listed companies, while section 2 contains the principles and provisions applicable to institutional shareholders in their relationships with companies.

corporate hospitality *Gen Mgt* entertainment provided by an organisation. Corporate hospitality was originally designed to help salespeople build relationships with customers, but it is now increasingly used as a staff incentive and in employee *team building* and training exercises.

corporate identity *Gen Mgt* the distinctive characteristics or personality of an organisation, including *corporate culture*, values, and philosophy as perceived by those within the organisation and presented to those outside. Corporate identity is expressed through the name, symbols, and logos used by the organisation, and the design of communication materials, and is a factor influencing the *corporate image* of an organisation. The creation of a strong corporate identity also involves consistency in the organisation's actions, behaviour, products, and brands, and often reflects the *mission statement* of an organisation. A positive corporate identity can promote a sense of purpose and belonging within the organisation and encourage *employee commitment* and involvement.

corporate image *Gen Mgt* the perceptions and impressions of an organisation by the public as a result of interaction with the organisation and the way the organisation presents itself. Organisations have traditionally focused on the design of communication and advertising materials, using logos, symbols, text, and colour to create a favourable impression on target groups, but a range of additional activities contribute to a positive corporate image. These include *PR* programmes such as *community involvement*, *sponsorship*, and environmental projects, participation in quality improvement schemes, and good practice in industrial relations.

corporate planning *Gen Mgt* the process of drawing up detailed action plans to achieve an organisation's aims and objectives, taking into account the resources of the organisation and the environment within which it operates. Corporate planning represents a formal, structured approach to achieving objectives and to implementing the *corporate strategy* of an organisation. It has traditionally been seen as the responsibility of senior management. The use of the term became predominant during the 1960s but has now been largely superseded by the concept of *strategic management*.

corporate portal *Gen Mgt* a single gateway to information and software applications held within an organisation that also allows links to information outside the organisation. A corporate portal is a development of *intranet* technology. Ideally, it should allow users to access groupware, e-mail, and desktop applications, and to customise both the way information is presented and the way it is used. It should also provide dynamic access to data held within an *MIS*, *decision support system*, or other corporate database, and enable *virtual team* working across an organisation. Like many purely technological solutions, a corporate portal still relies on good *internal communication* and a *corporate culture* that embraces openness and information sharing.

corporate restructuring *Gen Mgt* a fundamental change in direction and strategy for an organisation that affects the way in which the organisation is structured. Corporate restructuring may involve increasing or decreasing the layers of personnel between the top and the bottom of an organisation, or re-assigning roles and responsibilities. Invariably, corporate restructuring has come to mean reorganising after a period of unsatisfactory performance and poor results, and is often manifested in the *divestment* or closure of parts of the business and the *outplacement*, or shedding, of personnel. In this case, corporate restructuring is used as a euphemism for *delayering*, *rationalisation*, *downsizing*, or *rightsizing*.

corporate social accounting *Fin* the reporting of the social and environmental impact of an entity's activities upon those who are directly associated with the entity (employees, customers, suppliers, etc.) or those who are in any way affected by the activities of the entity, as well as an assessment of the cost of compliance with relevant regulations in this area

corporate strategy *Gen Mgt* the direction an organisation takes with the aim of achieving business success in the long term. A number of models such as **Michael Porter**'s Five Forces model and **Gary Hamel**'s and **C.K. Prahalad**'s model of **core competencies** have been used to develop corporate strategy. More recent approaches have focused on the need for companies to adapt to and anticipate changes in the business environment. The formulation of corporate strategy involves establishing the purpose and scope of the organisation's activities and the nature of the business it is in, taking the environment in which it operates, its position in the marketplace, and the competition it faces into consideration. **Corporate planning** and **business plans** are used to implement corporate strategy.

corporate university *HR* a centralised training and education facility within an organisation, offering **training** and development only to employees of that organisation. Traditionally, corporate universities only offered internal qualifications and were used as a means of channelling **employee development** towards meeting corporate goals, sharing corporate information or knowledge, and disseminating **corporate culture**. More recently, some corporate universities have established links with academic institutions in order to offer formal qualifications.

corporate veil *Gen Mgt* immunity granted to shareholders to protect them from legal action in the event of the failure of a business

corporate venturing *Gen Mgt* the undertaking of an investment initiative by a commercial organisation to gain experience of a new technology or an unfamiliar market

corporate vision *Gen Mgt* the overall goal of an organisation that all business activities and processes should contribute towards achieving. Ideally, the workforce should be committed to, and driven by, the vision, because it is they who make it happen. As the vision nears achievement, a new corporate vision or an evolution of the existing one should be established. Corporate vision is usually summed up in a formal **vision statement**.

corporation *(US) Fin* = **limited liability company**

corporation tax *Fin* tax chargeable on companies resident in the United Kingdom or trading in the United Kingdom through a branch or agency as well as on certain unincorporated associations

correlation *Stats* the interdependence between pairs of variables in data

correlation coefficient *Stats* an index of the linear relationship between two variables in data

cosmeceuticals *Gen Mgt* pharmaceuticals such as anti-ageing creams that have a cosmetic rather than a health-related purpose (*slang*)

cost[1] *Fin* the amount of expenditure (actual or notional) incurred on, or attributable to, a specified thing or activity

cost[2] *Fin* to ascertain the cost of a specified thing or activity

cost accounting *Gen Mgt* the maintaining and checking of detailed records of the costs involved in manufacturing a product or providing a service in order to provide the information required for **costing** purposes. Cost accounting tries to identify the costs of outputs. This information is useful for pricing, budgeting, control of manufacturing or service processes, and planning materials and labour.

cost and freight *E-com* indicates that a quoted price includes the costs of the merchandise and the transportation but not the cost of insurance. *Abbr* **CFR**

cost audit *Fin* the verification of cost records and accounts, and a check on adherence to prescribed cost accounting procedures and their continuing relevance

cost behaviour *Fin* the variability of input costs with activity undertaken. A number of cost behaviour patterns are possible, ranging from **variable costs**, whose cost level varies directly with the level of activity, to **fixed costs**, where changes in output have no effect upon the cost level.

cost-benefit analysis *Gen Mgt* a technique for comparing the tangible and intangible costs of a project with the resulting benefits. Cost-benefit analysis assigns monetary value to the costs and benefits (social, environmental, and monetary) associated with a project for the purpose of evaluating and selecting investment project opportunities.

cost centre *Gen Mgt* a department, function, section, or individual whose cost, overall or in part, is an accepted overhead of a business in return for services provided to other parts of the organisation. A cost centre is usually an **indirect cost** of an organisation's products or services.

cost classification *Fin* the arrangement of elements of cost into logical groups with respect to their nature (fixed, variable, value adding etc.), function (production, selling etc.), or use in the business of the entity

cost (at cost) concept *Fin* the practice of valuing assets with reference to their acquisition cost

cost control *Fin* the process which ensures that actual costs do not exceed acceptable limits

cost-cutting *Gen Mgt* the reduction of the amount of money spent on the operations of an organisation or on the provision of products and services. Cost-cutting measures such as budget reductions, salary freezes, and staff redundancies may be taken by an organisation at a time of *recession* or financial difficulty or in situations where inefficiency has been identified. Alternative approaches to cost-cutting include modifying organisational structures and redesigning organisational processes for greater efficiency. Excessive cost-cutting may affect *productivity* and quality or the organisation's ability to add value.

cost driver *Gen Mgt* a factor that determines the cost of an activity. Cost drivers are analysed as part of *activity-based costing* and can be used in *continuous improvement* programmes. They are usually assessed together as multiple drivers rather than singly. There are two main types of cost driver: the first is a **resource driver**, which refers to the contribution of the quantity of resources used to the cost of an activity; the second is an **activity driver**, which refers to the costs incurred by the activities required to complete a particular task or project.

cost-effective *Gen Mgt* offering the maximum benefit for a given level of expenditure. When limited resources are available to meet specific objectives, the cost-effective solution is the best that can be achieved for that level of expenditure and the one that provides good value for money. The term is also used to refer to a level of expenditure that is perceived to be commercially viable.

cost-effectiveness analysis *Gen Mgt* a method for measuring the benefits and effectiveness of a particular item of expenditure. Cost-effectiveness analysis requires an examination of expenditure to determine whether the money spent could have been used more effectively or whether the resulting benefits could have been attained through less financial outlay.

cost estimation *Fin* the determination of cost behaviour. This can be achieved by

engineering methods, analysis of the accounts, use of statistics, or the pooling of expert views.

cost function *Econ* a mathematical function relating a firm's or an industry's total cost to its output and factor costs

costing *Fin* the process of determining the costs of products, services, or activities

cost, insurance, and freight *E-com* indicates that a quoted price includes the costs of the merchandise, transportation, and insurance. *Abbr* **CIF**

cost management *Fin* the application of management accounting concepts, methods of data collection, analysis, and presentation, in order to provide the information required to enable costs to be planned, monitored, and controlled

cost of appraisal *Fin* costs incurred in order to ensure that outputs produced meet required quality standards

cost of capital *Fin* the minimum acceptable return on an investment, generally computed as a hurdle rate for use in investment appraisal exercises. The computation of the optimal cost of capital can be complex, and many ways of determining this opportunity cost have been suggested.

cost of conformance *Fin* the cost of achieving specified quality standards. *See also cost of appraisal, cost of prevention*

cost of entry *Mkting* the cost of introducing a new product to the market. Cost of entry calculations include the cost of all research, development, production, testing, marketing, advertising, and distribution of a product.

cost of external failure *Fin* the cost arising from inadequate quality discovered after the transfer of ownership from supplier to purchaser

cost of internal failure *Fin* the costs arising from inadequate quality which are identified before the transfer of ownership from supplier to purchaser

cost of non-conformance *Fin* the cost of failure to deliver the required standard of quality. *See also cost of external failure, cost of internal failure*

cost of prevention *Fin* the costs incurred prior to or during production in order to prevent substandard or defective products or services from being produced

cost of quality *Fin* the difference between

---

the actual cost of producing, selling, and supporting products or services and the equivalent costs if there were no failures during production or usage. *See also cost of conformance, cost of non-conformance*

cost of sales *Fin* the sum of variable cost (see *cost behaviour*) of sales plus factory overhead attributable to the sales

cost per action *E-com see CPA*

cost per click-through *E-com* a pricing model for online advertising, where the seller gets paid whenever a visitor clicks on an ad

cost-plus pricing *Mkting* a standard **mark-up** added to the cost of a product or service to establish a selling price. Many companies simply add a percentage of production costs to arrive at a selling price. The degree of mark-up depends on the level of anticipated sales. Low-volume luxury goods may have a high mark-up; high-volume goods may have a relatively lower mark-up.

cost pool *Fin* the point of focus for the costs relating to a particular activity in an activity-based costing system

cost reduction *Fin* the reduction in unit cost of goods or services without impairing suitability for the use intended

cost table *Fin* a database containing all the costs associated with the production of a product, broken down to include the costs of functions and/or components and sub-assemblies. Cost tables also incorporate the cost changes which would result from a number of possible changes in the input mix.

cost unit *Fin* a unit of product or service in relation to which costs are ascertained

cost-volume-profit analysis *Fin* the study of the effects on future profit of changes in fixed cost, variable cost, sales price, quantity and mix

Council of Australian Governments *Gen Mgt* a body consisting of the heads of the Australian federal, state, and territory governments that meets to discuss matters of national importance. *Abbr* **COAG**

Council of Trade Unions (*ANZ*) *Gen Mgt see* **CTU**

counselling *HR* the provision of help by a trained person to permit somebody to clarify concerns, come to terms with feelings, and take responsibility for and begin to resolve difficulties. Counselling is a technique inherent to the *mentoring* process.

counterfactual *Gen Mgt* untrue (*slang*)

counterfeit *Gen Mgt* to produce forged or imitation goods or money intended to deceive or defraud. Counterfeited goods of inferior quality are often sold at substantially lower prices than genuine products and may bear the **brand** or **trade name** of the company. Counterfeiting violates **trademark** and **intellectual property** rights and may damage the reputation of producers of authentic goods. National and international legislation provides some recourse to companies against counterfeiters, but strategies such as consumer warnings and labelling methods are also used to minimise the impact of counterfeiting. Efforts to eliminate counterfeiting are co-ordinated by the International Anti-Counterfeiting Coalition.

counterparty (*US*) *Fin* a person with whom somebody is entering into a contract

counterpurchase *Econ see countertrade*

countertrade *Econ* a range of reciprocal trading practices. This umbrella term encompasses the direct exchange of goods for goods (or **barter**) where no cash changes hands to more complex variations; **counterpurchase**, which involves a traditional export transaction plus the commitment of the exporter to buy additional goods or services from that country; and **buy-back**, in which the supplier of plant or equipment is paid from the future proceeds resulting from the use of the plant. Countertrade conditions vary widely from country to country and can be costly and administratively cumbersome.

country club management *Gen Mgt see Managerial Grid™*

country risk *Fin* the risk associated with undertaking transactions with, or holding assets in, a particular country. Sources of risk might be political, economic, or regulatory instability affecting overseas taxation, repatriation of profits, nationalisation, currency instability, etc.

coupon *Fin* **1.** a piece of paper that a bondholder presents to request payment **2.** the rate of interest on a bond **3.** an interest payment made to a bondholder
clip coupons to collect periodic interest on a bond (*slang*)

covariance *Stats* the value that is predicted from the product of the deviations of two variables from each of their means

covariate *Stats* a variable that is not crucial

---

in an investigation but may affect the crucial variables from which a model is being built

coverage *Mkting* the percentage of a target audience reached by different media

Coverdale training *HR* a system of training that concentrates on improving **teamwork** and methods of getting a job done. Coverdale training is concerned with management behaviour, including setting **objectives**, briefing subordinates, and tackling a job. Groups of people are put into **scenarios** reproducing everyday situations and encouraged to experiment and build up successful working practices.

covered option *Fin* an option whose owner has the shares for the option

covered warrant *Fin* a futures contract for shares in a company

covering letter *HR* a letter sent to a potential employer together with a curriculum vitae (CV). It is used when a jobseeker knows the exact position he or she is applying for, and the name of the person to whom the CV is being sent.

A covering letter is important because it is the first thing the recruiting manager will read, and is key to their forming first impressions of the jobseeker. It must, therefore, be well-presented, well-informed, concise, professional, and yet enthusiastic.

cover note *Fin* a document that an insurance company issues to a customer to serve as a temporary insurance certificate until the issue of the policy itself

Covey, Stephen (*b.* 1932) *Gen Mgt* US writer and consultant. Offers a holistic approach to life and work, based on Mormon principles, the self-drive philosophy of **Dale Carnegie**, and the self-help advice of Samuel Smiles. His message is enshrined in *The Seven Habits of Highly Effective People* (1989), which calls for a re-think of many fundamental assumptions and attitudes.

CPA *abbr* **1.** *E-com* cost per action: a pricing model for online advertising based on the number of times an Internet user clicks on a banner ad that is linked to a particular website **2.** *Fin* customer profitability analysis

CPD *abbr* *HR* continuing professional development: on-going training and education throughout a career to improve the skills and knowledge used to perform a job or succession of jobs. CPD should be a planned, structured process, involving the assessment of development needs and the tailoring of train-

ing to meet those needs. CPD is founded on the belief that the development of professionals should not finish after initial qualification, especially in a fast-changing business environment in which skills are likely to obsolesce quickly. CPD requires commitment and resources from the employee, the employer, and supportive agencies such as professional bodies. Advocates of CPD argue that it can enhance **employability** and **career development** by keeping skills up to date and broadening a person's skill base. **Dominic Cadbury** has said that CPD should be centred on the individual, who must take responsibility for the continuing assessment and satisfaction of his or her own development needs. Much can be found in support of the principle of CPD in the concepts of **David Kolb**'s **experiential learning** cycle, **Peter Honey**'s and **Alan Mumford**'s learning types, the **personal development** cycle, and **lifelong learning**.

CPF *abbr HR* Central Provident Fund

CPI *abbr Econ* consumer price index

CPIX (*ANZ*) *Econ* the **consumer price index** excluding interest costs, on the basis that these are a direct outcome of monetary policy

CPM *abbr E-com* cost per thousand impressions: a pricing model for online advertising. The M represents the Roman numeral for 1,000.

crash 1. *Fin* a precipitous drop in value, especially of the stocks traded in a market **2.** *E-com* a hardware failure or program error that stops a computer working. If data has not been backed up it can be lost as a result of a crash. **3.** *Econ* a sudden and catastrophic downturn in an economy. The crash in the United States in 1929 is one of the most famous.

creative accounting *Fin* the use of accounting methods to hide aspects of a company's financial dealings in order to make the company appear more or less successful than it is in reality (*slang*)

creative consultancy *Mkting* an organisation that plans and creates advertising on behalf of a client

creative director *Mkting* an employee of an advertising agency who is responsible for planning and managing the creative work of a campaign

creative strategy *Mkting* a technique for determining the most effective creative approach to reach a target audience

creative thinking *Gen Mgt see* **creativity**

---

creativity *Gen Mgt* the generation of new ideas by approaching problems or existing practices in innovative or imaginative ways. Psychologists have disagreed on the nature of creativity. Until about 1980, research concentrated on identifying the personality traits of creative people, but more recently psychologists have focused on the mental processes involved. Creativity involves re-examining assumptions and reinterpreting facts, ideas, and past experience. A growing interest in creativity as a source of *competitive advantage* has developed in recent years, and creativity is considered important, not just for the development of new products and services, but also for its role in organisational *decision-making* and *problem-solving*. Many organisations actively seek a *corporate culture* that encourages creativity. There are a number of techniques used to foster **creative thinking**, including *brainstorming* and *lateral thinking*. Creativity is linked to *innovation*, the process of taking a new idea and turning it into a market offering.

credit *Fin* the trust that people have in somebody's ability to repay a loan, or a loan itself

credit account *Fin see charge account*

credit available *Fin* the amount of money that somebody can borrow at a given time

credit balance *Fin* the amount of money that somebody owes on a credit account

credit bureau *Fin* a company that assesses the creditworthiness of people for businesses or banks in the United States. *See also mercantile agency*

credit capacity *Fin* the amount of money that somebody can borrow and be expected to repay

credit card *E-com, Fin* a card issued by a bank or financial institution and accepted by a merchant in payment for a transaction for which the cardholder must subsequently reimburse the issuer

credit ceiling *Fin* the largest amount that a lender will permit somebody to borrow, for example, on a credit card

credit committee *Fin* a committee that evaluates a potential borrower's creditworthiness

credit company *Fin* a company that extends credit to people

credit co-operative *Fin* an organisation of people who join together to gain advantage in borrowing

credit creation *Fin* the collective ability of lenders to make money available to borrowers

credit crunch *Fin* a situation in which money for borrowing is unavailable

credit deposit *E-com* the value of the credit-card purchases deposited in a merchant's bank account after the acquirer's fees are deducted

credit derivative *Fin* a financial instrument that transfers a lender's risk to a third party

credit entity *Fin* a borrower or lender

credit entry *Fin* an item on the asset side of a financial statement

credit exposure *Fin* the risk to a lender of a borrower defaulting

credit-granter *Fin* a person or organisation that lends money

credit history *Fin* a potential borrower's record of debt repayment

crediting rate *Fin* the interest rate paid on an insurance policy that is an investment

credit limit *Fin* the highest amount that a lender will allow somebody to borrow, for example, on a credit card

credit line *Fin see line of credit*

credit note *Fin* a document stating that a shop owes somebody an amount of money and entitling the person to goods to the specified value

creditor *Fin* a person or organisation that is owed money

creditor days *Fin* the number of days on average that a company requires to pay its creditors.

EXAMPLE To determine creditor days, divide the cumulative amount of unpaid suppliers' bills (also called trade creditors) by sales, then multiply by 365. For example, if suppliers' bills total £800,000 and sales are £9,000,000, the calculation is:

(800,000 / 9,000,000) × 365 = 32.44 days

The company takes 32.44 days on average to pay its bills.

Creditor days is an indication of a company's creditworthiness in the eyes of its suppliers and creditors, since it shows how long they are willing to wait for payment. Within reason, the higher the number the better, because all companies want to conserve cash. At the same time, a company that is especially slow to pay its bills (100 or more days, for example) may be a company having trouble generating cash,

or one trying to finance its operations with its suppliers' funds.
*See also **debtor days***

creditor days ratio *Fin* a measure of the number of days on average that a company requires to pay its creditors.
EXAMPLE To determine creditor days, divide the cumulative amount of unpaid suppliers' bills (also called trade creditors) by sales, then multiply by 365. For example, if suppliers' bills total £800,000 and sales are £9,000,000, the calculation is:

(800,000 / 9,000,000) x 365 = 32.44 days

This means the company takes 32.44 days on average to pay its bills.

creditor nation *Econ* a country that has a balance of payments surplus

creditors' committee *Fin* a group that directs the efforts of creditors to receive partial repayment from a bankrupt person or organisation. *Also known as **creditors' steering committee***

creditors' meeting *Fin* a meeting of those to whom a bankrupt person or organisation owes money

creditors' settlement *Fin* an agreement on partial repayment to those to whom a bankrupt person or organisation owes money

creditors' steering committee *Fin see **creditors' committee***

credit rating *or* **credit ranking** *Fin* **1.** an assessment of somebody's creditworthiness **2.** the process of assessing somebody's creditworthiness

credit rating agency *(US) Fin = **credit-reference agency***

credit rationing *Fin* the process of making credit less easily available or subject to high interest rates

credit-reference agency *Fin* a company that assesses the creditworthiness of people on behalf of businesses or banks. *US term **credit rating agency***

credit report *Fin* information about an individual or entity relevant to a decision to grant credit

credit risk *Fin* **1.** the chance that a borrower will default on a loan **2.** a borrower who may default on a loan **3.** the possibility that a loss may occur from the failure of another party to perform according to the terms of a contract

credit sale *Fin* a sale for which the buyer need not pay immediately

credit scoring *Fin* a calculation done in the process of credit rating

credit side *Fin* the part of a financial statement that lists assets

credit squeeze *Fin* a situation in which credit is not easily available or is subject to high interest rates

credit standing *Fin* the reputation that somebody has with regard to meeting financial obligations

credit system *Fin* a set of rules and organisations involved in making loans

credit union *Fin* a co-operative savings association that lends money to members at low rates of interest

creditworthy *Fin* regarded as being reliable in terms of meeting financial obligations

creeping takeover *Fin* a takeover achieved by the gradual acquisition of small amounts of stock over an extended period of time (*slang*)

creeping tender offer *Fin* an acquisition of many shares in a company by purchase, especially to avoid US restrictions on tender offers

CREST *Fin* the paperless system used for settling stock transactions electronically in the United Kingdom

crisis management *Mkting* actions taken by an organisation in response to unexpected events or situations with potentially negative effects that threaten resources and people or the success and continued operation of the organisation. Crisis management includes the development of plans to reduce the risk of a crisis occurring and to deal with any crises that do arise, and the implementation of these plans so as to minimise the impact of crises and assist the organisation to recover from them. Crisis situations may occur as a result of external factors such as the development of a new product by a competitor or changes in legislation, or internal factors such as a product failure or faulty *decision-making*, and often involve the need to make quick decisions on the basis of uncertain or incomplete information. *See also **risk management**, **disaster management***

critical mass *Gen Mgt* the point at which an organisation or *project* has gained sufficient momentum or *market share* to be either self-sustaining or worth the input of extra investment or resources

critical-path method *Gen Mgt, Ops* a *network analysis* planning technique used especially in *project management* to identify the activities within a project that are critical for its success. In critical-path method, individual activities within a project and their duration are recorded in a diagram or flow chart. A critical path is plotted through the diagram, showing the sequence in which activities must be completed in order to complete the project in the shortest amount of time, incurring the least cost.

critical-ratio analysis *Gen Mgt* a technique used in inventory control to calculate comparative priorities for the reordering of stock. Critical-ratio analysis requires the division of remaining stock items by the likely daily demand for them. This figure is then divided by the time taken to process an order, to derive the critical ratio. The smaller the ratio, the greater the reorder priority. A ratio of less than 1 indicates an imminent shortage. Critical ratios are also used in conjunction with *MRP II* systems to determine the sequence in which orders should be processed. In this case, a ratio of less than 1 indicates that the order is behind schedule.

critical region *Stats* the range of values of a test statistic that lead a researcher to reject the null hypothesis

critical restructuring *Gen Mgt* major economic or social changes that fundamentally reshape traditional patterns of organisation

critical success factors *Gen Mgt* the aspects of a business that are identified as vital for successful targets to be reached and maintained. Critical success factors are normally identified within such areas as production processes, employee and organisation skills, functions, techniques, and technologies. The identification and strengthening of such factors may be similar to identifying *core competences*, and is considered an essential element in achieving and maintaining *competitive advantage*.

critical value *Stats* the value with which a researcher compares a statistic from sample data in order to determine whether or not the null hypothesis should be rejected

CRM *abbr Mkting* customer relationship management

crony capitalism *Econ* a form of capitalism in which business contracts are awarded to the family and friends of the government in power rather than by open-market tender

Crosby, Philip (1926–2001) *Gen Mgt* US business executive and consultant *Quality* guru who introduced and popularised catch-phrases such as 'zero defects', 'get it right first time', and 'quality is free'. Crosby summarised his approach towards quality improvement as the Fourteen Steps, set down in *Quality is Free* (1979).

cross *Fin* a transaction in securities in which one broker acts for both parties

cross-border trade *Econ* trade between two countries that have a common frontier

cross-hedging *Fin* a form of hedging using an option on a different but related commodity, especially a currency

cross listing *Fin* the practice of offering the same item for sale in more than one place

crossposting *E-com* the act of posting the same Internet messages into several different news or discussion groups at the same time

cross-rate *Econ* the rate of exchange between two currencies expressed in terms of the rate of exchange between them and a third currency, for example, sterling and the peso in relation to the dollar

cross-sectional study *Stats* a statistical study in which a range of information is collected at the same time, for example, in a single telephone call

cross-sell *Mkting* to sell existing customers different products from the company's range

crowding out *Fin* the effect on markets of credit produced by extraordinarily large borrowing by a national government

crude annual death rate *Stats* the total number of deaths in a population in one year divided by the total population at the midpoint of the year

cryptography *E-com* a powerful means of restricting access to part or all of a website, whereby only a user with an assigned 'key' can request and read the information

crystallisation *Fin* the process whereby a floating charge relating to company assets becomes fixed to the assets to which it relates

CSIRO *abbr* (*ANZ*) *Gen Mgt* Commonwealth Scientific and Industrial Research Organisation: an Australian federal government body in charge of scientific research, established in 1949

CSP *abbr E-com* commerce service provider

CTI *abbr Gen Mgt* computer telephony integration

CTO *abbr Gen Mgt* chief technical officer

A good newspaper, I suppose, is a nation talking to itself. *Arthur Miller*

CTU *abbr Gen Mgt* Council of Trade Unions: New Zealand's national trade union organisation. It has 19 affiliated unions and represents approximately 200,000 workers.

cube farm *(US) Gen Mgt* an office that is divided into cubicles *(slang)*

cue *Gen Mgt* a factor that differentiates a high-value product from an ordinary commodity

CUL *abbr Gen Mgt* see you later *(slang)*

cultural creative *HR* somebody who values personal and spiritual development, enjoys change, likes learning about new cultures, and typically desires to live a simpler way of life

cultural synergy *Gen Mgt* the harmonisation of the direction and operation of separate organisations into a whole. Whether cultural synergy can be achieved lies in the degree to which there is congruence of vision, mission, values, strategy, and operational processes in the different organisations. The lack of cultural and *strategic fit* is the main cause of failure of *mergers*, sometimes because of the major partner imposing its own *corporate culture*, rather than developing a shared culture. Cultural integration, therefore, needs to be carefully analysed, planned, and implemented.

culture shock *Gen Mgt* the effects on an employee or organisation when faced with new, unfamiliar, or rapidly changing circumstances. Symptoms of culture shock include uncertainty, *stress*, confusion, disorientation, or simply not knowing how to act in the circumstances. Culture shock can occur in a number of scenarios, for example, when *expatriates* come across new cultures and customs in a foreign country, when new staff are thrown into the deep end of a busy department, when two organisations merge with poor strategic, operational, or *cultural synergy*, or when public sector organisations adopt private sector practices. The degree of shock can be reduced through careful analysis, planning, training, and consequent preparedness.

cum *Fin* with

cum rights *Fin* an indication that the buyer of the shares is entitled to participate in a forthcoming rights issue

cumulative method *Fin* a system in which items are added together

cumulative preference shares *Fin* shares which entitle the holders to a fixed rate of dividend, and the right to have any arrears of dividend paid out of future profits with priority over any distribution of profits to the holders of ordinary share capital

cumulative preferred stock *Fin* preferred stock for which dividends accrue even if they are not paid when due

currency *Fin* the money in circulation in a particular country

currency future *Fin* an option on currency

currency hedging *Fin* a method of reducing *exchange rate risk* by diversifying currency holdings and adjusting them according to changes in exchange rates

currency note *Fin* a bank note

currency risk *Fin* **1.** the risk that a currency used for a transaction may lose value **2.** the possibility of a loss or gain due to future changes in exchange rates

currency unit *Econ* each of the notes and coins that are the medium of exchange in a country

current account *Fin* a bank account in which deposits can be withdrawn at any time, but do not usually earn interest, except in the case of some online accounts. It is the most common type of bank account. *US term* **checking account**

current account equilibrium *Econ* a country's economic circumstances when its expenditure equals its income from trade and invisible earnings

current account mortgage *Fin* a long-term loan, usually for the purchase of a property, in which the borrower pays interest on the sum loaned in monthly instalments and repays the principal (see *mortgage*) in one lump sum at the end of the term. When calculating the interest payments, the lender takes into account the balance in the borrower's current and/or savings accounts. It is the borrower's responsibility to make provisions to accumulate the required capital during the period of the mortgage, usually by contributing to tax efficient investment plans such as Individual Savings Accounts or by relying on an anticipated inheritance. *See also* **mortgage**

current assets *Fin* cash or assets that are readily convertible to cash

current assets financing *Fin* the use of current assets as collateral for a loan

current cash balance *Fin* the amount, which excludes balances due soon for outstanding transactions, that a client has available for investment with a broker

---

Experience teaches slowly, and at the cost of mistakes.　　　　*J.A. Froude*

current-cost accounting *Fin* accounting based on the cost of items at the time of the financial statement

current earnings *Fin* the annual earnings most recently reported by a company

current liabilities *Fin* business liabilities that are to be cleared within the financial year

current principal factor *Fin* the portion of the initial amount of a loan that remains to be paid

current purchasing power accounting *Fin* a method of accounting in which the values of non-monetary items in the historical cost accounts are adjusted, using a general price index, so that the resulting profit allows for the maintenance of the purchasing power of the shareholders' interest in the organisation

current ratio *Fin* a ratio of *current assets* to *current liabilities*, used to measure a company's liquidity and its ability to meet its short-term debt obligations. *Also known as working capital ratio*

EXAMPLE The current ratio formula is simply:

Current assets /Current liabilities = Current ratio
Current assets are the ones that a company can turn into cash within 12 months during the ordinary course of business. Current liabilities are bills due to be paid within the coming 12 months.

For example, if a company's current assets are £300,000 and its current liabilities are £200,000, its current ratio would be:

300,000 / 200,000 = 1.5
As a rule of thumb, the 1.5 figure means that a company should be able to get hold of £1.50 for every £1.00 it owes.

The higher the ratio, the more liquid the company. Prospective lenders expect a positive current ratio, often of at least 1.5. However, too high a ratio is cause for alarm too, because it indicates declining receivables and/or inventory—which may mean declining liquidity.

current stock value *Fin* the value of all stock in a portfolio, including stock in transactions that have not yet been settled

current value *Fin* a ratio indicating the amount by which *current assets* exceed *current liabilities*

current yield *Fin* the interest being paid on a bond divided by its current market price, expressed as a percentage

curriculum vitae *HR see CV*

cushion bond *Fin* a bond that pays a high rate of interest but sells at a low premium because of the risk of its being called soon

customer *Mkting* a purchaser of a product or service. A customer is a person or organisation that purchases or obtains goods or services from other organisations such as manufacturers, retailers, wholesalers, or service providers. A customer is not necessarily the same person as the *consumer*, as a product or service can be paid for by one party, the customer, and used by another, the *consumer*.

customer capital *Gen Mgt* the value of an organisation's relationships with its customers, which involves factors such as market share, customer retention rates, and profitability of customers

customer care *Mkting see customer relations*

customer-centric model *Gen Mgt* a business model organised around the needs of the customer

customer complaint *Gen Mgt see complaint*

customer expectation *Gen Mgt* the needs, wants, and preconceived ideas of a customer about a product or service. Customer expectation will be influenced by a customer's perception of the product or service and can be created by previous experience, advertising, hearsay, awareness of competitors, and *brand image*. The level of *customer service* is also a factor, and a customer might expect to encounter efficiency, helpfulness, reliability, confidence in the staff, and a personal interest in his or her custom. If customer expectations are met, then *customer satisfaction* results. *Also known as buyer expectation*

customer flow *Mkting* the number and pattern of customers coming into a shop or passing through a railway or bus station, airport, or other large service, retail, or leisure area. Customer flow can be monitored by observation, time lapse or normal closed circuit television, or, less satisfactorily, by analysis of purchase data. This provides useful information about the number of customers, flow patterns, bottlenecks, areas not visited, and other aspects of consumer behaviour.

customer focus *Mkting* an organisational orientation towards satisfying the needs of potential and actual *customers*. Customer focus is considered to be one of the keys to business success. Achieving customer focus involves ensuring that the whole organisation, and not just front-line service staff, puts its customers first. All activities, from the planning of a new product to its production, marketing, and after-sales care, should be built around the customer. Every department and every employee should share the same customer-focused vision. This can be aided by practising good *customer relationship management* and maintaining a *customer relations* programme.

customer profitability *Mkting* the degree to which a *customer* or segment of customers contributes towards organisation profits. Customer profitability has been shown to be produced primarily by a small proportion of customers, perhaps 10% to 20%, who generate up to 80% of a company's profits. Up to 40% of customers may generate only moderate profits, and the other 40% may be loss-making. Such data enables companies to focus efforts on the most profitable segments.

customer profitability analysis *Fin* analysis of the revenue streams and service costs associated with specific customers or customer groups. *Abbr* **CPA**

customer recovery *Mkting* activities intended to win back customers who no longer buy from an organisation

customer relations *Mkting* the approach of an organisation to winning and retaining customers. The most critical activity of any organisation wishing to stay in business is its approach to dealing with its customers. Putting customers at the centre of all activities is seen by many as an integral part of quality, pricing, and product differentiation. On one level, customer relations means keeping customers fully informed, turning complaints into opportunities, and genuinely listening to customers. On another level, being a customer-focused organisation means ensuring that all activities relating to trading—for example, planning, design, production, marketing, and after-sales of a product or service—are built around the customer, and that every department and individual employee understands and shares the same vision. Only then can a company deliver continuous *customer satisfaction* and experience good customer relations. *Also known as* **customer care**

customer relationship management *Mkting* the cultivation of meaningful relationships with actual or potential purchasers of goods or services. Customer relationship management aims to increase an organisation's sales by promoting customer satisfaction, and can be achieved using tools such as relationship marketing.

CRM is particularly important in the sphere of e-commerce, as there is no personal interaction between the vendor and the customer. A website therefore has to work hard to develop the relationship with customers and demonstrate that their business is valued. A CRM system generally includes some or all of the following components: customer information systems, *personalisation* systems, *content management* systems, *call centre* automation, *data warehousing*, *data mining*, sales force automation, and campaign management systems. All these elements combine to provide the essentials of CRM: understanding customer needs; anticipating their information requirements; answering their questions promptly and comprehensively; delivering exactly what they order; making deliveries on time; and suggesting new products that they will be genuinely interested in. *Abbr* **CRM**

customer retention *Mkting* the maintenance of the custom of people who have purchased a company's goods or services once and the gaining of repeat purchases. Customer retention occurs when a customer is loyal to a company, *brand*, or to a specific product or service, expressing long-term commitment and refusing to purchase from competitors. A company can adopt a number of strategies to retain its customers. Of critical importance to such strategies are the wider concepts of *customer service*, *customer relations*, and relationship marketing. Companies can build loyalty and retention through the use of a number of techniques, including *database marketing*, the issue of loyalty cards, redeemable against a range of goods or services, preferential *discounts*, free gifts, special promotions, newsletters or magazines, members' clubs, or customised products in limited editions. It has been argued that customer retention is linked to employee loyalty, since loyal employees build up long-term relationships with customers.

customer satisfaction *Mkting* the degree to which customer expectations of a product or service are met or exceeded. Corporate and individual customers may have widely differing reasons for purchasing a product or service and therefore any measurement of satisfaction will need to be able to measure such differences. The quality of *after-sales service* can also be a crucial factor in influencing any purchasing decision. More and more companies are striving, not just for customer satisfaction, but for customer delight, that extra bit of added value that may lead to increased customer loyalty. Any extra added

---

People don't choose their careers; they are engulfed by them.   *John Dos Passos*

value, however, will need to be carefully costed.

customer service *Mkting* the way in which an organisation deals with its **customers**. Customer service is most evident in sales and **after-sales service**, but should infuse all the processes in the **value chain**. Good customer service is the result of adopting **customer focus**. Poor customer service can be a product of poor **customer relations**.

customisation *Gen Mgt* the process of modifying products or services to meet the requirements of individual customers

customised service *Gen Mgt* a service tailored to the requirements of an individual customer

cut-off *Fin* a date and procedure for isolating the flow of cash and goods, stocktaking and the related documentation, to ensure that all aspects of a transaction are dealt with in the same financial period

cutthroat *Mkting* aggressively ruthless, especially in dealing with competitors

cutting-edge *Gen Mgt* at the forefront of new technologies or markets

CV *HR* a document that provides a summary of somebody's career history, skills, and experience. A curriculum vitae is usually prepared to aid in a job application. A job advertisement may ask for a curriculum vitae or instead may require a candidate to complete an **application form**.

Every CV should include: the jobseeker's name and contact details; a clear and concise description of his or her career objective; some kind of outline of work experience; and a list of education and qualifications. It is important to customise a curriculum vitae to the type of job or career being applied for.

There are four basic types of curriculum vitae: the chronological, the functional, the targeted, and the capabilities curriculum vitae. A chronological curriculum vitae is useful for people who stay in the same field and do not make major career changes. They should start with and focus on the most recent positions held. A functional curriculum vitae is the preferred choice for those seeking their first professional job, or those making a major career change. It is based around 3–5 paragraphs, each emphasizing and illustrating a particular, important skill or accomplishment.

A targeted curriculum vitae is useful for jobseekers who are very clear about their job direction and need to make an impressive case for a specific job. Like a functional curriculum vitae, it should be based around several capabilities and accomplishments that are relevant to the job target, focusing on action and results. A capabilities curriculum vitae is used for people applying for a specific job within their current organisation. It should focus on 5–8 skills and accomplishments achieved with the company. *US term* **résumé**

cyberbole *E-com* hype about the Internet and the online world (*slang*)

cybercrud *E-com* confusing and useless computer jargon (*slang*)

cyber mall *E-com* a website shared by two or more commercial organisations, usually with some similarity in appearance, function, product, or service. *Also known as* **e-commerce mall, electronic mall, online shopping mall**

cybermarketing *E-com* the use of Internet-based promotions of any kind. This may involve targeted e-mail, bulletin boards, websites, or sites from which the customer can download files.

cybersales *E-com, Fin* sales made electronically through computers and information systems

cyberslacker *Gen Mgt* somebody who spends time surfing the Internet for personal purposes during office hours (*slang*)

cyberspace *E-com* the online world and its communication networks

cycle plot *Stats* a graphical representation of the behaviour of seasonal time series

cycle time *Ops* the period required to complete an operation on one unit of a **batch**. *See also* **lead time**

cyclical stock *Fin* a stock whose value rises and falls periodically, for example, according to the seasons of the year or economic cycles

cyclical unemployment *Econ* unemployment, usually temporary, caused by a lack of **aggregate demand**, for example, during a downswing in the business cycle

cyclic variation *Stats* the repeatable systematic variation of a variable over time

---

When two men always agree, one of them is unnecessary.
William Wrigley

daily price limit *Fin* the amount by which the price of an option can rise or fall within one trading day

daisy chaining *Fin* an illegal financial practice whereby traders create artificial transactions in order to make a particular security appear more active than it is in reality (*slang*)

dancing baloney *E-com* animated visual computer effects that serve little practical purpose but look impressive (*slang*)

dancing frog *E-com* a problem or image on somebody's computer screen that disappears when shown to somebody else (*slang*)

Darwin Trade Development Zone *Gen Mgt* a free trade zone in the city of Darwin in the Northern Territory of Australia. Companies operating within the zone, which is intended to facilitate trade with Asia, are exempt from certain state taxes and customs duties.

data *Stats* the measurements and observations collected during a statistical investigation

database *Gen Mgt* a structured collection of related information held in any form, especially on a computer. The creation of a database assists organisations in keeping records and facilitates the retrieval of specific facts or different categories of information as and when required. Databases of various kinds may form part of an organisation's *MIS*.

database management system *Stats* a dedicated computer program designed to manipulate a collection of information

database marketing *Mkting* the collection and analysis of information about customers and their buying habits, lifestyles, and other such data. Database marketing is used to build profiles of individual customers, who are then targeted with customised mailings, special offers, and other incentives to encourage spending. Database marketing is a form of relationship marketing.

data capture *Mkting* the acquisition of information through advertisement coupons, inquiry forms, or other response mechanisms

data cleansing *Mkting* the process of ensuring that data is up to date and free of duplication or error

data dredging *Stats* the process of making comparisons and drawing conclusions from data that was not part of the original brief for a study

data editing *Stats* the removal of keying or format errors from data

Data Encryption Standard *E-com see* **DES**

dataholic *Gen Mgt* somebody who is obsessed with obtaining information, especially on the Internet (*slang*)

data mining 1. *E-com* the process of using sophisticated software to identify commercially useful statistical patterns or relationships in online databases **2.** *Mkting* the extraction of information from a *data warehouse* to assist managerial *decision-making*. The information obtained in this way helps organisations gain a better understanding of their customers and can be used to improve customer support and marketing activities.

data protection *Mkting* the safeguards that govern the storage and use of personal data held on computer systems and in paper-based filing systems. The growing use of computers to store information about individuals has led to the enactment of legislation in many countries designed to protect the privacy of individuals and prevent the disclosure of information to unauthorised persons. In the United Kingdom, the Data Protection Act 1998 requires organisations that hold personal data in any form to register with a central authority and maintain standards of confidentiality and security. The legislation also stipulates what use may be made of the information and how it may be processed.

data reduction *Stats* the process of summarising large data sets into histograms or frequency distributions so that calculations such as means can be made

data screening *Stats* the process of assessing a set of observations to detect significant deviations such as *outliers*

data set *Stats* all of the measurements or observations collected in a statistical investigation

data smoothing algorithm *Stats* a procedure for removing meaningless data from a sequence of observations so that a pattern can be detected

data transfer *E-com* the amount of data downloaded from a website. This information can be useful, particularly for measuring the number of visitors to a website.

data warehouse *Gen Mgt* a collection of subject-orientated data collected over a period of time and stored on a computer to provide information in support of managerial *decision-making*. A data warehouse contains a large volume of information selected from different sources, including operational systems and organisational databases, and brought together in a standard format to facilitate retrieval and analysis. Like *EIS*s, data warehouses can be used to support *decision-making*, but the ways in which they can be searched are not predetermined. Organisations often use data warehouses for marketing purposes, for example, the analysis of customer information, or for market segmentation. *Data mining* techniques are used to access the information in a data warehouse.

DAX *abbr Fin* Deutscher Aktienindex: the principal German stock exchange, based in Frankfurt

day in the sun *Gen Mgt* the period of time during which a product is successful in the marketplace

day order *Fin* for dollar trading only, an order that is valid only during one trading day

day release *HR* the discharge of an employee from normal work to take part in education or training. Day release is normally for one day each week, fortnight, or month, and it enables an employee to study for further education or *vocational qualifications* on a part time basis.

days' sales outstanding *Fin see* **collection ratio**

day trader *Fin* somebody who makes trades with very close dates of maturity

day trading *Fin* the making of trades that have very close dates of maturity

DCM *abbr* (*S Africa*) *Fin* Development Capital Market

dead cat bounce *Fin* a short-term increase in the value of a stock following a precipitous drop in value (*slang*)

dead tree edition *E-com* the print version of a publication that is also available in electronic form (*slang*)

dead wood *HR* employees who are no longer considered to be useful to a company (*slang*)

deal

cut somebody a deal *Gen Mgt* to agree on terms for a business arrangement with somebody (*slang*)

dealership *Mkting* a retail outlet distributing, selling, and servicing products such as cars or construction plant on behalf of a manufacturer

death by committee *Gen Mgt* the prevention of serious consideration of a proposal by assigning a committee to look at it

Death Valley curve (*US*) *Gen Mgt* a point in the development of a new business when losses begin to erode the company's equity base, so that it becomes difficult to raise new equity (*slang*)

debenture *Fin* **1.** an unsecured bond backed only by the issuer's credit standing **2.** a bond, usually repayable at a fixed date

debit card *Fin* a card issued by a bank or financial institution and accepted by a merchant in payment for a transaction. Unlike the procedure with a *credit card*, purchases are deducted from the cardholder's account, as with a cheque, when the transaction takes place.

debit note *Fin* a document prepared by a purchaser notifying the seller that the account is being reduced by a stated amount, for example, because of an allowance, return of goods, or cancellation

de Bono, **Edward** (*b.* 1933) *Gen Mgt* Maltese-born academic and consultant. Creator of the concept of *lateral thinking*, which was introduced in *Lateral Thinking: a Textbook of Creativity* (1970).

debt *Fin* an amount of money owed to a person or organisation

debt capacity *Fin* the extent to which an entity can support and/or obtain loan finance

debt collection agency *Fin* a business that secures the repayment of debts for third parties on a commission or fee basis

debt counselling *Fin* a service offering advice and support to individuals who are financially stretched

debt/equity ratio *Fin* the ratio of what a company owes to the value of all of its outstanding shares

debt forgiveness *Fin* the writing off of all or part of a nation's debt by a lender

debt instrument *Fin* any document used or issued for raising money, for example, a bill of exchange, bond, or promissory note

debtnocrat *Fin* a senior bank official who specialises in lending extremely large sums, for example, to developing nations (*slang*)

debtor *Fin* a person or organisation that owes money

debtor days *Fin* the number of days on average that it takes a company to receive payment for what it sells.

EXAMPLE To determine debtor days, divide the cumulative amount of accounts receivable by sales, then multiply by 365. For example, if accounts receivable total £600,000 and sales are £9,000,000, the calculation is:

$$(600,000 / 9,000,000) \times 365 = 24.33 \text{ days}$$

The company takes 24.33 days on average to collect its debts.

Debtor days is an indication of a company's efficiency in collecting monies owed. Obviously, the lower the number the better. An especially high number is a telltale sign of inefficiency or worse. *See also* **creditor days**

debt rescheduling *Gen Mgt* the renegotiation of debt repayments. Debt rescheduling is necessary when a company can no longer meet its debt payments. It can involve deferring debt payments, deferring payment of interest, or negotiating a new loan. It is usually undertaken as part of **turnaround management** to avoid **business failure**. Debt rescheduling is also undertaken in less developed countries that encounter national debt difficulties. Such arrangements are usually overseen by the International Monetary Fund.

debt/service ratio *Econ* the ratio of a country's or company's borrowing to its equity or **venture capital**

debugging *Stats* the identification and removal of errors in a computer program or system

decentralisation *Gen Mgt* the dispersal of decision-making control. Decentralisation involves moving power, authority, and decision-making control within an organisation from a central headquarters or from high managerial levels to subsidiaries, branches, divisions, or departments. As an organisational concept, decentralisation implies **delegation** of both power and responsibility by top management in order to promote flexibility through faster decision-making and improved response times. Decentralisation is, therefore,

strongly related to the concept of **empowerment**, though the latter is perhaps more focused on direct working front-line staff.

decision lozenge *Gen Mgt see flow chart*

decision-maker *Gen Mgt* somebody with the responsibility and authority to make decisions within an organisation, especially those that determine future direction and strategy. **Decision theory** is used to assist decision-makers in the process of **decision-making**.

decision-making *Gen Mgt* the process of choosing between alternative courses of action. Decision-making may take place at an individual or organisational level. The process may involve establishing objectives, gathering relevant information, identifying alternatives, setting criteria for the decision, and selecting the best option. The nature of the decision-making process within an organisation is influenced by its culture and structure, and a number of theoretical models have been developed. One well-known method for individual decision-making was developed by **Charles Kepner** and **Benjamin Tregoe** in their book *The New Rational Manager* (1981). **Decision theory** can be used to assist in the process of decision-making. Specific techniques used in decision-making include **heuristics** and **decision trees**. Computer systems designed to assist managerial decision-making are known as **decision support systems**.

decision-making unit *Mkting* a group of people who directly or indirectly influence the purchase of a product or service

decision support system *Fin* a computer system whose purpose is to aid managers to make unstructured decisions, where the nature of the problem requiring resolution may be unclear. *Abbr* **DSS**

decision theory *or* **decision analysis** *Gen Mgt* a body of knowledge that attempts to describe, analyse, and model the process of **decision-making** and the factors influencing it. Decision theory encompasses both formal mathematical and statistical approaches to solving decision problems, using quantitative techniques such as probability and **game theory**, and more informal behavioural approaches. It is used to inform and assist decision-making in organisations.

decision tree *Fin* a pictorial method of showing a sequence of interrelated decisions and their expected outcomes. Decision trees can incorporate both the probabilities and values of expected outcomes, and are used in decision-making.

The truth is I started my own company because I could not fill out a job application.   *Terri Bowersock*

declaration date *Fin* in the United States, the date when the directors of a company meet to announce the proposed dividend per share that they recommend be paid

declaration of dividend *Fin* a formal announcement by a company's directors of the proposed dividend per share that they recommend be paid. It is subsequently put to a shareholders' vote at the company's annual general meeting.

declaration of solvency *Fin* in the United Kingdom, a document, lodged with the Registrar of Companies, that lists the assets and liabilities of a company seeking voluntary liquidation to show that the company is capable of repaying its debts within 12 months

declining balance method *Fin see accelerated depreciation*

decompilation *Ops see reverse engineering*

deconstruction *Gen Mgt* the breaking up of traditional business structures to meet the requirements of the modern economy

de-diversify *Gen Mgt* to sell off parts of a company or group that are not considered directly relevant to a corporation's main area of interest

deductible *Fin* the part of a commercial insurance claim that has to be met by the policyholder rather than the insurance company. A deductible of £500 means that the company pays all but £500 of the claim for loss or damage. *See also* **excess**

deduction at source *Fin* a UK term for the collection of taxes from an organisation or individual paying an income rather than from the recipient, for example, from an employer paying wages, a bank paying interest, or a company paying dividends

deed *Fin* a legal document, most commonly one that details the transfer or sale of a property

deed of assignment *Fin* a legal document detailing the transfer of property from a debtor to a creditor

deed of covenant *Fin* a legal document in which a person or organisation promises to pay a third party a sum of money on an annual basis. In certain countries this arrangement may have tax advantages. For example, in the United Kingdom, it is often used for making regular payments to a charity.

deed of partnership *Fin* a legal document formalising the agreement and financial arrangements between the parties that make up a partnership

deed of variation *Fin* in the United Kingdom, an arrangement that allows the will of a deceased person to be amended, provided certain conditions are met and the amendment is signed by all the original beneficiaries

deep discount bond *Fin* a bond that is issued at a discount of at least 15%, or 0.5% for each year of a bond's term, on its par value

deep-in-the-money call option *Fin* a call option that has become very profitable and is likely to remain so

deep-in-the-money put option *Fin* a put option that has become very profitable and is likely to remain so

deep market *Fin* a commodity, currency, or stock market where such is the volume of trade that a considerable number of transactions will not influence the market price

de facto standard *Gen Mgt* a standard set in a given market by a highly successful product or service

default notice *Fin* a formal document issued by a lender to a borrower who is in default. *US term* **notice of default**

defended takeover bid *Fin* a bid for a company takeover in which the directors of the target company oppose the action of the bidder

defensive stock *Fin* stock that prospers predictably regardless of external circumstances such as an economic slowdown, for example, the stock of a company that markets a product everyone must have

deferred coupon *Fin* a coupon that pays no interest at first, but pays relatively high interest after a specified date

deferred credit *or* **deferred income** *Fin* revenue received but not yet reported as income in the profit and loss account, for example, payment for goods to be delivered or services provided at a later date, or government grants received for the purchase of assets. The deferred credit is treated as a credit balance on the balance sheet while waiting to be treated as income. *See also* **accrual concept**

deferred month *Fin* a month relatively late in the term of an option

deferred ordinary share *Fin* **1.** a share, usually held by founding members of a com-

---

pany, often with a higher dividend that is only paid after other shareholders have received their dividends and, in some cases, only when a certain level of profit has been achieved **2.** a share that pays no dividend for a certain number of years after its issue date but that then ranks with the company's ordinary shares

deferred shares *Fin* a special class of shares ranking for dividend after preference and ordinary shares

deficit *Fin see* **budget deficit**

deficit financing *Fin* the borrowing of money because expenditures will exceed receipts

deficit spending *Fin* government spending financed through borrowing rather than taxation

deflation *Econ* a reduction in the general level of prices sustained over several months, usually accompanied by declining employment and output

deflationary fiscal policy *Econ* a government policy that raises taxes and reduces public expenditure in order to reduce the level of **aggregate demand** in the economy

deflationary gap *Econ* a gap between **GDP** and the potential output of the economy

de Geus, Arie (*b.* 1930) *Gen Mgt* Dutch business executive, adviser, and consultant. Former strategist for Royal Dutch Shell who, in *The Living Company* (1997), identified the characteristics of long-lived companies: financial conservatism, sensitivity to their environment, cohesiveness, and tolerance of unconventional thinking.

degree mill *HR* an establishment that offers to award a qualification for little or no work, often on payment of a large sum of money. Degree mills mostly operate on the edge of the law, often being unaccredited or unregistered as educational institutions. Most degree mills fail to offer any worthwhile education, and those that do lack the appropriate accreditation that makes their qualifications acceptable by employers, with the result that they award **bogus degree** certificates.

delayed settlement processing *E-com* a procedure for storing authorised transaction settlements online until after the merchant has shipped the goods to the purchaser

delayering *Gen Mgt* the removal of supposedly unproductive layers of middle management to make organisations more efficient

and customer-responsive. The term came into vogue during the 1980s. When taken to extremes, delayering can lead to an **anorexic organisation**.

del credere agent *Fin* an agent who agrees to sell goods on commission and pay the principal even if the buyer defaults on payment. To cover the risk of default, the commission is marginally higher than that of a general agent.

delegation *HR* the process of entrusting somebody else with the appropriate responsibility and authority for the accomplishment of a particular activity. Delegation involves briefing somebody else to carry out a task for which the delegator holds individual responsibility, but which need not be executed by him or her. It does not involve the delegate doing something he or she is already paid to do as part of his or her job. There are various degrees of delegation: for example, a manager may delegate responsibility, but not necessarily full authority, and continue to supervise the activity. Delegation should be a positive activity, for example, as an aid to **employee development**, rather than a negative one, for example, passing on an unpopular task. It should be accompanied by support and encouragement from the delegator to the delegatee. An extension of delegation is **empowerment**, in which complete authority for a task is passed to somebody else, who takes full responsibility for its objectives, execution, and results.

delist (*US*) *Fin* to remove a company from the list of companies whose stocks are traded on an exchange

delivery month *Fin see* **contract month**

delivery note *Fin* a document containing details of the quantity and specifications of accompanying goods. A signed copy of the delivery note often acts as proof of delivery. An **advice note** contains similar information, but is sent to inform a third party of delivery. *Also known as* **carrier's note, consignment note, despatch note**

Dell, Michael (*b.* 1965) *Gen Mgt* US business executive. Founder of Dell Computer Corporation and youngest CEO to run a **Fortune 500** company, whose business achieved success through building to order, **direct selling**, minimising **inventory**, and using **Internet** technology.

Delphi technique *Gen Mgt* a qualitative **forecasting** method in which a panel of experts respond individually to a questionnaire or series of questionnaires, before reaching a consensus. The Delphi technique requires individual submission of, and response to, the questionnaire on the topic under investigation, in order to avoid the effect of a dominant personality influencing a group discussion. A summary of the written replies is then distributed so that responses can be revised in the light of the views expressed. This cycle is repeated until the co-ordinator of the group is satisfied that the best possible consensus has been reached. The Delphi technique was developed at the Rand Corporation during the late 1940s and 1950s and owes its name to the Greek oracle at Delphi, which was believed to make predictions about the future.

demand forecasting *Gen Mgt* the activity of estimating the quantity of a product or service that consumers will purchase. Demand forecasting involves techniques including both informal methods, such as educated guesses, and quantitative methods, such as the use of historical sales data or current data from test markets. Demand forecasting may be used in making pricing decisions, in assessing future capacity requirements, or in making decisions on whether to enter a new market.

demarcation dispute *HR* an industrial *dispute* between *trade unions*, or between members of the same union, regarding the allocation of work between different types of workers. Demarcation disputes are much less prevalent than in the past because of *multiskilling* agreements between employers and unions and the greater use of *teamwork*.

demassifying *Gen Mgt* the process of changing a mass medium to a medium that is customised to meet the requirements of individual consumers

Deming, W. Edwards (1900–93) *Gen Mgt* US academic and statistician. A leading champion of the *quality* movement and the most influential catalyst for the economic resurgence of post-war Japan, Deming's approach is summarised in his 14 points, which form the central thesis to his book *Out of the Crisis* (1986).

Deming Prize *Gen Mgt* an annual award to a company that has achieved significant performance improvement through the successful application of company-wide *quality control*. The Deming Prize was set up in recognition of the work carried out by *W. Edwards Deming* in post-war Japan to improve manufacturing quality by reducing the potential for error. The Deming Prize has been awarded annually since 1951 by the Union of Japanese Scientists and Engineers.

Contenders have to be able to demonstrate that, by applying the disciplines outlined by the assessment components, the productivity, growth, and financial performance of the organisation have been improved. Entrants require a substantial resource in order to be able to submit their entry, which can take years to prepare. The focus of the Deming Prize reflects a rigour for the identification and elimination of defects through teamwork. The prize was also the first to apply the process of self-assessment, which has been adopted by other models such as the *Malcolm Baldrige National Quality Award* and the *EFQM Excellence Model*.

democracy *Gen Mgt* a form of government in which people govern themselves, usually by electing representatives from their own number who are charged with governing in the best interests of the people. Democracy enables participation by the electorate in *decision-making* and thus encourages *empowerment*. In an organisational context, it is known as *industrial democracy*.

demographics *Stats* the characteristics of the size and structure of a human population, such as its distribution and age range

denial of service attack *E-com* an attack on a computer system by a *hacker* or *virus* that does not seek to break into the system, but rather to crash a website by deluging it with phoney traffic. Such attacks are difficult to defend against, but *firewall*s can be designed to block repeated traffic from a particular source.

department *Gen Mgt* a section of an organisation, usually centred on a specialised function, under the responsibility of a head of department or team leader

departmental accounts *Fin* revenue and expenditure statements for departments of an entity. These usually take the form of a trading and profit and loss account for each department, or operating accounts for service departments.

departmental budget *Fin* see *functional budget*

departmentalisation *Gen Mgt* the division of an organisation into sections. Departmentalisation is usually based on operating function, and organisations will commonly have departments such as finance, personnel, or marketing. Such organisational structure is typical of a *bureaucracy*. It may be used in *centralisation*, when a particular activity is undertaken by one department in one

---

Always establish a paper trail to make sure others can't take credit for what you do. Dennis Stevenson

location on behalf of the whole organisation, but may equally be a feature of a ***decentralised*** organisation, in which departments are used as individual operating units responsible for their own management.

deposit account Gen Mgt *see* **savings account**

deposit protection *Fin* insurance that depositors have against loss

deposit slip *Fin* a US term for the slip of paper that accompanies money or cheques being paid into a bank account

depreciation *Gen Mgt* an allocation of the cost of an asset over a period of time for accounting and tax purposes. Depreciation is charged against earnings, on the basis that the use of capital assets is a legitimate cost of doing business. Depreciation is also a non-cash expense that is added into net income to determine cash-flow in a given accounting period.

EXAMPLE To qualify for depreciation, assets must be items used in the business that wear out, become obsolete, or lose value over time from natural causes or circumstances, and they must have a useful life beyond a single tax year. Examples include vehicles, machines, equipment, furnishings, and buildings, plus major additions or improvements to such assets. Some intangible assets also can be included under certain conditions. Land, personal assets, stock, leased or rented property, and a company's employees cannot be depreciated.

Straight-line depreciation is the most straightforward method. It assumes that the net cost of an asset should be written off in equal amounts over its life. The formula is:

(Original cost – scrap value) /Useful life (years)

For example, if a vehicle cost £30,000 and can be expected to serve the business for seven years, its original cost would be divided by its useful life:

(30,000 – 2,000) / 7 = 4,000 per year

The £4,000 becomes a depreciation expense that is reported on the company's year-end income statement under 'operation expenses'. In theory, an asset should be depreciated over the actual number of years that it will be used, according to its actual drop in value each year. At the end of each year, all the depreciation claimed to date is subtracted from its cost in order to arrive at its 'book value', which would equal its market value. At the end of its useful business life, any un-depreciated portion would represent the salvage value for which it could be sold or scrapped.

For tax purposes, some accountants prefer to use ***accelerated depreciation*** to record larger amounts of depreciation in the asset's early years in order to reduce tax bills as soon as possible. In contrast to the straight-line method, the **declining balance method** assumes that the asset depreciates more in its earlier years of use. The table below compares the depreciation amounts that would be available, under these two methods, for a £1,000 asset that is expected to be used for five years and then sold for £100 as scrap.

The depreciation method to be used for a particular asset is fixed at the time that the asset is first placed in service. Whatever rules or tables are in effect for that year must be followed as long as the asset is owned.

Depreciation laws and regulations change frequently over the years as a result of government policy changes, so a company owning property over a long period may have to use several different depreciation methods.

Straight-line Method

Year	Annual Depreciation	Year-end Book Value
1	£900 × 20% = £180	£1,000 – £180 = £820
2	£900 × 20% = £180	£820 – £180 = £640
3	£900 × 20% = £180	£640 – £180 = £460
4	£900 × 20% = £180	£460 – £180 = £280
5	£900 × 20% = £180	£280 – £180 = £100

Declining-balance Method

Year	Annual Depreciation	Year-end Book Value
1	£1,000 × 40% = £400	£1,000 – £400 = £600
2	£600 × 40% = £240	£600 – £240 = £360
3	£360 × 40% = £144	£360 – £144 = £216
4	£216 × 40% = £86.40	£216 – £86.40 = £129.60
5	£129.60 × 40% = £51.84	£129.60 – £51.84 = £77.76

Good listeners, like precious gems, are to be treasured.   *Walter Anderson*

depression *Econ* a high level of unemployment during a downturn in the business cycle, sustained for months or years

deprival value *Fin* a basis for asset valuation based on the maximum amount which an organisation would be willing to pay rather than forgo the asset. *Also known as **value to the business**, **value to the owner***

deregulation *Gen Mgt* the process of removing government regulations from an industry

derivative *Fin* a security, such as an option, the price of which has a strong correlation with an underlying financial instrument

Derivative Trading Facility *Fin* a computer system and associated network operated by the Australian Stock Exchange to facilitate the purchase and sale of exchange-traded options. *Abbr* **DTF**

DES *abbr E-com* Data Encryption Standard: the most widely used standard for encrypting sensitive business information

design audit *Mkting* an examination of the branding, style, and design of an organisation's marketing material. A design agency may carry out a design audit free of charge in the hope that an organisation will accept their recommendations and place design of material with them.

design consultancy *Mkting* an organisation that plans and carries out design work for clients, including packaging, corporate identity, products, and publication graphics

design for manufacturability, design for assembly, *or* **design for production** *Gen Mgt* the process of designing a product for best-fit with the manufacturing system of an organisation in order to reduce the problems of bringing a product to market. Design for manufacturability is a team approach to manufacturing that pairs those responsible for the design of a product with those who build it. The manufacturing issues that need to be taken into account in the design process may include using the minimum number of parts, selecting appropriate materials, ease of assembly, and minimising the number of machine set-ups. Design for manufacturability is one of the elements of **concurrent engineering** and is sometimes used as a synonym for it. *Also known as **engineering for excellence**, **manufacturing for excellence**, **producibility engineering***

design protection *Mkting see **copyright***

deskfast *Gen Mgt* breakfast eaten in the office at a desk *(slang)*

de-skilling *HR* the removal of the need for skill or judgment in the performance of a task, often because of new technologies. While it can be argued that de-skilling has adversely affected some **manual workers** in traditional manufacturing industries, the technologies used in modern production systems require a wider range and higher level of skill among the workforce as a whole.

desk jockey *Gen Mgt* somebody who works at a desk *(slang)*

desk research *Mkting* research carried out using documents, telephone interviews, or the Internet

despatch note *Fin see **delivery note***

Deutscher Aktienindex *Fin see **DAX***

devaluation *Econ* a reduction in the official fixed rate at which one currency exchanges for another under a fixed-rate regime, usually to correct a balance of payments deficit

developing country *Econ* a country, often a producer of primary goods such as cotton or rubber, that cannot generate investment income to stimulate growth and possesses a national income that is vulnerable to change in commodity prices

development capital *Gen Mgt* finance for the expansion of an established business

Development Capital Market *(S Africa)* *Fin* a sector on the JSE Securities Exchange for listing smaller developing companies. Criteria for listing in the Development Capital Market sector are less stringent than for the main board listing. *Abbr* **DCM**

development cycle *Mkting see **new product development***

Diagonal Street *(S Africa)* *Fin* an informal term for the financial centre of Johannesburg or, by extension, South Africa

dial and smile *(US)* *Mkting* to cold call potential customers of a product or service *(slang)*

dicing and slicing *Mkting* the analysis of raw data to extract information under different categories *(slang)*

differential cost *Fin* the difference in total cost between alternatives, calculated to assist decision-making. *Also known as **incremental cost***

differential pricing *Mkting* a method of pricing that offers the same product at different prices, for example, in different markets, countries, or retail outlets

differentiation *Mkting see* **product differentiation**

digerati *E-com* people who have or claim to have a sophisticated understanding of Internet or computer technology (*slang*)

digital cash *E-com* an anonymous form of **digital money** that can be linked directly to a bank account or exchanged for physical money. As with physical cash, there is no way to obtain information about the buyer from it, and it can be transferred by the seller to pay for subsequent purchases. *Also known as* **e-cash, electronic cash**

digital certificate *E-com* an electronic document issued by a recognised authority that validates a purchaser. It is used much as a driving licence or passport is used for identification in a traditional business transaction.

digital coins *E-com* a form of electronic payment authorised for instant transactions that facilitates the purchase of items priced in small denominations of **digital cash**. Digital coins are transferred from customer to merchant for a transaction such as the purchase of a newspaper using a **smart card** for payment.

digital coupon *E-com* a voucher or similar form that exists electronically, for example, on a website, and can be used to reduce the price of goods or services

digital Darwinism *E-com* the idea that the development of Internet companies is governed by rules similar to Darwin's theory of evolution, and that those that adapt best to their environment will be the most successful

digital economy *Econ* an economy in which the main productive functions are in electronic commerce, for example, trade on the Internet

digital goods *E-com* merchandise that is sold and delivered electronically, for example, over the Internet

digital hygienist *Gen Mgt* somebody within a company who is responsible for checking employees' e-mails and surfing habits for non-work-related activity (*slang*)

digital money *E-com* a series of numbers with an intrinsic value in some physical currency. Online digital money requires electronic interaction with a bank to conduct a transaction; offline digital money does not. Anonymous digital money is synonymous with **digital cash**. Identified digital money carries with it information revealing the identities of those involved in the transaction. *Also known as* **e-money, electronic money**

digital nervous system *Gen Mgt* an information system that allows an organisation to respond to external events through the accumulation, management, and distribution of knowledge

digital strategy *Gen Mgt* a business strategy that is based on the use of information technology

digital wallet *E-com* software on the hard drive of an online shopper from which the purchaser can pay for the transaction electronically. The wallet can hold in encrypted form such items as credit card information, digital cash or coins, a digital certificate to identify the user, and standardised shipping information. *Also known as* **electronic wallet**

digithead (*US*) *Gen Mgt* somebody who is very knowledgeable about technology and mathematics but has poor social skills (*slang*)

digitisable *E-com* capable of being converted to digital form for distribution via the Internet or other networks

dilberted (*US*) *HR* badly treated by your boss. The term derives from the same fictional character who gave his name to the **Dilbert principle**. (*slang*)

Dilbert principle (*US*) *HR* the principle that the most inefficient employees are moved to the place where they can do the least damage. Dilbert is the main character in a comic strip and cartoon series by Scott Adams that satirises office and corporate life.

dilution *Fin* a reduction in the earnings and voting power per share caused by an increase or potential increase in the number of shares in issue. For the purpose of calculating diluted earnings per share, the net profit attributable to ordinary shareholders and the weighted average number of shares outstanding should be adjusted for the effects of all dilutive potential ordinary shares.

DINKY *abbr Gen Mgt* Dual Income, No Kids (*slang*)

direct action marketing *Mkting see* **direct response marketing**

direct channel *Mkting* a method of selling and distributing products direct to customers. Direct channels include direct sales, sales force, mail order, and the Internet.

direct connection *E-com* a permanent connection between a computer system and the Internet

direct cost *Gen Mgt, Ops* a variable cost directly attributable to production. Items that are

---

If you wanted an easy job, you could be a gravedigger or run a graveyard. **Ted Turner**

classed as direct costs include materials used, labour deployed, and marketing budget. Amounts spent will vary with output. *See also* *indirect cost*

direct debit *Fin* a direct claim on an individual or organisation by a creditor, and paid by the individual's or organisation's bank. Variations in period claims are admissible.

direct labour *HR* personnel directly involved in the manufacturing of products or the provision of services. Direct labour includes blue-collar workers.

direct labour cost percentage rate *Fin* an *overhead absorption rate* based on direct labour cost

direct labour hour rate *Fin* an *overhead absorption rate* based on direct labour hours

direct mail *Mkting* the sending by post, fax, or e-mail of *advertising* communications addressed to specific prospective customers. Direct mail is one tool that can be used as part of a marketing strategy. The use of direct mail is often administered by third-party companies that own databases containing not only names and addresses, but also social, economic, and lifestyle information. It is sometimes seen as an invasion of personal privacy, and there is some public resentment of this form of advertising. This is particularly true of e-mailed direct mail, known derogatively as *spam*. By enabling advertisers to target a specific type of potential customer, however, direct mail can be more cost-efficient than other *advertising media*. It is frequently used as part of a relationship marketing strategy.

direct mail preference scheme *Mkting* an arrangement that allows individuals and organisations to refuse direct mail by having participating organisations remove them from their mailing lists

direct marketing *Mkting see* **direct response marketing**

directorate *Gen Mgt* the governing or controlling body of an organisation responsible for the organisation's *corporate strategy* and accountable to its *stakeholders* for business results. A directorate may also be known as a *board of directors* or council, or at an inner level, the executive or management committee.

director's dealing *Fin* the purchase or sale of a company's stock by one of its directors

direct product profitability *Fin* used primarily within the retail sector, DPP involves the attribution of costs other than the pur-

chase price (for example, distribution, warehousing, retailing) to each product line. Thus a net profit, as opposed to a gross profit, can be identified for each product. The cost attribution process uses a variety of measures (for example, warehousing space or transport time) to reflect the resource consumption of individual products.

direct response marketing *or* **direct response advertising** *Mkting* the use of direct forms of *advertising* to elicit enquiries or sales from potential customers directly to producers or service providers. Direct response marketing aims to bypass intermediaries such as retailers or wholesalers. Forms of communication used include *direct mail*, home shopping channels, and television and press advertisements. *Also known as* **direct action marketing, direct marketing**

direct selling *Mkting* the selling of products or services directly to customers without the use of intermediaries such as wholesalers, retailers, or brokers. Direct selling offers many advantages to the customer, including lower prices and shopping from home. Potential disadvantages include lack of *after-sales service*, an inability to inspect products prior to purchase, lack of specialist advice, and difficulties in returning or exchanging goods. Methods of direct selling include mail-order catalogues and door-to-door and telephone sales, and direct selling has increased with the growth of the Internet, which enables producers to make direct contact with potential customers.

direct tax *Fin* a tax on income or capital that is paid directly rather than added to the price of goods or services

dirty float *Econ* a floating exchange rate that cannot float freely because a country's central bank intervenes on foreign exchange markets to alter its level

dirty price *Fin* the price of a debt instrument that includes the amount of accrued interest that has not yet been paid

disaggregation *Gen Mgt* the breaking apart of an alliance of companies to review their strengths and contributions as a basis for rebuilding an effective business web

disaster management *Gen Mgt* the actions taken by an organisation in response to unexpected events that are adversely affecting people or resources and threatening the continued operation of the organisation. Disaster management includes the development of **disaster recovery plans**, for minimising the risk of disasters and for handling them when they do occur, and the implementation of such plans. Disaster management usually refers to the management of natural catastrophes such as fire, flooding, or earthquakes. Related techniques include *crisis management*, *contingency management*, and *risk management*.

disaster recovery plan *Gen Mgt see disaster management*

disbursing agent *Fin see paying agent*

disciplinary procedure *HR see discipline*

discipline *HR* standards of required behaviour or performance. Good practice requires an organisation to establish a **disciplinary procedure** in order to ensure just decisions. A disciplinary procedure should consist of a formal system of documented warnings and hearings, with rights of representation and appeal at each stage.

disclosure of information *Gen Mgt* the release of information that may be considered confidential to a third party or parties. The disclosure of information in the public interest may be prohibited, permitted, or required, by legislation in a variety of contexts. For example: *data protection* legislation restricts the disclosure of personal data held by organisations; *company law* requires the publication of certain financial and company data; and *whistleblowing* legislation entitles employees to divulge information relating to unethical or illegal conduct in the workplace. Restrictive covenants and *confidentiality agreements* also regulate the information that may be disclosed to third parties.

discount *Fin, Gen Mgt* a reduction in the price of goods or services in relation to the standard price. A discount is a selling technique that is used, for example, to encourage customers to buy in large quantities or to make payments in cash. It can also be used to improve sales of a slow-moving line. The greater the purchasing power of the buyer, the greater the discounts that can be negotiated. Some companies inflate original list prices to give the impression that discounts offer value for money; conversely too many genuine discounts may harm profitability.

discount broker *Fin* a broker who charges relatively low fees because he or she provides restricted services

discounted bond *Fin* a bond that is sold for less than its face value because its yield is not as high as that of other bonds

discounted cash flow *Fin* the discounting of the projected net cash flows of a capital project to ascertain its present value. The methods commonly used are: yield, or internal rate of return (IRR), in which the calculation determines the return in the form of a percentage; net present value (NPV), in which the discount rate is chosen and the present value is expressed as a sum of money; and discounted payback, in which the discount rate is chosen and the payback is the number of years required to repay the original investment. *See also capital investment appraisal*

discounted dividend model *Fin* a method of calculating a stock's value by reducing future dividends to the present value. *Also known as dividend discount model*

discount loan *Fin* a loan that amounts to less than its face value because payment of interest has been subtracted

discount rate *E-com* a percentage fee that an e-commerce merchant pays to an account provider or independent sales organisation for settling an electronic transaction

discount security *Fin* a security that is sold for less than its face value in lieu of bearing interest

discrete variable *Stats* a variable in a statistical study that has only a whole-number value, such as the number of deaths in a population

discretionary account *Fin* a securities account in which the broker has the authority to make decisions about buying and selling without the customer's prior permission

discretionary cost *Fin* a cost whose amount within a time period is determined by, and is easily altered by, a decision taken by the appropriate budget holder. Marketing, research, and training are generally regarded as discretionary costs. Control of discretionary costs is through the budgeting process.

discretionary order *Fin* a security transaction in which a broker controls the details, such as the time of execution

discriminant analysis *Gen Mgt* a statistical technique designed to predict the groups or categories into which individual cases will fall on the basis of a number of independent variables. Discriminant analysis attempts to identify which variables or combinations of variables accurately discriminate between groups or categories by means of a scatter diagram or classification table called a **confusion**

Big things and little things are my job. Middle level management can be delegated.

Konosuke Matsushita

matrix. Discriminant analysis has applications in finance, for example, credit risk analysis, or in the prediction of company failure, and in the field of marketing, for market segmentation purposes.

discriminating monopoly *Econ* a company able to charge different prices for its output in different markets because it has power to influence prices for its goods

discrimination *HR* unfavourable treatment in employment based on prejudice. Major forms of outlawed discrimination include sex discrimination, *racial discrimination*, disability discrimination, and, in some countries, *age discrimination*. Discrimination may also be practised through *indirect discrimination*.

discussion board *E-com* an area on a website that allows people to contribute opinions, ideas, and announcements. It is particularly suitable for casual, one-off interactions because little commitment is required from participants. They can generally review a discussion topic without subscribing, although they do have to subscribe if they want to contribute something themselves.

It is not essential for the website owner to moderate discussion boards, although it is important to watch out for the emergence of 'off-topic' subjects—contributions that are unnecessarily negative or perhaps libellous—and copyright infringement.

A prime example of the success of the discussion board approach is how Amazon.com uses it to allow its consumers to publish book reviews.

discussion list *E-com* an arrangement for sending e-mail messages to a number of people that also allows recipients to respond and everyone else on the list to see these responses. A discussion list is similar to a distribution list except that it is based on a two-way model. Discussion lists can be moderated or unmoderated. In a moderated list, all mail is screened by an intermediary, typically the individual or organisation that set up the list. Unmoderated lists involve no editorial process, so any subscriber can contribute anything he or she wants to the e-mail discussion. Unlike newsgroups, discussion lists do not provide a consolidated record of responses.

disequilibrium price *Econ* the price of a good set at a level at which demand and supply are not in balance

dishonour *Fin* to refuse payment of a cheque because the account for which it is written holds insufficient money. *Also known as bounce*

disinflation *Econ* the elimination or reduction of inflation or inflationary pressures in an economy by fiscal or monetary policies

disintermediation *E-com* the elimination of intermediaries, for example, the wholesalers found in traditional retail channels, in favour of direct selling to the consumer. *See also reintermediation*

dismissal *HR* the termination of an *employee's* employment by his or her *employer*. Dismissal may take place with or without notice, when a fixed-term contract expires and is not renewed, or when an employee leaves claiming *constructive dismissal*. The employer must show that the main reason for dismissal was for one of five fair reasons: incapability, misconduct, *redundancy*, legal restrictions, or some other substantial reason. In addition, the employer must have followed a reasonable procedure before deciding on dismissal. If any of these conditions is not met, the employee may be entitled to claim *unfair dismissal*.

dispersion *Stats* the amount by which a set of observations deviates from its mean

display advertising *Mkting* newspaper or magazine advertisements that use eye-catching typography and graphic images

disposable income *Fin* income that is left for spending after tax and other deductions

dispute *HR* a disagreement. An **industrial dispute** is a disagreement between an *employer* and an employees' representative, usually a *trade union*, over pay and conditions and can result in *industrial action*. A **commercial dispute** is a disagreement between two businesses, usually over a contract. There are three main types of dispute resolution: litigation, *arbitration*, and alternative dispute resolution.

dispute benefit *HR see strike pay*

distance learning *Gen Mgt* a course of study that involves minimal or no attendance at an academic institution, but relies instead on personal study, using books, audio-visual materials, and computer-based materials. Tutorial support may be available via the telephone or Internet, and attendance at weekend or summer schools may be required. The best-known provider of such courses in the United Kingdom is the Open University. Distance learning is similar to *open learning*.

distance sampling *Stats* a method of sampling in ecological statistics used to determine the number of animals that feed or plants that grow in a particular habitat

---

Never dump a good idea on a conference table. It will belong to the conference. **Jane Trahey**

distribution centre *Ops* a warehouse or storage facility where the emphasis is on processing and moving goods on to wholesalers, retailers, or consumers rather than on storage

distribution channel *Ops* the route by which a product or service is moved from a producer or supplier to customers. A distribution channel usually consists of a chain of intermediaries, including **wholesalers**, **retailers**, and distributors, that is designed to transport goods from the point of production to the point of consumption in the most efficient way.

distribution cost *Fin* the cost of warehousing saleable products and delivering them to customers

distribution list *E-com* a list of e-mail addresses given one collective title. Internet users can send a message to all the addresses on the list simultaneously by referring to the list title.

distribution management *Ops* the management of the efficient transfer of goods from the place of manufacture to the point of sale or consumption. Distribution management encompasses such activities as **warehousing**, **materials handling**, packaging, **stock control**, order processing, and transportation.

distribution resource planning *Ops* a computerised system that integrates distribution with manufacturing by identifying requirements for finished goods and producing schedules for **inventory** and its movement within the distribution process. Distribution resource planning systems receive data on sales forecasts, customer order and delivery requirements, available inventory, **logistics**, and manufacturing and purchasing **lead times**. This data is analysed to produce a time-phased schedule of resource requirements that is matched against existing supply sources and production schedules to identify the actions that must be taken to synchronise supply and demand. The effective integration of material requirements planning and distribution resource planning systems leads to the more effective and timely delivery of finished goods to the customer, and to reduced inventory levels and lower material costs. *Abbr* **DRP**

distributive network *E-com* a system or infrastructure that enables products and services to move around. Offline distributive networks include roads, telephone companies, electrical power grids, and the postal service. In the new economy, distributive networks include online banks and Web-enabled mobile telephones.

distributor *Mkting* an organisation that distributes products to retailers on behalf of a manufacturer

distributor support *Mkting* marketing or financial support by manufacturers aimed at improving the performance of organisations that distribute their products

diversification *Gen Mgt* a strategy to increase the variety of business, service, or product types within an organisation. Diversification can be a growth strategy, taking advantage of market opportunities, or it may be aimed at reducing risk by spreading interests over different areas. It can be achieved through **acquisition** or through internal research and development, and it can involve managing two, a few, or many different areas of interest. Diversification can also be a **corporate strategy** of investment in acquisitions within a broad portfolio range by a large **holding company**. One distinct type is **horizontal diversification**, which involves expansion into a similar product area, for example, a domestic furniture manufacturer producing office furniture. Another is **vertical diversification**, in which a company moves into a different level of the **supply chain**, for example, a manufacturing company becoming a retailer. A well-known example of diversification is the move of Bic, the ball-point pen manufacturer, into the production of disposable razors.

diversified investment company *Fin* a unit trust with a variety of types of investments

diversity *Gen Mgt* difference between people, for example, in race, age, gender, disability, geographic origin, family status, education, or personality, that can affect workplace relationships and achievement. Diversity management aims to value these differences and encourage each person to fulfil his or her potential in terms of organisational objectives. The approach goes beyond **equal opportunities**, which stresses the rights of particular disadvantaged groups rather than those of the individual.

diverted hours *Fin* the available hours of nominally direct workers who are diverted to indirect activities, for example, cleaning machines, and are therefore charged as indirect labour. This contrasts with the hours worked by indirect workers, whose entire time is charged as indirect.

I don't think that ambition is a bad word if you work hard yourself.   **Lynn Forrester**

divestment *Gen Mgt* the sale or closure of one or several businesses, or parts of a business. Divestment often takes place as part of a *rationalisation* effort to cut costs or to enable an organisation to concentrate on core business or competences, and may take the form of a *management buy-out*.

dividend *Fin* an amount payable to shareholders from profits or other distributable reserves. Dividends are normally paid in cash, but *scrip dividends*, paid by the issue of additional shares, are permissible. Listed companies normally pay two dividends per year, an interim dividend, based on interim profits reported during the accounting period, and a final dividend, based on the final audited accounts and approved at the *Annual General Meeting*.

dividend clawback *Fin* an agreement that dividends will be reinvested as part of the financing of a project

dividend cover *Fin* the number of times a company's dividends to ordinary shareholders could be paid out of its net after-tax profits. This measures the likelihood of dividend payments being sustained, and is a useful indication of sustained profitability.

EXAMPLE If the figure is 3, for example, a firm's profits are three times the level of the dividend paid to shareholders.

Dividend cover is calculated by dividing earnings per share by the dividend per share:

Earnings per share / dividend per share = dividend cover

If a company has earnings per share of £8, and it pays out a dividend of 2.1, dividend cover is:

$$8 / 2.1 = 3.80$$

An alternative formula divides a company's net profit by the total amount allocated for dividends. So a company that earns £10 million in net profit and allocates £1 million for dividends has a dividend cover of 10, while a company that earns £25 million and pays out £10 million in dividends has a dividend cover of 2.5:

$$10,000,000 / 1,000,000 = 10 \text{ and } 25,000,000 / 10,000,000 = 2.5$$

A dividend cover ratio of 2 or higher is usually adequate, and indicates that the dividend is affordable. A dividend cover ratio below 1.5 is risky, and a ratio below 1 indicates a company is paying the current year's dividend with retained earnings from a previous year: a practice that cannot continue indefinitely. On the other hand, a high dividend cover figure may disappoint an investor looking for

income, since the figure suggests directors could have declared a larger dividend.
See also payout ratio

dividend discount model *Fin see discounted dividend model*

dividend growth model *Fin* a financial model which can be used to value companies based on assumptions about their current and future dividend payments

dividend limitation *Fin* a provision in a bond limiting the dividends that may be paid

dividend payout ratio *Fin* a ratio which shows the proportion of earnings which are distributed to the ordinary shareholders by way of dividends. It is calculated as follows:

Ordinary dividends for the year / Earnings attributable to the ordinary shareholders

dividend per share *Fin* total amounts declared as dividends per share. The dividend per share is actually paid in respect of a financial year. Special rules apply if equity shares are issued during the year.

dividend reinvestment plan *Fin* a plan that provides for the reinvestment of dividends in the shares of the company paying the dividends. *Abbr* **DRIP**

dividend rights *Fin* rights to receive dividends

dividends-received deduction *Fin* a tax advantage on dividends that a company receives from a company it owns

dividend yield *Fin* dividends expressed as a percentage of a share's price

division of labour *Ops* the allocation of each task in a process to a different worker. Division of labour is a concept originated by *Adam Smith* in order to increase output. It enables workers to become highly skilled at one job, but they may lack transferable skills and find their work monotonous. To a certain extent, division of labour has been superseded by *multiskilling*.

document *E-com* an electronic file containing text, graphics, multimedia, or hyperlinks

documentary credit *Fin* an arrangement, used in the finance of international transactions, whereby a bank undertakes to make a payment to a third party on behalf of a customer

dog *Gen Mgt see Boston Box*
that dog won't hunt *Gen Mgt* that idea will not work (*slang*)

When you are through changing, you are through. *Percy Barnevik*

dog and pony show (*US*) *Gen Mgt* a national tour by the top staff of a company aimed at persuading investors to invest in the company (*slang*)

dog-eat-dog *Mkting* ruthless, especially in the marketplace (*slang*)

dogfood *E-com* temporary software used by an organisation for testing purposes

dogs of the Dow (*US*) *Fin* the stocks in the Dow Jones Industrial Average that pay the smallest dividends as a percentage of their prices (*slang*)

dole bludger (*ANZ*) *Gen Mgt* somebody who lives off social security payments and makes no attempt to find work (*slang*)

dollar cost averaging (*US*) *Fin* = *pound cost averaging*

dollar roll (*US*) *Fin* an agreement to sell a stock and buy it later for a specified price

dollars-and-cents (*US*) *Fin* considering money as the determining factor

domain name *E-com* the officially registered address of a website. Domain names typically contain two or more parts separated from each other by a dot, for example, www.yahoo.com. The domain name suffix (following the final dot) is intended to indicate either the nature or location of the website, for example, com for a commercial website and co.uk for a British website.

domicilium citandi et executandi (*S Africa*) *Fin* the address where a summons or other official notice should be served when or if necessary, which must be supplied by somebody applying for credit or entering into a contract

donut (*US*) *Mkting* the middle section of a commercial where the product information is usually placed (*slang*)

dot bam *E-com* a real-world business with a strong Web presence. The 'bam' stands for 'bricks and mortar'.

dot-bomb *or* **dot.bomb** *E-com* an e-commerce enterprise that has gone out of business (*slang*)

dot-com *or* **dot.com** *E-com* an e-commerce enterprise. It markets its products through the Internet, rather than through traditional channels.

dotted-line relationships *HR* the links, as shown on an organisational chart, that exist between managers and staff whom they over-see indirectly rather than on a day-to-day basis (*slang*)

double-blind *Stats* relating to an experiment, usually a medical one, in which neither the experimenter nor the subject knows whether the treatment being administered is genuine or a control procedure

double dipping (*US*) *Gen Mgt* the practice of receiving income from a government pension as well as social security payments

double indemnity *Fin* a provision in an insurance policy that guarantees payment of double its face value on the accidental death of the holder

double opt-in *E-com* a type of *subscription process* for users wanting to sign up to receive specific information or services via a website. The double opt-in approach is emerging as the industry standard for subscription management, as it protects the user from being maliciously subscribed to a service by a third party.

The user requests a subscription, via e-mail or web form. The vendor's system replies with a verification message, requesting an affirmative reply to the message. Only when an affirmative reply is received from the user is the subscription completed.

double taxation *Fin* the taxing of something twice, usually the combination of corporation tax and tax on the dividends that shareholders earn

double taxation agreement *Fin* an agreement between two countries intended to avoid a situation in which income is subject to taxation in both

doubtful debts provision *Fin* an amount charged against profit and deducted from debtors to allow for the estimated non-recovery of a proportion of the debts. *See also bad debt*

doughnut principle *Gen Mgt* a concept that likens an organisation to an **inverted doughnut** with a centre of dough—the core activities—surrounded by a hole—a flexible area containing the organisation's partners. The doughnut principle was originated by **Charles Handy** in *The Empty Raincoat* (1994). He saw organisations as having an essential core of jobs and people, surrounded by a space filled with flexible workers and flexible supply contracts. He maintained that organisations often neglect the core, developing the surrounding hole instead. The doughnut analogy is a way of helping a balance to be achieved between what has to be done and what could be done, by analysing the dough and the hole of a particular organisation. The principle has also been applied to personal life.

Dow Jones Averages *Fin* an index of the prices of selected stocks on the New York Stock Exchange compiled by Dow Jones & Company, Inc

downshifting *Gen Mgt* the concept of giving up all or part of your work commitment and income in exchange for improved quality of life. The term was coined by **Charles Handy**. Downshifting has increased in popularity because of rising *stress* in the workplace caused partly by the *downsizing* trend of the late 20th century, and may be contrasted with the concept of the *organisation man*. Downshifting is integral to the idea of *portfolio working*, in which individuals opt out of a formal employee relationship to sell their services at a pace and at a price to suit themselves.

Most people consider downshifting because of family demands, or because they have been asked to do something by their organisation that goes strongly against their values, pushing them to question why they are working so hard for that organisation. Others downshift as they approach retirement, in order to smooth the transition. People who downshift need to be very sure that that is what they really want and know why they want it, as it can be hard to reverse the decision.

Someone wanting to take the risk of downshifting should make a thorough assessment of his or her short-term and long-term financial situation by way of preparation. They will need to have a good bed of savings to rely on in the first year. It may be necessary to consider moving to a smaller, cheaper place. Deciding what to keep of the old life and what to let go is another important part of the preparation. Some downshifters will want to completely leave their old work life behind them, starting a new job in a slower-paced organisation, or setting up on their own. Others will want to stay with their organisation but perhaps move to a less demanding job. Once these things have been considered and decided upon, it is time for the downshifter to make an action plan with a schedule which includes regular re-assessment periods.

downsizing *HR* the reduction of the size of a business, especially by making staff redundant. Downsizing may be part of a *rationalisation* process, or *corporate restructuring*, with the removal of hierarchies or the closure of departments or functions either after a

period of unsatisfactory results or as a consequence of strategic review. The terms **upsizing** and **resizing** are applied when an organisation increases the number of staff employed.

downstream *Ops* later in the production process

downstream progress *Gen Mgt* movement by a company towards achieving its objectives that is easy because it involves riding a wave or trend and benefiting from favourable conditions. *See also* **upstream progress**

downtime *Ops* a period of time during which a machine is not available for use because of maintenance or breakdown

Dow Theory *Fin* the theory that stock market prices can be forecast on the basis of the movements of selected industrial and transport stocks

Doz, Yves (*b.* 1947) *Gen Mgt* French academic. Collaborator with **C.K. Prahalad** and **Gary Hamel** in researching *strategic models* to tackle the complexities and *globalisation* of markets. His *Alliance Advantage* (1998, co-author), focuses on *strategic partnering*.

draft *Fin* a written order to pay a particular sum from one account to another, or to a person. *See also* **sight draft**, **time draft**

drawee *Fin* the individual or institution to whom a bill of exchange or cheque is addressed

drawing account *Fin* an account that permits the tracking of withdrawals

dress-down day *HR* a day on which employees are allowed to wear informal clothes to work

drilling down *Mkting* a technique for managing data by arranging it in hierarchies that provide increasing levels of detail

DRIP *Fin see* **dividend reinvestment plan**

drip method *Mkting* a marketing method that involves calling potential customers at regular intervals until they agree to make a purchase (*slang*)

drive time *Mkting* the time of the day when most people are likely to be in their cars, usually early in the morning or late in the afternoon, considered to be the optimum time to broadcast a radio commercial (*slang*)

drop lock *Fin* the automatic conversion of a debt instrument with a floating rate to one

---

National and economic prosperity is created, not inherited. *Michael Porter*

with a fixed rate when interest rates fall to an agreed percentage

drownloading *E-com* the act of simultaneously downloading so many files that a computer crashes (*slang*)

DRP *Ops see* **distribution resource planning**

Drucker, Peter (*b.* 1909) *Gen Mgt* US academic. Recognised as the father of management thinking. His earlier works studied management practice, while later he tackled the complexities and the management implications of the post-industrial world. *The Practice of Management* (1954), best known perhaps for the introduction of **management by objectives**, remains a classic. He also anticipated other management themes such as the importance of marketing (see **marketing management**) and the rise of the **knowledge worker**.

DSO *abbr Fin* days' sales outstanding. *See* **collection ratio**

DTF *abbr* (*ANZ*) *Fin* Derivative Trading Facility

dual currency bond *Fin* a bond that pays interest in a currency other than the one used to buy it

dual economy *Econ* an economy in which the manufacturing and service sectors are growing at different rates

dual pricing *Fin* a form of transfer pricing in which the two parties to a common transaction use different prices

dual trading *Fin* the practice of acting as agent both for a broker's firm and its customers

duck
get your ducks in a row *or* **line up your ducks** *Gen Mgt* (*slang*) **1.** to get everything properly organised **2.** (*US*) to get all concerned parties to agree to a plan of action

due-on-sale clause *Fin* a provision requiring a homeowner to pay off a mortgage upon sale of the property

dumbsizing *HR* the process of reducing the size of a company to such an extent that it is no longer profitable or efficient (*slang*)

DUMP *Gen Mgt* Destitute Unemployed Mature Professional (*slang*)

dumping *Econ* the selling of a commodity on a foreign market at a price below its **marginal cost**, either to dispose of a temporary surplus or to achieve a monopoly by eliminating competition

Dunlap, Albert (*b.* 1937) *Gen Mgt* US business executive. He is noted for his **turnaround management** capabilities, based on **downsizing** and **cost-cutting**, which earned him the nickname 'Chainsaw Al' and which are described in his book *Mean Business* (1996).

duopoly *Econ* a market in which only two sellers of a good exist. If one decides to alter the price, the other will respond and influence the market's response to the first decision.

Dutch auction *Fin* an auction in which the lot for sale is offered at an initial price which, if there are no takers, is then reduced until there is a bid

duvet day *Gen Mgt* a day sanctioned by an employing organisation as a day when an employee may call in and say that they will not attend work that day because they do not feel like it. A duvet day does not form part of an employee's **leave** entitlement, but will be recorded as a sanctioned absence. Duvet days are more popular in the United States than in the United Kingdom, and those organisations that allow them do not usually make them part of written policy, limit them to two or three per year, and sometimes only offer them to key employees.

Dynamic HTML *E-com* a relatively limited animation tool for creating website graphics which, if properly designed, can be viewed by most **browsers**. Its major advantage is that it does not require a **plug-in** to view. *Abbr* **DHTML**

dynamic pricing *Gen Mgt* pricing that changes in line with patterns of demand

dynamic programming *Gen Mgt* a mathematical technique used in **management science** to solve complex problems in the fields of production planning and inventory control. Dynamic programming divides the problem into sub-problems or decision stages that can be addressed sequentially, normally by working backwards from the last stage. Applications of the technique include maintenance and replacement of equipment, resource allocation, and process design and control. The term comes from the work of Richard Bellman published in the late 1950s and early 1960s.

Join the union, girls, and together say Equal Pay for Equal Work. *Susan B. Anthony*

E2E *E-com see* **exchange** *(sense 1)*

EAI *E-com see* **enterprise application integration**

e-alliance *E-com* a partnership forged between organisations in order to achieve business objectives, for enterprises conducted over the Web. There has been a surge in such alliances since the Internet took off in the mid-1990s, and studies show that the most successful have been those involving traditional offline businesses and online entities—the *clicks-and-mortar* strategy—such as that between Amazon.com and Toys 'R' Us. Toys 'R' Us had the physical infrastructure and brand, while Amazon.com had the online infrastructure and experience of making e-commerce work.

E&O *abbr Fin* errors and omissions

EAP *(US) HR see* **employee assistance programme**

ear candy *HR* pleasant but meaningless noise or talk (*slang*)

early adopter *Gen Mgt* an individual or organisation that is among the first to make use of a new technology

early retirement *HR retirement* from work before the statutory retirement age or before the normal retirement age set by an employer. Early retirement may be taken because of ill health or at the request of the employee or employer. An employer may offer opportunities for early retirement on advantageous financial terms as a way of reducing staff numbers without *redundancies*. *Also known as* **premature retirement**

earned income *Fin* money generated by an individual's or an organisation's labour, for example, wages, salaries, fees, royalties, and business profits. *See also* **unearned income**

earnings 1. *Fin* income or profit from a business, quoted gross or net of tax, which may be retained and distributed in part to the shareholders **2.** *HR* a sum of money gained from paid employment, usually quoted before tax, including any extra rewards such as *fringe benefits*, allowances, or incentives. *Also known as* **pay**

earnings before interest and taxes *Ops abbr* **EBIT**. *See* **operating income**

earnings before interest, tax, depreciation, and amortisation *Fin see* **EBITDA**

earnings per share *Fin* a financial ratio that measures the portion of a company's profit allocated to each outstanding ordinary share. It is the most basic measure of the value of a share, and also is the basis for calculating several other important investment ratios.

EXAMPLE EPS is calculated by subtracting the total value of any preference shares from net income (earnings) for the period in question, then dividing the resulting figure by the number of shares outstanding during that period.

Net income – Dividends on any preference shares / Average number of shares outstanding

Companies usually use a weighted average number of shares outstanding over the reporting period, but shares outstanding can either be 'primary' or 'fully diluted'. Primary EPS is calculated using the number of shares that are currently held by investors in the market and able to be traded. Diluted EPS is the result of a complex calculation that determines how many shares would be outstanding if all exercisable warrants and options were converted into shares at the end of a quarter.

Suppose, for example, that a company has granted a large number of share options to employees. If these options are capable of being exercised in the near future, that could significantly alter the number of shares in issue and thus the EPS–even though the net income is the same. Often in such cases, the company might quote the EPS on the existing shares and the fully diluted version.
Abbr **EPS**

earnings report *(US) Fin* = *published accounts*

earnings retained *Fin see* **retained profits**

earnings surprise *Fin* a report by a company that its earnings vary considerably from expectations

earnings yield *Fin* money earned by a company during a year, expressed as a percentage of the price of one of its shares

earn-out arrangement *Fin* a procedure whereby owner/managers selling an organisation receive a portion of their consideration linked to the financial performance of the business during a specified period after the sale. The arrangement gives a measure of security to the new owners, who pass some of the financial risk associated with the purchase of a new enterprise to the sellers.

EASDAQ *abbr Fin* European Association of Securities Dealers Automated Quotations: a stock exchange for technology and growth companies based in Europe and modelled on *NASDAQ* in the United States

eased *Fin* used in stock market reports to describe a market that has experienced a slight fall in prices

easy money *Fin see* ***cheap money***

EBIT *abbr Ops* earnings before interest and taxes

EBITDA *abbr Fin* earnings before interest, tax, depreciation, and amortisation: The earnings generated by a business's fundamental operating performance, frequently used in accounting ratios for comparison with other companies. Interest on borrowings, tax payable on those profits, depreciation, and amortisation are excluded on the basis that they can distort the underlying performance.
EXAMPLE It is calculated as follows:
Revenue – Expenses (excluding tax and interest, depreciation, etc.) = EBITDA
It is important to note that EBITDA ignores many factors that impact true cash-flow, such as working capital, debt payments, and other fixed expenses. Even so, it may be useful in terms of evaluating firms in the same industry with widely different capital structures, tax rates, and depreciation policies.

EBQ *abbr Ops* economic batch quantity: the optimum batch size for the manufacture of an item or component, at the lowest cost. The batch size is a trade-off between unit costs that increase with batch size and those that decrease. The point of lowest combined or total cost indicates the most economic batch size for production. *Also known as* ***economic lot quantity****. See* ***economic order quantity***

EBRD *abbr Fin* European Bank for Reconstruction and Development: the bank, which was established in 1991, developed programmes to tackle a range of issues. These included: the creation and strengthening of infrastructure; privatisation; the reform of the financial sector, including the development of capital markets and the privatisation of commercial banks; the development of productive competitive private sectors of small and medium-sized enterprises in industry, agriculture, and services; the restructuring of industrial sectors to put them on a competitive basis; and encouraging foreign investment and cleaning up the environment.

The EBRD had 41 original members: the European Commission, the European Investment Bank, all the EEC countries, and all the countries of Eastern Europe except Albania, which finally became a member in October 1991, followed by all the republics of the former USSR in March 1992.

e-business *E-com* **1.** the conduct of business on the Internet, including the electronic purchasing and selling of goods and services, servicing customers, and communications with business partners. *Also known as* ***electronic business*** **2.** a company that conducts business on the Internet

e-cash *E-com see* ***digital cash***

ECB *abbr Fin* European Central Bank: the financial institution that replaced the European Monetary Institute (EMI) in 1998 and which is responsible for carrying out EU monetary policy and administering the euro

ECGD *abbr Mkting* Export Credit Guarantee Department

ECML *abbr E-com* electronic commerce modelling language

ecoconsumer *Gen Mgt* a customer who will only select from, or subscribe to, goods that meet environmentally sound considerations

ecolabel *Gen Mgt* a label used to characterise products that satisfy particular total ***environmental management*** considerations with regard to their production, usage, or disposal

ecological priority *Gen Mgt* the priority for organisations and governments to put as much emphasis on environmental protection as economic performance

ecological statistics *Stats* statistical studies in the field of ecology using such techniques as ***distance sampling***

ECO-Management Audit Scheme *Gen Mgt see* ***environmental management****. Abbr* **EMAS**

e-commerce *E-com* the exchange of goods, information products, or services via an electronic medium such as the Internet. Originally limited to buying and selling, it has evolved to include such functions as customer service, marketing, and advertising. *Also known as* ***electronic commerce****, **web commerce***

e-commerce mall *E-com see* ***cyber mall***

e-commerce processes *E-com* the flow of information through planning, design, manufacture, sales, order processing, distribution, and quality in an e-business

---

Whoever wants to accomplish great things must devote a lot of profound thought to details.
Paul Valéry (attrib.)

e-company *E-com* an e-commerce enterprise (*slang*)

econometric model *Econ* a way of representing the relationship between economic variables as an equation or set of equations with statistically precise parameters linking the variables

econometrics *Econ* the setting up of mathematical models to describe relationships in an economy, for example, between wage rates and levels of employment

Economic and Monetary Union *Fin see* **EMU**

economic assumption *Econ* an assumption built into an economic model, for example, that output will grow at 2.5% in the next tax year

economic batch quantity *Ops see* **EBQ**

Economic Development Board *Fin* an organisation established in 1961 that aims to promote investment in Singapore by providing various services and assistance schemes to foreign and local companies. *Abbr* **EDB**

economic goods *Econ* services or physical objects that can command a price in the market

economic growth *Econ* an increase in the national income of a country created by the long-term productive potential of its economy

economic indicator *Econ* a statistic that may be important for a country's long-term economic health, for example, rising prices or falling exports

economic life *Econ* the conditions of trade and manufacture in a country that contribute to its prosperity or poverty

economic lot quantity *Ops see* **EBQ**

economic miracle *Econ* the rapid growth after 1945 in countries such as Germany and Japan, where in ten years economies shattered by the Second World War were regenerated

economic order quantity *Ops* a re-order method that attempts to estimate the best order quantity by balancing the conflicting costs of holding stock and of placing replenishment orders. For large orders, the unit cost may be lower, but storage costs will be higher, because the average storage time will increase. For small orders, the cost of order processing and unit cost may be higher, but storage costs will be lower, because the average storage time is less. *Abbr* **EOQ**

economic paradigm *Econ* a basic unchanging economic principle

Economic Planning and Advisory Council *Fin* a committee of business people and politicians appointed to advise the Australian government on economic issues.

economic pressure *Econ* a condition in a country's economy in which economic indicators are unfavourable

economics *Econ* the study of the consumption, distribution, and production of wealth in a society

economic surplus *Econ* the difference between an economy's output and the costs incurred, for example, wages, raw material costs, and depreciation

economic theory of the firm *Gen Mgt* the theory that states the only duty that a company has to those external to it is financial. The economic theory of the firm holds that shareholders should be the prime beneficiaries of an organisation's activities. The theory is associated with **top-down leadership**, and **cost-cutting** through **rationalisation** and **downsizing**. With immediate share price dominating management activities, economic theory has been criticised as being too short term, as opposed to the longer-term thinking behind **stakeholder theory**.

economic value added *Fin* a way of judging financial performance by measuring the amount by which the earnings of a project, an operation, or a company exceed or fall short of the total amount of capital that was originally invested by its owners.

EXAMPLE EVA is conceptually simple: from net operating profit, subtract an appropriate charge for the opportunity cost of all capital invested in an enterprise—the amount that could have been invested elsewhere. It is calculated using this formula:

Net operating profit less applicable taxes – Cost of capital = EVA

If a company is considering building a new plant, and its total weighted cost over ten years is £80 million, while the expected annual incremental return on the new operation is £10 million, or £100 million over ten years, then the plant's EVA would be positive, in this case £20 million:

£100 million – £80 million = £20 million

An alternative but more complex formula for EVA is:

(% Return on invested capital – % Cost of capital) × original capital invested = EVA

An objective of EVA is to determine which business units best utilise their assets to generate returns and maximise shareholder value; it can be used to assess a company, a business unit, a single plant, office, or even an assembly line. This same technique is equally helpful in evaluating new business opportunities.

economic welfare *Econ* the level of prosperity in an economy, as measured by employment and wage levels

economies of scale *Fin* reductions in unit average costs caused by increasing the scale of production

economies of scope *Fin* reductions in unit average costs caused by the simultaneous production of a number of related products, permitting benefits such as the sharing of joint costs over a larger volume than would otherwise be possible

economist *Econ* somebody who studies the consumption, distribution, and production of wealth in a society

economy *Econ* the distribution of wealth in a society and the means by which that wealth is produced and consumed

economy efficiency principle *Econ* the principle that if an economy is efficient, no one can be made better off without somebody else being made worse off

ecopreneur *Gen Mgt* an entrepreneur who is concerned with environmental issues

EDB *abbr Fin* Economic Development Board

EDC *abbr E-com* electronic data capture

EDI *abbr E-com* electronic data interchange

EDI envelope *E-com see **electronic envelope***

EDIFACT *E-com see **UN/EDIFACT***

EDI for Administration, Commerce, and Trade *E-com see **UN/EDIFACT***

educational leave *HR special leave* granted to assist those undertaking a course of study

Edwardes, Sir Michael (*b.* 1930) *Gen Mgt* South African-born business executive. Chairman of British Leyland from 1977 to 1982, he was appointed to rescue the company from financial difficulties and industrial disruption. His re-assertion of the manager's right to manage led to the coining of the term ***macho management***. He recorded his experiences in *Back from the Brink* (1983).

e-economy *Econ* an economy that is characterised by extensive use of the Internet and information technology

effect *Stats* the change in a response that is created by a change in one or more of the explanatory *variables* in a statistical study

effective annual rate *Fin* the average interest rate paid on a deposit for a period of a year. It is the total interest received over 12 months expressed as a percentage of the principal at the beginning of the period.

effective capacity *Ops* the volume that a workstation or process can produce in a given period under normal operating conditions. Effective capacity can be influenced by the age and condition of the machine, the skills, training, and flexibility of the workforce, and the availability of ***raw materials***.

effective date *Fin* the date when an action, such as an issuance of new stock, is effective

effectiveness *Fin* the utilisation of resources such that the output of the activity achieves the desired result

effective price *Fin* the price of a share adjusted to take into account the effects of a rights issue. *See also **rights issue***

effective sample size *Stats* the remaining size of a sample after irrelevant or excluded factors have been removed

effective spread *Fin* the difference between the price of a newly issued share and what the underwriter pays, adjusted for the effect of the announcement of the offering

effective strike price *Fin* the price of an option at a specified time, adjusted for fluctuation since the initial offering

effective tax rate *Fin* the average tax rate applicable to a given transaction, whether it is income from work undertaken, the sale of an asset, or a gift, taking into account personal allowances and scales of tax. It is the amount of money generated by the transaction divided by the additional tax payable because of it.

effective yield *Fin see **gross yield to redemption***

efficiency *Gen Mgt* the achievement of goals in an economical way. Efficiency involves seeking a good balance between economy in terms of resources such as time, money, space, or materials, and the achievement of an organisation's aims and objectives. A distinction is often made between technical and

---

The trouble with a free market economy is that it requires so many policemen to make it work.
Dean Acheson

economic efficiency. **Technical efficiency** means producing maximum output with a minimum input, while economic efficiency means the production and distribution of goods at the lowest possible cost. In management, a further distinction is often made between efficiency and effectiveness, with the latter denoting performance in terms of achieving objectives. Achieving efficient performance is one of the key drivers behind *scientific management*.

efficiency ratio *Fin* a way of measuring the proportion of operating revenues spent on overhead expenses.

EXAMPLE Often identified with banking and financial sectors, the efficiency ratio indicates a management's ability to keep overhead costs low. In banking, an acceptable efficiency ratio was once in the low 60s. Now the goal is 50, while better-performing banks boast ratios in the mid 40s. Low ratings usually indicate a higher return on equity and earnings.

This measurement is also used by mature industries, such as steel manufacture, chemicals, or car production, that must focus on tight cost controls to boost profitability because growth prospects are modest.

The efficiency ratio is defined as operating overhead expenses divided by turnover. If operating expenses are £100,000, and turnover is £230,000, then:

100,000 / 230,000 = 0.43 efficiency ratio

However, not everyone calculates the ratio in the same way. Some institutions include all non-interest expenses, while others exclude certain charges and intangible asset amortisation.

A different method measures efficiency simply by tracking three other measures: accounts payable to sales, days' sales outstanding, and stock turnover. This indicates how fast a company is able to move its merchandise. A general guide is that if the first two of these measures are low and the third is high, efficiency is probably high; the reverse is likewise true.

To find the stock turnover ratio, divide total sales by total stock. If net sales are £300,000, and stock is £140,000, then:

300,000 / 140,000 = 2.14 stock turnover ratio

To find the accounts payable to sales ratio, divide a company's accounts payable by its annual net sales. A high ratio suggests that a company is using its suppliers' funds as a source of cheap financing because it is not operating efficiently enough to generate its own funds. If accounts payable are £42,000, and total sales are £300,000, then:

42,000 / 300,000 = 0.14 × 100 = 14% accounts payable to sales ratio

efficient capital market *Gen Mgt* a market in which share prices reflect all the information available to the market about future economic trends and company profitability

efficient markets hypothesis *Fin* the hypothesis that the stock market responds immediately to all available information, with the effect that an individual investor cannot, in the long run, expect to obtain greater than average returns from a diversified portfolio of shares. There are three forms: the weak form, in which security prices instantaneously reflect all information on past price and volume changes in the market; the semi-strong form, in which security prices reflect all publicly available information; and the strong form, in which security prices reflect instantaneously all information available to investors, whether publicly available or otherwise.

EFQM Excellence Model *or* **EFQM European Excellence Award** *Gen Mgt* a framework that can be used to assess a company's achievement of business *excellence*. The European Foundation for Quality Management (EFQM) was founded in the late 1980s by leading companies in Western Europe that saw a need for the implementation of a *quality award* in Europe. EFQM launched the **European Quality Award** in 1991. In the United Kingdom, the British Quality Foundation promoted the model, now often referred to as the **Business Excellence Model**. The model was revised in 1999 and renamed the EFQM European Excellence Model. The model focuses on all the key elements that sustain business success, and incorporates nine criteria that cover all aspects of business.

EFT *abbr Fin* electronic funds transfer

EGM *abbr Gen Mgt* extraordinary general meeting

egosurfing *Gen Mgt* the practice of surfing the Internet in search of references to yourself (*slang*)

EIB *abbr Fin* European Investment Bank: a financial institution whose main task is to further regional development within the EU by financing capital projects, modernising or converting undertakings, and developing new activities

86 *Gen Mgt* to discard something such as a proposal or a document (*slang*)

eighty-twenty rule *Gen Mgt* the principle that explores the natural balance between the

---

He that would govern others, first should be the master of himself.   *Philip Massinger*

causes and effects of business activities, and holds that all business activities display an 80%/20% split. Developed by **Vilfredo Pareto**, the eighty-twenty rule can be used to concentrate management control and identify problem areas. Examples of the eighty-twenty rule in practice might include: 20% of the workforce accounting for 80% of the salary bill; 80% of a company's profits coming from 20% of its products; 80% of the stock value being tied up in 20% of the inventory. The rule can be represented graphically in the form of a Pareto chart, which is a bar chart identifying the relationships between causes and effects of activities. *Also known as* **Pareto analysis**, **Pareto's principle**. *See also* **Pareto's Law**

EIS *abbr Gen Mgt* **1.** Environmental Impact Statement **2.** Environmental Impact Study **3.** executive information system: a computer system designed to collect, store, process, and provide access to information appropriate to the needs of senior management. Executive information systems combine internal organisational information with data from external sources. The emphasis of executive information systems is on supporting strategic *decision-making* by presenting information in accessible formats and enabling users to get an overview of trends, often through the use of advanced graphical capabilities. Decision-making at managerial levels is supported by *decision support systems*.

Eisner, Michael (*b.* 1942) *Gen Mgt* US business executive. CEO and chairman of Disney who *turned around* the company, by encouraging *creativity* while maintaining financial control and discipline. His autobiography *Work in Progress* (1998) explains his *leadership* philosophy.

either-way market *Fin* a currency market with identical prices for buying and selling, especially for the euro

e-lance *Gen Mgt* a type of *freelance* work that makes use of the *Internet*. It enables a freelancer to take up work opportunities anywhere in the world.

elasticity *Fin* the measure of the sensitivity of one variable to another.
EXAMPLE In practical terms, elasticity indicates the degree to which consumers respond to changes in price. It is obviously important for companies to consider such relationships when contemplating changes in price, demand, and supply.
Demand elasticity measures how much the quantity demanded by a customer changes when the price of a product or service is increased or lowered. This measurement helps companies to find out whether demand will remain constant despite price changes. Supply elasticity measures the impact on supply when a price is changed.

The general formula for elasticity is:
Elasticity = % change in x / % change in y
In theory, x and y can be any variable. However, the most common application measures price and demand. If the price of a product is increased from £20 to £25, or 25%, and demand in turn falls from 6,000 to 3,000, elasticity would be calculated as:
$$-50\% / 25\% = -2$$
A value greater than 1 means that demand is strongly sensitive to price, while a value of less than 1 means that demand is not price-sensitive.

eldercare (*US*) *HR* an organisation's approach towards care for employees' elderly relatives in the form of an *employee assistance programme*

e-learning *HR* the facilitation of learning through the *Internet* or an *intranet*. E-learning is a development from *computer-based training* and consists of self-contained learning materials and resources that can be used at the pace and convenience of the learner. An e-learning package normally incorporates some form of test that can demonstrate how much an e-learner has assimilated from a course, as well as some form of monitoring to enable managers to check the use of the system of e-learning. Successful e-learning depends largely on the self-motivation of individuals to study effectively. Because it is Internet-based, it has the potential to respond to a company's rapidly changing needs and offer new learning opportunities relevant to a company's new position very quickly. *Also known as electronic learning*

elected officers *HR* officials such as directors or union representatives chosen by a vote of the members or shareholders of an organisation, who hold a *decision-making* position on a committee or board

electronic business *E-com see* **e-business**

electronic cash *E-com see* **digital cash**

electronic catalogue *E-com* a listing of available products that can be viewed in an electronic format, for example, on a website, and can include information such as illustrations, prices, and product descriptions

electronic cheque *E-com* a payment system in which fund transfers are made electronically from the buyer's current account to the seller's bank account. *US term* **electronic check**

electronic commerce *E-com see* **e-commerce**

electronic commerce modelling language *E-com* a standardisation of field names to streamline the process by which e-merchants electronically collect information from consumers about order shipping, billing, and payment. *Abbr* **ECML**

electronic data capture *E-com* the use of a point-of-sale terminal or other data-processing equipment to validate and submit credit or debit card transactions. *Abbr* **EDC**

electronic data interchange *E-com* a standard for exchanging business documents such as invoices and purchase orders in a standard form between computers through the use of electronic networks such as the Internet. *Abbr* **EDI**

electronic envelope *E-com* the header and trailer information that precedes and follows the data in an electronic transmission to provide routing information and security. *Also known as* **communications envelope**, **EDI envelope**, **envelope**

electronic funds transfer *Fin* the system used by banking organisations for the movement of funds between accounts and for the provision of services to the customer. *Abbr* **EFT**

electronic funds transfer at point of sale *Fin* the payment for goods or services by a bank customer using a card that is swiped through an electronic reader on the till, thereby transferring the cash from the customer's account to the retailer's or service provider's account.

electronic learning *HR see* **e-learning**

electronic mail *E-com see* **e-mail**

electronic mall *E-com see* **cyber mall**

electronic money *E-com see* **digital money**

electronic office *Gen Mgt see* **paperless office**

electronic payment system *E-com* a means of making payments over an electronic network such as the Internet

electronic procurement *E-com see* **e-procurement**

electronic retailer *E-com see* **e-retailer**

electronic shopping *E-com* the process of selecting, ordering, and paying for goods or services over an electronic network such as the Internet. *Also known as* **online shopping**

electronic software distribution *E-com* a form of electronic shopping in which computer programs can be purchased and downloaded directly from the Internet

electronic store *E-com* a website that is specifically designed to provide product information and handle transactions, including accepting payments

electronic trading *Fin* the buying and selling of investment instruments using computers

electronic wallet *E-com see* **digital wallet**

elements of cost *Fin* the constituent parts of costs according to the factors upon which expenditure is incurred, namely, material, labour, and expenses

elephant *Gen Mgt* a large corporate institution (*slang*)

elevator pitch (*US*) *E-com* the practice of pitching dot-com business plans to investors in a short space of time

eligible paper *Fin* **1.** in the United Kingdom, bills of exchange or securities accepted by the Bank of England as security for loans to discount houses **2.** in the United States, first class paper (such as a bill of exchange or a cheque) acceptable for rediscounting by the Federal Reserve System. *See also* **lender of last resort**

eligible reserves *Fin* in the United States, the sum of the cash held by a bank plus the money it holds at its local Federal Reserve Bank

Eligible Service Period *Gen Mgt* the amount of time an employee works for one employer or contributes to a particular superannuation scheme. *Abbr* **ESP**

Eligible Termination Payment *Fin* a sum paid to an employee when he or she leaves a company, that can be transferred to a concessionally taxed investment account, such as an Approved Deposit Fund. *Abbr* **ETP**

Elvis year *Gen Mgt* the year in which the popularity of a product, service, or individual is at its peak (*slang*)

e-mail *E-com* electronic mail, a message sent across the Internet, or a system for transferring messages between computers, mobile phones, or other communications attached to the Internet

---

Money is better than poverty, if only for financial reasons.   *Woody Allen*

e-mail address *E-com* somebody's electronic address on the Internet or an intranet. An e-mail address is commonly formed by joining the user name and the mail server name, separating the two by an @ symbol.

e-mail mailing list *E-com* a marketing technique particularly suited to discussing complex topics over a period of time. Members can be drawn from anywhere in the world, and come together to share information and experience on a particular theme or subject area. It works as follows: a *moderator* compiles a list of e-mail addresses for possible members, and mails them with the theme for discussion. People then join up, via e-mail or *Web form*. The moderator invites contributions, which are duly published by e-mail; subscribers then react to the initial publication with their opinions and feedback. A selection of these reactions is published in the next e-mail sent out—and so on. If successful, a feedback and opinion loop is created, with new topics being introduced as older topics have received sufficient discussion.

e-mail signature *E-com* the text at the bottom of an e-mail that contains information about the sender.
    In general, the signature should be no longer than five lines, but it can be used in marketing to place a short, two-line ad. E-mail signature promotion was used very effectively when Andersen Consulting changed its name to Accenture. Every time one of its 60,000 employees sent an e-mail, there was a short e-mail signature ad notifying the recipient of the change of name.

e-mail system *E-com* the collective e-mail software that allows somebody to create, send, receive, and store e-mail messages

e-marketplace *E-com* an Internet-based environment that brings together business-to-business buyers and sellers so that they can trade more efficiently online.
    The key benefits for users of an e-marketplace are reduced purchasing costs, greater flexibility, saved time, better information, and better collaboration. However, the drawbacks include costs in changing procurement processes, cost of applications, set-up, and integration with internal systems, and transaction/subscription fees.
    There are three distinct types of e-marketplace: independent, in which public environments seek simply to attract buyers and sellers to trade together; consortium-based, in which sites are set up on an industry-wide basis, typically when a number

of key buyers in a particular industry get together; and private, in which e-marketplaces are established by a particular organisation to manage its purchasing alone.

EMAS *abbr Gen Mgt* ECO-Management Audit Scheme

embezzlement *Fin* the illegal practice of using money entrusted to an individual's care by a third party for personal benefit

emerging market *Fin* a country that is becoming industrialised

Emery, Frederick Edmund (1928–97) *Gen Mgt* Australian psychologist and sociologist. Contributor to the development of theories of *industrial democracy* in collaboration with *Einar Thorsrud* at the Tavistock Institute of Human Relations.

e-money *E-com see digital money*

emotag *E-com* a tag such as <smile> or <growl> used in an e-mail instead of an emoticon (*slang*)

emoticon *E-com* a symbol commonly used in e-mail and newsgroup messages to denote a particular emotion by representing a face on its side. For example,:-) indicates happiness by representing a smiley face. The word is a combination of 'emotion' with 'icon'.

emotional capital *Gen Mgt* the intangible organisational asset created by employees' cumulative emotional experiences, which give them the ability to successfully communicate and form interpersonal relationships. Emotional capital is increasingly being seen as an important factor in company performance. Low emotional capital can result in conflict between staff, poor *teamwork*, and poor *customer relations*. By contrast, high emotional capital is evidence of *emotional intelligence* and an ability to think and feel in a positive way that results in good *interpersonal communication* and self-motivation. Related concepts are *intellectual capital* and *social capital*.

emotional intelligence *HR* the ability to perceive and understand personal feelings and those of others. Emotional intelligence means recognising emotions and acting on them in a reflective and rational manner. It involves self-awareness, empathy, and self-restraint. In the workplace, this ability can greatly enhance *interpersonal communication* and people skills. Emotional intelligence was first broadly discussed by *Daniel Goleman*.

The vaster the power gained, the vaster the appetite for more.   Ursula K. Le Guin

employability *HR* the potential for obtaining and keeping fulfilling work through the development of skills that are transferable from one employer to another. Employability is affected by market demand for a particular set of skills and by personal circumstances. Employees may take responsibility for developing their own employability through learning and training, or as part of the *psychological contract*, employers may assist their employees in enhancing their employability. An important factor in employability is the concept of *lifelong learning*.

employee *HR* someone taken on by an employer under a *contract of employment* to carry out work on a regular basis at the employer's behest. An employee works either at the employer's premises or at a place otherwise agreed, is paid regularly, and enjoys *fringe benefits* and *employment protection*.

employee assistance programme (*US*) *HR* a structured and integrated support service that identifies and resolves the concerns of employees that may affect performance. Employee assistance programmes can range from support for staff during periods of intensive change, *counselling* to tackle the problem of *stress*, return-to-work, and *eldercare* initiatives, to defined organisational policies on substance abuse and bullying. Employee assistance programmes are set up by employers who recognise that providing professional support for their staff makes good business sense. Some organisations find it cost-effective to *outsource* the programme depending on the nature of the problem and on the size of the organisation. *Abbr* **EAP**

employee association *HR* a professional or social body of employees who work for the same organisation

employee attitude survey *HR* a systematic investigation of the views and opinions of those employed by an organisation on issues relating to the work of that organisation or their role within it. Employee attitude surveys may be conducted by means of questionnaires or interviews. They may be undertaken occasionally or at regular intervals and may be used to make a general assessment of employee morale or focus on a specific issue such as the introduction of a new policy. Aims may be to identify or gain an understanding of problems so that action to resolve them can be taken, to encourage employee involvement and commitment, or to assist in planning, implementing, and evaluating new initiatives.

employee commitment *HR* the psychological bond of an employee to an organisation, the strength of which depends on the degree of *employee involvement*, employee loyalty, and belief in the values of the organisation. Employee commitment was badly damaged in the late 20th century during corporate re-organisations and *downsizing*, which undermined job security and resulted in fewer *promotion* opportunities. This led to the re-negotiation of the *psychological contract* and the need to develop strategies for increasing commitment. These included *flexible working* and *work-life balance* policies, *teamwork*, *training* and development, *employee participation*, and *empowerment*.

employee development *HR* the enhancement of the skills, knowledge, and experience of employees with the purpose of improving performance. Employee development, unlike *personal development*, is usually co-ordinated by the employing organisation. It can use a range of *training* methods, and is usually conducted on a planned basis, perhaps as a result of a *performance appraisal*.

employee discount *HR* a reduction in the price of company goods or services offered to employees as one of their *fringe benefits*

employee handbook *HR* a reference document containing information on what an employee should know about his or her organisation or employment. Employee handbooks typically include information on terms and *conditions of employment*, organisational policies and procedures, and *fringe benefits*.

employee involvement *HR* a range of management practices centred on *empowerment* and trust that are designed to increase *employee commitment* to organisational objectives and performance improvement. The term employee involvement is often used interchangeably with *employee participation*, but employee involvement practices tend to take place at individual or workgroup level, rather than at higher *decision-making* levels.

employee ownership *HR* the possession of shares in a company, in whole or in part, by the workers. There are various forms of employee ownership that give employees a greater or lesser stake in the business. These include: *employee share schemes*, employee *buy-outs*, co-operatives, and employee trusts. Ownership does not necessarily lead to greater *employee participation* in *decision-making*, although the evidence suggests that

---

A woman is like a teabag—only in hot water do you realise how strong she is. Nancy Reagan

where employees are involved in this, the company is more successful.

employee participation *HR* the involvement of workers in *decision-making*. Employee participation can take either a representational or direct form. Representation takes place through bodies such as consultative committees or *works councils*. This type of direct participation can be achieved through communication methods such as newsletters, *employee attitude surveys*, *team briefing*, and *open-book management*, or through involvement initiatives such as self-managed teams, *suggestion schemes*, and *quality circles*.

employee referral programme *HR* a policy, popular in the United States, for encouraging employees, usually through cash incentives, to nominate potential job candidates as part of the recruiting process. Employee referral programmes have been developed in an attempt to address the recruitment difficulties experienced by organisations in times of full employment. Although they can be very successful, there is a danger that if a referral programme is relied on too heavily, only limited sectors of the potential labour force will be available for recruitment, which might lead to a reduction in the *diversity* of the workforce.

employee share ownership plan *HR* a scheme sponsored by a company by which a trust holds shares in the company on behalf of *employees* and distributes those shares to employees. In the United States, shares can only be sold when an employee leaves the organisation, and are thus thought of as a form of pension provision. In the United Kingdom, shares can be disposed of at any time. There are two types of employee share ownership plan in the United Kingdom: the case-law employee share ownership plan, which can benefit all or some employees but may not qualify for tax benefits; and the employee share ownership trust. *Abbr* **ESOP**

employee share scheme *HR* a plan to give, or encourage employees to buy, a stake in the company that employs them by awarding free or discounted shares. Employee share schemes may be available to some or all employees, and schemes approved by the Inland Revenue enjoy tax advantages. Types of scheme include *employee share ownership plans*, *share options*, *save as you earn*, and employee share ownership trusts. Among the potential benefits are improved *employee commitment* and productivity, but the success of a scheme may depend on linking it to employee performance and the performance of the share price.

employee stock fund *Fin* in the United States, a fund from which money is taken to buy shares of a company's stock for its employees

employer *HR* a person or organisation that pays people to carry out specified activities. An employer usually contracts an *employee* to fill a permanent or temporary position to carry out work on a regularly paid basis within the relevant legal framework of the country of residence. In the United Kingdom, employers are required to contribute towards employees' National Insurance Contributions, deduct their income tax, provide paid *leave*, and ensure compliance with regulations relevant to the work concerned and to health and safety requirements.

employers' association *HR* a body that regulates relations between employers and employees, represents members' views on public policy issues affecting their business to national and international policy makers, and supplies support and advice. An employers' association represents companies within one or many sectors at regional, national, or international level and is usually a non-profit, non-party-political organisation, funded by subscriptions paid by its members.

Employment Court *HR* a higher court in New Zealand responsible for arbitrating in industrial relations disputes. It hears cases relating to disputes between employers and employees or unions as well as appeals referred to the court by *employment tribunals*.

employment equity (*S Africa*) *HR* the policy of giving preference in employment opportunities to qualified people from sectors of society that were previously discriminated against, for example, black people, women, and people with disabilities

employment law *HR* the collection of statutes, common law rules, and decisions in court or employment tribunal cases that govern the rights and duties of employers and employees. The *contract of employment* forms the cornerstone of employment law, which also embraces *discrimination*, *unfair dismissal*, and *redundancy* rights, *collective bargaining*, health and safety, union membership, and *industrial action*.

employment pass (*S Africa*) *Gen Mgt* a visa issued to a foreign national who is a professional earning in excess of R1,500 per month

employment protection *HR* the legal framework for establishing and defending the rights of employees. Employment protection in the United Kingdom was greatly extended by the Employment Protection Act 1975 and the Employment Protection (Consolidation) Act 1978. Since then, UK legislation and case law has continued to develop. The Employment Rights Act 1996 consolidated most of the existing law on individual employment rights.

employment tribunal *HR* a government body responsible for hearing and adjudicating in disputes between employees and employers

empowerment *Gen Mgt* the redistribution of **power** and **decision-making** responsibilities, usually to **employees**, where such **authority** was previously a management prerogative. Empowerment is based on the recognition that employee abilities are frequently underused, and that, given the chance, most employees can contribute more. Empowered workplaces are characterised by managers who focus on energising, supporting, and **coaching** their staff in a blame-free environment of trust.

empty suit *Gen Mgt* a corporate executive who dresses very smartly and follows all procedures exactly without actually contributing anything of significance to the company (*slang*)

EMS *abbr* **1.** *Fin* European Monetary System: the first stage of economic and monetary union of the EU, which came into force in March 1979, giving stable, but adjustable, exchange rates **2.** *Gen Mgt* environmental management system

EMU *abbr* *Fin* Economic and Monetary Union, or European Monetary Union: the timetable for EMU was outlined in the Maastricht Treaty in 1991. The criteria were that national debt must not exceed 60% of GDP; budget deficit should be 3% or less of GDP; inflation should be no more than 1.5% above the average rate of the three best-performing economies of the EU in the previous 12 months; and applicants must have been members of the **ERM** for two years without having re-aligned or devalued their currency.

encryption *E-com* a means of encoding information, especially financial data, so that it can be transmitted over the Internet without being read by unauthorised parties.

Within an Internet security system, a secure server uses encryption when transferring or receiving data from the Web. Credit card information, for example, which could be targeted by a **hacker**, is encrypted by the server, turning it into special code that will then be decrypted only when it is safely within the server environment. Once the information has been acted on, it is either deleted or stored in encrypted form.

encryption key *E-com* a sequence of characters known to both or all parties to a communication, used to initiate the **encryption** process

end-around (*US, Canada*) *Gen Mgt* an approach to a problem that does not attack it directly but rather tries to avoid it

end consumer *Mkting see* **consumer**

endogenous variable *Stats* the dependent variable in an econometric study

endorsement *Gen Mgt* the public approval of a product by a person or organisation. The endorsement can be used to promote the product to other organisations that may be more cautious in their approach to adopting new products.

endowment assurance *Fin* life cover that pays a specific sum of money on a specified date, or earlier in the event of the policyholder's death. Part of the premium paid is for the life cover element, while the remainder is invested in property and stocks and shares (either a 'with-profits' or 'without-profits' policy) or, in the case of a unit-linked policy, is used to purchase units in a life fund. The sum the policyholder receives at the end of the term depends on the size of the premiums and the performance of the investments. *See also* **term assurance**

endowment fund *Fin* a unit trust that supports a non-profit institution

endowment mortgage *Fin* a long-term loan, usually for the purchase of a property, in which the borrower makes two monthly payments, one to the lender to cover the interest on the loan, and the other as a premium paid into an endowment assurance policy. At the end of the loan's term, the proceeds from the endowment policy are used to repay the principal. *See also* **mortgage**

endowment policy *Fin* an insurance policy that pays a set amount to the policyholder when the policy matures, or to a beneficiary if the policyholder dies before it matures

endpoint *Stats* a point at which a definable event in a study takes place, for example, the recovery of a patient in a medical study

---

Prosperity doth best discover vice; but adversity doth best discover virtue.   *Francis Bacon*

energy audit *Gen Mgt* a review, inspection, and evaluation of sources and uses of energy within an organisation to ensure efficiency and lack of waste

energy conservation *Gen Mgt* the minimisation of fuel consumption. Energy conservation, through the monitoring and control of the amounts of electricity, gas, and other fuels used in the workplace, can help reduce costs and damage to the environment. An energy management scheme provides a systematic method of assessing, evaluating, and improving an organisation's energy usage. This forms part of an organisation's approach to *environmental management*.

engineered cost *Fin* a cost which varies in proportion to a measure of activity. Direct materials and royalty payments are engineered costs. Control is through flexible budgeting or standard costing.

engineering for excellence *Ops see design for manufacturability*

English disease *Gen Mgt* the supposed predilection of British workers to opt for *strike* action. In the United Kingdom in the 1960s and 1970s, strikes were commonly used by workers for *dispute* resolution. Government legislation in the 1980s, however, made striking more difficult for workers.

enterprise *Gen Mgt* a venture characterised by *innovation*, *creativity*, dynamism, and risk. An enterprise can consist of one project, or may refer to an entire organisation. It usually requires several of the following attributes: flexibility, initiative, *problem-solving* ability, independence, and imagination. Enterprises flourish in the environment of *delayered*, non-hierarchical organisations but can be stifled by *bureaucracy*. Enterprises are often created by *entrepreneurs*.

enterprise application integration *E-com* the unrestricted sharing of data and business processes via integrated and compatible software programs. As businesses expand and recognise the need for their information and applications to be shared between systems, they are investing in enterprise application integration in order to streamline processes and keep all the elements of their organisations, for example, human resources and inventory control, connected. *Abbr* **EAI**

enterprise culture *Gen Mgt* an organisational or social environment that encourages and makes possible initiative and *innovation*. An organisation with an enterprise culture is usually more competitive and more profitable than a *bureaucracy*. Such an organisation is believed to be more rewarding and stimulating to work in. A society with an enterprise culture facilitates individuality and requires people to take responsibility for their own welfare. Conservative governments in the United Kingdom during the 1980s and 1990s promoted an enterprise culture by introducing market principles into all areas of economic and social life. These included policies of deregulation of financial services, *privatisation* of utilities and national monopolies, and commercialisation of the public sector.

enterprise portal *E-com* a website that assembles a wide range of content and services for employees of a particular organisation, with the aim of bringing together all the key information they need to do a better job. The key difference between an enterprise portal and an *intranet* is that an enterprise portal contains not just internal content, but also external content that may be useful—such as specialised news feeds, or access to industry research reports. Ensuring that content is relevant, current, and frequently refreshed is essential for such sites to succeed, and enterprise portals are thus expensive to maintain.

enterprise resource planning *Gen Mgt see* **ERP**

enterprise zone *Gen Mgt* an area in which the government offers financial incentives to new business activities

entertainment expenses *HR* costs, reimbursable by the *employer*, that are incurred by an *employee* in hosting social events for clients or suppliers in order to obtain or maintain their custom or goodwill

entitlement *Gen Mgt* the expectation that an organisation or individual will make large profits regardless of their contribution to the economy

entitlement offer *Fin* an offer that cannot be transferred to anyone else

entity *Fin* an economic unit that has a separate, distinct identity, for example, an industrial or commercial company, charity, local authority, government agency, or fund

entrapment *Fin* restrictions placed on an organisation due to the limitations of its existing resource base and management competencies, which prevent it from responding to changes in its environment

entreprenerd *Gen Mgt* an entrepreneur with computing skills, especially one who starts up an Internet business (*slang*)

Behind an able man there are always other able men. *Chinese proverb*

entrepreneur *Gen Mgt* somebody who sets up a business or *enterprise*. An entrepreneur typically demonstrates effective application of a number of enterprising attributes such as creativity, initiative, risk-taking, problem-solving ability, and autonomy, and will often risk his or her own capital to set up a business. *See also* **intrapreneur**

entropy *Stats* a measure of the rate of transfer of the information that a system such as a computer program or factory machine receives or outputs

entry barrier *Mkting* a perceived or real obstacle preventing a competitor from entering a market

envelope *E-com see* **electronic envelope**

environment *E-com* the different computers, *browsers*, or *bandwidth* access points from which a user may access a website. Web pages may download at very different speeds according to the environment, so when building a website, it is important to test its performance within as many different environments as possible.

environmental analysis *Gen Mgt see* **environmental scanning**

environmental audit *Gen Mgt* the regular systematic gathering of information to monitor the effectiveness of environmental policies. An environmental audit now often forms part of an organisation's *environmental management* systems, and is concerned with checking conformity with legislative requirements and environmental standards such as ISO 14001 (see *ISO 14000*), as well as with company policy. The audit may also cover potential improvements in environmental performance and systems.

Environmental Impact Statement *Gen Mgt* a report on the results of an Environmental Impact Study. *Abbr* **EIS**

Environmental Impact Study *Gen Mgt* an analysis of the potential effects of a building development or a similar project on the natural environment. *Abbr* **EIS**

environmental management *Gen Mgt* a systematic approach to minimising the damage created by an organisation to the environment in which it operates. Environmental management has become an issue in organisations because consumers now expect them to be environmentally aware, if not environmentally friendly. Senior managers and directors are increasingly being held liable for their organisations' environmental

performance, and the onus is on them to adopt a *corporate strategy* that balances economic growth with environmental protection.

Environmental management involves reducing pollution, waste, and the consumption of natural resources by implementing an environmental action plan. This plan brings together the key elements of environmental management, including an organisation's *environmental policy* statement, an *environmental audit*, *environmental management system*, and standards such as the EC **ECO-Management Audit Scheme** and *ISO 14000*.

environmental management system *Gen Mgt* a procedure to manage and control an organisation's impact on the environment. An environmental management system is part of an organisation's *environmental management* practice. It includes creation of an *environmental policy*, which sets objectives and targets a programme of implementation, effectiveness monitoring, problem correction, and system review. An environmental management system should also identify key resources and holders of responsibility for determining and implementing environmental policy. Systems for environmental management have been formalised in the *ISO 14000* quality standards. *Abbr* **EMS**

environmental policy *Gen Mgt* a statement of organisational intentions regarding the safeguarding of the environment. Clause 4.2 of the ISO 14001 (see *ISO 14000*) series of environmental management standards, which many organisations now either apply in full or make use of for guidance on environmental management, focuses on environmental policy and states the necessary themes and commitments for an environmental policy that conforms to ISO 14001 requirements.

environmental scanning *Gen Mgt* the monitoring of changes in the external environment in which an organisation operates in order to identify threats and opportunities for the future and maintain *competitive advantage*. The process of environmental scanning includes gathering information on an organisation's task environment of competitors, markets, customers, and suppliers, carrying out a *PEST analysis* of social, economic, technological, and political factors that may affect the organisation, and analysing the implications of this research. Environmental scanning may be undertaken systematically by a dedicated department or unit within an organisation or more informally by project groups and may be used in the planning and

---

development of **corporate strategy**. *Also known as **environmental analysis***

environmental statistics *Stats* statistical studies concerning environmental matters such as pollution

EOQ *abbr Fin* economic order quantity

epidemiology *Stats* the statistical study of the incidence of a particular disease in a given population

e-procurement *E-com* the business-to-business sale and purchase of goods and services over an electronic network such as the Internet. *Also known as **electronic procurement***

EPS *abbr Gen Mgt* earnings per share

equal opportunities *HR* the granting of equal rights, privileges, and status regardless of gender, age, race, religion, disability, or sexual orientation. Equality in employment is regulated by law in most Western countries. An organisational equal opportunities policy aims to go further than the regulatory framework demands. Such a policy should focus on preventing discriminatory or harassing behaviour in the workplace and achieving equal access to training, job, and promotion opportunities. *Positive discrimination*, which is referred to as affirmative action in the United States, is a controversial approach to encouraging the advancement of minorities. *Diversity* management builds on and goes beyond equal opportunities by looking at the rights of individuals rather than groups.

equal pay *HR* the principle and practice of paying men and women in the same organisation at the same rate for like work, or work that is rated as of equal value. Work is assessed either through an organisation's *job evaluation* scheme or by the judgment of an independent expert appointed by an industrial tribunal. Although many countries have legislation on equal pay, a gap still exists between men's pay and women's pay and is attributed to sexual discrimination in job evaluation and payment systems.

equal treatment *HR* a principle of the *EU* that requires member states to ensure that there is no *discrimination* with regard to employment, vocational training, and working conditions. The principle of equal treatment is applied through Europe-wide directives and national legislation of the member states.

equilibrium price *Econ* the price that regulates supply and demand. Suppliers increase prices when demand is high and reduce prices when demand is low.

equilibrium quantity *Econ* the quantity that regulates supply and demand. Suppliers increase quantity when demand is high and reduce quantity when demand is low.

equilibrium rate of interest *Econ* the rate at which the expected interest rate in a market equals the actual rate prevailing

equipment trust certificate *Fin* a bond sold for a 20% down payment and collateralised by the equipment purchased with its proceeds

equity *Fin* the issued ordinary share capital plus reserves, statutory and otherwise, which represent the investment in a company by the ordinary shareholders

equity claim *Fin* a claim on earnings that remain after debts are satisfied

equity contribution agreement *Fin* an agreement to provide equity under specified circumstances

equity dilution *Fin* the reduction in the percentage of a company represented by each share for an existing shareholder who has not increased his or her holding in the issue of new ordinary shares

equity dividend cover *Fin* an accounting ratio, calculated by dividing the distributable profits during a given period by the actual dividend paid in that period, that indicates the likelihood of the dividend being maintained in future years. *See also **capital reserves***

equity floor *Fin* an agreement to pay whenever some indicator of a stock market's value falls below a specified limit

equity multiplier *(US) Fin* a measure of a company's worth, expressed as a multiple of each dollar of its stock's price

equity share capital *Fin* a company's issued share capital less capital which carries preferential rights. Equity share capital normally comprises ordinary shares.

equivalent annual cash flow *Fin* the value of an annuity required to provide an investor with the same return as some other form of investment

equivalent bond yield *Fin see **bond equivalent yield***

equivalent taxable yield *Fin* the value of a taxable investment required to provide an investor with the same return as some other form of investment

---

There is nothing so easy but that it becomes difficult when you do it reluctantly.   **Terence**

equivalent units *Fin* notional whole units representing uncompleted work. Used to apportion costs between work in progress and completed output, and in performance assessment.

e-retailer *E-com* a business that uses an electronic network such as the Internet to sell its goods or services. *Also known as* **electronic retailer, e-tailer**

erf (*S Africa*) *Fin* a plot of rural or urban land, usually no larger than a smallholding

ergonomics *Gen Mgt, HR* the study of workplace design and the physical and psychological impact it has on workers. Ergonomics is about the fit between people, their work activities, equipment, work systems, and environment to ensure that workplaces are safe, comfortable, efficient, and that *productivity* is not compromised. Ergonomics may examine the design and layout of buildings, machines, and equipment, as well as aspects such as lighting, temperature, ventilation, noise, colour, and texture. Ergonomic principles also apply to working methods such as systems and *procedures*, and the allocation and scheduling of work.

ERM *abbr Fin* Exchange Rate Mechanism: a system to maintain exchange rate stability used in the past by member states of the European Community

ERP *abbr Gen Mgt* enterprise resource planning: a software system that co-ordinates every important aspect of an organisation's production into one seamless process so that maximum efficiency can be achieved

ERR *abbr Fin* expected rate of return

error account *Fin* an account for the temporary placement of funds involved in a financial transaction known to have been executed in error

errors and omissions *Fin* mistakes from incorrect record-keeping or accounting. *Abbr* **E&O**

ESC *abbr Fin* European Social Charter: a charter adopted by the European Council of the EU in 1989. The 12 rights it contains are: freedom of movement, employment, and remuneration; social protection; improvement of living and working conditions; freedom of association and collective bargaining; worker information; consultation and participation; vocational training; equal treatment of men and women; health and safety protection in the workplace; pension rights; integration of those with disabilities; protection of young people.

e-shock *E-com* the forward momentum of electronic commerce, considered as irresistible

ESOP *abbr HR* employee share ownership plan

ESP *abbr Gen Mgt* Eligible Service Period

establishment fee *Fin see* **commitment fee**

estate *Fin* **1.** a substantial area of land that normally includes a large house such as a stately home **2.** a deceased person's net assets

estimate *Gen Mgt* **1.** an approximate calculation of an uncertain value. An estimate may be a reasonable guess based on knowledge and experience or it may be calculated using more sophisticated techniques designed to forecast projected costs, profits, losses, or value. **2.** an approximate price quoted for work to be undertaken by an organisation

estimation *Stats* the provision of a numerical value for a parameter of a population that has been sampled

e-tailer *E-com see* **e-retailer**

e-tailing *E-com* the practice of doing business over an electronic network such as the Internet

ethical investment *Fin* investment only in companies whose policies meet the ethical criteria of the investor. *Also known as* **socially-conscious investing**

ethnic monitoring *HR* the recording and evaluation of the racial origins of employees or customers with the aim of ensuring that all parts of the population are represented. When ethnic monitoring is carried out as a part of the *recruitment* process, candidates are asked to indicate their ethnic origin on an anonymous basis. Information thus supplied is removed from the application as soon as it is received by the prospective employer.

ETP *abbr Fin* Eligible Termination Payment

EU *abbr Fin* European Union: a social, economic, and political organisation of European countries whose aim is integration for all member nations. So called since November 1993 under the Maastricht Treaty, before which it was known as the European Community (EC), and before that as the European Economic Community.

EUREX *abbr Fin* Eureka Research Expert System: EUREX was established by Eureka (European Research and Co-ordination Agency) in 1985 on a French initiative for non-military industrial research in advanced technologies in Europe

euro *Fin* the currency of 12 member nations of the European Union. The euro was introduced in 1999, when the first 11 countries to adopt it joined together in an Economic and Monetary Union and fixed their currencies' exchange rate to the euro. Notes and coins were brought into general circulation in January 2002, although banks and other financial institutions had before that time carried out transactions in euros.

Eurobank *Fin* a US bank that handles transactions in foreign currencies

Eurobond *Fin* a bond specified in the currency of one country and sold to investors from another country. *Also known as* **global bond**

Euro-commercial paper *Fin* short-term uncollateralised loans obtained by companies in foreign countries

Eurocredit *Fin* intermediate-term notes used by banks to lend money to governments and companies

Eurocurrency *Fin* money deposited in one country but denominated in the currency of another country

Eurodeposit *Fin* a short-term deposit of Eurocurrency

Eurodollar *Fin* a US dollar deposited in a European bank or other bank outside the United States

Euroequity issue *Fin* a note issued by banks in several countries

Euroland *Fin* the area of Europe comprising those countries that have adopted the euro

Euro-note *Fin* a note in the Eurocurrency market

European Association of Securities Dealers Automated Quotations *Fin see* **EAS-DAQ**

European Bank for Reconstruction and Development *Fin see* **EBRD**

European Central Bank *Fin see* **ECB**

European Economic Community *or* **European Community** *Fin see* **EU**

European Investment Bank *Fin see* **EIB**

European Monetary System *Fin see* **EMS**

European Monetary Union *Fin see* **EMU**

European option *Fin* an option that the buyer can exercise only on the day that it expires. *See also* **American option**

European Quality Award *Gen Mgt see* **EFQM Excellence Model**

European Social Charter *Fin see* **ESC**

European Union *Fin see* **EU**

Euroyen bond *Fin* a Eurobond denominated in yen

EVA *abbr Fin* economic value added

evaluation of training *HR* a continuous cycle consisting of defining training objectives, carrying out **training needs analysis**, delivering training, assessing reactions to training, and measuring the bottom-line effects of training

event marketing *Mkting* the promotion and marketing of a specific event such as a conference, seminar, exhibition, or trade fair. Event marketing may encompass **corporate hospitality** activities, business or charity functions, or sporting occasions. The planning, marketing, and managing of the function on the day are sometimes entirely **outsourced** to companies specialising in event management.

evergreen loan *Fin* a series of loans providing a continuing stream of capital for a project

ex *Fin* 'without', as in **ex dividend**, where security purchases do not include rights to the next dividend payment, and **ex-rights**, where rights attaching to share ownership, such as a scrip issue, are not transferred to a new purchaser

ex-all *Fin* having no right in any transaction that is pending with respect to shares, such as a split, or the issue of dividends

ex ante *Fin* before the event. An **ex ante** budget, or standard, is set before a period of activity commences, and is based on the best information available at **that time** on expected levels of cost, performance, etc.

excellence *Gen Mgt, Ops* a state of organisational performance achieved through the successful integration of a variety of operational and strategic elements that enables an organisation to become one of the best in its field. Excellence is initially evident when an organisation rises above its competitors, and it is usually measured by the ability to sustain a leading or significant market share. The strategic and operational elements contributing to excellence include the organisation's approach to **total quality management**, **quality**

---

assurance, *quality awards* and *quality standards*, core competency, *benchmarking*, *customer service*, the *balanced scorecard*, and *leadership*. Taken altogether, these components should produce an organisational approach to the generation, development, and delivery of products and services that is better, cheaper, and smarter than that of the competition. Attempts at becoming an excellent organisation have spawned terms such as *best practice*, *best-in-class*, and *world class manufacturing* and are usually associated with a holistic approach to *competitive advantage*.

exception reporting *Gen Mgt* the passing on of information only when it breaches or transcends agreed norms. Exception reporting is intended to reduce *information overload* by minimising the circulation of repetitive or old information. Under this system, only information that is new and out of the ordinary will be transmitted. *See also* *management by exception*

excess *Fin* **1.** the part of an insurance claim that has to be met by the policyholder rather than the insurance company. An excess of £50 means that the company pays all but £50 of the claim for loss or damage. *See also* *deductible* **2.** in a financial institution, the amount by which assets exceed liabilities

excess profits tax *Fin* a tax levied by a government on a company that makes extraordinarily large profits in times of unusual circumstances, for example, during a war. An excess profits tax was imposed in both the United States and the United Kingdom during the Second World War.

excess reserves *Fin* reserves held by a financial institution that are higher than those required by the regulatory authorities. As such reserves may indicate that demand for loans is low, banks often sell their excess reserves to other institutions.

exchange[1] **1.** *E-com* the main type of business-to-business marketplace. The **B2B exchange** enables suppliers, buyers, and intermediaries to come together and offer products to each other according to a set of criteria. **B2B web exchanges** provide constant price adjustments in line with fluctuations of supply and demand. In E2E or 'exchange-to-exchange' e-commerce, buyers and sellers conduct transactions not only within exchanges but also between them. **2.** *Fin* the conversion of one type of security for another, for example, the exchange of a bond for shares

exchange[2] *Fin* **1.** to trade one currency for another **2.** to barter

exchange controls *Econ* the regulations by which a country's banking system controls its residents' or resident companies' dealings in foreign currencies and gold

exchange equalisation account *Econ* the Bank of England account that sells and buys sterling for gold and foreign currencies to smooth out fluctuations in the exchange rate of the pound

exchange offer *Fin* an offer to trade one security for another

exchange rate *Fin* the rate at which one country's currency can be exchanged for that of another country

Exchange Rate Mechanism *Fin see* **ERM**

exchange rate parities *Fin* relationships between the values of various currencies

exchange rate risk *Fin* the risk of suffering loss on converting another currency to the currency of a company's own country.
EXAMPLE Exchange rate risks can be arranged into three primary categories. Economic exposure: operating costs will rise due to changes in rates and make a product uncompetitive in the world market. Little can be done to reduce this routine business risk that every enterprise must endure. Translation exposure: the impact of currency exchange rates will reduce a company's earnings and weaken its balance sheet. To reduce translation exposure, experienced corporate fund managers use a range of techniques known as *currency hedging*. Transaction exposure: there will be an unfavourable move in a specific currency between the time when a contract is agreed and the time it is completed, or between the time when a lending or borrowing is initiated and the time the funds are repaid. Transaction exposure can be eased by *factoring*: transferring title to foreign accounts receivable to a third-party factoring house.

Although there is no definitive way of forecasting exchange rates, largely because the world's economies and financial markets are evolving so rapidly, the relationships between exchange rates, interest rates, and inflation rates can serve as leading indicators of changes in risk. These relationships are as follows. Purchasing Power Parity theory (PPP): while it can be expressed differently, the most common expression links the changes in exchange rates to those in relative price indices in two countries:

Rate of change of exchange rate = Difference in inflation rates

International Fisher Effect (IFE): this holds that an interest-rate differential will exist only if the exchange rate is expected to change in such a way that the advantage of the higher interest rate is offset by the loss on the foreign exchange transactions. Practically speaking, the IFE implies that while an investor in a low-interest country can convert funds into the currency of a high-interest country and earn a higher rate, the gain (the interest-rate differential) will be offset by the expected loss due to foreign exchange rate changes. The relationship is stated as:

Expected rate of change of the exchange rate = Interest-rate differential

Unbiased Forward Rate Theory: this holds that the forward exchange rate is the best unbiased estimate of the expected future spot exchange rate.

Expected exchange rate = Forward exchange rate

exchange rate spread *Fin* the difference between the price at which a broker or other intermediary buys and sells foreign currency

exchequer *Fin* in the United Kingdom, the government's account at the Bank of England into which all revenues from taxes and other sources are paid

excise duty *Fin* a tax on goods such as alcohol or tobacco produced and sold within a particular country

exclusive economic zone *Econ* a zone in a country in which particular economic conditions apply. The Special Economic Zone (SEZ) in China, where trade is conducted free of state control, is an example.

execution only *Fin* used to describe a stock market transaction undertaken by an intermediary who acts on behalf of a client without providing advice

executive *Gen Mgt* an employee in a position of senior responsibility in an organisation. An executive is involved in planning, strategy, policy making, and *line management*. The term executive can also be used as an alternative to *manager*, *consultant*, *executive officer*, or *agent*.

executive chairman *Gen Mgt see chair*

executive coaching *HR* regular one-to-one *coaching* for leaders, designed as part of a *management development* programme to provide knowledge and skills in a particular area. Executive coaching involves giving *feedback* to a leader and assisting in the creation of a development plan, often using *360 degree appraisal*. It can include in-depth development coaching conducted by colleagues, superiors, or specialist trainers, lasting perhaps six to twelve months.

executive director *Gen Mgt* a senior employee of an organisation, usually with line responsibility for a particular function and usually, but not always, a member of the *board of directors*

executive information system *Gen Mgt see EIS*

executive officer *Gen Mgt see executive*

executive pension plan *Fin* in the United Kingdom, a pension scheme for senior executives of a company. The company's contributions are a tax-deductible expense but are subject to a cap. The plan does not prevent the executive being a member of the company's group pension scheme although the executive's total contributions must not exceed a certain percentage of his or her salary.

executive search *HR* the identification of suitable external candidates for senior positions on behalf of an organisation by recruitment agents or consultants, often using *headhunting* techniques. Executive search consultants work from personal recommendation and lists of their own contacts, and monitor rising stars or key personnel in particular organisations or professions. The number of potential candidates is usually limited because of the speciality or seniority of the post, so that the search takes place within upper salary ranges. Executive search consultants rarely advertise because the publicity may be unfruitful or detrimental to the organisation for which they are working, and they do not find posts for individual jobhunters.

executive share option scheme *Fin* a UK term for an arrangement whereby certain directors and employees are given the opportunity to purchase shares in the company at a fixed price at a future date. In certain jurisdictions, such schemes can be tax efficient if certain local tax authority conditions are met. *See also employee share ownership plan*

executor *Fin* the person appointed under a will to ensure the deceased's estate is distributed according to the terms of the will

exempt gift *Fin* a gift that is not subject to US gift tax

We find it easy to believe that praise is sincere: why should anyone lie in telling us the truth?

Jean Rostand

exempt investment fund *Fin* in the United Kingdom, a collective investment, usually a unit trust, for investors who have certain tax privileges, for example, charities or contributors to pension plans

exemption *Fin* an amount per family member that an individual can subtract when reporting income to be taxed

exempt purchaser *Fin* an institutional investor who may buy newly issued securities without filing a prospectus with a securities commission

exempt securities *Fin* securities that are not subject to a provision of law such as margin or registration requirements

exempt supplies *Fin* in the United Kingdom, items or services on which VAT is not levied, for example, the purchase of, or rent on, property and financial services

exercise notice *Fin* an option-holder's notification to the option's writer of his or her desire to exercise the option

exercise of warrants *Fin* the use of a warrant to purchase stock

exercise price *Fin* the price at which an option to purchase or to sell shares or other items, **call option** or **put option**, may be exercised

exercise value *Fin* the amount of profit that can be realised by cashing in an option

ex gratia *Fin* as an act of favour, without obligation

ex-gratia payment *HR* a one-off extra payment in addition to normal **pay**, made out of gratitude or courtesy, or in recognition of a special contribution

exhibition *Mkting* an event organised to bring together buyers and sellers at a single venue

Eximbank *abbr Fin* Export-Import Bank: a US bank founded in 1934 that provides loans direct to foreign importers of US goods and services

existential culture *Gen Mgt* a form of *corporate culture* in which the organisation exists to serve the individual, rather than individuals being servants of the organisation. Existential culture was identified by **Charles Handy**. It typically consists of a group of professionals who work together, but have no leader.

exit interview *HR* a meeting between an employee and a management representative on the employee's departure from an organisation. An exit interview is conducted in order to ascertain why an employee is leaving, either because of pull factors, such as better pay and conditions, or push factors, such as poor training or management. Another purpose of the exit interview is to capture information relating to the departing employee's knowledge and experience.

exit PE ratio *Fin* the price-earnings ratio when a company changes hands

exogenous variable *Stats* any variable in an econometric study that has an impact on it from outside

expatriate *HR* somebody who has left his or her home country to live or work abroad, either for a long period of time or permanently

expectancy theory *HR* a view that people will be motivated to behave in particular ways if they believe that doing so will bring them rewards they both seek and value. Expectancy theory was first applied in the context of the workplace by **Victor Vroom** in the 1960s. He defined the concepts of valence and expectancy to explain how people decide to act. Valence refers to somebody's perception of the value of the reward or outcome that might be obtained if he or she performs a task successfully.

expected rate of return *Fin* the projected percentage return on an investment, based on the weighted probability of all possible rates of return. *Abbr* **ERR**

EXAMPLE It is calculated by the following formula:

$$E[r]=\Sigma sP(s)rs$$

where E[r] is the expected return, P(s) is the probability that the rate rs occurs, and rs is the return at s level.

The following example illustrates the principle which the formula expresses.

The current price of ABC Ltd stock is trading at £10. At the end of the year, ABC shares are projected to be traded:

25% higher if economic growth exceeds expectations—a probability of 30%

12% higher if economic growth equals expectations—a probability of 50%

5% lower if economic growth falls short of expectations—a probability of 20%

To find the expected rate of return, simply multiply the percentages by their respective probabilities and add the results:

(30% × 25%) + (50% × 12%) + (25% × –5%) = 7.5 + 6 + –1.25 = 12.25% ERR

A second example:

if economic growth remains robust (a 20% probability), investments will return 25%

if economic growth ebbs, but still performs adequately (a 40% probability), investments will return 15%

if economic growth slows significantly (a 30% probability), investments will return 5%

if the economy declines outright (a 10% probability), investments will return 0%

Therefore:

(20% × 25%) + (40% × 15%) + (30% × 5%) + (10% × 0%) = 5% + 6% + 1.5% + 0% = 12.5% ERR.

*See also **capital asset pricing model***

expected value *Fin* the financial forecast of the outcome of a course of action multiplied by the probability of achieving that outcome. The probability is expressed as a value ranging from 0 to 1.

expenditure switching *Econ* government action to improve the attractiveness of home-produced goods at the expense of imports or to make domestic spending switch from imports to home-produced goods

expense *Fin* **1.** a cost incurred in buying goods or services **2.** a charge against a company's profit

expense account *HR* an amount of money that an employee or group of employees can draw on to reclaim personal *expenses* incurred in carrying out activities for an organisation

expenses *HR* personal costs incurred by an employee in carrying out activities for an organisation that are reimbursed by the employer

experience curve *Gen Mgt see **learning curve***

experience economy *Gen Mgt* an economy in which products are differentiated through the quality of the 'consumer experience' or level of added value (*slang*)

experiential learning *HR* a model that views learning as a cyclical process in four stages: concrete experience, reflective observation, abstract conceptualisation, and active experimentation. Experiential learning relates to participants' activities and reactions to a training event, in contrast to passive learning. Proposed by ***David Kolb*** in 1971, the model was later expanded by other practitioners including ***Peter Honey*** and ***Alan Mumford***. Experiential learning differs from ***action learning*** in that it can apply to an individual working alone while action learning is seen essentially as a group activity.

experimental design *Stats* the planning of the procedures to be used in an ***experimental study***

experimental study *Stats* a statistical investigation in which the researcher can influence events in the study

expert system *Gen Mgt* a computer program that emulates the reasoning and ***decision-making*** of a human expert in a particular field. The main components of an expert system are the knowledge base, which consists of facts and rules about appropriate courses of action based on the knowledge and experience of human experts; the inference engine, which simulates the inductive reasoning of a human expert; and the user interface, which enables users to interact with the system. Expert systems may be used by non-experts to solve well-defined problems when human expertise is unavailable or expensive, or by experts seeking to find solutions to complex questions. They are used for a wide variety of tasks including medical diagnostics and financial decision-making, and are an application of ***artificial intelligence***.

explicit knowledge *Gen Mgt see **knowledge***

exploding bonus *HR* a bonus offered to recent graduates that encourages them to sign for a job as quickly as possible as it reduces in value with every day of delay (*slang*)

exponential smoothing *Gen Mgt* a statistical technique used in quantitative ***forecasting***, particularly in the areas of inventory control and ***sales forecasting***, that adjusts data to give a clearer view of trends in the long term. In exponential smoothing, values are calculated using a formula that takes all previous values into account but assigns greatest weight to the most recent data.

exponential trend *Stats* a statistical trend that is revealed in a ***time series***

export agent *Gen Mgt* an intermediary who acts on behalf of a company to open up or develop a market in a foreign country. Export agents are often paid a commission on all sales and may have exclusive rights in a particular geographical area. A good agent will know or get to know local market conditions and will have other valuable information that can be used to mutual benefit.

Export Credit Guarantee Department *Mkting* a UK government department that provides financial and insurance assistance for exporters. The Export Credit Guarantee Department works to benefit organisations exporting UK goods and services and sets up insurance for UK companies investing overseas. *Abbr* **ECGD**

Export-Import Bank *Fin see **Eximbank***

exporting *Mkting* the process of selling goods to other countries. Exporting provides access to non-domestic markets and can be co-ordinated by an **export manager**. As with all business activities, careful *market research* needs to be undertaken. This can be carried out by the company itself or through an experienced *export agent*. Many companies produce goods almost entirely for export. Services also can be exported, but require different delivery mechanisms through subsidiary offices or local *franchise*, or *licensing agreements*.

export-led growth *Econ* growth in which a country's main source of income is from its export trade

export manager *Mkting see **exporting***

ex post *Fin* after the event. An ex post budget, or standard, is set after the end of a period of activity, when it can represent the optimum achievable level of performance in the conditions which were experienced. Thus the budget can be flexed, and standards can reflect factors such as unanticipated changes in technology and in price levels. This approach may be used in conjunction with sophisticated cost and revenue modelling to determine how far both the plan and the achieved results differed from the performance that would have been expected in the circumstances which were experienced.

exposure *E-com see **ad view***

ex-rights *Fin* for sale without rights, for example, voting or conversion rights. The term can be applied to transactions such as the purchase of new shares.

ex-rights date *Fin* the date when a stock first trades ex-rights

extendable bond *Fin* a bond whose maturity can be delayed by either the issuer or the holder

extendable note *Fin* a note whose maturity can be delayed by either the issuer or the holder

extended fund facility *Econ* a credit facility of the *IMF* that allows a country up to eight years to repay money it has borrowed from the Fund

external account *Fin* in the United Kingdom, a bank account at a UK branch held by a customer who is an overseas resident

external audit *Fin* an audit of a company done by people who are external to, and independent of, the organisation. *See also* ***internal audit***

external communication *Gen Mgt* the exchange of information and messages between an organisation and other organisations, groups, or individuals outside the formal structure of the organisation. The aims of external communication are to facilitate co-operation with groups such as suppliers, investors, and shareholders, and to present a favourable image of an organisation and its products or services to potential and actual customers and to society at large. A variety of channels may be used for external communication including face-to-face meetings, print or broadcast media, and electronic communication technologies such as the Internet. External communication includes the fields of *PR*, media relations, *advertising*, and *marketing management*.

external debt *Econ* the part of a country's debt that is owed to creditors who are not residents of the country

external finance *Fin* money that a company obtains from investors, for example, by loans or by issuing stock

external funds *Fin* money that a business obtains from a third party rather than from its own resources

external growth *Fin* business growth as a result of a merger, a takeover, or through a partnership with another organisation

extranet *E-com* a closed network of websites and e-mail systems that is open to people outside as well as inside an organisation. An extranet enables third-party access to internal applications or information—usually subject to some kind of signed agreement. This is useful for organisations that need to share internal systems and information with potential partners. As with *intranets*, extranets provide all the benefits of Internet technology (browsers, web servers, HTML, etc.) with the added benefit of security, being confined to an isolated network.

Because this is a work environment and partners enter it to access information as quickly as possible, extranet design generally focuses on minimal graphics and maximum content. Security being a key issue, it is generally password-protected in order to main-

---

Always be smart enough to hire people brighter than yourself. *Caroline Marland*

tain confidentiality. Content management is also essential, as the extranet is only as useful as the information it contains. Many extranets fall down because the content is not updated and managed properly.

extraordinary general meeting *Gen Mgt* any general meeting of an organisation other than the *AGM*. Directors can usually call an extraordinary general meeting at their discretion, as can company members who either hold not less than 10% of the paid-up voting shares, or who represent not less than 10% of the voting rights. Directors are obliged to call an EGM if there is a substantial loss of capital. Fourteen days' written notice must be given, or 21 days' written notice if a special resolution is to be proposed. Only special business can be transacted at the meeting, the general nature of which must be specified in the convening notice. *Abbr* **EGM**

extraordinary resolution *Fin* in the United Kingdom, an exceptional issue that is put to the vote at a company's general meeting, for example, a change to the company's articles of association. *Also known as* **special resolution**

extrapolate *Stats* to estimate from a data set values that lie beyond the range of the data collected

extreme value *Stats* either of the smallest or largest variate values in a sample of observations from a statistical study

eyeballing *Stats* the process of informally inspecting statistical data by simply looking at it to assess results (*slang*)

eyeballs *E-com* a measure of the number of visits made to a website (*slang*)

eyebrow management *Gen Mgt* a management style whereby a manager or top executive can change a course of action simply by implying his or her disapproval (*slang*)

eye candy *Gen Mgt* visually attractive material (*slang*)

eye service *HR* the practice of working only when a supervisor is present and able to see you (*slang*)

e-zine *E-com* a regular publication on a particular topic distributed in digital form, mainly via the Web but also by e-mail

---

Entrepreneurs have no frontier other than their own ambition.   *Robert Heller*

F2F *abbr Gen Mgt* face-to-face (*slang*)

face time *HR* time spent in face-to-face communication as opposed to time spent communicating electronically (*slang*)

facilitation *HR* the process of helping groups, or individuals, to learn, find a solution, or reach a consensus, without imposing or dictating an outcome. Facilitation aims to *empower* individuals or groups to learn for themselves or find their own answers to problems without control or manipulation. Facilitators need good *communication skills*, including listening, questioning, and reflecting. Facilitation is used in a range of contexts including *training*, *experiential learning*, conflict resolution, and *negotiation*.

facilities management *Gen Mgt* **1.** the management of an organisation's property **2.** the provision of equipment or services to an organisation by an agent or company

facility-sustaining activities *Fin* activities undertaken to support the organisation as a whole, which cannot be logically linked to individual units of output. Accounting is a facility-sustaining activity. *See also* **hierarchy of activities**

facing matter *Mkting* advertisements printed opposite editorial material in newspapers or magazines

factor *Stats* a variable investigated in a statistical study

factor analysis *Stats* the examination of the covariances, correlations, or relationships between the variables observed in a statistical study

factored goods *Fin* goods purchased for resale

factor four *Ops* a concept of environmentally-friendly production based on increasing the productivity of resources by a factor of four to reduce waste

factoring *Fin* the sale of debts to a third party (the factor) at a discount, in return for prompt cash. A factoring service may be with recourse, in which case the supplier takes the risk of the debt not being paid, or without recourse when the factor takes the risk. *See also* **invoice discounting**

factor market *Econ* a market in which factors of production are bought and sold, for example, the capital market or the labour market

factory *Gen Mgt* a building or set of buildings housing workers and equipment for the sole purpose of manufacturing goods, often on a large scale

factory gate price *Ops* the actual cost of manufacturing goods before any *mark-up* is added to give profit. The factory gate price includes direct costs such as labour, *raw materials*, and energy, and indirect costs such as interest on loans, plant maintenance, or rent.

failure *Gen Mgt see* **business failure**

failure mode effects analysis *Gen Mgt see* **FMEA**

fallen angel *Fin* a stock that was once very desirable but has now dropped in value (*slang*)

family business *Gen Mgt* a *small* or *medium-sized business*, run by a family owner, often with the help of other family members, and passed on within the family. If a family business grows, it may be run as an unregistered partnership or, more commonly, registered as a limited company, although in both cases the partners or the directors will be appointed from within the family to retain family control. In the case of larger, *public limited* family businesses, family members are usually majority shareholders and retain control of the *board of directors*, although non-family directors and shareholders will have an influence on the way the company is run. The most common cause of *business failure* in family-owned businesses is poor *succession planning*.

family-friendly policy *HR* a range of working practices designed to enable employees to achieve a satisfactory *work-life balance*. A family-friendly policy is often introduced by an organisation to facilitate the reintroduction of women with children into the workplace. *Equal opportunities* legislation and corporate good practice, however, require that such a policy is open to all employees. Typically, a family-friendly policy will allow for a range of *flexible working* practices and may go further by providing childcare or care for employees' elderly relatives, or paid time off for participation in community activities as part of a *community involvement* programme.

To succeed at reengineering, you have to be a missionary, a motivator, and a leg breaker.
Michael Hammer

Although the introduction of a family-friendly policy may initially be expensive, benefits to the organisation, including improved employee retention and higher **motivation** and **job satisfaction** levels, are believed to offset these costs.

Fannie Mae (*US*) *Fin see* **FNMA**

FAO *abbr Gen Mgt* the Food and Agriculture Organisation of the United Nations: the FAO's priority objectives include encouraging sustainable agriculture and rural development and ensuring the availability of adequate food supplies

FAQ *abbr E-com* frequently asked question: FAQ pages are often included on websites to provide first-time visitors with answers to the most likely questions they may have. FAQ pages are also used in newsgroups and software applications.

far month *Fin* the latest month for which there is a futures contract for a particular commodity. *See also* **nearby month**

FASB *abbr Fin* (*US*) Financial Accounting Standards Board: a body responsible for establishing the standards of financial reporting and accounting for US companies in the private sector. The Securities and Exchange Commission (SEC) performs a comparable role for public companies.

FASTER *Fin* Fully Automated Screen Trading and Electronic Registration, a computer-based clearing, settlement, registration, and information system operated by the New Zealand Stock Exchange

fast track *Gen Mgt* a rapid route to success or advancement. The fast track involves competition and a race to get ahead, and is associated with high ambition and great activity. An employee can be on a fast track, for example, to **promotion**, but an activity also can be said to take the fast track, for example, to rapid **product development**. The **horizontal fast track** is a variation on the idea of the fast track in which advancement is not upwards but sideways.

fat
trim the fat *Gen Mgt* to lay off unnecessary staff in an organisation during a time of economic difficulty (*slang*)

faxback *Mkting* a method of distributing information in which customers dial a dedicated fax machine that automatically sends information back to the customer's fax machine

Fayol, Henri Louis (1841–1925) *Gen Mgt* French engineer and industrialist. First European to define **management** as a process, consisting, he argued, of five activities—planning, organising, co-ordinating, commanding, and controlling—with further detail contained in 14 general principles. Fayol's ideas were published in *Administration Industrielle et Générale* (1916), and were practised by others, notably **Alfred Sloan, Jr**.

FCM *abbr Fin* futures commission merchant

FCOL *abbr Gen Mgt* for crying out loud (*slang*)

FDI *abbr Fin* foreign direct investment

feasibility study *Gen Mgt* an investigation into a proposed plan or project to determine whether and how it can be successfully and profitably carried out. Frequently used in **project management**, a feasibility study may examine alternative methods of reaching objectives or be used to define or redefine the proposed project. The information gathered must be sufficient to make a decision on whether to go ahead with the project or to enable an investor to decide whether to commit finances to it. This will normally require analysis of technical, financial, and market issues, including an estimate of resources required in terms of materials, time, personnel, and finance, and the expected return on investment.

feasible region *Fin* the area contained within all of the constraint lines shown on a graphical depiction of a linear programming problem. All feasible combinations of output are contained within, or located on, the boundaries of the feasible region.

Federal Funds *Fin* deposits held in reserve by the US Federal Reserve System

federal organisation *Gen Mgt* a form of **organisation structure**, identified by **Charles Handy**, in which subsidiaries federate to gain benefits of scale. In a federal organisation, the leader provides co-ordination and vision, and initiatives are generated from the component subsidiary organisations. Federal organisation is one of the many ways in which organisations **restructure** in order to deal with the dilemmas of power and control. According to Handy, federal organisation offers an enabling framework for autonomy to release corporate energy for people to do things in their own way, provided that it is in the common interest, and for people to be well informed so as to be able to interpret that common interest. Handy cites Royal Dutch Shell, Unilever, and ABB as exemplars of federalism.

Hindsight is good, foresight is better; but second sight is best of all. *Evan Esar (attrib.)*

Federal Reserve Bank *Fin* a bank that is a member of the US Federal Reserve System

Federal Reserve Board *(US) Fin* a body of seven governors appointed by Congress on the nomination of the President, that supervises the US Federal Reserve System. Appointees serve for 14 years. *Abbr* **FRB**

Federal Reserve note *Fin* a note issued by the US Federal Reserve System to increase the availability of money temporarily

Federal Reserve System *Fin* the central banking system of the United States, founded in 1913 by an Act of Congress. The board of governors, made up of seven members, is based in Washington DC and 12 Reserve Banks are located in major cities across the United States.

Fed pass *Fin* the US Federal Reserve's addition of reserves to the Federal Reserve System to increase credit availability

Fedwire *Fin* the US Federal Reserve System's electronic system for transferring funds

feedback *Gen Mgt* the communication of responses and reactions to proposals and changes, or of the findings of *performance appraisals* with the aim of enabling improvements to be made. Feedback can be either positive or negative. In the context of performance evaluation, or *performance appraisal*, positive feedback should be delivered to reinforce good performance, whereas negative feedback should be intended to correct or improve poor performance. Feedback that is delivered inappropriately can be very demotivating, so good communication skills are a prerequisite.

feedback control *Fin* the measurement of differences between planned outputs and actual outputs achieved, and the modification of subsequent action and/or plans to achieve future required results

feedforward control *Fin* the forecasting of differences between actual and planned outcomes, and the implementation of action, before the event, to avoid such differences

feeding frenzy *Fin* a period of frantic buyer activity in a market *(slang)*

feet
get your feet wet *Gen Mgt* to begin a new project or activity *(slang)*

fee work *Gen Mgt* work on a project carried out by independent workers or contractors, rather than employees of an organisation

Feigenbaum, Armand Vallin *(b.* 1920) *Gen Mgt* US manager and author. Originator of the concept of total *quality control*, the forerunner of *total quality management*. In *Quality Control* (1951), Feigenbaum argued that quality should be a company-wide process.

Ferguson, Sir Alex *(b.* 1941) *Gen Mgt* British football manager. Considered to be one of the most successful club managers of all time, whose management methods, particularly in the area of *motivation*, are studied by other business leaders. His approach is set out in *Managing My Life: My Autobiography* (1999).

FID *abbr (ANZ) Fin* Financial Institutions Duty

field plot *Stats* a statistical study, usually in agriculture, of the results of an operation such as planting GM crops

field research *Mkting* the collection of data directly from contact with customers and potential customers through surveys, interviews, and other forms of *market research*

field staff *HR* sales staff who cover a specific geographical region and who travel regularly to meet customers. The term field staff may also be applied to professional and technical staff who operate mainly on site, such as conservationists and archaeologists.

field trial *Mkting* a limited pilot test of a product under real conditions. A field trial is undertaken to test the physical or engineering properties of a product in order to identify and iron out any technical shortcomings prior to marketing. Customers may be involved in some trials, for example, in testing a new washing powder. Field trials should not be confused with *test marketing*, which is used to determine the likely market for, and likely consumer response to, a new product or service.

field work *Mkting* practical work, study, or research carried out in the real world away from the desk. In a marketing context, field work forms primary *market research* and involves obtaining customers' views and opinions on a face-to-face basis or through postal questionnaires or telephone surveys.

FIFO *abbr Ops* first in first out: a method of stock control where the stock of a given product first placed in store is used before more recently produced or acquired goods or materials

FIF Tax *abbr (ANZ) Fin* Foreign Investment Funds Tax

I have direct knowledge. I don't have to call someone to ask a question. *Nancy Peretsman*

file server *E-com* a computer that stores and makes software programs and data available to other computers on a network

file transfer protocol *E-com see* **FTP**

filter *Gen Mgt* a process for analysing large amounts of incoming information to identify any material that might be of interest to an organisation

Filthy Five *Gen Mgt* a list of companies with a poor environmental record, compiled annually by *Mother Jones Magazine* in the United States

final average monthly salary *(US) Fin* = *pensionable earnings*

finance *Fin* the money needed by an individual or company to pay for something, for example, a project or stocks

finance bill *Fin* an act passed by a legislature to provide money for public spending

finance company *Fin* a business that lends money to people or companies against collateral, especially to make purchases by hire purchase

finance house *Fin* a financial institution

finance lease *Fin* a lease that is treated as though the lessee had borrowed money and bought the leased assets.

If a lease agreement does not meet any of the criteria below, the lessee treats it as an *operating lease* for accounting purposes. If, however, the agreement meets one of the criteria below, it is treated as a finance lease.
1. The lease agreement transfers ownership of the assets to the lessee during the term of the lease.
2. The lessee can purchase the assets leased at a bargain price (also called a bargain purchase option), such as £1, at the end of the lease term.
3. The lease term is at least 75% of the economic life of the leased asset.
4. The present value of the minimum lease payments is 90% or more of the asset's value.

Finance leases are reported by the lessee as if the assets being leased were acquired and the monthly rental payments as if they were payments of principal and interest on a debt obligation. Specifically, the lessee capitalises the lease by recognising an asset and a liability at the lower of the present value of the minimum lease payments or the value of the assets under lease. As the monthly rental payments are made, the corresponding liability decreases. At the same time, the leased asset is depreciated in a manner that is con-

sistent with other owned assets having the same use and economic life.
US term **capital lease**. *See also* **operating lease**

financial *Fin* relating to finance

financial accounting *Fin* the classification and recording of the monetary transactions of an entity in accordance with established concepts, principles, accounting standards, and legal requirements, and their presentation, by means of profit and loss accounts, balance sheets, and cash flow statements, during and at the end of an accounting period

Financial Accounting Standards Board *(US) Fin see* **FASB**

financial adviser *Fin* somebody whose job is to give advice about investments

financial analyst *Fin see* **investment analyst**

financial control *Fin* the control of divisional performance by setting a range of financial targets and the monitoring of actual performance towards these targets

financial distress *Fin* the condition of being in severe difficulties over money, especially being close to bankruptcy

financial economies of scale *Fin* financial advantages gained by being able to do things on a large scale

financial engineering *Fin* the conversion of one form of financial instrument into another, such as the swap of a fixed-rate instrument for a floating-rate one

financial incentive scheme *Gen Mgt see* **incentive scheme**

Financial Institutions Duty *(ANZ) Fin* a tax on monies paid into financial institutions imposed by all state governments in Australia except for Queensland. Financial institutions usually pass the tax on to customers. *Abbr* **FID**

financial instrument *Fin* a document that has a cash face value or represents a financial transaction

financial leverage *Fin* the use of debt finance to increase the return on equity by deploying borrowed funds in such a way that the return generated is greater than the cost of servicing the debt. If the reverse is true, and the return on deployed funds is less than the cost of servicing the debt, the effect of financial leverage is to reduce the return on equity. *Also known as* **gearing**

financial liability *Fin* any liability that is a contractual obligation to either deliver cash or another financial asset to another entity or to exchange financial instruments with another entity under conditions that are potentially unfavourable

financial management *Fin* the management of all the processes associated with the efficient acquisition and deployment of both short- and long-term financial resources

Financial Ombudsman *Fin* the person responsible for investigating and resolving complaints involving money from members of the public against a company, institution, or other organisation

financial planning *Fin* planning the acquisition of funds to finance planned activities

Financial Planning Association of Australia *Fin* a national organisation representing companies and individuals working in the Australian financial planning industry. Established in 1992, the association is responsible for monitoring standards among its members. *Abbr* **FPA**

Financial Reporting Review Panel *Fin* a UK review panel established to examine contentious departures, by large companies, from accounting standards

Financial Reporting Standards Board (*ANZ*) *Fin* a peak body that is responsible for setting and monitoring accounting standards in New Zealand. *Abbr* **FRSB**

financial risk *Fin* the possibility of loss in an investment or speculation

financial statements *Fin* summaries of accounts to provide information for interested parties. The most common financial statements are: trading and profit and loss account; profit and loss appropriation account; balance sheet; cash-flow statement; report of the auditors; statement of total recognised gains and losses; and reconciliation of movements in shareholders' funds.

financier *Fin* somebody who provides financing

financing gap *Econ* the gap in funding for institutions such as the *IMF* caused by cancelling the debts of poorer countries such as those in West Africa

find time *Mkting* the time it takes a consumer to locate a company's product among other products on the shelf (*slang*)

finished goods *Ops* completed goods that are available for sale to customers

finite capacity plan *Ops* *see* *capacity requirements planning*

finite loading *Ops* the scheduling or *loading* of jobs onto a workstation so that the number of jobs matches the *effective capacity* of that station over a given time period. Finite loading is often used in a computerised operation of *loading*. *See also* *infinite loading*

finite population *Stats* a statistical population that has a limited size

FIRB *abbr* (*ANZ*) *Fin* Foreign Investment Review Board

firewall *E-com* a combination of hardware, software, and procedures that controls access to an intranet. Firewalls help to control the information that passes between an intranet and the Internet. A firewall can be simple or complex depending on how an organisation decides to control its Internet traffic. It may, for example, be set up to limit Internet access to e-mail only, so that no other types of information can pass between the intranet and the Internet.

firm *Gen Mgt* a *partnership* business. A firm is strictly the name for a business run by partners, but it is often used more generally as a synonym for a *company*, or *organisation*, usually in the *private sector*.

first in first out *Ops* *see* *FIFO*

first-line management *HR* *see* *supervisory management*

first mover *Mkting* the company that first introduces a new type of product or service to a market. Those organisations that follow a first mover to market are known as **followers** or **laggards**—terms that also describe companies that are not the recognised leaders in a sector.

first mover advantage *Gen Mgt* the benefit produced by being the first to enter a market with a new product or service. First mover advantages include becoming a market leader (see *market share*) in a new area establishing a new leading *brand*; being able to charge a premium until competitor products appear; enhanced reputation, design, and copyright protection; and possibly setting an industry standard to which other competitors may have to aspire. Disadvantages include: cheaper, and possibly better, **follower** products; the possibility of having to reduce prices or continuously having to add value to stay ahead; first mover development costs; a possible shift in consumer tastes away from the product; obsolescence; and a follower product being accepted as the industry standard.

first-round financing *Fin* the first infusion of capital into a project

fiscal *Fin* relating to financial matters, especially in respect of governmental collection, use, and regulation of money through taxation

fiscal balance *Econ* a taxation policy that keeps a country's employment and taxation levels in balance

fiscal drag *Fin* the effect that inflation has on taxation in that it raises the amount of tax collected as earnings rise without increasing tax rates

fiscal policy *Econ* the central government's policy on lowering or raising taxation or increasing or decreasing public expenditure in order to stimulate or depress *aggregate demand*

fishbone chart *Gen Mgt* a diagram resembling the skeleton of a fish that is used to identify and categorise the possible causes of problems. Within a fishbone chart, the topic or problem to be discussed is placed in a box at the right-hand side that corresponds to the fish's head, and the major elements to be investigated are shown as branches at an angle to the horizontal spine. Questions are asked to identify possible causes of problems in each area and the results are added to the diagram as additional layers of branches. This ensures that all aspects of the problem are considered systematically. The fishbone chart is also known as a **cause and effect diagram** or an **Ishikawa diagram** after the originator, Professor *Kaoru Ishikawa* of Tokyo University, and is frequently used in *brainstorming* and *problem-solving*.

5-S concept *Ops* a technique that evolved in Japan to establish and maintain a quality culture environment within an organisation. The 5-S concept has been associated with *total productive maintenance* and *industrial housekeeping* in both manufacturing and services. It is seen as being fundamental to quality and productivity. The 5-Ss relate to Japanese words that have been variously translated into English. The words are: Seiri, for sort; Seiton, for simplify or straighten; Seiso, for shine or sweep; Seiketsu, for standardise; and Shitsuke, for sustain or self-discipline. The application of these ideas can reduce waste, and increase efficiency, productivity, and quality.

fixed asset *Fin* a long-term asset of a business such as a machine or building that will not usually be traded

fixed budget *Fin* a budget which is normally set prior to the start of an accounting period, and which is not changed in response to subsequent changes in activity or costs/revenues. Fixed budgets are generally used for planning purposes.

fixed charge *Fin* a form of protection given to secured creditors relating to specific assets of a company. The charge grants the holder the right of enforcement against the identified asset (in the event of default on repayment) so that the creditor may realise the asset to meet the debt owed. Fixed charges rank first in order of priority in receivership or liquidation.

fixed cost *Fin see cost behaviour*

fixed exchange rate system *Fin* a system of currency exchange in which there is no change of rate

fixed-interest loan *Fin* a loan whose rate of interest does not change

fixed interval re-order system *Ops see periodic inventory review system*

fixed rate *Gen Mgt* an interest rate for loans that does not change with fluctuating conditions in the market

fixed-rate loan *Fin* a loan with an interest rate that is set at the beginning of the term and remains the same throughout

flagpole
let's run it up a flagpole and see who salutes *Gen Mgt* let's try this idea and see what level of support or popularity it commands (*slang*)

flame *E-com* a hostile or aggressive message sent via e-mail or posted into an online newsgroup. Typically, flame messages are sent in response to *spam* or unsolicited commercial e-mail. If a flame message is responded to in a similarly hostile manner, it can lead to a **flame war**.

flat organisation *Gen Mgt, HR* a slimmed-down *organisation structure*, with fewer levels between top and bottom than a traditional *bureaucracy*, that is supposedly more responsive and better able to cope with fast-moving change. A flat organisation can be the result of *delayering*. *Also known as* **horizontal organisation**

flat yield curve *Fin* a *yield curve* with the same interest rates for long-term bonds as for short-term bonds

flexecutive *HR* a multiskilled executive able to switch jobs or tasks easily (*slang*)

There is no merit in sowing dissension among subordinates; any beginner can do it.   Henri Fayol

flexed budget *Fin see budget cost allowance*

flexible benefit *HR see fringe benefits*

flexible budget *Fin* a budget which, by recognising different *cost behaviour* patterns, is designed to change as volume of activity changes

flexible exchange rate system *Fin* a system of currency exchange in which rates change from time to time

flexible manufacturing system *Ops* an integrated, computer-controlled production system which is capable of producing any of a range of parts, and of switching quickly and economically between them. *Abbr* **FMS**

flexible working *HR* a generic term for employment practices that differ from the traditional norm in terms of the hours worked, the length of contract, or the place of work. Flexible working practices can be divided into three categories: those that give flexibility in the management of time through *flexible working hours* schemes such as *flexitime* or *shiftwork*; those that allow employers to cater for peaks or troughs in demand through numerical flexibility, for example, by employing temporary staff; and those that give flexibility regarding the place of work, for example, teleworking.

flexible working hours *HR* flexibility in the management of working time. Flexible working hours are achieved through systems such as *annual hours*, *part-time work*, *flexitime*, or job sharing that are arranged to meet organisational requirements or to help employees reconcile the demands of work and personal circumstances.

flexilagger *HR* a company or organisation considered to put too little emphasis on flexibility in its employment practices (*slang*)

flexileader *HR* a company or organisation considered to put a great deal of emphasis on flexibility in its employment practices (*slang*)

flexitime *HR* a system of *flexible working hours* based on a set number of hours to be worked per week. Employees are able to determine their precise hours of work, provided business demands are met and attendance at work during core periods is achieved. A debit or credit of hours can be carried forward into the next accounting period.

flight risk *HR* an employee who may be planning to leave a company in the near future (*slang*)

flip *Gen Mgt* a start-up company that aims to build market share quickly and generate short-term personal wealth for its founders through flotation or sell-off

float¹ *Fin* to sell shares or bonds, for example, to finance a project

float² *Fin* the period between the presentation of a cheque as payment and the actual payment to the payee or the financial advantage provided by this period to the drawer of a cheque

floating charge *Fin* a form of protection given to secured creditors which relates to assets of the company which are changing in nature. Often current assets like stock or debtors are the subject of this type of charge. In the event of default on repayment, the chargeholder may take steps to enforce the charge so that it crystallises and becomes attached to the current assets to which it relates. Floating charges rank after certain other prior claims in receivership or liquidation.

floating debt *Fin* a short-term borrowing that is repeatedly refinanced

floating rate *Fin* an interest rate that is not fixed and which changes according to fluctuations in the market

floor *Fin* a lower limit on an interest rate, price, or the value of an asset

floor effect *Stats* the occurrence of clusters of scores near the lower limit of the data in a statistical study

flotation *Fin* the financing of a company by selling shares in it or a new debt issue, or the offering of shares and bonds for sale on the stock exchange

flow chart *or* **flow diagram** *Gen Mgt* a graphical representation of the stages in a process or system, or of the steps required to solve a problem. A flow chart is commonly used to represent the sequence of functions in a computer program or to model the movement of materials, money, or people in a complex process. Two primary symbols used in flow charts are the **process box**, indicating a process or action taking place, and the **decision lozenge**, indicating the need for a decision.

flow line production *or* **flow lines** *Ops see flow production*

flow on *Gen Mgt* a pay increase awarded to one group of workers as a result of a pay rise awarded to another group working in the same field

flow production *Ops* a production method in which successive operations are carried out on a product in such a way that it moves through the factory in a single direction. Flow production is most widely used in **mass production** on production lines. More recently, it has been linked with **batch production**. Under flow production, stock is often kept to the minimum necessary to ensure continued activity. Stoppages and interruptions to the flow indicate a fault, and corrective action can be taken. *Assembly line* production is an extreme version of flow production. *Also known as* **flow line production**

flow theory *Gen Mgt* a theory of the way in which people become engaged with, or disengaged from, change. Flow theory suggests that people harmonise in change situations, and open, honest, trusting relationships emerge. The theory recognises the unpredictability and rigidity of human nature when faced with change. *See also* **change management**

fluff it and fly it *Mkting* to make a product look good and then sell it (*slang*)

FMEA *abbr Gen Mgt* failure mode effects analysis: a technique for analysing the causes, risks, and effects of potential systems or component failures that is used as a basis for prevention and contingency planning. FMEA was developed by engineers primarily to prevent defects in electrical and mechanical systems. All possible failures and their potential effects are listed and ranked according to severity of impact and probability of occurrence so that prevention efforts can be focused on the most critical issues.

FMS *abbr Ops* flexible manufacturing system

FNMA *abbr* (*US*) *Fin* Federal National Mortgage Association: the largest source of housing finance in the United States, the FNMA trades in mortgages guaranteed by the Federal Housing Finance Board. Created in 1938, the FNMA is a shareholder-owned private company and its stock is traded on the New York Stock Exchange. It has two principal regulators; the Department for Housing and Urban Development (HUD) aims to make sure that liquidity in the residential mortgage finance market is increased, while the Office of Federal Housing Enterprise Oversight (OFHEO) monitors soundness of accounting practice and financial safety.

focus group *Mkting* a carefully selected representative range of consumers or employees used for the purposes of providing feedback on consumer preferences and responses to a selected range of products or marketing issues. A focus group usually operates with a *facilitator* to guide discussion. Although primarily used for marketing purposes, focus groups are also being more widely used to obtain employee feedback on a wide range of employment and other issues within an organisation.

followback survey *Stats* a further survey of a statistical population carried out a period of years after an original survey

follower *Mkting see* **first mover**

Fong Kong (*S Africa*) *Gen Mgt* a product with a fake designer label, especially sports shoes (*slang*)

Food and Agriculture Organisation *Gen Mgt see* **FAO**

footer *E-com* an information section at the bottom of a web page, usually containing a copy of the essential links, contact information, and links to copyright and privacy policy information

footfall *Mkting* a measure of the number of people who walk past a shop (*slang*)

Forbes 500 *Fin* a list of the 500 largest public companies in the United States, ranked according to various criteria by *Forbes* magazine

force field analysis *Gen Mgt* a technique for promoting change by identifying positive and negative factors and by working to lessen the negative forces while developing the positive ones. Force field analysis was developed by **Kurt Lewin** as an aid to **decision-making**, **problem-solving**, and conflict prevention.

Ford, Henry (1863–1947) *Gen Mgt* US industrialist. Founder of the Ford Motor Company, who organised the **assembly line** along the scientific management principles of **Frederick Winslow Taylor** and recorded his philosophy in *My Life and Work* (1922)

After spending time as a machinist's apprentice, a watch repairer, and a mechanic, Ford built his first car in 1896. He quickly became convinced of the vehicle's commercial potential and started his own company in 1903. His first car was the Model A. After a year in business he was selling 600 a month.

In 1907 Ford professed that his aim was to build a motor car for the masses. In 1908 his Model T was born. Through innovative use of new mass-production techniques, 15 million Model Ts were produced between 1908 and 1927.

To stay ahead, you must have your next idea waiting in the wings. *Rosabeth Moss Kanter*

At that time, Ford's factory at Highland Park, Michigan, was the biggest in the world. Over 14,000 people worked on the 57-acre site. He was quick to establish international operations as well. Ford's first overseas sales branch was opened in France in 1908 and, in 1911, Ford began making cars in the United Kingdom.

In 1919 Henry Ford resigned as the company's president, letting his son, Edsel, take over. By then the Ford company was making a car a minute and Ford's market share was in excess of 57%.

forecast *Fin* a prediction of future events and their quantification for planning purposes

forecasting *Gen Mgt* the prediction of outcomes, trends, or expected future behaviour of a business, industry sector, or the economy through the use of statistics. Forecasting is an *operational research* technique used as a basis for management planning and decision-making. Common types of forecasting include trend analysis, *regression analysis*, *Delphi technique*, time series analysis, *correlation*, *exponential smoothing*, and input–output analysis.

foreclosure *Gen Mgt see repossession*

foreign bill *Fin* a bill of exchange that is not payable in the country where it is issued

foreign currency *Econ* the currency or interest-bearing bonds of a foreign country

foreign currency translation *Fin* the restatement of the foreign currency accounts of overseas subsidiaries and associated companies into the domestic currency of the country in which the group is incorporated, for the purpose of producing consolidated group accounts

foreign debt *Fin* hard-currency debt owed to a foreign country in payment for goods and services

foreign direct investment *Fin* the establishment of new overseas facilities or the expansion of existing overseas facilities, by an investor. FDI may be inward (domestic investment by overseas companies) or outward (overseas investment by domestic companies). *Abbr* **FDI**

foreign dividend *Fin* in the United Kingdom, a dividend paid by another country, possibly subject to special rules under UK tax codes

foreign equity market *Fin* the market in one country for equities of companies in other countries

foreign exchange *Fin* the currencies of other countries, or dealings in these

foreign exchange option *Fin* a contract which, for a fee, guarantees a worst-case exchange rate for the future purchase of one currency for another. Unlike a *forward transaction*, the option does not obligate the buyer to deliver a currency on the settlement date unless the buyer chooses to. These options protect against unfavourable currency movements while allowing retention of the ability to participate in favourable movements.

foreign income dividend *Fin* a dividend paid from earnings in other countries

Foreign Investment Funds Tax (*ANZ*) *Fin* a tax imposed by the Australian government on unrealised gains made by Australian residents from offshore investments. It was introduced in 1992 to prevent overseas earnings being taxed at low rates and never brought to Australia. *Abbr* **FIF Tax**

Foreign Investment Review Board (*ANZ*) *Fin* a nonstatutory body that regulates and advises the federal government on foreign investment in Australia. It was set up in 1976. *Abbr* **FIRB**

foreign reserve *Fin* the currency of other countries held by an organisation, especially a country's central bank

foreign subsidiary company *Gen Mgt see subsidiary company*

foreign tax credit *Fin* a tax advantage for taxes that are paid to or in another country

forensic accounting *Fin* the use of accounting records and documents in order to determine the legality or otherwise of past activities

forfaiting *Fin* the purchase of financial instruments such as bills of exchange or letters of credit on a non-recourse basis by a forfaiter, who deducts interest (in the form of a discount) at an agreed rate for the period covered by the notes. The forfaiter assumes the responsibility for claiming the debt from the importer (buyer) who initially accepted the financial instrument drawn by the seller of the goods. Traditionally, forfaiting is fixed-rate, medium-term (one- to five-year) finance.

formica parachute *HR* unemployment insurance (*slang*)

Fortune 500 *Fin* a list of the 500 largest industrial companies in the United States, compiled annually by *Fortune* magazine

---

Chaos often breeds life, when order breeds habit.   *Henry Brooks Adams*

forum *E-com* a newsgroup, mailing-list discussion group, chat room, or other online area that enables Internet users to read, post, and respond to messages

forward contract *Fin* a private futures contract for delivery of a commodity

forward cover *Fin* the purchase for cash of the quantity of a commodity needed to fulfil a futures contract

forward integration *Ops* a means of guaranteeing **distribution channels** for products and services by building relationships with, or taking control of, **distributors**. Forward integration can free the supplier from the threat or influence of major buyers and can also provide a barrier to market entry by potential rivals. **Backward integration** can provide similar guarantees on the supply side. Forward integration is a feature of Japanese **keiretsu**.

forward interest rate *Fin* an interest rate specified for a loan to be made at a future date

forward-looking study *Stats* a survey of a statistical population carried out for a period such as a year after an original survey

forward pricing *Fin* the establishment of the price of a share in a unit trust based on the next asset valuation

forward rate *Fin* an estimate of what an interest rate will be at a specified future time

forward scheduling *Ops* a method for determining the start times for the various operations involved in a particular **job**. Forward scheduling is most often used when the operations department sets the delivery date for a job, rather than the sales or marketing departments. Jobs are scheduled for the various operations as the workstations are expected to become available. The customer can then be informed of the projected delivery date. *See also* **backward scheduling**

forward transaction *Fin* an agreement to buy one currency and sell another on a date some time beyond two business days. This allows an exchange rate on a given day to be locked in for a future payment or receipt, thereby eliminating exchange rate risk.

founders' shares *Fin see* **deferred shares**

fourth level of service *Gen Mgt* a very high rating in a system of measuring the added value in a product or service

fourth market *Fin* trading carried out directly without brokers, usually by large institutions

FPA *abbr Fin* Financial Planning Association of Australia

fractional currency *Fin* the paper money that is in denominations smaller than one unit of a standard national currency

frames *E-com* a feature of **HTML** that allows different web pages to be displayed in one window simultaneously. Frames enable websites to keep a standard navigation bar on the screen regardless of the web page a visitor decides to access. However, there are a number of problems with frames. For instance, pages can be more difficult to print and bookmark because browsers can often only recognise one frame at a time.

franchise *Mkting* an agreement enabling a third party to sell or provide products or services owned by a manufacturer or supplier. A franchise is granted by the manufacturer, or **franchisor**, to a **franchisee**, who then retails the product. The franchise is regulated by a **franchise contract**, or **franchise agreement**, that specifies the terms and conditions of the franchise. These may include an obligation for the franchisor to provide national advertising or training for sales staff in return for the meeting of agreed sales targets by the franchisee. The franchisee normally retains a percentage of sales income. In other cases, a franchise may involve the **licensing** of a franchisee to manufacture a product to the franchisor's specification, and the sale of this product to retailers. Franchises can also be organised by issue of a **master franchise**.

franchise agreement *Mkting see* **franchise**

franchise chain *Mkting* a number of retail outlets operating the same **franchise**. A franchise chain may vary in size from a few to many thousands of outlets and in coverage from a small local area to worldwide.

franchise contract *Mkting see* **franchise**

franchisee *Mkting see* **franchise**

franchisor *Mkting see* **franchise**

franked investment income *Fin* the total of dividends received plus their associated tax credit

franked payments *Fin* the total of dividends paid plus their associated tax credit

fraud *Gen Mgt* the use of dishonesty, deception, or false representation in order to gain a material advantage or to injure the interests of others. Types of fraud include false accounting, theft, third party or investment fraud, employee collusion, and computer fraud.

FRB *abbr* *(US)* *Fin* Federal Reserve Board

free agent *(US)* *HR* a worker who operates on a *freelance* or *e-lance* basis, offering skills and expertise to companies anywhere in the world. A free agent works independently and may follow a pattern of *portfolio working*.

freebie *Mkting* a product or service that is given away, often as a business promotion

free cash flow *Fin* cash flow from operations after deducting interest, tax, dividends, and ongoing capital expenditure, but excluding capital expenditure associated with strategic acquisitions and/or disposals

free coinage *Fin* a government's minting of coins from precious metals provided by citizens

free enterprise *Econ* the trade carried on in a free-market economy, where resources are allocated on the basis of supply and demand

free gold *Fin* gold held by a government but not pledged as a reserve for the government's currency

freelance *Gen Mgt* working on the basis of being self-employed, and possibly working for several employers at the same time, perhaps on a temporary basis. Freelance workers have been described by *Charles Handy* as ideally suited to *portfolio working*.

Freelancers must be good at *multitasking*; they require the skills of a manager, bookkeeper, and a promoter. People thinking about becoming freelance, should conduct plenty of research, not only into the industry in which they will be offering their services, but also into their own motivation for freelancing and their character-suitability. Before leaving their day job, they should put together a business plan plotting the first year's goals and activity, perhaps considering the possibility of starting their freelance business on a part-time basis, so that they can initially rely on their current income.

An important part of this first year will be in marketing and promoting the business. Freelancers should develop a target list of companies they wish to work for, learning all they can about each company before approaching them with marketing and proposals. Good customer service could be the thing to make or break their career. Being liked is as valuable as being prompt and doing a professional job, and will encourage future business. It is,

though, inevitable that a set of clients will change as time goes by. To protect themselves against this, freelancers should try to plan six months ahead, and create diversity in their client base.

free market *Econ* a market in which supply and demand are unregulated, except by the country's competition policy, and rights in physical and intellectual property are upheld

freephone *Mkting* a telephone service in which the cost of calls to an organisation is borne by the organisation rather than the caller

freepost *Mkting* a postal service in which the cost of postage to an organisation is borne by the organisation rather than the sender

free stock *Fin* stock on hand or on order which has not been scheduled for use

freeware *E-com* free software programs

free worker *HR* somebody who frequently moves from one job or project to another, transferring skills and ideas. The term free worker was coined by the Industrial Society in the United Kingdom in 2000. Free workers have knowledge or skills that organisations value. They do not subscribe to the idea of a job for life or long-term loyalty to any one organisation but instead work on short-term *personal contracts*. They depend largely on networking to find new assignments. They may be *freelance* or *e-lance* workers and may follow a pattern of *portfolio working*.

freeze-out *Gen Mgt* the exclusion of minority *shareholders* in a company that has been taken over. A freeze-out provision may exist in a *takeover* agreement, which permits the acquiring organisation to buy the non-controlling shares held by small shareholders. A fair price is usually set, and the freeze-out may take place at a specified time, perhaps two to five years after the takeover. A freeze-out can still take place, even if provision for it is not made in a corporate charter, by applying pressure to minority shareholders to sell their shares to the acquiring company.

freight *Ops* goods loaded for onward transport, most often by sea or by air

freight forwarder *Ops* an organisation that collects shipments from a number of businesses and consolidates them into larger shipments for economies of scale. A freight forwarder often also deals with route selection, price negotiation, and documentation of

---

Without work, all life goes rotten, but when work is soulless, life stifles and dies. **Albert Camus**

distribution, and can act as a distribution agent for a business. By consolidating loads, a freight forwarder can negotiate cheaper rates of transportation than the individual businesses and can pre-book space to ensure a more rapid delivery schedule.

frequency analysis *Mkting* a technique for comparing the number of opportunities to reach the same target audience in different media

frequency distribution *Stats* the process of dividing a sample of observations in a statistical study into classes and listing the number of observations in each class

frequency polygon *Stats* a diagrammatic representation showing the values in a *frequency distribution*

frequently asked question *E-com see FAQ*

frictional unemployment *Econ* a situation in which people are temporarily out of the labour market. They could be seeking a new job, incurring search delays as they apply, attending interviews, and relocating.

friction-free market *Gen Mgt* a market in which there is little differentiation between competing products, so that the customer has exceptional choice

fringe benefits *HR* rewards given or offered to employees in addition to their wages or salaries and included in the **contract of employment**. Fringe benefits range from share options, company cars, expense accounts, cheap loans, medical insurance, and other types of **incentive scheme** to discounts on company products, subsidised meals, and membership of social and health clubs. Many of these benefits are liable for tax. A **cafeteria benefits** scheme permits employees to select from a variety of such benefits, although usually some are deemed to be core and not exchangeable for others. Minor benefits, sometimes appropriated rather than given, are known as **perks**.

front end *Gen Mgt* the part of an organisation that deals with customers on a face-to-face basis

front-end loading *Fin* the practice of taking the commission and administrative expenses from the early payments made to an investment or insurance plan. *See also **back-end loading***

FRSB *abbr* (*ANZ*) *Fin* Financial Reporting Standards Board

FTP *abbr E-com* file transfer protocol: a set of communication rules that allow data or files to be transferred between computers over a network

FTSE index *Fin* established in 1984, the Financial Times–Stock Exchange 100 share index is based on the share prices of the 100 largest public companies in the United Kingdom

fulfilment *Mkting* the process of responding to customer inquiries, orders, or sales promotion offers

fulfilment house *Mkting* an organisation that specialises in responding to inquiries, orders, or sales promotion offers on behalf of a client

full bank *Fin* a local or foreign bank permitted to engage in the full range of domestic and international services

full coupon bond *Fin* a bond whose interest rate is competitive in the current market

full-text index *E-com* an index consisting of every single word of every document catalogued

full-time *HR* standard hours of **attendance** in an organisation, on the basis of a permanent **contract of employment**, for example, 9am–5pm, five days a week

full-time job *HR* a position of paid employment that occupies all somebody's normal working hours

Fully Automated Screen Trading and Electronic Registration (*ANZ*) *Gen Mgt see FASTER*

fully connected world *Gen Mgt* a world in which most people and organisations are linked by networks such as the Internet

fully diluted earnings per (common) share *Fin* earnings on a share that take into account commitments to issue more shares, for example, as a result of convertibles, share options, or warrants

fully distributed issue *Fin* an issue of shares sold entirely to investors rather than held by dealers

functional analysis *Fin* an analysis of the relationships between product functions, their perceived value to the customer, and their cost of provision

functional budget *Fin* a budget of income and/or expenditure applicable to a particular

---

function. A function may refer to a department or a process. Functional budgets frequently include the following: production cost budget (based on a forecast of production and plant utilisation); marketing cost budget; sales budget; personnel budget; purchasing budget; and research and development budget. *Also known as* ***departmental budget***

functional relationship *Stats* the relationship between the variables in a study, in which there is no bias or any other distorting factor

fund accounting *Fin* the preparation of financial statements for an entity which is a fund. Such statements are usually on a cash basis and are most commonly found in the public sector.

fundamental analysis *Fin* analysis of external and internal influences on the operations of a company with a view to assisting in investment decisions. Information accessed might include fiscal/monetary policy, financial statements, industry trends, competitor analysis etc. *See also* ***technical analysis***

funded debt *Fin* long-term debt or debt that has a maturity date in excess of one year. Funded debt is usually issued in the public markets or in the form of a private placement to qualified institutional investors.

funding risk *Fin* the risk that an entity will encounter difficulty in realising assets or otherwise raising funds to meet commitments associated with financial instruments

fund manager *Fin* somebody who manages the investments of a unit trust or large financial institution

fund of funds (*S Africa*) *Fin* a registered unit trust that invests in a range of underlying unit trusts and in which subscribers own units in the fund of funds, not in the underlying unit trusts

fungible *Fin* interchangeable and indistinguishable for business purposes from other items of the same type

funny money *Fin* an unusual type of financial instrument created by a company

future *Fin* a contract to deliver a commodity at a future date. *Also known as* ***futures contract***

future option *Fin* a contract in which somebody agrees to buy or sell a commodity, currency, or security at an agreed price for delivery in the future. *Also known as* ***futures option***

futures commission merchant *Fin* somebody who acts as a broker for futures contracts. *Abbr* **FCM**

futures contract *Fin see* ***future***

futures exchange *Fin* an exchange on which futures contracts are traded

futures market *Fin* a market for buying and selling securities, commodities, or currencies that tend to fluctuate in price over a period of time. The market's aim is to reduce the risk of uncertainty about future prices.

futures option *Fin see* ***future option***

futures research *Gen Mgt* the identification of possible future *scenarios* with the aim of anticipating and perhaps influencing what the future holds. Futures research is important to the process of *issues management*. It normally identifies several possible scenarios for any particular set of circumstances, and enables an informed decision to be made.

future value *Fin* the value that a sum of money will have in the future, taking into account the effects of inflation, interest rates, or currency values.
| EXAMPLE | Future value calculations require three figures: the sum in question, the percentage by which it will increase or decrease, and the period of time. In this example, these figures are £1,000, 11%, and two years.
At an interest rate of 11%, the sum of £1,000 will grow to £1,232 in two years:

£1,000 × 1.11 = £1,110 (first year) × 1.11 = £1,232 (second year, rounded to whole pounds)

Note that the interest earned in the first year generates additional interest in the second year, a practice known as compounding. When large sums are in question, the effect of compounding can be significant.
At an inflation rate of 11%, by comparison, the sum of £1,000 will shrink to £812 in two years:

£1,000 / 1.11 = £901 (first year) / 1.11 = £812 (second year, rounded to whole pounds)

In order to avoid errors, it is important to express the percentage as 1.11 and multiply and divide by that figure, instead of using 11%; and to calculate each year, quarter, or month separately. *See also* ***present value***

futurise *Gen Mgt* to ensure that an organisation is taking full advantage of the latest technologies

futuristic planning *Fin* planning for that period which extends beyond the planning

---

horizon in the form of future expected conditions which may exist in respect of the entity, products/services, and environment, but which cannot usefully be expressed in quantified terms. An example would be working out the actions needed in a future with no motor cars.

fuzzword *Gen Mgt* a piece of jargon that is obscure or difficult to understand (*slang*)

FWIW *abbr Gen Mgt* for what it's worth (*slang*)

FYI *abbr Gen Mgt* for your information (*slang*)

If you see a bandwagon, it's too late.   *James Goldsmith*

G7 *Fin* the group of seven major industrial nations established in 1985 to discuss the world economy, consisting of the United States, Canada, the United Kingdom, France, Germany, Italy, and Japan

G8 *Fin* the group of eight major industrial nations consisting of the *G7* plus Russia

GAB *abbr Fin* General Arrangements to Borrow: a fund financed by the Group of Ten that is used when the IMF's own resources are insufficient, for example, when there is a need for large loans to one or more industrialised countries

GAAP *abbr Fin* Generally Accepted Accounting Principles

gain sharing *HR* a group-based *bonus scheme* to share profits from improvements in production efficiency between employees and the company. There are many variants of gain sharing, the *Rucker* and *Scanlon plans* being the best known.

game theory *Gen Mgt* a mathematical technique used in *operational research* to analyse and predict the outcomes of games of strategy and conflicts of interest. Game theory is used to represent conflicts and problems involved in formulating marketing and organisational strategy, with the aim of identifying and implementing optimal strategies. It involves assessing likely strategies to be adopted by players in a given situation under a particular set of rules. It was initially developed by John Von Neumann, who later developed the theory further with Oskar Morgenstern to apply it to economics.

Gantt, Henry Laurence (1861–1919) *Gen Mgt* US mechanical engineer and consultant. Originated the *Gantt chart*, which was popularised by Wallace Clark in *The Gantt Chart: a Working Tool of Management* (1952).

Gantt chart *Gen Mgt* a graphic tool widely used in *project management* for planning and scheduling work, setting out tasks and the time periods within which they should be completed. The Gantt chart looks like a lateral bar chart and was initially developed by *Henry Gantt* during the 1900s. It is still used both in its traditional form and in the evolved form of programme evaluation and review technique.

gap analysis *Mkting* a marketing technique used to identify gaps in market or product coverage. In gap analysis, consumer informa-tion or requirements are tabulated and matched to product categories in order to identify product or service opportunities or gaps in product planning.

garage *Fin* **1.** a UK term meaning to transfer assets or liabilities from one financial centre to another to take advantage of a tax benefit. **2.** the annex to the main floor of the New York Stock Exchange (*slang*)

garbatrage (*US*) *Fin* stocks that rise because of a takeover but are not connected to the target company (*slang*)

garden leave *Gen Mgt* a clause in a *contract of employment* that allows the employer to send an employee home on full pay, but not require him or her to work, during the employee's contractual *notice period*. Garden leave thereby prevents the employee from working in competition with the employer until the notice period has expired, by which time any confidential information the employee holds is likely to have become commercially out of date and links with customers will have been broken. Such a clause may be unenforceable if judged by the courts to be in restraint of trade.

gatekeeper *Gen Mgt* somebody within an organisation who controls the flow of information and therefore influences policy

Gates, Bill (*b.* 1955) *Gen Mgt* US entrepreneur. Founder of the Microsoft™ Corporation, which led the information technology revolution and still dominates the world software market through the Windows™ operating system and the Web browser Internet Explorer. Microsoft has made Gates one of the richest men in the world, although anti-trust proceedings have forced him to step down as CEO. His book *Business@the Speed of Thought* (1999) focuses on the impact of technology on business.

gateway *E-com* a point where two or more computer networks meet and can exchange data

gateway page *E-com* a web page customised to each search engine with specific meta-tags and keywords. These pages are intended to appeal to search engine robots and are not always visible to customers who visit the website.

GATT *Fin* General Agreement on Tariffs and Trade: a treaty signed in Geneva in 1947 that

---

Global managers have exceptionally open minds. They respect how different countries do things.
Percy Barnevik

aimed to foster multilateral trade and settle trading disputes between adherent countries. Initially signed by 23 nations, it started to reduce trade tariffs and, as it was accepted by more and more countries, tackled other barriers to trade. It was replaced on 1 January 1995 by the World Trade Organization.

gazelle *Gen Mgt* a fast-growing and volatile new company (*slang*)

gazump *Fin* in the period between agreeing verbally to sell to one buyer but before the agreement becomes legally binding, to accept a higher offer from another buyer. Gazumping is normally associated with the property market, although it can occur in any market where the prices are rising rapidly.

gazunder *Fin* in the period between agreeing verbally to buy at one price but before the agreement is legally binding, to offer a lower price. Gazundering is normally associated with the property market, although it can occur in any market where the prices are falling rapidly.

GBE (*ANZ*) *Gen Mgt see* **Government Business Enterprise**

GDP *abbr Econ* gross domestic product: the total flow of services and goods produced by an economy over a quarter or a year, measured by the aggregate value of services and goods at market prices

GDP per capita *Econ GDP* divided by the country's population so as to achieve a figure per head of population

GEAR *abbr* (*S Africa*) *Fin* Growth, Employment, And Redistribution: the macroeconomic reform programme of the South African government, intended to foster economic growth, create employment, and redistribute income and opportunities in favour of the poor

geared investment trust *Fin* an investment trust that borrows money in order to increase its portfolio. When the market is rising, shares in a geared investment trust rise faster than those in an ungeared trust, but they fall faster when the market is falling.

gearing *Fin see* **financial leverage**

gearing ratios *Fin* ratios that indicate the level of risk taken by a company as a result of its capital structure. A number of different ratios may be calculated, for example, debt ratio (total debt divided by total assets), debt-to-equity or leverage ratio (total debt divided by total equity), or interest cover (earnings

before interest and tax divided by interest paid). *US term* **leverage ratios**

geisha bond *Fin see* **shogun bond**

Geneen, Harold (1910–97) *Gen Mgt* British-born business executive. CEO of International Telephone and Telegraph (ITT) in the 1960s and 1970s, who turned a moderately successful US company into a massive, international conglomerate. Geneen built a business machine that was almost without parallel in terms of its systematic efficiency. He explained his approach in *Managing* (1985). ITT was broken up following anti-trust proceedings during the 1980s and **taken over** in 1997.

General Agreement on Tariffs and Trade *Fin see* **GATT**

General Arrangements to Borrow *Fin see* **GAB**

General Commissioners *Fin* a body of unpaid individuals appointed by the Lord Chancellor in England, Wales, and Northern Ireland, and the Secretary of State for Scotland in Scotland, to hear appeals on tax matters

general ledger *Fin* a book that lists all of the financial transactions of a company

Generally Accepted Accounting Principles *Fin* a summary of best practice in respect of the form and content of financial statements, the form and content of auditor's reports, and best practice and acceptable alternatives in respect of accounting policies and disclosures adopted for the preparation of financial information. GAAP does not have any statutory or regulatory authority in the United Kingdom, unlike in a number of other countries where the term is in use, such as the United States, Canada, and New Zealand. *Abbr* **GAAP**

general manager *Gen Mgt, HR* a **manager** whose work encompasses all areas of an organisation. A general manager is traditionally non-specialist, has a working knowledge of all aspects of an organisation's activities, and oversees all operating functions. In large companies and the public sector, specialist managers with expert knowledge may control departments, while a general manager provides unifying **leadership** from the top.

Generation X *Gen Mgt, HR* the generation of people born between 1963 and 1981 who entered the workplace from the 1980s onwards, bringing new attitudes to working life that run contrary to traditional corporate expectations. The term was popularised by the writing of Douglas Coupland and also by **Bruce Tulgan** in *Managing Generation X* (1995). Those who belong to Generation X are said to be not solely motivated by money, but they look to a **work-life balance**, favour **flexible working**, embrace the concept of **employability**, and value opportunities for learning, self-advancement, and new challenges. Human resource management practices are increasingly being adapted to accommodate the favoured new ways of working.

generic strategy *Gen Mgt* a strategy for marketing products or services. Generic strategy is a term introduced by **Michael Porter**. He suggested there are three generic strategies for marketing products or services: cost leadership, differentiation, and focus. The first implies supplying products in a more cost-effective way than competitors; the second refers to adding value to products or services; and the third focuses on a specific product market segment with the aim of establishing a **monopoly**.

gensaki *Fin* the Japanese term for a bond sale incorporating a repurchase agreement at a later date

geographical information systems *Mkting* technology used to integrate maps and data to provide multidimensional marketing information. *Abbr* **GIS**

Ghoshal, Sumantra (*b.* 1946) *Gen Mgt* Indian-born academic. Author of work that has shifted its focus from international **strategy** to the importance of people and **creativity**. Ghoshal put forward a new model of transnational enterprise to cope with the complexities of **competition** and the growing global marketplace. He also suggested the **three Ps** of Purpose, Process, and People to replace the old model of Strategy, Structure, and Systems and proposed a new moral contract. He first came to prominence with *Managing Across Borders* (1989), coauthored with **Christopher Bartlett**.

ghost rider *Gen Mgt* somebody who claims to have been in a vehicle that was involved in an accident in order to claim compensation (*slang*)

GIF *Abbr E-com* Graphics Interchange Format: a type of file used to compress and store images for transfer via the Internet. The major advantage of GIF files is that you do not need a **plug-in** to view them, so almost any **browser** can display them. GIF is ideal for small, simple icons and basic images. More

complex images, including photographs, can be compressed using **JPEG** files.

gift-leaseback *Fin* the practice of giving somebody a property and then leasing it back, usually for tax advantage or charitable purposes

gift with reservation *Fin* a gift with some benefit retained for the donor, for example, the legal transfer of a dwelling when the donor continues in residence

gig *Gen Mgt* an individual project or assignment, typical of a working pattern made up of a series of one-off projects rather than a career with a single employer

gigabyte *Gen Mgt* a measure of the memory capacity of a computer. One gigabyte equals 1024 megabytes.

Gilbreth, Frank (1868–1924) *Gen Mgt* US consulting engineer. Formed a husband-and-wife team with **Lillian Gilbreth** and pioneered the principles of **motion study**, which embraced **work simplification**, and took a strong interest in **occupational psychology**. Their work, which straddled the **scientific management** and **human relations** schools of management, is recorded in *Writings of the Gilbreths* (1953), edited by William R. Spriegel and Clark E. Myers.

Gilbreth, Lillian (1878–1972) *Gen Mgt* US consulting engineer. *See* **Gilbreth, Frank**

gilt *Fin see* **gilt-edged security**

gilt-edged security *Fin* **1.** a security issued by the UK government that pays a fixed rate of interest on a regular basis for a specific period of time until the redemption date when the principal is returned. Their name, for example, Exchequer 10½% 2005 (abbreviated to Ex 10½% '05) or Treasury 11¾% 2003–07 (abbreviated to Tr 11¾% '03–'07) indicates the rate and redemption date. Thought to have originated in the 17th century to help fund the war with France, today they form a large part of the National Debt. *Also known as* **gilt**. *See also* **index-linked gilt 2.** a US term used to describe a security issued by a blue-chip company, which is therefore considered very secure

gilt repos *Fin* the market in agreed sales and repurchase of gilt-edged securities, launched in 1996 by the Bank of England to make gilts more attractive to overseas investors

gilt strip *Fin* a zero-coupon bond created by unbundling the interest payments from a gilt-edged security so that it produces a single cash payment at maturity

---

I would constructively rebel by changing the rules but, once agreed, I would observe them. Howard Davies

gilt unit trust *Fin* in the United Kingdom, a unit trust where the underlying investments are gilt-edged securities

Ginnie Mae *(US) Fin see GNMA*

giro *Fin* **1.** a European term for the transfer of money from one bank account to another. *Also known as bank giro* **2.** a benefit paid by the state *(slang)*

GIS *abbr Mkting* geographical information systems

Glacier studies *Gen Mgt* research experiments conducted at the Glacier Metal Company in London from 1948 to 1965 to investigate the development of group relations, the effects of *change*, and employee roles and responsibilities. The Glacier studies were conducted by the Tavistock Institute of Human Relations with the research being headed by *Elliot Jaques* and *Frederick Emery*. Findings from the initial study came from a methodology called 'working-through', which examined possible social and personal factors at play in any potential dispute. From this arose an early form of *works council* where employees could participate in setting policy for their department. It was also discovered that employees felt the need to have their role and status defined in a way acceptable to both themselves and their colleagues. This research into job roles led Jaques to come up with the notion of the *time span of discretion*, according to which all jobs, no matter how strictly defined, have some level of content that requires judgment and therefore discretion by the jobholder. Jaques then examined this phenomenon in bureaucratic organisations. In defining a *bureaucracy* as a hierarchical system in which employees are accountable to their bosses for the work they do, he took a different stance from *Max Weber*. Much like the *Hawthorne experiments*, the Glacier studies had far-reaching implications for the way organisations were managed. The initial findings were written up by Jaques in *The Changing Culture of a Factory* (1951). In 1965, Jaques published the *Glacier Project Papers* with *Wilfred Brown*, the managing director of Glacier.

glad-hand *Gen Mgt* to shake hands with and greet people at a business party or meeting *(slang)*

glamour stock *(US) Fin* a fashionable security with an investment following

glass ceiling *Gen Mgt* the level in an organisation beyond which women are supposedly unable to gain *promotion*. A glass ceiling often exists at *senior management* level and is perceived as an invisible barrier to career progression for women. *Equal opportunities* policies and legislation aim to break such ceilings to make equal career advancement opportunities available to both men and women.

Glass-Steagall Act *Fin* a US law that enforces the separation of the banking and brokerage industries

glaze *Gen Mgt* to doze or sleep with your eyes open during a business meeting *(slang)*

global bank *Fin* a bank that is active in the international markets and that has a presence in several continents

global bond *Fin see Eurobond*

global bond issue *Fin* an issue of bonds that incorporates a settlement mechanism allowing for the transfer of titles between markets

global brand *Mkting* the brand name of a product that has worldwide recognition. A global brand has the advantage of economies of scale in terms of production, recognition, and packaging. While the product or brand itself remains the same, the marketing must take into account the local market conditions and the resulting marketing campaign must be tailored accordingly. Care must also be taken to ensure that there is nothing offensive in terms of the name or packaging in the various cultures and languages. A problem with global branding is that if problems are experienced in one country, there could be worldwide repercussions for the brand. *Also known as global product*

global co-ordinator *Fin* the lead manager of a global offering who is responsible for overseeing the entire issue and is usually supported by regional and national co-ordinators

global custody *Fin* a financial service, usually only available to institutional investors, that includes the safekeeping of securities certificates issued in markets across the world, the collection of dividends, dealing with tax, valuation of the investments, foreign exchange, and the settlement of transactions

global hedge *Fin see macrohedge*

globalisation *Gen Mgt* the creation of international strategies by organisations for overseas expansion and operation on a worldwide level. The process of globalisation has been precipitated by a number of factors including rapid technology developments that make

---

Companies have to be socially responsible or the shareholders pay eventually. Warren Shaw

global communications possible, political developments such as the fall of communism, and transport developments that make travelling faster and more frequent. These produce greater development opportunities for companies with the opening up of additional markets, allow greater customer harmonisation as a result of the increase in shared cultural values, and provide a superior competitive position with lower operating costs in other countries and access to new raw materials, resources, and investment opportunities.

global marketing *Mkting* a marketing strategy used mainly by multinational companies to sell goods or services internationally. Global marketing requires that there is harmonisation between the marketing policies for different countries and that the **marketing mix** for the different countries can be adapted to the local market conditions. Global marketing is sometimes used to refer to overseas expansion efforts through **licensing**, **franchises**, and **joint ventures**.

global offering *Fin* the offering of securities in several markets simultaneously, for example, in Europe, the Far East, and North America

global pricing contract *Ops* a contract between a customer and a supplier whereby the supplier agrees to charge the customer the same price for the delivery of parts or services anywhere in the world. As **globalisation** increases, more customers are likely to press their suppliers for global pricing contracts. Through such contracts suppliers can benefit by gaining access to new markets and growing their business, achieving economies of scale, developing strong relationships with customers, and thereby gaining a **competitive advantage** that is difficult for competitors to break. There are risks involved, too, for example, being in the middle of a conflict between a customer's head office and its local business units, or being tied to one customer when there are more attractive customers to serve.

global product *Mkting see* **global brand**

glocalisation *Gen Mgt* the process of tailoring products or services to different local markets around the world. Glocalisation is a combination of globalisation and localisation. Improved communication and advancements in technology have made worldwide markets accessible to even small companies but, rather than being homogenous, the global market is in fact made up of many different localities. Success in a globalised environment

is more likely if products are not globalised or **mass marketed**, but glocalised and customised for individual local communities that have different needs and different cultural approaches.

glue *Gen Mgt* something such as information that unifies organisations, supply chains, and other commercial groups

GmbH *abbr Gen Mgt* Gesellschaft mit beschränkter Haftung: the German term for a private limited company

GNMA *abbr Fin* Government National Mortgage Association: a US-owned corporation that issues mortgage-backed bonds

gnomes of Zurich *Fin* a derogatory term for Swiss bankers and currency dealers (who have a reputation for secrecy), often used when unknown currency speculators cause havoc in the currency markets (*slang*)

GNP *abbr Econ* gross national product: GDP plus domestic residents' income from investment abroad less income earned in the domestic market accruing to foreigners abroad

GNP per capita *Econ* GNP divided by the country's population so as to achieve a figure per head of population

goal *Gen Mgt see* **objective**

goal congruence *Fin* in a control system, the state which leads individuals or groups to take actions which are in their self-interest and also in the best interest of the entity. Goal incongruence exists when the interests of individuals or of groups associated with an entity are not in harmony.

gofer *Gen Mgt* US term **gopher**

go-go fund *Fin* a unit trust that trades heavily and predominantly in high-return, high-risk investments

going concern concept *Fin* the assumption that an entity will continue in operational existence for the foreseeable future. The assumption that a particular entity is a going concern can now be operationally tested by statistical models for firms operating in well-defined business areas. *See also* **Z score**

going short *Fin* selling an asset one does not own with the intention of acquiring it at a later date at a lower price for delivery to the purchaser. *See also* **bear**

gold bond *Fin* a bond for which gold is collateral, often issued by mining companies

---

One man's wage increase is another man's price increase. *Harold Wilson*

goldbricker *or* **gold brick** (*US*) *HR* a lazy employee who attempts to get away with doing the least possible amount of work (*slang*)

gold card *Fin* a gold-coloured credit card, generally issued to customers with above average incomes, that may include additional benefits, for example, an overdraft at an advantageous interest rate, and may have an annual fee

gold certificate *Fin* a document that shows ownership of gold

golden goodbye *HR see* **golden handshake**

golden handcuffs *HR* a package of *fringe benefits* designed to tie an employee to an organisation, and prevent another organisation from successfully *headhunting* them. A golden handcuffs payment may be paid out only if an employee remains with an organisation for a specified period of time. (*slang*)

golden handshake *HR* a sum of money given to a senior executive on his or her involuntary departure from an employing organisation as a form of *severance pay*. A golden handshake can be offered when an executive is required to leave before the expiration of his or her contract, for example, because of a *merger* or *corporate restructuring*. It is intended as compensation for loss of office. It can be a very large sum of money, but often it is not related to the perceived performance of the executive concerned. (*slang*) *Also known as* **golden goodbye**

golden hello *HR* a welcome package for a new *employee* that may include a *bonus* and share options. A golden hello is designed as an incentive to attract employees. Some of the contents of the welcome package may be contingent on the performance of the employee.

golden parachute *HR* a clause inserted in the *contract of employment* of a senior employee that details a financial package payable if the employee is dismissed. A golden parachute provides an executive with a measure of financial security and may be payable if the employee leaves the organisation following a *takeover* or *merger*, or is dismissed as a result of poor performance. *Also known as* **golden umbrella**

golden rolodex (*US*) *Gen Mgt* the small group of experts who are most frequently quoted in news stories or asked to appear on television to give an opinion. 'Rolodex' is a trademark for a desktop card index. (*slang*)

golden share *Fin* a controlling shareholding retained by a government in a company that

has been privatised after having been in public ownership

golden umbrella *HR see* **golden parachute**

gold fix *Fin* the daily setting of the gold price in London and Zurich

Goldratt, Eliyahu (*b.* 1948) *Gen Mgt* Israeli author and educator. Disseminator of theories, through the medium of novels, on optimising *production* methods and *project management*. Goldratt explained the technique of *optimised production technology* in *The Goal* (1993, co-authored), and his theory later broadened into the *Theory of Constraints*. His third book applies the concept of the theory of constraints to *project management*.

gold reserve *Fin* gold coins or bullion held by a central bank to support a paper currency and provide security for borrowing

gold standard *Fin* a system in which a currency unit is defined in terms of its value in gold

Goleman, Daniel (*b.* 1946) *Gen Mgt* US psychologist and journalist. Developer of the concept of *emotional intelligence*, who is credited with making it generally accessible, initially through the book of the same name (1995). He was influenced by *Richard Boyatzis*.

good for the day *Fin* used to describe instructions to a broker that are valid only for the day given

good for this week/month *Fin* used to describe instructions to a broker that are valid only for the duration of the week/month given. *Abbr* **GTW/GTM**

Goods and Services Tax 1. *Fin* a 3% tax payable on all purchase transactions. *Abbr* **GST 2.** *Gen Mgt* a government-imposed consumption tax, currently of 10%, added to the retail cost of goods and services in Australia **3.** *Gen Mgt* a former Canadian tax on goods and services. It was a value-added tax and was replaced by the *harmonised sales tax*. *Abbr* **GST**

goods received note *Fin* a record of goods at the point of receipt

good 'til cancel *Fin* relating to an order to buy or sell a security that is effective until an investor cancels it, up to a maximum of 60 days

good title *Fin* the legally unquestionable title to property. *Also known as* **clear title**

Technology is our word for something that doesn't work yet.   *Douglas Adams*

goodwill *Fin* an intangible asset of a company that includes factors such as reputation, contacts, and expertise, for which a buyer of the company may have to pay a premium.

EXAMPLE Goodwill becomes an intangible asset when a company has been acquired by another. It then appears on a balance sheet in the amount by which the price paid by the acquiring company exceeds the net tangible assets of the acquired company. In other words:

Purchase price – net assets = goodwill

If, for example, an airline is bought for £12 billion and its net assets are valued at £9 billion, £3 billion of the purchase would be allocated to goodwill on the balance sheet.

The treatment of goodwill in accounts is determined by FRS10, 'Goodwill and Intangible Assets', issued by the Accounting Standards Board of the Institute of Chartered Accountants in England and Wales.

gopher *Gen Mgt* an employee who carries out menial duties for a manager or another employee (*slang*)

go plural *Gen Mgt* to engage in a form of *downshifting* by leaving full-time employment in order to undertake *part-time work* or *portfolio working* (*slang*)

go private *Fin* to revert from being a public limited company quoted on a stock exchange to a private company without a stock market listing

go public *Gen Mgt* to float the shares of a *company* on a stock exchange, thereby changing the company status to that of a *public limited company*

go-slow *HR* a protest in which employees demonstrate their dissatisfaction by carrying out their work slowly. A go-slow is a form of *industrial action* designed to inconvenience an employer without the more serious effects of an all-out *strike*.

Government Business Enterprise (*ANZ*) *Gen Mgt* an Australian business that is fully or partly owned by the state. *Abbr* **GBE**

government gazette (*ANZ*) *Gen Mgt* a journal published by the Australian federal government or a state or territory government that reports all actions and decisions made by that body

Government National Mortgage Association (*US*) *Fin see* **GNMA**

government secuities/stock *Fin* securities or stock issued by a government, for example, US Treasury bonds or UK gilt-edged securities

gradual retirement *HR see* **phased retirement**

graduated payments mortgage (*US*) *Fin* a low start mortgage. *Abbr* **GPM**

granny bond *Fin see* **index-linked savings certificate**

grant of probate *Fin* in the United Kingdom, a document issued by the Probate Court that pronounces the validity of a will and upholds the appointment of the executor(s)

grantor *Fin* a person who sells an option

grapevine *Gen Mgt* an informal communication network within an organisation that conveys information through unofficial channels independent of management control. Information travels much more quickly through the grapevine than through formal channels and may become distorted. A grapevine may reinterpret official corporate messages or spread gossip and rumour in the absence of effective organisation channels. It can, however, also complement official communication, provide feedback, and strengthen social relationships within the organisation.

graph *Gen Mgt* a diagram depicting the relationship between dependent and independent variables through the use of lines, curves, or figures on horizontal and vertical axes. Time is the most common independent variable, showing how the dependent variable has altered over a defined period.

graphical user interface *E-com* an easy-to-use interface or operating system that allows a user to give a computer instructions by using icons, menus, and windows. *Abbr* **GUI**

Graphics Interchange Format *E-com see* **GIF**

graphology *HR* the study of handwriting styles in an attempt to identify personality traits and to predict how somebody may react in particular situations. Graphology is sometimes used as part of the *recruitment* process. Because it cannot be substantiated, it is not recommended as a formal test and tends to be used informally.

grass ceiling *Gen Mgt* the set of social and cultural factors that discourage or prevent women from using golf to conduct business (*slang*)

graveyard market *Fin* **1.** a UK term for a

---

market for shares that are infrequently traded either through lack of interest or because they are of little or no value **2.** a bear market where investors who dispose of their holdings are faced with large losses, as potential investors prefer to stay liquid until the market shows signs of improving

greater fool theory *Fin* the investing strategy that assumes it is wise to buy a stock that is not worth its current price. The assumption is that somebody will buy it from you later for an even greater price.

great man theory *Gen Mgt* the idea that *leaders* possess innately superior qualities that distinguish them from other people, including the ability to capture the imagination and loyalty of the masses

green ban *(ANZ) HR* a ban imposed by unions on work that is perceived to pose a threat to the natural environment or an area of historical significance

greenfield site *Gen Mgt* a location for a new development, such as a factory, office, or warehouse, that has not been built on before

greenmail *Fin, Gen Mgt* the purchase of enough of a company's shares to threaten it with takeover, so that the company is forced to buy back the shares at a higher price to avoid the takeover *(slang)*

green marketing *Mkting* marketing that highlights an organisation's environmentally friendly policies or achievements

green pound *Econ* the fixed European Currency Unit (ECU) in which prices of agricultural goods in the European Union are set

green shoe *or* **greenshoe option** *Fin* an option, offered by the company raising the capital, for the issue of further shares to cover a shortfall in the event of over-allocation. It gets its name from the Green Shoe Manufacturing Company which was the first to include the feature in a public offering. *(slang)*

green taxes *Fin* taxes levied to discourage behaviour that will be harmful to the environment

greenwash *Gen Mgt* information produced by an organisation to present an environmentally responsible public image *(slang)*

greybar-land *Gen Mgt* a state of vagueness induced by staring at the grey bar that appears on a computer screen when the computer is processing something *(slang)*

grey knight *Gen Mgt see* **knight**

grey market *Mkting* **1.** a *market* in which goods are sold that have been manufactured abroad and imported. A grey market product is one that has been imported legally, in contrast to one on the *black market*, which is illegal. Such markets arise when there is a supply shortage, usually for exclusive goods, and offer goods for sale at lower prices than the equivalent goods manufactured in the home country. **2.** the market segment occupied by older members of a population **3.** the unofficial trading of securities that have not yet been formally issued

grey marketing *Mkting* marketing aimed at older age groups

grey matter *Gen Mgt* older and more experienced business experts who are hired by young companies to give an impression of seriousness and reliability *(slang)*

grey wave *Fin* used to describe a company that is thought likely to have good prospects in the distant future. It gets its name from the fact that investors are likely to have grey hair before they see their expectations fulfilled *(slang)*.

grievance procedure *HR* a process for settling or redressing employee complaints. A grievance procedure is part of an organisation's *personnel policy* and sets out how an employee with a work-related grievance can bring up the issue and how it may be addressed and resolved. Such a procedure should focus on settling the matter as soon as possible, so as to promote employee satisfaction and prevent the issue escalating into a *dispute*.

gross *Fin* total, before consideration of taxes

gross domestic fixed capital formation *Econ* investment in the fixed asset in an economy, including depreciation

gross domestic product *Econ see* **GDP**

gross interest *Fin* interest earned on a deposit or security before the deduction of tax. *See also* **net interest**

gross lease *Fin* a lease that does not require the lessee to pay for things the owner usually pays for. *See also* **net lease**

gross margin *Fin* **1.** the differential between the interest rate paid by a borrower and the cost of the funds to the lender **2.** the differential between the manufacturing cost of a unit of output and the price at which it is sold

gross misconduct *HR* behaviour in the workplace that may lead to a warning or to dismissal in extreme cases. Most contracts of employment provide guidelines on the type of behaviour that constitutes gross misconduct.

gross national product *Econ see* **GNP**

gross negligence *Gen Mgt see* **negligence**

gross profit *Gen Mgt* sales revenue less the cost of goods sold. *See also* **net profit**

gross profit margin *Gen Mgt see* **profit margin**

gross profit percentage *Fin* a ratio used to gain an insight into the relationship between production/purchasing costs and sales revenues. It is calculated as follows:

(Sales – cost of sales) × 100 /Sales for the period

gross receipts *Fin* the total revenue received by a business

gross redemption yield *Fin see* **gross yield to redemption**

gross yield *Fin* the share of income return derived from securities before the deduction of tax

gross yield to redemption *Fin* the total return to an investor if a fixed interest security is held to maturity, in other words, the aggregate of gross interest received and the capital gain or loss at redemption, annualised. *Also known as* **gross redemption yield**. *US term* **yield to maturity**

group *Fin* a parent company and all its subsidiaries

group capacity assessment *Gen Mgt* the application of **work measurement** techniques such as **activity sampling** and **standard time** data to clerical, administrative, and indirect staff to measure group effort and establish optimum performance levels. Group capacity assessment is used to plan and control payroll costs for groups of clerical and administrative workers.

group certificate *(ANZ) HR* a document provided by an employer that records an employee's income, income tax payments, and superannuation contributions during the previous financial year

group discussion *Mkting* a research technique in which groups of people discuss attitudes to a product or organisation

group dynamics *HR* the interaction and interpersonal relationships between members of a group and the ways in which groups form, function, and dissolve. Group dynamics is an important aspect of successful **teamwork** and is a factor influencing the outcome of any

form of group activity, including **training** courses. Issues of power, influence, and interpersonal conflict all affect dynamics and group performance. One means of helping people to create positive group dynamics is **sensitivity training**.

group incentive scheme *HR* a reward system giving **bonuses** to workers in a team. A group incentive scheme is designed to promote effective **teamwork**, as the bonus is dependent on the performance and output of the team as a whole.

group interview *HR see* **group selection**

group investment *Fin* an investment made by more than one person

group life assurance *Fin* a life assurance policy that covers a number of people, for example, members of an association or club, or a group of employees at a company

Group of Seven *Fin* the seven leading industrial nations: Canada, France, Germany, Italy, Japan, the United States, and the United Kingdom

Group of Ten *Fin* the group of ten countries who contribute to the General Arrangements to Borrow fund: Belgium, Canada, France, Germany, Italy, Japan, the Netherlands, Sweden, the United States, and the United Kingdom. Switzerland joined in 1984. *Also known as* **Paris Club**. *See also* **GAB**

group selection *HR* a method of **recruitment** in which candidates are assessed in groups rather than individually. Group selection can take place in an **assessment centre**. It should not be confused with a **panel interview**, which involves one candidate but several interviewers. *Also known as* **group interview**

group technology *Ops* the practice of gathering operations and resources for the manufacture of specific components or products into groups or cells with the aim of simplifying manufacturing operations. Group technology is an attempt to take advantage of the benefits of both **batch production** and **flow production**. Similar tasks or products are identified and are grouped into families. This requires a robust coding or classification scheme. The manufacturing resources, including workers, for each family are then grouped together into cells. The sense of ownership encouraged by such organisation has resulted in benefits including improved quality, **productivity**, and **motivation** of employees, as well as reductions in work in progress, inventory, and materials movement. *Also known as* **cellular manufacturing, cellular production**

A banker is a man who lends another man the money of a third man.   *Guy de Rothschild*

groupthink *Gen Mgt* a phenomenon that occurs during **decision-making** or **problem-solving** when a team's desire to reach an agreement overrides its ability to appraise the problem properly. It is similar to the **Abilene paradox** in that it is based on people's desire to conform and please others.

group tool *Gen Mgt* an electronic tool such as videoconferencing, networking, or electronic mail that allows people in different locations to collaborate on a project

groupware *Gen Mgt* software that enables a group whose members are based in different locations to work together and share information. Groupware enables collective working by providing communal diaries, address books, work planners, bulletin boards, newsletters, and so on, in electronic format on a closed network. This network may take the form of an **intranet**. Groupware can be used to facilitate collaborative **project management** or to co-ordinate any kind of work involving input from more than one person, and is particularly useful to those working in a **virtual team**.

Grove, Andrew (*b.* 1936) *Gen Mgt* US business executive. Chairman of Intel Corporation, which became the world's largest semiconductor manufacturer. He coined the term **strategic inflection point**, which he discusses in *Only the Paranoid Survive* (1996).

Growth, Employment, And Redistribution *Fin see* GEAR

growth and income fund *Fin* a unit trust that tries to maximise growth of capital while paying significant dividends

growth capital *Fin* funding that allows a company to accelerate its growth. For new start-up companies, growth capital is the second stage of funding after **seed capital**.

growth company *Econ* a company whose contribution to the economy is growing because it is increasing its workforce or earning increased foreign exchange for its exported goods

growth curve *Stats* a line plotted on a graph that shows statistically an increase over a period of time

growth equity *Fin* an equity that is thought to have good investment prospects

growth fund *Fin* a unit trust that tries to maximise growth of capital without regard to dividends

growth industry *Fin* an industry that has the potential to expand at a faster rate than other industries

growth rate *Econ* the rate of an economy's growth as measured by its technical progress, the growth of its labour, and the increase in its **capital stock**

growth share 1. *Fin* a share that offers investors the prospect of longer-term earnings, rather than a quick return **2.** *Gen Mgt* a share that has been rising greatly in value, relative to its industry or to the market as a whole

growth stock *Fin* stock that offers investors the prospect of longer-term earnings, rather than a quick return

grupo *Gen Mgt* a group of companies in Mexico, based on a parent company or central family. Grupos may be involved in a cross-section of industries, much like a **conglomerate company**. Some grupos are integrated financially, legally, and administratively, while others have a looser structure with stockholding interests and interrelated directorates.

GST *abbr Fin* Goods and Services Tax

guan xi *Gen Mgt* a Mandarin term for 'connections', used to describe the level of personal trust required between business partners

guarantee *Fin* a promise made by a third party, or guarantor, that he or she will be liable if one of the parties to a contract fails to fulfil their contractual obligations. A guarantee may be acceptable to a bank as security for borrowing provided the guarantor has sufficient financial means to cover his or her potential liability.

guaranteed bond *Fin* in the United States, a bond on which the principal and interest are guaranteed by a company other than the one who issues them, or a stock in which the dividends are similarly guaranteed. *See also* **guaranteed stocks**

guaranteed employment *HR* an arrangement to protect employees in the event of a shortage of work. Guaranteed employment requires the payment of a minimum wage for a maximum number of workless days or hours. In some cases, a worker may qualify for a legal right to a guaranteed payment. An employer cannot lay off workers without a term in the individual **contract of employment**.

The right to do so usually lies in a *collective agreement* incorporated into the contract of employment. *Also known as* **guaranteed wage**, **guaranteed week**

guaranteed fund *Fin* a fixed term investment where a third party promises to repay the investors' principal in full should the investment fall below the initial sum invested

guaranteed income bond *Fin* a bond issued by a UK life assurance company designed to provide an investor with a fixed rate of income for a specified period of time. Changes to the regulations now only permit those policies with an independent third party guarantee to receive this denomination.

guaranteed investment certificate *Fin* an investment instrument issued by an insurance company that guarantees interest but not the principal originally invested

guaranteed stocks *Fin* in the United Kingdom, bonds issued by nationalised industries that incorporate an explicit guarantee from the government. *See also* **guaranteed bond**

guaranteed wage *HR* *see* **guaranteed employment**

guaranteed week *HR* *see* **guaranteed employment**

guarantor *Fin* a person or organisation that guarantees repayment of a loan if the borrower defaults or is unable to pay

guard book *Mkting* a book or folder for storing copies of published advertisements

guerilla marketing *Mkting* a marketing technique, the aim of which is to damage the market share of competitors

GUI *abbr Gen Mgt* graphical user interface

Gulick, Luther (1892–1993) *Gen Mgt* US academic. Member of President Roosevelt's Committee on Administrative Management (1936–38), who, following the earlier work of *Henri Fayol*, coined the acronym *POSDCORB* to describe the functions of management.

gun jumping (*US*) *Fin* insider trading

GW *abbr E-com* payment gateway

gweeping *Gen Mgt* the activity of spending many hours at a time surfing the Internet (*slang*)

Unhappiness is best defined as the difference between our talents and our expectations. Edward de Bono

hacker *E-com* somebody who gains unauthorised access to computer systems, usually to corrupt or steal stored data

haggle *Fin* to negotiate a price with a buyer or seller by the gradual raising of offers and lowering of asking prices until a mutually agreeable price is reached

half-normal plot *Stats* a plot of statistical data used to check for the presence of **outliers** in the data

Hamel, Gary (*b.* 1954) *Gen Mgt* US academic. With **C.K. Prahalad**, introduced the concept of **core competences** and argued for an innovative approach to **corporate-strategy** creation, based on emotion as well as analysis. They co-authored *Competing for the Future* (1994), which set out their revolutionary but well-respected view of strategy.

Hamel believes that too many managers operate essentially on a hand-to-mouth basis, not devoting sufficient time to thinking about and planning for the future. He argues that developing strategy ('strategising' in his terminology) should be an ongoing, radical, and inclusive process that habitually challenges existing assumptions, involves as many people as possible, and looks for its inspiration as often outside the organisation as within it.

Hammer, Michael (*b.* 1948) *Gen Mgt* US academic and consultant. Advocate of re-engineering, a concept he explained in the book *Reengineering the Corporation* (1993), co-authored with **James Champy**.

hammering the market *Fin* used to describe a situation where there is intense selling (*slang*)

Hampel, Sir Ronald Claus (*b.* 1932) *Gen Mgt* British business executive. Former chairman of ICI and chairman of the Committee on **Corporate Governance** (1995–98).

hand-hold *HR* to reassure a nervous client or colleague (*slang*)

hand off (*US*) (*Canada*) *Gen Mgt* to transfer responsibility for a project

hand signals *Fin* the signs used by traders on the trading floors at exchanges for futures and options to overcome the problem of noise

hands-off *Gen Mgt* without continuing management attention

hands-on *Gen Mgt* favouring first-hand personal involvement in a task

Handy, Charles (*b.* 1932) *Gen Mgt* Irish-born academic, writer, and social commentator. Known for his work on **organisation structures**, the future of work, and the implications of change for people. Since his landmark book *Understanding Organizations* (1976), he has originated concepts such as the **shamrock organisation**, the **federal organisation**, the **doughnut principle**, and **portfolio working**.

After graduating from Oxford, Handy worked for Shell until 1972, when he left to teach at the London Business School. He also spent time at MIT where he came into contact with many of the leading lights in the human relations school of thinking, including **Ed Schein**.

hang-out loan *Fin* the amount of a loan that is still outstanding after the termination of the loan

Hang Seng index *Fin* an index of the prices of selected shares on the Hong Kong Stock Exchange

happy camper *Gen Mgt* somebody who has no grievances against his or her employer (*slang*)

hara-kiri swap *Fin* an interest rate swap made without a profit margin

hard commodities *Fin* metals and other solid raw materials. *See also* **commodity**, **soft commodities**

hard currency *Econ* a currency that is traded in a foreign exchange market and for which demand is persistently high relative to its supply. *See also* **soft currency** ·

hard disk *E-com* a thin rigid magnetised disk inside a computer, used for storing data and programs

hard landing *Econ* a sustained period of growth that ends with the economy moving rapidly into recession and business stagnation

hard sell *Mkting* a heavily persuasive and highly pressured approach used to sell a product or service. In a hard sell situation, salespeople may use incentives such as a limited special offer or a discount to encourage people to buy, or to sign an agreement to buy on the spot.

hard systems *Gen Mgt* see **systems method**

---

hardware *E-com* the physical components of a computer system such as the processor, keyboard, and monitor. **Software** is the name given to operating systems and applications.

harmonisation *Gen Mgt* **1.** the resolution of inequalities in the *pay* and *conditions of employment* between different categories of workers **2.** the alignment of the systems of pay and benefits of two companies on *merger*, acquisition, or takeover **3.** the convergence of social regulation in the European Union

harmonised sales tax *Fin* a Canadian tax on goods and services. It is a value-added tax that replaced the Goods and Services Tax. *Abbr* HST

Harrigan, Kathryn Mary Rudie (*b.* 1951) *Gen Mgt* US academic. Known for her work on mature and declining industries, and on *strategic alliances*.

harvesting strategy *Fin* a reduction in or cessation of marketing for a product prior to it being withdrawn from sale resulting in an increase in profits on the back of previous marketing and advertising campaigns

Harvey-Jones, Sir John (*b.* 1924) *Gen Mgt* British business executive. Chairman of ICI (1982–87), who recorded his reflections on leadership in *Making It Happen* (1987). After his retirement, he advised ailing British companies in a television series, 'Troubleshooter'.

hate site *Gen Mgt see anti-site*

Hawthorne effect *Gen Mgt see Hawthorne experiments*

Hawthorne experiments *Gen Mgt* a series of studies undertaken at the Hawthorne plant of Western Electric in the United States from which *Elton Mayo* concluded that an approach emphasising *employee participation* can improve *productivity*. The Hawthorne experiments began in 1924 as a study conducted by the National Research Council into the relationship between workplace lighting and employee efficiency, and was then extended to include *wage incentives* and *rest periods*. It was found that whatever variations were applied upwards or downwards, output rose, and this was termed the **Hawthorne effect**. The increased productivity was attributed to several causes, including small group size, earnings, the novelty of being part of an experiment, and the increased attention given to the employees being studied. The style of the supervisor, which was relaxed and friendly, in contrast to the then standard practice, was found to be particularly important. In a second group of employees, however, it was observed that, as the experiments progressed, output was restricted, and that whatever the incentive, the group showed a resistance to it. In 1929 and 1930, Elton Mayo visited Hawthorne. He linked supervisory style and levels of morale with productivity. High productivity resulted from an engaged supervisory style that encouraged participation. Low productivity resulted when a supervisor remained remote and retained a traditional supervisory role. The Hawthorne experiments established the importance of management style and interpersonal skills to organisational success.

Hayes, Robert (*b.* 1936) *Gen Mgt* US academic. Harvard professor who came to prominence following the publication in 1981 of his co-authored *Harvard Business Review* article, 'Managing Our Way to Economic Decline'. Hayes argued that US manufacturing companies were at a competitive disadvantage as a result of a too heavy reliance on detached, precisely structured analysis. A more positive future was foreseen by Hayes in the co-written *Restoring Our Competitive Edge* (1984), which examines the structural changes required of manufacturing in order to succeed and provides some guidance on how management practices need to change.

hazardous substance *Gen Mgt* a substance that creates a potential danger to people in the workplace. Employers have a duty to assess the risks from hazardous substances to personnel and customers, and to ensure that no one is endangered. Substances classed as hazards could be raw materials used in production, fumes, or other byproducts resulting from workplace activities. They may also be substances linked to seemingly innocuous activities, for example, cleaning fluids and toner for photocopiers. *Health and safety* policies must cover this area, and *risk assessments* must be carried out to ascertain the potential dangers.

head and shoulders *Fin* used to describe a graph plotting a company's share price that resembles the silhouette of a person's head and shoulders. Chartists see this as an early indication of a market fall.

headcount *HR* the total number of *employees* in an organisation

headhunting *HR* the practice of approaching people already working for one company with an offer of a job at another. Headhunting is usually carried out by a recruiter—either an employee within a company or an employment agency—who keeps an eye on the performance of targeted personnel. The recruiter then matches high-performing personnel with job vacancies, contacting individuals directly, without the knowledge of the employer, with a job offer. Headhunters most often perform *executive searches*, but they may also work at lower levels with the intention of picking out those with management potential. Headhunting is often seen as poaching, and it can create employee-retention problems, since a company's best staff can be tempted to leave by better job offers.

headline rate of inflation *Econ* a measure of inflation that takes account of home owners' mortgage costs

heads of agreement *Gen Mgt* the most important elements of a commercial agreement

health and safety *Gen Mgt, HR* the area of policy and legislation covering employee well-being. Health and safety within an organisation is often co-ordinated by a particular person, but it is the responsibility of all employees. Maintaining a safe working environment and safe working practices and ensuring that employees' health is not detrimentally affected by their work is a statutory duty of organisations. In the United Kingdom, it is co-ordinated by the Health and Safety Executive.

health screening *HR* the checking of employees' health to ensure they are fit for work. Health screening can take the form of **pre-employment screening**, which takes place after a new employee has been appointed, but before employment commences. It also is a feature of *occupational health* schemes and involves the monitoring of employee health at work. This is particularly important if the work involves hazardous substances or strenuous physical conditions. Health screening can also be used, for example, to detect substance abuse or to carry out eyesight tests for users of VDUs.

heatseeker *E-com* somebody who always buys the latest version of a software product as soon as it comes on the market (*slang*)

heavy hitter *Gen Mgt* an executive or company that performs extremely well (*slang*)

heavy site *E-com see* **sticky site** (*slang*)

hedge *Fin* a transaction to reduce or eliminate an exposure to risk

hedge fund *Fin* a unit trust that takes considerable risks, including heavy investment in unconventional instruments, in the hope of generating great profits

hedging against inflation *Fin* investing in order to avoid the impact of inflation, thus protecting the purchasing power of capital. Historically, equities have generally outperformed returns from savings accounts in the long term and beaten the Retail Price Index. They are thus considered as one of the best hedges against inflation, although it is important to bear in mind that no stock market investment is without risk.

held order *Fin* an order that a dealer does not process immediately, often because of its great size

Helgeson, Sally (*b*. 1948) *Gen Mgt* US consultant and author. Researcher on the effects of changing technology, demographics, and the knowledge economy on organisations and *leadership*. Her book *The Female Advantage* (1990) considers women's *management styles*.

helicopter view *Gen Mgt* an overview of a problem (*slang*)

helpline *Mkting* a telephone service operated by a company that offers customers product information, advice, or technical support

Henderson, Bruce (1915–92) *Gen Mgt* Australian engineer and consultant. Founder of the Boston Consulting Group (1963), a firm that has specialised in *corporate strategy* and conceived the *experience curve* and the *Boston Box*.

herding cats *Gen Mgt* a very difficult, or impossible, activity. The phrase is taken from the title of Warren Bennis's book, *Managing People is Like Herding Cats*. (*slang*)

Herzberg, Frederick (*b*. 1923) *Gen Mgt* US psychologist and academic. Took a particular interest in *motivation* and put forward the 'hygiene-motivation theory' of *job satisfaction*. Herzberg was a co-author of *The Motivation to Work* (1959) and the author of 'One More Time: How Do You Motivate Employees?' (1968), one of the most requested reprints of all time from *Harvard Business Review*. Through his work for the US Public Health Service, Herzberg became an influential figure in the human relations school of the 1950s.

heuristics *Gen Mgt* a method for *problem-solving* or *decision-making* that arrives at solutions through exploratory means such as experimentation, trial and error, or evaluation

HHOK *abbr Gen Mgt* ha ha only kidding (*slang*)

hidden tax *Fin* a tax that is not immediately apparent. For example, while a consumer may be aware of a tax on retail purchases, a tax imposed at the wholesale level, which consequently increases the cost of items to the retailer, will not be apparent.

hierarchy of activities *Fin* classification of activities according to the level within the organisation to which they relate, for example, product level activities, batch level activities, product sustaining activities, or facility sustaining activities

high concept *Gen Mgt* a compelling idea expressed clearly and economically

highdome (*US*) *Gen Mgt* a scientist. This term stems from the stereotype of scientists, who are often depicted as having high foreheads that are supposed to be a sign of intelligence. (*slang*)

high-end *Gen Mgt* relating to the most expensive, most advanced, or most powerful in a range of things, for example, computers

higher-rate tax *Fin* in the United Kingdom, the highest of the three bands of income tax. Most countries have bands of income tax with different rates applicable to income within each band.

high-flier *or* **high-flyer** *Fin* a heavily traded stock that increases in value quickly over a short period

high/low method *Fin* a method of estimating cost behaviour by comparing the total costs associated with two different levels of output. The difference in costs is assumed to be caused by variable costs increasing, allowing the unit variable cost to be calculated. From this, since total cost is known, the fixed cost can be derived.

high-premium convertible debenture *Fin* a convertible bond sold at a high premium that offers a competitive rate of interest and has a long term

high-pressure *Mkting* a selling technique in which the sales representative attempts to persuade a buyer very forcefully and persistently

high-risk company *Gen Mgt* a company that is exposed to high levels of business risk

high street *Gen Mgt* a main street considered as an important retail area

high yielder *Fin* a security that has a higher than average yield and is consequently often a higher risk investment

hip shooter *Gen Mgt* an executive who follows his or her immediate instinct when responding to a question or problem rather than considering it rationally (*slang*)

hired gun (*slang*) **1.** *Gen Mgt* an adviser, lawyer, or accountant brought into a company during a takeover battle **2.**(*US*) *HR* somebody who works for whoever will contract for his or her services for as long as he or she is needed for a particular project

hire purchase *Fin* a method of paying for a product or service in which the buyer pays by a series of instalments over a period of time. *US term* **instalment plan**. *Abbr* **HP**

historical cost *Fin* the original acquisition cost of an asset, unadjusted for subsequent price level or value changes

historical cost accounting *Fin* a system of accounting in which all values are based on the historical costs incurred. This is the basis prescribed in the Companies Act for published accounts.

historical pricing *Fin* basing current prices on prior period prices, perhaps uplifted by a factor such as inflation

historical summary *Fin* in the United Kingdom, an optional synopsis of a company's results over a period of time, often five or ten years, featured in the annual accounts

historic pricing *Fin* the establishment of the price of a share in a unit trust on the basis of the most recent values of its holdings

hit *E-com* a measure of the number of files or images that are sent to a browser from a website in response to a single request.

The measure is one of the most abused statistics on the Internet, as hits do not provide an accurate picture of website visitor activity. Every web page is made up of a number of components—graphics, text, programming elements—and many have anything from 10 to 20 components. Each component is counted as a hit. Therefore, the total number of hits is generally very high and bears little or no relation to the number of people visiting.

hit squad *Gen Mgt* a company's acquisitions team (*slang*)

hockey stick *Fin* a performance curve typical of businesses in their early stages that descends then rises sharply in a straight line, creating a shape similar to that of a hockey stick (*slang*)

Hofstede, Geert (*b.* 1928) *Gen Mgt* Dutch academic and business executive. Identified four work-related dimensions of national culture, thus providing a framework for understanding cultural differences within business. His work, first published in *Culture's Consequences* (1980), has been extended by **Fons Trompenaars**.

After spending time working in factories as a foreman and plant manager, Hofstede became chief psychologist on the international staff of IBM, and then joined IMEDE, the Swiss business school, in 1971. He has also worked at the European Institute for Advanced Studies in Management in Brussels and at the University of Limburg in Maastricht, where he is now emeritus professor of organisational anthropology and international management.

holdback *E-com* funds from a merchant's credit card transactions held in reserve for a predetermined time by the merchant account provider to cover possible disputed charges. *Also known as* **reserve account**

holder *Fin* the person who is in possession of a bill of exchange or promissory note

holding company *Gen Mgt* a parent organisation that owns and controls other companies. In the United Kingdom, a holding company has to own over half of the nominal share capital in companies that are then deemed to be its subsidiaries. A holding company may have no other business than the holding of shares of other companies.

holding cost *Fin* the cost of retaining an asset, generally stock. Holding cost includes the cost of financing the asset in addition to the cost of physical storage.

holiday *HR* a day of work on which an employee is not required to be at work but is paid by the employer. The number of days of holiday is agreed in the **contract of employment** and may be dependent on the employee's length of service. *US term* **vacation**

home loan *Fin* a mortgage

homepage *E-com* the first and/or main page on a website

home run 1. *Fin, Gen Mgt* a very great achievement **2.** *Fin, Gen Mgt* an investment that produces a high rate of return in a short time **3.** *Gen Mgt* the journey home at the end of the working day (*slang*)

home shopping *Mkting* the ordering of goods from home by telephone, Internet, mail order, or direct-response television

homeworker *HR* somebody who carries out paid work in his or her home for one or more businesses, but who is not **self-employed**. The method of working can be a permanent or occasional arrangement, or may involve a split of work between an employer's premises and home. *See also* **teleworker**

homogenisation *Gen Mgt* the removal of characteristic differences between separate markets and cultures. Globalisation is frequently blamed for homogenisation.

Honey, Peter *Gen Mgt* British psychologist and consultant. With **Alan Mumford**, he identified four types of **learning style** and devised an instrument to determine somebody's predominant style in their book, *The Manual of Learning Styles* (1982).

honorarium *HR* a token sum given in recognition of the recipient's performance of specific, non-onerous duties. An honorarium may take the form of an annual retainer.

HOPEFUL *abbr Gen Mgt* Hard-up Older Person Expecting Full Useful Life (*slang*)

HOQ *abbr Ops* house of quality

horizontal diversification *Gen Mgt see* **diversification**

horizontal fast track *Gen Mgt* a variation of **fast track** developed by **Charles Handy** in which talented people are moved around from task to task to test and develop their capability in different working situations

horizontal integration *Gen Mgt* the merging of functions or organisations that operate on a similar level. Horizontal integration involves the union of companies producing the same kinds of goods or operating at the same stage of the **supply chain**. It may also describe the merging of departments within an organisation that carry out similar tasks. *See also* **vertical integration**

horizontal keiretsu *Gen Mgt see* **keiretsu**

horizontal merger *Gen Mgt see* **merger**

horizontal organisation *Gen Mgt see* **flat organisation**

horizontal spread *Fin* a purchase of two options that are identical except for their dates of maturity

horse-trading *Fin* hard bargaining that results in one party giving the other a concession

hostile bid *Fin* a takeover bid that is opposed by the target company. *See also* **greenmail**, **knight**

hostile takeover *Gen Mgt see* **takeover**

hosting *E-com* the process of putting a website on the Internet so that people can visit it. There are two basic options: internal or external hosting. Internal hosting is often the option when dealing with an intranet, because most of the access to the intranet will be from within the organisation. For most public websites, it makes sense to use a third-party hosting company. Such companies have mastered the complexities of website hosting and can offer excellent service. Issues that need to be considered when deciding whether to outsource include: whether you need a **domain name**; how many visitors you expect each month; how much space and what access speeds are needed; whether you require **e-commerce** or special programming facilities; whether you need to deal with **e-mail**; what support is offered, and price and payment options. *See also* **hosting options**

hosting options *E-com* the different kinds of **hosting**, usually offered by third-party hosting companies. There are several options: **non-virtual hosting**, **virtual hosting**, **collocation hosting**, and **managed hosting**.

hot button *Mkting* a sales or marketing offer that particularly appeals to a buyer (*slang*)

hot card *Fin* a credit card that has been stolen

hot-desking *Gen Mgt* a flexible working practice enabling employees to occupy any vacant workspace instead of sitting at a permanent personalised desk. Organisations using a hot-desking system may have a set of standardised workspaces equipped with **information and communications technologies**, and employees may sit at a different desk each day. Alternatively, the majority of employees may have their own desks, but some employees, such as consultants or part-time workers, may sit at any desk that happens to be free that day. Most conventional offices are only full for a fraction of the time they are open because of sickness, holidays, or **teleworking** and this results in empty desks and wasted resources. Hot-desking enables expensive office space to be fully utilised and forms part of the concept of the **virtual office**. Although employees practising hot-desking may have limited storage space in the form of a filing cabinet or locker, most of their work and information will be stored electronically.

hotelling *Gen Mgt* the practice of occupying a desk or workspace in another employer's premises. Hotelling is normally carried out by employees such as consultants or sales people, who spend more time with customers than at their employers' offices and rely on their clients to provide desk space. Hotelling has developed through improved **information and communications technologies** and is an extension of the **virtual office**.

hot file *Fin* a list of stolen credit cards

hot issue *Fin* a new security that is expected to trade at a significant premium to its issue price. *See also* **hot stock**

hot money *Fin* **1.** money that has been obtained by dishonest means. *See also* **money laundering** **2.** money that is moved at short notice from one financial centre to another to secure the best possible return

hot stock *Fin* a share, usually a new issue, that rises quickly on the stock market. *See also* **hot issue**

hours of work **1.** *Gen Mgt* the actual hours worked by an employee, often well in excess of those stated in the **contract of employment** and sometimes without the payment of **overtime** **2.** *HR* the hours agreed between an employer and employee for which the employee is paid

house journal *Gen Mgt see* **newsletter**

house of quality *Ops* a **decision-making** and planning tool that brings customers and engineers together in the product design process. House of quality is one of the four houses or phases of **quality function deployment**. House of quality provides a structure for the design and development cycle. The name is derived from the use of matrices that explore the relationship between customer needs and design attributes. The matrices used in the analysis fit together to form a house-like structure. *Abbr* **HOQ**. *Also known as* **quality table**

HP *abbr Fin* hire purchase

HR *abbr HR* human resources

HREOC *abbr* (*ANZ*) *HR* Human Rights and Equal Opportunities Commission

HRIS *abbr HR* human resource information system

HRM *HR* **human resource management**, a model of **personnel management** that focuses on the individual rather than taking a collective approach. Responsibility for human resource management is often devolved to *line management*. It is characterised by an emphasis on strategic integration, *employee commitment*, workforce flexibility, and quality of goods and services.

HR service centre *HR* a *centralised* office that handles routine administration and answers enquiries from managers and staff throughout an organisation on *human resources*-related matters

HST *abbr Fin* harmonised sales tax

HTH *abbr Gen Mgt* hope this helps (*slang*)

HTML *abbr E-com* hypertext markup language: a computer code used to build and develop web pages. It is used to format the text of a document and indicate *hyperlinks* to other web pages and describes the layout of the web page.

HTTP *abbr E-com* hypertext transport (or transfer) protocol: the communications mechanism used to exchange information on the Internet

hub and spoke *Gen Mgt* any arrangement of component parts resembling a wheel, with a central hub and a series of spokes radiating outwards. The metaphor of the hub and spoke arrangement can be applied to any area. Examples include *organisation structure*, computer network design, work processes, service delivery methods, and transport systems.

humanagement *Gen Mgt* a style of management that emphasises the *empowerment* of people

human asset accounting *HR see human capital accounting*

human capital *HR* the *employees* of an organisation. The term builds on the concept of capital as an asset of an organisation, implying recognition of the importance and monetary worth of the skills and experience of its employees. It is measured through *human capital accounting*.

human capital accounting *HR* an attempt to place a financial figure on the knowledge and skills of an organisation's *employees* or *human capital*. *Also known as human asset accounting, human resource accounting*

human factors engineering *Gen Mgt* the analysis of human needs and abilities in the design of workplace activities, facilities, and systems in order to optimise employee performance. Human factors engineering uses *ergonomics* in the design of the workplace

and aims to offer a better choice of computer software by striving to obtain a fit between human operators and the equipment or technology that they are using. In this way, human factors engineering tries to reduce risk by raising safety levels, and to produce cost savings by improving performance.

human relations *HR* an interdisciplinary study of social relations in the workplace that embraces sociology, social anthropology, and social psychology. The human relations movement presents a counterpoint to the scientific management view that focuses on maximising the productivity and income of individual manual workers and on the separation of mental and physical work between management and workers. In contrast, supporters of the human relations movement believe that workers want to feel part of a team with socially supportive relationships and to grow and develop. *Motivation*, communication, *employee participation*, and *leadership* are significant issues.

human resource accounting *HR see human capital accounting*

human resource information system *HR* a data *MIS*, usually computerised, that facilitates strategic and operational *decision-making* for human resource management (see *HRM*). *Abbr* **HRIS**

human resource management *HR see HRM*

human resource planning *HR* the development of strategies for matching the size and skills of the workforce to organisational needs. Human resource planning assists organisations to recruit, retain, and optimise the deployment of the personnel needed to meet business objectives and to respond to changes in the external environment. The process involves carrying out a *skills analysis* of the existing workforce, carrying out *manpower forecasting*, and taking action to ensure that supply meets demand. This may include the development of training and retraining strategies. *Also known as manpower planning*

human resources *HR* **1.** the discipline of managing people in an organisation. *Abbr* **HR** **2.** the employees of an organisation

Human Rights and Equal Opportunities Commission (*ANZ*) *HR* an Australian federal government body that administers legislation relating to human rights, anti-discrimination, privacy, and social justice. It was set up in 1986, replacing the Human Rights Commission. *Abbr* **HREOC**

The public be damned. I am working for my stockholders.   ***William Henry Vanderbilt***

Humble, John William (*b*. 1925) *Gen Mgt* British consultant. Popularised **Peter Drucker**'s concept of **management by objectives**, which he explained in *Improving Business Results* (1967).

hunch marketing *Mkting* marketing based on instinct rather than research (*slang*)

hurdle rate *Fin* a rate of return which a capital investment proposal must achieve if it is to be accepted. Set by reference to the cost of the capital, the hurdle rate may be increased above the basic cost of capital to allow for different levels of risk.

hurry sickness *Gen Mgt* a state of anxiety caused by the feeling of not having enough time in the day to achieve everything that is required (*slang*)

hybrid *Fin* a combination of financial instruments, for example, a bond with warrants attached, or a range of cash and derivative instruments designed to mirror the performance of a financial market

hybrid financial instrument *Fin* a financial instrument such as a convertible bond that has characteristics of multiple types of instruments, often convertible from one to another

hygiene factors *Gen Mgt see* **job satisfaction**

hymn sheet

sing from the same hymn sheet *HR* to be in agreement about something with another person or group of people (*slang*)

hyperinflation *Econ* very rapid growth in the rate of inflation so that money loses value

and physical goods replace currency as a medium of exchange. This happened in Latin America in the early 1990s, for example.

hyperlink *E-com* an image or piece of text that enables the user, by clicking on it, to move directly to other web pages. Hyperlinks are most commonly found on web pages, and can be used to connect web pages within the same site, as well as to link to other websites. Hyperlinks can be added to web pages by using simple **HTML** commands. They can also be used in e-mail messages, for example, to include the address of a company's website. *Also known as* **hypertext link**

hyperpartnering *E-com* a form of commerce in which companies use Internet technology to form partnerships and execute transactions at high speed and low cost in order to take advantage of business opportunities as soon as they appear

hypertext link *E-com see* **hyperlink**

hypertext markup language *E-com see* **HTML**

hypertext transport protocol *or* **hypertext transfer protocol** *E-com see* **HTTP**

hyper time *E-com* the apparent fast pace and decentralised nature of Internet time

hypothecate *Fin* to use a property as collateral for a loan

hypothesis testing *Stats* the process of testing sample data from a statistical study to determine whether it is consistent with what is known about the sample population

Iacocca, Lee (*b.* 1924) *Gen Mgt* US business executive. President of the Ford Motor Company and subsequently Chairman and Chief Executive of the Chrysler Corporation. His experiences are described in *Iacocca: an Autobiography* (1985).

IANAL *abbr Gen Mgt* I am not a lawyer (*slang*)

IAP *abbr E-com* Internet access provider

IAS *abbr* (*ANZ*) *Fin* Instalment Activity Statement

IASC *abbr Fin* International Accounting Standards Committee: an organisation based in London that works towards achieving global agreement on accounting standards

IBOR *abbr Fin* Inter Bank Offered Rate: the rate of interest at which banks lend to each other on the interbank market

IBRC *abbr Fin* Insurance Brokers Registration Council: in the United Kingdom, a statutory body established under the Insurance Brokers Registration Act of 1977 that was deregulated following the establishment of the Financial Services Authority and the General Insurance Services Council. Its complaints and administration functions passed to the Institute of Insurance Brokers.

IBRD *abbr Fin* International Bank for Reconstruction and Development: a United Nations organisation that provides funds, policy guidance, and technical assistance to facilitate economic development in its poorer member countries

ICA *abbr* (*ANZ*) *Gen Mgt* Insurance Council of Australia

Icarus factor *Gen Mgt* the tendency of managers or executives to embark on overambitious projects which then fail. In Greek mythology, Icarus made himself wings of wax and feathers to attempt to escape from Crete, but flew too near the sun and drowned in the sea after the wax melted. (*slang*)

ICC *abbr Fin* International Chamber of Commerce: an organisation that represents business interests to governments, aiming to improve trading conditions and foster private enterprise

iceing *Gen Mgt* dismissal from employment. The first part of the word is derived from 'involuntary career event'. (*slang*)

ICSA *abbr Fin* Institute of Chartered Secretaries and Administrators: in the United Kingdom, an organisation that aims to promote the efficient administration of commerce, industry, and public affairs. Founded in 1891 and granted a Royal Charter in 1902, it represents the interests of its members to government, publishes journals and other materials, promotes the standing of its members, and provides educational support and qualifying schemes.

ICT *abbr Gen Mgt* information and communications technologies

IDA *abbr* **1.** *Fin* International Development Association: an agency administered by the IBRD to provide assistance on concessional terms to the poorest developing countries. Its resources consist of subscriptions and general replenishments from its more industrialised and developed members, special contributions, and transfers from the net earnings of the IBRD. **2.** *Gen Mgt* Infocomm Development Authority

idea
let's put some ideas on the ground and see if any of them walk *Gen Mgt* let's try some of these ideas and see whether any of them is successful (*slang*)

idea hamster *Gen Mgt* somebody who appears to have an endless supply of new ideas (*slang*)

Identrus *E-com* a consortium of financial institutions engaged in developing a standard for a network over which business-to-business e-commerce can be conducted securely

idle time *Gen Mgt* time spent waiting to continue working on a task while there is a delay (*slang*)

IEA *abbr Fin* International Energy Authority: an autonomous agency within the OECD whose objectives include improving global energy co-operation, developing alternative energy sources, and promoting relations between oil-producing and oil-consuming countries

IFC *abbr Fin* International Finance Corporation: a United Nations organisation promoting private sector investment in developing countries to reduce poverty and improve the

---

quality of people's lives. It finances private sector projects that are profit-oriented and environmentally and socially sound, and helps to foster development. IFC has a staff of 2,000 professionals around the world who seek profitable and creative solutions to complex business issues.

IIB *abbr Fin* Institute of Insurance Brokers: in the United Kingdom, the professional body for insurance brokers and the caretaker for the deregulated Insurance Brokers Registration Council's complaints scheme

ILG *abbr Fin* index-linked gilt

illegal parking *Fin* a stock market practice that involves a broker or company purchasing securities in another company's name though they are guaranteed by the real investor (*slang*)

illiquid *Fin* **1.** used to describe a person or business that lacks cash or assets such as securities that can readily be converted into cash **2.** used to refer to an asset that cannot be easily converted into cash

IMA *abbr (ANZ) Fin* Investment Management Agreement

image advertising *Mkting* a form of advertising that attempts to create a positive attitude to a product, brand, or company

imaginisation *Gen Mgt* an approach to *creativity* originated by *Gareth Morgan* in 1993. Imaginisation is concerned with improving our ability to see and understand situations in new ways, with finding new ways of organising, with creating shared understanding and personal *empowerment*, and with developing a capability for continuing self-organisation.

IMAP *abbr E-com* Internet Message Access Protocol: a protocol that enables e-mails to be received from any computer

IMF *abbr Fin* International Monetary Fund: the organisation that industrialised nations have established to reduce trade barriers and stabilise currencies, especially those of less industrialised nations

IMHO *abbr Gen Mgt* in my humble opinion (*slang*)

immediate holding company *Fin* a company with one or more subsidiaries but which is itself a subsidiary of another company (the holding company)

IMNSHO *abbr Gen Mgt* in my not so humble opinion (*slang*)

IMO *abbr Gen Mgt* in my opinion (*slang*)

impact day *Fin* the day when the terms of a new issue of shares are announced

impaired capital *Fin* a company's capital that is worth less than the par value of its stock

impairment of capital *Fin* the extent to which the value of a company is less than the par value of its stock

imperfect competition *Fin* a situation that exists in a market when there are strong barriers to the entry of new competitors

impersonal account *Fin* any account other than a personal account, being classified as either a real account, in which property is recorded, or a nominal account, in which income, expenses, and capital are recorded. *See also* **account, personal account**

implicit knowledge *Gen Mgt see* **knowledge**

import *Mkting* a product or service brought into another country from its country of origin either for sale or for use in manufacturing

import duty *Fin* a tax on goods imported into a country. Although it may simply be a measure for raising revenue, it can also be used to protect domestic manufacturers from overseas competition.

import penetration *Econ* a situation in which one country's imports dominate the market share of those from other industrialised countries. This is the case, for example, with high-tech imports to the United States from Japan.

imposed budget *Fin* a budget allowance which is set without permitting the ultimate budget holder to have the opportunity to participate in the budgeting process. *Also known as* **top-down budget**

impression *E-com* a measure of the number of times an online advertisement is viewed. One impression is equal to one *click-through*.

imprest account *Fin* a UK term for a record of the transactions of a type of petty cash system. An employee is given an advance of money, an imprest, for incidental expenses and when most of it has been spent, he or she presents receipts for the expenses to the accounts department and is then reimbursed with cash to the total value of the receipts.

imprest system *Fin* a method of controlling cash or stock: when the cash or stock has been reduced by disbursements or issues, it is restored to its original level

---

Some mistakes cost money, others have a more personal cost.   *Peter de Savary*

improvement curve *Gen Mgt see* **learning curve**

imputation system *Fin* a system in which recipients of dividends gain tax advantage for taxes paid by the company that paid the dividends

in box *(US) Gen Mgt, HR* = **in tray**

inc *abbr (US) Gen Mgt* incorporated

incentive programme *Mkting* an award or reward scheme designed to improve salesforce or retail performance

incentive scheme *HR* a programme set up to give benefits to employees to reward them for improved commitment and performance and as a means of motivation. An incentive scheme is designed to supplement **basic pay** and **fringe benefits**. A **financial incentive scheme** may offer share options or a cash bonus, whereas a **non-financial incentive scheme** offers benefits such as additional paid holidays. Awards from incentive schemes may be made on an individual or team basis.

incentive stock option *Fin* in the United States, an employee stock option plan that gives each qualifying employee the right to purchase a specific number of the corporation's shares at a set price during a specific time period. Tax is only payable when the shares are sold.

incestuous share dealing *Fin* transactions by companies within a group in the shares of the other companies within that group. The legality of such transactions depends on the objective of the deals.

inchoate instrument *Fin* a negotiable instrument that is incomplete because, for example, the date or amount is missing. The person to whom it is delivered has the prima facie authority to complete it in any way he or she considers fit.

incidence of tax *Fin* used to indicate where the final burden of a tax lies. For example, although a retailer pays any sales tax to the tax collecting authority, the tax itself is ultimately paid by the customer.

income *Fin* **1.** money received by a company or individual **2.** money received from savings or investments, for example, interest on a deposit account or dividends from shares. This is also known as unearned income. **3.** money generated by a business

income and expenditure account *Fin* a financial statement for non-profit entities such as clubs, associations, and charities. It shows the surplus or deficit, being the excess

of income over expenditure or vice versa, for a period, and is drawn up on the same accruals basis as a profit and loss account.

income bond *Fin* a bond that a company repays only from its profits

income distribution *Fin* **1.** the UK term for the payment to investors of the income generated by a collective investment, less management charges, tax, and expenses. It is distributed in proportion to the number of units or shares held by each investor. *US term* **income dividend** **2.** the distribution of income across a particular group, such as a company, region, or country. It shows the various wage levels and gives the percentage of individuals earning at each level.

income dividend *(US) Fin* = *income distribution*

income-linked gilt *Fin* a bond issued by the United Kingdom whose principal and interest track the retail price index

income redistribution *Econ* a government policy to redirect income to a targeted sector of a country's population, for example, by lowering the rate of tax paid by low-income earners

income shares/stock *Fin* **1.** ordinary shares sought because of their relatively high yield as opposed to their potential to produce capital growth **2.** fixed interest securities acquired for their relatively high yield as opposed to their potential to produce capital growth **3.** certain funds, for example, investment trusts, that issue split level funds where holders of the income element receive all the income (less expenses, charges, and tax), while holders of the capital element receive only the capital gains (less expenses, charges, and tax)

income smoothing *Fin* a UK term for a form of creative accounting that involves the manipulation of a company's financial statements to show steady annual profits rather than large fluctuations

incomes policy *Econ* a government policy that seeks to restrain increases in wages or prices by regulating the permitted level of increase

income statement *Fin see* **trading, profit and loss account**

income stream *Fin* the income received by a company from a particular product or activity

income tax *Fin* a tax levied directly on the income of a person and paid to the government

income tax return *Fin* a form used for reporting income and computing the tax due on it

income unit *Fin* a unit in a unit trust that makes regular payments to its unit holders

in-company training *HR* programmes of *employee development* that are delivered within an organisation by external training providers. In-company training allows programmes to be tailored to a company's specific needs. It is the opposite of **public training programmes**, which have a set syllabus and are open to employees of any organisation.

incomplete records *Fin* an accounting system which is not double-entry bookkeeping. Various degrees of incompleteness can occur, for example, **single-entry bookkeeping**, in which usually only a cash book is maintained.

incorporation *Fin* the legal process of creating a corporation or company. All incorporated entities have a legal status distinct from that of their owners and most have limited liability.

incremental analysis *Fin* analysis of the changes in costs and revenues caused by a change in activity. Normally the technique is used where a significant volume change occurs, causing changes to both variable and fixed costs, and possibly to selling prices. Incremental or differential costs and revenues are compared to determine the financial effect of the activity change.

incremental budgeting *Fin* a method of setting budgets in which the prior period budget is used as a base for the current budget, which is set by adjusting the prior period budget to take account of any anticipated changes

incremental cost *Fin see differential cost*

incrementalism *Gen Mgt* a collective term for the many initiatives of the 1980s and 1990s that took a small-step approach to improving quality and productivity and reducing costs. Incrementalism encompasses initiatives such as *total quality management*, *continuous improvement*, and *benchmarking*. Although incrementalism originally provided a source of *competitive advantage*, it is generally recognised today that a more radical approach is required.

indaba (*S Africa*) *Gen Mgt* a meeting or conference

indemnity *Fin* an agreement by one party to make good the losses suffered by another. *See also indemnity insurance, letter of indemnity*

indemnity insurance *Fin* an insurance contract in which the insurer agrees to cover the cost of losses suffered by the insured party. Most insurance contracts take this form except personal accident and life assurance policies where fixed sums are paid as compensation, rather than reimbursement, for a loss that cannot be quantified in monetary terms.

independent service organisation *E-com see ISO*

index *Fin* **1.** a standard that represents the value of stocks in a market, particularly a figure such as the Hang Seng, FTSE 100, or Nikkei average **2.** an amount calculated to represent the relative value of a group of things

indexation *Fin* the linking of a rate to a standard index of prices, interest rates, share prices, or similar items

index fund *Fin* a unit trust composed of companies listed in an important stock market index in order to match the market's overall performance. *See also managed fund. Also known as index-tracker, tracker fund*

index futures *Fin* a futures contract trading in one of the major stock market indices such as the FTSE 100. *See also Dow Jones Averages, FTSE index*

index-linked bond *Fin* a security where the income is linked to an index, such as a financial index. *See also index-linked gilt, index-linked savings certificate*

index-linked gilt *Fin* an inflation-proof UK government bond, first introduced for institutional investors in 1981 and then made available to the general public in 1982. It is inflation-proof in two ways: the dividend is raised every six months in line with the Retail Price Index and the original capital is repaid in real terms at redemption, when the indexing of the repayment is undertaken. The nominal value of the stock, however, does not increase with inflation. Like other gilts, ILGs are traded on the market. Price changes are principally dependent on investors' changing perceptions of inflation and real yields. *Abbr* **ILG**

index-linked savings certificate *Fin* a National Savings Certificate issued by the UK National Savings organisation with a return linked to the rate of inflation. *Also known as granny bond*

index number *Econ* a weighted average of a number of observations of an economic attribute such as retail prices expressed as a percentage of a similar weighted average calculated at an earlier period

index-tracker *Fin see index fund*

indicated dividend *Fin* the forecast total of all dividends in a year if the amount of each dividend remains as it is

indicated yield *Fin* the yield that an indicated dividend represents

indication price *Fin* an approximation of the price of a security as opposed to its firm price

indicative price *Fin* the price shown on a screen-based system for trading securities such as the UK Stock Exchange Automated Quotations system. The price is not firm, as the size of the bargain will determine the final price at which market makers will actually deal.

indirect channel *Mkting* the selling and distribution of products to customers through intermediaries such as wholesalers, distributors, agents, dealers, or retailers

indirect cost *Gen Mgt* a fixed or overhead cost that cannot be attributed directly to the production of a particular item and is incurred even when there is no output. Indirect costs may include the *cost centre* functions of finance and accounting, information technology, administration, and personnel. *See also direct cost*

indirect discrimination *HR* apparently *equal treatment* that in fact *discriminates* because the employment requirement can only be met by a proportion of those in the relevant group and cannot be justified on non-discriminatory grounds

indirect labour *HR* personnel not directly engaged in the manufacturing of products or the provision of services. Indirect labour includes *white-collar workers* and office and support staff.

individual retirement account *(US) Fin see IRA*

Individual Savings Account *Fin see ISA*

induction *HR* a process through which a new employee is integrated into an organisation, learning about its *corporate culture*, policies, and *procedures*, and the specific practicalities of his or her job. An induction programme should not consist of a one-day introduction, but should be planned and paced over a few days or weeks. In the United States there is a growing use of **boot camps**, which aim to assimilate a new employee rapidly into the culture of the employing organisation. *US term* **orientation**

industrial action *HR* concerted action taken by employees to pressurise an employer to accede to a demand, usually work-related, but sometimes of a political or social nature. Examples of industrial action include **strikes**, overtime bans, **go-slows**, and extended tea breaks.

industrial advertising *Mkting* the advertising of technical products and services to the industrial or business sectors

industrial co-operative *Gen Mgt* a group of individuals who together produce goods or provide services and share any profits that are made. Industrial co-operatives are an extension of the **co-operative movement** that developed during the 1800s.

industrial court *(ANZ) HR* a state body in Australia responsible for arbitrating in industrial disputes and setting wage awards

industrial democracy *HR* a way of running an organisation that involves employees in strategy and **decision-making**. Industrial democracy involves **employee participation** in management, which empowers employees and aids **motivation**. It can be facilitated by such set-ups as **works councils** and consultation committees. In an industrial democracy, workers should not only share in inputs to the running of the organisation but also in its outputs, for example, by taking part in a profit-sharing scheme.

industrial dispute *Gen Mgt see dispute*

industrial engineering *Gen Mgt* an applied science discipline concerned with the prediction, planning, evaluation, and improvement of company effectiveness. The purpose of industrial engineering is to maximise efficiency, quality, and production through the best use of personnel, materials, facilities, and equipment.

industrial espionage *Gen Mgt* the practice of spying on a business competitor in order to obtain their trade or commercial secrets. Information sought through industrial espionage will often refer to new products, designs, formulas, manufacturing processes, marketing surveys, research, or future plans. The aim of industrial espionage is either to injure the business prospects or market share of the target company, or to use the secrets discovered for another organisation's commercial benefit.

Too many people are on boards because they want to have nice-looking visiting cards. *Utz Fecht*

industrial goods *Ops* goods produced for industry, which include processed or **raw materials**, goods used to produce other goods, machinery, components, and equipment

industrial goods marketing *Mkting* the **industrial marketing** of products. Industrial goods marketing is different from the marketing of consumer goods in that it is directed at organisations, businesses, and other institutions, rather than at the individual end-user of a product. It may require different marketing strategies from those used in **consumer goods marketing** to be effective.

industrial housekeeping *Gen Mgt* the process of ensuring that the workplace is kept clean and tidy. Industrial housekeeping forms part of the general responsibility of managers. It includes the provision of adequate workspace, adequate storage arrangements, both around the workstation and within the unit, and the development of effective administration and procedures to ensure a culture of tidiness and cleanliness within the workforce. A lack of concern with housekeeping can result in an increase in accidents and machine failure and in a reduction in the overall efficiency of the unit. The introduction of the Japanese 5-S concept into Western companies has renewed management interest in industrial housekeeping.

industrialisation *Gen Mgt* the change from a society based on agriculture to one based on manufacturing. Industrialisation is the process undergone in much of the developed world during the Industrial Revolution. Features of the process include **automation**, scientific development, the introduction of factories, the **division of labour**, the replacement of barter with a money-based economy, a more mobile workforce, and the growth of urban centres. The phase of development following industrialisation is the **post-industrial society**.

industrial marketing *Mkting* the marketing of goods or services to companies, as opposed to individual consumers. Industrial marketing involves a number of key differences from selling to consumers. These include a smaller customer base with higher-value or larger-unit purchases, more technically complex or specially tailored products, professionally qualified purchasers, closer buyer-seller relationships, and possible group-purchasing decision-making. *Also known as* **B2B marketing**

industrial market research *Mkting* **market research** into the **marketing** of services and goods to industry, businesses, and other institutions. Industrial market research is used as an aid to **decision-making** and concerns the manufacture, selling, and distribution of products with the aim of reducing costs and increasing profits. It considers factors such as the available labour force, location of the firm, export market potential, and use of resources.

industrial production *Econ* the output of a country's productive industries. Until the 1960s, this was commonly iron and steel or coal, but since then lighter engineering in motor car or robotics manufacture has taken over.

industrial psychology *HR see* **occupational psychology**

Industrial Relations Commission *Gen Mgt see* **Australian Industrial Relations Commission**

Industrial Relations Court of Australia *HR* an Australian superior court responsible for enforcing industrial awards, hearing and ruling on claims for unfair dismissal, and ruling on points of industrial law. *Abbr* **IRCA**

industrial revenue bond *Fin* a bond that a private company uses to finance construction

industrial-sector cycle *Econ* a business cycle that reflects patterns of an old economy rather than the new electronic economy

industrial services marketing *Mkting* the **industrial marketing** of services. Industrial services marketing may promote services such as maintenance contracts, insurance, training, transportation, office cleaning, and advertising to industry, businesses, and other institutions. Many services offered to industry are also offered to the consumer, but promoting them to consumers requires strategies derived from **consumer services marketing**.

industry rules *Gen Mgt* the unwritten conventions that are considered to govern the interactions of organisations within an industry

inertia selling *Mkting* a method of selling that involves the sending of unsolicited goods on a sale or return policy. Inertia selling relies on the passive reaction of a potential purchaser to choose to pay for the goods received rather than undertake the effort to send them back. The receiver of the goods is not bound by law to pay for them but must keep them in good condition until they are collected or returned. Regarded by some as unethical,

---

inertia selling is the principle by which many postal book, record, and video clubs operate.

inference *Stats* a conclusion drawn by a researcher about a statistical population after observing individuals in the population

infinite capacity plan *Ops see capacity requirements planning*

infinite loading *Ops* the scheduling or loading of jobs onto a workstation as if it had a limitless capacity to handle them. *See also finite loading*

inflation *Fin* a general increase in the price level over time. *See also hyperinflation*

inflation accounting *Fin* the adjustment of a company's accounts to reflect the effect of inflation and provide a more realistic view of the company's position

inflationary *Econ* characterised by excess demand or high costs creating an excessive increase in the country's money supply

inflationary gap *Econ* a gap that exists when an economy's resources are utilised and *aggregate demand* is more than the full-employment level of output. Prices will rise to remove the excess demand.

inflationary spiral *Econ* the vicious circle in which, in inflationary conditions, excess demand causes producers to raise prices and workers to demand wage rises to sustain their living standards

inflation-proof security (*US*) *Fin* a security that is indexed to inflation

inflation rate *Econ* the rate at which general price levels increase over a period of time

inflation tax *Econ* an incomes policy that taxes companies that grant pay rises above a particular level

Infocomm Development Authority *Gen Mgt* a statutory board responsible for developing the information and communications sector in Singapore. It was formed in 1999 as a result of the merger of the Telecommunications Authority of Singapore and the National Computer Board. *Abbr* **IDA**

infoholic *Gen Mgt* somebody who is obsessed with obtaining information, especially on the Internet (*slang*)

infomatics *Gen Mgt* the process of automation using information systems

infomediary *E-com* a website that provides and aggregates relevant customer or industry information for other companies

infomercial *Mkting* a television or cinema commercial that includes helpful information about a product as well as advertising content

info rate *Fin* a money market rate quoted by dealers for information only

informal economy *Econ* the economy that runs in parallel to the formal economy but outside the reach of the tax system, most transactions being paid for in cash or goods

information and communications technologies *Gen Mgt* computer and telecommunications technologies considered collectively. Information and communications technology convergence has given rise to technologies such as the *Internet*, *videoconferencing*, *groupware*, *intranets*, and third-generation mobile phones. Information and communications technologies enable organisations to be more flexible in the way they are structured and in the way they work, and this has given rise to both the *virtual organisation* and the *virtual office*. *Abbr* **ICT**

information architecture *E-com* the means and methods of designing metadata, navigation, search, and content layout for a website

information management *Gen Mgt* the acquisition, recording, organising, storage, dissemination, and retrieval of information. Good information management has been described as getting the right information to the right person in the right format at the right time.

information overload *E-com* the problem caused by the excessive quantity of web and e-mail-based information and the Internet's inability to discriminate between useful and useless material. In 1997, the problem of information overload was identified in an influential report from the MCA (Marketing and Communication Agency). The report concluded that 'information overload is not simply the problem of too much information. It is the problem of too much *irrelevant* information caused by the heavy reliance on one medium (the Internet) to distribute information'.

information space *E-com* the abstract concept of all the knowledge, expertise, and information accessible on the Web

infotainment *Gen Mgt* television programmes that deal with serious issues or current affairs in an entertaining way

infrastructure *Gen Mgt* the basic elements that together support something, for example, the network and systems that support computing or the public services and facilities that support business activity

in-house newsletter *Gen Mgt see* **newsletter**

initial offer *Fin* the first offer that a company makes to buy the shares of another company

initial public offering *Fin* the first instance of making particular shares available for sale to the public. *Abbr* **IPO**

initial yield *Gen Mgt* the estimated yield at the launch of an investment fund

injunction *Fin* a court order forbidding an individual or organisation from doing something

inland bill *Fin* a UK term for a bill of exchange that is payable and drawn in the same country

Inland Revenue *Fin see* **Board of Inland Revenue**

Inland Revenue Department (*ANZ*) *Fin* the New Zealand government body responsible for the administration of the national taxation system. *Abbr* **IRD**

innovation *Gen Mgt* the creation, development, and implementation of a new product, process, or service, with the aim of improving efficiency, effectiveness, or **competitive advantage**. Innovation may apply to products, services, manufacturing processes, managerial processes, or the design of an organisation. It is most often viewed at a product or process level, where product innovation satisfies a customer's needs, and process innovation improves efficiency and effectiveness. Innovation is linked with **creativity** and the creation of new ideas, and involves taking those new ideas and turning them into reality through invention, research, and **new product development**.

input tax *Fin see* **VAT**

input tax credit (*ANZ*) *Fin* an amount paid as **Goods and Services Tax** on supplies purchased for business purposes, which can be offset against Goods and Services Tax collected

insert *Mkting* a loose piece of advertising material, for example, a card or brochure, placed inside a newspaper or magazine

insertion rate *Mkting* the cost of a single appearance of an advertisement

inside information *Fin* information that is of advantage to investors but is only available

to people who have personal contact with a company

inside quote *Fin* a range of prices for a security, from the highest offer to buy to the lowest offer to sell

insider *Gen Mgt* somebody who has access to information that is privileged and unavailable to most members of the public

insider trading *or* **insider dealing** *Fin* profitable, usually illegal, trading in securities carried out using privileged information

insolvency *Fin, Gen Mgt* the inability to pay debts when they become due. Insolvency will apply even if total assets exceed total liabilities, if those assets cannot be readily converted into cash to meet debts as they mature. Even then, insolvency may not necessarily mean **business failure. Bankruptcy** may be avoided through **debt rescheduling** or **turnaround management**.

insourcing *Gen Mgt* the use of in-house personnel or an internal department to meet an organisation's need for specific services. Insourcing is seen as a reaction to the growing popularity of **outsourcing** that has not always met expectations. An insourcing strategy is chosen where it appears that a better service can be provided from internal resources than from an external supplier. In some cases, organisations opt for a combination of outsourcing and insourcing in which external service providers work in co-operation with in-house personnel.

inspector of taxes *Fin* in the United Kingdom, an official who reports to the Board of Inland Revenue and is responsible for issuing tax returns and assessments, agreeing tax liabilities, and conducting appeals on matters of tax

instalment *Fin* one of two or more payments or repayments for the purchase of an initial public offering

Instalment Activity Statement (*ANZ*) *Fin* a standard form used in Australia to report **Pay-As-You-Go** instalment payments on investment income. *Abbr* **IAS**

instalment credit *Fin* the UK term for a loan that is repaid with fixed regular instalments, and with a rate of interest fixed for the duration of the loan. *US term* **instalment loan**

instalment loan (*US*) *Fin* = **instalment credit**

instalment plan (*US*) *Fin* = **hire purchase**

One man that has a mind and knows it can always beat ten men who haven't and don't.
George Bernard Shaw

instalment purchase *Fin* a financing arrangement in which the buyer pays by a series of instalments over a period of time

instant messaging *E-com see* **live chat**

Institute of Chartered Accountants *Fin* in the United Kingdom and the Republic of Ireland, one of three professional accountancy bodies that provide qualification by examinations, ensure high standards of education and training, and supervise professional conduct

Institute of Chartered Secretaries and Administrators *Fin see* **ICSA**

Institute of Financial Services *Fin* the trading name of the Chartered Institute of Bankers

Institute of Insurance Brokers *Fin see* **IIB**

institutional investor *Fin* an institution that makes investments

institutional survey *Stats* a statistical investigation in which an institution such as a company is the unit of analysis

instrument 1. *Fin* a generic term for either securities or derivatives. *See also* **financial instrument**, **negotiable instrument 2.** *Fin* an official or legal document **3.** *Fin* a means to an end, for example, a government's expenditure and taxation in its quest for reducing unemployment **4.** *HR see* **psychometric test**

insurable risk *Fin see* **risk**

insurance 1. *Fin* in financial markets, hedging or any other strategy that reduces risk while permitting participation in potential gains **2.** *Gen Mgt* an arrangement in which individuals or companies pay another company to guarantee them compensation if they suffer loss resulting from risks such as fire, theft, or accidental damage

insurance agent *Fin* in the United States, an individual who sells the insurance policies of a particular company

Insurance and Superannuation Commission *(ANZ) Gen Mgt* an Australian federal government body responsible for regulating the superannuation and insurance industries. *Abbr* **ISC**

insurance broker *Fin* a person or company that acts as an intermediary between companies providing insurance and individuals or companies who need insurance

Insurance Brokers Registration Council *Fin see* **IBRC**

Insurance Council of Australia *Gen Mgt* an independent body representing the interests of businesses involved in the insurance industry. It was set up in 1975 and currently represents around 110 companies. *Abbr* **ICA**

insurance intermediary *Fin* an individual or firm that provides advice on insurance or assurance and can arrange policies. *See also* **IIB**, **IBRC**

insurance policy *Gen Mgt* a document that sets out the terms and conditions for providing insurance cover against specified risks

insurance premium tax *Fin* a tax on household, motor vehicle, travel, and other general insurance

insured *Fin* covered by a contract of insurance

insured account *(US) Fin* an account with a bank or savings institution that belongs to a federal or private insurance organisation

insurer *Fin* the underwriter of an insurance risk

intangible asset *Fin* an asset such as **intellectual property** or **goodwill** that is not physical

integrated accounts *Fin* a set of accounting records which provides both financial and cost accounts using a common input of data for all accounting purposes

integrated implementation model *Gen Mgt see* **new product development**

Integrated Services Digital Network *E-com see* **ISDN**

intellectual assets *Gen Mgt* the knowledge, experience, and skills of its staff that an organisation can make use of

intellectual capital *Fin* knowledge which can be used to create value. Intellectual capital includes: human resources, the collective skills, experience, and knowledge of employees; intellectual assets, knowledge which is defined and codified such as a drawing, computer program, or collection of data; and intellectual property, intellectual assets which can be legally protected, such as patents and copyrights.

intellectual property *Gen Mgt* the ownership of rights to ideas, designs, and inventions, including **copyrights**, **patents**, and **trademarks**. Intellectual property is protected by law in most countries, and the World Intellectual Property Organisation is responsible for harmonising the law across different

---

Doubt is a necessary precondition to meaningful action. Fear is the great mover in the end.
Donald Barthelme

countries and promoting the protection of intellectual property rights.

intelligence test *HR see aptitude test*

intelligent e-mail *E-com* an automated e-mail system that is automatically able to analyse incoming messages without the need for criteria pre-set by each user

interactive *E-com* relating to a facility of an online service or software program that allows the user to enter data or issue commands

interactive planning *Gen Mgt* a process that promotes participation in both the design of a desirable future and the developments that enable this future to be achieved rather than waiting for it to happen. Interactive planning is associated with *Russell Ackoff*, and was outlined in *Creating the Corporate Future* (1981).

Inter Bank Offered Rate *Fin see IBOR*

interchange *E-com* a transaction between the acquiring bank and the issuing bank

interchangeable bond *Fin* a bond whose owner can change it at will between bearer and book-entry form

interchange fee *E-com* the charge on a transaction between the acquiring bank and the issuing bank, paid by the acquirer to the issuer

intercommodity spread *Fin* a combination of purchase and sale of options for related commodities with the same delivery date

intercompany pricing *Gen Mgt* the setting of prices by companies within a group to sell products or services to each other, rather than to external customers

interdependency concept *Fin* the principle that management accounting, in recognition of the increasing complexity of business, must access both external and internal information sources from interactive functions such as marketing, production, personnel, procurement, and finance. This assists in ensuring that the information is adequately balanced.

interest *Fin* the rate that a lender charges for the use of money that is a loan

interest arbitrage *Fin* transactions in two or more financial centres in order to make an immediate profit by exploiting differences in interest rates. *See also arbitrage*

interest assumption *Fin* the expected rate of return on a portfolio

interest charged *Fin* the cost of borrowing money, expressed as an absolute amount, or

as a percentage interest rate. *See also annual percentage rate, nominal interest rate, real interest rate*

interest cover *Fin* The amount of earnings available to make interest payments after all operating and non-operating income and expenses—except interest and income taxes—have been accounted for.

EXAMPLE Interest cover is regarded as a measure of a company's creditworthiness because it shows how much income there is to cover interest payments on outstanding debt.

It is expressed as a ratio, comparing the funds available to pay interest—earnings before interest and taxes, or EBIT—with the interest expense. The basic formula is:

EBIT / interest expense = interest coverage ratio

If interest expense for a year is £9 million, and the company's EBIT is £45 million, the interest coverage would be:

45 million / 9 million = 5:1

The higher the number, the stronger a company is likely to be. A ratio of less than 1 indicates that a company is having problems generating enough cash flow to pay its interest expenses, and that either a modest decline in operating profits or a sudden rise in borrowing costs could eliminate profitability entirely. Ideally, interest coverage should at least exceed 1.5; in some sectors, 2.0 or higher is desirable.

Variations of this basic formula also exist. For example, there is:

Operating cash flow + interest + taxes / interest = Cash-flow interest coverage ratio

This ratio indicates the firm's ability to use its cash flow to satisfy its fixed financing obligations. Finally, there is the fixed-charge coverage ratio, which compares EBIT with fixed charges:

EBIT + lease expenses / interest + lease expense = Fixed-charge coverage ratio

'Fixed charges' can be interpreted in many ways, however. It could mean, for example, the funds that a company is obliged to set aside to retire debt, or dividends on preferred stock.

interest-elastic investment *Fin* an investment with a rate of return that varies with interest rates

interest-inelastic investment *Fin* an investment with a rate of return that does not vary with interest rates

interest in possession trust *Fin* a trust that gives one or more beneficiaries an immediate right to receive any income generated by the trust's assets. It can be used for property, enabling the beneficiary either to enjoy the rent generated by the property or to reside there, or as a life policy, a common arrangement for Inheritance Tax planning.

interest-only mortgage *Fin* a long-term loan, usually for the purchase of a property, in which the borrower only pays interest to the lender during the term of the mortgage, with the principal (see *mortgage*) being repaid at the end of the term. It is thus the borrower's responsibility to make provisions to accumulate the required capital during the period of the mortgage, usually by contributing to tax efficient investment plans such as Individual Savings Accounts or by relying on an anticipated inheritance. *See also mortgage*

interest rate *Fin* the amount of interest charged for borrowing a sum of money over a specified period of time

interest rate cap *Fin* an upper limit on a rate of interest, for example, in an adjustable-rate mortgage

interest rate effect *Econ* the mechanism by which interest rates adjust so that investment is equal to savings in an economy

interest rate exposure *Fin* the risk of a loss associated with movements in the level of interest rates. *See also bond*

interest rate floor *Fin* a lower limit on a rate of interest, for example, in an adjustable-rate mortgage

interest rate future *Fin see future*

interest rate guarantee *Fin* **1.** an interest rate cap, collar, or cap and collar **2.** a tailored indemnity protecting the purchaser against future changes in interest rates

interest rate option *Fin see option*

interest rate parity theory *Fin* a method of predicting foreign exchange rates based on the hypothesis that the difference between the interest rates in two countries should offset the difference between the spot rates and the forward foreign exchange rates over the same period

interest rate swap *Fin* an exchange of two debt instruments with different rates of interest, made to tailor cash flows to the participants' different requirements

interest sensitive *Fin* used to describe assets, generally purchased with credit, that are in demand when interest rates fall but

considered less attractive when interest rates rise

interest yield *Fin* the annual rate of interest earned on a security, excluding the effect of any increase in price to maturity

interface *Gen Mgt* **1.** the point of contact between two or more things, for example, between a computer and user, or customer and seller **2.** a face-to-face meeting (*slang*)

interfirm comparison *Fin* systematic and detailed comparison of the performance of different companies generally operating in a common industry. Companies participating in such a scheme normally provide standardised, and therefore comparable, information to the scheme administrator, who then distributes to participating members only the information supplied by participants. Normally the information distributed is in the form of ratios, or in a format which prevents the identity of individual scheme members from coming to light.

interfirm co-operation *Gen Mgt* a formal or informal agreement between organisations to collaborate in achieving common or new aims more efficiently or effectively. Interfirm co-operation usually takes the form of a *joint venture*, *strategic alliance*, or *strategic partnering* arrangement.

interim certificate *Fin* a document certifying partial ownership of stock that is not totally paid for at one time

interim dividend *Fin* a dividend whose value is determined on the basis of a period of time of less than a full fiscal year

interim financial statement *Fin* a financial statement that covers a period other than a full financial year. Although UK companies are not legally obliged to publish interim financial statements, those listed on the London Stock Exchange are obliged to publish a half-yearly report of their activities and a profit and loss account which may either be sent to shareholders or published in a national newspaper. In the United States, the practice is to issue quarterly financial statements.

interim financing *Fin* financing by means of bridging loans

interim management *Gen Mgt* the temporary employment of an experienced manager by an organisation seeking to fill a temporary vacancy or co-ordinate a particular project. Interim managers are generally used to bring in skills not already present in an organisation. Sometimes they are employed when an

---

A self-made man is one who believes in luck and sends his son to Oxford. **Christina Stead**

organisation is facing *business failure*, but increasingly they are used as a strategic resource as and when required. **Interim managers** work on a *freelance* or *portfolio working* basis.

Interim managers differ from both temporary staff and consultants. In general, they are considerably senior to most other temporary workers, and fulfil assignments—often long term—that drive the future of the employing company. They also provide hands-on, day-to-day expertise, in contrast to the prescriptive, advisory support that management consultants deliver.

interim manager *Gen Mgt see* **interim management**

interim statement *Fin* a financial statement relating to a period of time of less than a full fiscal year

interlocking accounts *Fin* a system in which cost accounts are kept distinct from the financial accounts, the two sets of accounts being kept continuously in agreement by the use of control accounts or reconciled by other means. *Also known as* **non-integrated accounts**

intermarket spread *Fin* a combination of purchase and sale of options for the same commodity with the same delivery date on different markets

intermediary *Fin* somebody who makes investments for others

intermediate goods *Ops* goods bought for use in the production of other products

intern (*US*) *HR* a trainee working in a junior position in a company

internal audit *Fin* an audit of a company undertaken by its employees. *See also* **external audit**

internal check *Fin* the procedures designed to provide assurance that everything which should be recorded has been recorded; errors or irregularities are identified; assets and liabilities exist and are correctly recorded

internal communication *Gen Mgt* communication between employees or departments across all levels or divisions of an organisation. Internal communication is a form of *corporate communication* and can be formal or informal, upward, downward, or horizontal. It can take various forms such as *team briefing*, *interviewing*, employee or *works councils*, *meetings*, *memos*, an *intranet*, *newsletters*, *suggestion schemes*, the *grapevine*, and reports.

internal consultant *Gen Mgt* an employee who uses knowledge and expertise to offer advice or business solutions to another department or business unit within an organisation. **Internal consulting** is one aspect of work carried out by a *management services* department.

internal consulting *Gen Mgt see* **internal consultant**

internal cost analysis *Gen Mgt* an examination of an organisation's value-creating activities to determine sources of profitability and to identify the relative costs of different processes. Internal cost analysis is a tool for analysing the *value chain*. Principal steps include identifying those processes that create value for the organisation, calculating the cost of each value-creating process against the overall cost of the product or service, identifying the cost components for each process, establishing the links between the processes, and working out the opportunities for achieving relative cost advantage.

internal differentiation analysis *Gen Mgt* an examination of processes in the *value chain* to determine which of them create differentiation of the product or service in the customer's eyes, and thus enhance its value. Internal differentiation analysis enables an organisation to focus on improving the identified processes to maximise *competitive advantage*. Steps involve identification of value-creating activities, evaluation of strategies that can enhance value for the customer, and assessment of which differentiation strategies are the most sustainable.

internal growth *Fin* organic growth created within a business, for example, by inventing new products and so increasing its market share, producing products that are more reliable, offering a more efficient service than its competitors, or being more aggressive in its marketing. *See also* **external growth**

internal marketing *Mkting* the application of the principles of marketing within an organisation. Internal marketing involves the creation of an internal market by dividing departments into *business units*, with control over their own operations and expenditure, with attendant impacts on *corporate culture*, politics, and power. Internal marketing also involves treating employees as internal customers with the aim of increasing employees' motivation and *customer focus*.

internal rate of return *Fin* the annual percentage return achieved by a project, in which

---

A friend in power is a friend lost.   *Henry Brooks Adams*

the sum of the discounted cash inflows over the life of the project is equal to the sum of the discounted cash outflows. *Abbr* **IRR**

internal recruitment *HR recruitment* carried out within the existing workforce. Internal recruitment gives employees opportunities for *promotion* and to develop new skills.

Internal Revenue Code *(US)* *Fin* the complex series of federal tax laws

Internal Revenue Service *Fin see IRS*

internal versus external sourcing *Gen Mgt see purchasing versus production*

International Accounting Standards Board *Fin* an independent and privately funded accounting standards setter based in London. The Board, whose members come from nine countries and a range of backgrounds, is committed to developing a single set of high quality, understandable, and enforceable global standards that require transparent and comparable information in general purpose financial statements. It also works with national accounting standard setters to achieve convergence in accounting standards around the world. *Abbr* **IASB**

International Accounting Standards Committee *Fin see IASC*

International Bank for Reconstruction and Development *Fin see IBRD*

International Chamber of Commerce *Fin see ICC*

International Development Association *Fin see IDA*

International Energy Authority *Fin see IEA*

International Finance Corporation *Fin see IFC*

international fund *Fin* a unit trust that invests in securities both inside and outside a country

International Fund for Agricultural Development *Fin* a specialised United Nations agency with a mandate to combat hunger and rural poverty in developing countries. Established as an international financial institution in 1977 following the 1974 World Food Conference, it has financed projects in over 100 countries and independent territories, to which it has committed US$7.7 billion in grants and loans. It has three sources of finance (contributions from members, loan repayments, and investment income) and an

annual commitment level of approximately US$450 million.

international management *Gen Mgt* **1.** the maintenance and development of an organisation's *production* or market interests across national borders with either local or *expatriate* staff **2.** the process of running a *multinational business*, made up of formerly independent organisations **3.** the body of skills, knowledge, and understanding, required to manage cross-cultural operations

International Monetary Fund *Fin see IMF*

International Organization of Securities Commissions *Fin* an organisation of securities commissions from around the world, based in Madrid. Its objectives are to promote high standards of regulation, exchange information, and establish standards for and effective surveillance of international securities transactions. *Abbr* **IOSCO**

International Securities Market Association *Fin* the self-regulatory organisation and trade association for the international securities market. Its primary role is to oversee the fast-changing marketplace through the issuing of rules and recommendations relating to trading and settlement practices. Established in 1969, the organisation has over 600 members from 51 countries. *Abbr* **ISMA**

International Standards Organisation *Gen Mgt see ISO*

International Union of Credit and Investment Insurers *Fin* an organisation that works for international acceptance of sound principles of export credit and foreign investment insurance. Founded in 1934, the London-based Union has 51 members in 42 countries who play a role of central importance in world trade, both as regards exports and foreign direct investments. *Also known as* **Berne Union**

Internesia *E-com* the tendency to find interesting websites on the Internet and then forget how to locate them again (*slang*)

Internet *E-com* the global network of computers accessed with the aid of a modem. The Internet includes websites, e-mail, newsgroups, and other forums. It is a public network, though many of the computers connected to it are also part of *intranets*. It uses the **Internet Protocol** (IP) as a communication standard.

Internet access provider *E-com* a company or organisation that provides its customers with an entry point to the Internet via a dial-up connection, cable modem, or wireless application. *Abbr* **IAP**

Internet commerce *E-com* the part of *e-commerce* that consists of commercial transactions conducted over the Internet

Internet marketing *E-com* marketing of products or services over the Web.

Although similar in many ways to traditional marketing, Internet marketing is best suited to several particular purposes. It is ideal for marketing: products and services that require a lot of information to sell, such as travel and books; products and services that people feel strongly about, such as music and films (much of the success of *The Blair Witch Project* was credited to fans getting together on the Internet and promoting it through enthusiastic reviews and dialogue); products and services that are bought by the Internet demographic.

In terms of advertising, online advertisements do not have the same impact as television or glossy media, as consumers are generally unwilling to download them. However, due to extensive *personalisation* capabilities, Internet marketing has a unique ability to reach niche markets and target just the right consumer with just the right product.

Internet marketing is thus best used as an adjunct to a traditional offline marketing strategy. Offline marketing is used to raise consumer awareness and arouse interest; Internet marketing educates and answers questions by having comprehensive information on offer.

Internet merchant *E-com* a businessman or businesswoman who sells a product or service over the Internet

Internet Message Access Protocol *E-com* see **IMAP**

Internet payment system *E-com* any mechanism for fund transfer from customer to merchant or business to business via the Internet. There are many payment options available, including credit card payment, credit transfer, electronic cheques, direct debit, smart cards, prepaid schemes, loyalty scheme points-based approaches, person-to-person payments, and mobile phone schemes.

Getting the online payment system right is critical to the success of e-commerce. Currently, the most common form of online consumer payment is by credit card (90% in the United States; 70% in Europe). The most common business-to-business payments, however, are still offline—probably because

such transactions often involve large sums of money.

Good online payment systems share key characteristics: ease of use; robustness and reliability; proper authentication (to combat fraud); efficient integration with the vendor's own internal systems; security and assurance procedures which check that the seller gets the money and the buyer gets the goods.

Internet Protocol *E-com see* **Internet**

Internet security *E-com* the means used to protect websites and other electronic files from attack by **hacker**s and **virus**es. The Internet is, by definition, a network; networks are open, and are thus open to attack. A poor Internet security policy can result in a substantial loss of productivity and a drop in consumer confidence.

The essential elements of Internet security are: constant vigilance—the perfect Internet security system will be out of date the next day; a combination of software and human expertise—security software can only do so much, it must be combined with human experience; and internal as well as external security—many security breaches come from within an organisation.

Internet service provider *E-com see* **ISP**

interoperability *Gen Mgt* the ability of products from different manufacturers to be used in conjunction with each other

interpersonal communication *HR* all aspects of personal interaction, contact, and communication between individuals or members of a group. Effective interpersonal communication depends on a range of **interpersonal skills** including listening, asserting, influencing, persuading, empathising, sensitivity, and diplomacy. Important aspects of communication between people include *body language* and other forms of *non-verbal communication*.

interpersonal skills *HR see* **interpersonal communication**

interquartile range *Stats* the difference between the first and third quartiles of a statistical sample, used to measure the spread of variables in the data

interstate commerce *Fin* commerce that involves more than one US state and is therefore subject to regulation by Congress. *See also* **intrastate commerce**

interstitial *E-com* a Web advertisement that appears on its own page. This can either be sandwiched between content pages on a website, in a similar way to that used in traditional magazine advertising, or appear on its own

---

Power is not only what you have but what the enemy thinks you have.   **Saul Alinsky**

before the actual web page loads. The latter gets visitors' attention, but can be very frustrating.

intervention *Econ* government action to manipulate market forces for political or economic purposes

interviewer bias *Stats* distortion in the results of a statistical survey caused by actions of the interviewer such as cues given to the interviewee

interviewing *HR* the practice of asking questions of another person in order to gain information and make an assessment. Interviewing is a selection tool used in recruitment to assess somebody's suitability for a job. A **structured interview** relies on asking the same job-related questions of all candidates and systematically evaluating their responses. There are two principal models: the **behavioural interview**, which aims to find out how applicants have behaved in the past in similar situations; and the **situational interview**, in which they are asked hypothetical questions to determine how they might act in the future. Interviewing is a technique also used in *counselling*, *performance appraisal*, and as part of a disciplinary procedure. *See also discipline*

intranet *E-com* a corporate network of computers utilising Internet tools and technology for the purpose of communication and information sharing. Intranets have been introduced by many organisations as an aid to *internal communication*. Where an intranet is extended beyond the employees of an organisation, perhaps to suppliers, customer, or distributors, it is called an *extranet*.

At their best, intranets can combine internal and external information resources in a one-stop information shop, and become the intellectual capital library of an organisation, capturing staff knowledge, facilitating teamwork and collaboration, and providing an excellent induction vehicle for new employees. However, if not managed properly, intranets can easily evolve in a haphazard way with no clear objectives, and simply become information dumps. Consequently, staff do not use them and their potential is lost.

intrapreneur *Gen Mgt* an *employee* who uses the approach of an *entrepreneur* within an organisational setting. An intrapreneur must have freedom of action to explore and implement ideas, although the outcome of such work will be owned by the organisation rather than the intrapreneur, and it is the organisation that will take the associated risk.

Managers of organisations in which intrapreneurs are allowed to operate subscribe to the view that *innovation* can be achieved by encouraging *creative* and exploratory activity in semi-autonomous units.

intrastate commerce *Fin* commerce that occurs within a single state of the United States. *See also interstate commerce*

in tray *Gen Mgt, HR* a receptacle for documents and other items requiring the attention of an individual. An in tray is normally placed on the desk or in the office of the person responsible for dealing with the contents. *US term in box*

in-tray learning *HR* a training exercise in which the trainee plays the role of a manager dealing with the contents of an *in tray* within a set period of time. In-tray training is a form of *simulation* used to develop the *decision-making*, prioritising, and *time management* skills of managers and supervisors in the context of the normal working day.

intrinsic value *Fin* the extent to which an option is in the money

introducing broker *Fin* a broker who cannot accept payment from customers

intuitive management *Gen Mgt* a *management style* that relies on gut feeling or a sixth sense, rather than on analytical or objective reasoning. Intuitive management exploits the holistic, imaginative, spiritual skills of the right side of the brain, whereas the conventional school of management favours left side of the brain skills, which are logical, rational, linear, and mathematical in nature. Intuitive management is closely linked to a style of *decision-making* that encourages *creativity* and *innovation*. Because this style of decision-making has no rational basis, however, it can be difficult to justify decisions that turn out to be wrong.

inventory 1. (*US*) *Fin* the total of an organisation's commercial assets **2.** *Gen Mgt* the stock of finished goods, raw materials, and work in progress held by a company

inventory record *Ops* a record of the *inventory* held by an organisation. An inventory record forms an important part of material requirements planning systems. Such records usually make use of some form of part numbering or classification system, and include a description of the part, the quantity held, and the location of all the holdings. A **transaction file** keeps track of inventory use and replenishment.

---

inventory turnover *Fin* an accounting ratio of the number of times *inventory* is replaced during a given period. The ratio is calculated by dividing net sales by average inventory over a given period. Values are expressed as times per period, most often a year, and a higher figure indicates a more efficient manufacturing operation.

Its formula is:

Cost of goods sold / Inventory

For example, if COGS is £2 million, and inventory at the end of the period is £500,000, then:

2,000,000 / 500,000 = 4.

Also known as **stock turns**

inverse floating rate note *Fin* a note whose interest rate varies inversely with a *benchmark interest rate*

inverted doughnut *Gen Mgt see* **doughnut principle**

inverted market *Fin* a situation in which near-term futures cost more than long-term futures for the same commodity

inverted yield curve *Fin* a yield curve with lower interest rates for long-term bonds than for short-term bonds. *See also* **yield curve**

investment *Fin* any application of funds which is intended to provide a return by way of interest, dividend, or capital appreciation

investment analyst *Fin* an employee of a stock-exchange company who researches other companies and identifies investment opportunities for clients. *Also known as* **financial analyst**

investment bank *Fin* **1.** a bank that specialises in providing funds to corporate borrowers for start-up or expansion **2.** (*US*) = **merchant bank**

investment bill *Fin* a bill of exchange that is an investment

investment bond *Fin* in the United Kingdom, a product where the investment is paid as a single premium into a life assurance policy with an underlying asset-backed fund. The bondholder receives a regular income until the end of the bond's term when the investment—the current value of the fund—is returned to the bondholder.

investment borrowing *Econ* funds borrowed to encourage a country's economic growth or to support the development of particular industries or regions by adding to physical or human capital

investment centre *Fin* a profit centre with additional responsibilities for capital investment, and possibly for financing, whose performance is measured by its return on investment

investment club *Fin* a group of people who join together to make investments in securities

investment committee (*US*) *Fin* a group of employees of an investment bank who evaluate investment proposals

investment company (*US*) *Fin* a company that pools for investment the money of several investors by means of unit trusts

investment dealer (*Canada*) *Fin* a securities broker

investment fund *Fin* a savings scheme that invests its clients' funds in corporate start-up or expansion projects

Investment Management Agreement (*ANZ*) *Fin* a contract between an investor and an investment manager required under SIS legislation. *Abbr* **IMA**

investment manager *Fin see* **fund manager**

investment portfolio *Fin see* **portfolio**

investment properties *Fin* either commercial buildings (for example, shops, factories, or offices) or residential dwellings (for example, houses or apartments) that are purchased by businesses or individuals for renting to third parties

investment revaluation reserve *Fin* in the United Kingdom, the capital reserve where changes in the value of a business's investment properties when they are revalued are disclosed

investment tax credit (*US*) *Fin* a tax advantage for investment, available until 1986 in the United States

investment trust *Fin* an association of investors that invests in securities

investomer *Fin* a customer of a business who is also an investor (*slang*)

investor *Fin* a person or organisation that invests money in something, especially in shares of publicly owned corporations

investor relations research *Mkting* research carried out on behalf of an organisation in order to gain an understanding of how financial markets regard the organisation, its shares, and its sector

---

Investors in People *HR* a national programme in the United Kingdom for *employee development*. Investors in People is a UK government initiative in which organisations that meet the required standards are awarded the status of 'Investor in People'. The goal of the programme is to encourage organisations in all sectors to develop their staff in order to better achieve organisational objectives. Criteria are based on established best practice, and an organisation is assessed for evidence that it is actively developing the skills of its employees.

invisible asset *Fin see* **intangible asset**

invisible exports *Econ* the profits, dividends, interest, and royalties received from selling a country's services abroad

invisible imports *Econ* the profits, dividends, interest, and royalties paid to foreign service companies based in a country

invisibles *Econ* items such as financial and leisure services, as opposed to physical goods, that are traded by a country

invisible trade *Econ* trade in items such as financial and other services that are listed in the current account of the balance of payments

invitation to tender *Gen Mgt* a formal statement of requirements sent to short-listed suppliers, inviting the submission of a formal proposal for completing a particular piece of work. An invitation to tender should provide background information on the organisation and identify the key areas that suppliers need to address such as functionality and operating requirements. A timetable for the tendering process should also be included.

invoice *Fin* a document prepared by a supplier showing the description, quantities, prices, and values of goods delivered or services rendered. To the supplier this is a sales invoice; to the purchaser the same document is a purchase invoice.

invoice date *Fin* the date on which an invoice is issued. The invoice date may be different from the delivery date.

invoice discounting *Fin* the selling of invoices at a discount for collection by the buyer

invoicing *Fin* the process of issuing invoices

involuntary liquidation preference *Fin* a payment that a company must make to holders of its preference shares if it is forced to sell its assets when facing bankruptcy

inward investment *Fin* investment by a government or company in its own country or region, often to stimulate employment or develop a business infrastructure

IOSCO *abbr Fin* International Organization of Securities Commissions

IOU *Fin* a rendition in letters of 'I owe you' that can be used as legal evidence of a debt, although it is most commonly used by an individual as a reminder that small change has been taken, for example, from a float

IOW *abbr Gen Mgt* in other words (*slang*)

IP *E-com see* **Internet**

IP address *E-com* Internet protocol address, an identifier for a computer or other Internet-enabled device on the Internet and other *TCP/IP* networks. The format of an IP address is a numeric address written as four groups of numbers separated by dots. For example, 1.542.20.350 could be an IP address.

IPO *abbr Fin* initial public offering

IRA *abbr* (*US*) *Fin* individual retirement account: a pension plan, designed for individuals without a company pension scheme, that allows annual sums, subject to limits dependent upon employment income, to be set aside from earnings tax-free. Individuals with a company pension may invest in an IRA, but only from their net income. IRAs, including the Education IRA, designed as a way of saving for children's education, may invest in almost any financial security except property.

IRCA *HR see* **Industrial Relations Court of Australia**

IRD (*ANZ*) *Fin see* **Inland Revenue Department**

IRD number (*ANZ*) *Fin* a numeric code assigned to all members of the New Zealand workforce for the purpose of paying income tax

IRL *abbr Gen Mgt* in real life (*slang*)

IRR *abbr Fin* internal rate of return

irrevocable letter of credit *Fin see* **letter of credit**

irritainment *Gen Mgt* television programmes or other forms of entertainment that are irritating but nevertheless compulsive viewing (*slang*)

IRS *abbr Fin* Internal Revenue Service: in the United States, the branch of the federal government charged with collecting the majority of federal taxes

ISA *abbr Fin* Individual Savings Account: a portfolio created according to rules that exempt its proceeds, including dividends and capital gains, from taxes. It was launched in 1999 with the intention that it would be available for at least ten years. Individuals may invest up to £7,000 each year, £3,000 of which may be invested in a savings account and £1,000 in life assurance. Either the remaining £3,000, or the entire £7,000, may be invested in the stock market. A 'maxi' ISA is an investment of up to the maximum amount, whether divided or entirely in the stock market, that has been purchased from one provider only. A 'mini' ISA is one of the three individual components which may be purchased from different providers. Investors may therefore have up to three 'minis', but only one 'maxi'.

ISC (*ANZ*) *Gen Mgt see* **Insurance and Superannuation Commission**

ISDN *abbr E-com* Integrated Services Digital Network: a digital telephone network supporting advanced communications services and used for high-speed data transmission

Ishikawa, Kaoru (1915–89) *Gen Mgt* Japanese academic. Originator of *fishbone charts* and champion of other *quality control* tools such as *Pareto charts*, as explained in *Guide to Quality Control* (1976).

Ishikawa diagram *Gen Mgt see* *fishbone chart*

ISMA *abbr Fin* International Securities Market Association

ISO *abbr* **1.** *E-com* independent service organisation: a company that processes online credit card transactions for small businesses, usually in exchange for a fee or percentage of sales **2.** *Gen Mgt* International Standards Organisation: an organisation responsible for determining and managing common standards for products and for business and manufacturing processes

ISO 14000 *Gen Mgt* a series of internationally recognised *quality standards* providing a framework that organisations can use to regulate the environmental impact of their activities. ISO 14000 is a management system standard rather than a performance standard and can be applied to organisations of all shapes and sizes, wherever they may be located. The standard does not identify specific goals but presents a framework for carrying out environmental management. **ISO 14001** is the part of the standard that specifies the requirements that organisations must

meet if they are to obtain certification. ISO 14001 gives a framework for identifying operations, processes, and products that impact on the environment, for evaluating these impacts, for setting objectives and targets for reducing any negative impacts that have been identified, and for implementing activities to achieve targets. ISO 14000 provides a certified standard that can be seen as a reflection of an organisation's ethical achievements. It pays no attention, however, to cultural or human dimensions and disregards the fact that organisations will need to perceive bottom-line cost benefits if they are to implement the standard.

ISO 14001 *Gen Mgt see* *ISO 14000*

ISO 9000 *Fin* a quality system standard which requires complying organisations to operate in accordance with a structure of written policies and procedures that are designed to ensure the consistent delivery of a product or service to meet customer requirements

ISP *abbr E-com* Internet service provider: a company or organisation that not only provides an entry point to the Internet, like an *Internet access provider*, but also additional services such as website hosting and web-page development

issuance costs *Fin* the underwriting, legal, and administrative fees required to issue a debt. These fees are significant when issuing debt in the public markets, such as bonds. However, other types of debt, such as private placements or bank loans, are cheaper to issue because they require less underwriting, legal, and administrative support.

issue *Fin* a set of stocks or bonds that a company offers for sale at one time

issue by tender *Fin see* *sale by tender*

Issue Department *Fin* the department of the Bank of England that is responsible for issuing currency

issued share capital *Fin* the type, class, number, and amount of the shares held by shareholders

issued shares *Fin* those shares that comprise a company's authorised capital that has been distributed to investors. They may be either fully paid or partly paid shares.

issue price *Fin* the price at which securities are first offered for sale

issuer *E-com* a financial institution that issues payment cards such as credit or debit

---

cards, pays out to the merchant's account, and bills the customer or debits the customer's account. The issuer guarantees payment for authorised transactions using the payment card. *Also known as* **card-issuing bank**, **issuing bank**

issuer bid *Fin* an offer made by an issuer for its own securities when it is disappointed by the offers of others

issues management *Gen Mgt* the anticipation and assessment of key trends and themes of the next decade, and the relation of these to the organisation. Issues management is informed by *futures research* in order to formulate strategic plans and actions.

issuing bank *E-com see* **issuer**

issuing house *Fin* in the United Kingdom, a financial institution that specialises in the flotation of private companies. *See also* **investment bank**, **merchant bank**

itchy finger syndrome *E-com* the Internet user's need for interactivity. Sites can combat this by adding interactive elements such as *hyperlinks* and online *forums*.

item non-response *Stats* a refusal to respond to a question in a statistical survey or a response that cannot be fitted into the given response design

Japanese management *Gen Mgt, HR* a *management style* with particular emphasis on employees and manufacturing techniques, to which the Japanese economic miracle that began in the 1960s is attributed. Japanese management practices have been studied in the rest of the world in the hope that the economic success they brought to Japan can be recreated elsewhere. These practices emphasise forming collaborations, particularly in times of uncertainty, human resources, closer superior-subordinate relationships, and consensus as a means of facilitating implementation. *Richard Pascale* and *Anthony Athos* suggested that the Japanese *competitive advantage* stemmed from skills, staff, and superordinate goals, the softer features identified by the *McKinsey 7-S framework*. Other dominant characteristics include people-centred management, loyalty to employees, *just-in-time*, *kaizen*, *continuous improvement*, *quality control*, *total quality management*, and the ideas of *W. Edwards Deming*. *William Ouchi* expounded *Theory J* and *Theory Z*, which demonstrated the differences between US and Japanese styles of management. With the downturn in the Japanese economy in the 1990s, management practices were reappraised, and there emerged a focus on radical change as opposed to incremental improvement. Customers were offered less variety, there was a shift towards simplicity, and an alternative to consensus-based decision-making was adopted, with individuals making decisions based on high-tech information systems.

Japanese payment option *E-com* a series of extensions to the *SET* protocol to facilitate handling features unique to the Japanese market. *Abbr* **JPO**

Jaques, Elliot (*b.* 1917) *Gen Mgt* Canadian psychologist and writer. Best known for his participation in the *Glacier studies*, and for originating the *time span of discretion* theory.

Java *E-com* a programming language developed in the mid-1990s to enhance the visual appearance and interactive elements of web documents. Java is automatically translated using a Java-compatible web browser. For example, an Internet user can connect to a Java *applet* on the Web, download it, and run it, all at the click of a mouse.

jelly
like nailing jelly to a tree *Gen Mgt* used for describing a task that is considered impossible, especially when the difficulty arises from poor or sloppy specifications (*slang*)

JEPI *abbr E-com* joint electronic payment initiative

jikan *Fin* in Japan, the priority rule relating to transactions on the Tokyo Stock Exchange whereby the earlier of two buy or sell orders received at the same price prevails

JIT *abbr Ops* just-in-time

job 1. *HR* a position of employment **2.** *Ops* a batch of work that undergoes a specific action through a workstation or workshop

jobber's turn *Fin* formerly, a term used on the London Stock Exchange for a *spread*

jobbing *Ops see* **job production**

jobbing backwards *Fin* a UK term for the analysis of an investment transaction with a view to learning from mistakes rather than apportioning blame

job card *Fin see* **clock card**

job classification *HR* the listing of jobs in groups according to areas of similarity. The term job classification normally applies to a broad classification of work such as the schemes produced by the Office for National Statistics in the United Kingdom or the International Labour Office in Geneva. At an organisational level, job classification is more usually referred to as **job grading** and is used for *job evaluation* purposes.

job costing *Fin* a form of specific order costing in which costs are attributed to individual jobs

job cost sheet *Fin* a detailed record of the amount, and cost, of the labour, material, and overhead charged to a specific job

job design *HR* the process of putting together various elements to form a job, bearing in mind organisational and individual worker requirements, as well as considerations of health, safety, and *ergonomics*. The *scientific management* approach of *Frederick Winslow Taylor* viewed job design as purely mechanistic, but the later *human relations* movement rediscovered the importance of workers' relationship to their work and stressed the importance of *job satisfaction*.

job enlargement *HR* the addition of extra similar tasks to a job. In job enlargement, the job itself remains essentially unchanged, the employee rarely needs to acquire new skills to carry out the additional task, and the motivational benefits of job enrichment are not experienced. Job enlargement is sometimes viewed by employees as a requirement to carry out more work for the same amount of pay.

job evaluation *HR* a technique that aims to provide a systematic, rational, and consistent approach to defining the relative worth of jobs within an organisation. Job evaluation is a system for analysing and comparing different jobs and placing them in a ranking order according to the overall demands of each one. It is not concerned with the volume of work, or with the person doing it, or with determining pay. It is used in order to provide the basis for an equitable and defensible pay structure, particularly in determining *equal pay* for equal value. Job evaluation schemes can be divided into two main categories: non-analytical and analytical. In non-analytical schemes a job is compared with others as a whole, but such schemes have a limited use, because they are unlikely to succeed as a defence against an equal value claim. In an analytical scheme, a job is split up into a number of different aspects and each factor is measured separately. The main types of analytical schemes are factor comparison, point-factor rating, competency-based schemes, and the *profile method*.

job family *HR* a category of jobs in a similar area. Examples of job families might be engineering, agriculture, health, and sport and leisure. Job families are also found within an organisation, for example, clerical, sales, information technology, and so on. Such families are sometimes used when determining *pay scales* or for statistical analysis of the *workforce*.

job grading *HR see* **job classification**

job lock *Gen Mgt* the inability to leave a job because of a fear of losing the benefits associated with it (*slang*)

job lot *Fin* a UK term for a miscellaneous assortment of items, including securities, that are offered as a single deal

job process system *Ops see* **job production**

job production *Ops* the manufacture of different products in unit quantities or in very small numbers. In job production, a complete task may be handled by one worker and is often carried out in a *job shop*. A company may operate under a **job process system**, producing small batches of sometimes unique products and so becoming a job shop in itself. Job production is characterised by a functional grouping of equipment and staff and by the considerable variation in the time it takes to complete a given job. *Also known as* **jobbing**

job rotation *HR* the movement of employees through a range of jobs in order to increase interest and *motivation*. Job rotation can improve *multiskilling* but involves the need for greater *training*.

job satisfaction *HR* the sense of fulfilment and pride felt by people who enjoy their work and do it well. Various factors influence job satisfaction, and our understanding of the significance of these stems in part from *Frederick Herzberg*. He called elements such as remuneration, working relationships, status, and job security ' **hygiene factors**' because they concern the context in which somebody works. Hygiene factors do not in themselves promote job satisfaction, but serve primarily to prevent job dissatisfaction. **Motivators** contribute to job satisfaction and include achievement, recognition, the work itself, responsibility, advancement, and growth. An absence of job satisfaction can lead to poor *motivation*, *stress*, *absenteeism*, and high labour turnover.

job-share *HR* a form of employment in which two or more people occupy a single job. Each person works on a part-time basis and is paid pro-rata for the number of hours they work in the job.

job shop *Ops* a manufacturing facility designed to work on a *job production* basis, producing small quantities of what are often specialised or expensive items. A job shop can be a special facility within a factory, or a whole company can be run as a job shop. Job shops often have the ability to produce a wide variety of products.

job vacuum *Gen Mgt* an employee who voluntarily takes on extra duties (*slang*)

Johari window *HR* a *communication* model that facilitates analysis of both how someone gives and receives information and the dynamics of *interpersonal communication*. The Johari window was developed by Joseph Luft and Henry Ingram. It is normally represented in the form of a grid divided into four sections, each of which represents a type of communication exchange. First, there is the open self: you have awareness of the impact you have on the other and the impact they have on you, so that the risk of interpersonal conflict is minimised. The second sector covers the hidden self: you have awareness of your impact on others, but not of their impact on you. This leads to defensive behaviour in which you seek to hide what you want and increases the possibility of interpersonal conflict. In the third sector, or blind self, you have awareness of what the other wants, but you lack self-awareness of the impact of your communication or actions. Finally, there is the undiscovered self: you lack self-awareness and are either unaware of or cannot understand the other. Although the Johari window can be used in a number of situations, it is most frequently used as a tool for *training* or *coaching* purposes, in order to provide feedback on communication skills.

Johnson, Spencer *Gen Mgt* US writer and consultant. Collaborated with **Kenneth Blanchard** on the concept of one-minute management, but is also known for *Who Moved My Cheese?* (1998), a parable on *change management*.

joined-up *Gen Mgt* relating to an idea or initiative that involves both the community and government in an effort to improve the quality of life for everyone (*slang*)

joint account *Fin* an account, for example one held at a bank or by a broker, that two or more people own in common and have access to

joint and several liability *Fin* a legal liability that applies to a group of individuals as a whole and each member individually, so that if one member does not meet his or her liability, the shortfall is the shared responsibility of the others. Most guarantees given by two or more individuals to secure borrowing are joint and several. It is a typical feature of most partnership agreements.

joint cost *Fin* the cost of a process which results in more than one main product

joint electronic payment initiative *E-com* a proposed industry standard protocol for electronic payment in e-commerce transactions. *Abbr* **JEPI**

joint float *Econ* a situation in which a group of currencies maintains a fixed relationship relative to each other but moves jointly relative to another currency

joint life annuity *Fin* an annuity that continues until both parties have died. They are attractive to married couples as they ensure

that the survivor has an income for the rest of his or her life.

joint ownership *Gen Mgt* ownership by more than one party, each with equal rights in the item owned. Joint ownership is often applied to property or other assets.

Joint Photographics Experts Group *E-com* see *JPEG*

joint products *Fin* two or more products produced by the same process and separated in processing, each having a sufficiently high saleable value to merit recognition as a main product. *See also* **by-product**

joint return *Fin* a tax return filed jointly by a husband and a wife

joint stock bank *Fin* a term that was formerly used for a commercial bank (one that is a partnership), rather than a High Street bank (one that is a public limited company)

joint venture *Fin* a project undertaken by two or more persons/entities joining together with a view to profit, often in connection with a single operation

journal *Fin* a record of original entry, into which transactions are normally transferred from source documents. The journal may be subdivided into: sales journal/day book for credit sales; purchases journal/day book for credit purchases; cash book for cash receipts and payments; and the journal proper for transactions which could not appropriately be recorded in any of the other journals.

JPEG *E-com* Joint Photographics Experts Group: a file format used to compress and store photographic images for transfer over the Internet. *See also* **GIF**

JPO *abbr E-com* Japanese payment option

JSE *abbr Fin* Johannesburg Stock Exchange: the former unofficial name of the JSE Securities Exchange

judgment creditor *Fin* in a legal action, the individual or business who has brought the action and to whom the court orders the judgment debtor to pay the money owed. In the event of the judgment debtor not conforming to the court order, the judgment creditor must return to the court to request that the judgment be enforced.

judgment debtor *Fin* in a legal action, the individual or business ordered to pay the judgment creditor the money owed

jumbo mortgage (*US*) *Fin* a mortgage that is too large to qualify for favourable treatment by a US government agency

---

The market, whether stock, bond, or super, is a barometer of civilisation.   *Jason Alexander*

junior debt *Fin* a debt that has no claim on a debtor's assets, or less claim than another debt. *See also* **senior debt**. *Also known as* **subordinated debt**

junior mortgage *Fin* a mortgage whose holder has less claim on a debtor's assets than the holder of another mortgage. *See also* **senior mortgage**

junk bond *Fin* a bond with high return and high risk

Juran, Joseph Moses (*b*. 1904) *Gen Mgt* Romanian-born engineer and consultant. Introduced ideas on *total quality management* to Japan and later, like **W. Edwards Deming**, to the West. Juran's methods, first published in *Quality Control Handbook* (1951), centre on building a customer-focused organisation through planning, control and improvement, and good people management. Juran trained as an electrical engineer, worked for Western Electric in the 1920s, becoming quality manager at their Chicago plant, and later went to work for AT&T. In 1953, he made his first visit to Japan, where he spent two months observing Japanese practices and training managers and engineers in what he called managing for quality. For the next quarter of a century, Juran continued to give seminars on the subject of quality throughout the world. In 1979 he founded the Juran Institute to spread and facilitate the implementation of quality-management programmes worldwide.

just-in-time *Ops* a system whose objective is to produce or to procure products or components as they are required by a customer or for use, rather than for stock. A just-in-time system is a *pull system*, which responds to demand, in contrast to a *push system*, in which stocks act as buffers between the different elements of the system, such as purchasing, production, and sales. *Abbr* **JIT**

just-in-time production *Fin* a production system which is driven by demand for finished products, whereby each component on a production line is produced only when needed for the next stage

just-in-time purchasing *Fin* a purchasing system in which material purchases are contracted so that the receipt and usage of material coincide to the maximum extent possible

K *abbr Fin* a thousand

kaizen *Gen Mgt, Ops* the Japanese term for the **continuous improvement** of current processes. Kaizen is derived from the words 'kai', meaning 'change', and 'zen', meaning 'good' or 'for the better'. It is a philosophy that can be applied to any area of life, but its application has been most famously developed at the Toyota Motor Company, and it underlies the philosophy of **total quality management**. Under kaizen, continuous improvement can mean waste elimination, innovation, or working to new standards. The kaizen process makes use of a range of techniques, including small-group **problem-solving**, **suggestion schemes**, statistical techniques, **brainstorming**, and **work study**. Although kaizen forms only part of a strategy of continuous improvement, for many employees it is the element that most closely affects them and is therefore synonymous with continuous improvement.

kaizen budget *Fin* a budget into which is incorporated the expectation of continuous performance improvement throughout the budget period

kakaku yusen *Fin* in Japan, the price priority system operated on the Tokyo Stock Exchange whereby a lower price takes precedence over a higher price for a sell order, and vice versa for a buy order. *See also* **jikan**

kanban *Ops* a Japanese production management technique that uses cards attached to components to monitor and control workflow in a factory. The kanban system was first developed by the car manufacturer Toyota.

kanbrain *Gen Mgt* relating to the technology that is used in the transmission of knowledge (*slang*)

kangaroo *Fin* an Australian share traded on the London Stock Exchange (*slang*)

Kansas City Board of Trade *Fin* a commodities exchange, established in 1856, that specialises in futures and options contracts for red winter wheat, the Value Line® Index, natural gas, and the ISDEX® Internet Stock Index

Kanter, Rosabeth Moss (*b*. 1943) *Gen Mgt* US academic. Known for her interest in new **organisation structures**, with a focus on harnessing **change**, encouraging **innovation**, and increasing **empowerment** among employees.

Her research has also embraced **globalisation**. Among her many books is *The Change Masters* (1988).

Kaplan, Robert *Gen Mgt* US academic. Co-developer, with **David Norton**, of the **balanced scorecard**, which looks at intangible assets such as **customer satisfaction** alongside traditional financial measures. This concept, introduced in a *Harvard Business Review* article of 1992 with the saying 'What you measure is what you get', was explained in *The Balanced Scorecard* (1996).

KBG *Gen Mgt, Ops see* **keiretsu**

Keidanren *Fin* the Japanese abbreviation for the Japan Federation of Economic Organizations. Established in 1946, it aims to work towards a resolution of the major problems facing the Japanese and international business communities and to contribute to the sound development of their economies. The equivalent of the Confederation of British Industry, its members include over 1,000 of Japan's leading corporations (including over 50 foreign companies) and over 100 industry-wide groups representing such major sectors as manufacturing, trade, distribution, finance, and energy.

keiretsu *or* **keiretsu business group** *Gen Mgt, Ops* a Japanese loose **conglomerate company** that promotes interdependencies between firms with interlocking interests in each other and is characterised by close internal control, policy co-ordination, and cohesiveness. Keiretsu business groups are alliances between firms that share close buyer-supplier relationships. The issue of interlocking shares by group affiliated companies to member companies of the group keeps ownership in friendly hands, helps prevent foreign **takeovers**, and aids a company's long-term survival and growth. There are two sorts of keiretsu operation: **horizontal keiretsu**, in which member firms are involved in different industries, and **vertical keiretsu**, in which member firms in one industry form themselves into a hierarchy with a lead company. Vertical KBGs consist largely of manufacturing companies and their subcontractors. Some keiretsu are 350 years old, but most developed from the pre-war **zaibatsu**. The Korean equivalent of the keiretsu is the **chaebol**, and a Mexican equivalent is the **grupo**. *Abbr* **KBG**

Making a success of the job at hand is the best step toward the kind you want.   *Bernard Baruch*

Keough Plan *Fin* a pension subject to tax advantage in the United States for somebody who is self-employed or has an interest in a small company. *See also* **stakeholder pension**

Kepner, Charles Higgins (*b*. 1922) *Gen Mgt* US manager and consultant. Originator with **Benjamin Tregoe** of a methodological approach to **decision-making** based on information gathering, organisation, and analysis, which was first explained in *The Rational Manager* (1965).

kerb market *Fin* a stock market that exists outside the stock exchange. The term originates from markets held in the street.

Kets de Vries, Manfred Florian Robert (*b*. 1942) *Gen Mgt* Dutch psychoanalyst and academic. His principal academic interests focus on the interface between psychoanalysis/ dynamic psychiatry and **management, leadership, entrepreneurship**, and **family business**.

key account management *Mkting* the management of the customer relationships that are most important to a company. Key accounts are those held by customers who produce most **profit** for a company or have the potential to do so, or those who are of strategic importance. Development of these **customer relations** and **customer retention** is important to business success. Particular emphasis is placed on analysing which accounts are key to a company at any one time, determining the needs of these particular customers, and implementing procedures to ensure that they receive premium **customer service** and to increase **customer satisfaction**.

keyboard plaque *Gen Mgt* the build-up of dirt that becomes ingrained in computer keyboards (*slang*)

key factor *Fin see* **limiting factor**

key-man insurance *Gen Mgt see* **key-person insurance**

Keynesian economics *Econ* the economic teachings and doctrines associated with John Maynard Keynes

key-person insurance *Gen Mgt* an insurance policy taken out to cover the costs of replacing a key **employee**. Key-person insurance comes into play in the case of an employee's medium- to long-term illness or death. *Also known as* **key-man insurance**

keyword *E-com* a word used by a search engine to help locate and register a website. Companies need to think very carefully about the keywords they place in their **meta-tags** and in web pages in order to attract relevant search-engine traffic.

keyword search *E-com* a search for documents containing one or more words that are specified by a search-engine user

kiasu *Gen Mgt* a Hokkien word, used to describe the 'must win, never lose' mentality of Singaporeans

kickback *Fin* a sum of money paid illegally in order to gain concessions or favours (*slang*)

kicker *Fin* an addition to a standard security that makes it more attractive, for example, options and warrants (*slang*) *See also* **bells and whistles** (*sense 2*), **sweetener** (*sense 3*)

killer app *E-com* a computer application that is extremely effective or commercially successful

killerbee *Fin* somebody, especially a banker, who helps a company avoid being taken over

killfile *E-com* a list on an Internet newsreader of undesirable authors or threads that can be filtered out by the user (*slang*)

killing *Fin* a considerable profit on a transaction (*slang*)

Kim, W. Chan *Gen Mgt* Korean-born academic. INSEAD professor, Fellow of the World Economic Forum, writer on the knowledge economy and collaborator with **Renée Mauborgne** on research into **corporate strategy** and **value innovation**.

kimono
open the kimono *Gen Mgt* to inspect something that has not been open for examination before, especially a company's accounts (*slang*)

KISS *abbr Gen Mgt* keep it simple stupid (*slang*)

kiss up to sb (*US*) *Gen Mgt* to attempt to ingratiate yourself with somebody who is in a position of power (*slang*)

kite *Fin* a fraudulent financial transaction, for example, a bad cheque that is dated to take advantage of the time interval required for clearing
fly a kite 1. *Fin* to use a fraudulent financial document such as a bad cheque **2.** *Gen Mgt* to make a suggestion in order to test people's opinion of it

kite-flying *Fin* in the United States, a preliminary or pathfinder prospectus (*slang*)

---

kiwibond *Fin* a eurobond denominated in New Zealand dollars

knight *Fin* a term borrowed from chess strategy to describe a company involved in the politics of a *takeover* bid. There are three main types of knight. A **white knight** is a company that is friendly to the board of the company to be acquired. If the white knight gains control, it may retain the existing *board of directors*. A **black knight** is a former white knight that has disagreed with the board of the company to be acquired and has set up its own hostile bid. A **grey knight** is a white knight that does not have the confidence of the company to be acquired.

Knight, Phil (*b.* 1938) *Gen Mgt* US entrepreneur. Founder of Nike Inc, whose worldwide success is based on strong *brand building*, aggressive marketing, and the *outsourcing* of production to Asia.

knock-for-knock *Fin* used to describe a practice between insurance companies whereby each will pay for the repairs to the vehicle it insures in the event of an accident

knocking copy *Gen Mgt* advertising copy that consists of criticism of a competitor's product or company

knock-out option *Fin* an option to which a condition relating to the underlying security or commodity's present price is attached so that it effectively expires when it goes out of the money

knowledge *Gen Mgt* information acquired by the interpretation of experience. Knowledge is built up from interaction with the world and organised and stored in each individual's mind. It is also stored on an organisational level within the minds of employees and in paper and electronic records. Two forms of knowledge can be distinguished: **tacit knowledge** or **implicit knowledge**, which is held in a person's mind and is instinctively known without being formulated into words; and **explicit knowledge**, which has been communicated to others and is contained in written documents and procedures. Organisations are increasingly recognising the value of knowledge, and many employees are now recognised as *knowledge workers*. A major writer in this area is *Ikujiro Nonaka*,

co-author of *The Knowledge-creating Company* (1995), who asserted that knowledge is the greatest core capability (see *core competence*) that an organisation can have.

knowledge-based system *E-com* a specialised search facility on a website that enables a user to type in a question, rather than using keywords, or choosing from a list of frequently asked questions *FAQ*s. The response may involve the user being asked a series of questions in order to narrow down the area of interest. The Ask Jeeves website, www.askjeeves.com, is an example of this approach.

knowledge capital *Gen Mgt* knowledge that a company possesses and can put to profitable use

knowledge management *Gen Mgt* **1.** the process of acquiring, storing, distributing and using information within a company. The information is generally held on a powerful database and distributed via a communications network. **2.** the co-ordination and exploitation of an organisation's *knowledge* resources, in order to create benefit and *competitive advantage*

knowledge worker *Gen Mgt* an *employee* who deals in information, ideas, and expertise. Knowledge workers are products of the so-called information age, in which the emphasis is on *creativity* and *innovation* rather than on maintaining the status quo. According to *Peter Drucker*, in the new economy every employee is becoming a knowledge worker.

Kolb, David (*b.* 1939) *Gen Mgt* US academic. Originator of the concept of *experiential learning*, a model describing how adults learn, which he explained in the book of the same name (1984).

Kotler, Philip (*b.* 1931) *Gen Mgt* US academic. Acknowledged as an expert in **marketing** theory, which he has made a major business function and academic discipline, and which he explained in *Marketing Management* (first published 1980).

Krugerrand *Fin* a South African coin consisting of one ounce of gold, first minted in 1967, bearing the portrait of Paul Kruger on the obverse

laboratory training *Gen Mgt see* ***sensitivity training***

labor union *(US) Gen Mgt, HR* = ***trade union***

labour dispute *HR* **1.** a disagreement or conflict between an ***employer*** and ***employees*** or between the ***employers' association*** and ***trade union*** **2.** *see* ***strike***

labour force *HR* people of working age who are available for paid employment, including the unemployed looking for work, but excluding categories such as full-time students, carers, and the long-term sick and disabled

labour force survey *Stats* a survey carried out every quarter in the United Kingdom, covering such topics as unemployment and hours of work

labour-intensive *Fin* involving large numbers of workers or high labour costs

labour market *HR* a market that brings together employers and people who are looking for employment

labour shortage *HR* **1.** a lack of workers or potential workers to fill the jobs available **2.** a lack of suitably qualified and skilled workers to fill particular vacancies. This is more correctly described as a ***skills shortage***.

labour tourist *HR* somebody who lives in one country but works in another *(slang)*

Lady Macbeth strategy *Gen Mgt* a change of approach on the part of a presumed **white knight**, in which it becomes a black knight. A Lady Macbeth strategy is usually associated with ***takeover*** battles and has connotations of treachery.

laggard *Mkting see* ***first mover***

lagging indicator *(US) Econ* a measurable economic factor, for example, corporate profits or unemployment, that changes after the economy has already moved to a new trend, which it can confirm but not predict

LAN *E-com see* ***network***

land bank *Fin* the land that a builder or developer has that is available for development

land banking *(US) Fin* the practice of buying land that is not needed immediately, but with the expectation of using it in the future

land tax *Fin* a form of wealth tax imposed in Australia on the value of residential land. The level and conditions of the tax vary from state to state.

lapping *(US) Fin* = ***teeming and lading***

lapse *Fin* the termination of an option without trade in the underlying security or commodity

lapse rights *Fin* rights, such as those to a specified premium, owned by the person who allows an offer to lapse

large-sized business *Gen Mgt* an organisation that has grown beyond the limits of a ***medium-sized business*** and has 500 or more employees. It is usually from the ranks of large-sized businesses that ***multinational businesses*** arise.

last-in first-out *HR see* ***LIFO***

last survivor policy *Fin* an assurance policy covering the lives of two or more people. The sum assured is not paid out until all the policyholders are deceased. *See also* ***joint life annuity***

latent market *Mkting* a group of people who have been identified as potential consumers of a product that does not yet exist

lateral thinking *Gen Mgt* a creative method of problem-solving that ignores traditional logic and approaches problems from unorthodox perspectives. Lateral thinking was developed by ***Edward de Bono***, who distinguished two forms of thinking: vertical thinking, which is based on logic; and lateral thinking, which disregards apparently rational trains of thought and branches out at tangents. Lateral thinking involves the examination of a problem and its possible solutions from all angles. Seemingly intractable problems often can be solved in this manner, and it is a technique used in ***brainstorming***, or to help generate ***creativity*** and ***innovation*** within organisations.

launch *Mkting* the process of introducing a new product to the market

laundering *Fin* the process of making money obtained illegally appear legitimate by passing it through banks or businesses

law of diminishing returns *Gen Mgt* a rule stating that as one factor of production is increased, while others remain constant, the extra output generated by the additional input will eventually fall. The law of diminishing returns therefore means that extra workers, extra capital, extra machinery, or extra land may not necessarily raise output as much as expected. For example, increasing the supply of raw materials to a production line may allow additional output to be produced by using any spare capacity workers have. Once this capacity is fully used, however, continually increasing the amount of raw material without a corresponding increase in the number of workers will not result in an increase of output.

law of supply and demand *Gen Mgt see* **supply and demand**

lay-by *(ANZ) Gen Mgt* the reservation of an article for purchase by the payment of an initial deposit followed by regular interest-free instalments, on completion of which the article is claimed by the buyer

lay off *HR* **1.** to dismiss workers permanently **2.** to suspend workers temporarily because of lack of work

layoff *(US) Gen Mgt* = **redundancy**

layout by function *Ops see* **process layout**

LBO *abbr Fin* leveraged buyout

LCH *abbr Fin* London Clearing House

LCM *abbr Fin* lower of cost or market

LDC *abbr Econ* less developed country

lead *Fin* in an insurance policy from Lloyd's, the first named underwriting syndicate

leader **1.** *Gen Mgt, HR* a business executive who possesses exceptional leadership qualities as well as management skills **2.** *Mkting* the most successful product or company in a marketplace

leadership *Gen Mgt, HR* the capacity to establish direction and to influence and align others towards a common aim, motivating and committing them to action and making them responsible for their performance. Leadership theory is one of the most discussed areas of management, and many different approaches are taken to the topic. Some notions of leadership are related to types of *authority* delineated by *Max Weber*. It is often suggested that leaders possess innate personal qualities that distinguish them from others: *great man theory* and *trait theory* express this idea. Other theories, such as *Behaviourist Theories of Leadership*, suggest that leadership is defined by action and behaviour, rather than by personality. A related idea is that leadership style is not fixed but should be adapted to different situations, and this is explored in *contingency theory* and situational theory. A further branch of research that examines relationships between leaders and followers is found in *transactional*, *transformational*, *attribution*, and *power and influence theories of leadership*. Perhaps the most simple model of leadership is *action-centred leadership*, which focuses on what an effective leader actually does. These many approaches and differences of opinion illustrate the complexity of the leadership role and the intangibility of the essence of good leadership.

leading economic indicator *Econ* a factor such as private-sector wages that is used as a reference for public-sector wage claims

leading-edge *Gen Mgt* situated at the forefront of *innovation*. A leading-edge company is ahead of others in such areas as inventing or implementing new technologies, and in entering new markets.

lead manager *Fin* the financial institution with overall responsibility for a new issue including its co-ordination, distribution, and related administration

lead partner *Gen Mgt* the organisation that takes the lead role in an alliance

leads and lags *Fin* in businesses that deal in foreign currencies, the practice of speeding up the receipt of payments (leads) if a currency is going to weaken, and slowing down the payment of costs (lags) if a currency is thought to be about to strengthen, in order to maximise gains and reduce losses

lead time *Ops* **1.** in inventory control, the time between placing an order and its arrival on site. Lead time differs from delivery time in that it also includes the time required to place an order and the time it takes to inspect the goods and receive them into the appropriate store. Inventory levels can afford to be lower and orders smaller when purchasing lead times are short. **2.** in *new product development* and manufacturing, the time required to develop a product from concept to market delivery. Lead time increases as a result of the poor sequencing of dependent activities, the lack of availability of resources, poor quality in the component parts, and poor plant layout. The technique of *concurrent engineering* focuses on the entire concept-to-customer process with the aim of reducing lead time. Companies can gain a *competitive advantage*

A debt may get mouldy, but it never decays. *Chinua Achebe* by achieving a lead-time reduction and so getting products to market faster. *Also known as cycle time*

lead underwriter *(US) Fin* = *lead manager*

leaky reply *E-com* an e-mail response that is accidentally sent to the wrong recipient and causes embarrassment to the sender *(slang)*

lean enterprise *Ops* an organisational model that strategically applies the key ideas behind *lean production*. The concept of the lean enterprise was proposed by J.P. Womack and D.T. Jones in their 1994 *Harvard Business Review* article 'From lean production to the lean enterprise'. They view the lean enterprise as a group of separate individuals, functions, or organisations that operate as one entity. The aim is to apply lean techniques that create individual breakthroughs in companies and to link these up and down the *supply chain* to form a continuous value stream to raise the whole chain to a higher level.

lean manufacturing *Ops see lean production*

lean operation *Ops see lean production*

lean production *Ops* a methodology aimed at reducing waste in the form of overproduction, excessive *lead time*, or product defects in order to make a business more effective and more competitive. Lean production originates in the production systems established by Toyota in Japan in the 1950s. In the early 1980s there was a significant increase in the application of lean production in Western companies. Lean production is characterised by **lean operations** with low *inventories*, *quality management* through prevention of errors, small batch runs, *just-in-time* production, high commitment human resource policies, team-based working, and close relations with suppliers. The term lean production was popularised by researchers on the International Motor Vehicle Program of the Massachusetts Institute of Technology in their book *The Machine that Changed the World*. Concepts that can help an organisation move towards lean production include *continuous improvement* and *world class manufacturing*. *Also known as lean manufacturing*

LEAPS *Fin* long-term equity anticipation securities, options that expire between one and three years in the future

learning by doing *Gen Mgt* the acquisition of knowledge or skills through direct experience of carrying out a task. Learning by doing often happens under supervision, as part of a training or *induction* process, and is closely associated with the practical experience picked up by '**sitting with Nellie**'. It is an outcome of the research into learning of **David Kolb** and **Reg Revans**. A more formalised approach to learning by doing is *experiential learning*.

learning curve *Gen Mgt* **1.** a graphic representation of the acquisition of knowledge or experience over time. A steep learning curve reflects a substantial amount of learning in a short time, and a shallow curve reflects a slower learning process. The curve eventually levels out to a plateau, during which time the knowledge gained is being consolidated. **2.** the proportional decrease in effort when production is doubled. The learning curve has its origin in *productivity* research in the aeroplane industry of the 1930s, when **T.P. Wright** discovered that in assembling an aircraft, the time and effort decreased by 20% each time the cumulative number of planes produced doubled. **Bruce Henderson** of the Boston Consulting Group formulated the learning curve as a strategic planning device in the 1960s by plotting product costs against cumulative volume.

learning organisation *Gen Mgt* an organisational model characterised by a *flat* structure and *customer-focused* teams, that engenders the collective ability to develop shared visions by capturing and exploiting employees' willingness, commitment, and curiosity. The concept of the learning organisation was proposed by **Chris Argyris** and **Donald Schön** as part of their work on *organisational learning*, but was brought back to public attention in the 1990s by **Peter Senge**. For Senge, a learning organisation is one with the capacity to shift away from views inherent in a traditional hierarchical organisation, towards the ability of all employees to challenge prevailing thinking and gain a balanced perspective. Senge believes the five major elements of a learning organisation are mental models, personal mastery, *systems thinking*, shared vision, and team learning. Because of the requirement for an open, risk-tolerant culture, which is the opposite of the *corporate culture* of most organisations today, the learning organisation remains, for many, an unattainable ideal.

learning relationship *Gen Mgt* a relationship between a supplier and a customer in which the supplier modifies or customises a product as it learns more about the customer's requirements

learning style *Gen Mgt* the way in which somebody approaches the acquisition of knowledge and skills. Learning styles have been divided into four main types by **Peter Honey** and **Alan Mumford**, in their *Manual of Learning Styles* (1982). The types of learner are: the activist, who likes to get involved in new experiences and enjoys the challenges of change; the theorist, who likes to question assumptions and methodologies and learns best when there is time to explore links between ideas and situations; the pragmatist, who prefers practicality and learns best when there is a link between the subject matter and the job in hand and when he or she can try out what he or she has learned; and the reflector, who likes to take his or her time and think things through, and who learns best from activities where he or she can observe and carry out research. One person can demonstrate more than one learning style, and the category or categories that best describe somebody can be determined through use of a learning styles questionnaire.

leaseback *Fin see* **sale and leaseback**

leave *HR* work time when an employee is paid, but is not required to be at work. Leave takes several forms and includes **holiday** entitlement. The number of days of holiday is agreed in the **contract of employment** and may be dependent on the employee's length of service. It may also take the form of **sick leave**, **compassionate leave**, **garden leave**, **educational leave**, or **maternity** or **paternity leave**.

Leavitt, Harold (*b*. 1922) *Gen Mgt* US psychologist and academic. Researcher with an interest in **organisation behaviour** and psychology, and originator of **Leavitt's Diamond** and author of *Managerial Psychology* (1958).

Leavitt's Diamond *Gen Mgt* a model for analysing management change, developed by **Harold Leavitt**. Leavitt's Diamond is based on the idea that it is rare for any change to occur in isolation. Leavitt sees technology, tasks, people, and the organisational structure in which they function as four interdependent variables, visualised as the four points of a diamond. Change at any one point of the diamond will impact on some or all of the others. Thus, a changed task will necessarily affect the people involved in it, the structure in which they work, and the technology that they use. Failure to manage these interdependencies at critical times of change can create problems. *See also* **change management**

ledger *Fin* a collection of accounts, maintained by transfers from the books of original entry. The ledger may be subdivided as follows: the sales ledger/debtors ledger contains the personal accounts of all customers; the purchases ledger/creditors ledger contains all the personal accounts of suppliers; the private ledger contains accounts relating to the proprietor's interest in the business such as capital and drawings; the general ledger/nominal ledger contains all other accounts relating to assets, expenses, revenue, and liabilities.

legacy system *E-com* an existing computer system that provides a strategic function for a specific part of a business. Inventory management systems, for example, are legacy systems.

legal loophole *Gen Mgt* an area in the law that is insufficiently explicit or comprehensive and allows the law to be circumvented

legal tender *Fin* banknotes and coins that have to be accepted within a given jurisdiction when offered as payment of a debt. *See also* **limited legal tender**

legs *Gen Mgt* a longer-than-usual life for an advertising campaign, film, book, or other short-lived product (*slang*)

lekgotla (*S Africa*) *Gen Mgt see* **bosberaad**

lemon (*slang*) **1.** *Fin* an investment that is performing poorly **2.** *Gen Mgt* a product, especially a car, that is defective in some way

lender of last resort *Fin* a central bank that lends money to banks that cannot borrow elsewhere

length of service *HR* the period in which a person has been continually employed within an organisation, without breaks in the **contract of employment**. Length of service may determine entitlement to employment rights or **fringe benefits**, for example, the amount of annual leave allocated.

less developed country *Econ* a country whose economic development is held back by the lack of natural resources to produce goods demanded on world markets. *Abbr* **LDC**

lessee *Fin* the person who has the use of a leased asset

lessor *Fin* the person who provides the asset being leased

letter of agreement *Gen Mgt* a document that constitutes a simple form of contract

letter of allotment *Fin* a document that says how many shares have been allotted to a shareholder

---

Transformational change requires enormous energy.   Robert H. Miles

letter of comfort *Fin* a letter from a holding company addressed to a bank where one of its subsidiaries wishes to borrow money. The purpose of the letter is to support the subsidiary's application to borrow funds and offer reassurance—although not a guarantee—to the bank that the subsidiary will remain in business for the foreseeable future, often with an undertaking to advise the bank if the subsidiary is likely to be sold. *US term* **letter of moral intent**

letter of credit *Fin* a letter issued by a bank that can be presented to another bank to authorise the issue of credit or money

letter of indemnity *Fin* a statement that a share certificate has been lost, destroyed, or stolen and that the shareholder will indemnify the company for any loss that might result from its reappearance after the company has issued a replacement to the shareholder

letter of intent *Fin* a document in which an individual or organisation indicates an intention to do something, for example, buy a business, grant somebody a loan, or participate in a project. The intention may or may not depend on certain conditions being met and the document is not legally binding. *See also* *letter of comfort*

letter of licence *Fin* a letter from a creditor to a debtor who is having problems repaying money owed, giving the debtor a certain period of time to raise the money and an undertaking not to bring legal proceedings to recover the debt during that period

letter of moral intent (*US*) *Fin* = *letter of comfort*

letter of renunciation *Fin* a form used to transfer an allotment

level playing field *Gen Mgt* a situation in which all competitors are in a position of equal strength or weakness (*slang*)

level production *Gen Mgt see* *production smoothing*

level term assurance *Fin* a life assurance policy in which an agreed lump sum is paid if the policyholder dies before a certain date. A joint form of this life cover is popular with couples who have children.

leverage *Fin* a method of corporate funding in which a higher proportion of funds is raised through borrowing than share issue

leveraged bid *Fin* a takeover bid financed by borrowed money, rather than by an issue of shares

leveraged buyout *Fin* a takeover using borrowed money, with the purchased company's assets as collateral. *Abbr* **LBO**

leveraged required return *Fin* the rate of return from an investment of borrowed money needed to make the investment worthwhile

leverage ratios (*US*) *Fin* = *gearing ratios*

Levitt, Theodore (*b*. 1925) *Gen Mgt* German-born academic. Harvard professor, who wrote the landmark article 'Marketing myopia', *Harvard Business Review* (July/August 1960). In this article, which has sold over 500,000 reprints and genuinely changed basic perceptions of business practice, Levitt argued that the central preoccupation of corporations should be with satisfying their customers, rather than simply producing goods. According to Levitt, production-led thinking inevitably led to narrow perspectives, the ultimate result of which would be that customers would be overlooked.

Lewin, Kurt (1890–1947) *Gen Mgt* German-born social psychologist. Known for studies of *leadership* styles and group *decision-making*, developer of *force field analysis* with a linked *change management* model, pioneer of *action research* and the T-Group (see *sensitivity training*) approach.

Lewin was a professor of philosophy and psychology at Berlin University until 1932 when he fled from the Nazis to the United States. He was professor of child psychology at the Child Welfare Research Station in Iowa until 1944. After leaving Iowa, Lewin worked at MIT, with *Douglas McGregor* among others, founding a research centre for group dynamics.

liability *Fin* a debt that has no claim on a debtor's assets, or less claim than another debt

liability insurance *Fin* insurance against legal liability that the insured might incur, for example, from causing an accident

liability management *Fin* any exercise carried out by a business with the aim of controlling the effect of liabilities on its profitability. This will typically involve controlling the amount of risk undertaken, and ensuring that there is sufficient liquidity and that the best terms are obtained for any funding needs.

To tax and to please is no more given to man than to love and be wise.   **John Simon**

LIBID *abbr Fin* London Inter Bank Bid Rate

LIBOR *abbr Fin* London Inter Bank Offered Rate

licence *Gen Mgt* a contractual arrangement, or a document representing this, in which one organisation gives another the rights to produce, sell, or use something in return for payment

licensing *Mkting* the transfer of rights to manufacture or market a particular product to another individual or organisation through a legal arrangement or contract. Licensing usually requires that a fee, commission, or royalty is paid to the licensor. *See also* **franchise**

licensing agreement *Mkting* an agreement permitting a company to market or produce a product or service owned by another company. A licensing agreement grants a licence in return for a fee or royalty payment. Items licensed for use can include patents, trademarks, techniques, designs, and expertise. This kind of agreement is one way for a company to penetrate overseas markets in that it provides a middle path between direct export and investment overseas.

life annuity *Fin* an annuity that pays a fixed amount per month until the holder's death

life assurance *Fin* insurance that pays a specified sum to the insured person's beneficiaries after the person's death. *US term* **life insurance**. *Also known as* **life cover**

life assured *Fin* the person or persons covered by a life assurance policy. The *life office* pays out on the death of the policyholder.

lifeboat (*S Africa*) *Fin* a low-interest emergency loan made by a central bank to rescue a commercial bank in danger of becoming insolvent

life cover *Fin see* **life assurance**

life cycle *Gen Mgt* the sales pattern of a product or service over a period of time. Typically, a life cycle falls into four stages: introduction, growth, maturity, and decline.

life-cycle costing *Fin* the maintenance of physical asset cost records over the entire life of an asset, so that decisions concerning the acquisition, use, or disposal of the assets can be made in a way that achieves the optimum asset usage at the lowest possible cost to the entity. The term may be applied to the profiling of cost over a product's life, including the pre-production stage (**terotechnology**), and to both company and industry life cycles.

life-cycle savings motive *Econ* the reasons that a household or individual has for saving or spending in the course of life. These can include spending when starting a family or saving when near retirement.

life expectancy *Stats* the number of years that somebody of a given age is expected to live

life insurance (*US*) *Fin* = **life assurance**

lifelong learning *Gen Mgt* the continual acquisition of knowledge and skills throughout somebody's life. Lifelong learning occurs in preparation for, and in response to, the different roles, situations, and environments that somebody will encounter in the course of a lifetime. It is supported by formal and informal education systems, both within and outside the workplace, through which somebody can both learn and receive guidance and encouragement. The adoption of lifelong learning is seen as a key element in *CPD*, and as an important tool in maintaining *employability*.

life office *Fin* a company that provides life assurance

life policy *Fin* a life assurance contract

lifestyle business *Fin* a typically small business run by individuals who have a keen interest in the product or service offered, for example, handmade greetings cards or jewellery, antique dealing or restoring. Such businesses tend to operate during hours that suit the owners, and generally provide them with a comfortable living.

life table *Stats* a table that shows the probabilities of death, survival, and remaining years of life for people of given ages

lifetime customer value *Mkting* a measure or forecast of a customer's total expenditure on an organisation's products over a period of time

lifetime transfer *Fin see* **chargeable transfer**

lifetime value *Gen Mgt* a measure of the total value to a supplier of a customer's business over the duration of their transactions.

In a consumer business, customer lifetime value is calculated by analysing the behaviour of a group of customers who have the same recruitment date. The revenue and cost for this group of customers is recorded, by campaign or season, and the overall contribution for that period can then be worked out. Industry experience has shown that the benefits to

---

Don't worry about people stealing an idea. If it's original, you will have to ram it down their throats.
Howard Aiken

a business of increasing lifetime value can be enormous. A 5% increase in customer retention can create a 125% increase in profits; a 10% increase in retailer retention can translate to a 20% increase in sales; and extending customer life cycles by three years can treble profits per customer.

LIFFE *abbr Fin* London International Financial Futures and Options Exchange

LIFO *abbr HR* last in first out: a technique used when selecting employees for *redundancy*, where the most recent recruits are the first to be made redundant. The LIFO technique has the benefits of reducing redundancy costs and of being seen as fair by some employees. Its disadvantages, however, are increasingly being recognised. It can result in a serious imbalance in the age profile of the workforce and can remove recently acquired skills. It may also be discriminatory, as men are more likely to have built up periods of *continuous service* than women.

lift
let's put it in a lift and see what floor it stops at *Gen Mgt* let's try this idea and see what happens (*slang*)

lightning strike *HR* a *strike* that occurs at very short notice. It may be of short duration and may not be sanctioned by a *trade union*.

light pages *E-com* web pages that are under 50KB in size, enabling them to download quickly

Likert, Rensis (1903–81) *Gen Mgt* US psychologist and academic. Known for situational leadership research and in particular for establishing four systems of management to interpret the way managers behave towards others. In *New Patterns of Management* (1961), Likert described these systems as exploitive/authoritative, benevolent/authoritative, consultative, and participative. He later suggested a system 5 in which the authority of hierarchy disappears.

LIMEAN *abbr Fin* London Inter Bank Mean Rate

limit *Fin* an amount above or below which a broker is not to conclude the purchase or sale of a security for the client who specifies it

limit down *Fin* the most that the price of an option may fall in one day on a particular market

Limited *Fin* used to indicate that a UK company is a limited company when placed at the end of the company's name

limited by guarantee *Fin see* **public limited company**

limited company *Gen Mgt, HR see* **private company**, **public limited company**

limited legal tender *Fin* in some jurisdictions, low denomination notes and all coins that may only be submitted up to a certain sum as legal tender in any one transaction

limited liability *Fin* the restriction of an owner's loss in a business to the amount of capital he or she has invested in it

limited liability company *Fin* a company in which a number of people provide finance in return for shares. The principle of limited liability limits the maximum loss a shareholder can make if the company fails. *US term* **corporation**

limited market *Fin* a market in which dealings for a specific security are difficult to transact, for example, because it has only limited appeal to investors or, in the case of shares, because institutions or family members are unlikely to sell them

limiting factor *Fin* anything which limits the activity of an entity. An entity seeks to optimise the benefit it obtains from the limiting factor. Examples are a shortage of supply of a resource, or a restriction on sales demand at a particular price. *Also known as* **key factor**

limit up *Fin* the most that the price of an option may rise in one day on a particular market

linear programming *Fin* the use of a series of linear equations to construct a mathematical model. The objective is to obtain an optimal solution to a complex operational problem, which may involve the production of a number of products in an environment in which there are many constraints.

line item budget *Fin* the traditional form of budget layout showing, line by line, the costs of a cost object analysed by their nature (salaries, occupancy, maintenance, etc.)

line management *Gen Mgt, HR* a hierarchical *chain of command* from executive to front-line level. Line management is the oldest and least complex management structure, in which top management have total and direct authority and employees report to only one *supervisor*. Managers in this type of *organisation structure* have direct responsibility for giving orders to their subordinates. Line management structures are usually organised along functional lines, although

---

they increasingly undertake cross-functional duties such as *employee development* or strategic direction. The lowest managerial level in an organisation following a line management structure is *supervisory management*.

line manager *HR* an employee's immediate superior, who oversees and has responsibility for the employee's work. A line manager at the lowest level of a large organisation is a *supervisor*, but a manager at any level with direct responsibility for employees' work can be described as a line manager.

line of credit *Fin* an agreed finance facility that allows a company or individual to borrow money. *Also known as* **credit line**

line organisation *Gen Mgt* an *organisation structure* based on *line management*

link *E-com* a pointer to another record, embedded in a document. One or more documents can be connected by inserting links. On the Internet, a link is a reference either to another website or to another document.

linking *E-com* connecting two websites or documents by inserting *links*.

Linking is one of the simplest, yet most effective, Internet marketing devices available. It is like embedded word of mouth: if another website links to yours, it is essentially recommending you to its own visitors. Likewise, it is important to be certain that any other websites that you place links to within your own site are likely to be of interest to your own visitors.

link rot *E-com* the process by which links to websites become obsolete as the websites to which they refer change address or cease to function (*slang*)

liquid asset ratio *Fin* the ratio of liquid assets to total assets

liquid assets *Fin* financial assets that can be quickly converted to cash

liquidated damages *Fin* an amount of money somebody pays for breaching a contract

liquidation *Fin* a process in which a company ceases to be a legal entity, usually because it is insolvent. The company's assets are then sold by a *liquidator* to discharge debts.

liquidation value *Fin* the amount of money that a quick sale of all of a company's assets would yield

liquidator *Fin* the person appointed by a company, its creditors, or its shareholders to sell the assets of an insolvent company. The proceeds of the sale are used to discharge debts to creditors, with any surplus distributed to shareholders.

liquidity *Fin* the ability to convert an asset to cash quickly at its market value

liquidity agreement *Fin* an agreement to allow conversion of an asset into cash

liquidity preference *Econ* a choice made by people to hold their wealth in the form of liquid cash rather than bonds or stocks

liquidity ratio *Fin see* **cash ratio**

liquidity trap *Fin* a central bank's inability to lower interest rates once investors believe rates can go no lower

liquid market *Fin* a market in which an ample number of shares is being traded

list broker *Fin, Gen Mgt* a person or organisation that makes the arrangements for one company to use another company's direct mail list

listed company *Fin* a company whose shares trade on an exchange

listed security *Fin* a security listed on an exchange

listing requirements *Fin* the conditions that have to be met before a security can be traded on a recognised stock exchange. Although exact requirements vary from one exchange to another, the two main ones are that the issuing company's assets should exceed a minimum amount and that the required information about its finances and business should have been published.

list price *Ops* the price of goods or services published by a supplier. The list price of an item may be discounted to regular customers or for bulk purchases.

list renting *Gen Mgt* an arrangement in which a company that owns a direct mail list lets another company use it for a fee

litigation *Gen Mgt* the process of bringing a lawsuit against an individual or organisation

Little Board *Fin* the American Stock Exchange (*slang*). *See also* **Big Board**

live chat *E-com* a facility that enables two or more Web users to communicate with each other in real time, using text.

Live chat is frequently employed in customer support services. This is because one of its main benefits is that a customer does not need to disconnect from the Internet in order to telephone a support line: live chat means they can receive text-based support without having to disconnect. *Also called* **instant messaging**

livery *Mkting* a mark of corporate identity used on a company vehicle

living wage *HR* a level of *pay* that provides just enough income for normal day-to-day subsistence

LME *abbr Fin* London Metal Exchange

load *Fin* an initial charge in some investment funds. *See also* **load fund**

load fund *Fin* a unit trust that charges a fee for the purchase or sale of shares. *See also* **no-load fund**

loading 1. (*ANZ*) *HR* a payment made to workers over and above the basic wage in recognition of special skills or unfavourable conditions, for example, for overtime or shiftwork **2.** *Ops* the assignment of tasks or jobs to a workstation. The loading of jobs is worked out through the use of *master production scheduling*. Workstations may be loaded to *finite* or *infinite loading* levels.

loan *Fin* borrowing either by a business or a consumer where the amount borrowed is repaid according to an agreed schedule at an agreed interest rate, typically by regular instalments over a set period of years. However, the principal may be repayable in one instalment. *See also* **balloon loan**, *fixed-rate loan*, *interest-only mortgage*, *variable interest rate*

loanable funds theory *Fin* the theory that interest rates are determined solely by supply and demand

loanback *Fin* the ability of a holder of a pension fund to borrow money from it

loan capital *Fin* debentures and other long-term loans to a business

loan constant ratio *Fin* the total of annual payments due on a loan as a fraction of the amount of the principal

Loan Council (*ANZ*) *Fin* an Australian federal body made up of treasurers from the states and the Commonwealth of Australia that monitors borrowing by state governments

loan loss reserves *Fin* the money a bank holds to cover losses through defaults on loans that it makes

loan production cycle *Fin* the period that begins with an application for a loan and ends with the lending of money

loan schedule *Fin* a list of the payments due on a loan and the balance outstanding after each has been made

loan shark *Fin* somebody who lends money at excessively, and often illegally, high rates of interest

loan stock *Fin* bonds and debentures

loan to value ratio *Fin* the ratio of the amount of a loan to the value of the collateral for it

loan value *Fin* the amount that a lender is willing to lend a borrower

lobby *Gen Mgt* a pressure group that seeks to influence government or legislators on behalf of a particular cause or interest

localisation *E-com* the translation of a website into the language or idiom of the target user.

Studies have shown that if a vendor is serious about selling to foreign marketplaces, localising their website is essential: without it, sales will be minimal and returns very high because of misunderstanding by people who are purchasing in a foreign language.

lock-out *HR* a form of industrial action taken by an employer during a dispute in which employees are prevented from entering the business premises

logistics *Ops* the management of the movement, storage, and processing of materials and information in the *supply chain*. Logistics encompasses the acquisition of raw materials and components, manufacturing or processing, and the distribution of finished products to the end user. Each organisation focuses on a different aspect of logistics, depending on its area of interest. For example, one might apply logistics to find a way of linking *physical distribution management* with earlier events in the supply chain, another to plan its acquisition and storage, while a third might use logistics as a support operation.

logistics management *Ops* the management of the distribution of products to the market

logo *Gen Mgt* a graphic device or symbol used by an organisation as part of its corporate identity. A logo is used to facilitate instant recognition of an organisation and to reinforce *brand* expectations and public image.

The beginning is the most important part of any work.

log of claims *(ANZ) HR* a document listing the demands made by employees on an employer or vice versa, often submitted during industrial negotiations

LOL *abbr Gen Mgt* laugh out loud *(slang)*

London Bullion Market *Fin* the world's largest market for gold where silver is also traded. It is a wholesale market, where the minimum trades are generally 1,000 ounces for gold and 50,000 ounces for silver. Members typically trade with each other and their clients on a principal-to-principal basis so that all risks, including those of credit, are between the two parties to the transaction.

London Chamber of Commerce and Industry *Fin* in the United Kingdom, the largest chamber of commerce that aims 'to help London businesses succeed by promoting their interests and expanding their opportunities as members of a worldwide business network'. *See also* **ICC**

London Clearing House *Fin* an organisation that acts on behalf of its members as a central counterparty for contracts traded on the London International Financial Futures and Options Exchange, the International Petroleum Exchange, and the London Metal Exchange. When the LCH has registered a trade, it becomes the buyer to every member who sells and the seller to every member who buys, ensuring good financial performance. To protect it against the risks assumed as central counterparty, the LCH establishes margin requirements. *See also* **margining**. *Abbr* **LCH**

London Commodity Exchange *Fin* see *London International Financial Futures and Options Exchange*

London Inter Bank Bid Rate *Fin* on the UK money markets, the rate at which banks will bid to take deposits in eurocurrency from each other. The deposits are for terms from overnight up to five years. *Abbr* **LIBID**

London Inter Bank Mean Rate *Fin* the average of the London Inter Bank Offered Rate and the London Inter Bank Bid Rate, occasionally used as a reference rate. *Abbr* **LIMEAN**

London Inter Bank Offered Rate *Fin* on the UK money markets, the rate at which banks will offer to make deposits in eurocurrency from each other, often used as a reference rate. The deposits are for terms from overnight up to five years. *Abbr* **LIBOR**

London International Financial Futures and Options Exchange *Fin* an exchange for trading financial futures and options. Established in 1982, it offered contracts on interest rates denominated in most of the world's major currencies until 1992, when it merged with the London Traded Options Market, adding equity options to its product range. In 1996 it merged with the London Commodity Exchange, adding a range of soft commodity and agricultural commodity contracts to its financial portfolio. From November 1998, trading was gradually migrated from the floor of the exchange to screen-based trading. *Abbr* **LIFFE**

London Metal Exchange *Fin* one of the world's largest non-ferrous metal exchanges that deals in aluminium, tin, and nickel. The primary roles of the exchange are hedging, providing official international reference prices, and appropriate storage facilities. Its origins can be traced back to 1571, though in its present form it dates from 1877. *Abbr* **LME**

London Traded Options Market *Fin* see *London International Financial Futures and Options Exchange*

long *Fin* having more shares than are promised for sale

long-dated bond *Fin* a bond issued by the United Kingdom with a maturity at least 15 years in the future

long-dated gilt *Fin* see *gilt-edged security*

longitudinal study *Stats* a statistical study that produces data gathered over a period of time

long position *Fin* a situation in which dealers hold securities, commodities, or contracts, expecting prices to rise

long-service award *HR* a gift to recognise the *length of service* of an employee within an organisation. A long-service award may be cash or may take the form of something an employee will value. The tradition of a clock or watch for 25 or 40 years of service is being replaced by awards recognising shorter durations of employment and the greater mobility of employees.

long-service leave *(ANZ) HR* a period of paid leave awarded by some employers to staff who have completed several years of service

long-term *Gen Mgt* involving a long period of time, for example, years rather than weeks or months

long-term bond *Fin* a bond that has at least 10 years before its redemption date, or, in

---

some markets, a bond with more than seven years until its redemption date

long-term debt *Fin* loans that are due after at least one year

long-term equity anticipation securities *Fin see* **LEAPS**

long-term financing *Fin* forms of funding such as loans or stock issue that do not have to be repaid immediately

long-term lease *Fin* a lease of at least ten years

long-term liabilities *Fin* forms of debt such as loans that do not have to be repaid immediately

lookback option *Fin* an option whose price the buyer chooses from all of the prices that have existed during the option's life

loop
in the loop *Gen Mgt* up to date with what is happening currently (*slang*)

loss *Fin* a financial position in which costs exceed income

loss adjuster *Fin, Gen Mgt* a professional person acting on behalf of an insurance company to assess the value of an insurance claim. *Also known as* **claims adjuster**

loss assessor *Fin* in the United Kingdom, a person appointed by a insurance policyholder to assist with his or her claim. *See also* **loss adjuster**

loss control *Gen Mgt see* **total loss control**

lossmaker *Gen Mgt* a product or company that fails to make a profit or break even

lost time record *Fin* a record of the time a machine or employee is not producing, usually stating reasons and responsibilities. Lost time can include waiting time and maintenance.

lot *Fin* **1.** the minimum quantity of a commodity that may be purchased on an exchange, for example, 1,000 ounces of gold on the London Bullion Market **2.** an item or a collection of related items being offered for sale at an auction **3.** (*US*) a group of shares held or traded together, usually in units of 100 **4.** (*US*) a piece of land that can be sold

lottery *Fin* the random method of selecting successful applicants, occasionally used when a new issue is oversubscribed

lowball *Gen Mgt* to begin a sales negotiation by quoting low prices, and then raise them once a buyer appears interested (*slang*)

lower level domain *E-com* the main part of a domain name. For most e-business sites this is usually the company or brand name.

lower of cost or market *Fin* a method used by manufacturing and supply firms when accounting for their homogeneous stocks that involves valuing them either at their original cost or the current market price, whichever is lower. *Abbr* **LCM**

low-hanging fruit (*slang*) **1.** *Gen Mgt* something that is easy to obtain. Low-hanging fruit is highly visible, easily obtained, and provides good short-term opportunities for profit. Such fruit must be taken advantage of quickly, because it is accessible to anyone and there might be considerable competition. Picking low-hanging fruit may involve, for example, taking over a company or choosing the easiest tasks to do first, in order to achieve a quick result. **2.** *Mkting* people who are easy marketing targets because they are already thinking about buying a product or signing up for a service

low start mortgage *Fin* a long-term loan, usually for the purchase of a property, in which the borrower only pays the interest on the loan for the first few years, usually three. After that, the repayments increase to cover the interest and part of the original loan, as in a *repayment mortgage*. Low start mortgages are popular with first-time buyers as the lower initial costs may free up funds for furnishings or home improvements. *See also* **mortgage**

loyalty bonus *Fin* in the United Kingdom in the 1980s, a number of extra shares, calculated as a proportion of the shares originally subscribed, given to original subscribers of privatisation issues providing the shares were held continually for a given period of time

loyalty scheme *Mkting* a sales promotion technique to encourage customers to continue buying a product or using an organisation's services. It works by rewarding customers who spend more and/or stay longer with an organisation. Examples include a shopper card that gives discounts on purchases over a period of time.

There are several other loyalty scheme approaches: points systems—which give points to customers based on what they purchase; premium customer programmes—where customers who spend certain amounts of money and are repeat purchasers gain special status and receive benefits such as discounts, exclusive offers, and gifts; buyers' clubs—where a certain number of customers can club together to buy a particular product, at a special volume discount.

To accuse is so easy that it is infamous to do so where proof is impossible.   *Zoë Akins*

If implementing a loyalty scheme, it is important to remember that it must be there for the long term, and the level of incentive must be right. Offering too much will hurt your profits; offering too little will not attract members. Customers also need to be able to check up on their status easily—to see, for example, how many points they have currently accumulated.

Ltd *Fin see* **limited liability company**

lump sum *Fin* **1.** used to describe a loan that is repayable with one instalment at the end of its term. *See also* **balloon loan, interest-only mortgage 2.** an amount of money received in one payment, for example, the sum payable to the beneficiary of a life assurance policy on the death of the policyholder

lurk *E-com* to visit an Internet newsgroup without taking part. People wishing to promote their company's products or services within a newsgroup lurk to see whether the group accepts commercial messages or whether there are any questions they could answer. Lurking is important because inappropriate messages are likely to receive a hostile response from newsgroup members and may even be considered as *spam*. Lurking in relevant newsgroups can also be an effective means of online market research.

luxury tax *Fin* a tax on goods or services that are considered non-essential

M1 *Econ* the narrowest definition of the amount of money in the economy, including notes and coins in public circulation and sterling sight deposits held in the private sector

Ma and Pa shop *Gen Mgt* a small family-run business (*slang*)

Machiavelli, Niccolò (1469–1527) *Gen Mgt* Italian politician. Machiavelli's *The Prince* (1532) is one of the earliest works on political theory, embracing the concepts of **power**, **authority**, and **leadership**. In *Management and Machiavelli* (1967), Antony Jay sought to show the relevance of Machiavelli's philosophy to modern society.

Machiavelli was born in Florence, and served as an official in the Florentine government. His work brought him into contact with some of Europe's most influential ministers and government representatives. His chief diplomatic triumph occurred when Florence obtained the surrender of Pisa. But in 1512 when the Medicis returned to power, his career came to an abrupt end. He was accused of being involved in a plot against the government. For this he was imprisoned, tortured, and finally exiled.

He retired to a farm outside Florence and began a successful writing career, producing plays and a history of Florence as well as the books on politics for which he is now chiefly remembered.

machine code *E-com* a set of instructions to a computer in the form of a binary code

machine hour rate *Fin* an **overhead absorption rate** based on machine hours

macho management *Gen Mgt* an authoritarian management style that asserts a manager's right to manage. Macho management is a term coined by **Michael Edwardes**, and it was adopted by the media in the 1980s. Macho managers tend to take a tough approach to improving **productivity** and efficiency, and are unsympathetic to **trade unions**.

macroeconomics *Econ* the branch of economics that studies national income and the economic systems of national economies

macroeconomy *Econ* those broad sectors of a country's economic activity, for example, the financial or industrial sector, that are aggregated to form its economic system as a whole

macrohedge *Fin* a hedge that pertains to an entire portfolio. *See also* **microhedge**. *Also known as* **global hedge**

Macromedia Flash™ *E-com* a trademark for a type of web animation software. Its small file sizes and easy **scaleability** make Flash one of the more flexible animation packages, and it uses **streaming** technology so that animations can be viewed more quickly. Flash also allows sound to be added to an animation effectively.

mail form *E-com* a web page that requires the user to input data, for example, name, address, or order or shipping information, that is transmitted to an e-merchant via e-mail

mailing house *Mkting* an organisation that specialises in planning, creating, and implementing direct mail campaigns for clients

mailing list *Mkting* the names and addresses of a particular group of people compiled for marketing purposes. A mailing list may be compiled internally or bought or rented from an outside agency, and can be used for advertising, fundraising, news releases, or for **direct mail** or a **mailshot**. A mailing list is usually compiled for a selected group using one or more criteria, such as men between the ages of 15 and 20.

mail order *Mkting* a form of retailing in which consumers order products from a catalogue for delivery to their home

mail-out *Gen Mgt* a single instance of using direct mail

mail server *E-com* a remote computer enabling people and organisations to send and receive e-mail

mailshot *Mkting* the speculative targeting of a particular or specified group of people by mail. A mailshot normally contains **advertising**, fundraising requests, or **press releases**.

mailsort *Mkting* a sorting service offered to organisations by the Post Office, intended to reduce the cost and time spent on direct mail

mainframe *E-com* a powerful computer capable of supporting hundreds of thousands of users simultaneously

mainstream corporation tax *Fin* formerly the balance of corporation tax due after deducting ACT. *See also* **Advance Corporation Tax**

maintenance *Ops* the process of keeping physical assets in working order to ensure their availability and to reduce the chance of failure. An effective maintenance programme can enhance safety, increase reliability, reduce quality errors, lower operating costs, and increase the lifespan of assets. There are different maintenance approaches, including *reactive maintenance*, *predictive maintenance*, and *preventive maintenance*. Two strategies that have more recently become prominent are *reliability-centred maintenance* and *total productive maintenance*.

maintenance bond *Fin* a bond that provides a guarantee against defects for some time after a contract has been fulfilled

majority shareholder *Fin* a shareholder with a controlling interest in a company. *See also minority interest*

make or buy *Gen Mgt see* **purchasing versus production**

make-to-order *Ops* the production of goods or components to meet an existing order. Make-to-order products are made to the customer's specification, and are often processed in small batches.

Malcolm Baldrige National Quality Award *Gen Mgt* an award, given to US companies, recognising achievements in quality and business performance. The Malcolm Baldrige National Quality Award was launched by the US government in 1987 to encourage US companies to publicise successful quality and improvement strategies, to adopt *total quality management*, and to encourage competitiveness. In assessing companies for the Award, examiners allocate points in seven major areas: 1. Leadership, 2. Information and analysis, 3. Strategic planning, 4. Human resource development, 5. Process management, 6. Customer focus and satisfaction, 7. Business results. The Award also involves evaluation of companies according to three main factors: 1. What is the organisation's approach to achieving its goals: how does it attempt to achieve top-class performance? 2. How is this approach put into practice in the organisation, what resources are being brought to bear, and how widespread is this action throughout the organisation? 3. What evidence is there to demonstrate that improvements are really taking place?

managed currency fund *Fin* a unit trust that makes considered investments in currencies

managed economy *Fin* an economy directed by a government rather than the free market

managed float *Econ* the position when the exchange rate of a country's currency is influenced by government action in the foreign exchange market

managed fund *Fin* a unit trust that makes considered investments. *See also index fund*

managed hosting *E-com* a *hosting option* in which the hosting provider is principally responsible for a client's servers. This responsibility can range from the vendor supplying and managing the hardware only, to supplying the software as well. This type of vendor is called an *ASP* (application service provider).

managed rate *Fin* the rate of interest charged by a financial institution for borrowing, that is not prescribed as a margin over base rate, but is set from time to time by the institution

management *Gen Mgt, HR* the use of professional skills for identifying and achieving organisational objectives through the deployment of appropriate resources. Management involves identifying what needs to be done, and organising and supporting others to perform the necessary tasks. A manager has complex and ever-changing responsibilities, the focus of which shifts to reflect the issues, trends, and preoccupations of the time. At the beginning of the 20th century, the emphasis was both on supporting the organisation's administration and managing *productivity* through increased efficiency. Organisations following *Henri Fayol*'s and *Max Weber*'s models built the functional divisions of personnel management, production management, marketing management, operations management, and financial management. At the beginning of the 21st century, those original drivers are still much in evidence, although the emphasis has moved to the key areas of *competence* within the National Occupational Standards for Management, particularly people management. Although management is a profession in its own right, its skill-set often applies to professionals of other disciplines.

management accountant *Fin* a person who contributes to management's decision-making processes by, for example, collecting and processing data, relating to a business's costs, sales, and the profitability of individual activities

management accounting *Fin* the preparation and use of financial information to support management decisions

---

Strategy is not the consequence of planning but the opposite, its starting point. *Henry Mintzberg*

management audit *Gen Mgt see* **operational audit**

management buy-in *Gen Mgt* the purchase of an existing business by an individual manager or management group outside that business. In the United Kingdom, the unique company 3i is often involved in supporting management buy-ins. 3i has also promoted a hybrid form of management buy-in and **management buy-out**, given the acronym **BIMBO**, which involves an incoming chief executive sharing his or her investment with the company's existing management team. *Abbr* **MBI**

management buy-out *Gen Mgt* the purchase of an existing business by an individual manager or management group from within that business. *Abbr* **MBO**

management by exception *Gen Mgt* a system of management in which only deviations from the plan or the norm are to be reported to the manager, ensuring management attention is only given when necessary

management by objectives *or* **management by results** *Gen Mgt* a method of managing an organisation by setting a series of **objectives** that contribute towards the achievement of its goals. *Abbr* **MBO**

management by walking around *Gen Mgt* a hands-on style of management based on regularly walking around to speak to, question, and listen to employees, and to learn more about work processes

management company *Gen Mgt* a company that takes over responsibility from internal staff for managing facilities such as computer systems, telecommunications, or maintenance. The process is known as **outsourcing**.

management consultancy *Gen Mgt* **1.** the activity of advising on management techniques and practices. Management consultancy usually involves the identification of a problem, or the analysis of a specific area of one organisation, and the reporting of any resulting findings. The consultancy process can sometimes be extended to help put into effect the recommendations made. **2.** a firm of **management consultants**

management consultant *Gen Mgt* a person professionally engaged in advising on, and providing, a detached, external view about a company's management techniques and practices. A management consultant may be self-employed, a partner, or employed within a **management consultancy**. Consultants can

be called in for many reasons, but are employed particularly for projects involving business improvement, **change management**, information technology, and long-term planning.

management control *Fin* all of the processes used by managers to ensure that organisational goals are achieved and procedures adhered to, and that the organisation responds appropriately to changes in its environment

management control systems *Gen Mgt* measures, procedures, **performance indicators**, and other instruments used to systematically check and regulate operations. Management control systems are set up to maintain management **control** on a routine basis, and can include **budgets** and budgetary controls, credit control, working procedures, inventory control, production processes, and quality measures or controls.

management development *HR* the process of creating, and enhancing, the **competences** of **managers** and potential managers. Management development is usually thought of as a planned process, focusing on a long-term development programme to increase managerial effectiveness, but it also incorporates informal and unplanned elements such as learning from day-to-day experience. Management development programmes within an organisation aim to identify and recruit potential managers, and develop their knowledge and skills to meet organisational needs. They also equip managers for more senior posts. Management development activities include short courses, **management education** programmes, **management training**, **coaching**, and **mentoring**.

management education *HR* formal instruction in the principles and techniques of **management**, and in related subjects, leading to a qualification. Management education aims to develop management knowledge, understanding, and **competence** through classroom or distance-based methods. Management education is a main component of **management development**, and differs from **management training** in that the latter may exploit any one of a variety of formal or informal methods, tends to be focused on a specific skill, and does not result directly in a formal qualification.

management guru *Gen Mgt* an informal term for a **management theorist**

management information system *Gen Mgt see* **MIS**

management science *Gen Mgt* the application of scientific methods and principles to management *decision-making* and *problem-solving*. Management science encompasses the use of quantitative, mathematical, and statistical techniques. The term can be used to denote scientific management, which has origins in the work of *Frederick Winslow Taylor*, *Henry Gantt*, and *Frank* and *Lillian Gilbreth*. Management science lies at the opposite end of the spectrum to the *human relations* school.

management services *Gen Mgt* a department or team of internally employed technical and professional specialists offering services or advice to management. Management services can cover areas such as work study, legal, computer, information, economic intelligence, and similar specialist support services.

management standards *Gen Mgt* published guidelines to best practice, outlining the knowledge, understanding, and personal *competences* that managers need to develop and demonstrate if they are to be effective. Management standards form the core criteria on which management *National Vocational Qualifications* in the United Kingdom are based. They are split into seven key areas: manage activities; manage people; manage resources; manage information; manage energy; manage quality; and manage projects.

management style *Gen Mgt* the general manner, outlook, attitude, and behaviour of a manager in his or her dealings with subordinates. Organisations may have, or seek to have, distinctive management styles, and sometimes train employees to try to ensure that a preferred style, fitting in with the desired *corporate culture*, is always used. Management styles can vary widely between extremes of control and consultation. The latter are generally thought to encourage degrees of *employee participation* in management with consequently improved *employee commitment*, *employee involvement*, and *empowerment*. More participatory styles are also usually related to more open organisational cultures and flatter organisational structures. One well-known instrument for distinguishing individual management styles is *Robert Blake*'s and *Jane Mouton*'s *Managerial Grid*™.

management succession *Gen Mgt see succession planning*

management team *Gen Mgt see senior management*

management theorist *Gen Mgt* somebody who puts forward original ideas and theories about management. The work of a management theorist is usually presented through books or articles, and often has its base in practical or academic research, and consultancy or practical work experience.

management threshold *Gen Mgt* an outmoded term for a level of seniority in an organisation which somebody cannot surmount. The management threshold is reached by an *employee* who has risen to a certain level in an organisation and seems unable to rise any further. It can lead to plateauing, where an employee is unable to gain *promotion* and stays in the same role for many years. Failure to surmount the management threshold can be caused by lack of opportunities for advancement, lack of ambition, or lack of skills or ability.

management trainee *HR* an employee who holds a junior management position while undergoing formal training in management techniques

management training *HR* planned activities for *management development*. Management training methods include public or *in-company training* courses and *on-the-job training* designed to improve managerial *competences*. Management training tends to be practical and to focus on specific management techniques. Unlike *management education*, it does not result in a formal qualification.

manager *Gen Mgt* a person who identifies and achieves organisational objectives through the deployment of appropriate resources. A manager can have responsibilities in one or more of five key areas: managing activities; managing resources; managing information; managing people; and managing him- or herself at the same time as working within the context of the organisational, political, and economic business environments. There are managers in all disciplines and activities, although some may not bear the title of manager. Some specialise in areas such as personnel, marketing, production, finance, or project management, while others are *general managers*, applying *management* skills across all business areas. Very few jobs are entirely managerial, and very few exist without any management responsibilities. It is the capability to harness resources that largely distinguishes a manager from a non-manager.

All men who have turned out worth anything have had the chief hand in their own education. Walter Scott

Managerial Grid™ *Gen Mgt* a tool to measure and understand managerial behaviour which places concern for task and concern for people on two matrices against which a manager's style can be plotted. The Managerial Grid™ grades each matrix 1 to 9, and identifies five different managerial behaviour patterns: 1-1, or impoverished management, in which a minimum of concern for either people or task is displayed; 9-1, or **authority-compliance management**, in which a preoccupation with task is displayed; 5-5, or **middle of the road management**, in which a balance between task and people is striven for; 1-9, **country club management**, which is concerned with human relations to the detriment of output; and 9-9, **team management**, the ideal, in which production and human requirements are integrated in a team approach to achieving results.

managerialism *Gen Mgt* emphasis on efficient management, and the use of systems, planning, and management practice. Managerialism is often used in a critical sense, especially from the perspective of the public sector, to imply over-enthusiasm for efficiency, or private sector management techniques and systems, possibly at the expense of service or quality considerations. The term is also used to describe confrontational attitudes, or actions displayed by management towards trade unions.

managing director *Gen Mgt* a director of a company who has overall responsibility for its day-to-day operations. *Abbr* **MD**

M&A *abbr Fin* mergers and acquisitions

mandarin *Gen Mgt* a high-ranking and influential adviser, especially in government circles

mandatory quote period *Fin* a period of time during which prices of securities must be displayed in a market

manpower forecasting *Gen Mgt* the prediction of future levels of demand for, and supply of, workers and skills at organisational, regional, or national level. A range of techniques are used in manpower forecasting, including the statistical analysis of current trends and the use of mathematical models. At national level, these include the analysis of census statistics; at organisational level, projections of future requirements may be made from sales and production figures. Manpower forecasting forms part of the *manpower planning* process.

manpower planning *Gen Mgt* the development of strategies to match the supply of workers to the availability of jobs at organisational, regional, or national level. Manpower planning involves reviewing current manpower resources, forecasting future requirements and availability, and taking steps to ensure that the supply of people and skills meets demand. At a national level, this may be carried out by government or industry bodies, and at an organisational level, by human resource managers. A more current term for manpower planning at organisational level is *human resource planning*.

manual worker *HR* an employee who carries out physical work, especially in a factory or outdoors. *Also known as blue-collar worker*

manufacture *Ops* the large-scale production of goods from raw materials or constituent parts

manufacturer *Ops* a person or organisation involved in *production*

manufacturer's agent *Ops* a person or organisation with authority to act for a *manufacturer* in obtaining a *contract* with a third party

manufacturing *Gen Mgt see production*

manufacturing cost *Ops* the expenditure incurred in carrying out the *production* processes of an organisation. The manufacturing cost includes *direct costs*, for example, labour, materials, and expenses, and indirect costs, for example, *subcontracting* and overheads.

manufacturing for excellence *Gen Mgt see design for manufacturability*

manufacturing information system *Ops* an *MIS* designed specifically for use in a *production* environment

manufacturing management *Gen Mgt see production management*

manufacturing resource planning *Ops see MRP II*

manufacturing system *Ops* a method of organising *production*. Manufacturing systems include assembly and *batch production*, *flexible manufacturing systems*, *lean production*, *group technology*, *job production*, *kanban*, and *mass production*.

manufacturing to order *Ops* a production management technique in which goods are produced to meet firm orders, rather than being produced for stock

MAPS *abbr E-com* Mail Abuse Prevention System: the leading US organisation campaigning against unsolicited commercial e-mail messages, or *spam*

Marché des Options Négotiables de Paris *Fin* in France, the traded options market. *Abbr* **MONEP**

Marché International de France *Fin* in France, the international futures and options exchange

Margerison, Charles (*b.* 1940) *Gen Mgt* British business researcher and writer. *See McCann, Dick*

margin 1. *Fin, Gen Mgt* the difference between the cost and the selling price of a product or service **2.** (*ANZ*) *HR* a payment made to workers over and above the basic wage in recognition of special skills

margin account *Fin* an account with a broker who lends money for investments

marginal analysis *Econ* the study of how small changes in an economic variable will affect an economy

marginal cost *Econ* the amount by which the costs of a firm will be increased if its output is increased by one more unit, or if one more customer is served.

EXAMPLE If the price charged is greater than the marginal cost, then the revenue gain will be greater than the added cost. That, in turn, will increase profit, so the expansion in production or service makes economic sense and should proceed. The reverse is also true: if the price charged is less than the marginal cost, expansion should not go ahead.

The formula for marginal cost is:

Change in cost /change in quantity

If it costs a company £260,000 to produce 3,000 items, and £325,000 to produce 3,800 items, the change in cost would be:

£325,000 − £260,000 = £65,000

The change in quantity would be:

3,800 − 3,000 = 800

When the formula to calculate marginal cost is applied, the result is:

£65,000 /800 = £81.25

If the price of the item in question were £99.95, expansion should proceed.

Relying on marginal cost is not fail-safe, however; putting more products on a market can drive down prices and thus cut margins. Moreover, committing idle capacity to long-term production may tie up resources that could be directed to a new and more profitable opportunity. An important related principle is contribution: the cash gained (or lost) from selling an additional unit.

marginal costing *Fin* the accounting system in which variable costs are charged to cost units and fixed costs of the period are written off in full against the aggregate contribution. Its special value is in recognising cost behaviour, and hence assisting in decision-making. *Also known as* **variable costing**

marginal costs and benefits *Econ* the amount by which an individual or household will lose or benefit from a small change in a variable, for example, food consumption or income received

marginalisation *Gen Mgt* the process by which countries lose importance and status because they are unable to participate in mainstream activities such as industrialisation or the Internet economy

marginal lender *Fin* a lender who will make a loan only at or above a particular rate of interest

marginal private cost *Econ* the cost to an individual of a small change in the price of a variable, for example, petrol

marginal revenue *Gen Mgt* the revenue generated by additional units of production

marginal tax rate *Fin* the rate of tax payable on a person's income after business expenses have been deducted

margining *Fin* the system by which the London Clearing House (LCH) controls the risk associated with a London International Financial Futures and Options Exchange clearing member's position on a daily basis. To achieve this, clearing members deposit cash or collateral with the LCH in the form of initial and variation margins. The initial margin is the deposit required on all open positions (long or short) to cover short-term price movements and is returned to members by the LCH when the position is closed. The variation margin is the members' profits or losses, calculated daily from the marked-to-market-close value of their position (whereby contracts are revalued daily for the calculation of variation margin), and credited to or debited from their accounts.

margin of error *Ops* an allowance made for the possibility of miscalculation

margin of safety *Ops* the difference between the level of activity at which an organisation breaks even and the level of activity greater than this point. For example, a margin of safety of £200,000 is achieved when the breakeven point is £600,000 and sales reach £800,000. This measure can be

---

expressed as a proportion of sales value, as a number of units sold, or as a percentage of *capacity*.

margin of safety ratio *Fin* a ratio which indicates the percentage by which forecast turnover exceeds or falls short of that required to break even. It is calculated as follows:

(Forecast turnover – breakeven turnover) × 100 / Forecast turnover

mark-down *Fin* a reduction in the selling price of damaged or slow-selling goods

marked cheque *Fin* a certified cheque (*slang*)

marked price *Gen Mgt* the original displayed price of a product in a shop. In a sale, customers may be offered a saving on the marked price.

market **1.** *Fin* the rate at which financial commodities or securities are being sold **2.** *Gen Mgt* a grouping of people or organisations unified by a common need **3.** *Gen Mgt* a gathering of sellers and purchasers to exchange commodities

marketable *Mkting* possessing the potential to be commercially viable. To determine whether a new product or service is marketable, an assessment needs to be carried out to see if it is likely to make a profit. The assessment is often based on detailed *market research* analysing the potential market, and the projected financial returns and any other benefits for the company.

market analysis *Mkting* the study of a market to identify and quantify business opportunities

market area *Mkting* the geographical location of a market

market based pricing *Fin* setting a price based on the value of the product in the perception of the customer. *Also known as perceived value pricing*

market bubble *Fin* a stock market phenomenon in which values in a particular sector become inflated for a short period. If the bubble bursts, share prices in that sector collapse.

market coverage *Gen Mgt* the degree to which a product or service meets the needs of a market

market development *Mkting* marketing activities designed to increase the overall size of a market through education and awareness

market driven *Mkting* using market knowledge to determine the *corporate strategy* of an organisation. A market driven organisation has a *customer focus*, together with awareness of competitors, and an understanding of the *market*.

market economy *Econ* an economy in which a *free market* in goods and services operates

marketeer *Mkting* a small company that competes in the same market as larger companies. Examples of marketeers are restaurants, travel agents, computer software providers, garages, and insurance brokers.

marketer *Mkting* somebody who is responsible for developing and implementing marketing prices

marketface *Gen Mgt* the interface between suppliers and customers

market-facing enterprise *Gen Mgt* an organisation that aligns itself with its markets and customers

market-focused organisation *Mkting* an organisation whose strategies are determined by market requirements rather than organisational demands

market fragmentation *Mkting* a situation in which the buyers or sellers in a market consist of a large number of small organisations

market gap *Mkting* an opportunity in a market where no supplier provides a product or service that buyers need

market if touched *Fin* an order to trade a security if it reaches a specified price. *Abbr* **MIT**

marketing *Mkting see* **marketing management**
4 Ps of marketing *Gen Mgt see* **marketing mix**

marketing audit *Mkting* an analysis of either the external marketing environment or a company's internal marketing aims, objectives, operations, and efficiency. An external marketing audit covers issues such as economic, political, infrastructure, technological, and consumer perspectives; *market size* and *structure*; and competitors, suppliers, and distributors. An internal marketing audit covers aspects such as the company's *mission statement*, aims, and objectives; its structure, corporate culture, systems, operations, and processes; *product development* and pricing; profitability and efficiency; *advertising*; and deployment of the *salesforce*.

marketing consultancy *Mkting* an organisation that plans and develops marketing strategies and programmes on behalf of clients

marketing cost *Fin* the cost of researching potential markets and promoting a product or service

marketing information system *Mkting* an information system concerned with the collection, storage, and analysis of information and data for marketing *decision-making* purposes. Information for use in marketing information systems is gathered from customers, competitors and their products, and from the market itself.

marketing management *Mkting* one of the main management disciplines, encompassing all the strategic planning, operations, activities, and processes involved in achieving organisational objectives by delivering value to customers. Marketing management focuses on satisfying customer requirements by identifying needs and wants, and developing products and services to meet them. In seeking to satisfy customer requirements, **marketing** aims to build long-term relationships with customers and with other interested parties and to provide value to them. This begins with *market research*, which analyses needs and wants in society, and continues with attracting customers and the cultivation of mutually beneficial exchange processes with them. Tools used in this process are diverse and include market segmentation, *brand management*, *PR*, *logistics*, *direct response marketing*, *sales promotion*, and *advertising*.

marketing manager *Mkting* an employee of a client organisation who is responsible for planning and controlling its marketing activities and budgets

marketing mix *Mkting* the range of integrated decisions taken by a marketing manager to ensure successful marketing. These decisions are taken in four key areas known as the **4 Ps of marketing**—product, price, place, and promotion—and cover issues such as the type of product to be marketed, brand name, pricing, advertising, publicity, geographical coverage, retailing, and distribution.

marketing myopia *Mkting* the name given to the theory that challenged the assumption that organisations should be production-oriented by suggesting that to be successful, the wants of customers must be their central consideration. First promoted by *Theodore Levitt* in 'Marketing myopia', published in the *Harvard Business Review* during 1960, the theory has gained such widespread acceptance that it now appears commonplace.

marketing plan *Mkting* overall marketing objectives and the strategies and programmes of action designed to achieve those objectives

marketing planning *Mkting* the process of producing a *marketing plan*. Marketing planning requires a careful examination of all strategic issues, including the business environment, the markets themselves, competitors, the corporate *mission statement*, and organisational capabilities. The resulting marketing plan should be communicated to appropriate staff through an oral briefing to ensure it is fully understood.

market intelligence *Mkting* a collection of internal and external data on a given market. Market intelligence focuses particularly on competitors, customers, consumer spending, market trends, and suppliers.

market leader *Mkting see **market share***

market logic *Fin* the prevailing forces or attitudes that determine a company's success or failure on the stock market

market maker *Fin* **1.** somebody who works in a stock exchange to facilitate trade in one particular company **2.** a broker or bank that maintains a market for a security that does not trade on any exchange

market order *Fin* an order to trade a security at the best price the broker can obtain

market penetration *HR* a measure of the percentage or potential percentage of the market that a product or company is able to capture, expressed in terms of total sales or turnover. Market penetration is often used to measure the level of success a new product or service has achieved.

market penetration pricing *Mkting* the policy of pricing a product or service very competitively, and sometimes at a loss to the producer, in order to increase its *market share*

market position *Mkting* the place held by a product or service in a *market*, usually determined by its percentage of total sales. An ideal market position is often pre-defined for a product or service. Analysis of potential customers and competing products can be used with product differentiation techniques to formulate a product to fill the desired market position.

market potential *Mkting* a forecast of the size of a market in terms of revenue, numbers of buyers, or other factors

market power *Mkting* the dominance of a market either by customers, who create a buyer's market, or by a particular company, which creates a seller's market. Individuals or companies retain control of the market by fixing the pricing and number of products available.

market price *Econ* in economics, the theoretical price at which supply equals demand

market research *Mkting* research carried out to assess the size and nature of a market

market risk *Fin* risk that cannot be diversified away, also known as systematic risk. **Non-systematic** or **unsystematic risk** applies to a single investment or class of investments, and can be reduced or eliminated by diversification.

market risk premium *Fin* the extra return required from a share to compensate for its risk compared with the average risk of the market

market sector *Mkting* a subdivision of a *market*. Market sectors are usually determined by market segmentation, which divides a market into different categories. Car buyers, for example, could be put into sectors such as car fleet buyers, private buyers, buyers under 20 years old, and so on. The smaller the sector, the more its members will have in common.

market segment *Mkting* a part of a market that has distinctive characteristics. Sellers may decide to compete in the whole market or only in segments that are attractive to them or where they have an advantage.

market sentiment *Fin* the mood of those participating in exchange dealings that can range from absolute euphoria to downright gloom and despondency and tends to reflect recent company results, economic indicators, and comments by politicians, analysts, or opinion formers. Optimism increases demand and therefore prices, while pessimism has the opposite effect.

market share *Mkting* the proportion of the total market value of a product or group of products or services that a company, service, or product holds. Market share is shown as a percentage of the total value or output of a market, usually expressed in sterling or US dollars, by weight (tons or tonnes), or as individual units, depending on the commodity. The product, service, or company with a dominant market share is referred to as the **market leader**.

market site *E-com* a website shared by multiple e-commerce vendors, each having a different speciality, to conduct business over the Internet

market size *Fin* the largest number of shares that a market will handle in one trade of a particular security

market structure *Mkting* the make-up of a particular *market*. Market structure can be described with reference to different characteristics of a market, including its size and value, the number of providers and their *market share*, consumer and business purchasing behaviour, and growth forecasts. The description may also include a demographic and regional breakdown of providers and customers and an analysis of pricing structures, likely technological impacts, and domestic and overseas sales.

market targeting *Mkting* the selection of a particular market segment towards which all marketing effort is directed. Market targeting enables the characteristics of the chosen segment to be taken into account when formulating a product or service and its advertising.

market valuation *Fin* **1.** the value of a portfolio at market prices **2.** the opinion of an expert professional as to the current worth of a piece of land or property

market value *Fin* the price that buyers are willing to pay for a good or service

market value added *Fin* the difference between a company's market value (derived from the share price), and its economic book value (the amount of capital that shareholders have committed to the firm throughout its existence, including any retained earnings)

marking down *Fin* the reduction by market makers in the price at which they are prepared to deal in a security, for example, because of an adverse report by an analyst, or the announcement or anticipated announcement of a profit warning by a company

mark-up *Gen Mgt* the difference between the cost of a product or service and its selling price. Mark-up is often calculated as a percentage of the production and overhead costs, and represents the profit made on the product or service.

Marxism *Econ* a view of social development found in the writings of Karl Marx, stating that a country's culture is determined by how its goods and services are produced

marzipan *HR* belonging to the level of management immediately below the top executives (*slang*)

Education is when you read the fine print; experience is what you get when you don't. **Pete Seeger**

Maslow, Abraham (1908–70) *Gen Mgt* US psychologist and behavioural scientist. Known for his work on *motivation*, principally the hierarchy of needs, which was set out in his book, *Motivation and Personality* (1954). Maslow's concepts were originally offered as general explanations of human behaviour but are now seen as a significant contribution to workplace motivation theory. He is often mentioned in connection with his contemporaries **Douglas McGregor** and **Frederick Herzberg**, all part of the **human relations** movement in management.

massaging *Fin* the adjustment of financial figures to create the impression of better performance (*slang*)

mass customisation *Ops* a process that allows a standard, mass-produced item, for example, a bicycle, to be individually tailored to specific customer requirements

mass market *Mkting* a market that covers substantial numbers of the population. A mass market may consist of a whole population or just a segment of that population. *Mass customisation* of products has allowed a greater number of single products to satisfy a mass market.

mass medium *Mkting* an advertising medium such as television or national newspapers which reaches a very large audience

mass meeting *HR* the assembling of most or all of the members of a *trade union* in order to reach a decision on workforce policy. Mass meetings were frequently called during the 1960s and 1970s to determine whether or not *industrial action* would take place. In the United Kingdom, the most memorable examples occurred at British Leyland.

mass production *Ops* large-scale manufacturing, often designed to meet the demand for a particular product. Mass production methods were developed by **Henry Ford**, founder of the Ford Motor Company. Mass production involves using a moving production or assembly line on which the product moves while operators remain at their stations carrying out their work on each passing product. Mass production is now challenged by methods including *just-in-time* and *lean production*.

master budget *Fin* the budget into which all subsidiary budgets are consolidated, normally comprising budgeted profit and loss account, budgeted balance sheet, and budgeted cash flow statement. These documents, and the supporting subsidiary budgets, are used to plan and control activities for the following year.

master franchise *Mkting* a licence issued by the owner of a product or service to another party or master franchisee allowing them to issue further *franchise* licences. A master franchise can benefit the original franchisor, as the master franchisee effectively develops the *franchise chain* on their behalf. A master franchise usually grants further licences within a defined geographical area, and several master franchises may cover a country.

master limited partnership *Fin* a partnership of a type that combines tax advantages and advantages of liquidity

Master of Business Administration *Gen Mgt see* **MBA**

master production scheduling *Ops* a technique used in material requirements planning systems to develop a detailed plan for product manufacturing. The master production schedule, compiled by a master scheduler, takes account of the requirements of various departments, including sales (delivery dates), finance (inventory minimisation), and manufacturing (minimisation of set-up times), and it schedules production and the purchasing of materials within the capacity of and resources available to the production system.

masthead *E-com* the area at the top of a web page, usually containing the logo of the organisation, often with a *search* box and a set of essential links to important areas of the website

matador bond *Fin* a foreign bond in the Spanish domestic market (*slang*)

matched bargain *Fin* the linked sale and repurchase of the same security. *See also* **bed and breakfast deal**

material cost *Ops* the cost of the raw materials that go into a product. The material cost of a product excludes any *indirect costs*, for example, overheads or wages, associated with producing the item.

material facts *Fin* **1.** information that has to be disclosed in a prospectus. *See also* **listing requirements 2.** in an insurance contract, information that the insured has to reveal at the time that the policy is taken out, for example, that a house is located on the edge of a crumbling cliff. Failure to reveal material facts can result in the contract being declared void.

material news *Fin* price sensitive developments in a company, for example, proposed acquisitions, mergers, profit warnings, and the resignation of directors, that most stock exchanges require a company to announce immediately prior to the exchange. *US term material information*

material requirements planning (MRP I) *Fin* a system that converts a production schedule into a listing of the materials and components required to meet that schedule, so that adequate stock levels are maintained and items are available when needed

materials handling *Ops* the techniques employed to move, transport, store, and distribute materials, with or without the aid of mechanical equipment

materials management *Ops* an approach for planning, organising, and controlling all those activities principally concerned with the flow of materials into an organisation. The scope of materials management varies greatly from company to company and may include material planning and control, *production planning*, *purchasing*, inventory control and stores, in-plant materials movement, and *waste management*.

materials requisition *Fin* a document which authorises the issue from a store of a specified quantity of materials. *Also known as stores requisition*

materials returned note *Fin* a record of the return to stores of unused material

materials testing *Ops* the process of analysing the physical and chemical characteristics of materials against a specification

materials transfer note *Fin* a record of the transfer of material between stores, cost centres, or cost units

maternity leave *HR* time off work because of pregnancy and childbirth. All female *employees*, regardless of *length of service* and *hours of work*, are legally entitled to statutory maternity leave and to statutory *maternity pay*. Many *employers* offer improved maternity arrangements but these vary from organisation to organisation and often depend on length of service.

maternity pay *HR* earnings paid by an *employer* to *employees* who take *maternity leave*, or leave employment because of pregnancy, and who satisfy certain qualifying conditions

matrix *Gen Mgt* a chart showing data set out squarely, and symmetrically, in columns and rows with the potential to show both vertical and horizontal relationships. A matrix is often used as form of *organisation chart* to show reporting relationships for a *matrix organisation*, or within a *matrix management* context.

matrix management *Gen Mgt* management based on two or more reporting systems linked to the vertical organisation hierarchy, and to horizontal relationships based on geographic, product, or project requirements

matrix organisation *Gen Mgt* organisation by both vertical administrative functions and horizontal tasks, areas, processes, or projects. Matrix organisation originated in the 1960s and 1970s, particularly within the US aerospace industry, when *organisation charts* showing how the management of a given *project* would relate to *senior management* were often required to win government contracts. A two-dimensional *matrix* chart best illustrates the dual horizontal, and vertical, reporting relationships. Matrix organisation is closely linked to *matrix management*.

matrix structure *Gen Mgt* a form of *organisation structure* based on horizontal and vertical relationships. The matrix structure is linked closely to *matrix management*, and is related to *project management*. It emerged on an improvised rather than a planned basis as a way of showing how people work with or report to others in their organisation, project, geographic region, process, or team.

Matsushita, Konosuke (1894–1989) *Gen Mgt* Japanese entrepreneur, business executive, and philanthropist. Founder of Matsushita Electric, and owner of the Panasonic brand, noted for his humanistic approach to business, which was described by John Kotter in *Matsushita Leadership* (1997).

mature economy *Fin* an economy that is no longer developing or growing rapidly

maturity *Gen Mgt* the stage at which a financial instrument, such as a bond, is due for repayment

maturity date *Fin* the date when an *option* expires

maturity yield *Fin* see *yield*

Mauborgne, Renée *Gen Mgt* French academic. INSEAD professor, Fellow of the World Economic Forum, and collaborator of *W. Chan Kim* on research into *corporate strategy* and *value innovation*.

maximax criterion *Fin* an approach to decision-making under uncertainty in which an 'optimistic' view of the possible outcome is adopted. The favoured strategy is therefore to implement the course of action which leads to the highest possible profit, irrespective of (a) the probability of that profit actually being achieved, and (b) the outcome if it is not successful. A risk-taker may make decisions on this basis.

maximin criterion *Fin* an approach to decision-making under uncertainty in which a 'pessimistic' view of the possible outcome is adopted. The favoured strategy is therefore to implement the course of action whose worst possible outcome generates the highest profit. This basis for decision-making characterises risk-averse decision-makers.

maximum stock level *Fin* a stock level, set for control purposes, which actual stockholding should never exceed. It is calculated as follows:

((reorder level + EOQ) – (minimum rate of usage × minimum lead time))

Mayo, Elton (1880–1949) *Gen Mgt* Australian psychologist and academic. Responsible for finding, through the *Hawthorne experiments*, that *job satisfaction* increases through employee participation in decision-making, rather than through short-term incentives. The results of the Hawthorne studies were published in Mayo's *The Human Problems of an Industrial Civilization* (1933), and were further publicised by one of his collaborators, *Fritz Jules Roethlisberger*. Mayo is recognised as the founder of the *human relations* school of management.

In the early part of his career, Mayo studied in London and Edinburgh and taught at Queensland University. He arrived in the United States in 1923 and worked at the University of Pennsylvania before moving to Harvard. It was while he was at Harvard that Mayo became involved in the Hawthorne Studies.

MBA *abbr Gen Mgt* Master of Business Administration: a post-graduate qualification awarded after a period of study of topics relating to the strategic management of businesses. A Master of Business Administration course can be followed at a *business school* or university, and covers areas such as finance, personnel, and resource management, as well as the wider business environment and skills such as information technology use. The course is mostly taken by people with experience of managerial work, and is offered by universities worldwide. Part-time or distance learning MBAs are available, so that students can study while still working. There is an increasing number of MBA graduates, as an MBA is seen as a passport to a better job and higher salary. For many positions at a higher level within organisations, an MBA is now a prerequisite.

MBI *abbr Gen Mgt* management buy-in

MBIA *abbr Fin* Municipal Bond Insurance Association: a group of insurance companies that insure high-rated municipal bonds

MBO *abbr Gen Mgt* **1.** management buy-out **2.** management by objectives

McCann, Dick (*b.* 1943) *Gen Mgt* Australian business researcher and writer. Developer, with *Charles Margerison*, of the *Team Management Wheel*™, and the team management index/questionnaire, as originally reported in *How to Lead a Winning Team* (1985). Their work on team roles and work preferences compares with that of Carl Jung and *R. Meredith Belbin*.

McClelland, David Clarence (1917–98) *Gen Mgt* US academic. Initiator of research into the use of *competences* to predict effective job performance, later developed by *Richard Boyatzis*. Author of 'Testing for competence rather than for intelligence', *American Psychologist* (1973).

McCormick, Roger *Gen Mgt* UK business executive

McGregor, Douglas (1906–64) *Gen Mgt* US social psychologist and academic. Developer of *Theory X* and *Theory Y*, which describe two views of people at work and two opposing *management styles*. McGregor's writings on *motivation* and *leadership*, first published in *The Human Side of Enterprise* (1960), have been very influential. *William Ouchi* later developed the idea of *Theory Z*.

The son of a clergyman, McGregor graduated from the City College of Detroit (now Wayne University) in 1932. He then went on to Harvard to study for a PhD. After working at Harvard, MIT, and Antioch College in Ohio, McGregor returned to MIT in 1954 as a professor of management. At MIT he attracted some of the stars of the emerging generation of thinkers to work with him, including *Warren Bennis* and *Ed Schein*.

McKinsey 7-S framework *Gen Mgt* a model for identifying and exploiting an organisation's *human resources* in order to create *competitive advantage*. The McKinsey 7-S framework was developed by McKinsey consultants, including *Tom Peters* and *Robert*

If you can run one business well, you can run any business well.　　　　　　　*Richard Branson*

Waterman, with the academic partnership of **Richard Pascale** and **Anthony Athos** in the early 1980s. It sought to present an emphasis on human resources, rather than the traditional mass production tangibles of capital, infrastructure, and equipment. The 7-Ss are: Structure, Strategy, Skills, Staff, Style, Systems, and Shared values (see **core values**).

m-commerce *E-com* electronic transactions between buyers and sellers using mobile communications devices such as mobile phones, personal digital assistants (PDAs), or laptop computers

MD *Gen Mgt see* **managing director**

mean *Stats* a central value or location for a continuous variable in a statistical study

mean reversion *Fin* the tendency of a variable such as price to return towards its average value after approaching an extreme position

measurement error *Stats* an error in the recording, calculating, or reading of a numerical value in a statistical study

mechanical handling *Ops* the use of machines for moving and positioning materials in a warehouse or factory

mechanisation *Gen Mgt see* **automation**

medallion *E-com* the microprocessor chip in a *smart card*

media independent *Mkting* an organisation that specialises in planning and buying advertising for clients or advertising agencies

median *Stats* the value that divides a set of ranked observations into two parts of equal size

media plan *Mkting* an assessment and outline of the various **advertising media** to be used for a campaign

media planner *Mkting* an employee of an advertising agency or media independent who chooses the media, timing, and frequency of advertising

media schedule *Mkting* a document that sets out the choice of media, timing, and frequency for advertising

mediation *HR* intervention by a third party in a dispute in order to try to reach agreement between the disputing parties. Where a commitment or award is imposed on either party the process is known as **arbitration**. *Also known as* **conciliation**

Medicare 1. *Fin* a US health insurance programme in which the government pays part of the cost of medical care and hospital treatment for people over 65 **2.** (*ANZ*) *Gen Mgt* the Australian public health insurance system. It was created in 1983 and is funded by a levy on income.

medium of exchange *Fin* anything that is used to pay for goods. Nowadays, this always take the form of money (banknotes and coins), but in ancient societies, it included anything from cattle to shells.

medium-sized business *Gen Mgt* an organisation with between 100 and 500 employees. *See also* **small business**, **large-sized business**

medium-term bond *Fin* a bond that has at least five but no more than 10 years before its redemption date. *See also* **long-term bond**

meeting *Gen Mgt* a gathering of two or more people for a particular purpose. Meetings are convened for a variety of purposes, including planning, *decision-making*, *problem-solving*, communication, and the exchange of information. They may be informal, for example, a few people getting together to discuss ideas, or they may be formal, following strict procedures. Formal meetings are conducted by a chairperson (see *chair*) according to an *agenda* set in advance, and the proceedings are recorded in *minutes*. Some meetings, such as company board meetings and *AGMs*, are a legal requirement, and take place on a regular basis.

megacity *Gen Mgt* a very large city in which media and political power is concentrated because of its key role in global information networks

megacorporation *or* **megacorp** (*US*) *Gen Mgt* an informal term for an extremely large and powerful business organisation

megatrend *Gen Mgt* a general shift in thinking or approach affecting countries, industries, and organisations. The term was made popular by **John Naisbitt** in his bestseller *Megatrends* (1982).

MEGO *abbr Gen Mgt* my eyes glaze over: an often sarcastic exclamation of wonder at the complexity of what a person has just said (*slang*)

meltdown *Fin* an incidence of substantial losses on the stock market. Black Monday (19 October 1987) was described as Meltdown Monday in the press the following day.

member bank *Fin* a bank that is a member of the US Federal Reserve System

member firm *Fin* a firm of brokers or market makers that are members of the London Stock Exchange

---

In many walks of life, a conscience is a more expensive encumbrance than a wife or a carriage.
Thomas de Quincey

member of a company *Fin* in the United Kingdom, a shareholder whose name is recorded in the register of members

members' voluntary liquidation *Fin* in the United Kingdom, a special resolution passed by the members of a solvent company for the winding-up of the organisation. Prior to the resolution the directors of the company must make a declaration of solvency. Should the appointed liquidator have grounds for believing that the company is not solvent, the winding-up will be treated as compulsory liquidation. *See also* **voluntary liquidation**

memo *Gen Mgt* a documented note that acts as a reminder and is used for conveying and recording information. The memo has to some extent been displaced by e-mail, although it is still sometimes used for important communications.

memorandum of association *Gen Mgt* an official company document, registered with the *Registrar of Companies*. A memorandum of association sets out company name, status, address of the registered office, objectives of the company, statement of *limited liability*, amount of guarantee, and the amount of authorised share capital. The *articles of association* is a related document.

memory *E-com* the facility that enables a computer to store data and programs

mentoring *HR* a form of *employee development* whereby a trusted and respected person—the mentor—uses their experience to offer guidance, encouragement, career advice, and support to another person—the mentee. The aim of mentoring is to facilitate the mentee's learning and development and to enable them to discover more about their potential. Mentoring can occur informally or it can be arranged by means of an organisational scheme.

Mentor/mentee relationships can take any form that suits the individuals involved, but in practice there are a few rules that apply to most such arrangements—the most important of which is that anything discussed remains confidential. The relationship also needs to be based on trust and candid communication. A mentor does not have to belong to the same organisation as the mentee, but can come from any sphere of the mentee's life—trade association, college, local committee, for example—just as long as he or she is not the mentee's direct supervisor or working in the same department. Mentoring does not have to be paid for; in fact it is usually seen as an hon-

our by the mentor. . .many accomplished individuals consider it good professional citizenship to participate in the process of helping those coming up after them. It can also frequently be beneficial to volunteer to be a mentor, as many organisations consider mentoring a valuable hallmark of leadership material.

mercantile *Econ* relating to trading or commercial activity

mercantile agency *Fin* a company that evaluates the creditworthiness of potential corporate borrowers. *See also* **credit bureau**

mercantile paper *Fin see* **commercial paper**

mercantilism *Econ* the body of economic thought developed between the 1650s and 1750s, based on the belief that a country's wealth depended on the strength of its foreign trade

merchandising *Mkting* **1.** the process of increasing the market share of a product in retail outlets using display, stocking, and sales promotion techniques **2.** the promotion of goods associated with a particular *brand*, film, or celebrity. Merchandising based on a specific film, for example, may significantly add to its total revenues through appropriate *licensing* opportunities. Merchandising may include clothing, toys, food products, or music and often extends well beyond the *core business* of the producer of the original product.

merchant account *E-com* an account established by an e-merchant at a financial institution or *merchant bank* to receive the proceeds of credit card transactions

merchant bank 1. *E-com* a financial institution at which an e-merchant has opened a *merchant account* into which the proceeds of credit card transactions are credited after the institution has subtracted its fee **2.** *Fin* a bank that does not accept deposits but only provides services to those who offer securities to investors and also to those investors. *US term* **investment bank**

merger *Gen Mgt* the union of two or more organisations under single ownership, through the direct **acquisition** by one organisation of the net assets or liabilities of the other. A merger can be the result of a friendly *takeover*, which results in the combining of companies on an equal footing. After a merger, the legal existence of the acquired organisation is terminated. There is no standard definition of a merger, as each union is different, depending on what is expected from the merger, and on the negotiations, strategy, stock and assets, human resources, and shareholders of the players. Four broad types of mergers are recognised. A **horizontal merger** involves firms from the same industry, while a **vertical merger** involves firms from the same supply chain. A **circular merger** involves firms with different products but similar distribution channels. A *conglomerate company* is produced by the union of firms with few or no similarities in production or marketing but that come together to create a larger economic base and greater profit potential. *Also known as* **acquisition, one-to-one merger**. *See also* **consolidation, joint venture, partnership**

mergers and acquistions *Fin* a blanket term covering the main ways in which organisations change hands. *Abbr* **M&A**

merit rating *or* **merit pay** *HR* a payment system in which the personal qualities of an employee are rated according to organisational requirements, and a pay increase or bonus is made against the results of this rating. Merit rating has been in use since the 1950s. Unlike new *performance-related pay* systems, which focus rewards on the output of an employee, merit rating examines an employee's input to the organisation—for example, their attendance, adaptability, or aptitude—as well as the quality or quantity of work produced. In merit rating schemes, these factors may be weighted to reflect their relative importance and the resultant points score determines whether the employee earns a bonus or pay increase.

metadata *E-com* essential information on a document or web page, such as publication date, author, keywords, title, and summary. This information is used by search engines to find relevant websites when a user requests a search.

When designing metadata, there are several rules which it is useful to keep in mind. Always remember the type of person who will be looking for the content—how would they like the content classified? Only collect metadata that is genuinely useful—someone has to fill in all the metadata, and if you ask for too much, it will slow down the publishing process and make it more expensive. Make sure that all essential information is collected—if copyright information is needed, make certain that copyright is part of the metadata list. Check that people are not abusing metadata—some will put popular keywords in their metadata just to increase the chance of their

documents coming up in a search, whether relevant or not. Remember that metadata should be strongly linked with advanced search—the metadata form the parameters for refining an advanced search. *See also* *meta-tag*

meta-tag *E-com* any of the keyword and description commands used in a web page code that are used to help search engines index the website

Metcalfe's law *E-com* the proposition that networks dramatically increase in value with each additional user. Metcalfe's law was formulated by Robert Metcalfe, founder of 3Com, and has been instrumental in developing the concept of *viral marketing*.

methods-time measurement *Gen Mgt* a system of *standard times* for movements made by people in the performance of work tasks. Methods-time measurement was developed in the 1940s and is the most widely used of *predetermined motion-time systems* of *work measurement* designed to increase efficiency and consistency in work operations. Work operations are broken down into a set of basic motions such as reach, grasp, position, and release and standard times for each motion are calculated by analysing films of industrial operations. Simplified versions of the system called MTM2 and MTM3, approved in 1965 and 1970 respectively, use combinations of the basic motions, such as get and put. *Abbr* **MTM**

method study *Gen Mgt* the systematic recording, examination, and analysis of existing and proposed ways of carrying out work tasks in order to discover the most efficient and economical methods of performing them. The basic procedure followed in method study is as follows: select the area to be studied; record the data; examine the data; develop alternative approaches; install the new method; maintain the new method. Method study forms part of *work study* and is normally carried out prior to *work measurement*. The technique was initially developed to evaluate manufacturing processes but has been used more widely to evaluate alternative courses of action. It is based on research into *motion study* carried out by *Frank* and *Lillian Gilbreth* during the 1920s and 1930s.

Mickey Mouse *Gen Mgt* so simple as to appear silly or trivial (*slang*)

microbusiness *Gen Mgt* a very *small business* with fewer than ten employees

---

microcash *E-com* a form of electronic money with no denominations, permitting sub-denomination transactions of a fraction of a penny or cent

microeconomic incentive *Econ* a tax benefit or subsidy given to a business to achieve a particular objective such as increased sales overseas

microeconomics *Econ* the branch of economics that studies the contribution of groups of consumers or firms, or of individual consumers, to a country's economy

microeconomy *Econ* those narrow sectors of a country's economic activity that influence the behaviour of the economy as a whole, for example, consumer choices

microhedge *Fin* a hedge that relates to a single asset or liability. *See also* **macrohedge**

micromanagement *Gen Mgt* **1.** managing the finer details of a project or enterprise, for example, examining the operational minutiae of a task **2.** a style of management where a manager becomes over-involved in the details of the work of subordinates, resulting in the manager making every decision in an organisation, no matter how trivial. Micromanagement is a euphemism for meddling, and has the opposite effect to **empowerment**. Micromanagement can retard the progress of **organisational development** as it robs employees of their self-respect.

micromarketing *Mkting* marketing to individuals or very small groups. Micromarketing contrasts with mass marketing and targets the specific interests and needs of individuals by offering customised products or services. It is similar to **niche marketing**, but rather than targeting one large niche, a micromarketing company targets a large number of very small niches.

micromerchant *E-com* a provider of goods or services on the Internet in exchange for electronic money

micropayment *E-com, Fin* a payment protocol for small amounts of electronic money, ranging from a fraction of a cent or penny to no more than ten US dollars or euros

middleman *Gen Mgt* an intermediary in a transaction. With direct sales models, manufacturers cut out the middleman by dealing directly with end customers.

middle management *HR* the position held by managers who are considered neither senior nor junior in an organisation. Middle managers were subject to **delayering** and

downsizing in the 1980s as organisations sought to reduce costs by removing the layer of managers between those who had direct interface with customers and senior decision-makers.

middle price *Fin* a price, halfway between the bid price and the offer price, that is generally quoted in the press and on information screens

mid-range *Stats* the mean of the largest and smallest values in a statistical sample

migrate *Gen Mgt* to transfer data and applications from an existing computer system to a new one

millennium bug *Gen Mgt* the inability of some computer systems to recognise the year 2000 as a date. The millennium bug arose from the computer programming practice of using two digits to represent a year. It was thought that this could cause great problems when digital clocks turned from 1999 to 2000, because computers would read 00 and cease to function. The millennium bug was thought to affect any business system that used electronically generated date information. Speculation on what would happen sparked fears of global disaster. Much work was carried out in the late 1990s in order to correct the problem and systems that did not have the bug were referred to as **Y2K-compliant**, Y2K being shorthand for Year 2000. In the event, the anticipated disaster did not occur.

millionerd *E-com* somebody who has become a millionaire through working in a high-tech business (*slang*)

MIME *abbr E-com* multipurpose Internet mail extension: a standard Internet protocol enabling users to send binary files as e-mail attachments

Mind Map™ *Gen Mgt* a graphical tool that can be used to visualise and clarify thoughts or ideas. In a Mind Map, the central image or idea is drawn in the middle of a piece of paper with major branches radiating from it to denote related themes. Second and third levels of thought are connected by thinner branches. Mind Maps can include the use of colour or pictures. Developed by **Tony Buzan**, the Mind Mapping technique can be used to introduce order and rationality to thought processes, and develop the creative, artistic, logical, and mathematical elements of the brain.

mindshare *Mkting* the process of fostering favourable attitudes towards a product or organisation

---

minimax regret criterion *Fin* an approach to decision-making under uncertainty in which the opportunity cost (regret) associated with each possible course of action is measured, and the decision-maker selects the activity which minimises the maximum regret, or loss. Regret is measured as the difference between the best and worst possible payoff for each option.

minimum lending rate (*US*) *Fin* an interest rate charged by a central bank, which serves as a floor for loans in a country

minimum quote size *Fin* the smallest number of shares that a market must handle in one trade of a particular security

minimum salary *HR* the lowest amount of money that an employee is guaranteed to earn. A minimum salary is **basic pay**, which may be increased if an employee qualifies for a **bonus** by performing well. **Payment by results**, **performance-related pay**, and sales **commission** are paid on top of a minimum salary.

minimum stock level *Fin* a stock level, set for control purposes, below which stockholding should not fall without being highlighted. It is calculated as follows:

(reorder level – (average rate of usage × average lead time))

minimum subscription *Fin* the smallest number of shares or securities that may be applied for in a new issue

minimum wage *HR* an hourly rate of pay, usually set by government, to which all **employees** are legally entitled

minority interest *Fin* the nominal value of shares held in a subsidiary undertaking by members other than the parent company or its nominees plus the appropriate portion of the accumulated reserves, including share premium account

minority ownership *Fin* ownership of less than 50% of a company's ordinary shares, which is not enough to control the company

Mintzberg, Henry (*b.* 1939) *Gen Mgt* Canadian academic. Known for his views on **strategic management** and **strategic planning**, and for analysing managerial work. In *The Nature of Managerial Work* (1973), he showed that the work done by managers was substantially different from the way it was described in business theory.

Mintzberg graduated in mechanical engineering from McGill University in 1961 and later obtained a PhD in management from MIT. He is currently professor of management at McGill University, Montreal, and professor of organisation at INSEAD in Fontainebleau, France.

minutes *Gen Mgt* an official written record of the proceedings of a **meeting**. Minutes normally record points for action, and indicate who is responsible for implementing decisions. Good practice requires that the minutes of a meeting be circulated well in advance of the next meeting, and that those attending that meeting read the minutes in advance. Registered companies are required to keep minutes of meetings and make them available at their registered offices for inspection by company members and shareholders.

mirror *E-com* a copy of a website held on a different server and therefore available at a different location. Mirror sites can be used to accelerate download times by alleviating website congestion. Sites offering software downloads are the most common form of mirror site.

MIS *abbr Ops* management information system: a computer-based system for collecting, storing, processing, and providing access to information used in the management of an organisation. Management information systems evolved from early electronic data processing systems. They support managerial **decision-making** by providing regular structured reports on organisational operations. Management information systems may support the functional areas of an organisation such as finance, marketing, or production. **Decision support systems** and **EISs** are types of MIS developed for more specific purposes.

mismanagement *Gen Mgt* functional or ethical dereliction of duty due to ignorance, negligence, incompetence, avoidance, or criminality

missing value *Stats* an observation that is absent from a set of statistical data, for example, because a member of a population to be sampled was not at home when the researcher called

mission statement *Gen Mgt* a short memorable statement of the reasons for the existence of an organisation. *See also* **vision statement**

MIT *abbr Fin* market if touched

Mittelstand *Gen Mgt* a German term which incorporates the meaning of **small and medium-sized enterprises**

mixed economy *Econ* an economy in which both public and private enterprises participate

---

in the production and supply of goods and services

MMC *abbr Fin* Monopolies and Mergers Commission

mobile office *Gen Mgt* the practice of working on the move. Mobile office equipment would typically include a mobile phone, laptop computer, and a modem to link the computer to the Internet or a company's main office.

mobile worker *HR* an employee who does not have one fixed place of work. Mobile workers are linked to a central base by telephone and sometimes by computer technology. A *teleworker* is a form of mobile worker.

mode *Stats* the most frequently occurring value in a set of ranked observations

model building *Stats* the process of providing an adequate fit to the data in a set of observations in a statistical study

modem *E-com* a device that transforms computer data into signals that can be sent over telephone lines. The modem enables computers to transmit and receive data. The speed at which it can send and receive data is measured in BPS (bits per second).

moderator *E-com* somebody in charge of a newsgroup, mailing list discussion group, or similar forum

modernisation *Gen Mgt* investing in new equipment or upgrading existing equipment to bring resources up to date or improve efficiency

modified ACRS *Fin* a system used in the United States for computing the depreciation of some assets acquired after 1985 in a way that reduces taxes. The ACRS applies to older assets. *See also accelerated cost recovery system*

modified book value *Fin see adjusted book value*

modified cash basis *Fin* the bookkeeping practice of accounting for short-term assets on a cash basis and for long-term assets on an accrual basis

Moller, Claus (*b.* 1942) *Gen Mgt* Danish consultant. Founder of Time Manager International™ (1975), advocate of the theory that effective *customer service* is achieved through employees' personal development, he is the originator of the concepts 'Time Manager' and 'Putting People First'.

mom-and-pop operation (*US*) (*& Canada*) *Gen Mgt = Ma and Pa shop* (*slang*)

moment of conception *Gen Mgt* the point at which a new organisation takes shape in the mind of its founder

Monday-morning quarterback (*US*) (*& Canada*) *Gen Mgt* somebody who criticises a decision only when it is too late to change it (*slang*)

Mondex *E-com* an electronic cash system that uses a smart card for both traditional shopping and e-commerce transactions

Mondragon co-operative *Gen Mgt* a large, worker-ownership movement based in the town of Mondragon, in the Basque region of northwest Spain. The Mondragon co-operative movement started in 1956, and was founded on the teachings of *José Maria Arizmendietta*. It consists of worker-owned businesses, supported by a savings bank that raises money for the co-operative enterprises. Mondragon is not part of the traditional *co-operative movement*, and is instead based on ten principles: equality of opportunity; the democratic election of managers; sovereignty of labour; a requirement for capital to be used by labour rather than labour used by capital; participative management; low pay differentials; co-operation with other co-operative movements; social change; solidarity with those working for peace, justice, and development; and education.

MONEP *abbr Fin* Marché des Options Négotiables de Paris

monetarism *Econ* an economic theory that states that inflation is caused by increases in a country's money supply

monetary *Fin* relating to or involving money, cash, or assets

monetary assets *Fin* a generic term for accounts receivable, cash, and bank balances: assets that are realisable at the amount stated in the accounts. Other assets, for example, facilities and machinery, inventories, and marketable securities will not necessarily realise the sum stated in a business's balance sheet.

monetary base *Econ* the stock of a country's coins, notes, and bank deposits with the central bank

monetary base control *Econ* government measures to restrict the amount of stocks of *liquid assets* in an economy

monetary policy *Econ, Fin* government economic policy concerning a country's rate of interest, its exchange rate, and the amount of money in the economy

monetary reserve *Fin* the foreign currency and precious metals that a country holds, usually in a central bank

monetary system *Econ* the set of government regulations concerning a country's monetary reserves and its holdings of notes and coins

monetary unit *Fin* the standard unit of a country's currency

monetise *Econ* to establish a currency as a country's legal tender

money *Econ* a medium of exchange that is accepted throughout a country as payment for services and goods and as a means of settling debts

money at call and short notice *Fin* **1.** in the United Kingdom, advances made by banks to other financial institutions, or corporate and personal customers, that are repayable either upon demand (call) or within 14 days (short notice) **2.** in the United Kingdom, balances in an account that are either available upon demand (call) or within 14 days (short notice)

money broker *Fin* an intermediary who works on the money market

moneyer *Fin* somebody who is authorised to coin money

money illusion *Econ* the tendency of consumers to react to prices in monetary terms rather than taking account of factors such as inflation

money laundering *Fin* the process of making money obtained illegally appear legitimate by passing it through banks or businesses

moneylender *Fin* a person who lends money for interest

money market *Fin* the short-term wholesale market for securities maturing in one year, such as certificates of deposit, treasury bills, and commercial paper

money market account *Fin* an account with a financial institution that requires a high minimum deposit and pays a rate of interest related to the wholesale money market rates and so is generally higher than retail rates. Most institutions offer a range of term accounts, with either a fixed rate or variable rate, and notice accounts, with a range of notice periods at variable rates.

money market fund *Fin* a unit trust that invests in short-term debt securities

money market instruments *Fin* short-term (usually under 12 months) assets and securities, such as certificates of deposit, and commercial paper and treasury bills, that are traded on money markets

money national income *Econ* GDP measured using money value, not adjusted for the effect of inflation

money of account *Fin* a monetary unit that is used in keeping accounts but is not necessarily an actual currency unit

money order *Fin* a written order to pay somebody a sum of money, issued by a bank or post office

money purchase pension scheme *Fin* in the United Kingdom, a pension plan where the fund that is built up is used to purchase an annuity. The retirement income that the beneficiary receives therefore depends on his or her contributions, the performance of the investments those contributions are used to buy, the annuity rates, and the type of annuity purchased at retirement.

money-purchase plan *Fin* in the United States, a pension plan (a defined benefit plan) in which the participant contributes part and the firm contributes at the same or a different rate

money substitute *Econ* the use of goods as a medium of exchange because of the degree of devaluation of a country's currency

money supply *Econ* the stock of **liquid assets** in a country's economy that can be given in exchange for services or goods

money wages *Econ* wages that are expressed in terms of money units and are not adjusted for changes in price. *US term* **nominal wages**

Monopolies and Mergers Commission *Fin* in the United Kingdom, a commission that was replaced by the Competition Commission in April 1999. *Abbr* **MMC**

monopoly *Gen Mgt* a **market** in which there is only one producer or one seller. A company establishes a monopoly by entering a new market or eliminating all competitors from an existing market. A company that holds a monopoly has control of a market and the ability to fix prices. For this reason, governments usually try to avoid monopoly situations and in the United Kingdom the Competition Commission exists to regulate this

---

Few rich men own their own property. The property owns them.   *Robert Green Ingersoll*

area. Some monopolies, however, such as government-owned utilities, are seen as beneficial to *consumers*.

Monte Carlo method *Gen Mgt* a statistical technique used in business *decision-making* that involves a number of uncertain variables, such as capital investment and resource allocation. The name of the Monte Carlo method derives from the use of random numbers as generated by a roulette wheel. The numbers are used in repeated simulations, often performed by spreadsheet programs on computers, to calculate a range of possible outcomes. The technique was developed by mathematicians in the early 1960s for use in nuclear physics and *operational research* but has since been used more widely.

moonlighting *HR* undertaking a second job, often for cash and in the evenings, in addition to a full-time permanent job

Moore's law *E-com* the proposition that every 18 months computer chip density (and hence computer power) will double while costs remain constant, creating ever more powerful computers without raising their price. Moore's law was formulated by Intel founder Gordon Moore in the 1960s. IBM and Intel research published in 1997 corroborates it.

moral hazard *Fin* the risk that the existence of a contract will cause behavioural changes in one or both parties to the contract, as where asset insurance causes less care to be taken over the safeguarding of the assets

morality in business *Gen Mgt* see *business ethics*

moratorium *Fin* a period of delay, for example, additional time agreed by a creditor and a debtor for recovery of a debt

more bang for your buck (*US*) *Fin* a better return on your investment (*slang*)

Morgan, Gareth (*b*. 1943) *Gen Mgt* Canadian academic. Originator of the term *imaginisation*, which he described in the book of the same name (1993).

Morita, Akio (1921–99) *Gen Mgt* Japanese business executive. Co-founder and chairman of the electronics company Sony, whose global success has been based on product innovation, most famously the Walkman. The phrase 'Think global, act local' has been attributed to Morita. His experiences are recorded in his autobiography *Made in Japan* (1986).

mortgage *Fin* **1.** a financial lending arrangement whereby an individual borrows money from a bank, or another lending institution, in order to buy property or land. The original amount borrowed, the **principal**, is then repaid with interest to the lender over a fixed number of years. **2.** a borrowing arrangement whereby the lender is granted a legal right to an asset, usually a property, should the borrower default on the repayments. Mortgages are usually taken out by individuals who wish to secure a long-term loan to buy a home. *See also* ***current account mortgage***, ***endowment mortgage***, ***interest-only mortgage***, ***low start mortgage***, ***repayment mortgage***

mortgage-backed security *Fin* a security for which a mortgage is collateral

mortgage bond (*US*) *Fin* a debt secured by land or property

mortgage broker *Fin* a person or company that acts as an agent between people seeking mortgages and organisations that offer them

mortgagee *Fin* a person or organisation that lends money to a borrower under a mortgage agreement. *See also* ***mortgagor***

mortgage equity analysis *Fin* a computation of the difference between the value of a property and the amount owed on it in the form of mortgages

mortgage insurance *Fin* insurance that provides somebody holding a mortgage with protection against default

mortgage lien *Fin* a claim against a property that is mortgaged

mortgage note *Fin* a note that documents the existence and terms of a mortgage

mortgage pool *Fin* a group of mortgages with similar characteristics packaged together for sale

mortgage portfolio *Fin* a group of mortgages held by a mortgage banker

mortgage rate *Fin* the interest rate charged on a mortgage by a lender

mortgage tax *Fin* a tax on mortgages

mortgagor *Fin* somebody who has taken out a mortgage to borrow money. *See also* ***mortgagee***

Mosaic *E-com* the first web browser made available for Macintosh and Windows. It was developed by Netscape founder Marc Andreesen.

Capital must be propelled by self-interest; it cannot be enticed by benevolence.   *Walter Bagehot*

most distant futures contract *Fin* a futures option with the latest delivery date. *See also* **nearby futures contract**

MOTAS *abbr Gen Mgt* member of the appropriate sex (*slang*)

motion study *Gen Mgt* the observation of physical movements involved in the performance of work, and investigation of how these can be made more effective and cost efficient. Motion study was originally developed by **Frank** and **Lillian Gilbreth**, and is now often grouped with **time study**, to form **time and motion study**.

motion-time analysis *Gen Mgt see* **predetermined motion-time system**

motivate (*S Africa*) *Gen Mgt* to argue for a position or request, especially in a proposal

motivation *Gen Mgt* **1.** the creation of stimuli, incentives, and working environments which enable people to perform to the best of their ability in pursuit of organisational success. Motivation is commonly viewed as the magic driver that enables managers to get others to achieve their targets. In the 20th century, there was a shift, at least in theory, away from motivation by dictation and discipline, exemplified by **Frederick Winslow Taylor**'s scientific management, towards motivation by creating an appropriate corporate climate and addressing the needs of individual employees. Although it is widely agreed to be one of the key management tasks, it has frequently been argued that one person cannot motivate others but can only create conditions for others to self-motivate. Many **management theorists** have provided insights into motivation. **Elton Mayo**'s **Hawthorne experiments** identify some root causes of self-motivation, and **Abraham Maslow**'s hierarchy of needs provides insight into personal behaviour patterns. Other influential research has been carried out by **Frederick Herzberg**, who looked at **job satisfaction**, and **Douglas McGregor** whose **Theory X** and **Theory Y** suggest management styles that motivate and demotivate employees. **2.** (*S Africa*) a formal written proposal

motivators *HR see* **job satisfaction**

MOTOS *abbr Gen Mgt* member of the opposite sex (*slang*)

MOTSS *abbr Gen Mgt* member of the same sex (*slang*)

mouse milk *Gen Mgt* to do a disproportionately large amount of work on a project that yields very little return (*slang*)

mouse potato *E-com* a person who spends an excessive amount of time using a computer (*slang*)

mousetrap
build a better mousetrap *Mkting* to create a new or better product (*slang*)

Mouton, Jane (1930–87) *Gen Mgt* US psychologist. *See* **Blake, Robert**

mover and shaker *Gen Mgt* an influential and dynamic person within an organisation or group of people (*slang*)

move time *Fin* the time taken in moving a product between locations during the production process. *See also* **cycle time**

MRP II *abbr Ops* manufacturing resource planning: a computer-based manufacturing, inventory planning and control system that broadens the scope of production planning by involving other functional areas that affect production decisions. Manufacturing resource planning evolved from material requirements planning to integrate other functions in the planning process. These functions may include engineering, marketing, purchasing, production scheduling, business planning, and finance.

MSB *abbr Fin* mutual savings bank

MTM *abbr Gen Mgt* methods-time measurement

multi-channel *E-com* using a combination of online and offline communication methods to conduct business

multicurrency *Fin* relating to a loan that gives the borrower a choice of currencies

multi-employer bargaining *HR* the centralisation of **pay** negotiations at industry level, either nationally or regionally, usually conducted by **employers' associations** and **trade unions**. Multi-employer bargaining is a form of **collective bargaining**. Seen as having a moderating influence on pay rises, it hinders flexibility to link pay awards to company or individual employee performance.

multifunctional card *Fin* a plastic card that may be used for two or more purposes, for example, as a cash card, a cheque card, and a debit card

multilevel marketing *Gen Mgt see* **network marketing**

multimedia *Gen Mgt* a method of presenting information on a computer, CD-ROM, television, or games console. The presentation combines different media such as sound, graphics, video, and text.

Multimedia has had problems on the Web, due mainly to limited **bandwidth**. Web browsers are not designed to view most multimedia so extra software is required: a **plug-in**.

multimedia document *Gen Mgt* an electronic document that incorporates interactive material from a range of different media such as text, video, sound, graphics, and animation. Such documents can be viewed on a multimedia computer or transmitted via the Internet.

multinational business *or* **multinational company** *Gen Mgt* a company, or corporation, that operates internationally, usually with subsidiaries, offices, or production facilities in more than one country

multiparty auction *E-com* a method of buying and selling on the Internet in which prospective buyers make electronic bids

multiple application *Fin* the submission of more than one share application for a new issue which is expected to be oversubscribed. In most jurisdictions, this practice is illegal.

multiple exchange rate *Fin* a two-tier rate of exchange used in certain countries where the most advantageous rate may be for tourists or for businesses proposing to build a factory

multiple regression analysis *Gen Mgt see* **regression analysis**

multiple sourcing *Ops* a **purchasing** policy of using two or more suppliers for products or services. Multiple sourcing prevents reliance on any one supplier, as is the case in **single sourcing**. It encourages competition between suppliers, and ensures access to a wide range of goods or services. Dealing with more than one supplier can improve access to market information but can also entail more administration.

multiple time series *Stats* two or more **time series** that are observed simultaneously

multiskilling *HR, Ops* a process by which employees acquire new skills. Multiskilling is a form of **flexible working** in which employees are available to undertake a number of different jobs. It has led to a reduction in **demarcation disputes** and greater **employability** for employees.

multitasking *Gen Mgt* the practice of performing several different tasks simultaneously (*slang*)

multivariate analysis *Gen Mgt* any of a number of statistical techniques used in **operational research** to examine the characteristics and relationships between multiple variables. Multivariate analysis techniques include **cluster analysis**, **discriminant analysis**, and multiple **regression analysis**.

multivariate data *Stats* data for which each observation involves values for more than one random variable

mum and dad investors (*ANZ*) *Gen Mgt* people who hold or wish to purchase shares but have little experience or knowledge of the stock market (*slang*)

Mumford, Alan *Gen Mgt* British academic. *See* **Honey, Peter**

Mumford, Enid (*b.* 1924) *Gen Mgt* British academic. She adopted the socio-technical approach of the Tavistock Institute of Human Relations, applying it to the design and implementation of information technology. Mumford termed her method ETHICS (Effective Technical and Human Implementation of Computer-based Systems), which is explained in *Effective Systems Design and Requirements Analysis: The ETHICS Approach* (1995).

municipal bond *Fin* in the United States, a security issued by states, local governments, and municipalities to pay for special projects such as motorways

Murphy's Law (*US*) *Gen Mgt* = **Sod's Law**

mushroom job (*US*) *Gen Mgt* a job that is unpleasant (*slang*)

mutual *Fin* used to describe an organisation that is run in the interests of its members and that does not have to pay dividends to its shareholders, so surplus profits can be ploughed back into the business. In the United Kingdom, building societies and friendly societies were formed as mutual organisations, although in recent years many have demutualised, either by becoming public limited companies or by being bought by other financial organisations, resulting in members receiving cash or share windfall payments. In the United States, **mutual associations**, a type of savings and loan association, and state-chartered mutual savings banks are organised in this way.

mutual association (*US*) *Fin see* **mutual**

mutual company *Fin* a company that is owned by its customers who share in the profits

mutual fund (*US*) *Fin* = **unit trust**

---

mutual insurance *Fin* an insurance company that is owned by its policyholders who share the profits and cover claims with their pooled premiums

mutual savings bank *Fin* in the United States, a state-chartered savings bank run in the interests of its members. It is governed by a local board of trustees, not the legal owners. Some of these banks have recently begun offering accounts and services that are typical of commercial banks. *Abbr* **MSB**

Myers-Briggs type indicator *HR* a *psychometric test* that identifies four basic preferences in people's behaviour. The indicator was created in the 1940s by *Katherine Cook Briggs* and her daughter *Isabel Briggs-Myers*. It is based largely on the Jungian theory of personality types. The four preferences identified are made up of pairs of opposites: extraversion and introversion; sensing and intuition; thinking and feeling; and judgment and perception. The indicator provides a framework allowing people to understand themselves and others more fully, as well as encouraging the appreciation of different styles and perceptions. It is often used in *team building* and in the *recruitment* process.

MYOB *abbr Gen Mgt* mind your own business (*slang*)

mystery shopping *Mkting* the use of employees or agents to visit a store or use a service anonymously and assess its quality. Mystery shopping is used to assess such factors as the quality of customer service, including general and technical efficiency, and friendliness of staff, layout, and appearance of the premises, and quality and range of goods or services on offer. Mystery shoppers fill in a questionnaire based on their impressions and this information is then used to identify possible areas for business or service improvement.

Naisbitt, John (*b.* 1930) *Gen Mgt* US business executive and forecaster. Known for the publication of *Megatrends* (1982) in which he predicted ten main patterns of change that would shape the world.

naked debenture *Fin see* **debenture**

naked option *Fin* an option in which the underlying asset is not owned by the seller, who risks considerable loss if the price of the asset falls

naked writer *Fin* a writer of an option who does not own the underlying shares

name *Fin* an individual who is a member of Lloyd's of London

Napsterise *E-com* to distribute without charge something that somebody else owns. The term stems from the peer-to-peer business model pioneered by Napster, a software package for electronically distributing copies of copyrighted music without charge or payment of royalties. (*slang*)

narrowcasting *E-com* targeting information to a niche audience. Owing to its ability to personalise information to the requirements of individual users, the Internet is generally viewed as a narrowcast (rather than broadcast) medium.

narrow market *Fin* a market where the trading volume is low. A characteristic of such a market is a wide spread of bid and offer prices.

narrow range securities *Fin see* **trustee investment**

NASD *abbr Fin* National Association of Securities Dealers

NASDAQ *abbr Fin* National Association of Securities Dealers Automated Quotation system: a screen-based quotation system supporting market-making in US-registered equities. NASDAQ International has operated from London since 1992.

NASDAQ Composite Index *Fin* a specialist US share price index covering shares of high-technology companies

National Association of Investors Corporation (*US*) *Fin* a US organisation that fosters investment clubs

National Association of Securities Dealers *Fin* in the United States, the self-regulatory organisation for securities dealers that develops rules and regulations, conducts regulatory reviews of members' business activities, and designs and operates marketplace services facilities. It is responsible for the regulation of the NASDAQ Stock Market as well as the extensive US over-the-counter securities market. Established in 1938, it operates subject to the Securities Exchange Commission oversight and has a membership that includes virtually every US broker or dealer doing securities business with the public. *Abbr* **NASD**

national bank *Fin* **1.** a bank owned or controlled by the state that acts as a bank for the government and implements its monetary policies **2.** (*US*) a bank that operates under federal charter and is legally required to be a member of the Federal Reserve System

national debt *Econ, Fin* the total borrowing of a country's central government that is unpaid

national demand *Econ* the total demand of consumers in an economy

National Guarantee Fund *Fin* a supply of money held by the Australian Stock Exchange which is used to compensate investors for losses incurred when an exchange member fails to meet its obligations

national income *Econ* the total earnings from a country's production of services and goods in a particular year

national income accounts *Fin* economic statistics that show the state of a nation's economy over a given period of time, usually a year. *See also* **gross domestic product**, **gross national product**

National Insurance contributions *Fin* in the United Kingdom, payments made by both employers and employees to the government. The contributions, together with other government receipts, are used to finance state pensions and other benefits such as the dole. *Abbr* **NIC**

nationalisation *Gen Mgt* the taking over of privately owned companies by government. Nationalisation has strong political connotations. Recent global political trends have moved away from nationalisation by introducing more competition and liberalisation into markets. *See also* **privatisation**

National Market System *Fin* in the United States, an inter-exchange network system designed to foster greater competition between domestic stock exchanges. Legislated for in 1975, it was implemented in 1978 with the Intermarket Trading System that electronically links eight markets: American, Boston, Cincinnati, Chicago, New York, Pacific, Philadelphia, and the NASD over-the-counter market. It allows traders at any exchange to seek the best available price on all other exchanges that a particular security is eligible to trade on. *Abbr* **NMS**

National Occupational Health and Safety Commission (*ANZ*) *Gen Mgt* an Australian statutory body responsible for co-ordinating efforts to prevent injury, disease, and deaths occurring in the workplace. *Abbr* **NOHSC**. *Also known as* **Worksafe Australia**

National Savings *Fin* in the United Kingdom, a government agency accountable to the Treasury that offers a range of savings products directly to the public or through post offices. The funds raised finance the national debt.

National Savings Bank *Fin* in the United Kingdom, a savings scheme established in 1861 as the Post Office Savings Bank and now operated by National Savings. *Abbr* **NSB**

National Savings Certificate *Fin* in the United Kingdom, either a fixed-interest or an index-linked certificate issued for two or five year terms by National Savings with returns that are free of income tax. *Abbr* **NSC**

National Vocational Qualification *HR* a qualification awarded following *vocational training*. National vocational qualifications are based on national standards developed by leading bodies from industrial and commercial sectors, defining the skills or *competences* required in particular occupations. Work-based evidence to demonstrate competence is assessed, and a qualification is awarded on the basis of the assessment. There is no formal examination. Five levels of NVQs are awarded, with level 1 equating to GCSE qualifications and level 5 equating to a higher degree. *Abbr* **NVQ**

national wage agreement *HR* a country-wide *collective agreement* reached through *collective bargaining* between *trade unions* and employers, which sets a national rate of *pay* within an industry or for a particular job

natural capitalism *Gen Mgt* an approach to capitalism in which protection of the earth's resources is a strategic priority

NAV *abbr Fin* net asset value

navigate *E-com* to find your way around the Internet, a website, or an *HTML* document.

Research has shown that people navigate in a certain way when reading content in a website, and certain standards and conventions of navigation are emerging for website design. More important than anything else is functionality: visitors want to find the information they are seeking quickly and easily, and are not particularly interested in style.

The most basic design convention, termed 'essential' or 'global' navigation, holds that every web page should have a set of essential navigation tools that are visible when the first screen loads, linking to key areas within the website. Essential navigation should contain links such as Home, About, Products, Customers, and Contact.

It is also important to let visitors know where they are on a website, with each page clearly displaying what part of the overall *classification* it represents. If it is the home page, for example, this should be made clear; or if it is a page dealing with pricing information, the heading at the top of the page should say so.

Users also find it useful to know where they have been on a website—usually done by changing the colour of *hyperlink*s that have been clicked on from blue to purple.

NBV *abbr Fin* net book value

NDA *abbr Gen Mgt* non-disclosure agreement, non-disparagement agreement

NDP *abbr Econ* net domestic product

nearby futures contract *Fin* a futures option with the earliest delivery date. *See also* *most distant futures contract*

nearby month *Fin* the earliest month for which there is a futures contract for a particular commodity. *Also known as* **spot month**. *See also* **far month**

near money *Fin* assets that can quickly be turned into cash, for example, some types of bank deposit, short-dated bonds, and certificates of deposit

negative amortisation *Fin* an increase in the principal (see *mortgage*) of a loan due to the inadequacy of payments to cover the interest

negative carry *Fin* interest that is so high that the borrowed money does not return enough profit to cover the cost of borrowing

negative cash flow *Fin* a cash flow with higher outgoings than income

---

Men work but slowly, that have poor wages. *Thomas Fuller*

negative equity *Fin* a situation in which a fall in prices leads to a property being worth less than was paid for it

negative gearing *Fin* the practice of borrowing money to invest in property or shares and claiming a tax deduction on the difference between the income and the interest repayments

negative income tax (*US*) *Econ* payments such as tax credits made to households or individuals to make their income up to a guaranteed minimum level

negative pledge clause *Fin* a provision in a bond that prohibits the issuer from doing something that would give an advantage to holders of other bonds

negative yield curve *Fin* a representation of interest rates that are higher for short-term bonds than they are for long-term bonds

negligence *Gen Mgt* the breach of a duty of care, resulting in harm to one or more people. Negligence occurs when an organisation causes harm or injury through carelessness or inattention to the needs of the groups to which it owes a duty of care. These can include its customers, consumers of its product or service, shareholders, or the local community. Victims of negligence are entitled to claim compensation. Negligence is considered to be **gross negligence** if it is the result of excessively careless behaviour.

negotiable certificate of deposit *Fin* a certificate of deposit with a very high value that can be freely traded

negotiable instrument *Fin* a document of title which can be freely traded, such as a bill of exchange or other certificate of debt

negotiable order of withdrawal *Fin* a cheque drawn on an account that bears interest

negotiable security *Fin* a security that can be freely traded

negotiate *Fin* to transfer financial instruments such as bearer securities, bills of exchange, cheques, and promissory notes, for consideration to another person

negotiated budget *Fin* a budget in which budget allowances are set largely on the basis of negotiations between budget holders and those to whom they report

negotiated commissions *Fin* commissions that result from bargaining between brokers

and their customers, typically large institutions

negotiated issue *Fin see* **negotiated offering**

negotiated market *Fin* a market in which each transaction results from negotiation between a buyer and a seller

negotiated offering *Fin* a public offering, the price of which is determined by negotiations between the issuer and a syndicate of underwriters. *Also known as* **negotiated issue**

negotiated sale *Fin* a public offering, the price of which is determined by negotiations between the issuer and a single underwriter

negotiation *Gen Mgt* a discussion with the aim of resolving a difference of opinion or dispute, or to settle the terms of an agreement or transaction

Nellie
sitting with Nellie *HR see* **on-the-job training** (*slang*)

nest egg *Fin* assets, usually other than a pension plan or retirement account, that have been set aside by an individual for his or her retirement (*slang*)

nester *Mkting* in advertising or marketing, a consumer who is not influenced by advertising hype but prefers value for money and traditional products (*slang*)

net advantage of refunding *Fin* the amount realised by refunding debt

net advantage to leasing *Fin* the amount by which leasing something is financially better than borrowing money and purchasing it

net advantage to merging *Fin* the amount by which the value of a merged enterprise exceeds the value of the pre-existing companies, minus the cost of the merger

net assets *Fin* the amount by which the value of a company's assets exceeds its liabilities

net asset value *Fin* a sum of the values of all that a unit trust owns at the end of a trading day. *Abbr* **NAV**

NetBill *E-com* a micropayment system developed at Carnegie Mellon University for purchasing digital goods over the Internet. After the goods are delivered in encrypted form to the purchaser's computer, the money is debited from the purchaser's prefunded account and the goods are decrypted for the purchaser's use.

Power tires only those who do not have it.   *Giulio Andreotti*

net book value *Fin* the historical cost of an asset less any accumulated depreciation or other provision for diminution in value, for example, reduction to net realisable value, or asset value which has been revalued downwards to reflect market conditions. *Also known as* **written-down value**

net capital *Fin* the amount by which net assets exceed the value of assets not easily converted to cash

net cash balance *Fin* the amount of cash that is on hand

NetCheque *E-com* a trademark for an electronic payment system developed at the University of Southern California to allow users to write electronic cheques to each other

net current assets *Fin* the amount by which the value of a company's current assets exceeds its current liabilities

net dividend *Fin* the value of a dividend after the recipient has paid tax on it

net domestic product *Econ* the figure produced after factors such as depreciation have been deducted from **GDP**

net errors and omissions *Fin* the net amount of the discrepancies that arise in calculations of balances of payments

net fixed assets *Fin* the value of fixed assets after depreciation

net foreign factor income *Fin* income from outside a country, constituting the amount by which a country's gross national product exceeds its gross domestic product

nethead *E-com* somebody who is obsessed with the Internet (*slang*)

Net imperative *E-com* the idea that Internet business processes must be adopted by organisations for future success

net income *Fin* **1.** an organisation's income less the costs incurred to generate it **2.** gross income less tax **3.** a salary or wage less tax and other statutory deductions, for example, National Insurance contributions

net interest *Fin* gross interest less tax

netiquette *E-com* the etiquette of the Internet. The term is used mainly in the context of e-mail and newsgroup communication.

netizen *E-com* a regular user of the Internet

net lease *Fin* a lease that requires the lessee to pay for things that the owner usually pays for. *See also* **gross lease**

net liquid funds *Fin* an organisation's cash plus its marketable investments less its short-term borrowings, such as overdrafts and loans

net margin *Fin* the percentage of revenues that is profit

net operating income *Fin* the amount by which income exceeds expenses, before considering taxes and interest

net operating margin *Fin* net operating income as a percentage of revenues

net pay *HR see* **take-home pay**

net position *Fin* the difference between an investor's long and short positions in the same security

net present value *Fin* the value of an investment calculated as the sum of its initial cost and the **present value** of expected future cash flows. *Abbr* **NPV**

EXAMPLE A positive NPV indicates that the project should be profitable, assuming that the estimated cash flows are reasonably accurate. A negative NPV indicates that the project will probably be unprofitable and therefore should be adjusted, if not abandoned altogether.

NPV enables a management to consider the time-value of money it will invest. This concept holds that the value of money increases with time because it can always earn interest in a savings account. When the time-value-of-money concept is incorporated in the calculation of NPV, the value of a project's future net cash receipts in 'today's money' can be determined. This enables proper comparisons between different projects.

For example, if Global Manufacturing Ltd is considering the acquisition of a new machine, its management will consider all the factors: initial purchase and installation costs; additional revenues generated by sales of the new machine's products, plus the taxes on these new revenues. Having accounted for these factors in its calculations, the cash flows that Global Manufacturing projects will generate from the new machine are:

Year 1:	−100,000 (initial cost of investment)
Year 2:	30,000
Year 3:	40,000
Year 4:	40,000
Year 5:	35,000
Net Total:	145,000

At first glance, it appears that cash flows total 45% more than the £100,000 initial cost, a sound investment indeed. But time-value of money shrinks return on the project considerably, since future pounds are worth less than present pounds in hand. NPV accounts for these differences with the help of present-value tables, which list the ratios that express the present value of expected cash-flow pounds, based on the applicable interest rate and the number of years in question.

In the example, Global Manufacturing's cost of capital is 9%. Using this figure to find the corresponding ratios on the present value table, the £100,000 investment cost and expected annual revenues during the five years in question, the NPV calculation looks like this:

Year	Cash-flow	Table factor (at 9%)	Present value
1	(£100,000) ×	1.000000 =	(£100,000)
2	£30,000 ×	0.917431 =	£27,522.93
3	£40,000 ×	0.841680 =	£33,667.20
4	£40,000 ×	0.772183 =	£30,887.32
5	£35,000 ×	0.708425 =	£24,794.88
NPV =	£16,873.33		

NPV is still positive. So, on this basis at least, the investment should proceed.

net price *Fin* the price paid for goods or services after all relevant discounts have been deducted

net proceeds *Fin* the amount realised from a transaction minus the cost of making it

net profit *Fin gross profit* minus costs

net profit margin *Gen Mgt see profit margin*

net profit ratio *Fin* the ratio of an organisation's net profit to its total net sales. Comparing the net profit ratios of companies in the same sector shows which are the most efficient.

net realisable value *Fin* the value of an asset if sold, allowing for costs

net residual value *Fin* the anticipated proceeds of an asset at the end of its useful life, less the costs of selling it, for example, transport and commission. It is used when calculating the annual charge for the straight-line method of depreciation. *Abbr* **NRV**

net return *Fin* the amount realised on an investment, taking taxes and transaction costs into account

net salvage value *Fin* the amount expected to result from terminating a project, taking tax consequences into consideration

network[1] *E-com* a group of computers that are able to communicate with each other. There are two types of computer network:

LAN (a local area network) and **WAN** (a wide area network). LANs are typically used by organisations that have a large number of computers based in one location and connected to a single computer server. They are often used as the basis for private networks such as *intranets*. WANs are slower than LANs because they use telephone cables as well as computer servers. The Internet is the main WAN in existence.

network[2] *HR* to build up and maintain relationships with people whose interests are similar or whose friendship could bring advantages such as job or business opportunities.

It is important to network for the good of the organisation and the professional field in which the networker operates. The networker should know what they hope to accomplish by networking, and what they have to offer other people: it is a two-way process, as the more someone has to offer other people, the more those people will want to do things for them.

In order to network effectively, it is useful to make a list of organisations and events for networking, a *contact list*, and an action plan with a schedule. The organisations and events list helps the networker identify and target places and situations where they are likely to meet with people who may be of assistance to them in their career or with a particular project. The contact list allows the networker to keep track of the people they have met, or want to meet. It is a good idea to prioritise this list according to who is most likely to be helpful. Using these two lists, the networker can then put together a schedule for making or maintaining connections.

network analysis *Gen Mgt, Ops* any of a set of techniques developed to aid the planning, monitoring, and controlling of complex *projects* and project resources. Network analysis is a tool of *project management* that involves breaking down a project into component parts or individual activities and recording them on a network diagram or *flow chart*. The resulting chart shows the interaction and interrelations between activities and can be used to determine project duration, time and resource limitations, and cost estimates. Constituent techniques include the *critical-path method* and the programme evaluation and review technique. *Also known as **network flow analysis***

network culture *Gen Mgt* forms of culture that are heavily influenced by communication using global networks

network flow analysis *Gen Mgt, Ops see **network analysis***

---

network management *Gen Mgt* the co-ordinated control of computer systems and programs to allow access to and delivery of information to a number of users. Network management enables users to connect by means of cabling within a LAN (see *network*) or via telecommunications lines in a wide area network.

network marketing *Mkting* the selling of goods or services through a network of self-employed agents or representatives. Network marketing usually involves several levels of agents, each level on a different commission rate. Each agent is encouraged to recruit other agents. In genuine network marketing, in contrast to *pyramid selling*, there is an end product or service sold to customers. Another version of network marketing is the loose co-operative relationship between a company, its competitors, collaborators, suppliers, and other organisations affecting the overall marketing function. *Also known as* **multilevel marketing**

network organisation *Gen Mgt* a company or group of companies that has a minimum of formal structures and relies instead on the formation and dissolution of teams to meet specific objectives. A network organisation utilises *information and communications technologies* extensively, and makes use of know-how across and within companies along the *value chain*. *See also* **virtual organisation**

network revolution *Gen Mgt* the fundamental change in business practices triggered by the growth of global networks

network society *Gen Mgt* a society in which patterns of work, communication, and government are characterised by the use of global networks

net worth *Fin* the difference between the assets and liabilities of a person or company

net yield *Fin* the rate of return on an investment after considering all costs and taxes

neural network *Stats* a computer system designed to mimic the neural patterns of the human brain

neurolinguistic programming *Gen Mgt* an approach to recognising, applying, developing, and reproducing behaviour, thought processes, and ways of communicating that contribute to success. Neurolinguistic programming was developed by Richard Bandler and John Grinder through their observations of how therapists achieved excellent results with

clients. It is popular in the business environment, where its influencing techniques can help firms implement change initiatives, improve communication and management skills, and develop training techniques. *Abbr* **NLP**

newbie *Gen Mgt* a person who is new to using the Internet (*slang*)

new economy *Econ* firms in the e-commerce sector and in the *digital economy* that often trade online rather than in the bricks and mortar of physical premises in the high street

new entrants *Mkting* organisations or products that have recently come into a market or sector

new issue *Fin* **1.** a new security, for example, a bond, debenture, or share, being offered to the public for the first time. *See also* **float**[1], *initial public offering* **2.** a rights issue, or any further issue of an existing security

new issues market *Fin* the part of the market in which securities are first offered to investors by the issuers. *See also* **float**[1], *initial public offering*, *primary market*

newly industrialised economy *Econ* a country whose industrialisation has reached a level beyond that of a developing country. Mexico and Malaysia are examples of newly industrialised economies.

new product development *Mkting* the processes involved in getting a new product or service to market. The traditional **product development cycle**, the **stage-gate model**, embraces the conception, generation, analysis, development, testing, marketing, and commercialisation of new products or services. Alternative models of new product development fall into two broad categories: **accelerating time to market models** and **integrated implementation models**. These aim to achieve both flexibility and acceleration of development. All activities such as design, production planning, and test marketing are carried out in parallel rather than going through a sequential linear progression. *Abbr* **NPD**

newsgroup *E-com see* **bulletin board**

newsletter *Gen Mgt* an informal publication, issued periodically by an organisation or agency to provide information to a particular audience. A newsletter may be issued externally or it may take the form of an **in-house**

To change and to improve are two different things.   *German proverb*

newsletter, or **house journal**, used to aid the *internal communication* process. It is becoming more common for newsletters to be issued in electronic format.

newsreader *E-com* a program that enables Internet users to send and access newsgroup messages. Newsreader programs are contained within e-mail software available as independent programs.

New York Mercantile Exchange *Fin* the world's largest physical commodity exchange and North America's most important trading exchange for energy and precious metals. It deals in crude oil, petrol, heating oil, natural gas, propane, gold, silver, platinum, palladium, and copper. *Abbr* **NYMEX**

New York Stock Exchange *Fin see NYSE*

New Zealand Stock Exchange *Fin* the principal market in New Zealand for trading in securities. It was established in 1981, replacing the Stock Exchange Association of New Zealand and a number of regional trading floors. *Abbr* **NZSE**

New Zealand Trade Development Board *Fin* a government body responsible for promoting New Zealand exports and facilitating foreign investment in New Zealand. *Also known as* **TRADENZ**

next futures contract *Fin* an option for the month after the current month

NIC *abbr Fin* National Insurance contribution

nice guys finish last *Gen Mgt* an axiom used in business to suggest that people should think about themselves first (*slang*)

nice-to-haves *HR* benefits of a job, such as free parking or subsidised meals, that are good to have but not essential (*slang*)

niche market *Mkting* a very specific market segment within a broader segment. A niche market involves specialist goods or services with relatively few or no competitors. Niche consumers often look for exclusiveness or some other differentiating factor such as high status. Alternatively, they may have a specific requirement not satisfied by standard products. Allergy sufferers, for example, may require specially formulated soaps and detergents. Niche markets are often targeted by small companies that produce specialised goods and services. *See also* **micromarketing**

niche player *Fin* **1.** an investment banker specialising in a particular field, for example, management buyouts **2.** a broking house that

deals in securities of only one industry. *Also known as* **boutique investment house**

nickel (*US*) *Fin* five basis points (*slang*)

nifty fifty (*US*) *Fin* on Wall Street, the fifty most popular stocks among institutional investors (*slang*)

night shift *HR* a *shift* within a *shiftwork* pattern that takes place during the evening and overnight. Night shifts involve particular health and social issues, and the antisocial hours usually incur a pay premium.

NIH syndrome *Gen Mgt* a problem afflicting large old-fashioned companies which reject ideas that come from outside the company simply because they were 'not invented here' (*slang*)

Nikkei 225 *or* **Nikkei Index** *Fin* the Japanese share price index

nil paid *Fin* with no money yet paid. This term is used in reference to the purchase of newly issued shares, or to the shares themselves, when the shareholder entitled to buy new shares has not yet made a commitment to do so and may sell the rights instead.

NIMBY *abbr Gen Mgt* Not In My Back Yard (*slang*)

NLP *abbr Gen Mgt* neurolinguistic programming

NMS *abbr Fin* National Market System

no-brainer *Fin* a transaction that is so favourable, no intelligence is required when deciding whether to enter into it (*slang*)

node *E-com* any single computer connected to a network

NOHSC *abbr Gen Mgt* National Occupational Health and Safety Commission

noise *Fin* irrelevant or insignificant data which overload a feedback process. The presence of noise can confuse or divert attention from relevant information; efficiency in a system is enhanced as the ratio of information to noise increases.

Nolan, Lord Michael Patrick, Baron of Brasted (*b.* 1928) *Gen Mgt* British lawyer. Chairman of the Committee on Standards in Public Life 1994–97.

no-load fund *Fin* a unit trust that does not charge a fee for the purchase or sale of shares. *See also* **load fund**

nomadic worker *HR see* **mobile worker**

---

nominal account *Fin* a record of revenues and expenditures, liabilities and assets classified by their nature, for example, sales, rent, rates, electricity, wages, share capital

nominal annual rate *Fin see* **APR**

nominal capital *Fin* the total value of all of a company's stock

nominal cash flow *Fin* cash flow in terms of currency, without adjustment for inflation

nominal exchange rate *Fin* the exchange rate as specified, without adjustment for transaction costs or differences in purchasing power

nominal interest rate *Fin* the interest rate as specified, without adjustment for compounding or inflation

nominal ledger *Fin* a ledger listing revenue, operating expenses, assets, and capital

nominal price *Fin* the price of an item being sold when consideration does not reflect the value

nominal share capital *Fin see* **authorised share capital**

nominal value *Fin* the value of a newly issued share

nominal wages *(US) Econ =* **money wages**

nominee holding *Fin* a shareholding in a company registered in the name of a nominee, instead of that of the owner

nominee name *Fin* a financial institution, or an individual employed by such an institution, that holds a security on behalf of the actual owner. While this may be to hide the owner's identity, for example, in the case of a celebrity, it is also to allow an institution managing any individual's portfolio to carry out transactions without the need for the owner to sign the required paperwork.

non-acceptance *Fin* on the presentation of a bill of exchange, the refusal by the person on whom it is drawn to accept it

Nonaka, Ikujiro (*b.* 1935) *Gen Mgt* Japanese academic. Focuses on the creation of organisational **knowledge**, believing this to be the most meaningful **core competence** for a company, particularly because it leads to **innovation** and **competitive advantage**. His ideas on knowledge management, published in *The Knowledge-creating Company* (1995, co-authored by Hirotaka Takeuchi) draw on **Peter Drucker**'s earlier ideas of the **knowledge worker** and the knowledge society.

non-branded goods *Mkting* generic goods that are not linked to a particular **brand** name, manufacturer, or producer, such as food produce, floor coverings, furniture, computer keyboards, or hand tools. Non-branded goods are often widely available in street markets or by mail order and like **own brands** are often perceived to be of low quality.

non-business days *Fin* those days when banks are not open for all their business activities, for example, in the West, Saturdays, Sundays, and public holidays

non-conformance costs *Gen Mgt see* **quality costs**

non-conforming loan *Fin* a loan that does not conform to the lender's standards, especially those of a US government agency

non-contributory pension plan *(US) Fin =* **non-contributory pension scheme**

non-contributory pension scheme *Fin* a pension scheme to which the employee makes no contribution

non-current assets *Fin see* **fixed asset**

nondeductible *Fin* not allowed to be deducted, especially as an allowance against income taxes

non-disclosure agreement *HR* a legally enforceable agreement preventing present or past **employees** from disclosing commercially sensitive information belonging to the employer to any other party. A non-disclosure agreement can remain in force for several years after an employee leaves a company. In the event of a dispute, a company may be required to prove that the information in question belongs to the company itself, is not in the public domain, or cannot be obtained elsewhere. *Abbr* **NDA**

non-disparagement agreement *HR* an agreement that prevents present or past **employees** from criticising an employing organisation in public. Non-disparagement agreements are a relatively new type of agreement and have arisen primarily to prevent employees putting comments about their employing organisation onto the Internet. Case law has yet to determine whether such agreements are legally binding. *Abbr* **NDA**

non-executive director *Gen Mgt* a part-time, non-salaried member of the **board of directors**, involved in the planning, strategy, and policy-making of an organisation but not in its day-to-day operations. The appointment of a non-executive director to a board is normally made in order to provide independence and balance to that board, and to ensure that good *corporate governance* is practised. A non-executive director may be selected for the prestige they bring or for their experience, contacts, or specialist knowledge. *Also known as part-time director, outside director*

non-financial asset *Fin* an asset that is neither money nor a financial instrument, for example, real or personal property

non-financial incentive scheme *HR see incentive scheme*

non-financial performance measures *Fin* measures of performance based on non-financial information which may originate in and be used by operating departments to monitor and control their activities without any accounting input.

Non-financial performance measures may give a more timely indication of the levels of performance achieved than financial ratios, and they may be less susceptible to distortion by factors such as uncontrollable variations in the effect of market forces on operations.

Examples of non-financial performance measures:

The values expected may vary significantly between industries/sectors.

non-integrated accounts *Fin see interlocking accounts*

non-interest-bearing bond *Fin* a bond that is sold at a discount instead of with a promise to pay interest

non-judicial foreclosure *Fin* a foreclosure on property without recourse to a court

non-linear programming *Fin* a process in which the equations expressing the interactions of variables are not all linear but may, for example, be in proportion to the square of a variable

non-negotiable instrument *Fin* a financial instrument that cannot be signed over to anyone else

non-operational balances *Fin* accounts that banks maintain at the Bank of England without the power of withdrawal

non-optional *Fin* not subject to approval by shareholders

non-participating preference share *Fin* the most common type of preference share that pays a fixed dividend regardless of the profitability of the company. *See also participating preference share*

Area assessed	Performance measure
Service quality	Number of complaints
	Proportion of repeat bookings
	Customer waiting time
	On-time deliveries
Production performance	
	Set-up times
	Number of suppliers
	Days' inventory in hand
	Output per employee
	Material yield percentage
	Schedule adherence
	Proportion of output requiring rework
	Manufacturing lead times
Marketing effectiveness	
	Trend in market share
	Sales volume growth
	Customer visits per salesperson
	Client contact hours per salesperson
	Sales volume forecast v. actual
	Number of customers
	Customer survey response information
Personnel	
	Number of complaints received
	Staff turnover
	Days lost through absenteeism
	Days lost through accidents/sickness
	Training time per employee

The man who views the world at fifty the same as he did at twenty has wasted thirty years of his life.
Muhammad Ali

non-performing asset *Fin* an asset that is not producing income

non-profit organisation *Gen Mgt, HR* an *organisation* that does not have financial profit as a main strategic objective. Non-profit organisations include charities, professional associations, trade unions, and religious, arts, community, research, and campaigning bodies. These organisations are not situated in either the *public* or *private sectors*, but in what has been called the **third sector**. Many have paid staff and working capital but, according to *Peter Drucker*, their fundamental purpose is not to provide a product or service, but to change people. They are led by values rather than financial commitments to shareholders.

non-random sampling *Ops* a *sampling* technique which is used when it cannot be ensured that each item has an equal chance of being selected, or when selection is based on expert knowledge of the population. *See also random sampling*

non-recourse debt *Fin* a debt for which the borrower has no personal responsibility, typically a debt of a limited partnership

non-recoverable *Fin* relating to a debt that will never be paid, for example, because of the borrower's bankruptcy

non-recurring charge *Fin* a charge that is made only once

non-resident *Fin* used to describe an individual who has left his or her native country to work overseas for a period. Non-residency has tax implications, for example, while a UK national is working overseas only their income and realised capital gains generated within the United Kingdom are subject to UK income tax. During a period of non-residency, many expatriates choose to bank offshore.

Non-Resident Withholding Tax *Fin* a duty imposed by the New Zealand government on interest and dividends earned by a non-resident from investments. *Abbr* **NRWT**

non-store retailing *E-com* the selling of goods and services electronically without setting up a physical store

non-tariff barrier *Econ see* **NTB**

non-taxable *Fin* not subject to tax

non-verbal communication *Gen Mgt* any form of *communication* that is not expressed in words. Non-verbal communication is estimated to make up 65–90% of all communication, and understanding, interpreting, and using it are essential skills. Forms of non-verbal communication include actions and behaviour such as silence, failure or slowness to respond to a message, and lateness in arriving for a meeting. *Body language* is also an important part of non-verbal communication. Non-verbal elements of communication may reinforce or contradict a verbal message.

non-virtual hosting *E-com* the most basic *hosting option*, which is often provided free, and is advisable only for very small businesses. The client does not have their own domain name; instead, their address would be: www.hostingcompany.com/clientname. The most serious drawback of this kind of package is the lack of flexibility: the client cannot change their hosting company without changing their web address.

non-voting shares *Fin* ordinary shares that are paid a dividend from the company's profits, but that do not entitle the shareholder to vote at the Annual General Meeting or any other meeting of shareholders. Such shares are unpopular with institutional investors. *Also called* **A shares**

Nordström, Kjell (*b.* 1958) *Gen Mgt* Swedish academic. Known for a focus on *globalisation*, *innovation*, *agility*, and *product differentiation*. Co-author of *Funky Business* (2000), with *Jonas Ridderstråle*.

norm *Stats* a range of statistics that are normal for a population

normal capacity *Fin* a measure of the long-run average level of capacity that may be expected. This is often used in setting the budgeted fixed overhead absorption rate which gives it stability over time, although budgeted fixed overhead volume variances are generally produced as a consequence.

normal distribution *Stats* the probability distribution of a random variable

normal loss *Fin* an expected loss, allowed for in the budget, and normally calculated as a percentage of the good output from a process during a period of time. Normal losses are generally either valued at zero, or at their disposal values.

normal profit *Econ* the minimum level of profit that will attract an entrepreneur to begin a business or remain trading

normal yield curve *Fin* a yield curve with higher interest rates for long-term bonds than for short-term bonds. *See also* **yield curve**

Norton, David (*b.* 1941) *Gen Mgt* US consultant. *See* **Kaplan, Robert**

no-strike agreement *HR* a formal understanding between an *employer* and a *trade union* that the union will not call its members out on *strike*. A no-strike agreement is usually won by the employer in exchange for improved terms and *conditions of employment*, including pay, and sometimes *guaranteed employment*.

notch (*S Africa*) *HR* an increment on a salary scale

notes to the accounts *Fin* explanation of particular items in a set of accounts

notes to the financial statements *Fin* explanation of particular items in a set of financial statements

notice of default (*US*) *Fin* = *default notice*

notice period *HR* the amount of time specified in the terms and *conditions of employment* that an *employee* must work between resigning from an organisation and leaving the employment of that organisation. Part of a notice period may sometimes be waived while in other circumstances employees may be required to take *garden leave*.

notional cost *Fin* a cost used in product evaluation, decision-making, and performance measurement to represent the cost of using resources which have no conventional 'actual cost'. Notional interest, for example, may be charged for the use of internally generated funds.

notional principal amount *Fin* the value used to represent a loan in calculating *interest rate swaps*

not negotiable *Fin* wording appearing on a cheque or bill of exchange that it is deprived of its inherent quality of negotiability. When such a document is transferred from one person to another, the recipient obtains no better title to it than the signatory. *See also negotiable instrument*

NPD *abbr Mkting* new product development

NPV *abbr Fin* net present value

NRV *abbr Fin* net residual value

NRWT *abbr Fin* Non-Resident Withholding Tax

NSB *abbr Fin* National Savings Bank

NSC *abbr Fin* National Savings Certificate

NTB *abbr Econ* non-tariff barrier: a country's economic regulation on something such as safety standards that impedes imports, often from developing countries

nuisance parameter *Stats* a parameter in a statistical model that is insignificant in itself but whose unknown value is needed to make inferences about significant variables in a study

numbered account *Fin* a bank account identified by a number to allow the holder to remain anonymous

numerical control *Ops* the use of numerical data to influence the operation of equipment. Numerical control allows the operation of machinery to be automated and usually involves the use of computer systems. Data is generated, stored, manipulated, and retrieved while a process is in operation.

NVQ *abbr HR* National Vocational Qualification

NYMEX *abbr Fin* New York Mercantile Exchange

NYSE *abbr Fin* New York Stock Exchange: the leading stock exchange in New York which is self-regulatory but has to comply with the regulations of the US Securities and Exchange Commission

NZSE *abbr Fin* New Zealand Stock Exchange

NZSE10 Index *Fin* a measure of changes in share prices on the New Zealand Stock Exchange, based on the change in value of the stocks of the 10 largest companies

NZSE30 Selection Index *Fin* a measure of changes in share prices on the New Zealand Stock Exchange, based on the change in value of the stocks of the 30 largest companies. *Abbr* **NZSE30**

NZSE40 *Fin* the principal measure of changes in share prices on the New Zealand Stock Exchange, based on the change in value of the stocks of the 40 largest companies. The makeup of the index is reviewed every three months.

Obeng, Eddie (*b.* 1959) *Gen Mgt* Ghanaian-born academic and consultant. Pioneer of the first virtual business school. Obeng founded the school, named Pentacle, in 1994, to assist managers and organisations facing the pressures and challenges of the global economy, a situation described in his book *New Rules for the New World* (1997).

OBI *abbr E-com* open buying on the Internet

object and task technique (*US*) *Gen Mgt* a method of budgeting that involves assessing a project's objectives, determining the tasks required for their accomplishment, and then estimating the cost of each task

objective *Gen Mgt, HR* an end towards which effort is directed and on which resources are focused, usually to achieve an organisation's **strategy**. There is endless discussion on whether objective, **goal**, **target**, and **aim** are the same. In general usage, the terms are often used interchangeably, so it is important that if an organisation has a particular meaning for one of these terms, it must define it in its documentation. Sometimes an objective is seen as the desired final end result, while a goal is a smaller step on the road to it. Objective setting is given a practical application in **management by objectives**.

obscuranto *Gen Mgt* incomprehensible jargon used by large international organisations such as the European Commission (*slang*)

OBSF *abbr Fin* off-balance-sheet financing

obsolescence *Mkting* the decline of products in a market due to the introduction of better competitor products or rapid technology developments. Obsolescence of products can be a planned process, controlled by introducing deliberate minor cosmetic changes to a product every few years to encourage new purchases. It can also be unplanned, however, and in some sectors the pace of technological change is so rapid that the rate of obsolescence is high. This is the case particularly in consumer and industrial electronics, affecting computers, Internet-related products, telecommunications, and television, audio, and car technology. Obsolescence is part of the product **life cycle**, and if a product cannot be turned around, it may lead to **product abandonment**.

occupational health *HR* the well-being of **employees** at work. An occupational health service is concerned with reacting to and preventing work-related illness and injury, and with maintaining and improving employees' health. Occupational health may involve some or all of these elements: health screening, including pre-employment screening (see **health screening**); monitoring compliance with health and safety legislation; health promotion activities; and initiating and maintaining health-related policies. There may be some overlap with **employee assistance programmes**. An occupational health service aims to reduce **absenteeism** and improve employee morale and performance.

occupational illness *HR* an illness associated with a particular job. Occupational illnesses include lung disease, which can affect miners, **repetitive strain injury**, which can be suffered by keyboard users, and asbestosis, caused by working with asbestos. **Occupational health** policies must take all hazards into account and minimise the potential for these diseases to develop. Government benefits are sometimes available to people who are disadvantaged because of occupational illness.

occupational pension scheme *HR* a pension scheme, run by an organisation for its employees, which has satisfied the conditions allowing the employer to contract out of the state earnings related pension scheme. Occupational pensions are regarded as deferred pay and form part of the total compensation package. Until recently, most schemes were based on final salary but there has been a shift towards money purchase schemes, particularly amongst smaller companies. Alternatively, employers may choose to contribute to an employee's **personal pension**. Also known as **company pension scheme**

occupational psychology *HR* the branch of psychology concerned with the assessment of the well-being of **employees** within their work environment in order to improve performance and efficiency, **job satisfaction**, and **occupational health**. The eight main areas of occupational psychology include: human-machine interaction; design of working environment; **health and safety**; personnel **recruitment** and assessment; **performance appraisal** and career development; **counselling** and **personal development**; **training**; **motivation**; industrial relations; and organisation change and development. *Also known as* **industrial psychology**

Ever tried. Ever failed. No matter. Try again. Fail again. Fail better.   **Samuel Beckett**

OCR *abbr Fin* official cash rate

Odiorne, George Stanley *Gen Mgt* US academic. Known for his popularisation in the United States of *Peter Drucker*'s *Management by Objectives*. Odiorne is said to have coined the saying 'If you can't measure it, you can't manage it'.

OECD *abbr Fin* Organisation for Economic Co-operation and Development: a group of 30 member countries, with a shared commitment to democratic government and the market economy, that has active relationships with some 70 other countries via nongovernmental organisations. Formed in 1961, its work covers economic and social issues from macroeconomics to trade, education, development, and scientific innovation. Its goals are to promote economic growth and employment in member countries in a climate of stability; to assist the sustainable economic expansion of both member and non-member countries; and to support a balanced and even-handed expansion of world trade.

OEIC *abbr Fin* open-ended investment company

OEM *abbr Ops* original equipment manufacturer

off-balance-sheet financing *Fin* financing obtained by means other than debt and equity instruments, for example, partnerships, joint ventures, and leases. *Abbr* **OBSF**

offer *Fin* the price at which a market maker will sell a security, or a unit trust manager in the United Kingdom will sell units. It is also the net asset value of a mutual fund plus any sales charges in the United States. It is the price investors pay when they buy a security. *Also known as* **ask**, *offering price*, *offer price*

offer by prospectus *Fin* in the United Kingdom, one of the ways available to a lead manager of offering securities to the public. *See also* **float**, *initial public offering*, *new issue*, *offer for sale*

offer document *Fin* a description of the loan a lender is offering to provide

offer for sale *Fin* an invitation by a party other than the company itself to apply for shares in a company based on information contained in a prospectus

offering memorandum *Fin* a description of an offer to sell securities privately

offering price *Fin* see *offer price*

offeror *Fin* somebody who makes a bid

offer price *Fin* the price at which somebody offers a share of a stock for sale. *Also known as offering price*

office design *Gen Mgt* the arrangement of work space so that work can be carried out in the most efficient way. Office design incorporates both *ergonomics* and **work flow**, which examine the way in which work is performed in order to optimise layout. Office design is an important factor in *job satisfaction*. It affects the way in which employees work, and many organisations have implemented open-plan offices to encourage *teamwork*. The development of *information and communications technologies* has led to changes in traditional layouts and some offices are designed to facilitate *hot-desking* or *hotelling*. The design of work spaces must conform to health and safety legislation.

office-free *HR* used to refer to employees whose jobs do not require them to work in an office (*slang*)

office junior *HR* an employee with no responsibilities who carries out mundane or routine tasks in an office

office politics *Gen Mgt* interpersonal dynamics within a workplace. Office politics involves the complex network of power and status that exists within any group of people.

officer *Gen Mgt see executive*

officer of a company *HR* an individual who acts in an official capacity in a company, for example, the company secretary, a director, or a manager

official banks *Fin* banks that have charters from governments

official books of account *Fin* the official financial records of an institution

official cash rate *Fin* the current interest rate as set by a central bank. *Abbr* **OCR**

official development assistance *Fin* money that the Organisation for Economic Co-operation and Development's Development Assistance Committee gives or lends to a developing country

official list *Fin* in the United Kingdom, the list maintained by the Financial Services Authority of all the securities traded on the London Stock Exchange

official receiver *Gen Mgt* an officer of the court who is appointed to wind up the affairs of an organisation that goes bankrupt. In the United Kingdom, an official receiver is appointed by the Department of Trade and Industry and often acts as a *liquidator*. The job involves realising any assets that remain to repay debts, for example, by selling property. *Abbr* **OR**

off-line transaction processing *E-com* the receipt and storage of order and credit or debit card information through a computer network or point-of-sale terminal for subsequent authorisation and processing

offset *Fin* a transaction that balances all or part of an earlier transaction in the same security

offset clause *Fin* a provision in an insurance policy that permits the balancing of credits against debits so that, for example, a party can reduce or omit payments to another party that owes it money and is bankrupt

offshore bank *Fin* a bank that offers only limited wholesale banking services to non-residents

offshore company *Fin* a company that is registered in a country other than the one in which it conducts most of its business, usually for tax purposes. For example, many captive insurance companies are registered in the Cayman Islands.

offshore finance subsidiary *Fin* a company created in another country to handle financial transactions, giving the owning company certain tax and legal advantages in its home country. *US term* *offshore financial subsidiary*

offshore financial centre *Fin* a country or other political unit that has banking laws intended to attract business from industrialised nations

offshore financial subsidiary *(US) Fin* = *offshore finance subsidiary*

offshore holding company *Fin* a company created in another country to own other companies, giving the owning company certain legal advantages in its home country

offshore production *Ops* the manufacture of goods abroad for import to the domestic market

offshore trading company *Fin* a company created in another country to handle commercial transactions, giving the owning company certain legal advantages in its home country

off-the-shelf company *Fin* a company for which all the legal formalities, except the appointment of directors, have been completed so that a purchaser can transform it into a new company with relative ease and low cost

off-topic *Gen Mgt* irrelevant or off the subject (*slang*)

Ohmae, Kenichi (*b.* 1943) *Gen Mgt* Japanese consultant, writer, and politician. Herald of Japanese management techniques in the West, arguing that the success of Japanese companies could be attributed to Japanese strategic thinking based on *creativity* and *innovation*. In *The Mind of the Strategist* (1982), Ohmae identified key differences between the strategies adopted by Japanese managers and their Western counterparts. He later challenged all companies to take account of *globalisation* in their *strategic planning* and to focus on the relationship between business and the nation state. His recent work examines the relationship between old economy and *new economy* companies and identifies the basic forces influencing the new economy.

Ohmae is a graduate of Waseda University and the Tokyo Institute of Technology, and has a PhD in nuclear engineering from the Massachusetts Institute of Technology. He joined McKinsey in 1972, becoming managing director of its Tokyo office.

Ohno, Taiichi (*b.* 1912) *Gen Mgt* Japanese business executive. Responsible for much of the background work and thinking that created the *Toyota production system*, explained in the book of the same name (1988).

ohnosecond *Gen Mgt* the short time required to realise that you have made a serious mistake (*slang*)

oil
the good oil (*ANZ*) *Gen Mgt* accurate and useful information (*slang*)

OINK *Gen Mgt* One Income, No Kids (*slang*)

older worker *HR* generally considered to mean an employee aged 50 or over but in some industries, such as IT, an older worker is somebody over 30. Older workers can be subject to *age discrimination*.

Old Lady of Threadneedle Street *Fin* the Bank of England, which is located in Threadneedle Street in the City of London (*slang*)

old old *Mkting* the oldest age group, consisting of people over the age of 75

A stockbroker is someone who takes all your money and invests it until it's gone.   *Woody Allen*

oligarchy *Gen Mgt* an organisation in which a small group of managers exercises control. Within an oligarchy, the controlling group often directs the organisation for its own purposes, or for purposes other than the best interests of the organisation.

oligopoly *Econ* a market in which there are only a few, very large, suppliers

ombudsman *Gen Mgt* an official who investigates complaints against public departments, large organisations, or business sectors. *See also* **Financial Ombudsman**

omitted dividend *Fin* a regularly scheduled dividend that a company does not pay

omnibus account *Fin* an account of one broker with another that combines the transactions of multiple investors for the convenience of the brokers

omnibus survey *Mkting* a survey covering a number of topics usually undertaken on behalf of several clients who share the cost of conducting the survey. It is a cost-effective means of researching several subjects at the same time, and is also suitable for measuring attitudes and behaviour towards different types of products and services, or monitoring changes in attitude among groups of consumers.

on account *Fin* paid in advance against all or part of money due in the future

on demand *Fin* **1.** used to describe an account from which withdrawals may be made without giving a period of notice **2.** used to describe a loan, usually an overdraft, that the lender can request the borrower to repay immediately **3.** used to describe a bill of exchange that is paid upon presentation

one-stop shopping *Fin* the ability of a single financial institution to offer a full range of financial services

one-to-one marketing *Mkting* a marketing technique using detailed data, personalised communications, and customised products or services to match the requirements of individual customers

one-to-one merger *Gen Mgt see* **merger**

one-year money *Fin* money placed on a money market for a fixed period of one year, with either a fixed or variable rate of interest. It can only be removed during the fixed term upon payment of a penalty.

on-hold advertising *Mkting* telephone advertising aimed at consumers who are

being kept on hold while waiting to speak to somebody (*slang*)

online capture *E-com* a payment transaction generated after goods have been shipped, in which funds are transferred from issuer to acquirer to merchant account

online catalogue *E-com* a business-to-business marketplace that collects the catalogue data of every supplier in a particular industry and places it on one central web resource. Catalogues are important to companies for marketing purposes because they are one of the main ways to distribute product information to public marketplaces and private exchanges. *Also known as* **procurement portal**

online community *E-com* a means of allowing Web users to engage with one another and with an organisation through use of interactive tools such as e-mail, *discussion boards*, and *chat systems*.

They are a means by which a website owner can take the pulse of consumers to find out what they are thinking, and to generate unique content. As stand-alone businesses, online communities have been found to be weak: they work best when they are supporting the need for an organisation to collect ongoing feedback.

online shopping *E-com see* **electronic shopping**

online shopping mall *E-com see* **cyber mall**

online training *HR see* **computer-based training**

on-pack offer *Mkting* a sales promotion technique in which customers are offered a premium on the pack

on-target earnings *HR* the amount earned by a person working on *commission* who has achieved the targets set. *Abbr* **OTE**

on-the-job training *HR* *training* given to employees in the workplace as they perform everyday work activities. On-the-job training is based on the principle of *learning by doing* and includes demonstration and explanation by a more experienced employee, supervisor, or manager; performance of tasks under supervision; and the provision of appropriate *feedback*. On-the-job training is sometimes informally referred to as **sitting with Nellie**. Types of on-the-job training include *coaching*, *delegation*, *job rotation*, *secondment*, and participation in special projects.

OPEC *abbr Fin* Organization of the Petroleum Exporting Countries: an international organisation of 11 developing countries, each one largely reliant on oil revenues as its main source of income, that tries to ensure there is a balance between supply and demand by adjusting the members' oil output. The current members, Algeria, Indonesia, Iran, Iraq, Kuwait, Libya, Nigeria, Qatar, Saudi Arabia, the United Arab Emirates, and Venezuela, meet at least twice a year to decide on output levels and discuss recent and anticipated oil market developments.

open-book management *Gen Mgt* a *management style* in which everything is revealed to employees and there are no secrets. Open-book management involves not only revealing a company's full financial information to its employees but also making transparent all of the workings of the company. Open-book management has been viewed as enabling the *empowerment* and *involvement* of the workforce, increasing employee *motivation* and organisational efficiency.

open buying on the Internet *E-com, Fin* a standard built round a common set of business requirements for electronic communication between buyers and sellers that, when implemented, allows different e-commerce systems to talk to one another. *Abbr* **OBI**. *See also open trading protocol*

open cheque *Fin* **1.** a cheque that is not crossed and so may be cashed by the payee at the branch of the bank where it is drawn **2.** (*US*) a signed cheque where the amount payable has not been indicated

open-collar worker *HR* a person who works from home (*slang*)

open communication *Gen Mgt* a communications policy intended to ensure that employees have full information about their organisation

open-door policy *Gen Mgt* a receptive, listening approach to management characterised by a ready, informal availability on the part of the manager towards employees. Open-door management removes the need to make appointments or to show the deference traditionally associated with relationships between superiors and subordinates in hierarchies. The opposite management style is a **closed-door policy**, which is more formal. Open- and closed-door policies can reflect different kinds of *corporate culture*.

open economy *Econ* an economy that places no restrictions on the movement of capital, labour, foreign trade, and payments into and out of the country

open-end credit (*US*) *Fin* = *open-ended credit*

open-ended credit *Fin* a form of credit that does not have an upper limit on the amount that can be borrowed or a time limit before repayment is due

open-ended fund *Fin* a unit trust that has a variable number of shares. *US term* **open-end fund**

open-ended investment company *Fin* a unit trust, as distinguished from an investment trust, or **closed-end fund**. *See also open-ended fund*. *US term* **open-end investment company**

open-ended management company *Fin* a company that sells unit trusts. *US term* **open-end management company**

open-ended mortgage *Fin* a mortgage in which prepayment is allowed. *US term* **open-end mortgage**

open-end fund (*US*) *Fin* = *open-ended fund*

open-end investment company (*US*) *Fin* = *open-ended investment company*

open-end management company (*US*) *Fin* = *open-ended management company*

open-end mortgage (*US*) *Fin* = *open-ended mortgage*

opening balance *Fin* the value of a financial quantity at the beginning of a period of time, such as a day or a year

opening balance sheet *Fin* an account showing an organisation's opening balances

opening bell *Fin* the beginning of a day of trading on a market

opening price *Fin* a price for a security at the beginning of a day of trading on a market

opening purchase *Fin* a first purchase of a series to be made in options of a particular type for a particular commodity or security

opening stock *Fin* on a balance sheet, the closing stock at the end of one accounting period that is transferred forward and becomes the opening stock in the one that follows. *US term* **beginning inventory**

open interest *Fin* options that have not yet been closed

open learning *HR* a flexible approach to a course of study that allows individuals to learn at a time, place, and pace to suit their needs. A typical open learning programme might offer the student a range of delivery methods, including tutorials, workshops, formal lectures, and the Internet, supported by a variety of learning materials such as textbooks, workbooks, and video, audio, and computer-based materials. *See also distance learning*

open loop system *Fin* a management control system which includes no provision for corrective action to be applied to the sequence of activities

open-market operation *Fin* a transaction by a central bank in a public market

open-market value *Fin* the price that an asset or security would realise if it was offered on a market open to all

open standard *Gen Mgt* a standard for computers and related products that allows pieces of equipment from different manufacturers to operate with each other

open system *Fin* an operating system whose developer encourages the development of applications that use it

open systems thinking *Gen Mgt* a learning and *problem-solving* approach that involves describing the behaviour of a system, then exploring possibilities for improving it. Open systems thinking encourages *creativity* and is used by *learning organisations*.

open trading protocol *E-com* a standard designed to support Internet-based retail transactions that allows different systems to communicate with each other for a variety of payment-related activities. The *open buying on the Internet* protocol is a competing standard. *Abbr* **OTP**. *See also open buying on the Internet*

operating budget *Fin* a budget of the revenues and expenses expected in a forthcoming accounting period

operating cash flow *Fin* the amount used to represent the money moving through a company as a result of its operations, as distinct from its purely financial transactions

operating costing *Ops* a costing system that is applied to continuous operations in mass production or in the service industries. In the simplest form of operating costing, the costing period is set at a specific length of time, usually a calendar month or four weeks. The costs incurred over the period are related to the number of units produced, and the division of the first by the second gives the average unit cost for the period. *Also known as batch costing*

operating cycle *Ops* the cycle of business activity in which cash is used to buy resources which are converted into products or services and then sold for cash

operating income *Ops* revenue minus the cost of goods sold and normal operating expenses. *Also known as earnings before interest and taxes*

operating lease *Gen Mgt* a lease that is regarded by accountants as rental rather than as a *finance lease*. The monthly lease payments are simply treated as rental expenses and recognised on the income statement as they are incurred. There is no recognition of a leased asset or liability.

operating leverage *Fin* the ratio of a business's fixed costs to its total costs. As the fixed costs have to be paid regardless of output, the higher the ratio, the higher the risk of losses in an economic downturn.

operating margin *Fin see profit margin*

operating risk *Fin* the risk of a high operating leverage

operating statement *Fin* a regular report for management of actual costs and revenues, as appropriate. Usually compares actual with budget and shows variances.

operating system *Ops* a program that controls the basic operation of a computer and its communication with devices such as the keyboard, printer, and mouse

operational audit *Gen Mgt* a structured review of the systems and procedures of an organisation in order to evaluate whether they are being carried out efficiently and effectively. An operational audit involves: establishing performance *objectives*, agreeing the standards and criteria for assessment, and evaluating actual performance against targeted performance. *Also known as management audit, operations audit*

operational control *Gen Mgt* the management of daily activities in accordance with strategic and tactical plans

operational gearing *Fin* the relationship of the fixed cost to the total cost of an operating unit. The greater the proportion of total costs that are fixed (high operational gearing), the greater the advantage to the organisation of increasing sales volume. Conversely, should sales volumes drop, a highly geared organisation would find the high proportion of fixed costs to be a major problem, possibly causing

---

There's no such thing as bad publicity except your own obituary. Brendan Behan a rapid swing from profitability into significant loss-making. *See also* **leverage**

operational research *Gen Mgt* the application of scientific methods to the solution of managerial and administrative problems, involving complex systems or processes. Operational research aims to find the optimum plan for the control and operation of a system or process. It was originally used during the second world war as a means of solving logistical problems. It has since developed into a planning, scheduling, and *problem-solving* technique applied across the industrial, commercial, and public sectors.

operation planning *Ops see* **planning**

operations *Ops see* **operations management**

operations audit *Gen Mgt see* **operational audit**

operations management *Ops* the maintenance, control, and improvement of organisational activities that are required to produce goods or services for consumers. Operations management has traditionally been associated with manufacturing activities but can also be applied to the service sector. The measurement and evaluation of operations is usually undertaken through a process of business appraisal. Efficiency and effectiveness may be monitored by the application of *ISO 9001* quality systems, or *total quality management* techniques.

operations plans *Ops* the fully detailed specifications by which individuals are expected to carry out the predetermined cycles of operations to meet sectoral objectives

operation time *Ops* the period required to carry out an operation on a complete batch exclusive of set-up and breaking-down times

opinion leader *Mkting* a high-profile person or organisation that can significantly influence public opinion. An opinion leader can be a politician, religious, business or community leader, journalist, or educationalist. Show business and sports personalities can exert a great deal of influence on young people's leisure lifestyles and buying habits and are consequently frequently used in *advertising campaigns*.

opinion leader research *Mkting* the investigation of the perceptions of *corporate image* and reputation among the people at the top of a company, industry, or profession

opinion shopping (*US*) *Gen Mgt* the practice of searching for an auditor whose views are in line with those of a company being audited. Opinion shopping can take place when a company is about to be audited and has recently undertaken questionable dealings. Auditors are sought whose interpretation of the law matches the company's own, and who will approve the company's financial statements.

opinion survey *Stats* a survey carried out to determine what members of a population think about a given topic

opportunity cost *Fin, Gen Mgt* an amount of money lost as a result of choosing one investment rather than another

OPT *abbr Ops* optimised production technology

optimal portfolio *Fin* a theoretical set of investments that would be most profitable for an investor

optimal redemption provision *Fin* a provision that specifies when an issuer can call a bond

optimise *Fin* to allocate such things as resources or capital as efficiently as possible

optimised production technology *Ops* a sophisticated *production planning* and *control* system, based on *finite loading* procedures, that concentrates on reducing *bottlenecks* in the system in order to improve efficiency. The key task of OPT is to increase total systems throughput by realising existing capacity in other parts of the system. OPT is a practical application of the **theory of constraints**. *Abbr* **OPT**

optimum capacity *Ops* the level of output at which the minimum cost per unit is incurred

opt-in *E-com* a type of *subscription process* for users of a website wanting to sign up to receive specific information or services. An opt-in approach is where a user actively decides to provide their e-mail address, so the website owner can send them e-mail. However, the emerging convention is *double opt-in*.

option *Fin* a contract for the right to buy or sell an asset, typically a commodity, under certain terms. *Also known as* **option contract**

option account *Fin* a brokerage account used for trading in options

optionaire *Fin* a millionaire whose wealth consists of share options (*slang*)

option buyer *Fin* an investor who buys an option

---

option class *Fin* a set of options that are identical with respect to type and underlying asset

option contract *Fin see* **option**

option elasticity *Fin* the relative change in the value of an option as a function of a change in the value of the underlying asset

option income fund *Fin* a unit trust that invests in options

option premium *Fin* the amount per share that a buyer pays for an option

option price *Fin* the price of an option

option pricing model *Fin* a model that is used to determine the fair value of options

options clearing corporation *Fin* the organisation in the United States that is responsible for the listing of options and clearing trades in them

option seller *Fin see* **option writer**

option series *Fin* a collection of options that are identical in terms of what they represent

options market *Fin* the trading in options, or a place where options trading occurs

options on physicals *Fin* options on securities with fixed interest rates

option writer *Fin* a person or institution who sells an option. *Also known as* **option seller**

OR *abbr Fin* official receiver

order 1. *Fin* an occasion when a broker is told to buy or sell something for an investor's own account **2.** *Ops* a **contract** made between a customer and a supplier for the supply of a range of goods or services in a determined quantity and quality, at an agreed price, and for delivery at or by a specified time

order book *Ops* a record of the outstanding orders that an organisation has received. An order book may be physical, with the specifications and delivery times of orders recorded in it, or the term may be used generally to describe the health of a company. A full order book implies a successful company, while an empty order book can indicate an organisation at risk of **business failure**.

order confirmation *E-com* an e-mail message informing a purchaser that an order has been received

order picking *Ops* selecting and withdrawing goods or components from a store or warehouse to meet production requirements or to satisfy customer orders

order point *Fin* the quantity of an item that is on hand when more units of the item are to be ordered

order processing *Ops* the tracking of **orders** with suppliers and from customers

orders pending *Fin* orders that have not yet resulted in transactions

ordinary interest *Fin* interest calculated on the basis of a year having only 360 days

ordinary shares *Fin* shares that entitle the holder to a dividend from the company's profits after holders of preference shares have been paid

organigram *Gen Mgt see* **organisation chart**

organisation *Gen Mgt* an arrangement of people and resources working in a planned manner towards specified strategic goals. An organisation can be any structured body such as a business, company, or firm in the private or public sector, or in a non-profit association. *See also* **organisation structure**, **organisation theory**

organisational analysis *Gen Mgt* a type of internal business appraisal aimed at identifying areas of inefficiency and opportunities for streamlining and re-organisation

organisational change *Gen Mgt see* **change management**

organisational chart *Gen Mgt see* **organisation chart**

organisational commitment *Gen Mgt* **1.** the commitment of an organisation to given aims and objectives, as demonstrated through its stated aims and policies, and its actions and allocation of resources **2.** the degree of **employee commitment** within an organisational workforce

organisational culture *Gen Mgt see* **corporate culture**

organisational design *Gen Mgt see* **organisation structure**

organisational development *Gen Mgt* a planned approach to far-reaching, organisation-wide change designed to enable an organisation to respond and adapt to changing market conditions and to set a new agenda. Organisational development is frequently linked to **organisation structure**, which can act either as an enabling or restrictive mechanism for change. For organisational development to succeed, any policies or strategies introduced must fit with the **corporate culture**.

organisational federalism *Gen Mgt see federal organisation*

organisational learning *Gen Mgt* a culture of change and improvement within an organisation, characterised by employee enthusiasm, energy, and high levels of **creativity** and **innovation**. In their book *Organizational Learning* (1978), **Chris Argyris**, and **Donald Schön** suggest that if a number of employee development activities are in progress within an organisation, a sense of organisational movement and development can be achieved, and that with the right encouragement, support, and reward, this can become self-perpetuating. The concept of organisational learning was further developed by **Peter Senge**, and re-popularised as the **learning organisation**.

organisational planning *Gen Mgt* deciding on, and designing, the most appropriate structure for an organisation. Stages of the organisation planning process include: identifying and grouping activities or processes, setting out lines of authority and areas of responsibility, and possibly illustrating these through a formal organisation chart.

organisation behaviour *Gen Mgt* the study of human and group behaviour within organisational settings. The study of organisation behaviour involves looking at the attitudes, interpersonal relationships, performance, **productivity**, **job satisfaction**, and commitment of employees, as well as levels of **organisational commitment** and industrial relations. Organisation behaviour can be affected by **corporate culture**, **leadership**, and **management style**. Organisation behaviour emerged as a distinct specialism from **organisation theory** in the late 1950s and early 1960s through attempts to integrate different perspectives on human and management problems and develop an understanding of behavioural dynamics within organisations.

organisation chart *Gen Mgt* a graphic illustration of an **organisation's structure**, showing hierarchical authority and relationships between departments and jobs. The horizontal dimension of an organisation chart shows the nature of job function and responsibility and the vertical dimension shows how jobs are co-ordinated in reporting or authority relationships. Some charts include managers' names, others only job titles. Organisation charts are widely used to bring order and clarity to the way the organisation is structured. Despite this, they reflect little of the way organisations actually work and can appear complex, especially in highly **bureaucratic** organisations. The first recorded organisation chart was produced in the United States by David C. McCallum for the New York and Erie Railroad. *Also known as* **organigram**, **organisational chart**, **org chart**

Organisation for Economic Co-operation and Development *Fin see OECD*

organisation hierarchy *Gen Mgt* the vertical layers of ranks of personnel within an organisation, each layer subordinate to the one above it. Organisation hierarchy is often shown in the form of an **organisation chart**. An extended hierarchy is typical of a **bureaucracy**, but during the later 20th and early 21st centuries the layers of hierarchical positions within large organisations have often been reduced as part of **downsizing** exercises. These result in the shallow or non-existent hierarchies of flexible, **flat organisations** within which there is greater employee **empowerment** and autonomy.

organisation man *Gen Mgt* somebody who fully accepts and may be absorbed by organisational objectives and values. *The Organisation Man*, a best-selling novel by **William Whyte**, is the source of the phrase.

organisation structure *Gen Mgt* the form of an organisation that is evident in the way divisions, departments, functions, and people link together and interact. Organisation structure reveals vertical operational responsibilities, and horizontal linkages, and may be represented by an **organisation chart**. The complexity of an organisation's structure is often proportional to its size and its geographic dispersal. The traditional organisation structure for many businesses in the 20th century was the **bureaucracy**, originally defined by **Max Weber**. More recent forms include the **flat**, **network**, **matrix**, and **virtual organisations**. These forms have become more prevalent during the last decades of the 20th century as a result of the trend towards restructuring and downsizing and developments in telecommunications technology. According to **Harold Leavitt**, organisation structure is inextricably linked to the technology and people who carry out the tasks. **Charles Handy** has shown that it is also directly linked to **corporate culture**.

organisation theory *Gen Mgt* the body of research and knowledge concerning organisations. Organisation theory originally focused primarily on the organisation as a unit, as

---

No man can produce great things who is not thoroughly sincere in dealing with himself.
James Russell Lowell

opposed to *organisation behaviour*, which explored individual and group behaviour within the organisation. Organisation behaviour emerged as a separate discipline in the late 1950s and early 1960s but there remains a large amount of overlap between the two. Organisation theory covers a range of areas including *organisation structure* and organisational psychology.

Organization of the Petroleum Exporting Countries *Fin see OPEC*

org chart *Gen Mgt see organisation chart*

orientation *(US) HR = induction*

original equipment manufacturer 1. *Fin* a company that makes a product that works with a basic and common product, for example, a computer **2.** *Ops* a company that assembles components from other suppliers or subcontractors to produce a complete product such as a car or aircraft. *Abbr* **OEM**

original face value *Fin* the amount of the principal of a mortgage on the day it is created

original issue discount *Fin* the discount offered on the day of sale of a debt instrument

original maturity *Fin* a date on which a debt instrument is due to mature

origination fee *Fin* a fee charged by a lender for providing a mortgage, usually expressed as a percentage of the principal

orthogonal *Stats* statistically independent

OTC market *abbr Fin* over-the-counter market

OTE *abbr HR* on-target earnings

other capital *Fin* capital that is not listed in specific categories

other current assets *Fin* assets that are not cash and are due to mature within a year

other long-term capital *Fin* long-term capital that is not listed in specific categories

other prices *Fin* prices that are not listed in a catalogue

other short-term capital *Fin* short-term capital that is not listed in specific categories

OTOH *abbr Gen Mgt* on the other hand (*slang*)

OTP *abbr E-com* open trading protocol

Ouchi, William (*b.* 1943) *Gen Mgt* Japanese-US academic. Best known for *Theory Z* (1981) which developed the work of *Douglas McGregor*.

out box *(US) Gen Mgt = out tray*

outdoor advertising *Mkting* the use of outdoor advertising media in venues such as airports, shopping malls, bus shelters, and railway stations

outdoor training *HR see adventure training*

outlier *Stats* a statistical observation that deviates significantly from other members of a sample

out-of-date cheque *Fin* a cheque which has not been presented to the bank on which it is drawn for payment within a reasonable time of its date (six months in the UK) and which may therefore be dishonoured by the bank without any breach of the banker–customer contract

out of the loop *Gen Mgt* excluded from communication within a group. Somebody who is out of the loop may have been deliberately or inadvertently excluded from the decision-making process or the information flow around an organisation. That person is likely to feel isolated and will be unable to contribute fully to the organisation. Effective networking may help to prevent this from happening. (*slang*)

outplacement *HR* a programme of resources, information, and advice provided by an employing organisation for employees who are about to be made redundant. Outplacement agencies typically help by drafting *curricula vitae*, offering career guidance, providing practice interviews, and placing redundant employees in new jobs. Outplacement programmes are often put into place well before the redundant employees leave the employer and, in the case of large-scale redundancy programmes, may remain in place for several years.

output *Fin* anything produced by a company, usually physical products

output gap *Econ* the difference between the amount of activity that is sustainable in an economy and the amount of activity actually taking place

output method *Econ* an accounting system that classifies costs according to the *outputs* for which they are incurred, not the inputs they have bought

output tax *(ANZ) Fin* the amount of *GST* (goods and services tax) paid to the tax office after the deduction of *input tax credits*

outside director *Gen Mgt* a member of a company's *board of directors* neither cur-

---

rently, or formerly, in the company's employment. An outside director is sometimes described as being synonymous with a **non-executive director**, and as usually being employed by a holding or associated company. In the United States, an outside director is somebody who has no relationships at all to a company. In US public companies, compensation and audit committees are generally made up of outside directors, and use of outside directors to select board directors is becoming more common.

outsourcing *Gen Mgt* the transfer of the provision of services previously carried out by in-house personnel to an external organisation, usually under a **contract** with agreed standards, costs, and conditions. Areas traditionally outsourced include legal services, transport, catering, and security. An increasing range of activities, including IT services, training, and public relations are now being outsourced. Outsourcing, or **contracting out**, is often introduced with the aim of increasing efficiency and reducing costs, or to enable the organisation to develop greater flexibility or to concentrate on **core business** activities. The term **subcontracting** is sometimes used to refer to outsourcing.

outstanding share *Fin* a share that a company has issued and somebody has bought

outstanding share capital *Fin* the value of all of the stock of a company minus the value of retained shares

out tray *Gen Mgt* a receptacle for documents and other items that have been dealt with. An out tray is normally placed in the office or on the desk of the person responsible for dealing with the contents. Items are placed in the out tray before being filed or delivered to another person. *US term* **out box**

outward bound training *HR see* **adventure training**

outwork *Fin, Gen Mgt* work carried out for a company away from its premises, for example, by subcontractors or employees working from home

outworker *Fin, Gen Mgt* a sub-contractor or employee carrying out work for a company away from its premises

overall capitalisation rate *Fin* net operating income other than debt service divided by value

overall market capacity *Econ* the amount of a service or good that can be absorbed in a market without affecting the price

overall rate of return *Fin* the yield of a bond held to maturity, expressed as a percentage

overall return *Fin* the aggregate of all the dividends received over an investment's life together with its capital gain or loss at the date of its realisation, calculated either before or after tax. It is one of the ways an investor can look at the performance of an investment.

overbid *Fin* **1.** to bid more than necessary **2.** an amount that is bid that is unnecessarily high

overbought market *Fin* a market where prices have risen beyond levels that can be supported by fundamental analysis. The market for internet companies in 2001 was over-bought and subsequently collapsed when it became clear that their trading performance could not support such price levels.

overcapacity *Ops* an excess of capability to produce goods or provide a service over the level of demand

overcapitalised *Fin* used to describe a business that has more capital than can profitably be employed. An overcapitalised company could buy back some of its own shares in the market; if it has significant debt capital it could repurchase its bonds in the market; or it could make a large one-off dividend to shareholders.

overdraft *Fin* the amount by which the money withdrawn from a bank account exceeds the balance in the account

overdraft facility *Fin* a credit arrangement with a bank, allowing a person or company with an account to use borrowed money up to an agreed limit when nothing is left in the account

overdraft line *Fin* an amount in excess of the balance in an account that a bank agrees to pay in honouring cheques on the account

overdraft protection *Fin* the bank service, amounting to a line of credit, that assures that the bank will honour overdrafts, up to a limit and for a fee

overdraw *Fin* to withdraw more money from a bank account than it contains, thereby exceeding an agreed credit limit

overdrawn *Fin* in debt to a bank because the amount withdrawn from an account exceeds its balance

overdue *Fin* an amount still owed after the date due

The almighty dollar, that great object of universal devotion throughout our land. **Washington Irving**

over-geared *Fin* used to describe a company with debt capital and preference shares that outweigh its ordinary share capital

overhanging *Fin* a large amount of commodities or securities that has not been sold and therefore has a negative effect on prices, for example, the element of a new issue left in the hands of the underwriters

overhead absorption rate *Fin* a means of attributing overhead to a product or service, based for example on direct labour hours, direct labour cost, or machine hours. The choice of overhead absorption base may be made with the objective of obtaining 'accurate' product costs, or of influencing managerial behaviour, for example, overhead applied to labour hours or part numbers appears to make the use of these resources more costly, thus discouraging their use.

overhead cost *Gen Mgt* the indirect recurring costs of running a business

over-insuring *Fin* insuring an asset for a sum in excess of its market or replacement value. However, it is unlikely that an insurance company will pay out more in a claim for loss than the asset is worth or the cost of replacing it.

over-invested *Fin* used to describe a business that invests heavily during an economic boom only to find that when it starts to produce an income, the demand for the product or service has fallen

overnight position *Fin* a trader's position in a security or option at the end of a trading day

overprice *Mkting* to set the price of a product or service too high, with the result that it is unacceptable to the market

overrated *Fin* used to describe something that is valued more highly than it should be

overseas company *Fin* a branch or subsidiary of a business that is incorporated in another country

Overseas Investment Commission *Fin* an independent body reporting to the New Zealand government that regulates foreign investment in New Zealand. It was set up in 1973 and is funded by the Reserve Bank of New Zealand.

overseas taxation *Fin see* **double taxation**, **double taxation agreement**

oversold *Fin* used to describe a market or security that is considered to have fallen too

rapidly as a result of excessive selling. *See also* **bear market**

overstocked *Fin* used to describe a business that has more stock than it needs

over the counter (OTC) market *Fin* a market in which trading takes place directly between licensed dealers, rather than through an auction system as used in most organised exchanges

overtime *HR* extra time worked beyond normal **hours of work**. Overtime is a traditional form of **flexible working**, often used by employers to cover periods of peak demand without incurring a permanent increase in costs. Some workers are entitled to a higher rate of **overtime pay** for the extra hours, but salaried workers in particular can be expected to work overtime with no additional reward.

overtime pay *HR* remuneration for **overtime** worked. Overtime pay often comes at a premium rate but in some occupations overtime is paid at a lower rate than the standard rate of pay.

overtrading *Fin* the condition of a business which enters into commitments in excess of its available short-term resources. This can arise even if the company is trading profitably, and is typically caused by financing strains imposed by a lengthy operating cycle or production cycle.

Owen, Robert (1771–1858) *Gen Mgt* British industrialist, and social reformer. Owner of a factory at New Lanark that he ran on model lines, pioneering improved working and living conditions for his employees. Author of *A New View of Society* (1813).

own brand *Mkting* a product or range of products offered by a retailer under their own name in competition with branded goods. Own brand products, like **non-branded goods**, are normally cheaper than branded items but are often perceived to be of a lower quality. *Also known as* **own-label**. *US term* **private label**

owner *Gen Mgt* **1.** a person or organisation that has legal title to products or services **2.** the person who controls a private company

owner-operator *Gen Mgt see* **sole proprietor**

owners' equity *Fin* a business's total assets less its total liabilities. *See also* **capital**, **ordinary shares**

ownership of companies *Gen Mgt* the possession of shares in companies. Company ownership structures can differ widely.

When women ask for equality, men take them to be demanding domination.   *Elizabeth Janeway*

Owners of public companies may be institutions, or individuals, or a mixture of both. Directors are often offered company shares as incentives and more participative companies may offer shares to employees through *employee ownership* schemes. Private companies are usually owned by individuals, families, or groups of individual shareholders. Nationalised industries are publicly owned. Co-operatives are wholly owned by employees. A separation between the ownership and control of companies became a widely discussed issue during the 20th century, especially in the United States and the United Kingdom where shareholders have tended to be more passive. Managers were viewed as having come to occupy controlling positions as the scale of industry grew. From the 1980s, this position changed to some extent as *privatisation*, *management buyouts*, restructuring, and *share incentive schemes* led to greater share ownership among managers and produced less passive shareholders.

own-label *Mkting see* *own brand*

P2P *abbr E-com* peer-to-peer: a means of optimising the networking capabilities of the Internet among groups of computers. Effectively it puts every computer on an equal footing, in that each can be both a publisher and consumer of information. The traditional model on the Web is the client-server one: the client is a computer that is able only to receive information; the server, on the other hand, publishes information on a website. Peer-to-peer makes a computer both a server and a client. Perhaps the best-known example of peer-to-peer is Napster, which enabled person A to search for and download music from person B's computer, while person B could search for and download music from person A's computer.

There are several options for the use of peer-to-peer technologies. Information/content: where the content on your computer becomes accessible to everyone else in the peer-to-peer environment, and vice versa. Processing sharing: where computers with spare processing capacity network together in order to combine resources. Using a large number of computers, this can create very significant processing capabilities. Services: a computer user can offer services to other people in the peer-to-peer network. File sharing: if person A downloads a file from a central server (an e-learning course from the Internet, for example), other people can use it from person A's machine instead of having to download it again, significantly reducing strain on *bandwidth*.

The main problem with peer-to-peer is the issue of security, and therefore it is essential to authenticate users. Many peer-to-peer interactions also use *encryption*, which ensures that the communication is secure as it is being passed from computer to computer.

paced line *Ops* a production line that moves at a constant speed. A paced line, such as a car *assembly line*, moves partly finished products past a *workstation* or zone at a constant speed. Work is carried out on the product within each work zone as the line continues to move. The speed of movement of the line is set to match worker proficiency or machine processing speed.

packaging 1. *Fin* the practice of combining securities in a single trade. *See also* **bundling** **2.** *Ops* materials used for containing, protecting, and presenting goods during the delivery process from the producer to the consumer.

Packaging has evolved from the basic function of protection to become an important marketing tool for communicating brand values.

Packard, David (1912–96) *Gen Mgt* US entrepreneur and business executive. Co-founder of Hewlett-Packard. Hewlett-Packard was noted for its *corporate culture* and *management style* based on openness, and respect for its employees. See Packard's book *The HP Way* (1995).

Pac Man defence *Fin* avoiding purchase by making an offer to buy the prospective buyer

page counter *E-com* a utility program that registers the number of times a web page is visited, for example, by means of a *click-through*

page impressions *E-com* the number of customers who land on a web page, as in an *ad view*. *Also known as* **page views**

page pushing *E-com see* **co-browsing**

page views *E-com see* **page impressions**

paid cheque *Fin* a cheque which has been honoured by the bank on which it was drawn, and bears evidence of payment on its face

paid circulation *Mkting* the number of copies of a newspaper or magazine that are actually bought

paid-up policy *Fin* **1.** in the United Kingdom, an endowment assurance policy, for which the policyholder has decided not to continue paying premiums, that continues to provide life cover while the cost of the premiums is covered by the underlying fund. If the fund is sufficient to pay the premiums for the remainder of the term, the remaining funds will be paid to the policyholder at maturity. **2.** in the United States, an insurance policy on which all the premiums have been paid

paid-up share *Fin* a share for which shareholders have paid the full contractual amount. *See also* **call**, **called-up share capital**, **paid-up share capital**, **share capital**

paid-up share capital *Fin* the amount which shareholders are deemed to have paid on the shares issued and called up

painting the tape *Fin* an illegal practice in which traders break large orders into smaller units in order to give the illusion of heavy buying activity. This encourages investors to buy, and the traders then sell as the price of the stock goes up. (*slang*)

palmtop *Gen Mgt* a very small portable computer. Compared to a personal computer or laptop, the functionality of a palmtop is currently limited but it is increasing.

pandas *Fin* a series of Chinese gold and silver bullion/collector coins, each featuring a panda, that were first issued in 1982. Struck with a highly polished surface, the smallest gold coin weighs 0.05 ounces, the largest 12 ounces.

P & L *Fin see profit and loss account*

panel interview *HR* an interview that takes place before two or more interviewers who may be from different parts of the interviewing organisation or external to it.

Organisations tend to use panel interviews as they save time by bringing all the interviewers together rather than shuffling the applicant around from one office to the next. They are also used for their consistency of information: from the applicant and from the organisation.

As with any job interview, it is important beforehand for applicant to find out not only about the position they are applying for, but the organisation to which they are applying. It may also help them to mentally rehearse the panel interview situation. With several interviewers, the applicant may feel bombarded by questions. He or she should aim to answer all the questions, taking one at a time, and if necessary, ask for clarification where a question is not clear.

The interview is an opportunity for the applicant to showcase his or her strengths to several interviewers at once, and so while it is not wise to interrupt the interviewers, he or she should resist the temptation to let them do most of the talking. Making meaningful eye contact with all members of the panel when talking is a good way for the applicant to convey a sense of confidence and calm—the key to success in the panel interview.

Panel on Takeovers and Mergers *Fin see City Code on Takeovers and Mergers*

panel study *Stats* a study that surveys a selected group of people over a period of time

panic buying *Fin* an abnormal level of buying caused by fear or rumours of product shortages or by severe price rises

PANSE *Gen Mgt* Politically Active and Not Seeking Employment (*slang*)

pants
drop your pants *Mktg* to lower the price of a product in order to sell it (*slang*)

put some pants on something (*US*) *Gen Mgt* to supply the missing details of a plan or idea (*slang*)

paper *Fin* **1.** a certificate of deposits and other securities **2.** a rights issue or an issue of bonds launched by a company to raise additional capital (*slang*) **3.** all debt issued by a company (*slang*)

paper architecture *Gen Mgt* an ambitious business project that never gets beyond the planning stage, because of lack of funding or because it is not feasible (*slang*)

paper company *Fin* a company that only exists on paper and has no physical assets

paperless office *Gen Mgt* a workplace in which as much communication and as many procedures as possible have been computerised. The paperless office was predicted in the 1960s. The recent widespread availability of *e-mail*, the *Internet*, and word processing, file transfer, and *intranet* systems means that it is beginning to become achievable for those organisations that wish to pursue it. In a truly paperless office, document storage is on computer rather than in filing cabinets and written communication is not circulated in hard copy but e-mailed. This is largely unattainable, as most people still prefer paper to electronic copy, especially when faced with reading more than one page. Encouraging employees to cut down on paper usage can help achieve *environmental management* targets, and storing information electronically can lead to greater communication efficiency which may result in *competitive advantage*.

paper millionaire *Fin* an individual who owns shares that are worth in excess of a million in currency, but which may fall in value. In 2001, many of the founders of dot-com companies were paper millionaires. *See also paper profit*

paper money *Fin* **1.** banknotes **2.** payments in paper form, for example, cheques

paper profit *Fin* an increase in the value of an investment that the investor has no immediate intention of realising

paper trail *Gen Mgt* all of the documentation of an event, especially a decision (*slang*)

par *Fin* the nominal value of a bond, being the price denominated for the purpose of setting the interest rate (coupon) payable

PAR *abbr Fin* prime assets ratio

paradigm shift *Gen Mgt* a change in an accepted pattern of thought or behaviour

---

parallel engineering *Ops see concurrent engineering*

parallel pricing *Fin* the practice of varying prices in a similar way and at the same time as competitors, which may be done by agreement with them

paralysis by analysis *Gen Mgt* the inability of managers to make decisions as a result of a preoccupation with attending meetings, writing reports, and collecting statistics and analyses. Paralysis of effective *decision-making* in organisations can occur in situations where there is horizontal conflict, disagreement between different hierarchical levels, or unclear objectives.

parameter *Stats* a quantity that is numerically characteristic of a whole model or population

parameter design *Stats* a process aimed at reducing variation in processes or products

parent company *Fin* a company that owns or controls a number of other companies

Pareto, Vilfredo Frederico Damaso (1848–1923) *Gen Mgt* Italian economist, mathematician, and sociologist. Originator of the *eighty-twenty rule*, and of the law of income distribution known as *Pareto's Law*, which he explained in *Cours d'Économie Politique* (1896–97).

Pareto analysis *Gen Mgt see eighty-twenty rule*

Pareto chart *Gen Mgt see eighty-twenty rule*

Pareto's Law *Econ* a theory of income distribution. Developed by *Vilfredo Pareto*, Pareto's Law states that regardless of political or taxation conditions, income will be distributed in the same way across all countries.

Pareto's principle *Gen Mgt see eighty-twenty rule*

pari passu *Fin* ranking equally

Paris Club *Fin see Group of Ten*

Paris Inter Bank Offered Rate *Fin* the French equivalent of the London Inter Bank Offered Rate. *Abbr* **PIBOR**

parity *Fin* a situation when the price of a commodity, foreign currency, or security is the same in different markets. *See also **arbitrage***

parity bit *E-com* an odd or even digit used to check binary computer data for errors

parity value *Fin see conversion value*

park *Fin* to place owned shares with third parties to disguise their ownership, usually illegally

Parker Follett, Mary (1868–1933) *Gen Mgt* US academic. Applied psychological and social science insights to the study of industrial organisation at a time when the *scientific management* methods of *Frederick Winslow Taylor* were predominant. Recent interest in her work owes much to Pauline Graham's writings, including *Mary Parker Follett: Prophet of Management* (1995). Follett's career was largely spent in social work, though her books appeared regularly—*The New State* (1918) was an influential description of her own brand of dynamic democracy, and *Creative Experience* (1924) was her first business-oriented book. In her later years she was in great demand as a lecturer.

parking *Fin* **1.** the transfer of shares in a company to a nominee name or the name of an associate, often for non-legitimate or illegal reasons (*slang*) **2.** (*US*) putting money into safe investments while deciding where to invest the money

Parkinson, C. Northcote (1909–93) *Gen Mgt* British academic. Known for *Parkinson's Law* (1957).

Parkinson's Law *HR* the facetious assertion that work will expand to fill the time available

Parquet *Fin* the Paris Bourse (*slang*)

partial retirement *HR see phased retirement*

participating bond *Fin* a bond that pays the dividends that stockholders receive as well as interest

participating insurance *Fin* insurance in which policy holders receive a dividend from the insurer's profits

participating preference share *Fin* a type of preference share that entitles the holder to a fixed dividend and, in addition, to the right to participate in any surplus profits after payment of agreed levels of dividends to ordinary shareholders has been made. *See also **nonparticipating preference share***

participative budgeting *Fin* a budgeting system in which all budget holders are given the opportunity to participate in setting their own budgets. *Also known as **bottom-up budgeting***

partly-paid share *Fin* a share for which shareholders have not paid the full contractual amount. *See also **call**, **share capital***

partnering *Gen Mgt see strategic partnering*

partnership *Gen Mgt* a contractual relationship between two or more people who agree to share in the profits and losses of a business. A partnership is not an incorporated company and the individual partners are responsible for decisions and debts. A partnership at the organisational level is known as a *joint venture* or *strategic alliance*.

partnership accounts *Fin* the capital and current accounts of each partner in a partnership, or the accounts recording the partnership's business activities

partnership agreement *Fin* the document that sets up a partnership, detailing the capital contributed by each partner, whether an individual partner's liability is limited, the apportionment of the profit, salaries, and possibly procedures to be followed, for example, in the event of a partner retiring or a new partner joining. In the United Kingdom, when a partnership agreement is silent on any matter, the provisions of the Partnership Act 1890 apply. *Also known as* **articles of partnership**

part-time director *Gen Mgt see* **non-executive director**

part-time work *Gen Mgt* work that occupies fewer hours than *full-time* work. Traditionally, part-time simply meant working fewer hours a day, or fewer days a week, than a full-time employee, but part-time working is now seen as one of several *flexible working hours* alternatives to the 9–5 working day.

party plan *Mkting* a sales technique in which local agents host parties to demonstrate or sell products to customers

Pascale, Richard Tanner (*b.* 1938) *Gen Mgt* US academic and consultant. Co-developer of the *McKinsey 7-S framework* of corporate success, and co-author, with **Anthony Athos**, of *The Art of Japanese Management* (1981). Pascale also originated the concept of organisational *agility*. Pascale and Athos collaborated with **Tom Peters** and **Bob Waterman** on the 7-S model at the management consultancy company McKinsey. Peters and Waterman cited US examples of success in *In Search of Excellence*, but it was Pascale and Athos who explored the model in greater depth, tracing many of its origins to working practice in Japanese organisations.

passbook *Fin* a small booklet issued by banks, building societies, and other financial institutions to record deposits, withdrawals, interest paid, and the balance on savings and deposit accounts. In all but the smaller building societies, it has now largely been replaced by statements.

passing off *Fin* a form of fraud in which a company tries to sell its own product by deceiving buyers into thinking it is another product

passive investment management *Fin* the managing of a unit trust or other investment portfolio by relying on automatic adjustments such as indexation instead of making personal judgments. *See also* **active fund management**

passive portfolio strategy *Fin* the managing of an investment portfolio by relying on automatic adjustments or tracking an index

password *E-com* a series of characters that enables a user to access a private file, website, computer, or application

patent *Mkting* a type of *copyright* granted as a fixed-term monopoly to an inventor by the state to prevent others copying an invention, or improvement of a product or process.

The granting of a patent requires the publication of full details of the invention or improvement but the use of the patented information is restricted to the patent holder or any organisations licensed by them.

A patent's value is usually the sum of its development costs, or its purchase price if acquired from someone else. It is generally to a company's advantage to spread the patent's value over several years. If this is the case, the critical time period to consider is not the full life of the patent (20 years in the United Kingdom), but its estimated useful life.

For example, in January 2000 a company acquired a patent issued in January 1995 at a cost of £100,000. It concludes that the patent's useful commercial life is 10 years, not the 15 remaining before the patent expires. In turn, patent value would be £100,000, and it would be spread (or amortised in accounting terms) over 10 years, or £10,000 each year.

patent attorney *Gen Mgt* a lawyer who specialises in the type of intellectual property called a patent

paternity leave *HR* time off work given to a new father on the birth of his child. Paternity leave is a form of *special leave*, and is granted at an organisation's discretion. It may be paid, or unpaid. Paternity leave forms an important part of an organisation's *family-friendly policies*.

path analysis *Stats* a means of showing the correlation between variables in a statistical study

path diagram *Stats* a diagram that shows the correlation between variables in a statistical study

pathfinder prospectus *Fin* a preliminary prospectus used in initial public offerings to gauge the reaction of investors

pawnbroker *Fin* a person who lends money against the security of a wide range of chattels, from jewellery to cars. The borrower may recover the goods by repaying the loan and interest by a certain date. Otherwise, the items pawned are sold and any surplus after the deduction of expenses, the loan, and interest is returned to the borrower.

pay *HR* a sum of money given in return for work done or services provided. Pay, in the form of *salary* or *wages*, is generally provided in weekly or monthly fixed amounts, and is usually expressed in terms of the total sum earned per year. It may also be allocated using a *piece-rate system*, where workers are paid for each unit of work they carry out.

payable to order *Fin* on a bill of exchange or cheque, used to indicate that it may be transferred. *See also* **endorsement**

Pay As You Earn *HR* in the United Kingdom, a system for collecting direct taxes that requires employers to deduct taxes from employees' *pay* before payment is made. *Abbr* **PAYE**

pay-as-you-go *(Canada) HR* a means of financing a pension system whereby benefits of current retirees are financed by current workers

Pay-As-You-Go *(ANZ) Fin* a system used in Australia for paying income tax instalments on business and investment income. PAYG is part of the new tax system introduced by the Australian government on 1 July 2000. *Abbr* **PAYG**

payback *Fin* the time required for the cash inflows from a capital investment project to equal the cash outflows

payback period *Fin* the length of time it will take to earn back the money invested in a project.

EXAMPLE The straight payback period method is the simplest way of determining the investment potential of a major project. Expressed in time, it tells a management how many months or years it will take to recover the original cash cost of the project. It is calculated using the formula:

cost of project / annual cash revenues = payback period

Thus, if a project cost £100,000 and was expected to generate £28,000 annually, the payback period would be:

100,000 / 28,000 = 3.57 years

If the revenues generated by the project are expected to vary from year to year, add the revenues expected for each succeeding year until you arrive at the total cost of the project. For example, say the revenues expected to be generated by the £100,000 project are:

	Revenue	Total
Year 1	£19,000	£19,000
Year 2	£25,000	£44,000
Year 3	£30,000	£74,000
Year 4	£30,000	£104,000
Year 5	£30,000	£134,000

Thus, the project would be fully paid for in Year 4, since it is in that year the total revenue reaches the initial cost of £100,000. The precise payback period would be calculated as:

((100,000 – 74,000) /(1000,000 – 74,000)) × 365 = 316 days + 3 years

The picture becomes complex when the time-value-of-money principle is introduced into the calculations. Some experts insist this is essential to determine the most accurate payback period. Accordingly, the annual revenues have to be discounted by the applicable interest rate, 10% in this example. Doing so produces significantly different results:

	Revenue	Present value	Total
Year 1	£19,000	£17,271	£17,271
Year 2	£25,000	£20,650	£37,921
Year 3	£30,000	£22,530	£60,451
Year 4	£30,000	£20,490	£80,941
Year 5	£30,000	£18,630	£99,571

This method shows that payback would not occur even after five years.

Generally, a payback period of three years or less is desirable; if a project's payback period is less than a year, some contend it should be judged essential.

PAYE *abbr HR* Pay As You Earn

payee *Fin* **1.** the person or organisation to whom a cheque is payable. *See also* **drawee** **2.** the person to whom a payment has to be made. *See also* **endorsement**

payer *Fin* the person making a payment

PAYG *abbr (ANZ) Fin* Pay-As-You-Go

paying agent *Fin* the institution responsible for making interest payments on a security

---

and repaying capital at redemption. *Also known as* **disbursing agent**

paying banker *Fin* the bank on which a bill of exchange or cheque is drawn

paying-in book *Fin* book of detachable slips that accompany money or cheques being paid into a bank account

payload *Fin* the amount of cargo that a vessel can carry

paymaster *Fin* the person responsible for paying an organisation's employees

payment by results *HR* a system of *pay* that directly links an employee's *compensation* to their work output. The system is based on the view put forward by *Frederick Winslow Taylor* that payment by results will increase workers' productivity by appealing to their materialism. The concept is closely related to *performance-related pay* which rewards employees for behaviour and skills rather than quantifiable productivity measures.

payment gateway *E-com* a company or organisation that provides an interface between a merchant's point-of-sale system, *acquirer* payment systems, and *issuer* payment systems. *Abbr* **GW**

payment in advance *Fin* payment made for goods when they are ordered but before they are delivered. *See also* **prepayment**

payment in due course *Fin* the date on which a bill of exchange becomes payable

payment-in-kind *HR* an alternative form of *pay* given to employees in place of monetary reward but considered to be of equivalent value. A payment in kind may take the form of use of a car, purchase of goods at cost price, or other non-financial exchange that benefits the employee. It forms part of the total pay package rather than being an extra benefit.

payment-in-lieu *HR* payment that is given in place of an entitlement

payment terms *Fin* the stipulation by a business as to when it should be paid for goods or services supplied, for example, cash with order, payment on delivery, or within a particular number of days of the invoice date

payout ratio *Fin* an expression of the total dividends paid to shareholders as a percentage of a company's net profit in a given period of time. This measures the likelihood of dividend payments being sustained, and is a useful indication of sustained profitability. The lower the ratio, the more secure the dividend, and the company's future.

The payout ratio is calculated by dividing annual dividends paid on ordinary shares by earnings per share:

Annual dividend / earnings-per-share = payout ratio

Take the company whose earnings per share is £8 and its dividend payout is 2.1. Its payout ratio would be:

2.1 / 8 =.263 or 26.3%

A high payout ratio clearly appeals to conservative investors seeking income. However, when coupled with weak or falling earnings it could suggest an imminent dividend cut, or that the company is short-changing reinvestment to maintain its payout. A payout ratio above 75% is a warning. It suggests the company is failing to reinvest sufficient profits in its business, that the company's earnings are faltering, or that it is trying to attract investors who otherwise would not be interested. *See also* **dividend cover**

Pay Pal *E-com* a web-based service that enables Internet users to send and receive payments electronically. To open a Pay Pal account, users register and provide their credit card details. When they decide to make a transaction via Pay Pal, their card is charged for the transfer.

pay-per-click *E-com* a website that charges a *micropayment* to see digital information, for example, an e-book or e-magazine

pay-per-play *E-com* a website that charges a *micropayment* to play an interactive game over the Internet

pay-per-view 1. *E-com* a website that charges a *micropayment* to see digital information, for example, an e-book or e-magazine **2.** *Fin* a method of collecting revenue from television viewers. The viewer pays a fee for watching an individual programme, typically a sports or entertainment event.

payroll *HR* the organisational function that is responsible for the payment of employees. Payroll also can refer to the list of employees and their *pay* details, or to the total cost of pay to an organisation.

payroll analysis *Fin* an analysis of a payroll for cost accounting purposes, giving, for example, gross pay by department or operation, gross pay by class of labour, gross pay by product, or constituent parts of gross pay, such as direct pay and lost time

pay scale *HR* a framework that groups together jobs of broadly equivalent worth into job grades, based on *job evaluation*, with a *pay* range given to each grade. Although pay scales are still widely used, other pay structures such as *broadbanding* are replacing the traditional approach. Some organisations do not have a formal structure and instead rely on *personal contracts*. *Also known as* **salary scale**, **wage scale**. *See also* **job family**

payslip *HR* a document given to employees when they are paid, providing a statement of *pay* for that period. A payslip includes details of deductions such as *income tax*, national insurance contributions, pension contributions, and trade union dues.

PDA *abbr E-com* personal digital assistant: a handheld mobile device that can access the Internet and act as a personal organiser

PDF *Gen Mgt, Mkting* an electronic document format that allows all elements of a document, including page layout, text, photographs, and colours to be viewed on different computers or systems

PDR *abbr Fin* price-dividend ratio

P/E *abbr Fin* price-earnings ratio

peer-to-peer *E-com see* **P2P**

peg *Fin* **1.** to fix the exchange rate of one currency against that of another or of a basket of other currencies **2.** to fix wages and salaries during a period of inflation to help prevent an inflationary spiral

penalty *Fin* an arbitrary pre-arranged sum that becomes payable if one party breaks a term of a contract or an undertaking. The most common penalty is a high rate of interest on an unauthorised overdraft. *See also* **overdraft**

penalty rate *(ANZ) HR* a higher than normal rate of pay awarded for work performed outside normal working hours

pencil-whip *Gen Mgt* to criticise somebody in writing (*slang*)

penetrated market *Mkting* the existing customers within a market

penetration pricing *Fin* setting prices low, especially for new products, in order to maximise market penetration

penny shares *Fin* very low-priced stock that is a speculative investment

pension *Fin* money received regularly after *retirement*, from a *personal pension* scheme, *occupational pension scheme*, or state pension scheme. *Also known as* **retirement pension**

pensionable earnings *Fin* in an occupational pension scheme with a defined benefit, the earnings on which the pension is based. Generally, overtime payments, benefits in kind, bonuses, and territorial allowances, for example, payments for working in a large city, are not pensionable earnings. *US term* **final average monthly salary**

people churner *HR* a bad boss with a reputation for losing talented staff (*slang*)

PEP *abbr Fin* personal equity plan

P/E ratio *Fin* the price/earnings ratio, calculated by dividing a company's share price by its earnings per share

per capita income *Econ* the average income of each of a particular group of people, for example, citizens of a country

perceived value pricing *Fin see* **market based pricing**

percussive maintenance *Gen Mgt* the practice of hitting or shaking an electronic device in order to make it work (*slang*)

per diem *HR* a rate paid per day, for example, for expenses when an employee is working away from the office

perfect capital market *Econ* a capital market in which the decisions of buyers and sellers have no effect on market price

perfect competition *Econ* a market in which no buyer or seller can influence prices. In practice, perfect markets are characterised by few or no barriers to entry and by many buyers and sellers.

perfect hedge *Fin* a hedge that exactly balances the risk of another investment

performance appraisal *HR* a face-to-face discussion in which one employee's work is discussed, reviewed, and appraised by another, using an agreed and understood framework. Usually, line managers conduct the appraisals of their staff, although peers can appraise each other, and line managers can themselves be appraised by their staff through **360 degree appraisal**. The appraisal process focuses on behaviours and outcomes, and aims to improve **motivation**, growth, and performance of the appraisee. Performance appraisals should be carried out at least once per year. *Also known as* **performance evaluation**

performance bond *Fin* a guarantee given by a bank to a third party stating that it will pay a sum of money if its customer, the account holder, fails to complete a specified contract

performance criteria *Fin* the standards used to evaluate a product, service, or employee

performance evaluation *HR see performance appraisal*

performance fund *Fin* an investment fund designed to produce a high return, reflected in the higher risk involved

performance indicator *HR* a key measure designed to assess an aspect of the qualitative or quantitative performance of a company. Performance indicators can relate to operational, strategic, confidence, behavioural, and ethical aspects of a company's operation and can help to pinpoint its strengths and weaknesses. They are periodically monitored to ensure the company's long-term success.

performance management *Gen Mgt* the facilitation of high achievement by employees. Performance management involves enabling people to carry out their work to the best of their ability, meeting and perhaps exceeding targets and standards. Performance management can be co-ordinated by an inter-related framework between manager and employee. Key areas of the framework to be agreed are *objectives*, human resource management (see *HRM*), standards and *performance indicators*, and means of reward. For successful performance management, a culture of collective and individual responsibility for the continuing improvement of business processes needs to be established, and individual skills and contributions need to be encouraged and nurtured. One tool for monitoring performance management is *performance appraisal*. For organisations, performance management is usually known as company performance and is monitored through business appraisal.

performance measurement *Fin* the process of assessing the proficiency with which a reporting entity succeeds, by the economic acquisition of resources and their efficient and effective deployment, in achieving its objectives. Performance measures may be based on non-financial as well as on financial information.

performance-related pay *HR* a *compensation* system in which the level of *pay* is dependent on the employee's performance. Performance-related pay can be entirely dependent or only partly dependent on performance. There are usually three stages to a

performance-related pay system: determining the criteria by which the employee is assessed, establishing whether the employee has met the criteria, and linking the employee's achievements to the pay structure. Performance measures can incorporate skills, knowledge, and behavioural indicators. The system can be compared to *payment by results*, which is based solely on quantitative productivity measures.

period bill *Fin* a bill of exchange payable on a certain date rather than on demand. *Also known as **term bill***

period cost *Fin* a cost which relates to a time period rather than to the output of products or services

periodic inventory review system *Ops* a system for placing orders of varying sizes at regular intervals to replenish *inventory* up to a specified or target inventory level. A periodic inventory review system fixes a specific reorder period, but the reorder quantity can vary according to need. The quantity reordered is calculated by subtracting existing inventory and on-order inventory from the target inventory level. *Also known as **fixed interval re-order system***

periodicity concept *Fin* the requirement to produce financial statements at set time intervals. This requirement is embodied, in the case of UK corporations, in the Companies Acts.

perk *HR see fringe benefits*

permalancer *HR* a freelance worker who has worked in one company for so long that he or she is virtually a permanent member of staff (*slang*)

permanent interest-bearing shares *Fin* shares issued by a building society to raise capital because the law prohibits it from raising capital in more conventional ways. *Abbr* **PIBS**

permission marketing *E-com* any form of online direct marketing that involves gaining each recipient's permission. This type of marketing typically involves sending promotional material via e-mail to an opt-in list of subscribers. The term was popularised by business author Seth Godin, who has written a book on the subject, *Permission Marketing* (1999).

Perot (*US*) *Gen Mgt* to leave, fail, or give up something unexpectedly. The term comes from the sudden withdrawal from the US presidential race of candidate Ross Perot in the 1990s. (*slang*)

perpetual bond *Fin* a bond that has no date of maturity

perpetual debenture *Fin* a debenture that pays interest in perpetuity, having no date of maturity

perpetual inventory *Fin* the daily tracking of inventory

perpetuity *Fin* a periodic payment continuing for a limitless period. *See also* ***annuity***

per se *Gen Mgt* by itself or in itself

personal account *Fin* a record of amounts receivable from or payable to a person or an entity

personal allowances *Fin* the amount of money that an individual can earn without having to pay income tax. The allowances vary according to age, marital status, and whether the person is a single parent.

personal contract *HR* a ***contract of employment*** that is negotiated on an employee by employee basis, rather than using a traditional structured system that gives identical contracts to groups of workers

personal development *HR* the acquisition of knowledge, skills, and experience for the purpose of enhancing individual performance and self-perception. Personal development is usually led by the individual, in contrast to ***employee development***, which is initiated by an employing organisation. To be effective, it should follow a personal development cycle: establish the purpose or the reason for development; identify the skills or knowledge areas that need developing; look at development opportunities; formulate an action plan; undertake the development; record the outcomes of the development activity; review and evaluate the outputs and benefits. Personal development is an important aspect of ***CPD***. *Also known as* ***self-development***

personal digital assistant *Gen Mgt see* **PDA**

Personal Equity Plan *Fin* a scheme sponsored by the UK government to promote investment in company shares, unit trusts, and equity-based investment trusts by offering tax benefits to investors. The arrival of ISAs in 1999 meant that no new personal equity plans could be opened, but existing plans carry on as before. *Abbr* **PEP**

personal financial planning *Fin* short- and long-term financial planning by an individual,

either independently or with the assistance of a professional adviser. It will include the use of tax efficient schemes such as Individual Savings Accounts, ensuring adequate provisions are being made for retirement, and examining short- and long-term borrowing requirements such as overdrafts and mortgages.

Personal Identification Number *Fin see* **ATM**. *abbr* **PIN**

Personal Investment Authority *Fin* a self-regulatory organisation responsible for supervising the activities of financial intermediaries selling financial products to individuals. *Abbr* **PIA**

personalisation *E-com* the process by which a website presents customers with selected information on their specific needs. To do this, personal information is collected on the individual user and employed to customise the website for that person. Used properly, personalisation is a powerful tool that allows customers to access the right content more quickly, thus saving them valuable time. Personalisation is particularly useful if a website contains a very large quantity of material, meaning that a visitor is slow in finding the information they seek. It also requires a large number of visitors to the website, because personalisation systems are complex and expensive to install.

Information on the customer is usually collected in one of two ways. Either the individual is asked to fill out a personal profile, perhaps informing the organisation of the type of product and service he or she is interested in, or the organisation uses software that tracks the way a customer uses the website. For example, a customer interested in Product X last week, might receive details of an update for Product X upon their next visit to the website. A popular method by which such tracking is carried out is the use of ***cookies***, which reside on an individual's browser and collect information on that person's web behaviour. Because it requires the collection of personal information, personalisation raises key ***privacy policy*** issues.

personality promotion *Mkting* a method of promoting a product or service by fronting the campaign with a famous person. For example, the footballer David Beckham is employed to promote a variety of products.

personality test *HR see* ***psychometric test***

personal pension *HR* a pension taken out by an individual with a private sector insurance company or bank. A personal pension usually takes the form of a scheme in which an individual regularly contributes money to a pension provider who invests it in a pension fund. On retirement, a lump sum is available for the purchase of an annuity that provides weekly or monthly payments. Under the Finance Act (1987), all employees have the right to arrange their own pensions. *Stakeholder pensions* have recently been introduced that are government regulated but are administered by private sector companies.

personnel *HR* **1.** the people employed in an organisation, considered collectively **2.** the department of an organisation that deals with the employment of staff and staffing issues

personnel management *HR* the part of management that is concerned with people and their relationships at work. Personnel management is the responsibility of all those who manage people, as well as a description of the work of specialists. *Personnel managers* advise on, formulate, and implement *personnel policies* such as *recruitment*, *conditions of employment*, *performance appraisal*, *training*, industrial relations, and *health and safety*. There are various models of personnel management, of which human resource management (see *HRM*) is the most recent.

personnel manager *HR* a professional specialist and manager responsible for advising on, formulating, and implementing personnel or human resources strategy and personnel policies. The nature of the personnel manager's job is dependent on the size of the organisation and the extent to which personnel responsibilities are devolved to *line managers*.

personnel planning *HR see human resource planning*

personnel policy *HR* a set of rules that define the manner in which an organisation deals with a *human resources* or *personnel*-related matter. A personnel policy should reflect good practice, be written down, be communicated across the organisation, and should adapt to changing circumstances.

PEST analysis *Gen Mgt* a management technique that enables an analysis of four external factors that may impact on the performance of the organisation. These factors are: Political, Economic, Social, and Technological. PEST analysis is often carried out using *brainstorming* techniques. It offers an environment-to-organisation perspective as opposed to the organisation-to-environment perspective offered by *SWOT analysis*.

PESTLE *Mkting* an acronym that describes the six influences to which a market is subject, namely, political, economic, social, technological, legal, and environmental

Peter, Laurence (1919–90) *Gen Mgt* Canadian academic. Founder of the *Peter Principle*, described in the book of the same name (co-authored with Raymond Hull, 1970).

Peter Principle *HR* a tenet holding that all employees tend to rise to their level of incompetence within an organisation, at which point it is too late to move them down or sideways

Peters, Tom (*b.* 1942) *Gen Mgt* US consultant, writer, and lecturer. Co-developer of the *McKinsey 7-S framework* of corporate success, and co-author, with *Bob Waterman*, of *In Search of Excellence* (1982), which identified eight characteristics of successful companies. Peters moved the discussion of *management* away from the established structure of *bureaucracy* towards a more innovative, intuitive, and people-centred approach in which change is to be embraced, not resisted. *In Search of Excellence* was one of the first books to make management ideas generally accessible and his seminar presentations have earned Peters a reputation as an energetic, entertaining performer.

petites et moyennes entreprises *Gen Mgt* French for small and medium-sized businesses. *Abbr* **PME**

petty cash *Fin* a small store of cash used for minor business expenses

PFI *abbr Fin* Private Finance Initiative

phantom bid *Fin* a reported but non-existent attempt to buy a company

phantom income *Fin* income that is subject to tax even though the recipient never actually gets control of it, for example, income from a limited partnership

phased retirement *HR* a gradual reduction in hours of work, typically through working a three- or four-day week in the last six months leading up to *retirement*. Phased retirement is a *personnel policy* introduced by organisations to try to ease the transition between employment and retirement, which for many employees can prove to be a traumatic change. *Also known as gradual retirement*

Phillips curve *Stats* a graphical representation of the relationship between unemployment and the rate of inflation

phone lag *Gen Mgt* tiredness caused by having to conduct business on the telephone with people who are based in different time zones (*slang*)

physical asset *Fin* an asset that has a physical embodiment, as opposed to cash or securities

physical distribution management *Ops* the planning, monitoring, and control of the distribution and delivery of manufactured goods

physical market *Fin* a market in futures that involves physical delivery of the commodities involved, instead of simple cash transactions

physical price *Fin* the price of a commodity for immediate delivery

physical retail shopping *Gen Mgt* shopping carried out by visiting high-street shops rather than buying online

physicals *Fin* commodities that can be bought and used, as contrasted with commodities traded on a futures contract

physical stocktaking *Fin* the ascertainment of stocks held (by counting physical objects) for comparison with accounting records. Modern practice is to stocktake different items with different frequencies, classifying items according to the degree of control required. **Periodic stocktaking** is a process whereby all stock items are counted and valued at a set point in time, usually the end of an accounting period. **Continuous stocktaking** is the process of counting and valuing selected items at different times, on a rotating basis.

physical working conditions *HR* the surroundings within which somebody works, taking into account aspects such as temperature, air quality, lighting, safety, cleanliness, and noise

PIA *abbr Fin* Personal Investment Authority

PIBOR *abbr Fin* Paris Inter Bank Offered Rate

PIBS *abbr Fin* permanent interest-bearing shares

pick and shovel work *Gen Mgt* boring and detailed work such as the examination of documents for mistakes (*slang*)

picture *Fin* the price and trading quantity of a particular stock on Wall Street, used for example, in the question to a specialist dealer 'What's the picture on ABC?'. The response would give the bid and offer price and number of shares for which there would be a buyer and seller. (*slang*)

piece-rate system *or* **piece work** *HR* a system of payment through which an employee

is paid a pre-determined amount for each unit of output. The rate of **pay**, or piece rate, is usually fixed subjectively, rather than by a more objective technique such as **work study**. Rates are said to be tight when it is difficult for an employee to earn a bonus and loose when bonuses are easily earned. Piece-rate systems, or **piece work**, are a form of **payment by results** or **performance-related pay**.

pie chart *Stats* a chart drawn as a circle divided into proportional sections like portions of a pie

piggyback advertising *Mkting* an offer or promotion that runs in parallel with another campaign and incurs no costs

piggyback loan *Fin* a loan that is raised against the same security as an existing loan

piggyback rights *Fin* the permission to sell existing shares in conjunction with the sale of like shares in a new offering

pig in a python *Gen Mgt* the large increase in the birth rate between 1946 and 1964 (*slang*)

pilot fish *HR* a junior executive who follows close behind a more senior executive (*slang*)

pilot survey *Mkting* a preliminary piece of research carried out before a complete survey to test the effectiveness of the research methodology

PIN *abbr Fin* personal identification number

pin-drop syndrome *HR* stress induced by extreme quietness in a working environment (*slang*)

pink advertising *Mkting* advertising aimed at the gay and lesbian community

pink-collar job *HR* a sexist term for a position normally held by a woman, especially a young one (*slang*)

pink dollar (*US*) *Fin* = **pink pound**

pink form *Fin* in the United Kingdom, a preferential application form at an initial public offering that is reserved for the employees of the company being floated

pink pound *Fin* money spent by gays and lesbians. US term **pink dollar**

pink slip
get your pink slip (*US*) *HR* to be dismissed from employment (*slang*)

pink slipper (*US*) *HR* a person who has been dismissed from employment (*slang*)

Pink 'Un *Fin* the Financial Times (*slang*)

piracy *Gen Mgt* illegal copying of a product such as software or music

pit *Fin* the area of an exchange where trading takes place. It was traditionally an octagonal stepped area with terracing so as to give everyone a good view of the proceedings during open outcry.

pit broker *Fin* a broker who transacts business in the pit of a futures or options exchange

pitch *Gen Mgt* an attempt to win business from a customer, especially a *sales presentation*

placement *Fin see placing, private placing*

placement fee *Fin* a fee that a stockbroker receives for a sale of shares

placing *Fin* a method of raising share capital in which there is no public issue of shares, the shares being issued, rather, in a small number of large 'blocks', to persons or institutions who have previously agreed to purchase the shares at a predetermined price

plain text e-mail *E-com* a basic format option for e-mails, which is simple and cheap to produce. The advantage is that even older e-mail systems will be able to read plain text, whereas they may be unable to receive more heavily designed *HTML* messages.

If conducting an e-mail marketing campaign, the appearance of the e-mail is important. With plain text layout, it is best to keep the line length between 65 and 70 characters (to avoid lines breaking), and to keep paragraphs short—five or six lines at most. Because plain text does not allow the use of bold type or font sizing, capitalising is the only way to add emphasis.

plain vanilla *Fin* a financial instrument in its simplest form (*slang*)

plan comptable *Fin* in France, a uniformly structured and detailed bookkeeping system that companies are required to comply with

plank
make somebody walk the plank *HR* to dismiss somebody from employment (*slang*)

planned maintenance *Ops see preventive maintenance*

planned obsolescence *Ops* a policy of designing products to have a limited lifespan so that customers will have to buy replacements

planning *Fin* the establishment of objectives, and the formulation, evaluation, and selection of the policies, strategies, tactics, and action required to achieve them. Planning comprises long-term/strategic planning and short-term operation planning. The latter is usually for a period of up to one year.

planning horizon *Fin* the furthest time ahead for which plans can be quantified. It need not be the planning period. *See also planning, futuristic planning*

planning period *Fin* the period for which a plan is prepared and used. It differs according to product or process life cycle. For example, forestry requires a period of many years whereas fashion garments require only a few months.

plant *Ops* the capital assets used to produce goods, typically factories, production lines, and large equipment

plant layout *Ops* the grouping of equipment and operations in a factory for the greatest degree of efficiency. *See also process layout, product layout*

plastic *or* **plastic money** *Fin* a payment system using a plastic card (*slang*). *See also credit card, debit card, multifunctional card*

plateauing *HR* the process of reaching a phase where performance is stable. Plateauing may be experienced by an employee due to a lack of ambition or ability or a lack of opportunity for *promotion* within the organisational hierarchy. One form of plateau is the *management threshold*.

platform *Gen Mgt* a product used as a basis for building more complex products or delivering services. For example, a communications network is a platform for delivering knowledge or data.

plc *or* **PLC** *abbr Fin see public limited company*

plentitude *Econ* a hypothetical condition of an economy in which manufacturing technology has been perfected and scarcity is replaced by an abundance of products

plough back *Fin* to reinvest a company's earnings in the business instead of paying them out as dividends

ploughed back profits *Fin* retained profits

plug and play *HR* relating to a new member of staff who does not require training (*slang*)

plug-in *E-com* a software application that can be added to a web browser to enable added functionality, for example, the receipt of audio or multimedia files

---

The market has no morality. *Michael Heseltine*

plum *Fin* a successful investment (*slang*)

PME *abbr Gen Mgt* petites et moyennes entreprises

PMTS *abbr Gen Mgt* predetermined motion-time system

poaching *HR* the practice of recruiting people from other companies by offering inducements

point (*US*) *Fin* a unit used for calculation of a value, such as a hundredth of a percentage point for interest rates

point and click agreement *E-com see* **click wrap agreement**

point-factor system *HR see* **points plan**

point of presence *Gen Mgt* an access point to the **Internet**. A point of presence is usually controlled by an Internet service provider. Subscribers can use this to gain access to the Internet, normally by dialling a local number, and thereby saving the cost of a national phone call. A point of presence has a unique **IP address**.

point of purchase *Gen Mgt see* **point of sale**

point-of-purchase display *Gen Mgt* the physical arrangement of products and marketing material at the place where an item is bought. A point-of-purchase display is designed to encourage sales. It can include posters, showcards, leaflets, and dispensers to attract customers.

point of sale *Gen Mgt* the place at which a product is purchased by the customer. The point of sale can be a retail outlet, a display case, or even a particular shelf. Retailers refer to both point of sale and to **point of purchase**. The distinction is a fine one, but a sale and a purchase do not always take place at the same time. The difference becomes relevant where they are clearly separate, for example, with **mail order** and **Internet** shopping. *Abbr* **POS**

points plan *HR* a method of **job evaluation** that uses a points scale for rating different criteria. *Also known as* **point-factor system**

poison pill *Fin* a measure taken by a company to avoid a hostile takeover, for example, the purchase of a business interest that will make the company unattractive to the potential buyer (*slang*)

policy *Fin* an undated, long-lasting, and often unquantified statement of guidance regarding the way in which an organisation will seek to behave in relation to its stakeholders

policyholder *Fin* a person or business covered by an insurance policy

political economy *Econ* a country's economic organisation

political price *Gen Mgt* the negative impact on a government of a business or economic decision such as raising interest rates

political risk *Gen Mgt* the potential negative impact on a government of a business or economic decision

politics *Gen Mgt* the theory of government, the making of policy, or the power struggles within an organisation

POP *abbr E-com* Post Office protocol: the most common Internet standard for e-mail. Once POP is in use, all new incoming messages are downloaded from the server as soon as the e-mail account is accessed. All POP e-mails are stored on the server until the user removes them.

population *Stats* the entire collection of units such as events or people from which a sample may be observed in a statistical study

population pyramid *Stats* a graphical presentation of data in the form of two histograms with a common base, showing a comparison of a human population in terms of sex and age

pop-under ad *E-com* a Web advertisement that launches in a separate browser window from the rest of a website

portable document format *Gen Mgt, Mkting see* **PDF**

portable pension *Fin* in the United Kingdom, a pension plan that moves with an employee when he or she changes employer. *See also* **personal pension**, **stakeholder pension**

portal *E-com* a website that provides access and links to other sites and pages on the Web. **Search engines** and directories are the most common portal sites.

Porter, Michael (*b.* 1947) *Gen Mgt* US academic and consultant. Known for his theories such as the **value chain** designed to help businesses examine their competitive capabilities. In *Competitive Strategy* (1980), Porter argued that to gain **competitive advantage**, an organisation needs to perform the activities in the value chain more cheaply or in a better way than its competitors. More recently, in response to thinkers such as **Gary Hamel**, he advised on using the value chain to achieve differentiation from other players in a market. Porter studied at Harvard, and at the age of 26 he became one of the youngest tenured professors in the school's history. He has served

---

The man who is activated by love of power is more apt to inflict pain than to permit pleasure.
Bertrand Russell

as a counsellor on competitive strategy to many leading US and international companies and plays an active role in economic policy with the US Congress, business groups, and as an advisor to foreign governments.

portfolio *Fin* the range of investments, such as stocks and shares, owned by an individual or an organisation

portfolio career *HR* a career based on a series of varied shorter-term jobs—either concurrently or consecutively—as opposed to one based on a progression up the ranks of a particular profession. The portfolio worker is frequently self-employed, offering his or her services on a *freelance* or consultancy basis to one or more employers at the same time. However, a portfolio approach can also be taken to full-time employment with a single employer, if the employee chooses to expand his or her experience and responsibilities through taking different roles within the organisation.

To critics, the portfolio approach to career development may appear unfocused and directionless. However, it is an excellent opportunity to experience the many different avenues available in modern life. It is important, in general, for the portfolio worker to maintain some overall sense of purpose or strategic direction in the work they undertake, and to view their portfolio career as a unified whole rather than a collection of 'odd jobs'.
See portfolio working

portfolio immunisation *Fin* measures taken by traders to protect their share portfolios (*slang*)

portfolio insurance *Fin* options that provide hedges against stock in a portfolio

portfolio investment *Fin* a form of investment that aims for a mixture of income and capital growth

portfolio manager *Fin* a person or company that specialises in managing an investment portfolio on behalf of investors

portfolio working *HR* the working pattern of following several simultaneous career pursuits at any one time. Portfolio working was coined by *Charles Handy* to describe a style of working life which no longer involves working full-time for one employer. *See also down-shifting. Also known as portfolio career*

POS *abbr Gen Mgt* point of sale

POSDCORB *abbr Gen Mgt* Planning, Organising, Staffing, Directing, Co-ordinating, Reporting, and Budgeting: coined in 1935 by *Luther Gulick* to describe the functional elements of the work of a *chief executive*. It is based on the functional analysis of management of *Henri Fayol*.

position *Fin* the number of shares of a security that are owned

position audit *Fin* part of the planning process which examines the current state of an entity in respect of the following: resources of tangible and intangible assets and finance; products, brands, and markets; operating systems such as production and distribution; internal organisation; current results; and returns to stockholders

position limit *Fin* the largest amount of a security that any group or individual may own

positive discrimination *HR* preferential treatment, usually through a quota system, to prevent or correct discriminatory employment practices, particularly relating to recruitment and promotion. The term positive discrimination is widely used in the United Kingdom, whereas in the United States **affirmative action** is the preferred term.

positive economics *Econ* the study of economic propositions that are capable of being verified by observing economic events in the real economy

possessor in bad faith *Fin* somebody who occupies land even though they do not believe they have a legal right to do so

possessor in good faith *Fin* somebody who occupies land believing they have a legal right to do so

possessory action *Fin* a lawsuit over the right to own land

post a credit *Fin* to enter a credit item in a ledger

postal survey *Mkting* a research technique in which questionnaires are sent and returned by post

Post Big Bang *Fin* used to describe the trading mechanism on the London Stock Exchange after 26 October 1986. *See also Big Bang*

postdate *Fin* to put a later date on a document or cheque than the date when it is signed, with the effect that it is not valid until the later date

post-industrial society *Gen Mgt* a society in which the resources of labour and capital are replaced by those of knowledge and information as the main sources of wealth creation. The post-industrial society involves a shift in focus from manufacturing industries to service industries and is enabled by technological advances. The idea is associated with sociologist Daniel Bell, who wrote *The Coming of Post-Industrial Society: A Venture in Social Forecasting* (1973).

post-purchase costs *Fin* costs incurred after a capital expenditure decision has been implemented and facilities acquired. These costs may include training, maintenance, and the cost of upgrades.

potential GDP *Econ* a measure of the real value of the services and goods that can be produced when a country's factors of production are fully employed

potentially exempt transfer *Fin* see *chargeable transfer*

pot trust *Fin* a trust, typically created in a will, for a group of beneficiaries

pound cost averaging *Fin* investing the same amount at regular intervals in a security regardless of its price. *US term* **dollar cost averaging**

poverty trap *Fin* a situation whereby low income families are penalised by a progressive tax system: an increase in income is either counteracted by a loss of social benefit payments or by an increase in taxation

power *Gen Mgt* the ability to compel others to obey. Power refers to an authority or influence over others which, in an organisational context, may be derived from the holder's rank or status, or from their personality. According to **Max Weber**, power refers to the probability of imposing your own will despite resistance. It is closely linked to, but not the same as, **leadership**, **authority**, and **responsibility**. Organisational power is linked to **organisation structure** and is an inherent part of any hierarchy or **bureaucracy**.

power and influence theory of leadership *Gen Mgt* the idea that **leadership** is based on the form of relationships between people rather than on the abilities of a single person. The power and influence theory of leadership sees a network of interaction between people, shaped by the power and influence emanating from the leader. Leadership and followership are products of the flow of power between individuals.

power centre *Gen Mgt* the part of an organisation that has the strongest influence on policy

power lunch *Gen Mgt* see *working lunch*

power of attorney *Fin* a legal document granting one person the right to act on behalf of another

power structure *Gen Mgt* the way in which power is distributed among different groups or individuals in an organisation

pp *Fin* used beside a signature at the end of a letter meaning 'on behalf of'

PPP *abbr Econ* purchasing power parity

PR *abbr Mkting* public relations: the presentation of an organisation and its activities to target audiences with the aim of gaining awareness and understanding, influencing public opinion, generating support, and developing trust and co-operation. Public relations programmes aim to create and maintain a positive **corporate image** and enhance an organisation's reputation. The work of a public relations department includes research into current perceptions of the organisation, the production of publicity material, the organisation of events and **sponsorship** programmes, and the evaluation of responses to these activities. Target audiences include the media, government bodies, customers and suppliers, investors, the wider community, or an organisation's own employees. Public relations practice originated in the United States in the mid-19th century. Public relations forms part of an organisation's overall **external communication** strategy.

Prahalad, C.K. (*b.* 1941) *Gen Mgt* Indian-born academic. Developer with **Gary Hamel** of a new view of competitiveness, **strategy**, and **organisations** in reaction to traditional strategic thinking. Prahalad and Hamel originated the ideas of strategic intent, **core competences**, and strategy as stretch, and published them in *Competing for the Future* (1994).

prairie dogging (*US*) *Gen Mgt* in an office that is divided into cubicles, the sudden appearance of people's heads over the top of the cubicle walls when something interesting or noisy happens (*slang*)

pre-acquisition profits/losses *Fin* the profits or losses of a subsidiary undertaking, attributable to a period prior to its acquisition by a parent company. Such profits are not available for distribution as dividends by the parent company unless the underlying value of the subsidiary undertaking is at least equal to its net carrying value in the books of the parent company.

The modern history of economic theory is a tale of evasions of reality. *Thomas Balogh*

preauthorised electronic debit *Fin* a scheme in which a payer agrees to let a bank make payments from an account to somebody else's account

prebilling *Fin* the practice of submitting a bill for a product or service before it has actually been delivered

precious metals *Fin* gold, silver, platinum, and palladium

predatory pricing *Fin* the practice of setting prices for products that are designed to win business from competitors or to damage competitors. This may involve dumping, which is selling a product in a foreign market at below cost or below the domestic market price (subject to adjustments for taxation differences, transportation costs, specification differences etc.).

predetermined motion-time system *Gen Mgt* a *work measurement* technique that uses a set of established times for basic human motions to build up *standard times* for jobs and processes at a specific level of performance. The predetermined motion-time system is based on the idea, first conceived by *Frederick Winslow Taylor* and later developed by *Frank* and *Lillian Gilbreth*, that the same length of time is required for basic human motions in whatever context they are performed. These standard times are established using *time study* techniques and can then be combined to provide a standard time for specific work tasks. The first PMTS, called **motion time analysis**, was developed in 1927, and others appeared in the United States during the 1930s. Interest in the use of PMTS increased during and after the second world war. The most widely used system is *methods-time measurement*. *Abbr* **PMTS**

predictive maintenance *Ops* a set of techniques used to manage the *maintenance* of high-cost equipment that experiences extremely low failure rates. Statistical techniques for predicting service before failure are not effective for equipment with extremely low failure rates. Predictive maintenance uses the techniques of surveillance, diagnosis, and remedy to manage the maintenance of such equipment. It is based on the premise that most equipment will give indications of impending failure well in advance of it actually happening.

pre-employment screening *HR see* **health screening**

pre-emptive right *Fin* the right of a stockholder to maintain proportional ownership in a corporation by purchasing newly issued stock

preference shares *Fin* shares that entitle the owner to preference in the distribution of dividends and the proceeds of liquidation in the event of bankruptcy. *US term* **preferred stock**

preferential creditor *Fin* a creditor who is entitled to payment, especially from a bankrupt, before other creditors

preferential form *Fin see* **pink form**

preferential issue *Fin* an issue of stock available only to designated buyers

preferential payment *Fin* a payment to a preferential creditor

preferred position *Fin* the particular position in which an advertiser wants an advertisement to appear, for example, in a publication or on a website

preferred risk *Fin* somebody considered by an insurance company to be less likely to collect on a policy than the average person, for example, a non-smoker

preferred stock (*US*) *Fin* = **preference shares**

pre-financing *Fin* the practice of arranging funding for a project before the project begins

prelaunch *Mkting* the activities that precede the launch of a new product

preliminary prospectus *Fin* a document issued prior to a share issue that gives details of the shares available

premarket *Fin* used to describe transactions between market members carried out prior to the official opening of the market. *Also known as* **pretrading**

premature retirement *HR see* **early retirement**

Premiers' Conference *Gen Mgt* an annual meeting at which the premiers of the states and territories of Australia meet with the federal government to discuss their funding allocations

premium 1. *Fin* the price a purchaser of an option pays to its writer **2.** *Fin* the difference between the futures price and the cash price of an underlying asset **3.** *Fin* the consideration for a contract of insurance or assurance **4.** *Gen Mgt* a higher price paid for a scarce product or service **5.** *Gen Mgt* a pricing method that uses high price to indicate high quality

---

By creating conversation, we let our customers spread our message by word of mouth.   *Anita Roddick*

at a premium *Fin* **1.** of a fixed interest security, at an issue price above its par value **2.** of a new issue, at a trading price above the one offered to investors **3.** at a price that is considered expensive in relation to others

Premium Bond *Fin* in the United Kingdom, a non-marketable security issued by National Savings at £1 each that pays no interest but is entered into a draw every month to win prizes from £50 to £1 million. There are many lower value prizes, but only one £1 million prize. The bonds are repayable upon demand.

premium income *Fin* the income earned by a life company or insurance company from premiums

premium offer *Mkting* a sales promotion technique in which customers are offered a free gift

premium pay plan *HR* an enhanced pay scale for high performing employees. A premium pay plan can be offered as an incentive to motivate employees, rewarding such achievements as high productivity, long service, or completion of training with increased pay.

premium pricing *Mkting* the deliberate setting of high prices for a product or service to emphasise its quality or exclusiveness. *Also known as* **prestige pricing**

prepackaged choice *Gen Mgt* a package of multimedia computer material that cannot be customised by the user

prepaid interest *Fin* interest paid in advance of its due date

prepayment *Fin* the payment of a debt, for example, a payment on a mortgage or other loan, before it is due to be paid

prepayment penalty (*US*) *Fin* a charge that may be levied against somebody who makes a payment before its due date. The penalty compensates the lender or seller for potential lost interest.

prepayment privilege *Fin* the right to make a prepayment, for example, on a loan or mortgage, without penalty

prepayment risk *Fin* the risk that a debtor will avoid interest charges by making partial or total prepayments, especially when interest rates fall

prequalification *Mkting* a sales technique in which the potential value of a prospect is carefully evaluated through research

prescribed payments system (*ANZ*) *Fin* a system under which employers are obliged to deduct a certain amount of tax from cash payments made to casual workers. The system was introduced in Australia in 1983.

presentation *Gen Mgt* an event at which preplanned material is shown to an audience for a specific purpose. Although a presentation is a verbal form of communication, it is often supported by other media, such as computer software, slides, printed handouts, and so on and to be successful, appropriate *body language* and good *interpersonal communication* skills are required. A presentation is normally intended to either introduce something new to the audience, to persuade them of a viewpoint, or to inform them. *Sales representatives* use presentations when introducing a product to a potential customer. Presentations are also used in *team briefing* and other business contexts.

presenteeism *HR* an employee or organisation subscribing to the view that the hours spent at work have more value than *productivity* or results. Presenteeism is often displayed by *workaholics*. At its most extreme, presenteeism can be seen in a worker who reports for work even when sick, for fear of letting the company down or of losing their job. (*slang*) *See also* **absenteeism**

present value *Fin* **1.** amount that a future interest in a financial asset is currently worth, discounted for inflation **2.** the value now of an amount of money somebody expects to receive at a future date, calculated by subtracting any interest that will accrue in the interim

preservation of capital *Fin* an approach to financial management that protects a person's or company's capital by arranging additional forms of finance

president *Gen Mgt see* **chair**

press advertising *Mkting* advertising in newspapers or magazines

press clipping (*US*) *Gen Mgt* = **press cutting**

press communications *Mkting* communications activities designed to improve press awareness and attitudes to a product or an organisation

press conference *Mkting* a meeting to which journalists are invited to hear about a new product or other news about an organisation

press cutting *Gen Mgt* a copy of a news item kept by a company because it contains important business information or is a record of news published about the company. *US* term **press clipping**

press date *Mkting* the date on which a newspaper or magazine is printed

press release *Mkting* an item of news about an organisation, its staff, products, or services that is sent to selected members of the press

press the flesh *Gen Mgt* to shake hands with people at a business function (*slang*)

pressure group *Gen Mgt* a body of people who have banded together to campaign on one or more issues of importance to them. A pressure group usually has a formal constitution and co-ordinates its activities to influence the attitudes or activities of business or government. One area in which pressure groups operate is the environment and some large companies that have failed to practise good *environmental management* have been targeted by campaigners. Pressure groups often represent widespread views, so it is important for a company to maintain good relations with them.

prestige pricing *Mkting see* **premium pricing**

pre-syndicate bid *Fin* a bid made before a group of buyers can offer blocks of shares in an offering to the public

pretax *Fin* before tax is considered or paid

pretax profit *Fin* the amount of profit a company makes before taxes are deducted

pretax profit margin *Fin* the profit made by a company, calculated as a percentage of sales, before taxes are considered

pretesting *Mkting* the practice of assessing the effectiveness of an advertising campaign or marketing activity in a small sector or single region before running the full campaign

pretrading *Fin see* **premarket**

prevalence *Stats* a measure of the number of people with a particular quality in a statistical population

preventive maintenance *or* **preventative maintenance** *Ops* the scheduling of a programme of planned *maintenance* services or equipment overhauls. The aim of preventive maintenance is to reduce equipment failure and the need for corrective maintenance. It can be carried out at regular time intervals, after a specified amount of equipment use, when the opportunity arises, for example, at a factory's annual shutdown, or when certain pre-set conditions occur to trigger the need for action. *Also known as* **planned maintenance**. *See also* **reactive maintenance**

price *Fin* an amount of money that somebody charges for a good or service

price-book ratio *Fin see* **price-to-book ratio**

price ceiling *Fin* the highest price that a buyer is willing to pay

price competition *Gen Mgt* a form of competition based on price rather than factors such as quality or design

price control *Econ* government regulations that set maximum prices for commodities or control price levels by credit controls

price differentiation *Gen Mgt* a pricing strategy in which a company sells the same product at different prices in different markets

price discovery *Fin* the process by which price is determined by negotiation in a free market

price discrimination *Econ* the practice of selling of the same product to different buyers at different prices

price-dividend ratio *Fin* the price of a stock divided by the annual dividend paid on a share

price-earnings ratio *Fin* a company's share price divided by earnings per share (EPS). EXAMPLE While EPS is an actual amount of money, usually expressed in pence per share, the P/E ratio has no units, it is just a number. Thus if a quoted company has a share price of £100 and EPS of £12 for the last published year, then it has a historical P/E of 8.3. If analysts are forecasting for the next year EPS of, say, £14 then the forecast P/E is 7.1.

The P/E ratio is predominantly useful in comparisons with other shares rather than in isolation. For example, if the average P/E in the market is 20, there will be many shares with P/Es well above and well below this, for a variety of reasons. Similarly, in a particular sector, the P/Es will frequently vary from the sector average, even though the constituent companies may all be engaged in similar businesses. The reason is that even two businesses doing the same thing will not always be doing it as profitably as each other. One may be far more efficient, as demonstrated by a history of rising EPS compared with the flat EPS picture of the other over a series of years, and the market might recognise this by awarding the more profitable share a higher P/E.

price effect *Econ* the impact of price changes on a market or economy

---

Retail has been described as selling things which don't come back to customers who do.   **Tom Farmer**

price elasticity of demand *Econ* the percentage change in demand divided by the percentage change in price of a good

price elasticity of supply *Econ* the percentage change in supply divided by the percentage change in price of a good

price escalation clause *Gen Mgt* a contract provision that permits the seller to raise prices in response to increased costs

price fixing *Fin* an often illegal agreement between producers of a good or service in order to maintain prices at a particular level

price floor *Fin* the lowest price at which a seller is prepared to do business

price index *Fin* an index, such as the consumer price index, that measures inflation

price indicator *Econ* a price that is a measurable variable and can be used, for example, as an index of the cost of living

price instability *Econ* a situation in which the prices of goods alter daily or even hourly

price leadership *Mkting* the establishment of price levels in a market by a dominant company or brand

price list *Gen Mgt* a document that sets out the prices of different products or services

price range *Gen Mgt* the variety of prices at which competitive products or services are available in the market

price ring *Fin* a group of traders who make an agreement, often illegally, to maintain prices at a particular level

prices and incomes policy *Econ* a policy of using government regulations to limit price or wage increases

price-sensitive *Fin* describes a good or service for which sales fluctuate depending on its price, often because it is a nonessential item

price-sensitive information *Fin* as yet unpublished information that will affect a company's share price. For example, the implementation of a new manufacturing process that substantially cuts production costs would have a positive impact, whereas the discovery of harmful side effects from a recently launched drug would have a negative impact.

price stability *Fin* a situation in which there is little change in the price of goods or services

price support *Econ* the use of government regulations to keep market prices from falling below a minimum level

price tag *Gen Mgt* **1.** a label attached to an item being sold that shows its price **2.** the value of a person or thing

price-to-book ratio *Fin* the ratio of the value of all of a company's stock to its *book value*. *Also known as* **price-book ratio**

price-to-cash-flow ratio *Fin* the ratio of the value of all of a company's stock to its cash flow for the most recent complete fiscal year

price-to-sales ratio *Fin* the ratio of the value of all of a company's stock to its sales for the previous twelve months, a way of measuring the relative value of a share when compared with others.

EXAMPLE The P/S ratio is obtained by dividing the market capitalisation by the latest published annual sales figure. So a company with a capitalisation of £1 billion and sales of £3 billion would have a P/S ratio of 0.33.

P/S will vary with the type of industry. You would expect, for example, that many retailers and other large-scale distributors of goods would have very high sales in relation to their market capitalisations—in other words, a very low P/S. Equally, manufacturers of high-value items would generally have much lower sales figures and thus higher P/S ratios.

A company with a lower P/S is cheaper than one with a higher ratio, particularly if they are in the same sector so that a direct comparison is more appropriate. It means that each share of the lower P/S company is buying more of its sales than those of the higher P/S company.

It is important to note that a share which is cheaper only on P/S grounds is not necessarily the more attractive share. There will frequently be reasons why it has a lower ratio than another similar company, most commonly because it is less profitable.

price war *Mkting* a situation in which two or more companies each try to increase their own share of the market by lowering prices. A price war involves companies undercutting each other in an attempt to encourage more customers to buy their goods or services. In the long term, this can devalue a market and lead to loss of profits, but it can sometimes have short-term success.

price-weighted index *Fin* an index of production or market value that is adjusted for price changes

pricing *Fin* the determination of a selling price for a product or service

pricing policy *Mkting* the method of *decision-making* used for setting the prices for a company's products or services. A pricing policy is usually based on the costs of production or provision with a margin for profit, such as, for example, *cost-plus pricing*.

primary account number *Fin* an identifier for a credit card used in secure electronic transactions

primary data *or* **primary information** *Mkting* original data derived from a new research study and collected at source, as opposed to previously published material

primary earnings per (common) share (*US*) *Fin see* **earnings per share**

primary liability *Fin* responsibility to pay before anyone else, for example, for damages covered by insurance

primary market *Fin* the part of the market on which securities are first offered to investors by the issuer. The money from this sale goes to the issuer, rather than to traders or investors as it does in the secondary market. *See also* **secondary market**

primary sector *Econ* the firms and corporations of the productive sector of a country's economy

prime *Fin see* **prime rate**

prime assets ratio *Fin* the proportion of total liabilities which Australian banks are obliged by the Reserve Bank to hold in secure assets such as cash and government securities. *Abbr* **PAR**

prime cost *Fin* the total cost of direct material, direct labour, and direct expenses

prime rate *or* **prime interest rate** *Fin* the lowest interest rate that commercial banks offer on loans

principal *Fin see* **mortgage**

principal budget factor *Fin* a factor which will limit the activities of an undertaking and which is often the starting-point in budget preparation

principal shareholders *Fin* the shareholders who own the largest percentage of shares in an organisation

print farming *Mkting* the management of an organisation's print requirements, including choosing printers and overseeing production

prior charge capital *Fin* capital which has a right to the receipt of interest or of preference dividends in precedence to any claim on distributable earnings on the part of the ordinary shareholders. On winding up, the claims of holders of prior charge capital also rank before those of ordinary shareholders.

prior charge percentage *Fin see* **priority percentage**

priority-based budgeting *Fin* a method of budgeting in which budget requests are accompanied by a statement outlining the changes which would occur if the prior period budget were to be increased or decreased by a certain amount or percentage. These changes are prioritised.

priority percentage *Fin* the proportion of a business's net profit paid in interest to preference shareholders and holders of debt capital. *Also known as* **prior charge percentage**

prior lien bond *Fin* a bond whose holder has more claim on a debtor's assets than holders of other types of bonds

privacy policy *E-com* the means by which an organisation reassures customers that personal information they supply—usually over the Internet—will be securely protected, and used only for the stated purpose.

Most customers are willing to give personal information if they know that it will benefit them. However, privacy is a major concern on the Internet, and needs to be addressed comprehensively. The use of customer information is legislated separately by individual countries, and collecting it and—in particular—moving it between countries can be very complicated, because different countries have different laws.

However, a basic principle is for an organisation to tell the individual clearly why it is collecting the information, and what that information will be used for. If the organisation wishes to use the information for other purposes, such as sending out e-mails on special offers, or sharing with partners, the individual should be specifically informed of that intention, and given the opportunity to opt out.

It is good policy for organisations to allow individuals to check the information held on them, and to delete information if they wish to do so. A proper security procedure is essential. Internet security breaches are increasing, and hackers are particularly interested in breaking into systems that contain personal information.

private bank *Fin* **1.** a bank that is owned by a single person or a limited number of private shareholders **2.** a bank that provides banking facilities to high net worth individuals. *See also* **private banking 3.** a bank that is not state-

---

Show me a man who enjoys firing people and I'll show you a charlatan or a sadist.   *Tony O'Reilly*

owned in a country where most banks are owned by the government

private banking *Fin* a service offered by certain financial institutions to high net worth individuals. In addition to standard banking services, it will typically include portfolio management and advisory services on taxation, including estate planning.

private company *Fin* a company which has not been registered as a public company under the Companies Act. The major practical distinction between a private and public company is that the former may not offer its securities to the public.

private cost (*US*) *Econ* the cost incurred by individuals when they use scarce resources such as petrol

private debt *Fin* money owed by individuals and organisations other than governments

private enterprise *Econ* the parts of an economy that are controlled by companies or individuals rather than the government

Private Finance Initiative *Fin* a policy which is designed to harness private sector management and expertise in the delivery of public services. Under PFI, the public sector does not buy assets, it buys the asset-based services it requires, on contract, from the private sector, the latter having the responsibility for deciding how to supply these services, the investment required to support the services, and how to achieve the required standards. *Abbr* **PFI**

private label (*US*) *Mkting* = **own brand**

private placement (*US*) *Fin* = **private placing**

private placing *Fin* the sale of securities directly to institutions for investment rather than resale. *US term* **private placement**

private sector *Econ* the organisations in the section of the economy that is financed and controlled by individuals or private institutions, such as companies, shareholders, or investment groups. *See also* **public sector**

private sector investment *Econ* investment by the private enterprise sector of the economy

private treaty *Fin* the sale of land without an auction

privatisation *Fin* the transfer of a company from ownership by either a government or a

few individuals to the public via the issuance of stock

probability *Stats* the quantitative measure of the likelihood that a given event will occur

probability distribution *Stats* a mathematical formula showing the probability for each value of a variable in a statistical study

probability plot *Stats* a graphic plot of data that compares two probability distributions

probability sample *Stats* a sample in which every individual in a finite statistical *population* has a known chance, but not necessarily an equal chance, of being included

probability sampling *Stats* sampling in which every individual in a finite *population* has a known but not necessarily equal chance of being included in the sample

probation *HR* a trial period in the first months of employment when an employer checks the suitability and capability of a person in a certain role, and takes any necessary corrective action. An employee's performance during a probation period may be evaluated informally, for example, by means of conversations with a supervisor. If a probationary period is included in a **contract of employment**, formal documented assessment is required.

problem child 1. (*US*) *Fin* a **subsidiary company** that is not performing well or is damaging the **parent company** in some way 2. *Mkting* a product with a low market share but high growth potential. Problem children often have good long-term prospects, but high levels of investment may be needed to realise the potential, thereby draining funds that may be needed elsewhere. *See also* **Boston Consulting Group matrix**

problem-solving *Gen Mgt* a systematic approach to overcoming obstacles or problems in the management process. Problems occur when something is not behaving as it should, when something deviates from the norm, or when something goes wrong. A number of problem-solving methodologies exist, but the most widely used is that proposed by **Charles Kepner** and **Benjamin Tregoe**. Steps in their problem-solving process include: recognising a problem exists and defining it; generating a range of solutions; evaluating the possible solutions and choosing the best one; implementing the solution and evaluating its effectiveness in solving the problem. Various techniques can aid problem-solving, such as **brainstorming**, **fishbone charts**, and **Pareto charts**.

I try to avoid experience if I can. Most experience is bad.   *E.L. Doctorow*

procedure *Gen Mgt* a set of step-by-step instructions designed to ensure that a task is efficiently and consistently carried out. Procedures regulate the conduct of an organisation's activities and ensure that *decision-making* is undertaken fairly and with due consideration, as, for example, in the case of disciplinary and complaints procedures. In the context of formal quality management systems, procedures are used to control and monitor work processes and to ensure that standards are met.

procedure manual *Gen Mgt* a document containing written rules and regulations that govern the conduct of *procedures* within an organisation. Procedure manuals are often used in the induction and training of new recruits.

proceeds *Fin* the income from a transaction

process *Gen Mgt* a structured and managed set of work activities designed to produce a particular output

process box *Gen Mgt see* **flow chart**

process chart *Gen Mgt* a diagrammatic representation of the sequence of work and the nature of events in a *process*. A process chart provides the basis for visualising the different stages for evaluation and possible improvement.

process control *Ops* the inspection of work-in-progress to provide feedback on, and correct, a production process. First developed as a mechanical feedback mechanism, process control is now widely used to monitor and maintain the quality of output. *See also* **statistical process control**

process layout *Ops* a type of office or *plant layout* that groups together workstations or equipment that undertake similar processes. Within a process layout organisation, the partly finished product moves from process to process and each batch may follow a different route. *Also known as* **process-oriented layout**, **layout by function**. *See also* **product layout**

process management *Ops* the operation, *control*, evaluation, and improvement of interconnected tasks, with the aim of maximising effectiveness and efficiency

processor *E-com see* **acquirer**

process-oriented layout *Ops see* **process layout**

process production *Ops* the continuous production of a product in bulk, often by a chemical rather than mechanical *process*

process time *Gen Mgt* the period which elapses between the start and finish of one process or stage of a process

procurement *Gen Mgt see* **purchasing**

procurement exchange *E-com* a group of companies that act together to buy products or services they need at lower prices

procurement manager *Gen Mgt see* **purchasing manager**

procurement portal *E-com see* **online catalogue**

producer price index *Econ* a statistical measure, the weighted average of the prices of commodities that firms buy from other firms

producibility engineering *Ops see* **design for manufacturability**

product *Mkting* anything that is offered to a market that customers can acquire, use, interact with, experience, or consume, to satisfy a want or need. Early *marketing* tended to focus on tangible physical goods and these were distinguished from *services*. More recently, however, the distinction between products and services has blurred, and the concept of the product has been expanded so that in its widest sense it can now be said to cover any tangible or intangible thing that satisfies the consumer. Products that are marketed can include services, people, places, and ideas.

product abandonment *Mkting* the ending of the manufacture and sale of a product. Products are abandoned for many reasons. The market may be saturated or declining, the product may be superseded by another, costs of production may become too high, or a product may simply become unprofitable. Product abandonment usually occurs during the decline phase of the *product life cycle*.

product assortment *Mkting see* **product mix**

product bundling *Fin* a form of discounting in which a group of related products is sold at a price which is lower than that obtainable by the consumer were the products to be purchased separately

product churning *Gen Mgt* the flooding of a market with new products in the hope that one of them will become successful. Product churning is especially prevalent in Japan, where pre-launch *test marketing* is often replaced by multiple product launches. Most of these products will decline and disappear, but one or more of the new products churned out may become profitable.

The higher our income, the more resources we control and the more havoc we wreak. Paul Carter Harrison

product development *Mkting* the revitalisation of a product through the introduction of a new concept or consumer benefit. Product development is part of the **product life cycle**. The concepts or benefits that can be implemented range from modification of the product to simply introducing new packaging.

product development cycle *Mkting* see *new product development*

product differentiation *Mkting* a marketing technique that promotes and emphasises a product's difference from other products of a similar nature. Product differentiation is one of the aspects of **Michael Porter's generic strategy** theory and it has been described by **Anita Roddick** as being the key to the success of the Body Shop. *Also known as* **differentiation**

product family *Mkting* a group of products or services that meet a similar need in the market

production *Ops* the processes and techniques used in making a product. *Also known as* **manufacturing**

production control *Ops* the control of all aspects of **production**, according to a predetermined production plan. **Production planning** and production control are closely linked, and sometimes the terms are used interchangeably. Nevertheless, they differ in focus: production planning focuses on the scheduling of the production process; production control focuses on the application of the plan which results from the production planning. Computerised techniques, such as material requirements planning and **optimised production technology** combine elements of planning and control.

production cost *Fin* prime cost plus absorbed production overhead

production levelling *Ops* see **production smoothing**

production management *Ops* the management of those resources and activities of a business that are required to produce goods for sale to consumers or to other organisations. Production management is concerned with the manufacturing industry. The growing interest in the production management task in service industries has led to the use of **operations management** as a more general term. *Also known as* **manufacturing management**

production planning *or* **production scheduling** *Ops* the process of producing a specification or chart of the manufacturing operations to be carried out by different functions and workstations over a particular time period. Production scheduling takes account of factors such as the availability of plant and materials, customer delivery requirements, and maintenance schedules.

production smoothing *Ops* the smoothing, or levelling, of **production scheduling** so that mix and volume are even over time. Production smoothing is an important condition for production by **kanban**, and is key to the **Toyota production system**. The aim is to minimise idle time. *Also known as* **production levelling**

production versus purchasing *Ops* see **purchasing versus production**

productive capacity *Ops* the maximum amount of output that an organisation or company can generate at any one time

productivity *Gen Mgt, Ops* a measurement of the efficiency of production, taking the form of a ratio of the output of goods and services to the input of factors of production. **Labour productivity** takes account of inputs of employee hours worked; **capital productivity** takes account of inputs of machines or land; and **marginal productivity** measures the additional output gained from an additional unit of input. Techniques to improve productivity include greater use of new technology, altered working practices, and improved training of the workforce.

productivity agreement *HR* see **productivity bargaining**

productivity bargaining *HR* a form of **collective bargaining** leading to a **productivity agreement** in which management offers a pay rise in exchange for alterations to employee working practices designed to increase **productivity**

product launch *Mkting* the introduction of a new product to a market. A product launch progresses through a number of important stages: internal communication, which encourages high levels of awareness and commitment to the new product; pre-launch activity, which secures distribution and makes sure that retailers have the resources and knowledge to market the product; launch events at national, regional, or local level; post-event activity, which helps salesforce and retailers make the most of the event; and launch advertising and other forms of customer communication.

product layout *Ops* the organisation of a

People ask you for criticism but they only want praise.   W. Somerset Maugham

factory or office so that the position of the **workstations** is optimised to suit the product. Product layout ensures that products follow an **assembly line** where the different operations are undertaken in a logical sequence. *Also known as* **product-oriented layout**. *See also* **process layout**

product leader *Mkting see* **brand leader**

product liability *Mkting* a manufacturer's, producer's, or service provider's obligation to accept responsibility for defects in their products or services. Faulty products may result in personal injury or damage to property, in which case product liability may result in the payment of compensation to the purchaser.

product life cycle *Mkting* the life span of a product from development, through testing, promotion, growth, and maturity, to decline and perhaps regeneration. A new product is first developed and then introduced to the market. Once the introduction is successful, a growth period follows with wider awareness of the product and increasing sales. The product enters maturity when sales stop growing and demand stabilises. Eventually, sales may decline until the product is finally withdrawn from the market or redeveloped.

product line *Mkting* a family of related products. Products within a line may be the same type of product, they may be sold to the same type of customer, or through similar outlets, or they may all be within a certain price range.

product management *Mkting* a system for the co-ordination of all the stages through which a product passes during its life cycle. Product management involves control of a product from its innovation and development to its decline. The process is co-ordinated by a **product manager** who focuses on the marketing of the product but may also be responsible for pricing, packaging, branding, research and development, production, distribution, sales targets, and product performance appraisal. This cross-departmental approach is based on the theory that a dedicated product management system will lead to tighter control over the product, and thus higher sales and profits. A **brand manager** fulfils a similar function to a product manager, concentrating on products within one brand.

product market *Mkting* the **market** in which products are sold, usually to organisations rather than consumers. The product market is concerned with **purchasing** by organisations for their own use, and includes such items as raw materials, machinery, and equipment

which may in turn be used to manufacture items for the consumer market.

product mix *Mkting* the range of product lines that a company produces, or that a retailer stocks. Product mix usually refers to the length (the number of products in the product line), breadth (the number of product lines that a company offers), depth (the different varieties of product in the product line), and consistency (the relationship between products in their final destination) of product lines. Product mix is sometimes called **product assortment**.

product-oriented layout *Ops see* **product layout**

product placement *Mkting* a form of advertising in which an identifiable branded product is seen by the audience during a film or television programme

product portfolio *Mkting* a range of products manufactured or supplied by an organisation

product positioning *Mkting see* **brand positioning**

product range *Mkting* all of the types of product made by one company

product recall *Ops* the removal from sale of products that may constitute a risk to consumers because of contamination, **sabotage**, or faults in the production process. A product recall usually originates from the product manufacturer but retailers may act autonomously, especially if they believe their outlets are at particular risk. *See* **brand positioning**

product-sustaining activities *Fin* activities undertaken in support of production, the costs of which are linked to the number of separate products produced rather than to the volume of output. Engineering change is a product-sustaining activity. *See* **hierarchy of activities**

profession *HR* an occupational group characterised by extensive education and specialised training, the use of skills based on theoretical knowledge, a **code of conduct**, and an association that organises its members. Members of a profession are normally well paid and derive social status and prestige from their occupation. They have substantial autonomy and tend to be highly resistant to control or interference in their affairs by outside groups. As many professionals now work within organisations rather than independently, there may be a conflict of interests between professional and corporate values, and between professional autonomy and bureaucratic direction.

War is capitalism with the gloves off.   *Tom Stoppard*

professional 1. *Gen Mgt* somebody who shows a high level of skill or **competence 2.** *HR* a member of a particular **profession 3.** *HR* somebody paid to do a job, rather than working as a volunteer or pursuing a hobby

professionalism *HR* the skill, **competence**, or standards expected of a member of a **profession**

profile *Fin* a description of a company, including its products and finances

profile method *HR* an analytical form of **job evaluation** used by management consultants. The most well-known version of the profile method is the Hay Guide Chart and Profile Methodology.

profitability index *Fin* the present value of the money an investment will earn divided by the amount of the investment

profitability threshold *Fin* the point at which a business begins to make profits

profitable *Fin* used to refer to a product, service, or organisation which makes money

profit and loss *Fin* the difference between a company's income and its costs

profit and loss account *or* **profit and loss statement** *Fin* the summary record of a company's sales revenues and expenses over a period, providing a calculation of profits or losses during that time. *Abbr* **P & L**

EXAMPLE Companies typically issue P&L reports monthly. It is customary for the reports to include year-to-date figures, as well as corresponding year-earlier figures to allow for comparisons and analysis.

There are two P&L formats, multiple-step and single-step. Both follow a standard set of rules known as *Generally Accepted Accounting Principles* (GAAP). These rules generally adhere to requirements established by governments to track receipts, expenses, and profits for tax purposes. They also allow the financial reports of two different companies to be compared.

The multiple-step format is much more common, because it includes a larger number of details and is thus more useful. It deducts costs from revenues in a series of steps, allowing for closer analysis. Revenues appear first, then expenses, each in as much detail as management desires. Sales may be broken down by product line or location, while expenses such as salaries may be broken down into base salaries and commissions.

Expenses are then subtracted from revenues to show profit (or loss). A basic multiple-step P&L looks like this:

MULTIPLE-STEP PROFIT & LOSS ACCOUNT		(£)
NET SALES	750,000	
Less: cost of goods sold	450,000	
Gross profit		300,000
LESS: OPERATING EXPENSES		
Selling expenses		
Salaries & commissions	54,000	
Advertising	37,500	
Delivery/transportation	12,000	
Depreciation/store equipment	7,500	
Other selling expenses	5,000	
Total selling expenses		116,000
General & administrative expenses		
Administrative/office salaries	74,000	
Utilities	2,500	
Depreciation/structure	2,400	
Misc. other expenses	3,100	
Total general & admin expenses		82,000
Total operating expenses		198,000
OPERATING INCOME		102,000
LESS (ADD): NON-OPERATING ITEMS		
Interest expenses	11,000	
Interest income earned	(2,800)	8,200
Income before taxes		93,800
Income taxes		32,360
Net Income		**61,440**

If you can't change your fate change your attitude.   *Amy Tan*

P&Ls of public companies may also report income on the basis of earnings per share. For example, if the company issuing this statement had 12,000 shares outstanding, earnings per share would be £5.12, that is, £61,440 divided by 12,000 shares.

profit before tax *Fin* the amount that a company or investor has made, without taking taxes into account

profit centre *Gen Mgt* a person, unit, or department within an organisation that is considered separately when calculating profit. Profit centres are used as part of *management control systems*. They operate with a degree of autonomy with regard to marketing and pricing, and have responsibility for their own costs, revenues, and profits.

profit distribution *Fin* the allocation of profits to different recipients such as shareholders and owners, or for different purposes such as research or investment

profit from ordinary activities *Fin* profits earned in the normal course of business, as opposed to profits from extraordinary sources such as windfall payments

profit margin *Gen Mgt* the amount by which income exceeds expenditure. The profit margin of an individual product is the sale price minus the cost of production and associated costs such as *distribution* and *advertising*. On a larger scale, the profit margin is an accounting ratio of company income compared with sales. The profit margin ratio can be used to compare the efficiency and profitability of a company over a number of years, or to compare different companies. The **gross profit margin** or **operating margin** of a company is its operating, or gross, profit divided by total sales. The **net profit margin** or **return on sales** is net income after taxes divided by total sales.

profit motive *Fin* the desire of a business or service provider to make profit

profit per employee *Fin* an indication of the effectiveness of the employment of staff. When there are full- and part-time employees, full-time equivalents should be used. It is calculated as follows:
Profit for the year before interest and tax /
Average number of employees
See also ***sales per employee***

profit-related pay *HR* a *profit sharing* scheme, approved by the Inland Revenue, in which employees received tax-free payments

in addition to their basic salary. Profit-related pay was phased out during 2000.

profit retained for the year *Fin* non-distributed profit retained as a distributable reserve

profit sharing *HR* a scheme giving *employees* a payment that is conditional on the company's profits. Profit sharing takes the form of a ***share incentive scheme***, or a pay ***bonus***. The purpose of relating payment to company performance is to increase *employee commitment* and *motivation*.

profit-sharing debenture *Fin* a debenture, held by an employee, whose payouts depend on the company's financial success

profits tax *Fin* a tax on profits, for example, corporation tax (*slang*)

profit–volume/contribution graph *Fin* a graph showing the effect on contribution and on overall profit of changes in sales volume or value

profit warning *Fin* a statement by a company's executives that the company may realise less profit in a coming quarter than investors expect

pro-forma *Gen Mgt* a document issued before all relevant details are known, usually followed by a final version

pro-forma financial statement *Fin* a projection showing a business's financial statements after the completion of a planned transaction

pro-forma invoice *Fin* an invoice that does not include all the details of a transaction, often sent before goods are supplied and followed by a final detailed invoice

program *E-com* a set of instructions for a computer to act upon

programme trading *Fin* the trading of securities electronically, by sending messages from the investor's computer to a market

programming *Fin see **dynamic programming**, **linear programming**, **non-linear programming***

progressive tax *Fin* a tax with a rate that increases proportionately with taxable income. *See also **proportional tax**, **regressive tax***

project *Gen Mgt* a set of activities designed to achieve a specified goal, within a given period of time. Projects focus on activities outside the routine operations of an organisation. They vary immensely in size, scope, and complexity and often involve drawing together resources from different parts of an organisation for the duration of the project. The process of planning and completing projects is known as *project management*.

project costing *Fin see costing, contract costing*

project finance *Fin* money, usually non-recourse finance, raised for a specific self-contained venture, usually a construction or development project

projection *Fin* an expected future trend pattern obtained by extrapolation. It is principally concerned with quantitative factors, whereas a forecast includes judgments.

project management *Gen Mgt* the co-ordination of resources to ensure the achievement of a *project*. Project management includes the planning and allocation of financial, material, and human resources and the organisation of the work needed to complete a project. Formal, structured approaches to project management began to emerge in the late 1950s in the construction and military industries, where methods such as **PRINCE**—PRojects IN Controlled Environments—developed to facilitate the process. ·

promissory note *Fin* a contract to pay money to a person or organisation for a good or service received

promotion 1. *HR* the award to an employee of a job at a higher grade, usually offering greater responsibility and more money **2.** *Mkting see* **sales promotion**

proof-of-purchase *Mkting* a sales receipt or other document that can be used to show that someone has bought a product

property *Fin* assets, such as land or goods, that somebody owns

property bond *Fin* a bond, especially a bail bond, for which a property is collateral

property damage insurance *Fin* insurance against the risk of damage to property

proportional tax *Fin* a tax whose amount is strictly proportional to the value of the item being taxed, especially income. *See also* **progressive tax**, **regressive tax**

proprietary ordering system *E-com* a family of computer programs, usually interactive and online, that is developed and owned by a supplier and made available to its customers to facilitate ordering

ProShare *Fin* a group that acts in the interests of private investors in securities of the London Stock Exchange

prospect *Mkting* a person or organisation considered likely to buy a product or service

prospecting *Mkting* the process of identifying people or organisations that are likely to buy a product or service

prospectus *Fin* a document that sets out corporate and financial information for prospective shareholders. A prospectus is usually issued when a company is offering new shares to the market.

prosuming *Gen Mgt* acting both as producer and consumer, as, for example, when a person plays an interactive computer game (*slang*)

protected class *HR* an employee with skills that are currently in short supply (*slang*)

protectionism *Econ* a government economic policy of restricting the level of imports by using measures such as tariffs and *NTBs*

protective put buying *Fin* the purchase of *puts* for stocks already owned

protective tariff *Econ* a tariff imposed to restrict imports into a country

protocol *Fin* a set of rules that govern and regulate a process

prototype *Gen Mgt* an initial version or working model of a new product or invention. A prototype is constructed and tested in order to evaluate the feasibility of a design and to identify problems that need to be corrected. Building a prototype is a key stage in *new product development*.

provision *Fin* a sum set aside in the accounts of an organisation in anticipation of a future expense, often for doubtful debts. *See also* **bad debt**

provisional tax *Fin* tax paid in advance on the following year's income, the amount being based on the actual income from the preceding year

proxy *Gen Mgt* somebody who votes on behalf of another person at a company meeting

proxy fight *Fin* the use of proxy votes to settle a contentious issue at a company meeting

proxy server *E-com* a program added to an intranet to provide one-way (outward) access to the Internet. In addition to providing Internet access for those within the intranet, the proxy server creates a *firewall* to prevent external users from accessing the private network.

proxy statement *Fin* a notice that a company sends to stockholders allowing them to vote and giving them all the information they need to vote in an informed way

PSBR *abbr Econ* Public Sector Borrowing Requirement

psychic income *HR* the level of satisfaction derived from a job rather than the salary earned doing it (*slang*)

psychological contract *HR* the set of unwritten expectations concerning the relationship between an *employee* and an *employer*. The psychological contract addresses factors that are not defined in a written *contract of employment* such as levels of *employee commitment*, *productivity*, *quality of working life*, *job satisfaction*, attitudes to *flexible working*, and the provision and take-up of suitable training. Expectations from both employer and employee can change, so the psychological contract must be re-evaluated at intervals to minimise misunderstandings.

psychometric test *HR* a series of questions, problems, or practical tasks that provide a measurement of aspects of somebody's personality, knowledge, ability, or experience. There are three main categories of psychometric test: ability or *aptitude tests*, *achievement tests*, and *personality tests*. A test should be both valid—it should measure what it says it measures—and reliable—it should give consistent scores. However, no test can ever be 100% accurate, and should be viewed more as a useful indicator than a definitive verdict on a person's skills or potential. Tests are used in *recruitment*, to ascertain whether or not a candidate is likely to be a good fit for a job, and in *employee development*, and their administration and interpretation must be carried out by qualified people. Tests are increasingly taken, scored, and interpreted with the aid of computer-based systems. A test may also be referred to as an **instrument**, and tests can be grouped into a **test battery**.

Pty *abbr* (*S Africa*) *Fin* used in company names to indicate a private limited liability company

public corporation *Fin* a state owned organisation established to provide a particular service, for example, the British Broadcasting Corporation. *See also **corporation***

public debt *Fin* the money that a government or a set of governments owes

public deposits *Fin* in the United Kingdom, the government's credit monies held at the Bank of England

public expenditure *Econ* spending by the government of a country on things such as pension provision and infrastructure enhancement

public finance law *Fin* legislation relating to the financial activities of government or public sector organisations

public issue *Fin* a way of making a new issue of shares by offering it for sale to the public. An issue of this type is often advertised in the press. *See also **offer for sale**, **offer by prospectus***

public-liability insurance *Fin* insurance against the risk of being held financially liable for injury to somebody

public limited company *Gen Mgt* a company in the United Kingdom that is required to have a minimum authorised capital of £50,000 and to offer its shares to the public. A public limited company has the letters 'plc' after its name. In the United Kingdom, only public limited companies can be listed on the London Stock Exchange. *Abbr* **plc** or **PLC**. *US term **publicly held corporation***

publicly held corporation (*US*) = *public limited company*

public monopoly *Gen Mgt* a situation of limited competition in the public sector, usually relating to nationalised industries

public offering *Fin* a method of raising money used by a company in which it invites the public to apply for shares

public placing *Fin* placing shares in a public company. *See also **private placing***

public relations *Mkting* see **PR**

public relations consultancy *Mkting* an organisation specialising in planning and implementing public relations strategies

public sector *Gen Mgt* the organisations in the section of the economy that is financed and controlled by central government, local authorities, and publicly funded corporations. *See also **private sector***

public sector borrowing requirement *Fin abbr* **PSBR**. *See **public sector cash requirement***

public sector cash requirement *Econ* the difference between the income and the expenditure of the public sector. It was formerly called the **public sector borrowing requirement**.

public servant *Gen Mgt* a person employed by a government department or agency

public service *Gen Mgt* the various departments and agencies that carry out government policies and provide government-funded services

public spending *Econ* spending by the government of a country on publicly-provided goods and services

public training programme *HR see* **in-company training**

published accounts *Fin* a company's financial statements that must by law be published. *US term* **earnings report**

puff *Fin* to overstate the virtues of a product, especially a stock (*slang*)

puffery *Mkting* exaggerated claims made for a product or service. In general, puffery does not constitute false advertising under law. (*slang*)

puff piece *Mkting* an article in a newspaper or magazine promoting a product, person, or service (*slang*)

pull strategy *Mkting see* **push and pull strategies**

pull system *Ops* a production planning and control system in which the specification and pace of output of a delivery, or supplier, workstation is set by the receiving, or customer, **workstation**. In pull systems, the customer acts as the only trigger for movement. The supplier workstation can only produce output on the instructions of the customer for delivery when the customer is ready to receive it. Demand is therefore transferred down through the stages of production from the order placed by an end customer. Pull systems are far less likely to result in work-in-progress inventory, and are favoured by just-in-time or **lean production** systems. *See also* **push system**

pull technology *E-com* technology that enables users to seek out and then pull in information, rather than having it pushed their way. Understanding the 'pull' nature of the Internet is often considered to be one of the key factors in determining a website's success. The Internet is essentially a pull technology, though direct outbound e-mail can be classified as a **push technology**.

pull the plug on something *Gen Mgt* to bring something such as a business project to an end, especially by cutting off its financial support (*slang*)

pump priming *Gen Mgt* the injection of further investment in order to revitalise a company in stagnation, or to help a **start-up** over a critical period. Pump priming has a similar effect to the provision of **seed capital**.

punt (*US & Canada*) *Gen Mgt* to stop trying to accomplish something and just try to avoid losing any more resources (*slang*)

purchase contract *Fin* a form of agreement to buy specified products at an agreed price

purchase history *Mkting* a record of a customer's transactions with an organisation

purchase ledger *Gen Mgt* a record of all purchases made by an organisation

purchase money mortgage (*US*) *Fin* a mortgage whose proceeds the borrower uses to buy the property that is collateral for the loan

purchase order *Gen Mgt* a document that authorises a person or an organisation to deliver goods or perform a service and that guarantees payment

purchase price *Fin* the price that somebody pays to buy a good or service

purchase requisition *Gen Mgt* an internal instruction to a buying office to purchase goods or services, stating their quantity and description and generating a purchase order

purchasing *Gen Mgt* the acquisition of goods and services needed to support the various activities of an organisation, at the optimum cost and from reliable suppliers. Purchasing involves defining the need for goods and services; identifying and comparing available supplies and suppliers; negotiating terms for price, quantity, and delivery; agreeing contracts and placing orders; receiving and accepting delivery; and authorising the payment for goods and services. *Also known as* **procurement**

purchasing by contract *Ops see* **contract purchasing**

purchasing manager *Gen Mgt* an individual with responsibility for all activities concerned with **purchasing**. The responsibilities of a purchasing manager can include ordering, commercial negotiations, and delivery chasing. *Also known as* **buying manager**, **procurement manager**

purchasing power *Gen Mgt* a measure of the ability of a person, organisation, or sector to buy goods and services

purchasing power parity *Econ* a theory stating that the exchange rate between two currencies is in equilibrium when the purchasing power of currency is the same in each country. If a basket of goods costs £100 in the United Kingdom and $150 for an equivalent in the United States, for equilibrium to exist, the exchange rate would be expected to be £1 = $1.50. If this is were not the case, **arbitrage** would be expected to take place until equilibrium was restored.

purchasing versus production *Ops* a decision on whether to produce goods internally or to buy them in from outside the organisation. The aim of purchasing versus production is to secure needed items at the best possible cost, while making optimum use of the resources of the organisation. Factors influencing the decision may include: cost, spare **capacity** within the organisation, the need for tight quality and scheduling control, flexibility, the enhancement of skills that can then be used in other ways, volume and economies of scale, utilisation of existing personnel, the need for secrecy, capital and financing requirements, and the potential reliability of supply. *Also known as* **buy or make, make or buy, internal versus external sourcing**

pure competition *Fin* a situation in which there are many sellers in a market and there is free flow of information

pure endowment *Fin* a gift whose use is fully prescribed by the donor

pure play *E-com* a company that conducts business only over the Internet, provides only Internet services, or sells only to other Internet companies (*slang*)

purpose credit *Fin* credit used for trade in securities

push and pull strategies *Mkting* approaches used as part of a marketing strategy to encourage customers to purchase a product or service. Push and pull strategies are contrasting approaches and tend to target different types of consumer. A **pull strategy** targets the end consumer, using *advertising*, *sales promotions*, and *direct response marketing* to pull the customer in. This approach is common in consumer markets. A **push strategy** targets members of the *distribution channel*, such as *wholesalers* and *retailers*, to push the promotion up through the channel to the consumers. This approach is more common in industrial markets.

push system *Ops* a *production control* and planning system in which demand is predicted centrally and each *workstation* pushes work out without considering if the next station is ready for it. While the central control aspect of a push system can achieve a balance across workstations, in practice a particular station can suffer from any one of a number of problems that delays work flow, so affecting the whole system. Push systems are characterised by work-in-progress inventory, queues, and idle time. *See also* **pull system**

push technology *E-com see* **pull technology**

push the envelope *Gen Mgt* to exceed normal limits. Pushing the envelope is a term adapted from aviation. The term implies a sense of risk at transcending normal safe limits of operation.

put *or* **put option** *Fin* an option to sell stock within a specified time at a specified price

pyramid selling *Mkting* the sale of the right to sell products or services to distributors who in turn recruit other distributors. Sometimes ending with no final buyer, pyramid selling is a form of multilevel marketing, and often involves a system of franchises. It is similar to *network marketing*, but in many cases no end products are actually sold. Unscrupulous instigators of a pyramid marketing scheme profit from the initial fees paid to them by distributors in advance of promised sales income. Pyramid selling is now illegal in the United Kingdom.

I'm all in favour of free expression, provided it's kept strictly under control.   *Alan Bennett*

QFD *abbr Ops* quality function deployment

qualification payment (*ANZ*) *Gen Mgt* an additional payment sometimes made to employees of New Zealand companies, who have gained an academic qualification relevant to their job

qualified auditor's report *Fin see adverse opinion*

qualified lead *Fin* a sales prospect whose potential value has been carefully researched

qualified listed security *Fin* a security that is eligible for purchase by a regulated entity such as a trust

qualitative analysis *Fin* the subjective appraisal of a project or investment for which there is no quantifiable data. *See also chartist, fundamental analysis, quantitative analysis, technical analysis*

qualitative factors *Fin* factors which are relevant to a decision, but which are not expressed numerically

qualitative lending guideline *Fin* a rule for evaluating creditworthiness that is not objective

qualitative research *Mkting* research that focuses on 'soft' data, for example, attitude research or focus groups. *See also quantitative research*

quality *Gen Mgt* all the features and characteristics of a product or service that affect its ability to meet stated or implied needs. Quality can be assessed in terms of conforming to specification, being fit for purpose, having zero defects, and producing *customer satisfaction*. Quality can be managed through *total quality management*, *quality standards*, and *performance indicators*.

quality assurance *Gen Mgt* all the methods used to ensure compliance with a *quality standard*. Quality assurance is recognised by the international standard *ISO 9000*.

quality audit *Gen Mgt* an independent and systematic examination to establish whether quality activities and related results comply with planned arrangements. A quality audit is a form of internal *audit* useful in the maintenance of *quality control*. A quality audit needs to look at effective implementation of quality arrangements and whether they are suitable for the achievement of objectives. It is an integral part of working towards a *quality standard* or a *quality award*.

quality award *Gen Mgt* a formal recognition of quality and business *excellence*. The best-known quality awards include the *Malcolm Baldrige National Quality Award*, the *Deming Prize*, and the *EFQM Excellence Model*.

quality bond *Fin* a bond issued by an organisation that has an excellent credit rating

quality circle *Gen Mgt* a group of employees who meet voluntarily and on a regular basis to discuss performance and problems evident in their working environment. A quality circle is usually made up of employees from the shop floor, led by a supervisor. The group has responsibility for implementing solutions to identified problems. Participants are trained in the necessary leadership, *problem-solving*, and *decision-making* skills to enable them to contribute fully to the group. The quality circle is a form of *employee involvement* derived from a Japanese idea widely adopted in the United Kingdom in the late 1970s. By the end of the 1980s, however, many organisations had abandoned the idea.

quality control *Gen Mgt* an inspection system for ensuring that pre-determined *quality standards* are being met. Quality control measures the progress of an activity by means of a quality inspection checking for and identifying non-conformance. *Also known as quality inspection*

quality control plan *Ops* a means of setting out practices, resources, and sequences of activities relevant to the *quality control* of a particular product, service, contract, or project

quality costs *Gen Mgt* costs associated with the failure to achieve conformance to requirements. Quality costs accrue when organisations waste large sums of money because of carrying out the wrong tasks, or failing to carry out the right tasks *right first time*. *Also known as non-conformance costs*

quality equity *Fin* an equity with a good track record of earnings and dividends. *See also blue chip*

quality function deployment *Ops* a *quality* technique used to design services or products based on customer expectations. Quality function deployment is an approach that sees quality as something that can be designed into

---

a product or service at an early stage. It involves converting customers' demands into quality characteristics of the finished product. The four phases of the approach are design or *house of quality*, detail, process, and production. Each phase helps to steer a design team towards *customer satisfaction*. Quality function deployment is based on methods developed by *Genichi Taguchi*. *Abbr* **QFD**

quality inspection *Gen Mgt see* **quality control**

quality loss *Ops see* **Taguchi methods**

quality management *Gen Mgt* the use of a programme to ensure the production of high-quality products. *See also* **total quality management**

quality manual *Gen Mgt* a document containing the quality policy, quality objectives, structure chart, and description of the quality system of an organisation. A quality manual often explains how the requirements of a *quality standard* are to be met and identifies the person responsible for *quality management* functions.

quality of design *Ops* the degree to which the design of a product or service meets its purpose. Quality of design is an important factor in *customer satisfaction*.

quality of life *HR* **1.** at a personal level, the degree of enjoyment and satisfaction experienced in everyday life, embracing health, personal relationships, the environment, *quality of working life*, social life, and leisure time **2.** at community level, a set of social indicators such as nutrition, air quality, incidence of disease, crime rates, health care, educational services, and divorce rates

quality of working life *HR* the degree of personal satisfaction experienced at work. Quality of working life is dependent on the extent to which an employee feels valued, rewarded, motivated, consulted, and empowered. It is also influenced by factors such as job security, opportunities for *career development*, work patterns, and *work-life balance*.

quality standard *Gen Mgt* a framework for achieving a recognised level of *quality* within an organisation. Achievement of a quality standard demonstrates that an organisation has met the requirements laid out by a certifying body. Quality standards recognised on an international basis include *ISO 9000* and *ISO 14000*.

quality table *Ops see* **house of quality**

quality time *Gen Mgt* time that is set aside for activities which you consider important, for example, time spent with your family (*slang*)

quango *Fin* in the United Kingdom, an acronym derived from quasi-autonomous non-governmental organisation. Established by the government and answerable to a government minister, some, but not all, are staffed by civil servants and some have statutory powers in a specified field.

quantitative analysis *Fin* the appraisal of a project or investment using econometric, mathematical, and statistical techniques. *See also* **chartist, fundamental analysis, qualitative analysis, technical analysis**

quantitative factors *Fin* factors which are relevant to a decision and which are expressed numerically

quantitative research *Fin* the gathering and analysis of data that can be expressed in numerical form. Quantitative research involves data that is measurable and can include statistical results, financial data, or demographic data. *See also* **qualitative research**

quantum meruit *Fin* a Latin phrase meaning 'as much as has been earned'

quarterback (*US*) (*Canada*) *Gen Mgt* to give directions on a project (*slang*)

quarterly report *Fin see* **interim statement**

quartile *Stats* any of the values in a frequency or probability distribution that divide it into four equal parts

quasi-contract *Fin* a decree by a UK court stipulating that one party has a legal obligation to another, even though there is no legally binding contract between the two parties

quasi-loan *Fin* an arrangement whereby one party pays the debts of another, on the condition that the sum of the debts will be reimbursed by the indebted party at some later date

quasi-money *Fin see* **near money**

quasi-public corporation (*US*) *Gen Mgt* an organisation that is owned partly by private or public shareholders and partly by the government

quasi-rent *Econ* the short-run excess earnings made by a firm, the difference between production cost (the cost of labour and materials) and selling cost

question mark company Gen Mgt see Boston Box

questionnaire Gen Mgt a collection of structured questions designed to elicit information for a specific purpose. Questionnaires are commonly used in *market research* and make use of two types of question: multiple choice questions, which are designed to produce a limited response, and open questions, which allow respondents the opportunity to air their views freely.

queuing theory Gen Mgt techniques developed by the study of people waiting in queues to determine the optimum level of service provision. In queuing theory, mathematical formulae, or *simulations*, are used to calculate variables such as length of time spent waiting in queues and average service time, which depend on the frequency and number of arrivals and the facilities available. The results enable decisions to be made on the most cost-effective level of facilities and the most efficient organisation of the process. Early developments in queuing theory were applied to the provision of telephone switching equipment but the techniques are now used in a wide variety of contexts, including machine maintenance, production lines, and air transport.

queuing time Fin the time between the arrival of material at a workstation and the start of work on it

quick asset Fin see *near money*

quick ratio Fin 1. a measure of the amount of cash a potential borrower can acquire in a short time, used in evaluating creditworthiness 2. the ratio of liquid assets to current debts

quid pro quo Fin a Latin phrase meaning 'something for something'

quorum Fin the minimum number of people required in a meeting for it to be able to make decisions that are binding on the organisation. For a company, this is stated in its Articles of Association, for a partnership, in its partnership agreement.

quota Fin 1. the maximum sum to be contributed by each party in a joint venture or joint business undertaking 2. the maximum number of investments that may be purchased and sold in a given situation or market 3. the maximum amount of a particular commodity, product, or service that can be imported into or exported out of a country

quote Fin a statement of what a person is willing to accept when selling, or willing to pay when buying

quoted company Fin a company whose shares are listed on a stock exchange

quote driven Fin used to describe a share dealing system where prices are initially generated by dealers' and market makers' quotes before market forces come into play and prices are determined by the interaction of supply and demand. The London Stock Exchange's dealing system, as well as those of many over-the-counter markets, have quote driven systems.

quoted securities Fin securities or shares that are listed on a stock exchange

---

R150 Bond *Fin* the benchmark South African government bond which has a fixed interest rate of 12% and matures in 2005

racial discrimination *HR* the practice of making unfavourable distinctions between the members of different groups of people on the grounds of colour, race, nationality, or ethnic origin. In the United Kingdom, anti-discrimination law is provided by the Race Relations Act 1976. The Act established the Commission for Racial Equality to work towards the elimination of racial discrimination by promoting equality of opportunity and race relations. In 1999, measures to combat institutional racism, especially in the police force, were recommended in a report on the murder of a black student, Stephen Lawrence. *See also* **indirect discrimination**

radio button *Gen Mgt* a device on a computer screen that can be used to select an option from a list

raid *Fin* the illegal practice of selling shares short to drive the price down. *Also known as* **bear raid**

raider *Fin* a person or company that makes hostile takeover bids

rainmaker *HR* somebody, especially a lawyer, who procures clients who spend a lot of money on their firm's business

rake it in *Fin* to make a great deal of money (*slang*)

rake-off *Fin* commission (*slang*)

rally *Fin* a rise in share prices after a fall

ramp *Fin* to buy shares with the objective of raising their price. *See also* **rigged market**

rand *Fin* the South African unit of currency, equal to 100 cents

R & D *abbr Ops* research and development

Randlord *Fin* originally a Johannesburg-based mining magnate or tycoon of the late 19th or early 20th centuries, now used informally for any wealthy or powerful Johannesburg businessman

random *Stats* not part of a pattern but governed by chance

random observation method *Gen Mgt see* **activity sampling**

random sampling *Ops* an unbiased *sampling* technique in which every member of a population has an equal chance of being included in the sample. Based on probability theory, random sampling is the process of selecting and canvassing a representative group of individuals from a particular population in order to identify the attributes or attitudes of the population as a whole. Related sampling techniques include: **stratified sampling**, in which the population is divided into classes, and random samples are taken from each class; **cluster sampling**, in which a unit of the sample is a group such as a household; and **systematic sampling**, which refers to samples chosen by any system other than random selection. *See also* **non-random sampling**

range *Stats* the difference between the smallest and the largest observations in a data set

range pricing *Fin* the pricing of individual products so that their prices fit logically within a range of connected products offered by one supplier, and differentiated by a factor such as weight of pack or number of product attributes offered

ranking *Stats* the ordered arrangement of a set of variable values

ratable value *Fin* the value of something as calculated with reference to a rule

ratchet effect *Econ* the result when households adjust more easily to rising incomes than to falling incomes, as, for example, when their consumption drops by less than their income in a recession

rate cap *Fin see* **cap**

rate of exchange *Fin see* **exchange rate**

rate of interest *Fin* a percentage charged on a loan or paid on an investment for the use of the money

rate of return *Fin* an accounting ratio of the income from an investment to the amount of the investment, used to measure financial performance. *Also known as* **return**

EXAMPLE There is a basic formula that will serve most needs, at least initially:

[(Current value of amount invested – Original value of amount invested) / Original value of amount invested] × 100% = rate of return

If £1,000 in capital is invested in stock, and one year later the investment yields £1,100,

---

the rate of return of the investment is calculated like this:

[(1100 – 1000) / 1000] × 100% = 100 /1000 × 100%
= 10% rate of return

Now, assume £1,000 is invested again. One year later, the investment grows to £2,000 in value, but after another year the value of the investment falls to £1,200. The rate of return after the first year is:

[(2000 – 1000) / 1000] × 100% = 100%

The rate of return after the second year is:

[(1200 – 2000) / 2000] × 100% = – 40%

The average annual return for the two years (also known as average annual arithmetic return) can be calculated using this formula:

(Rate of return for Year 1 + Rate of return for
Year 2) / 2 = average annual return

Accordingly:

(100% + – 40%) / 2 = 30%

The average annual rate of return is a percentage, but one that is accurate over only a short period, so this method should be used accordingly.

The geometric or compound rate of return is a better yardstick for measuring investments over the long term, and takes into account the effects of compounding. This formula is more complex and technical.

The real rate of return is the annual return realised on an investment, adjusted for changes in the price due to inflation. If 10% is earned on an investment but inflation is 2%, then the real rate of return is actually 8%.

ratings *Mkting* the proportion of a target audience who are exposed to a television or radio commercial

ratio analysis *Fin* the use of ratios to measure financial performance

ratio-delay study *Gen Mgt see* **activity sampling**

rationalisation *Gen Mgt* the application of efficiency or effectiveness measures to an organisation. Rationalisation can occur at the onset of a downturn in an organisation's performance or results. It usually takes the form of cutbacks aimed at bringing the organisation back to profitability and may involve **redundancies**, plant closures, and cutbacks in supplies and resources. It often involves changes in **organisation structure**, particularly in the form of **downsizing**. The term is also used in a cynical way as a euphemism for mass redundancies.

ratio pyramid *Fin* the analysis of a primary

ratio into mathematically linked secondary ratios

raw materials *Ops* items bought for use in the manufacturing or development processes of an organisation. While most often referring to bulk materials, raw materials can also include components, subassemblies, and complete products.

RBA *abbr Fin* Reserve Bank of Australia

RBNZ *abbr Fin* Reserve Bank of New Zealand

RDO *abbr (ANZ) HR* rostered day off: a day of leave allocated under certain employment agreements to staff in lieu of accumulated overtime

RDP *abbr Fin* Reconstruction and Development Program: a policy framework by means of which the South African government intends to correct the socio-economic imbalances caused by apartheid

RDPR *abbr Fin* refer to drawer please represent

reactive maintenance *Ops* a form of **maintenance** in which equipment and facilities are repaired only in response to a breakdown or a fault. Because of the potential for loss of production, reactive maintenance is at odds with **just-in-time**. *See also* **preventive maintenance**

readership *Mkting* a detailed profile of the readers of a newspaper or magazine

Reaganomics *Econ* the policy of former US President Reagan in the 1980s, who reduced taxes and social security support and increased the national budget deficit to an unprecedented level

real *Fin* after the effects of inflation are taken into consideration

real asset *Fin* a non-movable asset such as land or a building

real balance effect *Econ* the effect on income and employment when prices fall and consumption increases

real capital *Fin* assets that can be assigned a monetary value

real estate *(US) Gen Mgt* property consisting of land or buildings

real estate developer *(US) Gen Mgt* a person or company that develops land or buildings to increase their value

real exchange rate *Fin* an exchange rate that has been adjusted for inflation

---

That action is best which provides the greatest happiness for the greatest numbers. **Francis Hutcheson**

real GDP *Econ GDP* adjusted for changes in prices

real growth *Econ* the growth of a country or a household adjusted for changes in prices

real interest rate *Fin* interest rate approximately calculated by subtracting the rate of inflation from the nominal interest rate

real investment *Fin* the purchase of assets such as land, property, and plant and machinery as opposed to the acquisition of securities

realisation concept *Fin* the principle that increases in value should only be recognised on realisation of assets by arm's-length sale to an independent purchaser

reality check *Gen Mgt* a consideration of limiting factors such as cost when discussing or contemplating an ambitious project. In other words, a test to see if something that works in theory will also work in practice. (*slang*)

real purchasing power *Econ* the purchasing power of a country or a household adjusted for changes in prices

real time company *Gen Mgt* a company that uses the Internet and other technologies to respond immediately to customer demands

real time credit card processing *E-com* the online authorisation of a credit card indicating that the credit card has been approved or rejected during the transaction

real time data *Fin* information received very soon after a company comes into existence

real time EDI *E-com* online electronic data interchange, the online transfer and processing of business data, for example, purchase orders, customer invoices, and payment receipts, between suppliers and their customers

real time manager *Gen Mgt* a manager who is responsible for delivering the immediate service that customers expect using the Internet and other technologies

real time transaction *E-com* an Internet payment transaction that is approved or rejected immediately when the customer completes the online order form

rebadge *Fin* to buy a product or service from another company and sell it as part of your own product range

rebate *Fin* **1.** money returned because a payment exceeded the amount required, for example, a tax rebate **2.** a discount **3.** of a broker, to reduce part of the commission charged to the client as a promotional offer

rebating *Mkting* a sales promotion technique in which the customer is offered a rebate for reaching volume targets

recd *abbr Fin* received

receipt *Fin* a document acknowledging that something, for example, a payment, has been received

receipts and payments account *Fin* a report of cash transactions during a period. It is used in place of an income and expenditure account when it is not considered appropriate to distinguish between capital and revenue transactions or to include accruals.

receiver *Fin* the person appointed to sell the assets of a company that is insolvent. The proceeds of the sale are used to discharge debts to creditors, with any surplus distributed to shareholders.

Receiver of Revenue *Fin* **1.** a local office of the South African Revenue Service **2.** an informal term for the South African Revenue Service as a whole

receivership *Fin* the control of a receiver, who is appointed by secured creditors or by the court to take control of company property. The most usual reason for the appointment of a receiver is the failure of a company to pay principal sums or interest due to debenture holders whose debt is secured by fixed or floating charges over the assets of the company.

recession *Econ* a stage of the *business cycle* in which economic activity is in slow decline. Recession usually follows a boom, and precedes a *depression*. It is characterised by rising unemployment and falling levels of output and investment.

recessionary gap *Econ* the shortfall in the amount of *aggregate demand* in an economy needed to create full employment

reciprocal cost allocation *Fin* a method of secondary cost allocation generally used to reallocate service department costs over the user departments. Service department costs are recharged over user departments (including other service departments) in a number of iterations until all of the service department costs have been re-charged to users.

reconciliation *Fin* adjustment of an account, such as an individual's own record of a bank account, to match more authoritative information

Reconstruction and Development Program *Fin see RDP*

record date *Gen Mgt* the date when a computer data entry or record is made

recourse *Fin* a source of redress should a debt be dishonoured at maturity

recourse agreement *Fin* an agreement in a hire purchase contract whereby the retailer repossesses the goods being purchased in the event of the hirer failing to make regular payments

recovery *Econ* the return of a country to economic health after a crash or a depression

recovery fund *Fin* a fund that invests in recovery stock

recovery stock *Fin* a share that has fallen in price because of poor business performance, but is now expected to climb due to an improvement in the company's prospects

recruitment *HR* the activity of employing workers to fill vacancies or enrolling new members. Employment recruitment is composed of several stages: verifying that a vacancy exists; drawing up a job specification; finding candidates; selecting them by *interviewing* and other means such as carrying out a *psychometric test*; and making a job offer. Effective recruitment is important in achieving high organisational performance and minimising labour turnover. Employees may be recruited either externally or internally.

recurring billing transaction *E-com* an electronic payment facility based on the automatic charging of a customer's credit card in each payment period

recurring payments *E-com* an electronic payment facility that permits a merchant to process multiple authorisations by the same customer either as multiple payments for a fixed amount or recurring billings for varying amounts

red *Fin* the colour of debit or overdrawn balances in some bank statements
in the red *Fin* in debt, or making a loss (*slang*)

Red Book *Fin* in the United Kingdom, a copy of the Chancellor of the Exchequer's speech published on the day of the Budget. It may be regarded as the country's financial statement and report.

Reddin, William James (*b.* 1930) *Gen Mgt* British-born Canadian academic. Best known for his research on *three-dimensional man-*

agement, a development of the work of *Robert Blake* and *Jane Mouton* explained in *Managerial Effectiveness* (1970).

redeemable bond *Fin see bond*

redeemable gilt *Fin see gilt-edged security*

redeemable shares *Fin* shares which are issued on terms which may require them to be bought back by the issuer at some future date, at the discretion of either the issuer or of the holder. Redemption must comply with the conditions of the Companies Act 1985.

redemption *Fin* **1.** the purchase by a company of its own shares from shareholders **2.** the repayment of a security on a specific date, usually specified when the security is issued

redemption yield *Fin* the rate of interest at which the total of the discounted values of any future payments of interest and capital is equal to the current price of a security

redeployment *HR* the movement of employees by their employer from one location or task to another. Redeployment is often used to minimise redundancies, ensure the fulfilment of a specific order, or ensure the most cost-effective use of employees.

red eye (*US*) *Fin* a pathfinder prospectus (*slang*)

redistributive effect *Fin* an effect of a progressive tax or benefit that tends to equalise people's wealth

red screen market *Fin* in the United Kingdom, a market where the prices are down and are being shown as red on the dealing screens

red tape *Fin* excessive bureaucracy (*slang*)

reducing balance depreciation *Fin see depreciation*

redundancy *HR* dismissal from work because a job ceases to exist. Redundancy occurs most frequently when an employer goes out of business, suffers a drop in business necessitating a cutback in the workforce, or relocates part, or all, of the company. Redundancy may also be due to a reduced requirement for employees to carry out work of a particular kind. Employees who are made redundant may qualify for a *redundancy payment*. If the redundancy process is handled incorrectly, the employer may be faced with claims for *unfair dismissal*. In the United Kingdom, redundancy is defined by the Employment Rights Act 1996. *US term* **layoff**

redundancy package *HR* a package of benefits that an employer gives to somebody who is made redundant. *US term* **severance package**

redundancy payment *HR* a one-off payment given to a worker who has been made **redundant**, usually calculated with reference to age, length of service, and weekly rate of pay. In the United Kingdom, redundancy payments are regulated by the Employment Rights Act 1996. Some redundancy payments are made in excess of the statutory minimum and also are supplemented by other benefits, such as a car and **outplacement** support. *US term* **severance pay**

redundant capacity *Ops see* **surplus capacity**

re-engineering *Gen Mgt see* **business process re-engineering**

reference 1. *HR* a statement of facts and opinions concerning the qualifications, skills, capabilities, personal qualities, conduct, and attitudes of a person, usually a job applicant. Employers supplying references have a legal obligation to take reasonable care that the information provided is accurate. **2.** *Fin see* **banker's reference**

reference population *Stats* a standard against which a statistical population under study can be compared

reference rate *Fin* a benchmark rate, for example, a bank's own base rate or LIBOR. Lending rates are often expressed as a margin over a reference rate.

reference site *E-com* a customer site where a new technology is being used successfully

referred share *Fin* a share that is ex dividend

refer to drawer *Fin* to refuse to pay a cheque because the account from which it is drawn has too little money in it

refer to drawer please represent *Fin* in the United Kingdom, written on a cheque by the paying banker to indicate that there are currently insufficient funds to meet the payment, but that the bank believes sufficient funds will be available shortly. *See also* **refer to drawer**. *Abbr* **RDPR**

refinance *Fin* to replace one loan with another, especially at a lower rate of interest

refinancing *Fin* the process of taking out a loan to pay off other loans, or loans taken out for that purpose

reflation *Econ* a government policy of reducing unemployment by increasing an

economy's **aggregate demand**. *See also* **recession**

refugee capital *Fin* people and resources that come into a country because they have been forced to leave their own country for economic or political reasons

refund *Mkting* the reimbursement of the purchase price of a good or service, for reasons such as faults in manufacturing or dissatisfaction with the service provided

regeneration *Gen Mgt* the redevelopment of industrial or business areas that have suffered decline, in order to increase employment and business activity

regional fund *Fin* a unit trust that invests in the markets of a geographical region

registered bond *Fin* a bond whose ownership is recorded on the books of the issuer

registered broker *Fin* a broker registered on a particular exchange

registered capital *Fin see* **authorised capital**

registered company *Gen Mgt* in the United Kingdom, a company that has lodged official documents with the **Registrar of Companies** at Companies House. A registered company is obliged to conduct itself in accordance with company law. All organisations must register in order to become companies.

registered name *Fin* in the United Kingdom, the name of a company as it is registered at Companies House. It must appear, along with the company's registered number and office on all its letterheads and orders. *See also* **company, corporation**

registered number *Fin* in the United Kingdom, a unique number assigned to a company registered at Companies House. It must appear, along with the company's registered name and office on all its letterheads and orders. *See also* **company, corporation**

registered office *Gen Mgt* the official address of a company, which is reproduced on its letterheads and lodged with Companies House, to which all legal correspondence and documents must be delivered

registered security *Fin* a security where the holder's name is recorded in the books of the issuer. *See also* **nominee name**

registered share *Fin* a share the ownership of which is recorded on the books of the issuer

registered share capital *Fin see* **authorised share capital**

registered trademark *Gen Mgt see trademark*

register of companies *Fin* in the United Kingdom, the list of companies maintained at Companies House. *See also **company**, **corporation***

register of directors and secretaries *Fin* in the United Kingdom, a record that every registered company must maintain of the names and residential addresses of directors and the company secretary together with their nationality, occupation, and details of other directorships held. Public companies must also record the date of birth of their directors. The record must be kept at the company's registered office and be available for inspection by shareholders without charge and by members of the public for a nominal fee.

register of directors' interests *Fin* in the United Kingdom, a record that every registered company must maintain of the shares and other securities that have been issued by the company and are held by its directors. It has to be made available for inspection during the company's Annual General Meeting.

Registrar of Companies *Gen Mgt* the official charged with the duty of holding and registering the official start-up and constitutional documents of all *registered companies* in the United Kingdom

registration statement *Fin* in the United States, a document that corporations planning to issue securities to the public have to submit to the Securities and Exchange Commission. It features details of the issuer's management, financial status, and activities, and the purpose of the issue. *See also **shelf registration***

regression analysis *Gen Mgt* a *forecasting* technique used to establish the relationship between quantifiable variables. In regression analysis, data on dependent and independent variables is plotted on a scatter graph or diagram and trends are indicated through a line of best fit. The use of a single independent variable is known as **simple regression analysis**, while the use of two or more independent variables is called **multiple regression analysis**.

regressive tax *Fin* a tax whose percentage falls as the value of the item being taxed, especially income, rises. *See also **progressive tax**, **proportional tax***

regulated price *Fin* a selling price set within guidelines laid down by a regulatory authority, normally governmental

regulated superannuation fund (*ANZ*) *Fin* an Australian superannuation fund that is regulated by legislation and therefore qualifies for tax concessions. To attain this status, a fund must show that its main function is the provision of pensions, or adopt a corporate trustee structure.

regulation *Fin* laws or rules stipulated by a government or regulatory body, such as the Financial Services Authority or the Securities and Exchange Commission, to provide orderly procedures and to protect consumers and investors

regulator *Gen Mgt* an official or body that monitors the behaviour of companies and the level of competition in particular markets, for example, telecommunications or energy

regulatory body *Fin, Gen Mgt* an independent organisation, usually set up by government, that regulates the activities of all companies in an industry

regulatory framework *Fin* the set of legal and professional requirements with which the financial statements of a company must comply. Company reporting is influenced by the requirements of law, of the accountancy profession, and of the stock exchange (for listed companies).

regulatory pricing risk *Fin* the risk an insurance company faces that a government will regulate the prices it can charge

reinsurance *Fin* a method of reducing risk by transferring all or part of an insurance policy to another insurer

reintermediation *E-com* the reintroduction of intermediaries found in traditional retail channels. *See also **disintermediation***

reinvestment rate *Fin* the interest rate at which an investor is able to reinvest income received from another investment

reinvestment risk *Fin* the risk that it will not be possible to invest the proceeds of an investment at as high a rate as they earned

reinvestment unit trust *Fin* a unit trust that uses dividends to buy more shares in the company issuing them

rejects *Ops* units of output which fail a set quality standard and are subsequently rectified, sold as sub-standard, or disposed of as scrap

relational database *Gen Mgt* a computer database in which different types of data are linked for analysis

---

Teamwork is a constant balancing act between self-interest and group interest.   *Susan Campbell*

relationship management *Mkting* the process of fostering good relations with customers to build loyalty and increase sales

relative income hypothesis *Econ* the theory that consumers are concerned less with their absolute living standards than with consumption relative to other consumers

relaxation allowance *Gen Mgt see* **standard time**

release *E-com* a version of a software program that has been modified. Release 1.0 would be followed by release 1.1 after minor modification, or release 2.0 after major changes to the program.

relevancy concept *Fin* the principle that management accounting must ensure that flexibility is maintained in assembling and interpreting information. This facilitates the exploration and presentation, in a clear, understandable, and timely manner, of as many alternatives as are necessary for impartial and confident decisions to be taken. The process is essentially forward-looking and dynamic. Therefore, the information must satisfy the criteria of being applicable and appropriate.

relevant costs/revenues *Fin* costs and revenues appropriate to a specific management decision. These are represented by future cash flows whose magnitude will vary depending upon the outcome of the management decision made. If stock is sold by a retailer, the relevant cost, used in the determination of the profitability of the transaction, would be the cost of replacing the stock, not its original purchase price, which is a sunk cost. Abandonment analysis, based on relevant cost and revenues, is the process of determining whether or not it is more profitable to discontinue a product or service than to continue it.

relevant interest *(ANZ)* *Fin* the legal status held by share investors who can legally dispose of, or influence the disposal of, shares

relevant range *Fin* the activity levels within which assumptions about cost behaviour in breakeven analysis remain valid

reliability *Gen Mgt* the quality of being fit for an intended purpose over a continued period of time

reliability-centred maintenance *Ops* a *maintenance* system that focuses on ensuring equipment is always functioning reliably. Reliability-centred maintenance involves assessing each piece of equipment or other asset individually and in the context of how it is being used, for example, frequency of use and volume of output. Analysis is made of its weak points and a *preventive maintenance* schedule is drawn up taking them into account.

reliability concept *Fin* the principle that management accounting information must be of such quality that confidence can be placed in it. Its reliability to the user is dependent on its source, integrity, and comprehensiveness.

relocation *Gen Mgt* the transfer of a business from one location to another. Relocation occurs for a variety of reasons, including the need for more space, the desire to centralise operations, or to be nearer to suppliers, customers, or raw materials.

remuneration *HR see* **earnings**

remuneration package *HR* the salary, pension contributions, bonuses, and other forms of payment or benefit that make up an employee's remuneration

renounceable document *Fin* written proof of ownership for a limited period, for example, a letter of allotment. *See also* **letter of renunciation**

renting back *Fin see* **sale and leaseback**

renunciation *Fin see* **letter of renunciation**

reorder level *Ops* a level of stock at which a replenishment order should be placed. Traditional 'optimising' systems use a variation on the following computation, which builds in a measure of safety stock and minimises the likelihood of a stock out.

reorganisation bond *Fin* in the United States, a bond issued to creditors of a business that is undergoing a Chapter 11 form of reorganisation. Interest is normally only paid when the company can make the payments from its earnings.

repayment mortgage *Fin* a long-term loan, usually for the purchase of a property, in which the borrower makes monthly payments, part of which cover the interest on the loan and part of which cover the repayment of the principal (see *mortgage*). In the early years, the greater proportion of the payment is used to cover the interest charged but, as the principal is gradually repaid, the interest portion diminishes and the repayment portion increases. *See also* **mortgage**

repeat business *Mkting* the placing of order after order with the same supplier. Repeat business can be implemented by an agreement between the customer and supplier for purchase on a regular basis. It is often used where there are small numbers of customers, or high volumes per product and low product variety. There is only market competition for the first order, and customisation is usually only available for the initial purchase. Sales and marketing have a diminished role once the business has been gained.

repertory grid *Gen Mgt* a technique for gathering information on an individual's personal constructs or perceptions of their environment through mapping interview responses to a matrix. The repertory grid was initially used and developed by clinical psychologists in the 1930s. It has business applications in job analysis, performance measurement, *evaluation of training*, questionnaire design, and *market research*.

repetitive strain injury *Gen Mgt* damage caused to muscles or tendons as the result of prolonged repetitive movements or actions. Repetitive strain injury is most commonly associated with injury to the wrist or arms through the use of computer keyboards. *Abbr* **RSI**

replacement cost *Fin* the cost of replacing an asset or service with its current equivalent

replacement cost accounting *Fin* a method of valuing company assets based on their replacement cost

replacement price *Fin* the price at which identical goods or capital equipment could be purchased at the date of valuation

replacement ratio *Econ* the ratio of the total resources received when unemployed to those received when in employment

replenishment system *Ops* an inventory control system that relies on accurate estimates of usage rates and delivery lead times to allow orders to be completed and to ensure stock does not run out. The timing of a replenishment order is crucial, as *buffer stock* should not be allowed to run out during the time it takes for a delivery to arrive.

repo *Fin* **1.** repurchase agreement (*slang*) **2.** in the United States, an open market operation undertaken by the Federal Reserve to purchase securities and agree to sell them back at a stated price on a future date

report *Gen Mgt* a written or verbal statement analysing a particular issue, incident, or state of affairs, usually with some form of recommendations for future action

repositioning *Mkting* a marketing strategy that changes aspects of a product or brand in order to change *market position* and alter consumer perceptions

repossession *Fin* the return of goods bought on hire purchase when the purchaser fails to make the required regular payments. *Also known as* **foreclosure**. *See also* **recourse agreement**

repudiation *Fin* a refusal to pay or acknowledge a debt

repurchase *Fin* of a fund manager, to buy the units in a unit trust when an investor sells

repurchase agreement *Fin* in the bond and money markets, a spot sale of a security combined with its repurchase at a later date and pre-agreed price. In effect, the buyer is lending money to the seller for the duration of the transaction and using the security as collateral. Dealers finance their positions by using repurchase agreements. *Also known as* **repo**

request form *E-com* an interactive web page that accepts user-provided data, for example, name, address, or shipping information, that can be saved for recurring use or sent by e-mail to the page owner

required rate of return *Fin* the minimum return for a proposed project investment to be acceptable. *See also* **discounted cash flow**

required reserves (*US*) *Fin* the minimum reserves that member banks of the Federal Reserve System have to maintain

requisition *Fin* an official order form used by companies when purchasing a product or service

resale price maintenance *Mkting* an agreement between suppliers or manufacturers and retailers, restricting the price that retailers can ask for a product or service. Resale price maintenance was designed to enable all retailers to make a profit. The Resale Prices Act now prevents this practice on the grounds that it is uncompetitive. Now, unless they can prove that resale price maintenance is in the public interest, manufacturers can only recommend a retail price. *Abbr* **RPM**

research *Fin* the examination of statistics and other information regarding past, present, and future trends or performance that enables analysts to recommend to investors which shares to buy or sell in order to maximise their return and minimise their risk. It may be used either in the top-down approach (where the investor evaluates a market, then an industry, and finally a specific company) or the bottom-up approach (where the investor selects a company and confirms his or her findings by evaluating the company's sector and then its market). Careful research is likely to help investors find the best deals, in particular *value shares* or *growth equities*. *See also fundamental analysis, technical analysis*

research and development *Ops* the pursuit of new knowledge and ideas and the application of that knowledge to exploit new opportunities to the commercial advantage of a business. The research and development functions are often grouped together to form a division or department within an organisation. *Abbr* **R & D**

research park *(US) Gen Mgt* = *science park*

reserve account *E-com see* **holdback**

reserve bank *Fin* a bank such as a US Federal Reserve Bank that holds the reserves of other banks

Reserve Bank of Australia *Fin* Australia's central bank, which is responsible for managing the Commonwealth's monetary policy, ensuring financial stability, and printing and distributing currency. *Abbr* **RBA**

Reserve Bank of New Zealand *Fin* New Zealand's central bank, which is responsible for managing the government's monetary policy, ensuring financial stability, and printing and distributing currency. *Abbr* **RBNZ**

reserve currency *Fin* foreign currency that a central bank holds for use in international trade

reserve for fluctuations *Fin* money set aside to allow for changes in the values of currencies

reserve price *Fin* a price for a particular lot, set by the vendor, below which an auctioneer may not sell

reserve ratio *Fin* the proportion of a bank's deposits that must be kept in reserve.
EXAMPLE In the United Kingdom and in certain European countries, there is no compulsory ratio, although banks will have their own internal measures and targets to be able to repay customer deposits as they forecast they will be required. In the United States, specified percentages of deposits—established by the Federal Reserve Board—must be kept by banks in a non-interest-bearing account at one of the twelve Federal Reserve Banks located throughout the country.

In Europe, the reserve requirement of an institution is calculated by multiplying the reserve ratio for each category of items in the reserve base, set by the European Central Bank, with the amount of those items in the institution's balance sheets. These figures vary according to the institution.

The required reserve ratio in the United States is set by federal law, and depends on the amount of checkable deposits a bank holds. The first $44.3 million of deposits are subject to a 3% reserve requirement. Deposits in excess of $44.3 million are subject to 10% reserve requirement. These breakpoints are reviewed annually in accordance with money supply growth. No reserves are required against certificates of deposit or savings accounts.

The reserve ratio requirement limits a bank's lending to a certain fraction of its demand deposits. The current rule allows a bank to issue loans in an amount equal to 90% of such deposits, holding 10% in reserve. The reserves can be held in any combination of till money and deposit at a Federal Reserve Bank.

reserve requirements *Fin* the requirements an agency levies on a nation's banks to hold reserves

reserves *Fin* the money that a bank holds to ensure that it can satisfy its depositors' demands for withdrawals

residual income *Fin* pretax profits less an imputed interest charge for invested capital. Used to assess divisional performance.

residuary legatee *Fin* the person to whom a testator's estate is left after specific bequests have been made

resignation *HR* the act of voluntarily leaving a job. Resignation is normally signalled by a formal letter of resignation. On acceptance, a *notice period* is usually served before the employee can leave.

resizing *HR see* **downsizing**

resolution *Fin* a proposal put to a meeting, for example, an Annual General Meeting of shareholders, on which those present and eligible can vote. *See also* **extraordinary resolution, special resolution**

resource allocation *Ops* the process of assigning human and material resources to projects to ensure that they are used in the optimum way. Resource allocation is used in conjunction with *network analysis* techniques such as *critical-path method*. Basic data assembled for a project is displayed as a

---

bar chart with start and finish times and resources required for each day of the project being easily identifiable. If there is a mismatch between planned resources and those available, resources can be reallocated or smoothed by manipulating start and finish times, or changing activities around. Resource allocation is usually computerised.

resource driver *Gen Mgt see* **cost driver**

resource productivity *Gen Mgt* an environmentally-friendly approach to production based on increasing the productivity of resources to reduce waste

resources *Ops* anything that is available to an organisation to help it achieve its purpose. Resources are often categorised into finance, property, premises, equipment, people, and raw materials.

response bias *Stats* the disparity between information that a survey respondent provides and data analysis, for example, a person claiming to watch little television but giving answers showing 30 hours' weekly viewing

response level *Mkting* a measurement of response to an advertising or marketing campaign

response marketing *E-com* in e-marketing, the process of managing responses or leads from the time they are received through to conversion to sale

response mechanism *Mkting* a means of reply such as a coupon or reply card in an advertisement or mail shot by which customers can request further information

response rate *Stats* the proportion of subjects in a statistical study who respond to a researcher's questionnaire

response surface methodology *Stats* mathematical and statistical techniques that are used to improve product design systems

responsibility *Gen Mgt* the duty to carry out certain activities and be accountable for them to others

responsibility accounting *Fin* the keeping of financial records with an emphasis on who is responsible for each item

responsibility centre *Fin* a department or organisational function whose performance is the direct responsibility of a specific manager

restated balance sheet *Fin* a balance sheet reframed to serve a particular purpose, such as highlighting depreciation on assets

rest break *HR* a period of time during the working day when an employee is allowed to be away from their workstation for a rest or meal break. Many countries have statutory regulations governing the frequency and length of rest breaks related to the hours worked in a day. Regulations also may cover the requirement for a **rest period** over a working week or month.

rest period *HR* the length of time between periods of work that an employee is entitled to have for rest. Many countries have statutory regulations governing the rights of employees to periods of rest over daily, weekly, and, sometimes, monthly timescales. Different allowances may be given to younger workers. In addition, employees may be entitled to **rest breaks** during the working day.

restraint of trade *Gen Mgt, HR* a term in a contract of employment that restricts a person from carrying on their trade or profession if they leave an organisation. Generally illegal, it is usually intended to prevent key employees from leaving an organisation to set up in competition.

restricted tender *Fin* an offer to buy shares only under specified conditions

restructuring *Gen Mgt see* **corporate restructuring**

result-driven *Gen Mgt* relating to a form of **corporate strategy** focused on outcomes and achievements. A result-driven organisation concentrates on meeting objectives, delivering to the required time, cost, and quality, and holds performance to be more important than **procedures**.

résumé *(US) HR* = **CV**

retail banking *Fin* services provided by commercial banks to individuals as opposed to business customers, that include current accounts, deposit and savings accounts, as well as credit cards, mortgages, and investments. In the United Kingdom, although this service was traditionally provided by high street banks, separate organisations, albeit offshoots of established financial institutions, are now providing Internet and telephone banking services.

retail co-operative *Gen Mgt* a concern for the collective purchase and sale of goods by a group who share profits or benefits.

Retail co-operatives were the first off-shoot of the **co-operative movement** and profits were originally shared among members through dividend payments proportionate to a member's purchases.

retailer *Mkting, Ops* an outlet through which products or services are sold to customers. Retailers can be put into three broad groups: independent traders, multiple stores, or *retail co-operatives*.

retail investor *Fin* an investor who buys and sells shares in retail organisations

retail management *Mkting* marketing or financial support aimed at improving the performance of retail outlets

retail price *Mkting* a price charged to customers who buy in limited quantities

retail price index *Econ* a listing of the average levels of prices charged by retailers for goods or services. The retail price index is calculated on a set range of items, and usually excludes luxury goods. It is updated monthly, and provides a running indicator of changing costs. *Abbr* **RPI**

retained profits *or* **retained earnings** *Fin* the amount of profit remaining after tax and distribution to shareholders that is retained in a business and used as a reserve or as a means of financing expansion or investment. *Also known as* **earnings retained**

retention money or payments withheld *Fin* an agreed proportion of a contract price withheld for a specified period after contract completion as security for fulfilment of obligations

retirement *HR* the voluntary or forced termination of employment because of age, illness, or disability. **Retirement age** is often stipulated in the *contract of employment*. Differences between the retirement ages of men and women are no longer allowed in many countries. Employees may take *early retirement* from their employer, or may, with the agreement of their employer, take gradual, or *phased retirement*. A *pension* may be drawn on reaching retirement age. The current policy of a national retirement age, when a statutory pension entitlement is drawn, is under debate in the United Kingdom.

retirement age *HR see* **retirement**

retirement pension *Fin see* **pension**

retraining *HR* **training** designed to enable employees to perform a job that their previous training has not equipped them for or to adapt to changes in the workplace. Retraining may be needed when new methods or equipment are introduced or when jobs for which employees have trained are phased out. It

may also be provided by employers or governments for employees who have been made **redundant** and are no longer able to find employment using the skills they already possess. The need for retraining may arise because of a decline in a particular industry sector or because of rapid technological change.

retrenchment *Fin* the reduction of costs in order to improve profitability

retrospective study *Stats* a study that examines data collected before it began, for example, to measure the risk factors that predispose people to disease

return *Fin* **1.** the income derived from an activity **2.** *see* **rate of return 3.** *see* **tax return**

return on assets *Fin* a measure of profitability calculated by expressing a company's net income as a percentage of total assets.
☐EXAMPLE Because the ROA formula reflects total revenue, total cost, and assets deployed, the ratio itself reflects a management's ability to generate income during the course of a given period, usually a year.

To calculate ROA, net income is divided by total assets, then multiplied by 100 to express the figure as a percentage:

Net income / total assets × 100 = ROA

If net income is £30, and total assets are £420, the ROA is:

30 / 420 = 0.0714 × 100 = 7.14 %

A variation of this formula can be used to calculate return on net assets (RONA):

Net income / fixed assets + working capital = RONA

And, on occasion, the formula will separate after-tax interest expense from net income:

Net income + interest expense / total assets = ROA

It is therefore important to understand what each component of the formula actually represents.

Some experts recommend using the net income value at the end of the given period, and the assets value from beginning of the period or an average value taken over the complete period, rather than an end-of-the-period value; otherwise, the calculation will include assets that have accumulated during the year, which can be misleading.

return on capital *Fin* a ratio of the profit made in a financial year as a percentage of the capital employed

return on capital employed *Fin* indicates the productivity of capital employed.

The denominator is normally calculated as the average of the capital employed at the beginning and end of year. Problems of seasonality, new capital introduced, or other factors may necessitate taking the average of a number of periods within the year. The ROCE is known as the primary ratio in a ratio pyramid. *See also* **capital employed**

return on equity *Fin* the ratio of a company's net income as a percentage of shareholders' funds.

Return on equity (ROE) is easy to calculate and is applicable to a majority of industries. It is probably the most widely used measure of how well a company is performing for its shareholders.

It is calculated by dividing the net income shown on the income statement (usually of the past year) by shareholders' equity, which appears on the balance sheet:

Net income / owners' equity × 100% = return on equity

For example, if net income is £450 and equity is £2,500, then:

450 / 2,500 = 0.18 × 100% = 18 % return on equity

Return on equity for most companies should be in double figures; investors often look for 15% or higher, while a return of 20% or more is considered excellent. Seasoned investors also review five-year average ROE, to gauge consistency.

return on investment *Fin* a ratio of the profit made in a financial year as a percentage of an investment

EXAMPLE The most basic expression of ROI can be found by dividing a company's net profit (also called net earnings) by the total investment (total debt plus total equity), then multiplying by 100 to arrive at a percentage:

Net profit / Total investment × 100 = ROI

If, say, net profit is £30 and total investment is £250, the ROI is:

30 / 250 = 0.12 × 100 = 12%

A more complex variation of ROI is an equation known as the Du Pont formula:

(Net profit after taxes / Total assets) = (Net profit after taxes / Sales) × Sales / Total assets

If, for example, net profit after taxes is £30, total assets are £250, and sales are £500, then:

30 / 250 = 30 / 500 × 500 / 250 =12% = 6% × 2 = 12%

Champions of this formula, which was developed by the Du Pont Company in the 1920s, say that it helps reveal how a company has both deployed its assets and controlled its costs, and how it can achieve the same percentage return in different ways.

For shareholders, the variation of the basic ROI formula used by investors is:

Net income + (current value – original value) / original value × 100 = ROI

If, for example, somebody invests £5,000 in a company and a year later has earned £100 in dividends, while the value of the shares is £5,200, the return on investment would be:

100 + (5,200 – 5,000) / 5,000 × 100 (100 + 200) / 5,000 × 100 = 300 / 5,000 =.06 × 100 = 6% ROI

It is vital to understand exactly what a return on investment measures, for example, assets, equity, or sales. Without this understanding, comparisons may be misleading. It is also important to establish whether the net profit figure used is before or after provision for taxes.

return on net assets *Fin* a ratio of the profit made in a financial year as a percentage of the assets of a company

return on sales *Fin* a company's operating profit or loss as a percentage of total sales for a given period, typically a year. *See also* **profit margin**

EXAMPLE Return on sales shows how efficiently management uses the sales income, thus reflecting its ability to manage costs and overheads and operate efficiently. It also indicates a firm's ability to withstand adverse conditions such as falling prices, rising costs, or declining sales. The higher the figure, the better a company is able to endure price wars and falling prices. It is calculated using the basic formula:

Operating profit / total sales × 100 = Percentage return on sales

So, if a company earns £30 on sales of £400, its return on sales is:

30 / 400 = 0.075 × 100 = 7.5%

Some calculations use operating profit before subtracting interest and taxes; others use after-tax income. Either figure is acceptable as long as ROS comparisons are consistent. Using income before interest and taxes will produce a higher ratio.

Return on sales has its limits, since it sheds no light on the overall cost of sales or the four factors that contribute to it: materials, labour, production overheads, and administrative and selling overheads.

returns to scale *Econ* the proportionate increase in a country's or firm's output as a result of proportionate increases in all its inputs

revaluation *Econ* the restoration of the value of a country's depreciated currency, for example, by encouraging exports to increase foreign exchange

revaluation of currency *Fin* an increase in the value of a currency in relation to others. In situations where there is a floating exchange rate, a currency will normally find its own level automatically but this will not happen if there is a fixed exchange rate. Should a government have persistent balance of payment surpluses, it may exceptionally decide to revalue its currency, making imports cheaper but its exports more expensive.

revaluation reserve *Fin* money set aside to account for the fact that the values of assets may vary due to accounting in different currencies

revalue *Fin* to change the exchange rate of a currency

Revans, Reginald William (*b.* 1907) *Gen Mgt* British educator and academic. Originator of *action learning*, explained in the book of the same name (1980), which rejected the traditional approach to *management education* in favour of learning from sharing problems with others.

revenue *Fin* the income generated by a product or service over a period of time

revenue anticipation note *Fin* a government-issued debt instrument for which expected income from taxation is collateral

revenue bond *Fin* a bond that a government issues, to be repaid from the money made from the project financed with it

revenue centre *Fin* a centre devoted to raising revenue with no responsibility for costs, for example, a sales centre

revenue ledger *Fin* a record of all income received by an organisation

revenue sharing *Fin* **1.** distribution to states by the US federal government of money that it collects in taxes **2.** the distribution of income within limited partnerships

revenue stamp *Fin* a stamp that a government issues to certify that somebody has paid a tax

revenue tariff *Fin* a tax levied on imports or exports to raise revenue for a national government

reversal stop *Fin* a price at which a trader stops buying and starts selling a security, or vice-versa

reverse bear hug *Gen Mgt see* **bear hug**

reverse commuter *Gen Mgt* a commuter who travels to work in the opposite direction to the majority of people (*slang*)

reverse engineering *Ops* the taking apart of a product to establish how it was put together. Reverse engineering enables a company to redesign a product. It also enables competitors to analyse the composition, technology, and development of rival products. *Also known as* **decompilation**

reverse leverage *Fin* the negative flow of cash, or borrowing money at a rate of interest higher than the expected rate of return on investing the money borrowed

reverse mortgage *Fin* a financial arrangement in which a lender such as a bank takes over a mortgage then pays an annuity to the homeowner

reverse split *Fin* the issuing to shareholders of a fraction of one share for every share that they own. *See also* **split**

reverse takeover *Gen Mgt* the **takeover** of a large company by a smaller one, or the takeover of a public company by a private one

revolving charge account *Fin* a charge account with a company for use in buying that company's goods with **revolving credit**

revolving credit *Fin* a credit facility which allows the borrower, within an overall credit limit and for a set period, to borrow or repay debt as required

revolving fund *Fin* a fund the resources of which are replenished from the revenue of the projects that it finances

revolving loan *Fin* a loan facility where the borrower can choose the number and timing of withdrawals against their bank loan and where any money repaid may be reborrowed at a future date. Such loans are available both to businesses and personal customers.

reward management *HR* the establishment, maintenance, and development of a system that rewards the work done by employees. Reward management involves offering not only **basic pay**, but also an **incentive scheme** and **fringe benefits**. Levels of reward may be based on different criteria. Some involve **performance appraisal** to determine whether an employee merits a certain reward, while others may be dependent on length of service, type of job, or team or company performance. The notion of a reward system is gradually replacing the traditional idea of a standard pay system, as it

---

Advertising is what you do when you can't go see somebody. That's all it is.   *Fairfax Cone*

incorporates all aspects of employee compensation into one package.

Ricardo, David (1772–1823) *Gen Mgt* British economist. Developer of the concept of *comparative advantage*, as explained in his book *Principles of Political Economy* (1820).

rich media *E-com* technology that can integrate audio, video, and high-resolution graphics

Ridderstråle, Jonas (*b.* 1966) *Gen Mgt* Swedish academic. See **Nordström, Kjell**

ride the curve *E-com* to take advantage of rapid growth in demand for a new technology as it becomes widely adopted (*slang*)

rigged market *Fin* a market where two or more parties are buying and selling securities among themselves to give the impression of active trading with the intention of attracting investors to purchase the shares. This practice is illegal in the majority of jurisdictions.

right first time *Ops* a concept integral to *total quality management*, where there is a commitment to customers not to make mistakes. The approach requires employees at all levels to commit to, and take responsibility for, achieving this goal. *Quality circles* are sometimes used as a method to help in this process.

rights issue *Fin* an issue of new shares to existing holders who have the right to buy them at a discount

rightsizing *Gen Mgt corporate restructuring*, or *rationalisation*, with the aim of reducing costs and improving efficiency and effectiveness. Rightsizing is often used as a euphemism for *downsizing*, or *delayering*, with the suggestion that it is not as far-reaching. Rightsizing can also be used to describe increasing the size of an organisation, perhaps as an attempt to correct a previous downsizing, or delayering, exercise.

rights letter *Fin see **letter of allotment***

rights offer *Fin see **rights issue***

rights offering *Fin* an offering for sale of a *rights issue*

ring *Fin* **1.** a trading pit **2.** a concert party **3.** a trading session on the London Metal Exchange

ring-fence *Fin* **1.** to set aside a sum of money for a specific project **2.** to allow one company within a group to go into liquidation without affecting the viability of the group as a whole or any other company within it

ring member *Fin* a member of the London Metal Exchange

ring trading *Fin* business conducted in a trading pit

rising bottoms *Fin* a pattern on a graph of the price of a security or commodity against time that shows an upward price movement following a period of low prices (*slang*) See also *chartist*

risk *Gen Mgt* the possibility of suffering damage or loss in the face of uncertainty about the outcome of actions, future events, or circumstances. Organisations are exposed to various types of risk including damage to property, injury to personnel, financial loss, and legal liability. These may affect profitability, hinder the achievement of objectives, or lead to business interruption or failure. Risk may be deemed high or low depending on the probability of an adverse outcome. Risks that can be quantified on the basis of past experience are insurable and those that cannot be calculated are uninsurable.

risk-adjusted return on capital *Fin* return on capital calculated in a way that takes into account the risks associated with income.
⌐EXAMPLE¬ Being able to compare a high-risk, potentially high-return investment with a low-risk, lower-return investment helps answer a key question that confronts every investor: is it worth the risk?

There are several ways to calculate risk-adjusted return. Each has its strengths and shortcomings. All require particular data, such as an investment's rate of return, the risk-free return rate for a given period, and a market's performance and its standard deviation.

The choice of calculation depends on an investor's focus: whether it is on upside gains or downside losses.

Perhaps the most widely used is the **Sharpe ratio**. This measures the potential impact of return volatility on expected return and the amount of return earned per unit of risk. The higher a fund's Sharpe ratio, the better its historical risk-adjusted performance, and the higher the number the greater the return per unit of risk. The formula is:

(Portfolio return – Risk-free return) / Std deviation of portfolio return = Sharpe ratio

Take, for example, two investments, one returning 54%, the other 26%. At first glance, the higher figure clearly looks like the better choice, but because of its high volatility it has a Sharpe ratio of .279, while the investment with a lower return has a ratio of .910. On a risk-adjusted basis the latter would be the wiser choice.

The Treynor ratio also measures the excess of return per unit of risk. Its formula is:

(Portfolio return – Risk-free return) / Portfolio's beta = Treynor ratio

In this formula (and others that follow), **beta** is a separately calculated figure that describes the tendency of an investment to respond to marketplace swings. The higher beta the greater the volatility, and vice versa.

A third formula, Jensen's measure, is often used to rate a money manager's performance against a market index, and whether or not a investment's risk was worth its reward. The formula is:

(Portfolio return – Risk-free return) – Portfolio beta × (Benchmark return – Risk-free return) = Jensen's measure

risk analysis *Gen Mgt* the identification of risks to which an organisation is exposed and the assessment of the potential impact of those risks on the organisation. The aim of risk analysis is to identify and measure the risks associated with different courses of action in order to inform the *decision-making* process. In the context of business decision-making, risk analysis is especially used in investment decisions and capital investment appraisal. Techniques used in risk analysis include sensitivity analysis, probability analysis, *simulation*, and modelling. Risk analysis may be used to develop an organisational *risk profile*, and also may be the first stage in a *risk management* programme.

risk arbitrage *Fin arbitrage* without certainty of profit

risk assessment *Gen Mgt* the determination of the level of risk in a particular course of action. Risk assessments are an important tool in areas such as *health and safety* management and *environmental management*. Results of a risk assessment can be used, for example, to identify areas in which safety can be improved. Risk assessment can also be used to determine more intangible forms of risk, including economic and social risk, and can inform the *scenario planning* process. The amount of risk involved in a particular course of action is compared to its expected benefits to provide evidence for decision-making.

risk-bearing economy of scale *Fin* conducting business on such a large scale that the risk of loss is reduced because it is spread over

so many independent events, as in the issuance of insurance policies

risk capital *Fin see venture capital*

risk factor *Gen Mgt* the degree of risk in a project or other business activity

risk-free return *Fin* the profit made from an investment that involves no risk

risk management *Gen Mgt* the range of activities undertaken by an organisation to control and minimise threats to the continuing efficiency, profitability, and success of its operations. The process of risk management includes the identification and analysis of risks to which the organisation is exposed, the assessment of potential impacts on the business, and deciding what action can be taken to eliminate or reduce risk and deal with the impact of unpredictable events causing loss or damage. Risk management strategies include taking out insurance against financial loss or legal liability and introducing safety or security measures.

risk profile *Gen Mgt* **1.** an outline of the risks to which an organisation is exposed. An organisational risk profile may be developed in the course of *risk analysis* and used for *risk management*. It examines the nature of the threats faced by an organisation, the likelihood of adverse effects occurring, and the level of disruption and costs associated with each type of risk. **2.** an analysis of the willingness of individuals or organisations to take risks. A risk profile describes the level of risk considered acceptable by an individual or by the leaders of an organisation, and considers how this will affect *decision-making* and *corporate strategy*.

ROA *abbr Fin* return on assets

robot *Ops* a programmable machine equipped with sensing capabilities used in *production* environments. Robots are used in automatic assembly and *automated handling* situations.

robotics *Gen Mgt* the industrial use of robots to perform repetitive tasks. Robotics is an application of artificial intelligence.

rocket scientist *Fin* an employee of a financial institution who creates innovative securities that usually include derivatives (*slang*)

Roddick, Anita Lucia (*b.* 1942) *Gen Mgt* British business executive. Founder of the Body Shop, whose principles, reflected in the company's *core values* of *social responsibility* and care for the environment, are explained in her autobiography *Business as Unusual* (2000).

The only reason to invest in the market is because you think you know something others don't.
R. Foster Winans

rodo kinko *Fin* in Japan, a financial institution specialising in providing credit for small businesses

ROE *abbr Fin* return on equity

Roethlisberger, Fritz Jules (1898–1974) *Gen Mgt* US academic. Collaborated with *Elton Mayo* in the *Hawthorne experiments*, leading the research and data analysis and publicising the findings in *Management and the Worker* (1939).

rogue trader *Fin* a dealer in stocks and shares who uses illegal methods to make profits

ROI *abbr Fin* return on investment

role ambiguity *Gen Mgt* a lack of clarity on the part of an employee about the expectations of colleagues concerning his or her role within an organisation. Role ambiguity may occur in newly created posts or in positions that are undergoing change. When role ambiguity extends to responsibilities or priorities it can lead to *role conflict*.

role conflict *Gen Mgt* a situation in which two or more job requirements are incompatible. Role conflict can arise from others' misperceptions of what the priorities of a role holder should be. It may also be caused by a division of loyalties between departmental peers and the organisation, or between personal professional ethics and those of the organisation.

role culture *Gen Mgt* a style of *corporate culture*, identified by *Charles Handy*, which assumes that employees are rational and that roles can be defined and discharged within clearly defined procedures. An organisation with a role culture is believed to be generally very stable but poor at implementing *change management*.

role playing *HR* performing either as yourself in a contrived situation, in order to analyse how you react, or in the manner expected of another person. The role playing technique is a useful *training* tool, as it enables trainees to gain a better understanding of themselves, other people, new situations, and different jobs.

rolling budget *Fin* a budget continuously updated by adding a further accounting period (month or quarter) when the earliest accounting period has expired. Its use is particularly beneficial where future costs and/or activities cannot be forecast accurately. *Also known as* **continuous budget**

rolling forecast *Fin* a continuously updated forecast whereby each time actual results are reported, a further forecast period is added and intermediate period forecasts are updated

roll-out *Mkting* the full-scale implementation of an advertising campaign or marketing programme

roll up *Fin* the addition of interest amounts to principal in loan repayments

root cause analysis *Gen Mgt* a technique used in *problem-solving* to identify the underlying reason why something has gone wrong or why a difficulty has arisen. The root cause of a problem may be identified by repeatedly asking the question 'Why?', by examining relationships of cause and effect, or by defining the distinctive features of the problem and developing a number of hypotheses that can be tested. Root cause analysis has been criticised on the grounds that it presupposes a single source for a problem, while in reality the situation may be more complex.

rootless capitalism *Gen Mgt* a form of capitalism that is not tied to a specific country or economy

rort (*ANZ*) *Gen Mgt* an illegal or underhand strategy

ROS *abbr Fin* return on sales

RosettaNet *E-com* a consortium focusing on the development of e-business interfaces and a common global business language that would permit sharing of efficient e-business processes, for example, manufacturing, distribution, and sales

rostered day off *HR see RDO*

ROTFL *abbr Gen Mgt* rolling on the floor laughing (*slang*)

round figures *Fin* figures that have been adjusted up or down to the nearest 10, 100, 1,000, and so on

rounding *Stats* the practice of reducing the number of significant digits in a number, for example, expressing a figure that has four decimal places with only two decimal places

router *Gen Mgt* a telecommunications device used to transfer calls to an alternative network that may offer cheaper rates

routing number (*US*) *Fin* = *sort code*

royalties *Fin* a proportion of the income from the sale of a product paid to its creator, for example, an inventor, author, or composer

RPI *abbr Econ* retail price index

Technology—the knack of so arranging the world that we need not experience it. *Max Frisch*

RPIX *Fin* an index based on the Retail Price Index that excludes mortgage interest payments and is commonly referred to as the underlying rate of inflation

RPIY *Fin* an index based on the Retail Price Index that excludes mortgage interest payments and indirect taxation

RPM *abbr Mkting* resale price maintenance

RSI *abbr Gen Mgt* repetitive strain injury

RTM *abbr Gen Mgt* read the manual (*slang*)

RTSC *abbr Gen Mgt* read the source code (*slang*)

RUBBY *Mkting* Rich Urban Biker (*slang*)

Rucker plan *Ops* a type of *gain sharing* scheme that is concerned with the value added by labour. The Rucker plan was developed in the 1950s by Allen Rucker. A typical Rucker plan includes a *suggestion scheme*, a committee system, and a *bonus* formula, based on *value added*. It assesses the relationship between the value added to goods as they pass through the manufacturing process, and the total labour costs. Bonuses are earned when the current ratio is better than the base ratio over a given time period. A Rucker plan usually has a far less elaborate structure than the similar *Scanlon plan*.

rule of 78 *Fin* a method used to calculate the rebate on a loan with front-loaded interest that has been repaid early. It takes into account the fact that as the loan is repaid, the share of each monthly payment related to interest decreases, while the share related to repayment increases.

rumortrage (*US*) *Fin* speculation in securities issued by companies that are rumoured to be the target of an imminent takeover attempt (*slang*)

run 1. *Fin* an incidence of bank customers en masse and simultaneously withdrawing their entire funds because of a lack of confidence in the institution **2.** *Fin* an incidence of owners of holdings in a particular currency selling en masse and simultaneously usually because of a lack of confidence in the currency **3.** *Stats* an uninterrupted sequence of the same value in a statistical series

running account credit *Fin* an overdraft facility, credit card, or similar system that allows customers to borrow up to a specific limit and reborrow sums previously repaid by either writing a cheque or using their card

running yield *Fin see* yield

run with something *Gen Mgt* to pursue an idea or project (*slang*)

rust belt (*US*) *Gen Mgt* the manufacturing areas in the US Midwest that have experienced severe decline following the move away from manufacturing to service industries (*slang*)

One of the most important tasks of a manager is to eliminate his people's excuses for failure.
                                                              Robert Townsend

SA *abbr Fin* Société Anonyme, Sociedad Anónima, Sociedade Anónima

sabbatical *HR* a period of *special leave*, traditionally a year, granted to an employee for the purpose of study, work experience, or travel

sabotage *Gen Mgt* a deliberate action to damage property or equipment. In an industrial context sabotage may be undertaken by employees who have a grievance against an employer in order to halt production or undermine the efficiency of an organisation. Sabotage of this type may include time wasting or other measures designed to reduce *productivity*. Sabotage against organisations is also undertaken by terrorist or political groups in protest against their actions or policies. Security measures may be necessary to prevent sabotage.

SADC *abbr Fin* Southern African Development Community: an organisation that aims to harmonise economic development in countries of Southern Africa. Member countries are Angola, Botswana, Democratic Republic of Congo, Lesotho, Malawi, Mauritius, Mozambique, Namibia, South Africa, Seychelles, Swaziland, Tanzania, Zambia, Zimbabwe.

safe custody *Fin see safe keeping*

safe hands *Fin* **1.** investors who buy securities and are unlikely to sell in the short- to medium-term **2.** securities held by friendly investors

safe keeping *Fin* the holding of share certificates, deeds, wills, or a locked deed box on behalf of customers by a financial institution. Securities are often held under the customer's name in a locked cabinet in the vault so that if the customer wishes to sell, the bank can forward the relevant certificate to the broker. A will is also normally held in this way so that it may be handed to the executor on the customer's death. Deed boxes are always described as 'contents unknown to the bank'. Most institutions charge a fee for this service. *Also known as* **safe custody**

safety stock *Fin* the quantity of stocks of raw materials, work in progress, and finished goods which are carried in excess of the expected usage during the lead time of an activity. The safety stock reduces the probability of operations having to be suspended due to running out of stocks.

salad
let's toss it around and see if it makes a salad *Gen Mgt* let's try this idea and see if it is successful (*slang*)

salaried partner *Fin* a partner, often a junior one, who receives a regular salary, detailed in the partnership agreement

salary *HR* a form of *pay* given to employees at regular intervals in exchange for the work they have done. Traditionally, a salary is a form of remuneration given to professional employees on a monthly basis. In modern usage, the word refers to any form of pay that employees receive on a regular basis, and it is often used interchangeably with the term *wages*. A salary is normally paid straight into an employee's account.

salary ceiling *HR* **1.** the highest level on a *pay scale* that a particular employee can achieve under their contract **2.** an upper limit on *pay* imposed by government or according to *trade union* and employer agreements

salary review *HR* a reassessment of an individual employee's rate of *pay*, usually carried out on an annual basis

salary scale *HR see pay scale*

sale and leaseback *Fin* the sale of an asset, usually buildings, to a third party that then leases it back to the owner. It is used by a company as a way of raising finance. *Also known as* **renting back**

sale by instalments *Fin see hire purchase*

sale by tender *Fin* the sale of an asset to interested parties who have been invited to make an offer. It is sold to the party that makes the highest offer. *See also* **issue by tender**

sales *Mkting* the activity of selling a company's products or services, the income generated by this, or the department that deals with selling

sales channel *Gen Mgt* a means of distributing products to the marketplace, either directly to the end customer, or indirectly through intermediaries such as retailers or dealers

sales conference *Mkting* a conference at which the members of a sales team are brought together for a review or a significant announcement, such as a product launch.

The race is over, but the work never is done while the power to work remains. Oliver Wendell Holmes, Jr

Sales conferences are also useful for ensuring that sales representatives are fully aware of company policies, products, and support; without these, time spent with customers may be unproductive. They also play a key role in motivating sales teams and building team spirit, an important factor for people who spend most of their time working alone. In addition, conferences can be used to reward high achievement. Many organisations run annual incentive and recognition programmes for sales employees, and using a national conference as the occasion for the award ceremony can confer real status on the winner and raise the profile of the programme among the whole salesforce, encouraging high levels of participation and effort.

sales contest *Mkting* a prize competition for salespeople, often part of an ***incentive scheme***, designed to increase sales. A sales contest winner is usually the person who has achieved the most sales for a particular time period.

salesforce *Mkting* a group of salespeople or sales representatives responsible for the sales of either a single product or the entire range of an organisation's products. A salesforce normally reports to a ***sales manager***. *Also known as **sales team***

salesforce communications *Mkting* communications aimed at improving the performance and market awareness of a salesforce

sales forecast *Mkting* a prediction of future sales, based mainly on past sales performance. Sales forecasting takes into account the economic climate, current sales trends, company capacity for production, ***company policy***, and ***market research***. A sales forecast can be a good indicator of future sales in stable market conditions, but may be less reliable in times of rapid market change.

sales manager *Mkting* the manager directly responsible for the planning, organisation, and performance of the ***salesforce***

sales network *Mkting* the distribution network by which goods and services are sold. A sales network will include both independent agents and retailers.

sales office *Mkting* the department responsible for selling a company's products or services, or the office in the company's premises that this department occupies

sales order *Fin* an acknowledgement by a supplier of a purchase order. It may contain terms which override those of the purchaser.

sales outlet *Mkting* a company's office that deals with customers in a particular region or country

sales per employee *Fin* an indicator of labour productivity. *See also **profit per employee***

sales plan *Gen Mgt* the development of the future objectives of a sales department in order to improve performance and increase sales. A sales plan is a form of ***business plan*** that sets out the short- and long-term opportunities for the sales department, concentrating on building on the department's strengths and analysing and avoiding weaknesses. It also includes the setting of future sales objectives, based on realistic projections, looking at future costs, and taking into account the objectives of other departments.

sales presentation *Mkting* a structured product presentation using a binder, flipchart, or laptop computer

sales promotion *Mkting* activities, usually short-term, designed to attract attention to a particular product and to increase its sales using ***advertising*** and publicity. Sales promotion usually runs in conjunction with an advertising campaign that offers free samples or money-off coupons. During the period of a sales promotion, the product may be offered at a reduced price and the campaign may be supported by additional telephone or door-to-door selling or by competitions. *Also known as **promotion***

sales promotion agency *Mkting* an organisation that specialises in planning, creating, and implementing sales promotion activities

sales quota *Gen Mgt* a target set for the ***salesforce*** stating the number and range of products or services that should be sold

sales representative *Mkting* a salesperson selling the products or services of a particular organisation or manufacturer. Sales representatives are sometimes employed directly by a company as part of the ***salesforce***, or they may work independently and be employed by contract. Sales representatives are often paid on a commission basis.

sales resistance *Mkting* a potential customer's refusal to allow a ***sales representative's*** sales pitch to persuade them to buy. Sales resistance may be caused, for example, by lack of interest in, or determined dislike of, the product or service offered.

Lack of confidence is not the result of difficulty; the difficulty comes from lack of confidence.   **Seneca**

sales statistics *Mkting* data relating to the sales of a particular **product**, service, or **brand**. Sales statistics include numbers and types of products sold, areas where they are sold, calls and visits made, contacts established, categories of customers, costs and time spent on sales activities, and administration. These statistics are often used in conjunction with the **sales plan** and for sales forecasting. They can also be used to identify areas of weakness in sales support staff and to identify areas for training. Statistics can also contribute to the identification of profitable product lines or products to **abandon**.

sales team *Mkting see* **salesforce**

sales territory *Mkting* a defined area within which a designated salesperson is responsible for selling a product or service. A sales territory is usually organised along geographical lines, for example, counties or regions, but it can also be defined by **market sector** or by product group.

sales turnover *Mkting* the total amount sold within a specified time period, usually a year. Sales turnover is often expressed in monetary terms but can also be expressed in terms of the total amount of stock or products sold.

salmon day *Gen Mgt* a day spent making a great deal of effort to achieve something but getting nowhere (*slang*)

sample *Stats* a subset of a population in a statistical study chosen so that selected properties of the overall population can be investigated

sample size *Stats* the number of individuals included in a statistical survey

sample survey *Stats* a statistical study of a sample of individuals designed to collect information on specific subjects such as buying habits or voting behaviour

sampling 1. *Mkting* a sales promotion technique in which customers and prospects are offered a free sample of a product **2.** *Ops* the selection of a small proportion of a set of items being studied, from which valid inferences about the whole set or population can be made. Sampling makes it possible to obtain valid research results when it is impracticable to survey the whole population. The size of the sample needed for valid results depends on a number of factors, including the uniformity of the population being studied and the level of accuracy required. The technique is based on the laws of probability, and a number of different sampling methods can be used, including **random sampling** and **non-**

random sampling. Specialised applications of sampling include **activity sampling**, **acceptance sampling**, and **attribute sampling**.

sampling design *Stats* the procedure by which a particular sample is chosen from a population

sampling error *Stats* the difference between the population characteristic being estimated in a statistical study and the result produced by the sample investigated

sampling units *Stats* the elements chosen to be sampled by a sampling design

sampling variation *Stats* variation between different samples of the same size taken from the same population

samurai bond *Fin* a bond issue denominated in yen and issued in Japan by a foreign institution

sandbag *Fin* in a hostile **takeover** situation, to enter into talks with the bidder and attempt to prolong them as long as possible, in the hope that a white **knight** will appear and rescue the target company (*slang*)

S&L *abbr Fin* savings and loan association

S&P 500 *abbr Fin* Standard & Poor's Composite 500 Stock Index

S&P Index *abbr Fin* Standard & Poor's Composite 500 Index

sanity check *Gen Mgt* a check to verify that no obvious mistakes have been made (*slang*)

Santa Claus rally (*US*) *Fin* a rise in stock prices in the last week of the year

sarakin *Fin* the Japanese term for a finance company that charges high interest rates to personal customers

SARL *abbr Fin* Société à responsabilité limitée

SARS *abbr Fin* South African Revenue Service

SAS *abbr Fin* Statement of Auditing Standards

satellite centre *Gen Mgt* a **telecentre** that houses employees from a single organisation

save as you earn *HR* a system for saving on a regular basis that is encouraged by the government through tax concessions. *Abbr* **SAYE**

savings *Fin* money set aside by consumers for a particular purpose, to meet contingencies, or to provide an income during retirement. Savings, money in deposit and savings accounts, differ from investments, for example, on the stock market, in that they are not subject to price fluctuations and are thus considered safer.

The world is filled with unsuccessful men of talent.   *Ray Kroc*

savings account *Fin* an account with a financial institution that pays interest. *See also fixed rate, gross interest, net interest*

savings and loan association *Fin* a chartered bank that offers savings accounts, pays dividends, and invests in new mortgages. *See also thrift institution*

savings bank *Fin* a bank that specialises in managing small investments. *See also thrift institution*

savings bond *Fin* a US bond that an individual buys from the federal government

savings certificate *Fin see National Savings Certificate*

savings function *Econ* an expression of the extent to which people save money instead of spending it

savings ratio *Econ* the proportion of the income of a country or household that is saved in a particular period

SAYE *abbr HR* save as you earn

SC *abbr Fin* Securities Commission

scaleability *E-com* the capability of the hardware and software that support an e-business to grow in capacity as transaction demand increases

Scanlon plan *HR* a type of *gain sharing* plan that pays a *bonus* to employees for incremental improvements. The Scanlon plan was developed by Joseph Scanlon in the 1930s. A typical Scanlon plan includes an employee *suggestion scheme*, a committee system, and a formula-based bonus system. The simplest formula is: base ratio = HR payroll costs divided by net sales or production value. A Scanlon organisation is characterised by *teamwork* and *employee participation*. A bonus is paid when the current ratio is better than that of the base period. A Scanlon plan focuses attention on the variables over which the organisation and its employees have some control. *See also Rucker plan*

scatter *Stats* the amount by which a set of observations deviates from its mean

scatter chart *or* **scatter diagram** *Stats* a chart or diagram that plots a sample of bivariate observations in two dimensions

scenario *Gen Mgt* a possible future state of affairs or sequence of events. Scenarios are imagined or projected on the basis of current circumstances and trends and expectations of change in the future.

scenario planning *Gen Mgt* a technique that requires the use of a scenario in the process of *strategic planning* to aid the development of *corporate strategy* in the face of uncertainty about the future. Scenario planning was developed in a military context during the 1940s. Its use in a business context was pioneered at Royal Dutch Shell during the 1960s and increased after the 1972 oil crisis. The process of identifying alternative scenarios of the future, based on a range of differing assumptions, can help managers anticipate changes in the business environment and raise awareness of the frame of reference within which they are operating. The scenarios are then used to assist in both the development of strategies for dealing with unexpected events and the choice between alternative strategic options.

Schein, Edgar (*b*. 1928) *Gen Mgt* US academic. The first to define *corporate culture* in *Organizational Culture and Leadership* (1985), and the developer of the notion of the *psychological contract*, originated by *Chris Argyris*.
  Schein completed a PhD in social psychology at Harvard and, after graduating in 1952, carried out research into leadership as part of the Army Program. He joined MIT in 1956 and has remained there ever since. At MIT Schein researched the similarities between the brainwashing of POWs and the techniques of indoctrination used by corporations. Out of this came Schein's book *Coercive Persuasion*. His subsequent work and writing has mainly been on organisational culture, organisation development, and career development.

schmooze *Gen Mgt* to behave flatteringly during a social event towards somebody who might be in a position to benefit your career (*slang*)

Schön, Donald (1931–97) *Gen Mgt* US academic. Co-author, with Chris Argyris, of *Organizational Learning* (1978). *See also Argyris, Christopher*

Schonberger, Richard (*b*. 1937) *Gen Mgt* US industrial engineer and writer. Known for showing how techniques such as *total quality management* and *just-in-time* can be used to achieve *world class manufacturing*. Author of *World Class Manufacturing* (1986).

Schumacher, Ernst Friedrich (1911–77) *Gen Mgt* German economist. Author of *Small is Beautiful* (1973), a counterblast to the dominance of big companies. Schumacher developed his people-centred approach to life and business working alongside *Reg Revans*.

The least one can say about power is that a vocation for it is suspicious.   *Jean Rostand*

science park *Gen Mgt* an area developed as a location for high-tech or research-based companies. Usually developed by a university or local authority, a science park is often in the same locality as a higher education establishment. *US term* **research park**

scientific management *Gen Mgt, HR* an analytical approach to managing activities by optimising efficiency and **productivity** through measurement and control. Scientific management theories, attributed to **Frederick Winslow Taylor**, dominated the 20th century, and many management techniques such as **benchmarking**, **total quality management**, and **business process re-engineering** result from a scientific management approach. Other figures such as **Henry Gantt** and **Frank and Lillian Gilbreth** were firmly in the scientific school and furthered its influence, particularly through the **time and motion study**. Such was the dominance of Taylor's influence that scientific management is also known as Taylorism. The main criticism of Taylorism is that it degenerated into an inhumane and mechanistic approach to working, treating people like machines.

scorched earth policy *Gen Mgt* destructive actions taken by an organisation in defence against a hostile **takeover**. Extreme actions under a scorched earth policy may include voluntary liquidation or selling off critical assets. A scorched earth policy may come into play if the value of the company to be acquired exceeds the value of the company making a hostile bid. (*slang*)

scrap *Fin* discarded material that has some value

screen-based activity *Gen Mgt* a task that requires access to a computer

screening study *Stats* a medical statistical study of a population carried out to investigate the prevalence of a disease

screen popping *Gen Mgt see* **computer telephony integration** (*slang*)

screensaver *E-com* a program that displays a series of moving images, designed to prevent a static image being burnt into the phosphor monitor screen when a computer is idle

scrip dividend *Fin* a dividend that shareholders can accept in the form of possibly fractional shares of the company instead of cash

scrip issue *Fin* a proportional issue of free shares to existing shareholders. *US term* **stock split**. *Also known as* **bonus shares**, **share split**

scripophily *Fin* the collection of valueless share or bond certificates

scroll bar *E-com* a bar at the right-hand side and/or bottom of a window that enables users to view more information on a web page

SCUM *abbr Gen Mgt* Self-Centred Urban Male (*slang*)

Sdn *abbr Fin* Sendirian

seagull manager *HR* a manager who is brought in to deal with a project, makes a lot of fuss, achieves nothing, and then leaves (*slang*)

SEAQ *abbr Fin* Stock Exchange Automated Quotations System: the London Stock Exchange's system for UK securities. It is a continuously updated computer database containing quotations that also records prices at which transactions have been struck.

SEAQ International *abbr Fin* Stock Exchange Automated Quotations System International: the London Stock Exchange's system for overseas securities. It is a continuously updated computer database containing quotations that also records prices at which transactions have been struck.

search *E-com* the facility that enables visitors to a website to look for the information they want.

Search is one of the most common activities that people carry out on a website, and therefore needs to be prominently displayed—preferably on every page, near the top. There are essentially two approaches to website search: basic search, suitable for small websites of 50 pages or under, and advanced search, for larger websites, which allows a user to refine their search on the basis of various parameters.

In either case, because search is an exclusively functional activity, the search results should be very clear and contain no distractions. Each set of results should include: the title of the web page that it refers to, shown in bold type and hyperlinked to that page; a two-line summary describing the content on that page; the URL for the page, and its date of publication.

search engine *E-com* a website that enables users to conduct **keyword** searches of indexed information on its database

search engine registration *E-com* the process of enlisting a website with a **search engine**, so that the website is selected when a user requests a search. The process involves choosing the right **keywords** and **metadata** for the documents, in order for them to be selected in as many appropriate circumstances as possible.

When registering a website with search engines, it is important to consider which will be of most benefit. Of the hundreds of search engines and directories, only a few really matter in terms of mass appeal—such as Yahoo, Google, and Alta Vista. However, there may well be specialist search engines for your particular industry, which should be on your list. All search engines used to be free to register with, but many are now charging, so consider whether they are worth the fee. An increasing number sell special placements in their search results: you choose a keyword, and when that keyword is input by a searcher, a short promotion for your website will appear. Search engines also need to be monitored regularly, as they can change the rules by which search results are presented. If your website is dropping down the results page, you may need to re-register.

seasonal adjustment *Fin* an adjustment made to accounts to allow for any short-term seasonal factors, such as Christmas sales, that may distort the figures

seasonal business *Fin* trade that is affected by seasonal factors, for example, trade in goods such as suntan products or Christmas trees

seasonal products *Mkting* products that are only marketed at particular times of the year, for example, Christmas trees or fireworks

seasonal variation *Stats* the variation of data according to particular times of the year such as winter months or a tourist season

seasoned equity *Fin* shares that have traded long enough to have a well-established value

seasoned issue *Fin* an issue for which there is a pre-existing market. *See also* **unseasoned issue**

SEATS *Fin* Stock Exchange Automatic Trading System, the electronic screen-trading system operated by the Australian Stock Exchange. It was introduced in 1987.

SEC *abbr Fin* Securities and Exchange Commission

secondary issue *Fin* an offer of listed shares that have not previously been publicly traded

secondary market *Fin* a market that trades in existing shares rather than new share issues, for example, a stock exchange. The money earned from these sales goes to the dealer or investor, not to the issuer.

secondary offering *Fin* an offering of securities of a kind that is already on the market

secondary sector *Econ* the sector of the labour force with employment options other than the wage earned in the market, consisting of married women, the semi-retired, and young people

Secondary Tax on Companies *(S Africa) Fin* see **STC**.

secondment *HR* a UK term for the temporary transfer of a member of staff to another organisation for a defined length of time, usually for a specific purpose. Secondment has grown in popularity in recent years, primarily for *career development* purposes. Secondments have been carried out between the public and private sectors as a mechanism to share management techniques and to disseminate *best practice*.

second mortgage *Fin* a loan, that uses the equity on a mortgaged property as security, taken out with a different lender than the first mortgage. As the first mortgagee holds the deeds, the second mortgagee has to register its interest with the Land Registry and cannot foreclose without the first mortgagee's permission.

second-tier market *Fin* a market in stocks and shares where the listing requirements are less onerous than for the main market, as in, for example, London's Alternative Investment Market

secretary of the board *Gen Mgt* see **company secretary**

Section 21 Company *(S Africa) Fin* a company established as a *non-profit organisation*

sector index *Fin* an index of companies in particular parts of a market whose shares are listed on a general or specialist stock exchange

secular trend *Stats* the underlying smooth movement of a *time series* over a time period of several years

secured *Fin* **1.** used to describe borrowing when the lender has a charge over an asset or assets of the borrower, for example, a mortgage or floating charge **2.** used to describe a creditor who has a charge over an asset or assets of the borrower, for example, a mortgage or floating charge. *See also* **collateral**, **security**

secured bond *Fin* a collateralised bond

secured creditors *Fin* creditors whose claims are wholly or partly secured on the assets of a business

---

secured debenture *Fin see* **debenture**

secure electronic transaction protocol *E-com see* **SET**

secure server *E-com* a combination of hardware and software that secures e-commerce credit card transactions so that there is no risk of unauthorised people gaining access to credit card details online

secure sockets layer *E-com see* **SSL**

securities account *Fin* an account that shows the value of financial assets held by a person or organisation

securities analyst *Fin* a professional person who studies the performance of securities and the companies that issue them

Securities and Exchange Commission *Fin* the US government agency responsible for establishing standards of financial reporting and accounting for public companies. *Abbr* **SEC**

Securities and Futures Authority *Fin* a self-regulatory organisation responsible for supervising the activities of institutions advising on corporate finance activity, or dealing, or facilitating deals, in securities or derivatives. *Abbr* **SFA**

Securities and Investment Board *Fin* a private company, limited by guarantee, which, along with the Bank of England, is responsible for regulating the conduct of a wide range of investment activities under the 1986 Financial Services Act. These responsibilities have been delegated to a number of self-regulatory organisations whose effectiveness is monitored by the SIB. *Abbr* **SIB**

Securities Commission *Fin* a statutory body responsible for monitoring standards in the New Zealand securities markets and for promoting investment in New Zealand. *Abbr* **SC**

securities deposit account *Fin* a brokerage account into which securities are deposited electronically

Securities Institute of Australia *Fin* a national professional body that represents people involved in the Australian securities and financial services industry. *Abbr* **SIA**

Securities Investor Protection Corporation *Fin* in the United States, a corporation created by Congress in 1970 that is a mutual insurance fund established to protect clients of securities firms. In the event of a firm being closed because of bankruptcy or financial difficulties, the SIPC will step in to recover cli-

ents' cash and securities held by the firm. The corporation's reserves are available to satisfy cash and securities that cannot be recovered up to a maximum of US$500,000, including a maximum of US$100,000 on cash claims. *Abbr* **SIPC**

securities lending *Fin* the loan of securities to those who have **sold short**

securitised paper *Fin* the **bond** or **promissory note** resulting from securitisation

security *Fin* **1.** a tradable financial asset, for example, a bond, stock, a share, or a warrant **2.** the collateral for a loan or other borrowing

security deposit *Fin* an amount of money paid before a transaction occurs to provide the seller with recourse in the event that the transaction is not concluded and this is the buyer's fault

security investment company *Fin* a financial institution that specialises in the analysis and trading of securities

seed capital *Gen Mgt* a usually modest amount of money used to convert an idea into a viable business. Seed capital is a form of **venture capital**. *US term* **seed money**

seed money (*US*) *Gen Mgt* = **seed capital**

segmentation *Stats* the division of the data in a study into regions

selection bias *Stats* the effect on a statistical or clinical trial of unmeasured variables that are unknown to the researcher

selection board *HR see* **panel interview**

selection instrument *HR see* **psychometric test**

selection interviewing *HR see* **interviewing**

selection of personnel *HR see* **recruitment**

selection test *HR see* **psychometric test**

selective pricing *Fin* setting different prices for the same product or service in different markets. This practice can be broken down as follows: category pricing, which involves cosmetically modifying a product such that the variations allow it to sell in a number of price categories, as where a range of brands is based on a common product; customer group pricing, which involves modifying the price of a product or service so that different groups of consumers pay different prices; peak pricing, setting a price which varies according to the level of demand; and service level pricing, setting a price based on the particular level of service chosen from a range.

If civilisation has risen from the Stone Age, it can rise again from the Wastepaper Age. *Jacques Barzun*

self-actualisation *HR* the maximisation of your skills and talents. Self-actualisation was considered by *Abraham Maslow* as the pinnacle of his hierarchy of needs. *Also known as self-fulfilment*

self-appraisal *HR* an assessment carried out by an individual on his or her own ability or understanding. Self-appraisal is sometimes part of the *performance appraisal* process but is also carried out as part of *continuing professional development* or *career development*.

self-assessment 1. *Ops* a systematic and regular review of the activities of an organisation and the referencing of the results against a model of *excellence* that is carried out by the organisation itself. Self-assessment allows an organisation to identify its strengths and weaknesses and to plan improvement activities. The technique came to prominence with the spread of the *EFQM Excellence Model*. **2.** *Fin* in the United Kingdom, a system that enables taxpayers to assess their own income tax and capital gains tax payments for the fiscal year

self-certification *HR* in the United Kingdom, the notification and recording of the first seven days of an employee's *sick leave*. Self-certification requires the completion of a form by the employee on their return to work, indicating the nature and duration of their illness and countersigned by a manager.

self-development *HR see personal development*

self-directed team *HR see autonomous work group*

self-employment *HR* being in business on one's own account, either on a *freelance* basis, or by reason of owning a business, and not being engaged as an *employee* under a *contract of employment*. The distinction between the self-employed and the employed is not always clear in law, but has a crucial bearing on matters such as the tax treatment of pay and the applicability of *employment protection*. A self-employed person may be an *employer* of others.

self-fulfilment *HR see self-actualisation*

self-insurance *Fin* the practice of saving money to pay for a possible loss rather than taking out an insurance policy against it

self-liquidating *Fin* providing enough income to pay off the amount borrowed for financing

self-liquidating premium *Mkting* a sales promotion technique that pays for itself, in which customers send money and vouchers or proof of purchase to obtain a premium gift

self-liquidating promotion *Mkting* a sales promotion in which the cost of the campaign is covered by the incremental revenue generated by the promotion

self-managed team *HR see autonomous work group*

self-managed work team *HR see autonomous work group*

self-managing team *HR see autonomous work group*

self-regulatory organisation *Gen Mgt* an organisation that polices its members, for example, an exchange

self-tender *Fin* in the United States, the repurchase by a corporation of its stock by way of a tender

sell and build *Gen Mgt* an approach to manufacturing in which the producer builds only when a customer has placed an order and paid for it, rather than building products for stock

seller's market *Fin* a market in which sellers can dictate prices, typically because demand is high or there is a product shortage

selling cost *Fin* cost incurred in securing orders, usually including salaries, commissions, and travelling expenses

selling season *Fin* a period in which market conditions are favourable to sellers

sell short *Fin* to sell commodities, currencies, or securities that one does not own in the expectation that prices will fall before delivery to the seller's profit. *See also bear*

seminar *Gen Mgt* a small business meeting at which participants present information or exchange ideas

semi-variable cost/semi-fixed cost/mixed cost *Fin* a cost that contains both fixed and variable components and is thus partly affected by a change in the level of activity

Semler, Ricardo (*b.* 1957) *Gen Mgt* Brazilian business executive. Owner of Semco, which he *turned around*, using three main strategies: *employee democracy*, *open-book management*, and self-setting salaries. His methods were written up in *Maverick!* (1993).

Sendirian *Gen Mgt* Malay term for 'limited'. Companies can use 'sendirian berhad' or 'Sdn Bhd' in their name instead of 'Pte Ltd'. *Abbr* **Sdn**

Bureaucracies indicate a lack of trust and mutual regard and respect.   *Shiv Nadar*

Senge, Peter (*b.* 1947) *Gen Mgt* US academic. Popularised the theory of the **learning organisation**, first suggested by **Chris Argyris** and **Donald Schön**. Senge studied how organisations develop adaptive capabilities in a world of increasing complexity and change. His work culminated in the publication of *The Fifth Discipline: The Art and Practice of the Learning Organization* (1990).

Senge studied engineering at Stanford before doing a PhD on social systems modelling at the Massachusetts Institute of Technology. He is currently director of the Center for Organizational Learning at MIT, and is also a founding partner of the training and consulting company, Innovation Associates, now part of Arthur D. Little.

senior debt *Fin* a debt whose holder has more claim on the debtor's assets than the holder of another debt. *See also* **junior debt**

senior management *Gen Mgt* the managers and executives at the highest level of an organisation. Senior management includes the **board of directors**. Senior management has responsibility for **corporate governance**, **corporate strategy**, and the interests of all the organisation's **stakeholders**. *Also known as* **management team**

senior mortgage *Fin* a mortgage whose holder has more claim on the debtor's assets than the holder of another mortgage. *See also* **junior mortgage**

sensitivity analysis *Fin* a modelling and risk assessment procedure in which changes are made to significant variables in order to determine the effect of these changes on the planned outcome. Particular attention is thereafter paid to variables identified as being of special significance.

sensitivity training *HR* group-based training designed to help participants develop interpersonal skills (see **interpersonal communication**). Sensitivity training is a form of human relations training, and was developed by **Kurt Lewin**, and others at the National Training Laboratory in the United States during the 1940s. The format most commonly used is a **training group**, or **T-Group**, consisting of between 7 and 12 people who meet together over a period of about two weeks, normally at a residential training centre. The aims are to develop sensitivity and awareness of participants' own feelings and reactions, to increase their understanding of **group dynamics**, and to help them learn to adapt

their behaviour in appropriate ways. Group activities may include discussion, games, and exercises but may also be relatively unstructured. The provision of **feedback** is a key feature. This type of training has been controversial, as the group interactions can be confrontational, and some have suggested that participants could suffer emotional harm. The popularity of T-Groups has declined since the 1960s and 1970s. Sensitivity training is also known as **laboratory training**. This term emphasises the way participants are placed in an environment in which different ways of interacting can be tried out. Lewin's early work in this field was developed at the National Training Laboratories, founded in 1947, in the United States.

separation *HR* a term used mainly in the United States to refer to **termination of service** or **resignation**

serial entrepreneur *Gen Mgt* an **entrepreneur** who sets up a string of new ventures, one after the other

seriation *Stats* the process of arranging a set of objects in a series on the basis of similarities or dissimilarities

SERPS *abbr Fin* State Earnings-Related Pension Scheme: in the United Kingdom, a state scheme designed to pay retired employees an additional pension to the standard state pension. Contributions, collected through National Insurance payments, and benefits are related to earnings. Individuals may opt out of SERPS and have their contributions directed to an occupational or personal pension.

server *E-com* a computer that provides services to another computer. Typically, a server stores data to be shared over a computer network. The computers receiving services are called **clients**.

server farm *E-com* a place where a number of server computers are located, usually providing server functions for a number of different organisations

server log *E-com see* **web log**

service *Mkting* any activity with a mix of tangible and intangible outcomes that is offered to a market with the aim of satisfying a customer's need or desire. Early **marketing** tended to distinguish a service from a physical good, but more recently these two have been seen as interrelated because service delivery frequently has physical aspects. For example, in a restaurant, service is provided by a waiter

---

No task is a long one but the task on which one dare not start. It becomes a nightmare. **Charles Baudelaire**

but physical goods, such as the food and the dining room, are also involved. In modern marketing, all forms of services and goods can be seen as *products*.

service charge 1. *Fin* a fee for any service provided, or additional fee for any enhancements to an existing service. For example, banks may charge a fee for obtaining foreign currency for customers. Residents in blocks of flats may pay an annual maintenance fee that is also referred to as a service charge. **2.** *Mkting* a gratuity usually paid in restaurants and hotels. A service charge may be voluntary or may be added as a percentage to the bill.

service contract *HR* a *contract of employment* for *executive directors* which lays down the *conditions of employment* and details of any *bonus* which may be paid, and outlines the procedure for *termination of service*

service cost centre *Fin* a cost centre providing services to other cost centres. When the output of an organisation is a service, rather than goods, an alternative name is normally used, for example, support cost centre or utility cost centre.

service/function costing *Fin* cost accounting for services or functions, for example, canteens, maintenance, personnel

service level agreement *Mkting* an agreement drawn up between a customer or client and the provider of a service or product. A service level agreement can cover a straightforward provision of a service, for example, office cleaning, or the provision of a complete function such as the *outsourcing* of the administration of a payroll or the maintenance of plant and equipment for a large company. The agreement lays down the detailed specification for the level and quality of the service to be provided. The agreement is essentially a legally binding contract.

services *Fin* value-creating activities which in themselves do not involve the supply of a physical product. Service provision may be subdivided into: pure services, where there is no physical product, such as consultancy; services with a product attached, such as the design and installation of a computer network; and products with services attached, such as the purchase of a computer with a maintenance contract.

servicing borrowing *Fin* paying the interest due on a loan

SET *abbr E-com* secure electronic transaction protocol: a payment protocol that permits secure credit card transactions over open networks such as the Internet, developed by Visa and MasterCard

set-off *Fin* an agreement between two parties to balance one debt against another or a loss against a gain

set the bar *HR* to motivate staff by setting targets that are above their current level of achievement

settlement 1. *E-com* the portion of an electronic transaction during which the customer's credit card is charged for the transaction and the proceeds are deposited into the merchant account by the acquirer **2.** *Fin* the payment of a debt or charge

settlement date *Fin* the date on which an outstanding debt or charge is due to be paid

set-up costs *Gen Mgt* the costs associated with making a workstation or equipment available for use. Set-up costs include the personnel needed to set up the equipment, the cost of down time during a new set-up, and the resources and time needed to test the new set-up to achieve the specification of the parts or materials produced.

set-up fees *E-com* the costs associated with establishing a *merchant account*, for example, application and software licensing fees and point-of-sale equipment purchases

set-up time *Ops* the time it takes to prepare, calibrate, and test a piece of equipment to produce a required output

set-up time reduction *Ops see single minute exchange of dies*

seven-day money *Fin* funds that have been placed on the money market for a term of seven days

severance package (*US*) *HR* = *redundancy package*

severance pay (*US*) *HR* = *redundancy payment*

sexual discrimination *HR* unfavourable treatment or *discrimination*, especially in employment, based on prejudice against a person's sex. Legislation against sexual discrimination is in place in many countries and many organisations have specific *personnel policies* to prevent sexual discrimination in the workplace.

sexual harassment *HR* a form of *discrimination* through the unwelcome and unwanted

---

sexual conduct of one employee towards another. Most of the victims of sexual harassment are women, and the most common forms are physical, verbal, suggestive gesturing, written messages, graphic or pictorial displays, or the emotional isolation of an individual. The effective promotion of a policy to protect employees and customers from such harassment is good organisational practice.

SFA *abbr Fin* Securities and Futures Authority

SFAS *abbr Fin* Statement of Financial Accounting Standards

SFE *abbr Fin* Sydney Futures Exchange

SGX *abbr Fin* Singapore Exchange

shadow market *Gen Mgt see* **black market**

shadow price *Fin* an increase in value which would be created by having available one additional unit of a limiting resource at its original cost. This represents the opportunity cost of not having the use of the one extra unit. This information is routinely produced when mathematical programming (especially linear programming) is used to model activity.

shakeout *Fin* the elimination of weak or cautious investors during a crisis in the financial market (*slang*)

shamrock organisation *Gen Mgt* a form of *organisation structure* with three bases on which people can be employed and on which organisations can be linked to each other. The shamrock organisation was identified by *Charles Handy*. The three bases or groups are professional managers, contracted specialists such as advertising, computing, or catering personnel, and a flexible labour force discharging part-time, temporary, or seasonal roles. *See also* **Handy, Charles**

shape up or ship out (*US*) *HR* an order to improve your performance at work or else be fired (*slang*)

share *Fin* any of the equal parts into which a company's capital stock is divided, whose owners are entitled to a proportionate share of the company's profits

share account *Fin* **1.** in the United Kingdom, an account at a building society where the account holder is a member of the society. Building societies usually offer another type of account, a deposit account, where the account holder is not a member. A share account is generally paid a better rate of interest but, in the event of the society going into liquidation, deposit account holders are given preference. **2.** in the United States, an account with a credit union that pays dividends rather than interest

share capital *Fin* the amount of capital that a company raises by issuing shares

share certificate *Fin* a document that certifies ownership of a share in a company. *US term* **stock certificate**

shared drop *Mkting* a sales promotion technique in which a number of promotional offers are delivered by hand to **prospects** at the same time

shared services *Fin* a business strategy which involves centralising certain business activities such as accounting and other transaction-oriented activities in order to reduce costs and provide better customer service

shared values *Gen Mgt see* **core values**

share exchange *Fin* a service provided by certain collective investment schemes whereby they exchange investors' existing individual shareholdings for units or shares in their funds. This saves the investor the expense of selling holdings, which can be uneconomical when dealing with small shareholdings.

share-for-share offer *Fin* a *takeover bid* where the bidder offers its own shares, or a combination of cash and shares, for the target company

shareholder *Fin* a person or organisation that owns shares in a limited company or partnership. A shareholder has a stake in the company and becomes a member of it, with rights to attend the *annual general meeting*. Since shareholders have invested money in a company, they have a vested interest in its performance, can be a powerful influence on company policy, and should consequently be considered *stakeholders* as well as shareholders. Some *pressure groups* have sought to exploit this by becoming shareholders in order to get a particular viewpoint or message across. At the same time, managers must, in order to maintain or increase the company's market value, consider their responsibility to shareholders when formulating strategy. It has been argued that on some occasions the desire to make profits to raise returns for shareholders has damaged companies because it has limited the amount of money spent in other areas, such as the development of facilities or health and safety.

shareholders' equity *Fin* a company's share capital and reserves

shareholders' perks *Fin* benefits offered to shareholders in addition to dividends, often in the form of discounts on the company's products and services

shareholder value *Fin* total return to the shareholders in terms of both dividends and share price growth, calculated as the present value of future free cash flows of the business discounted at the weighted average cost of the capital of the business less the market value of its debt

shareholder value analysis *Gen Mgt* a calculation of the value of a company by looking at the returns it gives to its shareholders. Shareholder value analysis, like the *economic theory of the firm*, assumes that the objective of a company director is to maximise the wealth of the company's shareholders. It is based on the premise that discounted cash flow principles can be applied to the business as a whole. SVA is calculated by estimating the total net value of a company and dividing this figure by the value of shares. Shareholder value analysis can be applied to assess the contribution of a business unit or to evaluate individual projects. *Abbr* **SVA**

shareholding *Fin* the shares in a limited company owned by a shareholder. *US term* **stockholding**

share incentive scheme *HR* a type of financial *incentive scheme* in which employees can acquire shares in the company in which they work and so have an interest in its financial performance. A share incentive scheme is a type of *employee share scheme*, in which employees may be given shares by their employer, or shares may be offered for purchase at an advantageous price, as a reward for personal or group performance. A *share option* is a type of share incentive scheme.

share index *Fin see* **index**

share issue *Fin* an occasion when shares in a business are offered for sale. The *capital* derived from share issues can be used for investment in the core business or for expansion into new commercial ventures.

share of voice *Mkting* an individual company's proportion of the total advertising expenditure in a sector

share option *Fin, HR* a type of *share incentive scheme* in which an employee is given the option to buy a specified number of shares at a future date, at a price agreed at the present time. Share options provide a financial benefit to the recipient only if the share price rises over the period the option is available. If the share price falls over the period, the employee is under no obligation to buy the shares. There

may be a tax advantage to the employees who participate in such a scheme. Share options may be available to all employees or operated on a discretionary basis.

shareowner *Fin* somebody who owns a share of stock

share premium *Fin* **1.** the amount by which the price at which a company sells a share exceeds its par value **2.** the amount payable for a share above its nominal value. Most shares are issued at a premium to their nominal value. Share premiums are credited to the company's *share premium account*.

share premium account *Fin* the special reserve in a company's balance sheet to which *share premiums* are credited. Expenses associated with the issue of shares may be written off to this account.

share register *Fin* a list of the shareholders in a particular company

share shop *Fin* the name given by some financial institutions to the office open to the public where shares may be bought and sold

share split *Fin see* **scrip issue**

Share Transactions Totally Electronic *(S Africa) Fin see* **STATE**

shareware *E-com* software distributed free of charge, but usually with a request that users pay a small fee if they like the program

shark repellent *Gen Mgt* provisions in a company's bye-laws that make it more difficult for a proposition such as a change of status or the acceptance of a hostile *takeover* bid to succeed. Elements of shark repellent may include: requiring a vote that is substantially higher than that required by law; creating different voting rights attached to different stocks; very long notice for special business meetings; or requiring certain shareholders to waive rights to any capital gains resulting from a takeover. *(slang)*

shark watcher *Fin* in the United States, a firm specialising in monitoring the stock market for potential takeover activity *(slang)*

Sharpe ratio *Fin see* **risk-adjusted return on capital**

shelf registration *Fin* a registration statement, lodged with the Securities and Exchange Commission two years before a corporation issues securities to the public. The statement, which has to be updated periodically, allows the corporation to act quickly when it considers that the market conditions are right without having to start the registration procedure from scratch.

Flextime is the essence of respect for and trust in people.   *David Packard*

shelfspace *Mkting* the amount of space allocated to a product in a retail outlet

shell company *Fin* a company that has ceased to trade but is still registered, especially one sold to enable the buyer to begin trading without having to set up a new company

Shewhart, Walter Andrew (1891–1967) *Gen Mgt* US statistician. Pioneer of the development and application of statistical techniques for the control of variation in industrial production, in particular **statistical process control**. Mentor of **W. Edwards Deming**.

shibosai *Fin* the Japanese term for a private placing

shibosai bond *Fin* a **samurai bond** sold direct to investors by the issuing company as opposed to being sold via a financial institution

shift *HR* **1.** a designated period during a working day when a group of employees work continuously. Shifts are arranged in a variety of different patterns during a day or over a week or month, to enable a business to make more effective use of its equipment, and to enable a greater level of output to be achieved. **2.** a group of employees working for a designated period during a working day. Where a shift pattern changes, the hours of work for the whole group of employees alters.

shift differential *HR* payment made to employees over and above their basic rate to compensate them for the inconvenience of the pattern of **shiftwork**. A shift differential usually takes account of the time of day when the shift is worked, the duration of the shift, the extent to which weekend working is involved, and the speed of rotation within the shift.

shiftwork *HR* an arrangement whereby the working day is divided into a number of **shifts**, and a separate group of employees works for each period

shingle
hang out your shingle (*US*) *Gen Mgt* to start a business or announce the start-up of a new business (*slang*)

Shingo, Shigeo (1909–90) *Gen Mgt* Japanese researcher and consultant. Inventor of the **single minute exchange of dies** and a developer of the **Toyota production system**. Methods to achieve **zero defects** were explained in *Zero Quality Control* (1985).

shinyo kinku *Fin* in Japan, a financial institution that provides financing for small businesses

shinyo kumiai *Fin* in Japan, a credit union that provides financing for small businesses

shipping confirmation *E-com* an e-mail message informing the purchaser that an order has been shipped

shogun bond *Fin* a bond denominated in a currency other than the yen that is sold on the Japanese market by a non-Japanese financial institution. *Also known as* **geisha bond**. *See also* **samurai bond**

shopbot *E-com* an automated means of searching the Internet for particular products or services, allowing the user to compare prices or specifications

shopping cart *or* **shopping basket** *E-com* a software package that collects and records items selected for purchase along with associated data, for example, item price and quantity desired, during shopping at an electronic store. *Also known as* **shopping trolley**

shopping experience *E-com* the virtual environment in which a customer visits an e-merchant's website, selects items and places them in an electronic **shopping cart**, and notifies the merchant of the order. The experience does not include a payment transaction, which is initiated by a message generated to the point-of-sale program when the customer signals the experience is completed.

shopping trolley *E-com see* **shopping cart**

shop steward *HR* a representative elected by **trade union** members within an office or factory to represent their feelings, wishes, and grievances to management. A shop steward is often the first point of contact for supervisors and personnel officers in their industrial relations dealings with an outside trade union.

shop window website *E-com* a website which provides information about an organisation and its products, but without encouraging any significant visitor interaction—rather like an online company brochure

short *Fin* **1.** a short-dated gilt (*slang*) **2.** an asset in which a dealer has a short position

short covering *Fin* the purchase of foreign exchange, commodities, or securities by a firm or individual that has been **selling short**. Such purchases are undertaken when the market has begun to move upwards, or when it is thought to be about to do so.

short-dated gilt *Fin see* **gilt-edged security**

shorthand *Gen Mgt* a system of rapid note-taking, using abbreviations and symbols to represent words and phrases

shorting *Fin* the act of *selling short*

short-interval scheduling *Ops* a technique for assigning a planned quantity of work to a workstation, to be completed in a specific time. Short-interval scheduling was pioneered during the 1930s by large mail-order houses in the United States and was widely used in the 1950s to provide greater control of routine and semi-routine processes through regular checks of individual performance over short spans of time. Short-interval scheduling enables *productivity* to be improved, as all delays can be identified and corrected at an early stage.

short messaging service *E-com see SMS*

short-run production *Ops* a production system designed to produce one-off or small batches of a product

short selling *Fin see sell short*

short-term bond *Fin* a bond on the corporate bond market that has an initial maturity of less than two years

short-term capital *Fin* funds raised for a period of less than 12 months. *See also working capital*

short-term debt *Fin* debt with a term of one year or less

short-term economic policy *Fin* an economic policy with objectives that can be met within a period of months or a few years

short-termism *Gen Mgt* an approach to business that concentrates on short-term results rather than long-term objectives

shovelware *E-com* a derogatory term for the materials produced by converting existing materials from a traditional medium, for example, a catalogue, without taking advantage of the digital medium's audiovisual and linking possibilities (*slang*)

show stopper *Fin* another form of *poison pill*

shrink wrap agreement *or* **shrink wrap licence** *E-com see click wrap agreement*

shutdown of production *Ops* the action of stopping production due to a lack of resources or components, equipment failure or installation, or *industrial action* by workers. Shutdown of production may also be instigated by management to reduce output. A shutdown can be a temporary measure, for example, in holiday periods, but it can also be permanent, for example, when a manufacturing company closes down after *business failure*.

SIA *abbr Fin* Securities Institute of Australia

SIB *abbr Fin* Securities and Investment Board

sickie *HR* a day of sick leave, often implying that the sickness is not genuine (*slang*)

sick leave *or* **sickness absence** *HR* absence from work caused by illness

sickness and accident insurance *Fin* a form of permanent health insurance that may be sold with some form of credit, for example a credit card or personal loan. In the event of the borrower being unable to work because of accident or illness, the policy covers the regular payments to the credit card company or lender.

sickout (*US*) *HR* a form of protest by a group of employees who attempt to achieve their demands by absenting themselves from work on the grounds of ill-health (*slang*)

sight bill *Fin* a bill of exchange payable on sight

sight deposit *Fin* a bank deposit against which the depositor can immediately draw

sight draft *Fin* a bill of exchange that is payable on delivery. *See also time draft*

signature *E-com* the name, position, and full contact details of the sender of an e-mail, added to the end of a business message. Some e-mail programs enable users to automatically add a signature to all sent messages.

signature guarantee *Fin* a stamp or seal, usually from a bank or a broker, that vouches for the authenticity of a signature

signature loan *Fin see unsecured loan*

silent partner (*US*) *Fin = sleeping partner*

silversurfer *E-com* an Internet user aged between 45 and 65 (*slang*)

silvertail (*ANZ*) *Gen Mgt* a wealthy person of high social standing (*slang*)

Simon, Herbert (1916–2001) *Gen Mgt* US economist, and political and social scientist. Respected for his work on *problem-solving*, *decision-making*, and *artificial intelligence*. He began developing his ideas in *Administrative Behavior* (1946).

simple interest *Fin* interest charged simply as a constant percentage of principal and not compounded. *See also compound interest*

Grab a chance and you won't be sorry for a might have been. *Arthur Ransome*

simple mail transfer protocol *E-com see* *SMTP*

simple moving average *Stats* the selection of units from a population in such a way that every possible combination of selected units is equally likely to be in the sample chosen

simple regression analysis *Gen Mgt see* *regression analysis*

simulation *Gen Mgt* the construction of a mathematical model to imitate the behaviour of a real-world situation or system in order to test the outcomes of alternative courses of action. Simulation was used in a military context by the Chinese as many as 5,000 years ago and has applications in the fields of science, research and development, economics, and business systems. The use of simulation has become more widespread since the development of computers in the 1950s, which facilitated the manipulation of large quantities of data and made it possible to model more complex systems. Simulation techniques are used in situations where real-life experimentation would be impossible, costly, or dangerous, and for training purposes.

simulation game *Gen Mgt* an interactive game based on a simulation of a real-life situation, where participants role-play, make decisions, and receive *feedback* on the results of their actions. A simulation game is used for training purposes and enables trainees to put theory into practice in a risk-free environment. Simulation games are used to increase business awareness and develop management skills such as *decision-making*, *problem-solving*, and team working. An element of competition between individuals or teams of players is normally involved. Formats used include board games and computer-based simulations of the running of a business.

simulation model *Gen Mgt* a mathematical representation of the essential characteristics of a real-world system or situation, which can be used to predict future behaviour under a variety of different conditions. The process of developing a simulation model involves defining the situation or system to be analysed, identifying the associated variables, and describing the relationships between them as accurately as possible.

simultaneous engineering *Ops see concurrent engineering*

simultaneous management *Gen Mgt* a *management style* in which managers organise competing demands in an integrated way, rather than sequentially. Simultaneous management reflects the increasingly rapid changes of the business environment, which create conflicting demands on a manager's attention. It involves integrating tasks, people, and procedures and handling them in an interactive way, rather than tackling problems individually and one at a time.

SINBAD *abbr Mkting* Single Income, No Boyfriend, And Absolutely Desperate: one of many humorous acronyms used in UK advertising to help define the market of a product or service (*slang*)

Singapore dollar *Fin* Singapore's unit of currency, whose exchange rate is quoted as S$ per US$

Singapore Exchange *Fin* a merger of the Stock Exchange of Singapore and the Singapore International Monetary Exchange, established in 1999. It provides securities and derivatives trading, securities clearing and depository, and derivatives clearing services. *Abbr* **SGX**

Singapore Immigration and Registration *Gen Mgt* the department responsible for all entry and immigration issues relating to Singapore. *Abbr* **SIR**

single currency *Fin* denominated entirely in one currency

single customs document *Fin* a standard universally used form for the passage of goods through customs

single-employer bargaining *HR see collective bargaining*

single entry *Fin* a type of bookkeeping where only one entry, reflecting both a credit to one account and a debit to another, is made for each transaction

single market *Fin see EU*

single minute exchange of dies *Ops* a technique for reducing the *set-up times* of equipment. Single minute exchange of dies was developed by *Shigeo Shingo* to improve set-up times in the *Toyota production system*. It is a simple technique that divides the elements of a set-up task into internal activities (those that can only be carried out when the machine is stopped) and external activities (those that can be carried out in advance). Single minute refers to making the changes in less than ten minutes, while exchange of dies comes from the steel presses that were the focus of Shingo's attention. By converting as many internal activities to external activities as possible, Shingo was able to reduce a four-hour set-up time on a large press to less than ten minutes. *Abbr* **SMED**

single-payment bond *Fin* a bond redeemed with a single payment combining principal and interest at maturity

single premium assurance *Fin* life cover where the premium is paid in one lump sum when the policy is taken out, rather than in monthly instalments

single premium deferred annuity *Fin* an annuity that gives tax advantage, paid for with a single payment at inception, and paying returns regularly after a set date

single sourcing *Ops* the *purchasing* policy of using one supplier for a particular component or service. Single sourcing can result in higher quality and a greater level of co-operation in *product development* than the traditional Western approach of *multiple sourcing*. Single sourcing has risen in prominence in the West following the introduction of Japanese production techniques, particularly *just-in-time*, which encourage manufacturers to establish closer relationships with a smaller number of suppliers.

single tax *Fin* a tax that supplies all revenue, especially on land

SINK *abbr Mkting* Single, Independent, No Kids (*slang*)

SIPC *abbr Fin* Securities Investor Protection Corporation

SIR *abbr Gen Mgt* Singapore Immigration and Registration

SIS *abbr Gen Mgt* strategic information systems

site analysis *E-com* analysis of information about a website stored on web servers. Typically, this information details how many page views they serve, as well as more specific data about the site's performance such as how long visitors stayed on the site and which pages they looked at when they were there.

situational interview *HR see interviewing*

six-month money *Fin* funds invested on the money market for a period of six months

Six Sigma *Ops* a data-driven method for achieving near perfect quality. Sigma is the Greek letter used to denote *standard deviation*, or the measure of variation from the mean, which in production terms is used to imply a defect. The greater the number of sigmas, the fewer the defects. In true Six Sigma environments, companies operate at a quality level of six standard deviations from the mean, or at a defect level of 3.4 per mil-

lion. Six Sigma analysis can be focused upon any part of production or service activities, and has a strong emphasis on statistical analysis in design, manufacturing, and customer-oriented activities. It is based on statistical tools and techniques of quality management developed by *Joseph Juran*.

size of firm *Gen Mgt* method of categorising companies according to size for the purposes of government statistics. Divisions are typically *microbusiness*, *small business*, *medium-sized business*, and *large-sized business*.

skeleton staff *HR* the minimum number of employees needed to keep a business running, for example, during a holiday period

skewness *Stats* a lack of symmetry in a probability distribution

skill *HR* the ability to do something well, gained through training and experience. *See also competence*

skills analysis *HR* the process of obtaining information on employees' technical and behavioural *skills*. Skills analysis is used to define the skills or *competencies* required in a particular job. It is also used to identify those skills that are not being deployed at all or could be utilised by another part of the organisation. *Also known as skills mapping*

skills mapping *HR see skills analysis*

skills shortage *HR* a shortfall in the number of workers with the *skills* needed to fill the jobs currently available. A skills shortage may be caused by a lack of education and *vocational training*, or by wider social and economic factors such as new technological developments. A skills shortage may affect a region, an industry, or a whole country. Skills shortages of this type need to be addressed at national level through effective *manpower planning* and the development of strategies for adult education and vocational training. An organisation may suffer from a skills shortage as a result of poor *recruitment* and employee retention policies, or through inadequate provision of training and employee development opportunities.

skunkworks (*US*) *Gen Mgt* a fast-moving group, working at the edge of the *organisation structure*, which aims to accelerate the *innovation* process without the restrictions of organisational policies and procedures. Skunkworks can operate unknown to an organisation, or with its tacit acceptance. With the organisation's acceptance, skunkworks are an extreme form of **intrapreneurialism**. The term skunkworks was popularised by **Tom Peters** and **Bob Waterman** in *A Passion for Excellence* (1984).

slack variables *Fin* the amount of each resource which will be unused if a specific linear programming solution is implemented

sleeping partner *Gen Mgt* a person or organisation that invests money in a company but takes no active part in the management of the business. Although a sleeping partner is inactive in the operation of the business, they have legal obligations and benefits of ownership and are therefore fully liable for any debts. *US term* **silent partner**

Sloan, Alfred Pritchard (1875–1966) *Gen Mgt* US industrialist. Chairman and CEO of General Motors, which he built into the largest company in the world by developing *decentralised organisation structure* and adopting the theories of *Henri Fayol*. Sloan's divisional structure, which became the model for organising large business, is described in *My Years with General Motors* (1963).

slowdown *Econ* a fall in demand that causes a lowering of economic activity, less severe than a *recession* or *slump*

slump *Econ* a severe downturn phase in the business cycle

slumpflation *Econ* a collapse in all economic activity accompanied by wage and price inflation. This happened, for example, in the United States and Europe in 1929. (*slang*)

slush fund *Fin* a fund used by a company for illegal purposes such as bribing officials to obtain preferential treatment for planned work or expansion

small and medium-sized enterprises *Gen Mgt* organisations that are in the *start-up* or growth phase of development and have between 10 and 500 employees. This definition of small and medium-sized enterprises is the one adopted by the United Kingdom's Department of Trade and Industry for statistical purposes. *Abbr* **SME**

small business *Gen Mgt* an organisation that is small in relation to the potential market size, managed by its owners, and not part of a larger organisation. There is no single official definition of what constitutes a small business. A standard definition for the size of small business, adopted by the UK Department of Trade and Industry for purposes of examining trends and for distinguishing from *microbusiness*, *medium-sized business*, and

large-sized business, is an organisation of between 10 and 99 employees.

small change *Fin* a quantity of coins that a person might carry with them

Small Order Execution System *Fin* on the NASDAQ, an automated execution system for bypassing brokers when processing small order agency executions of Nasdaq securities up to 1,000 shares

small print *Gen Mgt* details in an official document such as a contract that are usually printed in a smaller size than the rest of the text and, while often important, may be overlooked. Items often referred to as 'small print' can include terms and conditions or penalty clauses.

smart card *E-com* a small plastic card containing a microprocessor that can store and process transactions and maintain a bank balance, thus providing a secure, portable medium for electronic money. Financial details and personal data stored on the card can be updated each time the card is used.

smart market *E-com* a market in which all transactions are carried out electronically using network communications

smartsizing *HR* the process of reducing the size of a company by laying off employees on the basis of incompetence and inefficiency (*slang*)

SME *abbr Gen Mgt* small and medium-sized enterprises

SMED *abbr Ops* single minute exchange of dies

Smith, Adam (1723–90) *Gen Mgt* Scottish political economist and philosopher. Author of *The Wealth of Nations* (1776), one of the most influential books written about political economy, Smith did much to promulgate the theory of free trade in a society based on *mercantilism*. He is recognised for his use of the expression 'the invisible hand', which he used to describe the important role of self-interest in a free market.

smoking memo *Gen Mgt* a memo, letter, or e-mail message containing evidence of a corporate crime (*slang*)

smoko (*ANZ*) *Gen Mgt* a break taken by employees during working hours, traditionally to smoke cigarettes but often to take tea or other refreshments (*slang*)

smoothing methods *Stats* procedures used in fitting a model to a set of statistical observations in a study, often by graphing the data to highlight its characteristics

SMS *abbr E-com* short messaging service: the system used to send text messages via mobile phone networks

SMTP *abbr E-com* simple mail transfer protocol: an e-mail protocol used to help pass messages along their route. SMTP is understood by e-mail software and by the server computers that each e-mail message passes.

snail mail *E-com* a derogatory term for the off-line postal service, viewed as slow in comparison to e-mail

snowball sampling *Stats* a form of sampling in which existing sample members suggest potential new sample members, for example, personal acquaintances

snowflake *Stats* a graph that shows *multivariate data*

SO *abbr Gen Mgt* significant other (*slang*)

social audit *Gen Mgt* a process for evaluating, reporting on, and improving an organisation's performance and behaviour, and for measuring its effects on society. The social audit can be used to produce a measure of the *social responsibility* of an organisation. It takes into account any internal *code of conduct* as well as the views of all *stakeholders* and draws on *best practice* factors of *total quality management* and human resource development. Like *internal auditing*, social auditing requires an organisation to identify what it is seeking to achieve, who the stakeholders are, and how it wants to measure performance.

social capital *Gen Mgt* the asset to an organisation produced by the cumulative social skills of its employees. Social capital, like *intellectual* and *emotional capital*, is intangible and resides in the employees of the organisation. It is a form of capital produced by good interpersonal skills (see *interpersonal communication*), which can be considered an asset as they are an important factor in organisational success. Key components of social capital include: trust; a sense of community and belonging; unrestricted and participative communication; democratic decision-making; and a sense of collective responsibility. Evidence of social capital can be seen, for example, in trust relationships, in the establishment of effective personal networks, in efficient *teamwork*, and in an organisation's exercise of *social responsibility*.

social cost *Fin* tangible and intangible costs and losses sustained by third parties or the general public as a result of economic activity, for example, pollution by industrial effluent

socialism *Econ* a way of organising society in which the use and production of goods are in collective (usually government) ownership

socially-conscious investing *Fin see* **ethical investment**

social marginal cost *Econ* the additional cost to a society of a change in an economic variable, for example, the price of petrol or bread

social responsibility *Gen Mgt* the approach of an organisation to managing the impact it has on society. Social responsibility involves behaving within certain socially acceptable limits. These limits may not always take the form of written laws or regulations but they amount to an accepted organisation-wide moral or ethical code. Organisations that transgress this code are viewed as irresponsible. In order to determine levels of social responsibility, organisations may choose to undertake a *social audit* or more specifically an *environmental audit*. Social responsibility, along with *business ethics*, has grown as a strategic issue as *empowerment* and the *flat organisation* have pushed decision-making down to a wider range of employees at the same time as green or caring consumers are becoming a more powerful market segment.

social responsibility accounting *Fin* the identification, measurement, and reporting of the social costs and benefits resulting from economic activities

Sociedad Anónima *Fin* the Spanish equivalent of a private limited company. *Abbr* **SA**

Sociedade Anónima *Fin* the Portuguese equivalent of a private limited company. *Abbr* **SA**

Società a responsabilità limitata *Fin* an Italian limited liability company that is unlisted. *Abbr* **Srl**

Società per azioni *Fin* an Italian public limited company. *Abbr* **Spa**

Société anonyme *Fin* the French equivalent of a private limited company. *Abbr* **SA**

Société à responsabilité limitée *Fin* a French limited liability company that is unlisted. *Abbr* **SARL**

Société d'investissement à capital variable *Fin* the French term for collective investment. *Abbr* **SICAV**

I am extraordinarily patient, provided I get my own way in the end.   *Margaret Thatcher*

Society for Worldwide Interbank Financial Telecommunication *Fin see* **SWIFT**

socio-cultural research *Mkting* exploration of social and cultural trends which identifies how they are likely to impact on different *market sectors*

socio-economic *Econ* involving both social and economic factors. Structural unemployment, for example, has socio-economic causes.

socio-economic environment *Gen Mgt* the combination of external social and economic conditions that influence the operation and performance of an organisation. The socio-economic environment is part of the overall business environment.

socio-economic segmentation *Mkting* the division of a market by socio-economic categories

Sod's Law *Fin* the principle that if something can go wrong, it will. *US term* **Murphy's Law**

soft benefits *HR* non-monetary benefits offered to employees (*slang*)

soft commissions *Fin* brokerage commissions that are rebated to an institutional customer in the form of, or to pay for, research or other services

soft commodities *Fin* commodities, such as foodstuffs, that are neither metals nor other solid raw materials. *Also known as* **softs**. *See also* **future**, **hard commodities**

soft-core radicalism *Mkting* a marketing technique that plays on people's concerns about environmental and ethical issues in order to sell them a product (*slang*)

soft currency *Fin* a currency that is weak, usually because there is an excess of supply and a belief that its value will fall in relation to others. *See also* **hard currency**

soft landing *Econ* a situation in which a country's economic activity slows down but demand does not fall far enough or rapidly enough to cause a recession

soft loan *Fin* a loan on exceptionally favourable terms, for example, for a project that a government considers worthy

soft market *Fin* a market in which prices are falling

softs *Fin see* **soft commodities**

soft systems *Gen Mgt see* **systems method**

software *E-com see* **hardware**

sole practitioner *Gen Mgt* the sole proprietor of a professional practice

sole proprietor *Gen Mgt* somebody who owns and runs an unincorporated business by themselves. In the United Kingdom, a sole proprietor does not have to register the company or publish annual accounts and is taxed as an individual. They are personally liable, however, for all business losses or debts and in the event of **bankruptcy** personal possessions may be forfeited. *Also known as* **sole trader**

sole trader *Fin* a person carrying on business with total legal responsibility for his/her actions, neither in partnership nor as a company

solus position *Mkting* the condition of being the only advertisement to appear on a page

solution brand *Gen Mgt* a combination of products and related services, for example, a computer system with pre-sales consultancy, installation, and maintenance, that meets a customer's needs more effectively than a product alone

solvency margin *Fin* **1.** a business's liquid assets that are in excess of those required to meet its liabilities **2.** in the United Kingdom, the extent to which an insurance company's assets exceed its liabilities

solvency ratio *Fin* **1.** a ratio of assets to liabilities, used to measure a company's ability to meet its debts **2.** in the United Kingdom, the ratio of an insurance company's net assets to its non-life premium income

solvent *Fin* able to pay off all debts

sort code *Fin* a combination of numbers that identifies a bank branch on official documentation, such as bank statements and cheques. *US term* **routing number**

sort field *E-com* a computer field used to identify data in such a way that it can be easily categorised and arranged in sequence

source and application of funds statement *Fin see* **cash-flow statement**

source document *Fin* a document upon which details of transactions or accounting events are recorded and from which information is extracted to be subsequently entered into the internal accounting system of an organisation, for example, a sales invoice or credit note

sources and uses of funds statement *Fin see* **cash-flow statement**

Southern African Development Community *Fin see* **SADC**

sovereign loan *Fin* a loan by a financial institution to an overseas government, usually of a developing country. *See also* **sovereign risk**

sovereign risk *Fin* the risk that an overseas government may refuse to repay or may default on a **sovereign loan**

Spa *abbr Fin* Società per azioni

spam 1. *E-com* unsolicited bulk e-mail, usually sent for commercial purposes. Spam is used by some companies as a cheap form of advertising, although it is generally considered offensive and unwelcome by the Internet community. Sending spam is regarded as unethical because the cost is paid by the recipient's site or server, not the sender's. Various Internet bodies campaign against spam and those individuals or organisations accused of spamming. The term originates from a sketch in an episode of *Monty Python* in which customers at a 'greasy spoon' café are served the tinned meat Spam with everything, regardless of whether it was part of their order. **2.** *Mkting see* **direct mail**

spamkiller software *E-com* software that can block e-mail messages from companies sending unsolicited commercial e-mail

span of control *Gen Mgt* the number and range of subordinates for whom a manager is responsible. The span of control can be calculated by various methods which take into account such factors as whether those supervised are doing the same or different jobs and their levels of seniority, **empowerment**, experience, and qualification.

spare parts *Ops* a stock of components of machinery or plant held in store in case of breakdown

spatial data *Stats* variables that are measured at different locations to illustrate the spatial organisation of data

SPC *abbr Ops* statistical process control

speako *Gen Mgt* a mistake made by a computer while using a speech-recognition program (*slang*)

spear carrier *HR* somebody who is in the second tier of command in an organisation and is responsible for carrying out the commands and communicating the messages of the top-level executives (*slang*)

special clearing *Fin see* **special presentation**

special deposit *Fin* an amount of money set aside for the rehabilitation of a mortgaged house

special leave *HR* exceptional **leave** that may be granted to an **employee**. Special leave includes **sabbaticals**, leave granted for study (also known as **educational leave**), leave for jury service, for volunteer forces training, leave granted to candidates for local or national elections, or for trade union duties and activities, and for **community involvement** purposes. Special leave can also refer to **maternity leave** and **paternity leave**.

special presentation *Fin* the sending of a cheque directly to the paying banker rather than through the clearing system. *Also known as* **special clearing**. *See also* **advice of fate**

special purpose bond *Fin* a bond for one particular project, financed by levies on the people who benefit from the project

special resolution *Fin see* **extraordinary resolution**

specie *Fin* coins, as opposed to banknotes, that are legal tender

specification *Ops* documentation relating to the required quantity and quality of materials, and the order of the work to be carried out to complete a task

specific charge *Fin* a fixed charge as opposed to a floating charge

specific order costing *Fin* the basic cost accounting method applicable where work consists of separately identifiable contracts, jobs, or batches

speculation *Fin* a purchase made solely to make a profit when the price or value increases

speech *Gen Mgt* a formal spoken address made to an audience by a speaker. Speeches are made in the context of a meeting or conference or on other occasions such as after a business dinner. The aim of a speech may be to motivate, inspire, or entertain as well as to inform. In contrast to **presentations**, speeches are a form of public speaking normally made without the assistance of audio-visual aids, and may be wide-ranging rather than focusing on a well-defined topic or proposal. Jokes, humorous anecdotes, and quotations are frequently used in speeches. To give a speech successfully requires good **communication skills**.

spider food *E-com* words that are embedded in a web page to attract search engines

spiffs (*US*) *Mkting* gifts or money offered to store managers in exchange for promoting a product (*slang*)

If disorder is the rule with you, you will be penalised for installing order.   Paul Valéry

spin-off *Gen Mgt* a company or subsidiary formed by splitting away from a parent company. A spin-off company can, for example, be created when research and development yields a new product that does not fit into the company's current portfolio, or when a company wants to explore a new venture related to its current activities. It can also be formed from a demerger, in which acquired companies or parts of a business are separated in order to create a more streamlined parent organisation. A spin-off is often entrepreneurial in spirit, but the backing of the parent company can provide financial stability.

splash page *E-com* an introductory or initial page, usually containing advertisements, presented to visitors to a website before they get to the *homepage*

split *Fin* an issuance to shareholders of more than one share for every share owned. *See also reverse split.* US term **stock split**

split-capital investment trust *Fin* an investment trust set up for a specific time-scale where the shares are divided at launch into two different classes: income shares and capital shares. Income shareholders receive all or most of the income generated by the trust and a predetermined sum at liquidation, while capital shareholders receive no interest but the remainder of the capital at liquidation. *Also known as* **split-level trust, split trust**

split commission *Fin commission* that is divided between two or more parties in a transaction

split coupon bond *Fin see* **zero coupon bond**

split-level trust *Fin see* **split-capital investment trust**

split trust *Fin see* **split-capital investment trust**

sponsorship *Mkting* a form of advertising in which an organisation provides funds for something such as a television programme, music concert, or sports event in return for exposure to a target audience

Spoornet *Gen Mgt* the rail division of the state-owned South African transport company, Transnet Ltd

spot *Mkting* a TV or radio commercial (*slang*)

spot colour *Mkting* single colour overprinted on a black-and-white advertisement

spot exchange rate *Fin* the exchange rate used for immediate currency transactions

spot goods *Fin* a commodity traded on the spot market

spot interest rate *Fin* an interest rate that is determined when a loan is made

spot market *Fin* a market that deals in commodities or foreign exchange for immediate rather than future delivery

spot month *Fin see* **nearby month**

spot price *Fin* the price for immediate delivery of commodities or foreign exchange

spot transaction *Fin* a transaction in commodities or foreign exchange for immediate delivery

spread *Fin* **1.** the difference between the buying and selling price of a share on a stock exchange **2.** the range of investments in a portfolio

spreadsheet *Fin* a computer program that provides a series of ruled columns in which data can be entered and analysed

sprinkling trust *Fin* a trust with multiple beneficiaries whose distributions occur at the trustee's total discretion

spruik (*ANZ*) *Gen Mgt* to publicise goods or services, typically by standing at the door of a shop and addressing passersby using a microphone (*slang*)

squatter (*ANZ*) *Gen Mgt* a wealthy landowner (*slang*)

squattocracy (*ANZ*) *Gen Mgt* a derogatory term for wealthy landowners, who are considered a powerful social class (*slang*)

squeaky wheel *Gen Mgt* somebody who gets good results by being extremely assertive in their dealings with other people (*slang*)

squeeze *Econ* a government policy of restriction, commonly affecting the availability of credit in an economy

squirt the bird *Gen Mgt* to transmit a signal to a satellite (*slang*)

Srl *abbr Fin* Società a responsabilità limitata

SSADM *abbr Gen Mgt* structured systems analysis and design method

SSAP *abbr Fin* Statement of Standard Accounting Practice

SSL *abbr E-com* secure sockets layer: a widely used protocol for encrypting data that permits the transmission of credit card transactions in a secure fashion

stabilisation fund *Econ* a fund created by a government as an emergency savings account for international financial support

staff costs *Fin* the costs of employment which include gross pay, paid holidays, and

---

employer's contributions to national insurance, pension schemes, sickness benefit schemes, and other benefits, for example, protective clothing and canteen subsidies

staffing level *HR* the number and type of personnel employed by an organisation for the performance of a given workload. The ideal staffing level for an organisation depends on the amount of work to be done and the skills required to do it. If the number and quality of staff employed are greater than necessary for the workload, an organisation may be deemed to be over-staffed; if the number of staff is insufficient for the workload, an organisation is deemed to be under-staffed. Effective **human resource planning** will determine the appropriate staffing level for an organisation at any given point in time.

stage-gate model *Mkting see* **new product development**

stagflation *Econ* the result when both inflation and unemployment exist at the same time in an economy. There was stagflation in the United Kingdom in the 1970s, for example.

stakeholder *Gen Mgt* a person or organisation with a vested interest in the successful operation of a company or organisation. A stakeholder may be an employee, customer, supplier, partner, or even the local community within which an organisation operates.

stakeholder pension *Fin, HR* a pension, bought from a private company, in which the retirement income depends on the level of contributions made during a person's working life. Stakeholder pensions are designed for people without access to an **occupational pension scheme**, and are intended to provide a low-cost supplement to the state earnings related pension scheme. A stakeholder pension scheme can either be trust-based, like an occupational pension scheme, or contract-based, similar to a personal pension. Subject to certain exceptions, employers must provide access to a stakeholder pension scheme for employees, although they are not required to establish a stakeholder pension scheme themselves. Membership of a stakeholder pension scheme is voluntary. *See also* **Keough Plan**

stakeholder theory *Gen Mgt* the theory that an organisation can enhance the interests of its shareholders without damaging the interests of its wider **stakeholders**. Stakeholder theory grew in response to the **economic theory of the firm**, and contrasts with **Theory E**. One of the difficulties of stakeholder theory is

allocating importance to the values of different groups of stakeholders, and a solution to this is proposed by **stakeholder value analysis**.

stakeholder value analysis *Gen Mgt* a method of determining the values of all **stakeholders** within an organisation for the purposes of making strategic and operational decisions. Stakeholder value analysis is one method of justifying an approach based on **stakeholder theory** rather than the **economic theory of the firm**. It involves identifying groups of stakeholders and eliciting their views on particular issues in order that these views may be taken into account when making decisions.

stamp duty *Fin* in the United Kingdom, a duty that is payable on some legal documents and is shown to have been paid by a stamp being fixed to the document

standard *Fin* a benchmark measurement of resource usage, set in defined conditions.
    Standards can be set on the following bases: an ex ante estimate of expected performance; an ex post estimate of attainable performance; a prior period level of performance by the same organisation; the level of performance achieved by comparable organisations; and the level of performance required to meet organisational objectives.
    Standards may also be set at attainable levels which assume efficient levels of operation, but which include allowances for normal loss, waste, and machine downtime, or at ideal levels, which make no allowance for the above losses and are only attainable under the most favourable conditions.

Standard 8 *Fin* a standard used in Internet commerce

Standard & Poor's 500 *Fin* a US index of 500 general share prices selected by the Standard & Poor agency. *Abbr* **S&P 500**, **S&P index**

Standard & Poor's rating *Fin* a share rating service provided by the US agency Standard & Poor

standard business transaction *E-com* any business procedure conducted between trading partners, characterised by a paper document or its equivalent EDI transaction set or message

standard cost *Fin* the planned unit cost of the products, components, or services produced in a period. The main uses of standard costs are in performance measurement, control, stock valuation, and in the establishment of selling prices.

standard cost card *Fin* a document or other record detailing, for each individual product, the standard inputs required for production as well as the standard selling price. Inputs are normally divided into material, labour, and overhead categories, and both price and quantity information is shown for each.

standard costing *Fin* a control technique which compares standard costs and revenues with actual results to obtain variances which are used to stimulate improved performance

standard deviation *Ops* a measure of how dispersed a set of numbers are around their mean

standard direct labour cost *Fin* the planned average cost of direct labour

standard of living *Econ* a measure of economic well-being based on the ability of people to buy the goods and services they desire

standard performance–labour *Fin* the level of efficiency which appropriately trained, motivated, and resourced employees can achieve in the long run

standard time *Gen Mgt* 1. the length of time taken by a worker to complete a particular motion, such as reaching or grasping 2. the total time required to complete a specific task for an employee working at the expected rate. The standard time for any particular task is derived through *work measurement* and *time study* techniques, and takes into account **relaxation allowances**, which allow employees time to recover from the psychological or physiological effects of carrying out a task, and **contingency allowances**, which recognise that there may be legitimate causes of delay before a task can be completed. *Predetermined motion-time systems* may be used to help determine a standard time.

standby credit *Econ* credit drawing rights given to a developing country by an international financial institution, to fund industrialisation or other growth policies

standby loan *Econ* a loan given to a developing country by an international financial institution, to fund technology hardware purchase or other growth policies

stand down *(ANZ)* *HR* to suspend an employee without pay *(slang)*

standing instructions *Fin* instructions, that may be revoked at any time, for a particular procedure to be carried out in the event of a certain occurrence, for example, for the monies from a fixed term account that has just matured to be placed on deposit for a further fixed period

standing order *Fin* an instruction given by an account holder to a bank to make regular payments on given dates to the same payee. *US term* **automatic debit**

standing room only *Mkting* a sales technique whereby customers are given the impression that there are many other people waiting to buy the same product at the same time *(slang)*

staple commodities *Fin* basic food or raw materials that are important in a country's economy

star 1. *Gen Mgt see* **Boston Box** 2. *Fin* an investment that is performing extremely well *(slang)*

start-up *Gen Mgt* a relatively new, usually small business, particularly one supported by venture capital and within those sectors closely linked to new technologies

start-up costs *Fin* the initial sum required to establish a business or to get a project underway. The costs will include the capital expenditure and related expenses before the business or project generates revenue.

start-up model *Gen Mgt* a business model based on rapid short-term success. Typically, the aim is to acquire venture capital, grow rapidly, and float or sell off quickly, generating profit for the founders but not necessarily for the business.

state bank *Fin* a bank chartered by a state of the United States

state capitalism *Econ* a way of organising society in which the state controls most of a country's means of production and capital

State Earnings-Related Pension Scheme *Fin see* **SERPS**

state enterprise *Gen Mgt* an organisation in which the government or state has a controlling interest

statement of account *Fin* a list of sums due, usually relating to unpaid invoices, items paid on account but not offset against particular invoices, credit notes, debit notes, and discounts

statement of affairs *Fin* a statement, usually prepared by a receiver, in a prescribed form, showing the estimated financial position of a debtor or of a company which may

---

be unable to meet its debts. It contains a summary of the debtor's assets and liabilities. The assets are shown at their estimated realisable values. The various classes of creditors, such as preferential, secured, partly secured, and unsecured, are shown separately.

Statement of Auditing Standards *Fin* an auditing standard, issued by the Auditing Practices Board, containing prescriptions as to the basic principles and practices which members of the UK accountancy bodies are expected to follow in the course of an audit. *Abbr* **SAS**

statement of cash flows *Fin* a statement that documents actual receipts and expenditures of cash

statement-of-cash-flows method *Fin* a method of accounting that is based on flows of cash rather than balances on accounts

statement of changes in financial position *Fin* a financial report of a company's incomes and outflows during a period, usually a year or a quarter

Statement of Financial Accounting Standards *Fin* in the United States, a statement detailing the standards to be adopted for the preparation of financial statements. *Abbr* **SFAS**

statement of source and application of funds *Fin see* **cash-flow statement**

Statement of Standard Accounting Practice *Fin* an accounting standard issued by the Accounting Standards Committee (ASC). *Abbr* **SSAP**

state of balance *Gen Mgt* an approach to capitalism that balances ecological and economic priorities

state planning *Econ* the regulation of a sector of an economy by administrators rather than by the price system

statistic *Fin* a piece of information in numerical form

statistical expert system *Stats* a computer program used to conduct a statistical analysis of a set of data

statistical model *Stats* the particular methods used to investigate the data in a statistical study

statistical process control *Ops* a means of monitoring a *process* to assist in identifying causes of variation with the aim of improving process performance. Statistical process control consists of three elements: data gathering;

determining control limits; and variation reduction. The tools used include process *flow charts*, tally charts, histograms, graphs, *fishbone charts*, and control charts. The thinking behind SPC has been attributed to *Walter Shewhart* in the 1920s. *Abbr* **SPC**

statistical quality control *Stats* the process of inspecting samples of a product to check for consistent quality according to given parameters

statistical significance *Fin* the level of importance at which an event influences a set of *statistics*

statistics *Fin* information in numerical form and its collection, analysis, and presentation

statute-barred debt *Fin* a debt that cannot be pursued as the time limit laid down by law has expired

statutory auditor *Fin* a professional person qualified to carry out an audit required by the Companies Act

statutory body *Fin* an entity formed by Act of Parliament

STC *abbr* (*S Africa*) *Fin* Secondary Tax on Companies: a secondary tax levied on corporate dividends

STEP analysis *Gen Mgt see* **PEST analysis**

Stewart, Rosemary Gordon *Gen Mgt* British academic. Respected for her research on managerial work and behaviour, including the essential aspects of becoming an effective manager, published in *The Reality of Management* (1963).

Stewart, Thomas (*b.* 1948) *Gen Mgt* US publisher and writer. A leader in the *knowledge management* debate who, in *Intellectual Capital: The New Wealth of Organizations* (1997), encouraged organisations to exploit their untapped knowledge.

stickiness *E-com* a website's ability to hold visitors and to keep them coming back

stick to the knitting *Gen Mgt* an exhortation to organisations to concentrate on the activities, products, and services that are key to their *core business* and consequently to their success. Stick to the knitting was popularised by *Tom Peters* and *Bob Waterman* in their book *In Search of Excellence* (1984).

sticky site *E-com* a website that holds the interest of visitors for a substantial amount of time and is therefore effective as a marketing vehicle (*slang*) *Also known as* **heavy site**

If you are capable of displaying energy, hold office, if not resign. *Zhou Ren*

stipend *HR* a regular remuneration or allowance paid to an individual holding a particular office

stock *Fin* **1.** a form of security that offers fixed interest **2.** the *capital* made available to an organisation after a *share issue*

stockbroker *Fin* somebody who arranges the sale and purchase of stocks

stock certificate (*US*) *Fin* = *share certificate*

stock control *Fin see inventory*

stockcount *Fin* profit gained from ownership of a stock or share

stock exchange *Fin* an organisation that maintains a market for the trading of stock

Stock Exchange Automated Quotations System *Fin see SEAQ*

Stock Exchange Automated Quotations System International *Fin see SEAQ International*

Stock Exchange Automatic Trading System *Fin see SEATS*

stockholding (*US*) *Fin* = *shareholding*

stock market *Fin* the trading of stocks, or a place where this occurs

stock option *Fin* **1.** *see option* **2.** *see employee share ownership plan*

stockout *Ops* the situation where the stock of a particular component or part has been used up and has not yet been replenished. Stockouts result from poor inventory control or the failure of a *just-in-time* supply system. They can result in delays in the delivery of customer orders and can damage the reputation of the business.

stock split (*US*) *Fin* = *scrip issue*

stock symbol *Fin* a shortened version of a company's name, usually made up of two to four letters, used in screen-based trading systems

stocktaking *Ops* the process of measuring the quantities of stock held by an organisation. Stock, or *inventory*, can be held both in stores and within the processes of the operation. Better *materials management* and inventory systems have made annual stocktaking less important.

stock turns *or* **stock turnover** *Ops see inventory turnover*

stokvel (*S Africa*) *Fin* an informal, widely-used co-operative savings scheme that provides small-scale loans

stop-go *Econ* the alternate tightening and loosening of fiscal and monetary policies. This characterised the UK economy in the 1960s and 1970s.

stop limit order *Fin* in the United States, an order to trade only if and when a security reaches a specified price

stop loss *Fin* an order to trade only if and when a security falls to a specified price

stop order *Fin* in the United States, an order to trade only if and when a security rises above or falls below its current price

stop-work meeting (*ANZ*) *HR* a meeting held by employees during working hours to discuss issues such as wage claims and working conditions with union representatives or management

stores requisition *Fin see materials requisition*

story stock *Fin* a stock that is the subject of a press or financial community story that may affect its price

straight-line depreciation *Fin* a form of depreciation in which the cost of a fixed asset is spread equally over each year of its anticipated lifetime

Straits Times Industrial Index *Fin* an index of 30 Singapore stocks, the most commonly quoted indicator of stock market activity in Singapore

strata title (*ANZ*) *Gen Mgt* a system for registering ownership of space within a multilevel building, under which a title applies to the space and a proportion of the common property

strata unit (*ANZ*) *Gen Mgt* an apartment or office within a multilevel building that has been registered under the *strata title* system

STRATE (*S Africa*) *Fin* Share Transactions Totally Electronic: the electronic share transactions system of the Johannesburg Stock Exchange

strategic alignment *Gen Mgt see strategic fit*

strategic alliance *Gen Mgt* an agreement between two or more organisations to co-operate in a specific business activity, so that each benefits from the strengths of the other, and gains *competitive advantage*. The formation of strategic alliances has been seen as a response to *globalisation* and increasing uncertainty and complexity in the business environment. Strategic alliances involve the sharing of knowledge and expertise between partners as well as the reduction of risk and costs in areas such as relationships with suppliers and the development of new products and technologies. A strategic alliance is sometimes equated with a *joint venture*, but an alliance may involve competitors, and generally has a shorter life span. *Strategic partnering* is a closely related concept.

strategic analysis *Gen Mgt* the process of conducting researching on the business environment within which an organisation operates and the organisation itself, in order to formulate *strategy*. A number of tools are used in the process of strategic analysis, including *PEST*, *SWOT analysis*, and *Michael Porter*'s five forces model.

strategic business unit *Fin* a section within a larger organisation, responsible for planning, developing, producing, and marketing its own products or services

strategic financial management *Fin* the identification of the possible strategies capable of maximising an organisation's net present value, the allocation of scarce capital resources among the competing opportunities, and the implementation and monitoring of the chosen strategy so as to achieve stated objectives

strategic fit *Gen Mgt* the extent to which the activities of a single organisation or of organisations working in partnership complement each other in such a way as to contribute to *competitive advantage*. The benefits of good strategic fit include cost reduction, due to economies of scale, and the transfer of knowledge and skills. The success of a *merger*, *joint venture*, or *strategic alliance* may be affected by the degree of strategic fit between the organisations involved. Similarly, the strategic fit of one organisation with another is often a factor in decisions about acquisitions, mergers, *diversification*, or *divestment*. *Also known as strategic alignment*

strategic goal *Gen Mgt* the overall aim of an organisation in terms of its market position in the medium or long-term. A strategic goal forms part of an organisation's *corporate strategy* and should act as a motivating force as well as a measure of performance and achievement for those working in an organisation.

strategic inflection point *Gen Mgt* the time at which an organisation takes a decision to change its *corporate strategy* to pursue a different direction and avoid the risk of decline. The term was coined by *Andy Grove* of Intel

to describe the period of change that affects an organisation's competitive position. It also concerns the ability of organisations to recognise and adapt to change factors of major significance.

strategic information systems *Gen Mgt* an information system established with the aim of creating *competitive advantage* and improving the competitive position of an organisation. A strategic information system supports and shapes the *corporate strategy* of an organisation, often leading to innovation in the way the organisation conducts its business, the creation of new business opportunities, or the development of products and services based on information technology. Strategic information systems represent a development in organisational use of information systems, following in the wake of *MISs*, *EISs*, and *decision support systems*.

strategic investment appraisal *Fin* a method of investment appraisal which allows the inclusion of both financial and non-financial factors. Project benefits are appraised in terms of their contribution to the strategies of the organisation, either by their financial contribution or, for non-financial benefits, by the use of index numbers or other means.

strategic management *Gen Mgt* the development of *corporate strategy*, and the management of an organisation according to that strategy. Strategic management focuses on achieving and maintaining a strong *competitive advantage*. It involves the application of corporate strategy to all aspects of the organisation, and especially to *decision-making*. As a discipline, strategic management developed in the 1970s, but it has evolved in response to changes in *organisation structure* and *corporate culture*. With greater *empowerment*, strategy has become the concern not just of directors but also of employees at all levels of the organisation.

strategic management accounting *Fin* a form of management accounting in which emphasis is placed on information which relates to factors external to the firm, as well as non-financial information and internally generated information

strategic marketing *Mkting* a method of selling products directly to customers, bypassing traditional retailers or distributors

strategic partnering *Gen Mgt* structured collaboration between organisations to take joint advantage of market opportunities, or to

---

The only conclusive evidence of a man's sincerity is that he gave himself for a principle.

James Russell Lowell

respond to customers more effectively than could be achieved in isolation. Strategic partnering occurs both in and between the public and private sectors. Besides allowing information, skills, and resources to be shared, a strategic partnership also permits the partners to share risk. *See also **strategic alliance***

strategic plan *Fin* a statement of long-term goals along with a definition of the strategies and policies which will ensure achievement of these goals

strategic planning *Gen Mgt see **planning***

strategy *Gen Mgt, HR* a planned course of action undertaken to achieve the aims and objectives of an organisation. The term was originally used in the context of warfare to describe the overall planning of a campaign as opposed to tactics, which enable the achievement of specific short-term objectives. The overall strategy of an organisation is known as *corporate strategy*, but strategy may also be developed for any aspect of an organisation's activities such as *environmental management* or production and manufacturing strategy.

stratified sampling *Ops see **random sampling***

straw man *Gen Mgt* a first proposal for a solution to a problem, offered more as a place to start looking for a solution than as a serious suggestion for final action

streaming *E-com* Web technology used for simultaneous downloading and viewing of large amounts of material. For example, with a *multimedia* file, the user can download just enough of the file to start viewing or listening to it, while the rest of the file is downloaded in the background, reducing, but not eliminating, download time.

street *(US) Fin* used to describe somebody who is considered to be well informed about the market *(slang)*

street name *(US) Fin* a broker who holds a customer's security in the broking house's name to facilitate transactions

stress *HR* the psychological and physical state that results when perceived demands exceed an individual's ability to cope with them

stress puppy *(US) HR* somebody who complains a lot and seems to enjoy being stressed *(slang)*

strike *HR* a concerted refusal to work by employees, with the aim of improving wages or employment conditions, voicing a grievance, making a protest, or supporting other workers in such an endeavour. A strike is a form of *industrial action*.

strike pay *or* **strike benefit** *HR* a benefit or allowance paid by a *trade union* to its members during the course of official *strike* action to help offset loss of earnings. *Also known as **dispute benefit***

strike price *Fin* the price for a security or commodity that underlies an option

stripped bond *Fin* a bond that can be divided into separate zero-coupon bonds to represent its principal repayment and its interest

stripped stock *Fin* stock whose rights to dividends have been separated and sold

strips *Fin* the parts of a bond that entitle the owner only to interest payments or only to the repayment of principal

structural change *Econ* a change in the composition of output in an economy that means that resources have to be reallocated

structural inflation *Fin* inflation that naturally occurs in an economy, without any particular triggering event

structural unemployment *Econ* the situation where demand or technology changes so that there is too much labour in particular locations or skills areas

structured interview *HR see **interviewing***

structured systems analysis and design method *Gen Mgt* a technique for the analysis and design of computer systems. The structured systems analysis and design method was developed by the Central Computer and Telecommunications Agency in the United Kingdom in the early 1980s. The technique adopts a structured methodology towards systems development through the use of data flow, logical data, and entity event modelling. Core development stages include: *feasibility study*; requirements analysis; requirements specification; logical system specification; and physical design. All the steps and tasks within each stage must be complete before subsequent stages can begin. *Abbr* **SSADM**

stub equity *Fin* the money raised through the sale of high risk bonds in large amounts or quantities, as in a leveraged takeover or a leveraged buy-out

subcontract *Gen Mgt* a *contract* under which all, or part, of the work specified in an existing contract is delegated to another person or organisation

subcontracting *Gen Mgt, Ops* the delegation to a third party of some, or all, of the work that one has **contracted** to do. Subcontracting usually occurs where the contracted work, for example, the construction of a building, requires a variety of skills. Responsibility for the fulfilment of the original **contract** remains with the original contracting party. Where the fulfilment of a contract depends on the skills of the person who has entered into the contract, for example, in the painting of a portrait, then the work cannot be subcontracted to a third party. The term subcontracting is sometimes used to describe **outsourcing** arrangements.

subject line *E-com* the field at the top of an e-mail template in which the title or subject of the e-mail can be typed. The subject line is the only part of the e-mail—apart from the name of the sender—which can be read immediately by the recipient. It is important to have a strong subject line, particularly if using e-mail for advertising or promotional purposes, or the recipient may well simply delete the e-mail.

subject to collection *Fin* dependent upon the ability to collect the amount owed

subliminal advertising *Mkting* advertising intended to influence an audience subconsciously, especially through images shown very briefly on a film or television screen

subordinated debt *Fin see junior debt*

subordinated loan *Fin* a loan that ranks below all other borrowings with regard to both the payment of interest and repayment of the principal. *See also pari passu*

subscribed share capital *Fin see issued share capital*

subscriber *Fin* **1.** a buyer, especially one who buys shares in a new company or new issues **2.** a person who signs a company's Memorandum of Association

subscription-based publishing *E-com* content or a selection of content from a website, magazine, book, or other publication, delivered regularly by e-mail or other means to a group of people who have subscribed to received this content

subscription process *E-com* the means by which users of a website sign up to receive specific information, content, or services via that website. Someone may become a subscriber as a result of giving personal informa-

tion such as an e-mail address, or of making a payment if the subscription service is directly revenue-generating.

The early Internet promoted a culture that encouraged the free transfer of information, so subscription processes were relatively rare. However, it is becoming clear that, in general, websites must pay for themselves, either directly through subscription or advertising revenues, or indirectly by delivering valuable information that will further the organisation's objectives. As the Internet evolves, many more websites will become subscription based.

Subscription processes are also used to limit access to certain information. An extranet, for example, may contain confidential material, and a subscription process will be required to ensure that the right people have access to the right information.

subscription share *Fin* a share purchased by a subscriber when a new company is formed

subsidiary account *Fin* an account for one of the individual people or organisations that jointly hold another account

subsidiary company *Gen Mgt* a company that is controlled by another. A subsidiary company operates under the control of a parent or **holding company**, which may have a majority on the subsidiary's **board of directors**, or a majority shareholding in the subsidiary, giving it majority voting rights, or it may be named in a contract as having control of the subsidiary. If all of the stock in a company is owned by its parent, it is known as a **wholly-owned subsidiary**. A subsidiary that is located in a different country from the parent is a **foreign subsidiary company**.

subsistence allowance *HR expenses* paid by an **employer**, usually within pre-set limits, to cover the cost of accommodation, meals, and incidental expenses incurred by employees when away on business

subtreasury *Fin* a place where some of a nation's money is held

succession planning *Gen Mgt* the preparation for the replacement of one postholder by another, usually prompted by **retirement** or **resignation**. Succession planning involves preparing the new postholder before the old one leaves, possibly with training or through work shadowing. At a senior level, **management succession** should be accomplished as smoothly as possible in order to avoid organisational crises caused by absent or inadequate top management. General Electric

---

Men are quite humourless about their own businesses.   *Betty MacDonald*

is held to be an exemplar of succession planning for its preparation for the retirement of **Jack Welch**.

suggestion scheme *HR* a policy designed to encourage employees to generate ideas or proposals that improve work processes, for which they receive a gift or cash reward. The objective of a suggestion scheme is to promote **employee involvement**, creative thinking, and continuous improvement. Its success can be evaluated in terms of the participation rate or by the level of cost savings, but there may be an incalculable beneficial effect on sales, customer loyalty, retention of employees, and **motivation**.

suit *Gen Mgt* somebody who works for a large corporation and is required to wear a suit for work (*slang*)

sum *Fin* an amount or total of any given item, such as money, stocks, or securities

sum at risk *Fin* an amount of any given item, such as money, stocks, or securities that an investor may lose

sum insured *Fin* the maximum amount that an insurance company will pay out in the event of a claim

sum-of-the-year's-digits depreciation *Fin* accelerated depreciation, conferring tax advantage by assuming more rapid depreciation when an asset is new

Sunday night syndrome *Gen Mgt* feelings of depression experienced by employees when they consider their return to work on Monday morning

sunshine law *Fin* a law that requires public disclosure of a government act

super (*ANZ*) *Fin* an informal term for superannuation (*slang*)

superannuation plan *HR* a pension plan in Australia

superannuation scheme *HR* a pension plan in New Zealand

superindustrial society *Gen Mgt* a society in which technology dominates both the personal and working lives of its members

superstitial *E-com* a form of web-based advertisement that is run while new web pages are loading onto a user's computer. Unlike **interstitials**, superstitials are loaded onto the computer using a 'cache-and-play' delivery system that works while the Internet user is browsing the Web. Superstitials are mainly used during business-to-consumer advertising campaigns.

supervisor *Gen Mgt, HR* an employee who is given authority and responsibility for planning and controlling the work of a group through close contact. A supervisor is the first level of management in an organisation. The subordinates he or she controls are usually at a non-managerial level and the supervisor is wholly responsible for their work.

supervisory management *Gen Mgt, HR* the most junior level of management within an organisation. Supervisory management activities include staff **recruitment**, handling day-to-day grievances and staff discipline, and ensuring that quality and production targets are met. *Also known as* **first-line management**

supplier *HR, Ops* an organisation that delivers materials, components, goods, or services to another organisation

supplier appraisal *Ops see* **vendor rating**

supplier development *HR* the development of close and long-term relationships between a customer and a **supplier**. Supplier development tends to be associated with **Japanese management** practices and has only recently been introduced to the West. Various approaches to customer-supplier relations have emerged, including co-makership, partnership sourcing, collaborative sourcing, and co-operative sourcing. All these forms of supplier development are characterised by a long-term commitment, an integration of key functions and activities, a structured framework for determining price and sharing cost and profit, a proactive approach to **problem-solving**, and the adoption of both a win-win philosophy and a culture of continuous improvement.

supplier evaluation *Ops* the process of screening and evaluating potential suppliers of materials, goods, or services. Supplier evaluation involves establishing a set of requirements, which may include basic business robustness, performance elements specific to the product or service, and the key order winning criteria for final selection. Existing and potential suppliers are screened against these criteria, prior to placing a new order. When this process is undertaken after the fulfilment of an order, it is known as **vendor rating**.

supplier rating *Ops see* **vendor rating**

supply and demand *Gen Mgt, Ops* the quantity of goods available for sale at a given price, and the level of consumer need for those

---

Alignment is not about the management of quality. It is about the quality of management. **George Labovitz**

goods at a given price. The balance of supply and demand fluctuates as external economic factors such as the cost of materials and the level of competition in the marketplace influence the level of demand from consumers and the desire and ability of producers to supply the goods. Supply and demand is recognised as an economic principle, and is often referred to as the **law of supply and demand**.

supply chain *Gen Mgt, Ops* the network of *manufacturers*, *wholesalers*, distributors, and *retailers*, who turn *raw materials* into *finished goods* and services and deliver them to *consumers*. Supply chains are increasingly being seen as integrated entities, and closer relationships between the organisations throughout the chain can bring *competitive advantage*, reduce costs, and help to maintain a loyal customer base.

supply chain management *Ops* the management of the movement of goods and flow of information between an organisation and its *suppliers* and *customers*, to achieve strategic advantage. Supply chain management covers the processes of *materials management*, *logistics*, *physical distribution management*, and *purchasing*, as well as *information management*.

supply-side economics *Econ* the study of how economic agents behave when supply is affected by changing price

support *Mkting* help, advice, and services offered to customers by a seller after a sale

support price *Econ* the price of a product that is fixed or stabilised by a government so that it cannot fall below a certain level

surety *Fin* **1.** a guarantor **2.** the collateral given as security when borrowing

surplus *Fin see budget surplus*

surplus capacity *Ops* the capability of a factory or workstation to produce output over and above the level required by consumers or subsequent processes. Surplus capacity is a product of materials, personnel, and equipment that are superfluous, or not working to maximum *capacity*. Some surplus capacity is required in any production system to deal with fluctuations in demand, and as a backup in case of failure. Excessive surplus capacity, however, adds to the cost of the production process as work-in-progress inventory or finished-goods storage increases, and can result in *overcapacity*. If a workstation has no surplus capacity its workloads cannot be increased, so it is at risk of becoming a *bottleneck*. *Also known as redundant capacity*

surrender value *Fin* the sum of money offered by an insurance company to somebody who cancels a policy before it has completed its full term

surtax *Fin* a tax paid in addition to another tax, typically levied on an a corporation with very high income

survey *Stats* the collection of data from a given population for the purpose of analysis of a particular issue. Data is often collected only from a sample of a population, and this is known as a *sample survey*. Surveys are used widely in research, especially in *market research*.

survivalist enterprise *(S Africa) Gen Mgt* a business that has no paid employees, generates income below the poverty line, and is considered the lowest level of micro-enterprise

sushi bond *Fin* a derogatory name for a bond that is not denominated in yen and is issued in any market by a Japanese financial institution. This type of bond is often bought by Japanese institutional investors.

sustainable advantage *Gen Mgt* a competitive advantage that can be maintained over the long term, as opposed to one resulting from a short-term tactical promotion

sustainable development *Gen Mgt* development that meets the needs of the present without compromising the ability of future generations to meet their own needs. The concept of sustainable development was introduced by the Brundtland Report, the first report of the World Commission on Environment and Development, set up by the United Nations in 1983. It advocates the integration of social, economic, and environmental considerations into policy decisions by business and government. Particular emphasis is given to social, cultural, and ethical implications of development. Sustainable development can be achieved through *environmental management* and is a feature of a socially responsible business.

SVA *abbr Gen Mgt* shareholder value analysis

swap *Fin* an exchange of credits or liabilities. *See also asset swap, bond swap, interest rate swap*

swap book *Fin* a broker's list of stocks or securities that clients wish to swap

---

swaption *Fin* an option to enter into a *swap* contract (*slang*)

sweat equity *Gen Mgt* an investment of labour rather than cash in a business enterprise (*slang*)

sweep facility *Fin* the automatic transfer of sums from a current account to a deposit account, or from any low interest account to a higher one. For example, a personal customer may have the balance transferred just before receipt of their monthly salary, or a business may stipulate that when a balance exceeds a certain sum, the excess is to be transferred.

sweetener 1. *Gen Mgt* an incentive offered to somebody to take a particular course of action **2.** *Fin* a feature added to a security to make it more attractive to investors **3.** *Fin* a security with a high yield that has been added to a portfolio to improve its overall return. *See also* **kicker**

sweetheart agreement (*ANZ*) *HR* an agreement reached between employees and their employer without recourse to arbitration

SWELL *abbr Mkting* Single Woman Earning Lots in London (*slang*)

SWIFT *abbr Fin* Society for Worldwide Interbank Financial Telecommunication: a non-profit cooperative organisation whose mission is to create a shared worldwide data processing and communications link and a common language for international financial transactions. Established in Brussels in 1973 with the support of 239 banks in 15 countries, it now has over 7,000 live users in 192 countries, exchanging millions of messages valued in trillions of dollars every business day.

swing trading *Fin* the trading of stock by individuals that takes advantage of sudden price movements that occur especially when large numbers of traders have to cover short sales

swipe box *E-com* an electronic device used for reading the magnetic data on a credit card during a card-present transaction

switch *Fin* **1.** to exchange a specific security with another within a portfolio, usually because the investor's objectives have changed **2.** a swap exchange rate. *See also* **swap 3.** to move a commodity from one location to another

Switch *Fin* a debit card widely used in the United Kingdom

switching *Fin* the simultaneous sale and purchase of contracts in futures with different expiration dates, for example, when a business

decides that it would like to take delivery of a commodity earlier or later than originally contracted

switching discount *Fin* the discount available to holders of collective investments who move from one fund to another offered by the same fund manager. This is usually a lower initial charge compared to the one made to new investors or when existing investors make a further investment.

SWOT analysis *Gen Mgt* an assessment of Strengths, Weaknesses, Opportunities, and Threats. SWOT analysis is used within organisations in the early stages of strategic and *marketing planning*. It is also used in *problem-solving*, *decision-making*, or for making staff aware of the need for change. It can be used at a personal level when examining your *career path* or determining possible *career development*.

Sydney Futures Exchange *Fin* the principal market in Australia for trading financial and commodity futures. It was set up in 1962 as a wool futures market, the Sydney Greasy Wool Futures Exchange, but adopted its current name in 1972 to reflect its widening role. *Abbr* **SFE**

symmetrical distribution *Stats* a distribution of statistical data that is symmetrical about a central value

syndicated research *Mkting* trend data supplied by research agencies from their regularly operated retail audits or consumer panels

sysop *E-com* systems operator, somebody who manages a website or bulletin board (*slang*)

systematic sampling *Ops see* **random sampling**

system attack *E-com* a deliberate attack on an e-mail system, usually in the form of a barrage of messages sent to one address simultaneously

systems administrator *E-com* the person responsible for the management of an e-mail system

systems analysis *Gen Mgt* the examination and evaluation of an operation or task in order to identify and implement more efficient methods, usually through the use of computers. Systems analysis can be broken down into three main areas: the production of a statement of objectives; determination of the methods of best achieving these objectives in

---

Basing our happiness on our ability to control everything is futile.   **Stephen Covey**

a cost-effective and efficient way; and the preparation of a **feasibility study**. *Also known as systems planning*

systems approach *Gen Mgt* a technique employed for organisational **decision-making** and **problem-solving** involving the use of computer systems.

The systems approach uses **systems analysis** to examine the interdependency, interconnections, and interrelations of a system's components. When working in synergy, these components produce an effect greater than the sum effects of the parts. System components might comprise departments or functions of an organisation or business which work together for an overall objective.

systems audit *Gen Mgt* an approach to **auditing** which utilises the **systems method**. By using a systems audit to assess the internal control system of an organisation, it is possible to assess the quality of the accounting system and the level of testing required from the financial statements. One shortcoming of systems audit is that it does not consider audit **risk**. Consequently, risk-based audit is now considered more effective.

systems design *Gen Mgt* the creation of a computer program to meet predetermined functional, operational, and personnel specifications. The systems design process involves the use of **systems analysis** and flow-charting of organisational functions and operations. It can be split into four stages: definition of the system's goals; preparation of a conceptual model of how these goals will be achieved; development of a physical design; and preparation of a system specification.

systems dynamics *Gen Mgt* a computer-based tool, developed at the Massachusetts Institute of Technology, designed to model the behaviour of constantly changing systems. Systems dynamics investigates the combined effects of individual changes made at different points in a system, and uses **simulation** to design information feedback structures.

systems engineering *Gen Mgt* the process of planning, designing, creating, testing, and operating complex systems. Systems engineering can be viewed as a continuous cycle, aimed at developing alternative strategies for effective systems utilisation. It is concerned with the definition, planning, and deployment of future systems.

systems method *Gen Mgt* a widely used group of methodologies which explore the nature of complex business situations by mapping activities in a model. The systems method can be applied to systems that are either **hard systems**, where precise objectives are expressed in mathematical terms, or **soft systems**, where a human factor is involved and situations often do not involve such precise objectives. A range of **systems approaches** are available including **operational research**, **systems analysis**, and **systems dynamics**.

systems planning *Gen Mgt see systems analysis*

T+ *Fin* an expression of the number of days allowed for settlement of a transaction

TA *abbr Gen Mgt* transactional analysis

tacit knowledge *Gen Mgt see* **knowledge**

tactical campaign *Mkting* a series of marketing activities designed to achieve short-term targets

tactical plan *Gen Mgt* a short-term plan for achieving an entity's objectives

TAFN *abbr Gen Mgt* that's all for now (*slang*)

Taguchi, Genichi (*b.* 1924) *Gen Mgt* Japanese academic and consultant. Known for his contribution to quality engineering and founder of the *Taguchi method*, which seeks to integrate **quality control** into product design using experiment and statistical analysis. His concepts, including quality loss (see *Taguchi methods*), are explained in publications such as *Introduction to Quality Engineering* (1986).

Taguchi methods *Ops* the pioneering techniques of **quality control** developed by **Genichi Taguchi**, which focus on improving the quality of a product or process at the design stage rather than after manufacture or delivery. Taguchi's philosophy is that a quality approach that focuses on the parameters or factors of design produces a design that is more robust and is capable of withstanding variations from unwanted sources in the production or delivery process. He developed methods for both offline (design) and online (production) quality control. He developed the concepts of **quality loss** and the signal to noise ratio, and a product design improvement process based on three steps: system design, parameter design, and tolerance design.

tailgating *Fin* the practice of buying or selling a security by a broker, immediately after a client's transaction, in order to take advantage of the impact of the client's deal

tailormade promotion *Mkting* a promotional campaign that is customised for a particular customer

take a flyer *Fin* to speculate (*slang*)

take a hit *Fin* to make a loss on an investment (*slang*)

takeaway *Gen Mgt* the impressions that a consumer forms about a product or service

take-home pay *HR* the amount of *pay* an employee receives after all deductions, such as income tax, national insurance, or pension contributions. *Also known as* **net pay**

takeout financing *Fin* loans used to replace bridge financing

takeover *Fin* the acquisition by a company of a controlling interest in the voting share capital of another company, usually achieved by the purchase of a majority of the voting shares

takeover approach *Fin* the price at which a suitor offers to buy a corporation's shares. *US term* **tender offer**

takeover battle *Fin* the result of a hostile takeover bid. The bidder may raise the offer price and write to the shareholders extolling the benefits of the takeover. The board may contact other companies in the same line of business hoping that a white knight may appear. It could also take action to make the company less desirable to the bidder. *See also* **poison pill**

takeover bid *Mkting* an attempt by one company to acquire another. A takeover bid can be made either by a person or an organisation, and usually takes the form of an approach to **shareholders** with an offer to purchase. The bidding stage is often difficult and fraught with politics, and various forms of **knight** may be involved.

takeover ratio *Fin* the book value of a company divided by its market capitalisation. If the resulting figure is greater than one, then the company is a candidate for a takeover. *See also* **appreciation**, **asset-stripping**

taker *Fin* **1.** the buyer of an option **2.** a borrower

takings *Fin* a retailer's net receipts

talent *HR* people with exceptional abilities, especially a company's most valued employees (*slang*)

talk offline *Gen Mgt* **1.** to continue a particular line of discussion outside the original context. A person may wish to talk offline about an issue tangential to the current discussion, or may carry on that branch of the conversation at a later time, using different media. (*slang*) **2.** to express an opinion in opposition to an employing organisation's official position

tall organisation *Gen Mgt* an *organisation structure* with many levels of management. A tall organisation contrasts with a *flat organisation*, since it has an extended vertical structure with well-defined but long reporting lines. The number of different levels may cause *communication* problems and slow *decision-making*. It is for this reason that many companies are converting to flatter structures more suited to the fast responses needed in a rapidly changing business environment.

tall poppy (*ANZ*) *Gen Mgt* a prominent member of society (*slang*)

tall poppy syndrome (*ANZ*) *Gen Mgt* an inclination in the media and among the general public to belittle the achievements of prominent people (*slang*)

talon *Fin* a form attached to a bearer bond that the holder of the bond uses when the coupons attached to the bond have been depleted to order new coupons

tangible assets *Fin* assets that are physical, such as buildings, cash and stock, as opposed to intangible assets. Leases and securities, although not physical, are classed as tangible assets because the underlying assets are physical.

tangible book value *Fin* the book value of a company after intangible assets, patents, trademarks, and the value of research and development have been subtracted

tangible fixed asset statement *Fin* a summary of the opening and closing balances for tangible fixed assets and acquisitions, disposals, and depreciation in the period

tank *Fin* to fall precipitously. This term is used especially in reference to stock prices. (*slang*)

tap CD *Fin* the issue of certificates of deposit, normally in large denominations, when required by a specific investor

tape
don't fight the tape *Fin* don't go against the direction of the market (*slang*)

target *Gen Mgt see* *objective*

target audience *Mkting* a group of people considered likely to buy a product or service

target cash balance *Fin* the amount of cash that a company would like to have in hand

target company *Fin* a company that is the object of a takeover bid

target cost *Fin* a product cost estimate derived by subtracting a desired profit margin from a competitive market price. This may be less than the planned initial product cost, but will be expected to be achieved by the time the product reaches the mature production stage.

targeted repurchase *Fin* a company's purchase of its own shares from somebody attempting to buy the company

target population *Stats* the collection of individuals or regions that are to be investigated in a statistical study

target savings motive *Econ* the motive that people have not to save when their families are growing up but to save when they are in middle age and trying to build up a pension

target stock level *Ops* the level of *inventory* that is needed to satisfy all demand for a product or component over a specified period

tariff 1. *Econ* a government duty imposed on imports or exports to stimulate or dampen economic activity **2.** *Fin* a list of prices at which goods or services are supplied

Tariff Concession Scheme *Fin* a system operated by the Australian government in which imported goods that have no locally produced equivalent attract reduced duties. *Abbr* **TCS**

tariff office *Fin* an insurance company whose premiums are determined according to a scale set collectively by several companies

task analysis *HR* a methodology for identifying and examining the jobs performed by users when interacting with computerised, or non-computerised, systems. Task analysis employs a range of techniques to help analysts collect information, organise it, and use it to integrate the human element in systems. It assists in the achievement of higher safety, *productivity*, and maintenance standards.

task culture *Gen Mgt* a form of *corporate culture* based on individual projects carried out by small teams. Task culture was identified by *Charles Handy*. It draws resources from different parts of the organisation to form study groups, working parties, and ad hoc committees to take on problems, projects, and initiatives as they arise.

task group *HR* a group of employees temporarily brought together to complete a specific project or task. A task group can take the form of an *autonomous work group* if it is responsible for its own management.

Monopoly is a terrible thing, till you have it.   *Rupert Murdoch*

taste space *Mkting* a community of consumers identified as having similar tastes or interests, for example, in music or books, enabling companies to recommend purchases or target advertising at them (*slang*)

tax *Fin* a governmental charge that is not a price for a good or service

taxability *Fin* the extent to which a good or individual is subject to a tax

taxable *Fin* subject to a tax

taxable base *Fin* the amount subject to taxation

taxable income *Fin* income that is subject to taxes

taxable matters *Fin* goods or services that can be taxed

tax and price index *Econ* an index number measuring the percentage change in gross income that taxpayers need if they are to maintain their real disposable income

tax avoidance *Fin* strategies to ensure the payment of as little in taxes as is legally possible. *See also* **tax evasion**

tax bracket *Fin* a range of income levels subject to marginal tax at the same rate

tax break *Fin* an investment that is tax efficient or a legal arrangement that reduces the liability to tax. *See also* **tax avoidance**, **tax shelter**

tax consultant *Fin* a professional who advises on all aspects of taxation from tax avoidance to estate planning

tax-deductible *Fin* able to be subtracted from taxable income before tax is paid

tax-deductible public debt *Fin* debt instruments exempt from US federal income tax

tax-deferred *Fin* not to be taxed until a later time

tax domicile *Fin* a place that a government levying a tax considers to be a person's home

tax-efficient *Fin* financially advantageous by leading to a reduction of taxes to be paid

tax evasion *Fin* the illegal practice of paying less money in taxes than is due. *See also* **tax avoidance**

tax evasion amnesty *Fin* a governmental measure that affords those who have evaded a tax in some specified way freedom from punishment for their violation of the tax law

tax-exempt *Fin* not subject to tax

Tax Exempt Special Savings Account *Fin* a UK savings account in which investors could save up to £9,000 over a period of five years and not pay any tax provided they made no withdrawals over that time. The advent of the ISA in 1999 meant that no new accounts of this type could be opened, but those opened prior to 1999 will continue under their original premise until their expiry date. *Abbr* **TESSA**

tax exile *Fin* a person or business that leaves a country to avoid paying taxes, or the condition of having done this

tax-favoured asset *Fin* an asset that receives more favourable tax treatment than some other asset

tax file number *Fin* an identification number assigned to each taxpayer in Australia. *Abbr* **TFN**

tax-free *Fin* not subject to tax

tax harmonization *Fin* the enactment of taxation laws in different jurisdictions, such as neighbouring countries, provinces, or states of the United States, that are consistent with one another

tax haven *Fin* a country that has generous tax laws, especially one that encourages non-citizens to base operations in the country to avoid higher taxes in their home countries

tax holiday *Fin* an exemption from tax granted for a specified period of time. *See also* **tax subsidy**

taxi industry *Fin* the privately owned mini-bus taxi services, which constitute the largest sector of public transport in South Africa

tax incentive *Fin* a tax reduction afforded to people for particular purposes, for example, sending their children to college

tax inspector *Fin* a government employee who investigates taxpayers' declarations

tax invoice (*ANZ*) *Fin* a document issued by a supplier which stipulates the amount charged for goods or services as well as the amount of **GST** payable

tax law *Fin* the body of laws on taxation, or one such law

tax loophole *Fin* a provision in a tax law that permits some individuals and companies to avoid or reduce taxes

tax loss *Fin* a loss of money that can serve to reduce tax liabilities

---

You don't go to a poker table with no money in your pocket. *Barbara Thomas*

tax loss carry-back *Fin* the reduction of taxes in a previous year by subtraction from income for that year of losses suffered in the current year

tax loss carry-forward *Fin* the reduction of taxes in a future year by subtraction from income for that year of losses suffered in the current year

tax obligation *Fin* the amount of tax a person or company owes

tax on capital income *Fin* a tax on the income from sales of capital assets

tax payable *Fin* the amount of tax a person or company has to pay

taxpayer *Fin* an individual or corporation who pays a tax

tax rate *Fin* a percentage of a taxable amount that is due to be paid in taxes

tax refund *Fin* an amount that a government gives back to a taxpayer who has paid more taxes than were due

tax relief *Fin* **1.** the reduction in the amount of taxes payable, for example, on capital goods a company has purchased **2.** (*US*) money given to a certain group of people by a government in the form of a reduction of taxes

tax return *Fin* an official form on which a company or individual enters details of income and expenses, used to assess tax liability. *Also known as* **return**

tax revenue *Fin* money that a government receives in taxes

tax sale (*US*) *Fin* a sale of an item by a government to recover overdue taxes on a taxable item

tax shelter *Fin* a financial arrangement designed to reduce tax liability. *See also* **abusive tax shelter**

tax subsidy *Fin* a tax reduction given by a government to a business for a particular purpose, usually to create jobs. *See also* **tax holiday**

tax system *Fin* the system of taxation adopted by a country

tax treaty *Fin* an international treaty that deals with taxes, especially taxes by several countries on the same individuals

tax year *Fin* a period covered by a statement about taxes

Taylor, Frederick Winslow (1856–1917) *Gen Mgt* US engineer. Acknowledged as the father of *scientific management*, which is sometimes referred to as 'Taylorism'. Taylor's methods, recorded in *The Principles of Scientific Management* (1911), have been criticised as too mechanistic, treating people like machines rather than human beings to be motivated. They were later counterbalanced by the *human relations* school of management.

Taylor grew up in an affluent Philadelphia family. He worked as chief engineer at the Midvale Steel Company, and later became general manager of the Manufacturing Investment Company's paper mills in Maine. In 1893 he moved to New York and began business as a consulting engineer.

T-bill *abbr Fin* Treasury bill

TCO *abbr Gen Mgt* total cost of ownership

T-commerce *E-com* business that is conducted by means of interactive television (*slang*)

TCP/IP *abbr E-com* transmission control protocol/Internet protocol: the combination of protocols that enables the Internet to function. TCP deals with the process of sending packets of information from one computer to another. IP is the process of passing each packet between computers until it reaches its intended destination.

TCS *abbr Fin* Tariff Concession Scheme

TDB *abbr Fin* Trade Development Board

team briefing *HR* a regular meeting between managers or supervisors and their teams to exchange information and ideas. The idea of team briefing evolved from the concept of **briefing groups** which was developed in the United Kingdom in the 1960s and promoted by the Industrial Society as a means of communicating systematically with managers and employees throughout an organisation. The aim was to reduce misunderstandings and rumours and increase co-operation, *employee commitment*, and *team building*. Team briefings are characterised as being regular face-to-face meetings of small teams which are led by a team leader and are relevant to the work of the group, providing an opportunity for questions.

team building *Gen Mgt* the selection and grouping of a mix of people and the development of skills required within the group to achieve agreed objectives. Effective team building can be achieved through a number of models, one of the most established of which

---

Let us never negotiate out of fear, but let us never fear to negotiate.   *John F. Kennedy*

was created by **R. Meredith Belbin**.

team management *Gen Mgt see Managerial Grid™*

Team Management Wheel™ *Gen Mgt* a visual aid for the efficient co-ordination of *teamwork*, which can be used to analyse how teams work together, assist in *team building*, and aid self-development and training. The Team Management Wheel outlines eight main team roles. Team members can determine the main functions of their jobs (what they have to do), by using the 'Types of Work Index', and can determine their own work preferences (what they want to do), using the 'Team Management Index'. They are then assigned one major role and two minor roles on the Team Management Wheel. At the centre of the Wheel are the linking skills common to all team members. The Team Management Wheel was developed by **Charles Margerison** and **Dick McCann** in 1984.

team player *Gen Mgt* somebody who works well within a team (*slang*)

teamwork *Gen Mgt* collaboration by a group of people to achieve a common purpose. Teamwork is often a feature of day-to-day working, and is increasingly used to accomplish specific projects, in which case it may bring together people from different functions, departments, or disciplines. A team should ideally consist of people with complementary skills; **R. Meredith Belbin** has established nine personality types that are needed in every team. One tool aimed at effective *team building* is the *Team Management Wheel*™. There are various types of teamworking, including the *autonomous work group* and the *virtual team*.

teaser rate *Fin* a temporary concessionary interest rate offered on mortgages, credit cards, or savings accounts in order to attract new customers

technical analysis *Fin* the analysis of past movements in the prices of financial instruments, currencies, commodities, etc., with a view to predicting future price movements by applying analytical techniques. *See also fundamental analysis*

technical rally *Fin* a temporary rise in security or commodity prices while the market is in a general decline. This may be because investors are seeking bargains, or because analysts have noted a support level.

technical reserves *Fin* the assets that an insurance company maintains to meet future claims

technocracy *Gen Mgt* an organisation controlled by technical experts. *See also bureaucracy*

techno-determinist *Gen Mgt* somebody who believes that technological progress is inevitable

technographics *Gen Mgt* a research process that evaluates the attitudes of consumers towards technology. The process was introduced by Forrester Research.

technological risk *Fin* the risk that a newly designed plant will not operate to specification

technology adoption life cycle *Gen Mgt* a model used to describe the adoption of new technologies, typically including the stages of innovators, early adopters, early majority, late majority, and *technology laggards*

Technology and Human Resources for Industry Programme *(S Africa) Fin see THRIP*

technology laggard *Gen Mgt* an organisation that is very slow or reluctant to adopt new technology

technology stock *Fin* stock issued by a company that is involved in new technology

teeming and lading *Fin* a fraud based on a continuous cycle of stealing and later replacing assets (generally cash), each theft being used in part, or in full, to repay a previous theft in order to avoid detection

telcos *(ANZ) Gen Mgt* an informal term for telecommunications companies (*slang*)

telebanking *Fin* electronic banking carried out by using a telephone line to communicate with a bank

telecentre *Gen Mgt* a building offering office space and facilities outside the home but away from the main workplace to enable remote working. A telecentre may be owned by one employer—in which case it is known as a *satellite centre*—or may be independently run on behalf of a number of organisations. Employees avoid long commuting times but work in an office rather than at home; employers avoid having to equip several homes with expensive office equipment. *Also known as telecottage*

telecommute *Gen Mgt* to work without leaving your home by using telephone lines to carry data between your home and your employer's place of business

telecommuter *Gen Mgt see teleworker*

telecommuting *Gen Mgt see teleworking*

teleconferencing *Gen Mgt* the use of telephone or television channels to connect people in different locations in order to conduct group discussions, meetings, conferences, or courses

telecottage *Gen Mgt see* **telecentre**

telegraphic transfer *Fin* a method of transferring funds from a bank to a financial institution overseas using telegraphs. *Abbr* **TT**

telemarketing *Mkting see* **telephone selling**

telephone banking *Fin* a system in which customers can access their accounts and a range of banking services up to 24 hours a day by telephone. Apart from convenience, customers usually benefit from higher interest rates on savings accounts and lower interest when borrowing as providers of telephone banking have lower overheads than traditional high street banks.

telephone interview survey *Stats* a method of sampling a population by telephoning its members

telephone number salary *HR* a six- or seven-figure salary (*slang*)

telephone selling *Mkting* the sale of products or services to customers over the telephone. Telephone selling may be used as an alternative, cheaper, method than door-to-door selling, or may be used to obtain an initial appointment for a salesperson to visit a potential customer. *Also known as* **telemarketing**, **telesales**

telephone survey *Mkting* a research technique in which members of the public are asked a series of questions on the telephone

telephone switching *Fin* the process of connecting telephones to one another

telephone tag *Gen Mgt* the reciprocal calling and leaving of messages by two people who wish to speak to each other but are never available to speak on their telephones when the other calls (*slang*)

telesales *Mkting see* **telephone selling**

teleshopping *E-com* the use of telecommunications and computers to shop for and purchase goods and services

television audience measurement *Mkting* the recording of the viewing patterns of a sample of the population, used as the basis for estimating national viewing figures for individual programmes

teleworker *Gen Mgt* an employee who spends a substantial amount of working time away from the employer's main premises and communicates with the organisation through the use of computing and telecommunications equipment. A teleworker may be based at home, in which case the worker is known as a **homeworker**, or in a **telecentre**, or on a variety of sites, in which case he or she may be known as a **mobile worker**. *Also known as* **telecommuter**

teleworking *Gen Mgt* a geographically dispersed work environment where workers can work at home on a computer and transmit data and documents to a central office via telephone lines. As people become accustomed to working via e-mail and the Internet, teleworking is proving ever more popular.

The advantages of teleworking are considerable, offering as it does an excellent compromise between the security of full-time employment and the liberty and privacy of self-employment. However, it also has disadvantages—the most important of which is the danger of being left behind, forgotten, or overlooked when new assignments or promotions come up within the organisation. It is therefore supremely important for teleworkers to build a plan for staying visible and connected with the people they work with, even if they spend much of their working life in their home office. *Also known as* **telecommuting**

teller *Fin* a bank cashier

tender 1. *Fin* to bid for securities at auction. The securities are allocated according to the method adopted by the issuer. In the standard auction style, the investor receives the security at the price they tendered. In a Dutch style auction, the issuer announces a strike price after all the tenders have been examined. This is set at a level where all the issue is sold. Investors who submitted a tender above the strike price only pay the strike price. The Dutch style of auction is increasingly being adopted in the United Kingdom. US Treasury Bills are also sold using the Dutch system. *See also* **offer for sale**, **sale by tender 2.** *Gen Mgt* to make or submit a bid to undertake work or supply goods at a stated price. A tender is usually submitted in response to an invitation to bid for a work contract in competition with other suppliers.

tender offer (*US*) *Fin* = **takeover approach**

tenor *Fin* the period of time that has to elapse before a bill of exchange becomes payable

---

The goals on which hope are based have to be realistic.   *Arthur Lydiard*

term *Fin* the period of time that has to elapse from the date of the initial investment before a security, or other investment such as a term deposit or endowment assurance, becomes redeemable or reaches its maturity date

term assurance *Fin* a life policy that will pay out upon the death of the life assured or in the event of the death of the first life assured with a joint life assurance

term bill *Fin see* **period bill**

term deposit *Fin* a deposit account held for a fixed period. Withdrawals are either not allowed during this period, or they involve a fee payable by the depositor.

terminal date *Fin* the day on which a futures contract expires

terminal identification number *E-com see* **TIN**

terminal market *Fin* an exchange on which futures contracts or spot deals for commodities are traded

termination interview *HR* a meeting between an employee and a management representative in order to **dismiss** the employee. A termination interview should be brief, explaining the reasons for the dismissal, and giving details of whether a **notice period** should be worked, and whether, especially in the case of **redundancy**, additional assistance will be forthcoming from the employer.

termination of service *HR* the ending of an employee's **contract of employment** for a reason such as **redundancy**, employer **insolvency**, or **dismissal**

term insurance *Fin* insurance, especially life assurance, that is in effect for a specified period of time

term loan *Fin* a loan for a fixed period, usually called a personal loan when it is for non-business purposes. While a personal loan is normally at a fixed rate of interest, a term loan to a business may be at either a fixed or variable rate. Term loans may be either secured or unsecured. An early repayment fee is usually payable when such a loan is repaid before the end of the term. *See also* **balloon loan**, **bullet loan**

term shares *Fin* in the United Kingdom, a share account in a building society that is for a fixed period of time. Withdrawals are usually not allowed during this period. However, if they are, then a fee is normally payable by the account holder.

terms of trade *Econ* a ratio to determine whether the conditions under which a country conducts its trade are favourable or unfavourable

terotechnology *Ops* a multidisciplinary technique that combines the areas of management, finance, and engineering with the aim of optimising life-cycle costs for physical assets and technologies. Terotechnology is concerned with acquiring and caring for physical assets. It covers the specification and design for the reliability and maintainability of plant, machinery, equipment, buildings, and structures, including the installation, commissioning, maintenance, and replacement of this plant, and also incorporates the feedback of information on design, performance, and costs.

tertiary sector *Econ* the part of the economy made up of non-profit organisations such as consumer associations and self-help groups

TESSA *abbr Fin* Tax Exempt Special Savings Account

testacy *Fin* the legal position of a person who has died leaving a valid will

testate *Fin* used to refer to a person who has died leaving a valid will

testator *Fin* a man who has made a valid will

testatrix *Fin* a woman who has made a valid will

test battery *HR see* **psychometric test**

testimonial advertising *Mkting* advertising in which customers or celebrities recommend the product

test marketing *Mkting* the use of a small-scale version of a **marketing plan**, usually in a restricted area or with a small group, to test the marketing strategy for a new product. Test marketing gauges both the success of the marketing strategy and the reactions of consumers to a new product by giving an indication of the potential response to a product nationwide. Test marketing avoids the costs of a full-scale launch of an untested product, but a drawback is that both the product and marketing plan are exposed to competitors.

TFN *abbr Fin* tax file number

TFN Withholding Tax (*ANZ*) *Fin* Tax File Number Withholding Tax: a levy imposed on financial transactions involving an individual who has not disclosed his or her tax file number

We feel the spear of the marketplace in our back. *Tony O'Reilly*

TGIF *abbr Gen Mgt* thank God it's Friday (*slang*)

T-Group *HR see sensitivity training*

Theory E *Gen Mgt* a mechanism for bringing about change in an organisation through the creation of economic value and improved profits for the shareholders. Theory E has the single goal of satisfying the financial markets with a *top-down approach* style of *leadership* from the *chief executive*. Theory E contrasts with *Theory O*, which involves employee *empowerment* and *employee participation* in leadership. *See also alphabet theories of management*

Theory J *Gen Mgt* the *Japanese* form of management. Theory J is closely related to *Theory Z*, and was expounded by *William Ouchi*. *See also alphabet theories of management*

Theory O *Gen Mgt* a mechanism for organisational **change** based on developing *corporate culture* and human capability through personal and *organisational learning*. Theory O involves fostering a culture that encourages employees to find their own solutions to problems through *empowerment* and participative *leadership*. Theory O contrasts with *Theory E*, which involves a *top-down approach* style of leadership rather than *employee participation*. *See also alphabet theories of management*

theory of constraints *Fin* an approach to production management which aims to maximise sales revenue less material and variable overhead cost. It focuses on factors such as bottlenecks which act as constraints to this maximisation. *Abbr* **TOC**

theory of the horizontal fast track *Gen Mgt* a variation of *fast track* coined by *Charles Handy*. The theory of the horizontal fast track describes the development of talented people who are moved around from task to task to test and develop their capability in different working situations.

Theory W *Gen Mgt* an extreme extension of *Douglas McGregor's Theory X*, which proposes that not only should employees be coerced into action but that force is often required. Theory W is a humorous contribution to the *alphabet theories of management*. Theory W stands for Theory Whiplash.

Theory X *Gen Mgt* a management theory based on the assumption that most people are naturally reluctant to work and need discipline, direction, and close control if they are to meet work requirements. Theory X was coined by *Douglas McGregor* in *The Human*

Side of Enterprise, and it was considered by him to be an implicit basis for traditional hierarchical management. McGregor rejected Theory X as an appropriate management style and favoured instead his proposed alternative, *Theory Y*. *See also alphabet theories of management*

Theory Y *Gen Mgt* a management theory based on the assumption that employees want to work, achieve, and take responsibility for meeting their work requirements. Theory Y was coined by *Douglas McGregor* in *The Human Side of Enterprise*. Although he recognised that Theory Y could not solve all human resource management (see *HRM*) problems, McGregor favoured it over his *Theory X*, which required an autocratic management style. *See also alphabet theories of management*

Theory Z *Gen Mgt* a management theory based on the assumption that greater employee involvement leads to greater productivity. Theory Z was proposed by *Douglas McGregor* shortly before his death in an attempt to address the criticisms of his *Theory X* and *Theory Y*. McGregor's ideas were expanded by *William Ouchi* in his book *Theory Z*, reflecting the Japanese approach to human resource management (see *HRM*). Theory Z advocates greater *employee participation* in management, greater recognition of employees' contributions, better career prospects and security of employment, and greater mutual respect between employees and managers. *See also alphabet theories of management*

think tank *Gen Mgt* an organisation or group of experts researching and advising on issues of society, science, technology, industry, or business

thin market *Fin* a market where the trading volume is low. A characteristic of such a market is a wide spread of bid and offer prices.

third market *Fin* a market other than the main stock exchange in which stocks are traded

third-party network *or* **third-party service provider** *E-com see value-added network*

third-party service provider *E-com see value-added network*

third sector *HR see non-profit organisation*

Thorsrud, Einar (1923–85) *Gen Mgt* Norwegian academic. Researcher at the Tavistock Institute of Human Relations and collaborator with *Fred Emery*. Thorsrud set up an institute

---

in Oslo which became the centre of Scandinavian exploration of the concept of *industrial democracy*.

three-dimensional management *or* **3-D management** *Gen Mgt* a theory outlining eight *management styles* that differ in effectiveness. Three-dimensional management was coined by *Bill Reddin* and was a development of the work of *Robert Blake* and *Jane Mouton*. Reddin described four managerial styles that he considered effective, and four that he considered less effective. These can be plotted in grids, showing how each style approaches relationships and tasks. The least effective type of manager is called the Deserter, the most effective is the Executive. Reddin believed that different styles are used in different types of work settings and that managers modify their style to suit different circumstances.

three generic strategies *Fin* strategies of differentiation, focus, and overall cost leadership outlined by Porter as offering possible means of outperforming competitors within an industry, and of coping with the five competitive forces

three martini lunch (*US*) *Gen Mgt* a business lunch involving a lot of alcohol to relax the client (*slang*)

three Ps *Gen Mgt* a model proposed by *Sumantra Ghoshal* to succeed the *three Ss*, which refers to the three foundations of today's leading companies: purpose, process, and people

360 degree appraisal *HR* the *management style* adopted depending on the location of a manager on the *Managerial Grid*™, indicating a preference for focusing on the task or people side of management

360 degree branding *Mkting* taking an inclusive approach in branding a product by bringing the brand to all points of consumer contact

three Ss *Gen Mgt* a classification of *decision-making* relating to strategy, structure, and systems. *Sumantra Ghoshal* has suggested replacing the three Ss model with the *three Ps*.

three steps and a stumble *Fin* a rule of thumb used on the US stock market that if the Federal Reserve increases interest rates three times consecutively, stock market prices will go down (*slang*)

threshold company *Gen Mgt* a company that is on the verge of becoming well established in the business world (*slang*)

thrift institution *or* **thrift** *Fin* a bank that offers savings accounts. *See also* **savings and loan association**, **savings bank**

THRIP *abbr* (*S Africa*) *Fin* Technology and Human Resources for Industry Programme: a collaborative programme involving industry, government, and educational and research institutions that supports research and development in technology, science, and engineering

throughput accounting *Fin* a management accounting system which focuses on ways by which the maximum return per unit of bottleneck activity can be achieved

throw somebody a curve ball (*US*) *Gen Mgt* to do or say something unexpected, for example during a meeting or a project. The metaphor is from baseball. (*slang*)

TIBOR *abbr Fin* Tokyo Inter Bank Offered Rate

Tichy, Noel *Gen Mgt* US academic. Known for his research on the *transformational theory of leadership*, which developed the work of *James Burns*. See *The Transformational Leader* (1986, co-author).

tick *Fin* the least amount by which a value such as the price of a stock or a rate of interest can rise or fall. This could be, for example, a hundredth of a percentage point.
have ticks in all the right boxes *Gen Mgt* to be on course to meet a series of objectives (*slang*)

tied loan *Fin* a loan made by one national government to another on the condition that the funds are used to purchase goods from the lending nation

tie-in *Mkting* an advertising campaign in which two or more companies share the costs by combining their products or services (*slang*)

tigers *Fin* the most important markets in the Pacific Basin region, excluding Japan, including Hong Kong, South Korea, Singapore, and Taiwan

tight money *Econ* a situation where it is expensive to borrow because of restrictive government policy or high demand

TILA *abbr Fin* Truth in Lending Act

time and material pricing *Fin* a form of cost plus pricing in which price is determined by reference to the cost of the labour and material inputs to the product/service

---

I'm the boss. I'm allowed to yell.   *Ivan Boesky*

time and motion study *HR* the measurement and analysis of the motions or steps involved in a particular task and the time taken to complete each one. Time and motion study can be broken down into two distinct techniques: *method study*, the analysis of how people work and how jobs are performed, and *work measurement*, the time taken to complete each job. It can be used to set job standards, simplify work, and check and improve the efficiency of workers. Time and motion study is similar to the broader concept of *work study*.

time bargain *Fin* a stock market transaction in which the securities are deliverable at a future date beyond the exchange's normal settlement day

time deposit *Fin* a US savings account or a certificate of deposit, issued by a financial institution. While the savings account is for a fixed term, deposits are accepted with the understanding that withdrawals may be made subject to a period of notice. Banks are authorised to require at least 30 days' notice. While a certificate of deposit is equivalent to a term account, passbook accounts are generally regarded as funds readily available to the account holder.

time draft *Fin* a bill of exchange drawn on and accepted by a US bank. It is either an after date or after sight bill.

time keeping *HR* the activity of recording the amount of time an employee works. Time keeping may involve a formal *clock in* system or it may be an informal arrangement based on trust.

time management *Gen Mgt* conscious control of the amount of time spent on work activities, in order to maximise personal efficiency. Time management involves analysing how time is spent, and then prioritising different work tasks. Activities can be reorganised to concentrate on those that are most important. Various techniques can be of help in carrying out tasks more quickly and efficiently: information handling skills; verbal and written communication skills; *delegation*; and daily time planning. Time management is an important tool in avoiding *information overload*.

time off in lieu *HR leave* given to compensate an employee for additional hours worked. Time off in lieu is often given instead of a payment for *overtime*. *Abbr* **TOIL**

timeous (*S Africa*) *Gen Mgt* done or happening in good time

time series *Gen Mgt* a series of measurements, observations, and recordings of a set of variables at successive points in time. The time series forecasting technique is commonly used to track long-term trends and seasonal fluctuations and variations in data or statistics. It can be applied in an economic context in the review of sales, production, and investment performance, or in a sociological context in the compilation of census or panel study statistics. It can include the use of input-output analysis and *exponential smoothing*.

time sovereignty *Gen Mgt* control over the way you spend your time. Time sovereignty gives employees the ability to arrange their working lives to suit their own situations. It involves handing decisions on working hours to employees, enabling them to work flexibly, so that they can better juggle the *work-life balance*. Time sovereignty is more than just good *time management*, as it gives people control over the way they arrange their lives, rather than having to manage time within the decreed hours. It has been argued that rather than viewing work and home as separate lives, employees should see that they are living just one life that integrates both parts. Time sovereignty gives mastery over managing life as a whole.

time span of discretion *HR* the time between starting and completing the longest task within a job, used as a measure of the level of a job within an organisation. The time span of discretion was originated by *Elliot Jaques* as part of the *Glacier studies*. He saw two components to any job: prescribed and discretionary. The time span of the discretionary component refers to the longest span of time that employees spend working on a task on their own initiative, and often unsupervised. This reflects the amount of responsibility an individual has, and Jaques found that the time span of discretion rises steadily with the position of an employee in the company hierarchy. An hourly worker may have a one-hour time span of discretion, a middle manager may have one year, and a chief executive of a large company may have 20 years.

time spread *Fin* the purchase and sale of options in the same commodity or security with the same price and different maturities

time study *Gen Mgt* a *work measurement* technique designed to establish the time taken to complete work tasks in order to set a *standard time* for each task

---

Economy: cutting down other people's wages.   J.B. Morton (attrib.)

time value *Fin* the premium at which an option is trading relative to its **intrinsic value**

timing difference *Fin* a difference between the balances held on related accounts which is caused by differences in the timing of the input of common transactions. For example, a direct debit will appear on the bank statement before it is entered into the bank account. Knowledge of the timing difference allows the balances on the two accounts to be reconciled.

TIN *abbr E-com* terminal identification number: a bank-provided identification number that uniquely identifies a merchant for point-of-sale transactions

tip *Fin* a piece of useful expert information. Used in the sense of a 'share tip', it is a share recommendation published in the financial press, usually based on research published by a financial institution.

tip-off *Fin* a warning based on confidential information. *See also insider trading, money laundering*

TISA *abbr Fin* TESSA Individual Savings Account. *See TESSA*

title *Fin* a legal term meaning ownership. Deeds to land are sometimes referred to as title deeds. If a person has good title to a property, their proof of ownership is beyond any doubt.

title inflation *HR* the practice of giving an employee a job title that implies status and importance. Title inflation renames an employee's job with a title that sounds more elevated or grand than the old one even though the nature of the job has not changed. This is sometimes used as a form of **motivation** or incentive to make employees feel rewarded and more valued.

TLS *abbr E-com* transaction layer security: a payment protocol based on **SSL** that offers improved security for credit card transactions

TNA *abbr HR* training needs analysis

toasted *Fin* used to refer to someone or something that has lost money (*slang*)

TOC *abbr Fin* theory of constraints

toehold (*US*) *Fin* a stake in a corporation built-up by a potential bidder which is less than 5 per cent of the corporation's stock. It is only when a 5 per cent stake is reached that the holder has to make a declaration to the Securities and Exchange Commission.

Toffler, Alvin (*b.* 1928) *Gen Mgt* US futurist and social commentator. Known for his analyses of the future which embraced the impact of the Information Society and the wired age, and the knowledge economy. His first book was *Future Shock* (1970).

Toffler studied English at New York University. In the early stages of his journalistic career, he was commissioned by IBM to write a report on the long-term social and organisational implications of the computer. He worked as Washington correspondent for a Pennsylvania newspaper and as associate editor of *Fortune* before being employed as a visiting professor at Cornell University, a visiting scholar at the Russell Sage Foundation, and a teacher at the New School for Social Research.

TOIL *abbr HR* time off in lieu

Tokyo Inter Bank Offered Rate *Fin* on the Japanese money markets, the rate at which banks will offer to make deposits in yen from each other, often used as a reference rate. The deposits are for terms from overnight up to five years. *Abbr* **TIBOR**

tombstone *Fin* a notice in the financial press giving details of a large lending facility to a business. It may relate to a management buy-out or to a package that may include interest rate cap and collars to finance a specific package. More than one bank may be involved. Although it may appear to be an advertisement, technically in most jurisdictions it is regarded as a statement of fact and therefore falls outside the advertisement regulations. The borrower generally pays for the advertisement, though it is the financial institutions that derive the most benefit.

top-down approach *Gen Mgt* an autocratic style of **leadership** in which strategies and solutions are identified by **senior management** and then cascaded down through the organisation. The top-down approach can be considered a feature of large **bureaucracies** and is associated with a **command and control approach** to management. A number of management gurus, particularly **Gary Hamel**, have criticised it as an out-of-date style that leads to stagnation and **business failure**. It is the opposite of a **bottom-up approach**.

top-down budget *Fin see imposed budget*

top level domain *E-com* the concluding part of a domain name, for example, the .com, .net, or .co.uk suffixes.

top management *HR* an informal term for **senior management** or a **board of directors**

top slicing *Fin* **1.** selling part of a shareholding that will realise a sum that is equal to the original cost of the investment. What remains therefore represents potential pure profit. **2.**

Whenever you fall, pick up something. *Oswald Avery*

in the United Kingdom, a complex method used by the Inland Revenue for assessing what tax, if any, is paid when certain investment bonds or endowment policies mature or are cashed in early

total absorption costing *Fin* a method used by a cost accountant to price goods and services, allocating both direct and indirect costs. Although this method is designed so that all of an organisation's costs are covered, it may result in opportunities being missed because of high prices. Consequently sales may be lost that could contribute to overheads. *See also* *marginal costing*

total assets *Fin* the total net book value of all assets

total asset turnover ratio *Fin* a measure of the use a business makes of all its assets. It is calculated by dividing sales by total assets.

total cost of ownership *Gen Mgt* a structured approach to calculating the **costs** associated with buying and using a product or service. Total cost of ownership takes the purchase cost of an item into account but also considers related costs such as ordering, delivery, subsequent usage and maintenance, supplier costs, and after-delivery costs. Originally designed as a process for measuring IT expense after implementation, total cost of ownership considers only financial expenses and excludes any **cost-benefit analysis**. *Abbr* **TCO**

total-debt-to-total-assets *Fin* the premium at which an option is trading relative to its *intrinsic value*

total environmental management *Gen Mgt see environmental management*

total loss control *Gen Mgt* the implementation of safety procedures to prevent or limit the impact of a complete or partial loss of an organisation's physical assets. Total loss control is based on safety audit and prevention techniques. It is concerned with reduction or elimination of losses caused by accidents and occupational ill health. The extent to which it is implemented is usually decided by calculating the total organisational asset cost and weighing this against the likelihood of failure and its worst possible effects on the organisation. Total loss control was developed in the 1960s as an approach to *risk management*.

total productive maintenance *Ops* a Japanese approach to maximising the effectiveness of facilities used within a business. Total productive maintenance, or TPM, aims to improve the condition and performance of particular facilities through simple, repetitive maintenance activities. Based on a culture of teamworking and consensus, TPM teams are encouraged to take a proactive approach to maintenance. A team is made up of operators and those involved in the setting up and maintenance of the facilities. TPM can be compared to *reliability-centred maintenance*. *Abbr* **TPM**

total quality management *Gen Mgt* a philosophy and style of management that gives everyone in an organisation responsibility for delivering quality to the customer. Total quality management views each task in the organisation as a process that is in a customer/supplier relationship with the next process. The aim at each stage is to define and meet the customer's requirements in order to maximise the satisfaction of the final consumer at the lowest possible cost. Total quality management constitutes a challenge to organisations that have to manage the conflict between **cost-cutting** and the commitment of employees to **continuous improvement**. Achievement of quality can be assessed by **quality awards** and **quality standards**. *Abbr* **TQM**

total return *Gen Mgt* the total percentage change in the value of an investment over a specified time period, including capital gains, dividends, and the investment's appreciation or depreciation

EXAMPLE The total return formula reflects all the ways in which an investment may earn or lose money, resulting in an increase or decrease in the investment's net asset value (NAV):

(Dividends + Capital gains distributions +/- Change in NAV) / Beginning NAV = Total return × 100%

If, for instance, you buy a stock with an initial NAV of £40, and after one year it pays an income dividend of £2 per share and a capital gains distribution of £1, and its NAV has increased to £42, then the stock's total return would be:

(2 + 1 + 2) / 40 = 5 / 40 = 0.125 × 100% = 12.5%

The total return time frame is usually one year, and it assumes that dividends have been reinvested. It does not take into account any sales charges that an investor paid to invest in a fund, or taxes they might owe on the income dividends and capital gains distributions received.

touch *Fin* the difference between the best bid and the best offer price quoted by all market makers for a particular security, the narrowest spread

---

Consultants eventually leave, which makes them excellent scapegoats for major management blunders.
Scott Adams

touchdown centre (*US*) *Gen Mgt* a centre where business people can make calls and use computers and the Internet whilst travelling (*slang*)

touch price *Fin* the best bid and offer price available

tourist *HR* somebody who takes a training course in order to get away from his or her job (*slang*)

Townsend, Robert (*b*. 1920) *Gen Mgt* US business executive. One time chairman of Avis Rent-a-car, who built up the company into an international organisation. Best known for his book *Up the Organization* (1970), a humorous A-Z of management practices.

toxic employee *HR* a disgruntled and resentful employee who spreads discontent within a company or department (*slang*)

Toyota production system *Ops* a *manufacturing system*, developed by Toyota in Japan after the second world war, which aims to increase production efficiency by the elimination of waste in all its forms. The Toyota production system was invented, and made to work, by *Taiichi Ohno*. Japan's fledgling car-making industry was suffering from poor *productivity*, and Ohno was brought into Toyota with an initial assignment of catching up with the productivity levels of Ford's car plants. In analysing the problem, he decided that although Japanese workers must be working at the same rate as their American counterparts, waste and inefficiency were the main causes of their different productivity levels. Ohno identified waste in a number of forms, including over-production, waiting time, transportation problems, inefficient processing, *inventory*, and defective products. The philosophy of TPS is to remove or minimise the influence of all these elements. In order to achieve this, TPS evolved to operate under *lean production* conditions. It is made up of soft or cultural aspects, such as automation with the human touch— *autonomation*— and hard, or technical, aspects, which include *just-in-time*, *kanban*, and *production smoothing*. Each aspect is equally important and complementary. TPS has proved itself to be one of the most efficient manufacturing systems in the world but although leading companies have adopted it in one form or another, few have been able to replicate the success of Toyota. *Abbr* **TPS**

TPM *abbr Ops* total productive maintenance

TPS *abbr Ops* Toyota production system

TQM *abbr Gen Mgt* total quality management

tracker fund *Fin see* **index fund**

tracking *Mkting* research designed to monitor changes in the public perception of a product or organisation over a period of time

tracking error *Fin* the deviation by which an index fund fails to replicate the index it is aiming to mirror

tracking stock *Fin* a stock whose dividends are tied to the performance of a subsidiary of the corporation that owns it

trade balance *Fin see* **balance of trade**

trade barrier *Econ* a condition imposed by a government to limit free exchange of goods internationally. *NTBs*, safety standards, and tariffs are typical trade barriers.

trade bill *Fin* a bill of exchange between two businesses that trade with each other. *See also* **acceptance credit**

trade credit *Fin* credit offered by one business when trading with another. Typically this is for one month from the date of the invoice, but it could be for a shorter or longer period.

trade creditors *Fin* money owed to suppliers for goods and services. Other money owed, including employers' national insurance and taxation, is to be shown under the heading other creditors.

trade debt *Fin* a debt that originates during the normal course of trade

trade delegation *Mkting* a group of manufacturers or suppliers who visit another country to increase export business

Trade Development Board *Fin* a government agency that was established in 1983 to promote trade and explore new markets for Singapore products, and offers various schemes of assistance to companies. *Abbr* **TDB**

traded option *Fin* an option that is traded on an exchange that is different from the one on which the asset underlying the option is traded

tradefair *Mkting* a commercial exhibition designed to bring together buyers and sellers from a particular market sector. For the publishing industry, for example, the annual Frankfurt Book Fair is a key trade fair.

trade gap *Fin* a balance of payments deficit

trade investment *Fin* the action or process of one business making a loan to another, or buying shares in another. The latter may be the first stages of a friendly takeover.

The worst mistake a boss can make is not to say 'Well done'. John Ashcroft

trademark *Gen Mgt* an identifiable mark on a product that may be a symbol, words, or both, that connects the product to the trader or producer of that product. In the United Kingdom, a trademark can be registered at the Register of Trademarks, giving the producer or trader protection from fraudulent use. Any use of the trademark without permission gives the owner the right to sue for damages.

trade mission *Fin* a visit by businessmen from one country to another for the purpose of discussing trade between their respective nations

trade name *Mkting* the proprietary name given by the producer or manufacturer to a product or service. A trade name occasionally becomes the generic name for products of a similar nature, for example, 'Thermos' is often applied to all insulated flasks, and 'Hoover' to all vacuum cleaners.

Tradenet *Gen Mgt* an electronic system for applying for import or export licences from *Trade Development Boards*

TRADENZ *abbr Fin* New Zealand Trade Development Board

trade-off analysis *Gen Mgt see conjoint analysis*

trade point *Fin* a stock exchange that is less formal than the major exchanges

trade press *Mkting* specialist publications aimed at people in particular industries or business sectors

trades and labour council *(ANZ) HR* a collective organisation that represents unions at a level such as that of a state or territory

trade union *Gen Mgt, HR* an organisation of *employees* within a trade or profession that has the objective of representing its members' interests, primarily through improving pay and conditions, and provides a variety of services. *US term* **labor union**

trade union recognition *HR* the acknowledgment by an *employer* of the right of a *trade union* to conduct *collective bargaining* on behalf of *employees* in a particular bargaining unit. The Employment Relations Act 1999 grants a statutory right to recognition under certain conditions.

trade war *Econ* competition between two or more countries for a share of international or domestic trade

trade-weighted index *Econ* an index that measures the value of a country's currency in relation to the currencies of its trading partners

trading account *Fin see profit and loss account*

trading halt *Fin* a stoppage of trading in a stock on an exchange, usually in response to information about a company, or concern about rapid movement of the share price

trading partner *E-com* the merchant, customer, or financial institution with whom an EDI (*electronic data interchange*) transaction takes place. Transactions can be either between senders and receivers of EDI messages or within distribution channels in an industry, for example, financial institutions or wholesalers.

trading pit *Fin see pit*

trading profit *Fin see gross profit*

trading, profit and loss account *Fin* an account which shows the gross profit or loss generated by an entity for a period (trading account), and after adding other income and deducting various expenses shows the profit or loss of the business (the profit and loss account). Some small entities combine the two accounts.

traffic *E-com* the number of visitors to a website measured in any of several ways, for example, *click-throughs*, hits, or page views

traffic builder *Mkting* a marketing promotion that is designed to generate an increase in customers (*slang*)

training *HR* activities designed to facilitate the learning and development of new and existing skills, and to improve the performance of specific tasks or roles. Training may involve structured programmes or more informal and interactive activities, such as group discussion or *role playing*, which promote *experiential learning*. A wide range of activities, including classroom-based courses, *on-the-job training*, and business or *simulation games*, are used for training. Audio-visual and multimedia aids such as videos and CD-ROMs may also be employed. Training may be carried out by an internal training officer or department, or by external training organisations. The effectiveness of training can be maximised by conducting a *training needs analysis* beforehand, and following up with *evaluation of training*. Training should result in individual learning and enhanced organisational performance.

training group *HR see **sensitivity training***

training needs *HR* a shortage of skills or abilities which could be reduced or eliminated by means of training and development. Training needs hinder employees in the fulfilment of their job responsibilities and prevent an organisation from achieving its objectives. They may be caused by a lack of skills, knowledge, or understanding, or arise from changes in the workplace. Training needs are identified through *training needs analysis*.

training needs analysis *HR* the identification of *training needs* at employee, departmental, or organisational level, in order for the organisation to perform effectively. The aim of training needs analysis is to ensure that training addresses existing problems, is tailored to organisational objectives, and is delivered in an effective and cost-efficient manner. Training needs analysis involves: monitoring current performance using techniques such as observation, interviews, and questionnaires; anticipating future shortfalls or problems; identifying the type and level of training required; and analysing how this can best be provided. *Abbr* **TNA**

trait theory *Gen Mgt* the belief that all leaders display the same key personality traits. Trait theory developed from the **great man theory** of leadership as researchers attempted to identify universally applicable characteristics that distinguish leaders from other people. During the 1920s and 1930s, theorists compiled lists of traits, but these were often contradictory and no single trait was consistently identified with good leadership.

tranche CD *Fin* one of a series of certificates of deposit that are sold by the issuing bank over time. Each tranche CD has a common maturity date.

transaction 1. *E-com* any item or collection of sequential items of business that are enclosed in encrypted form in an electronic envelope and transmitted between trading partners **2.** *Fin* a trade of a security

transactional analysis *Gen Mgt* a theory that describes sets of feelings, thoughts, and behaviour or ego-states that influence how individuals interact, communicate, and relate with each other. The theories of transactional analysis were developed between the 1950s and 1970s by Eric Berne, a US psychiatrist who studied the behaviour patterns of his patients. Berne identified three ego states, parent, adult, and child, and examined how these affected interactions or transactions between individuals. Transactional analysis is used in psychotherapy but also has applica-

tions in education and training. In *human relations* training, transactional analysis is used to help people understand and adapt their behaviour and develop more effective ways of communicating. *Abbr* **TA**

transactional theory of leadership *Gen Mgt* the idea that effective *leadership* is based on a reciprocal exchange between leaders and followers. Transactional leadership involves giving employees something in return for their compliance and acceptance of authority, usually in the form of incentives such as pay rises or an increase in status. The theory was propounded by **James MacGregor Burns**, and is closely linked with his *transformational theory of leadership*, which involves moral, rather than tangible, rewards for compliance.

transaction e-commerce *E-com* the electronic sale of goods and services, either business-to-business or business-to-customer

transaction exposure *Fin* the susceptibility of an organisation to the effect of foreign exchange rate changes during the transaction cycle associated with the export/import of goods or services. Transaction exposure is present from the time a price is agreed until the payment has been made/received in the domestic currency.

transaction file *Ops see **inventory record***

transaction history *Fin* a record of all of an investor's transactions with a broker

transaction layer security *E-com see **TLS***

transaction message *or* **transaction set** *E-com* the EDI (*electronic data interchange*) equivalent of a paper document, exchanged as part of an e-commerce transaction, comprising at least one data segment representing the document sandwiched between a header and a trailer. It is called a transaction message within the *UN/EDIFACT* protocol and a transaction set within the ANSI X.12 protocol.

transactions motive *Econ* the motive that consumers have to hold money for their likely purchases in the immediate future

transfer *Fin* **1.** the movement of money from one account to another at the same branch of the same bank **2.** the movement of money through the domestic or international banking system. *See also **BACS**, **Fedwire**, **SWIFT** **3.** the change of ownership of an asset

transferable skill *HR* a skill typically considered as not specifically related to a particular job or task. Transferable skills are usually those related to relationship, leadership,

---

The task of the leader is to get people from where they are to where they have not been. **Henry Kissinger**

communication, critical thinking, analysis, and organisation.

transfer of training *HR* the appropriate and continued application of skills learned during a training course to the working environment. A measure of the transfer of training should form part of any *evaluation of training* carried out, as it can help demonstrate the cost-effectiveness of a training programme. It is normally measured between three to six months after the training course in order to allow trainees to apply their newly learned skills in the workplace.

transfer of value *Fin see chargeable transfer*

transferor *Fin* a person who transfers an asset to another person

transfer-out fee *Fin* a fee for closing an account with a broker

transfer price *Fin* the price at which goods or services are transferred between different units of the same company. If those units are located within different countries, the term **international transfer pricing** is used.

The extent to which the transfer price covers costs and contributes to (internal) profit is a matter of policy. A transfer price may, for example, be based upon marginal cost, full cost, market price or negotiation. Where the transferred products cross national boundaries, the transfer prices used may have to be agreed with the governments of the countries concerned.

transfer pricing *Mkting* a pricing method used when supplying products or services from one part of an organisation to another. The transfer pricing method can be used to supply goods either at cost or at profit if profit targets are to be achieved. This can cause difficulties if an internal customer can buy more cheaply outside the organisation. Multi-national businesses have been known to take advantage of this pricing policy by transferring products from one country to another in order for profits to be higher in the country where corporation tax is lower.

transfer stamp *Fin* the mark embossed onto transfer deeds to signify that stamp duty has been paid

transfer value *Fin* the value of an individual's rights in a pension when they are lost in preference to rights in a new pension. *See also vested rights*

transformational theory of leadership *Gen Mgt* the idea that effective *leadership* is based on inspiring and enthusing subordinates with a **corporate vision** in order to gain their commitment. Transformational leadership theory was developed by *James MacGregor Burns*, and is similar to his *transactional theory of leadership*. Both involve an exchange between leaders and followers, but while the transactional leader offers tangible rewards for compliance, the transformational leader offers moral rewards.

transformative potential *Gen Mgt* the ability of a force such as information technology to transform the economy, society, and business

transit time *Fin* the period between the completion of an operation and the availability of the material at the succeeding workstation

translation *Fin see foreign currency translation*

translation exposure *Fin* the susceptibility of the balance sheet and income statement to the effect of foreign exchange rate changes

transmission *E-com* digital data sent electronically from one trading partner to another, or from a trading partner to a *value-added network*

transmission control protocol *E-com see TCP/IP*

transmission control standards *E-com* the defined format by which to address the *electronic envelopes* used by trading partners to exchange business data

Transnet *Gen Mgt* a state-owned holding company that controls the main South African transport networks

transparency *Fin* a situation where nothing is hidden. This is an essential situation for a free market in securities. Prices, the volume of trading, and factual information must be available to all.

travel accident insurance *Fin* a form of insurance cover offered by some credit card companies when the whole or part of a travel arrangement is paid for with the card. In the event of death resulting from an accident in the course of travel, or the loss of eyesight or a limb, the credit card company will pay the cardholder or his or her estate a pre-stipulated sum. *See also travel insurance*

travel insurance *Fin* a form of insurance cover that provides medical cover while abroad as well as covering the policyholder's possessions and money while travelling. Many travel insurance policies also reimburse

---

Conscience: self-esteem with a halo.   *Irving Layton*

the policyholder if a holiday has to be cancelled and pay compensation for delayed journeys. *See also* **travel accident insurance**

treasurer *Fin* somebody who is responsible for an organisation's funds

Treasurer (*ANZ*) *Fin* the minister responsible for financial and economic matters in a national, state, or territory government

treasuries *Fin* the generic name for negotiable debt instruments issued by the US government. *See also* **Treasury bill**, **Treasury bond**, **Treasury note**

treasury *Fin* **1. Treasury** in some countries, the government department responsible for the nation's financial policies as well as the management of the economy **2.** the department of a company or corporation headed by the treasurer

Treasury bill *Fin* a short-term security issued by the government. *Also known as* **T-bill**

Treasury bill rate *Fin* the rate of interest obtainable by holding a treasury bill. Although Treasury bills are non-interest bearing, by purchasing them at a discount and holding them to redemption, the discount is effectively the interest earned by holding these instruments. The Treasury bill rate is the discount expressed as a percentage of the issue price. It is annualised to give a rate per annum.

Treasury bond *Fin* a long-term bond issued by the US government that bears interest

treasury management *Gen Mgt* the management functions responsible for the custody and investment of money, cashflow forecasting, capital provision, credit management, **risk management**, and the collection of accounts. Treasury management has a strategic role in the management of an organisation's finances.

Treasury note *Fin* **1.** a note issued by the US government **2.** a short-term debt instrument issued by the Australian federal government. Treasury notes are issued on a tender basis for periods of 13 and 26 weeks.

treaty *Fin* **1.** a written agreement between nations, such as the Treaty of Rome that was the foundation of the European Union **2.** a contract between an insurer and the reinsurer whereby the latter is to accept risks from the insurer **3.** *see* **private treaty**

Tregoe, Benjamin Bainbridge (*b.* 1927) *Gen Mgt* US manager and consultant. *See* **Kepner, Charles Higgins**

trend *Stats* the movement in a particular direction of the values of a variable in a statistical study over a period of time

trendline *Stats* the tendency to move in a particular direction shown by data variables over a period of time such as a month or year

Treynor ratio *Fin* see **risk-adjusted return on capital**

trial balance *Fin* a list of account balances in a double-entry accounting system. If the records have been correctly maintained, the sum of the debit balances will equal the sum of the credit balances, although certain errors such as the omission of a transaction or erroneous entries will not be disclosed by a trial balance.

trickle-down theory *Econ* the theory that if markets are open and programmes exist to improve basic health and education, growth will extend from successful parts of a developing country's economy to the rest

triple I organisation *Gen Mgt* a type of **corporate culture** identified by **Charles Handy** in which the focus is on three areas: Information, Intelligence, and Ideas. The triple I organisation recognises the value of information and learning. It minimises the distinction between managers and workers, concentrating instead on people and the need to pursue learning, both personal, **lifelong learning**, and **organisational learning**, in order to keep up with the pace of change.

triple tax exempt (*US*) *Fin* exempt from federal, state, and local income taxes

Trist, Eric Lansdown (1909–93) *Gen Mgt* British social psychologist. Known for research into socio-technical systems, particularly in the UK coal-mining industry, with associates such as **Fred Emery**, at the Tavistock Institute of Human Relations.

Trojan horse *E-com* a computer **virus** that pretends to serve a useful function, such as a screen saver. However, as soon as it is run, it carries out its true purpose, which can be anything from using the computer as a host to infect other computers to wiping the entire hard drive of the computer.

troll *Gen Mgt* a posting on a website that is designed to provoke a large number of responses, especially from inexperienced Internet users (*slang*)

trolling (*US*) *Mkting* making cold calls in an effort to solicit new business (*slang*)

Trompenaars, Fons (*b.* 1952) *Gen Mgt* Dutch academic. Known for his research into how national cultures influence **corporate cultures**. His work owes much to that of **Geert Hofstede**, and is published in *Riding the Waves of Culture* (1993).

trophy wife *Gen Mgt* the young wife of an older executive (*slang*)

troy ounce *Fin* the traditional unit used when weighing precious metals such as gold or silver. It is equal to approximately 1.097 ounces avoirdupois or 31.22 grams.

true interest cost *Fin* the effective rate of interest paid by the issuer on a debt security that is sold at a discount

trump *Mkting* to make something such as a competitor's product appear useless because what you have is so much better (*slang*)

trust 1. *Econ* a company that has a **monopoly** **2.** *Fin* a collection of assets held by somebody for another person's benefit

trust account *Fin* a bank account that is held in trust for somebody else

trust bank *Fin* a Japanese bank that acts commercially in the sense of accepting deposits and making loans and also in the capacity of a trustee

trust company *Fin* a company whose business is administering trusts

trust corporation *Fin* a US state-chartered institution that may also undertake banking activities. A trust corporation is sometimes known as a non-bank bank.

Trusted Third Party *E-com see* **TTP**

trustee *Fin* somebody who holds assets in trust

trustee in bankruptcy *Fin* somebody appointed by a court to manage the finances of a bankrupt person or company

trustee investment *Fin* an investment that is made by a trustee and is subject to legal restrictions

trusteeship *Fin* the holding of a trust, or the term of such a holding

trust fund *Fin* assets held in trust by a trustee for the trust's beneficiaries

trust officer *Fin* somebody who manages the assets of a trust, especially for a bank that is acting as a trustee

Truth in Lending Act *Fin* in the United States, a law requiring lenders to disclose the terms of their credit offers accurately so that consumers are not misled and are able to compare the various credit terms available.

The Truth in Lending Act requires lenders to disclose the terms and costs of all loan plans, including the following: annual percentage rate, points and fees; the total of the principal amount being financed; payment due date and terms, including any balloon payment where applicable and late payment fees; features of variable-rate loans, including the highest rate the lender would charge, how it is calculated and the resulting monthly payment; total finance charges; whether the loan is assumable; application fee; annual or one-time service fees; pre-payment penalties; and, where applicable, confirm the address of the property securing the loan.

tshayile time (*S Africa*) *Gen Mgt* an informal term for the end of the working day (*slang*)

TT *abbr Fin* telegraphic transfer

TTFN *abbr Gen Mgt* ta ta for now (*slang*)

TTP *abbr E-com* Trusted Third Party: an independent, trustworthy organisation that verifies individuals, companies, and organisations over the Internet

Tulgan, Bruce Lorin (*b.* 1967) *Gen Mgt* US lawyer, writer, and consultant. Pioneer of the concept that young people have a different attitude to work than their forebears and need to be managed differently. He explores this in *Managing Generation X* (1995).

turbulence *Gen Mgt* unpredictable and swift changes in an organisation's external or internal environments which affect its performance. The late 20th century was considered a turbulent environment for business because of the rapid growth in technology and globalisation, and the frequency of restructuring and merger activity.

turkey *Fin* a poorly performing investment or business (*slang*)

turkey trot (*US*) *HR* the practice of transferring a difficult, incompetent, or nonessential employee from one department to another (*slang*)

turn *Fin* the difference between a market maker's bid and offer prices

turnaround management *Gen Mgt* the implementation of a set of actions required to save an organisation from **business failure** and return it to operational normality and financial solvency. Turnaround management usually requires strong **leadership** and can include **corporate restructuring** and **redundancies**, an investigation of the root causes of failure, and long-term programmes to revitalise the organisation.

Companies worry too much about the cost of doing something. They should worry about the cost of not doing it.
                   Philip Kotler

turnkey contract *Gen Mgt* an agreement in which a contractor designs, constructs, and manages a *project* until it is ready to be handed over to the client and operation can begin immediately

turnover ratio *Fin* stock or inventory turnover ratio, a measure of the number of times in a year that a business's stock or inventory is turned over. It is calculated as the cost of sales divided by the average book value of inventory/stock.

24 *E-com* the American National Standards Institute accepted protocol for the electronic interchange of business transactions

24/7 *Gen Mgt* twenty-four hours a day, seven days a week. Businesses often advertise themselves as being 'open 24/7'. (*slang*)

2L8 *abbr Gen Mgt* too late (*slang*)

twenty-four hour trading *Fin* the possibility of trading in currencies or securities at any time of day or night. It is not a reference to one trading floor being continually open, but instead refers to operations being undertaken at different locations in different time zones. A financial institution with offices in the Far East, Europe, and the United States can offer its clients 24-hour trading either by the client

contacting their offices in each area, or by the customer's local office passing the orders on to another centre.

two-tier tender offer *Fin* in the United States, a takeover bid in which the acquirer offers to pay more for shares bought in order to gain control than for those acquired at a later date. The ploy is to encourage shareholders to accept the offer. Bidding of this type is outlawed in some jurisdictions, including the United Kingdom.

type I error *Stats* an error arising from incorrectly rejecting the null hypothesis in a statistical study

type II error *Stats* an error arising from incorrectly accepting the null hypothesis in a statistical study

tyrekicker (*US*) *Mkting* a prospective customer who asks for a lot of information and requires a lot of attention but does not actually buy anything (*slang*)

Tzu, Sun (*b.* uncertain) *Gen Mgt* Chinese general. Although he lived over 2,400 years ago, he is said to have an influence on modern business thinking, based on his thoughts on *strategy* recorded in *The Art of War* (various translations).

UCE *abbr E-com* unsolicited commercial e-mail: the official term for **spam**

UIF *abbr (S Africa) Fin* Unemployment Insurance Fund: a system administered through payroll deductions that insures employees against loss of earnings through being made unemployed by such causes as retrenchment, illness, or maternity

UITF *abbr Fin* Urgent Issues Task Force

ultra vires activity *Fin* an act that is not permitted by applicable rules, such as a corporate charter. Such acts may lead to contracts being void.

unbalanced growth *Econ* the result when not all sectors of an economy can grow at the same rate

unbundling *Fin* dividing a company into separate constituent companies, often to sell all or some of them after a takeover

uncalled share capital *Fin* the amount of the nominal value of a share which is unpaid and has not been called up by the company

uncertainty *Fin* the inability to predict the outcome from an activity due to a lack of information about the required input/output relationships or about the environment within which the activity takes place

uncertainty analysis *Stats* a study designed to assess the extent to which the variability in an outcome variable is caused by uncertainty at the time of estimating the input parameters of the study

uncollected funds *Fin* money deriving from the deposit of an instrument that a bank has not been able to negotiate

uncollected trade bill *Fin* an account with an outstanding balance for purchases made from the company that holds it

unconditional bid *Fin* in a takeover battle, a situation in which a bidder will pay the offered price irrespective of how many shares are acquired

unconsolidated *Fin* not grouped together, as of shares or holdings

uncontested bid *Fin* an offering of a contract by a government or other organisation to one bidder only, without competition

UNCTAD *abbr Fin* United Nations Conference on Trade and Development: the focal point within the UN system for the integrated treatment of development and interrelated issues in trade, finance, technology, and investment

underbanked *Fin* without enough brokers to sell a new issue

underlying asset *Fin* an asset that is the subject of an option

underlying inflation *Fin* the rate of inflation that does not take mortgage costs into account

underlying security *Fin* a security that is the subject of an option

undermargined account *Fin* an account that does not have enough money to cover its margin requirements, resulting in a margin call

undervalued *Fin* used to describe an asset that is available for purchase at a price lower than its worth

undervalued currency *Fin* a currency that costs less to buy with another currency than its worth in goods

underwrite *Fin* to assume risk, especially for a new issue or an insurance policy

underwriter *Fin* a person or organisation that buys an issue from a corporation and sells it to investors

underwriters' syndicate *Fin* a group of organisations that buys an issue from a corporation and sells it to investors

underwriting *Fin* the buying of an issue from a corporation for the purpose of selling it to investors

underwriting income *Fin* the money that an insurance company makes because the premiums it collects exceed the claims it pays out

underwriting spread *Fin* an amount that is the difference between what an organisation pays for an issue and what it receives when it sells the issue to investors

undistributable reserves *Fin* in the United Kingdom, reserves that are not legally available for distribution to shareholders as dividends according to the Companies Act (1985)

UNDP *abbr Fin* United Nations Development Programme: the world's largest source of grants for sustainable human development. Its aims include the elimination of poverty, environmental regeneration, job creation, and advancement of women.

---

unearned income *Fin* income received from sources other than employment

unearned increment *Fin* an increase in the value of a property that arises from causes other than the owner's improvements or expenditure

unearned premium *Fin* the amount of premiums paid on a policy that an insurance company refunds when the policy is terminated

uneconomic *Econ* not profitable for a country, firm, or investor in the short or long term

UN/EDIFACT *E-com* a standard for *electronic data interchange* widely used in Western Europe and very similar to the *ANSI X.12 standard*. *Also known as* **EDIFACT**, **EDI For Administration, Commerce, and Trade**

unemployment *Econ* the situation when some members of a country's labour force are willing to work but cannot find employment

Unemployment Insurance Fund *(S Africa) Fin see* **UIF**

uneven playing field *Mkting* a situation in which some competitors have an unfair advantage over others *(slang)*

unfair dismissal *HR* the *dismissal* of an *employee* that cannot be shown to be fair by the *employer*. An employee has the right not to be unfairly dismissed, and to bring a claim to an industrial tribunal provided he or she has one year's *continuous service*, although there are certain reasons for dismissal that are automatically unfair. If a finding of unfair dismissal is reached, a tribunal can make a reinstatement or re-engagement order, or it can order a basic and compensatory award to be paid. Statutory protection does not apply to members of certain groups of employees, such as the police.

unfranked investment income *Fin* amounts received by a company net of basic rate tax, for example, patent royalties

unfunded debt *Fin* short-term debt requiring repayment within a year from issuance

ungluing *Gen Mgt* the process of breaking up traditional supply chains or groups of co-operating organisations by taking control of the element of mutual interest that holds the partners together

unhappy camper *HR* somebody who has grievances against his or her employer *(slang)*

uniform accounting *Fin* a system by which different organisations in the same industry adopt common concepts, principles, and assumptions in order to facilitate interfirm comparison, or a system of classifying financial accounts in a similar manner within defined business sectors of a national economy, to ensure comparability

uniform costing *Fin* the use by several undertakings of the same costing methods, principles, and techniques

uniform resource locator *E-com see* **URL**

unimodal *Stats* describes a frequency or probability distribution that has only one mode

uninstalled *HR* dismissed from employment *(slang)*

uninsurable *Fin* considered unsuitable for insurance, especially because of being a poor risk

unique selling point *or* **unique selling proposition** *Mkting, Ops* a specific feature that differentiates a product from similar products. *Abbr* **USP**

unique visitor *E-com* somebody who visits a website more than once within a specified period of time. Tracking software that monitors site traffic can distinguish between visitors who only visit the site once and unique visitors who return to the site. Unique visitor statistics are considered to be the most accurate measurement of a website's popularity because they reflect the number of people who want to be there rather than those who have arrived there by accident. Furthermore, unlike hits (which are measured by the number of files that are requested from a site) unique visitors are measured according to their unique *IP addresses*. This means that no matter how many times they visit the site, they are only counted once.

unissued share capital *Fin* stock that is authorised but has not been issued. *US term* **unissued stock**

unissued stock *(US) Fin* = **unissued share capital**

unit *Fin* a collection of securities traded together as one item

unit cost *Fin* the cost to a company of producing one item that it markets

United Nations Conference on Trade and Development *Fin see* **UNCTAD**

United Nations Development Programme *Fin see* **UNDP**

unit of account *Econ* a unit of a country's currency that can be used in payment for goods or in a firm's accounting

unit of trade *Fin* the smallest amount that

can be bought or sold of a share of stock, or a contract included in an option

unit trust *Fin* an investment company that sells shares to investors and invests for their benefit. *US term* **mutual fund**

universe *Mkting* the total market for a product or service

unlimited liability *Fin* full responsibility for the obligations of a general partnership

unlisted *Fin* used to refer to security that is not traded on an exchange

unlisted securities market *Fin* a market for stocks that are not listed on an exchange. *Abbr* **USM** *See also* **AIM**

unofficial strike *HR* a **strike** that is called without the approval or recognition of a trade union. An unofficial strike, also known as a **wildcat strike**, is a form of **industrial action** often associated with the activities of shop stewards. Any workers involved do not receive **strike pay**.

unquoted *Fin* having no publicly stated price, usually referring to an unlisted security

unrealised capital gain *or* **unrealized gain** *Fin* a profit from the holding of an asset worth more than its purchase price, but not yet sold

unrealised profit/loss *Fin* a profit or loss that need not be reported as income, for example, deriving from the holding of an asset worth more/less than its purchase price, but not yet sold

unreason *Gen Mgt* the process of thinking the unlikely and doing the unreasonable that can be a means by which an organisation or individual achieves success

unremittable gain *Fin* a capital gain that cannot be imported into the taxpayer's country, especially because of currency restrictions

unseasoned issue *Fin* an issue of shares or bonds for which there is no existing market. *See also* **seasoned issue**

unsecured *Fin* used to refer to something without collateral

unsecured debt *Fin* money borrowed without supplying collateral

unsecured loan *Fin* a loan made with no collateral. *Also known as* **signature loan**

unsocial hours *HR* the working hours of an employee outside the socially recognised working day, for which an additional payment is sometimes made

unsolicited commercial e-mail *E-com see* **UCE**

unstable equilibrium *Econ* a market situation in which if there is a movement (of price or quantity) away from the equilibrium, existing forces will push the price even further away

upsell *Mkting* to sell customers a higher-priced version of a product they have bought previously

upsizing *HR see* **downsizing**

upstairs market *Fin* the place where traders for major brokerages and institutions do business at an exchange

upstream progress *Gen Mgt* advancement against opposition or in difficult conditions. A company or project can make upstream progress if it moves towards achieving its objectives despite impediments. *See also* **downstream progress**

Urgent Issues Task Force *Fin* in the United Kingdom, an organisation whose aim is to assist the ASB in areas where unsatisfactory or conflicting interpretations of an accounting standard have developed, or seem likely to develop. *Abbr* **UITF**

URL *abbr E-com* uniform resource locator: a full web address, for example, http://www.yahoo.com

Urwick, Lyndall Fownes (1891–1983) *Gen Mgt* British educator and consultant. Promulgator of the theories of **Frederick Winslow Taylor** and **Henri Fayol**, which he developed in *Elements of Administration* (1944). Urwick was a founder of the British Institute of Management (1947), and of the management consultancy firm, Urwick Orr (1934).

usability *E-com* the suitability of a website design from the user's perspective. The term has been popularised by web design guru Jakob Nielsen who has stressed that a website must be simple to use. One of the main points of usability relates to download times. For Nielsen, 'fast response times are the most important criterion for web pages'. Nielsen also believes usability involves a human approach. He states that 'what constitutes a good site relates to the core basis of human nature and not to technology'.

usenet *E-com* the vast information space encompassed by the thousands of publicly available newsgroups

USM *abbr Fin* unlisted securities market

USP *Mkting, Ops see* **unique selling point**

utopian socialism *Econ* a form of socialism in which the use and production of all services and goods are held collectively by the group or community, rather than by a central government

---

Some people use research like a drunkard uses a lampost: for support not illumination. **David Ogily**

vacation *(US) HR = holiday*

valence *HR see expectancy theory*

value added *Gen Mgt* **1.** originally, the difference between the cost of bought-in materials and the eventual selling price of the finished product **2.** loosely, the features that differentiate one product or service from another and thus create value for the customer. Value added is a customer perception of what makes a product or service desirable over others and worth a higher price. Value added is more difficult to measure without a physical end product, but value can be added to services as well as physical goods, through the process of *value engineering*. *Also known as added value*

value-added network *E-com* an organisation that provides messaging-related functions and EDI communications services, for example, protocol matching and line-speed conversion, between trading partners. *Abbr* **VAN**. *Also known as third-party network, third-party service provider*

value-added reseller *Fin* a merchant who buys products at retail and packages them with additional items for sale to customers. *Abbr* **VAR**

value-added services *Mkting* services that enhance a basic product, such as the design in engineering components or technical support for software

value-added tax *Fin see* **VAT**

value-adding intermediary *Gen Mgt* a distributor who adds value to a product before selling it to a customer, for example, by installing software or a modem in a computer

value analysis *Ops* a cost reduction and *problem-solving* technique that analyses an existing product or service in order to reduce or eliminate any costs that do not contribute to value or performance. Value analysis usually focuses on design issues relating to the function of a product or service, looking at the properties that make it work, or which are *unique selling points*.

value-based management *Fin* a management team preoccupation with searching for and implementing the activities which will contribute most to increases in shareholder value

value chain 1. *Gen Mgt* the sequence of activities a company performs in order to design, produce, market, deliver, and support its product or service. The concept of the value chain was first suggested by **Michael Porter** in 1985, to demonstrate how value for the customer accumulates along the chain of organisational activities that make up the final customer product or service. Porter describes two different types of business activity: primary and secondary. Primary activities are concerned principally with transforming inputs, such as raw materials, into outputs, in the form of products or services, delivery, and after-sales support. Secondary activities support the primary activities and include procurement, technology development, and human resource management. All of these activities form part of the value chain and can be analysed to assess where opportunities for *competitive advantage* may lie. To survive competition and supply what customers want to buy, the firm has to ensure that all value chain activities link together, even if some of the activities take place outside the organisation. **2.** *HR* the most traditional approach to exploring career prospects, which involves identifying the next, most obvious, move in a career path. The next step is usually assumed to be the role occupied by a manager.

value engineering *Ops* the practice of designing a product or service so that it gives as much value as possible to the consumer. Value engineering analyses a developing product so that the focus is on those attributes that make the product appeal to the consumer over competing items and produce *customer satisfaction*. Value engineering also concentrates on eliminating costs that do not contribute to the creation of customer value.

value for customs purposes only *Fin* what somebody importing something into the United States declares that it is worth

value for money audit *Fin* an investigation into whether proper arrangements have been made for securing economy, efficiency, and effectiveness in the use of resources. *Abbr* **VFM**. *Also known as comprehensive auditing*

value innovation *Gen Mgt* a strategic approach to business growth, involving a shift away from a focus on the existing competition to one of trying to create entirely new markets. Value innovation can be achieved by implementing a focus on *innovation* and creation of new marketspace. The term was coined by **W. Chan Kim** and **Renée Mauborgne** in 1997.

value map *Gen Mgt* the level of value that the market recognises in a product or service and that helps to differentiate it from competitors

value mesh *HR* an expanded look at the positioning of a job in the overall marketplace. Seen as a way of helping employees identify their next move, a value mesh encourages them to consider all opportunities within their organisation and others.

value proposition 1. *Mkting* a statement by an organisation of the way in which it can provide value for a prospective customer. A value proposition is a marketing tool that explains why customers can benefit from a company's products or services. It can also be created for **recruitment** purposes, to show applicants the value of becoming an employee of the company. **2.** *Gen Mgt* a proposed scheme for making a profit (*slang*)

value share *Fin* a share that is considered to be currently underpriced by the market and therefore an attractive investment prospect

value to the business *or* **value to the owner** *Fin see* **deprival value**

VAN *abbr E-com* value-added network

VAR *abbr Fin* value-added reseller

variable *Stats* an element of data whose changes are the object of a statistical study

variable annuity *Fin* an annuity whose payments depend either on the success of investments that underlie it, or on the value of an index

variable cost *Fin see* **cost behaviour**

variable costing *Fin see* **marginal costing**

variable cost of sales *Fin* the sum of direct materials, direct wages, variable production overhead, and variable selling and distribution overhead

variable interest rate *Fin* an interest rate that changes, usually in relation to a standard index, during the period of a loan

variable rate note *Fin* a note the interest rate of which is tied to an index, such as the prime rate in the United States or the London InterBank Offering Rate (LIBOR) in the United Kingdom. *Abbr* **VRN**

variance *Ops* a measure of the difference between actual performance and forecast, or standard, performance. Variance is a key measure in **statistical process control**.

variance accounting *Fin* a method of accounting by means of which planned activities (quantified through budgets and standard costs and revenues) are compared with actual results. It provides information for **variance analysis**.

variance analysis *Fin* a standard costing technique involving the comparison, calculation, and explanation of **variances** between actual and standard costs. Variance analysis is used to evaluate success in conforming to plans and budgets.

variance components *Stats* the changes in random effect terms such as error terms in a linear statistical model

variety reduction *Ops* the process of controlling and minimising the range of new parts, equipment, materials, methods, and procedures that are used to produce goods or services. Variety reduction aims to minimise the variety of all elements in the production or service delivery process. Variety adds costs to any organisation and variety management and reduction can immediately benefit profitability. The main techniques of variety reduction are simplification, standardisation, and specialisation.

VAT *abbr Fin* value added tax: a tax added at each stage in the manufacture of a product. It acts as a replacement for a sales tax in almost every industrialised country outside North America. It is levied on selected goods and services, paid by organisations on items they buy and then charged to customers.

VAT collected *Fin* with the VAT already collected by a taxing authority

VAT paid *Fin* with the VAT already paid

VAT receivable *Fin* with the VAT for an item not yet collected by a taxing authority

VAT registration *Fin* listing with a European government as a company eligible for return of VAT in certain cases

VCM *abbr Fin* Venture Capital Market

velocity of circulation of money *Fin* the rate at which money circulates in an economy

vendor placing *Fin* the practice of issuing shares to acquire a business, where an agreement has been made to allow the vendor of the business to place the shares with investors for cash

vendor rating *Ops* a system for recording and ranking the performance of a supplier in terms of a range of issues, which may include delivery performance and the quality of the items. A process of vendor rating is essential to effective **purchasing**. When carried out before an order is placed, it is known as **supplier evaluation**. When undertaken after the fulfilment of an order, it is called **supplier rating**, or **supplier appraisal**.

Venn diagram *Stats* a diagram in which overlapping circles are used to show how two or more items in a statistical study are mutually inclusive or exclusive

venture capital *Fin* **1.** money used to finance new companies or projects, especially those with high earning potential and high risk. *Also known as* **risk capital 2.** the money invested in a new company or business venture

Venture Capital Market *Fin* a sector on the *JSE* Securities Exchange for listing smaller developing companies. Criteria for listing in the VCM sector are less stringent than for the DCM (**Development Capital Market**) sector. *See also* **Development Capital Market**. *Abbr* **VCM**

venture funding *Fin* the round of funding for a new company that follows seed funding, provided by venture capitalists

venture management *Gen Mgt* the collaboration of various sections within an organisation to encourage an **entrepreneurial** spirit, increase **innovation**, and produce successful **new products** more quickly. Venture management is used within large organisations to create a small-firm, entrepreneurial atmosphere, releasing innovation and talent from promising employees. It cuts out **bureaucracy** and bypasses traditional management systems. The collaboration is generally between research and development, corporate planning, marketing, finance, and purchasing functions.

venturer *Fin* one of the parties involved in a *joint venture*

verbal contract *Gen Mgt* an agreement that is oral and not written down. It remains legally enforceable by the parties who have agreed to it.

verification *Fin* in an audit, a substantive test of the existence, ownership, and valuation of a company's assets and liabilities

versioning *Mkting* the practice of offering information to customers in different versions to suit particular customer groups (*slang*)

vertical diversification *Gen Mgt see* **diversification**

vertical equity *Fin* the principle that people with different incomes should pay different rates of tax

vertical form *Fin* the presentation of a financial statement in which the debits and credits are shown in one column of figures

vertical integration *Gen Mgt* the practice of combining some or all of the sequential operations of the **supply chain** between the sourcing of **raw materials** and sale of the final product. Vertical integration can be pursued as a strategy through the acquisition of **suppliers**, **wholesalers**, and **retailers** to increase control and reliability. It can also be achieved when a company gains strong control over suppliers or distributors, usually by exercising purchasing power.

vertical keiretsu *Gen Mgt see* **keiretsu**

vertical linkage analysis *Gen Mgt* a tool that enables analysis of the **value chain** in order to determine where opportunities for enhancing **competitive advantage** may lie. Vertical linkage analysis extends the value chain beyond the organisation to incorporate the suppliers and users who are at either end of the chain. This maximises the number of locations where value can be created for customers. Vertical linkage analysis incorporates three steps: working out the value chain for the industry and costing value-creating activities; determining cost drivers for each of these activities; and evaluating opportunities for competitive advantage.

vertical market *E-com* a market that is oriented to one particular speciality, for example, plastics manufacturing or transportation engineering

vertical merger *Gen Mgt see* **merger**

vertical thinking *Gen Mgt see* **lateral thinking**

vested employee benefits *Fin* employee benefits that are not conditional on future employment

vested rights *Fin* the value of somebody's rights in a pension in the United States if he or she leaves a job

VFM *abbr Fin* value for money audit

v-form *Fin* a graphic representation that something had been falling in value and is now rising

videoconferencing *Gen Mgt* the use of a live video link to connect people in different locations so that they can see and hear one another and conduct real-time *meetings*. Videoconferencing is a useful tool for managing *communication* with remote workers, between staff at geographically dispersed offices, including those who form a *virtual team*, or with clients at remote locations. It is also used in *distance learning* courses.

There are two basic options for videoconferencing. The more expensive option is full-blown videoconferencing using *ISDN* lines, dedicated equipment, and large screens, which guarantee a higher quality experience. Cheaper and more common is the PC/web-based videoconferencing, which piggybacks on existing PC and Internet technology, and occupies a small box window on a PC. However, it is less reliable, and still requires an ISDN line to achieve any degree of quality.

viewing figures *Mkting* the number of people who watch a particular television programme or channel

viewtime *E-com* the length of time an advertising banner is visible on a web page

viral marketing *Mkting* the rapid spread of a message about a new product or service, in a similar way to the spread of a virus. Viral marketing can be by word of mouth, but it is particularly common on the Internet, where messages can be spread easily and quickly to reach millions of people. Products can become household names in this way with very little advertising expenditure.

Viral marketing works well in the following circumstances: when a product is genuinely new and different, and it is something that opinion leaders want to associate with; when the benefits of the product are real; when the product is relevant to a large number of people, and the benefits are easy to communicate.

Some viral marketing campaigns use an incentive-based approach, rewarding people if, for example, they inform their friends and a percentage of these friends make a purchase. Because the Internet is perceived as an information resource, it is also useful to publish on a website information that users are allowed to quote and redistribute, perhaps by means of an 'e-mail-to-a-friend' button. *Linking* is also an effective viral marketing tool, as is the provision of free products or services. The Hotmail free e-mail service, for example, grew quickly with little marketing spend.

virement *Fin* authority to apply saving under one subhead to meet excesses on others

virtual hosting *E-com* a type of *hosting option*, suitable for small and medium-sized businesses, in which the customer uses space on a network vendor's server that is also used by other organisations. The hosting company agrees to deliver minimum access speeds and *data transfer* rates, and to carry out basic hardware maintenance, but the customer is responsible for managing the content and software.

virtualisation *Gen Mgt* the creation of a product, service, or organisation that has an electronic rather than a physical existence

virtual office *Gen Mgt* a workplace that is not based in one physical location but consists of employees working remotely by using *information and communications technologies*. A virtual office is characterised by the use of *teleworkers*, *telecentres*, *mobile workers*, *hot-desking*, and *hotelling*, and promotes the use of *virtual teams*. A virtual office can increase an organisation's flexibility, cost effectiveness, and efficiency.

virtual organisation *Ops* a temporary network of companies, suppliers, customers, or employees, linked by *information and communications technologies*, with the purpose of delivering a service or product. A virtual organisation can bring together companies in *strategic partnering* or *outsourcing* arrangements, enabling them to share expertise, resources, and cost savings until objectives are met and the network is dissolved. Such organisations are virtual not only in the sense that they exist largely in cyberspace, but also that they employ various forms of flexibility unconstrained by the traditional barriers of time and place, such as *virtual teams*. A greater level of trust is required between employer and employee or co-workers, or partner organisations, because they will be working out of one another's sight for the majority of the time. *See also* *network organisation*

virtual team *Gen Mgt* a group of employees using *information and communications technologies* to collaborate from different work bases. Members of a virtual team may work in different parts of the same building or may be scattered across a country or around the world. The team can be connected by technology such as *groupware*, e-mail, an *intranet*, or *videoconferencing* and can be said to inhabit a *virtual office*. Although virtual teams can work efficiently, occasional face-to-face meetings can be important to avoid feelings of isolation and to enable *team building*.

The strategist's method is very simply to challenge the prevailing assumptions with a single question: Why?
                                                                    Kenichi Ohmae

virus *E-com* a computer program designed to damage or destroy computer systems and the information contained within them. The fact that extremely destructive viruses can be attached to, and even embedded within, e-mail messages means that anyone with an e-mail account is a potential target. Although there is no single foolproof way to eradicate the risk of viruses, the threat they pose can be reduced in a number of ways. The main precaution that should be taken is to invest in anti-virus software that can check e-mail messages and attachments automatically.

visible trade *Econ* trade in physical goods and merchandise

vision statement *Gen Mgt* a statement giving a broad, aspirational image of the future that an organisation is aiming to achieve. Vision statements express *corporate vision*. They are related to *mission statements*.

visit *E-com* the first entry in a given time period into a website by a web user as identified by a unique web address. A visit is considered to be concluded when the user has not viewed any page at the website in a given time period.

vocational qualification *HR* a qualification awarded after a period of *vocational training* has been successfully completed. Vocational qualifications provide the knowledge and skills for a particular trade or profession and may lead to full membership of a professional body. In the United Kingdom, a Scottish or *National Vocational Qualification* is the most common form of vocational qualification.

vocational training *HR training* that equips somebody for a specific trade or profession. Vocational training may lead to a recognised *vocational qualification*, or it may form part of in-company *employee development*. It might take the form of a short course, practical training, or part-time or full-time study at a college or university.

voetstoots *(S Africa)* *Fin* purchased at the buyer's risk or without warranty

volume of retail sales *Econ* the amount of trade in goods carried out in the retail sector of an economy in a particular period

volume variances *Fin* differences in costs or revenues compared with budgeted amounts, caused by differences between actual and budgeted levels of activity

voluntary arrangement *Fin* an agreement the terms of which are not legally binding on the parties

voluntary bankruptcy *Gen Mgt* see *bankruptcy*

voluntary liquidation *Fin* liquidation of a solvent company that is supported by the shareholders

voluntary registration *Fin* in the United Kingdom, registration for *VAT* by a trader whose turnover is below the registration threshold. This is usually done in order to reclaim tax on inputs.

vortal *E-com* a portal website devoted to one specific industry. These sites enable business-to-business e-commerce transactions by bringing businesses at different points of the supply chain together. Vortal is formed from 'vertical portal'.

vostro account *Fin* an account held by a local bank on behalf of a foreign bank

votes on account *Fin* in the United Kingdom, money granted by Parliament in order to continue spending in a fiscal year before final authorisation of the totals for the year

voting shares *Fin* shares whose owners have voting rights. *US term voting stock*

voting stock *(US)* *Fin* = *voting shares*

voting trust *Fin* a group of individuals who have collectively received voting rights from shareholders

voucher *Fin* documentary evidence supporting an accounting entry

vouching *Fin* an auditing process in which documentary evidence is matched with the details recorded in accounting records in order to check for validity and accuracy

Vredeling Directive *Fin* a proposal, presented to the European Council of Ministers in 1980, for obligatory information, consultation, and participation of workers at headquarters level in multinational enterprises

VRN *abbr Fin* variable rate note

Vroom, Victor Harold *(b. 1932)* *Gen Mgt* Canadian academic. An authority on the psychological analysis of behaviour in organisations, whose work includes contributions on *motivation, leadership* styles and *decision-making*. He described his *expectancy theory* in *Work and Motivation* (1964).

Vulcan nerve pinch *Gen Mgt* the uncomfortable hand position required to reach all the keys for certain computer commands *(slang)*

vulture capitalist *Fin* a venture capitalist who structures deals on behalf of an entrepreneur in such a way that the investors benefit rather than the entrepreneur *(slang)*

The only people who never make mistakes are those who have never taken a decision.   *Jack Straw*

wage earner *HR* a person in paid employment

wage freeze *HR* government policy of preventing *pay* rises in order to combat inflation

wage incentive *HR* a monetary benefit offered as a reward to those employees who perform well in a specified area

wages *HR* a form of *pay* given to employees in exchange for the work they have done. Traditionally, the term wages applied to the weekly pay of manual, or non-professional workers. In modern usage, the term is often used interchangeably with *salary*.

wage scale *HR see pay scale*

waiting time *Fin* the period for which an operator is available for production but is prevented from working by shortage of material or tooling, or by machine breakdown

waiver of premium *Fin* a provision of an insurance policy that suspends payment of premiums, for example, if the insured suffers disabling injury

walk (*US*) *Gen Mgt* to resign from a job (*slang*)

wall
let's throw it at the wall and see if it sticks
Gen Mgt let's try this idea and see if it is successful (*slang*)

walled garden *E-com* an environment on the Internet in which customers can access only e-merchants selected by the owner of the environment (*slang*)

wallet technology *E-com* a software package providing *digital wallets* or purses on the computers of merchants and customers to facilitate payment by digital cash

Wall Street *Fin* the US financial industry, or the area of New York City where much of its business is done

WAN *E-com see network*

WAP *abbr E-com* wireless application protocol: the mobile equivalent of *HTML*, enabling websites to be accessed via mobile devices

warehousing *Ops* the storage and protection of *raw materials* and *finished goods* in a dedicated building or room

war for talent *Gen Mgt* competition between organisations to attract and retain the most able employees

warrants risk warning notice *Fin* a statement that a broker gives to clients to alert them to the risks inherent in trading in options

waste *Fin* discarded material having no value

waste management *or* **waste control** *Gen Mgt* a sustainable process for reducing the environmental impact of the disposal of all types of materials used by businesses. Waste management aims to avoid excessive use of resources and damage to the environment and may be carried out through processes such as recycling. It focuses on efficiency in the use of materials and on disposing of rubbish in the least harmful way. Waste management also involves compliance with the legislation and regulations covering this area.

wasting asset *Fin* an asset that will cease to have any value at all at a date in the future, such as an option or a short-term lease

water
let's put it in the water and see if it floats
Gen Mgt let's try this idea and see if it is successful (*slang*)

Waterman, Robert (*b.* 1936) *Gen Mgt* US consultant. Former McKinsey consultant, who, with *Tom Peters*, wrote the best-selling work *In Search of Excellence* (1984).

Watson, Jr, Thomas (1914–93) *Gen Mgt* US industrialist. CEO of IBM, 1956–70, who gave the company a strong core philosophy and led it through a period of complete domination of the computer industry. His beliefs, which centred on consideration for the employee, care for the customer, and taking time to get things right, are described in *A Business and its Beliefs: The Ideas that Helped Build IBM* (1963).

wealth *Econ* physical assets such as a house or financial assets such as stocks and shares that can yield an income for their holder

wealth tax *Fin* a tax on somebody's accumulated wealth, as opposed to their income

wear a hat *Gen Mgt* to fulfil a specified role at a particular moment in time. Somebody may be required to wear several hats within the same company. (*slang*)

wear and tear *Fin* the deterioration of a tangible fixed asset as a result of normal use. This is recognised for accounting purposes by *depreciation*.

---

web bug *E-com* a small file sent to reside in a website user's browser, in order to track that consumer the next time he or she visits the website—in much the same manner as a *cookie*.

Web bugs, however, are not generally detectable by standard browsers, although there is software that can be downloaded to spot them. They are therefore controversial, as their very design reflects a desire not to let a person know that they are being tracked, and they have sometimes been used in a surreptitious manner. This has added fuel to the fear that people's privacy rights are being abused on the Internet.

webcast *E-com* use of the Web to broadcast information. A webcast event is intended to be viewed simultaneously by numerous people connecting to the same website. Webcast events often use *rich media* technology.

web commerce *E-com see e-commerce*

Weber, Max (1864–1920) *Gen Mgt* German sociologist. Remembered for his work on *power* and *authority*, published in *Theory of Social and Economic Organization* (1924), where he proposed *bureaucracy* as the most efficient form of *organisation*.

After studying legal and economic history, Weber was a law professor at the University of Freiburg and later at the University of Heidelberg. He studied the sociology of religion and in this area he produced his best-known work, *The Protestant Work Ethic and the Spirit of Capitalism*. In political sociology he examined the relationship between social and economic organisations. Towards the end of his life, Weber developed his political interests and was on the committee that drafted the constitution of the Weimar Republic in 1918.

web form *E-com* a means of collecting information from a visitor to a website in a structured manner. Once the consumer has filled in the form, it is usually returned to the owner of the website via e-mail.

There are several golden rules to follow when designing a web form. It should be short or, if necessary, split into clear sections. Mandatory fields—such as e-mail addresses—should be clearly marked, conventionally with red type or red asterisks. Consumers should be given an alternative for information they cannot give—for example: 'If you don't have a ZIP code, please write "None".' Errors should be isolated: if the consumer makes an error in the form, they should be asked to correct that specific error, not simply have the form returned to them. Fields should be of suf-

ficient size for all the requested information. Alternative means of providing the information should be made available for people with disabilities.

web log *E-com* a means of tracking activity on a website or computer system. It can provide important marketing information such as how many users are visiting the site, how they behave, and what they are interested in, as well as highlighting useful technical issues such as whether there are page errors occurring, or whether spikes in visitor behaviour are causing *bandwidth* shortages. *Also called server log*

web marketing *E-com* the process of creating, developing, and enhancing a website in order to increase the number of visits by potential customers

web marketplace *E-com* a business-to-business web community that brings business buyers and sellers together. Although their exact nature can vary considerably, there are essentially three types of web-based B2B marketplace: *online catalogues*, *auctions*, and *exchanges*.

webmaster *E-com* the person responsible for managing the content of a website and monitoring traffic through the site. The role of webmaster may be shared between numerous individuals within an organisation.

web response form *E-com see WRF*

web server *E-com* **1.** the physical computer that supports a website **2.** the software that runs on web servers. Web server software delivers web pages to browsers on Internet-based computers.

website classification *E-com* the organisation of content on a website into different categories, so that it can be identified and found easily by a user. Classification is a particularly important form of *metadata*, as a website with poor classification will be difficult to navigate and of little use to the visitor.

The top-level classification of a website expresses, in the fewest and simplest words possible, the nature of the business. For example, is it selling 'products', 'services', or 'solutions'? Are its customers 'home users', 'small businesses', 'large businesses'? It is important, if possible, to avoid going more than five levels deep in further classification. The more levels there are, the more clicks will be required from visitors to find what they are looking for. It is also best to avoid having too many documents under one classification: more than 50 becomes confusing, and it would probably be better to break down the classification further.

weighted average *Stats* an average of quantities that have been adjusted by the addition of a statistical value to allow for their relative importance in a data set

weighted average number of ordinary shares *Fin* the number of ordinary shares at the beginning of a period, adjusted for shares cancelled, bought back, or issued during the period, multiplied by a time-weighting factor. This number is used in the calculation of *earnings per share*.

weighting *Stats* the assigning of greater importance to particular items in a data set

weightlessness *Gen Mgt* a quality considered to characterise an economy that is based on knowledge or other intangibles rather than on physical assets

Welch, Jack (*b.* 1935) *Gen Mgt* US business executive. Turned around General Electric in the 1980s by making *redundancies*, *divesting* and acquiring (see *merger*) businesses, and introducing 'Work-Out', a programme centred on *communication* and *innovation*.

welfare *HR* the physical and mental well-being of employees, and the provision of help for those in need of assistance. Welfare embraces: *physical working conditions*, such as hygiene, sanitation, temperature, humidity, ventilation, lighting, physical comfort, and refreshments; *occupational health* or wellness promotion; *counselling* and advice on personal problems, such as bereavement, drug abuse, or *stress*; and working time, covering matters such as *hours of work*, rest periods, paid holidays, and *shiftwork*. *Employee assistance programmes* are a modern form of welfare policy, although not common outside the United States.

well
let's drop it down the well and see what kind of splash it makes *Gen Mgt* let's try this idea and see if it is successful (*slang*)

wellness program (*US*) *HR* a company programme offering benefits, activities, or training, to improve and promote employees' health and fitness. A wellness programme can include **wellness benefits** such as fitness training, company sponsored athletics and sports teams, health education, and life improvement classes. It also includes prevention of mental health problems by *stress* management.

wet signature *Gen Mgt* a signature on paper rather than a faxed or e-mailed copy (*slang*)

wharfie (*ANZ*) *Gen Mgt* a docker (*slang*)

Wheat Report *Fin* a report produced by a committee in 1972 that set out to examine the principles and methods of accounting in the United States. Its publication led to the establishment of the Financial Accounting Standards Board.

whisper stock *Fin* a stock about which there is talk of a likely change in value, usually upwards and often related to a takeover

whistle
blow the whistle on somebody or something *Gen Mgt* to speak out publicly about malpractice or incompetence within an organisation

whistleblowing *Gen Mgt* speaking out to the media or the public on malpractice, misconduct, corruption, or mismanagement witnessed in an organisation. Whistleblowing is usually undertaken on the grounds of morality or conscience or because of a failure of *business ethics* on the part of the organisation being reported.

white coat rule *Mkting* a US Federal Trade Commission rule prohibiting the use of actors dressed as doctors to promote a product in TV commercials (*slang*)

white-collar crime *Gen Mgt* a crime committed by somebody doing a white-collar job

white-collar job *HR* a position that does not involve physical labour. *See also* **blue-collar job**

white-collar worker *HR* an office worker. Office workers traditionally wore a white shirt and a tie.

white goods *Mkting* large household electrical appliances such as cookers, fridges, and freezers

white knight *Fin see* **knight**

white squire *Gen Mgt* a *shareholder* who purchases a significant, but not controlling, number of shares in order to prevent a *takeover bid* from succeeding. A white squire is often invited to purchase the shares by the company to be acquired, and may be required to sign an agreement to prevent them from later becoming a black *knight*.

whizz kid *Fin* a young, exceptionally successful person, especially one who makes a lot of money in large financial transactions, including takeovers

---

Business? It's quite simple. It's other people's money. *Alexandre Dumas*

wholesale price *Fin* a price charged to customers who buy large quantities of an item for resale in smaller quantities to others

wholesale price index *Fin* a government-calculated index of wholesale prices, indicative of inflation in an economy

wholesaler *Mkting, Ops* an intermediary who buys in bulk from manufacturers for resale to *retailers* or other traders. Some wholesalers sell directly to the public. One type of wholesaler is a **cash and carry**, which offers discounted prices for bulk purchases that are paid for and taken away at the time of sale. Cash and carries traditionally serve the business community, but many now allow the general public to buy from them.

wholesale trade *Fin* trade at wholesale prices

wholly-owned subsidiary *Fin* a company that is completely owned by another company. A wholly-owned subsidiary is a *registered company* with board members who all represent one *holding company* or corporation. Board members may be directly from the holding company or acting as its nominees, or they may be from other wholly-owned subsidiaries of the holding company.

Whyte, William Hollingsworth (1917–99) *Gen Mgt* US urban theorist. Author of *The Organization Man* (1956), a study of the impact of the power of *corporate culture* on individuals from the suburban middle class.

Wickens, Peter (*b.* 1938) *Gen Mgt* British business executive. Personnel director at Nissan UK, where he helped to introduce Japanese working practices, such as *continuous improvement*, into the UK car industry. Wickens's employee relations philosophy at Nissan was based on job flexibility, *single status*, and a single union deal. His book, *The Ascendant Organisation* (1995), brings together his experience and knowledge of *best practice*.

widow-and-orphan stock (*US*) *Fin* a stock considered extremely safe as an investment

wiggle room *Gen Mgt* flexibility in matters relating to contracts or deadlines (*slang*)

wildcat strike *HR see* **unofficial strike**

Willie Sutton rule *Gen Mgt* the maxim that it is most logical to concentrate on areas that yield most profit. The Willie Sutton rule is based on an alleged remark made by bank robber Willie Sutton. He was reputedly asked why he robbed banks and replied 'Because that's where the money is'. A person or organisation following this rule will focus their effort on those activities that give the greatest return.

windfall gains and losses *Fin* unexpected gains and losses

windfall profit *Fin* a sudden large profit, subject to extra tax

windfall tax *Fin* the tax a government levies on a company that makes extraordinarily large profits in times of unusual circumstances, for example, during a war

winding-up *Fin* the legal process of closing down a company

winding-up petition *Fin* a formal request to a court for the compulsory liquidation of a company

window dressing *Fin* a creative accounting practice in which changes in short-term funding have the effect of disguising or improving the reported liquidity position of the reporting organisation

win win situation *Gen Mgt* a business situation in which all parties stand to gain something (*slang*)

WIP *abbr Fin* work in progress

wired company *Gen Mgt* a company that makes full use of information technology to run its business (*slang*)

wireless application protocol *E-com see* **WAP**

witching hour (*US*) *Fin* the time when a type of derivative financial instrument such as a *put*, a *call*, or a contract for advance sale becomes due (*slang*)

withdrawal *Fin* regular disbursements of dividend or capital gain income from an open-end unit trust

withholding tax *Fin* **1.** in the United States, the money that an employer pays directly to the government as a payment of the income tax on the employee **2.** the money deducted from a dividend or interest payment that a financial institution pays directly to the government as a payment of the income tax on the recipient

WOMBAT *abbr Gen Mgt* waste of money, brains, and time (*slang*)

wood

put wood behind the arrow *Gen Mgt* to provide resources or money for a project or enterprise (*slang*)

Woodward, Joan (1916–71) *Gen Mgt* British academic. Originator of what subsequently became known as the *contingency theory* of

---

organisations, based on research inspired by **Elton Mayo** and which was written up in *Industrial Organization* (1965).

word of mouse *E-com* word-of-mouth publicity on the Internet. Owing to the fast-paced and interactive nature of online markets, word of mouse can spread much faster than its off-line counterpart. (*slang*)

work *Gen Mgt* the expenditure of physical or mental energy to achieve a purposeful task. Work is usually performed by *employees* within organisations, where it involves completion of a particular activity that contributes to the achievement of organisational goals.

workaholic *HR* somebody who is addicted to working. A workaholic spends long hours in the workplace and probably suffers from *presenteeism*. While workaholics may be very productive, workaholism is sometimes a sign of *stress* or personal problems. The term was coined in the 1960s.

work cell *Fin* a group of employees or machines dedicated to performing a specific manufacturing task or a group of related tasks

worker control *Gen Mgt* participation by employees in the management of an organisation. Worker control can involve *worker directors*, *works councils*, or a *management buy-out*.

worker director *HR* an *employee* raised to executive status within an organisation, usually as part of a structured programme of *employee participation* in management. A worker director usually represents the views of staff at board level.

workers' co-operative *Gen Mgt* see *industrial co-operative*

work ethic *Gen Mgt* the belief that *work* itself is as important and fulfilling as the end result. The work ethic originated among Protestants and was central to the views of Martin Luther and John Calvin. It played an important role in the achievements of the Industrial Revolution.

work experience *HR* the temporary placement of young people in organisations to give them a taste of the work environment. Successful work experience programmes require adequate preparation by schools and employing organisations, together with follow-up activities to monitor the outcomes of a placement.

work flow *Gen Mgt* see *office design*

workforce *HR* the whole body of employees, either in an organisation or across an industry

working capital *Fin* the funds that are readily available to operate a business.

EXAMPLE Working capital comprises the total net current assets of a business minus its liabilities.

Current assets – current liabilities

Current assets are cash and assets that can be converted to cash within one year or a normal operating cycle; current liabilities are monies owed that are due within one year.

If a company's current assets total £300,000 and its current liabilities total £160,000, its working capital is:

£300,000 – £160,000 = £140,000

working capital cycle *Fin* the period of time which elapses between the point at which cash begins to be expended on the production of a product, and the collection of cash from the purchaser

working capital ratio *Fin* see *current ratio*

working hours *HR* see *hours of work*

working lunch *Gen Mgt* a lunchtime meal during which business is transacted. A working lunch can occur either when an employee continues to work through their lunch hour, or when clients or colleagues are entertained and business is conducted at the same time, when it is also known as a **power lunch**.

work in process *(US)* *Fin* = *work in progress*

work in progress *Fin* products that are in the process of being made. They are included in stocks and usually valued according to their production costs. *US term* **work in process**

work-life balance *HR* the equilibrium between the amount of time and effort somebody devotes to work and that given to other aspects of life. Work-life balance is the subject of widespread public debate on how to allow *employees* more control over their working arrangements in order to better accommodate other aspects of their lives, while still benefiting their organisations. The agenda consists primarily of *flexible working* practices and *family-friendly policies*, although good practice demonstrates that flexibility should be open to all, including those without caring responsibilities. The work-life balance debate has arisen through social and economic changes, such as greater numbers of women in the workforce, the expectations of the younger *Generation X*, a growing reluctance to accept the longer hours culture, the rise of the 24/7 society, and technological advancements. It has been supported by government and by organisations which see it as a means

---

Preparation is everything. Noah did not start building the ark when it was raining. **Warren Buffett**

of aiding **recruitment** and employee retention.

work measurement *Gen Mgt* the establishment of **standard times** for the completion of particular work tasks to a particular level of performance. In work measurement, tasks are broken down into elements. The time required for each is established and an assessment of relaxation and contingency allowances is made. Work measurement forms part of **work study** and is normally carried out subsequent to **method study** with the aim of increasing efficiency and **productivity**. Work measurement was developed in the context of industrial **production management** but has recently become more widely used. **Time study** and **predetermined motion-time systems** are used in work measurement.

work permit *HR* a licence granted to a foreign national in order that they may perform a specific job for a limited period. A work permit scheme is intended to safeguard the interests of the resident labour force while enabling employers to recruit or transfer skilled workers from abroad. It is the responsibility of the employing organisation to obtain permits from its national government.

workplace bullying *HR* persistent intimidation or harassment at work which demoralises and humiliates a person or group. There are no universally agreed definitions of what constitutes workplace bullying, as there are many kinds of bullying behaviour or tactics. As a general guideline to distinguish between workplace bullying and legitimate criticism, comments should follow the principles for offering **feedback**: it should be properly conducted, non-personal, and constructive, and should not be abusive, aiming to help people to improve their behaviour or performance rather than cause them anxiety or distress.

work profiling *HR see profile method*

work rage *Gen Mgt* an expression of irrational anger felt by an employee in the workplace (*slang*)

Worksafe Australia *HR see National Occupational Health and Safety Commission*

work sampling *Gen Mgt see activity sampling*

works council *HR* a body of representatives of management and employees who meet to exchange opinions, information and advice on matters concerning the efficiency of the organisation and the interests of staff. A works council is a form of joint consultation, or

employee participation. The idea was first introduced by **Wilfred Brown** at the **Glacier Metal Company** as a genuine attempt at **industrial democracy**. The European Works Council Directive, approved in 1994, makes it compulsory for larger employers in Europe to implement a European works council, or EWC, if operations span two or more countries. An EWC enables employees to be informed and consulted across national boundaries.

work shadow *HR* somebody who observes a jobholder in action with the aim of learning something about how that role is performed. Work shadowing has traditionally been seen as a way of giving **work experience** to school students or graduates but it is also a means of offering employees the opportunity to find out more about other jobs within their own or other organisations. It can be used, for example, as a form of **secondment**, or as a preliminary to a sideways move for somebody experiencing **plateauing**.

work simplification *Gen Mgt* an idea pioneered by **Frank** and **Lillian Gilbreth** and favoured by practitioners of **scientific management**. Any work that does not add value to an idea or process is seen as reducible waste. Tasks in a procedure are analysed to see if unnecessary steps can be eliminated, thereby reducing complexity as much as possible. This should enable workers to complete tasks more quickly. Work simplification is most suited to manufacturing processes and low-skilled jobs. It can lead to cost savings and better use of resources but it has been criticised for resulting in workers specialising in only one task and for making work repetitive and monotonous.

works manager *HR* the person in charge of a factory, plant, or area of operations in a manufacturing company. A works manager is usually a **general manager**, with responsibility not just for the manufacturing operation but also for personnel, finance, marketing, etc.

workstation 1. *E-com* a powerful, single-user computer. A workstation is like a personal computer, but it has a more powerful microprocessor and a higher-quality monitor. **2.** *Gen Mgt* the place where a person or small group carries out their particular work tasks. A workstation might take the form of an individual unit where a stage of the manufacturing process is carried out. A factory may contain many workstations, organised to optimise the production process. In an office environment, a workstation may refer to a desk with a computer, telephone, and other equipment at which one person sits.

work structuring *HR* the design of work processes. Work structuring involves arranging the factors that make up employees' jobs in the most efficient way. Factors to be engineered include *hours of work*, duties performed, and level of *empowerment*. Work structuring can make use of practices such as *flexible working*, *teamwork*, job enrichment, *job enlargement*, and *job rotation*. It is similar to *job design*.

work study *Gen Mgt, HR, Ops* the analysis of activities of employees within an organisational context. Work study comprises a set of techniques that are used to examine a work process and determine where improvements can be made. It usually involves *method study* followed by *work measurement*, and is an important tool in *total quality management*. It is similar to *time and motion study*.

work-to-rule *HR* a form of *industrial action* in which employees work strictly according to the terms of their *contract of employment*. A work-to-rule usually involves refusal to do any extra tasks and an overtime ban, causing production to slow down.

world class manufacturing *Ops* the capability of a manufacturer to compete with any other manufacturing organisation in a chosen market, with the aspiration of achieving world-beating standards in all organisational aspects. World class manufacturing encompasses the practices of *total quality management*, *continuous improvement*, international *benchmarking*, and *flexible working*.

world economy *Econ* the global marketplace that has grown up since the 1970s in which goods can be produced wherever production cost is cheapest

wrap fund (*S Africa*) *Fin* a registered fund, not itself a unit trust but with similar status to that of a stockbroker's portfolio, which invests in a range of underlying unit trusts, each of which is treated as a discrete holding

WRF *abbr E-com* web response form: a web-based form designed to collect site-visitor contact and other information. A WRF often forms part of a landing page or termination point of a website address intended to funnel response not just from a website but also from traditional direct marketing material.

Wright, T.P. *Gen Mgt* originator of a mathematical model describing a *learning curve*, introduced in an article entitled 'Factors Affecting the Cost of Airplanes' in *the Journal of Aeronautical Science* (February 1936)

write-down *Fin* a reduction in the recorded value of an asset to comply with the concept of prudence. The valuation of stock at the lower of cost or net realisable value may require the values of some stock to be written down.

write off *Fin* a reduction in the recorded value of an asset, usually to zero

writing down allowances *Fin* in the United Kingdom, the annual depreciation of fixed assets for tax purposes. These allowances form part of the capital allowance system.

written-down value *Fin see net book value*

wrongful trading *Fin* the continuation of trading when a company's directors know that it cannot avoid insolvent liquidation

WRT *abbr Gen Mgt* with respect to (*slang*)

WYSIWYG *abbr E-com* what you see is what you get: refers to web creation software that enables users to design content on their computer that will look exactly the same when transferred to the Web. Before the advent of the Internet, the term was also used in reference to word processing software that allowed the user to see exactly how a document would look when it was printed.

Blameless people are always the most exasperating.   *George Eliot*

X.12 *E-com see ANSI X.12 standard*

XBRL *abbr E-com, Fin* Extensible Business Reporting Language: a computer language for financial reporting. It allows companies to publish, extract, and exchange financial information through the internet and other electronic means.

XML *E-com* extensible mark-up language, a meta-language that describes rules for defining tagged mark-up languages. XML is similar to **HTML**, except that it is intended to deliver data to a variety of applications and is designed to be read by the applications run by a system, whereas HTML is intended to be read from a web browser by a person.

XML is an emerging world standard for **metadata**, delivering a common approach by which metadata for content is collected. So in order to achieve a common standard, organisations in a particular industry would agree to structure their documents in the same way. For example, finance companies would agree to use the same methods of creating documentation such as morning notes, which are short analyses issued daily. The morning notes would all use the same layout structure, and have the same metadata such as author name, date, ticker symbols, buy, and sell rating. Because of this common structure, anyone receiving these morning notes would be able to search and interrogate them in a far more comprehensive manner.

Y2K-compliant *Gen Mgt see* **millennium bug**

yakka *(ANZ) HR* an informal term for work

Yankee bond *Fin* a bond issued in the US domestic market by a non-US company

YAPPY *abbr Mkting* Young Affluent Parent *(slang)*

year-end *Fin* relating to the end of a financial or fiscal (tax) year

year-end closing *Fin* the financial statements issued at the end of a company's fiscal (tax) year

Yellow Book *Fin* a book, *Admission of Securities to Listing*, which sets out the regulations for admission to, and continuing membership of, the official list of quoted companies on the London Stock Exchange *(slang)*

yield *Fin* a percentage of the amount invested that is the annual income from an investment.

It is calculated by dividing the annual cash return by the current share price and expressing that as a percentage.

Yields can be compared against the market average or against a sector average, which in turn gives an idea of the relative value of the share against its peers. Other things being equal, a higher yield share is preferable to that of an identical company with a lower yield.

An additional feature of the yield (unlike many of the other share analysis ratios), is that it enables comparison with cash. Cash placed in an interest-bearing source like a bank account or a government stock, produces a yield—the annual interest payable. This is usually a safe investment. The yield from this cash investment can be compared with the yield on shares, which are far riskier. This produces a valuable basis for share evaluation.

Share yield is less reliable than bank interest or government stock interest yield, because unlike banks paying interest, companies are under no obligation at all to pay dividends. Frequently, if they go through a bad patch, even the largest companies will cut dividends or abandon paying them altogether.

yield curve *Fin* a representation of relative interest rates of short- and long-term bonds. It may be normal, flat, or inverted.

yield gap *Fin* an amount representing the difference between the yield on a very safe investment and the yield on a riskier one

yield to call *Fin* the yield on a bond at a date when the bond can be called.

Bond issuers reserve the right to 'call', or redeem, the bond before the maturity date, at certain times and at a certain price. Issuers often do this if interest rates fall and they can issue new bonds at a lower rate. Bond buyers should obtain the yield-to-call rate, which may, in fact, be a more realistic indicator of the return expected.

yield to maturity *(US) Fin* = **gross yield to redemption**

YK *abbr Fin* yugen kaisha

young old *Mkting* the group of people aged between 55 and 75

yugen kaisha *Fin* in Japan, a private limited liability corporation. Usually, the number of shareholders must be less than 50. The minimum capital of a limited liability corporation is 3,000,000 yen. The par value of each share must be 50,000 yen or more. *Abbr* **YK**

YUPPY *abbr Gen Mgt* Young Urban Professional *(slang)*

zaibatsu *Gen Mgt* Japanese mining-to-manufacture conglomerates dating from before the second world war. At the end of the second world war, zaibatsu were disbanded because of their involvement in the war effort. When post-war restrictions were relaxed, these groups of companies reformed as *keiretsu*.

Zaleznik, Abraham (*b*. 1924) *Gen Mgt* US academic. Author of the landmark article *Managers and Leaders: Are They Different?* published in the 'Harvard Business Review' (1977), which influenced the ideas of *Warren Bennis* on the key elements found in effective *leaders*.

ZBB *abbr Fin* zero-based budgeting

Z bond *Fin* a bond whose holder receives no accrued interest until all of the holders of other bonds in the same series have received theirs

zero-balance account *Fin* a bank account that does not hold funds continuously, but has money automatically transferred into it from another account when claims arise against it

zero-based budgeting *Fin* a method of budgeting which requires each cost element to be specifically justified, as though the activities to which the budget relates were being undertaken for the first time. Without approval, the budget allowance is zero. *Abbr* **ZBB**

zero coupon bond *Fin* a bond that pays no interest and is sold at a large discount.
Zero coupon bonds increase in value until maturity. A buyer might pay £3,000 for a 25-year zero bond with a face value of £10,000. This bond will simply accrue value each year, and at maturity will be worth £10,000, thus earning £7,000. These are high-risk investments, however, especially if they must be sold on the open market amid rising interest rates. *Also known as* **accrual bond**

zero defects *Ops* a *quality* philosophy according to which organisations aim to produce goods that are 100% perfect. Zero defects was developed during the early 1960s in the United States by *Philip Crosby* while he was working for the Martin-Marietta Corporation. The aim is to eliminate the smallest defects at each process stage. It requires a high level of *employee participation*. When introduced in Japan it merged with *quality circle* concepts.

zero fund *Gen Mgt* to assign no money to a business project without actually cancelling it (*slang*)

zero growth *Econ* a fall in output for two successive quarters

zero out *Gen Mgt* to dial zero when using an automated call system in the hope of finding a live person to speak to (*slang*)

zero-rated supplies *or* **zero-rated goods and services** *Fin* in the United Kingdom, taxable items or services on which VAT is charged at zero rate, such as food, books, public transport, and children's clothes

Z score *Fin* a single figure, produced by a financial model, which combines a number of variables (generally financial statements ratios), whose magnitude is intended to aid the prediction of failure. A Z score model may predict that a company with a score of 1.8 or less is likely to fail within 12 months. Individual companies are scored against this benchmark.

MULTILINGUAL GLOSSARY

AAA[1]
(验证; 授权; 和清算)
authentification, autorisation et
comptabilité
Authentifizierung, Autorisierung
und Buchhaltung
autenticación, autorización y
contabilidad
認証・認可・課金

AAA[2]
债券最高信誉等级
évaluation de toute sécurité
donnée par Standard & Poor's
AAA
máxima clasificación de Standard
& Poor's
最優良の社債格付け

AAMOF
事实上
en fait
eigentlich
con toda naturalidad
実は...

abandonment option
废弃期权
option d'abandon
Aufgabeoption
opción de abandono
放棄オプション

abandonment value
废弃价值
valeur à l'abandon
Aufgabewert
valor de abandono
廃棄価値

Abilene paradox
阿比林悖论
paradoxe d'Abilene
Paradox von Abilene
paradoja de Abilene
アベリーンの逆説

ABN
澳大利亚商业号
numéro d'identification de
compagnie en Australie
Australische Steuernummer
código de identificación fiscal
australiano
オーストラリア法人登記番号

abnormal loss
非正常损失
perte anormale
anormaler Verlust
pérdida anormal
異常損失

abnormal spoilage
非正常损耗
détérioration anormale
abnormale Abnahme

reducción anormal
異常仕損

above-the-line[1]
广告佣金
dépenses (en publicité-média)
großangelegte Werbekampagne
proporcional
広告用(のマーケティング予算)

above-the-line[2]
线上项目
au-dessus de la ligne
über der Linie
partidas extracontables
広告用(のマーケティング予算)

above-the-line[3]
经常 项目
au-dessus de la ligne
makroökonomisches
Landeseinkommen
por encima de la línea
広告用(のマーケティング予算)

absenteeism
缺席; 缺勤; 旷工
absentéisme
Absentismus
absentismo
ausentismo
欠勤

absorbed account
分摊帐户; 附属帐
compte absorbé
verrechnete Faktura; absorbierte
Forderung
cuenta absorbida
配賦勘定

absorbed business
附属企业
entreprise absorbée
übernommenes Unternehmen
negocio absorbido
吸収企業

absorbed costs
已吸收成本; 已分摊成本
coûts absorbés
absorbierte Kosten
costes absorbidos
costos absorbidos
配賦原価

absorbed overhead
已吸收的间接费用
frais généraux ventilés
verrechnete Gemeinkosten
tasa de gasto absorbido
配賦済経費

absorption costing
分担成本计算
évaluation de coût d'absorption
Vollkostenrechnung
cálculo de costes de absorción
cálculo de costos de absorción
全部原価計算

abusive tax shelter
滥用税收掩蔽所
avantage fiscal illégal
mißbräuchliche
Steuerbegünstigung
refugio tributario abusivo
タックス・シェルターの乱用,
不法な節税手段

ACCC
澳大利亚竞争及消费者委员会
commission australienne de la
concurrence et du consommateur
Australische Wettbewerbs- und
Verbraucherbehörde
comisión australiana reguladora de
las prácticas comerciales
オーストラリア競争消費者委員会

**accelerated cost recovery
system**
加速成本回收系统
système accéléré de recouvrement
de coût
beschleunigte Abschreibung
sistema acelerado de recuperación
de costes
sistema acelerado de recuperación
de costos
加速度原価回収制度,
加速償却制度

accelerated depreciation
加速折旧
dépréciation accélérée
beschleunigte
Sonderabschreibung
amortización acelerada
加速償却, 加速償却制度,
超過償却

acceptable quality level
可 接 受 质 量 水 平
niveau de qualité acceptable
Annahmegrenze
nivel aceptable de calidad
合格品質水準, AQL

acceptance
承诺
acceptation
Akzept
aceptación
手形引受

acceptance bonus
任职奖金
prime d'acceptation (d'emploi)
Einstiegsbonus
plus por aceptar
新規採用賞与金

acceptance credit
承兑信用
crédit d'acceptation
Akzeptkredit
línea de crédito
引受信用

Translations appear in the following order: Chinese, French, German, Spanish/Latin American Spanish, and Japanese

acceptance house
承兑商行; 期票承兑行
banque d'acceptation
Akzeptbank
casa de aceptaciones
(手形)引受業者, 引受商社(英)

acceptance region
容忍区间
région d'acceptation
Annahmebereich
región de aceptación
許容範囲

acceptance sampling
可接受样例
technique d'échantillonnage à
réception
Abnahmekontrolle mittels
Stichproben
muestreo para aceptación
受入サンプリング, 受入抜取検査

accepting bank
承兑行
banque d'acceptation
akzeptierende Bank
banco de aceptación
引受銀行

acceptor
承诺人
accepteur
Remittent(in)
aceptante de una letra de cambio
手形引受人

access bond
一种允许将未来额外收入作为
抵押的房屋按揭
obligation hypothécaire avec accès
à emprunt sur capital
supplémentaire
Hypothekenart
bono de acceso
アクセスボンド(担保の一種)

account¹
帐; 帐目; 帐户
compte-client
Konto
cuenta
会計

account²
客户
client
Kunde(-in); Kundenetat
cliente
顧客, 得意先

accountability
负责
(prise de) responsabilité
Verantwortlichkeit;
Rechenschaftpflicht
responsabilidad
アカウンタビリティ(説明責任)

accountability concept
责任概念
concept de la responsabilité
Verantwortlichkeitskonzept
presentación de logros y proyectos
説明責任

accountancy
会计
comptabilité
Rechnungswesen; Buchhaltung;
Buchführung
contabilidad
会計業務

accountancy bodies
会计师团体
organismes comptables
professionnels
professionelle Institute und
Verbände für Buchhalter
organismos contables
会計士団体

accountancy profession
会计员
profession de comptable
Buchhalterverbände
profesión de contables
会計士業

accountant
会计师; 会计
comptable
Wirtschaftsprüfer(in)
contable
contador(a)
会計士

accountant's letter
查账意见书
lettre de comptable
Schreiben des Rechnungsprüfers
carta de contable
carta de contador(a)
会計報告書

account day
结算日; 结帐日
jour de liquidation (boursière)
Liquidationstermin (Bö)
día de liquidación
受渡日

account debtor
债务人
débiteur de compte
Kunde(-in); Abnehmer(in)
deudor(a) a cuenta
借方

account director
帐户经理; 营业主管; 客户经理
directeur du budget (publicitaire)
Key-Asset Manager(in)
director (a) de cuentas
アカウント・ディレクター

account executive
帐户管理员; 业务员; 营业经理;
客户经理
responsable du budget publicitaire
Sachbearbeiter(in)
ejecutivo(-a) de cuentas
アカウント・エグゼクティブ

accounting cost
会计成本
coût de comptabilité
Buchungskosten
coste contable
costo contable
会計処理費用

accounting cycle
会计周期
cycle d'exercice comptable
Buchungsdurchlauf;
Umschlagzyklus
ciclo contable
会計サイクル

accounting equation
会计等式
échéance comptable
Bilanzgleichung
ecuación contable
差引勘定期日平均法

accounting exposure
会计风险
risque comptable
beschleunigte
Sonderabschreibung
riesgo comptable
(為替リスク等の)
会計上のエクスポージャー

accounting insolvency
会计周转不灵
insolabilité comptable
Überschuldung
insolvencia contable
会計上の支払不能

accounting period
会计结算期
période comptable
Abrechnungszeitraum
período contable
会計期間

accounting principles
会计原理
principes comptables
Bilanzierungsgrundsätze
principios de contabilidad
会計原則

accounting profit
会计利润
bénéfice comptable
rechnerischer Gewinn;
Buchgewinn
beneficio contable
会計利益

Translations appear in the following order: Chinese, French, German, Spanish/Latin American Spanish, and Japanese

accounting rate of return
会计 收益 率
recettes comptables
rechnerische Rendite
tasa de rendimiento
contable
会計収益率

accounting ratio
会计比率
rapport de comptabilité
rechnerisches Verhältnis
relación de cuenta
会計比率

accounting reference date
会计期间截止日
date de référence comptable
Stichtag
fecha de cierre del ejercicio
会計参照期間の末日

accounting reference period
会计期
exercice comptable de référence
Bezugszeitraum; für die
Rechnungsführung;
Abrechnungsperiode/zeitraum;
Bilanzierungszeitraum
período contable de referencia
会計年度

accounting system
会计 系统
système de comptabilité
Buchführungssystem;
Buchungssystem
sistema contable
会計制度

accounting year
会计 年度
exercice comptable
Geschäftsjahr; Wirtschaftsjahr
año contable
会計年度

account reconciliation[1]
调解帐户; 协调帐户
ajustement des écritures
Kontoabstimmung
conciliación de cuentas
勘定尻の調整

account reconciliation[2]
账目调和
ajustement des écritures
Kontoabstimmung
conciliación de cuentas
勘定尻の調整

account sales
承销帐，承销清单
compte de vente(s)
Verkaufskonto;
Verkaufsabrechnung
ventas en cuenta
売上計算書

accounts payable
应 付 帐款; 应 付 帐
comptes payables
Verbindlichkeiten; Kreditoren
cuentas por pagar
買掛金

accounts receivable
应收帐款; 应收帐
comptes de créances recouvrables
Forderungen; Debitoren;
Außenstände
cuentas por cobrar
売掛金

accounts receivable ageing
应收帐款赊欠期间帐龄分析
comptes de créances arrivant à
maturation
fällige Forderungen
ordenación cronológica de las
cuentas por cobrar
売掛金報告書

accounts receivable factoring
应收帐款让售
comptes de créances d'affacturage
Forderungsankauf; Factoring von
Forderungen
factoraje de cuentas por cobrar
売掛金買収業

accounts receivable financing
应收帐款融通
financement par créances
Finanzierung durch Abtretung von
Geschäftsforderungen; Factoring
financiación basada en cuentas
por cobrar
売掛金(担保)金融

accounts receivable turnover
应收帐目周转率
rapport de rotation des effets à
recevoir
Debitoren-Umschlag
razón de ventas a crédito
売掛金回転率

accreditation of prior learning
以往学历认可
accréditation des qualifications
préalables
Anerkennung; von
Qualifikationen; offizielle
Akkreditierung; früherer;
Qualifikationen und Erfahrungen
certificación de estudios propios
習得認証, 習熟認定制

accredited investor
信用投资商
investisseur accrédité
zugelassene/r Anleger(in) od.
Investor(in)
inversor(a) acreditado(-a)

有資格投資家, 適格投資家,
自衛力認定投資家

accreted value
债券增值
valeur accumulée
Zuwachswert
valor teórico
付加価値, 増加価値, 自然増価

accretion
自然増値; 増殖
accroissement
Wertzuwachs;
Vermögenszuwachs
acrecentamiento; aumento
価値増価, 合併太り

accrual
増 加; 増长; 积累
accumulation
Anfall; Rechnungs-;
Abgrenzungsposten
devengo; acumulación
未収支勘定

accrual concept
应付 应 收 概念; 应 计 概念
concept d'accumulation
Konzept der antizipativen
Abgrenzung von Aufwendungen
und Erträgen
criterio del devengo
発生主義会計

accrual method
应计法
méthode d'accumulation
Methode des
Betriebsvermögensvergleichs
método de acumulación
発生主義

accrual of discount
折价债券增值
accumulation due à l'escompte
Disagio-Zuwachs
plusvalía de descuento
割引増加額

accrue
逐渐 増长; 自然 増长
courir; s'accumuler
anfallen; auflaufen; rückstellen
devengar; acumular
見越計上する

accrued expense
应记费用
frais cumulés
antizipative Passiva
gasto acumulado
未払費用

accrued income
应计收入; 应收收益
effets à recevoir
antizipative Aktiva
ingreso acumulado
未払収益

Translations appear in the following order: Chinese, French, German, Spanish/Latin American Spanish, and Japanese

accrued interest
应计利息
intérêt couru
Stückzinsen; aufgelaufene Zinsen
interés acumulado
未払利子, 未収利子, 経過利子,
経過利息

accruing
增殖
accumulation (d'intérêts)
fällig werdend; entstehend
devengo; acumulación
利子を付ける

accumulated depreciation
累积折旧
dépréciation accumulée
ansteigende Abschreibung;
Wertberichtigung auf das
Sachanlagevermögen
depreciación acumulada
減価償却累積額

accumulated dividend
累积股息; 累积红利
dividendes accumulés
aufgelaufene Dividende;
kumulative Dividende
dividendo acumulado
累積配当, 未払配当

accumulated earnings tax
累计收益税
impôt sur les bénéfices non
distribués
Körperschaftssteuer auf nicht
ausgeschüttete Gewinne
impuesto sobre ingresos
acumulados
留保利益税, 不当留保税(米)

accumulating shares
累计股
actions cumulatives
aufgelaufene Stammaktien,
emittiert anstelle der
Nettodividende
acciones ordinarias emitidas por
una empresa, que son
equivalentes y sustituyen al
dividendo neto pagadero a
accionistas ordinarios
累積配当株

accumulation unit
累积单位
unité avec accumulation de
dividende
Aufzinsungsanteil
unidad de acumulación
積立累積ユニット

accuracy
精度
exactitude
Treffgenauigkeit
exactitud
正確さ

acid-test ratio
酸性测试比率
ratio de liquidité immédiate
Liquiditätsquote
ratio de liquidez inmediata
当座比率

acquiescence bias
默认偏差
distorsion d'assentiment
Verzerrung durch widersprüchliche
Zustimmung
sesgo de aquiescencia
黙従バイアス

acquirer
票据交换所
acquéreur
Erwerbsbank
adquiriente
アクワイアラー, 取得銀行

acquisition accounting
购置会计
comptabilité des acquisitions
Übernahmebilanzierung
contabilidad de adquisiciones
買収会計

acquisition rate
获得率
taux d'acquisition
die Erfolgsrate bei der Akquise,
Neugewinnung, von Kunden
tasa de adquisición
新規顧客取得率

action-centred leadership
行动中心式领导
leadership basé sur l'action
handlungsorientierter Führungsstil
liderazgo centrado en la acción
行動中心リーダーシップ

action learning
行动学习
apprentissage par l'action
praktisches Lernen
aprendizaje práctico
アクション学習

action research
行动研究
étude des plans d'action et du
changement
anwendungsbezogene Forschung
investigación acción
アクション調査研究

active asset
活动资产; 流动资产
capital productif
produktiver Vermögenswert
activo
生産資産

active fund management
活动资金管理

gestion de trust
aktive Vermögensverwaltung
gestión activa de fondos
アクティブ資産運用,
積極的資産運用

active listening
积极倾听; 有效倾听
écoute active
aktives Hinhören; od. Zuhören
escucha activa
アクティブ・リスニング,
意欲的傾聴

active portfolio strategy
主动投资组合策略
gestion de portefeuille proactive
aktive Portefeuille-Strategie
estrategia activa de cartera de
valores
アクティブ・ポートフォリオ戦略,
積極的ポートフォリオ運用

activist fiscal policy
积极的财政政策
politique fiscale activiste
aktivitstische Fiskalpolitik
política fiscal activista
積極(的)財政政策

activity-based budgeting
以活动为基础的预算
prévisions budgétaires par activité
Erstellung; eines
Prozesskostenbudgets
elaboración de presupuestos
basada en la actividad
活動基準予算

activity-based costing
产量成本法
calcul des coûts selon les activités
aktivitätsorientierte
Kostenrechnung;
Prozesskostenrechnung;
Vorgangskalkulation
cálculo de costes basado en la
actividad
cálculo de costos basado en la
actividad
活動基準原価計算

activity-based management
作业管理
gestion basée sur l'analyse des
activités
beschäftigungsorientierte
Geschäftsführung
gestión de costes basada en las
actividades
gestión de costos basada en las
actividades
活動基準経営管理

activity indicator
活动指标

indice d'activité
Aktivitätsindikator;
betriebswirtschaftliche Kennziffer
indicador de actividad
経済活動指標, 活動指標

activity sampling
工作的抽样检验
observations instantanées
(d'activités)
Multimomentverfahren
muestreo de una actividad
アクティビティー・サンプリング

actuals
实际货物; 现货
chiffres réels
effektive Stücke; sofort verfügbare
Ware; Ist-Zahlen
disponibilidades; mercancías físicas
現実現物

actual to date
盘现
chiffres réels à ce jour
Istwert bis dato
a fecha fija
現在までの実価

actual turnover
实际周转率
rotation réelle
Effektivumsatz
política fiscal activista; cifras de
ventas reales
現実の取引, 実務取引

actuarial age
精算年龄
espérance de vie
Versicherungsalter
edad actuarial
保険数理年齢

actuarial analysis
精算分析
analyse actuarielle
aktuarielle Analyse;
versicherungsmathematische
Auswertung
análisis actuarial
保険数理分析

actuarial science
保险统计学, 保险统计计算科学
science actuarielle
Versicherungstechnik;
Versicherungskunde
ciencia actuarial
保険数理学

actuary
保险精算师, 保险(业务)计算员
actuaire
Aktuar(in);
Versicherungsmathematiker(in)
actuario(-a)
保険計理士

ad
标题广告
pub sur écran
Werbebanner
anuncio
アド, (eコマースの)広告

adaptive control
自适应控制
commande adaptative
Folgeregelung
control adaptativo
適応制御

adaptive measure
适合度度量
mesure d'adaptation
adaptives Maß
medida adaptativa
適応方法

added value
增值; 附加价值
valeur ajoutée
Mehrwert
valor añadido
付加価値

address book
地址本
carnet d'adresse
Adressbuch
agenda de direcciones
アドレス帳

address verification
地址核对; 地址验证
vérification d'adresse
Adressprüfung
verificación de la dirección
アドレス・ベリフィケーション,
アドレス検証

ad hoc research
一次性研究
étude au cas par cas
situative Forschung;
Gelegenheitsforschung
investigación ad hoc
単一特別調査

adjusted book value
调整后帐面值
valeur comptable ajustée
berichtigter Buchwert
valor contable ajustado
調整(修正)後帳簿価額

adjusted futures price
调整后期货价格
prix ajusté des transactions à terme
Tageswert eines Terminkontrakts;
bereinigter Terminkurs
precio de futuros ajustado
調整済先物価格, 調整後先物相場

adjusted gross income
调整后总收入
revenu brut ajusté

berichtigtes Bruttoeinkommen
beneficio bruto ajustado
调整粗所得, 調整総所得

adjusted present value
调整后现值
valeur actuelle ajustée
bereinigter Barwert;
Gegenwartswert od. Zeitwert
valor presente ajustado
調整済現在価値または市場価格,
修正現在価値

adminisphere
行政官僚
sphère-admin
Administrativ-Sphäre
esfera administrativa
管理職の空域

administration
行政管理; 管理; 经营; 遗产管理
administration
Verwaltung;
Unternehmensführung
administración
管理

administrative expenses
管理费用
frais d'administration et gestion
Verwaltungskosten
gastos de administración
経営費

administrivia
琐碎的网络维护工作
tâches souvent banales et
ennuyeuses associées au maintien
d'un site Web
triviale Administrationsaufgaben
im Zusammenhang mit
Internet-Ressourcen
actualización cansina de
información
退屈な(インターネット関連の)
管理仕事

admissibility
最优性
admissibilité
Zulässigkeit
aceptabilidad
許容性

ADR
美国存券收据; 美国保管收据;
美国预托收据
certificat américain de dépôt
American Deposit Receipt
recibo de depósito de valores
extranjeros
ADR(米国預託証券)

Adshel
广告栏候车站
abri bus spécifiquement conçu
pour l'affichage de posters

Translations appear in the following order: Chinese, French, German, Spanish/Latin American Spanish, and Japanese

publicitaires
Bushaltestellenwerbung
tipo de marquesina publicitaria
広告表示用のバスシェルター

ADSL
非对称数字用户环线
ADSL
ADSL
ADSL
非対称デジタル加入者回線

ad valorem
从价，按价
(taxe) selon la valeur
im Wert von; nach Wert
al valor
従価

Advance Corporation Tax
预付公司税
impôt préalable sur les sociétés
Körperschaftssteuer-Vorauszahlung
auf ausgeschüttete Gewinne
impuesto que ha de pagar una
sociedad consistente en un
porcentaje de un dividendo u otro
dispositivo de distribución de
ganancias pagaderas a los
accionistas
前渡法人税

**advanced manufacturing
technology**
高新生产技术
technologie de fabrication de
pointe
moderne Fertigungstechnologie
tecnología avanzada de
fabricación
高度製造技術

advance payment
预付; 预付费
paiement préalable
Vorauszahlung; Vorschusszahlung;
Anzahlung
pago por adelantado
前金

advance payment guarantee
预付保证
garantie de paiement anticipé
Anzahlungsgarantie
garantía de pago a cuenta
前渡金支払い保証

adventure training
冒险培训; 室外培训
formation avec activités (de plein
air) multiples
Abenteuertraining
formación en actividades al aire
libre
冒険トレーニング

adverse balance
逆差，入超

balance déficitaire
passive Zahlungsbilanz
saldo negativo
貿易の逆調

adverse opinion
查账报告中的反面意见
avis contraire d'expert
ablehnendes Gutachten
dictamen desfavorable
否定的監査意見

advertisement
广告
publicité; annonce
Annonce; Inserat; Werbung;
Reklame
anuncio
广告

advertising
广告; 广告业广告学
publicité
Werbung; Reklame
publicidad
广告

advertising agency
广告公司; 广告代理行; 广告社
agence de publicité
Werbeagentur
agencia de publicidad
广告代理店

advertising campaign
广告运动; 广告战; 广告宣传活动
campagne publicitaire
Werbekampagne; Werbefeldzug
campaña publicitaria
广告キャンペーン

advertising department
广告部
service de la publicité
Werbeabteilung
departamento de publicidad
广告部

advertising expenditure
广告费
frais de publicité
Werbekosten; Werbeaufwand
gastos publicitarios
广告費

advertising manager
广告经理
directeur de la publicité
Werbeleiter(in)
gerente(-a) de publicidad
广告マネージャー

advertising media
广告媒体
supports publicitaires
Werbemittel
medios publicitarios
广告媒体、広告メディア

advertising research
广告研究
études publicitaires
Marktforschung
investigación en publicidad
広告前後の世論調査

advertorial
广告宣传文章; 社论式广告;
广告编辑
publireportage
Werbung in Form von
Zeitschriften-oder Zeitungsartikeln
artículo publicitario;
publirreportaje
記事体広告

advice of fate
支票能否兑现通知书
notification de décision sur chèque
Bezahltmeldung
notificación de los resultados de
gestión
引き受け通知

advid
宣传录象带; 广告录像
vidéo pub
Werbevideo
vídeo publicitario
広告用ビデオ

ad view
广告浏览数量
nombre de téléchargements de
pub
Seitenaufrauf
impresión; hit
アド・ビュー, アド閲覧回数

affiliate
关系企业; 联营公司; 附属公司;
建立密切联系; 加入成为成员
affilié
Schwestergesellschaft
afiliar
関連会社

affiliate directory
加盟名录
répertoire associé
zugehöriges Verzeichnis
directorio de programas de
afiliación
加盟ディレクトリー

affiliate marketing
联合营销
marketing d'affiliation
Anwendung von assoziierten
Programmen zu
Vermarktungszwecken
marketing de empresas afiliadas
アフィリエイト・
マーケティング、
アフィリエイト・
プログラムの利用

Translations appear in the following order: Chinese, French, German, Spanish/Latin American Spanish, and Japanese

affiliate partner
网上营销伙伴
partenaire apparenté
angeschlossener Partner
compañía afiliada
ネット上の商業提携サイト

affiliate programme
联合营销方案
programme affilié
assoziiertes Programm
programa de afiliación
アフィリエイト・プログラム

affinity card
关系信用卡
carte d'affinité
Kreditkarte: ausgegeben an die
Mitglieder einer bestimmten
Gruppe. Die jeweilige Organisation
erhält bei Benutzung der Karte
einen kleinen Prozentsatz des
Kartenumsatzes als Spende.
tarjeta de crédito distribuida entre
miembros de un grupo específico.
La organización en cuestión
obtiene una donación al emitirse la
tarjeta o utilizarse por primera vez,
así como un pequeño porcentaje
de la facturación posterior
社会貢献型カード

affluent society
手裕社会
société affluente
Wohlstandsgesellschaft
sociedad opulenta
豊かな社会

affluenza
富贵病
stress de la prospérité
Wohlstandskrankheit
agotamiento producido por la
ambición de riqueza
金持ちの鬱病

after-acquired collateral
抵押后担保条款; 取后条款.
nantissement après emprunt
Nacherwerbssicherheit
garantía pignoraticia de
adquisiciones posteriores
契約後取得抵当または担保

after-sales service
售后服务
service après-vente
Kundendienst
servicio posventa
アフター・サービス

after-tax
税后
après impôts
nach Steuern
después de impuestos
税引き後

AG
代理; 代理人
AG
Bilanzbuchhalter(in);
Generalbevollmächtigte/r
jefe(-a) de contabilidad
株式会社

against actuals
兑现货
contre chiffres réels
gegen effektive Ware; gegen
Kassainstrumente
contado(-a) contra futuros
現物受渡し

age analysis of debtors
债务人债龄分析
analyse des débiteurs selon l'âge
des dettes
Debitorenanalyse nach dem Alter;
Schuldneranalyse nach
Altersstruktur
análisis de deudores por
antigüedad
債務額年数分析

aged debt
过期债务
dette échue
fällige Forderung
deuda vencida
期限経過売掛金

aged debtor
过期债务人
débiteur échu
fällige Forderung
deudor(a); vencido(-a)
期限経過借方

age discrimination
年龄歧视
âgisme
Altersdiskriminierung
discriminación por edad
年齢(による)差別

agency
代理; 代理处; 代理商; 代理机构
agence
Niederlassung; Stelle; Behörde;
Organ
agencia
代理権

agency commission
广告商佣金
commission d'agence
Agenturkommission
comisión de la agencia
広告代理店のコミッション

agency mark-up
广告商佣金; 广告商手续费
majoration de frais d'agence
Agenturaufschlag

tarifa de gestión de la agencia
広告代理店の管理手数料

agency theory
委托代理理论
théorie des agences
Theorie der Vertretung
teoría de agencia
代理人理論

agenda
议事日程; 会议议程
ordre du jour
Tagesordnung; Punkte zur
Erörterung
orden del día; programa
協議事項

agent
代理商; 代理人
agent
Vertreter(in); Beauftragte/r
agente
代理人, 代理店

agent bank
代理银行
banque représentante
Konsortialbank;
Korrespondenzbank;
Zweigniederlassung
banco agente
エージェント・バンク

age pension
年龄养老金
retraite vieillesse
Rente
pensión de jubilación
老齢年金

aggregate demand
总需求
demande globale
Gesamtnachfrage
demanda agregada
総需要

aggregate income
总收入
revenu global
Gesamteinkommen;
Volkseinkommen
ingresos totales
総所得

aggregate output
总产值; 总产出
production globale
Gesamtergebnis; Sozialprodukt
rendimiento total
総産出額

aggregate planning
总计划
planification globale
mittelfristige Gesamtplanung
planificación global
総生産計画

Translations appear in the following order: Chinese, French, German, Spanish/Latin American Spanish, and Japanese

aggregate supply
总供给; 供给总量
offre globale
Gesamtangebot
oferta agregada
総供給

aggregator
网络公司联盟中介
organisation d'agrégation
Internet-Händler
intermediario en la red
アグリゲータ

aggressive
大胆的; 进攻性的; 进取性的;
积极进取的
agressif
angriffslustig; aggressiv
agresivo(-a)
攻撃的

aggressive growth fund
高盼增长基金
fonds à croissance agressive
risikoreicher Wachstumsfonds;
hochspekulativer
fondo de crecimiento agresivo
積極運用型(ミューチュアル)
ファンド

agile manufacturing
敏捷制造
fabrication habile
agile Herstellung
fabricación ágil
柔軟生産システム

agility
企业的灵活性
agilité
Agilität; Wendigkeit;
Beweglichkeit
agilidad
柔軟性

AGM
年度(股东)大会
AG
Jahreshauptversammlung
junta general anual
年次総会

agora
网上市场
marché sur Internet
eMarket
mercado agora en la red
ネット上の広場・市場

agreement of sale
销售协议
contrat de vente
Kaufvertrag
acuerdo de venta
売買契約

AHI
一个非洲商会 组织
chambre de Commerce des
entreprises afrikaans
Afrikaans Handelskammer
cámara de comercio bóer
アフリカーンス商工会議所

AIM
伦敦另 项 投 资 市 场
(即：二板市场)
AIM
Wachstumsmarkt an der Londoner
Börse, für Unternehmen, die zu
jung oder zu klein sind, um die
Bedingungen anderer Märkte zu
erfüllen
mercado de la Bolsa londinense
para pequeñas o nuevas empresas
ＡＩＭ(代替投資市場)

air bill
空运货单
bordereau descriptif
Luftfrachtbrief
carta de porte aéreo
航空運送状

airtime
广告时间
temps d'antenne
Sendezeit
tiempo de emisión
エアタイム

air waybill
空运货单
bordereau descriptif
Luftfrachtpapier; Luftfrachtbrief
talón de porte aéreo
航空運送受託証

alignment
公司文化建设
alignement
Unternehmenskulturentwicklung
reorganización estratégica
企業の全部門を
戦略的に整列すること

all equity rate
通用合理费率(保险)
taux tout capital
Risikoprämie
tasa de riesgos extra mercado
(危険の高い案件に対する)
オール・エクイティ・レート

All Industrials Index
所有工业指数
indice toutes industries:
sous-indice de l'indice ordinaire
australien des compagnies autres
que minières et de ressources
Industrieindex
índice bursátil australiano de
empresas industriales

オール・インダストリアル
株価指数

All Mining Index
所有矿产工业指数
indice minier: sous-indice de
l'indice ordinaire australien
comprenant toutes les compagnies
minières
Bergbauindex
índice bursátil australiano de
empresas mineras
オール・マイニング株価指数

**All Ordinaries Accumulation
Index**
(澳大利亚) 所有普通股指数
accumulation sur actions de
l'indice ordinaire
Gesamtaktienindex
índice australiano de acumulación
de las acciones ordinarias
オール・オーディナリー
累計株価指数

All Ordinaries Index
所有普通指数
Indice des actions ordinaires
Gesamtindex der Stammaktien
índice de acciones ordinarias
(豪)全普通株指数

all-or-none underwriting
必须全部投保
garantie d'émission tout ou rien
Alles-oder-Nichts-Versicherung
reaseguro todo o nada
全株引き受け

All Resources Index
所有资源指数
indice toutes ressources:
sous-indice de l'indice ordinaire
australien comprenant les
compagnies de ressources
minérales
Ressourcenindex
índice bursátil australiano de
empresas de explotación de
recursos
オール・リソース株価指数

**alphabet theories of
management**
字顺管理理论
théories alphabétiques de gestion
Alphabet-Theorien der
Unternehmensleitung
teorías de administración E, J, O,
W, X, Y y Z
経営アルファベット理論

alpha geek
计算机通
crack de l'informatique
Oberstreber
experto(-a) en informática
部門内の情報技術おたく

---

*Translations appear in the following order: Chinese, French, German, Spanish/Latin American
Spanish, and Japanese*

alpha rating
阿尔法比率
coefficient alpha
Risikofaktor
tasa de ganancia relativa a un
alfa cero
実績リターンと予想リ
ターンとの
違いを示すアルファ値

alpha test
阿尔法 测试
test alpha
Alphatest
prueba alfa
アルファテスト

alpha value
阿尔法 值
valeur alpha
Alpha-Wert
valor alfa
アルファ値

alternate director
代理董事
directeur remplaçant
stellvertretender Direktor
director(a) accidental
代替役員

alternative investment
选择投资
investissement alternatif
alternative Investition
inversión alternativa
(非主流の株や債券への)
代替的投資

**alternative mortgage
instrument**
可选择性抵押工具
instrument d'hypothèque
alternatif
alternatives
Hypothekeninstrument
instrumento hipotecario
alternativo
代替モーゲージ証券

amalgamation
兼并; 合并
fusionnement
Unternehmenszusammenschluss
fusión
融合

Amazon
亚马逊效应
perdre une grande part des ventes
d'un détaillant traditionnel au
profit d'un concurrent sur-ligne dû
à un manquement à développer
une stratégie de e-commerce
efficace
Amazon-Strategie
perder cuota de mercado ante una
empresa en Internet por no tener

una estrategia definida de
comercio electrónico
アマゾン

ambit claim
仲裁索赔
revendication ambit
beim Schiedsgericht eingereichte
Arbeitnehmerforderung
reivindicación intencionalmente
exagerada
超過請求

American option
美国式期权
option américaine
amerikanische Option
opción americana
アメリカン・オプション

AMEX
美国证券交易所
Bourse newyorkaise listant des
compagnies plus petites et plus
jeunes que la Bourse newyorkaise
principale
AMEX
Bolsa de valores estadounidense
アメリカ証券取引所

amortisation¹
摊销
amortissement
Amortisierung
amortización
割賦償還, 割賦償却, 割賦償還額

amortisation²
摊还
amortissement
Tilgung; Amortisierung;
Rückzahlung
amortización
債務償還

amortise
分期清偿
amortir
amortisieren
amortizar
部分償還

amortised value
分期偿还值
valeur amortie
Restwert; Nettobuchwert;
getilgter Wert
valor amortizado
償却引価額, 償却調整後額

analysis of variance
方差分析
analyse de variance
Varianzanalyse
análisis de varianza
分散分析法

analysis of variance table
方差分析表
tableau d'analyse de variance
Varianzanalysentafel
tabla de análisis de varianza
分散分析表

analytical review
分析性评估
bilan analytique
analytische Revision od.
Bestandsaufnahme
revisión analítica
会計分析法

angel investor
天使投资人
ange investisseur
stille Teilhaber
inversor(a) dispuesto a respaldar
un nuevo proyecto de comercio
electrónico
エンジェル投資家

angry fruit salad
愤怒的水果沙拉，喻指过分装饰
的计算机界面
interface visuelle peu attrayante et
criarde sur un ordinateur
userunfreundliche Eingabemaske
interfaz amarga
破壊的な色合いの
インタフェース

angular histogram
圆形直方图
histogramme angulaire
Winkelhistogramm
histograma angular
円形グラフ

announcement
公告
déclaration
Aktionärsbrief
anuncio
公告

annoyware
骚扰件
programme de logiciel qui
interrompt le fonctionnement
normal régulièrement pour
rappeler aux utilisateurs qu'ils
utilisent une copie non enregistrée
Shareware, die in nervender Art
und Weise an die Registrierung
erinnert
programa de fastidio
頻繁に支払を催促する
シェアウェア

annual hours
年度工作小时
heures de travail sur l'année
Jahresstunden
horas por año
年間平均就業時間, 変形勤務時間

---

*Translations appear in the following order: Chinese, French, German, Spanish/Latin American
Spanish, and Japanese*

annual percentage yield
年度受益百分比
rendement annuel en pourcentage
jährliche Gesamtrendite
rendimiento porcentual anual
年利回り

annual report
年度报告
rapport annuel
Jahresabschluss; Jahresbericht
informe anual; memoria anual
reporte anual
年次報告書

annuity
年金; 年金保险; 年金债券
annuité
Annuität; Rente; Zeitrente
anualidad; renta anual
年金, 年金収受権

annuity in arrears
拖欠年金
annuité en arriéré
Nachzahlungsannuität
anualidad pagada al final del
período de pago
未払年金, 後払い年金,
据え置き年金

anorexic organisation
萎缩型组织
organisation anorexique
magersüchtige Organisation
organización esquelética
衰弱化企業,
(極端なダウンサイジングの結
果の)
アノレクシア(拒食症)的 組織

ANSI X.12 standard
美国国家标准协会x.12标准
ANSI X.12: protocole de l'Institut
des Normes américaines pour
l'échange électronique de
transactions commerciales
ANSI X.12 Standard
estándar X.12 del ANSI
全米規格協会支援プロトコル

anticipation note
提前付款债券
bon par anticipation
Vorauszahlungsschein
bono previo a una emisión
長期債借り換え予定証券

anticipatory hedging
预期套期交易
opération d'arbitrage par
anticipation
antizipatorisches
Sicherungsgeschäft
cobertura anticipada
先行ヘッジング

anticipointment
大失所望

expectation déçue
Enttäuschung hochgeschraubter
Erwartungen
expectativas decepcionadas
期待外れ

anti-dumping
反倾销
antidumping
Antidumping-; gegen das
Dumping gerichtet
antidumping
反ダンピング、ダン
ピング防止措置

anti-site
敌视网站
site web dédié aux attaques contre
des compagnies ou organisations
Hass-Seite
sitio web en el que se ataca a otro
sitio
アンチ-サイト

antitrust
反托拉斯; 反垄断
antitrust
Antitrust-; Kartell-; kartell-
antimonopolio
反トラスト

APEC
亚太地区经济合作
APEC: coopération économique
pacifico-asiatique
Wirtschaftskooperations-
abkommen in Pazifisch-Asien
foro para la cooperación entre los
países asiáticos del Pacífico y
Australia
アジア太平洋経済協力会議

applet
小型应用程序; Applet程序
applet: mini programme
habituellement écrit en langage
Java que l'on peut télécharger et
intégrer dans des pages Web
Applet
subprograma
アプレット

application form
工作申请表; 申请表
formulaire de demande d'emploi
Bewerbungsformular
formulario
就職申込書

application program interface
应用程序
interface de programme
d'application
Schnittstelle für das
Anwendungsprogramm
interfaz de aplicación del
programa

アプリケーション・プログラム
・インターフェース

application server
应用服务器
serveur d'application
Anwendungsserver
servidor de aplicaciones
アプリケーション・サーバー

applied economics
应用经济学
économie appliquée
angewandte Wirtschaftstheorie
economía aplicada
応用経済学

appointment[1]
约会
rendez-vous
Verabredung; Termin;
Anberaumung
cita
アポ

appointment[2]
职位
nomination
Posten; Stelle; Amt
puesto
任命

apportion
分摊, 分配
ventiler ou répartir
umlegen; zurechnen; gleichmäßig
zuteilen; kontingentieren
prorrateo
配賦

appreciation[1]
增值
plus-value monétaire
Wertzuwachs; Wertsteigerung
apreciación
騰貴

appreciation[2]
升值
plus-value monétaire
Aufwertung
apreciación
相場上昇

appropriation
拨款; 挪用; 占用; 偿债
dotation de fonds
buchmäßige Gewinnverteilung;
Konkretisierung;
Zweckbestimmung
consignación; asignación
充当金

appropriation account
分拨帐，拨款帐户
compte d'affectation (aux réserves
ou fonds)
Bereitstellungskonto;
Rückstellungskonto

cuenta de aplicación; cuenta de
dotación
処分勘定

Approved Deposit Fund
核实的存款基金
caisse de dépôt agréé
zertifizierter Sparfonds
fondo autorizado de depósitos
認可デポジット基金

APR
年度百分利率
taux annuel
Effektivzins;
TAE (Tasa anual equivalente)
APR年率

aptitude test
能力测试
test d'aptitude
Eignungsprüfung; Eignungstest
prueba de aptitud
能力適性試験

arb
套利者; 投机分子
arbitragiste
Arbitrageur
arbitrajista
裁定取引者, 鞘取り業者

arbitrage
套利; 套汇; 差价
arbitrage
Arbitrage
arbitraje
裁定取引, 鞘取り売買

arbitrage pricing theory
套利定价理论; 差价定价理论
théorie de fixation des prix
Arbitragepreis-Theorie
teoría de los precios en
operaciones de arbitraje
裁定価格決定理論

arbitrageur
套利者; 套汇者
arbitragiste
Arbitrageur
árbitro; arbitrajista
鞘取り売買人

arbitration
仲裁; 公断
arbitrage
Schiedsverfahren; Schlichtung
arbitraje
仲裁, 裁定

arbitrator
套利者; 套汇者
médiateur/médiatrice
Schiedsrichter(in)
árbitro(-a)
仲裁人

area sampling
面积抽样法, 分布区取样,
地区取样
échantillonnage par secteur
Flächenstichprobenverfahren
muestreo por áreas
地域抜取調査

area under a curve
曲线下方区域
série sous courbe
Fläche unter einer Kurve
área bajo una curva
曲線下の面積

arithmetic mean
算术法
moyenne arithmétique
arithmetisches Mittel
media aritmética
単純平均

armchair economics
扶手椅经济; 尤指根据不完全信息
作出的经济预测或经济理论
économie de chambre
Lehnstuhlökonomie
economía de salón
素人の経済学

arm's-length price
彼此独立的价格
prix fixé indépendamment
Marktpreis
precio de mercado
商業ベース価格, 独立企業間価格

ARPAnet
ARPA网; (美国国防部的)
高级研究计划局网
réseau militaire expérimental
qui reliaient les scientifiques
engagés dans la recherche
militaire
ARPAnet
Red ARPANET (Agencia de
proyectos de investigación
avanzados)
アーパネット(米国防総省高等
研究計画局が開発したインター
ネットの原形)

arrow shooter
有远见之明的人
tireur de flèche
Visionär im Unternehmen
visionario(a)
アイデアマン, ビジョナリー,
発想人, クリエーター

art director
艺术设计总监
directeur artistique
Chefdesigner
director(a) de arte
アート・ディレクター

articles of association
公司(组织)章程
statuts (d'une société)
Gesellschaftsvertrag; Satzung
einer Kapitalgesellschaft
estatutos; acta de fundación;
estatutos sociales
株式会社の定款

articles of incorporation
公司条例; 公司章程
acte de constitution (d'une société)
Gründungsurkunde; Satzung
escritura de constitución
私会社の定款

artificial intelligence
人工智能
intelligence artificielle
künstliche Intelligenz
inteligencia artificial
人口知能, AI

ASEAN Free Trade Area
东南亚国家联盟自由贸易区
zone de libre échange d'ASEAN
(association des nations de l'Asie
du Sud-Est)
asiatische Freihandelszone
área asiática de libre comercio
アジア諸国自由貿易地域

A share[1]
'A' 股; 甲级普通股
action A
Aktie der Kategorie A
acción de clase A
無議決権株

A share[2]
A 股
action de type A
A Share
participación
無議決権株

Asian Currency Unit
亚洲货币单位
unité de devise asiatique
asiatische Währungseinheit
unidad contable de divisas en Asia
アジア通貨単位

ask[1]
问价
demande
Forderungspreis
precio de venta de un instrumento
マーケット・メーカーが提示する
証券, 通貨, その他の金融商品の
売り値

ask[2]
出价
cours de l'offre
Angebotspreis
precio de oferta
売り呼値

*Translations appear in the following order: Chinese, French, German, Spanish/Latin American
Spanish, and Japanese*

asking price
开价; 要价; 问价; 索价
prix de départ
geforderter Preis; ursprüngliche
Preisforderung; Briefkurs
precio de oferta
売り指値

ASP
动态服务器主页
fournisseur de services
d'application
ASP
proveedor de servicios de
aplicaciones
アプリケーション・サービス・
プロバイダー

assembly
装配
montage
Montage; Zusammenbau
montaje
組み立て

assembly line
装配线; 装配流水线
chaîne de montage
Fließband; Montagestraße
cadena de montaje
組み立てライン

assembly plant
装配车间
usine de montage
Montagewerk; Montageanlage
planta de montaje
組立工場

assessed loss
估计损失
perte évaluée pour impôts directs
Verlustvortrag
arrastre de pérdidas evaluadas
査定損失

assessed value
估价值
valeur évaluée
veranlagter Wert; geschätzter
Wert; Einheitswert
valor catastral
(特に課税のための不動産の)
査定価額, 評価額

assessment centre
评估中心
centre d'évaluation
Personalauswahlverfahren; A.C.
centro de evaluación
(職能考課のための)能
力査定センター

assessment of competence
能力评估
évaluation de compétence
Kompetenzbewertung
evaluación de la competencia
コンピタンス評価

asset
财产; 资产; 有作用的人或物; 优势
actif
Vermögenswert; Aktivposten
activo; bien
資産

asset allocation
财产分配; 资产分配
allocation de l'actif
Portefeuille-Strukturierung
asignación de activos
資産配分

asset-backed security
资产担保证券
nantissement garanti par actif
durch Vermögenswerte gesicherte
Sicherheit
valor respaldado por activo
アセット・バック証券

asset-based lending
以资产为基础的借款
prêt basé sur actif
besichertes Darlehen
préstamos respaldados por activos
資産担保貸付

asset conversion loan
资产转换放款
emprunt de conversion d'actif
Wandlungsdarlehen
préstamo para la conversión de
activos
資産転換ローン

asset coverage
资产保障率
couverture de l'actif
akzessorische Sicherheit;
Vermögensdeckung
cobertura de activos
資産担保率, 資産倍率

asset demand
资产需求
demande d'actif (liquide)
Geldnachfrage; Kapitalnachfrage
demanda de activo
貨幣の資産需要, 貨幣の投機的
需要

asset financing
资产融资
financement par l'actif
Anlagenfinanzierung
financiamiento respaldado por
activo
資産担保貸付,
資産を担保にした資金調達

asset for asset swap
资产互换
échange d'une dette de débiteur
pour celle d'un autre
Forderungstausch

asset management
资产管理; 财产管理
gestion de l'actif
Vermögensverwaltung;
Aktiv-Management
administración de activos
資産管理

asset play
资产炒作
opération d'ordre spéculatif
Investition in ein Unternehmen,
das als unterbewertet angesehen
wird
activo infravalorado
アセット・プレー

asset pricing model
资产定价模型
modèle de prix d'actif
Modell zur Bestimmung des ROI
einer Investition
modelo de fijación de precios de
los activos
資産価格評価モデル

asset protection trust
资产保护信托
fonds de protection d'actif
Vermögensschutztrust
fideicomiso de protección de los
activos
資産保護信託

asset restructuring
资产重组
restructuration de l'actif
Vermögensumschichtung
reestructuración de activos
資産再編成

asset side
资产方
colonne des actifs
Aktivseite
columna del activo
資産側

assets requirements
资产要求
exigences en actif
Finanzbedarf
requisitos de los activos
必要資産

asset-stripper
资产拆卖者; 资产剥割者
récupérateur d'entreprises (en
faillite)
Firmenausschlachter(in)
liquidador(a) de activos
アセット・ストリッパー

asset-stripping
资产剥夺
récupération d'entreprise

Ausschlachten von Firmen
liquidación de activos
アセット・ストリッピング

asset substitution
资产替代
substitution d'actif
Aufkauf von Risikoanteilen
sustitución de activos
(貸し手が懸念する)危険度の-
高い資産購入,アセット・
サブスティテューション

asset swap
资产互换
échange d'actif
Wandlung einer festverzinslichen
Anleihe, die in eine Variable
umgewandelt wird
intercambio de activos
アセット・スワップ

asset turnover
资产周转率
rotation des capitaux
Kapitalumschlag
movimiento or rotación de activos
資産に対する売上

asset valuation
资产估值
provision pour évaluation d'actif
Anlagenbewertung
evaluación de activos
資本資産価値

asset value per share
每股资产价值
valeur de l'actif par action
Anlagenwert pro Aktie
valor activo por acción
一株当りの資産価値

assign
分配; 把...转让给
assigner
übertragen; abtreten; bestellen
traspasar; ceder
財産権の委託譲渡

assignable cause of variation
变异的非机遇原因
cause de variation attribuable
zurechenbare
Abweichungsursache
causa imputable de la variación
ばらつきの見逃せない原因

assigned risk
转让风险
risque attribué
Zwangszuteilung von Risiken
riesgo asignado
割当危険分担(保険)

associate
加入; 与...有联系; 合伙人
associé(e)
Mitarbeiter(in); Kollege; Kollegin;

Gesellschafter(in); Partner(in)
socio(a)
関連会社

Association of British Insurers
英国保险家协会
Association des assureurs
britanniques
Verband britscher
Versicherungsgesellschaften
Asociación de Aseguradores
Británicos
英国保険会社協会

assumable mortgage
可承继抵押
hypothèque assumable
übernehmbare Hypothek;
übernahmefähige Hypothek
hipoteca asumible
アシューマブル・モーゲージ,
引継ぎモーゲージ

assumed bond
承担债券; 承继债券
obligation assumée
übernommene
Schuldverschreibung
bono asumido
保証社債, 引継ぎ社債

assumption
假设
présomption
Voraussetzung
supuesto
前提

assured shorthold tenancy
确定性短期租赁
contrat de location à court terme
garanti
preisüberwachtes kurzfristiges
Mietverhältnis
arrendamiento corto protegido
短期テナント保証

assured tenancy
确定性租赁
contrat de location garanti
preisüberwachtes Mietverhältnis;
preisüberwachter Mietbesitz
contrato de alquiler indefinido
テナント保証

ASX 100
澳大利亚证券交易100指数
ASX 100: indice des 100
compagnies australiennes les plus
importantes
ASX 100 Aktienindex
índice 100 de la Bolsa australiana
ASX100

asymmetrical distribution
非对称分布
distribution asymétrique
asymmetrische Verteilung

distribución asimétrica
非对称分布

asymmetric taxation
不对称征税
imposition asymétrique
asymmetrische Besteuerung
fiscalidad asimétrica; impuestos
asimétricos
非対照的課税,
アシンメトリック課税

asynchronous transmission
异步传输
transmission asynchrone
asynchrone Übertragung
transmisión asíncrona
非同期伝達

at best
最佳价格，最获利的价格
transaction de titres au meilleur
prix
bestens; billigst
al mejor precio
アット・ベスト注文

at call
按通知付款，即期付款
sur demande
sofort verfügbar
con obligación
短期融資

at limit
限定价格
avec limites
limitiert
dentro de determinados límites
指値

ATM
自动出纳机
DAB (distributeur automatique de
billets)
Geldautomat; Bankautomat
cajero automático
自動現金引き出し

atom
传统式信息传播
atome
nichtdigitale Informationspolitik
entrega a domicilio
(電子的でない)従来のメディア

atomise
化整为零; 分解
atomiser
Aufteilung in Geschäftsbereiche
descentralización
大きな組織を
小さい営業単位に分ける

attachment[1]
附件
annexe
Anhang

Translations appear in the following order: Chinese, French, German, Spanish/Latin American Spanish, and Japanese

archivo adjunto
添付ファイル

attachment²
附件
saisie
Pfändung; dinglicher Arrest
embargo
差押え

attendance
出勤
(bonne) présence
Anwesenheit
asistencia
勤務記録

attendance bonus
出勤奖励
prime de bonne présence
Anwesenheitsprämie
prima por asistencia
定時出勤を促進する
インセンティブ

attention management
注意力管理
gestion de la concentration
Aufmerksamkeits-Management
gestión de la atención
注目管理法

at-the-money
平値
à parité
am Geld; Optionspreis
al precio de contado
アット・ザ・マネー

attitude
态度
attitude
Einstellung; Haltung
actitud
態度, 意見, 姿勢, 受け止め方

attitude research
态度研究
recherche sur les attitudes
Erfragung der öffentlichen
Meinung
estudio de actitudes
意識調査

attitude survey
态度调查
étude de comportement
Imageanalyse
sondeo de actitudes
世論調査

attribute sampling
品质抽样检验
échantillonnage par attributs
Attributenverfahren
muestreo de atributos
帰属サンプリング

**attribution theory of
leadership**
归因领导理论

théorie de l'attribution par les
dirigeants
verhaltenstheoretischer
Managementansatz
teoría atributiva del liderazgo
リーダーシップの帰属理論

auction
拍卖
vente aux enchères
Versteigerung; Auktion
subasta
remate
競売

**auction market preferred
stock**
拍卖市场优先股
titre privilégié sur marché indexé
auktionsmarktbevorzugte Aktien
valores que siguen el mercado
monetario y reportan dividendos
オークション式優先株式

audience
观众
assistance
Audienz; Anhörung; Publikum;
Hörerschaft; Leserschaft
audiencia
視聴者

audience research
观众(听众)研究
études d'opinion
Zielgruppenforschung
estudio de audiencia
広告対象者調査

audit
审计
audit; vérification des comptes
Buchprüfung; Wirtschaftsprüfung;
Abschlussprüfung
auditoría
監査

audit committee
查账委员会
comité de commissaires aux
comptes
Finanzrevisionskomitee
comité de auditoría
監査委員会

Auditing Practices Board
审计工作委员会
commission des bonnes pratiques
pour audits
Gremium, 1991 gebildet. Seine
Aufgabe ist die Entwicklung und
Herausgabe von Standesnormen
für Rechnungsprüfer im
Vereinigten Königreich und der
Republik Irland.
consejo regulador de las prácticas
de auditoría
監査実行委員会

Auditor-General
审计总监
vérificateur comptable officiel
Staatsrechnungsprüfer
auditor(a) del tribunal de cuentas
de un estado australiano
会計監査長官

auditor's report
审计报告
rapport du vérificateur comptable
Prüfungsbericht des
Abschlussprüfers
informe del auditor
reporte del auditor
監査報告書

audit trail
查账索引
trace d'audit
Prüfungspfad
rastro de auditoría
監査証跡

aural signature
品牌听觉标志
signature musicale
Kennmelodie
sintonía de una marca
ブランドのテーマ曲

Aussie Mac
澳洲抵押证书
Aussie Mac: titre garanti sur
hypothèque émis en Australie par
la Corporation nationale du
marché des hypothèques
eine per Hypothek gesicherte
Anleihe
certificado respaldado por una
hipoteca emitido por el organismo
australiano del mercado de
hipotecas
オージー・マック

Austrade
澳大利亚贸易委员会
commission commerciale
australienne
Australische Handelskommission
organismo de fomento del
comercio australiano
オーストラリア貿易促進庁

**Australia and New Zealand
Closer Economic Relations
Trade Agreement**
澳大利亚和新西兰邻邦经济关系
贸易协定
accord commercial
australo-néo-Zélandais pour des
relations économiques plus
étroites
Australisch-Neuseeländisches
Handelsabkommen
acuerdo comercial entre Australia
y Nueva Zelanda

---

*Translations appear in the following order: Chinese, French, German, Spanish/Latin American
Spanish, and Japanese*

オーストラリア・ニュージー
ランド経済関係緊密化協定

**Australian Accounting
Standards Board**
澳大利亚会计标准局
comité australien des normes
comptables
Australische
Wirtschaftsprüfungskammer
organismo australiano regulador
de los estándares de contabilidad
オーストラリア会計基準審議会

**Australian Bureau of
Statistics**
澳洲统计局
bureau australien des statistiques
Australisches Statistiksbüro
departamento australiano de
estadísticas
オーストラリア統計局

**Australian Chamber of
Commerce and Industry**
澳大利亚工商会
Chambre australienne du
commerce et de l'industrie
Australische Industrie- und
Handelskammer
cámara australiana de comercio e
industria
オーストラリア商工会議所

**Australian Chamber of
Manufactures**
澳大利制造亚商会
chambre de fabricants d'Australie
Australische Kammer des
produzierendes Gewerbes
cámara australiana de fabricantes
オーストラリア製造業会議所

**Australian Communications
Authority**
澳大利亚通讯局
organisme australien des
communications
Australische
Telekommunikationsbehörde
organismo australiano regulador
de la industria de las
comunicaciones
オーストラリア通信庁

Australian Council of Trade
澳大利亚贸易委员会
conseil du commerce australien
Australische Handelskammer
consejo comercial australiano
オーストラリア労働組合協議会

**Australian Industrial
Relations Commission**
澳大利亚工业关系委员会
commission australienne des
relations industrielles
Australischer Ausschuss für

Beziehungen zwischen
Arbeitsgebern und
Gewerkschaften
comisión australiana reguladora de
las relaciones industriales
オーストラリア労使関係委員会

**Australian Prudential
Regulation Authority**
澳大利亚谨慎管制当局
organisme australien de
réglementation des institutions
financières
Australische
Finanzaufsichtsbehörde
Organismo Regulador de partida
automática
オーストラリア健全性規制機関

**Australian Securities and
Investments Commission**
澳大利亚证券投资委员会
commission australienne des
investissements et titres
Australischer Wertpapier- und
Investmentausschuss
comisión australiana reguladora de
los productos financieros
オーストラリア証券投資委員会

Australian Stock Exchange
澳大利亚证券交易所
Bourse australienne
Australische Börse
Bolsa australiana
オーストラリア証券取引所

Australian Taxation Office
澳大利亚税务局
office australien du fisc
Australisches Finanzamt
agencia tributaria australiana
オーストラリア国税局

authentication
认证; 鉴定; 证实
authentification
Authentifizierung
autenticación
オーセンティケーション,
認証用ソフトウエア

authorisation
授权; 许可; 特许
autorisation
Autorisierung
autorización
オーソリゼーション, 認証, 認可

authorised capital
法定资本; 核定资本; 额定资本
capital nominal
autorisiertes (Aktien-) Kapital
capital autorizado
授権資本

authorised share
法定股票; 核定股票; 额定股票
capital (actions) autorisé

genehmigte Aktie; genehmigtes
Wertpapier
acción autorizada
授権株式(数)

authorised share capital
核定股本, 法定股本
capital social
eingetragenes Kapital
capital social autorizado
授権, 記名割当株式資本

authorised signatory
授权签署人
signataire social
Unterschriftsberechtigte/r
firmante autorizado(-a)
認定署名者

authority
权力; 职权
autorité
Befugnis; Kompetenz;
Weisungsbefugnis; Autorität
autoridad
権限

authority chart
职权图
organigramme d'autorité
hiérarchique
Firmenhierarchie;
Kompetenzenüberblick;
Organogramm
gráfico de jerarquías
権限系統, 会社機構図

automated clearing house
自动清算所; 自动票据交换所
chambre de compensation
informatisée
automatische Abrechnungsstelle
cámara de compensación
electrónica
オートメーテッド・クリアリン
グハウス, 自動手形交換所

**Automated Direct Debit
Amendments and
Cancellation Service**
自动直接借记修改和取消服务
service de modification ou
d'annulation de prélèvement
automatisé
automatischer
Überweisungsdienst
servicio automatizado para la
anulación y modificación de la
domiciliación de pagos
自動直接借り方変更
キャンセルサービス

automated handling
自动控制; 自动处理
manutention automatisée
automatisierte Handhabung
manipulación automatizada
自動処理, 自動操作

---

*Translations appear in the following order: Chinese, French, German, Spanish/Latin American
Spanish, and Japanese*

Automated Order Entry System
订单自动进入系统
système de saisie d'ordre automatisé
automatisches Auftragseingangssystem
sistema de orden de entrada automática
(米国の取引所における)自動注文入力システム

automated screen trading
自动屏幕贸易
transactions automatisées sur écran
Computerbörse
contratación bursátil automatizada por pantalla
自動電子取引

automated storage and retrieval systems
自动储存检索系统
systèmes informatisés pour entreposage et extraction
automatisierte Lagersysteme
sistema automatizado de almacenamiento y recuperación
自動保管回収システム

automatic assembly
自动组装
construction automatisée
vollautomatische Fertigung
montaje automatizado
自動組み立て

automatic guided vehicle system
自动指示车辆系统
système de véhicules téléguidés
automatisches spurgeführtes Fahrzeugleitsystem
sistema de vehículos guiados automáticamente
自動無人車システム

automatic rollover
自动到期转期
investissement automatique renouvelable
automatische Erneuerung von Festgeldanlagen bei Fälligkeit
reinversión automática de un depósito a plazo fijo
自動借り換え

automation
自动化
automisation
Automatisierung
automatización
自動化

autonomation
自动化
autonomation
Autonomatisierung
autonomación
オートノメーション

autonomous work group
自治工作组
groupe de travail autonome
autonome Arbeitsgruppe
grupo de trabajo autónomo
自律の作業集団

Auto Pact
美加汽车协定
terme informel pour l'accord sur les produits automobiles entre le Canada et les Etats-Unis
Fahrzeugprodukteabkommen
pacto sobre productos automovilísticos
オートパクト

autoresponder
自动回复
messages de réponse automatiques
Autoresponder
emisor de respuestas automáticas
オートレスポンダー

availability float
未指定用于保留支出或抵押的可用的资产
caisse de disponibilité
Verfügbarkeitskasse; Dispositionsbesitz
fondos disponibles en cuenta(s)
アベイラビリティ・フロート, 浮動手形交換前の利用可能金

available hours
heures de travail disponibles
verfügbare Arbeitszeit
horas disponibles
使用可能時間

average
平均, 平均数
moyenne
Mittelwert
promedio; media
平均

average accounting return
应收账款收益
pourcentage comptable moyen de revenu
geschätzter Gewinn einer Investition
beneficio contable medio
平均収益率, 平均利潤率

average collection period
平均收款期
durée moyenne d'encaissement
durchschnittliche Abholungszeit; Durchschnittsdauer der Außenstände

tiempo medio de cobro
平均回収期間

average cost of capital
资本平均成本
coût de capital moyen
durchschnittliche Kapitalkosten
coste medio de capital
costo medio de capital
平均資本コスト

average deviation
平均偏差
déviation par rapport à la moyenne
mittlere Abweichung
desviación media
平均偏差

average nominal maturity
平均名义到期日
échéance nominale moyenne
durchschnittliche nominelle Laufzeit od. Nominallaufzeit
vencimiento nominal medio
(ミューチュアル・ファンド等の)平均所定満期

average option
平均期货
option de valeur moyenne
Durchschnittsoption
opción media
アヴェレージ・オプション, 平均値ベースの商品オプション

Average Weekly Earnings
周平均收入
revenu hebdomadaire moyen
durchschnittliches wöchentliches Einkommen
sueldo semanal medio
平均週収

Average Weekly Ordinary Time Earnings
普通周平均收入
revenu hebdomadaire moyen des heures de travail ordinaires
durchschnittlicher einfacher Stundenlohn
sueldo semanal medio bruto
残業外平均週収

avoidable costs
可避免成本
frais évitables
vermeidbare Kosten
costes evitables
回避可能原価

award[1]
裁决
adjudication
Arbeitsbedingungen
adjudicación
職業別アワード制度

award[2]
裁决; 授予; 奖励; 判定
décision arbitrale

Translations appear in the following order: Chinese, French, German, Spanish/Latin American Spanish, and Japanese

Schiedsspruch; Verleihung;
zuerkannter Betrag; zuschlagen;
erteilen
fallo
審判

award wage
裁决工资
montant de salaire adjugé
durch Arbeitsgericht festgesetztes
Gehalt
sueldo mínimo sectorial
アワード賃金

axis
轴
axe
Achse
eje
軸

B2B
商家对商家; 企业对企业
entre entreprises
zwischenbetrieblich
relaciones comerciales entre
empresas
ビー・トゥ・ビー,
ビジネス・ツー・ビジネス,
企業対企業

B2B advertising
商家对商业广告; 企业对企业广告
publicité entreprise-à-entreprise
b2b Werbung
publicidad entre empresas
Ｂ２Ｂ広告

B2B agency
商业对商业广告代理商;
企业对企业广告代理商
agence de publicité pour b2b
b2b Webeagentur
agencia especializada en
publicidad entre empresas
Ｂ２Ｂ広告代理店

B2B auction
b2b拍卖
vente aux enchères b2b
b2b Versteigerung
subasta electrónica de servicios
B2Bオークション

B2B commerce
b2b商务
commerce entre entreprises
Handel von Unternehmen zu
Unternehmen
comercio de empresa a empresa
Ｂ２Ｂ取引

B2B marketing
商业对商业营销; 企业对企业营销
marketing entre empresas
Marketing von Unternehmen zu
Unternehmen

marketing de empresa a empresa
Ｂ２Ｂマーケティング

B2C
商家对消费者; 企业对消费者
entreprise à consommateur
Geschäft zu Verbraucher
relaciones comerciales entre
empresa y consumidor
ビジネス・ツー・コンシューマー,
企業対個人, ビー・ツー・シー

B4N
回见
salut pour l'instant
Aufwiedersehen
hasta luego
じゃあまた

back duty
拖欠税款
arriéré d'impôt
Steuerschuld
impuestos atrasados
遡及的納税義務

back-end loading
后端加载，喻指阻碍投资人卖
出的收费
droit à payer au moment de la
vente
Strafgebühr
comisión por cancelación
anticipada
解約手数料

backflush costing
回流成本计算
méthode d'évaluation des coûts
alignée sur la production ou
d'évaluation des coûts à
contre-courant
retrograde Entnahmekalkulation
coste regresivo calculado
バックフラッシュ・コスティング

backlink checking
相关网站检索
vérification de liaisons en aval
Backlink-Prüfung
comprobación del origen de las
visitas
バックリンク・チェック

backlog
积压的工作
commandes en carnet
Auftragsrückstand;
Arbeitsrückstand
acumulación de pedidos
納入残, 手持ち注文, 受注残

backlog depreciation
附加折旧
dépréciation en arriéré
Verlustabschreibung
depreciación acumulada
遡及的減価償却

back office
事务部; 后勤部门
arrière-boutique
Buchhaltung; Abrechnung;
Back-Office
trastienda; back-office
バック・オフィス

back pay
欠款; 补发
rappel de salaire
Nachzahlung
atrasos
遡及的賃金賠償

back-to-back loan
双向贷款
charge dos-à-dos
Parallelkredit
cargamento de vuelta
バック・ツー・バック・ローン

back-to-school sale
开学大降价
soldes de rentrée scolaire
Ausverkauf zum Schulbeginn nach
den Sommerferien
rebajas de vuelta al colegio
秋の進級・進学セール

back-up
(证券市场)退缩时期
sauvegarde
Deckung; sichern; unterstützen
respaldo
バックアップ期

back-up facility
备份
système de sauvegarde
Deckungsfazilität;
Deckungsmöglichkeit;
Deckungslinie
sistema para respaldo
バックアップ・ファシリティ

back-up withholding
代扣所得税
retenue fiscale de garantie
Anschlussquellensteuern
retención de impuestos
予備源泉徴収

backward integration
后向联合
intégration à contre-courant;
intégration par l'amont
Rückwärtsintegration
integración regresiva
後進的統合, 後向きの統合

backward scheduling
后向工作计划
planification à contre-courant
Rückwärtsterminierung
horario regresivo
後向き作業日程,
逆スケジューリング

Translations appear in the following order: Chinese, French, German, Spanish/Latin American Spanish, and Japanese

BACS
银行自动清算系统
services de crédits bancaires automatisés
elektronisches Clearingsystem für Posten mit geringem Wert oder Wiederholungsposten wie Daueraufträge, Einzugsverfahren und automatisierte Guthaben wie Gehaltszahlungen
sistema automático de compensación bancaria
銀行自動手形交換サービス

bad debt
坏帐; 倒帐; 倒帐者; 坏帐者
créance irrécouvrable
uneinbringliche Forderung
deuda incobrable
不良債権, 貸し倒れ損失

bad debt reserve
坏帐储备
réserves pour créances irrécouvrables
Rückstellung für uneinbringliche Forderungen;
Forderungsabschreibung;
Wertberichtigung auf notleidende Kredite
reserva para deudas incobrables
貸し倒れ引当金

bad debts ratio
coefficient de créances irrécouvrables
Quote der uneinbringlichen Forderungen
proporción (ratio) de deudas fallidas
貸倒率

bad debts recovered
坏帐收回
créances douteuses récupérées
dennoch eingebrachte Außenstände
deudas incobrables recuperadas
償却債権取立益

badwill
坏声誉
survaleur négative
schlechter Ruf
mala voluntad
負ののれん

bailment
寄托
acte de dépôt ou de gage
Gewahrsam; Aufbewahrung
caución
一時寄託

bait and switch
上钩销售法; 饵诱推销法
stratagème pour transfert d'achat
Lockvogelwerbung
artículo gancho
おとり商法

balance[1]
结余
solde (d'un compte)
positiver oder negativer Saldo
balance
残高

balance[2]
平衡
balance, solde ou reliquat
Saldo
saldo
差額

balance billing
追收保险赔偿以外的余额
facturation du solde
den von der Versicherung ungedeckten Betrag berechnen
facturación del balance
(保険会社の)調整的請求

balanced budget
平衡预算
budget équilibré
ausgeglichenes Budget
presupuesto equilibrado
均衡予算, 均衡財政, 財政均衡, 均衡予算

balanced design
平衡设计
conception équilibrée
symmetrischer Aufbau
diseño equilibrado
均衡デザイン

balanced fund
平衡基金; 资金平衡
fonds à placements équilibrés
Stabilitätsfonds; gemischter Investmentfonds
fondo equilibrado
バランス・ファンド, 分散投資による安全投資

balanced investment strategy
平衡投资策略
stratégie d'investissement équilibré
ausgeglichene Investitionsstrategie;
ausgewogene Anlagestrategie
estrategia de inversión equilibrada
均衡型投資戦略

balanced line
平衡流水线
chaîne de montage à cycle équilibré
abgeglichenes Fließband;
ausgewogenes Montageband fac

cadena de montaje equilibrada
バランスド・ライン

balanced quantity
平衡数量
quantité équilibrée
ausgeglichene Menge
cantidad equilibrada
バランスド・クオンティティ

balanced scorecard
平衡记分卡
fiche de mesure d'indicateurs
Balanced Scorecard
medición del desempeño
均衡採点カード

balance off
结算
arrêter (un compte)
Bilanz ziehen
saldar
帳尻を合わせる

balance of payments
国际收支差额; 国际收支平衡表; 国际收支
balance des paiements
Zahlungsbilanz
balanza de pagos
balance de pagos
国際収支

balance of payments on capital account
资本帐户的国际收支差额
balance des paiements sur compte de capital
Kapitalverkehrsbilanz;
Kapitalbilanz
balanza de pagos en operaciones de capital
資本勘定国際収支

balance of payments on current account
经常项目国际收支差额
balance des paiements sur compte courant
Leistungsbilanz;
Kontokorrentsaldo
balanza de pagos en cuenta corriente
当座勘定国際収支

balance of trade
贸易差额; 贸易收支
balance commerciale
Bezugszeitpunkt
balanza comercial
balance comercial
貿易収支

balance sheet
决算表; 平衡表; 资产负债表
bilan (d'entreprise)
Bilanz; Jahresabschluss
balance; balance general
貸借対照表

balance sheet audit
资产负债表审计
vérification de bilan
Geschäftsbilanzrevision
auditoría de balances
貸借対照表監査

balance sheet total
总资产负债表
total de bilan
Bilanzsumme
totales del balance
貸借対照表上の資産合計

balancing figure
配平数字
chiffre rectificatif (pour
comptabilité)
Fehlbetrag
saldo
調整差額

balloon loan
气球式贷款
prêt-ballon
Darlehen; mit hoher
Abschlusszahlung
préstamo amortizable en su mayor
parte al vencimiento
バルーン・ローン,
毎月の利息支払いと満期に一
括返済を必要とする銀行ローン

balloon payment
期末整付; 期末大笔还清
versement forfaitaire et final
hohe Abschlusszahlung
pago final
(返済期日の)元利合計支払い

ballpark
估略数字; 大约; 大概
fourchette (d'estimation)
grobe Schätzung
cifra estimada
大凡の

BALO
法国官方出版物
publication financière du
gouvernement français
finanzieller Bericht der
französischen Regierung
publicación del gobierno francés
sobre hechos y cifras de empresas
públicas
公開会社の財務諸表を含む
フランス政府の刊行物

banded pack
捆绑式包装
vente jumelée
Warenprobenbeilage
paquete conjunto
おまけ付き商品

bandwidth
灵活上班时间幅度
largeur de bande

Bandbreite
ancho de banda
带域幅

bang for the buck
投资回报
maximum de profits de ses
investissements
Kapitalrendite
ganancias de inversión
投資利益率

bangtail
插页定单
fourchette
Bang-Tail-Rückumschlag
formulario en la solapa de un
sobre
封筒に付けられた,
切り離して使える注文書

bank
银行; 存...银行; 在银行开帐户;
依赖于
banque
Bank
banco
銀行

bank bill¹
银行汇票; 银行票据
billet de banque
Wechsel
letra bancaria
銀行引受手形

bank bill²
钞票
billet de banque
Banknote; Papiergeld
billete de banco
I银行券,
(イングランド銀行の)銀行券

bank card
银行卡
carte bancaire
Bankkarte
tarjeta bancaria
バンク・カード,銀行発行カード

bank certificate
银行证明书
certificat bancaire
Kontostandserklärung
certificado bancario
銀行が作成する
企業口座残高などの証明書

bank charge
银行手续费用，银行收费
frais de banque
Bankgebühr
gastos bancarios
銀行手数料

bank confirmation
银行确认书
confirmation bancaire écrite

Bankbestätigung
confirmación bancaria
監査役が銀行に依頼する
企業口座残高の確認

bank credit
银行信贷; 银行担保; 银行放款
crédit bancaire
Bankkredit
crédito bancario
銀行信用状

bank discount
银行贴现
escompte bancaire
Wechseldiskont; Damnum,
Darlehensabgeld
descuento bancario
銀行割引料,银行手形割引

bank discount basis
银行贴现基础
base d'escompte bancaire
Bankdiskontbasis
interés bancario abonado al
descuento
銀行割引率方式

bank-eligible issue
银行合格(适宜)发行
émission éligible pour les banques
de commerce
bankfähige Emission
obligación del tesoro lista para ser
comprada por bancos comerciales
適格発行

banker
银行(家); 从事银行工作的人
banquier
Bankier; Bank
banquero(-a)
銀行経営者

banker's credit
银行信用状; 银行信用证
crédit bancaire
Akkreditiv
crédito bancario
銀行信用(状)

banker's draft
银行汇票
traite bancaire
Bankwechsel; Banktratte;
Bankscheck
giro bancario
銀行為替手形

bankers' hours
银行营业时间
horaires bancaires
kurzer Arbeitstag: Anspielung auf
Öffnungszeiten der Banken von 9
Uhr bis 3 Uhr und die kurzen
Arbeitstage ihrer Angestellten
horario de apertura
銀行の営業時間

Translations appear in the following order: Chinese, French, German, Spanish/Latin American Spanish, and Japanese

banker's order
银行代付通知
prélèvement bancaire
Dauerauftrag
domiciliación bancaria
銀行為替

banker's reference
银行推荐信
référence bancaire
Kreditauskunft; Bonitätsprüfung
referencia del banco
銀行による顧客信用報告書

bank fee
银行费
frais bancaires
Bankgebühr
comisión bancaria
銀行手数料

bank guarantee
银行担保; 银行担保 书
garantie bancaire
Bankgarantie; Bankbürgschaft;
Bankaval
garantía bancaria
銀行支払保証

bank holding company
银行的母公司
société de portefeuille bancaire
Bankholding
compañía propietaria de bancos
銀行持ち株会社

banking insurance fund
银行保险基金
caisse d'assurance des banques
(Etats-Unis)
Bankversicherungsfonds
fondo de seguridad de depósitos
para bancos
米国の連邦預金保険公社が
維持する銀行保険ファンド

Banking Ombudsman
银行事物调查官
médiateur bancaire
Bankombudsmann
defensor(a) de los clientes
bancarios
銀行業界オンブズマン

banking passport
银行证明书
faux passeport bancaire
Bankpass
pasaporte bancario
バンキング・パスポート

banking syndicate
银行业协会
syndicat bancaire
Bankenkonsortium
consorcio bancario
銀行団

banking system
银行体系; 银行制度
système bancaire
Bankensystem; Bankenapparat
sistema bancario
銀行制度

bank investment contract
银行投资合同
contrat d'investissement bancaire
Bankinvestitionsvertrag
contrato de inversión bancaria
銀行の出資契約

bankmail
银行同意文
chantage bancaire
Stillhalteabkommen
acuerdo entre un banco y una
empresa que lanza una OPA para
que aquel no apoye ninguna otra
oferta
バンクメール

Bank of England
英格兰银行
la Banque d'Angleterre
Bank von England
banco central del Reino Unido
イングランド銀行

bank overdraft
银行透支
découvert sur compte bancaire
Überziehungskredit; Kreditlinie;
Banküberziehung
descubierto bancario; sobregiro
bancario
当座借越し

bank reconciliation
apurement comptable
Kontenabstimmung zwischen dem
Konto einer Bank und einem
Kundenkonto
reconciliación de extractos/estados
bancarios
银行勘定调整

bank reserve ratio
银行储备金比率
taux de réserves bancaires
Bankreservenquote
coeficiente de reserva de caja
預金支払準備率

bank reserves
银行储备
réserves bancaires
Bankreserven; Bankrücklagen
reservas bancarias
準備預金, 支払準備

bankroll
货币储蓄; 手头资金
fonds
Banknotenbündel
fortuna
資金源

bankrupt
破产
failli(e)
zahlungsunfähig sein
quiebra
破産者

bankruptcy
倒闭; 破产
faillite
Konkurs; Bankrott
bancarrota; quiebra
破産

bank statement
银行对帐单，银行结帐表
relevé de compte
Kontoauszug; Bankauszug
extracto de cuenta bancario
銀行報告書

bank term loan
银行中长期分期偿还贷款
prêt bancaire à terme
mittelfristiges Bankdarlehen;
mittelfristiger Bankkredit
préstamo bancario a plazo
銀行のターム・ローン,
期限付き貸出

banner
标题广告
bannière
Transparent
banner; pancarta; anuncio
バナー, バナー広告

banner advertising
大字标题广告
pub avec des bandes publicitaires
Bannerwerbung
publicidad con banners
バナー広告

banner exchange
标题广告互换
programme d'échange de bandes
publicitaires sur Internet
ein Werbeprogramm, mit dem ein
Händler andere dazu bringt, seine
Fahneninserate und Schaltflächen
auf ihren Webseiten einzustellen,
im Gegenzug für die Darstellung
ihrer eigenen auf seiner Seite
intercambio de banners
バナー交換

bar
百万英镑
un million de livres sterling
eine Million Pfund Sterling
un millón de libras esterlinas
百万英ポンド

bar chart
柱形图; 条状图
graphe à batonnets
Säulendiagramm

Translations appear in the following order: Chinese, French, German, Spanish/Latin American Spanish, and Japanese

gráfico de barras
棒図表

bar coding
条形码
codage à barres
Strichcodierung
codificación con barras
バー・コード

barefoot pilgrim
赤脚朝圣者
investisseur peu sophistiqué qui a
tout perdu par ses transactions sur
titres
geprellter Kleinaktionär
peregrino descalzo (pérdida total)
裸足の巡礼者(株ですべてを失っ
てしまった素人投資家)

bargain
交易
marché ou transaction boursière
Börsengeschäft
transacción
売買

bargaining chip
讨价还价筹码
argument de négociation
Verhandlungspfand
baza
交渉チップ

bargain tax date
交易日
date d'impôt sur transaction
Abschlusstermin
fecha de una transacción a efectos
fiscales
売買日付

barometer stock
代表性股票
titre baromètre
Standardwerte
barómetro bursátil
景気指標として見なされる
人気証券, 標準株

barren money
银行货币
argent stérile
totes Kapital
deuda sin intereses
(金庫内の現金のような)
不妊貨幣

barrier option
挡板期权
option avec plafond de protection
Grenzoption
opción barrera
バリア・オプション

barrier to entry
进入(市场的)壁垒(障碍)
obstacle à pénétration (d'un
marché)

Marktzutrittsschranke
barrera de entrada
市場参入障壁

barrier to exit
退出(市场)壁垒(障碍)
obstacle à sortie (d'un marché)
Marktaustrittsschranke
barrera de salida
市場退散障壁

barter
易货
échanger ou troquer (des biens)
Tauschgeschäft
trueque
物々交換

base currency
基准货币
devise de base
Basiswährung; Grundwährung
moneda base
基準通貨

base date
基准日期
date de base
Basisdatum; Bezugszeitpunkt
fecha base
基準日

base interest rate
基本利率
taux d'intérêt de base
Eckzins; Leitzins
tipo de interés básico
基準利子

base rate
基本利率; 基础利率
taux de base
Kreditzins für erste Adressen
tipo básico
基準貸出金利

base rate tracker mortgage
基础利率抵押
hypothèque indexée dépendant
du taux de base
periodisch (normalerweise jährlich)
variabel verzinste Hypothek, deren
Zinssatz um einen Festbetrag
höher ist als ein bestimmter
Eckzins
hipoteca de interés variable
基準金利トラッカー・モーゲージ

base year
基年
année de base
Basisjahr
año base
基準年

basic pay
基本工资
salaire de base

Grundlohn
salario base
基本給

basic wage
基本工资
salaire de base
Mindestlohn
salario mínimo sectorial
職業別最低賃金

basic wage rate
基本工资率
taux de base des salaires
Wochengrundtarif
tasa de sueldo base
基本給

basis of apportionment
分配基础
base de répartition ou ventilation
Aufteilungsbasis; Zuweisungsbasis
bases de prorrateo
配賦基準

basis point
基本点
point de base ou centième de
point
Basispunkt
punto básico
ベーシス・ポイント

basis risk
基础风险
risque de base
Basisrisiko; Grundrisiko
riesgo de base
ベーシス・リスク

basket case
不可救药
cas pour la corbeille
hoffnungsloser Fall
caso perdido
助けようのない人会社

basket of currencies
一篮子货币
panier de devises
Währungskorb
cesta de monedas
通貨バスケット

batch
批，批量
lot
Stapel; Stoß; Bündel; Charge
remesa; lote
バッチ

batch costing
分批成本计算法
estimation de prix groupé
Loskostenkalkulation
coste por lotes
costo por lotes
バッチ原価計算

Translations appear in the following order: Chinese, French, German, Spanish/Latin American Spanish, and Japanese

batch-level activities
批量生产活动
activités liées aux lots de
production
Arbeiten auf Stapelebene
actividades clasificadas a nivel de
remesa
バッチ方式活動

batch production
成批生产; 分批生产; 批量生产
production par lots
Mengenproduktion;
Losfabrikation;
Kleinserienfertigung
producción en lotes
バッチ生産

baud
波德(电脑)
baud
Baud
baudio
ボー

Bayesian theory
贝叶斯理论
théorie bayésienne; théorie de
Bayes
Bayesianische Theorie;
Bayes-Regel
teoría bayesiana
ベイエシアン理論

Bayes' theorem
贝叶斯定理
théorème de Bayes
Theorem von Bayes
teoría de Bayes
ベイズの定理

BBS
电子布告栏系统
système de tableau d'affichage
Mailboxsystem
BBS
電子掲示板システム

bcc
隐蔽副本; 暗抄送
fonction informatique permettant
à l'utiisateur d'envoyer un
message E-mail à un nombre
quelconque d'adresses E-mail, tout
en dissimulant l'adresse de chaque
destinataire du message E-mail
Blinddurchschlag
control de llamadas de difusión
(bcc)
ブラインド・カーボン・コピー

BCNU
一会儿见
à la revoyure
wir sehen uns noch
hasta pronto
またね

bean counter[1]
喻指无足轻重的人
menu fretin
Ugs. Schütze Arsch
empleado de bajo rango
ぺいぺい

bean counter[2]
精于计算的人
petit comptable
abfällige Bezeichnung für
Wirtschaftsprüfer in großem
Unternehmen
cabeza contable
経理担当者を侮って指す言葉

bear
承受; 负担; 具有; 显示; 对...负责;
迫使价格下降; 空头; 卖空;
空头投资者
baissier
Baissespekulant
bajista
ベア, 弱気筋

bearer bond
持票人债券; 不记名债券
obligation au porteur
Inhaberschuldverschreibung;
Inhaberobligation
obligación al portador
無記名債権

bearer instrument
来人票据
document au porteur
Inhabercheck
papel al portador
無記名証券, 持参人払証券

bearer security
持有人证券
titre au porteur
Inhaberpapier
título al portador
無記名証券

bear hug
熊之拥抱
étreinte intéressée
Versuch das Board einer
Zielgesellschaft dazu zu bewegen
seinen Aktionären die Annahme
des Ubernahmeangebots zu
empfehlen
abrazo del oso
ベアー・ハッグ

bearish
熊市; 行情看跌
(tendance) à la baisse
fallend baisse-tendenziös in
Baissestimmung
a la baja; bajista
先安

bear market
熊市; 空头市场; 跌风市场

marché à la baisse
Baissemarkt; Börsenbaisse;
fallende Kurstendenz
mercado a la baja; mercado bajista
下げ相場

bear spread
空头差价
éventail de transactions à la baisse
Baisse-Spread
diferencial bajista
ベア・スプレッド

bear tack
熊市
louvoiement vers la baisse
Baisse
tendencia bajista del mercado de
valores
相場の下落傾向

bed and breakfast deal
暮售朝购式交易
aller et retour
kurzfristiger An- und Verkauf von
Aktien aus Steuergründen
venta de valores y compra al día
siguiente
ベッド・アンド・ブレックファー
スト取引

beepilepsy
寻呼机振动症
avoir un haut le bip
'Piepileptik' plötzliches Aufzucken
einer Person, deren Piepser losgeht
susto dado por el busca
susto dado por el localizador
ポケベルがなった時に起きる「
発作」

before-tax profit margin
暮售朝购式交易
marge bénéficiaire brute
Gewinnspanne vor Steuern
margen de beneficio antes de
impuestos
税込み利ザヤ

behavioural accounting
行为会计学
comptabilité behavioriste (de
comportement)
verhaltenstheoretisch orientierte
Kosten- und Leistungsrechnung
estudio contable analítico,
sociológico, psicológico y técnico
行動会計

behavioural implications
行为影响
implications dues au
comportement
Verhaltensimplikationen
repercusiones derivadas de la
conducta
行動会計理論

Translations appear in the following order: Chinese, French, German, Spanish/Latin American Spanish, and Japanese

behavioural modelling[1]
行为模型
modélisation du comportement
Verhaltensmodellbildung;
Erstellung; eines
Verhaltensmodells
modelo de conducta
人間の潜在的な
ノウハウを記録し, 符号化する
モデル化方法

behavioural modelling[2]
行为模型
modèles d'imitation de
comportement
Verhaltensmodell
modelo de la técnica de formación
モデルに従い, 習った行動を
維持する訓練方法

behavioural science
行为科学
science du comportement
Verhaltensforschung
ciencia del comportamiento
行動科学

**behaviourist theories of
leadership**
行为领导学理论
théories béhavioristes du
leadership
verhaltensorientierte
Führungstheorien
teorías conductistas del liderazgo
リーダーシップの行動原理

bell cow
主导产品
bonne laitière
Produkt, das sich gut verkauft und
relativ gute Gewinne einbringt
gallina de los huevos de oro
小金のなる木,
銀の卵を産むガチョウにな
ぞらえた利益の上がる商品

bells and whistles[1]
华而不实的产品特点
gadgets périphériques
Schnickschnack
parafernalia; accesorios
ベル・アンド・ウィッスル

bells and whistles[2]
华而不实的产品特点
caractéristiques fantaisies
(attachées à un instrument de
produits dérivés ou à une émission
de titres)
Blendwerk
rasgos de atracción al inversor y
reducción de costes
ベル・アンド・ウィッスル

bellwether
牵头羊(作为市场变化反向指示器)
indicateur

Schlüssel
indicador de tendencias
指標

below-the-line[1]
线下项目
en dessous de la ligne
unter dem Strich
no promocional
広告以外
(のマーケティング予算)

below-the-line[2]
线下项目
hors bilan
Schlüsselwerte
desglose de cuentas de resultados
ビロー・ザ・ライン

below-the-line[3]
资本项目
budget hors bilan
unter der Linie; unter dem Strich
transacciones capital país
ビロー・ザ・ライン

benchmark
基准; 基准数据; 基准程序
point de référence (pour
évaluation de performance)
Bezugspunkt; Bezugsmarke;
Maßstab; Benchmark; Eckwert
punto de referencia
ベンチマーク

benchmark accounting policy
基准会计政策
politique comptable de référence
steuerrechtliche Bilanzbildung
norma
国際会計基準内の
ベンチマーク会計方針

benchmarking
基准对照
étude comparative selon référence
Benchmarking
criterio de referencia
ベンチマーキング

benchmark interest rate
基准利率
taux d'intérêt de référence
Bezugszins; Referenzzins;
Vergleichszins
tipo de interés de referencia
基準金利, 指標金利

beneficial owner
受益权所有人
usufruitier
wirtschaftliche/r Eigentumer(in)
usufructuario(-a)
受益者

beneficiary bank
受益人银行
banque de gestion de legs
Empfängerbank

banco beneficiario
(口座を持つ受取人への)支
払銀行

benefit
利益; 津贴; 保险赔偿 费; 抚恤金;
救济金
prestation
Nutzen; Beihilfe; Leistung
beneficio
共済

benefit in kind
实物津贴; 额外福利
avantage en nature
Sachleistung
prestación en especie
現物給付

benefits plan
福利计划
programme d'intérêt général
Programm zur Steigerung
kanadischer
Wettbewerbsfähigkeit
plan de beneficios
便益プラン

bequest
遗产, 遗赠
legs
Vermächtnis
legado
遺産

Berhad
(马来西亚语)私有
privé
Privat
sociedad anónima en Malasia
会社

best-in-class
行业最佳
meilleur dans sa catégorie
Klassenbeste/r
empresa líder en eficacia
ベスト・イン・ クラス

best practice
最佳实践
meilleure pratique
beste Praxis; beste
Vorgehensweise; optimales
Verfahren
las mejores iniciativas prácticas
最良実施法

best value
最优价值方针
de la meilleure valeur
zur größter Nutzen
plan de incremento de la calidad
en los servicios públicos británicos;
uso eficiente de los recursos para
obtener los mejores resultados
ベストバリュー計画

---

*Translations appear in the following order: Chinese, French, German, Spanish/Latin American
Spanish, and Japanese*

beta
贝塔
bêta
Beta; Beta-Faktor; Beta-Koeffizient
beta
(統計)ベータ値

beta coefficient
变异系数, 贝它系数
coefficient bêta
Beta-Koeffizient
coeficiente beta
市場全体との連動性を示す
ベータ係数

beta factor
贝塔系数
facteur bêta
Betafaktor
factor beta
ベータ値

beta rating
贝塔率
bêta
Rendite-Risiko Vergleich
medida de volatilidad en
comparación con el mercado
市場指数に対し
何倍の値動きをするか
というベータ値

beta software
贝塔测试软件
logiciel bêta
Beta-Software
software gratis en proceso de
prueba
ベータ版ソフトウェア

beta test
贝塔检验
test bêta
Betatest
prueba beta
ベータテスト

BFH
德国税务最高法院
en Allemagne, la Cour suprême
pour les affaires concernant la
taxation
BFH
tribunal supremo sobre temas
fiscales
ドイツ連邦財政裁判所

BHP
澳大利亚最大的制造企业
la plus grosse compagnie de
fabrication d'Australie
die 'großen Australischen'
el mayor fabricante australiano
(豪)BHP社

bias
偏差
distorsion

Verzerrung
error sistemático; desvío;
propensión; sesgo; desviación
バイアス

bid
递盘; 投标; 招标; 出价; 报价
offre
Submissionsangebot; Gebot;
Kostenvoranschlag; bieten;
steigern; ein Angebot machen
oferta; puja
買い値

bid-ask quote
卖出买入报价
devis d'offre et de demande
Geld-Brief-Notierung
estado de precios de oferta y
demanda de valores u opciones
買い呼び値と売り呼び値

bid-ask spread
买卖价差
écart entre prix d'offre et de
demande
Geld-Brief-Spanne
diferencial comprador–vendedor
気配値差額

bid bond
投标保证金
caution de soumission
Bietungsgarantie
fianza de oferta
入札保証金

bidding war
报价战
guerre de la surenchère
Übernahmeschlacht;
Angebotskrieg
guerra de ofertas
競争入札, せり上げ競争

bid form
报价表; 投标表
bulletin de soumission
Angebotsformula
modelo de oferta
(英米地方債の)入札様式

bid-offer spread
最高买卖价差
écart entre enchère/offre
Spanne zwischen Ausgabe- und
Rücknahmekurs
diferencial de demanda y oferta
買い値と売り値の差

bid price
出价; 递盘价
prix de l'offre
gebotener Preis; Angebotspreis;
Geldkurs
precio de oferta
買い呼び値, 入札価格

bid-to-cover ratio
国库券购买率; 国库券出价与实际
购买比率
(国库券出价与实际购买比率)
coefficient offre-provision
Interessenten-Anzahl
proporción entre ofertas recibidas
y aceptadas
応札倍率

bid up
哄抬标价
faire une offre à la hausse
den Preis künstlich in die Höhe
bieten
puja
せり上げる

Big Bang
(证券市场)大震动, 大冲击
informatisation de la Bourse de
Londres mise en oeuvre en octobre
1986
Urknall
Big Bang
1986年のロンドン版ビッグバン

big bath
冲销
pratique qui consiste à donner un
aspect encore pire à la déclaration
de revenus d'une année médiocre
en accroissant les dépenses et en
vendant des biens corporels
umfassende Bilanzbereinigung
資産を売却して
赤字をわざと計上し, 来期に
「回復」をはかる会計処理

Big Board
纽约证券交易所的别称
la Bourse de New York
New Yorker Börse
Bolsa de Nueva York
ニューヨーク証券取引所

big business
大企业; 大商界; 巨型企业
de la grosse affaire
Großbetrieb; Großunternehmen;
Großindustrie; großbetriebliche
Wirtschaftsform; Big Business
grandes empresas
大企業, 巨大組織, 財閥

Big Four
澳大利亚四大银行
les quatre plus grosses banques
australiennes
die großen Vier
os cuatro gigantes bancarios
australianos
オーストラリア四大銀行

Big GAAP
大公司公认会计准则
principes comptables
généralement acceptés applicables

Translations appear in the following order: Chinese, French, German, Spanish/Latin American Spanish, and Japanese

aux grosses sociétés
US Bilanzrichtlinien für
Großunternehmen
principios contables para grandes
empresas
大企業に適用されるＧＡＡＰ(一
般に認められた会計原則)

big picture
大形势; 大环境
tableau d'ensemble
hohe Warte; Überblick
panorama global
全体像

big swinging dick
大金融贸易商
opérateur financier très prospère
ausgesprochen erfolgreicher
Wertpapierhändler;
Erfolgsmensch
intermediario(-a) financiero(-a) de
éxito
凄腕ブローカー

bilateral facility
双边贷款
système de prêt bilatéral
bilaterale Einrichtung
facilidad bilateral
双務的融資供与

bilateral monopoly
双边垄断
monopole bilatéral
bilaterales Monopol
monopolio bilateral
双方独占

bilateral trade
双边贸易
commerce bilatéral
bilateraler Handel
comercio bilateral
双務貿易、二国間貿易

bill¹
票据
traite; note; facture
Rechnung
factura; pagaré; efecto; cuenta
請求書

bill²
开具票据
facturer
in Rechnung stellen; berechnen
envíar una factura
請求する

bill broker
票据经纪人; 汇票经纪人;
贴现经纪人
courtier d'escompte
Wechselmakler(in)
corredor(a) de descuentos
ビル・ブローカー, 手形仲買人,
証券仲買業者

bill discount
票据贴现
escompte sur facture
Wechseldiskont
descuento de efectos
割引手形

bill discounting rate
票据贴现率
taux d'escompte de bon du Trésor
Wechseldiskontsatz
tipo de descuento de efectos
(英大蔵省,
米財務省証券の)割引レート

billing cycle
开票周期
cycle de facturation
Rechnungszyklus; Inkassozyklus;
Fakturierungszyklus
ciclo de facturación
請求書発送周期

bill of entry
报关单; 入港申报表; 报税通知单
déclaration (d'entrée) en douane
Einfuhrerklärung; Zolldeklaration
conocimiento de entrada
通関申告書

bill of exchange
汇票
lettre de change
Wechsel
letra de cambio

bill of goods
货单
connaissement de produits
Warenwechsel
relación de mercancías
商品証明書

bill of lading
提单; 提货单; 运货证
connaissement
Konnossement
carta de porte; conocimiento de
embarque
船荷証券

bill of materials
材料清单
nomenclature
Stückliste
cuenta de materiales
材料仕様書

bill of sale
销售确认单
acte de vente
Verkaufsnote
cuenta de ventas
売買証書

bill payable
应付票据
effet à payer
Wechselverbindlichkeit;

Schuldwechsel; Akzeptobligo
efectos a pagar (cuenta; factura;
pagaré; letra de cambio, etc.)
支払い手形

bill receivable
应收票据
effet à encaisser
Wechselforderung; Besitzwechsel
efectos a cobrar (cuenta; factura;
pagaré; letra de cambio, etc.)
受け取り手形

binary thinker
绝对思维; 极端思维
penseur en noir et blanc
Schwarzweißmaler
persona que piensa en blanco y
negro
二者択一的に考える人

bin card
存料卡
fiche de prélèvement (d'article)
Materialbestandskarte;
Lagerfachkarte
ficha de almacén
棚卸表

bingo card
宾戈卡; 指出版者随杂志发出的
已付邮资的明信片;
读者可凭卡免费函索
广告中有关产品的信息
carte à renvoyer
Antwortkarte in
Veröffentlichungen
encarte publicitario en forma de
postal
折込の返信用葉書広告

biodata¹
个人信息; 个人情报
biodonnées
Personaldaten
datos biográficos
就職希望者の履歴書などから
抜粋したデータ

biodata²
传记资料
biodonnées: biographie placée
dans un document de conférence
ou article dans une publication
périodique
Kurzbiografie
datos biográficos
論文などに添付される
簡略履歴書

biological assets
生物资产
biens biologiques (bétail et plantes
de culture)
biologisches Vermögensanteile
activos biológicos
生物的資産(収穫・屠殺前の動
植物)

biometrics
生物统计学
biométrie
Biometrie
estudio de características
biológicas
生体測定学

biomimicry
生物拟态
biomimétisme
Natürliche Produktion
reducción de desperdicio e
impacto ecológico
生物模倣法

biorhythm
个体生物规律
biorythme
Biorhythmus
biorritmo
バイオリズム

BiRiLiG
德国1985会计指示法
loi allemande sur les directives
pour pratiques comptables
BiRiLig
legislación contable alemana
(1985)
ドイツ財務諸表指令法

birth-death ratio
生死率
rapport natalité-mortalité
Verhältnis Geburten zu
Sterblichkeit
razón de nacimientos-defunciones
生死比率

BIS
国际清算银行
Banque des Règlements
Internationaux
BIS
Asociación de Bancos de Pagos
Internacionales
国際決済銀行

bit[1]
比特; 位; 二进制位
élément binaire
Bit
bit
ビット

bit[2]
比特, 喻指零散信息
morceau (d'information)
Bit
información binaria
少しの情報

bivariate data
双变量数据
données à deux variables
zweidimensionale Daten

datos bivariantes
二変量データ

bivariate distribution
二维(元)分布
distribution à deux variables
zweidimensionale
Normalverteilung
distribución bivariante
二変量分布

black-box engineering
黑箱工程
fabrication d'un composant où le
fournisseur a un contrôle absolu
sur la conception et le contenu du
composant
Schwarzer Kasten;
Blackbox-Ingenieurstechnik;
Blackbox-Engineering
fabricación tipo caja negra
ブラックボックス·エンジニア

black chip
黑人控制公司
compagnie détenue ou gérée par
des noirs
schwarzes Unternehmen
empresa de propiedad o dirigida o
controlada por accionistas negros
黑人会社

**black economic
empowerment**
黑人经济强化
délégation du pouvoir
économique aux noirs
Förderung der schwarzen
Wirtschaft
fomento de propiedad y control de
la economía sudafricana por
negros
ブラック経済推進

black economy
黑市经济; 黑色经济
économie souterraine
Schattenwirtschaft;
Untergrundwirtschaft
economía sumergida
地下経済、非合法的経済活動

black hole
黑洞
trou noir
schwarzes Loch
agujero negro
資源を無限に吸収しながら
利益を出さない企画

black market
黑市
marché noir
Schwarzmarkt
mercado negro
ヤミ市場

black market economy
黑市经济

économie de marché noir
Untergrundwirtschaft;
Schattenwirtschaft
economía sumergida or paralela
闇経済

Black Monday
黑钱; 暗款; 匪报收入
le lundi noir
Schwarzer Montag
lunes negro
ブラック·マンデー

black money
暗款; 黑钱
argent noir
nicht versteuertes; illegal
verdientes Geld
dinero negro
(地下経済で流通する非合法資金,
ブラックマネー

Black Tuesday
黑色星期二
le Mardi noir
Schwarzer Dienstag
martes negro
ブラック·チューズデー

blamestorming
责任追究风暴
séance de blâme-storming
gegenseitige Schuldzuweisung in
der Gruppe
tormenta de culpabilidad
責任追及のための
グループ·ディスカッション

blame-time
责任追究时刻
moment d'attribution du blâme
Zeit der öffentlichen
Bezichtigungen wegen des
Misslingens eines Vorhabens
hora de repartir culpas
責任追及の瞬間

blanket bond
总括式保证保险; 一篮子保险契约
garantie de couverture totale
Sicherungsabtretung;
Pauschalvertrauensschadenver-
sicherung
fianza colectiva
総括抵当権付債券, 包括保証

bleed
打印出界
coupe à vif
Plakat ohne Rand
sangrado
塗り足し

blended rate
混合利率
taux fusionné
Mischzin

---

*Translations appear in the following order: Chinese, French, German, Spanish/Latin American
Spanish, and Japanese*

tasa combinada; tipo combinado
ブレンデッド・レート, 混合金利

blind certificate
不记名调查
pastille d'information de laquelle le
nom de l'utilisateur est omis afin
de protéger sa vie privée, tout en
mettant à disposition des données
collectées aux fins d'études de
marketing
blindes Zertifikat: Cookie, aus dem
der Name der Benutzerin oder des
Benutzers ausgelassen wurde, um
ihre oder seine Privatsphäre zu
schützen, aber gleichzeitig
gesammelte Daten für
Marketingerhebungen verfügbar
zu machen
cookie sin el nombre del usuario
ブラインド・サーティフィケート,
無点検証明

blind entry[1]
无说明分录; 失实的记录
document de consignation en
aveugle
Eingangsrechnung
entrada ciega
盲目記入

blind entry[2]
不加说明的分录
entrée en aveugle
unvollständige Buchung
asiento negro
盲目記入

blind offer
虚盘
offre faite sans connaître le
montant des offres concurrentes
anonymes Angebot
oferta ciega
ブラインド・オファー

blind pool
委任企业同盟
syndicat de placement qui
n'informe de la manière dont il
investit
blindes Kartell; anonymes
Konsortium
sociedad de especulación
秘密企業連合

blindside
突袭
attaque masquée (que la personne
ne peut anticiper)
Ugs. aus dem toten Winkel
angreifen
lado ciego
無防備なところを襲う

blind trust
盲目信托
trust dont le contenu n'est pas
connu du fidéicommissaire

Treuhänder-Verwaltung
fideicomiso ciego
白紙委任

block diagram
方块图,方框图,柱状图,立体图,
结构图
bloc-diagramme
Blockdiagramm
diagrama de bloques
ブロック線図

blocked account
冻结帐户; 限制帐户
compte bloqué
Sperrkonto; gesperrtes Konto
cuenta congelada
閉鎖勘定

blocked currency
封锁货币; 冻结货币
devise bloquée
bewirtschaftete Währung
moneda bloqueada
封鎖通貨

blocked funds
封锁资金
fonds consignés
eingefrorener Fonds
fondos bloqueados
外国為替取引管理のために
封鎖された資金

block grant
分类财政补贴或拨款;
划区限制使用拨款
dotation gouvernementale
pauschale Finanzzuweisung
subvención global
包括補助金, ブロック交付金

blockholder
大户股东
détenteurs de tranches de titres
Aktienpaketinhaber; Blockinhaber
tenedor de paquete de acciones o
títulos
大量株式保持者

block investment
大宗投资
investissement en bloc
Blockinvestition;
Gruppeninvestition
inversión en bloque
ブロック投資

block release
脱产学习
période de libération du travail
alternierende Ausbildung;
Dualsystem
licencia para estudios
勤務者の集中型通学

block trade
大宗交易; 大宗贸易
commerce de (gros) blocs

d'actions
Pakethandel
contratación de bloques de
acciones
大口取引, ブロック・トレード

blow-in
插页广告
inserts de pub
Werbe-Antwortkarte in Zeitschrift
oder Zeitung
encarte publicitario en forma de
postal
折込の返信用葉書広告

blow-off top
止跌回升
montagnes russes boursières
Talfahrt nach rasantem Anstieg
einer Kursnotierung
ascenso y caída súbitos
折込の返信用葉書広告

bludge
逃避工作或靠别人生活
flemmarder ou vivre aux crochets
des autres
sich vor Arbeit drücken
escaquearse; gorronear
(他人の)寄生虫

blue chip
蓝筹股; 热门股票; 大公司股票
de premier ordre
Spitzenwert; Standartpapier;
erstklassige Aktie
de gran liquidez
優良株, 一流株

blue-chip stocks
蓝筹股
titres de premier ordre
Spitzenwerte; erstklassige Aktien;
Standardpapiere
acciones punteras or de primera
clase
優良銘柄

blue-collar job
蓝领工作
travail manuel
Arbeiter, Ugs. Blaumann
trabajo manual
肉体労働職

blue-collar worker
蓝领; 蓝领阶级
travailleur manuel
Arbeiter(in)
obrero(-a)
肉体労働者

blue hair
老年妇女
clientes à la chevelure bleutée
Blauspülungen, in der Werbung
und im Marketing verwendet zur
Beschreibung von Kundinnen im

Seniorenalter
clientela femenina de edad
avanzada
お客様としてのオバタリアン

blueshirt
IBM公司雇员
employé de IBM
Mitarbeiter der Computerfirma
IBM
empleado(-a) de IBM
ＩＢＭ社の社員

blue-sky ideas
突破传统的观念
idées sans but pratique
unrealistische Ideen
propuestas idealistas, no realistas
非現実的なアイデア

blue-sky law
青天法; 证券交易管理法;
股票买卖法
législation protégeant les
investisseurs contre les vendeurs
d'actions sans valeur
Gesetz, dass Investoren gegen
Betrug schützt
leyes estatales estadounidenses
reguladoras de los intercambios
bursátiles
青空法,
ブルースカイ(不正証券取
引禁止)法

blue-sky securities
无价值股票
titres douteux
wertlose Papiere
títulos mobiliarios sin valor
価値のない証券

blur
模糊阶段
période de confusion
Branchenumbruch
transición comercial borrosa, con
cambios rápidos y a gran escala
目が眩むほどの速さで
事業変革が起こること

board dismissal
董事会解职决定
dissolution du conseil
d'administration
Pauschalentlassung; des gesamten
Board of Directors; d.h. aller
Direktoren
cese del consejo de administración
取締役総免職, 役員会の解散

**Board of Currency
Commissioners**
新加坡貨币委员会
organisme d'émission de devises
unique à Singapoure
Währungsbehörde

casa de la moneda
シンガポール紙幣管理局

Board of Customs and Excise
关税与消费税局
Office des douanes
Zollamt
departamento de aduanas y
tributos
英国関税消費税庁

board of directors
董事会
conseil d'administration
Board
junta directiva; consejo de
administración
重役会

Board of Inland Revenue
国内税务局
Office du fisc
Finanzamt
dirección general de tributos
英国内国歳入庁

board of trustees
受托人董事会
conseil des administrateurs
Treuhänderausschuss;
Treuhandgremium; Kuratorium
patronato
(財団などの)理事会

boardroom
(董事会) 会议室
salle du conseil
Vorstandszimmer; Sitzungssaal
sala de juntas
取締役会議室

boardroom battle
董事会内部斗争
conflit interne au conseil
Schlacht; in der Führungsetage
lucha en el consejo de
administración
取締役会内紛,
ボードルーム・バトル

board seat
董事会席位
siège au conseil d'administration
Position im Board of Directors;
Direktorenposition
puesto en el consejo de
administración
取締役の資格権利, 役員議席

body corporate
法人团体
personne morale
juristische Person; Körperschaft
sociedad
法人

body language
体态语言
langage du corps
Körpersprache

lenguaje corporal
ボディー・ランゲージ

body of creditors
债权人委员会
organisation de créanciers
Gesamtheit der Gläubiger
masa de acreedores
債権者団体

body of shareholders
股东大会
organisation d'actionnaires
Gesamtheit der Anleger
accionariado
株主団体

BOGOF
买一赠一
deux pour le prix d'un
Zwei zum Preis von einem
compre dos por el precio de uno
奉仕品

bogus degree
虚假文凭
qualification bidon
betrügerisch gehandeltes Diplom
titulación fantasma
偽学位

boilerplate
样板文件
version passe-partout
standard Vertragsformular
modelo
契約のテンプレート

bona fide
真诚地
(de) bonne foi
in gutem Glauben; z. B.
Bona-Fide-Verkauf bzw. -Kauf
de buena fe
善意の

bona vacantia
无主财产
biens sans maître
bona vacantia
bienes vacantes
無主物

bond[1]
债券; 公债
obligation
Obligation; Anleihe; Rentenwert
bono
支払保証契約, 債務証書, 債券,
拘束

bond[2]
债券契约
obligation
Obligation
bono
債券

Translations appear in the following order: Chinese, French, German, Spanish/Latin American
Spanish, and Japanese

bond³
押金
caution
Kaution
fianza
敷金

bond⁴
抵押債券
obligation hypothécaire
Verpflichtung
obligación
物上担保付き社債

bond anticipation note
債券先期本票
bon d'anticipation sur obligation
Obligationengutschein
vale por pronto pago de bono
長期債借り換え予定証券

bond covenant
債券契約
convention de stipulation
d'obligation
Obligationsverpflichtung
contrato de bono
債券約款

bonded warehouse
保険倉庫
entrepôt des douanes
Freilager; Zolllager
depósito aduanero
保税倉庫

bond equivalent yield
債券等値収益
rendement équivalent sur
obligations
Jahresrendite kurzfristiger
unverzinslicher Wertpapiere;
Rentenertrags-Äquivalent
rentabilidad equivalente a la de los
bonos
債券換算利回り、債券に引き直
した場合の利回り

bond fund
債券基金
société d'investissement à capital
variable
Rentenfonds
fondo de bonos
ボンド(ミューチュアル)ファンド,
債券ファンド

bondholder
債券持有人
porteur d'obligation
Obligationär(in);
Anleihegläubiger(in);
Pfandbriefgläubiger(in)
obligacionista
債権持有者

bond indenture
債券契約

contrat synallagmatique pour
obligations
Anleihevertrag
escritura de emisión de bonos
債券信託証書, 社債契約(書)

bond indexing
債券指数
investissement en obligations
indexé
Anleiheindexierung Anpassung
von Obligationen an die
Lebenshaltungskosten
cotización de bonos
ボンド・インデクシング,
インデックス債投資

bond issue
債券発行
émission d'obligations ou de bons
Obligationsausgabe;
Anleiheemission
emisión de bonos
債券発行

bond quote
債券価格
cours d'obligation
Rentennotierung; Rentenpreis
cotización de bono
債券相場

bond swap
債券交換
échange d'obligations
Anleihe-Swap; Rentenswap
permuta de bonos
債券スワップ, 債券入替取引

bond value
債券値
valeur d'obligation
Anleihebewertung
valor del bono
ボンド・バリュー,
(社債の)転換価格

bond-washing
債券清洗; 剥夺債券紅利
vente d'une obligation du Trésor
américain avec coupon attaché et
son rachat ex-coupon pour obtenir
des avantages fiscaux
Steuerausweichung bei
Wertpapieren
venta y compra de los mismos
valores para no pagar impuestos
納税回避のための債券洗浄

bond yield
債券年収益率
rendement d'obligation
Renditespannen
rendimiento del bono
債券利回り

bonus
奖金

prime
Prämie; Bonus
prima; bonificación
賞与

bonus dividend
紅利股
superdividende
Sonderdividende
dividendo extraordinario
特別配当金

bonus issue
发行红(利)股
émission de prime
Ausgabe von Gratisaktien
dividendo en acciones
無償配当株

bonus offer
有奖促销
offre promotionnelle avec
pourcentage de produit gratuit en
plus
gratis Zugabe
oferta de mayor cantidad por el
mismo precio
お買い得商品

bonus scheme
奖金计划
système de prime
Prämienlohnsystem
sistema de primas
賞与制度

bonus shares
奖励股份(英)
actions gratuites
Gratisaktien
acciones gratuitas
決まった期間以内に
最初の株式を売却しなかった
株主に対して英国政府が
発行した特別株式

book-building
股票定价研究
recherche sur carnet d'ordres (pour
déterminer le prix d'offre de titres
nouvellement émis)
Emissionsverfahren (Emission), bei
dem die Investoren direkt in die
Preisfindung eingebunden werden
precio óptimo de oferta para
nueva emisión
ブック・ビルディング方式,
新規公開株式を決めるために
募集価格を決めるために
行われる需要予測

book cost
帐面成本
coût comptable
Buchwert
coste contable
costo contable
帳簿原価

Translations appear in the following order: Chinese, French, German, Spanish/Latin American Spanish, and Japanese

book-entry
帐面记录; 帐簿记录
écriture (comptable)
buchungsmäßig verwaltet
asiento (contable)
帳簿記入, 記帳

book inventory
帐面盘存
inventaire comptable
Buchinventur
inventario contable
帳簿棚卸し

bookkeeper
簿记员
comptable ou aide-comptable
Buchhalter
contable
簿記係

bookkeeping
簿记
comptabilité
Buchhaltung; Buchführung
teneduría de libros
簿記

bookkeeping barter
簿记易货
troc de comptabilité
bargeldloser Warenaustausch
contabilidad de trueque
記録用として
金額を使う物々交換

bookmark[1]
书签
marque-page informatique
Lesezeichen
marcapáginas; marcador
ブックマーク

bookmark[2]
书签, 喻指信息记忆
faire une pense-bête mentale
vermerken, mit Lesezeichen
versehen
tratar de recordar
覚えておく

book of account
帐簿
registre de comptabilité
Kontobuch; Geschäftsbuch
registro contable
会計帳簿

book of prime/original entry
原始序时分录簿
livre d'écriture originale/première
Kassenbuch
registro de asiento de apertura
原始記入簿

books of prime entry
原始分录簿
livre de première écriture
Kassenbücher

libros de primera partida
原始記入簿

book-to-bill ratio
账面与到款比率
coefficient commandes-factures
Verhältnis von Auftragseingang zu
Ausgangsrechnung
relación entre semiconductores
encargados y facturados
BBレシオ, 帳簿対請求額比率

book transfer
帐面转让
transfert comptable
Umbuchung
transferencia cuenta a cuenta
台帳上の名義書換、有価証券
の帳簿上の譲渡

book value
帐面值
valeur comptable
Buchwert; Nettobuchwert;
buchmäßiger Wert
valor contable
(株式の)帳簿価額、簿価

book value per share
每股帐面值
valeur comptable par action
Buchwert pro Aktie
valor contable por acción
一株当り純資産(額)

Boolean search
逻辑搜索
recherche booléenne
Boolesche Suche
búsqueda booleana
ブール・サーチ

boomerang worker
还巢雇员
employé qui revient travailler chez
son employeur préalable
Bumerang-Arbeiter(in)
trabajador(a) que vuelve a una
antigua empresa
前の会社に戻る人

boot camp
新员工培训
camp d'entraînement pour
nouvelles recrues
Einarbeitungsprogrammen, die
neue Angestellte bis an die
Grenzen ihrer Belastbarkeit
bringen sollen
programa de introducción
exhaustivo
ブート・キャンプ(新入社員
訓練プログラム)

bootstrapping
创业阶段
période de démarrage d'entreprise
Frühphase einer

Firmenneugründung, wo man sich
am Riemen reißen muss
arranque
企業を立ち上げる時期

border crosser
多面手
employé avec transcompétences
Grenzgänger
trabajador(a) polivalente
社内の各部署を超えて多様な
仕事をこなす有能社員

borderless world
无国界世界; 全球一体化
monde sans frontières
globalisierte Internetökonomie
comercio sin barreras
国境なき世界

border tax adjustment
边境税调整
redressement fiscal frontalier
steuerlicher Grenzausgleich
ajuste fiscal en la frontera
国境税調整

borrowing costs
借款成本
frais d'emprunt
Kreditkosten
costes de un préstamo
costos de un préstamo
借入コスト

bosberaad[1]
高层首脑会议
cellule de réflexion stratégique
Planungsstab
estrategia de grupo de expertos
長期戦略を考えるグループ

bosberaad[2]
高层灌木会议
réunion de leaders dans un endroit
isolé
Besprechung
cumbre Bush
ブッシュサミット(指導者会議)

boss
老板; 上级
patron/patronne
Chef(in); Vorgesetzte/r;
Vorarbeiter(in)
jefe(-a)
上司

Boston Box
波士顿箱
modèle utilisé pour analyser le
potentiel d'une compagnie en
établissant la courbe de sa part de
marché par rapport à son taux de
croissance
Boston-Box
matriz de Boston
ボストン・ボックス

Translations appear in the following order: Chinese, French, German, Spanish/Latin American Spanish, and Japanese

Boston Consulting Group matrix
波士顿顾问集团矩阵
matrice du groupe consultatif de Boston
Darstellung der Angebote an Produkten oder Dienstleistungen einer Organisation, die den Wert aller Produktverkäufe (abgebildet in Form einer Kreisfläche) in Beziehung zum Wachstum am jeweils bedienten Markt und zum Marktanteil der Organisation zeigt. Die
grupo de consultoría de Boston sobre métodos de análisis de carteras
ボストン・コンサルティング・グループ・マトリックス

bottleneck
瓶颈; 增产障碍; 薄弱环节
goulet d'étranglement
Engpass
atasco
ボトルネック

bottom fisher
水底捕鱼人; 尤指底价求利的人
investisseur pêcheur de fond
Anleger, der unter Aktien, die vor kurzem an Wert verloren haben, nach Schnäppchen sucht
inversor(a) de oportunidades
バーゲン探し派の投資家

bottom line[1]
帐本底行; 盈亏一览 结算行; 最终结果
résultat financier
Grundgeschäft;;Saldo; buchstäblich unter dem Strich letzte Zeile der Gewinn- und Verlustrechnung; Endverlust; Endgewinn
resultado; saldo final; beneficio
当期損益

bottom line[2]
底线
travail essentiel
Grundgeschäft; mit dem die Organisation den Reingewinn erwirtschaftet
trabajo rentable
純利益損失ライン

bottom-of-the-harbour scheme
一种通过分批变卖资产的逃税方式
stratégie d'évasion fiscale
Steuerumgehungsstrategie
estrategia de evasión legal de impuestos consistente en la liquidación de activos de una empresa y su venta varias veces
「港の底」税金回避策

bottom out
止跌回升
atteindre son niveau le plus bas
den tiefsten Stand (erreichen, die Talsohle verlassen)
tocar fondo
底打ち

bottom-up
筛选; 自下而上
ascendante
von unten nach oben; partizipativ
de abajo a arriba; invertido
ボトム・アップ方式

bottom-up approach
参与式领导
leadership consultatif de la base au sommet
partizipativer Ansatz
enfoque ascendente
下からのアプローチ

bought-in goods
买进部件
composants ou produits achetés tout fait
fremdbezogene Güter; od. Teile
mercancías adquiridas
購入部品, 外注部品

bounce
退支票; (支票)拒付退回出票人; 突然上涨; 股价上扬
refuser
einen Scheck platzen lassen
rechazar
不渡小切手の支払い拒否

bounced cheque
退回的支票
chèque sans provision
geplatzter Scheck
cheque devuelto
不渡り小切手

bourse
证券交易所; 股票交易所; 商品交易所; 货币市场
la Bourse
(europäische) Börse
Bolsa
(特にパリの)株式取引所

box spread
箱型差价交易
stratagème d'arbitrage qui élimine le risque par la vente et l'achat de la même chose
Box Spread
arbitraje en el que se establece una posición beneficiosa con riesgo cero utilizando opciones de compra y de venta
(リスク低減目的の裁定取引における)ボックス・スプレッド

bracket creep
税档潜升; 税级上升
augmentation sur tranche (de taux d'imposition)
schleichende Steuerprogression
tramo del impuesto progresivo
ブラケット・クリープ, 所得階層の漸昇

Brady bond
股升升降指数理论
obligation émise par une nation émergeante ayant comme nantissement des bons du Trésor américains
Brady Bond
bono Brady
ブレディ・ボンド

braindrain
人才外流; 人才流失
exode des cerveaux
Abwanderung; von Wissenschaftlern; Braindrain
fuga de cerebros
頭脳流出

brainiac
奇才; 怪才
zarbi intelligent
Superhirn
cerebro imprevisible
予想できない行動を取る天才社員

brainstorming
头脑风暴
remue-méninges ou brainstorming
Brainstorming; gemeinsame Problembewältigung
tormenta de ideas
ブレーン・ストーミング

branch accounts
分类帐
comptabilité de filiale
finanztechnische Geschäftsbereichsabgrenzung
cuentas de sucursal
支社帳簿

branch office
分店; 分公司; 分支结构 分部; 分会
(agence) succursale
Zweigstelle; Niederlassung; Zweigbüro
agencia; sucursal
支店

branch tax
外国分公司税
impôt sur les filiales (Afrique du Sud)
Zweigstellensteuer
impuestos de sucursal no residente
支店税

Translations appear in the following order: Chinese, French, German, Spanish/Latin American Spanish, and Japanese

brand
品牌
marque (de fabrique)
Marke; Warenzeichen;
Handelsname
marca
ブランド

brand awareness
品牌知名度
notoriété d'une marque (auprès du consommateur)
Markenbewusstsein
reconocimiento de marca;
conciencia de la marca
ブランド認知

brand building
树立品牌
établissement d'une marque
Aufwertung des Warenzeichens
creación de una marca
ブランド確立

brand champion
品牌主管
champion d'une marque
Brand-Manager
responsable de marca
ブランド・マネージャー

brand equity
品牌价值
valeur estimée d'une marque
Markenwert
valor de una marca
ブランド価値

brand extension
品牌扩展
agrandissement d'une marque
Produktdiversifikation
extensión de la marca
ブランド蘇生

brand image
品牌形象
image de marque
Markenprofil; Markenimage;
Markenbild
imagen de la marca
商標イメージ,
ブランド・イメージ

branding
创品牌
attribution de marque
Vertrieb von Markenwaren
asignación de marca
ブランディング

brand leader
主导品牌
marque leader
führende Marke; Spitzenmarke;
Markenführer
marca líder

市場占有率トップのブランド,
ブランドリーダー

brand life cycle
品牌生命周期
cycle de vie d'une marque
Lebensdauer od. Lebenszyklus von Marken; Dreiphasenzyklus von Marken
ciclo vital de una marca
ブランド・ライフ・サイクル

brand loyalty
品牌忠诚度;
(消费者)对牌子的信任
fidélité envers une marque
Markentreue; Markenloyalität
fidelidad a la marca
ブランド忠実度

brand management
商标或厂牌管理
gestion des marques
(commerciales)
Produktmanagement;
Markenpflege
gestión de la marca
(個別製品ごとの
マーケティング
計画策定等の)ブランド管理

brand positioning
品牌定位
positionnement de marque
Markenpositionierung;
Markenausrichtung
posicionamiento de marca
ブランド位置付け

brand recognition
品牌识别
sensibilisation à une marque
Markenerkennung;
Markenassoziation
reconocimiento de la marca
ブランド認識評価

brand value
品牌价值
valeur d'une marque
Wert des Warenzeichens;
Markenwert
valor de la marca
ブランドの価値

brand wagon
品牌策略
tendance de l'utilisation des marques en vogue pour le marketing
Markeneinfluss
utilización de nombres de marca
ブランド重視のマーケティング傾向

brandwidth
品牌知名度
amplitude de marque
Markenerkennung

reconocimiento de marca
ブランドの認知度

BRB
马上回来
je reviens tout de suite
ich komm' gleich zurück
vuelvo enseguida
ちょっと失礼します

breach of contract
违约;违反合同
rupture de contrat
Vertragsverletzung; Vertragsbruch;
Nichterfüllung; eines Vertrags
incumplimiento de contrato
契約違反

breadth-of-market theory
市场幅度理论
théorie de l'ampleur du marché
Analyse der Marktbreite
teoría de la anchura del mercado
(市場の価格変動幅を
ベースとする)ブレドス・
オブ・マーケット理論

breakeven
持平
seuil de rentabilité
Gewinnschwelle
análisis del punto crítico
損益分岐点

breakeven analysis
损益两平分析; 保本分析
analyse du seuil de rentabilité
Gewinnschwellenanalyse;
Break-even-Analyse
análisis del punto crítico
損益分岐(点)分析

breakeven chart
损益两平图; 保本图; 盈亏平衡图
organigramme du seuil de rentabilité
Gewinnschwellen-Diagramm
gráfico del punto crítico
損益分岐(点)図表

breakeven point
收支平衡点; 盈亏临界点;
损益两平点
seuil de rentabilité
Kostendeckungspunkt;
Rentabilitätsgrenze
punto crítico
損益分岐点

breaking-down time
中止时间
temps de remise en état (poste de travail)
Ausfallzeit
tiempo de arranque normal
ワークステーションを
元に戻すための「解体」時間

Translations appear in the following order: Chinese, French, German, Spanish/Latin American Spanish, and Japanese

breakout¹
暴涨或暴跌
décomposition (de données)
Aufgliederung einer Summe
ruptura
内訳

breakout²
突破
évasion (du prix d'un titre
au-dessus de son prix préalable le
plus élevé)
Kursausbruch
ruptura
相場の持ち合い放れ

breakthrough strategy
突破性策略
stratégie (de découverte) capitale
Durchbruchstrategie
estrategia de resultados nuevos e
importantes
現状打破戦略

break-up value
财产清理价值; 拆卖价值
valeur de liquidation
Liquidationswert; Eigenkapital
valor de disolución
清算価値

Bretton Woods
布雷顿森林协定
accord Bretton Woods
Bretton Woods Vereinbarung
acuerdo Bretton Woods
ブレトン・ウッズ

bribery
行贿; 贿赂
corruption
Bestechung; Angebot; od.
Zahlung; von Schmiergeld
soborno
贈収賄

bricks-and-mortar
传统型企业; 传统式操作公司
terme qui décrit les biens
d'équipement et les
immobilisations
Ziegelsteine und Mörtel
comercio tradicional
ブリック・アンド・モルタル

bricolage
利用手头东西制成的物品
bricolage
Bricolage
bricolaje informático
ブリコラージュ

bridge financing
过渡性融资; 临时贷款
financement par prêts-relais
Zwischenfinanzierung
financiación puente
つなぎ資金調達

bridging
过渡
prêt-relais
Überbrückung
financiación transitoria
ブリッジ・ローン

bridging loan
过渡贷款; 临时贷款
prêt de relais
Überbrückungskredit;
Zwischenkredit
préstamo puente
橋渡し融資(借り手の売買間の
時間的ずれを橋渡しする)

brief
摘要; 简介
mission
Thesenpapier
informe
概要

brightsizing
人才流失
réduction des effectifs par
élimination du personnel le plus
brillant
Ausmusterung der intelligentesten
Mitarbeiter beim Personalabbau
reducción de plantilla eliminando a
los trabajadores más inteligentes
優秀な社員を解雇し
人員整理をする

bring forward
承前页
reporter (une somme)
vorbringen; vorverlegen
arrastrar; pasar a cuenta nueva
繰越す

Brisch system
伯瑞奇系统
système de Brisch
Brisch-System
sistema Brisch
ブリスキ・システム

**British Accounting
Association**
英国会计学会
Association des comptables
britanniques
Britischer
Wirtschaftsprüferverband
asociación de contables británicos
英国会計学会

broadband
宽(频)带
bande large
Gehaltsstruktur mit wenigen
Stufen
banda ancha
ブロードバンド通信

broadbanding
加宽等级宽度; 缩减等级层数
élargissement des tranches de
salaires
Umgestaltung der Gehaltsstruktur
in weniger und Stufen
reducción del número de escalas
salariales
ブロードバンド(広帯域給
与体系)

brochure
小册子
brochure
Broschüre; Prospekt
folleto; prospecto
パンフレット

brochureware
产品宣传网页
brochure électronique
Brochureware
folleto electrónico
ブロシャーウエア

broker¹
经纪人
négocier
Handelsmakler; Broker;
Börsenmakler
corredor(a); broker
ブローカー

broker²
经纪人
courtier (de commerce)
Broker
broker
ブローカー

brokerage¹
手续费; 经纪费; 佣金; 回扣
maison de courtage
Maklergeschäft; Courtage;
Maklerprovision
correduría; corretaje
証券会社

brokerage²
经纪人业务
courtage
Aktienmakler
corretaje
株式仲買人

brokerage³
佣金，手续费
courtage
Maklergebühr
comisión de corretaje
委託手数料

brokered market
经纪人操作市场
marché de courtage
von Maklern vermittelter Markt
mercado a través de intermediarios
ブローカー市場

---

*Translations appear in the following order: Chinese, French, German, Spanish/Latin American
Spanish, and Japanese*

broker loan rate
经纪人贷款利率
taux d'emprunt de courtier
kurzfristiges Darlehen
tasa de préstamo a corredores de
Bolsa
証券担保貸付金利,
ブローカー・ローン金利

brownfield site
被遗弃的工业区
site de nouveau développement
industriel ou commercial
Industriestandort; Ödland
zona industrial abandonada
再開発用地

brown goods
家庭娱乐消费品
produits audiovisuels
Unterhaltungselektronik
línea marrón
AV機器

browser
浏览器
outil de navigation
Browser; Suchmaschine
navegador
ブラウザー

B share
'B' 股; 乙级普通股
action B
Aktie mit Bewertung B
acción de clase B
B株

BTW
顺便说一句
au fait
übrigens
a propósito
ちなみに...

bubble economy
泡沫经济
économie de chimère
Seifenblasenkonjunktur
economía de burbuja
バブル経済

bucket shop
投机商号
bureau de courtier marron
Winkelbörse; nicht
konzessionierter Makler
corredores que venden valores
dudosos
株式のノミ屋

bucket trading
投机交易
opérations de courtier marron
Betreiben betrügerischer
Maklergeschäfte; Winkelhandel
mala práctica de intermediarios
financieros
闇売買

budget
预算
budget
Budget; Etat; Haushalt;
Haushaltsplan
presupuesto
予算

budget account
赊销帐; 预算帐户
compte crédit
Kundenkreditkonto
cuenta presupuestaria
予算勘定

budgetary
预算
budgétaire
Haushalts-; Planungs-;
haushaltsmäßig
presupuestario(-a)
予算

budgetary control
预算控制
contrôle budgétaire
Etatkontrolle; Haushaltskontrolle
control de presupuestos
予算統制

budget centre
预算中心，预算单位
centre budgétaire
Planstelle
centro de presupuestos
予算センター

budget committee
预算委员会
comité budgétaire
Haushaltsausschuss
comisión de presupuestos
予算委員会

budget cost allowance
预算成本额度
coûts budgétisés
Plankostenvorgabe; flexibles
Budget
flexibilidad del coste
presupuestario
flexibilidad del costo
presupestario
原価割当予算

budget deficit
预算赤字
déficit budgétaire
Haushaltsdefizit;
Haushaltsfehlbetrag
déficit presupuestario
財政赤字, 予算の赤字

budget director
预算主管
directeur du budget
Finanzdirektor

administrador(a) de presupuestos
予算担当ディレクター

budgeted capacity
预算生产量
capacité prévisionnelle
eingeplante Kapazität
capacidad de presupuesto
計画能力

budgeted revenue
预算收入
revenu budgétisé
eingeplantes Einkommen
ingresos presupuestados
計画収入

budget lapsing
预算退回
caducité de budget
Budgetverfall; Haushaltsverfall
caducidad de presupuesto
(年度末における未使用)
予算の一時削減

budget management
预算管理
gestion de budget
Haushaltsführung
gestión presupuestaria
予算管理

budget manual
预算手册
manuel budgétaire
Budgetvorschrift; Haushaltsplan
manual de presupuestos
予算マニュアル

budget period
预算期
période budgétaire
Haushaltsperiode
período del presupuesto
予算期間

budget slack
预算松弛
relâchement dans la gestion
budgétaire
Haushaltsreserven; Spielraum im
Budget
flojedad presupuestaria
怠慢予算

budget surplus
预算盈余
excédent budgétaire
Budgetüberschuss;
Haushaltsüberschuss
superávit de presupuesto
財政黒字, 予算の黒字,
予算の余剰

buffer inventory
缓冲存货
inventaire tampon
Ausgleichslager
inventario regulador o de

Translations appear in the following order: Chinese, French, German, Spanish/Latin American Spanish, and Japanese

seguridad
缓冲存庫

buffer stock
缓冲存货，保险储备物资
stock tampon
Pufferbestand
fondo de regulación
緩衝在庫

building society
房屋建筑协会; 房屋互助协会
société immobilière
Bausparkasse
banco de crédito hipotecario
住宅共済組合

bulk handling
散货装卸
manutention de produits en vrac
Massenguthandhabung
manipulación a granel
大量債権処理

bull
买空人; 买空的证券投机者; 多头
haussier
Haussier; Haussespekulant(in)
alcista; al alza
買方, 強気筋

bulldog
无情进攻
s'acharner contre un problème
ein Problem unaufhaltsam
angehen
atacar un problema sin respiro
がむしゃらに問題に取り組む

bulletin board
公告牌
tableau d'affichage
Anschlagtafel; schwarzes Brett
tablón de anuncios
電子掲示板

bullet loan
一次还本贷款; 一次性偿还的贷款;
子弹式贷款
emprunt remboursable
uniquement à l'échéance
Anleihe mit Endfälligkeit
préstamo reembolsable de una
sola vez al vencimiento
一括返済ローン

bullish
看涨的
haussier
steigend; haussierend;
optimistisch
alcista; al alza
先高観

bull market
牛市; 多头市场
marché haussier
Haussemark
mercado alcista o al alza
強気相場, 上向き相場, 強気市場

bullshit bingo
难懂术语游戏
loto du charabia
Spiel, bei dem man alle abstrusen
Jargon – Begriffe zählt
juego consistente en identificar el
uso de jerga incomprensible
わけの分からない造語の
出る回数を数えて遊ぶゲーム

bull spread
多头价差
marge à la hausse
Hausse-Spread
diferencial alcista
ブル・スプレッド

bump up
升级
faire monter d'un cran
jdn. höher einstufen
cambiar a alguien a una categoría
superior
ホテル・飛行機などで
乗客を上のクラスに上げる

bundle
配置; 免费配置
intégrer
Paket
agrupamiento
多数の商品やサービスを
一つのバンドルとして売る

bundling
搭配; 捆绑销售
mise en forfait
Bündelung
agrupamiento en paquetes
多数の商品やサービスを
一つのバンドルとして売る

Bundy
出勤记时
Bundy: système de pointage qui
enregistre les heures d'arrivée et
de départ du personnel sur le lieu
de travail
Stempeluhr
sistema de control de la hora de
entrada y salida de los empleados
勤務時間記録のタイムレコーダー

Bundy off
签到签退
pointer quand on quitte son lieu
de travail
stempeln
fichar a la salida
marcar tarjeta a la salida
タイムカードを押す

Bundy on
签到签退
pointer quand on arrive sur son
lieu de travail
stempeln
fichar a la entrada

marcar tarjeta a la entrada
タイムカードを押す

bureaucracy
官僚机构; 官僚政治; 官僚体制
bureaucratie
Bürokratie
burocracia
官僚主義

bush telegraph
小道消息
téléphone de brousse
Buschtelegramm
radio macuto
口コミ, 情報網

**Business Accounting
Deliberation Council**
企业会计商议协会(日本)
comité de délibération de
comptabilité d'entreprise
Kartellamt
comisión reguladora de
contabilidades consolidadas
企業会計審議会

Business Activity Statement
商业活动说明
déclaration d'activité commerciale
Geschäftsaktivitätenbericht
informe sobre ingresos y
pagos fiscales de una
empresa
営業活動報告書

business administration[1]
行政管理业务行政
administration des affaires
Betriebswirtschaft
administración de empresas
経営管理

business administration[2]
业务行政
administration commerciale
Unternehmensführung
administración de empresas
経営管理

business card
名片
carte de visite (professionnelle)
Visitenkarte
tarjeta de visita
名刺

business case
商业价值
cas commercial
Geschäftsfall
valor comercial de una propuesta
ビジネス・ケース(実情に基づ
いたビジネス提案)

business cluster
商务联盟
groupement commercial
Firmenallianz; Firmengruppierung

Translations appear in the following order: Chinese, French, German, Spanish/Latin American Spanish, and Japanese

alianza entre empresas de un
sector
ビジネス・クラスター(集団)

business combinations
商业合并
combinaisons d'entreprises
Fusion
fusión de empresas
企業結合

business continuity
企业的持久性
continuité des activités
commerciales
Unternehmenskontinuität;
Kontinuität der Geschäftstätigkeit
continuidad de la actividad
empresarial
ビジネス継続性

Business Council of Australia
澳大利亚商业委员会
Conseil australien des affaires
Geschäftsrat von Australien
consejo australiano de la empresa
オーストラリア商業協議会

business cycle
商业周期
cycle commercial
Konjunkturzyklus;
Konjunkturverlauf;
Konjunkturphase
ciclo económico
景気循環, 景気変動

business efficiency
经营效率
efficacité commerciale
Leistungsfähigkeit;
Wirtschaftlichkeit; Produktivität
eines Unternehmens
eficacia empresarial
ビジネス効率

business entity concept
经营单位概念
concept de l'entité commerciale
Business Entity Concept
concepto del negocio como
persona jurídica
説明責任

business ethics
商业道德
code moral ou éthique
commerciale
Unternehmensethik; ethische
Unternehmenspolitik
ética empresarial
ビジネス倫理

business failure
倒闭
entreprise en échec ou en difficulté
Unternehmenspleite; Insolvenz
quiebra
企業倒産

business game
交易模仿游戏
jeu de simulation commerciale
Unternehmensspiel
juego de empresas
ビジネス・ゲーム

business gift
商务礼品
cadeau d'entreprise
Werbegeschenk
regalo comercial
企業贈答品

business intelligence
商业情报; 商业机密
RG d'entreprise
Geschäftsinformationen, die von
strategischem Nutzen sein können
información estratégica
戦略的ビジネス情報

**business interruption
insurance**
业务中断保险
assurance en cas d'interruption
d'activités commerciales
Betriebsunterbrechungsversicherung
seguro de lucro cesante; seguro
contra interrupción de negocios
営業利益保険

business name
公司名称
nom d'entreprise ou nom
commercial
eingetragener Firmenname
razón social
英国での法人の登録名称

business objective
业务目标
objectif commercial
Unternehmensziel; Betriebszweck
objetivo de negocios
営業目標

business plan
商务计划; 业务计划
plan de développement
Geschäftsplan;
Unternehmensplanung
plan comercial
経営計画

**business process
re-engineering**
业务流程重组
procédé commercial réinventé
Umgestaltung der
Geschäftsprozesse
reingeniería de procesos
empresariales
BPR(リエンジニアリング)

business property relief
运营资产继承税免除

dégrèvement sur immobilier
commercial
Steuervergünstigung
exención fiscal patrimonial de
empresa
英国での事業用資産の控除

business rates
商业税
impôt indirect sur les entreprises
Britische Gewerbesteuer
impuestos comerciales locales
ビジネス・レート
(法人事業税に相当)

business risk
商务风险; 业务风险
risque commercial
unternehmerisches Risiko;
Geschäftsrisiko; Investitionsrisiko
riesgo comercial
ビジネス・リスク

business school
商业管理学院; 商学院
école de commerce
Handelshochschule;
wirtschaftswissenschaftliche/
betriebswirtschaftliche Fakultät
escuela de negocios
ビジネス・スクール

business segment
营业部门
segment commercial ou
d'entreprise
Geschäftssegment
segmento del negocio
事業部門

business strategy
企业战略; 经营战略; 商务战略
stratégie d'entreprise
Unternehmensstrategie
estrategia comercial
営業戦略

**Business Times Industrial
index**
商业时代工业指数
indice de 40 actions de Singapour
et de Malaysie
Industrieaktienindex
Índice 40 (acciones de Singapur y
Malasia)
ビジネスタイムズ工業指標

business transfer relief
企业并购税务减免
allègement fiscal pour transfert
commercial
Steuererleichterung bei
Unternehmensübergängen
descuento fiscal por venta
de un negocio a cambio de
acciones
(英米の)資産取引税控除

Translations appear in the following order: Chinese, French, German, Spanish/Latin American Spanish, and Japanese

business unit
业务单位
unité commerciale
Sparte; Geschäftsbereich
unidad de negocios
事業体, 事業部門

bust-up proxy proposal
替代破产协议
proposition de faillite par
procuration
Bankrott-Vollmachtanweisung
propuesta hostil
バストアップ・プロクシー提案

busymeet
业务会议
séance de travail
Geschäftagung
reunión de negocios
ビジネス・ミーティング

butterfly spread
价差; 蝶形差幅
marge papillon
Butterfly Spread; Stellagegeschäft
auf der Basis von drei
Terminkontrakten
margen de mariposa
バタフライ・スプレッド

button
交互式按纽
case-pub sur une page Web
Werbe-Schaltfläche
botón
ボタン

buy and hold
购买和控股
stratégie de l'achat-conservation
auf lange Sicht investieren;
langfristig investieren
compra y retención
購入保持戦略

buy and write
期权买卖
stratégie de l'achat sans
décote
Buy and Write Strategy
compra y suscripción
バイライト

buy-back
回购股票
rachat (de titres)
Rückkauf
rescate; recompra
バイバック, 買戻し

buy-down
买低
remboursement de montants du
capital sur une hypothèque
außerordentliche Tilgung
tasa de interés reducida mediante

el pago de puntos de descuento
adicionales
バイダウン, 金利買い下げ

buyer¹
买方; 买主; 采购员
acquéreur
Käufer(in); Kunde; Kundin;
Abnehmer(in)
comprador(a)
買い手

buyer²
采购员
acheteur professionnel
Einkäufer
comprador(a)
バイヤー

buyer's guide
买方指南
guide d'acheteur
Katalog
guía de compradores
購入ガイド

buyer's market
买方市场
marché à la baisse
Käufermarkt
mercado de compradores
買い手市場

buy in
买回; 买进
acheter pour le compte du
vendeur
sich eindecken; ankaufen
comprar
バイ・イン, 処分買い

buying economies of scale
购买经济规模
économies d'échelle d'achat
Kostendegression; Skalenerträge;
Größenvorteile im Einkauf
economías de escala compradoras
購買規模の経済性

buy on close
收盘时买入
achat à la clôture
Kauf zum Schlusskurs
comprar al cierre
引け値買い注文

buy on opening
开盘时买入
achat à l'ouverture
Kauf zum Eröffnungskurs
comprar a la apertura
寄り付き買い注文

buy out¹
全部买下(一家企业的全部权益;
股份)
racheter
Aufkauf

comprar la parte de
買占め

buy out²
买下产权; 买下股权
désintéresser quelqu'un
aufkaufen (von Unternehmen)
comprar la parte de
バイ・アウト, 買取

buy-out¹
收购
rachat d'une entreprise active;
aussi appelé une acquisition
Aufkauf; Übernahme
adquisición
バイ・アウト

buy-out²
购入全部股权
rachat de la totalité des titres d'une
entreprise détenus par quelqu'un
d'autre, aussi appelé une
acquisition
Übernahme; Akquisition
adquisición de todas las acciones
バイ・アウト, 企業買収

buy-out³
职业退休金离职转移权
rachat: option de transfert des
prestations d'un plan de retraite
professionnelle, quand un
employé quitte une entreprise
Möglichkeit der Übertragung eines
betrieblichen Pensionsplans bei
Verlassen eines Unternehmens
propuesta de comprar de control
バイ・アウト(離職に当り企業
年金を書換えるオプション)

buy stop order
限价下订购单
ordre d'achat sur prix limite
Kauf-Stopp-Auftrag
orden de compra de pérdida
limitada
逆指値買い注文

buzz group
研讨小组(头脑风暴的一种)
petit groupe de discussion formé
pour une mission spécifique
Fachgruppe
grupo de discusión
小グループの合議体,
バズセッションのグループ,
創造的思考集団

buzzword-compliant
因特网最新术语行家
familier avec le tout dernier jargon
Internet
der neuesten Internetsprache
mächtig
al día de la jerga de Internet
インターネット関係の
流行語が話せる人

Translations appear in the following order: Chinese, French, German, Spanish/Latin American Spanish, and Japanese

BV
船级协会; 维里他斯船级社
SARL
GmbH
término holandés para una
sociedad limitada
(デンマーク)株式会社

b-web
网上商务
groupe d'entreprises
complémentaires qui se
rassemblent sur Internet
eMarket; Extranet
negocios web (varios negocios
complementarios en la Internet)
ビジネス・ウェブ

by-bidder
伪装成顾客的人
sous-enchérisseur
Scheinbieter(in)
licitante ficticio
空せり人

bylaws
细则，公司章程
statuts
Satzungen
estatutos
定款

bypass trust
继承信托
trust qui fait administrer un legs
par fidéicommis à l'intention de
personnes autres que le
bénéficiaire principal, en vue
d'obtenir des avantages fiscaux
Erbschaftssteuerumgehungsanlage
fideicomiso para reducir la
cantidad de impuestos sucesorios
バイパス信託, 迂回的信託

by-product
副产品
dérivé ou sous-produit
Nebenprodukt; Kuppelprodukt;
Koppelprodukt
subproducto
副産物

byte
字节; 位元组
octet
Byte
byte
バイト

cache
高速缓冲存储器
cachette; cache
Pufferspeicher; Cachespeicher
caché; memoria caché
キャッシュ

Cadbury Report
开德波瑞报告
rapport Cadbury
Bericht des Cadbury-Ausschusses
über die finanziellen
Gesichtspunkte der
Unternehmensführung
Informe Cadbury de 1992 sobre
los aspectos financieros, contables
y de gobierno en general de las
sociedades
キャドベリー報告書

CAD/CAM
电脑辅助设计和制造
CA/FA (conception automatisée/
fabrication automatisée)
CAD/CAM; computergestützte
Konstruktion; und Fertigung
CAD/CAM
キャド(CAD)キャム(CAM),
コンピュータ援用設計
コンピュータ援用製造(生産)

call
股票购买权; 购买选择权
appel de fonds
Kaufoption
obligación
コール, 株式買付選択権

callable
可赎回的; 可收回的
avec provision d'achat
abrufbar; kündbar
exigible
コーラブル,
(債券)の繰上げ償還ができる,
(優先株の)任意償還ができる

call centre
电话咨询中心
centre d'appel
Anrufzentrale; Telefonzentrale;
Kundendienstzentrale
centro de atención telefónica
コールセンター

called-up share capital
催缴股本
capital-actions appelé
eingefordertes Kapital
capital social exigido
払込資本

call money
短期放款
argent au jour le jour
tägliches Geld; Tagesgeld
dinero exigible
コールマネー, 借入金,
当座借入金

call off
取消
système de stock facturé sur
utilisation
Abrufsystem: Lagerbestände

werden beim Kunden aufbewahrt
und erst bei Einsatz in Rechnung
gestellt
inventario en poder de clientes que
se factura a su utilización /
cancelación
コール・オフシステム

call payment
通知付款
paiement appelé
Teilzahlung für Aktien
pago parcial por valores
償還支払い

call provision
提前收回条款
provision d'achat
Rückkaufklausel;
Kündigungsklausel
estipulación de rescate
任意償還条項

campaign
运动; 一系列行动
campagne (publicitaire)
Werbekampagne
campaña
キャンペーン

camp on the line
持电话长期等待
poireauter au bout du fil
in der Warteschleife hängen
larga espera en línea
電話で長く保留にされる

can
解雇; 辞退
virer quelqu'un
jemanden eindosen
echar a alguien
首にする

**Canadian Institute of
Chartered Accountants**
加拿大执业会计师协会
Institut canadien des
experts-comptables agréés
Kanadisches Institut für vereidigte
Wirtschaftsprüfer
instituto canadiense de contables
colegiados
カナダ勅許会計士協会

cap
利率上限
limite maximale
Obergrenze; Höchstsatz
techo; cap
(貸付利息の)上限, キャップ

CAPA
亚太会计师组织
organisation parapluie pour un
certain nombre d'organismes
comptables d'Asie et du Pacifique
CAPA

Translations appear in the following order: Chinese, French, German, Spanish/Latin American Spanish, and Japanese

conjunto de organismos contables
de Asia Pacífico
アジア太平洋会計士連盟

capacity
生产能力; 设备能力
capacité
Kapazität
capacidad
生産能力

capacity planning
生产能力规划
planification des moyens de
production
Kapazitätsplanung
planificación de la capacidad
許容工数計画

capacity ratios
coefficients de capacité ou de
potentiel
Kapazitätskennzahlen;
Kennziffern für die
Leistungsfähigkeit
índice de capacidad, razón de
capacidad
設備利用率

**capacity requirements
planning**
生产需求规划
planification des exigences des
moyens de production
Kapazitätsbedarfsplanung
planificación de los requisitos de la
producción
能力所要量計画

capacity usage variance
生产能力用量差异
écarts dus à la capacité utilisée
Varianz der Kapazitätsauslastung
diferencia en pérdida o ganancia
respecto a las expectativas
設備稼働変動

capacity utilisation[1]
生产能力利用
utilisation de la capacité
Kapazitätsauslastung
capacidad
稼働率、設備稼働率

capacity utilisation[2]
生产能力利用
utilisation de la capacité
Kapazitätsauslastung
capacidad utilizada
生産能力利用

Caparo case
开普罗案例
en Angleterre, décision juridique
prise par la chambre des Lords en
1990, comme quoi les vérificateurs
de comptes ont un devoir de bon
soin envers les actionnaires actuels

(et non potentiels) en tant que
groupe, et non en tant
qu'individus
Caparo-Fall
decisión de la Cámara de los Lores
de 1990 (RU) recordando a los
auditores su deber con los
accionistas como colectivo y no
como individuos
現在の株主全体に対する
監査役の義務を定めた
英国貴族院の判決

capital
资本; 资金
capital
Kapital; Vermögen; Eigenkapital
capital
純資産

capital account
资本帐户
compte de capital
Kapitalkonto; Kapitalbilanz
cuenta de capital
資本勘定, 出資金勘定

capital allowances
资本减免额，投资免税优惠
déductions fiscales pour
investissements
Abschreibung für Abnutzung
AfA
desgravaciones sobre bienes de
capital
英国および
アイルランドにおける
税務上の固定資産の減価償却

capital appreciation
资本升值
plus-value de capital
Vermögenszuwachs
revalorización del capital
資本増加, キャピタルゲイン

capital appreciation fund
资本增值基金
SICAV (société d'investissements à
capital variable) de plus-value de
capital
Thesaurierungsfonds
fondo de revalorización del capital
(元本順次増価型の)キャピタ
ル・アプレシエーション・ファ
ンド

capital asset
资本资产; 固定资产
valeur immobilisée
Kapitalanlagegegenstand
activo permanente o fijo
固定資産, 資本資産, 基本資産

capital asset pricing model
固定资产定价模式
modèle de fixation de prix de
valeurs immobilisées

Kapitalanlagepreis-Modell
modelo de fijación de precios del
activo fijo
資本資産価格モデル

capital budget
资本预算
budget d'investissement
Investitionsbudget; Kapitalbudget;
Investitionsplanung
presupuesto de capital
資本予算, 資本支出予算

capital budgeting
资本预算, 投资预算
budgétisation d'investissement
Investitionsrechnung
presupuestación del capital
設備投資計画

capital commitment
资本承诺
engagement des capitaux
Kapitalbindung
asunción de capital; suscripción de
capital
資本支出

capital consumption
资本消耗
consommation de capital
Kapitaleinforderung
consumo de capital
資本減耗

capital controls
资本控制法规
réglementations de capital
Kapitallenkung;
Investitionslenkung
controles sobre el capital
資本規制

capital cost allowance
资本成本减免额;
资本折旧免税优惠
déduction fiscale pour coût
d'investissement (Canada)
steuerliche Abschreibung für
Kapitalanlagegegenstände
desgravación de los costes de
inversión
desgravación de los costos de
inversión
(カナダの)資本コスト控除

capital costs
资产成本
coûts d'investissement
Kapitalkosten
coste de capital
costo de capital
資本費用

capital deepening
资本深化
intensification du capital
Verbesserungsinvestition

---

*Translations appear in the following order: Chinese, French, German, Spanish/Latin American
Spanish, and Japanese*

intensificación del capital
資本深化

capital employed
动用的资本，运用的资本总额
capitaux utilisés (valeurs
immobilisées plus actif réalisable,
moins le passif exigible à court
terme)
eingesetztes Kapital
activos netos; capital en uso
投下資本純資産

capital expenditure
资本支出; 资本开支
mise de fonds
Kapitalaufwand;
Investitionsausgaben
gastos de capital
資本的支出, 設備投資,
投資的経費

capital flight
资本外逃; 资本抽离
fuite des capitaux
eingesetztes Kapital;
Nettogesamtvermögen
fuga de capitales
資本逃避

capital formation
资本形成
formation du capital
Anlageinvestitionen;
Bestandsveränderungen;
Kapitalbildung; Vermögensbildung
formación de capital
資本形成

capital funding planning
资本基金规划
planification de financement des
investissements
Kapitalfinanzierungsplanung
plan de financiación de capital
資本金プラン

capital gain
资本收益; 资本利得
plus-value
Kapitalflucht;
Kapitalabwanderung
ganancia de capital; plusvalía
売却益

capital gains distribution
资本收益分配
distribution des plus-values
Ausschüttung realisierter
Kursgewinne
distribución de ganancias de
capital
資本利得配分

capital gains reserve
资本收益储备
réserve sur les plus-values
(avantage fiscal canadien)

Kapitalzuwachsreserve
reserva de las ganancias de capital
(カナダの)資本利得留保

capital gains tax
资本收益税
impôt sur les plus-values
Veräußerungsgewinn;
Kapitalgewinn; realisierter
Kursgewinn
impuesto sobre ganancias de
capital
譲渡課税

capital gearing
资本杠杆率; 资本结合率
rapport d'endettement sur capital
Kapitalstruktur; Leverage-Effekt
apalancamiento de capital
梃子操作,
キャピタル・ギアリング

capital goods
生产资料; 资本货物
biens d'équipement
Kapitalgüter; Anlagegüter
bienes de capital
資本財

capital inflow
资本内流; 资本流入
afflux de capital
Kapitalzufluss
afluencia de capital
資本流入

capital instruments
资本工具
instruments de financement de
capital
Finanzinstrumentarium
instrumentos de capital
資本調達手段

capital-intensive
资本集约的; 资本密集的;
需大量资本的
à forte intensité de capital
kapitalintensiv; anlagenintensiv
que requiere mucho capital
資本集約的な

capital investment appraisal
资本投资鉴定
évaluation du capital engagé ou
investi
Investitionsrechnung
evaluación de la inversión de
capital
資本投資評価

capitalisation[1]
股票资本市值; 市场资本总额
capitalisation
Kapitalausstattung;
Kapitalisierung
capitalización
資本、資本構成、時価総額

capitalisation[2]
资本化
capitalisation
Kapitalisierung
capitalización
資本化

capitalisation issue
资本流出; 发行股票
attribution d'actions gratuites
Ausgabe von Gratisaktien
dividendo en acciones
資本組入れ発行、無償増資、
無償発行

capitalisation rate
资本收益比
taux de capitalisation
Kapitalisierungsfaktor
tasa de capitalización
資本化率

capitalisation ratio
资本化比率
coefficient de capitalisation
Kapitalisierungsquote
coeficiente de capitalización
資本化比率

capitalise[1]
提供资金; 投资
capitaliser
kapitalisieren
capitalizar
資本供給する, 投資する

capitalise[2]
变成资本
capitaliser
kapitalisieren
capitalizar
資産計上する

capitalism
资本主义
capitalisme
Kapitalismus
capitalismo
資本主義

capitalist
资本家
capitaliste
Kapitalist(in)
capitalista
資本家、資本主義者

capital levy
资本税; 财产税
prélèvement sur le capital
Vermögensabgabe
impuesto sobre el capital
資本課徴, 資本税

capital loss
资本损失
moins-value
Kapitalverlust;
Kapitalveräußerungsverlust

Translations appear in the following order: Chinese, French, German, Spanish/Latin American Spanish, and Japanese

pérdida de capital
売却損

capital maintenance concept
资本维护概念
concept de maintenance du capital
Kapitalerhaltungskonzept
concepto que determina la
definición del beneficio con
distintos sistemas contables
資本維持概念

capital market
资本市场; 资金市场
marché des capitaux
Kapitalmarkt
capital de mercados
資本市場、起債市場

capital project management
投资方案管理
gestion de projet à capital
Investitionsprojektleitung
gestión de proyectos con inversión
de capital
資本プロジェクト管理

capital property
资本财产
biens de capital
Kapitalvermögen
propiedad del capital
(カナダ税法上の)資本資産

capital ratio
资本比率
rapport sur capital: revenu qu'a
une compagnie, sous forme de
fractions des immobilisations
corporelles
Eigenkapitalquote
razón de capital; razón capital;
razón efectiva
資本比率、自己資本比率

capital rationing
资金合理分配; 资金限额
rationnement de capital
Kapitalzuteilung
racionamiento del capital
資本の配分, 資本の割当,
資本制限

capital redemption reserve
资本偿还储备
réserve pour amortissement de
capital
Rückkaufeinlage;
Einlösungsrücklage
reserva para redención o rescate
de sus propias acciones
資本償還準備金

capital reserves
资本存量
réserves et provisions
Kapitalreserve; Reservekapital

reservas de capital
資本準備金

capital resource planning
资本性资源规划
planification des ressources en
capital
Eigenmittelplanung
planificación de recursos a largo
plazo
資本資源プラン

capital stock
股本
capital-actions
Aktienkapital; Grundkapital
capital social; accionariado
資本金,
株式額面資本総額、資本ストック

capital structure
资本结构; 资本构成
structure de capital
Kapitalstruktur
estructura de capital
資本構成

capital sum
本金总额; 退赔额
capital global
Kapitalsumme
suma de capital
傷害保険の約定給付金、一
時払い保険金

capital surplus
资本盈余
excédent de capital
Kapitalrücklage
superávit
資本余剰金

capital transactions
资本交易
transactions en capital
Kapitaltransaktionen
transacciones de capital
資本取引

capital transfer tax
资本转账税
impôt sur le transfert de capitaux
Vermögenssteuer
impuesto sobre las transferencias
de capital
資本譲渡税

capital turnover
资本周转率
chiffre d'affaires sur capital
Kapitalumschlag
rotación del capital
資本回転(率)

capital widening
资本扩大
augmentation de capital
Erweiterungsinvestition
ampliación del capital
資本拡張

captive finance company
附属金融公司
compagnie financière captive
Unternehmensbank
sociedad financiera cautiva
金融子会社

captive insurance company
附属保险公司
compagnie d'assurance captive
Captive Insurance Company
empresa de seguros cautiva
保険子会社

capture
资金的划转
saisie
Erfassung
captura
キャプチャー

cardholder
持卡人
titulaire de carte (de crédit)
Kreditkarteninhaber(in)
titular de una tarjeta
カードホルダー, カード保有者

**card-not-present merchant
account**
不需卡商业帐户
compte commercial sans présence
physique nécessaire pour
transactions par cartes de crédit
Bankkonto, das es Händlern im
elektronischen Geschäftsverkehr
gestattet,
Kreditkartentransaktionen zu
bearbeiten, ohne dass der Käufer
dabei persönlich anwesend ist
cuenta que permite transacciones
sin la presencia física del titular
カード・ナット・プレゼント・
マーチャント口座

career anchor
职业指南
point d'ancrage professionnel
Karriere-Anker
factores cruciales en la carrera
キャリア・アンカー(職業信念)

career break
职业间断
interruption de vie professionnelle
planifiée et soutenue par
l'employeur, en principe pour une
période prédéterminée
Unterbrechung der Berufstätigkeit
interrupción de la carrera
就業中止

career change
职业变换
étape dans un plan de carrière
Arbeitsplatzwechsel; berufliche
Veränderung

---

*Translations appear in the following order: Chinese, French, German, Spanish/Latin American
Spanish, and Japanese*

cambio profesional
職種変更

career development
职业发展
déroulement de carrière;
développement professionnel
beruflicher Aufstieg; Aufbau einer
Karriere
desarrollo profesional
キャリア開発

career ladder
职业生涯阶梯
échelle professionnelle
Karriereleiter
escala de promoción
出世階段

career path
职业路线
progression de carrière
(professionnelle)
beruflicher Werdegang
trayectoria profesional
昇進ルート

career pattern
职业模式
structure de carrière
Muster der beruflichen
Entwicklung
perfil de la carrera profesional
キャリア・パターン

careline
电话咨询服务
ligne d'assistance (téléphonique)
Hotline
servicio de asistencia
お客様相談センター

caring economy
关爱型经济
économie bienveillante
soziale Marktwirtschaft
economía con toques humanos
人と企業の友好的な関係に
基いた経済

carriage inwards
购货运费
frais de port pour achat
Frachtkosten
gastos de entrega de bienes
comprados
購買時運送費

carriage outwards
销货运费
frais de port pour vente
Versandkosten
gastos de entrega de bienes
vendidos
販売時運送費

carrier
通讯网络提供商
fournisseur de services
d'infrastructure de réseau

Telekommunikationsunternehmen
operador de telecomunicaciones
通信事業者

carrying cost
持有成本
frais de stockage
Versandkosten inkl. Lagerung und
Versicherung
coste incidental
costo incidental
保管費

cartel
卡特尔; 卡泰尔; 同业联合垄断
cartel
Kartell
cártel
カルテル

cartogram
比较统计地图，统计图; 统计地图
cartogramme
Kartogramm
cartograma
統計地図

cash
现金
espèces
Kasse; Bargeld; liquide Mittel
efectivo; metálico
現金

cash account
现金帐; 现金帐目
compte de caisse
Kassakonto
cuenta de caja
現金勘定

cash accounting[1]
现金会计
comptabilité de caisse
Kassenkontoführung
contabilidad de caja
現金主義会計

cash accounting[2]
现金会计学
comptabilité de caisse
zahlungsorientiertes
Rechnungswesen
contabilidad de caja
英国付加価値税制度における
現金会計方式

cash advance
预付现金
crédit de caisse
Barkredit
anticipo de caja
現金前貸し

cash at bank
活期存款，银行现金
fonds en banque
Bankguthaben
saldos disponibles en cuentas

bancarias
当座預金

cash available to invest
可投资的现有现金
liquidités disponibles pour
investissement
investitionsfähiges Kapital
activo disponible para invertir
投資用現金

cashback
退款
remboursement promotionnel
Cashback
reintegro en efectivo tras la
compra de un producto
キャッシュバック

cash basis
现金基础
comptabilité basée sur caisse
Istsystem; Buchführung auf
Einnahmen- und Ausgabenbasis
base de efectivo
現金主義

cash bonus
现金红利; 现金分红
prime sur dividende
Bardividende
dividendo extraordinario
現金払配当金

cashbook
现金出纳簿
livre de caisse
Kassenbuch
diario de caja
現金出納帳

cash budget
现金(收支)预算
budget de trésorerie
Kassenbudget
presupuesto de caja
現金予算

cash contract
现金合同
contrat en espèces
Liefervertrag
contrato en efectivo
当日決済取引、即日決済取引

cash conversion cycle
现金周转期
cycle de conversion en espèces
Umschlagszeit
ciclo de conversión de efectivo
現金循環

cash cow[1]
现金牛; 稳赚项目; 奶牛; 摇钱树
poule aux oeufs d'or
Goldesel
gallina de los huevos de oro;
producto chollo

Translations appear in the following order: Chinese, French, German, Spanish/Latin American Spanish, and Japanese

キャッシュ・カウ(投資や広告をせずに確実に安定した現金収入を生み出すもの)

cash cow²
现金牛 , 稳赚项目
vache à lait
Unternehmen mit hohen Liquiditätsreserven
fuente de ingresos
キャッシュ・カウ(確実で安定した収入を生み出す事業)

cash crop
经济作物; 商品化农作物; 现金作物
culture commerciale
Agrarprodukt für den Export; Cash-Crop; Verkaufsproduktion
cultivo comercial
换金作物

cash deficiency agreement
现金短缺协议
accord d'avance de fonds en numéraires
Fehlbetragsausgleich
acuerdo de inversión para cubrir deficiencias de capital
キャッシュ補塡契約

cash discount
现金折扣 , 付现折扣
remise au comptant
Skonto
descuento por pronto pago
现金割引

cash dividend
现金红利(股息)
dividende en espèces
Bardividende
dividendo en efectivo
现金配当

cash equivalents
现金等价物
équivalent en espèces
Barwertepapiere
equivalentes de caja
现金同等物

cash float
现金浮动
fonds de caisse
Wechselgeld
cambio disponible para vueltas en caja
釣り銭用の小銭

cash flow
现金流动; 资金流动
marge brute d'autofinancement
Barmittelfluss; Cashflow
cash-flow; flujo de caja
キャッシュ・フロー

cash-flow coverage ratio
现金流量担保比率
coefficient de couverture de trésorerie
Kassenbestandsdeckung; Cashflow-Deckungsquote
coeficiente de cobertura de obligaciones financieras por ingresos
キャッシュフロー・カバレッジ・レシオ、(所得に対する)キャッシュフロー倍率

cash-flow life
非固定收入生活方式
style de vie cash-flow
Cashflow
estilo de vida de autónomo
キャッシュフロー生活(終身雇用と対称的)

cash flow per common share
每普通股现金流量
cash-flow par action ordinaire
Liquidität od. Cashflow pro Stammaktie
flujo de efectivo por acción
flujo de efectivo por acción común
一株当りキャッシュフロー

cash-flow risk
现金流量 , 资金
risque associé aux liquidités
Cashflow-Risiko
riesgo por insuficiencia de efectivo
キャッシュフロー・リスク

cash-flow statement
现金流动 表; 资金流动表
état de trésorerie
Kapitalflussrechnung
origen y aplicación de fondos
现金収支一覧表

cash-generating unit
现金流生成单位
unité générant des liquidités
Berichtseinheit
minimo grupo de activos que genera flujos de entrada o salida de efectivo
キャッシュフロー創出単位

cashless pay
非现式支付工资; 银行转帐支付工资
paiement par transfert électronique
bargeldlose Lohn- und Gehaltszahlung
domiciliación de la paga
キャッシュレス給与

cashless society
无现金的社会
société sans argent: dans laquelle tout se paie en argent électronique

bargeldlose Gesellschaft
sociedad en la que no se maneja dinero en efectivo
キャッシュレス社会

cash loan company
短期无抵押贷款公司
compagnie de prêt de liquidés à court terme
Kredithai
empresa que presta dinero a corto plazo sin colateral y a altos tipos de interés
现金ローン会社(サラリーマン金融)

cash management models
现金管理模式
modèles de gestion de trésorerie
Modelle für die kurzfristige Finanzwirtschaft; Kassenhaltungsmodelle
modelos de gestión de caja
现金管理モデル

cash offer
现金报价
offre d'achat avec paiement au comptant
Barangebot
oferta en efectivo
キャッシュオファー、企業買収時の対価支払の申し出

cash payments journal
现金支付记录
livre des règlements en espèces
Kassenbuch
diario de pagos al contado
现金支払帳

cash ratio
现金比率; 现金储备率
taux d'espèces; coefficient de trésorerie
Barreservesatz; Liquidität ersten Grades
coeficiente de caja
现金比率

cash receipts journal
现金收取记录
livre des recettes en espèces
Kassenbuch
diario de cobros al contado
现金受入帳

cash sale
现卖 , 现沽 , 现金销售
vente au comptant
Barverkauf
venta al contado
现金販売

cash settlement¹
现金结算; 现汇结算
paiement au comptant
Barausgleich

Translations appear in the following order: Chinese, French, German, Spanish/Latin American Spanish, and Japanese

liquidación en efectivo
现金决济、即日决济, 现物决济

cash settlement[2]
现金结算
règlement au comptant
Barverrechnung
transacción liquidada al contado
現金決済

cash surrender value
保险单的退保价值; 退保金额
valeur de rachat au comptant
Rückkaufwert
valor de rescate en efectivo
(保険の)解約返戻金

casual worker
临时工
employé temporaire; ouvrier
temporaire
Gelegenheitsarbeiter(in)
trabajador(a) eventual
臨時工日雇い労働者

category management
产品类型管理
gestion de catégorie
Kategorien-Management
gestión de categorías
カテゴリー・マネジメント

causality
因果关系
causalité
Kausalität
causalidad
因果関係

CBD
商务中心区
quartier d'une ville où la plupart
des sièges d'entreprise est située
Hauptgeschäftsviertel
centro comercial de una ciudad
ビジネス中心街

cc
复送
copie conforme
Durchschlag, Kopie an
envío de mensajes electrónicos a
varios receptores todos visibles
カーボン・コピー

ccc
公共有限公司
sarl
GmbH
término galés para Sociedad
Anónima
ピーエルシー(plc)の
ウェールズ語版

ceiling effect
上端效应
effet de plafond
Obergrenzeneffekt
efecto tope
シーリング現象

cellular organisation
蜂窝式机构
organisation cellulaire
zellulare Organisation
organización celular
セル組織

census
人口普查
recensement
Zensus
censo
センサス

central bank
中央银行
banque centrale
Zentralbank
banco central
中央銀行

centralisation
集权化
centralisation
Zentralisierung
centralización
中央集権化

centralised purchasing
集中采购; 集中购置
service d'achat centralisé
Zentraleinkauf; zentrale
Beschaffung
compras centralizadas
集中購買方式

Central Provident Fund
中央准备基金
(新加坡的一种退休金安排)
plan de caisse de retraite
Rentensystem
fondo de pensiones al que
contribuyen el empleado y la
empresa
国民年金基金

Centrelink
澳大利亚政府机构;
主要负责介绍劳工福利及就业机会
agence gouvernementale
australienne responsable de
fournir l'accès aux services
gouvernementaux
Australisches Sozialamt
organismo australiano que
permite el acceso a servicios como
beneficios de la seguridad social
センターリンク

CEO churning
首席行政官更迭迅速
débit des PDG en série
schneller Wechsel von
geschäftsführenden Direktoren
tasa rápida de movimiento de los
consejeros delegados
取締役が激しく交代すること

certainty equivalent method
机会均等法则
méthode d'espérance
mathématique
Äquivalenzziffernmethode
método equivalente sin riesgo
確実性等価法

certificate
股份证书
certificat
Zertifikat
certificado
証書

certificate authority
证书发行机构
autorité de certification
Zertifizierungsstelle
autoridad de certificación
サーティフィケート・オーソ
リティ,(独立系の)電
子証明書発行機関

certificate of deposit
定期存款单，存单
certificat de dépôt
festverzinsliches Wertpapier;
Einlagenzertifikat; Depositenkonto
certificado de depósito
預金証明

certificate of incorporation
公司登记执照
certificat d'enregistrement de
société
Handelsregisterauszug
certificado de constitución de una
sociedad
会社設立許可書

**certificate to commence
business**
营业证书
certificat d'autorisation de
démarrage d'un commerce
Gründungszertifikat
certificado de inscripción
英国における事業開始許可書

certified accountant
注册会计师
expert-comptable
amtlich zugelassener
Wirtschaftsprüfer
censor(a) jurado(-a) de cuentas
contador(a) público(-a)
autorizado(-a)
公認会計士

certified public accountant
公证会计师
expert-comptable (agréé)
geprüfter Buchhalter
contable público(-a) certificado(-a)

Translations appear in the following order: Chinese, French, German, Spanish/Latin American Spanish, and Japanese

contador(a) público(-a)
certificado(-a)
公認会計士

cessation
停止
cessation
Geschäftsaufgabe
cesación
停止

CGI Joe
缺乏社交能力和魅力的电脑程序员
troufion de l'informatique
Computer-Programmierer, dem es
an gangsformen und Charisma
gebricht
programador(a) inadaptado(-a)
人間付き合いの下手なプ
ログラマー

chain of command
指挥链; 管理系统; 指挥系统
chaîne de commande
Kontrollspanne; Befehlskette
cadena de mando
指令連鎖, 指揮系統, CC

chainsaw consultant
裁员顾问
consultant élagueur de personnel
Kettensäge-Berater
consultor(a) eliminador(a) de
personal
人員整理用の外部コンサルタント

chair
主席
présidence
Vorsitzende/r; Chair
presidente(-a)
会長理事長

chairman's report
总裁寄语
rapport du président
Jahresbericht des
Aufsichtsratvorsitzenden
carta del presidente
年次報告内の会長挨拶文

change management
变革管理
gestion du changement
Change Management;
Handhabung; von
Veränderungen; od. Umstellung
gestión del cambio
改革的経営, 経営の刷新,
チェンジ・マネージメント

changeover time
(生产设备,
生产方法)的转换时间
temps de changement (de poste
de travail)
Benutzerwechselzeit
tiempo de cambio entre

operaciones
段取り時間

channel
渠道; 销售渠道
organe de distribution
Distributionskanal
canal
チャネル

channel communications
销售渠道交流
communications pour organes de
distribution
Händlerwerbung
comunicaciones con los canales
チャネルコミュニケーション

channel management
渠道管理
marketing des organes de
distribution
Vertriebskanalmanagement;
Vertriebskanalverwaltung
gestión de los canales
流通販売経路管理

channel strategy
销售渠道策略
stratégie de gestion d'organe (de
distribution ou vente)
Distributionskanal-Management
estrategia de canales
チャネル戦略

channel stuffing
渠道激励
gonflage artificiel
Anreizangebote an Vertreiber und
Händler zum Jahresende, sodass
diese mehr Güter kaufen, als sie
brauchen; künstliche
Absatzankurbelung
saturación del canal de
distribución
年度末における販売店への
過剰充填

channel support
销售渠道支持
support d'organe de distribution
Verkaufsförderung
apoyo a los canales
チャネルサポート

chaos¹
無秩序
chaos
Chaos
caos
無秩序

chaos²
混乱状态
chaos
Chaos
caos
カオス, 混沌

CHAPS
票据交换所自动支付系统
système de virements automatisés
entre banques
Clearing House Automated
Payment System: Methode zur
schnellen elektronischen
Überweisung von Geldern
zwischen Mitgliedsbanken im
Namen großer Gewerbekunden,
wo die Überweisungen generell
von beträchtlicher Höhe sind
(sistema CHAPS) cámara de
compensación electrónica europea
con sede en Londres; se encarga
de la compensación electrónica de
transferencias bancarias
internacionales
手形交換自動支払いシステム

Chapter 11
第11章
Chapitre 11
Chapter 11
ley de reforma de la bancarrota
en EE.UU. para facilitar la salvación
米国連邦破産法の第11条

charge
有权取得偿付
charge
Grundschuld
cargo sobre los bienes
債権者の法的権利

chargeable assets
可征税资产
actif soumis à l'impôt sur les
plus-values
steuerpflichtiges Vermögen
activos imponibles
英国でのキャピタルゲイン課税-
対象の資産

chargeable gain
可征税收益
profit soumis à l'impôt sur les
plus-values
steuerpflichtiger Gewinn
impuestos sobre la plusvalía
英国でのキャピタルゲイン課税-
対象の資産の売却による利益

chargeable transfer
可征税转让
transfert soumis à des droits de
succession
Schenkungssteuer
transferencia para evitar el
impuesto de sucesión
英国での相続税対象資産等の
譲渡

charge account
记帐，赊购帐户
compte-crédit d'achat
Anschreibekonto

Translations appear in the following order: Chinese, French, German, Spanish/Latin American
Spanish, and Japanese

cuenta de cargo
小売店における信用口座

charge and discharge accounting
赊销及销账
comptabilité avec port au débit et au crédit
(Bar-)Einnahmen und Ausgaben-Buchhaltung;
mittelalterliche Buchhaltung
sistema contable medieval anterior a la contabilidad por partida doble, basado en el autocargo
複式簿記以前の中世の簿記法

charismatic authority
领袖威望
autorité charismatique
charismatische Autorität;
Charisma
autoridad carismática
カリスマ的権威

charitable contribution
慈善捐款，公益捐款
contribution charitable
Spende an mildtätige Einrichtung
donativo de una empresa a una obra benéfica
慈善的寄付

charity accounts
慈善机构帐户
compte d'une organisation caritative
Konten mildtätiger Einrichtungen
libros de contabilidad de una obra benéfica
慈善事業の会計

chartered accountant
特许会计师
comptable agréé
vereidigter Wirtschaftsprüfer
censor(a) jurado(-a) de cuentas;
auditor(a) externo
contador(a) público(-a) autorizado(-a)
勅許会計士

Chartered Association of Certified Accountants
执业合格会计师协会
ancien nom de l'Association des comptables agréés
Verband vereidigter Wirtschaftsprüfer
asociación autorizada de contables colegiados
英国公認会計士勅許協会
(以前の勅許公認会計士協会)

chartered company
特许公司, 特许实体
compagnie à charte
durch Hoheitsakt geschaffene Gesellschaft

organismo formado por cédula real
勅許組織

Chartered Institute of Taxation
特许税务协会(英国)
Institut des agents du fisc agréés
Institut für beeidigte Steuerberater
instituto colegiado para asuntos fiscales
英国勅許税理士協会

chartist
图表分析家
prévisionniste
Analyst
persona que estudia tendencias pasadas de los mercados de valores por medio de cuadros y gráficos para pronosticar el futuro
罫線分析家

chart of accounts
账目表
plan comptable
Kontenrahmen; Kontenplan
cuadro de cuentas; plan contable
勘定課目表

chase demand plan
跟踪需求计划
plan d'harmonisation demande-capacité
variabler Produktionsplan
producción en función de la demanda
需要追求プラン

chat system
聊天系统
système de bavardage en temps réel
Internet Relay Chat (IRC)-System
sistema de charla
チャット・システム

cheap money
低息借款
facilité d'escompte
billiges Geld wegen billiger Zinsen
dinero a tipos de interés bajos para estimular la economía
低金利政策

cheque
支票
chèque
Scheck
cheque
小切手

cherry picking
摘樱桃原则
sélectionner ce qui est perçu comme étant le meilleur dans une série d'idées ou d'options

aus mehreren Ideen oder Möglichkeiten die auswählen, die am besten oder wertvollsten erscheint.
selección de lo mejor
チェリーピッキング(最善の選択)

CHESS
票据交换电子注册分系统
système électronique de transfert et paiements de titres
elektronischer Börsenhandel
sistema de contratación electrónica de la Bolsa australiana
クリアリング・ハウス電子サブレジスター・システム

chief executive
总经理; 总裁; 董事长
directeur général
Aufsichtsratsvorsitzende/r;
geschäftsführende/r Direktor(in)
director(a) ejecutivo(-a);
consejero(-a) delegado(-a)
総務部長

chief executive officer
首席执行官
directeur général
Chief Executive Officer;
geschäftsführende/r Direktor(in)
director(a) ejecutivo(-a);
consejero(-a) delegado(-a)
最高経営責任者(CEO)

chief financial officer
首席财务官
directeur financier
Finanzdirektor(in); Finanzleiter(in)
director(a) financiero(-a)
最高財務責任者(CFO)

chief information officer
首席信息官
directeur de l'information
CIO
director(a) de información
最高情報責任者(CIO)

chief operating officer
首席运营官
directeur des opérations
Betriebsleiter(in)
director(a) de operaciones
最高執行責任者(COO)

chief technology officer
技术总监
technicien en chef
CTO
encargado(-a) de la investigación y el desarrollo, y acaso de planes para nuevos productos
最高技術責任者

childcare provision
幼儿福利
politique d'aide envers la garde

---

d'enfants
betriebliche Kinderbetreuung
servicio de cuidado de los hijos
保育施設提供

Chinese wall
严重障碍; 难以逾越的壁垒
muraille de Chine
Chinesische Mauer:
Informationssperre zwischen
Unternehmensteilen zur
Vermeidung von
Interessenskonflikten
muralla china
チャイニーズ・ウォール

churn[1]
过多地买进卖出; 挤油交易;
刮皮买卖交易
faire tourner
aufwühlen; strudeln; wirbeln
agitar
回転売買

churn[2]
高人事变动率
avoir un taux élevé de
remplacement de personnel
Fluktuation der Arbeitnehmer
erleiden
padecer un alto movimiento de
personal
高離職率に苦しむ

churn[3]
(顾客购买)频变
acheter en série
beim günstigsten Anbieter kaufen,
ohne Markenpräferenz
comprar sin lealtad a ninguna
marca
目移り購買

churn rate[1]
挤油率
taux de débit des titre et valeurs
Abwanderungsquote
tasa de frecuencia en la cuenta de
corretaje
回転売買率

churn rate[2]
动摇率
taux de vitesse d'intérêt qu'a un
consommateur pour un produit ou
service, puis qui s'en désintéresse
ensuite
Churn-Rate
tasa de uso de un producto o
servicio que luego cesa
回転売買率

CIMA
特许管理会计师协会
Institut des comptables agréés et
de gestion
Institut für beeidigte
Finanzbuchhalter

colegio oficial de contables
gestores
管理会計特化の
公認管理会計士協会

CIPFA
特许公共财务及会计协会
un des organismes professionnels
leader pour les comptables
CIPFA
organismo contable especializado
en servicios públicos que regula las
normas de la profesión
公益事業特化の
公認公共会計士協会

circle the drain
在失败的边缘
être sur le point d'un échec total
vor dem Abgrund stehen
ser al borde del fracaso
失敗直前の状態

circuit breaker
股市中的)下限条款
disjoncteur boursier
Sicherungsunterbrecher, Regel der
großen amerikanischen Börsen
und der Börsenaufsichtsbehörde,
nach der bei extremen
Kursschwankungen der Handel
unterbrochen wird
mecanismo de control de los
cambios diarios
取引所内の価格が極端に変動し
た時に作動する停止措置

circular file
废纸篓
circulaire: terme américain pour
poubelle de bureau
Papierkorb
papelera de oficina
事務所内のごみ箱

circular flow of income
收入循环流转; 收入周转过程
flux circulaire des revenus
Einkommenskreislauf
modelo de economía de país
mostrando flujo de recursos en
torno a los sueldos
所得の循環

circularisation of debtors
资产核实通知
envoi de circulaires aux débiteurs
Kunden-Kontoauszug
cartas de los auditores a los
deudores para verificar datos
企業の債務者に対する残高確認

circulation
发行量; 销售量
tirage
Auflage
estrategia de canales
発行部数

**City Code on Takeovers and
Mergers**
并购城市法
code de la City sur les rachats et
fusions d'entreprises (lequel
protège les actionnaires)
Richtlinien für
Unternehmenszusammenschlüsse
código de la City sobre
absorciones y fusiones
合併および買収に関するロンド
ン・シティの自主規制

class action
共同起诉
action en justice d'une portée
générale
Sammelklage
acción judicial contra un individuo
o entidad jurídica
集団訴訟

classical economics
古典经济学
économie classique
klassische Nationalökonomie
economía clásica
古典派経済学

**classical system of
corporation tax**
企业税的传统体制
système classique d'imposition sur
les sociétés
klassisches System der
Körperschaftssteuer
doble imposición: impuesto de
sociedades y de individuos
法人税の古典的制度

classification
分类
classification
Klassifikation
clasificación; catalogación
分類

classified advertising
分类广告
petites annonces
Zielgruppenwerbung
anuncios por palabras
項目別広告

classified stock
分类股票
titres classifiés
Aktieneinteilung in Anteile mit
unterschiedlichen Rechten
acciones clasificadas
分類株式

class interval
类区间
intervalle de classe
Klassenbreite
intervalo de clase
部類間隔

Translations appear in the following order: Chinese, French, German, Spanish/Latin American Spanish, and Japanese

class of assets
资产种类
catégories d'éléments de l'actif
Vermögensgattung
clases de activos
資産区分

clean float
自由浮动; 清洁浮动
flottement libre
sauberes Floaten
flotación limpia
クリーン・フロート

clean opinion
标准无保留意见的审计报告
opinion non garantie + rapport
non garanti
Aussage eines Wirtschaftsprüfers,
die nicht mit der des
Unternehmens übereinstimmt
informe limpio
適正意見

clean surplus concept
净盈余观念
concept du surplus net ou sans
réserves
bereinigtes Geschäftsergebnis
idea de la totalidad de pérdidas
y ganancias sin incidir en el
capital
クリーン・サープラス関係

clearing bank
清算银行; 结关银行
banque qui appartient à une
chambre de compensation
Clearingbank; Geschäftsbank
banco de compensación
(ロンドンの)手形交換所加盟銀
行, クリアリング・バンク

clearing house
票据交换所，交换所
chambre de compensation
Abrechnungsstelle;
Verrechnungsstelle
cámara de compensación
クリアリング・ハウス

clearing system
交换系统
système de compensation (entre
banques)
Clearing-System;
Verrechnungssystem
sistema de compensación
決済機関,
クリアリング・システム

**clerical work improvement
programme**
行政工作改进计划
programme d'amélioration de
travail de bureau

Verbesserungsprogramm für
Verwaltungstätigkeiten
programa de medida del trabajo
de oficina
事務作業改善プログラム

clerical work measurement
行政工作检测法
mesures de travail de bureau
Zeitmessung od. Messung von
Verwaltungstätigkeiten
medida del trabajo de oficina
事務作業測定

clickable corporation
可点击企业; 即网上商务
compagnie que l'on peut cliquer
(sur Internet)
anklickbares Unternehmen
empresa que opera en la Internet
ネット上の企業

clicks-and-mortar
传统与网络并行机构
entreprise vendant sur le net et
dans un magasin; organisation
'clique-brique': organisation
traditionnelle avec pignon sur rue,
qui a également une présence
virtuelle sur Internet
eCommerce Erweiterung eines old
economy Unternehmens
comercio tradicional y electrónico
クリック・アンド・モルタル

clickstream
点击流; 路径, 点击路线
série de cliquage
Klickstrom
rastro de clics
ウェブサイト・ユーザの
クリック跡追跡

click-through
点击(率)
clic de sélection de pub (sur le Net)
Werbe-Klick; Click-Through
clic en un anuncio
クリックスルー

click-through rate
点击通过率
taux de cliquage: pourcentage des
pubs visualisées qui aboutissent à
un cliquage par le client potentiel;
une mesure du succès de la pub à
inciter les utilisateurs à accéder au
site web publicitaire
Quote der Webseitenaufrufe, die
einen Click-Through zur Folge
haben
coeficiente de clics en anuncios
クリックスルー・レート,
クリックスルー回数

click wrap agreement
点击开包协议
accord par cliquage: contrat
entièrement présenté sur Internet,
l'acheteur indiquant son
consentement à être lié par les
termes du contrat en cliquant sur
une case 'Je consens'
Klick-Wrap-Vereinbarung: Vertrag,
der ausschließlich per Internet
abgewickelt wird, wo der Käufer
den Vertragsbedingungen durch
Anklicken der entsprechenden
Schaltfläche zustimmt
contrato electrónico
クリック・ラップ契約

client[1]
客户; 顾客; 委托人
client
Kundin; Kunde; Klient(in);
Mandant(in); Käufer(in)
cliente
顧客

client base
老客户; 基本客户
clientèle de base
Kundenstamm
base de clientes
顧客ベース

clientele effect
顾客效应
effet clientèle
Kundenbindung
preferencia de compra del cliente
顧客効果

clinical trial
临床实验
étude en laboratoire
klinischer Versuch
ensayo clínico; ensayo clínico
comparativo
臨床試験

Clintonomics
克林顿经济政策
économie clintonnienne: politique
du comité de conseil économique
du président américain Clinton,
avec intervention dans l'économie
pour corriger les insuffisances de
marché et redistribuer les revenus
Clintonomics: die durch den
Sachverständigenrat des
amerikanischen Präsidenten
Clinton verfolgte Politik der
Wirtschaftsintervention zur
Korrektur von Marktmängeln und
Einkommensumverteilung
política económica de Clinton
クリントノミックス

---

*Translations appear in the following order: Chinese, French, German, Spanish/Latin American
Spanish, and Japanese*

CLM
找小鞋穿
auto-sabotage de carrière
Karrierestopper
mal paso profesional
自分のキャリアを
危うくする行動

CLOB International
新加坡自动撮
合国际股市(CLOB)
à Singapour, mécanisme pour
acheter et vendre des actions
étrangères
Mechanismus für den Kauf und
Verkauf ausländischer Aktien in
Singapur
mecanismo de compraventa de
acciones extranjeras en Singapur
外国株式取引機関

clock card
考勤记时卡
carte de pointage
Stechkarte; Uhrenstechkarte
ficha de control de asistencia
出勤票

clock in¹
出勤登记; 出勤报到; 上班记时
pointer
(vor Arbeitsbeginn) stempeln;
Arbeitsbeginn registrieren
fichar a la entrada
marcar tarjeta a la entrada
出勤登録

clock in²
出勤登记; 出勤报到
pointer: arriver au travail sans
physiquement pointer une carte
sich zu Arbeitsbeginn melden
anunciar la llegada al trabajo
出勤登録

close company
股份不公开的公司
société au nombre limité
d'actionnaires
Kapitalgesellschaft mit geringer
Mitgliederzahl
compañía cerrada
閉鎖会社

close corporation¹
不公开公司, 股份不公开公司,
股票全部或大部为少数人控制一
般不公开上市的公司
corporation au nombre limité
d'actionnaires
Kapitalgesellschaft mit
beschränkter Mitgliederzahl
compañía cerrada
非公開会社

close corporation²
不开发雇佣企业;
只雇佣工会会员的企业
corporation au nombre limité

d'actionnaires
eingetragene Unternehmen
compañía cerrada
非公開会社

closed economy
封闭式经济
économie fermée
geschlossene Volkswirtschaft
economía cerrada
封鎖経済、閉鎖(的)経済

closed-end credit
封闭式信贷
crédit à montant fixe
geschlossener Kredit
crédito limitado
クローズド・エンド型クレジット

closed-end fund
封闭式基金; 限额基金
société d'investissement à capital
fixe
geschlossener Investmentfonds;
geschlossener Fonds
fondo de inversión cerrado; fondo
con acciones limitadas
クローズドエンド型ファンド

closed-end mortgage
闭口抵押
prêt hypothécaire à montant fixe
abgeschlossene Hypothek
hipoteca que no permite pagos
anticipados
クローズドエンド・モーゲージ

**closed-loop production
system**
闭合生产系统
système de production en boucle
fermée
voll recyclebare Produktion
sistema de producción ecológico
en el que un producto industrial
puede ser reciclado para crear otro
producto
閉ループ形生産方式

closed loop system
闭环系统
système en boucle fermée
geschlossener Regelkreis;
geschlossenes Regelsystem
sistema de curva cerrada o
autosuficiente
閉鎖ループ式

closed shop
只雇用工会会员的工厂(商店);
不开放雇佣企业
atelier ou organisation qui
n'admet que les travailleurs
syndiqués
gewerkschaftspflichtiger Betrieb
acuerdo de afiliación a un
sindicato específico
労働組合員だけを雇う事業所

closely-held corporation
股东人数有限的公司,
封闭型控股公司
compagnie aux actions détenues
par peu de personnes
Aktiengesellschaft mit sehr
wenigen Anteilseignern
sociedad cuyas acciones se venden
al público pero solo las tienen unos
pocos
閉鎖的な会社

closely-held shares
股东人数有限的股票
actions détenues par peu de
personnes
Wertpapiere mit kleinem
Aktionärskreis
acciones estrechamente
controladas
少数者に握られた株式,
非公開株式

closing balance¹
期末余额
solde de clôture
täglicher Endsaldo
saldo de cierre
営業時間終了後の口座残高

closing balance²
终结余额
solde de fin d'exercice
Endbestand
suma y sigue
期末残高

closing bell
收盘铃声
cloche de clôture
Börsenschlussglocke
campana de cierre
取引終了

closing entries
结帐分录[记录]
entrées de fin d'exercice
Abschlussbuchungen
asientos de cierre
決算仕訳

closing price
收盘价
prix de clôture
Schlusskurs; Schlussnotierung
precio de cierre; cotización al cierre
引け値

closing quote
收盘价
cote en clôture
Schlusskurs; Schlussnotierung
cotización de cierre
終値

closing rate
期末汇率
taux de change en clôture

Translations appear in the following order: Chinese, French, German, Spanish/Latin American Spanish, and Japanese

Schlusskurs
cambio de cierre
期末為替率

closing-rate method
结算日记账法
méthode du taux de change en
clôture
Stichtagskursmethode
método del cambio de cierre
期末日レート法

closing sale
收盘销售; 最后销售
vente en clôture
Börsenschlussverkauf
venta de cierre
販売成立のテクニック;
クロージング売り取引

closing stock
期末存货
stock à l'inventaire
Endbestand
situación de las existencias al cierre
決算在庫

club culture
俱乐部文化
culture d'entreprise selon laquelle
toutes les lignes de
communication mènent à la
direction
Klubkultur
cultura empresarial en la que la
comunicación está centrada en
torno al líder
クラブ・カルチャー(企業文化)

cluster analysis
聚类分析
analyse par groupement
Clusteranalyse
análisis de conglomerados
クラスター分析

clustered data
集束数据
données en grappes
Datencluster
datos agrupados
クラスターデータ

coaching
指导; 辅导
coaching ou formation individuelle
Einzelausbildung
formación
コーチ

co-browsing
共同浏览
système de co-surfing
CoBrowsing
sincronización de páginas web
コ・ブラウズ

cobweb site
过时的网页
site miteux
lange nicht aktualisierte Seite
sitio anquilosado
長い間アップデートされていな-
いウェブサイト

code
编码
code
Code; Kennzahl; Schlüssel
código; codificación; clasificación
コード

codec
多媒体数字信号编解码器
codeur-décodeur
Codec
codificador-decodificador
コデック

code of conduct
行为准则; 业务规程
code de (bonne) conduite
Verhaltenskodex
código de conducta
業務法規

code of practice
工作守则; 工作规章制度
déontologie ou réglements et
usages
Verhaltenskodex; praktische
Verhaltensregeln; Verhaltensnorm
código de conducta
業務規定

coefficient of variation
变异 [变差] 系数
coefficient de variation
Variationskoeffizient
coeficiente de variación
変動係数

co-financing
共筹资金
cofinancement
Mitfinanzierung; Kofinanzierung;
gemeinsame Finanzierung
cofinanciación; cofinanciamiento
協調融資

coherence
相干性
cohérence
Kohärenz
coherencia
一貫性

cohesion fund
结合基金
fonds de cohésion
Kohäsionsfonds
fondo de cohesión
統合基金

cohort
群组
cohorte
Kohorte
cohorte; grupo humano
グループ

cohort study
群组调查
étude de cohorte
Kohortenstudie
estudio de grupo humano
グループ研究

coin analysis
工资分析
analyse des numéraires
Münzanalyse
cantidad y denominación de
monedas y billetes
賃金分析

coincidence
重合, 巧合
coïncidence
Koinzidenz
coincidencia
同時発生

cold calling
冷不防访问
appeler à froid (sans y être sollicité)
Kundenwerbung per Telefon
llamadas sin previo aviso
訪問販売

cold transfer
冷呼叫转移，被动呼叫转移
transfert d'appel (téléphonique) à
froid
automatische Weitervermittlung
transferencia de llamada sin
explicación alguna
通話切り替え

collaborative working
电子化通讯合作
travail fait en collaboration
Collaborative Working
trabajo colectivo electrónico
電子連携作業

collar
对冲
tunnel de taux
Collar
contrato de cobertura
カラー

collateral
不动产的)抵押; 抵押品; 担保品
nantissement
Sicherheit; Sicherungsgegenstand;
akzessorische Sicherheit
colateral
抵当、担保、担保財産

Translations appear in the following order: Chinese, French, German, Spanish/Latin American Spanish, and Japanese

collateral trust certificate
担保信托债券购买证
titres remis en nantissement
durch Wertpapiere gesicherte
Obligation
certificado con garantía prendaria
担保付証券、信託担保証券
付き証書

collection ratio
回收率
rapport d'encaissement
durchschnittliche
Schuldeneinziehungszeit
media de días para el cobro de
cuentas
代金回収率

collective agreement
劳资协议
convention collective
Tarifvereinbarung; Tarifvertrag
convenio colectivo
団体協約

collective bargaining
劳资谈判; 集 体 谈 判
(négotiations pour une)
convention collective de travail
Tarifverhandlungen
negociación colectiva
団体交渉

collocation hosting
服务器托管
option pour collocation d'hôte
Colocation-Hosting
coubicación de servidores
コロケーション・ホスティング

colour supplement
彩页期刊
supplément illustré
Zeitungsbeilage
suplemento en color
新聞に折り込まれるカラー雑誌

combination bond
联合债券
obligation combinée
Obligation mit doppelter
Absicherung
bono con combinación
重複担保公債

**combined financial
statement**
联合财政表
état financier global
Konzernbilanz; kombinierter
Abschluss
estado financiero combinado
総財務諸表

comfort letter[1]
安慰函
lettre pour rassurer des bonnes
pratiques comptables

Verwaltungsschreiben
carta de recomendación
コンフォート・レター

comfort letter[2]
安慰函
lettre de réconfort
Bürgschaft
carta de ratificación
コンフォート(幇助)レター

**command and control
approach**
命令管制方式
leadership de type commande et
instructions
Management by Exception
enfoque de mando y control
支配管理アプローチ

command economy
中央管制经济
économie planifiée
Kommandowirtschaft mit
zentraler Planung
economía dirigida
統制経済、指令経済

commerce
开始; 商业; 贸易; 商务
commerce
Handel; Wirtschaftsverkehr;
Handelsverkehr
comercio
商業, 貿易

commerce integration
商务一体化
intégration de commerce
Handelsintegration
integración comercial
商業統合

commerce server[1]
商务服务器
serveur (informatique) de
commerce
eCommerce Datenserver
servidor comercial por ordenador
servidor comercial por computador
コマース・サーバー

commerce server[2]
商业服务器
serveur commercial
eCommerce Applikationsserver
servidor de comercio electrónico
コマース・ サーバー

commerce service provider
电子商务服务商
fournisseur de service commercial
Handelsdiensteanbieter
proveedor de servicios de comercio
electrónico
商用サービス・ プロバイダー

commercial[1]
商业的; 贸易的; 商业广告
commercial
kaufmännisch; gewerblich;
handelsüblich; Geschäfts-
comercial
商業

commercial[2]
商业广告
publicité
Werbung
anuncio
商業, コマーシャル

commercial bank
商业银行
banque de commerce
Geschäftsbank
banco comercial
商業銀行、市中銀行、コマー
シャル・バンク

**commercial exposure
potential**
商务风险
potentiel de couverture
commerciale
wirtschaftliches Risikopotenzial;
Unternehmerwagnis
potencial de exposición comercial
広告物潜在的注目率

commercial hedger
商业套利者
société en couverture commerciale
Commercial Hedger
cubridor comercial; operador(a) de
cobertura comercial
コマーシャル・ヘッジャー

commercialisation
商品化; 商业化
commercialisation
geschäftliche Nutzung;
Kommerzialisierung
comercialización
商業化

commercial law
商法
droit commercial
Handelsrecht; Recht der Wirtschaft
derecho mercantil
商法

commercial loan
商业贷款
prêt commercial
Warenkredit; gewerblicher Kredit
préstamo comercial o mercantil
銀行貸付

commercial paper
商业票据
effet commercial
kurzfristiger Titel; Wertpapier

Translations appear in the following order: Chinese, French, German, Spanish/Latin American Spanish, and Japanese

papel comercial; èfectos
comerciales
コマーシャルペーパー,
無担保の短期持参人払約束手形,
CP

commercial report
商業報告
rapport commercial
Auskunft (einer Auskunftei)
informe comercial
reporte comercial
商業報告

commercial substance
商業実質
substance commerciale
Firmensubstanz
sustancia de venta
商業実態

commercial time
商業時間
heures de commerce
Werbezeit
tiempo comercial
コマーシャル時間

commercial version
软件商业版
version commerciale
Verkaufsversion
programa de software en versión
comercial
販売用ソフトバージョン

commercial year
商業年
année commerciale
Geschäftsjahr
año comercial
営業年度

commission
佣金; 手续费
commission; commande;
pourcentage
Kommission; Provision; Courtage
comisión
コミッション

Commission des Opérations de Bourse
(法国)证券和交易所委员会
Commission des Opérations de
Bourse
Französische
Börsenüberwachungsbehörde
comisión nacional del mercado de
valores
(仏)証券取引委員会

Commissioners of the Inland Revenue
英国税务局专员
agents du fisc
Steuerfachangestellte
comisarios de apelaciones en

materia de impuestos
内国税収入管理官

commitment accounting
承诺会计
comptabilité d'engagement
Bereitstellungsrechnung
contabilidad de compromisos;
contabilidad de créditos
comprometidos
支出勘定

commitment document
委任状; 任职令; 委员会; 佣金;
手续费
document d'engagement
Verpflichtungsdokument
documento de compromiso
約定書

commitment fee
承约费用
commission d'engagement
Bereitstellungsprovision;
Zusageprovision
comisión por compromiso
約定料、融資枠維持手数料

commitment letter
承诺信
lettre d'engagement
Kreditzusage
carta de compromiso
融資契約書

commitments basis
承诺起计制
base de l'engagement financier
Verpflichtungs-Bem essungs-
grundlage
registro de compromisos en su
momento inicial
委託ベース

commitments for capital expenditure
资本支出承诺
engagements financiers pour
investissement
Rückstellungen für
Kapitalausgaben
compromisos de gastos de capital
資本支出額

committed costs
承诺成本
frais engagés
bereitgestellte Kosten
costes obligados
支出原価

committee
委员会
comité
Ausschuss; Komitee
comité
委員会

Committee on Accounting Procedure
(美国)会计程序委员会
Comité sur les procédures
comptables (Etats-Unis)
Komitee geprüfter Buchhalter
comisión de principios contables
会計手続調査委員会

commodities exchange
商品交易所
bourse des matières premières et
denrées
Warenbörse; Produktenbörse
bolsa de comercio
商品取引

commodity
商品; 貨物
denrée ou produit
Ware; Wirtschaftsgut; Artikel
producto básico
商品, 生産品

commodity-backed bond
商品保证债券
titre gagé sur matières premières
Warenanleihe
bono vinculado a un producto
コモディティ・バックド・ボンド

commodity contract
商品合同
contrat pour denrées ou produits
Lieferschein
contrato para la entrega de
mercaderías
商品契約

commodity exchange
商品交易所
bourse des matières premières et
denrées
Warenbörse
bolsa de comercio
(特に米国の)商品取引所

commodity future
商品期货
opération à terme sur
marchandises
Warentermingeschäft
futuro sobre productos básicos
商品先物

commodity paper
商品票据
emprunts garantis par produits de
base
durch Konossement besicherter
Wechsel
efectos garantizados por
productos
商品手形

commodity pool
商品联营组织
groupement pour transactions

Translations appear in the following order: Chinese, French, German, Spanish/Latin American Spanish, and Japanese

d'options
Warentermin-Investmentfonds;
Futures Fonds; Sammelkonto
consorcio de bienes tangibles
コモディティ・プール

commodity pricing
商品定价
fixation du prix d'un article, d'un
produit d'usage ou d'un service
Massenpreisstellung
fijación de precios de los productos
básicos
商品価格決定

commodity-product spread
商品生产价差
éventail de transactions matières
premières-produits finis
Waren-bezogener Spread
compra (o venta) de un bien
tangible y venta (o compra) de sus
productos derivados
商品生産受け渡し契約,
コモディティ・プロダクト・
スプレッド

common cost
共同成本，联合成本
coût en commun
Gemeinkosten
coste común
共通原価

common market
共同市场
marché commun
gemeinsamer Markt
mercado común
共同市場

common seal
公章
cachet commun
Siegel
sello oficial
社印

**common-size financial
statements**
同比财务报告
rapports financiers avec éléments
sous forme de pourcentages du
total
Finanzbenchmarks
estados financieros expresados en
porcentajes
共通型財務諸表

common stock
普通股
actions ordinaires
Stammaktien
acción ordinaria
普通株

common stock ratio
普通股比率

coefficient d'actions ordinaires
Verhältnis der Stammaktien zur
Summe aller Aktien u.
Obligationen
coeficiente de acciones comunes
持ち株比率

Commonwealth of Australia
澳大利亚联邦公告
le commonwealth d'Australie
australischer Bund
gobierno federal de Australia
オーストラリア連邦

**Commonwealth of Australia
Gazette**
澳大利亚联邦公报
journal publié depuis 1901
rapportant les actions et décisions
du gouvernement australien
Staatsanzeiger des australischen
Bunds
boletín oficial del gobierno federal
australiano
オーストラリア連邦会報

commorientes
同时死亡
comourants
2 gleichzeitig sterbende Mensche;
Begriff des Erbrechts
conmorientes
同一事故死亡者

communication
交流
communication
Kommunikation;
Nachrichtenübermittlung;
Nachrichtenübertragung
comunicación
コミュニケーション

communications¹
交流系统; 交流方式; 交流信息;
通信; 通讯
systèmes de communications
Kommunikation;
Kommunikationswesen;
Nachrichtenwesen;
Informationsaustausch
comunicaciones
通信システム技術

communications²
通信
communications
Kommunikationen
comunicaciones
通信内容

communications channel
交流渠道
voie de communication
Übertragungskanal;
Informationskanal;
Nachrichtenkanal

canal de comunicaciones
通信チャンネル

communication skills
交流技巧
techniques de communication
Kommunikationsfähigkeit
dotes para la comunicación
通信技法

**communications
management**
交流管理
gestion des communications
Kommunikationsmanagement
gestión de las comunicaciones
コミュニケーション・
マネジメント

communications strategy
交流策略
stratégie de communication
Kommunikationsstrategie
estrategia de las comunicaciones
コミュニケーション戦略

communication technology
通讯技术
technologie des communications
Nachrichtentechnik;
Telekommunikationstechnik
tecnología de las comunicaciones
通信技術

Communism
共产主义
communisme
Kommunismus
comunismo
共産主義

community
社团
communauté
Gemeinschaft
comunidad
コミュニティ

community involvement
社区参与
participation communautaire
soziale Initiative;
Gemeindeinitiative; Mitwirkung in
der Gemeinde
participación en la comunidad
地域社会参加

**Compagnie Nationale des
Commissaires aux Comptes**
(法国)国家外部审计管理委员会
Compagnie Nationale des
Commissaires aux Comptes
Organisation, die
außerbetriebliche Revision regelt
organización francesa que regula
la auditoría externa
外部監査委員会

Translations appear in the following order: Chinese, French, German, Spanish/Latin American Spanish, and Japanese

companion bond
随利率涨落的抵押
titre qui va de pair
Unteranleihe
bono que se paga al caer los tipos
de interés
コンパニオン・ボンド

company
公司 , 企业
股份有限公司 , 法人团体
compagnie; société
(Kapital-) Gesellschaft;
Unternehmen
empresa; compañía
会社

company law
公司法
droit des sociétés
Gesellschaftsrecht; Recht über
Kapitalgesellschaften; Aktienrecht
derecho de sociedades
会社法

company limited by guarantee
担保有限公司
société limitée par cautionnement
Gesellschaft mit beschränkter
Nachschusspflicht
organización normalmente
constituida sin afán de lucro
保証責任会社

company limited by shares
股份有限公司
société à responsabilité limitée
Aktiengesellschaft/Kapitalgesells-
chaft; Abk. AG; Gesellschaft mit
beschränkter Nachschusspflicht
sociedad limitada; sociedad en
comandita por acciones
株式会社

company policy
公司政策
politique de l'entreprise
Unternehmensgrundsatz
política de la empresa
企業方針

company report
公司报告
rapport d'entreprise
Gesellschaftsbericht
informe empresarial
会社営業報告書

company secretary
公司秘书
secrétaire général(e)
Leiter(in) Allgemeine Verwaltung
jefe(-a) de administración
会社秘書役

comparative advantage
比较优势
avantage comparatif
komparativer Vorteil
ventaja comparativa
比較優位

comparative advertising
比较广告
publicité comparative
vergleichende Werbung
publicidad comparativa
比較広告

comparative balance sheet
比较决算表
bilan comparatif
Vergleichsbilanz
balance de situación comparado
比較貸借対照表

comparative credit analysis
比较信贷分析
analyse de crédit comparatif
vergleichende Risiko-Analyse
análisis del crédito comparativo
信用比較分析

comparative management
比较管理研究
gestion comparée
vergleichende Verwaltung
gestión comparativa
比較管理

compassionate leave
特准假期; 恩恤假期
congé exceptionnel (pour raisons
familiales)
Sonderurlaub aus familiären
Gründen; Beurlaubung aufgrund
dringender
Familienangelegenheiten
permiso por causa personal grave
慈悲休職

compensating balance[1]
补偿余额; 最低应存数
solde d'indemnisation
Deckungsguthaben
saldo compensatorio;, balance de
compensación
補償預金

compensating balance[2]
补偿性余额
solde de rémunération
Deckungsguthaben
saldo compensatorio
補償預金

compensation[1]
劳务报酬补偿金
rémunération
Vergütung
compensación
報酬

compensation[2]
补偿金
indemnité compensatrice

Abfindung; Entschädigung;
Ersatzleistung; Schadensersatz;
Wiedergutmachung
compensación
賠償

compensation package
工资待遇
contrat de rémunération
Gesamtleistungspaket;
Vergütungsleistungen
paquete de prestaciones
補償パッケージ

competence
水平
compétence
Kompetenz
competencia
コンピタンス

competency
才能
aisance
Fähigkeit
habilidad innata
コンピテンシー(
本来備わっている特性)

competition
竞争
concurrence
Mitbewerber; Wettbewerb
competencia
競争

competitive advantage
竞争优势
avantage concurrentiel
Wettbewerbsvorteil;
Wettbewerbsvorsprung
ventaja competitiva
競争の優位性

competitive analysis
竞争分析
analyse de concurrence
Wettbewerbsanalyse
análisis de la competitividad
競争分析

competitive equilibrium price
均衡价格
prix équilibré compétitif
konkurrenzfähiger
Gleichgewichtspreis
precio de equilibrio competitivo
競争均衡価格

competitive forces
竞争力
forces concurrentielles
Konkurrenz
fuerzas competitivas
競争力

competitive intelligence
竞争情报
informations sur la concurrence

Wettbewerbs-Intelligence;
Wettbewerberanalyse
información sobre la competencia
競合相手情報

competitiveness index
竞争力指数
indice de compétitivité
internationaler Index der
Wettbewerbsfähigkeit
índice de competitividad
競争力指標

competitive pricing
竞争性定价
fixation de prix basée sur la
concurrence
wettbewerbsfähige od.
konkurrenzfähige Preisgestaltung
precios competitivos
競争価格

competitive saw
竞争锯
dent de scie concurrentielle
‚Konkurrenz-Säge': Bezeichnung
für das Prinzip, dass jede
Investition in ein Produkt, obgleich
sie zunächst die ausgewiesene
Leistung im Vergleich zu
Mitbewerbern steigert, irgend
wann an Wert verliert und dass ihr
weitere Investitionen folgen
müssen, dam
medidas para mantener la
competitividad
競争原理

competitor analysis
竞争对手分析
analyse des concurrents
Wettbewerberanalyse; Analyse der
Mitbewerber
análisis de la competencia
競合相手分析

complaint
投诉; 抱怨
réclamation
Beschwerde; Reklamation;
Beanstandung; Mängelrüge
queja; reclamación
reclamo
苦情

complaints management
投诉管理; 意见管理
gestion des réclamations
Beschwerdemanagement
gestión de las quejas o
reclamaciones
苦情処理マネジメント

complementary goods
互补性产品; 相辅性产品
produits complémentaires
komplementäre Güter;
ergänzende Güter

bienes complementarios
補完商品

complementor
相辅性公司; 互补性公司
fournisseur de produits
complémentaires
Assemblierer
proveedor de productos
complementarios
相補会社

complex adaptive system
复杂适应性系统
système adaptatif complexe
komplex-adaptives System
sistema complejo de adaptación
複合適応システム

complexity theory
复杂理论
théorie de la complexité
Komplexitätstheorie
teoría de la complejidad
複雑理論

compliance audit
履约审计
audit de bonne conformité
Übereinstimmungsprüfung;
Erfüllungsprüfung
auditoría de cumplimiento
準拠監査

compliance documentation
履约文件
documentation de conformité
Compliance-Dokumentation
documentos de cumplimiento
準拠性証明書,
コンプライアンス(法令等遵
守)書類

compliance officer
履约主管
conseiller fiscal (pour conformité)
Compliance Officer
encargado(-a) del cumplimiento
コンプライアンス・オフィサー,
業務監査役

compounding
复利
encaissement des intérêts
composés
aufzinsen
incremento exponencial de la
inversión debido al interés
compuesto
複利計算, 複利利回り

compound interest
复利
intérêt composé
Zinseszins
interés compuesto
複利

compressed workweek
压缩工作周
semaine de travail condensée
komprimierte Arbeitswoche
semana laboral comprimida
コンプレス・ワークウィーク

compulsory acquisition
征购; 强制性收购
acquisition forcée
Zwangsübernahme
adquisición forzosa
義務取得

computer-aided design
电脑辅助设计
conception automatisée
computergestützte Konstruktion;
computergestütztes Design; CAD
diseño asistido por ordenador
diseño asistido por computador o
computadora
コンピュータ援用設計

computer-aided diagnosis
计算机辅助诊断
diagnostic automatisé (par
ordinateur)
computergestützte Diagnose
diagnóstico asistido por ordenador
コンピューター診断

computer-aided engineering
计算机辅助工程
ingénierie automatisée (ou assistée
par ordinateur)
rechnergestützte
Ingenieurtechnik;
computergestütztes Engineering;
CAE
ingeniería asistida por ordenador
ingeniería asistida por
computadora
コンピューター利用エンジニア

**computer-aided
manufacturing**
电脑辅助制造
fabrication assistée par ordinateur
computergestützte Fertigung;
CAM
sistema de fabricación por
ordenador
sistema de fabricación por
computador
コンピュータ援用生産(製造)

**computer-aided production
management**
电脑辅助生产管理
gestion de production automatisée
computergestützte
Fertigungsleitung; CAPM
gestión de la producción por
ordenador
gestión de la producción por
computador
コンピュータ援用生産管理

Translations appear in the following order: Chinese, French, German, Spanish/Latin American Spanish, and Japanese

computer-assisted interview
计算机辅助调查
enquête assistée par ordinateur
computergestützte Befragung
entrevista asistida por ordenador
コンピューターインタビュー

computer-based training
利用或借助电脑的培 训
formation basée sur ordinateur
computergestützte Ausbildung;
od. Schulung
formación por ordenador
capacitación por computador o
computadora
コンピューター支援教育,
コンピューター援用研修

computer telephony integration
电脑电话集成
intégration de téléphonie informatisée
Computer-Telephonie-Integration
integración informática de la telefonía
コンピューター・
電話システム統合

computer worm
计算机蠕虫
ver informatique
Computerwurm
virus de ordenador que infecta
pero no daña, aunque obstruye
virus de computador que infecta
pero no daña, aunque obstruye
ワーム

concentration services
服务集中
services de groupement de comptes
Sammelservice; Sammeldienste
servicios de concentración
(銀行の)資金集中サービス

concept board
构思论坛
panneau conceptuel
Konzepttafel
tablero para presentar ideas innovadoras
コンセプト・ ボード

concept search
概念搜索
recherche par concept
Konzeptssuche
búsqueda conceptual
コンセプト・ サーチ

concept testing
构思测定
étude d'évaluation de concept publicitaire

Werbe-Pre-Test
pruebas de conceptos
コンセプト・ テスト

concession[1]
让步减让
concession
Zugeständnis; Konzession
concesión
讓步

concession[2]
减让
réduction
Preiszugeständnis; Vorteil
descuento
割引

concession[3]
特许权
concession
Konzession; Lizenz
concesión
営業免許

concession[4]
差异协议
dérogation ou compromis (sur la qualité, etc.)
Zugeständnis; Konzession
concesión
特権付与

conciliation
调停; 调解
conciliation
Schlichtung; Vermittlung
conciliación
和解

concurrent engineering
并行工程
ingénierie en parallèle
Simultanentwicklung; verzahnte
od. parallele Ingenieurstechnik
ingeniería concurrente o simultánea
(製造の準備, 設計,
開発を同時進行させる)最適化-技術,
コンカレント・ エンジニアリング

conditional distribution
条件分布
distribution conditionnelle
bedingte Verteilung
distribución condicional
条件付き分布

conditions of employment
雇佣条件
conditions d'emploi
Arbeitsbedingungen
condiciones de empleo
雇用条件

conference
会议; 大会
conférence

Konferenz; Tagung; Besprechung;
Verhandlung; Beratung
conferencia
会議

conference call
电话会议
téléconférence
Konferenzschaltung;
Konferenzgespräch
multiconferencia
会議通話

confidence indicator
信心指标
indice de confiance
Verbrauchervertrauens-Indikator
indicador de confianza
信頼度指標

confidence interval
置信区间, 可靠区间
intervalle d'assurance
Vertrauensintervall;
Konfidenzbereich
intervalo de confianza
信頼間隔

confidentiality agreement
保密协定
accord de confidentialité
Vertraulichkeitsvereinbarung
acuerdo de confidencialidad
機密保持協定

conflict management
冲突管理
gestion de conflit
Konfliktmanagement;
Konfliktlösung
coonflicto
紛争管理

conflict of interests
利益冲突
conflit d'intérêts
Interessenskonflikt
conflicto de intereses
利害の衝突

conglomerate
跨行业公司 , 集团企业
association d'entreprises aux
activités diversifiées
Großkonzern; Konglomerat
conglomeración; conglomerado;
conglomerado de empresas
複合企業

conglomerate company
集 团 公 司; 跨行业公司; 多 种 经
营 大 公 司
conglomérat
Konglomerat
conglomerado de empresas
コングロマリット, 複合企業

conglomerate diversification
集团多样化
diversification de conglomérat
Diversifizierung eines
Konglomerats
diversificación de conglomerado
コングロマリットの多角化

conjoint analysis
联合分析
analyse conjointe
gemeinsame Analyse
análisis conjunto
共同分析

connectivity
电子互联性
connectivité
Interoperabilität; Kompabilität
conectividad
連結性

connexity
世界互联性
connexité
Online sein
condición de conexión con redes
de comunicación mundial
連結網

consol
统一公债，不能偿还的债券
titres non amortissables (consols)
konsolidierte staatliche
Rentenanleihen; nicht
rückzahlbare Rente
bono a largo plazo del gobierno
británico
コンソル, 無償還債券

consolidated balance sheet
统一结算表
bilan consolidé
Konzernbilanz; konsolidierte
Bilanz
balance consolidado
連結貸借対照表

consolidated debt
合并债务
dette consolidée
Schuldenkonsolidierung
deuda consolidada
連結債務総額, 整理借入金

**consolidated financial
statement**
统一财务报告书
résultats financiers consolidés
Konzernabschluss; konsolidierter
Abschluss; Gruppenabschluss
estado financiero consolidado
連結財務諸表

consolidated fund
统一基金; 国库基金
fonds consolidé
zentraler Haushaltsfonds

fondo consolidado
連結資金, 整理公債基金

consolidated invoice
联合发票
facture consolidée
Sammelrechnung
factura consolidada
連結送り状, 合併整理送り状

consolidated loan
统一信贷
emprunt consolidé
konsolidiertes Darlehen;
konsolidierte Anleihe
préstamo consolidado
併合ローン,
コンソリデーション・ ローン

consolidated tape
综合记录带
bande des cours consolidée
Consolidated Tape
cinta consolidada
(米証券取引所の)コンソリ
デーテッド・ テープ

consolidated tax return
综合所得税报表
déclaration fiscale consolidée
gemeinsame Steuererklärung
declaración de la renta
consolidada
連結納税申告書

consolidation¹
合并; 联合
consolidation; fusion;
regroupement
Fusion durch Neugründung;
Firmenkonsolidierung
consolidación
合併, 連結, 統合, 整理

consolidation²
合并，整合
consolidation
Konsolidierung
consolidación
合併

consortium
联合体; 财团; 联营公司
consortium
Konsortium; Joint Venture
consorcio
コンソーシアム(経済援助の
ための資本家連合)

constitutional strike
符合宪法的罢工
grève constitutionnelle
Verfassungsstreik
huelga legal
合法ストライキ

constraint
限制
contrainte; obligation

Beschränkung; Einschränkung;
Auflage; Zwang
área de contención
制約

constructive dismissal
推定解雇
démission forcée
fingierte Entlassung
despido constructivo
法定解雇

consultant
顾问; 咨询员; 专家顾问
expert-conseil ou consultant
Berater(in); Beratungsfirma;
Unternehmensberater(in)
consultor(a); asesor(a)
コンサルタント

consultative committee
咨询委员会
comité consultatif
beratender Ausschuss;
Beratungsausschuss
comité consultivo
諮問委員会

consultative management
咨询管理
gestion consultative
Unternehmensführung; od.
Management; nach dem
Beratungsprinzip
gestión consultiva
ボトムアップ経営管理方式

consumer
消费者
consommateur
Verbraucher(in); Konsument(in)
consumidor(a)
消費者

consumer advertising
消费者广告
publicité destinée aux
consommateurs
Verbraucherwerbung;
Konsumentenwerbung
publicidad para el consumidor
消費者広告

consumer demand
客户需求
demande des consommateurs
Verbrauchernachfrage;
Konsumentennachfrage;
Haushaltsnachfrage
demanda de los consumidores
顧客要求

consumer goods marketing
消费品营销
marketing des biens de
consommation
Konsumgüter-Marketing

marketing de bienes de consumo
消費財マーケティング

consumerism
消费者主义
consumérisme
Konsumerismus
consumerismo
コンシューマリズム

consumer market research
消费者市场研究
études de marché (des consommateurs)
Verbraucherforschung; Konsumforschung
estudio del mercado de consumo
消費者市場調査

consumer panel
消费者意见调研小组
jury de consommateurs
Verbraucherpanel; Verbrauchergruppe
panel de consumidores
消費者パネル

consumer price index
消费品价格指数
indice des prix à la consommation
Index der Verbraucherpreise
índice de precios al consumo
消費者物価指数

consumer profile
消费者简历
profil du consommateur
Verbraucherprofil
perfil del consumidor
消費者プロフィール

consumer protection
保护消费者利益
protection du consommateur
Verbraucherschutz
protección del consumidor
消費者保護

consumer services marketing
消费者服务营销
marketing de services des consommateurs
Vermarktung von Verbraucherdienstleistungen
marketing de servicios al consumidor
消費者サービス・マーケティング

consumer spending
消费者消费能力
dépenses du consommateur
Verbraucherausgaben
consumo privado
個人消費, 消費者支出

consumer-to-consumer commerce
消费者之间进行的商务
commerce consommateur-à-consommateur: transactions

effectuées électroniquement entre deux particuliers
C2C
comercio de consumidor a consumidor
コンシューマー・ツー・コンシューマー・コマース, 個人対個人取引

consumption
消费量; 消费总量
consommation
Verbrauch; Konsum
consumo
消費

contact card
接触式卡
carte intelligente par contact
Kontaktkarte
tarjeta de contacto
コンタクト・カード

contactless card
非接触式卡
carte intelligente sans contact
kontaktlose Karte
tarjeta sin contactos
コンタクトレス・カード

content
内容
contenu
Inhalt
contenido
コンテンツ

content management
内容管理
gestion de contenu
Inhaltsverwaltung
gestión del contenido
コンテンツ管理

contestable market
竞争性市场
marché attaquable
Markt ohne Zutritts- und Austrittsschranken wie beim vollständigen Wettbewerb
mercado accesible
競合可能な市場、コンテスタブル・マーケット

context
因特网产品资料
contexte
informeller Mehrwert
contexto
コンテクスト(インターネット上の商品情報)

contingency management
应变管理
gestion des situations inattendues
Eventualitätsmanagement; Management im Eventualfall; Alternativmanagement

administración de contingencias
不測事態対応管理

contingency plan
应变计划; 应急计划
plan de contingence
Ausweichplan; Alternativplan; Schubladenplan
plan de emergencia
不測事態対応計画

contingency table
列联表
tableau de contingence
Vierfeldertafel
tabla de contingencia
分割表

contingency tax
应急税
impôt extraordinaire
Eventualsteuer; Steuer im Fall unvorhergesehener Ereignisse
impuesto de contingencia
コンティンジェンシー税、偶発損失税

contingency theory
权变理论
théorie des contingences
Eventualfallprinzip
teoría de contingencia
状況理論

continuous disclosure
连续性信息披露
divulgation (d'information) en continu
offene Informationspolitik
información completa y continua para accionistas
連続開示

continuous improvement
持续改善
amélioration continue
kontinuierliche Verbesserung
mejora continua
継続改善

continuous operation costing
连续营运成本法
évaluation de coût d'exploitation en continu
Kontinuekalkulation
costes medios de explotación
costos medios de explotación
連続操業原価計算, 連続操業

continuous service
连续工作年限; 连续服务年限
service continu
ununterbrochenes Dienstverhältnis; ununterbrochene Dienstzeit; kontinuierliche Dienstzeit
período en el puesto de trabajo
永年勤続

Translations appear in the following order: Chinese, French, German, Spanish/Latin American Spanish, and Japanese

continuous shiftwork
连续倒班; 24小时连续倒班
travail par roulement
ininterrompu: système de travail
conçu pour fournir une couverture
continue sept jours sur sept et 24
heures sur 24. Il peut être effectué
selon la formule trois-huit ou deux
fois 12 heures
kontinuierliche od. fortlaufende
Schichtarbeit
turno continuo
連続交替制

contour plot
等高图
tracé des courbes de niveaux
Konturdiagramm
representación gráfica de datos
mediante la cual se trazan tres
variables en un mapa topográfico
等高線プロット

contra
抵销，相对，抵冲
contrepartie; contre-écriture
entlasten; gegenbuchen
contrapartida
反対の側

contract
合同; 合约; 契约
contrat
Vertrag; Kontrakt; Abschluss;
Vertragsurkunde; Auftrag
contrato
契約

contract broker
合同经纪人
courtier par contrat
Vertragsmakler
corredor que rellena el pedido
hecho por otros
契約ブローカー

contract cost
合同成本
coût de contrat
Vertragskosten
coste global de contrato
契約高

contract costing
合同成本计算
évaluation de coûts par contrat
Vertragskostenermittlung;
Vertragskostenrechnung
costes de contratación
costos de contratación
契約原価計算

contract distribution
合同分销; 外包合同分销
distribution sous-traitée
Drittvertrieb
distribución subcontratada

契约物流,
サードパーティ・ロジスティッ
ク, 提案型総合物流受託

contract hire
合同租赁
contrat de location
mittelfristiger Mietvertrag;
Mietvertrag; über bewegliche
Sachen
alquiler contratado
短期リース契約

contracting
签订合同
engagement par contrat
Auftragsvergabe
contratación
請負, 契約

contracting out[1]
退出合约; 另签订养老金计划
arrêt de cotisation à une caisse de
retraite: retraite, par l'employeur,
des employés du système de
retraite calculée sur les salaires
(SERP en Angleterre), l'employeur
les ayant inscrit à un plan de
retraite professionnel qui satisfait à
des normes spécif
Befreiung von der
entgeltbezogenen Zusatzrente
abandono del plan de pensiones
público por suscripción de uno
privado
公的年金等の適用除外

contracting out[2]
外包退休金
arrêt de cotisation à une caisse de
retraite
Ausstieg od. Ausscheiden aus der
entgeltbezogenen Zusatzrente
abandono del plan de pensiones
público por suscripción de uno
privado
公的年金等の適用除外

contract manufacturing
外承包生产
fabrication en sous-traitance
Vertragsfertigung; Außenvergabe;
der Fertigung
subcontratación de la fabricación
契約製造

contract month
到期月份; 交货月份
mois d'exécution
Kontraktmonat;
Andienungsmonat
mes de vencimiento de un
contrato
限月

contract note
股票买卖通知单
bordereau d'achat ou de vente
Schlussschein
notificación de transacción
契約書

contract of employment
雇佣合同
contrat de travail
Arbeitsvertrag
contrato laboral
雇用契約

contract purchasing
分期购买租赁商品
achat en sous-traitance
Außenvergabe; des
Einkaufswesens; Mechanismus
zum Kauf von Leasinggütern
compra a plazos
契約購買

contractual obligation
合同义务
obligation contractuelle
Vertragspflicht; vertragliche
Verpflichtung;
rechtsgeschäftliches
Schuldverhältnis
obligación contractual
契約責任

contributed content website
内容参与型网站
site Web avec apport de contenu
(par ses visiteurs)
Webseite mit Userbereich
contribución al contenido de un
sitio web
寄稿ウェブサイト

contributed surplus
股票买卖通知单
excédent contribué
eingebrachter Überschuss
excedente aportado
拠出剰余金

contribution
贡献，毛利
contribution
Deckungsbeitrag; Kostenbeitrag
producto de ventas neto, total,
unitario o porcentual
拠出金

contribution centre
贡献中心，利润中心
centre de contribution
Deckungskostenstelle
centro de producción que con la
renta casa los costes marginales o
directos
拠出センター

Translations appear in the following order: Chinese, French, German, Spanish/Latin American Spanish, and Japanese

contribution margin
贡献毛益,贡献值,差益额,边际
贡献,创利额
marge de contribution
Deckungsbeitrag
margen de contribución
貢献利益

contributions holiday
免供期
période d'exemption de
contributions
Ferien' für
Sozialversicherungsbeiträge
cese temporal de contribuciones
por suficiencia financiera
年金負担停止期間

control
控制; 支配
contrôle
Steuerung; Leitung;
Überwachung; Kontrolle
control
管理

control account
统制帐户，控制帐户
compte de contrôle
Sammelkonto;
Abstimmungskonto;
Mitbuchkonto
cuenta total de saldos; cuenta de
control
統制勘定

controllability concept
控制能力概念
concept du contrôle d'influence
Konzept von der Steuerbarkeit
concepto de los elementos de
evaluación gestión y control
管理可能性理論

controllable cost
可控制成本
coût contrôlable
beeinflussbare Kosten
coste controlable
管理可能原価

controlled circulation
构思测定
tirage gratuit planifiée
Testauflage
tirada controlada
コントロールド・サー
キュレーション

controlled disbursement
受控支付款
débours contrôlé
Controlled Disbursement System
desembolso controlado
コントロールド・ディスバー
スメント, 管理支出

control limits
控制限度
seuils de contrôle
Eingriffsgrenzen; siehe auch
Unternehmensführung nach dem
Ausnahmeprinzip
límites de control
管理限界

conversion¹
转换; 证券转换
conversion (d'instrument financier)
Wandlung; Konvertierung
conversión
交換, 兑换, 切り替え

conversion²
基金转换
conversion (d'actions)
Umtausch v. Wertpapieren
conversión
転換

conversion price
调换价格
prix de conversion
Wandlungskurs;
Umrechnungskurs
precio de conversión
転換価格

conversion rate
实购率
taux de conversion
Umwandlungsverhältnis von
Besuchern zu Käufern bzw.
Kunden
porcentaje de compras sobre el
total de visitas
転換比率

conversion ratio
转换率
coefficient de conversion
Konversionsquote;
Umtauschverhältnis
coeficiente de conversión
転換係数, 転換比率

conversion value
转换值
valeur de conversion
Umwandlungswert;
Konversionswert
valor de conversión
転換価格

convertible ARM
可转换的可调息抵押贷款
hypothèque à taux flexible
convertible: hypothèque que
l'emprunteur peut convertir en
hypothèque à taux fixe selon des
termes spécifiés
wandelbare variabel verzinsliche
Hypothek

hipoteca de tasa ajustable
convertible
転換変動利付きモーゲージ,
転換ARM

convertible bond
可转换债券
obligation convertible
Wandelanleihe;
Wandelschuldverschreibung
bono convertible
転換社債

convertible loan stock
可转换(公司)债券
emprunt avec titres convertibles en
actions ordinaires
Wandelanleihe;
Wandelschuldverschreibung
valores de empréstitos
convertibles
転換ローン株式

convertible preference shares
可兑换外币
actions privilégiées convertibles
Vorzugsaktien mit Umtauschrecht;
wandelbare Vorzugsaktien
acciones preferentes convertibles
転換優先株

convertible security
可转换证券
titre convertible
umtauschbares Wertpapier
título convertible
転換証券

convertible share
可转换股
action convertible
umtauschbare Aktie;
umtauschbares Wertpapier
acción convertible
転換株

convertible term insurance
可转换定期(人寿)保险; 转换保险
assurance à terme convertible
Risiko-Umtauschversicherung
seguro de vida ampliable
可変定期保険

cookie
点心文件
pastille d'informations
Cookie
galletita; cookie
クッキー

cooling-off period
冷却期
délai de réflexion
Bedenkzeit
período de reflexión
冷却期間

Translations appear in the following order: Chinese, French, German, Spanish/Latin American Spanish, and Japanese

co-operative
合作社
coopérative
Genossenschaft
cooperativa
協同事業

co-operative advertising
联合广告
publicité collective
Gemeinschaftswerbung
publicidad cooperativa
協同広告

co-operative movement
合作社运动
mouvement coopératif
Genossenschaftsbewegung
cooperativismo
協同(組合)運動

co-opetition
对手间合作
coopération entre entreprises
rivales
Kooperation zwischen
Wettbewerbern
cooperación entre la competencia
提携

copyright
版权
droit d'auteur
Urheberrecht; urheberrechtlich
geschützt
derechos de autor
コピーライト, 著作権

copy testing
广告效益测定
étude de tirage publicitaire
Werbeerfolgsmessung
pruebas de ideas publicitarias
コピー・テスト

copywriter
广告撰稿人
rédacteur publicitaire
Werbetexter(in)
creativo(-a) de publicidad;
redactor(a) creativo(-a)
コピーライター

core business
核心业务
activité (commerciale) clé
Hauptgeschäftsbereich;
Kerngeschäft
actividad básica
コア・ビジネス

core competence
核心竞争力
compétence essentielle
Kernkompetenz
competencia principal; capacidad
clave
コア・コンピタンス

core values[1]
核心价值观
valeurs fondamentales
Kernwerte
principios fundamentales
コアー・バリュー
(中心的価値観)

core values[2]
核心价值观
valeurs fondamentales
persönliche Werte
valores esenciales
コアー・バリュー
(中心的価値観)

corpocracy
企业官僚作风
gestion d'entreprise excessive
résultant de la fusion de plusieurs
sociétés
schwerfälliges
Unternehmensmanagement
gestión empresarial excesiva por
fusión de muchas empresas
コーポクラシー

corporate action
公司举措; 股东决议
mesure d'entreprise (concernant
les titres et actions)
Kapitalmaßnahme
acción de la empresa
企業決定

corporate amnesia
公司历史失落症
amnésie d'entreprise
Gedächtnisschwund eines
Unternehmens
amnesia empresarial
企業健忘症

corporate appraisal
公司鉴定
évaluation critique d'entreprise
Bestandsaufnahme
análisis de fuerzas, debilidades,
oportunidades y amenazas
diversas
企業査定

corporate bond
公司债券
obligation de société
Industrieschuldverschreibung
obligación societaria
社債

corporate brand
公司品牌
(image de) marque d'une
entreprise
Markenimage; eines
Unternehmens; Firmenimage
marca corporativa
企業ブランド

corporate climate
企业气氛
climat d'entreprise
Unternehmensklima
clima corporativo
企業環境

corporate communication
企业内外交流; 公司内外交流
communications professionnelles
ou d'entreprise
Unternehmenskommunikation
comunicación corporativa
企業コミュニケーション

corporate concierge
跑腿的; 打杂的; 勤杂工
larbin d'entreprise
Mädchen für Alles
trabajador(a) que hace de botones
para otros
使い走り社員

corporate culture
企业文化; 机构文化
culture d'entreprise
Unternehmenskultur
cultura corporativa
コーポレート・カルチャー,
企業文化

corporate evolution
公司演变; 公司发展
évolution (informatique) des
entreprises
Unternehmensentwicklung
evolución empresarial con la
informática
企業革新

corporate giving
企业捐赠
dons d'entreprise
Spendentätigkeit von
Organisationen
ayudas corporativas; donaciones
empresariales
企業贈与,
コーポレート・ギビング,
企業の社会貢献

corporate governance
公司管理方式
contrôle directorial d'entreprise
Unternehmensführung
control corporativo
企業統治

**Corporate Governance
Combined Code**
公司治理联合准则
code combiné de gouvernement
d'entreprise
Nachfolge-Kodex zum
Cadbury-Code, umfasst u.a.
Grundsätze der
Unternehmensführung

Translations appear in the following order: Chinese, French, German, Spanish/Latin American Spanish, and Japanese

principios de gobierno empresarial de conjunto y relación sociedad–accionista
企業統治共同コード

corporate hospitality
公司款待
hospitalité d'entreprise
Corporate Hospitality
actividades de entretenimiento a cargo de la empresa
企業接待サービス

corporate identity
公司标志; 企业标志
identité d'entreprise
Corporate Identity;
Unternehmensidentität
identidad corporativa
コーポレート・アイデンティティ

corporate image
公司形象; 企业形象
image de marque (d'une entreprise)
Unternehmens-Image
imagen corporativa
企業イメージ

corporate planning
公司规划; 总体规划
organisation des entreprises
Unternehmensplanung
planificación empresarial
(企業の中枢レベルでの)
事業計画

corporate portal
公司信息端口
portail d'accès d'entreprise
zentrales Unternehmensportal
portal corporativo
企業ポータル

corporate restructuring
机构重组; 公司重组
restructuration d'entreprise
Umstrukturierung;
Unternehmens-Neuordnung;
Neuorganisation
reestructuración empresarial
企業リストラクチャリング,
企業構造改革, 企業再構築,
体質改善

corporate social accounting
公司社会会计学
comptabilité des charges sociales d'entreprise
betriebliche Sozialbilanz
contabilidad social empresarial
企業社会会計

corporate strategy
公司战略; 公司总体战略
stratégie d'entreprise
Unternehmensstrategie

estrategia corporativa o empresarial
企業戦略, 経営戦略

corporate university
公司大学; 公司培训中心
université d'entreprise
industrieeigene Universität od. Ausbildungsstätte
centro de formación de una empresa
企業研修施設

corporate veil
公司面纱
voile d'immunité des actionnaires
Beschränkte Haftung
encubrimiento corporativo
企業ヴェール

corporate venturing
公司风险投资
nouvelle entreprise commerciale;
initiative d'investissement dans un projet risqué
Investitionsinitiative von Unternehmen in neue Technologien oder ihnen bislang unbekannte Märkte
aportación de capital de riesgo;
inversiones empresariales en nuevos mercados
ビジネス・ベンチャー

corporate vision
公司前景展望; 公司远景
optique d'entreprise
Unternehmensvision;
Zukunftsvorstellung; eines Unternehmens
visión corporativa
経営ビジョン, 経営構想,
企業の将来展望

corporation tax
公司税, 法人税
impôt sur les sociétés
Körperschaftssteuer
impuesto de sociedades
法人税

correlation
相关
corrélation
Korrelation
correlación
相関

correlation coefficient
相关系数
coefficient de corrélation
Korrelationskoeffizient
coeficiente de correlación
相関係数

cosmeceuticals
药用化妆品; 美容用品
produits cosméticiels

Kosmetika wie Crèmes gegen das Altern, die kosmetische und nicht so sehr gesundheitliche Zwecke haben
productos farmacéuticos con finalidad cosmética
美容用の薬品

cost[1]
成本
coût; frais
Kosten; Aufwand
coste
costo
費用

cost[2]
确定成本
coûter
Kosten ermitteln
establecer el precio de
原価, 経費

cost, insurance, and freight
成本; 保险及运费
coût, assurance et fret
Kosten, Versicherung und Fracht
coste seguro y flete
costo seguro y flete
運賃保険料込値段(条件), CIF

cost accounting
成本会计
comptabilité analytique;
comptabilité d'exploitation
Kostenrechnung;
Betriebskalkulation
contabilidad de costes
contabilidad de costos
原価会計

cost and freight
成本加运费价; 运费在内价;
离岸成本加运费价
coût et fret
Kosten und Fracht
coste y flete
costo y flete
運賃込値段(条件)、C&F

cost audit
成本审计
contrôle des coûts
Kostenprüfung
auditoría de costes
原価監査

cost behaviour
成本行为
comportement des coûts
Kostenverhalten
evolución del coste
原価動向

cost-benefit analysis
成本效益分析
analyse coûts-avantages
Kosten-Nutzen-Analyse

Translations appear in the following order: Chinese, French, German, Spanish/Latin American Spanish, and Japanese

análisis de costes
análisis de costos
費用・便益分析

cost centre
成本中心
centre de coût(s)
Kostenstelle
centro de costes
centro de costos
コスト・センター

cost classification
成本分类
classification des coûts
Kostenklassifizierung
clasificación del coste
clasificación del costo
原価分類

cost (at cost) concept
成本概念
concept du prix coûtant
Bewertung zu Einstandskosten
concepto de valoración de activos
en relación con el coste de
adquisición
原価概念

cost control
成本控制
maîtrise des coûts
Kostenkontrolle; Kostenlenkung
control de costes
control de costos
原価管理

cost-cutting
降低成本
compression des coûts
Kostensenkung
reducción de gastos
経費節減

cost driver
成本拉动因素
facteur qui détermine le coût
Kostenfaktor; Kostentreiber;
Zählgröße
factor determinante del coste
factor determinante del costo
原価決定要素

cost-effective
有成本效益的
d'un bon rapport coût-efficacité
ou coût-performance; rentable
rentabel; kosteneffizient
rentable
費用効果

cost-effectiveness analysis
成本效率分析
analyse coûts-efficacité
Kostenwirksamkeitsanalyse
análisis de rentabilidad
費用・効果分析

cost estimation
成本估算
estimation des coûts
Kalkulation
factor que determina la evolución
del coste
原価見積

cost function
费用函数
fonction coût
Kostenfunktion
función de costes
función de costos
費用関数

costing
成本计算
évaluation du coût ou du prix de
revient
Kostenermittlung;
Kostenbewertung;
Kostenerfassung
cálculo de costes
cálculo de costos
原価計算

cost management
成本管理
gestion des coûts
Kostenmanagement;
Kostenwirtschaft
gestión del coste
gestión del costo
原価管理

cost of appraisal
鉴定成本
coût d'évaluation de production
Prüfkosten
coste de evaluación
costo de evaluación
評価原価

cost of capital
资本成本
coût du capital
Kapitalkosten
coste de capital; coste de
oportunidad de capital
資本コスト

cost of conformance
质量达标成本
Coût de bonne conformité
Ausführungskosten;
Konformitätskosten
costes para el logro de las normas
de calidad
costos para el logro de las normas
de calidad
適合コスト

cost of entry
市场进入成本
coût de pénétration (d'un marché)

Einstandskosten; Einfuhrpreis;
Buchungspreis;
Markteintrittskosten
coste de entrada; coste de
introducción
costo de entrada; costo de
introducción
参入コスト

cost of external failure
外部故障成本
coût de défaillance externe
externe Fehlerkosten
coste del fallo externo
costo del fallo externo
外部欠陥商品コスト

cost of internal failure
内部故障成本
coût de défaillance interne
interne Fehlerkosten
coste del fallo interno
costo del fallo interno
内部欠陥商品コスト

cost of non-conformance
质量不达标成本
coût de non-conformité
nonkonformante Kosten; Kosten
der Qualitätserhaltung
coste por fallo en la calidad
costo por fallo en la calidad
不適合コスト

cost of prevention
预防成本
coût de prévention des
défectuosités
Fehlerverhütungskosten
costes de prevención de defectos
costos de prevención de defectos
防止予防費用

cost of quality
质量成本
coût de la qualité
Qualitätskosten; Gütekosten
coste de la calidad
品質コスト

cost of sales
销售成本
coût (de production) des ventes
Selbstkosten; Wareneinsatz
coste de bienes vendidos
costo de producción de ventas
売上原価

cost per click-through
按点击率收费基准
coût par clic (par visite sur site
Web)
Kosten pro Klick
modelo de precios para publicidad
en línea
コスト・パー・クリック

Translations appear in the following order: Chinese, French, German, Spanish/Latin American Spanish, and Japanese

cost-plus pricing
成本加成定价
prix de revient majoré
Erheben eines
Standard-Gewinnzuschlags auf die
Selbstkosten eines Produkts oder
einer Dienstleistung zur Ermittlung
des Verkaufspreises; Zuschlag auf
die Selbstkosten zur Ermittlung des
Verkaufspreises
fijación del coste incrementado
fijación del costo incrementado
原価プラス価格決定法

cost pool
成本积聚
pool des dépenses
Kostenblock
coste de una actividad específica
コスト・プール

cost reduction
成本降低
réduction du coût
Kostendämmung; Kostensenkung
reducción del coste
原価切下げ

cost table
成本表
tableau des coûts
Kostentabelle;
Kostenaufschlüsselung
desglose de gastos
原価表, 原価表

cost unit
成本单位
unité de coût
Kostenträger
unidad de coste
原価単位

cost-volume-profit analysis
成本-总额-利润分析
analyse du rapport coût-volume
des ventes-bénéfices
Kosten-Nutzen-Analyse; Abk. NKA
análisis de
coste-volumen-beneficio (ACVB)
原価・操業度・利益分析

Council of Australian Governments
澳大利亚政府委员会
Conseil des gouvernements
australiens: réunion des têtes des
gouvernements d'Australie
fédéral, des états et territoires
concernant les questions
d'importance nationale
Rat australischer
(Landes)-Regierungen
consejo representativo de las
autoridades nacionales y federales
australianas
オーストラリア政府間協議会

counselling
咨询; 咨询服务
assistance socio-psychologique
Counselling; Orientierungshilfe;
geben
asesoramiento
カウンセリング、相談制度

counterfactual
反事实德，无实际根据，
与事实相反
non factuel
unwahr
falso
条件法的叙述

counterfeit
伪造品; 赝品
contrefaire (produire des
contrefaçons)
fälschen
falsificar
偽造

counterparty
签约方, 对手方
contrepartie
Gegenpartei
contraparte
契約相手

countertrade
补偿贸易; 对销贸易; 反向贸易
troc commercial
Tauschgeschäft;
Kompensationshandel;
Gegenlieferungsgeschäft
contracomercio; comercio por
compensación
(相互に有利な条件や恩恵
を図りあう)互恵の取引,
交換取引,
カウンター・トレード,
バーター取引, 見返り輸入

country risk
国家风险
risque associé aux transactions
dans un pays
Länderrisiko
riesgo de país
カントリー・リスク

coupon¹
息票
coupon
Anleihezins; Kupon; Coupon;
Zinsschein
cupón
クーポン, 表面利率,
クーポンレート

coupon²
封面信(同附件一并发出)
coupon
Anleihezins; Coupon; Kupon;
Zinsschein
tasa de interés de un cupón
クーポン, 表面利率,
クーポンレート

coupon³
债券利息
taux nominal
Anleihezins; Coupon; Kupon;
Zinsschein
interés pagado a un tenedor de
bono
クーポン, 表面利率,
クーポンレート

covariance
协方差
covariance
Kovarianz
covarianza
共分散

covariate
协变量
covariable aléatoire
Kovariate
covariable
共変数

coverage
覆盖率
taux (de cible) couvert
Abdeckung
cobertura
カバレッジ

Coverdale training
科弗代尔培训
système de formation qui se
concentre sur l'amélioration du
travail d'équipe et des méthodes
pour que le travail soit effectué
Coverdale-Schulung
sistema de formación para la
mejora del trabajo en equipo
カバデール・トレーニング

covered option
有保障的期权
option couverte
gedeckte Option
opción cubierta
カバード・オプション

covered warrant
备兑权证
warrant couvert
Optionsschein auf Aktien
garantía cubierta
カバード・ワラント

covering letter
lettre d'accompagnement
Anschreiben
carta de presentación
carátula

Translations appear in the following order: Chinese, French, German, Spanish/Latin American Spanish, and Japanese

cover note
封面信(同附件一并发出)
attestation provisoire d'assurance
Deckungsbestätigung
nota o aviso de cobertura
カバーノート，添え状

CPA[1]
单位行动成本
coût par action
Kosten pro Click
precio por clic
CPA(コスト・パー・アクション)

CPD
员工综合发展计划
système de formation et
d'éducation continue durant une
carrière pour améliorer ses
compétences
kontinuierliche (berufliche)
Weiterbildung
Desarrollo profesional colegiado
個人開発トレーニング

CPIX
纯消费者物价指数
indice des prix à la consommation
sans les coûts d'intérêt
Verbraucherpreisindex
índice de precios al consumo (tasa
de inflación)
消費者物価指数(ローンの利子
除く)

CPM
千人次访问价格
coût par millier d'impressions
Kosten pro 1000 Kontakte
coste por mil impresiones
costo por mil impresiones
CPM(コスト・バー・サウザンド)

crash[1]
死机
krach
Krach; Zusammenbruch; Absturz
crack; quiebra
クラッシュ，暴落，恐慌，急落

crash[2]
电脑崩溃，死机
crash (d'ordinateur)
Absturz
crack; quiebra
クラッシュ

crash[3]
经济崩溃
krach
(Börsen)-Krach; wirtschaftlicher
Zusammenbruch
crack
大崩壊，暴落

creative accounting
作手脚会计
magouillage des comptes
kreative Rechnungslegung

contabilidad creativa
創造的会計

creative consultancy
创意广告咨询公司
cabinet-conseil en création
publicitaire
Werbeagentur
asesoría creativa
クリエイティブ・
コンサルタント事務所

creative director
创意广告主管
directeur de la création
Werbeleiter(in)
director(a) creativo(-a)
クリエイティブ・ディレクター

creative strategy
创造策略
stratégie de création publicitaire
Werbestrategie
estrategia creativa
クリエイティブ戦略

creativity
创造力
créativité
Kreativität
creatividad
創造性

credit
信贷; 信用
solvabilité
Kreditwürdigkeit; Kredit
crédito
信用, 信用貸し, 掛売

credit available
可用信贷
crédit disponible
verfügbarer Kredit
crédito disponible
利用可能な信用, 借入枠

credit balance
贷余; 贷差; 贷方余额; 结欠
solde créditeur
Saldo; Sollsaldo
saldo acreedor
貸方残高

credit bureau
征信所
bureau créditeur: compagnie
d'évaluation de la solvabilité
d'emprunteurs particuliers
potentiels
Auskunftei
agencia de clasificación de crédito
信用調査機関，
個人信用情報センター

credit capacity
信贷能力
capacité de crédit
Kreditfähigkeit

capacidad de crédito
信用力

credit card
信用卡
carte de crédit
Kreditkarte
tarjeta de crédito
クレジットカード

credit ceiling
信贷最高额
plafond de crédit
Kredithöchstgrenze; Kreditplafond
límite de crédito
貸出限度額

credit committee
信贷委员会
comité créditeur: comité
d'évaluation de la solvabilité d'un
emprunteur potentiel
Kreditausschuss
comité de crédito
審査委員会

credit company
信贷公司
compagnie de crédit
Kreditunternehmen
compañía de crédito
金融会社

credit co-operative
信用合作社; 信贷合作社
coopérative de crédit
Genossenschaftsbank
cooperativa de crédito
信用協同組合

credit creation
信用创造
création de crédit
Kreditschöpfung
creación de crédito
信用創造

credit crunch
信用压缩
écrasement du crédit
Kreditknappheit; Kreditrestriktion
restricción del crédito; crisis
crediticia
信用逼迫, クレジット・クランチ

credit deposit
信用押金
dépôt au crédit
Krediteinlage
depósito del crédito
クレジット・デポジット

credit derivative
信贷衍生工具
dérivation de crédit
Kreditderivat
derivado crediticio
信用派生商品

credit entity
信贷双方
entité de crédit: emprunteur ou prêteur
Darlehensgeber(in) od. Darlehensnehmer(in)
entidad o institución de crédito
借入(貸出)者

credit entry
贷方分录
écriture au crédit
Gutschrift; Habenbuchung
abono; asiento de crédito
貸付記入, 貸記

credit exposure
信用风险
exposition au risque de créancier
Kreditrisiko
riesgo crediticio
信用リスク, 与信リスク

credit-granter
信用让与人; 借方
fournisseur du crédit
Darlehensgeber(in); Kreditgeber(in)
que concede créditos; crediticio(a)
与信者, 融資者

credit history
信用记录
historique de solvabilité
Überprüfung der Kreditwürdigkeit
historial de crédito
クレジット・ヒストリー

crediting rate
贷款利率
taux créditeur: taux d'intérêt payé sur une police d'assurance qui est un investissement
Kreditrate
tipo de interés en una poliza de seguros sobre la inversión
(保険契約での)支払利息

credit limit
信贷限额
limite de crédit
Kreditlinie; Kreditrahmen
límite de crédito
掛貸し限度額, 信用限度

credit note
付款通知; 贷项清单
note d'avoir
Gutschrift; Gutschriftsanzeige
nota de crédito
貸方票, 入金済み通知書

creditor
债权人
créancier
Gläubiger(in)
acreedor(a)
債権者

creditor days
债权人日
jours requis pour paiement des créances
Kreditorenziel
plazo de pago a los acreedores
貸方への支払期限日数

creditor days ratio
债权人日均信贷比率
coefficient du créancier ou du fournisseur au quotidien
Kreditorentage-Quotient
proporción de días para el pago de compras a crédito
日常貸方取引

creditor nation
债权国
nation créditrice
Gläubigernation; Gläubigerland
nación acreedora
債権国

creditors' committee
债权人委员会
comité des créanciers
Gläubigerausschuss
comisión de acreedores
債権者委員会

creditors' meeting
债权人会议
réunion des créanciers
Gläubigerversammlung
junta de acreedores
債権者会議

creditors' settlement
债权人清算协议
concordat de créanciers
reduzierte Gläubigerabfindung
convenio de acreedores
債権者決済

credit rating[1]
信用定额; 信用能力; 信用地位
réputation de solvabilité
Kreditwürdigkeit; Bonität
calificación de solvencia crediticia
信用格付け, 信用評価, クレジット・レーティング

credit rating[2]
信用评级
évaluation de solvabilité
Einschätzung der Kreditfähigkeit; Bonitätseinschätzung
evaluación de crédito
信用格付け

credit rationing
贷款分配
rationnement du crédit
Kreditrationisierung
racionamiento del crédito
信用制限

credit-reference agency
资信调查机构
agence d'évaluation (de crédit)
Auskunftei
agencia de calificación crediticia o de riesgos
信用照会機関

credit report
信贷报告
rapport de crédit
Kreditauskunft
informe crediticio
信用報告書

credit risk[1]
信贷风险
risque de crédit
Kreditrisiko
riesgo de crédito
信用リスク

credit risk[2]
信贷风险
risque de crédit (emprunteur qui pourrait cesser de payer un prêt)
Risikokunde
riesgo crediticio
信用リスクのある借用者

credit risk[3]
信用风险，信贷风险
risque de crédit (possibilité de perte due au manquement d'une autre partie d'effectuer sa performance)
Kreditrisiko
riesgo crediticio
カウンターパーティー・リスク

credit sale
赊销
vente à crédit
Kreditkauf; Zielkauf
venta a crédito
掛け売り, 信用販売

credit scoring
信用评分
notation de solvabilité
Kreditwürdigkeitsprüfung
calificación de solvencia crediticia; calificación de riesgo crediticio
信用評価, クレジット・スコアリング

credit side
贷方
avoir
Habenseite; Kreditseite
haber
貸方欄

credit squeeze
信用紧缩; 银根紧缩
resserrement du crédit
Kreditrestriktion; Kreditdrosselung

Translations appear in the following order: Chinese, French, German, Spanish/Latin American Spanish, and Japanese

restricción del crédito
金融引締め

credit standing
资信状况; 信用状况
situation de solvabilité
Kreditwürdigkeit; Bonität
reputación crediticia; solvencia
信用状態

credit system
信贷系统
système de crédit
Kreditwesen
sistema de crédito
掛売制度、クレジット・システム

credit union
信贷互助会; 存款互助会
société de crédit
Kreditgenossenschaft
cooperativa de crédito
信用組合、消費者信用組合

creditworthy
信用可靠的
solvable
kreditwürdig
solvente
信用度の高い, 信用力のある

creeping takeover
缓慢的接管
rachat insidieux
schleichende Übernahme
absorción gradual o subrepticia
ある会社の株を徐々に
買い取ること

creeping tender offer
爬行的股权收购
soumission d'offre rampante
schleichender Erwerb
OPA encubierta
こそ泥的企業乗っ取り

CREST
一种电子运行的股票交易系统
système informatique utilisé au
Royaume Uni pour le règlement
électronique des opérations de
Bourse
britisches System zur
Wertpapierabwicklung
sistema de contratación
electrónica británico
CREST(電子株取引システム)

crisis management
危机管理
gestion de crise
Krisenmanagement
gestión de crisis
危機管理

critical mass
(公司发展的)临界点
masse critique
kritische Masse

masa crítica
限界量

critical-path method
统筹方法; 关键路线法
méthode du chemin critique
CPM-Methode; kritische
Pfadmethode
método del camino crítico
クリティカルパス・メソッド,
危機経路手法, CPM

critical-ratio analysis
关键比例分析
analyse de coefficient critique
Analyse des kritischen
Koeffizienten
análisis de la demanda crítica
臨界率分析

critical region
判域
région critique
Verwerfungsbereich
región crítica
臨界範囲

critical restructuring
关键性重组
restructuration critique
große Umstrukturierung
reestructuración crítica
重大リストラ

critical success factors
关键成功因素
facteurs de succès critiques
kritsche Erfolgsfaktoren
factores del éxito crítico
(企業の主要目標達成に必須の)
副次目標, 成功の決定要因, CSF

critical value
临界值
valeur critique
kritischer Wert
valor crítico
臨界値

crony capitalism
裙带资本主义; 关系资本主义
capitalisme de copinage
Vetternwirtschaft; Nepotismus;
Günstlingswirtschaft
capitalismo de camarilla
クローニー資本主義,
血縁者・親しい知人に利権を配-
分し経済発展する手法

cross
交叉操作
transaction croisée
Wertpapier Austausch
cruce
両建て, クロス売買

cross-border trade
过境贸易
commerce interfrontalier
grenzüberschreitender

Warenverkehr
comercio transfronterizo
国際取引、クロスボーダー・
トレード

cross-hedging
交叉避险
couverture de risques croisée
Cross-Hedging;
Ersatz-Sicherungsgeschäft
cobertura cruzada
クロス・ヘッジング,
クロス・ヘッジ取引

cross listing
交叉挂牌
listage croisé
Cross Listing
venta simultánea en varios lugares
クロス・リスティング

crossposting
多点发布, 交叉发布
expédition de messages croisée
Crossposting
envío masivo y cruzado de
mensajes
クロスポスティング

cross-rate
套汇汇率; 交叉汇率; 套价
taux de change entre devises
tierces
Kreuzparität; indirekte Parität
tipo cruzado
クロス・レート

cross-sectional study
横切研究
étude avec section transversale
d'informations
Querschnittsstudie
análisis de sección transversal
横断的調査

cross-sell
交叉销售
vendre en croisé
Cross-Sell
vender a cruzada
クロス・セリング

crowding out
电脑崩溃, 死机
effets sur le marché du crédit
produit par un emprunt de taille
extraordinaire par un
gouvernement national
Crowding Out
exclusión; desplazamiento
クローディング・アウト

crude annual death rate
概约年死亡率
taux de mortalité annuel brut
allgemeine jährliche Sterbeziffer
tasa anual bruta de mortalidad
生の年間死亡率

Translations appear in the following order: Chinese, French, German, Spanish/Latin American Spanish, and Japanese

cryptography
经济崩溃
cryptographie
Kryptografie
criptografía
暗号化(によるセキュリティ)

crystallisation
固定化
cristallisation
Herauskristallisieren
fiJación de activos relativos;
cristalización
クリスタライゼーション

CSIRO
联邦科学及工业研究局
organisme du gouvernement
fédéral australien chargé de la
recherche scientifique
Wissenschaftliche und
Industrieforschungsorganisation
des Australischen Bunds
organismo responsable de la
investigación científica; CSIC
オーストラリア連邦科学産業
研究機構

CTU
新西兰国家工会委员会
organisme national des syndicats
néo-zélandais
Australischer Gewerkschaftsbund
confederación nacional de
sindicatos neozelandeses
ニュージーランド労働組合協議会

cube farm
格子间式办公室
boîte à cubes
Büro, das in würfelförmige Zellen
unterteilt ist
oficina compartimentalizada en
cubículos
オープンプランでない,
区切られた事務所空間

cue
区分因素
facteur de différenciation (d'un
produit de haute valeur par
rapport à un produit normal)
besondere Eigenschaft
factor diferencial
キュー(差別化の印)

CUL
创造力
à plus tard
bis bald
hasta luego
また, 後で

cultural creative
可用信贷
créatif culturel
Kosmopolit
persona con grandes inquietudes

culturales
創造的な自由人

cultural synergy
机构文化协调; 企业文化的整合
synergie culturelle
kulturelle Synergie; Kultursynergie
sinergia cultural
文化共働作用

culture shock
文化休克
choc culturel
Kulturschock
choque cultural
カルチャー・ショック

cum
附带
avec
mit
con
付き

cum rights
附带认股权; 附带权力
avec les droits de souscription
mit Bezugsrechten
con derechos
権利付き

cumulative method
积累法
méthode cumulative
kumulative Methode
método acumulativo
累加法, 累積法

cumulative preference shares
债权人日
actions privilégiées
kumulative Vorzugsaktien
acciones preferentes de dividendo
acumulable
累化優先株

cumulative preferred stock
累积股息优先股; 累积优先股
actions privilégiées à dividende
cumulatif
kumulative Vorzugsaktien
acciones preferidas acumulativas
累積の優先株

currency
貨币; 流通貨币; 通币
devise
Währung; umlaufende
Bargeldmenge
moneda; divisa
通貨

currency future
貨币期权
option à terme sur une devise
Devisenterminkontrakt
futuro sobre divisa
通貨先物取引, 外国為替先物

currency hedging
信用风险, 信贷风险
couverture des devises
Devisen-Hedging
cobertura de riesgo de cambio
為替ヘッジ取引

currency note
纸币
billet de banque
papiergeld
activo realizable
政府通貨

currency risk[1]
貨币风险
risque de devise
Währungsrisiko
riesgo de una divisa
為替リスク

currency risk[2]
多点发布, 交叉发布
risque associé aux devises
Währungsrisiko
riesgo cambiario
為替リスク

currency unit
貨币单位
unité monétaire
Währungseinheit
unidad monetaria
通貨単位

current account
活期存款帐户; 往来帐户
compte courant
Girokonto; Kontokorrentkonto
cuenta corriente
当座預金, 経常収支

current account equilibrium
经常项目平衡; 经常帐户平衡
équilibre de compte courant
Leistungsbilanzgleichgewicht
equilibrio de la cuenta corriente
経常収支の均衡

current account mortgage
交叉销售
emprunt immobilier sur compte
courant
Girokonto-Hypothek
cuenta corriente hipotecaria
当座預金モーゲージ

current assets
流动资产
actif de roulement
Umlaufvermögen; Gegenstände d.
Umlaufvermögens
activo circulante or corriente
流動資産

current assets financing
流动资产融资
financement par actif de
roulement

Translations appear in the following order: Chinese, French, German, Spanish/Latin American Spanish, and Japanese

Umlaufvermögensfinanzierung
financiación con activo circulante
流動資産資金調達,
流動資産ファイナンス

current cash balance
现金周转余额
solde de caisse actuel
aktueller Kassenbestand
saldo de caja actualizado
当座現金残高

current-cost accounting
现行成本会计; 当期成本会计
comptabilité analytique actuelle
Gegenwartsbewertung;
Rechnungslegung zum Marktwert
contabilidad de costes corrientes
contabilidad de costos corrientes
现在原価会计,
カレント・コスト会計

current earnings
当期收益
bénéfices de l'exercice
laufende Erträge; aktuelle
Ertragslage
ingresos corrientes
当期所得, 経常所得, 経常利益

current liabilities
流动债务; 短期债务; 流动负债
passif exigible
laufende od. kurzfristige
Verbindlichkeiten
pasivo circulante or corriente
流動負債

current principal factor
未付本金部分
proportion de capital principal en
souffrance
Restbetrag
parte que queda por pagar
カレント・プリンシパル・
ファクター, 流動負債元本

current purchasing power accounting
现行购买力会计
comptabilité de pouvoir d'achat
actuel
kaufkraftindizierte
Rechnungslegung
contabilidad del poder adquisitivo
actual
当座購買力勘定

current ratio
流动比率
coefficient de liquidité
Liquidität dritten Grades
coeficiente de solvencia
relación corriente
流動比率

current stock value
当前股票价值

valeur de titres actuelle
laufender Anlagenwert
valor actual
現在の総株資産

current value
现值; 时价
coefficient de valeur actuelle
derzeitiger Wert; Marktwert;
Tageswert; Zeitwert
valor actualizado
現在価値, 時価

current yield
本期收益率; 现时收益实得率;
盈利率
proportion de rendement actuel
laufende Rendite
rendimiento corriente
直接利回り, 現行利回り

cushion bond
缓冲债券
obligation (à valeur) atténuée
hochverzinsliche Anleihe
bono amortiguador
クッション・ボンド

customer
顾客; 买主; 客户
client
Kundin; Kunde; Käufer(in);
Auftraggeber(in)
cliente(-a)
顾客

customer capital
客户资本
capital clients
Kundenkapital
capital del cliente
顧客資本

customer-centric model
以客户为中心模式
modèle centré sur le client
kundenorientiertes
Geschäftsmodell
modelo en torno al consumidor
顧客志向モデル

customer expectation
顾客期望值; 顾客预期值
attentes du client
Kundenerwartungen
expectativas del consumidor
顧客期待度

customer flow
顾客流动
flux de la clientèle
Kundenverkehr; Kundenströme
flujo de clientela
顧客の流れ

customer focus
客户至上; 以客户为中心
concentration sur la clientèle
Kundenorientierung;

Kundenfokus
foco en el cliente
顧客焦点システム

customer profitability
顾客盈利率
rentabilité du client
Kundenrentabilität
rentabilidad de los clientes
利益顧客層

customer profitability analysis
顾客群获利能力分析
analyse de rentabilité des clients
Analyse der Kundenrentabilität
análisis de la corriente de
rentabilidad del cliente
顧客利益分析

customer recovery
客户恢复
récupération d'anciens clients
Erinnerungswerbung
recuperación de clientela
カスタマー・リカバリー

customer relations
客户关系; 顾客关系
relations-clients
Kundenbetreuung; Kundendienst
relaciones con los clientes
カスタマー・リレーションズ,
対顧客広報活動

customer relationship management
客户关系管理
gestion des relations clients;
gestion de relations avec la
clientèle
Customer Relationship
Management
gestión de las relaciones con los
clientes; gestión de la atención al
cliente
カスタマー・リレーションシップ・
マネジメント

customer retention
客户维持
conservation de la clientèle;
maintien de clientèle
Kundenloyalität; Beibehalten von
Kunden
retención de clientes
顧客保持

customer satisfaction
客户满意度; 顾客满意度
satisfaction du client
Kundenzufriedenheit
satisfacción del cliente
顧客満足度

customer service
客户服务; 顾客服务
service clientèle

Kundendienst
atención al cliente
顧客サービス

customisation
按客户要求定制改制
personnalisation (de produits ou
services)
Customization
personalización
顧客特注制度

customised service
客户需求化服务
service sur mesure ou personnalisé
kundengerechter Service
servicio personalizado
カスタマイゼーション

cut-off
截止日期，中止
limite ou accord de règlement
Abbrechen; Stichtag;
Abgrenzungstermin
cierre de libros para inventario
会計締切り

cutthroat
残酷的
acharné(e) (dans ses transactions
avec la concurrence)
unbarmherzig; mörderisch
salvaje
殺人的

cutting-edge
前沿; 前卫
à l'avant-garde: à l'avant-garde ou
au premier plan des nouvelles
technologies ou nouveaux
marchés
zur vordersten Front
a la vanguardia
技術革新, 市場最先端

CV
可兑换的; 可转换的; 履历
Curriculum Vitae
Lebenslauf
currículum vitae
経歴書

cyberbole
网络炒作
cyberbole
Internet-Hype
revuelo en torno a Internet
サイバーボール

cybercrud
计算机行话
cyberjargon
Leuten, die Computer benutzen,
etwas überzustülpen
jerga informática inútil
サイバークラッド

cyber mall
联合网站
cybergalerie: site Web partagé par
deux ou plus organisations
commerciales, souvent avec des
similarités quant à leur apparence,
fonction, produits ou services
Cyber-Einkaufszentrum;
Internet-Einkaufszentrum
centro comercial electrónico
サイバーモール

cybermarketing
电子化营销
cybermarketing
Cyber-Marketing;
Internet-Marketing
cibermarketing; marketing
electrónico
サイバーマーケティング,
サイバー広告

cybersales
电子销售
cyberventes
Verkauf über das Intenet;
Internetverkauf; elektronischer
Hande; Cyber-Verkauf
ciberventas; ventas electrónicas
サイバーセールズ

cyberslacker
上班时间因私上网者
cyberglandeur
Internet-Bummelant
trabajador(a) que navega en horas
de trabajo
仕事時間内に私用で
ネット・サーフをする人

cyberspace
电子空间
cyberespace
Cyberspace
ciberespacio
サイバースペース

cycle plot
循环图
tracé graphique des cycles
Zyklusdiagramm
representación gráfica del
comportamiento de series
temporales estacionales
サイクルプロット

cycle time
周期
durée de cycle
Arbeitszyklus
plazo de producción
サイクルタイム

cyclical stock
周期性产业股票,股价循环股，
敏感性股票
stock cyclique
zyklische Wertpapiere

valor cíclico
周期的在庫

cyclical unemployment
周期性失业
chômage cyclique
zyklische Arbeitslosigkeit;
konjunkturbedingte
Arbeitslosigkeit
desempleo cíclico
景気的失業、循環的失業

cyclic variation
循环变差
permutation cyclique
zyklische Variation
variación cíclica
巡回変動

daily price limit
每日价格限幅
limite de prix quotidienne
tägliche Preisobergrenze; täglicher
Preisplafond
límite de precio diario
値幅制限, 一日の価格変動限度額

daisy chaining
菊花链
chapelet de transactions: pratique
illégale par laquelle les opérateurs
créent des transactions artificielles
pour qu'un titre particulier semble
beaucoup plus actif qu'il ne l'est
dans la réalité
Illegale Kursmanipulation
cadena de compra y venta para
manipular el mercado
デイジー・チェーン

dancing baloney
动画效果
inepties visuelles sur ordinateur
Computer-Trickeffekte, die kaum
praktischen Wert haben, aber
Eindruck machen
informática vacua pero
espectacular
格好いいけれども役に立たない
画面上ＳＦＸ

dancing frog
跳动的青蛙
problème ou image sur un écran
d'ordinateur qui disparaît quand
on le montre à quelqu'un d'autre
Vorführeffekt
problema en el ordenador que
desaparece al mostrarlo a otra
persona
problema en el computador que
desaparece al mostrarlo a otra
persona
ダンシング・フロッグ
(他人に見せると消えてしま
う問題)

Translations appear in the following order: Chinese, French, German, Spanish/Latin American
Spanish, and Japanese

Darwin Trade Development Zone
达尔文贸易发展特区
zone de développement commercial de la ville de Darwin
Darwinsche Freihandelsentwicklungszone
zona de libre comercio en el área de Darwin
ダーウィン貿易開発地域

data
数据
données
Daten
datos
データ

database
数据库
base de données
Datenbank
base de datos
データベース

database management system
数据库管理系统
système de gestion de base de données
Datenverwaltungssystem
sistema de gestión de base de datos
データベース管理システム

database marketing
数据库营销
marketing (de base) de données
Datenbankmarketing
marketing utilizando bases de datos
データベース・マーケティング

data capture
数据扑捉
saisie de données
Datenerfassung
captura de datos
データ収集

data cleansing
数据清理
nettoyage de données
Datenaufbereitung
limpieza de datos
データ・クレンジング

data dredging
数据挖掘
fait de ressortir des données
das Ziehen von Vergleichen und von Schlüssen aus Daten, die nicht zum urspünglichen Studienauftrag gehörten
proceso mediante el cual se realizan comparaciones y se sacan conclusiones a partir de datos que no forman parte de las

instrucciones originales del estudio
データ浚渫

data editing
数据编辑
correction de données
Dateneditierung
edición de datos
データ編集

dataholic
数据迷
accro des données informatiques
Datensüchtige/r, insbesondere nach Informationen aus dem Internet
infoadicto(-a)
データ中毒

data mining[1]
数据挖掘
extraction de données
Datamining
extracción de datos
データ・マイニング

data mining[2]
数据挖掘
extraction de données
Datamining
extracción de datos
データ・マイニング

data protection
数据 保护
protection de données
Datenschutz
protección de datos
データ保護

data reduction
数据处理
compression de données
Datenreduktion
reducción de datos; compresión de datos
データ整理

data screening
数据筛选
filtrage ou tri de données
Datenüberpüfung
selección de datos
データスクリーニング

data set
数据集
ensemble des données
Datensatz
conjunto de datos
データセット

data smoothing algorithm
数据加工算法, 数据平整算法
algorithme de lissage de données
Datenglättungsalgorithmus
algoritmo de alisado de datos;
algoritmo de suavización de datos
データスムーズアルゴリズム

data transfer
数据传送
transfert de données
Traffic
transferencia de datos
データトランスファー

data warehouse
数据仓库
entrepôt informatique de données
Datenspeicherung
almacenamiento de datos
データウェアハウス

DAX
德国的主要股票交易所
(位于法兰克福）
DAX: la Bourse allemande principale, à Francfort
Deutscher Aktienindex
índice de la bolsa de Fráncfort
DAX(フランクフルト株式市場)

day in the sun
产品旺季
temps au soleil
Zeit des Markterfolgs
período de éxito
ブーム期

day order
当日有效委托书; 当日订单;
当日订货
ordre valable pour la journée
Tagesorder
orden de compra de un día
当日限り有効注文

day release
脱产进修日
journée de stage ou de formation pendant les heures de travail
Freistellung für einen Tag
permiso para acudir a un curso de formación un día a la semana
デイ・リリース

day trader
作短线者; 当日交易者
opérateur boursier qui initie et liquide ses transactions au cours d'une seule journée
Tageshändler(in);
Tagesspekulant(in)
operador(a) del día o a corto plazo
デイ・トレーダー,
日計り商いの投機家

day trading
日间交易; 当日交易
opérations initiées et dénouées au cours d'une seule journée de Bourse
Leerverkauf mit Deckung am selben Tag; An- und Verkauf am selben Tag; Tageshandel
compra y venta de la misma cantidad de un valor el mismo día

Translations appear in the following order: Chinese, French, German, Spanish/Latin American Spanish, and Japanese

デイ・トレーディング、日計り商
い、日計り取引

dead cat bounce
死猫弹
sursaut de chat mort
Todeszuckungen
subida breve después de un
desplome
急落後の短期反発

dead tree edition
印刷版本
édition bois mort
Papierversion einer
Veröffentlichung, die auch in
elektronischem Format vorliegt
versión en papel
電子文章の印刷版

dead wood
闲置人员
employé redondant
Totholz; Ballast
empleados que sobran
不必要となった社員

dealership
代理商; 商品特许经销商;
商品经销特许权
concession
Vertragshändler(in)
concesionario
特約販売権

death by committee
委员会致死
mort par comité
eine Idee durch den Einsatz eines
Komitees stoppen
paralización a través de un comité
委員会監視体制

Death Valley curve
死亡曲线
descente dans la vallée de la mort
Todestal-Kurve
caída producida cuando las
pérdidas no permiten hacer frente
a los gastos
新しい企業の損失が
経営困難を来す時期

debenture[1]
债券; 公司债券
obligation (non garantie)
ungesicherte Verbindlichkeit;
ungesichertes Darlehen;
ungesicherte Schuldverschreibung
bono de dueda; certificado de
deuda
債券、社債、無担保社債

debenture[2]
债券
emprunt obligataire
ungesicherte Verbindlichkeit
bono de dueda; certificado de

deuda
無担保社債

debit card
结算卡; 借方卡
carte de débit
plastische Kontokarte, die das
Konto des Benutzers bei
Transaktionen sofort belastet
tarjeta de débito
デビットカード

debit note
付款通知书
bordereau de débit
Lastschriftanzeige;
Belastungsanzeige
nota de cargo
買付換票

debt
债务; 负债
dette
Schuld; Forderung; Verbindlichkeit
deuda
負債

debt capacity
负债能力
potentiel de la dette
Kreditwürdigkeit; Fähigkeit der
Kreditaufnahme
capacidad de endeudamiento
借方能力

debt collection agency
债务托收机构，收债代理行
agence de recouvrement de
créances
Inkassobüro
agencia de cobro de deudas
借金取り

debt counselling
债务咨询
assistance sociopsychologique
pour les personnes endettées
Schuldnerberatung
asesoramiento en fórmulas para la
liquidación de deudas
債務アドバイス

debt/equity ratio
负债与权益比率; 债务产权率
coefficient endettement-capital
actions
Verschuldungsgrad;
Eigenkapitalquote;
Verschuldungskoeffizient
coeficiente de endeudamiento;
relación deuda-capital
負債(対)資本比率、負債比率

debt forgiveness
债务赦免
abandon de créances
Schuldenerlass
condonación de la deuda;

cancelación de la deuda
債務帳消し

debt instrument
债务票据
instrument de créance
Schuldurkunde; schuldrechtliches
Wertpapier
instrumento de la deuda
借入証書

debtnocrat
高级拨款官员
detnocrate
obere/r Bankangestellte/r, deren
oder dessen Spezialgebiet die
Kreditvergabe extrem hoher
Summen ist, beispielsweise an
Entwicklungsländer
alto funcionario de un banco que
está especializado en los
préstamos de grandes cantidades
de dinero
デトノクラット

debtor
债务人; 负债人
débiteur
Schuldner(in); Kreditnehmer(in)
deudor(a)
借方、借主、債務者

debtor days
债务人日
nombre de jours débiteurs
Debitorenziel
plazo de pago de los deudores
借方の支払期限日数

debt rescheduling
债务重新安排
restructuration de dette
Umschuldung
reprogramación de la deuda
債務の繰り延べ

debt/service ratio
偿债比率
ratio endettement/fonds propres
Schuldendienstquote
coeficiente del servicio de la deuda
デット・サービス・レシオ、
債務返済比率

debugging
排错
mise au point ou élimination des
défauts
Austesten, Fehlersuche und
-entfernung
depuración
デバッギング

decentralisation
分散化; 分权化
décentralisation
Dezentralisierung;
Dezentralisation

Translations appear in the following order: Chinese, French, German, Spanish/Latin American Spanish, and Japanese

descentralización
各部門分権化,
(経営等の)分散化, 分権管理

decision-maker
決策人
décideur
Entscheidungsträger(in); Person;
die Entscheidungen; trifft
responsable de tomar decisiones
政策担当者, 意思決定者

decision-making
決策
prise de décision; prendre les
décisions
Entscheidungsfindung;
Willensbildung; Beschlussfassung
toma de decisiones
意思決定, 政策決定

decision-making unit
決策組
cellule décisionnaire
entscheidungsrelevante Personen
unidad con capacidad de decisión
意思決定主体

decision support system
決策支持系統
système de support de décision
Entscheidungs-Unterstützungs-
system
sistema de apoyo en la toma de
decisiones
意思決定支援システム

decision theory
決策理論
théorie de la décision
Entscheidungstheorie
teoría de las decisiones
決定理論, 意思決定論

decision tree
決策樹, 決策圖表
arbre décisionnel; graphique des
décisions
Entscheidungsbaum
secuencia de decisiones; árbol de
decisión
樹状図

declaration date
宣告日
date de déclaration
Verkündung der
Dividendenausschüttung
fecha de la declaración
(米)配当金支払発表日

declaration of dividend
分红宣告
déclaration de dividende
Erklärung der Dividende
anuncio de dividendos
配当の発表

declaration of solvency
偿付能力宣告
déclaration de solvabilité
Solvenzerklärung
declaración de solvencia
支払い能力宣告

deconstruction
打破传统结构
déconstruction
Reengineering
desconstruccionismo
デコンストラクション

de-diversify
反多样化
dé-diversifier
auf Kernkompetenzen
Konzentrieren
abandonar la diversificación
非多角化

deductible
绝对免赔额, 免赔额
déductible
Selbstbehalt
franquicia
保険金控除

deduction at source
税款代缴
retenue à la source
Quellenabzug;
Quellenbesteuerung
deducción del impuesto realizada
por el pagador
源泉徴収

deed
契约
acte notarié
Vertrag; Übertragungsurkunde
escritura
捺印証書, 不動産権利証書

deed of assignment
转让契约
acte attributif
Abtretungsurkunde
escritura/acta de cesión de la
propiedad del deudor al acreedor
不動産譲渡証書

deed of covenant
捐款契据, 定期捐款协议
contrat d'engagement à payer une
somme fixe à un tiers sur une base
annuelle
Schenkungsurkunde
escritura de garantía
支払約款証書

deed of partnership
合伙契据
acte d'association
Gesellschaftsvertrag
escritura/acta de constitución de
una sociedad colectiva; contrato

de asociación
パートナーシップ契約証書

deed of variation
变更契据
accord de variation
Abwandlungsurkunde
escritura de modificación de un
testamento
遺言変更証書

deep discount bond
大幅折价债券
grosse décote
Anleihe mit ungewöhnlich hohem
Disagio
bono con alto descuento
高割引債

**deep-in-the-money call
option**
深价买入期权; 大有价选择权
option d'achat 'poches pleines'
Tief-im-Geld-Kaufoption
opción de compra muy dentro del
dinero; opción de compra cuando
el precio es muy superior al del
ejercicio
ディープ・イン・ザ・マネー・
コール・オプション

**deep-in-the-money put
option**
深价卖出期权
option de vente 'poches pleines'
Tief-im-Geld-Verkaufsoption
opción de venta fuera del dinero;
opción de venta cuando el precio
es muy inferior al del ejercicio
ディープ・イン・ザ・プット・
オプション

deep market
纵深市场
marché profond
'tiefer Markt': Waren-,
Währungs-, oder
Wertpapierbörse, wo das
Handelsvolumen so groß ist, dass
selbst eine große Menge
Transaktionen den Marktpreis/Kurs
nicht beeinflussen kann.
mercado profundo
ディープ・マーケット

de facto standard
事实标准
norme 'de facto'
de-facto Standard
estándar común
デファクト・スタンダード
(事実上の基準)

default notice
违约通知
notification de manquement
d'engagement
Säumnisanzeige

---

*Translations appear in the following order: Chinese, French, German, Spanish/Latin American
Spanish, and Japanese*

comunicación de incumplimiento
不履行通告

defended takeover bid
防御式并购出价
offre publique d'achat opposée
abgewiesenes
Übernahmeangebot; verteidigter
Übernahmeversuch
oferta pública de adquisición (OPA)
defendida
企業乗取り防御

defensive stock
防卫性股
stock défensif
risikoarme Aktie
valores defensivos o seguros
防衛株

deferred coupon
递延债息
coupon à longue échéance
Verzugskupon; Kupon od.
Zinsschein mit verzögerter
Verzinsung
cupón diferido o aplazado
金利繰り延べ債,
ディファード・クーポン債

deferred credit
递延信贷
crédit différé
transitorische Passiva;
zurückgestelltes Einkommen
crédito diferido
繰延貸方

deferred month
迟延月(用于期权交易)
mois reporté
entfernter Monat
mes más distante
期先物

deferred ordinary share[1]
递延普通股份
action ordinaire à dividende
différé
Gründeraktie; Nachzugsaktie
acción ordinaria diferida
利益後受普通株

deferred ordinary share[2]
递延普通股份
action ordinaire à dividende
retardé
Nachzugsaktie
acción ordinaria diferida
後配普通株

deferred shares
滞后分红股票
actions à dividende différé
Nachzugsaktie
acciones diferidas
利益後受株発起人株

deficit financing
赤字财政
financement par déficit budgétaire
Defizitfinanzierung
financiación del déficit
赤字財政、赤字資金調達

deficit spending
赤字开支
dépenser plus que son budget
Deficit Spending;
Defizitfinanzierung
gasto financiado mediante déficit
赤字支出、超過支出

deflation
(通貨) 紧缩; 减缩
déflation
Deflation; Deflationierung
deflación
デフレーション

deflationary fiscal policy
通货紧缩财政方针
politique fiscale déflationniste
deflatorische Fiskalpolitik;
Finanzpolitik
política fiscal deflacionista
デフレ政策

deflationary gap
通货紧缩差额; 通货紧缩缺口
écart déflationniste
deflatorische Lücke
brecha deflacionista
デフレ・ギャップ

degree mill
学位工厂; 学位磨坊
établissement qui offre de donner
une qualification pour un travail
non existant ou peu important,
souvent contre le paiement d'une
somme d'argent substantielle
Diplom-Mühle
institución educativa que ofrece un
título a cambio de dinero
学位提供機関

**delayed settlement
processing**
延期结算处理
traitement pour règlement à
retardement
verzögerte Verrechnung
procesamiento aplazado de pagos
ディレイド・セトルメント・
プロセッシング, 遅延決済処理

delayering
减少中介; 取消中间机构;
精简领导层
écrasement des niveaux
hiérarchiques
Managementebenen abbauen
desjerarquización; eliminación de
capas intermedias
ディレヤリング,

(過剰な中間管理層に対応する)
組織の水平化

del credere agent
保付代理人
agent ducroire
Delkredereagent(in)
agente del credere
買主支払能力保証代理人

delegation
委派; 指派; 授权
délégation
Delegation
delegación
権利の委譲

delist
除名
radier du registre (des compagnies
cotées en Bourse)
eine Gesellschaft aus der
Börsenliste streichen, die
Börsennotierung einer
Gesellschaft zurücknehmen
suspender la cotización de
上場廃止

delivery note
发货单，交货单
bon de réception
Lieferschein
albarán; nota de entrega
貨物引渡し通知書

Delphi technique
德尔斐预测法
technique de Delphes (Méthode
de prévision qualitative selon
laquelle une commission d'experts
répond individuellement à un
questionnaire, ou à une série de
questionnaires, avant d'atteindre
un consensus. La technique de
Delphes nécessite une soumission i
Delphi-Methode;
Delphi-Progrosetechnik
técnica Delphi
(定性的予測の)デルファイ技法

demand forecasting
需求预测
prévisions de demande
Erstellung von Bedarfsprognosen
predicción de la demanda
需要予測

demarcation dispute
分工争议; 分界争议
conflit d'attributions
Kompetenzstreitigkeiten
enfrentamiento entre sindicatos
por la adjudicación de trabajo a
diferentes grupos
組合員境界紛争

demassifying
非大众化

Translations appear in the following order: Chinese, French, German, Spanish/Latin American Spanish, and Japanese

démassifier
Individualisierung
abandono de la masificación
広告媒体の的絞り

Deming Prize
岱明奖
Prix Deming: prix annuel décerné
aux entreprises qui ont réalisé une
amélioration substantielle de leurs
performances, par le biais de
l'application réussie d'un contrôle
de qualité dans toute l'entreprise
Deming-Preis
premio Deming a la mejora del
rendimiento
デミング賞

democracy
民主
démocratie
Demokratie
democracia
民主主義

demographics
人口統計学
données démographiques
Bevölkerungsstatistiken
demografía
人口統計学

denial of service attack
拒接服务攻击
dénégation d'attaque de système
(informatique)
DOS Attacke
ataque para colapsar un sitio
コンピューター・
アタックによるサービス停止

department
部门
service (dans une entreprise)
Abteilung; Dienststelle;
Kostenstelle
departamento
部門, 課

departmental accounts
部门帐户
comptes des services;
départements (d'une entité)
Abteilungsbücher; Bücher einer
Kostenstelle
cuenta departamentales de
operaciones y resultados
部門勘定

departmentalisation
部门化
organisation en départements
Aufgliederung in Abteilungen
oder Kostenstellen
departamentalización
部門化主義

deposit protection
存款保护
protection de dépôt de garantie
Einlagensicherung
protección del depósito
預金保険

deposit slip
存款单
bulletin de versement
Einzahlungsschein
recibo de depósito
預入れ伝票

depreciation
折旧; 贬值; 降值; 损值
dépréciation
Wertminderung; Abschreibung;
Kursverlust
depreciación; amortización
減価償却(有形資産の)

depression
萧条; 不景气; 衰退
récession; dépression
Depression; Konjunkturtiefstand;
Wirtschaftskrise
depresión
不景気, 不況, 大恐慌

deprival value
剥夺价值
valeur de privation
Entziehungswert
valor de privación
剥奪価値

deregulation
取消管理规则; 放松管理;
放弃管理
déréglementation
Deregulierung; Liberalisierung
desregulación
規制緩和

derivative
派生的
dérivé
nachgeordnetes Finanzinstrument
derivado
金融派生商品

Derivative Trading Facility
一种衍生工具交易系统
système informatique d'opérations
boursières et réseau dérivé
Handelseinrichtung für Derivate
sistema informático de
contratación de opciones
negociadas
デリバティブ取引ファシリティー

DES
数据加密标准
DES ou NED: norme d'encryptage
de données
Datenverschüsselungsnorm
estándar estadounidense de

cifrado de datos
DES(データ暗号規格)

design audit
设计审计
audit de conception commerciale
Designprüfung
auditoría de diseño
デザイン監査

design consultancy
设计咨询公司
cabinet-conseil concepteur
Werbeagentur
consultoría de diseño
デザイン・コンサルタント事務所

design for manufacturability
生产设计
conception pour productibilité
Fertigungstechnik
diseño orientado a la fabricación
製造最適化デザイン

deskfast
办公桌早餐
p'tit dèj-bureau
Frühstück am Schreibtisch
desayuno en la mesa del trabajo
デスクで事務に携わる人

de-skilling
降低技术要求的
déqualification
Qualifikationsrückgang;
Qualifikationsabbau
pérdida de la aportación humana
como resultado de la utilización de
nuevas tecnologías
技術不必要化

desk jockey
办公人员
personne qui travaille assise à une
table ou bureau
Schreibtischhengst
oficinista
デスクで事務に携わる人

desk research
桌面研究; 办公室内调查研究
étude sur table
Sekundärforschung
investigación realizada desde la
oficina
デスク・リサーチ

devaluation
贬值; 降值
dévaluation
Abwertung
devaluación
通貨切り下げ, 通貨安

developing country
发展中国家
pays en voie de développement
Entwicklungsländer

país en vías de desarrollo
発展途上国, 開発途上国

development capital
发展资金
capital de développement
Entwicklungskapital;
Anlagekapital
capital de desarrollo
開発資本

Development Capital Market
发展资本市场
marché des capitaux de
développement
Entwicklungskapitalmarkt
sección de pequeñas empresas en
desarrollo de la Bolsa de
Johanesburgo
開発資本市場(証券取引所のー
セクター)

Diagonal Street
对角线街; 南非金融中心
terme informel désignant le centre
financier de Johannesburg et donc
d'Afrique du Sud
Bankenviertel in Johannesburg
el centro financiero de
Johanesburgo
ヨハネスブルグ金融センター

dial and smile
冷不防访问; 敲门微笑式访问
appel sourire de démarchage
potenzielle Kunden unangemeldet
besuchen/anrufen
llamar sin previo aviso pero con
amabilidad
見込客にいきなりセールスコー
ルを掛ける

dicing and slicing
数据析取
analyse par découpage et
catégorisation (de données)
Fachbegriff der Datenanalyse
análisis compartimentalizado de
datos
ダイシング及びスライシング

differential cost
差别增量成本
coût différentiel
Mehrkosten
coste diferencial; coste marginal
原価差異原価

differential pricing
差别定价
fixation de prix différentiels
Preispolitik
fijación de precios diferencial
差別価格

digerati
计算机网络行家
connaisseur (réel ou prétendu) en
technologies de l'information

Leute, die hochentwickelte
Kenntnisse der Internet- und
Computertechnologie haben oder
vorgeben
gurús informáticos
ITエキスパート(自称も含む)

digital cash
数字现金; 数字化现钞
argent numérique (espèces)
digitales Bargeld; digitales Cash
dinero electrónico
デジタル・キャッシュ,
電子マネー,
インターネット・キャッシュ

digital certificate
数字证书; 数字化证书
certificat électronique; certificat
numérique
digitales Zertifikat
certificado digital
デジタル・サーティフィケイト,
電子的(印鑑)証明書

digital coins
电子货币
pièces de monnaie numérique
digitale Münzen
dinero electrónico
デジタル・コイン, 電子的支払

digital coupon
数字优待券
coupon électronique
digitaler Gutschein; digitaler Bon
vale electrónico
電子クーポン,
デジタル・クーポン

digital Darwinism
IT产业进化论
Darwinisme numérique
digitaler Darwinismus
darwinismo digital
デジタル進化論

digital economy
数字经济
économie numérique
digitale Ökonomie;
Internetwirtschaft
economía digital
デジタル経済, 電子的経済

digital goods
数字商品交易
biens numériques
Digitalgüter; digitale Waren
mercancías digitales
デジタル商品, 電子商品,
インターネット商品

digital hygienist
网络监察员
hygiéniste du net
Digitalhygieniker(in)
censor(a) del correo electrónico y

la navegación
社内メールやサーフィンを検
関する人

digital money
数字化貨币; 电子貨币
argent numérique
digitales Geld
dinero electrónico
デジタル・マネー, 電子マネー

digital nervous system
数字化神经系统
système nerveux numérique
Digital Nervous System
sistema nervioso digital
デジタル・ナーバス・システム

digital strategy
数字策略
stratégie numérique
digitale Strategie
estrategia digital
デジタル企業戦略

digital wallet
数字钱包; 电子钱包
porte-monnaie numérique
digitale Geldbörse
monedero electrónico
デジタル・ウオレット,
電子ウオレット

digithead
数字脑袋
ringard technumérique
Person, die viel von Technologie
und Mathematik versteht, aber im
zwischenmenschlichen Bereich
versagt
informático(-a) inadaptado(-a)
人付き合いの下手な技術おたく

digitisable
可数字化处理的
numérisable
digitalisierbar
digitalizable
デジタル化可能な

dilberted
轻视; 蔑视
traité comme Dilbert
vom Chef schlecht behandelt
werden, wie im Comic „Dilbert'
maltratado(-a) por el jefe
上司のいじめを受けた人

Dilbert principle
迪尔伯特原则; 即最无能的工人
被换到最无足轻重的岗位
principe de Dilbert
Dilbert-Prinzip el principio según el
cual cuanto más inútil el
empleado, más probable es que
acabe en el puesto desde el que
puede hacer más daño
ディルバートの原理

Translations appear in the following order: Chinese, French, German, Spanish/Latin American Spanish, and Japanese

dilution
稀释，淡化
dilution
Verwässerung
dilución; debilitamiento
希薄化

DINKY
丁克一族
double revenu, pas d'enfant
Dinks, zwei Einkommen, keine
Kinder
pareja con dos ingresos y sin hijos
二重所得, 子供なし

direct channel
直销渠道
réseau (de distribution) direct
direkter Distributionskanal
canal directo
ダイレクト・チャネル

direct connection
直接连接
connexion directe
Direktverbindung
conexión directa
ダイレクト・コネクション

direct cost
直接成本
coût direct
Einzelkosten; leistungsabhängige
Kosten; direkte Kosten
coste directo
costo directo
直接原価, 可変費用

direct debit
直接付款
prélèvement bancaire
automatique
Einzugsverfahren; direkte
Lastschrift
cargo directo; débito directo;
domiciliación bancaria
直接借方記入

direct labour
直接劳动力
main-d'œuvre directe
direkt im Produktionsprozess
involviertes Personal
mano de obra directa
直接労働者

**direct labour cost percentage
rate**
直接劳动力成本百分比
taux de pourcentage des frais basé
sur le coût de la main d'oeuvre
directe
Stundensatz direkter
Arbeitskosten
porcentaje del costo directo de la
mano de obra
直接労働費率

direct labour hour rate
直接劳动小时比率
taux de pourcentage des frais basé
sur les heures de travail directes
Rate von indirekter zu direkter
Arbeit
coeficiente de horas de trabajo
directo
直接労働時間率

direct mail
直接邮寄广告; 直接信函广告
(publicité par) courrier individuel;
courrier direct
Postwurfsendung; Direktversand;
Direct-Mail
correo directo
ダイレクトメール

**direct mail preference
scheme**
直销邮件消名方案
système de choix pour refuser le
courrier individuel
Direct Mail Preference Scheme
plan para borrarse de los mailings
organizados por las empresas
ダイレクトメール・プ
レファレンス・サービス

directorate
董事会; 理事会
conseil d'administration
Direktorium; Direktion;
Verwaltungsrat
consejo de administración; junta
directiva
重役会, 理事会, 役員会

director's dealing
董事交易
transaction d'administrateur
Aktienhandel eines Mitglieds des
Board of Directors
compra o venta de acciones por un
miembro del consejo de
administración
役員取引

direct product profitability
产品直接利润率
rentabilité de produit directe
direkter Deckungsbeitrag
rentabilidad neta directa del
producto
直接製品利益

direct response marketing
直接反映营销
marketing de réaction directe
Direktrücklauf-Marketing;
Direktantwortwerbung
marketing de respuesta directa
直接リスポンス・マーケティング

direct selling
直销
vente directe

Direktvertrieb
venta directa
直販

direct tax
直接税
impôt direct
direkte Steuer
impuesto directo
直接税

dirty float
干预浮动; 不洁浮动;
有干预的浮动
taux de flottement muselé: taux de
change ne flottant pas librement
parce que la banque centrale d'un
pays intervient sur les marchés de
change étrangers pour altérer son
niveau
schmutziges Floaten
flotación sucia
ダーティー・フロート

dirty price
不洁价格
prix flottant
Barwert
precio sucio
不正価格、ダーティー・プライス

disaggregation
打破联盟
désintégration
Disaggregation
desagregación
ディスアグリゲーション

disaster management
灾难管理; 事故管理
actions prises par une organisation
en réponse à des événements
imprévus
Katastrophenmanagement
gestión de desastres
災害管理, 災害防止措置

discipline
纪律
discipline
Disziplin
disciplina
規律, 懲戒, 訓練, 教練

disclosure of information
信息披露
divulgation d'informations
Offenlegung von Informationen;
Preisgabe od. Weitergabe von
Informationen
revelación de información
情報開示

discount
折扣
escompte; ristourne
Preisnachlass; Diskont; Rabatt;
Nachlass; Skonto; Disagio

---

*Translations appear in the following order: Chinese, French, German, Spanish/Latin American
Spanish, and Japanese*

descuento
割引

discount broker
贴现(票据)经纪人;
贴现承兑票据经纪
courtier d'escompte
Diskontmakler(in);
Wechselmakler(in)
corredor(a) de préstamos
手形割引仲買人、割引ブローカー

discounted bond
折价债券
obligation au-dessous du pair
diskontierter Wechsel
bono descontado
割引債、ディスカウント債

discounted cash flow
现金流量折现法，扣息估利法
prévision du rapport à terme d'un
investissement
Ertragswert
flujo de efectivo descontado
キャッシュ・フロー割引法

discounted dividend model
折扣股息模式
modèle de dividende escompté
Dividendenmodell
modelo de descuento de
dividendos
配当割引モデル

discount loan
折价贷款
emprunt à l'escompte
Diskontkredit
préstama rebajado
ディスカウント・ローン、
割引融資

discount rate
折扣率
taux d'escompte
Diskontsatz
tipo de descuento
割引率, ディスカウント・レート

discount security
折价证券
titre au-dessous du pair
Diskontpapier
obligación cupón cero; activo al
tirón
割引証券

discrete variable
离散变量
variable discrète
diskrete Variable
variable discreta
ディスクリートな変数

discretionary account
自由支配帐户
compte avec procuration (géré par
une banque ou maison de

courtage)
Diskretionskonto; mit Vollmacht
geführtes Konto treuhänderisch
verwaltetes Konto
cuenta discrecional
売買一任勘定

discretionary cost
自定成本
coût sur appréciation
diskretionäre od. im Ermessen
stehende Kosten
coste discrecional
回避可能原価

discretionary order
由委托人付给经纪人一笔款项;
由经纪人决定买什么股票的委托
ordre à appréciation
interessewahrender Auftrag
orden discrecional
自由裁量注文、売買一任注文

discriminant analysis
判别分析
analyse des discriminants
Diskriminanzanalyse
análisis discriminant
判別式分析

discriminating monopoly
歧视性垄断; 差别取价垄断
monopole discriminatoire
diskriminierendes Monopol
monopolio discriminador
差別独占

discrimination
歧视
discrimination
Diskriminierung
discriminación
差別

discussion board
论坛
forum de discussion (sur Internet)
Forum
foro de discusión
ディスカッション・ボード

discussion list
研讨邮件单
liste de destinataires sur E-mail
pour discussion
Discussion List
lista de discusión
ディスカッション・リスト

disequilibrium price
非均衡价
prix déséquilibré
Ungleichgewichtspreis
precio de desequilibrio
不均衡価格

dishonour
拒付; 拒兑
ne pas honorer

nicht bezahlen
rechazar
(手形等の)引受拒否、不渡りにする

disinflation
通货紧缩; 通货收缩; 反通货膨胀
désinflation
Desinflation
desinflación
ディスインフレ

disintermediation
脱媒
désintermédiarisation
Ausschalten von Mittelsmännern
zum direkten Verkauf an
Verbrauch; Einlagenabzug
eliminación de intermediarios
仲介業者排除

dismissal
解雇
renvoi ou licenciement
Entlassung
despido
解雇

dispersion
离差
dispersion
Streuung
dispersión
ばらつき

display advertising
展示广告
publicité accrocheuse
Anzeigenwerbung
publicidad en anuncios
意匠広告

disposable income
税后所得; 可自由支配的收入;
纳税后个人可用收入
revenu net; revenu disponible
verfügbares Einkommen
renta o ingreso disponible
可処分所得

dispute
意见分歧; 纠纷; 劳资纠纷; 争议;
争论
conflit; litige
Streit; Streitfall; Streitigkeit
conflicto
係争, 争議

distance learning
远距离教学
téléenseignement
Tele-Learning; Fernunterricht
educación a distancia
通信教育, オープン・ラーニング

distance sampling
远距(离)采样
échantillonnage par distance
Entfernungs-Auswahlverfahren
método de muestreo utilizado en

estadística ecológica para
determinar el número de animales
que se alimentan en un habitat
específico o el número de plantas
que crecen en el mismo
距離サンプリング

distribution centre
销售中心
centre de distribution
Auslieferungszentrale;
Absatzzentrum
centro de distribución
流通センター

distribution channel
分配渠道; 销售渠道
voie de distribution
Vertriebskanal
canal de distribución
流通チャンネル

distribution cost
销售成本
frais de distribution
Vertriebskosten
coste de distribución
流通経費

distribution list
分发列表
liste de distribution
Verteiler
lista de distribución
ディストリビューション・リスト

distribution management
销售管理
gestion de la distribution
Verteilungswirtschaft;
Absatzwirtschaft;
Vertriebsmanagement
gestión de la distribución
物流管理、流通管理

**distribution resource
planning**
销售资源规划
planification des ressources de
distribution
vertriebsorientierte
Betriebsmittelplanung
planificación de la distribución de
recursos
流通リソース計画

distributive network
销售网络商
réseau de distribution
Distributionsnetzwerk
red distributiva
ディストリビュー
ション・ネットワーク

distributor
分销商
distributeur
Vertriebspartner; Händler(in);

Vertriebsstelle; Großhändler(in);
Generalvertretung
distribuidor(a)
卸売業者

distributor support
分销商支持
soutien au distributeur
Vertriebspartnerunterstützung
apoyo al distribuidor
ディストリビューター・
サポート

diversification
多样化; 分散化; 多角经营
diversification
Diversifizierung; Diversifikation;
Anlagenstreuung
diversificación
多角化

**diversified investment
company**
分散投资公司
société d'investissement à capital
variable et diversifié
Investmentgesellschaft mit
gesetzlicher Risikostreuung
compañía de inversiones
diversificada
分散型投資会社

diversity
多样化
diversité
Vielfalt
diversidad
多様性

diverted hours
转移时间
heures de travail dérivées (sur des
activités indirectes)
Zeit für auftragsfremde
Tätigkeiten
mano de obra indirecta; trabajo
indirecto
転用時間

divestment
撤销; 放弃; 减少投资
dépouillement (d'entreprise)
Veräußerung; Abtrennung
desinversión
会社分割, 事業の売却や譲渡

dividend
股息，红利，股利
dividende
Dividende
dividendo activo
配当

dividend clawback
股利弥补方式融资
récupération de dividendes
Dividendenrücklage;
Dividendenrückforderung
reinversión del dividendo

(資金調達目的の)配当金再投資,
配当金クローバック

dividend cover
股利保证倍数; 盈利对股息的比率;
净利与股息比率
garantie de dividende
Verhältnis Gewinn: Dividende
cobertura del dividendo; beneficio
por acción
配当倍率

dividend growth model
股息成长模式
modèle de croissance de dividende
Dividenden-Wachstumsmodell
modelo de crecimiento basado en
el dividendo
配当成長モデル

dividend limitation
股息限制; 红利限度
limitation de dividendes
Dividendenbeschränkung;
Dividendenreinvestitionsplan
limitación de dividendos
配当制限

dividend payout ratio
Rapport de pourcentage du
bénéfice net distribué en dividende
Ausschüttungssatz
índice de desembolso de
dividendos
配当支払率

dividend per share
每股股息
dividende par action
Dividende pro Aktie
dividendo activo por acción
株当り配当

dividend reinvestment plan
股息再投资计划
plan de réinvestissement de
dividendes
Wiederanlagenplan der Dividende
plan de reinversión de dividendos
配当金株式再投資制度

dividend rights
股息要求权
droit aux dividendes
Dividendenrechte
derecho a dividendos
配当請求権

dividends-received deduction
所得股息税项扣减
dégrèvement sur dividendes
Steuerabzug für Dividenden die
ein Unternehmen von
Tochterunternehmen bezieht
exención fiscal en los dividendos
por participación en otras
sociedades
受取配当金の控除

---

*Translations appear in the following order: Chinese, French, German, Spanish/Latin American
Spanish, and Japanese*

dividend yield
红利收益; 股利收益率;
股息收益报酬率
taux de rendement (en dividendes)
Dividendenrendite;
Dividendenertrag; Effektivrendite
rendimiento de dividendos
配当利回り

division of labour
(劳动)分工
répartition des tâches
Arbeitsteilung
reparto del trabajo
分業

document
文件
document
Dokument
documento
ドキュメント

documentary credit
扣汇信用证，跟单信用证
crédit documentaire
Dokumentenakkreditiv
crédito documentario
荷為替信用状

dog and pony show
引资演讲团; 引资演说团
tournée des manitous
Werbetour, mit der leitende
Angestellte Anleger zur Investition
in ihr Unternehmen überreden
sollen
gira de los directivos para atraer
inversores
幹部が投資を勧誘するために行-
う全国ツアー

dog-eat-dog
狗咬狗，竞争激烈
les loups se mangent entre eux
rücksichtslos, schonungslos
despiadado
熾烈競争

dogfood
狗食，测试版软件
logiciel temporaire utilisé par une
organisation aux fins de tests
Prototyp
software de pruebas
テストソフト

dogs of the Dow
道琼斯指数内的狗股
titres du Dow Jones qui paient les
plus petits dividendes
Dogs of the Dow
las acciones del Dow Jones que
pagan los dividendos más
pequeños
ダウジョーズ最小配当金株

dole bludger
靠救济金的懒惰虫
parasite de l'ANPE
Drückeberger
persona que vive del subsidio del
paro
福祉の寄生虫

dollar roll
美元滚动
accord d'opérations sur titres:
accord de vente de titres à un
moment donné avec son rachat
ultérieur pour un prix spécifié (en
dollars)
Dollar Roll Depot
acuerdo para vender un título y
comprar uno similar en el futuro
ドル・ロール

dollars-and-cents
以货币计算
calculé en espèces
Geldpolitik
dinero
金銭面だけを考慮した

domain name
域名
nom de domaine
Domänenname
nombre de dominio
ドメイン名

**domicilium citandi et
executandi**
法定正式地址
adresse où une sommation à
comparaître
Adresse, an die eine Vorladung
oder anderer offizieller Bescheid zu
liefern ist
domicilio
ビジネスの公告住所

donut
广告中产品信息部分
section au milieu d'une publicité
où l'information produit est
généralement placée
Feuerspatz
parte central
ＣＭの中央部分

dot bam
网上实务
entreprise réelle physique avec
forte présence sur Internet
bezeichnet eine online-Plattform
eines 'Old'-economy
Unternehmens
empresa con presencia física y en
Internet
ドット・ブリック・アンド・
モルタル

dot-bomb
互联网炸弹
point.bombe: entreprise sur le Net
qui a fait faillite
Dot.Bombe: ein
Internet-Unternehmen, das
bankrott gegangen ist
puntocom que ha quebrado
ドット・ボム

dot-com
互联网公司
point.com: entreprise sur le Net
Dot.com
puntocom
ドットコム企業

dotted-line relationships
间接上下级关系
relations entre managers et
personnel, comme sur un
organigramme, selon lequel ils
n'ont pas de contacts directs
quotidiens
Verbindung zwischen
Geschäftsleiter und Mitarbeitern
die ihnen indirekt unterstehen,
aber nicht im Arbeitsalltag; in
einem Organigramm durch
gestrichelte Linien dargestellt
relaciones indirectas
組織内での間接的な監督関係

double-blind
双方盲动
en double aveugle
doppelblind
estudio de doble ciego; ensayo a
doble ciego
ダブルブラインド

double dipping
双重领款
double pioche
Rente und Sozialunterstützung
beziehen
cobro simultáneo de subsidios de
la seguridad social y pagos de un
fondo de pensiones
(年金と社会保障の)二重取り

double indemnity
双倍赔偿金
double indemnité
Verdoppelung der
Versicherungssumme in
bestimmten Fällen, wie Unfalltod
acuerdo para vender un título y
comprar uno similar en el futuro
(事故による死亡時の)
災害倍額支払特約

double opt-in
二度确认加入
double processus d'inscription
(pour recevoir des informations via
un site Web)

---

*Translations appear in the following order: Chinese, French, German, Spanish/Latin American
Spanish, and Japanese*

'double-opt-in'-Verfahren
doble confirmación
ダブル・オプトイン

double taxation
双重课税
double imposition
Doppelbesteuerung
doble imposición
二重課税

double taxation agreement
双重征税协议
convention relative aux doubles
impositions
Doppelbesteuerungsabkommen
acuerdo de doble tributación
二重課税協定

doubtful debts provision
坏帐准备
provision pour créance douteuse
Delkredere-Rückstellung
provisión para deudas de cobro
dudoso; provisión para deudas
dudosas; provisión para
insolvencias
貸倒れ予想引当金

doughnut principle
环型原理
concept qui compare les
organisations à un beignet inversé,
avec un centre plein – les activités
essentielles – entouré d'un trou –
une zone flexible qui contient les
partenaires de l'organisation
Kernkompetenzen-Konzept
principio que asimila a las
organizaciones a un dónut con el
agujero fuera y la masa en el
medio
ドーナツ原理

Dow Jones Averages
道琼斯指数; 道琼斯平均指数
indice Dow-Jones
Dow-Jones Aktienindex
índices del Dow Jones
ダウジョーンズ平均(株価)

downshifting
为过有质量的生活而降薪降职
réduction des activités
professionnelles
Downshifting; 'Herunterschalten'
relajación de la entrega al trabajo
ダウン・シフト
(生活の質向上のための仕事量,
収入の下方修正)

downsizing
减 编; 裁员
réduction d'effectif (par
licenciement)
Stellenabbau; Verringerung; des
Personalbestands
reajuste de plantillas

ダウンサイジング,
従業員解雇を伴う経営合理化

downstream
下游
en aval
späte Produtionsstufe
más adelante
川下部門

downstream progress
借势取得成功
progrès dans le sens du courant
Fortschritt; mit dem Strom
avance a favor de la corriente
下流に向かう進歩

downtime
窝工时间; 停工时间
temps d'arrêt
Ausfallzeit
paro técnico
ダウンタイム(作業中止時間)

Dow Theory
道氏理论
théorie de Dow: théorie selon
laquelle seul un mouvement
similaire et simultané des titres
industriels et de transports indique
une tendance dans le prix des titres
et valeurs à la Bourse new-yorkaise
Dow-Theorie
teoría de Dow
ダウ理論

draft
汇票
traite
Tratte; Wechsel; Bankscheck
letra de cambio
手形振出し, 支払指図書

drawee
受票人，付款人
acceptant
Bezogene/r; Trassat
librado; girado; aceptante
手形名宛人

drawing account
提款帐户
compte d'associé
Girokonto; Kontokorrentkonto;
Spesen- u. Vorschusskonto
cuentacorriente
(経営者の)現金引出記入勘定,
引出勘定

dress-down day
便装日
journée décontractée au bureau
Tag, an dem Arbeitnehmer lässig
gekleidet am Arbeitsplatz
erscheinen können
día de ropa informal
カジュアルデー

drilling down
渐深数据陈列
forage de données
Detailgrad runterbrechen
organización jerárquica de la
información
ドリル・ダウン

drip method
定期电话提醒促销法
méthode de la guerre d'usure
Tropfmethode
método de goteo
購入が決まるまで見込客に定期
的に電話を掛ける商法

drive time
行车时间
heure d'encombrement
Tageszeit, zu der die meisten
Menschen im Auto sitzen, daher
für Radiowerbung am günstigsten
erachtet
hora punta
自動車通勤者のラッシュアワー

drop lock
利息保值债券，锁定下限债券
verrouillage sur taux fixe quand les
taux d'intérêts chutent sur un
pourcentage convenu
Drop-Lock-Floater
congelación del interés en un nivel
mínimo
ドロップ・ロック

drownloading
下载性死机，下载淹机
télénoyade
Saugen
descarga masiva que bloquea el
ordenador
descarga masiva que bloquea la
computadora
ダウンローディング

dual currency bond
双轨货币债券
obligation en double devise
Doppelwährungsanleihe
bono de doble divisa
二重通貨建て債,
デュアル・カレンシー債

dual economy
二元经济; 双重经济
économie double
duale Volkswirtschaft
economía dual
二重構造経済

dual pricing
双重定价
système de prix double
deglomerative Preisdifferenzierung
doble fijación de precios
二重価格表示

Translations appear in the following order: Chinese, French, German, Spanish/Latin American Spanish, and Japanese

dual trading
双轨交易
opérerations en double
Dual Trading
transacciones simultáneas para
cuentas ajenas y propias
二重取引, 二者取引

due-on-sale clause
转售即还交易
clause d'échéance d'hypothèque à
vente
'fällig bei Verkauf' – Klausel, nach
der beim Hauskauf die Hypothek
umgehend fällig wird
cláusula de préstamo pagadero a
la venta
デュー・オン・セール条項

dumbsizing
无效精简
réduction d'entreprise suicidaire
totverschlanken
reajuste de plantilla
contraproducente
過剰な人員整理

DUMP
贫困失业的成年工作者
chômeur cadre sans ressources et
d'un certain âge
mittellose, arbeitlose Person
reiferen Alters aus dem höheren
Berufsstand
profesional adulto pobre en el paro
貧困無職成人専門家

dumping
倾销
dumping
Dumping
dumping
ダンピング

duopoly
双头垄断; 双占
duopole
Duopol
duopolio
複占, 二人占

Dutch auction
荷兰式拍卖
enchères au rabais
holländische Auktion: Abgabe von
Wertpapieren zum Einheitspreis
subasta holandesa; subasta a la
baja
せり下げ競売

duvet day
事假
journée de congé prise par un
employé qui n'a pas envie de se
rendre au travail
ein Tag, an dem Personal
krankfeiern darf
día de baja sin necesidad de

justificación
許可休日

Dynamic HTML
动态超文本链接标示语言
HTML dynamique
Dynamic HTML
HTML dinámico
ダイナミックHTML(ホームペー
ジ記述言語)

dynamic pricing
动态定价
fixation de prix dynamique
dynamische Preisgestaltung
fijación dinámica de precios
動的価格決定

dynamic programming
动态规划; 动态程序设计
programmation dynamique
dynamisches Programmieren
programación dinámica
ダイナミック・プログラミング
(動的計画法)

e-alliance
网络联盟
partenariat entre entreprises pour
affaires sur Internet
Online Joint Venture
alianza electrónica
e 同盟, e 連合

ear candy
悦耳的甜蜜小曲
susurrement inepte
Süßholz; Ohrenschmaus
música intranscedente para los
oídos
聞こえはいいが中身がない話

early adopter
大胆尝试者
personne ou organisation qui est
une des premières à adopter une
nouvelle technologie
eine Technologie früh
annehmende Person oder
Unternehmen
pionero en la utilización de una
tecnología
新技術早期採用

early retirement
提前退休; 早退
retraite anticipée
Vorruhestand; Frührente
jubilación anticipada
早期退職

earned income
已赚收入
revenu provenant du travail
Arbeitseinkommen; realisierter
Gewinn
ingresos por trabajo; rentas del
trabajo
勤労所得

earnings[1]
报酬; 收入
salaire
Einkommen
ingresos
勤労所得

earnings[2]
收入
profits ou bénéfices (d'une
entreprise)
Ertrag; Reingewinn; Gewinn;
Einkommen
ganancias; beneficios
收益

earnings per share
每股收益
bénéfice par action
Gewinn je Aktie
beneficios por acción; dividendo
por acción; ganancia por acción
株当り利益

earnings surprise
收益突变
variation surprise des bénéfices
Ertragsüberraschungen
informe de ingresos que difiere de
la previsión
利益の意外性

earnings yield
盈余报酬率; 收益率; 值利率
rendement spéculatif
Gewinnrendite
rendimiento de ingresos
益回り

earn-out arrangement
多赚多交协议
accord de révision de
rémunération
an den Erfolg gekoppelte
Abfindung
acuerdo de remuneración por la
venta dependiente del
rendimiento en un período
específico posterior
アーン・アウト協定

EASDAQ
欧洲证券经纪商协会自动报价系统
bourse européenne pour les
compagnies technologiques et de
croissance, basée sur le NASDAQ
américain
EASDAQ; European Association of
Securities Dealers Automated
Quotation
EASDAQ
イースダック市場

eased
略为下迭
(marché) affaibli

Translations appear in the following order: Chinese, French, German, Spanish/Latin American
Spanish, and Japanese

nachgegeben; abgeschwächt; abgebröckelt
distendido; relajado
軟化傾向

EBITDA
利息，税收，折旧及摊还前收益
abréviation de revenus avant intérêts, impôts, dépréciation et amortissement
Abk. für earnings before interest, tax, depreciation, and amortisation
resultado antes de intereses e impuestos y sin la depreciación y amortización de intereses
利子，税，減価償却，
部分償還込み収益

EBQ
最优单批规模
taille de lot optimale pour la fabrication d'un produit ou composant au coût le plus bas
optimale Losgröße
cantidad económica por lote
最適バッチサイズ

EBRD
欧洲复兴开发银行
banque européenne pour la reconstruction et le développement
Europaïsche Bank für Wiederaufbau und Entwicklung
Banco Europeo para Reconstrucción y Desarrollo
欧州復興開発銀行

e-business[1]
电子商务
e-business: transactions commerciales sur Internet, y compris l'achat et la vente électronique de biens et services, les services clients et les communications avec les partenaires commerciaux
e-Business
negocios electrónicos
電子取引，Eビジネス，
エレクトロニック・コマース

e-business[2]
电子商务
e-entreprise: entreprise qui conduit ses affaires sur Internet
e-Business
empresa electrónica
eビジネス

ECB
欧洲中央银行
banque centrale européenne
ECB
BCE
欧州中央銀行

ecoconsumer
关注生态环境的客户
éco-consommateur
Öko-Verbraucher(in);
Ökokonsument(in);
umweltbewusste/r Verbraucher(in)
ecoconsumidor(a)
環境問題重視の消費者，
エコ・コンシューマー

ecolabel
生态标签
éco-label
Öko-Etikett; Ökokennzeichnung
ecoetiqueta
エコラベル，
(欧州連合の)環境保護認定印

ecological priority
环境保护优先政策
priorité écologique
ökologische Priorität
prioridad ecológica
生態優先権

ecological statistics
生态统计学
statistiques écologiques
Ökostatistik
estadística ecológica
生態統計学

e-commerce
电子商业活动
e-commerce
elektronischer Geschäftsverkehr;
elektronischer Handel
comercio electrónico
Eコマース

e-commerce processes
电子商业运作
procédés du e-commerce
Prozesse im E-Commerce
procesos del comercio electrónico
eコマース(電子取引)プロセス

e-company
电子商业公司
e-compagnie: entreprise de e-commerce ou commerce électronique sur Internet
Internet-Firma
empresa electrónica; ciberempresa
電子商取引会社，Eコマース会社

econometric model
计量经济学模式
modèle économétrique
ökonometrisches Modell
modelo econométrico
エコノメトリック・
モデル、計量経済モデル

econometrics
计量经济学
économétrie
Ökonometrie

econometría
計量経済学

economic assumption
经济假设
présomption économique
wirtschaftliche Annahme
hipótesis económica
経済見通し

Economic Development Board
经济发展局
Comité de développement économique (pour promouvoir les investissements à Singapour)
Wirtschaftsentwicklungsausschuss
consejo de desarrollo económico en Singapur
シンガポール経済開発局

economic goods
有价物品; 经济财货
produits économiques
Wirtschaftsgüter
bienes económicos
経済財

economic growth
经济增长
croissance économique
Wirtschaftswachstum
crecimiento económico
経済成長(率)

economic indicator
经济指标
indicateur économique
Konjunkturindikator
indicador económico
経済指標

economic life
经济生命
vie économique
Erwerbstätigkeit
vida económica
経済生活、経済的耐用年数、
経済的寿命

economic miracle
经济奇迹
miracle économique
Wirtschaftswunder
milagro económico
経済の奇跡

economic order quantity
经济定货数量
quantité de commandes économique
optimale Bestellmenge;
wirtschaftliche Bestellmenge
cantidad de orden económico;
valoración del orden económico
経済的注文量

Translations appear in the following order: Chinese, French, German, Spanish/Latin American Spanish, and Japanese

economic paradigm
经济经典理论
paradigme économique
Ökonomieprinzip
paradigma económico
基本経済原理

Economic Planning and Advisory Council
经济规划咨询委员会
comité de conseil et planification économique
Wirtschaftsplanungs- und Beratungsausschuss
comité asesor del gobierno australiano en asuntos económicos
経済企画諮問協議会

economic pressure
经济压力
pression économique
wirtschaftlicher Druck; Konjunkturdruck
presión económica
経済的圧力

economics
经济学
science économique
Volkswirtschaftslehre; Wirtschaftswissenschaft
economía
経済学、経済状態

economic surplus
经济过剩
excédent économique
ökonomischer Überschuss
superávit económico
経済余剰

economic theory of the firm
公司经济理论
théorie économique d'entreprise
Wirtschaftstheorie von der Firma
teoría económica de la empresa
企業の経済理論

economic value added
经济附加值
valeur ajoutée économique
zusätzlicher Mehrwert
valor añadido económico
経済付加価値

economic welfare
经济福利
bien-être économique
materielle Lebenslage; Wohlstandsniveau
bienestar económico
経済の厚生、経済的福祉

economies of scale
规模经济
économies d'échelle
Größenvorteile; Größeneffekt; Größendegression; Economies of Scale
economías de escala
規模の経済

economies of scope
范围经济
économies d'envergure
Umfangsvorteile; Diversifikationsvorteile
economías de alcance
エコノミー・オブ・スコープ

economist
经济学家
économiste
Wirtschaftswissenschaftler(in); Volkswirt(in); Wirtschaftler(in)
economista
経済学者、エコノミスト

economy
经济体系
économie
Wirtschaft; Volkswirtschaft
economía
経済機構、経済、倹約

economy efficiency principle
经济效率原则
principe de l'efficacité économique
Pareto Effizienz
principio de eficacia en la economía
経済効率原理

ecopreneur
生态企业家
entrepreneur vert
Unternehmer(in) mit ökologischen Anliegen
ecoempresario(-a)
環境意識の高い実業家

educational leave
学习假
congé pour raisons d'éducation ou de stage
Bildungsurlaub
permiso por estudios
就学休職

e-economy
电子经济
e-économie
Internetwirtschaft
economía electrónica
e 経済

effect
效果
effet
Wirkung
efecto
影響

effective annual rate
实际年利率
taux annuel effectif
jährliche Effektivverzinsung
tipo de interés efectivo anual
実効年利率

effective capacity
有效生产能力
capacité efficace
Grundkapazität; effektive Kapazität
capacidad efectiva
有効生産能力

effective date
有效日期
date d'entrée en vigueur
Stichtag
fecha efectiva
有効期日

effectiveness
有效性
efficacité
Effektivität; effektives Leistungsmaß
eficacia
有効性

effective price
有效价格
prix réel
Effektivkurs; tatsächlicher Kurs
precio efectivo
実効価格

effective sample size
有效试样量
taille d'échantillon efficace
effektiver Stichprobenumfang
tamaño efectivo de la muestra
有効サンプルサイズ

effective spread
有效差价
écart effectif
effektiv gezahlter Spread
margen de suscripción efectivo
実効スプレッド

effective strike price
有效买进期权价
prix d'accord effectif
Durchschnittspreis
precio de ejercicio efectivo
実効権利行使価格

effective tax rate
实际税率
taux d'imposition effectif
tatsächlicher Steuersatz
tipo impositivo efectivo
実効税率

efficiency
效率; 效能
efficacité
Wirtschaftlichkeit; Rentabilität; Leistungsfähigkeit; Produktivität
eficiencia
効率性、能率, 有効性

Translations appear in the following order: Chinese, French, German, Spanish/Latin American Spanish, and Japanese

efficiency ratio
效能比率
taux d'efficacité
Wirksamkeitsverhältnis;
Effizienzverhältnis
factor de rendimiento
效率

efficient capital market
有效的资本市场
marché financier efficace
wirtschaftlicher; rationeller
Kapitalmarkt
mercado de valores eficiente
能率的資本市場、効率的資本市場

efficient markets hypothesis
hypothèse de l'efficacité des
marchés
Markteffizienzhypothese
hipótesis de mercado eficiente
有効市場仮説

EFQM Excellence Model
欧洲质量管理基金会卓越表现
模式
modèle d'excellence européen de
la FEGQ
EFQM Modell und European
Excellence Award
modelo EFQM de calidad europeo
欧州品質管理基金最優秀モデル

egosurfing
自我浏览
surfer le Net à la recherche de
références sur soi-même
Ego-Surfing
navegación vanidosa
自名探しのサーフィン

EIB
欧洲投资银行
banque européenne
d'investissements
EIB: Europäische Investitionsbank
BIE
欧州投資銀行

86
抛弃
86: abandonner quelque chose
comme une proposition ou un
document
verwerfen
Rechazo
破棄する

eighty-twenty rule
8020法则; 帕累托最优;
帕累托法则
principe de Pareto
Pareto Prinzip (80/20-Regel)
regla del 80–20; principio de
Pareto
8020規則

EIS
执行资讯系统
système informatique conçu pour
la collecte, le stockage, le
traitement et la fourniture
d'informations pour cadres de
direction
Führungsinformationsysteme
sistema de información para
ejecutivos
エグゼクティブ

either-way market
两可市场
marché d'égalité monétaire
Devisenmarkt ohne Gebühren
mercado con tipos idénticos
両方向市場

e-lance
网络自由执业者
type de travail indépendant, ou
freelance, qui utilise l'Internet
freiberufliche Tätigkeit unter
Nutzung des Internets
trabajo de freelance a través de
Internet
eランス

elasticity
弹性
élasticité
Elastizität
elasticidad
弹力性, 融通性

eldercare
老年人福利
programme d'aide aux personnes
âgées
Altenfürsorge; Versorgung älterer
Verwandter von Arbeitnehmern
cuidado de los mayores
高齢者医療介護

e-learning
电子化学习; 通过网络学习
acquisition de connaissances par le
biais d'Internet ou d'un système
Intranet
elektronisches Lernen; das
Erwerben von Kenntnissen über
das Internet oder ein Intranet.
aprendizaje electrónico
インターネット学習

elected officers
当选官员
membres élus (du comité directeur
ou d'un syndicat, etc.)
Funktionärinnen; Funktionäre;
gewählte Vertreter(in)nen
representantes electos
選任役員

electronic catalogue
电子化目录
catalogue électronique

elektronischer Katalog
catálogo electrónico
電子カタログ

electronic cheque
电子化支票
chèque électronique/téléchèque
elektronischer Scheck; E-Scheck
cheque electrónico
電子小切手

electronic commerce modelling language
电子商业模式语音
langage de modélisation de
commerce électronique
Modelliersprache für den
elektronischen; Geschäftsverkehr
lenguaje de modelado de
comercio electrónico
Eコマースモデリング言語

electronic data capture
电子授权清算
saisie de données électroniques
elektronische Datenerfassung
captura electrónica de datos
POSシステム

electronic data interchange
电子数据交换
échange de données électronique
elektronischer Datenaustausch
intercambio electrónico de datos
電子データ交換

electronic envelope
电子信封
enveloppe électronique
elektronische Briefumschlag;
elektronische Brieftasche
sobre electrónico
電子封筒

electronic funds transfer
电子资金转帐
transfert de fonds électronique
belegloser Zahlungsverkehr;
elektronischer
Überweisungsverkehr
sistema de transferencia de fondos
electrónica
電子資金移動

electronic funds transfer at point of sale
电子基金即时划转
transfert de fonds électronique au
point de vente
elektronischer Zahlungsverkehr in
Verbindung mit einem
POS-Terminal; elektronische
Abbuchung am POS-Terminal
transferencia electrónica de
fondos en el punto de venta
販売時電子資金移動

Translations appear in the following order: Chinese, French, German, Spanish/Latin American Spanish, and Japanese

electronic payment system
电子付款系统
système de paiement électronique
elektronisches Zahlungssystem
sistema electrónico de pago
電子決済システム

electronic shopping
网络购物; 电子购物; 网上购物
shopping électronique
elektronischer Einkauf;
Computer-Shopping
compras en línea; compras
electrónicas
電子ショッピング

electronic software distribution
电子软件分销
distribution de logiciel
électronique
elektronischer Software-Vertrieb
distribución electrónica de
software
電子ソフトウェア配信

electronic store
电子商店
magasin électronique
elektronischer Laden;
Internetladen
tienda electrónica; cibertienda
電子商店,
エレクトロニック・ストア

electronic trading
电子贸易
opérations électroniques
elektronischer Handel
contratación electrónica
電子取引, システム売買

elements of cost
成本要素
éléments du prix
Kostenelemente
elementos de coste
原価要素

elephant
大型企业
mastodonte
Elefant; Unternehmenskoloss
gigante empresarial
自名探しのサーフィン

elevator pitch
(对投资者) 简短的公司介绍
pratique qui consiste à promouvoir
des plans d'entreprises point-com
à des investisseurs en très peu de
temps
kurzfristiges Anbieten von
Internet-Geschäftsplänen
charla comercial breve
エレベーター・ピッチ

eligible paper[1]
合格票据
effet de commerce accepté par la
banque centrale 'Bank of England'
comme garantie de prêts aux
maisons d'escompte (Royaume
Uni)
zentralbankfähiger Wechsel
efectos/valores negociables/
descontables
割引適格手形

eligible paper[2]
合格票据
effet de première catégorie
accepté pour être réescompté par
le système de réserve fédérale
(U.S.A)
rediskontfähiges Wertpapier
efectos/valores negociables/
descontables
割引適格手形

eligible reserves
合法储备
réserves bancables
Mindestbestand plus
Reserveguthaben
reservas bancarias totales
割引適格準備金

Eligible Service Period
合格服务期
période de service avec éligibilité
anzurechnende Verdienstjahre
tiempo computable
対象勤続年数

Eligible Termination Payment
合格停职金
versement de fin de contrat
d'emploi avec éligibilité
Abfindung, die in einem
zugelassenen Sparfonds investiert
werden kann
finiquito depositable en una
cuenta de inversiones
対象退職金

Elvis year
高峰年
année où la popularité de
quelqu'un ou quelque chose est à
son summum
Popularitätsspitze
año de éxito
人気高騰の年

e-mail
电子邮件
e-mail
EMail; elektronische Post
correo electrónico
Eメール

e-mail address
电子邮件地址
adresse e-mail

EMail-Adresse
dirección de correo electrónico
Eメール・アドレス

e-mail mailing list
电子邮件邮件发送清单
liste pour envoi de messages
e-mail
Mailing-List
lista de correo
eメール・メーリングリスト

e-mail signature
电子邮件签名
signature e-mail
digitale Signatur
firma en el correo electrónico
eメール署名(電子署名)

e-mail system
电子邮件系统
système de mail électronique
Email-System
sistema de correo electrónico
eメール・システム

e-marketplace
网上交易市场
e-marché
Elektronischer Marktplatz
mercado de trabajo electrónico
eマーケットプレース

embezzlement
盗用
détournement de fonds
Unterschlagung; Veruntreuung
desfalco de fondos/apropiación
indebida; malversación de fondos/
apropiación indebida
横領

emerging market
新兴市场
marché émergent
aufstrebender Markt;
aufstrebendes Land
mercado emergente
急成長市場, 新興市場,
エマージング・マーケット

emotag
情绪标签; 表情标签
émotag
Zeichen für Lächeln oder
Stirnrunzeln, in E-Mail anstelle von
Emoticons verwendet
palabra que hace de emoticono
エモティコン(感情・顔表現文字)
の代りに使われるHTMLタグ型
感情表現

emoticon
表情符号
émoticône
Emoticon
emoticono
顔文字(エモティコン)

Translations appear in the following order: Chinese, French, German, Spanish/Latin American Spanish, and Japanese

emotional capital
情感资本
capital émotionnel
emotionales Kapital
capital emocional
感性資本

emotional intelligence
情商
intelligence de cœur
emotionale Intelligenz
inteligencia emocional
感情知識

employability
可雇用性
susceptibilité d'être employé
Vermittlungsfähigkeit;
Arbeitsvermittlungsfähigkeit;
Beschäftigungsfähigkeit
potencia de conseguir empleo
エンプロイアビリティー

employee
雇员; 职工; 员工
salarié
Arbeitnehmer(in); Mitarbeiter(in);
Angestellte/r
empleado(-a)
被雇用者

**employee assistance
programme**
雇员支持计划
programme d'aide aux employés
Unterstützungsprogramm; für
Arbeitnehmer(in)nen
programa de ayuda a los
empleados
被雇用者支援プログラム

employee association
职工协会
association d'employés
Arbeitnehmerverband
asociación de empleados
従業員連合

employee attitude survey
雇员态度调查
étude sur l'attitude des employés
Arbeitsklimaerhebung;
Arbeitsmileustudie
encuesta de satisfacción entre los
empleados
従業員意識調査

employee commitment
员工忠诚度
degré de loyauté d'un employé
Engagement der
Arbeitnehmer(in)nen;
Arbeitnehmerloyalität
compromiso del empleado
従業員の忠誠心

employee development
职工发展

développement des employés
Mitarbeiterförderung
formación de los trabajadores
従業員能力開発

employee discount
内部职工价; 内部职工折扣
ristourne aux employés
Angestelltenrabatt
descuento para empleados
従業員割引

employee handbook
雇员手册; 员工手册
manuel du salarié
Handbuch; für
Arbeitnehmer(in)nen
manual del empleado
従業員便覧, 職員ハンドブック

employee involvement
职工参与
degré de participation des
employés
Beteiligung od. Einbindung der
Arbeitnehmer(in)nen
participación del empleado
従業員参加システム

employee ownership
职工所有权
participation par les employés
Mitarbeiter-Beteiligung;
Beteiligung; der Angestellten; am
Aktienkapital; der Gesellschaft
participación de los empleados en
la empresa
従業員持ち株

employee participation
职工参与
participation des employés
Mitbestimmung der
Arbeitnehmer(in)nen;
Arbeitnehmerbeteiligung
participación de los trabajadores
従業員参加

**employee referral
programme**
雇员推荐计划; 员工推荐政策
système de recommandation
d'employé
Arbeitnehmervorschlagsprogramm;
Arbeitnehmervermit-
tlungsprogramm
programa de recomendación de
futuros candidatos por parte de los
trabajadores
従業員による求職者回付
プログラム

**employee share ownership
plan**
员工持股计划
plan d'actionnariat des salariés
Mitarbeiterbeteiligungsplan;
Aktienerwerbsplan für

Arbeitnehmer(in)nen
plan de compra acciones para los
empleados
従業員持株制

employee share scheme
职工参股计划
système selon lequel les salariés
peuvent acheter des parts dans
l'entreprise qui les emploient,
laquelle leur offre des actions
gratuites ou à prix réduit
Belegschaftsaktienplan
plan de compra de acciones para el
personal
従業員株式システム

employee stock fund
职工股票基金
fonds d'actions pour salariés
Belegschaftsaktienfonds
fondo de inversión de los
empleados
従業員持株基金

employer
雇主
employeur
Arbeitgeber(in)
empresario(-a)
雇用者

employers' association
雇主联合会
association patronale
Arbeitgeberverband
organización patronal
雇用者連合

Employment Court
雇佣法庭
cour de justice pour l'emploi
Arbeitsgericht
tribunal laboral neozelandés;
magistratura de trabajo
neozelandesa
雇用裁判所

employment equity
平等雇佣; 平等就业
équité devant l'emploi
Beschäftigungsgleichheit
discriminación positiva en el
empleo
公正雇用政策

employment law
就业法; 雇佣法
droit du travail
Arbeitsrecht
legislación laboral
雇用法

employment pass
就业准证
visa d'emploi
Arbeitserlaubnis

Translations appear in the following order: Chinese, French, German, Spanish/Latin American Spanish, and Japanese

permiso de trabajo
雇用パス

employment protection
职业保护
protection de l'emploi
Kündigungsschutz
protección del empleo
雇用保護

employment tribunal
雇佣特别法庭
tribunal d'instance arbitral pour l'emploi
Arbeitstribunal
magistratura de trabajo neozelandesa; tribunal laboral neozelandés
雇用法廷

empowerment
授权
octroi de pouvoir et responsabilités
Ermächtigung; Empowerment
delegación de competencias
エンパワーメント(権限委譲)

empty suit
草包经理
pantin en costard
eine Führungskraft, die sich gut kleidet und alle Verfahren exakt befolgt, ohne jedoch eigentlich zur Geltung der Firma beizutragen
ejecutivo(-a) que es sólo fachada
タマネギ幹部(几帳面なだけで
能力のない幹部)

EMS
欧洲货币体系
système monétaire européen
EWG
SME
環境管理システム

EMU
经济和货币联盟
union monétaire et économique
EWG-Kriterien
UEM
EUの経済通貨統合

encryption
加密
encryptage
Datenverschlüsselung
encriptación
暗号化

encryption key
加密译本
code d'encryptage
Verschlüsselungscode
llave de encriptación
暗号キー, 暗号化鍵

end-around
回避
tourner autour du pot
Problemvermeidung, Aussitzen

enfoque evasivo
問題回避策

endogenous variable
内生变量
variable endogène
endogene Variable
variable endógena
内因性変数

endorsement
签署; 签名; 内容 简介; 违例记录; 签注; 背书; 新产品技术认可书
aval
Vermerk; Indossament; Bestätigung
endoso
裏書, 商品の保証宣伝

endowment assurance
人寿(定期)保险，储蓄保险，养老保险单
assurance à capital différé
gemischte Lebensversicherung
seguro dotal
養老保険

endowment fund
捐赠基金
société d'investissement à capital variable et différé soutenant une institution à but non lucratif
Stiftungsfonds; (unselbständige) Stiftung
fondo de beneficiencia
寄贈基金,
エンドーメント・ファンド

endowment mortgage
以养老保险单作抵押的贷款
hypothèque liée à une assurance-vie
Hypothek mit Tilgungssicherung über Lebensversicherungsvertrag
hipoteca inversión
養老モーゲージ

endowment policy
养老保险单; 人寿(定期)险; 储蓄保险
assurance à capital différé
Versicherungspolice; Versicherungsschein
póliza de seguro total
養老保険証券

endpoint
端点
point limite ou fin
Endpunkt
punto final
端点

energy audit
能源审计
audit d'énergie
Energiebilanz; Energieflusserfassung

auditoría energética
エネルギー監査、燃料費の
厳密検査

energy conservation
节省能源
conservation de l'énergie
Energiesparen
ahorro de energía
エネルギー節減(省エネ)

engineered cost
工程造价
coût généré
mitwachsende Kosten
coste elaborado
可変コスト

English disease
英国罢工病
prédilection du personnel d'entreprise anglais à choisir la grève comme première option dans les conflits industriels
englische Krankheit
la predisposición de los trabajadores británicos a la huelga
英国病

enterprise
企业精神; 事业心; 进取心
entreprise
Unternehmen; Unternehmung
empresa
企業

enterprise application integration
企业应用软件整合
intégration d'application d'entreprise
SAP
integración empresarial de aplicaciones
企業アプリケーション統合

enterprise culture
企业文化
culture d'entreprise
Unternehmenskultur
cultura empresarial
企業文化

enterprise portal
企业入口
site Web qui rassemble une vaste gamme de contenus et services pour les employés d'une organisation particulière
Unternehmensportal
portal empresarial
エンタープライズ・ポータル

enterprise zone
企业特区; 企业园区
zone d'entreprise
Industriefördergebiet; Wirtschaftsentwicklungsgebiet

Translations appear in the following order: Chinese, French, German, Spanish/Latin American Spanish, and Japanese

zona de desarrollo industrial
事業区域

entertainment expenses
招待費; 交際費
frais d'hospitalité
Bewirtungskosten;
Repräsentationsspesen
gastos de representación
交際費

entitlement
权力
droit aux gros profits
Erwartung
expectativa de obtener grandes
ingresos
福祉受給特典

entitlement offer
不可转让的要约
offre de droit à prestation
nicht übertragbares Angebot
oferta personal e intransferible
非譲渡金融商品の売り値

entity
实体
entité
Organisation; Einheit;
Rechtssubjekt; Unternehmen
entidad; institución; organismo;
órgano
経済組織

entrapment
约束
piège des restrictions
Einbau von Schwachstellen;
Einbau von Fallen
limitaciones impuestas por su
propia capacidad
足かせ

entreprenerd
精通电脑的企业家
ringard entrepreneur du Net
Unternehmer(in) mit
Computerkenntnissen,
insbesondere Neugründer eines
Internetgeschäfts
empresario(-a) experto en la
informática
コンピュータ技能に優れた起業家

entrepreneur
创业者; 企业家
entrepreneur
Unternehmer(in)
empresario(-a)
起業家

entropy
熵(平均信息量)
entropie
Entropie
entropía
エントロピー

entry barrier
市场进入障碍
entrave à la pénétration
Einstiegsbarriere
barrera de entrada
参入障壁

environment
环境，工作平台
environnement
Umgebung
entorno
環境

environmental audit
环境审计
audit sur l'environnement;
éco-audit
Umweltbetriebsprüfung;
Öko-Audit; Umweltprüfung
auditoría medioambiental
環境監査

**Environmental Impact
Statement**
环境影响报告
rapport d'impact sur
l'environnement
Umweltauswirkungsanalyse
declaración de impacto ambiental
環境影響報告

Environmental Impact Study
环境影响研究
étude d'impact sur
l'environnement
Umweltauswirkungsstudie
estudio de impacto
medioambiental
環境変化研究

environmental management
环境管理
gestion de l'environnement
Umweltmanagement;
Umweltpflege; Umweltschutz
gestión medioambiental
環境管理

**environmental management
system**
环境管理系统
système de gestion de
l'environnement
Umweltmanagementsystem
sistema de gestión
medioambiental
環境管理システム

environmental policy
环境政策; 环境方针
politique en matière
d'environnement
Umweltpolitik; umweltpolitische
Grundsätze
política medioambiental
環境政策

environmental scanning
环境扫描调查
balayage d'environnement
strategische Frühaufklärung
exploración medioambiental
詳しい環境調査,
環境スキャンニング

environmental statistics
环境统计学
statistiques environnementales
Umweltstatistik
estadísticas sobre medio ambiente
環境統計

epidemiology
流行病学
épidémiologie
Epidemiologie
epidemiología
疫学

e-procurement
网络采购
e-transactions
elektronische Beschaffung
adquisición electrónica; compra
electrónica
(企業間の)電子調達,
eプロキュアメント

equal opportunities
机会平等; 机会均等
égalité des chances
Chancengleichheit
igualdad de oportunidades
機会均等

equal pay
(同工)同酬
salaire égal
gleicher Lohn; gleiches Entgelt
igualdad salarial
同一賃金

equal treatment
平等对待
traitement égalitaire
Gleichbehandlung
igualdad de derechos
平等待遇制度

equilibrium price
均衡价格
prix d'équilibre
Gleichgewichtspreis
precio de equilibrio
均衡価格

equilibrium quantity
均衡质量
quantité d'équilibre
Gleichgewichtsmenge
cantidad de equilibrio
均衡量

equilibrium rate of interest
均衡利率
taux d'intérêt d'équilibre

---

*Translations appear in the following order: Chinese, French, German, Spanish/Latin American
Spanish, and Japanese*

Gleichgewichtszins
tipo de interés de equilibrio
均衡利子率

equipment trust certificate
设备信托债券
titre d'investissement nanti par
équipement
Durch Maschinen und
Ausrüstungsgegenstände
gesichertes Zertifikat
certificado de fideicomiso de
equipo
設備信託証書

equity
股本，权益，产权
actions ordinaires ou fonds propres
Aktienkapital
acción; activo neto; fondos
propios; equidad; neto patrimonial
株式，株主資本

equity claim
权益求偿权
créance sur bénéfices (après
paiement des dettes)
Forderungsüberschuss
solicitud de participación en el
capital social
(銀行に対する)株式請求権

**equity contribution
agreement**
产权资本提供协议
accord de contribution aux fonds
propres
Kapitaleinlagenvereinbarung
aporte de capital social
出資契約

equity dilution
产权稀释
dilution du capital actions
Kapitalverwässerung;
Verwässerung des Aktienkapitals
dilución de capital; disminución del
valor de las acciones ordinarias
持分希薄化

equity dividend cover
股利支付率
couverture de dividende du capital
actions
Verhältnis Gewinn zu Dividenden
cobertura de dividendos de las
acciones
持分配当倍率

equity floor
权益下限
plancher de valeur d'actions
Equity Floor
valor mínimo de las acciones
エクイティ・フロア，
最低限確保すべき下限値

equity multiplier
产权乘数
multiplicateur de fonds propres
Marktwertmulitplikato
multiplicador de capital propio
エクイティ・マルティプライ
ヤー，株価収益率による会社評価

equity share capital
权益股本
capital-actions
Eigenkapital; Grundkapital
capital en acciones ordinarias
衡平資本

equivalent annual cash flow
等值的年现金流量
cash-flow annuel équivalent
ausgeglichener jährlicher Cash
Flow
flujo de caja anual equivalente
均等年間キャッシュフロー

equivalent taxable yield
相等课税收益率
rendement équivalent imposable
gleichwertige steuerpflichtige
Einkünfte
rendimiento gravable equivalente
課税債券相当利回り

equivalent units
约当产量
unité équivalente
äquivalente Einheiten
unidades equivalentes
等価単位

e-retailer
网络零售商
e-commerçant
elektronischer Einzelhändler
tienda electrónica; cibertienda
電子小売業，
エレクトロニック・リテーラー

erf
小块土地
lopin de terrain rural ou urbain
ein kleines Stück Land
parcela urbana
小規模農地

ergonomics
工效学；人机工程学；
工作环境改造学
ergonomie
Ergonomie; Arbeitswissenschaft
ergonomía
人間工学(人にやさしい技術)

ERM
汇率机制
mécanisme du taux de change
Wechselkursmechanismus
mecanismo de tipos de cambio
為替相場メカニズム

ERP
企业资源规划
système logiciel
ERP Software
planificación de los recursos
empresariales
エンタープライズ・リソー
ス・プラニング

error account
错误账户
compte pour transactions erronées
Fehlerkonto
cuenta de error
エラー・アカウント，相殺勘定

errors and omissions
错误与遗漏
erreurs et omissions
Restposten der Zahlungsbilanz
errores y omisiones
過失及び怠慢

ESC
欧洲社会宪章
charte sociale européenne
europäische Sozialcharta
Carta Social Europea
EUの経済社会委員会

e-shock
电子商务潮流
élan vers l'avant du commerce
électronique, considéré comme
irrésistible
E-Commerce Boom
avance imparable de comercio
electrónico
eショック

estate[1]
地产
propriété /domaine
Ländereien
finca
私有地

estate[2]
遗产
masse des biens
Nachlass
masa hereditaria
純資産

estimate[1]
预测; 估计; 估算
estimation
Schätzung; Überschlag; Ermittlung
estimación; cálculo aproximado
予測, 概算, 推定、評価、見積

estimate[2]
估计,估价单,报价单
estimation
Kostenvoranschlag
presupuesto
概算、見積り

---

*Translations appear in the following order: Chinese, French, German, Spanish/Latin American
Spanish, and Japanese*

estimation
估计
estimation
Hochrechnung
estimación
概算する

e-tailing
网络
e-vente
elektronischer Handel
venta electrónica
eテーリング,
インターネット小売業

ethical investment
伦理投资
investissement de bonne éthique
ethische Investition; ethische
Anlagepolitik
inversión ética
倫理的投資

ethnic monitoring
人员种族监控
surveillance ethnique
ethnische Statistik
control de la composición étnica
民族監視システム

EU
欧洲联盟, 欧盟
Union Européenne
EU
UE
欧州連合

EUREX
欧洲交易所
EUREX
European Exchange
EUREX
ユーレックス市場

euro
欧洲; 欧洲共同体
euro
Euro
euro
ユーロ通貨

Eurobank
欧洲银行
eurobanque
Eurobank
eurobanco
ユーロバンク, ユーロ銀行

Eurobond
欧洲债券
euro-obligation
Eurobond; Euroanleihe
Eurobono
ユーロ債, ユーロボンド

Euro-commercial paper
欧洲商业票据; 欧洲商业本票
euro-effet commercial
Euro-Commercial-Paper;

Euronotes
europapelcomercial
ユーロ・コマーシャルペーパー,
ユーロCP

Eurocredit
欧洲信贷
eurocrédit
Euro-Kredit
eurocrédito
ユーロクレジット,
ユーロによる貸出

Eurocurrency
欧洲货币
euro-devise
Eurowährung
eurodivisa
ユーロカレンシー,
ユーロマネー, ユーロ市場で
取引される各国通貨

Eurodeposit
欧洲货币短期存款
euro-dépôt
Euroeinlage
eurodepósito
(短期の)ユーロ預金

Eurodollar
殴元
eurodollar
Eurodollar
eurodólar
ユーロダラー

Euroequity issue
欧洲股票发行
émission d'euro-actions
Euro-Equity-Emission
emisión de euroacciones
ユーロ原株発行

Euroland
欧元区
Euroland
Euroland; die Teilnehmerstaaten
der europäischen
Währungsunion; Eurozone
Eurolandia
ユーロ圏

Euro-note
欧洲票据
euronote
Euronote
europagaré
ユーロノート

European option
欧洲式期权
option européenne
Europäische Option; Option, die
nur zu einem vereinbarten
Endfälligkeitstermin ausgeübt
werden kann
opción (a la) europea

ヨーロッパ型オプション,
ヨーロピアン・オプション

Euroyen bond
欧洲日元债券
euro-obligation en yen
Euroyen Bond
bono euroyen
ユーロ円債

evaluation of training
培训评估
évaluation de la formation
Ausbildungsbewertung
evaluación de la formación
トレーニング評価

event marketing
活动宣传
marketing d'événement
Veranstaltungsmarketing;
Event-Marketing
marketing de acontecimientos
イベント・マーケティング

evergreen loan
长年有效贷款
emprunt par acceptation
renouvelable
Revolvingkredit
crédito o descubierto permanente
エバーグリーン融資

ex
无, 不包括
ex ou ex-dividende
ex; abzüglich
sin
配当落ち

ex-all
无权股票
sans aucun droit
ausschließlich aller Rechte
sin derechos
エクス・オール

ex ante
事前
anticipé ou souhaité
ex ante; vorab
desde antes
事前

excellence
卓越; 优秀; 杰出
excellence
Excellence
excelencia
エクセレンス

exception reporting
异常报告, 例外报告
rapport d'exception
Berichterstellung nur im
Ausnahmefall
información sobre las excepciones
例外報告制

Translations appear in the following order: Chinese, French, German, Spanish/Latin American Spanish, and Japanese

excess[1]
超出额
franchise (d'une assurance)
Selbstbehalt; Mehrbetrag;
Ekzedent
excedente
超過保険

excess[2]
超出额
excédent (de l'actif par rapport au passif)
Überhang; Mehrbetrag
exceso
過剰

excess profits tax
不当利得税
impôt sur les bénéfices exceptionnels
Überschussgewinnsteuer;
Kriegsgewinnsteuer
impuesto sobre beneficios extraordinarios
超過利得税

excess reserves
超额储备
réserves excédentaires
Überschussreserven;
Sonderrücklagen
exceso de reservas
過剰準備金

exchange[1]
交换; 交易; 兑换; 汇兑; 兑换率;
兑换 费; 交易所; 网上交易所;
échange
elektronischer Marktplatz; Börse
intercambios
オンライン交易市場

exchange[2]
交换
échange
Devisen; Umtausch; Austausch
canjear
為替

exchange[3]
兑换
changer
wechseln
cambiar
両替

exchange[4]
易货贸易, 物物交换
troquer
tauschen
cambiar
交换

exchange controls
外汇管理; 外汇管制
contrôles des changes
Devisenkontrollmaßnahmen;
Devisenbewirtschaftungs-

Maßnahmen
controles de cambio
為替管理、外国為替管理

exchange equalisation account
外汇平衡帐户; 外汇平准帐户
fonds de stabilisation des changes
Währungsausgleichsfonds
cuenta de igualación de tipos de cambio
(英)為替平衡勘定

exchange offer
交换发行
offre d'échange
Umtauschangebot
oferta cambiaria o de canje
交换オファー

exchange rate
汇率
taux de change
Wechselkurs; Devisenkurs
tipo de cambio
為替レート, 為替相場,
外国為替相場

exchange rate parities
汇率各方
parités du taux de change
Wechselkursparitäten
paridad de los tipos de cambio
為替交换比率, 為替評価

exchange rate risk
汇率风险
risque du taux de change
Kursrisiko; Wechselkursrisiko
riesgo cambiario
為替リスク, 為替相場上のリスク

exchange rate spread
汇率价差
écart du taux de change
Devisenhandel; Devisenaufschlag
tasa de cambio real efectiva/tipo de cambio efectivo real
換算率差

exchequer
财政部帐户(英)
compte de trésorerie du gouvernement à la Bank of England dans lequel tous les revenus provenant de l'impôt ou d'autres sources sont payés
Staatskasse; Schatzamt
erario público (del Reino Unido)
国庫

excise duty
国内消费税; 货物税
impôt indirect
Verbrauch- und Aufwandssteuer
impuesto sobre el consumo
国内消費税, 物品税

exclusive economic zone
专营经济区; 专属经济区
zone économique exclusive
ausschließliche Wirtschaftszone
área económica exclusiva
排他的経済ブロック、排他的経済水域

execution only
交易执行
uniquement exécution de transaction
lediglich Ausführung
sólo ejecución
執行のみ

executive
主管; 总经理; 行政长官;
行政人员; 行政部门;
cadre/chef de service
Führungskraft; leitende/r
Angestellte/r;
Leitungsbeauftragte/r
ejecutivo(-a)
経営幹部, マネジャー

executive coaching
行政主管辅导
formation individuelle pour cadres (supérieurs)
Einzelausbildung; für Führungskräfte
formación de ejecutivos
管理職コーチング

executive director
常务董事; 执行董事
directeur (général)
Exekutivdirektor(in)
director(a) ejecutivo(-a)
常勤ディレクター

executive pension plan
主管退休金计划
plan de retraite pour membres dirigeants d'une entreprise
Pensionskasse od.
Altersversorgung für Führungskräfte
plan especial de pensiones para ejecutivos
重役年金制度

executive search
人才物色; 猎头公司
recherche de cadres supérieurs
Suche; nach Führungskräften;
Kopfjagd;
Führungskräfte-Marketing
búsqueda de ejecutivos
エグゼキュティブ・サーチ,
ヘッド・ハンティング

executive share option scheme
主管股票购买选权方案
plan d'option de participation à une entreprise par ses membres

dirigeants et cadres
Aktienbezugsprogramm für
Führungskräfte
plan de compra de acciones de la
empresa por los ejecutivos de la
misma
重役株式オプション制度

executor
遗嘱执行人
exécuteur
Testamentvollstrecker(in)
albacea
遺言執行者

exempt gift
免税赠与
don exempt (d'impôt)
steuerfreies Geschenk
regalo sin retención fiscal
非課税贈与

exempt investment fund
豁免投资基金
fonds d'investissement exempté
(de certains impôts)
steuerbefreiter Investmentfonds
plan de inversiones exento
非課税投資基金

exemption
豁免; 免除
exonération
Freistellung; Befreiung; Freibetrag
exención
免除されるもの(人), 所得控除

exempt purchaser
豁免认购者; 免办登记认购者
acheteur exempt
befreite/r Auftraggeber(in)
comprador(a) exento(-a)
免除証券購買者

exempt securities
豁免证券
titres exemptés
gesetzlich freigestellte
Wertpapiere
valores exentos
免除証券, 適用除外証券

exempt supplies
免税品, 免税
produits francs de droits
steuerbefreite Hilfs- und
Betriebsstoffe
mercancía exenta
非課税供与

exercise notice
期权执行通知
notification de levée de prime
Erklärung über die Ausübung einer
Option
notificación de ejercicio
買収告知

exercise of warrants
用股份证书购买股票
exercice de droit d'achat de titres
Ausübung von Optionsscheinen
ejercicio de las garantías
株式買収権の行使

exercise price
执行价
cours de base
Basispreis; Ausübungskurs
precio de ejercicio
行使価格

exercise value
执行价格; 履约价格
valeur d'une levée
Ausübungswert
valores de ejercicio
(オプションを行使できる)権利,
行使価格

ex gratia
优惠, 通融
(paiement) de faveur
freiwillig; Kulanz-
ex gratia; discrecional
任意

ex-gratia payment
优惠付款; 通融付款
paiement à titre gracieux
Kulanzentschädigung
pago ex gratia
見舞金

exhibition
展销会
exposition
Messe; Ausstellung; Stipendium
exhibición
展示会

Eximbank
美国进出口银行
banque américaine qui fournit des
prêts aux importateurs étrangers
Eximbank
banco estadounidense que ofrece
préstamos a importadores de
productos estadounidenses
輸出入銀行

existential culture
存在文化
culture existentielle
Existenzkultur
cultura empresarial de servicio al
individuo y no a la empresa
実存文化

exit interview
离职面谈
entrevue de départ (d'un membre
du personnel d'une entreprise)
Abgangsgespräch
entrevista de salida
退職面接

exit PE ratio
换手市盈率
coefficient de capitalisation des
résultats en sortie (quand une
compagnie change de mains)
Ausstiegs-Ex-Pit-Verhältnis
relación precio-ganancia de salida
譲渡時の株価収益率

exogenous variable
外生变量
variable exogène
exogene Variable
variable exógena
外因性変数

expatriate
国外雇员; 外来雇员
expatrié/ressortissant d'un pays
travaillant à l'étranger
im Ausland Lebende/r; ehemalige/r
Staatsangehörige/r
emigrado(-a)
海外駐在員

expectancy theory
期望理论
théorie de l'attente et des espoirs
Motivationstheorie; der
Anwartschaft
teoría de las espectativas
期待理論

expected rate of return
预期报酬率
taux de rendement prévu
erwartete Rendite
tasa de rendimiento prevista
予定収益率

expected value
预期价值获利
Espérance/règlement
mathématique
Erwartungswert; erwarteter Wert
valor esperado/resultado final;
beneficio; retribución
期待価値

expenditure switching
支出转向
report de dépenses
Ausgabenumschichtung
reorientación del gasto
支出転換政策、支出切替政策

expense[1]
费用
dépense
Kosten; Aufwand
gasto
支出, 費用, 所要経費

expense[2]
支出
dépense
Ausgaben
gasto
経費

---

*Translations appear in the following order: Chinese, French, German, Spanish/Latin American
Spanish, and Japanese*

expense account
费用帐; 开支帐
notes de frais professionnels
Spesenkonto; Konto für
Geschäftsausgaben
cuenta de gastos
費用勘定

expenses
费用; 开支; 经费
frais
Auslagen
gastos
所要経費

experience economy
经验经济
économie d'expérience
Erfahrungswirtschaft
economía basada en la experiencia
positiva que un producto causa al
consumidor
消費者が「体験」する質で商品
を差別化する経済原理

experiential learning
实验性教学
enseignement qui résulte de
l'expérience; apprendre en se
basant sur l'expérience
Lernen durch Erfahrung; auf
Erfahrung beruhendes Lernen
aprendizaje experimental
経験習熟モデル

experimental design
实验设计
conception expérimentale
Versuchsanordnungn
diseño experimental
実験的デザイン

experimental study
实验性研究
étude expérimentale
Versuchsstudie
estudio experimental
実験的調査

expert system
专家系统
système informatique de
simulation d'expert
Expertensystem
sistema experto
エキスパート・システム

exploding bonus
毕业生就职奖金
prime dégonflante
Explosivprämie, die
Universitätsabgängern angeboten
wird, damit sie so schnell wie
möglich eine Stelle antreten, da
die Prämie mit jedem Tag
Verzögerung an Wert verliert

prima menguante
新卒者を勧誘するための
時限付きボーナス

exponential smoothing
指数型平滑
technique de lissage exponentiel
Exponentialglättung
suavizado exponencial
指数平滑法

exponential trend
指数趋势
tendance exponentielle
Exponentialtendenz
tendencia exponencial
指数傾向

export agent
出口代理商
commissionnaire exportateur
Exportvertretung; Exportagent;
Ausfuhragent
agente de exportación
輸出代理店

**Export Credit Guarantee
Department**
出口信用担保署
service gouvernemental de
garantie financière à l'exportation
staatliche
Exportkreditversicherung
departamento británico de crédito
para las exportaciones
輸出信用保証局

exporting
出口
exportation
Export
exportaciones
輸出

export-led growth
出口带来的增长
croissance dominée par
l'exportation
exportinduziertes Wachstum
crecimiento impulsado por las
exportaciones
輸出先行型成長、輸出主導型成長

ex post
事后
rétroactif
ex post; im Nachhinein
ex post
事後

ex-rights
无新股权; 无权认购新股; 除权
droits exclus; sans droits (de
souscription future)
ex Bezugsrechte; ohne
Bezugsrechte
sin derecho de suscripción; ex
derecho; acción sin derecho de

subscripción
权利落ちで(の),
新株引受権の付かない, 権利落ち

ex-rights date
除权日
date de transaction droits exclus
Neuemission
fecha de vencimiento de los
derechos
権利落ち期日

extendable bond
延期偿还债券
obligation à échéance prorogée
Obligation od. Anleihe mit
Möglichkeit der
Laufzeitverlängerung
bono de vencimiento ajustable
延長可能債

extendable note
可延期票据
effet à échéance prorogée
Wechsel mit Möglichkeit der
Laufzeitverlängerung
bono con vencimiento prorrogable
延長可能手形

extended fund facility
中期贷款; 中期放款
facilité de crédit prolongé FMI
erweiterte Fondsfazilität
servicio ampliado de financiación
(IMFの)拡大信用供与制度

external account
境外帐户
compte extérieur
Ausländerkonto; externes Konto
cuenta de no residente
海外口座

external audit
外来审计
audit extérieur
Betriebsprüfung
auditoría externa
外部監査

external communication
对外交流
communications externes
externe Komunikation;
außerbetriebliche Kommunikation
comunicación externa
対外的情報交換,
対外コミュニケーション

external debt
外债; 对外债务
dette extérieure
Auslandsschuld
deuda exterior
対外債務、外部負債

external finance
外部财务
financement extérieur

Fremdkapital
financiación externa
外部資金, 外部調達

external funds
外来资金
fonds extérieurs
Fremdmittel
recursos ajenos
外部資金

external growth
外部成长
croissance externe
externes Wachstum
crecimiento externo
外在的成長

extranet
外联网，外部网
extranet
Extranet
extranet
エクストラネット

extraordinary general meeting
临时总会; 特别股东大会;
(公司)临时股东大会
assemblée extraordinaire
außerordentliche
Hauptversammlung
junta o asamblea general
extraordinaria
臨時総会

extraordinary resolution
特别决议
question à l'ordre du jour d'une
assemblée générale extraordinaire
außerordentlicher Beschluss
resolución extraordinaria
特別決議

extrapolate
外推，外插
extrapoler
extrapolieren
extrapolar
外挿する

extreme value
极值
valeur extrême
Extremum
valor extremo
極値

eyeballing
目測(法)，目视检查
zieutage
durchsehen, prüfen
(proceso de inspección informal de
los datos estadísticos simplemente
estudiándolos a fin de evaluar los
resultados) (fam)
目測

eyeballs
(网址) 光顾人数
zieutage
Besucheranzahl
visitantes
アイボール

eyebrow management
表情管理
management par froncement des
sourcils
Geschäftsleitung per
Augenbrauensignal
gestión dominada por los
ejecutivos
眉毛で感情を表現することだけ-
で経営方針を決める

eye candy
眼睛糖果，吸引人的东西
visuellement attrayant
attraktives Material, Material mit
guter Optik, Ugs. Augenschmaus
gráficos bonitos
目の保養

eye service
干面子活
travail pour les châsses du patron
Augendienerei
trabajar sólo cuando está el jefe
上司に見られている時だけ働く

e-zine
电子杂志
magazine sous forme numérique
Web-Zeitung; Newsletter
revista electrónica
ｅザイン

F2F
面对面
face à face
von Angesicht zu Angesicht
cara a cara
面と向かって

face time
面谈时间; 面对面交流
pow-wow
Zeit, die in persönlicher
Kommunikation verbracht wird, im
Gegensatz zur Zeit, die auf
elektronische Kommunikation
verwendet wird
tiempo de contacto personal
directo
対面コミュニケーションの時間

facilitation
协调
facilitation
Förderung; Erleichterung;
Moderation
facilitación
ファシリテーション(トーレー-
ニング推進)

facilities management¹
设备管理
gestion des moyens
Betriebsmittelverwaltung;
Anlagenverwaltung;
Fazilitätenverwaltung
gestión de instalaciones
設備管理

facilities management²
设施管理
fourniture de matériel ou services à
une entreprise par un agent ou
une autre société
Haustechnik
gestión de prestaciones
設備管理

facility-sustaining activities
机构维持活动
activités de soutien d'organisation
unternehmenstragende
Tätigkeiten
actividades de sostenimiento a la
organización
組織支持活動

facing matter
封面广告
publicité en vis-à-vis
Anzeige gegenüber von
redaktionellem Text
anuncio en la página opuesta al
editorial
記事の対称面に印刷される広告

factor
因子，因数
facteur
Faktor
factor
因子

factor analysis
因子分析
analyse factorielle
Faktorenanalyse
análisis factorial
因子分析法

factored goods
转售商品
produits affacturés
Kommissionsware
bienes adquiridos para la reventa
再販用製品

factor four
因素4
concept de production écologique
qui vise à augmenter la production
par quatre pour réduire le rebut et
les déchets
Faktor Four
factor cuatro
ファクター4

factoring
货款保收法，货款让售法，
代收帐款
affacturage
Factoring
descuento de facturas, factoring
債権金融

factor market
生产要素市场
marché factoriel
Faktormarkt
mercado de factores de
producción
要素市場

factory
工厂
usine
Werk; Fabrik; Betrieb
fábrica
工場

factory gate price
出厂价
prix départ usine
Preis ab Werk
precio de fábrica
工場引渡し価格

fallen angel
跌股
ange déchu
gefallener Engel, ehemals als gute
Investition erachtetes Wertpapier,
das an Wert verloren hat
ángel caído
フォールン・エンジェル
（堕天使）

family business
家族企业; 家庭经营的商业;
个体工商业
entreprise familiale
Familienbetrieb
negocio familiar
家族ビジネス, 同族会社

family-friendly policy
关注职工家庭生活的政策
politique favorable à la vie de
famille
familienfreundliche
Unternehmenspolitik
política de facilidades para los
empleados con familias
家族にやさしい政策

FAO
联合国粮农组织
organisation des Nations Unies
pour l'alimentation et l'agriculture
Ernährungs-und
Landwirtschaftsorganisation der
Vereinten Nationen
Organización de las Naciones
Unidas para la Agricultura y
Alimentación
国連食糧農業機構

FAQ
常见问题
FAQ
häufig gestellte Fragen
preguntas más comunes
FAQ(頻繁な問い合わせと回答)

far month
远到月
mois éloigné
letzter Monat
mes más lejano
期先

FASB
美国财务会计标准委员会
organisme responsable de
l'établissement des normes de
rapport et comptabilité financière
Financial Accounting Standards
Board
organismo normalizador de los
informes financieros y de
contabilidad de las empresas del
sector privado
財務会計基準審議会

FASTER
(新西兰）一种全自动股票交
易系统
système informatique automatisé
d'opérations boursières pour
compensation, acquittement,
règlement, inscription et
information
voll automatisierter
Bildschirmhandel und
elektronische Registrierung
sistema de contratación
electrónica de la bolsa
neozelandesa
ファスター(全自動画面上取引,
電子登録システム)

fast track
捷径; 快速通道
filière ultra-rapide
schneller Aufstieg
vía rápida
ファースト・トラック(出生街道)

faxback
自动传真信息法
renvoi automatique par télécopie
Fax-Abruf
solicitud y envío de información a
través del fax
ファックスバック

FCOL
岂有此理! 嗳呀! 我的天啊!
(表惊奇, 愤怒)
oh, purée!
das darf doch wohl nicht wahr
sein!
como para llorar
嘆き落胆する

feasibility study
可行性研究
étude de faisabilité
Durchführbarkeitsstudie;
Planungsstudie; Projektstudie;
Vorstudie
estudio de viabilidad
事業化調査,
フィージビリティ・スタディ

feasible region
可行域
zone de faisabilité
zulässige Region
región posible
使用可能領域

Federal Funds
联邦基金
réserves de Trésorerie de la Fed
Tagesgeld
fondos federales
フェデラル・ファンズ

federal organisation
联邦组织; 联邦机构
organisation fédérale
föderale Organisation
organización federal
連合組織

Federal Reserve Bank
联邦储备银行
Réserve fédérale (la Fed)
Bank, die Mitglied des
Zentralbanksystems der
Vereinigten Staaten ist
Banco de la Reserva Federal
(米)連邦準備加盟銀行

Federal Reserve Board
联邦储备局; 联邦储备委员会
Comité directeur de la Réserve
fédérale
Zentralbankvorstand
Junta de la Reserva Federal
連邦準備制度理事会, FRB

Federal Reserve note
联邦储备兑换券
billet de la Fed
Nachricht an die Banken, die
Mindestreserven zu verringern
billete de la Reserva Federal
連邦準備券

Federal Reserve System
联邦储备系统
système de la Réserve fédérale
Zentralbanksystem der Vereinigten
Staaten
sistema de la Reserva Federal
連邦準備制度

Fed pass
额外储备金(英美联邦储备局）
réserves supplémentaires de la Fed

Mindestreserven werden erhöht
colocación de reservas en el
mercado bancario
FEDバス, 連邦準備バス

Fedwire
联邦联线系统; 联邦储备通讯系统
le Fedwire (système de transfert
électronique de la Réserve fédérale
aux USA)
elektronisches Clearingsystem des
amerikanischen
Zentralbanksystems
red de transferencias entre
instituciones con cuentas en el
sistema de la Reserva Federal
米のフェッドワイヤ,
連邦電信決済通信網

feedback
反馈
informations en retour
Feedback; Rückmeldung;
Reaktionen
retroalimentación; feedback
(情報, 質問,
サービス等の受け手側からの)-
反応, 意見, 感想,
フィードバック,

feedback control
反馈控制
maîtrise de prévision rétroactive
Regelung; selbsttätige Regelung;
Regelungstechnik
medida de reacción para lograr
resultados
フィードバック制御

feedforward control
预测控制
contrôle des informations en
prévision
Optimalwertsteuerung;
Vorwärtsregelung
intercambio de información para
prever y evitar diferencias
フィードフォワード制御

feeding frenzy
买主疯狂竞争时期
frénésie d'achat
Kaufmanie
fiebre compradora
投資家が飢えたサメのように
買い狂うこと

fee work
付费工作
travail payé par honoraires
Auftragsarbeit
trabajo subcontratado
手数料請負仕事

field plot
田间小区(试验)
étude graphique des champs
Feldgrafik

estudio estadístico, normalmente
utilizado en la agricultura, de los
resultados de una operación tal
como la plantación de cultivos
transgénicos
フィールドプロット

field research
实地研究; 现场研究
recherche sur le terrain; étude sur
le terrain
Feldforschung
investigación de campo
実地調査

field staff
外勤(推销)人员; 现场工作人员
personnel sur le terrain
Außendienstmitarbeiter(in)nen;
Mitarbeiter(in)nen im Außendienst
personal de campo
外勤職員

field trial
试销
essai sur le terrain
Feldversuch
prueba sobre el terreno
現地トライアル

field work
现场工作; 实地工作
travail sur le terrain
Feldarbeit
trabajo de campo
実地調査

FIFO
先入先出法
premier entré, premier sorti
Fifo-Methode der Vorratshaltung;
bei der früher gelagerte Güter vor
den später produzierten/
erworbenen verwendet werden
el más viejo sale primero
先入先出

file server
文件服务器
serveur de fichiers
Datei-Server
servidor de archivos
ファイル・サーバー

filter
过滤; 筛选
filtrer
Filter
filtro
フィルターに掛ける(選別)

Filthy Five
环境纪录最差的五家公司
liste de compagnies avec un
historique médiocre quant à leur
attitude envers l'environnement
die Fünf umweltversmutzensten
Firmen in den USA

las cinco empresas menos
respetuosas con el medio
ambiente
公害企業ワースト5

finance
基金筹措
financer
finanzieren; Mittel beschaffen
finanzas
ファイナンス, 資金調達

finance bill
财政法案; 拨款法案
projet de loi de finances
Finanzvorlage; Haushaltsvorlage
letra financiera
財政法案, 金融手形

finance company
金融公司; 财务公司
société de prêts
Finanzierungsgesellschaft
entidad financiera; financiera
金融会社

finance house
金融公司; 财务公司; 贷款公司
compagnie financière
Kundenkreditbank; Kreditinstitut
für die Kundenfinanzierung
entidad financiera; financiera
金融会社

finance lease
金融租赁
location financière
Finanz-Leasingvertrag
arrendamiento financiero
資金調達リース

financial
财务的
financier
finanziell; geldlich; Finanz-
financiero(-a)
財政上の, 金融上の

financial accounting
财务会计
comptabilité financière
Finanzbuchführung;
Finanzbuchhaltung
contabilidad financiera
財務会計

financial adviser
财务顾问
conseiller financier
Finanzberater(in)
asesor(a) financiero(-a)
ファイナンシャル・
アドバイザー, 財務顧問

financial control
财务控制
contrôle financier
Finanzkontrolle
control financiero
財務管理

Translations appear in the following order: Chinese, French, German, Spanish/Latin American Spanish, and Japanese

financial distress
财务困境
détresse financière
finanzielle Notlage;
ahlungsschwierigkeiten
dificultades financieras
財政困難, 経営難, 金融危機

financial economies of scale
财政规模经济
économies d'échelle financières
finanzielle Größenvorteile;
finanzielle Größendegression
economías financieras de escala
規模の経済の金融の有利性,
スケールメリットの金融
上の優位性

financial engineering
金融工程
ingénierie financière
Financial Engineering
ingenería financiera
金融エンジニアリング

Financial Institutions Duty
财务机构税
taxe des institutions financières
Finanz- und Kreditinstitutsteuer
impuesto sobre instituciones
financieras
金融機関税

financial instrument
财务票据
instrument financier
Finanzierungsinstrument;
Finanztitel; Kreditinstrument;
Finanzpapier
instrumento financiero
金融商品

financial leverage
财务杠杆作用
endettement financier
Fremdkapitalaufnahme
apalancamiento financiero;
relación entre deudas y activos
totales
金融レバレッジ, ギアリング

financial liability
财务债务
passif financier exigible
finanzielle Verpflichtung;
Finanzobligo
responsabilidad pecuniaria o
económica
金融負債

financial management
财务管理
gestion financière
Finanzverwaltung;
Finanzbuchhaltung; Treasuring;
Ausgabenverwaltung

gestión financiera; administración
o dirección financiera
財務管理

Financial Ombudsman
财务调查官
médiateur financier
Finanzombudsmann
Defensor(a) de los inversores
金融行政監察専門員,
金融関連苦情調査官

financial planning
财务计划, 财政规划
planification financière
Finanzdisposition; Finanzplanung
planificación financiera
財務プラン, 財務計画

**Financial Planning
Association of Australia**
澳大利亚经济规划协会
association australienne de
planification financière
Australischer
Finanzplanungsverband
confederación de empresas
australianas de planificación
financiera
オーストラリア・ファイナ
ンシャル・プランニング協会

**Financial Reporting Review
Panel**
财务报告审议小组
comité d'examination de rapports
financiers
britisches Financial Reporting
Review Panel
organismo británico que examina
los casos de irregularidades
contables por parte de grandes
empresas
財務報告審査パネル

**Financial Reporting
Standards Board**
(新西兰)财务报告标准委员会
conseil néo-zélandais pour les
normes financières
neuseeländisches
Finanzstandardinstitut
organismo neozelandés regulador
de los estándares de contabilidad
財務報告基準審議会

financial risk
财务风险
risque financier
Kreditrisiko
riesgo financiero
財務リスク, 金融リスク

financial statements
bilans financiers ou situation de
trésorerie
estados financieros; balance
general o financiero; memoria

financiera
財務諸表

financier
金融家; 金融业者
financier
Finanzier; Kapitalgeber
financiero(a)
財政家, 金融業者, 融資家

financing gap
财政缺口
déficit commercial
Finanzierungslücke
brecha de financiación
金融的ギャップ

find time
寻找时间
temps de trouve
Zeit, die Verbraucher zum
Auffinden eines Produktes im
Regal benötigen
tiempo de localización
棚上の商品を
発見するまでの時間

finished goods
成品
produits finis
Fertigerzeugnissse; Fertigware;
Fertiggüter; Fertigfabrikate
productos acabados
完成品, 最終財, 製品

finite loading
有限上载
charge limitée
Maschinenbelastung mit
Kapazitätsgrenze
carga finita
有限作業プラン

finite population
有限人口
population de nombre limité
endliche Grundgesamtheit
población finita
有限母集団

firewall
防火墙
mur de protection
Brandmauer
cortafuegos
ファイアーウォール

firm
公司企业; 厂商; 确定的; 明确的;
坚挺的; 稳定的; 确定地; 稳固地
maison de commerce; entreprise
Firma; Unternehmen; Betrieb
firma; empresa
(合資経営の)会社

first mover
首先进入市场的公司;
引进新产品的公司
compagnie qui est la première

introduire un nouveau type de
produit ou de service sur le marché
ökonomischer Nischenentdecker,
Innovator
pionero(-a)
新規参入

first mover advantage
先入者优势
avantage du premier qui bouge
Vorteil des Ersteintritts in einen
Markt
ventaja del pionero
市場第一参入の利点

first-round financing
第一轮资金投入
financement de premier tour
erste Kapitalspritze für ein
Vorhaben; Finanzierung der ersten
Runde
primera inversión externa
第一次ファイナンス,
第一回資金調達

fiscal
财政的; 国库的; 金钱的
fiscal
fiskalisch; Finanz-; Steuer-
fiscal
财政上の, 会計の,
(政府の)財政操作による
経済運営をはかる

fiscal balance
财政平衡
équilibre fiscal
fiskalisches Gleichgewicht;
steuerliche Ausgewogenheit
balance fiscal
财政收支

fiscal drag
财政拖累; 财政障碍
lourdeur du poids fiscal
fiskalpolitische Bremse;
Fiscal-Drag-Effekt
lastre o freno fiscal
財政的歯止め, 財政の障害

fiscal policy
财政政策; 赋税政策
politique fiscale
Fiskalpolitik
política fiscal
財政政策、フィスカル・ポリシー

fishbone chart
鱼骨图
schéma en forme de squelette de
poisson qui est utilisé pour
identifier et classer les causes
possibles d'un problème
Ursache-Wirkungs-Diagramm
diagrama en forma de esqueleto
de pez
(石川式)魚骨図,
フィッシュボーン・チャート

5-S concept
5-S概念
concept japonais de culture
d'entreprise
5-S Konzept
Concepto 5-S
5 S原則

fixed asset
固定资产
valeur immobilisée
Anlagegegenstand; Gegenstand
des Anlagevermögens
activo fijo or inmovilizado; capital
fijo or inmovilizado
固定資産

fixed budget
固定预算
budget fixe
starres Budget
presupuesto fijo
固定予算

fixed charge
固定费用
frais fixes
fundierte Schuld; feste Belastung
cargo fijo preferencial; gasto fijo
固定費

fixed exchange rate system
固定汇率系统
système de change à taux fixe
System der festen Wechselkurse
mecanismo de tipos de cambio
fijos
固定為替相場制

fixed-interest loan
定息贷款
emprunt à intérêt fixe
festverzinsliches Darlehen
préstamo a interés fijo
確定利子ローン

fixed rate
固定利率
taux fixe
festverzinst
interés fijo
定率, 固定相場

fixed-rate loan
定息贷款
prêt à taux fixe
zinsgebundener Kredit; Darlehen
mit Festverzinsung
empréstito a tipo de interés fijo
定率ローン

flame
火舌，火焰(flame
message不良信息，flame
war火焰战，火舌战)
message hostile
Beschimpfung

llamarada; desahogo
フレーム

flat organisation
扁平式结构或机构
organisation à plat
abgeflachte Organisation
organización plana
平面組織

flat yield curve
统扯收益率曲线
courbe de revenu à taux fixe
flache Renditenkurve; flache
Zinskurve
curva de rendimiento plana
水平型利回り曲線

flexecutive
多面手主管
cadre flexi
mehrfach qualifizierte
Führungskraft, die leicht zwischen
Aufgaben hin- und herschalten
kann
ejecutivo(-a) polivalente
仕事を自由に切り替えられる
多才な管理職

flexible budget
弹性预算
budget flexible
variables Budget oder Etat
presupuesto flexible
弾力の予算

flexible exchange rate
system
弹性汇率系统
système de change à taux variables
System der flexiblen od. frei
schwankenden Wechselkurse
mecanismo de tipos de cambio
flexibles
伸縮為替相場制度, 屈伸相場制

flexible manufacturing
system
弹性生产系统
système de fabrication flexible
flexible Fertigung; flexibles
Fertigungssystem
sistema flexible de producción
フレキシブル製造システム

flexible working
弹性工作安排; 弹性制工作
travail flexible
flexibles Arbeiten; flexible
Arbeitsmethoden;
od.-bedingungen
trabajo flexible
裁量労働制度

flexible working hours
弹性工作时间
horaire de travail flexible
gleitende Arbeitszeit; Gleitzeit

Translations appear in the following order: Chinese, French, German, Spanish/Latin American Spanish, and Japanese

horario de trabajo flexible
時間伸縮出勤制,
フレキシブル・タイム

flexilagger
僵硬式管理
entreprise à la traîne de la flexi
Firma oder Organisation, die im
Ruf steht, nicht genügend Wert
auf Flexibilität in ihren
Beschäftigungspraktiken zu legen
empresa inflexible con los
trabajadores
雇用条件がフレキシブルでない
企業

flexileader
灵活式管理
entreprise leader en flexi
Firma oder Organisation, die im
Ruf steht, besonderen Wert auf
Flexibilität in ihren
Beschäftigungspraktiken zu legen
empresa flexible con los
trabajadores
雇用条件がフレキシブルである
企業

flexitime
弹性工作时间; 弹性时间
horaire à la carte
Gleitzeit; gleitende Arbeitszeit
horario flexible
フレックスタイム

flight risk
计划跳槽
oiseau prêt à s'envoler
fluchtgefährdeter Arbeitnehmer;
Fluchtrisiko
empleado9a) con riesgo de que se
marche
近いうちに退社する危険性のあ
る社員

flip
短期利润导向型公司
start-up qui travaille pour établir
rapidement sa part de marché
et crée de la richesse à court
terme pour ensuite péricliter
lorsqu'elle est cotée en Bourse
ou vendue
Flip
empresa nueva cuyo objetivo
es crear riqueza a corto plazo
para sus fundadores a través
de una flotación o una
venta
フリップ企業

float¹
流通股票
émettre
Ugs. Geld in die Kassen spülen
flotar
株式の償還

float²
未达帐期
période de flottement
Wertstellungsdifferenz;
schwebende Einzugswerte;
Valutierungsgewinn
flotación
フロート期間

floating charge
不固定抵押
frais mobiles ou flottants
schwebende Schuld; nicht
spezifiziertes Globalpfandrecht;
ungesicherte Verbindlichkeit
garantía, cargo u obligación
flotante; préstamo comercial
garantizado con el patrimonio
entero; cesión del activo total
como garantía de una deuda
浮動担保

floating debt
流动债务
dette flottante
kurzfristige Verbindlichkeiten
deuda flotante
流動負債, 一時借入金, 短期公債

floating rate
浮动利率
taux flottant
variabler Zins
tipo variable
変動相場

floor
价格下限; 最低限价
plancher
Mindestpreis; Minimalsatz;
Mindestsumme
suelo
最低価格、底値, 下限

floor effect
地板效应
effet de plancher
Bodeneffekt
efecto mínimo; efecto tope
inferior; efecto límite inferior
フロア現象

flotation
开办; 创立; 发行
émission
Börsenbegebung einer Anleihe;
Gründung eines Unternehmens
lanzamiento
債券発行, 新規債券の募集

flow chart
流程图; 程序图
organigramme ou graphique
d'évolution
Flussdiagramm;
Arbeitsablaufdiagramm;
Datenflussplan

organigrama
フローチャート

flow on
工资随长
report d'augmentation
Lohnerhöhung einer Gruppe, die
sich positiv auf eine andere
auswirkt
subida de sueldo de un grupo
de trabajadores asociada a la de
otro
波及効果

flow production
流水线生产
production à flot unique
Fließfertigung; Reihenfertigung
producción a gran escala
流れ作業生産

flow theory
流动理论
théorie du fleuve
Flusstheorie
teoría del flujo
流れ理論

fluff it and fly it
先包装再销售
faire mousser un produit pour le
vendre
ein Produkt aufbauschen, sodass
es sich gut macht und dann
verkaufen
ponlo bonito y véndelo
商品を格好良くし、売り捌く

FMEA
失效模式与效应分析
technique d'analyse des causes,
risques et effets des défaillances
potentielles de système ou de
composants
FMEA
análisis de las causas y efectos de
los fallos
故障モード影響分析

FNMA
联邦国民抵押协会
plus grosse source de
financement de logement aux
Etats-Unis
FNMA
la mayor empresa de crédito
hipotecario en los Estados Unidos
米連邦住宅抵当金庫

focus group
讨论组
groupe d'intérêt spécifique
Zielgruppe;
Untersuchungsgruppe;
Fokusgruppe

Translations appear in the following order: Chinese, French, German, Spanish/Latin American
Spanish, and Japanese

grupo estudiado; grupo muestra
フォーカス・グループ

followback survey
返回调查
étude statistique de suivi de
population dans le temps
nachfassende Untersuchung
encuesta de seguimiento adicional
de una población estadística que
se lleva a cabo una serie de años
después de realizarse la encuesta
original
追跡調査

Fong Kong
冒牌产品
produit dont la marque sur
l'étiquette est une contrefaçon, en
particulier pour les chaussures de
sport
imitierte Designerkleidung
producto con una marca
falsificada
偽ブランド商品

footer
页脚
section en bas de page
Fußnote
pie de página
フッター(脚注)

footfall
路过人数
mesure du passage des gens
devant un magasin
Einzelhandelsmaß für die Anzahl
der an einem Laden
vorbeigehenden Passanten
personas que pasan por delante de
una tienda
小売店の前を通る人数

Forbes 500
福布斯500家
Forbes 500 (les 500 compagnies
américaines les plus importantes
selon les critères du magazine
Forbes)
Forbes 500
índice Forbes 500
(米経済専門誌)フォーブス
(の選ぶ)５００種

force field analysis
力场分析
analyse de champ (de force)
Ursachenanalyse
análisis del campo de fuerzas
フォース・フィールド分析

forecast
预测
prévision
Prognose; Voraussage
pronóstico; previsión
予想

forecasting
预测
prévisions; faire des prévisions
Prognose; Vorhersage
pronóstico; previsión
予測、予想、見込み

foreign bill
外国汇票
traite payable à l'étranger
Auslandswechsel;
Fremdwährungswechsel; im
Ausland zahlbarer Wechsel
letra extranjera
外国(為替)手形

foreign currency
外币
devise étrangère
Devisen; Fremdwährung;
ausländisches Geld
divisa; moneda extranjera
外貨、外国通貨

foreign currency translation
外币转换
transposition des devises
étrangères
Umrechnung von
Fremdwährungen
conversión de divisas
外貨翻訳

foreign debt
国外债务
endettement extérieur
Auslandsverschuldung;
Auslandsschulden
deuda exterior
外債、対外債務

foreign direct investment
外国直接投资
investissement étranger direct
ausländische Direktinvestition
inversión extranjera directa
国外直接投資

foreign dividend
外国股利
dividende étranger
Auslandsdividende
dividendo extranjero
外国利益配当

foreign equity market
外国股份交易市场
marché des actions étrangères
Markt für ausländische
Wertpapiere
mercado de valores extranjeros
対外株式市場

foreign exchange
外汇
devises étrangères
Devisen
divisas; cambio de divisas
外国為替、外貨

foreign exchange option
外汇期权
option de change
Devisenoption; Währungsoption
opción cambiaria
外国為替オプション

foreign income dividend
外国红利收入
dividende sur revenus étrangers
Dividende von Gewinnen im
Ausland
dividendo de ingresos del exterior
外国配当収入

Foreign Investment Funds Tax
海外投资基金税
impôt sur les fonds
d'investissement à l'étranger
Auslandinvestitions-Fondsteuer
impuesto australiano sobre los
fondos de inversión en el
extranjero
外国投資基金税

**Foreign Investment Review
Board**
外国投资评估局
conseil de révision des
investissements étrangers
Auslandinvestitions-
Überprüfungskammer
organismo asesor del gobierno
australiano sobre la inversión
extranjera
外国投資審査委員会

foreign reserve
外汇储备
réserves en devises étrangères
Devisenreserven;
Währungsreserven
reservas en divisas
外貨準備高

foreign tax credit
国外税额的检出; , 外国税收抵免
avoir fiscal pour paiement
d'impôts à l'étranger
Anrechnung ausländischer
Steuern
desgravación por pago de
impuestos en el extranjero
外国税額控除

forensic accounting
法庭会计学
comptabilité pour expertise légale
forensische Rechnungsführung
od. Rechnungslegung
contabilidad que determina la
legalidad de las actividades
法廷会計

forfaiting
福费廷

---

*Translations appear in the following order: Chinese, French, German, Spanish/Latin American
Spanish, and Japanese*

affacturage à forfait
Forfaitierung
forfetización; técnica de cobertura
de riesgo en operaciones a largo
plazo; financiación de una
operación con descuento
金融商品の買取

formica parachute
失业保险
parapluie en béton
Arbeitslosenversicherung
seguro de desempleo
失業保険

Fortune 500
财富500家
Fortune 500 (compilation annuelle
par le magazine Fortune des 500
plus grosses compagnies
industrielles américaines)
Jahresverzeichnis der 500
größtenKapitalgesellschaften =
der Vereinigten Staaten in der
Zeitschrift Fortune
índice Fortune 500
(米経済誌の)フォーチュー
ン500社

forum
论坛
forum
Forum
foro
フォーラム

forward contract
期货合同; 远期合同
contrat de transactions à terme
Terminkontrakt
contrato a plazo
先物契約、先物予約

forward cover
远期弥补; 远期抛补
couverture à terme
Kurssicherung durch
Devisentermingeschäft
cobertura futura o a término
先物カバー

forward integration
向前合并; 前向扩展
intégration par l'aval: moyen de
garantir des voies de distribution
pour des produits et services en
construisant des relations avec les
distributeurs ou en les contrôlant.
L'intégration par l'aval est une
caractéristique du keiretsu
japonais
Vorwärtsintegration
integración progresiva
前進的統合

forward interest rate
远期利率; 期货利率
taux pour opérations à terme

Terminzinssatz
tipo de interés a plazo
先渡し金利

forward-looking study
前瞻性调研[分析]
étude statistique de population
projetée dans le temps
vorausblickende Untersuchung
estudio prospectivo
事後調査

forward pricing
远期定价
fixation de prix d'action de SICAV à
terme
Geplante Preisfestsetzung
fijación de un precio en el futuro
先物価格、先物値段

forward rate
远期利率
taux à terme
Devisenterminkurs; Terminkurs
cambio a plazo
先物相場

forward scheduling
前导式排程
programmation en aval
Vorwärtsterminierung
planificación en función de la
disponibilidad
起算スケジュール方式

forward transaction
期货交易
transaction à terme
Devisentermingeschäft
operación a plazo
先物取引

fourth level of service
第四级价值
quatrième niveau de service
Top-Service
nivel de calidad muy alto
レベル4サービス

fourth market
第四市场
quatrième marché (faire des
transactions directes, sans
courtiers, comme peuvent le faire
les grosses institutions)
Vierter Markt
cuarto mercado
(ブローカーを介さない機関投-
資家どうしが
直接売買する)第四市場

fractional currency
辅币
devise fractionnaire
Scheidemünze
moneda fraccionaria
小額通貨、補助通貨

frames
帧; 框架
trames
Frames
marcos
HTMLのフレーム

franchise
专营权; 特(许)权
franchise
Franchise; Konzession;
Alleinverkaufsrecht
franquicia
フランチャイズ

franchise chain
特许经营连锁店
chaîne de magasins en franchise
Franchisekette
cadena de tiendas con franquicia
フランチャイズ・チェーン，
契約チェーン

franked investment income
免税投资收入
crédit d'impôt attaché au
dividende reçu
Dividendenerträge nach Steuern
und Vergünstigungen
dividendo más los impuestos
asociados
税引後投資利益

franked payments
免税股息
dividendes distribués
Dividendenausschüttung nach
Steuern und Vergünstigungen
total de dividendos pagados más
los impuestos asociados
税引後支払

fraud
舞弊; 诈骗; 欺诈
fraude
Betrug; betrügerisches Verhalten;
Veruntreuung; arglistige
Täuschung
fraude
詐欺

free agent
自由职业者
personne qui travaille en freelance
ou en e-lance (sur Internet)
unabhängige Handelsvertreter(in)
autónomo(-a)
フリーランス・エージェント

freebie
免费赠品
(produit ou service) gratis
Werbegeschenk
regalito
無料頒布品, 無料提供

free cash flow
活动现金流

Translations appear in the following order: Chinese, French, German, Spanish/Latin American Spanish, and Japanese

trésorerie après déductions ou en
franchise
freier Barmittelfluss; freier Cash
Flow; freie
Brutto-Eigenfinanzierungsspanne
reserva de fondos disponibles; caja
operativa generada
自由现金收支

free coinage
自由铸币
frappe de monnaie gratuite: pour
le gouvernement, à matière
première fournie par les citoyens
d'un pays
aus von Bürgern gestellten
Edelmetallen geprägte Münzen
acuñación libre
自由鑄貨

free enterprise
自由企业
libre entreprise
freie Marktwirtschaft
libre empresa
自由企業

free gold
自由黄金
or libre
nicht als Währungsreserve
gehaltenes Gold
oro libre
無拘束金塊、自由金

freelance
自由执业; 兼职
free-lance/indépendant
(travailleur); travail en indépendant
ou à son compte
Freischaffende/r; freiberuflich
freelance; de freelance
フリーランス

free market
自由市场
marché libre
freier Markt
mercado libre
自由市場、実勢市場

freephone
免费电话
numéro vert
kostenlose Rufnummer
teléfono gratuito
フリーダイヤル

freepost
免邮费邮递
port payé
Gebühr zahlt der Empfänger
franqueo pagado en destino
フリーポスト

free stock
自由库存
stock libre

verfügbarer Lagerbestand
existencias o valores, incluyendo
nuevos pedidos
自由在庫品

freeware
免费软件
logiciels gratuits
Freware
freeware
フリーウェア

free worker
自由执业人
une personne qui passe
fréquemment d'un emploi ou d'un
projet à un autre, transférant
Person, die häufig Tätigkeiten oder
Projekte wechselt, und damit
Fertigkeiten und Ideen überträgt
trabajador(a) cualificado que
cambia frecuentemente de trabajo
フリー・ワーカー(短期契約ワー
カー)

freeze-out
逼走小股东的政策
exclusion des actionnaires
minoritaires dans une compagnie
qui a été rachetée
Verdrängen von
Minderheitsaktionären
exclusión de pequeños accionistas
フリーズアウト

freight
货物; 货物运送; 运费
fret
Fracht; Frachtgut
flete; carga
貨物

freight forwarder
转运行; 货运代理行; 货运承揽行
transporteur
Spediteur; Spedition
transportista; agente de
transportes
小口運送業

frequency analysis
频率; 次数
technique des fréquences
Anzahl der Kontakte
análisis de frecuencia
フリクエンシー分析

frequency distribution
频数分布
distribution des fréquences
Häufigkeitsverteilung
distribución de frecuencias
頻度分布

frequency polygon
频数多边图
polygone de fréquence
Häufigkeitspolygon

polígono de frecuencias
頻度多角形グラフ

frictional unemployment
摩擦性失业; 暂时性失业
chômage frictionnel
Fluktuationsarbeitslosigkeit
desempleo friccional
摩擦的失業

friction-free market
无价格争斗市场
marché sans friction
homogener Markt
mercado sin fricciones
無摩擦市場

fringe benefits
附加福利
avantages en nature
Gehaltsnebenleistungen
beneficio adicional; extra
付加給付、厚生給付、賃金外諸給付,
フリンジ・ベネフィット

front end
直接对外服务部门
partie d'une organisation qui a
affaire à la clientèle face à face
direkter Kundenkontakt
parte que trata con los clientes
接客部門

front-end loading
前端销售费
méthode de prélèvement des frais
sur versements initiaux
Front-End-Loading; Inventory
Loading
utilización de parte de los primeros
pagos de un plan para cubrir los
gastos administrativos del mismo
幹事手数料事前徴収制度

FTP
文件传输协议
PTF protocole de transfert de
fichiers
Dateitransferprotokoll; FTP
FTP (protocolo de transferencia de
archivos)
ファイル転送プロトコル

FTSE index
纽约金融时报100指数
indice FTSE
FTSE-Index
índice FTSE
FT100種指数

fulfilment
履行, 实现; 实物兑现
réalisation
Bearbeitung von Kundenanfragen
cumplimiento
フルフィルメント

Translations appear in the following order: Chinese, French, German, Spanish/Latin American Spanish, and Japanese

fulfilment house
履行机构
centre de réalisation
Verkaufszentrale
agencia de servicios de atención al
cliente y promociones
フルフィルメント業者

full bank
全能银行
banque universelle
Universalbank
banco completo
完全銀行

full coupon bond
自由黄金
obligation avec coupon intégral
Anleihe mit marktgerechter
Verzinsung
bono por el que se paga el interés
del mercado
カレント・クーポン債,
パー・イールド債

full-text index
全文索引
indice de texte complet
Volltext Index
índice de todo el texto
フルテキスト・インデックス

full-time
全天
(à) plein temps
Vollzeitarbeit; Ganztagsarbeit
a tiempo completo
フル・タイム

full-time job
全职工作
emploi à plein temps
Voll-Zeit-Job
trabajo a tiempo completo
フルタイムの仕事

fully connected world
完全网络化世界
monde entièrement connecté (via
Internet)
vernetzte Welt
mundo completamente
interconectado
完全連結世界(インター
ネット等で)

**fully diluted earnings per
(common) share**
完全摊薄每股收益
bénéfices par action (ordinaire)
entièrement dilués
Gewinn je Aktie einschließlich
jeglicher Umtauschrechte
remuneración por acción
(ordinaria) con dilución/dilución
total del beneficio por acción
(ordinaria)
株当たり完全希薄利益

fully distributed issue
全部分配股票
émission entièrement distribuée
vollständig verteilte Emission
emisión de valores vendida en su
totalidad a inversores
完全配賦発行株

functional analysis
功能分析
analyse fonctionnelle
Funktionsanalyse
análisis funcional
機能分析

functional budget
部门功能预算
budget fonctionnel
Abteilungsbudget; Stellenplan;
Funktionsbudget
presupuesto departamental o
funcional
機能別予算

functional relationship
功能关系, 函数关系
relation fonctionnelle
funktionelle Beziehung
relación funcional
機能的関係

fund accounting
基金会计
comptabilité d'un fonds
Rechnungslegung für Fonds;
Fondsrechnung
contabilidad de fondos
資金勘定

fundamental analysis
基本分析
analyse fondamentale
Fundamental-Analyse
análisis fundamental
基礎要因分析

funded debt
固定债务, 长期债务
dette à long terme
fundierte Anleihe
deuda consolidada
固定債務, 長期公債

funding risk
筹资风险
risque de financement
Liquiditätsrisiko
riesgo de financiamiento
流動リスク, 金融リスク

fund manager
基金经理; 基金管理人;
投资信托业务经理
gestionnaire de fonds de SICAV
Disponent(in); Fondsverwalter(in);
Verwaltungsgesellschaft
gestor(a) or administrador(a) de
fondos
ファンド・マネージャー

fund of funds
一种注册单位基金
(专用于投资其它基层单位基金-
type de fonds de placement ouvert
qui investit dans une gamme de
fonds de placement sous-jacents
Dachfonds
fondo de fondos
ファンド・オブ・ファンズ

fungible
替代物
fongible
austauschbar
fungible
代替可能な

funny money
怪异资金
type d'instrument financier
inhabituel créé par une compagnie
Aktienoptionen statt Cash
dinero de mentira
通常ではない金融商品

future
期货选择权
à terme
Termingeschäft; Terminware;
Terminkontrakt
futuro
先物

future option
期货选择权，期权
option à terme
Terminoption; Future-Option
opción sobre futuros
先物オプション

futures commission merchant
期货合同佣金商人;
期货合同代理商
courtier de transactions à terme
Terminkommissionär; FCM-Firma
comisionista comercial de futuros
先物取引業者、先物ブローカー

futures exchange
期货外汇
change sur transactions à terme
Terminbörse
mercado de futuros; bolsa a plazo
先物取引

futures market
期货市场
marché à terme
Terminmarkt
mercado de futuros
先物市場

futures research
未来研究
étude des scénarios potentiels
futurs
Erforschung möglicher

Zukunftsversionen
prospectiva
未来調査

future value
终值
valeur à terme
abgezinster, zukünftiger Wert
valor futuro
将来価値

futurise
现代意识; 未来意识
s'assurer qu'une organisation tire
pleinement avantage des toutes
dernières technologies
sich der Internetökonomie
anpassen
prepararse para el futuro
未来化する(最新技術の駆使)

futuristic planning
未来性规划
planification futuriste
futuristische Planung
planificación futurística
未来プラン

fuzzword
难懂的术语
mot nébuleux
abstruser und obskurer Jargon
palabra incomprensible
分かり難い業界用語、隠語、
ジャーゴン

FWIW
物有所值
pour ce que cela vaut
wie das auch sein mag
si sirve de algo
(俗)はっきり知らないが

FYI
特此通告
pour votre information
zu Ihrer Information
para tu información
参考に

G7
七国集团
G7
G-7
G7
先進7ケ国

G8
八国集团
G8
G-8
G8
先進8ケ国

GAB
借款总协定，一般借款协定
fonds financé par le groupe des
Dix et utilisé quand les ressources
du Fonds monétaire international

sont insuffisantes
GAB
AGP
一般借入れ取決め

gain sharing
利润分成
partage des bénéfices
Beteiligung an
Produktivitätszuwächsen
participación en los beneficios
derivados de un incremento en la
productividad
利益分配制度

game theory
博弈论
théorie des jeux
Spieltheorie
teoría de juegos
ゲームの理論

Gantt chart
甘特表
graphique de Gantt
Gantt-Karte; Gantt-Chart
diagrama de Gantt
ガント・チャート

gap analysis
缺口分析; 差距分析
analyse de créneaux
Lückenanalyse
análisis de huecos en el mercado;
análisis de deficiencias
Gap分析

garage[1]
转移资产以降低税负
transférer l'actif ou le passif dans
un autre centre financier pour tirer
profit d'avantages fiscaux
Transfer von Vermögenswerten
oder Schuldtitel von einem
Finanzplatz zu einem anderen, um
Steuervergünstigungen zu nutzen
transferir activos o pasivos de un
centro financiero a otro a fin de
beneficiarse de desgravaciones
fiscales
ガレージ

garage[2]
纽约证券交易所附属楼
annexe du parquet de la Bourse
new-yorkaise
Nebenraum des Hauptparketts der
New Yorker Börse
anexo de la planta principal de la
Bolsa de Valores de Nueva York
NY証券取引所別館

garbatrage
哄炒抬高的股票
titres qui prennent de la valeur à
cause d'un rachat d'entreprise,
sans être connectés à l'entreprise
cible

Aktienwerte, die wegen einer
Übernahme steigen, aber nicht mit
dem Zielunternehmen zusammen
hängen
operaciones basura
企業買収がらみで上昇する関係
のない株

garden leave
带薪停职
congé de jardin
Vorruhestand
permiso retribuido a un empleado
que se marcha a otra empresa para
evitar que saque partido de los
últimos días en el trabajo
自宅待機、待機命令、出勤停止

gatekeeper
信息员
garde-barrière
Informationsmanager
controlador(a) de información
ゲートキーパー(情報の流れを
統制する人々)

gateway
接口; 网关; 网间连结器
passerelle
Rechtfertigungsgrund; Gateway;
Netzübertragungseinheit
pasarela
ゲートウェー

gateway page
网关页
page-passerelle
Gateway-Seite
página pasarela
ゲートウエー・ページ

GATT
关(税)贸(易)总协定
accord général sur les tarifs
douaniers et le commerce
GATT; Allgemeines Zoll- und
Handelsabkommen
GATT
関税と貿易に関する一般協定

gazelle
羚羊企业
entreprise gazelle
Gazellen-Firma mit schnellem
Wachstum und hoher Volatilität
nueva empresa en ascenso
急成長中の新しい企業

gazump
成交后再接受别人更高的报价
revenir sur une promesse de vente
pour accepter un prix plus élevé
Nachträgliches Erhöhen von Haus-
oder Grundstückspreisen
entgegen vorheriger Zusage, oder
Verkauf an einen Höherbietenden
trotz mündlicher Zusage
vender un inmueble a un mejor

Translations appear in the following order: Chinese, French, German, Spanish/Latin American Spanish, and Japanese

postor rompiendo el acuerdo de
venta
ガザンブ

gazunder
成交后再提出降价
revenir sur une promesse de vente
pour accepter un prix moins élevé
trotz mündlicher Einigung über
den Kaufpreis für ein Haus oder
Grundstück, doch bevor die
Vereinbarung rechtskräftig wird,
ein niedrigeres Angebot machen
en el período entre el acuerdo
verbal de compra a un precio
determinado, antes de que el
acuerdo sea legalmente
vinculante, ofrecer un precio más
bajo
ガザンダー

GDP
国内生产总值
PIB
Bruttoinlandsprodukt
producto interno bruto
国内総生産

GDP per capita
人均国内生产总值
PIB par habitant
Bruttoinlandsprodukt pro Kopf
PIB por habitante
1人当りの国内総生産

GEAR
增长; 就业及再分配
programme de réforme
macro-économique sud-africain
Wachstums-, Beschäftigungs- und
Umverteilungsprogramm
programa de reforma
macroeconómica del gobierno
sudafricano
成長雇用再分配政策

geared investment trust
联合投资信托公司
société d'investissement indexée
Anlagefonds, der zur
Portfolioerweiterung Darlehen
aufnimmt
sociedad de inversión mobiliaria de
capital variable
他人資本をてこに自己資本利益-
率を高める投資信託

gearing ratios
资本结合率
ratios d'autonomie financière ou
d'endettement
Verschuldungsquotienten;
Verschuldungskennzahlen
relación préstamos razón deuda/
capital; desembolsados y
pendientes-capital y reservas; nivel
de endeudamiento en relación con

el capital propio; razón préstamos
obtenidos/capital; coeficiente de
apalancamiento
ギャリング率

General Commissioners
总税务专员
commissaires généraux
Laienrichter(in)nen in England,
Wales und Nordirland, zuständig
für Berufungsfälle in Steuersachen
órgano de individuos no
remunerados que son designados
por el Ministro de Hacienda en
Inglaterra, Gales e Irlanda del
Norte, y por el Ministro para
Escocia en Escocia, a fin de
conocer de las apelaciones sobre
asuntos fiscales
一般税監督官

general ledger
普通分类帐; 总分类帐; 总帐
grand livre
Hauptbuch
libro mayor
総勘定元帳、一般元帳

**Generally Accepted
Accounting Principles**
(美国)公认会计准则
principes comptables
généralement acceptés
allgemein anerkannte Grundsätze
der Rechnungslegung
principios de contabilidad
generalmente aceptados
一般承認会計実務

general manager
总经理
directeur général
Hauptgeschäftsführer(in);
leitende/r Angestellte/r
director(a) general
ジェネラル・マネージャー

Generation X
X代
génération X
Generation X
generación X
世代X

generic strategy
总策略
stratégie générique
Marketingstrategie
estrategia genérica
ジェネリック戦略

gensaki
吉萨基 (日)
gensaki: terme japonais pour la
vente de titres incluant un accord
de rachat à date ultérieure
Gensaki: japanischer Begriff für
den Verkauf festverzinslicher

Wertpapiere mit
Rückkaufvereinbarung zu einem
späteren Zeitpunkt
gensaki
现先取引

**geographical information
systems**
地理信息系统
systèmes d'information
géographique
geographische Marketing-Analyse
sistemas de información
geográfica
地理情報システム

ghost rider
(伪称乘坐了出事故车辆而索赔的)
幽灵乘客
passager fantôme
Person, die vorgibt, in einem
Fahrzeug gewesen zu sein, das in
einen Unfall verwickelt war, um
Entschädigung zu fordern
pasajero(a) fantasma
事故に遭った車に乗った振りを-
して補償金を請求する人

GIF
图象交换格式
GIF
Grafisches Format u.a. für das
Internet
GIF
GIF(データ圧縮形式)

gift-leaseback
赠予式回租
cession-bail par donation
Geschenk Leasing
regalo y compra posterior
財産贈与リースバック制度

gift with reservation
有保留条件的赠予
donation avec réserves
Schenkung mit Vorbehalt
donación con reservas
保留条件付贈与

gig
作项目; 项目性工作
projet ou mission temporaire
Projektarbeit
proyecto individual
ギグ(短中期契約プロジェクト)

gigabyte
千兆字节
gigaoctet
Gigabyte
gigabyte
ギガバイト

gilt-edged security[1]
金边证券
titre de premier choix /placement
de tout repos

---

*Translations appear in the following order: Chinese, French, German, Spanish/Latin American
Spanish, and Japanese*

staatliche Obligation;
Regierungsanleihe; Staatspapier;
mündelsicheres Staatspapier
valor de primera clase
一流債權優良株

gilt-edged security[2]
金边证券
investissement de tout repos, sans
risque
Top Aktie
valor de primer orden
ギルト・エッジ証券, 優良証券

gilt repos
优良证券市场
marché des placements de tout
repos
Markt für Verkauf und Rückkauf
von mündelsicheren
Staatspapieren
recompra de valores de primera
clase; recompra de valores de
primer orden
優良証券レポ取引

gilt strip
零息债券到期收益
titre de premier choix à coupon
zéro
Nullkupon-Anleihe mit einmaliger
Auszahlung bei Fälligkeit
bono cupón cero creado mediante
la separación de los pagos de
intereses procedentes de una
obligación de primer orden, de
modo que produzca un solo pago
al contado cuando venza
ギルト・ストリップス債

gilt unit trust
金边单位投资信托
société d'investissement de titres
de premier choix
Gilt Unit Trust
fondo de inversión colectiva en
bonos del Estado/valores de
primera clase
一流債權ユニット信託

giro[1]
转帐
système de virement de compte à
compte
Giroverkehr; Banküberweisung
giro bancario
口座振替

giro[2]
社会福利
chèque (postal) d'indemnité
chômage ou maladie
in Großbritannien: staatliche
Beihilfezahlung
cheque de giro/estatal
ジャイロ

Glacier studies
格萊史尔研究
études Glacier
Glacier-Studien;
Glacier-Erhebungen
estudios en la empresa Glacier
グラシア研究

glad-hand
握手致意
serrer les pinces
Händeschütteln und Begrüßungen
bei einer Geschäftsparty
apretar los manos
ビジネス・パーティで大勢の人-
たちと握手する

glamour stock
热门股票
actions de prestige
Aktien, die sich lebhafter
Nachfrage erfreuen
acciones favoritas
花形株, 魅力株

glass ceiling
玻璃顶; 看不见的限制
plafond invisible: niveau
professionnel où les femmes ont
tendance à plafonner
gläserne Decke
barreras profesionales contra las
mujeres
ガラスの天井

Glass-Steagall Act
葛塞法案; 格拉斯-斯蒂格尔法案
loi Glass-Steagall: loi des Etats-Unis
qui distingue les industries
bancaire et de courtage
Gesetz über das Trennbankwesen
in den Vereinigten Staaten
ley Glass-Steagall
グラス・スティーガル法

glaze
上班时间睁着眼睛睡觉
dormir avec les yeux vitreux
mit offenen Augen dösen, geistig
abwesend sein
dormitar
グレーズ(会議中の居眠り)

global bank
全球银行
banque planétaire
globale Bank; globales Bankhaus
banca global
世界的銀行

global bond issue
全球债券发行
émission de titres pour marchés
planétaires
globale Anleiheemission
emisión global de bonos
グローバル社債発行

global brand
世界性品牌
marque mondiale
globale Marke
marca reconocida mundialmente
グローバル・ブランド

global co-ordinator
全球协调员
responsable de la coordination
planétaire
globale/r Koordinator(in)
coordinador global
グローバル・コーディネーター

global custody
全球保管
service financier de bonne garde
planétaire
Globaldepot
custodia global
グローバル・カストディー

globalisation
全球化
globalisation
Globalisierung
globalización
グローバル化

global marketing
全球销售
marketing mondial
globales Marketing; globale
Vermarktung
marketing global
グローバル・マーケティング

global offering
全球发行
nouvelle émission au niveau
planétaire
globales Emissionsangebot
oferta global
グローバル・オファリング

global pricing contract
全球统一定价合同
contrat de prix similaires à l'échelle
planétaire
globale Preisvereinbarung;
Vereinbarung über globale
Preisfixierung
contrato con los mismos precios
para todo el mundo
グローバルプライス契約

glocalisation
全球化市场定位
glocalisation: processus
d'adaptation des produits ou des
services aux divers marchés locaux
à travers le monde. Le terme
glocalisation est une synthèse des
mots globalisation et localisation
regionale Produktanpassung
adaptación de productos a los
diferentes mercados mundiales
グローカライゼーション

Translations appear in the following order: Chinese, French, German, Spanish/Latin American Spanish, and Japanese

glue
共同利益
mortier
gemeinsame Interessen, die
Unternehmen
zusammenschweißen
factor unificador
結合要素(のり)

GmbH
私人有限公司
GmbH
Gesellschaft mit beschränkter
Haftung
S.A.
(独)有限責任会社

GNMA
政府国民抵押协会
corporation américaine qui émet
des obligations garanties par
hypothèque
GNMA
agencia del gobierno
estadounidense que compra
hipotecas de instituciones de
préstamo y las vende a inversores
(米)政府住宅抵当金庫

gnomes of Zurich
苏黎世魔鬼，苏黎世金融大亨
gnomes de Zurich: terme péjoratif
pour les courtiers en devises et
banquiers suisses
Züricher 'Gnome'; Finanzexperten
gnomos de Zurich
チューリッヒの小鬼

GNP
国民生产总值
PNB
Bruttosozialprodukt
PNB
国民総生産

GNP per capita
人均国民生产总值
PNB par habitant
Bruttosozialprodukt pro Kopf
PNB por habitante
1人当りの国民総生産

goal congruence
目标一致
Harmonie des objectifs
Zielharmonie
congruencia de objetivos
目標一致

go-go fund
赌博性投资，速利基金
fonds de placement spéculatif
Risikofonds
valor de bolsa que promete
rápidos beneficios
(米)ゴーゴー・ファンド

going concern concept
继续经营假设
concept de l'entreprise prospère
Grundsatz der
Unternehmensfortführung
concepto de empresa que
funciona bien
継続企業概念

going short
卖空
vente à découvert (un bien dont on
n'est pas encore propriétaire avec
l'intention de l'acheter
ultérieurement au rabais pour
livraison à l'acheteur)
Baissespekulation; Leerverkauf
especular a la baja
売り持ち

gold bond
黄金债券
obligation or
Goldanleihe
bono respaldado por oro
金貨債券、金価格債券

goldbricker
偷懒雇员
tire-au-flanc
arbeitsunlustiger Arbeitnehmer,
der nur ein Minimum an Arbeit
verrichtet
empleado(-a) vago(-a)
怠け者の社員

gold card
金卡
carte de crédit Gold Card
Gold Card
tarjeta de crédito oro
ゴールド・カード

gold certificate
黄金债券
certificat de propriété aurifère
Goldzertifikat
certificado de oro
金証券、金貨証券

golden handcuffs
金手铐
contrat alléchant: contrat global
offrant toutes sortes d'avantages
en nature, dont le but est de lier un
employé à l'organisation et
d'empêcher les autres
organisations de réussir à l'attirer
goldene Handschellen
contrato blindado
ゴールデン・ハンドカフ，
社員に対する特別優遇措置

golden handshake
(大笔)退职金; 解雇费
(grosse) prime de départ
goldener Handschlag
baja involuntaria con

compensación en metálico
ゴールデン・ハンドシェイク

golden hello
调职补偿金
prime d'embauche
Einstellungsprämie
prima por incorporación
ゴールデン・ハロー

golden parachute
金降落伞; 高级职员去职补偿费
indemnité de départ: clause dans
le contrat d'emploi d'un cadre
supérieur qui lui garantit une
grosse prime en cas du rachat de
l'entreprise, d'une fusion ou d'un
congédiement dû à sa
performance médiocre
goldener Fallschirm
contrato blindado
ゴールデン・パラシュー
ト(A&Mに伴う高額退職補償
契約)

golden rolodex
媒介专家发言人; 媒介评论专家
élite dorée d'experts
die kleine Gruppe von
Sachverständigen, die am
häufigsten in den Nachrichten
zitiert oder im Fernsehsendungen
um ihre Meinung gebeten werden.
Rolodex ist das Warenzeichen für
eine Schreibtischkartei
los expertos más reconocidos
マスコミに持て囃される
専門家群

golden share
金股
action privilégiée
Anteil eines privatisierten
Unternehmens, der von der
Regierung zurückbehalten wird,
um nicht allen Einfluss zu verlieren
acción de oro
黄金株

gold fix
黄金定价
fixation quotidienne du cours de
l'or
Goldfixing; Festsetzung des
Goldpreises
precio del oro
金の建値決定

gold reserve
黄金储备
réserve d'or
Goldbestand; Goldreserve
reserva de oro
金準備、正貨準備金

gold standard
黄金本位; 金本位(制)
l'étalon-or

---

*Translations appear in the following order: Chinese, French, German, Spanish/Latin American
Spanish, and Japanese*

Goldwährung; Goldstandard
patrón oro
金本位制

good for the day
当天有效
bon pour aujourd'hui
Auftrag, der nur am angegebenen
Tag gültig ist
sólo para hoy
その日有効な指値注文

good for this week/month
本周月有效
bon pour cette semaine/ce mois-ci
Auftrag, der nur für die
angegebene Woche oder den
angegebenen Monat gültig ist
orden para la semana/el mes
今週月有効な指値注文

Goods and Services Tax[1]
商品和劳务税
taxe sur les biens et services
Vorsteuer
impuesto sobre bienes y servicios
物品 / サービス税

Goods and Services Tax[2]
(进口)货物和劳务税
taxe sur les biens et services
Mehrwertsteuer
impuesto sobre bienes y servicios
物品 / サービス税

Goods and Services Tax[3]
(加拿大)货物和劳务税
taxe sur les biens et services
Waren- und Dienstleistungssteuer
impuesto sobre bienes y servicios
カナダの財貨・用役に課税
される)一般消費税

goods received note
已收货物通知
bordereau de réception de produit
Wareneingangsschein
albarán; aviso de recibo de
mercancías; nota de recepción;
nota de recepción de mercancías
品目受領書

good 'til cancel
GTC; 长期有效委托书;
注销前有效
bon jusqu'à annulation
Auftrag bis auf Widerruf
vigente hasta su cancelación
解約まで有効

good title
有效的所有权
titre de propriété valable
unbestreitbares Eigentum;
hinreichender Rechtstitel; gültiger
Rechtsanspruch
título válido
優良権原, 完全所有権

goodwill
商誉; 信誉; 无形资产
actif incorporel
Goodwill
fondo de comercio
のれん代, 営業権

gopher
跑腿的; 打杂的
larbin
Laufbursche; Kalfaktor
gopher
使い走り従業員

go plural
同时从事若干种不同的工作
se diversifier
in die Teilzeitarbeit wechseln
pasar a trabajar a tiempo parcial
複数雇用者を持つ

go private
民营化
repasser au statut de société privée
Börsenzulassung aufgeben
salir de Bolsa
株式を非公開とする

go public
上市
porter quelque chose à la
connaissance du public
an die Börse gehen
cotizar en bolsa
株式を公開する, 公開企業となる

go-slow
怠工
grève perlée
Bummelstreik
huelga de celo
怠業戦術

**Government Business
Enterprise**
政府企业
entreprise commerciale
gouvernementale
staatliches Unternehmen
empresa con participación del
Estado
政府関係企業

government gazette
政府公报
gazette gouvernementale
Amtsblatt
boletín oficial del gobierno o de un
estado australiano
官報

government secuities/stock
政府证券, 政府债券
titres d'Etat; fonds
Staatsanleihen; Staatspapiere
títulos públicos; títulos del Estado
国債

**graduated payments
mortgage**
累进付款抵押
hypothèque à paiements
progressifs
Hypothek mit gestaffelten, aber
steigenden Tilgungsleistungen
préstamo hipotecario de
reembolso progresivo
累進的不動産抵当

grant of probate
遗嘱检验文件
document homologué d'un
testament
Erbschein
adveración testamentaria
遺言検認証書

grantor
让与人
octroyeur ou vendeur d'option
Optionsverkäufer(in)
otorgante, cesionista
オプション売却者

grapevine
非正式交流渠道
sources personnelles
d'information
Nachrichtendienst; Gerüchteküche
comunicación informal
(うわさや評判の)伝達路、
情報網、口こみ

graph
坐标图; 图表; 图解
graphique
Diagramm; Schaubild; Graph
gráfico
グラフ, 図表

graphical user interface
图形用户界面;
图象用户接口(界面)
interface utilisateur graphique
(IUG)
grafische Benutzeroberfläche
interfaz gráfica de usuario
グラフィカル・ユーザー・
インターフェース

graphology
笔记学
graphologie
Handschriftendeutung
grafología
筆跡観相法

grass ceiling
高尔夫行业的妇女歧视
facteurs socioculturels qui
empêchent ou découragent les
femmes d'utiliser le golf comme
endroit où mener leurs affaires
soziale und kulturelle Faktoren, die
Frauen davon abhalten, auf dem
Golfplatz Geschäfte zu machen

Translations appear in the following order: Chinese, French, German, Spanish/Latin American Spanish, and Japanese

las barreras que hacen que las
mujeres no utilicen el golf para
llevar a cabo negocios
女性をビジネス・ゴルフから
遠ざけている障壁

graveyard market[1]
坟墓市场
marché de transactions peu
fréquentes (d'actions qui suscient
peu d'intérêt ou qui n'ont aucune
ou très peu de valeur)
'Friedhofsmarkt':Markt für Aktien,
die nur selten gehandelt werden
cementerio
墓地市場

graveyard market[2]
坟墓市场
marché baissier à grosses pertes
'Friedhofsmarkt': Baissemarkt, wo
Anleger, die ihre Anteile
veräußern, mit hohen Verlusten zu
rechnen haben
cementerio
弱気相場

greater fool theory
大傻瓜理论
théorie du plus grand idiot
Greater Fool Theory
la teoría de que vale la pena
comprar acciones sobrevaloradas
porque siempre habrá alguien que
querrá comprarlas incluso más
caras
より高く買上げてくれる人が必
ずいると言う投資戦略理論

great man theory
伟人理论
théorie des grands hommes
Theorie vom großen Mann
teoría de los grandes hombres
偉大な人物理論

green ban
绿色禁令
interdiction pour raison écologique
Umweltauflage
boicot sindical a proyectos con
impacto ambiental negativo
労働組合による,
公害事業などへの就労拒否

greenfield site
绿地场地; 无建筑物场地
site en dehors d'une ville, en
général en ceinture verte
grüne Wiese
terreno edificable en el campo
更地

greenmail
绿票讹诈; 反购回
chantage financier
erpresserischer Kauf eines
Aktienpakets; Maßnahme zur

Vermeidung einer Übernahme,
wobei das gefährdete
Unternehmen seine eigenen
Aktien von einem Mitbewerber
zurückkauft, der die Aktien
angekauft hat
recompra de acciones para evitar
una OPA
グリーンメール

green marketing
环境意识营销
marketing vert
Öko-Marketing
marketing ecológico
グリーン・マーケティング

green pound
绿色英镑
livre verte
grünes Pfund; grüner Dollar
libra verde, unidad de contabilidad
de los productos agrícolas en la UE
グリーン・ポンド

green shoe
增售条款
option à rallonge
Mehrzuteilungsoption;
Platzierungsreserve
'zapato verde'
追加発行条項

green taxes
绿色税收
impôts écologiques
grüne Steuern
ecotasas
緑税

greenwash
绿色外衣(指公司为树立保护环
境的形象而作的捐赠或公关活动)
couleur écolo d'entreprise
Ökotünche: Informationen, die
eine Organisation herausgibt, um
sich in der Öffentlichkeit ein
umweltbewusstes Image zu geben
lavado verde de imagen
環境派を意識した企業情報

greybar-land
灰条区状态
vapes de la grisaille informatique
der vage Zustand, in den man
versetzt wird wenn man lange den
grauen Balken anstarrt, der auf
dem Bildschirm erscheint,
während der Rechner etwas
verarbeitet
la eterna espera a que el
ordenador acabe una tarea
la eterna espera a que el
computador or la computadora
acabe una tarea
グレーバー・ランド

grey market[1]
灰(色)市(场); 灰色市场
marché dans lequel les produits
vendus ont été fabriqués à
l'étranger puis importés
Markt, an dem im Ausland
gefertigte Importgüter verkauft
werden
mercado gris
品薄品のヤミ市場

grey market[2]
中老年人市场; 银发市场
segment de marché occupé par
des membres plus âgés de la
population
Markt der ältesten Leute in der
Bevölkerung
segmento de mercado ocupado
por las personas de edad avanzada
老齢企業市場

grey market[3]
未正式发行证券的非官方交易
commerce non officiel de titres (en
Bourse) qui n'ont pas encore été
émis officiellement
der nichtamtliche Handel mit noch
nicht offiziell emittierten
Wertpapieren
mercado gris
品薄品のヤミ市場

grey marketing
中老年市场
marketing destiné aux groupes de
personnes plus âgées
Seniorenmarketing
marketing dirigido a la tercera
edad
シルバー市場

grey matter
权威顾问; 高级顾问
têtes expertes grisonnantes
ältere und erfahrene
Firmenberater; graue Gehirnzellen
expertos veteranos
外見上経験豊かな老年専門家

grey wave
灰波
compagnie faisant partie de la
vague cendrée
Unternehmen, das in ferner
Zukunft gute Erfolgschancen hat.
Der Name beruht auf der Tatsache,
dass die Investoren bis dahin wohl
graue Haare haben werden
sociedad que se considera tiene
buenas perspectivas en un futuro
lejano
グレー・ウエイブ

grievance procedure
员工投诉程序
procédure d'arbitrage

Translations appear in the following order: Chinese, French, German, Spanish/Latin American Spanish, and Japanese

Beschwerdeverfahren;
Schlichtungsverfahren
procedimiento de quejas
苦情処理手続き

gross
毛的; 总的
brut
brutto
bruto
総体

gross domestic fixed capital formation
国内固定资产形成总值
formation de capital fixe intérieur brut
Bruttoinlandsinvestitionen
formación bruta interior del capital fijo
国内総固定資本形成

gross interest
总利息，毛利
intérêt brut
Zins; Bruttozins
interés bruto
粗利子

gross lease
毛额租金; 一般租赁契约
bail brut
Dienstleistungs-Leasing
arriendo bruto
諸経費家主(地主)持ち賃貸借

gross margin[1]
毛利，边际收益
marge brute
Rohgewinn; Bruttogewinn
margen comercial bruto; tasa de beneficio bruto
委託証拠金

gross margin[2]
毛利，边际收益
marge brute
Bruttospanne
margen comercial bruto; tasa de beneficio bruto
総売買差益

gross misconduct
严重违纪
mauvaise gestion flagrante
grobe Verletzung der Amtspflicht; schweres Fehlverhalten; schwere Verfehlung
falta grave
重大な不当経営, 監督不十分

gross profit
毛利，总利润
bénéfice brut
Bruttogewinn
beneficio bruto
総利益

gross profit percentage
pourcentage de bénéfice brut
Bruttogewinnanteil
porcentaje del beneficio bruto
総利益率

gross receipts
总收入，经营总收入
recettes brutes
Bruttoeinnahmen
ingresos brutos
総収入

gross yield
毛收益
rendement brut
Bruttoertrag
rendimiento bruto
総利回り

gross yield to redemption
偿还总收益，赎回总收益
rendement brut à remboursement
jährlicher Bruttoertrag
rendimiento bruto al vencimiento
年率換算

group
集团
groupe
Konzern; Unternehmensgruppe
grupo
グループ(系列会社)

group capacity assessment
小组能力评价
évaluation de capacité de groupe
Bewertung der Gruppenkapazität
evaluación de la capacidad de trabajo del grupo
グループ能力査定

group certificate
雇员收入证明
certificat groupé
Steuerkarte
documento en el que se detallan los ingresos y pago de impuestos anuales de un empleado
収入証明書

group discussion
分组讨论
discussion de groupe
Gruppendiskussion
discusión en grupo
グループ・ディスカッション

group dynamics
团队内部关系
dynamique de(s) groupe(s)
Gruppendynamik
dinámica de grupo
集団力学

group incentive scheme
集体奖励计划
système de prime par équipe
Gruppen-Anreizplan

plan de incentivos para el trabajo en grupo
グループ奨励制

group investment
集团投资
investissement en groupe
Gemeinschaftsinvestition
inversión en grupo
団体投資

group life assurance
集团人寿保险单，集体人寿保险单
assurance-vie de groupe
Gruppenlebensversicherung
seguro de vida colectivo
団体生命保険

Group of Seven
七大工业先进国家，七国集团
le groupe des Sept (les sept nations industrialisées leaders: Canada, France, Allemagne, Italie, Japon, Etats-Unis et Royaume Uni)
Gruppe der Sieben; Abk. G7
grupo de los siete
先進7ヶ国

Group of Ten
十国集团，十国财团组织
le groupe des Dix (groupe des dix pays qui contribuent aux arrangements généraux du fonds d'emprunt: Canada, France, Allemagne, Italie, Japon, Pays-Bas, Suède, Etats-Unis et Royaume Uni. La Suisse s'y est jointe en 1984)
Zehnergruppe; Abk. G10
grupo de los diez
先進10ヶ国

group selection
分组挑选
sélection de groupe
Gruppenauswahl; Gruppenauslese
selección en grupos
集団採用テスト

group technology
成组技术; 成组工艺
technologie de groupe
Inselfertigung
tecnología de grupos
グループ・テクノロジー
(多種少量生産における生産管理技術)

groupthink
群体迷思，群体思维
pensée en groupe
Gruppendenken
pensamiento grupal
集団思考

group tool
集团工具
outil de groupe
Workgroup Tool

Translations appear in the following order: Chinese, French, German, Spanish/Latin American Spanish, and Japanese

herramienta para trabajo en grupo
グループ・ツール

groupware
组件; 群件
logiciel qui permet à un groupe,
dont les membres se trouvent dans
des endroits divers, de travailler
ensemble et de partager des
informations
Groupware
software para el trabajo en grupo
グループウェア

growth and income fund
资本增长和收入基金
société d'investissement (SICAV)
de croissance et revenus
Wachstums- und
Einkommensfonds
fondo de crecimiento e ingresos
グロース・アンド・インカム・
ファンド

growth capital
增长资本
capital de croissance
Wachstumskapital
capital de desarrollo
成長資本

growth company
发展迅速的公司; 发展公司
compagnie en expansion
Wachstumgesellschaft
empresa en crecimiento
(高度)成長会社

growth curve
增长[生长]曲线
courbe de croissance ou de
grandissement
Wachstumskurve
curva de crecimiento
成長曲線

growth equity
成长性资产
fonds propres de croissance
Wachstumspapiere
acciones prometedoras
潜在成長株式

growth fund
资本增长基金
société d'investissements à
croissance maximisée
Wachstumsfonds
fondo de crecimiento
グロース(ミューチュアル)
ファンド, 成長目当ての投資信託

growth industry
成长型行业，发展迅速的行业
industrie (au bon potentiel) de
croissance
Wachstumsbranche;
Wachstumsindustrie

industria en expansión
成長産業

growth rate
增长率
taux d'expansion
Wachstumsrate; Zuwachsrate;
Expansionsrate
índice de crecimiento
経済成長率、伸び率

growth share[1]
成长股票; 增长股票; 发展股票;
热门股
valeur de croissance
Wachstumsaktie; Wuchsaktie
acciones de crecimiento
成長株

growth share[2]
成长股
action de croissance
Wachstumsaktie
acciones de crecimiento
成長株

growth stock
成长股票; 增长股票; 发展股票;
热门股
valeur de croissance; valeur
haute-croissance
Wachstumsaktie; Wuchsaktie
acciones de crecimiento
成長株

grupo
卢普集团
groupe de compagnies au
Mexique
Grupo, mexikanische
Firmengruppe
grupo
グルーボ(メキシコの複合企業)

guan xi
关系
connexions
persönliches Vertrauen zum
Geschäftspartner
contactos
(中)個人的信頼

guarantee
担保
garantie ou cautionnement
Garantie; Bürgschaft; Delkredere;
Aval
garantía; aval
支払保証

guaranteed bond
担保债券
bon ou obligation garantie
durch Bürgschaft gesicherte
Schuldverschreibungen
bono garantizado
支払債券, 保証債権

guaranteed employment
保证就业
emploi garanti
garantierte Beschäftigung;
Garantielohn
empleo garantizado
雇用保証(制), 保証賃金

guaranteed fund
保证基金
fonds d'investissement garanti
Garantiefonds
fondo garantizado
保証準備積立金

guaranteed income bond
收入保证债券
titre à revenu garanti: émis par une
compagnie d'assurance-vie avec
un taux de revenu fixe pour une
période spécifique
Anleihe mit Garantie eines festen
Ertrags über eine bestimmte
Zeitspanne hinweg
póliza de prima única
保証所得債権

**guaranteed investment
certificate**
有保障投资
contrat d'investissement à intérêts
garantis
Guaranteed Investment Contract
certificado de inversión
garantizado
利付き保険証券

guaranteed stocks
有担保的债券
titres garantis
Wertpapiere mit Garantie einer
Regierung
valores con dividendo garantizado
配当の保証株

guarantor
担保人; 保证人
garant/avaliste
Garantiegeber(in); Garant(in);
Bürge; Bürgin
fiador(a)
保証人

guard book
剪贴簿
livre de garde
Anzeigenakte; Inseratsmappe
libro de anuncios
ガード・ブック

guerilla marketing
游击营销
marketing sauvage
Guerrilla Marketing
marketing agresivo
ゲリラ・マーケティング

Translations appear in the following order: Chinese, French, German, Spanish/Latin American Spanish, and Japanese

gun jumping
枪跳
gun jumping: terme américain
pour délits (d'opérations
boursières) d'initiés (littéralement:
couper l'herbe sous le pied)
amerikanischer Begriff für
Insiderhandel; voreiliges Handeln
delito de iniciados
ガンジャンプ(自社株売買)

gweeping
长时间因特网漫游
lanternage sur le Net
stundenlanges Surfen im Internet
pasarse las horas surfeando
長時間のインターネット・
サーフィン

hacker
黑客; 计算机窃贼
pirate informatique
Hacker
pirata informático(-a)
ハッカー

haggle
大肆讨价还价
marchander
feilschen
regatear
値切り交渉

half-normal plot
半正常图
courbe semi-normale
half-normal plot
gráfico de probabilidad
seminormal
半正規プロット

hammering the market
抛售证券打击市场，打压市场
martèlement de marché
intensive Leerverkäufe tätigen
martilleo del mercado
売り集中

hand-hold
安慰; 吃定心丸
tenir la menotte
Händchenhalten
tranquilizar
安心させること

hand off
离职
transférer la responsabilité d'un
projet
delegieren
delegar responsabilidad
ハンドオフ(引継ぎ)

hand signals
手势
signes de la main
Handzeichen

señales manuales
手ぶり

hands-off
无为而治
sans intervention continue (de la
direction)
unbeachtet weiterarbeiten lassen
no intervencionista
無干渉主義

hands-on
实践; 实习
pratique/sur le terrain
praktisch; intensiv; straff;
interventionistisch
práctico(a); directo(a)
実践主義

hang-out loan
期限超过租赁期的贷款
emprunt avec somme rémanente
Restdarlehen
balance de un préstamo cuando el
plazo termina
ハングアウト・ローン，
融資残存額

Hang Seng index
恒生指数
Indice Hang Seng
Hang-Seng-Index
índice Hang Seng
ハンセン指数

happy camper
乐天派，乐天的人
quelqu'un qui n'a aucune
récrimination envers son
employeur
zufriedener Arbeitnehmer
trabajador(a) satisfecho(-a)
ハッピー・キャンバー(上司に
不満のない人)

hara-kiri swap
无利交换
échange croisé de type hara-kiri
Harakiri-Swap
swap haraquiri
腹切スワップ

hard commodities
硬商品，金属及其它原材料商品
biens durables
metallischer Rohstoff
mercaderías duras
硬金属商品

hard currency
硬通货; 硬币
devise forte
harte Währung
moneda fuerte
硬貨, ハードカレンシー

hard disk
硬盘
disque dur
Festplatte

disco duro
ハードディスク

hard landing
硬着陆
se dit d'une période de croissance
soutenue qui finit par un passage
soudain de l'économie à une
situation de récession et de
stagnation commerciale
Rezession; harte Landung
aterrizaje brusco
硬着陆

hard sell
硬性推销; 强行推销
vente agressive
aggressive Verkaufstechnik;
Hardselling
venta agresiva
押しの強い売り方法

hardware
硬件
hardware
Hardware; Eisenwaren;
Maschinenausrüstung
hardware
ハードウェア

harmonisation[1]
协调
harmonisation: résolutions
d'inégalités de salaires et de
conditions d'emploi entre ouvriers
et cadres. Aussi appelé statut
unique
Harmonisierung; Abstimmung
armonización
利害調整策

harmonisation[2]
协调
harmonisation: alignement des
systèmes de paiement de salaires
et de prestations de deux
entreprises qui fusionnent ou sont
rachetées
Harmonisierung; Abstimmung
armonización
利害調整策

harmonisation[3]
协调
harmonisation: convergence des
réglementations sociales de
l'Union européenne
Harmonisierung; Abstimmung
armonización
(加)一般消費税

harmonised sales tax
协调营业税
impôt commercial harmonisé
(Canada)
harmonisierte Umsatzsteuer
IVA
(カナダの)一般消費税

Translations appear in the following order: Chinese, French, German, Spanish/Latin American Spanish, and Japanese

harvesting strategy
收获战略
stratégie du moissonneur
Reduzierung oder Einstellung des
Marketings für ein Produkt bevor
es aus dem Verkehr gezogen wird,
mit dem Resultat einer
Gewinnsteigerung durch frühere
Werbekampagnen
estrategia de recogida de
beneficios
市場収穫戦略

Hawthorne experiments
霍桑实验
expériences de Hawthorne
Hawthornsche Versuche
experimentos de Hawthorne
ホーソーンの実験

hazardous substance
隐患性材料; 危险性材料
substance dangereuse
Gefahrstoff
sustancia tóxica
危険物質

head and shoulders
头肩式走势
la tête et les épaules (décrit une
courbe traçant les prix des actions
d'une compagnie qui ressemble à
la tête et aux épaules d'une
personne. Ceci est perçu comme la
première indication d'une chute de
marché)
'Kopf und Schultern':
Aktienkursgraphik, deren Form der
von Kopf und Schultern eines
Menschen gleicht.
Chart-Analysten sehen dies als
Indiz für einen Marktabschwung
cabeza y hombros
ヘッド・アンド・ショルダー,
三尊

headcount
总人数; 人头数
effectif (d'une organisation)
Personalbestand
total de empleados
総従業員数

headhunting
物色人才; 猎头
chasse aux têtes
Kopfjagd; Abwerbung von
Führungskräften
caza de talentos
人材スカウト

headline rate of inflation
头条通货膨胀率
(将购房分期付款利率含在内)
taux d'inflation indicateur de cap:
mesure du taux d'inflation qui
tient compte des frais

hypothécaires des propriétaires
immobiliers
Inflationsrate unter
Berücksichtigung von
Hypothekenzinsen
tasa global de inflación
インフレ率総合指数

heads of agreement
协议要点草案
dirigeants d'un accord
Hauptpunkte eines Vertrages
encabezados del acuerdo
契約書の最重要項目

health and safety
健康与安全
réglementations relatives à la santé
et sécurité sur le lieu de travail
Arbeitsschutz
seguridad e higiene
健康と安全

health screening
体检
test de dépistage médical (au
travail)
medizinische Untersuchung; am
Arbeitsplatz
examen médico
健康診断

heatseeker
求新者
quelqu'un qui achète toujours la
toute dernière version d'un produit
logiciel dès qu'elle apparaît sur le
marché
Heatseeker
persona que compra
sistemáticamente la última versión
de un software
ヒート・シーカー

heavy hitter
业绩卓越
gros joueur
Spitzenunternehmen; Spitzenkraft
empresa o
ejecutivo(-a)arrollador(-a)
実績の良い幹部

hedge
对冲
couverture ou arbitrage
Sicherungsgeschäft;
Kurssicherung
cobertura contra cambios de
precios de los mercados
financieros; protección; resguardo
ヘッジ取引

hedge fund
套利基金; 套头基金
société d'investissements (de type
SICAV) par arbitrage
stark spekulierender
Investmentfonds

fondo de inversión de alto riesgo
ヘッジ・ファンド

hedging against inflation
对付通货膨胀的套头交易
(investissement avec) couverture
contre l'inflation
Inflationssicherung
cobertura contra la inflación
インフレ・ヘッジ

held order
延迟订单
ordre détenu
Auftrag, der dem Händler
bezüglich Preis und Zeitpunkt der
Ausübung eine gewisse Freiheit
einräumt
orden paralizada
注文保留

helicopter view
纵观
vue d'hélico
Übersicht über ein Problem;
Hubschrauberblick
visión panorámica de conjunto
問題の全体像

helpline
帮助热线; 热线
ligne d'assistance (téléphonique)
Hotline
servicio de asistencia telefónica
お客様電話相談

herding cats
放牧猫群; 艰巨任务
rassembler les chats en troupeau
Flöhe hüten, eine schwierige oder
unmögliche Aufgabe
tarea imposible; trabajo imposible
難題(猫の群れを見守る)

heuristics
启发式
heuristique
Heuristik
heurística
発見的解決法

HHOK
哈哈，开个玩笑而已
ha, ha, je plaisante!
war nur ein Witz! Ugs. Ich hab'
dich auf den Arm genommen
era broma
冗談だよ

hidden tax
隐蔽税
taxe cachée
verdeckte Steuer
impuesto encubierto
隠れた税

hierarchy of activities
活动等级
hiérarchie des activités

Translations appear in the following order: Chinese, French, German, Spanish/Latin American Spanish, and Japanese

Tätigkeitshierarchie;
Arbeitshierarchie
clasificación jerárquica de las
actividades
体形的分類活動

high concept
高见
concept noble
gut durchdachtes Konzept
idea convincente, clara y sucinta
ハイ・コンセプト

highdome
科学家
scientifique
Bezeichnung für Wissenschaftler;
Intelligenzbestie; Großkopf
científico(-a)
知的な科学者

high-end
高价品
haut de gamme
obere Preisklasse
de gama alta
最高級仕様

higher-rate tax
较高税率的税
impôt de tranche supérieure
höchste Einkommenssteuerklasse
in Großbritannien
banda más alta de impuestos
高税率

high-flier
高价位投机性股票
titre craquant
Überflieger
acción especulativa con un precio
muy alto
ハイ・フライヤー(短期高収益株)

high/low method
高低法
méthode d'estimation de coût
basée sur une production forte/
faible
mathematische Kostenauflösung
método comparativo para estimar
la conducta del coste
ハイロー方法

**high-premium convertible
debenture**
高溢价可转换债券
obligation convertible de prime
élevée
weit über dem Nennwert
verkaufte
Wandelschuldverschreibung mit
gutem Zinsertrag und langer
Laufzeit
obligación convertible de prima
alta
ハイプレミアム転換社債

high-pressure
高压销售; 高压; 高压力
de choc/agressif (vendeur)
zielbewusst
agresivo(a); de alta presión
高圧的販売

high-risk company
高风险公司
compagnie à haut risque
risikoreiches od. hochriskantes
Unternehmen
empresa de alto riesgo
ハイリスク企業

high street
高街; 主街; 主要街道
grand-rue /petit commerce
Hauptstraße; Haupteinkaufsstraße
calle principal
本通り

high yielder
高收益股票
(valeur ou titre) de rendement
supérieur
hochverzinsliches Wertpapier
valor de alto rendimiento
高利回り債権

hip shooter
凭直觉判断的领导;
反应敏捷果断的人
dégaineur rapide
Führungskraft, die von der Hüfte
schießt; impulsiv reagiert
ejecutivo(-a) que se deja guiar por
su instinto
(俗)ヒップシューター

hired gun[1]
枪手
personne embauchée pour durée
de projet
Zeitarbeiter
experto(-a) a sueldo
企業買収の時に雇われる外部の者

hired gun[2]
公司接管中的外聘顾问
aide à gages
Scherge
persona incorporada para
defenderse de una OPA
導入武器(企業買収戦で
の人の装備)

hire purchase
分期付款(购买)
achat à crédit
Mietkauf; Teilzahlungskauf;
Ratenkauf
compra a plazos
分割払式購買

historical cost
历史成本会计
coût primitif d'acquisition

historische Kosten; Istkosten der
Vergangenheit; Anschaffungs-
oder Herstellungskosten
coste histórico
取得原価

historical cost accounting
历史成本会计
comptabilité basée sur les coûts
primitifs d'acquisition
Istkostenrechnung
contabilidad del coste histórico o
de adquisición
取得原価勘定

historical pricing
历史定价
fixation de prix historique
historische Preisbildung od.
Preisgestaltung
cálculo de precios históricos
取得価格決定

historical summary
历史概括
résumé historique (des résultats)
Firmengeschichte
resumen histórico
歴代収益概要

historic pricing
历史定价
fixation de prix historique
Preisverfahren auf Grundlage der
jüngsten Anteilsbestände
fijación histórica de precios
実際価格

hit
点击; 选中
résultat; coup réussi
Treffer; sofort bei Börsenbegin
ausgeführter Auftrag; aufprallen
auf
acceso; impresión; hit
ヒット

hit squad
采购部
commando des acquisitions
Akquisitionsteam eines
Unternehmens
equipo de adquisiciones
企業買収チーム

hockey stick
曲棍球棒型曲线
performance en crosse de hockey
Leistungskurve in Form eines
Hockeyschlägers, typisch in der
Gründungsphase von
Unternehmen, erst absteigend,
dann steil und geradlinig
ansteigend
curva descendente con un rápido
repunte al final
新しい企業の業績が下がってか
ら直線で伸びる傾向

---

*Translations appear in the following order: Chinese, French, German, Spanish/Latin American
Spanish, and Japanese*

holdback
预留金
fonds de réserve
Rückstellungen
fondos retenidos
ホールドバック, 支払保留金

holder
持有人，持票人
porteur
Inhaber(in)
tenedor
流通証券の所持人

holding company
控股公司; 股权公司; 持股公司
société de portefeuille
Dachgesellschaft;
Muttergesellschaft;
Holdinggesellschaft; Holding
sociedad de cartera
持ち株会社

holding cost
持币成本
coût de rétention
Lagerkosten; Kosten der
Lagerhaltung
coste de retención
財産保有費

holiday
假期
(jour de) congé
Feiertag; arbeitsfreier Tag
vacaciones
休日、休業日、祝日、休暇

home loan
住房贷款
prêt immobilier
Hypothek
préstamo hipotecario
住宅ローン

homepage
主页
page accueil
Homepage
página inicial; portada
ホームページ

home run¹
短期巨额回报
coup de circuit: terme américain
venant du baseball et signifiant
une réussite extraordinaire. Ce
terme s'applique souvent à des
investissements fructueux, qui
produisent un taux de rendement
élevé en peu de temps
Homerun
exitazo
大成功

home run²
全垒打，获得暴利的投资
beau coup

das große Los ziehen:
amerikanischer Begriff aus dem
Baseball, bezeichnet eine
herausragende Errungenschaft.
Wird häufig für erfolgreiche
Investitionen benutzt, die in kurzer
Zeit hohe Erträge erzielen.
exitazo
短期高収益投資

home run³
回家; 下班
trajet de retour: trajet de retour à
la maison après une journée de
travail
Heimfahrt am Ende eines
Arbeitstags
el camino de vuelta a casa
帰宅

home shopping
家中购物
shopping à domicile
Home Shopping
telecompra
ホーム・ショッピング

homeworker
在家工作者
domo-employé (employé qui
travaille chez lui, mais en tant que
salarié et non en travailleur
indépendant. Les arrangements
varient).
Heimarbeiter(in);
Hausgewerbebetreibende/r
teletrabajador(a)
在宅勤務者

homogenisation
统一化; 单一化
homogénéisation
Homogenisierung
homogeneización
均一化

honorarium
酬金; 谢礼金; 谢仪
honoraires
Honorar
honorarios
謝礼金

horizontal fast track
平行速成
filière ultra-rapide horizontale
Personalentwicklung per
Job-Zirkulation
teoría del desarrollo de personas
con talento trabajando en
diferentes tareas
水平ファースト・トラック

horizontal integration
横向一体化; 横向结合; 横向联合
intégration horizontale
horizontale Integration

integración horizontal
水平統合

horizontal spread
横向分布
opération horizontale: achat de
deux options identiques, sauf pour
leurs dates d'échéance
horizontaler Spread
diferencial horizontal
水平購買

horse-trading
精明的讨价还价
négociations féroces
Kuhhandel
duras negociaciones que acaban
con una parte otorgando
concesiones
熾烈な駆引きで片方が妥協すること

hostile bid
敌意收购
offre publique d'achat adverse
feindliches Übernahmeangebot
OPA hostil
敵対的入札

hosting
托管
être l'hôte d'un site sur Internet
Web-Hosting
alojamiento, hospedaje
ホスティング

hosting options
托管选择
options disponibles pour être hôte
sur Internet
Hosting Options
opciones de alojamiento
hospedaje
ホスティング・オプション

hot button
热键; 热销产品
touche spéciale/spécifique
spezielles Sonderangebot
botón caliente
目玉商品(ホットボタン)

hot card
丢失的信用卡
carte de crédit volée
gestohlene Kreditkarte
tarjeta caliente
盗難クレジットカード

hot-desking
共享办公桌安排
occupation multiple d'espaces de
travail
Schleuderschreibtischsystem
utilización intercambiable de
mesas de trabajo
ホットデスキング

hotelling
旅馆式安排
hôtelling: occuper un bureau ou

Translations appear in the following order: Chinese, French, German, Spanish/Latin American Spanish, and Japanese.

un espace de travail dans les
locaux d'un autre employeur.
L'hôtelling est une pratique utilisée
entre autres par des employés tels
que les experts-conseils ou le
personnel commercial
Hotelling
trabajo en los locales de otra
empresa
ホテリング

hot file
丢失的信用卡列单
liste avec cartes de crédit volées
Auflistung gestohlener
Kreditkarten
lista caliente
盗難クレジットカードリスト

hot issue
热门股票的发行
émission de nouvelle valeur
brûlante
Spekulationswert
emisión caliente
ホット債券

hot money[1]
烫手的钱，不義之才
argent volé
heißes Geld
capital especulativo; dinero
caliente
不正入手金

hot money[2]
游资，热钱
capitaux spéculatifs
vagabundierende Gelder
capital especulativo; dinero
caliente
ホットマネー

hot stock
热门股票
valeurs boursières brûlantes
gefragte Aktie
acción caliente
ホットストック

hours of work
工作时间
heures de travail
Arbeitszeit
horario de trabajo
労働時間

hours of work
工作时间
heures de travail
tatsächliche Arbeitsstunden
horas de trabajo
労働時間

house of quality
质量屋
phase de gestion de la qualité
Qualitätsphase

casa de la calidad
品質フェーズ

HRM
人力资源管理
gestion des ressources humaines
Personalmanagement
gestión de los recursos humanos
人的資源管理

HR service centre
人事处; 人事服务中心
centre des ressources humaines
HR Service-Zentrum;
Personal-Versorgungszentrale;
Personal-Dienstleistungszentrum
centro de recursos humanos
人的資源サービス・センター

HTH
希望能对您有所帮助
j'espère que cela t'aidera
hoffe, dass dies hilft
espero que esto sirva
これが役に立てばよいが

HTML
HTML语言; 超文本标记语言
HTML
HTML
HTML
HTML,
ハイパーテキスト・マー
クアップ・ランゲージ

HTTP
HTTP协议; 超文本传输协议
protocole de communications sur
Internet
HTTP
HTTP
情報の送受信方を規定する
インターネット・プロトコール

hub and spoke
中枢辐射式
agencement moyeu-rayon
Speichennetz
estructura en forma radial
ハブ・アンド・スポーク

humanagement
人性化管理
gestion humaine
Humanagement
gestión humanizada
エンパワーメント管理法

human capital
人力资本
capital humain
Humankapital
capital humano
人的資本

human capital accounting
人力资本会计; 人力资本核算
comptabilité du capital humain
Humankapitalrechnung

contabilidad del capital humano
人的資本勘定

human factors engineering
人力工程
application des facteurs humains
Anthropotechnik; Ergonomie
ingeniería de los factores humanos
人間要素工学

human relations
人事关系
relations humaines
Human Relations;
zwischenmenschliche
Beziehungen
relaciones humanas
人間関係研究、人事関係論ヒュー
マン・リレーションズ, HR

**human resource information
system**
人力资源信息系统
système d'informations des
ressources humaines
Personalinformationssystem;
Informationssystem für das
Personalwesen; HRIS
sistema de información sobre
recursos humanos
人的資源情報システム

human resource planning
人力资源规划
planification des ressources
humaines
Personalplanung;
Arbeitskräfteplanung
planificación de los recursos
humanos
人的資源計画

human resources[1]
人力资源; 人员管理; 人事管理
ressources humaines
Personal; Humankapital;
Humanvermögen;
Humanressourcen
recursos humanos
人的資源

human resources[2]
人力资源; 人员管理
ressources humaines
HR, Personal, Belegschaft
recursos humanos
人的資源

**Human Rights and Equal
Opportunities Commission**
人权及平等机会委员会
commission sur l'égalité des
chances et les droits de l'homme
Menschenrechte- und
Chancengleichheitskommission
comisión australiana de los
derechos humanos y la igualdad

Translations appear in the following order: Chinese, French, German, Spanish/Latin American Spanish, and Japanese

de oportunidades
人権機会均等委員会

hunch marketing
直觉性市场营销
marketing d'instinct
instinktgeleitetes Marketing;
Marketing nach innerem Gefühl
marketing instintivo
第六感に基いたマーケティング

hurdle rate
保底收益率
taux de rejet /d'actualisation
erwartete Mindestrendite
Basisrendite
tasa crítica de rentabilidad
ハードル率

hurry sickness
急迫症
maladie du pas le temps
Angstzustand aufgrund des
Gefühls, dass der Tag nicht lang
genug ist, um alles Erforderliche zu
erreichen
ansiedad que produce la falta de
tiempo
大慌て症候群, 恐慌症候群

hybrid
混合
(instruments financiers) hybrides
Mischformen von Finanzpapieren
híbrido
混成金融商品

hybrid financial instrument
混合金融工具
instrument financier hybride
hybrides Finanzinstrument
instrumento financiero combinado
ハイブリッド金融商品

hyperinflation
恶性通貨膨胀;
失去控制的通貨膨胀;
极度通貨膨胀
hyperinflation
Hyperinflation
hiperinflación
ハイパーインフレ,
超インフレーション

hyperlink
超级链接
hyperlink
Hyperlink
hiperenlace
ハイパーリンク

hyperpartnering
超级合伙
forme de commerce dans laquelle
des entreprises utilisent la
technologie d'Internet pour
former des partenariats et exécuter
des transactions à haute vitesse et

pour un faible coût
Hyperpartnering
alianzas comerciales en las que las
empresas participantes se
conectan en red usando Internet
para aprovechar las oportunidades
comerciales
ハイパー・パートナリング

hyper time
急速
hyper-temps
Hyperzeit
tiempo en Internet
ハイパータイム

hypothecate
财产抵押
hypothéquer
lombardieren
hipotecar
担保契約

hypothesis testing
假设检验[检定]
analyse d'hypothèse
Durchführung eines
Hypothesentests
verificación de hhipótesis;
contraste de hipótesis
仮説テスト

IANAL
我不是律师
je ne suis pas avocat(e)
ich bin kein Rechtsanwalt
no soy abogado
弁護士ではない

IASC
国际会计准则委员会
organisme basé à Londres qui
travaille envers la réalisation d'un
accord global sur les normes
comptables
IASC; International Accounting
Standards
organismo internacional de
armonización de las prácticas
contables
国際会計基準委員会

IBOR
银行同业拆借利率
I.B.O.R.: abréviation de taux
interbancaire offert
Interbankenangebotssatz
IBOR/TOI (Tasa de oferta
interbancaria)
銀行間出し手レート

IBRC
保险经纪人注册委员会
I.B.R.C.: abréviation de conseil
d'inscription des courtiers
d'assurance
Registrierungsausschuss der
Versicherungsmakler

IBRC
保険仲介人登録審査会

IBRD
国际复兴开发银行
banque internationale pour la
reconstruction et le
développement
IBRD; International Bank for
Reconstruction and Development
BIRD
国際復興開発銀行

Icarus factor
阿卡若斯因素
syndrome d'Icare
Ikarusfaktor
tendencia a embarcarse en
proyectos demasiado ambiciosos
幹部が高望みのプロジェクトを
手掛ける傾向

ICC
国际商务委员会
chambre de commerce
internationale
ICC; Internationale
Handelskammer
organismo de fomento del
comercio y la empresa privada
国際商工会議所

iceing
炒鱿鱼
aïcing
auf Eis gelegt werden, der erste Teil
ist eine engl. Abkürzung für
,,unfreiwilliges Karriereereignis''
pérdida del trabajo
首になる

ICSA
皇家特许状秘书和管理员学会
I.C.S.A: abréviation pour institut
des secrétaires et administrateurs
agréés
Institut der Sekretärinnen/
Sekretäre und
Verwaltungsfachleute
organización que promueve la
administración eficaz en el
comercio, la industria y la vida
pública
公認会社秘書管理者協会

IDA[1]
国际开发协会
association internationale de
développement
IDA; International Development
Association
AID
国際開発協会

idea hamster
点子库
lapin aux idées
Ideenhamster(in)

saco sin fondo de ideas
新発想の泉

Identrus
电子商务安全协会
Identrus: consortium d'institutions
financières développant une
norme pour un réseau sur lequel le
e-commerce d'entreprise à
entreprise peut être effectué en
toute sécurité
Identrus
consorcio Identrus
アイデントラス

idle time
等待时间
temps de latence
ungenutzte Zeit; Leerlaufzeit
tiempo muerto o inactivo
空回り時間, あき時間,
手すき時間, 遊休時間

IEA
国际能源署
agence internationale pour
l'énergie
IEA; OECD internationale
Energieagentur
OIE
国際エネルギー機関

IFC
国际金融公司
société financière internationale
IFC; Internationale
Finanzkorporation
CFI
国際金融公社

IIB
保险经纪人协会
I.I.B.: abréviation pour institut des
courtiers d'assurance
Institut der Versicherungsmakler
colegio profesional de agentes de
seguros británicos
保険仲介人協会

illegal parking
冒名顶替交易
stationnement interdit
Praxis an der Börse, wo ein Makler
oder ein Unternehmen Aktien im
Namen einer anderen Gesellschaft
ankauft, obgleich diese vom
echten Anleger gesichert sind
compra de valores a nombre de
otra compañia
他社名義での株購入

illiquid¹
非流动的，缺乏流动性
à court de capitaux liquides
illiquide; nicht flüssig;
zahlungsunfähig
ilíquido; irrealizable
非流動的

illiquid²
非流动资产
non-liquide: difficilement
convertible en liquidités
illiquide
ilíquido; irrealizable
非流動資産

image advertising
形象广告
publicité en image
Imagewerbung
publicidad con imágenes
イメージ広告

imaginisation
创新想象法
concept lié à la créativité qui se
soucie d'améliorer nos capacités à
visualiser et à comprendre les
situations sous de nouveaux angles
Anregung der Phantasie
enfoque creativo para comprender
y abordar mejor las diversas
situaciones
イマジナイゼーション

IMAP
因特网信息访问协议
protocole qui permet aux
messages e-mail d'être reçus sur
n'importe quel ordinateur
IMAP
IMAP
IMAPプロトコール

IMF
国际货币基金组织
FMI (fonds monétaire
international)
IWF; Internationaler
Währungsfonds
FMI
国債通貨基金

IMHO
个人浅见
selon mon humble avis
meiner bescheidenen Meinung
nach
en mi modesta opinión
私の愚かな意見では

immediate holding company
直接控股公司
société de portefeuille immédiate
unmittelbare Holdinggesellschaft
sociedad que cuenta con una o
más filiales, pero que es en sí filial
de otra sociedad: la sociedad
matriz
直持ち株会社

IMNSHO
我冒昧地认为
selon mon avis pas si humble que
ça
meiner nicht so bescheidenen

Meinung nach
en mi opinión no tan modesta
私のそれほど愚かでない意見では

IMO
我认为
à mon avis
meiner Meinung nach
en mi opinión
私の意見では

impact day
股票发行公告日
jour de l'impact
erster Handelstag einer Emission
día de impacto
インパクト・デイ

impaired capital
弱势资本; 资本不足的资本
capital affaibli
vermindertes od. verringertes
Kapital
capital no respaldado por un activo
equivalente
資本の欠損

impairment of capital
资本亏损; 资本损失
affaiblissement de capital
Kapitalminderung; Verminderung
des Kapitals
deterioro o menoscabo del capital
資本の欠損(額), 債務超過額

imperfect competition
不完全竞争
concurrence imparfaite
unvollkommener od.
unvollständiger Wettbewerb
competencia imperfecta
不完全競争

impersonal account
不记名帐户
compte anonyme
Sachkonto
cuenta impersonal, nominal o de
orden
物的勘定

import
进口
importation
Einfuhr; Import; Importartikel
importación
輸入, 輸入品

import duty
进口税
droit d'entrée ou d'importation
Einfuhrzoll; Importzoll
derecho de importación; derecho
de aduana
輸入関税

import penetration
进口渗透; 进口侵入
pénétration des importations

Importanteil; Importquote
penetración de las importaciones
輸入浸透度

imposed budget
强加预算自上而下的预算
budget imposé/budget du sommet
vers la base
auferlegtes Budget; angeordneter
Haushalt
presupuesto de enfoque/
descendente impuesto
強制トップダウン予算

impression
广告收视次数
mesure du nombre de fois qu'une
pub sur ligne est visualisée.
Online-Werbekontakt
impresión
インプレッション

imprest account
定额备用金帐户
compte d'avance de fonds (pour
frais divers)
Vorschusskonto
cuenta de anticipos
前払金勘定

imprest system
定额备用金制度
système d'avance de fonds (à
montant fixe)
Vorschuss-Kassensystem
sistema con saldo de caja positivo;
sistema de fondo fijo
定額資金前渡制

imputation system
避免重复课税制度; 估算制税收法
système d'imputation
Anrechnungsverfahren
sistema de imputación
インピュテーション・システム,
インピュテーション方式

incentive programme
奖励计划
programme de récompense avec
primes (pour employés)
Verkaufssonderaktion
programa de incentivos
奨励プログラム

incentive scheme
刺激机制; 奖励机制
système de primes
Anreizsystem; Anreizprogramm
plan de incentivos
(従業員に対する)生産性向
上目的の奨励金制度,
特別手当制度

incentive stock option
奖励股票期权
option d'encouragement d'achat
de titres

Aktienbezugsprogramm als Anreiz
für Arbeitnehmer
opcción de compra de acciones
奨励株式買取選択権

incestuous share dealing
自相股票交易
transactions d'actions
incestueuses
inzestuöser Aktienhandel
compraventa de acciones mutuas
近親株取引

inchoate instrument
不完整的票据
instrument (négociable) incomplet
Blankoakzept
instrumento financiero incompleto
記入漏れ証券

incidence of tax
税负担方
incidence de l'impôt
Steuerinzidenz
incidencia fiscal/tributaria
課税負担者

income[1]
收入; 所得; 收益
revenu
Einkommen
ingresos; renta
所得

income[2]
非劳动收入，非经营收入
revenu
Einkommen
renta
所得

income[3]
利润，收益
Recettes
Gewinn; Ertrag
ingresos
収益

**income and expenditure
account**
收支帐户，收支表
comptes de pertes et profits
Gewinn- und Verlustrechnung;
Abk. GuV
cuenta de ingresos, entradas y
gastos /salidas, sin ánimo de lucro
y similar a la cuenta de explotación
収支勘定

income bond
收益债券
obligation à revenu variable
Gewinnschuldverschreibung
bono cuyo pago depende de los
ingresos
収益債権

income distribution[1]
收益分配
distribution du revenu
Einkommensverteilung
distribución de la renta
所得分配

income distribution[2]
收益分配
distribution des revenus
Einkommensverteilung
distribución de los ingresos
所得分布

income-linked gilt
有益金边债券
placement sûr de valeur liée à
l'indice des prix
britische Schatzobligation, deren
Kapitalsumme und Zinssatz dem
Einzelhandelspreisindex folgen
bono del Tesoro vinculado al IPC
収益連携優良株

income redistribution
收入再分配
redistribution des revenus
Einkommensumverteilung
redistribución de la renta
所得再配分

income shares/stock[1]
收益股，稳定股利的普通股
actions ou titres ordinaires
recherchés, avec gros dividendes
Einkommensaktien
acciones de dividendos elevados
資産株, 優良銘柄

income shares/stock[2]
收益股，固定利率债券
titres à intérêt fixe acquis, avec
gros dividendes
Einkommensaktien
valores a interés fijo que dan
dividendos elevados
資産債権

income shares/stock[3]
收益型股票
actions ou titres avec revenus:
certains trusts ou fonds
d'investissement qui émettent des
fonds à niveau partagé où les
détenteurs de l'élément revenu
reçoivent tous les revenus (moins
les frais, charges et impôts), alors
que les détenteurs de l'élément
Einkommensaktien
fondo con capital dividido
資産株

income smoothing
收益滤波
atténuation des fluctuations de
revenu
Einkommensglättung

Translations appear in the following order: Chinese, French, German, Spanish/Latin American Spanish, and Japanese

ajuste de ingresos
收益平準化

incomes policy
收入政策
politique des revenus
Einkommenspolitik
política de rentas
所得政策

income stream
收入流; 收益来源
flot/section/niveau de revenu
Einkommensstrom
flujo de ingresos
所得の流れ

income tax
所得税
impôt sur le revenu
Einkommensteuer
impuesto sobre la renta
所得税, 法人(所得)税

income tax return
所得税纳税申报单
déclaration d'impôts sur le revenu
Einkommensteuererklärung
declaración del impuesto sobre la
renta
所得税申告(書), 法人税申告書

income unit
收益单位; 收益份额; 收入单元
investissement à revenus réguliers
regelmäßige Dividende
participación en un fondo de
inversión que produce
regularmente pagos
収益ユニット

in-company training
在本公司进行的培训
formation au sein de l'entreprise
innerbetriebliche Ausbildung oder
Weiterbildung
formación interna
capacitación interna
社内トレーニング

incomplete records
不完全记录
écritures incomplètes
unvollständige Aufzeichnungen
contabilidad de partida simple,
como lo opuesto a la contabilidad
de partida doble
未完了記録

incorporation
组成公司
constitution (d'une société ou
corporation)
Gründung einer juristischen
Person, z. B. einer
Kapitalgesellschaft
constitución de una sociedad
法人化

incremental analysis
增量分析
analyse incrémentielle
Zuwachsanalyse
análisis comparativo del
incremento por cambio de
actividad
増分分析

incremental budgeting
增量预算
budgétisation incrémentielle (sur
plusieurs exercices)
inkrementale Budgetierung
actualización de presupuestos
anteriores
増分予算

incrementalism
递增主义, 递变式
incrémentalisme
Philosophie der schrittweisen
Verbesserungen
gradualismo
増分主義

indaba
大会; 会议
réunion
Besprechung
reunión
会議

indemnity
赔偿, 补偿
dédommagement
Schadenersatz
indemnización
賠償

indemnity insurance
赔偿保险
assurance de compensation
Schadenversicherung
seguro de indemnización
傷害保険

index[1]
指数
indice
Index
índice
指数, インデックス

index[2]
指数
indice
Index
índice
指数

indexation
指数化
indexation
Indexierung
indexación
インデクセーション

index fund
指数基金
fonds de placement basé sur indice
Index-Fonds
fondo indexado
インデックス・ファンド, 指標債

index futures
指数期货
opérations à terme indexées sur un
indice des valeurs
Aktienindex-Terminkontrakt
futuros sobre índices
株価指数の先物取引

index-linked bond
与指数相连的债券
obligation indexée
indexierte Anleihe
obligación indexada; obligación
vinculada a un índice
指数連動債

index-linked gilt
与指数相连的金边债券
titre d'Etat indexé
indexierte Staatsanleihe
obligación vinculada a un índice;
valor de primer orden indexado
物価連動金ぶち国債

**index-linked savings
certificate**
与物价指数挂钩的储蓄券,
祖母债券
certificat d'épargne indexé
indexierter Sparbrief
obligación indexada
インフレ連動預金証書

index number
指数
(nombre) indice
Indexziffer
número índice
指数

indicated dividend
公开股息; 已表明的股息
dividende indiqué
angegebene Dividende
dividendo indicado
仮配当金, 予備配当額

indicated yield
预测的收益率
rendement indiqué
angegebener Ertrag
rendimiento indicado
仮利回り, 予想利回り

indication price
预期价格
prix approximatif d'un titre
Richtkurs
precio aproximado
表示価格

---

indicative price
指示价格
prix indicatif
Indikativkurs
precio indicativo
指標価格

indirect channel
间接销售渠道
organe de distribution indirecte
indirekter Vertriebsweg
canal indirecto
インダイレクト・チャネル

indirect cost
间接成本
coût indirect
Gemeinkosten; indirekte Kosten
coste indirecto
costo indirecto
間接費、間接原価

indirect discrimination
间接歧视
discrimination indirecte
indirekte Diskriminierung
discriminación indirecta
間接差別

indirect labour
间接劳动力
main-d'œuvre indirecte
indirekte Arbeitskosten
mano de obra indirecta
間接労働者

induction
就职介绍; 介绍
insertion ou intégration
Einarbeitung
iniciación; introducción
就業ガイダンス

industrial action
劳工行动
action revendicative
Arbeitskampfmaßnahmen
acciones reivindicativas
(労働者の)講義行為, 労働争議

industrial advertising
工业广告
publicité industrielle
Industriewerbung
publicidad industrial
工業広告、生産財広告、ビジネス
広告

industrial co-operative
工业合作社
coopérative industrielle
Industriegenossenschaft
cooperativa industrial
産業共同システム

industrial court
工业法庭
tribunal industriel et du commerce
Arbeitsgericht

tribunal laboral; magistratura de
trabajo
産業裁判所

industrial democracy
工业民主
démocratie industrielle
Demokratie im Betrieb
democracia industrial
産業民主主義,
(労働者の)経営参加

industrial engineering
经营工程学; 工业工程学
ingénierie industrielle
Produktions- und
Fertigungstechnik
ingeniería industrial
経営工学, 生産工学

industrial espionage
工业间谍活动
espionnage industriel
Industriespionage
espionaje industrial
産業スパイ

industrial goods
工业产品; 工业用品
biens d'équipement
Investitionsgüter
bienes industriales
生産財, 工業製品

industrial goods marketing
工业用品营销
marketing des biens d'équipement
Industriegüter-Marketing
marketing de bienes industriales
生産財マーケティング

industrial housekeeping
工业后勤管理
entretien industriel
Gewerbehygiene
orden y limpieza del lugar de
trabajo
職場整理整頓雑務

industrialisation
工业化
industrialisation
Industrialisierung
industrialización
工業化

industrial marketing
工业营销
marketing industriel
Industriegüter-Marketing;
Investitionsgüter-Marketing
marketing industrial
生産財マーケティング,
インダストリアル・マー
ケティング

industrial market research
工业市场研究
étude de marché industrielle
Marktforschung für

Investitionsgüter
estudios de mercado sobre el
marketing industrial de servicios y
productos
生産財マーケット・リサーチ

industrial production
工业产品
production industrielle
Industrieproduktion
producción industrial
鉱工業生産, 工業出荷額,
工業生産額

**Industrial Relations Court of
Australia**
工业法庭
cour suprême d'Australie pour les
relations industrielles
Australisches Arbeitsgericht
tribunal laboral australiano;
magistratura de trabajo
australiana
オーストラリア労使関係裁判所

industrial revenue bond
工业收益债券
obligation de revenu industriel
Schuldverschreibung zur
Finanzierung von gewerblichen
Bauvorhaben
bono a largo plazo pagadero con
ingresos industriales
産業歳入担保債, 産業振興債

industrial-sector cycle
工业部门周期
cycle de secteur industriel
Industriesektorzyklus
ciclo del sector industrial
工業部門ビジネスサイクル

industrial services marketing
工业服务营销
marketing de services industriels
Industriedienstleistungs-Marketing
marketing de servicios
empresariales
生産サービス・マーケティング

industry rules
工业(内部不成文)规则;
产业(内部不成文)规则
règles de l'industrie
betrauenübliche Konventionen
normas de la industira
産業規則

inertia selling
惰性推销(术); 惯性销售术;
被动推销(术)
vente forcée par correspondance
Trägheits-Verkauf
venta por inercia
惰性(押し付け)販売

inference
推论

---

*Translations appear in the following order: Chinese, French, German, Spanish/Latin American
Spanish, and Japanese*

inférence
Inferenz
inferencia
命題

infinite loading
无限配置
mise à charge illimitée
Endlosladen
carga infinita
無限作業プラン

inflation
通貨膨脹
inflation
Inflation
inflación
インフレーション

inflation accounting
通貨膨脹会计
comptabilité d'inflation
inflationsneutrale
Rechnungslegung
contabilidad en períodos de
inflación
インフレ会計

inflationary
通貨膨脹的
inflationniste
inflationär
inflacionario
インフレーションの,
インフレ傾向の, 通貨膨張の

inflationary gap
通貨膨脹差额; 通貨膨脹缺口;
通貨膨脹间隙
déficit inflationniste
inflatorische Lücke
brecha inflacionista
インフレ・ギャップ

inflationary spiral
恶性循环的通貨膨脹;
螺旋式通貨膨脹; 通貨膨脹螺旋
spirale inflationniste
Inflationsspirale
espiral inflacionista
悪性インフレ, インフレの悪循環

inflation-proof security
防通貨膨脹证券
titre indexé sur l'inflation
inflationssicheres Wertpapier
valor protegido contra la inflación
インフレ・ヘッジ証券

inflation rate
通貨膨脹率
taux d'inflation
Inflationsrate
tasa de inflación
インフレ率

inflation tax
通貨膨脹税
taxe sur l'inflation des salaires

Inflationssteuer
impuesto sobre la inflación
インフレ税

Infocomm Development Authority
国际开发协会
comité de développement
d'Infocomm à Singapour
Telekommunikations-
Entwicklungsbehörde
organismo que regula el sector de
la información y las
comunicaciones en Singapur
インフォコム開発局

infoholic
信息癖
accro de l'info
Informationssüchtige/r
infoadicto(-a)
情報中毒の人

infomatics
信息学; 信息科学
infomatique
Informatik
infomática
インフォマテイック・システム

infomediary
信息中介
infomédiaire
Fachportal
suministrador electrónico de
información
インフォミディアリー

infomercial
信息性商业广告; 商品信息电视片;
专题广告片
publi-information
Infomercial
publirreportaje
インフォマーシャル

info rate
信息率
cours pour info
Info-Satz: von Maklern nur zu
Informationszwecken genannter
Geldmarktsatz
tasa informativa
市场金利情报

informal economy
非正规经济; 非正式经济
économie parallèle
Schattenwirtschaft
economía informal
インフォーマル経済,
正式でないか政府への届出のな
い経済活動

information and communications technologies
信息通信技术

technologies de l'information et
des communications ou
technologie informatique
Informations- und
Kommunikationstechnik
tecnologías de la información y las
comunicaciones
情報通信技術

information architecture
信息体系
architecture d'information
Webdesign
arquitectura de la información
情報アーキテクチャー

information management
信息管理
gestion de l'information
Informationsmanagement
gestión de la información
情報管理

information overload
信息超载
surcharge d'information
Informationsüberschuss
sobrecarga de información
報過負荷

information space
信息空间
espace information (sur Internet)
Datenraum
espacio de la información
情報スペース

infotainment
讽刺幽默节目
émission d'info-loisirs
Fernsehsendungen, die ernste
Themen unterhaltsam aufbereiten
programa informativo de
entretenimiento
インフォテインメント

infrastructure
基础结构; 基本设施
infrastructure
Infrastruktur
infraestructura
インフラストラクチュア

initial offer
起始报价
offre initiale
Erstangebot zur Zeichnung von
Anteilen
oferta inicial
初期指値

initial public offering
首次公开发行;
初次公开销售股票(美)
offre publique initiale
IPO = erstes öffentliches
Zeichnungsangebot
salida a bolsa
株式新規公開, 新規公募

Translations appear in the following order: Chinese, French, German, Spanish/Latin American Spanish, and Japanese

initial yield
初始收益
rendement initial
Anfangsertrag
rendimiento inicial
初期利回り

injunction
禁止令
arrêt de suspension
einstweilige Verfügung
requerimiento
差止命令

inland bill
国内汇票
lettre de change sur l'intérieur
Inlandswechsel
letra de cambio interior
内国手形

Inland Revenue Department
国内税收部
service du fisc
Finanzamt
Agencia Tributaria
Dirección General Impositiva
国税局

innovation
创新; 革新
innovation
Innovation
estrategia genérica
革新

input tax credit
投入税收信贷
crédit d'impôt sur dépenses à fins
commerciales
Vorsteuergutschrift
desgravación de impuestos de
bienes y servicios
仕入税額控除

insert
插入广告
insert
Werbebeilage
encarte
折込広告

insertion rate
插入广告收费率
prix d'insertion
Einschaltpreis
tarifa de inserción
一回当たりの広告料

inside information
内部信息
information à la source
Insiderinformationen
bono a largo plazo pagadero con
ingresos industriales
インサイダー情報, 内部情報

inside quote
内部报价; 报价区间
cotation d'initié
inside quote
precios de compra y de venta
内輪値

insider
内线; 内部人员; 知情人; 内幕人
initié(e)
Insider(in)
persona con información
confidencial
部内者, 内輪筋

insider trading
内线交易; 就内部人交易;
知情人交易
délit d'initiés
Insidergeschäfte
especulación en bolsa
aprovechando información
privilegiada
インサイダー取引

insolvency
无偿付能力; 无偿债能力; 破产;
资不抵债
insolvabilité
Insolvenz; Zahlungsunfähigkeit
insolvencia
支払不能, 債務超過, 破産

insourcing
内部资源开发
approvisionnement en interne
Einsatz interner Mitarbeiter(in)nen
utilización de recursos internos
インソーシング

inspector of taxes
税务员, 税务稽查员
inspecteur des impôts
Steuerprüfer(in)
inspector de Hacienda
税検査官

instalment
分期付款
versement partiel
Teilzahlung
plazo; pago parcial; entrega
賦払金

**Instalment Activity
Statement**
分期付款活动说明
déclaration d'activité de
versements échelonnés: formulaire
standard en Australie pour
déclarer les versements échelonnés
de type 'Pay As You Go' sur les
revenus sur investissements
Ratenaktivitätsformular
formulario australiano para pagos
por ingresos derivados de
inversiones
投資活動報告書

instalment credit
分期付款信贷
prêt avec remboursements
échelonnés
Teilzahlungskredit
crédito para compras a plazos
分割払込金

instalment purchase
分期付款购买
achat à crédit/à plusieurs
versements/à traites échelonnées
Ratenkauf
compra a plazos
割賦仕入, 賦払購買

**Institute of Chartered
Accountants**
皇家特许会计师学会
Institut des experts-comptables
agréés au Royaume Uni et en
République d'Irlande
Institut der Wirtschaftsprüfer
Colegio de Censores Jurados de
Cuentas
英国勅許会計士協会

Institute of Financial Services
金融服务协会
Institut des services financiers
Institut der Bankier
organismo que ofrece servicios de
formación para el sector de
servicios financieros
財務サービス協会

institutional investor
机构性投资者
investisseur institutionnel
Kapitalsammelstelle
inversor(a) institucional
機関投資家, 保険仲介人協会

institutional survey
机构调查
étude institutionnelle
institutionelle Erhebung
encuesta institucional
組織調査

instrument²
投资工具
instrument: terme générique pour
titres ou produits dérivés
Handelspapier
instrumento
商業証券

instrument³
票据, 文件
acte juridique ou document officiel
Urkunde
instrumento
証書

instrument⁴
达到目的的手段
acte instrumental: un moyen qui

---

*Translations appear in the following order: Chinese, French, German, Spanish/Latin American
Spanish, and Japanese*

justifie une fin, par exemple une dépense ou imposition du gouvernement visant à réduire le chômage
Mittel
instrumento
金融政策手段

insurance[1]
保险; 保险业
assurance
Versicherung
seguro
保険, 保険契約

insurance[2]
保险
assurance financière (pour se couvrir contre le risque tout en permettant d'obtenir des gains potentiels)
Absicherung: Sicherungsgeschäfte oder sonstige risikomindernde Strategien
seguro
保険, 保険契約

insurance agent
保险代理人
agent d'assurances
Versicherungsvertreter
agente de seguros
保険代理人

Insurance and Superannuation Commission
保险及养老退休金委员会
commission des caisses de retraite et d'assurance en Australie
australischer Versicherungs- und Rentenanstalt
Comisión Australiana Reguladora de Seguros y Fondos de Pensiones
保険年金委員会

insurance broker
保险经纪人
assureur
Versicherungsmakler(in)
agente or corredor(a) de seguros
保険仲介人

Insurance Council of Australia
澳大利亚保险委员会
conseil des compagnies d'assurance d'Australie
australischer Versicherungsrat
organismo independiente representante del sector seguros
オーストラリア保険協議会

insurance intermediary
保险中介
agent intermédiaire d'assurance
Versicherungsvermittler(in)
mediador de seguros
保険仲介人

insurance policy
保(险)单
police d'assurance
Versicherungspolice
póliza de seguros
保険証書, 保険契約証券

insurance premium tax
保险费税
taxe sur les primes d'assurance
Versicherungsprämiensteuer
impuesto sobre las primas de seguro
保険料税

insured
投保人，受保人
assuré
versichert
asegurado
被保険者

insured account
保险帐户
compte assuré (aux Etats-Unis, compte bancaire ou d'épargne appartenant à un organisme d'assurance privé ou fédéral)
versichertes Konto
cuenta con una institución financiera que pertenece al sector de seguros
預金保険

insurer
保险人，保险商
assureur
Versicherer(in)
asegurador
保険業者

intangible asset
无形资产
actif incorporel ou immobilisations incorporelles
Immaterialgut
activo intangible, bien inmaterial
無形資産

integrated accounts
完整账目
comptes intégrés
integriertes Rechnungswesen
cuentas integradas
統合勘定

intellectual assets
智能资本
capital intellectuel
geistiges Vermögen
activos intelectuales
知的財産

intellectual capital
知识资本
capital intellectuel
intellektuelles Kapital
capital intelectual
知的資本

intellectual property
知识产权
propriété intellectuelle
geistiges Eigentum
propiedad intelectual
知的財産

intelligent e-mail
智能电子邮件系统
message e-mail intelligent
intelligente E-Mail
correo electrónico inteligente
知能eメール

interactive
可对话式
interactif
interaktiv
interactivo(-a)
双方向

interactive planning
互促式计划
planification interactive
interaktives Planen
planificación interactiva
双方向計画

interchange
互换
échange: transaction entre la banque d'acquisition et la banque émettrice
Interchange
intercambio
インターチェンジ, 交換

interchangeable bond
可互换债券
obligation interchangeable
austauschbare Schuldverschreibung
bono intercambiable
切り替え債券, 交換債券

interchange fee
互换费用
frais d'échange
von Kreditkarte-Emittentbank an Erwerbsbank erhobene Gebühren gegen Autorisierungsanfrage
tarifa de intercambio
インターチェンジ・フィー

intercommodity spread
跨商品差价
gamme d'options sur marchandises apparentées
Inter-Lieferungs-Spread
diferencia entre los activos
異商品間スプレッド

intercompany pricing
公司间定价
fixation de prix intersociétés
Verrechnung konzerninterner Leistungen

Translations appear in the following order: Chinese, French, German, Spanish/Latin American Spanish, and Japanese

precios entre empresas
会社間価格決定

interdependency concept
相互依頼关系
concept de l'interdépendance
Hypothese von der gegenseitigen
Abhängigkeit
concepto de la interdependencia
相互依存概念

interest
利息
intérêt
Zinsen
interés
利子

interest arbitrage
套利，套汇
arbitrage sur les intérêts
Zinsarbitrage
arbitraje de interés
利子裁定

interest assumption
假定利息
intérêt présumé
Zinsannahme
asunción de interés
予定収益

interest charged
已付利息
intérêt porté au débit
Zinsbelastung
tipo o tasa de interés cargado
利子賦課

interest cover
可付息收入
taux de couverture des frais
financiers
Zinsabdeckungsgrad
cubrimiento de intereses
金利負担率

interest-elastic investment
利率弹性投资
investissement à intérêt élastique
zinselastische Investition
inversión con interés elástico
利子弾力的投資

interest-inelastic investment
利率非弹性投资
investissement à intérêt rigide
zinsunelastische Investition
inversión con interés no elástico
利子非弾力的投資

interest in possession trust
利益财产信托
participation dans un trust de
possession de propriétés
Trustfonds, der einem oder
mehreren Begünstigten ein
unmittelbares Anrecht auf Erhalt
jeglicher durch den Fonds

erwirtschafteten Mittel gibt
fideicomiso que confiere a uno o
más beneficiarios el derecho
inmediato a recibir los ingresos
generados por el activo del
fideicomiso
信託資産に対し利害を持つ

interest-only mortgage
只付利息式抵押
hypothèque à paiements
uniquement de l'intérêt
Hypothek, bei der über die Laufzeit
lediglich die Zinsen bezahlt werden
hipoteca en la que el prestatario
únicamente paga interés al
prestamista durante el plazo de la
hipoteca, y el pago del capital se
realiza al finalizar el plazo
利子支払い住宅ローン

interest rate
利率对等理论
taux d'intérêt
Zinssatz
tipo de interés
金利

interest rate cap
利率上限; 帽子利率
plafond de taux d'intérêt
Zinsobergrenze
techo del tipo de interés
利率上限

interest rate effect
利率效应
effet du taux d'intérêt
Zinseffekt
efecto de los tipos de interés
有効利子率

interest rate exposure
利率风险
risque sur les taux d'intérêt
Zinsrisiko
riesgo de los tipos de interés
利率危険度

interest rate floor
利率下限
plancher de taux d'intérêt
Zinsuntergrenze
suelo de tipo de interés; límite
mínimo
金利フロア

interest rate guarantee[1]
利率担保
garantie de taux d'intérêt:
étranglement ou fixation de
plafond pour taux d'intérêt
Zinsgarantie
techo de tipo de interés
金利保証, キャップ, カラー

interest rate guarantee[2]
利率保障

garantie de taux d'intérêt
Höchstzins für variabel verzinsliche
Wertpapiere
garantía a la medida que protége
al comprador de los cambios de
tipo de interés que se produzcan
en el futuro
利率保証

interest rate parity theory
利率评价理论
théorie de la parité des taux
d'intérêt
Theorie von der Zinsparität
teoría de paridad del tipo de
interés
利率等価理論

interest rate swap
利率交换
échange de taux d'intérêt; taux
d'intérêt croisés
Zinsswap
swap de tipos de interés
スワップ

interest sensitive
对利率敏感的
(actif ou biens) sensibles aux taux
d'intérêt
zinsempfindlich
sensible al tipo de interés; sensible
a la tasa de interés
利率敏感資産

interest yield
利息收益率
intérêt produit/rapport sur intérêt
Zinsertrag
rendimiento de los intereses
利子利回り

interface[1]
接口; 接口程序; 连接; 接合; 对接;
面对面交流; 交谈
interface
Schnittstelle
interface
対面での交流

interface[2]
界面
face à face
persönliches Treffen
encuentro cara a cara
インターフェース, (俗)面談

interfirm comparison
公司间比较
comparaison inter-entreprises
zwischenbetrieblicher Vergleich
comparación entre empresas
会社間比較F

interfirm co-operation
公司间合作
coopération inter-entreprises
zwischenbetriebliche

Translations appear in the following order: Chinese, French, German, Spanish/Latin American Spanish, and Japanese

Zusammenarbeit
cooperación entre empresas
企業間協力

interim certificate
临时证券书
certificat provisoire
Zwischenschein
título provisional de acciones;
certificado provisional
仮証書

interim dividend
期中股息
dividende provisoire
Zwischendividende
dividendo a cuenta
中間配当

interim financial statement
期中财务报告
bilan financier intermédiaire
Zwischenbilanz
estado financiero provisional
中間会計報告書

interim financing
临时筹资办法
financement par crédits
provisoires
Zwischenfinanzierung
financiación temporal
つなぎ資金調達

interim management
临时管理
gestion intérimaire
Interimsmanagement
administración provisional
臨時職管理

interim statement
期中声明
bilan intermédiaire
Halbjahresergebnis
informe provisional
中間報告書

interlocking accounts
连锁账户非一体化账户
comptes interdépendants/
comptes non-intégrés
Verflechtung des
Rechnungswesens
cuentas mancomunadas
系列勘定非統合勘定

intermarket spread
市场间差价
gamme d'options intermarchés
Marktstreuung
venta de una posición con la
compra de otra en un mercado
diferente
(先物取引の)インターマーケッ
ト・スプレッド

intermediary
中介; 中间人
remisier
Vermittler(in)
intermediario(-a)
仲介投資

intermediate goods
中间产品; 半成品
biens intermédiaires
Zwischenerzeugnisse
bienes intermedios
中間生産物

intern
学徒; 受训人员
interne/interner
Praktikant(in)
aprendiz(a)
インターン

internal audit
内部审计
audit interne
Innenrevision
auditoría interna
内部監査

internal check
内部检查
vérification interne
interne Überprüfung
control interno
内部牵制制度

internal communication
内部交流
communications internes
innerbetriebliche Kommunikation
comunicaciones internas
社内コミュニケーション

internal consultant
内部咨询员
expert-conseil interne
innerbetriebliche(r) Berater(in)
consultor(a) interno(-a)
社内コンサルタント

internal cost analysis
内部成本分析
analyse de coût interne
interne Kostenanalyse
análisis de costes internos
análisis de costos internos
社内原価分析

internal differentiation analysis
内部差异分析
analyse de différenciation interne
interne Differenzierungsanalyse
análisis de los procesos internos
que crean diferenciación
社内製品差別化分析

internal growth
内部增长
croissance interne

internes Wachstum
crecimiento interno
内在的成長

internal marketing
机构内部市场营销
marketing interne
betriebsinternes Marketing
marketing interno
社内マーケティング

internal rate of return
内部收益率
intérêt d'un investissement interne
exprimé en pourcentage
interner Zinsfuß
índice de rendimiento interno
内部収益率

internal recruitment
内部聘用; 内部招聘
recrutement interne
interne Personalbeschaffung
contratación interna
社内募集

Internal Revenue Code
国内税法
code général des impôts
Überbegriff für die komplexen
Steuergesetze des amerikanischen
Bundes
Ley del Impuesto sobre la Renta
内国歳入法

International Accounting Standards Board
国际会计标准委员会
commission internationale des
normes comptables
Internationaler Ausschuss zur
Erarbeitung von Empfehlungen für
die Grundsätze der
Rechnungslegung
Comisión Internacional de normas
contables
国際会計基準委員会

international fund
国际基金
société d'investissements (SICAV)
internationaux
internationaler Fonds
fondo internacional
インターナショナル(ミュー
チュアル)ファンド,
国際ミューチュアル・ファンド

International Fund for Agricultural Development
国际农业发展基金会
Fonds International pour le
Développement Agricole (F.I.D.A.)
Internationaler Fonds für
landwirtschaftliche Entwicklung
Fondo Internacional para el
Desarrollo Agrícola (FIDA)
国際農業開発基金

Translations appear in the following order: Chinese, French, German, Spanish/Latin American Spanish, and Japanese

international management[1]
国际企业管理
gestion internationale
internationales Management
gestión de operaciones a nivel
internacional
国際管理業務

international management[2]
国际企业管理
gestion internationale
internationale
Unternehmensleitung
gestión internacional
国際管理業務

international management[3]
国际企业管理
gestion internationale
internationales Management
gestión de operaciones a nivel
internacional
国際管理業務

**International Organization of
Securities Commissions**
国际证券业委员会
organisation internationale de
contrôle des opérations boursières
(I.O.S.C.O)
Internationale Organisation der
Börsenaufsichtsbehörden
Organización Internacional de
Comisiones de Valores (OICV)
国際証券委員会機構

**International Securities
Market Association**
国际证券市场协会
association du marché des valeurs
et titres internationaux
Internationaler Verband für den
Wertpapiermarkt
Asociación Internacional del
Mercado de Valores
国際証券取引所協会

**International Union of Credit
and Investment Insurers**
国际信用证和投资保险公司协会
syndicat international des
assureurs d'investissements
étrangers et des crédits
d'exportation
Internationale Vereinigung der
Kredit- und Anlagenversicher
Unión Internacional de
Aseguradores de Crédito e
Inversiones
国際信用投資保険業者連合

Internesia
网络健忘症
tendance à trouver des sites Web
intéressants puis à oublier où ils se
trouvent
Internesia

el problema de encontrar páginas
interesantes en Internet y olvidarse
más tarde de su localización
インターネジア(インター
ネットと健忘症の造語)

Internet
因特网; 互联网; 国际互联网
internet
Internet
Internet
インターネット

Internet access provider
因特网上网服务商
fournisseur d'accès à Internet
Internet-Service-Provider
proveedor de acceso a Internet
インターネット・アクセス・
プロバイダー

Internet commerce
因特网商务
commerce sur Internet
Internet-Commerce
comercio por Internet
インターネット・コマース,
eコマース, 電子商取引

Internet marketing
网络营销
marketing sur Internet
Internetmarketing
marketing por Internet
インターネット・マーケティング

Internet merchant
因特网商人
commerçant sur Internet
Internethändler
empresa en Internet
インターネット・マーチャント,
電子商人

Internet payment system
因特网付款系统
système de paiement sur Internet
Internet-Zahlungssystem
sistema de pago por Internet
インターネット決済システム

Internet security
网络安全
sécurité sur Internet
Internetsicherheit
securidad en Internet
インターネット・セキュリティ

interoperability
兼容性
inter-capacité de fonctionnement
Kompatibilität
interoperabilidad
情報処理相互運用性

interpersonal communication
人与人之间的交流; 人际交流
communication interpersonnelle
zwischenmenschliche

Kommunikation
comunicación interpersonal
人間相互コミュニケーション

interquartile range
四分位数间范围
écart interquartile
interquartile Spannweite
amplitud intercuartillo
四分位数範囲

interstate commerce
跨州贸易
commerce entre états (aux
Etats-Unis)
zwischenstaatlicher Handel
comercio interestatal
州際通商

interstitial
插页广告
interstitiel
Interstitial
anuncio entre páginas
インタースティシャル

intervention
干预
intervention
Intervention
intervención
(政府の)介入

interviewer bias
调查员偏差
distorsion due à l'enquêteur
Verzerrung durch den Interviewer
bias de empadronadores
インタビュアのかたより

interviewing
面试
avoir un entretien avec
Interview
entrevistas
インタービューイング

intranet
企业内部网; 公司内部网
intranet
Intranet
intranet
イントラネット

intrapreneur
有创新能力的雇员
intrapreneur
interne/r Unternehmer(in)
empleado(-a) emprendedor(a)
社内起業家

intrastate commerce
州际商务
commerce inter-états (USA)
innerstaatlicher Handel
comercio dentro de los estados
(米)州内商業

---

*Translations appear in the following order: Chinese, French, German, Spanish/Latin American
Spanish, and Japanese*

in tray
公文筐
casier 'arrivée': pour le courrier ou les nouveaux documents à traiter
Eingangskorb; Ablage
bandeja de trabajos pendientes
未決書類入れ

in-tray learning
收件箱学问
formation en gestion de casier 'arrivée' (des nouveaux documents à traiter)
Ablagenschulung
ejercicio de formación para desarrollar la capacidad de toma de decisiones y de gestión del tiempo
未決問題解決トレーニング

intrinsic value
隐含价值
valeur intrinsèque
innerer Wert
valor intrínseco
実在価値

introducing broker
中介经纪商
courtier de présentation
Einführungsmakler(in)
corredor(-a) que puede aceptar dinero; títulos o propiedad de un cliente
紹介ブローカー

intuitive management
直觉性管理
gestion intuitive; gestion d'intuition
intuitive Geschäftsführung
gestión intuitiva
直観マネージメント

inventory¹
财产目录; 存货(清单); 存货; 盘存; 库存
inventaire
Bestände
inventario
在庫品, 棚卸資産

inventory²
存货
inventaire
Inventar
existencias
在庫品, 棚卸資産

inventory record
存货记录
registre d'inventaires
Lagerbuch
registro del inventario
在庫品記録

inventory turnover
存货周转量; 存货值销售值比率

rotation des stocks
Lagerumschlag
rotación del inventario
棚卸資産回転率

inverse floating rate note
反向浮动利率票据
effet à taux flottant inversé
inverser variabel verzinslicher Schuldschein
bono con interés variable inverso a la tasa de referencia
逆変動金利付約束手形

inverted market
反转市场
marché inversé
invertierter Markt
mercado invertido
逆先物市場, 逆ざや

inverted yield curve
反向收益率曲线
courbe de rendement inversée
invertierte Ertragskurve
curva de rendimiento invertida
逆利回り曲線, 長短金利の逆転

investment
投资
investissement
Investition
inversión
投資

investment analyst
投资分析员
analyste en placements
Investitionsanalyst(in)
analista de inversiones
投資アナリスト

investment bank
投资银行
banque d'investissement
Investmentbank
banco de inversiones
投資銀行, 商業銀行

investment bill
投资票据
traite-investissement
Wechsel, der nicht vor Fälligkeit diskontiert wird
letra comprada para invertir
投資手形

investment bond
投资债券
contrat d'assurance-vie à cotisation unique
festverzinsliches Anlagepapier
bono de inversión
投資債権

investment borrowing
投资借款
emprunts pour investissements
Kreditaufnahme zu Zwecken der

Investition
préstamos para inversiones
投資刺激目的の借入

investment centre
投资中心
centre d'investissement
Investitionskostenstelle
centro de inversiones
投資センター

investment club
投资俱乐部
club d'investissement
Vereinigung von Privatleuten zur Tätigung von Wertpapiere
club de inversiones
投資クラブ

investment committee
投资委员会
comité d'investissement
Anlageausschuss
comité de inversiones
投資委員会

investment company
投资公司
société d'investissement
Investmentgesellschaft
sociedad de inversión
投資(信託)会社

investment dealer
投资经纪人
courtier en placements
Wertpapiermakler(in)
corredor(a) de inversiones
投資ディーラー, 証券ブローカー

investment fund
投资基金
fonds d'investissement
Investmentfonds
fondo de inversión
投資信託

Investment Management Agreement
投资管理协议
contrat de gestion d'investissement
Investmentmanagementabkommen
acuerdo para la gestión de inversiones
投資顧問契約

investment properties
投资房地产
immeubles d'investissement
Anlageobjekte
inversiones inmobiliarias
投資不動産

investment revaluation reserve
投资资产重估储备
provision de réévaluation d'investissement

Translations appear in the following order: Chinese, French, German, Spanish/Latin American Spanish, and Japanese

Wertberichtigung auf
Beteiligungen
reserva de revalorización de la
inversión
投資再評価積立金

investment tax credit
投资税抵免; 投资减税额
avoir fiscal pour investissement
Steuergutschrift für
Neuinvestitionen
descuento fiscal por inversiones
投資税控除, 投資税額控除

investment trust
投资信托
société d'investissement
Investmentgesellschaft
sociedad de inversión (mobiliaria)
or cartera
投資信託, 会社型投資信託

investomer
投资顾客
client-investisseur
Kunde eines Unternehmens, der
gleichzeitig Investor ist
cliente inversor(a)
顧客投資家

investor
投资者; 投资商
investisseur
Investor(in); Kapitalanleger(in);
Anleger(in)
inversor(a); inversionista
投資家, 資本家

investor relations research
投资者关系研究
études sur les relations avec les
investisseurs
Aktionärsplfege-Forschung
estudio de las relaciones con el
inversor
投資筋関係調査

Investors in People
人力投资者
norme nationale au Royaume Uni
pour le développement des
employés
britische Norm für die
Mitarbeiterförderung
iniciativa del gobierno británico
para el desarrollo de las
habilidades de los trabajadores
インベスター・イン・ピープル
（人材投資家）

invisible exports
无形出口
exportation invisible
unsichtbare Ausfuhr
exportaciones invisibles
貿易外輸出, 無形の輸出

invisible imports
无形进口
importation invisible
unsichtbare Einfuhr
importaciones invisibles
貿易外輸入, 無形の輸入

invisibles
无形项目; 无形收支
invisibles
unsichtbare Ein- und Ausfuhren
invisibles
貿易外収支計上項目

invisible trade
无形贸易
commerce invisible
unsichtbarer Handel
comercio invisible
貿易外取引, 見えざる貿易

invitation to tender
投标邀请; 招标
appel d'offres; appel à soumission
d'offre
Ausschreibung
llamada a licitación; llamada a
concurso
入札募集

invoice
发票
facture
Rechnung; Faktura
factura
送り状, 請求書

invoice date
开发票日期; 发票日期
date de facture
Rechnungsdatum
fecha de facturación
送り状の日付

invoice discounting
把發票債權賣給別人或別的財
務公司
escompte sur facture
Bevorschussung von Rechnungen
descuentos en facturas
送り状の割引売却

invoicing
开发票
facturation
Fakturierung
facturación
送り状発行

**involuntary liquidation
preference**
强制清算優先权
préférence sur liquidation
involontaire
unfreiwilliger Liquidationsvorzug
preferencia por liquidación
involuntaria
強制破産選択

inward investment
投资吸纳; 对内投资; 内向投资
investissement étranger
ausländische Direktinvestition
inversión interna
对内投资

IOU
借据，欠条
abbréviation anglaise phonétique
de 'I owe you': 'Je vous dois. . .',
reconnaissance de dette
Schuldschein
pagaré
略式借用証書

IOW
换句话说
en d'autres termes
anders gesagt
en otras palabras
つまり

IP address
IP地址; 网际互连协议地址
adresse IP
IP-Adresse
dirección IP
IPアドレス

IRA
个人退休金帐户
I.R.A.: abbréviation de compte de
retraite individuel
steuerfreies Rentensparkonto
IRA
個人退職勘定

IRD number
劳动力号码
numéro IRD
Steuernummer
número de identificación fiscal
ニュージーランド納税者番号

IRL
在现实生活中
dans la vie réelle
in der Realität
en la vida real
実生活では

irritainment
愤怒娱乐节目
émissions-crispo
Medienbeiträge oder sonstige
Unterhaltungsformen, die einem
auf die Nerven gehen, einen aber
dennoch in ihren Bann ziehen
entretenimiento irritante pero
absorbente
病み付きになる,
苛立つエンターテインメント

IRS
国内税务署
I.R.S.: abbréviation anglaise de
Inland Revenue Service: service du
fisc

---

*Translations appear in the following order: Chinese, French, German, Spanish/Latin American
Spanish, and Japanese*

amerikanische
Bundessteuerbehörde
IRS
内国歳入庁

ISA

投資儲蓄帳戶
compte épargne individuel
Individualsparkonto
cuenta de ahorros individual
個人貯蓄口座

ISDN

综合服务数字网
réseau téléphonique numérique
diensteintegrierendes digitales
Nachrichtennetz, ISDN
RDSI
ISDN(総合デジタル通信網)

ISO¹

独立服务机构
OSI/ISO: abbréviation de
organisation de service
indépendante
Unternehmen, das
Online-Kreditkartentransaktionen
für kleine Unternehmen
bearbeitet, normalerweise für eine
geringe Gebühr
empresa de procesado de
transacciones electrónicas
インディペンデント・サービス・
オーガニゼーション

ISO²

国际标准化组织
OSI/ISO: abbréviation de
organisation de service
indépendante
Internationale
Normungsorganisation
ISO
国際標準化機構,
独立サービス組織

ISO 14000

国际标准化组织环境
管理质量标准14000
ISO 14000
ISO-Norm 14000
ISO 14000
ISO14000,
国際標準化機構品質保証規格
14000

ISO 9000

ISO9000
norme de qualité
ISO 9000:
Qualitätssicherungsnorm
Organización de Normas
Internacionales 9000 sobre
Productos y Servicios
ISO9000,
国際標準化機構品質保証規格
9000

ISP

因特网服务商
FSI: abbréviation de fournisseur de
service indépendant
Internet-Diensteanbieter
isp; proveedor de acceso
インターネット・サービス・
プロバイダー

issuance costs

发行成本
frais d'émission
Ausgabekosten
gastos de emisión
(債務証券)発行手数料

issue

发行
émission
Begebung
emisión
発行, 振り出し

Issue Department

发行部
service des émissions
Abteilung Notenemission
departamento de emisión
(イングランド銀行にある)
造幣局

issued share capital

已发行股票资本
capital-actions émis
ausgegebenes Aktienkapital
capital en acciones emitido
発行済株式資本

issued shares

已发行股票
actions émises (entièrement ou
non libérées)
ausgegebene Aktien
acciones emitidas
発行済株式

issue price

发行价格
prix d'émission
Ausgabekurs
precio de emisión
(証券類の)発行価格

issuer

信用卡发行银行
institution émettrice; banque
émettrice
Kreditkarten-Organisation
emisor
(カードの)発行人

issuer bid

发行人报价
offre par l'émetteur
Emittenten-Angebot
oferta del emisor
発行者指値

issues management

问题管理
gestion des sujets relatifs à
l'organisation
Problembewältigung
gestión de asuntos centrales
イシュー・マネージメント

issuing house

证券发行公司
banque de placement
Emissionshaus
casa de emisión
幹事会社

itchy finger syndrome

交互性需求
syndrome du doigt qui démande
de faire quelque chose
Fingerjucksyndrom
síndrome de la interactividad
イッチィ・フィンガー症候群

item non-response

无反应项
données de non-réponse
keine Antwort auf eine Frage
falta de respuesta
非応答項目

Japanese management

日式管理风格
gestion à la japonaise
Unternehmensführung nach
japanischer Art
gestión japonesa
ジャパニーズ・マネジメント
(日本型経営)

Japanese payment option

日本付款选择
option de paiement à la japonaise:
série d'extensions du protocole
SET pour faciliter les
caractéristiques de traitement
spécifiques au marché japonais
japanische Zahlungsoption: eine
Reihe von Erweiterungen des
SET-Protokolls, die die spezifischen
Abwicklungsmerkmale des
japanischen Markts ermöglichen
opción para pagos japoneses
日本型決済オプション,
ジャパニーズ・ペイメント・オ
プション

Java

一种网络编程语言; Java语言
Java
Java
Java
Java(オブジェクト指向プロ
グラム言語)

jikan

优先权规则
règle de priorité relative à la Bourse
de Tokyo

Translations appear in the following order: Chinese, French, German, Spanish/Latin American Spanish, and Japanese

Prioritätsregelung an der Börse
von Tokio
jikan
時間優先

job¹
职位
emploi
Stelle
trabajo; puesto de trabajo
地位

job²
工作
lot de tâches
Arbeitsaufgabe
tarea
仕事

jobber's turn
中间商利差
bénéfice que fait un intermédiaire
sur la vente de valeurs
ehemals an der Londoner Börse
verwendeter Begriff für
Händlerspanne
término utilizado antiguamente en
la Bolsa de Londres para referirse a
un margen
中継人利ザヤ

jobbing backwards
历史记录分析
analyse rétrospective de
spéculation
rückblickender Effekten- od.
Wertpapierhandel
análisis de una transacción de
inversión a fin de aprender de los
errores en lugar de buscar al
culpable
投資取引分析

job classification
工作分类
classification des emplois
Einteilung von Tätigkeiten;
Lohngruppeneinteilung
clasificación de un puesto de
trabajo
職務分類

job costing
工作成本核算，分批成本核算
évaluation du coût des tâches
Auftragskostenrechnung
cálculo de costes por trabajo
cálculo de costos por trabajo
個別原価計算

job cost sheet
工作成本清单
fiche de coût d'un emploi
Auftragskostensammelblatt
hoja de costos laborales por
trabajo
個別原価表

job design
职务设计; 工作设计
conception d'un emploi
Arbeitsgestaltung
diseño de un puesto de trabajo
職務設計

job enlargement
扩大工作量
élargissement des tâches
(professionnelles)
horizontale
Arbeitsfeldvergrößerung
ampliación del trabajo
職務範囲の拡大

job evaluation
工作评估
évaluation d'emploi
Arbeitsplatzbewertung
evaluación del trabajo
職務評価

job family
工作群; 工作系
catégorie d'emplois relevant d'un
même domaine
Kategorie beruflicher Tätigkeiten
in jeweils ähnlichen Bereichen
familia de trabajos
類似作業分野

job lock
福利牵制
être coincé dans son job pour
raisons financières
Stellensperre
permanencia en el trabajo por
miedo a la pérdida de prestaciones
sociales
福利を失うことを恐れて
仕事を止められない状態

job lot
小批交易
forfait pour articles divers
Restposten
lote irregular/partida de saldo
小口取引

job production
工作成果
production à la tâche
Einzelfertigung
producción individual en pequeñas
cantidades
注文生産

job rotation
工作轮班; 职务转换
rotation des tâches
(professionnelles)
systematischer Aufgabenwechsel
rotación de trabajos
職場の配置転換

job satisfaction
工作满足感; 工作乐趣
épanouissement professionnel
Arbeitszufriedenheit
satisfacción en el trabajo
職務満足度

job-share
工作分担; 职务分摊
partage de poste
Arbeitsplatzteilung
trabajo compartido
ジョブ・シェアリング

job shop
车间
atelier pour travaux particularisés
Betrieb mit Einzelfertigung
taller de producción de series
pequeñas
注文製作工場

job vacuum
任劳任怨
employé aspirateur
Arbeitnehmer, der freiwillig
zusätzliche Pflichten übernimmt
(wie ein Staubsauger)
trabajador(a) que asume tareas
adicionales voluntariamente
余計な仕事まで受け持つ社員

Johari window
乔哈利人际沟通模型
fenêtre de Johari: modèle de
communication qui facilite
l'analyse de la façon dont une
personne donne et reçoit des
informations, et la dynamique des
communications
interpersonnelles. La fenêtre de
Johari est habituellement
représentée sous forme d'une g
Johari-Fenster
ventana de Johari
ジョハリ・ウィンドー

joined-up
政府联合社会力量
conjoint
gemeinsam, unter Mitarbeit der
Gemeinde und der Regierung zur
Verbesserung der allgemeinen
Lebensqualität
en colaboración entre la
comunidad y el gobierno
官民共同の

joint account
联合帐户
compte joint
gemeinsames Konto
cuenta conjunta
共同預金口座

joint and several liability
各自连带责任
responsabilité conjointe et séparée
gesamtschuldnerische Haftung
responsabilidad conjunta y

---

*Translations appear in the following order: Chinese, French, German, Spanish/Latin American
Spanish, and Japanese*

solidaria
連帯責任

joint cost
联成本
coût joint
Gemeinkosten
coste conjunto; coste compartido
costo conjunto; costo compartido
個別原価

joint electronic payment initiative
联合电子支付联盟
initiative de paiement électronique commune
gemeinsame Initiative für elektronische Zahlung
iniciativa de pagos electrónicos conjuntos
ジョイント・エレクトロニック・ペイメント・イニシャティブ，
共同電子決済イニシャティブ

joint float
联合浮动
flottement conjoint
Gruppenfloating
flotación conjunta
ジョイント・フロート，
変動相場制への共同移行

joint life annuity
联合终生年金
rente viagère commune
gemeinsame Rentenversicherung
anualidad vitalicia conjunta
共同生命確定給付

joint ownership
共同所有
co-propriété
gemeinschaftliches Eigentum
copropiedad
共同所有権

joint products
联产品
produits liés
Kuppelprodukt
productos conjuntos o mancomunados; subproductos
連産品

joint return
共同纳税申报单
déclaration d'impôt commune
gemeinsame Steuererklärung
declaración conjunta de la renta
夫婦合算納税申告書

joint stock bank
股份银行，合股银行
société de dépôt
Aktienbank
banco por acciones
株式銀行

joint venture
合资经营，联营企业
Co-entreprise
Joint Venture
alianza estratégetica
合弁企業

journal
livre-journal
Journal; Geschäftsbuch; Hauptbuch; Grundbuch

JPEG
联合图象专家小组规范；
静止图象压缩规范；
压缩图形文件格式
JPEG
Joint Photographic Experts Group
= komprimiertes grafisches Datenformat
JPEG
JPEG
(圧縮アルゴリズムの勧告自体-名)

JSE
约翰内斯堡股票交易所
Bourse des titres JSE
ehemaliger inoffizieller Name der Wertpapierbörse JSE (Johannesburger Börse)
Bolsa de Johanesburgo
ヨハネスブルグ株式取引所

judgment creditor
判(决确)定债权人
plaignant qui a obtenu satisfaction
Vollstreckungsgläubiger(in)
acreedor por fallo
判決債権者

judgment debtor
判定债务，裁决债务
personne ou société devant payée la somme attribuée par le tribunal à un plaignant qui a obtenu satisfaction
Vollstreckungsschuldner(in)
deudor por fallo
判決債務

jumbo mortgage
巨额抵押
hypothèque géante
Großhypothek
hipoteca gigante
ジャンボ・モーゲージ，
米の大型住宅ローン

junior debt
低级债务
dette de deuxième rang
nachrangige Schuld
deuda subordinada
劣後債務，ジュニア・デット

junior mortgage
低级抵押

hypothèque en second
nachrangige Hypothek
hipoteca secundaria; segunda hipoteca
後順位先取権特権担保、下位抵当

junk bond
风险债券；低资信度债券
obligation aléatoire (à rendement et risque élevés)
Risikopapier
bono basura
ジャンクボンド、ジャンク債

just-in-time
及时
juste-à-temps
Justintime-System
por pedido justo a tiempo
カンバン方式

just-in-time production
及时生产
production juste-à-temps
Justintime-Fertigung
producción justo a tiempo, sólo para satisfacer la demanda
カンバン生産

just-in-time purchasing
及时采购
achat juste-à-temps
Justintime-Beschaffung
compra de coincidencia justo a tiempo
カンバン購買

kaizen
持续改善
amélioration continue des procédés actuels
Kaizen
mejora continua de los procesos
改善

kaizen budget
改善式预算
Budget de type kaizen
Kaizen-Budget
presupuesto con esperanza de mejoras continuas durante el período
カイゼン予算

kakaku yusen
价格优先权制度
système de priorité ou préférence de prix à la Bourse de Tokyo
japanisches Kurs-Prioritätssystem an der Börse in Tokio
kakaku yusen
価格優先

kanban
准时管理控制系统
Kanban
Kanban-System
ficha de reposición
かんばん方式

Translations appear in the following order: Chinese, French, German, Spanish/Latin American Spanish, and Japanese

kanbrain
知识传播技术
se dit de la technologie utilisée
dans la transmission de
connaissances
bezüglich der zur Übertragung von
Kenntnissen genutzten
Technologie
tecnología de transmisión de
conocimientos
知識伝達の技術

kangaroo
澳大利亚的公司股票
kangourou: terme argotique
désignant les actions et valeurs
autraliennes à la Bourse de
Londres
an der Londoner Börse gehandelte
australische Wertpapiere
canguro
カンガルー

Kansas City Board of Trade
堪萨斯城同业工会
Bourse de commerce de Kansas
City
Warenbörse zum Handel von
Terminkontrakten für den roten
Winterweizen, für den Value
Line® Gesamtwertindex, für
Erdgas und für den
Internet-Aktienindex ISDEX®
lonja de contratación de Kansas
City
カンザス市商品取引委員会

Keidanren
日本经济组织联合会
abbréviation japonaise de la
fédération japonaise des
organismes économiques
japanischer Verband der
Wirtschaftsorganisationen
Keidanren
経団連

keiretsu
株式会社
keiretsu
Keiretsu
conglomerado económico japonés
系列

Keough Plan
柯奥夫计划
plan Keough:plan de retraite avec
avantages fiscaux pour travailleur
indépendant ou avec un intérêt
dans une petite entreprise aux
Etats-Unis
steuerbegünstigter Pensionsplan
für Selbständige
pensión con ventajas fiscales para
autonómos o pequeños

empresarios
キオ・プラン,
米自営業者退職プラン

kerb market
场外(证券)市场
marché après clôture (de la Bourse)
nachbörslicher/außerbörslicher
Markt
mercado extrabursátil
場外市場, カーブ市場

key account management
关键客户管理 重要客户管理
gestion des comptes-clients clé
Großkundenbetreuung
gestión de cuentas clave
上顧客マネージメント

keyboard plaque
電脳键盘污渍
tartre de clavier
Tastaturbelag
mugre en el teclado
キーボード上の垢

Keynesian economics
凯恩斯经济学
keynésianisme
Keynessche Wirtschaftstheorie
economía keynesiana
ケインズ経済学

key-person insurance
关键人保险
assurance contre la perte de
personnel clé
Versicherung für eine
Schlüsselkraft
seguro de vida de un trabajador
clave
主要人物保険

keyword
关键字
mots clé
Schlüsselwort
palabra clave
キーワード

keyword search
关键字搜索
recherche par mots clé
Schlüsselwortsuche
búsqueda por palabras clave
キーワード・サーチ

kiasu
怕输
terme hokkien qui décrit la
mentalité 'je dois gagner et ne
jamais perdre' typique des
singapouriens
immer gewinnen, niemals verlieren
la mentalidad de siempre ganar,
nunca perder
キアス

kickback
贿赂
commission clandestine
Schmiergeld
soborno
キックバック(収賄)

kicker
诱饵，甜头，促销品
kicker: terme argotique anglais:
avantage supplémentaire à un titre
standard le rendant plus alléchant,
par exemple avec des options et
garanties
Zusatzangebot auf eine Aktie
kicker; incentivo
キッカー

killer app
極有效的電腦程式;
極成功的電腦程式
appareil avec l'instinct gagnant
Killer-Anwendung
programa revolucionario;
aplicación rompedora
キラー・アプ

killerbee
协助公司抵挡收购行为的银行
bourdon dissuasif
Investmentbank, die Unternehmen
dabei hilft, Übernahmeangebote
abzuwehren
inversor anti-opa; inversor(a) que
ayuda a repeler una OPA; abeja
asesina; 'cazatiburones'
買収阻止者

killfile
过滤单
crève-fichiers
Filterdatei
archivo de indeseables
削除リスト

killing
斩获
(réussir) un beau coup: faire un
bénéfice important sur une
transaction
ungewöhnlich hoher
Spekulationsgewinn
gran negocio; gran jugada
キリング(巨額利益)

KISS
长话短说
garde les choses simples, imbécile
Halte es einfach, Dummchen
no te compliques la vida, imbécil
シンプルにしておけ

kiss up to sb
巴结; 讨好
lécher les bottes à quelqu'un
sich einschleimen
hacer la pelota a alguien
ぺこぺこする

Translations appear in the following order: Chinese, French, German, Spanish/Latin American Spanish, and Japanese

kite
空头支票
transaction frauduleuse: par
exemple un chèque en bois
Kellerwechsel
transacción fraudulenta
空手形

kite-flying
试飞
prospectus pour tâter le terrain
(Etats-Unis)
Wechselreiterei
libranza de letras de cortesía
融通手形振り出し

kiwibond
新西兰债券，几维鸟债券
obligation kiwi: une
euro-obligation en dollars
néozélandais
Eurobond, dessen Stückelung
neuseeländische Dollar ist
bono kiwi
キーウィ・ボンド

knight
白马骑士
compagnie impliquée dans une
offre publique d'achat
Anleger, der eine
Unternehmensübernahme
beabsichtigt
caballero
騎士

knock-for-knock
汽车互撞免赔协定
accord entre compagnies
d'assurance pour dédommager
séparément les clients respectifs
Schadenteilungsvereinbarung
convenio de compensación mutua
自社引き受け自動車の損害賠償

knocking copy
中伤他人; 讲坏话
contre-publicité
herabsetzende Werbung
anuncio que descalifica a la
competencia
批判広告

knock-out option
拍卖时不出价的期权;
联手拍卖期权
option 'de type knock-out'
Knock-out-Option
opción acompañada de una
condición relativa al precio actual
del producto o activo subyacente,
de manera que en realidad expira
al cotizar fuera de dinero
ノックアウト・オプション

knowledge
知识，学问
savoir; connaissances

Kenntnisse
conocimiento
知識

knowledge-based system
基于知识的系统
système expert
wissensbasiertes System
sistema experto
ナレッジ・ベース・システム

knowledge capital
知识资本
capital de connaissances
Wissenskapital
capital intelectual
知識資本

knowledge management[1]
知识管理
gestion des connaissances
Wissensmanagement
gestión del conocimiento
知識情報管理,
ナレッジ・マネジメント

knowledge management[2]
知识管理
gestion des connaissances
Wissensmanagement
gestión del conocimiento
知識管理

knowledge worker
知识工人
travailleur avec connaissances
Informationsarbeiter(in)
trabajador(a) del conocimiento
知識労働者

Krugerrand
富格林金币(南非)
Krugerrand
Krügerrand
krugerrand
クルーガランド・コイン

labour dispute
劳资争端; 罢工; 怠工; 劳资纠纷
conflit des employés
Arbeitsstreitigkeiten
conflicto laboral
労使争議

labour force
劳动力
main-d'œuvre
Arbeiterschaft
población activa
労働力

labour force survey
'劳动力'调查
étude des effectifs et
main-d'œuvre
Erhebung zur Erwerbstätigkeit
encuesta de población activa
労働調査

labour-intensive
劳动集约型的; 劳动密集的;
使用大量劳力的
qui nécessite une main-d'œuvre
importante; dépendant d'une
main-d'œuvre considérable
arbeitsintensiv
que requiere mucha mano de obra
労働集約型

labour market
劳务市场
marché du travail
Arbeitsmarkt
mercado de trabajo
労働市場

labour shortage[1]
劳动力短缺
pénurie de main-d'œuvre: manque
de travailleurs, ou de travailleurs
potentiels pour remplir les postes
disponibles
Arbeitskräftemangel
escasez de mano de obra
労働力不足

labour shortage[2]
劳动力不足
pénurie de main-d'œuvre: manque
de travailleurs aux qualifications et
compétences adéquates pour
remplir des postes spécifiques. Un
terme plus exact serait 'pénurie de
compétences'
Fachkräftemangel
escasez de mano de obra
労働力不足

labour tourist
旅行工作者
travailleur touriste
Beschäftigungstourist(in)
persona que vive en un país pero
trabaja en otro
労働旅行者

Lady Macbeth strategy
麦克白策略
changement de tactique de la part
d'un cavalier blanc présumé, qui
fait qu'il se révèle être un cavalier
noir
Kehrtwende im Ansatz eines
Anlegers, der vom 'Retter in der
Not' zum unfreundlichen
Übernehmer wird
cambio de estrategia de un
caballero blanco que pasa a ser
caballero negro
レディ・マクベス戦略

lagging indicator
拉后指标; 后行指标
indicateur décalé
Spätindikator

Translations appear in the following order: Chinese, French, German, Spanish/Latin American Spanish, and Japanese

indicador atrasado
遅行指標

land bank
地产银行
terres d'investissement
Grundbesitz
terreno que una empresa
constructora o una inmobiliaria
tiene disponible para urbanizar
土地抵当銀行

land banking
土地储备
investissement dans propriété
foncière
Aufkauf von Boden, der nicht
unmittelbar benötigt wird, aber in
der Zukunft von Nutzen sein soll
compra de tierras para utilizarlas
en el futuro
土地抵当銀行業

land tax
住房占地税
impôt foncier
Grundsteuer
número de identificación fiscal
neozelandés
土地税

lapse
因未履行义务而引起的权利终止
caducité ou déchéance
Ablauf
caducidad
失効

lapse rights
终止权
droits de déchéance
Verfallrechte
derechos de caducidad
失効権

large-sized business
大型企业
grosse entreprise
Großunternehmen
gran empresa
大企業

last survivor policy
最后倖存者保险单
politique du dernier survivant
Überlebensrente
seguro de vida conjunto a favor del
último superviviente
最終生存者約款

latent market
潜在市场
marché latent
latenter Markt
mercado latente
予想商品の見込客

lateral thinking
横向思维
la pensée latérale

unkonventionelle Problemlösung
pensamiento lateral
水平思考

launch
启动; 起动; 开设; 开办; 投入; 推出
lancer
Markteinführung
lanzamiento
発売

laundering
洗黑钱; 洗钞
blanchiment
(Geld-) Wäsche
blanqueo; lavado
資金洗浄

law of diminishing returns
递减报酬律; 报酬递减律;
报酬递减法则
loi des rendements décroissants
Ertragsgesetz
ley del rendimiento decreciente
限界収穫逓減の法則

lay-by
保留
achat d'un produit avec paiement
d'un acompte puis par traites sans
intérêts
Ratenkauf bei dem ein Artikel mit
einer Anzahlung reserviert wird
compra a plazos sin pagar
intereses
商品予約購入制度

lay off[1]
解雇; (暂时)停工
licencier (de façon permanente)
entlassen
despedir
解雇,

lay off[2]
临时解雇
débaucher (temporairement par
manque de travail à donner)
Personal vorübergehend freisetzen
despedir
自宅待機

lead
首要承保人
(syndicat de garantie) chef de file
Erstversicherer (in)
consorcio asegurador principal
リード(ロイズ保険約款)

leader[1]
领袖人物; 主导产品; 主导公司
chef de file
Führer(in); Vorgesetzte/r;
Konsortialführerin
líder
リーダー, 主力商品会社

leader[2]
领袖人物; 主导产品; 主导公司
numéro un sur le marché
Leitartikel
líder
リーダー, 主力商品会社

leadership
领导能力
leadership; direction
Führungsqualitäten
liderazgo
リーダーシップ

leading economic indicator
先导经济指标; 主要经济指标
principal indicateur économique
Frühindikator
indicador económico anticipado
主要景気指標, 先行指標

leading-edge
前卫; 前锋; 先导; 开创; 创新; 先驱
avant-garde
am vorderste Front
vanguardia
最先端

lead manager
牵头经营, 主办
institution financière chef de file
(responsable d'une nouvelle
émission, y compris sa
coordination, distribution et
administration apparentée)
Konsortialführer(in)
jefe de fila
主幹事, 引受主幹事

lead partner
牵头合作者; 主导合作者
partenaire principal
federführender Partner
socio(-a) principal
先導パートナー

leads and lags
提前结算与拖后结算
jeu de termes de paiement
Vorauszahlungen und Stundungen
im Auslandszahlungsverkehr
adelantos y atrasos
リーズ・アンド・ラグズ
(投機取引の一種)

lead time[1]
订货至交货间隔期
délai d'exécution
Beschaffungszeit
plazo de entrega
リード・タイム,
(企画から実現までの)準備期間

lead time[2]
前置时间
délai de production
Vorlaufzeit
plazo de producción

リード・タイム,
(企画から実現までの)準備期間

leaky reply
露饴回覆
réponse divulguée par erreur
Leck-Antwort
correo enviado a la persona
equivocada
返答先違い

lean enterprise
精益企业
entreprise amincie
verschlanktes od. schlankes
Unternehmen
grupo de individuos o grupos que
actúan como una empresa
リーン・エンタープライズ

lean production
精益生产
production dégraissée
verschlankte Produktion
producción ajustada
リーン・プロダクション

LEAPS
长期证券
options expirant dans entre un et
trois ans
Optionen, die innerhalb von einem
Jahr bis zu drei Jahren ablaufen
opciones sobre acciones a largo
plazo
個別銘柄に対応した
長期的オプション契約

learning by doing
实践中学习; 幹中学
apprentissage par l'action
praktisches Lernen
aprendizaje práctico
実践学習

learning curve¹
学习曲线
courbe d'apprentissage
Lernkurve
curva de aprendizaje
学習曲線, 習熟曲線

learning curve²
学习曲线
courbe d'apprentissage
Lernkurve
curva de aprendizaje
学習曲線, 習熟曲線

learning organisation
学习型机构
organisation avec mentalité
apprenante
lernende Organisation
modelo empresarial con una
estructura plana y equipos
centrados en los clientes
学習する組織

learning relationship
学习关系
relation d'apprentissage (pour
connaître les exigences de sa
clientèle)
Lernbeziehung
relación de aprendizaje
学習関係

learning style
学习模式
style d'apprentissage
Lernstil
estilo de aprendizaje
習得スタイル

leave
假期; 假日; 准許離開崗位
congé
Urlaub
permiso
休職

Leavitt's Diamond
黎维尔钻石模式
modèle d'analyse de gestion
Leavitts Diamant
modelo de análisis de la gestión de
Leavitt
リービットのダイアモンド

ledger
元帳, 原簿

legacy system
既有系统
système informatique légataire
Altsystem
sistema heredado
レガシーシステム

legal loophole
法律漏洞; 法律空子
point faible légal/lacune dans la
législation
Rechtslücke
vacío legal
法的抜け穴

legal tender
法定货币，法币
monnaie ayant cours légal
gesetzliches Zahlungsmittel
moneda de curso legal
法貨

legs
超长
vie à tiroirs pour une campagne de
pub
ungewöhnlich lange Lebenszeit
einer Werbekampagne, eines
Films, eines Buchs oder sonstiger
kurzlebiger Produkte
duración prolongada
広告などが普通より長く続くこと

lemon¹
残次品(尤指汽车)
camelote
Schüssel
patata; producto defectuoso
不良品(特に車)

lemon²
不好的投资(俚语)
Lemon: terme argotique
américain: un investissement qui
est une fumisterie
minderwertige Investition
limón
レモン(儲からない投資)

lender of last resort
最后贷款者; 最后融资银行
prêteur de dernier recours
letzte Refinanzierungsinstanz
prestamista en última instancia
(中央銀行や世銀などの)
最後の貸し

length of service
服务年资
temps de service
Dienstzeit
antigüedad
在職期限

less developed country
不发达国家
pays moins développé (PMD)
Entwicklungsland
país en vías de desarrollo
低開発国、発展途上国

lessee
承租人，租户
locataire
Mieter(in)
arrendatatorio
借主

lessor
出租人
bailleur
Vermieter(in)
arrendador
貸主

letter of agreement
协议书
lettre de contrat
Einverständnisschreiben
carta de acuerdo
約定書

letter of allotment
认股分配书; 核定认股书
avis de répartition ou d'attribution
Zuteilungsanzeige
carta de adjudicación
株式割当文書

letter of comfort
支持函，告慰信
lettre de confort

Translations appear in the following order: Chinese, French, German, Spanish/Latin American Spanish, and Japanese

Patronatserklärung
carta de seguridades
念書

letter of credit
信用证
lettre de crédit
Akkreditiv; Kreditbrief
carta de crédito
信用状, LC

letter of indemnity
赔偿保证书; 赔偿担保书
lettre de garantie
Schadloshaltungserklärung
carta de indemnización
損失証書免責状

letter of intent
意向书
lettre d'intention
Absichtserklärung
carta de intenciones
趣意書

letter of licence
允许延期还债书
accord entre un débiteur défaillant
et ses créanciers lui octroyant une
période donnée pour lever des
fonds et l'assurant qu'aucune
action en justice de recouvrement
de dette ne sera entamée contre
lui durant cette période
Brief von einem Gläubiger an
einen Schuldner, mit dem diesem
ein gewisser Zahlungsaufschub
gewährt und zugesagt wird, dass
während dieser Zeitspanne kein
Verfahren eingeleitet wird, um die
Schulden einzutreiben
escritura de concordato/moratoria
支払期日延期書面

letter of renunciation
放弃股份分配权证书; 弃权声明
lettre de renoncement
Abtretungsformular für eine
Zuteilung
carta de renuncia
放棄承認状

level playing field
平级竞争状态
équipe de force égale
gleiche Voraussetzungen
igualdad de condiciones
公平な競争状態

level term assurance
标准条款人寿险
assurance à paiement forfaitaire (si
le détenteur de la police meurt
avant une certaine date)
abgekürzte Todesfallversicherung
carta de seguridades
平準定期保険

leverage
杠杆; 举债经营; 杠杆作用
effet de levier
Hebelwirkung; Leverage
apalancamiento
レバレッジ

leveraged bid
融资投标; 借款购买股票;
杠杆接管投标
offre financée par l'endettement
fremdfinanziertes
Submissionsangebot
oferta apalancada
レバレッジ・ビッド

leveraged buyout
借款买股; 杠杆购股
rachat financé par l'endettement
fremdfinanziertes
Übernahmeangebot
compra apalancada
レバレッジ・バイアウト

leveraged required return
借贷应得报酬
revenu requis pour financer
l'endettement
erforderlicher Ertrag aus einer
Fremdfinanzierung
rendimiento requerido apalancado
予定投資収益率

liability
债务
obligation ou dette
Verbindlichkeit
pasivo; deuda
債務

liability insurance
责任(保)险
assurance responsabilité civile
Haftpflichtversicherung
seguro de responsabilidad
賠償責任保険

liability management
债务管理
gestion des risques et
responsabilités
Verschuldungspolitik
gestión del pasibo
負債管理

licence
许可; 批准; 特许; 发放 许可证;
执照; 牌照
licence
Lizenz
licencia
ライセンス, 免許

licensing
许可证交易; 發牌
cession de licence
Lizenzerteilung

concesión de licencia
ライセンスを与える

licensing agreement
许可协议
accord de licence
Lizenzvereinbarung
acuerdo de licencia
ライセンス契約

life annuity
终身年金
rente viagère
Leibrente
renta vitalicia
終身年金、生命年金

life assurance
人寿保险
assurance-vie
Lebensversicherung
seguridad de vida
生命保険

life assured
人寿保险投保人，人寿保险受保人
assuré sur la vie
Lebensversicherte/r
asegurado de vida
生命保険でカバーされている人物

lifeboat
救济金; 救生艇
prêt d'urgence avec taux d'intérêt
bas par une banque centrale à une
banque commerciale pour lui
éviter de devenir insolvable
Niedrigzinsenkredit einer
Zentralbank für eine Handelsbank,
der sonst Insolvenz drohen würde
préstamo de emergencia a bajo
interés emitido por el banco
central para rescatar un banco
comercial
ライフボート(低金利緊急ロー
ン)

life cycle
生命周期
cycle de vie
Produktlebenszyklus
vida útil
ライフ・サイクル

life-cycle costing
生命(或寿命)周期成本核算
évaluation des prix de revient sur le
cycle de vie
Lebenszykluskalkulation
cálculo de costes durante el ciclo
de vida
ライフ・サイクル原価計算

life-cycle savings motive
生命周期储蓄动机
raison de l'épargne sur cycle de vie
Lebenszyklus-Sparmotiv
motivo para los ahorros en el ciclo
vital

Translations appear in the following order: Chinese, French, German, Spanish/Latin American Spanish, and Japanese

ライフサイクル貯蓄動機,
ライフ・サイクル理論

life expectancy
预期寿命
espérance de vie
Lebenserwartung
esperanza de vida
平均余命

lifelong learning
终生学习; 继续学习
apprentissage au cours de la vie
lebenslanges Lernen
aprendizaje a cualquier edad
生涯学習

life office
人寿保险公司
bureau d'assurance-vie
Lebensversicherungsgesellschaft
entidad de seguros de vida
生命保険会社

life policy
人寿保险单
police d'assurance-vie
Lebensversicherungspolice
póliza de seguro de vida
生命保険証券

lifestyle business
生活方式业务
entreprise mode de vie
Kleinunternehmen, von Personen
betrieben, die besonders lebhaftes
Interesse am eigenen Produkt-
oder Dienstleistungsangebot
haben
negocio normalmente pequeño
que llevan individuos muy
interesasdos en el producto o
servicio ofrecido, por ejemplo,
tarjetas de felicitación hechas a
mano, joyas, antiguedades, o
restauración de alfombras
orientales
ライフスタイル・ビジネス

life table
(人寿保险的)生命统计表 ,
死亡率表
tableau de probabilité de vie ou
tableau de survie
Sterbetafel
tabla de mortalidad; tabla de vida
死亡生残表

lifetime customer value
顾客终极消费值
valeur des dépenses d'un client sur
toute une vie
Kundenwert nach Lebenszeit, der
die Summe der Käufe des Kunden
darstellt
valor vitalicio del cliente
ライフタイム・バリュー

lifetime value
一生价值
valeur sur durée de vie
Lebenszeit-Wert
valor vitalicio
終身価値

LIFO
后进先出法
DAPS: voir dernier arrivé – premier
sorti
Lifo-Methode zur Auswahl von
Mitarbeitern zur Entlassung, nach
der die zuletzt eingestellten
Mitarbeiter als erste entlassen
werden
técnica de regulación de empleo
según la cual los trabajadores con
menos tiempo en el puesto son los
primeros en ser despedidos
後入先出(リストラの順序)

lightning strike
闪电式罢工
grève éclair
Blitzstreik
huelga relámpago
電撃ストライキ

light pages
光页
pages Web faisant moins de 50
kilo-octets
Webseiten von einer Größe unter
50 kB, schnell herunterladbar
páginas pequeñas
ライト・ページ

limit
限价
limite
Grenze
límite
指値

limit down
最低价
limite à la baisse
maximale zugestandene
Preisschwankung nach unten pro
Tag
límite mínimo
下限指値

Limited
有限公司
Limited: terme anglais signifiant
qu'une société est anonyme ou à
responsabilité limitée
als Teil des Firmennamens
britischer Unternehmen:
bezeichnet diese als
Gesellschaften mit
Haftungsbeschränkung
sociedad anónima
有限の

limited legal tender
有限法定货币; 辅币使用限额
(billets) à cours légal limité
begrenzt einsetzbares gesetzliches
Zahlungsmittel
moneda de curso legal limitada
有限法貨

limited liability
有限责任
responsabilité limitée
beschränkte Haftung
responsabilidad limitada
有限責任

limited liability company
股份有限公司; 责任有限公司
société à responsabilité limitée
Gesellschaft mit beschränkter
Haftung; GmbH
sociedad de responsabilidad
limitada
有限責任会社

limited market
有限(交易)市场
marché limité
begrenzter Markt
mercado restringido
限定市場

limiting factor
限制因素或关键因素
facteur restrictif
Beschränkungsfaktor
factor restrictivo
限定要素

limit up
最高价
limite à la hausse
maximale zugestandene
Preisschwankung nach oben pro
Tag
límite máximo
上限指値

linear programming
线性规划
programmation linéaire
lineare Programmierung
programación linear
線型計画法(LP)

line item budget
分项预算
budget d'articles ligne par ligne
Einzelpostenbudget
presupuesto del coste de partidas
en línea
品目予算

line management
各级负责管理; 垂直管理
direction de type hiérarchique
Linienmanagement
gestión de línea
ライン管理

Translations appear in the following order: Chinese, French, German, Spanish/Latin American Spanish, and Japanese

line manager
各级生产线管理人员
supérieur hiérarchique
Linienmanager(in)
jefe(-a) de línea
ライン・マネジャー

line of credit
信用额度
ligne de crédit
Kreditlinie
línea de crédito
信用供与限度, 融資限度

line organisation
各级负责管理组织; 垂直组织
organisation de type hiérarchique
Linienorganisation
organización lineal
ライン組織

link
链接
lien
Link
enlace
リンク(連携)

linking
链接
relier (deux sites Web ou
  documents)
Kettung
conexión por enlaces
リンキング(連携する)

link rot
连接失败; 登陆失败
liaison pourrie
Verknüpfungsfäule
caducidad de enlaces
リンク腐敗

liquid asset ratio
流动资产比率
coefficient d'actif liquide
Umlaufvermögensquote
coeficiente de activos líquidos
流動資産レシオ, 流動資産比率

liquid assets
流动资产
actif disponible ou disponibilités
liquide Mittel
activo líquido
流動資産

liquidated damages
现金赔偿
dommages-intérêts préalablement
  fixés
(vereinbarte) Vertragsstrafe
estimación de daños y perjuicios
損害賠償額の予定, 定額損害賠償

liquidation
清算; 清理(资产)变现; 清盘
liquidation/amortissement (dette);
mobilisation (de capitaux); dépôt
de bilan
Liquidation
liquidación
清算, 破産

liquidation value
清算价值
valeur de liquidation
Liquidationswert
valor de liquidación
清算価値, 即時処分価値

liquidator
清理人; 清算人; 清理员; 清算员
liquidateur
Liquidator(in)
liquidador(a)
清算人

liquidity
清偿能力; 流动性; 流动资产;
清偿手段; (尤指资产)流动性;
liquidité
Liquidität
liquidez
流動性

liquidity agreement
为保持资金流动性而作的安排
accord de liquidité
Liquiditätsvereinbarung
acuerdo de liquidez
流動性契約

liquidity preference
流动性偏好; 灵活(资产)偏好
préférence pour les liquidités
Liquiditätsneigung;
Liquiditätspräferenz
preferencia de liquidez
流動性選好

liquidity trap
流动性陷阱
piège de liquidité
Liquiditätsfalle
trampa de la liquidez
流動性のワナ

liquid market
流动市场
marché fluide
Markt mit ausreichenden
  Umsätzen
mercado fluido
流動市場

list broker
邮件经纪人
courtier en listes
Adressenverlag
agente de direcciones
リスト・ブローカー

listed company
上市公司; 挂牌公司;
股票上市的公司
compagnie cotée en Bourse
börsennotiertes Unternehmen
sociedad anónima
上場企業

listed security
上市证券; 挂牌证券
valeur cotée
börsennotiertes Wertpapier
valor cotizado
上場証券、上場株、上場有価証券

listing requirements
挂牌(上市)要求
exigences pour cotation
Zulassungsvorschriften
requisitos de cotización en Bolsa
上場条件

list price
目录价格
prix catalogue
Listenpreis
precio de catálogo
カタログ表記定価

list renting
邮件单租赁; 邮寄名单租赁
prêt de liste
Adressenvermietung
alquiler de listas
リスト・レンタル

litigation
诉讼; 打官司; 提出诉讼; 打官司
litige
Prozessführung
litigio
訴訟

Little Board
美国股票交易所, 小牌
la cote officielle ou Bourse
américaine
die amerikanische Börse
Little Board
リトル・ボード(アメリカ株
式取引所)

live chat
聊天室
discussion en temps réel (sur
Internet)
Live Chat
charla en tiempo real
ライブ・チャット

livery
公司车上的公司标志; 公司标志
couleurs (produit/compagnie)
Firmenfarben
distintivo
商標社名入り車

living wage
生计工资
salaire permettant de vivre
décemment
Existenzminimum
salario de subsistencia
生活賃金

Translations appear in the following order: Chinese, French, German, Spanish/Latin American
Spanish, and Japanese

load
费用
charge/charger
Aufschlag
comisión de entrada; carga
販売手数料

load fund
负担基金
fonds de placement avec frais
d'acquisition
Investmentfonds mit
Gebührenberechnung beim
Verkauf von Anteilen
fondo mutuo que cobra comisión
ローン・ファンド,
販売手数料込価格の
オープンエンド型投資信託

loading¹
负荷
allocation de charge
Belastung
carga
特別手当

loading²
附加工资
prime sur salaire
Prämie
paga adicional
特別手当

loan
贷款
emprunt
Anleihe
préstamo
ローン

loanable funds theory
可贷放资金理论
théorie des fonds empruntables:
selon laquelle les taux d'intérêt
sont déterminés uniquement par
l'offre et la demande
Zinstheorie
teoría de fondos de préstamo
貸付資金説

loanback
回贷
prêt en cession: retour d'une
somme donnée, sous forme de
prêt, souvent pour dissimuler, à
des fins illégales, l'identité du vrai
propriétaire de la somme
Fähigkeit des Inhabers einer
Pensionskasse, sich von dieser
Geld zu leihen
préstamo con garantía de póliza
ローンバック

loan capital
债务资本, 借入资本
capital d'emprunt
Anleihekapital
capital en préstamo; recursos

ajenos a largo plazo; fondos
ajenos; obligaciones y otros
empréstitos a largo plazo
借入資本

loan constant ratio
贷款利息本金比率
taux constant d'emprunt
Gesamtheit der fälligen
Darlehenstilgung für ein Jahr als
Bruchteil der Kapitalsumme
relación constante de préstamos
貸付定数比率

Loan Council
贷款委员会
Conseil de l'emprunt: organisme
australien qui détermine combien
les états peuvent emprunter au
cours de l'année prochaine
Australisches Komitee für den
Kreditbedarf der öffentlichen
Hand
consejo australiano supervisor de
los préstamos federales y estatales
(オーストラリアの)貸付委員会

loan loss reserves
坏帐准备基金
réserves pour pertes sur emprunts
Rückstellungen für Verluste aus
Kreditgeschäften
reservas para pérdidas de
préstamos
貸倒れ準備金、貸倒れ引当金

loan production cycle
贷款生产周期
cycle de production de l'emprunt
Kreditproduktionszyklus
ciclo de producción de préstamos
融資申込から資金貸出までの
期間, ローン・プロダクション・
サイクル

loan schedule
贷款还款计划
nomenclature d'emprunt
Tilgungsplan
tabla de pagos de préstamo
融資計画

loan shark
高利贷者; 贵利
usurier escroc
Kredithai
usurero(-a); prestamista
extorsionador(-a)
高利貸し、サラ金業者

loan stock
信用贷款(公司)债券股，
借款债券
obligation
festverzinsliche Wertpapiere
título de préstamo
転換社債

loan to value ratio
贷款价值比率
rapport emprunt-valeur
Beleihungsquote
relación préstamo-valor or del
préstamo al valor total
貸付比率、融資比率

loan value
抵借金额; 抵借价值
valeur de prêt
Beleihungswert
valor del préstamo
貸出額、貸付価額

lobby
游说组织
groupe de pression; faire pression
ou faire du lobbying
Lobby; Interessengruppe
lobby; grupo de presión
圧力団体

localisation
本土化
localisation
Lokalisierung
localización
ウェブサイトの翻訳

lock-out
停工; 关厂
lock-outer/grève patronale
Aussperrung von Arbeitnehmern
cierre patronal
ロックアウト, 作業所閉鎖

logistics
后勤工作; 后勤管理; 后勤;
产品配送
logistique
Logistik
logística
ロジスティックス

logistics management
产品配送管理
gestion de logistique
Versorgungswirtschaft
gestión logística
ロジスティックス(物的流通)
管理

logo
机构标志; 单词符号; 单词图案;
标志; 商标; 标识语
logo
Logo
logotipo
ロゴ, 意匠文字

log of claims
要求记录
liste de revendications
aufgelistete Ansprüche
listado de reivindicaciones
請求一覧表

Translations appear in the following order: Chinese, French, German, Spanish/Latin American Spanish, and Japanese

LOL
大声地笑
ris tout haut
laut lachen
me desternillo
大きな声で笑う

London Bullion Market
伦敦黄金市场
marché londonien de l'or et de l'argent
Londoner Goldmarkt
London Bullion Market (Mercado de oro de Londres)
ロンドン金市場

London Chamber of Commerce and Industry
伦敦工商会
chambre de commerce et d'industrie de Londres
Londoner Industrie- und Handelskammer
Cámara de Comercio de Londres
ロンドン商工会議所

London Clearing House
伦敦清算所
banque centrale de compensation de Londres
Londoner Clearingzentrale
Cámara de Comercio e Industria de Londres
ロンドン手形交換所

London Inter Bank Bid Rate
伦敦银行同业优惠利率
taux interbancaire demandé à Londres (LIBBID)
Zinssatz, zu dem die Londoner Großbanken bereit sind, Geldbankkredite am internationalen Interbankenmarkt aufzunehmen
tasa de demanda interbancaria de Londres (LIBID)
ロンドン銀行間取り手金利（ライビッド）

London Inter Bank Mean Rate
伦敦银行同业平均利率
moyenne entre le taux interbancaire offert et le taux demandé (LIMEAN)
Durchschnittssatz zwischen LIBID und LIBOR
tasa media interbancaria de Londres (LIMEAN)
ロンドン銀行間仲値金利

London Inter Bank Offered Rate
伦敦银行同业拆放利息(优惠利息),-伦敦银行同业拆息
taux interbancaire des eurobanques de Londres (taux LIBOR)

Londoner Interbanken-Angebotssatz
tasa de oferta interbancaria de Londres (LIBOR)
ロンドン銀行間出し手金利（ライボー）

London International Financial Futures and Options Exchange
伦敦国际金融期货交易所
Marché international de Londres des transactions et options sur contrat à terme (LIFFE)
Londoner Börse für Finanztermingeschäfte
Mercado de Futuros de Londres (LIFFE)
ロンドン国際金融先物オプション取引所

London Metal Exchange
伦敦金属交易所
Bourse londonienne des métaux non-ferreux (L.M.E.)
Londoner Metallbörse
Mercado de Metales de Londres (LME)
ロンドン金属取引所

long
多头; 超买
(position) longue
Hausse-
largo(-a)
強気筋

long-dated bond
长期债券
à longue échéance
langfristige Anleihe
a largo plazo
長期債権

longitudinal study
纵向研究
étude longitudinale
Längserhebung
estudio longitudinal
経年調査

long position
多头头寸
position longue
Hausseposition
posición larga
ロング・ポジション

long-service award
长期服务奖
récompense pour service de longue date
Dienstzeitvergütung
regalo por antigüedad en el puesto
勤続賞

long-service leave
长期服务带薪假期

congé payé pour employé de longue date
Sonderurlaub für langjährige Mitarbeiter
baja con sueldo para empleados con varios años de trabajo
長期勤続休暇

long-term
长期
à long terme
langfristig
largo plazo
長期

long-term bond
长期债券
titres ou obligations à long terme
langfristige Anleihe
obligaciones a largo plazo
長期手形

long-term debt
长期债务
dette à long terme
langfristige Verbindlichkeiten
deuda a largo plazo
長期負債、長期借入

long-term financing
长期资金筹措; 长期融资
financement à long terme
langfristige Finanzierung
financiación a largo plazo
長期融資

long-term lease
长期租赁
bail à long terme
langfristiger Mietvertrag
arrendamiento a largo plazo
長期リース，長期賃借契約

long-term liabilities
长期债务; 长期负债
dettes à long terme
langfristige Verbindlichkeiten
pasivo a largo plazo
長期負債

lookback option
回顾期权
option dont le prix est choisi par l'acheteur parmi tous les prix qui existaient pendant la vie de l'option
Option, deren Kurs der Käufer aus allen über den Bestand der Option hinweg existenten Preise auswählt
opción retrospectiva
ルックバック・オプション，オプションの有効期間中一番有利な価格で売買する権利のある

loss
亏损; 损失
perte

Translations appear in the following order: Chinese, French, German, Spanish/Latin American Spanish, and Japanese

Verlust
pérdida
損失

loss adjuster
损失清算人; 保险索赔调处人;
理赔理算人
expert en assurances
Schadensregulierer(in)
tasador(a) de pérdidas
損害評価人

loss assessor
估价员
évaluateur de sinistre
Schadensgutachter(in)
tasador de siniestros
損害評価人

lossmaker
亏损企业; 亏损产品; 亏损公司
entreprise en déficit chronique/
article vendu à perte
unrentables Produkt od. Projekt
productor(a) de pérdidas
赤字商品会社

lost time record
停工时期记录
consignation des temps morts
Fehlzeitenaufzeichnung
registro detallado del tiempo
improductivo
損失時間記録

lot[1]
固定数量 ，一手
quantité minimale d'une denrée
ou produit qui peut être achetée
sur une Bourse
Paket
lote
最小口

lot[2]
一批货 ，一组货品
article ou collection d'articles
offerts pour vente aux enchères
Los
lote
一組

lot[3]
成交单位
lot (groupe d'actions)
Los
lote
ロット

lot[4]
一块地
lot (terrain)
Grundstück
terreno
土地の一区画

lottery
抽彩票
tirage au sort

Lotterie
sorteo
抽選

lowball
向(买主)虚报低价
commencer bas (en citant des prix
bas au départ pour une
négociation de vente)
Käufer mit Niedrigpreisen
anlocken und diese anheben,
sobald ein Käufer Interesse zeigt
comenzar ofreciendo un precio
bajo para subirlo cuando aparece
un comprador
ローボール(値の吊り上げ)

lower level domain
低级域; 基層網址
domaine de bas niveau
Lower-Level-Domain
dominio de bajo nivel
ローワーレベルドメイン

lower of cost or market
成本和市场价孰低法则
le plus bas: soit le coût initial, soit
le prix de marché actuel (L.C.M)
Niederstwert
método del precio de mercado
低価主義

low-hanging fruit[1]
垂手可得且易逝的赢利机会;
易中目标用户; 挂在低处的果实
fruit facile à cueillir
leichter Fang
clientes a punto de caramelo
マーケティングの対象にな
り易い人

low-hanging fruit[2]
低果先摘
fruit facile à cueillir
leichter Fang
objetivo a punto de caramelo
入手し易いもの

low start mortgage
低开抵押贷款
emprunt hypothécaire à faibles
remboursements initiaux
langsam anlaufende Hypothek
hipoteca en la que durante los
primeros años sólo se paga el
interés
ロースタート(初期低額支払)
モーゲージ

loyalty bonus
忠诚股
prime de fidélité
Treueprämie
bonificación por fidelidad
(英)ロイヤリティ・ボーナス

loyalty scheme
老顾客优惠计划; 忠诚度营销计划

programme visant à conserver la
loyauté de la clientèle
Loyalitätsprogramm
plan de fidelización
ロイヤルティー(固定客)制度

lump sum[1]
整笔，一次总付的钱
montant forfaitaire
Pauschal-
tanto alzado; precio global
総括金額

lump sum[2]
一次总付的钱，总额
règlement global (de capital)
Pauschale
tanto alzado; precio global
一時金

lurk
匿名访问
rôder
leuern
estar de mirón
ラーク(潜伏する)

luxury tax
奢侈品税
impôt sur les produits de luxe
Luxussteuer
impuesto de lujo
奢侈品税

M1
基本货币供应量的量度
M1: définition la plus étroite de la
quantité d'argent présente dans
l'économie britannique, y compris
les billets et pièces en circulation
publique et dépôts à vue en
sterling détenus dans le secteur
privé
Geldvolumen M1
agregado monetario
狭義のマネーサプライ,
民間非金融部門の保有する
現金通貨に
対象金融機関の要求払預
金を加えたもの

Ma and Pa shop
家庭生意; 夫妻店
boutique familiale
Tante-Emma-Laden
pequeño negocio familiar
地元の小規模小売店

machine code
机器代码; 電腦碼
code machine
Maschinencode
código máquina
マシン・コード

machine hour rate
机器小时比率
taux de ventilation du coût horaire

de machine
Maschinenstundensatz
coeficiente máquina hora
機械時間率

macho management
硬性管理
gestion macho
Macho-Management
estilo de gestión a lo macho
マッチョ(権威主義的)管理

macroeconomics
宏观经济学; 总体经济学
macroéconomie
Makroökonomie
macroeconomía
マクロ経済学、巨視的経済学

macroeconomy
宏观经济体制
macroéconomie
Makroökonomie
macroeconomía
マクロ経済, 巨視的経済

macrohedge
宏观套头 整体套期
macro-arbitrage
Makro-Sicherungsgeschäft
macrocerca
マクロ·ヘッジ

Macromedia Flash™
Macromedia动画
Macromedia Flash™
Macromedia Flash™
Macromedia Flash™
マクロミディア·フラッシュ

mail form
邮件表格
formulaire de mail électronique
Mail-Formular
formulario por correo electrónico
メール·フォーム,
(ウエッブサイト上の)記入欄

mailing house
促销邮件公司
organisation spécialisée en
publipostage
Postwerbungszentrale
empresa de mailings
ダイレクトメール業者

mailing list
直接促销邮件名单
liste d'adresses
Adressenliste
lista de direcciones
メーリング·リスト

mail order
邮递订物; 邮购订单; 邮购
achat ou vente par
correspondance
Versandhandel

compra por correo
通信販売

mail-out
邮寄活动; 使用直接邮寄广告
envoi extérieur par mail
Sendung
mailing
ダイレクトメールを送付する

mail server
邮件服务器
serveur e-mail
Mailserver
servidor de correo
メールサーバー

mailshot
推销信; 直接促销或籌款邮件
publipostage
Postwurfsendung
mailing
メールショット

mailsort
促销邮件分编服务
service de tri postal
Postsortierdienst
servicio de correo directo ofrecido
por el Correo británico
メールソート

mainframe
主机; 大型机
gros ordinateur
Hauptrechner
ordenador central
computador central
メインフレーム

mainstream corporation tax
公司总税
impôt sur les sociétés intégré
ehemals
Körperschaftsabschlusszahlung
impuesto societario total
主要法人税

maintenance
维护; 维修
maintenance
Wartung
mantenimiento
メンテナンス

maintenance bond
维持债券
obligation de maintenance
Leistungsgarantie
garantía de mantenimiento
(請負工事の)瑕疵保証(証書),
メンテナンス·ボンド

majority shareholder
控股股东
actionnaire majoritaire
Mehrheitsaktionär(in)
accionista mayoritario
多数株主

make-to-order
按订单生产; 度身訂造
fabriquer sur commande
in Auftragsfertigung herstellen
producción bajo pedido
注文生产

**Malcolm Baldrige National
Quality Award**
马尔科姆。拜尔格瑞国家质量奖
Prix national Malcolm Baldrige de
la qualité: prix accordé aux
entreprises américaines en
reconnaissance de leur réussite en
ce qui concerne la qualité et les
performances commerciales
amerikanische Auszeichnung für
Qualität
premio estadounidense a la
calidad Malcolm Baldrige
マルカム·ボールドリッジ全国
品質賞

managed currency fund
管理通货基金
fonds de placement en devises
dirigé
gesteuerter Währungsfonds
fondo de moneda controlada
マネージド·カレンシー·
ボンド, 管理通貨基金

managed economy
管理经济; 计划经济
économie dirigée
Planwirtschaft
economía dirigidao
管理经济

managed float
管理浮动
flottement dirigé
schmutziges Floaten
flotación dirigida
管理フロート,
マネージド·フロート

managed fund
管理基金
société d'investissement dirigée
Investmentfonds mit
auswechselbarem
Wertpapierbestand
fondo administrado
マネージド·ファンド

managed hosting
代管
options d'infogérance pour hôte
informatique
verwaltete Wirtsfunktion
alojamiento or hospedaje
gestionado
ホスティング·オプション

managed rate
管理利率
taux dirigé

Translations appear in the following order: Chinese, French, German, Spanish/Latin American Spanish, and Japanese

verwalteter Zinssatz
tipo de interés controlado; tipo de interés regulado
管理利率

management
管理
gestion; management
Management
gestión; administración
マネジメント

management accountant
管理会计 师
comptable gestionnaire
betriebliche/r Rechnungsprüfer(in)
contable de gestión
管理会計士

management accounting
管理 会计
comptabilité de gestion
entscheidungsorientiertes Rechnungswesen
contabilidad de gestión
管理会計

management buy-in
买下管理权
achat d'une entreprise par un cadre ou un groupe de gestion extérieur
Management-Buy-in
adquisición de una empresa por directivos de otra empresa
マネジメント・バイ・イン

management buy-out
高级管理人员买公司全部股票
rachat d'une entreprise par sa direction ou ses cadres
Management-Buy-out
adquisición de una empresa por sus directivos
マネジメント・バイ・アウト

management by exception
例外管理法; 按例外原则管理
gestion par exception
Management im Ausnahmefall
dirección por excepción
例外管理

management by objectives
目标管理
gestion par objectifs
zielorientiertes/ergebnisorientiertes Management
gestión por objetivos
目的管理

management by walking around
走动式管理
gestion par consultation auprès des employés
Management durch Kontakt mit den Arbeitnehmern

dirección por paseo; dirección conociendo de cerca los procesos
歩き回り管理

management company
管理公司
société de gestion
auswärtiges Unternehmen
compañía administradora or de gestión
管理会社

management consultancy[1]
管理咨询
conseil en gestion d'entreprise
Unternehmensberatung
asesoría de gestión de empresas
経営コンサルタント業

management consultancy[2]
管理咨询公司
cabinet de conseil
Unternehmensberatung
asesoría de gestión de empresas
経営コンサルタント業

management consultant
管理顾问; 管理咨询员
conseiller en gestion d'entreprise
Unternehmensberater(in)
asesor(a) en administración de empresas
経営コンサルタント

management control
管理控制, 经营控制
contrôle de gestion
Geschäftsführungskontrolle
control de gestión
経営管理

management control systems
管理控制系统
systèmes de contrôle de gestion
Management-Kontrollsysteme
sistemas de control de gestión
マネジメント・コントロール・システム

management development
管理發展
développement des cadres (ou de la direction)
Weiterbildung von Führungskräften
desarrollo del personal de gestión
管理開発

management education
管理教育
études d'administration
Ausbildung von Führungskräften
enseñanza de la gestión
管理教育

management guru
管理学家
gourou de la gestion
Betriebswirtschaftstheoretiker(in)

gurú de la gestión
管理理论家

management science
管理科学
science de la gestion
Management-Wissenschaft
ciencia administrativa
管理科学

management services
内部管理咨询服务
service de gestion
Managementdienste
servicios administrativos
経営指導

management standards
管理准则
normes de gestion
Managementrichtlinien
criterios de gestión
管理基準

management style
管理风格; 管理方式
style de management
Führungsstil
estilo de gestión
経営スタイル

management theorist
管理理论家
théoricien en gestion et management
Managementtheoretiker(in)
teórico(-a) de la gestión
経営理論家

management threshold
升迁瓶颈; 升迁極限
statut limite possible dans une entreprise
Managementschwelle
umbral de gestión
管理職しきい(到達限界)

management trainee
接受管理培训的初级管理人员
cadre stagiaire
Managementtrainee
aprendiz de gestión
管理研修生

management training
管理培训
formation des cadres
Management-Schulung
formación administrativa
管理トレーニング

manager
经理; 主管
directeur/gérant; cadre ou dirigeant
Manager(in)
director (a); gerente
マネジャー

Translations appear in the following order: Chinese, French, German, Spanish/Latin American Spanish, and Japanese

Managerial Grid™
管理网
Managerial Grid; grille de gestion
Verhaltensgitter
parrilla de gestión
マネジリアル・グリッド

managerialism
管理主义
directorialisme
Managerwirtschaft
énfasis excesivo en la gestión
管理統制第一主義

managing director
总经理; 管理董事; 常务董事
directeur général; P.D.G.
Geschäftsführer(in)
consejero(-a) delegado(-a),
director(a) gerente
専務常務取締役, 専務理事

mandarin
普通话; 有影響力的官員
euphémisme décrivant un
conseiller de haut rang ayant
beaucoup d'influence, utilisé en
particulier dans les cercles
gouvernementaux
hoher Funktionär
mandarín
マンダリン(シナの官吏)

mandatory quote period
强制报价阶段
période de cotation obligatoire
obligatorischer
Notierungszeitraum
período obligatorio de cotización
強制相場告知期間

manpower forecasting
劳动力预测
prévisions concernant la
main-d'œuvre
Prognostizierung od.
Vorausplanung des
Arbeitskräftebedarfs
predicción de la mano de obra
人的資源予測

manpower planning
劳动力规划
planification de la main-d'œuvre
Arbeitskräfteplanung
planificación de la mano de obra
人的資源計画

manual worker
体力劳动者
travailleur manuel
Arbeiter(in)
trabajador(a) manual
肉体労働者

manufacture
制造; 生产
fabriquer
Fertigung

manufactura
製造

manufacturer
生产商
fabricant
Hersteller(in)
fabricante
製造者, 製造元

manufacturer's agent
生产商代理人
agent du fabricant
Handelsvertreter(in)
representante del fabricante
製造業者代理商

manufacturing cost
生产成本
frais de fabrication
Fertigungskosten
coste de fabricación
costo de fabricación
工場原価製造費

manufacturing information system
生产信息系统
système d'information pour la
fabrication
Fertigungs-Informationssystem
sistema de información sobre la
fabricación
製造情報システム

manufacturing system
生产系统
système de fabrication
Fertigungssystem
sistema de fabricación
製造システム

manufacturing to order
按计货需求生产; 按订单生产
fabrication sur commande/selon
commande
Sonderanfertigung
fabricación bajo pedido
注文製造

MAPS
邮件误用保护系统
organisation principale de lutte
contre les message e-mail non
solicités
führende britische Organisation
gegen unerwünschte Werbung
über E-Mail und gegen Spam
organización que lucha contra el
correo electrónico basura
MAPS(スパムメール防止
キャンペーン会社)

Marché des Options Négotiables de Paris
期货交易市场
Marché des Options Négotiables
de Paris (MONEP)

Markt für handelbare Optionen
Marché des Options Négotiables
de Paris (MONEP)
(仏)オプション取引市場

Marché International de France
法国国际期货交易
Marché International de France
internationaler
Termingeschäftemarkt in
Frankreich
Marché International de France;
MATIF
フランス国際先物オプション取
引所,フランス国際市場

margin¹
补贴; 津贴; 赚头; 盈利; 利润率;
余裕额; 利润; 成本与售价差额;
利差; 价差; 边际; 垫头; 边缘;
边界; 限度; 差数; 幅度
marge
Handelsspanne
margen
職能手当

margin²
奖金
marge
Prämie
complemento salarial
職能手当

margin account
保证金账户
compte de marge
Einschusskonto
cuenta de adelantos
証拠金取引口座, 証拠金勘定,
マージン・アカウント

marginal analysis
边际分析
analyse de marginalité
Marginalanalyse
análisis marginal
限界分析

marginal cost
边际成本
coût marginal
Grenzkosten
coste marginal
costo marginal
限界原価、限界費用

marginal costing
边际成本计算 , 边际成本法
évaluation des coûts marginale
Grenzkostenrechnung
cálculo de costes marginales
cálculo de costos marginales
限界原価計算

marginal costs and benefits
边际成本及受益
coûts et bénéfices marginaux

---

*Translations appear in the following order: Chinese, French, German, Spanish/Latin American
Spanish, and Japanese*

Grenzkosten und -nutzen
costes y beneficios marginales
costos y beneficios marginales
限界費用便益

marginalisation
排斥; 淘汰
marginalisation
Marginalisierung
marginalización
限界化(国が工業化やインター
ネット経済に乗り遅れること)

marginal lender
边际贷款人
prêteur sur marge minimale
Grenzanbieter(in) v. Kapital
prestamista marginal
限界貸し手

marginal private cost
边际私人成本
coût marginal pour l'individu
private Grenzkosten
coste privado marginal
costo privado marginal
私的限界費用

marginal revenue
边际收入
revenu marginal
Grenzeinnahmen
ingreso marginal
限界収入

marginal tax rate
边际税率
taux d'imposition marginal
Lohnsteuer nach Abzug der
Spesen
tipo impositivo marginal
限界税率

margining
边际, 限度规则
système selon lequel la chambre
de compensation de Londres
(L.C.H.) contrôle le risque associé
au Marché International de
Londres des transactions et
options à terme
System des Londoner
Clearingzentrales zur täglichen
Risikokontrolle bei den Positionen
der Mitglieder von LIFFE
constitución de márgenes
委託証拠金システム

margin of error
差错限度; 误差边际
marge d'erreur
Fehlerspanne
margen de error
誤差

margin of safety
安全边际
marge de sécurité

Sicherheitsspanne
margen de seguridad
MS比率, 安全余裕率

margin of safety ratio
marge du coefficient de sécurité
Sicherheitskennziffer;
Sicherheitskoeffizient
coeficiente de margen de
seguridad
安全率

mark-down
降价
baisse du prix de vente
Preisabschlag
rebaja
定価引き下げ

marked cheque
保兑支票
chèque visé
bestätigter Scheck
cheque certificado; cheque
marcado
記号承認小切手

marked price
标价
prix fixé/coté/prix (d'actions)
estampillé
ausgezeichneter Preis
precio marcado
表示価格

market¹
市场; 集市; 销路; 需求
marché
Markt
mercado
市場

market²
市场
marché
Börse
mercado
市場

market³
市场
marché
Preis
mercado
市場

marketable
有销路的; 可出售的; 畅销的
commercialisable
marktgängig
comercializable
市場性のある

market analysis
市场分析
analyse de marchés
Marktanalyse
análisis de mercado
市場分析

market area
市场区
zone/région de marché
Marktgebiet
zona comercial
市場エリア

market based pricing
市场定价
fixation de prix basée sur le marché
marktbezogene Preissenkung
fijación de precios del valor
percibido
市場基準価格決定

market bubble
市场泡沫
bulle du marché boursier (qui peut
éclater à tout moment)
Markt-Seifenblase
burbuja bursátil
市場バブル

market coverage
市场覆盖面
couverture de marché
Abdeckung des Marktes
cobertura de mercado
市場カバー率

market development
市场开发; 市场发展
développement des marchés
Marktentwicklung
desarrollo de mercado
市場開拓

market driven
市场驱动
(organisation) dirigée par le
marché
marktorientiert
que se deja llevar por el mercado
市場率先型

market economy
市场经济
économie de marché
Marktwirtschaft
economía de mercado
市場経済

marketeer
小商家
mercateur: petite entreprise qui est
concurrente dans le même marché
que des compagnies plus
importantes
Anbieter(in)
pequeña empresa en competencia
con empresas más grandes
市場商人

marketer
市场开拓人员; 市场营销人员
commercialisant/mercateur
Marketing-Spezialist(in)

Translations appear in the following order: Chinese, French, German, Spanish/Latin American Spanish, and Japanese

responsable de marketing
マーケティング担当者

marketface
市场对话
interface du marché
Schnittstelle zwischen Anbietern
und Kunden
interacción entre consumidores y
proveedores
市場でのインターフェース

market-facing enterprise
面对市场的企业
entreprise alignée sur son marché
et sa clientèle
marktorientiertes Unternehmen
empresa volcada al mercado y sus
clientes
市場直面企業

market-focused organisation
市场导向型组织
organisation dirigée par les
exigences de marché
marktbezogene Organisation
organización dependiente de los
movimientos del mercado
市場中心の企業

market fragmentation
市场断层; 细分市场
fragmentation de marché
Marktzersplitterung
fragmentación del mercado
市場破砕化

market gap
市场缺口; 市场短缺
créneau
Marktlücke
hueco en el mercado
市場ギャップ

market if touched
指定价格交易
vendre si prix spécifié atteint
Auftrag, ein Wertpapier beim
Erreichen eines bestimmten Kurses
zu kaufen oder zu verkaufen
orden de compra venta cuando se
alcanza el precio solicitado
条件付成り行き注文, MIT注文

marketing audit
营销审计
audit marketing
Marketing-Audit
auditoría de marketing
マーケティング監査

marketing consultancy
营销咨询公司
cabinet-conseil en marketing
Marketing-Beratungsdienst
consultoría de marketing
マーケティング・コンサルタン
ト事務所

marketing cost
市场营销成本
coût du marketing
Absatzkosten
gastos de marketing
販売費

**marketing information
system**
市场营销信息系统
système d'informations marketing
Marketing-Informationssystem
sistema de información de
marketing
マーケティング情報システム

marketing management
营销管理
gestion du marketing
Marketing-Management
gestión del marketing
マーケティング管理

marketing manager
营销经理
directeur du marketing
Marketing-Manager(in)
director(a) de marketing
マーケティング・マネジャー

marketing mix
营销组合
marketing mix
Marketing-Mix
marketing mix
マーケティング・ミックス

marketing myopia
行销近视
myopie de marketing
kurzsichtige Marketingpolitik
miopía en el marketing
近視眼的マーケティング

marketing plan
销售计划
plan de marketing
Marketingplan
plan de marketing
マーケティング・プラン

marketing planning
市场计划; 营销计划
planification marketing
Marketingplanung
planificación del marketing
マーケティング・プラン

market intelligence
市场情报
information sur les marchés
Marktinformationen
información sobre el mercado
市場知識

market logic
市场逻辑
logique du marché
Marktlogik

lógica del mercado
市場論理

market maker[1]
证券经纪人
teneur de marché
Market Maker
creador(a) de mercados
マーケット・メーカー,
市場開拓者, 市場形成者

market maker[2]
交易指令
faiseur de marché
Market Maker
creador(a) de mercados
マーケット・メーカー,
自己責任で顧客の
証券注文に応じる業者

market order
交易指令
ordre de marché
Bestens-Auftrag
orden al mercado
成り行き注文, 市場取引注文

market penetration
市场渗透; 市场侵入
pénétration de marché
Marktdurchdringung
penetración en el mercado
市場浸透

market penetration pricing
市场渗透定价
fixation de prix pour pénétration
de marché; pénétration de marché
Preispolitik zur Förderung der
Marktdurchdringung
fijación de precios de penetración
en el mercado
市場浸透価格決定

market position
市场地位
position sur le marché
Marktstellung
posición en el mercado
市場位置

market potential
市场潜力
potentiel sur le marché
Marktpotenzial
potencial del mercado
市場潜在性

market power
市场势力; 市场支配力
puissance du marché
Marktmacht
poder de mercado
市場力

market price
市场销售价格; 市场价格
prix du marché/cours (de la Bourse)
Marktpreis

---

*Translations appear in the following order: Chinese, French, German, Spanish/Latin American
Spanish, and Japanese*

precio de mercado
市場価格

market research
市場研究
étude de marché
Marktforschung
investigación de mercado
市場調査

market risk
市場风险
risque du marché
Marktrisiko
riesgo de mercado
市場変動リスク

market risk premium
市場风险报酬
prime de risque du marché
Marktrisikoprämie
prima por riesgo de mercado
市場リスクプレミアム

market sector
细分市场
secteur de marché
Marktsektor
sector del mercado
市場セクター

market segment
市场分割
segment de marché
Marktsegment
sector de mercado
市場区分

market sentiment
市场气氛
humeur des marchés financiers
Börsenstimmung
psicología del mercado
市場心理

market share
市场份额; 市场占有率
part de marché
Marktanteil
cuota de mercado
市場占有率

market site
市场网址
site multiservice
Markt-Seite
centro comercial electrónico
(ウエブサイト上の)電子市場,
ショッピングモール

market size
市场规模
volume du marché
Marktumfang
tamaño del mercado
市場規模

market structure
市场结构
structure de marché

Marktstruktur
estructura del mercado
市場構造

market targeting
确定营销目标
ciblage de marché
gerichtete Vermarktung
selección de sectores de
mercado
マーケット・ターゲット

market valuation[1]
市场价值
valeur de portefeuille aux prix du
marché
Wert eines Wertpapierbestandes
zu Marktkursen
valor de una cartera a precios de
mercado
市場価値

market valuation[2]
市场估价
évaluation de la valeur marchande
d'une terre ou propriété
Schätzung
valoración/tasación de mercado
市場評価額

market value
时价; 市场价值
valeur marchande
Verkehrswert
valor de mercado
市場価値

market value added
市场附加值
valeur marchande ajoutée
Wertschöpfung zu Marktpreisen
valor de mercado añadido
市場付加値

marking down
削价，降价
inscription en baisse
Kursabwertung
reajuste a la baja
下口銭定価引き下げ

mark-up
加在成本价上的金额，成本加利
marge (bénéficiaire)
Preisaufschlag
margen comercial; beneficio del
producto o servicio; aumentar
マークアップ, 利益

Marxism
马克思主义
marxisme
Marxismus
marxismo
マルクシズム、マルクス主義

marzipan
杏仁蛋白奶糖; 次層行政人員
désigne quelqu'un qui appartient

au niveau de direction juste
en-dessous de l'équipe de haute
direction
Begriff für Mitglieder der
Geschäftsleitung direkt unter der
Unternehmensspitze
de mandos intermedios
トップの次の管理者層

massaging
弄虚作假; 篡改; 作假帐
manipulation (des chiffres)
Frisieren; Manipulieren
maquillaje
(俗)マッサージする会計操作

mass customisation
批量产品个性化
fabrication de série adaptée sur
mesure
anwenderspezifische Anpassung
eines Massenartikels
personalización en masa
マス・カスタマイズ商品

mass market
大众市场; 批量市场
marché grand public
Massenmarkt
mercado de masas
大衆市場

mass medium
大众传播媒介; 大众媒介
véhicule de masse
Massenmedium
medio de comunicación de masas
マスメディア

mass meeting
群众大会
grand meeting: réunion de la
plupart, si ce n'est de tous les
membres d'un syndicat afin
d'arriver à une décision sur une
politique concernant les salariés
Vollversammlung
reunión de todos los sindicalistas
大衆集会

mass production
批量生产; 大量生产
fabrication en série
Massenproduktion;
Massenfertigung
fabricación en serie
大量生産

master budget
总预算
budget prévisionnel principal
Gesamtetat; Hauptbudget
presupuesto maestro; presupuesto
original; presupuesto principal
総合予算

master franchise
特许经营区域授权
特许经营区域授权

franchise maîtresse
Hauptfranchise
franquicia principal
マスター・フランチャイズ

master limited partnership
总合伙有限公司
société en commandite maîtresse
Personengesellschaft
sociedad limitada principal
マスター・リミテッド・パート
ナーシップ, MLP

master production scheduling
总作业计划
programmation de production maîtresse
Hauptfertigungsplanung;
Erstellung der Hauptfertigungsliste od. des Hauptfertigungsfahrplans
programa de producción
生産主計画ルーチン

masthead
刊头
zone-titre (sur page Web)
Masttop
cabecera
(マストヘッド)ウェブページの
トップ部

matador bond
外国债券(西班牙)
obligation de matador (obligation étrangère sur le marché intérieur espagnol)
Matador-Anleihe
bono matador
スペインの外国債

matched bargain
回购交易
transaction alignée
Wertpapierpensionsgeschäft
casación
マッチド・バーゲン

material cost
原材料成本
coût de matériau
Materialkosten
coste de materiales
costo de materiales
原材料費

material facts[1]
重要事实
information devant être divulguée dans un prospectus
materielle Tatsache
hechos pertinentes
要綱重要事実

material facts[2]
重要事实
faits essentiels
wesentliche rechtserhebliche

Tatsache
hechos pertinentes
保険必須情報

material news
重要新闻
informations essentielles
materielle Neuigkeiten
noticias pertinentes
重要ニュース

material requirements planning (MRP I)
物料需求计划
planifications des exigences de matérielles
Materialbedarfsplanung
planificación para disponer del nivel necesario de materiales
材料要求計画

materials handling
物质搬运; 材料搬运
manutention des matériaux
betriebsinterner Materialtransport;
Transport- und Lagerwesen
movimiento y almacenamiento de materiales
材料管理

materials management
物质管理; 材料管理
gestion des matériaux
Materialwirtschaft; Steuerung des Materialdurchflusses
gestión de materiales
原材料管理
マテリアル・マネジメント

materials requisition
材料需求
requête de matériaux/ de fournitures
Entnahmeauftrag;
Materialanforderung
solicitud u orden de entrega; pedido
材料出庫請求

materials returned note
材料回收簿
bon de retour des matériaux en magasin
Materialrückgabeschein
registro de los materiales devueltos
原料返還票

materials testing
材料测试
essai de matériaux
Materialprüfung
prueba de materiales
材料テスト

materials transfer note
材料转移记录
bordereau de transfert de matériaux

Materialübergabeschein
registro de traspaso de materiales
材料移動票

maternity leave
产假
congé de maternité
Mutterschaftsurlaub
baja por maternidad
出産休暇

maternity pay
产假工资
allocation de maternité (payée par l'employeur); congé de maternité
Mutterschaftsgeld
paga por maternidad
産休手当て

matrix
矩阵
matrice
Matrix
matriz
マトリックス

matrix management
矩阵式管理
gestion matricielle
Matrixmanagement
gestión por matrices
マトリックス管理

matrix organisation
矩阵结构组织
organisation matricielle
Matrixorganisation
organización matriz
マトリックス組織

matrix structure
矩阵结构
structure matricielle
Matrixstruktur
estructura matricial
マトリックス構造

mature economy
成熟经济
économie en pleine maturité
reife Volkswirtschaft
economía madura
成熟経済

maturity
到期日
échéance
Fälligkeit; Fristigkeit; Laufzeit;
Verfalltag
madurez
満期, 償還期間

maturity date
期货到期日
date d'échéance
Einlösungsfrist; Verfallstag;
Fälligkeitsdatum
fecha de vencimiento
満期(日), 期日、最終期日

Translations appear in the following order: Chinese, French, German, Spanish/Latin American Spanish, and Japanese

maximax criterion
最大化原则
critère maximax
Maximax-Kriterium;
Maximax-Regel
criterio máximo de optimismo
(asunción de riesgos)
マキシマックス規準

maximin criterion
最大最小化原则
critère maximini
Maximin-Kriterium;
Maximin-Regel
criterio pesimista e incierto
(aversión al riesgo)
マキシミニ規準

maximum stock level
最高持股水平
niveau de stock maximum
Höchstbestand
nivel máximo de existencias
最高手持ちレベル

MBA
工商管理硕士
abbréviation de Master of Business
Administration, l'équivalent d'une
maîtrise de gestion
betriebswirtschaftlicher Abschluss
MBA
経営管理修士号

MBIA
市政债券保险协会
MBIA: Municipal Bonds Insurance
Association ou association
américaine des assurances qui
assurent des bons du Trésor
municipaux de taux élevé
Versicherungverband, der
hochprozentige od.
hochverzinsliche
Kommunalanleihen versichert
grupo de empresas que aseguran
bonos municipales
地方债保険連合

McKinsey 7-S framework
麦克肯森7S框架
structure des 7-S de McKinsey
pour identifier et exploiter des
ressources humaines
7-S Rahmenbedingungen von
McKinsey
modelo McKinsey de
aprovechamiento de los recursos
humanos
マッケンジー7-Sフレームワーク

m-commerce
移动电子商业; 移动商务
m-commerce
mobiler Handel
comercio por teléfono móvil
comercio por teléfono celular
Mコマース

mean
平均值
moyenne
arithmetisches Mittel
media; promedio
期待值

mean reversion
平均逆转趋势
réversion vers la moyenne
mittlere Umkehrung
reversión a la media
平均回帰

measurement error
测量误差
erreur de mesure
Messfehler
error de medición
測定エラー

mechanical handling
机械处理
manutention mécanique
Einsatz mechanischer Fördermittel;
mechanische Förderung
manipulación mecánica
機械資材管理

medallion
微处理锌片
médaillon
Medaillon
micromódulo
(スマートカード搭載マイクロ
プロセッサー・ チップ)
メダリオン

media independent
独立媒体机构
organisation publicitaire
indépendante
medienübergreifende
Werbeagentur
agencia de compra y venta de
publicidad
独立系メディア事務所

median
中值
médiane
Median
mediana
メジアン

media plan
媒体计划
plan médiatique
Medienplanung
plan de medios publicitarios
メディア・プラン

media planner
媒介策划人
responsable du planning
médiatique de la publicité
Medien-Manager
planificador(a) de publicidad
メディア・ プランナー

media schedule
媒介日程表
programme médiatique de la
publicité
Mediaplan
programa de publicidad
メディア・ スケジュール

mediation
调解; 调停
médiation
Vermittlung; Schlichtung
mediación
仲裁

Medicare[1]
国家医疗照顾制
programme américain d'assurance
maladie avec soin gratuit pour les
personnes de plus de 65 ans
amerikanischer Gesundheitsdienst
für Rentner(in)nen
seguro médico para ancianos
老齢者医療保険制度, メディケア

Medicare[2]
医疗保险
système d'assistance médicale
publique
öffentliche Krankenversicherung
seguridad social australiana
国民健康保険

medium of exchange
交换媒介
moyen d'échange
Tauschmittel
instrumento de cambio
交换手段, 流通貨幣

medium-sized business
中型企业
entreprise de taille moyenne
mittleres Unternehmenm;
mittelgroßes Unternehmen
empresa mediana
中規模企業

medium-term bond
中期债券
obligation à moyen terme
mittelfristige Anleihe
bono a plazo medio
中期債

meeting
会议; 会
réunion
Treffen; Tagung; Sitzung;
Zusammenkunft; Versammlung
reunión
会合

megacity
特大城市
méga-cité

Translations appear in the following order: Chinese, French, German, Spanish/Latin American Spanish, and Japanese

Megastadt
megalópolis
メガシティー(巨大都市)

megacorporation
巨型企业
mégacorporation
Mega-Unternehmen;
Unternehmensriese
superempresa
超大型企業

megatrend
大趋势
méga-tendance: modification
générale de la façon de voir les
choses ou de les aborder, qui
affecte les pays et les industries,
ainsi que les organisations. Le
terme anglais 'megatrend' a été
popularisé par John Naisbett dans
son best-seller *Megatrends*.
Megatrend
gran tendencia
メガトレンド

MEGO
这事太没劲了
interjection anglophone souvent
sarcastique pour indiquer qu'on
est ébloui par la complexité de ce
que quelqu'un vient de dire
häufig sarkastischer Ausruf des
Erstaunens über die Komplexität
des gerade von jemandem
Geäußerten
pero ¡qué dices!
想像を絶する

meltdown
暴跌
pertes substantielles sur les
marchés boursiers
Meltdown am Markt
momento en que se producen
pérdidas importantes en Bolsa
メルトダウン(大暴落)

member bank
会员银行
banque membre
Bank, die Mitglied des
amerikanischen Federal Reserve
System ist
banco miembro
米連邦準備制度加盟銀行

member firm
会员公司
firme d'agents de change membre
de la Bourse de Londres
Börsenmitglied
agencia de Bolsa afiliada
取引所の会員会社

member of a company
公司成员
sociétaire

Aktionär(in)
asociado
会社役員メンバー

**members' voluntary
liquidation**
成员自愿清偿
liquidation volontaire par les
sociétaires
freiwillige Auflösung einer
Gesellschaft
liquidación voluntaria
任意破産

memo
备忘录
note de service; mémo
Memo
memorándum
メモランダム

memorandum of association
公司设立章程，公司组织大纲
acte de constitution d'une
société
Gründungsurkunde;
Gründungsvertrag;
Gründungsurkunde einer AG;
Satzung; Statut;
Gründungsurkunde
escritura de constitución de una
sociedad
基本約款

memory
内存; 记忆体; 存储体
mémoire
Speicher;
Erinnerungsvermögen
memoria
メモリー

mentoring
指导
système de 'parrainage' au sein
d'une entreprise par lequel un
membre du personnel
expérimenté, ou mentor, offre ses
conseils, encouragements, etc, à
un nouveau, ou relativement
nouveau membre du personnel
Begleitung am Arbeitsplatz durch
erfahrenere Kolleginnen und
Kollegen
sistema por el cual un trabajador
con experiencia aconseja a un
principiante
公的メンター

mercantile
商业的; 商人的
mercantile
kaufmännisch
mercantil
商業の、重商主義の

mercantile agency
商业代理人
agence commerciale
Handelsagentur
agencia mercantil
商業興信所, 信用調査機関

mercantilism
重商主义
mercantilisme: doctrine
économique développée entre les
années 1650 et 1750, selon
laquelle la prospérité d'un pays
dépend de la puissance de son
commerce extérieur
Merkantilismus
mercantilismo
重商主義

merchandising[1]
销售策划; (零售)销售
merchandising
Verkaufsförderung
merchandising
商品活動,

merchandising[2]
宣传
merchandising
Merchandising
merchandising
販売促進

merchant account
商业帐户
compte d'affaires
Händlerkonto
cuenta empresarial
マーチャント・アカウント

merchant bank[1]
商业银行
banque d'affaires
Handelsbank; Merchantbank
banco comercial
商業銀行,
マーチャント・バンク,
電子商人取引銀行

merchant bank[2]
商人(业)银行
banque d'affaires
Merchant Bank
banco de inversiones
商業銀行, マーチャント・バンク

merger
合并; 兼并; 融合
fusion
Firmenzusammenschluss; Fusion
fusión
合併

mergers and acquistions
并购
fusions et acquisitions
Fusionen und Übernahmen

Translations appear in the following order: Chinese, French, German, Spanish/Latin American Spanish, and Japanese

fusiones y adquisiciones
企业合并·买收

merit rating
功绩等级评定
système de paiement
méritocratique
Leistungsbeurteilung
valoración de méritos
人事考查

metadata
元数据; Meta数据
méta-données
Metadaten
metadatos
メタデータ

meta-tag
其中标签
méta-tag
Metatag
metamarcador
メタ-タッグ

Metcalfe's law
麦特卡非法规
Loi de Metcalfe
Metcalfesche Gesetz
principio según el cual las redes
aumentan drásticamente en valor
con cada usuario adicional que se
incorpora
メトカーフの法則

methods-time measurement
方法时间测量
mesure cadences-méthodes
MTM-Verfahren; MTM3-Verfahren
método de medición de tiempos
方法時間測定

method study
方法研究
étude de méthodologie
Arbeitsablaufstudie; Arbeitsstudie;
Betriebsstudie;
Arbeitsmethodenstudie
estudio de métodos
方法研究

Mickey Mouse
米老鼠
enfantin ou sans valeur
lächerlich einfach
supersencillo
ミッキーマウス
(単純過ぎて馬鹿げてつまらな
い)

microbusiness
微型企业
micro-entreprise
Kleinstunternehmen
microempresa
極小ビジネス

microcash
微型电子货币
micro-argent

Mikro-Cash
microdinero
(1，10円という)小さ
な価格単位, マイクロキャッシュ

microeconomic incentive
个体经济税收优惠
remise fiscale microéconomique
mikroökonomischer Anreiz
incentivo microeconómico
微视经济的措置,
ミクロ経済的インセンティブ

microeconomics
微观经济
science microéconomique
Mikroökonomik
microeconomía
ミクロ経済学、微視的経済学

microeconomy
微观经济体系
microéconomie
Mikroökonomie
microeconomía
ミクロ経済、微視的経済

microhedge
微观套期; 个别套期
micro-arbitrage
Mikro-Sicherungsgeschäft
microcerca
ミクロヘッジ

micromanagement[1]
微观式管理，微管理
microgestion
Mikro-Management
microgestion
微視的管理学

micromanagement[2]
微观式管理，微管理
microgestion
Mikro-Management
microgestion
微視的管理法

micromarketing
微观营销学
micro-marketing
Mikro-Marketing
micromarketing
マイクロ·マーケティング

micromerchant
网上商家
microcommerçant
Mikro-Händler(in)
empresa en Internet que opera con
dinero electrónico
(インターネット上で小単位の
財· サービスを提供する)
小額商品業者,
マイクロマーチャント

micropayment
微额付款; 小额电子付款协议;
小额网络付款

micropaiement
Mikrozahlung
micropago
小額取引

middleman
中介; 中间人
intermédiaire ou revendeur
Vermittler(in)
intermediario
仲介人

middle management
中层领导
cadres moyens
mittlere Leitungsebene; mittleres
Management
mandos intermedios
中間管理職

middle price
中间价格
cours moyen
Einheitskurs
precio medio
中値

mid-range
中间值，平均数
moyenne des valeurs les plus
grandes et les plus petites dans un
échantillon statistique
Spannweitenmitte
centro de la amplitud; mitad del
rango
最大, 最小値の平均値

migrate
转换; 转移; 移植; 迁移
migrer
abwandern
migrar
転送

millennium bug
千年虫
bug du millénaire
Jahr-2000-Problem
efecto 2000
Y2Kバグ(2000年問題)

millionerd
高科技富豪
techno-ringard millionnaire
jemand, der durch die Arbeit in
einem Unternehmen der
Hochtechnologie zum Millionär
oder zur Millionärin geworden ist
millonario(-a) del sector de la alta
tecnología
ハイテクビジネスの億万長者

MIME
多用途的网际邮件扩充协议
MIME: extension de courrier
Internet pour usages multiples
Methode zum Anhängen von
binären Dateien an E-Mails

Translations appear in the following order: Chinese, French, German, Spanish/Latin American Spanish, and Japanese

protocolo MIME
MIME(多目的インターネット
メールエクステンション)

Mind Map™
心智图
outil pour trier les idées
Mind Map
herramienta para la representación
gráfica de ideas
マインド・マップ(思考地図)

mindshare
心理认同
un processus visant à augmenter le
nombre d'attitudes favorables
envers un produit ou une
organisation
ein Produkt zum Allgemeingut
aufwerten
mejora de la imagen
マインドシェア

minimax regret criterion
最小最大遗憾原则
critère de regret minimax
Minimax-Regel zu den
Alternativkosten;
Minimax-Entscheidungsfunktion
zu den Alternativkosten
criterio de decisión incierto que
mide al máximo el valor de
oportunidad
ミニマックス後悔規準

minimum lending rate
最低贷款利率
taux d'emprunt minimum
Mindestzins; Diskontsatz einer
Zentralbank
tipo de descuento
イングランド銀行の最低貸出金利,
MLR

minimum quote size
最小开盘规模
volume de cotation minimum
Mindestnotierungsgröße
cotización mínima
最小相场规模

minimum salary
最低工资
salaire minimum
Mindestgehalt
salario mínimo
最低賃金

minimum stock level
最低持股水平
niveau de stock minimum
Mindestbestand
nivel mínimo de existencias
最低手持ちレベル

minimum subscription
最低认购
souscription minimale

Mindestzeichnung
subscripción mínima
株式最小应募額

minimum wage
最低工资
salaire minimum
(garantierter) Mindestlohn
salario mínimo
最低賃金

minority interest
少数股东权益
intérêt minoritaire
Minderheitsbeteiligung;
Fremdbeteiligung
participación minoritaria
少株主持分

minority ownership
少数拥有权; 少数股所有权
détention minoritaire de propriété
Minderheitsbesitz
propiedad minoritaria
少数所有権

minutes
会议记录
procès-verbal (d'une réunion)
Protokoll; Niederschrift
actas
議事録

mirror
镜子网址; 镜象
miroir
Spiegelseite
espejo
ミラーサイト

MIS
管理信息系统
système de gestion des
informations
Management-Informationssystem
sistema de gestión de la
información
管理情報システム

mismanagement
管理失误; 管理失当
mauvaise gestion
Misswirtschaft; Missmanagement
mala gestión
ミスマネージメント欠陥経営

missing value
遗漏值，漏测值
valeur manquante
fehlender Wert
valor ausente
不明値

mission statement
宗旨说明
déclaration de mission
Grundsatzerklärung eines
Unternehmens; Auftragsbericht

declaración de objetivos
ミッション声明文

Mittelstand
密特尔斯坦公司
Mittelstand: terme allemand
signifiant entreprise de taille
moyenne et qui signifie également
petites et moyennes entreprises
Mittelstand
PYME
中小企业

mixed economy
混合经济
économie mixte
Mischwirtschaft;
gemischtwirtschaftliches System
economía mixta
混合经济

mobile office
流动办公室; 移动办公
bureau mobile
tragbares Büro
oficina móvil
移動事務所

mobile worker
流动工作人员
employé mobile: salarié d'une
entreprise sans base fixe qui
voyage beaucoup ou qui fait du
télétravail
mobile/r Arbeiter(in)
trabajador(a) itinerante
移動労働者

mode
众数
mode
Modus, dichtester Wert
modo
並数最頻数

model building
建立模型, 建模
élaboration de modèle
Modellbildung
construcción de modelos
モデル設定(経)

modem
调制解调器
modem
Modem
módem
モデム

moderator
斑竹，版主
modérateur
Moderator
moderador(a)
モデレーター

modernisation
现代化
modernisation
Modernisierung; Rationalisierung

modernización
近代化

modified ACRS
修改后的加速成本回收制度
système utilisé aux Etats-Unis pour calculer la dépréciation de certaines valeurs acquises après 1985 de façon à réduire les impôts
flexible Vollkostenrechnung
método de cálculo de la depreciación de activos comprados después de 1985
修正加速度償却制度,
修正加速度原価回収制度

modified cash basis
改进的收付实现值
base de caisse modifiée
modifizierte Einnahmen-Ausgaben-Rechnung
método de acumulación para activos a largo plazo
修正現金主義

moment of conception
初具规模; 初步成形
moment de la conception
Gründungsmoment
momento de la concepción
概念化の瞬間

Monday-morning quarterback
星期一早晨的四分卫，马后炮
quelqu'un qui critique une décision uniquement quand il est trop tard pour la changer
jemand, der eine Entscheidung erst dann kritisiert, wenn sich nichts mehr daran ändern lässt
persona que critica cuando ya es demasiado tarde para hacer algo
他人のしたことをあと知識で批判する人

Mondex
英国银行界研制开发的一种智能卡型电子现金系统
Mondex: système d'argent électronique qui utilise une carte à puce pour le shopping traditionnel et les transactions de e-commerce
Mondex: elektronisches Bargeldsystem
sistema de pago Mondex
モンデックス

Mondragon co-operative
曼曳根合作社
coopérative de Mondragon
Mondragon-Kooperative
movimiento cooperativo de Mondragón
モンドラゴン共同組合

monetarism
货币主义; 货币主义者
monétarisme
Monetarismus
monetarismo
マネタリズム、通貨主義

monetary
货币的; 与货币有关的
monétaire
geldlich; monetär; Geld-; Währungs-; Münz-
monetario(-a)
金銭上の, 金融の、通貨の

monetary assets
货币资产
actifs monétaires
Geldvermögen
activos monetarios
通貨資産

monetary base
货币基础
base monétaire
Geldbasis; monetäre Basis
base monetaria
貨幣的ベース、マネタリー・ベース

monetary base control
货币基础控制
contrôle de base monétaire
Steuerung der Geldbasis
control de la base monetaria
ベース・マネー管理、ハイパワード・マネー管理

monetary policy
货币政策
politique monétaire
Geld- und Kreditpolitik; Währungspolitik
política monetaria
金融政策、通貨政策

monetary reserve
货币储备
réserve monétaire
Währungsreserven
reserva monetaria
通貨準備, 外貨準備

monetary system
货币系统
système monétaire
Währungssystem; Geld- und Währungsordnung
sistema monetario
通貨制度、貨幣制度

monetary unit
货币单位
unité monétaire
Währungseinheit
unidad monetaria
通貨単位、貨幣単位

monetise
规定法定币值
monétiser
monetisieren; zum gesetzlichen Zahlungsmittel machen
monetizar
貨幣化する、貨幣と定める

money
货币
monnaie
Geld; Münze
dinero
貨幣、交換の仲介物

money at call and short notice[1]
短期通知放款，短期内可收回的贷款
argent remboursable sur demande et à court terme
kurzfristiges Geld
dinero a la vista y con poca antelación
コールローン

money at call and short notice[2]
临时与短期资金余额
argent remboursable sur demande et à court terme: soldes sur un compte, soit disponibles sur demande, soit dans les 14 jours (à court terme)
kurzfristiges Geld
dinero a la vista y con poca antelación
コールマネー

money broker
借贷经纪人
intermédiaire ou courtier de change
Geldmakler(in)
cambista
マネー・ブローカー

moneyer
铸币者
monnayeur
Münzer(in)
persona autorizada para acuñar dinero
(英の)貨幣鋳造者

money illusion
货币幻觉
illusion monétaire
Geldillusion; Geldschleier
ilusión monetaria
貨幣錯覚、マネー・イリュージョン

money laundering
洗(黑)钱
blanchiment d'argent
Geldwäsche; Geldwäscherei

Translations appear in the following order: Chinese, French, German, Spanish/Latin American Spanish, and Japanese

lavado de dinero
資金洗浄

moneylender
放款人; 放债人
bailleur de fonds
Geldverleiher(in); Geldgeber(in)
prestamista
金貸し業者、金融業者

money market
货币市场
marché financier ou monétaire
Geldmarkt; Markt für kurzfristige
Gelder
mercado monetario o de dinero
金融市場

money market account
货币市场帐户
compte sur marché monétaire
Geldmarkteinlage
cuenta del mercado monetario
金融市場勘定

money market fund
货币市场基金
société d'investissement sur le
marché monétaire (en titres de
créance)
Geldmarkt-Investmentfonds
fondo de inversión en activos del
mercado monetario
短期金融資産投資信託,
マネー・マーケット・ファンド

money market instruments
货币市场票据
instruments financiers sur marché
monétaire (actifs et titres à court
terme)
Geldmarktinstrumente
instrumentos del mercado
monetario
金融市場証書

money national income
国民收入货币总值
revenu national monétaire
effektives Volkseinkommen
ingreso monetario nacional
貨幣国民所得

money of account
计帐货币
monnaie de compte
Buchgeld; Giralgeld
moneda de una cuenta
(通貨として発行されない)
計算貨幣

money order
汇票
mandat-poste
indossierbare Anweisung
orden de pago
為替、送金為替、郵便為替

**money purchase pension
scheme**
退休金享受权购买计划
plan de retraite avec rente viagère
constituée à titre onéreux
auf eingezahlten Beiträgen
basierender Pensionsplan
plan de pensiones según
cotizaciones
保険料建て年金制度

money-purchase plan
现金购买退休金计划
plan de prévoyance de retraite
auf eingezahlten Beiträgen
basierender Pensionsplan
plan de pensiones con
contribuciones de empleado y
empresa
(米)保険料建て制度

money substitute
货币代用品
substitut monétaire
Geldersatzstoff
sustituto monetario
貨幣代替物

money supply
货币供给; 货币供应量
masse monétaire
Geldmenge; Geldvolumen;
Geldversorgung der Wirtschaft
oferta monetaria
マネー・サプライ、貨幣供給量

money wages
货币工资
salaire monétaire
Barlohn
salarios monetarios
貨幣賃金、名目賃金

**Monopolies and Mergers
Commission**
垄断与合并委员会
Commission d'enquête sur les
monopoles et la concurrence, au
Royaume Uni (M.M.C.)
Kartellaufsicht
Comisión de Monopolios y
Fusiones (MMC)
独占合併委員会

monopoly
垄断; 独占; 专卖; 专利
monopole
Monopol
monopolio
専売独占

Monte Carlo method
蒙逖卡洛法
méthode Monte Carlo
Monte-Carlo-Methode
método de Montecarlo
モンテ・カルロ法

moonlighting
兼职
travail au noir
Schwarzarbeit; Nebentätigkeit;
Doppelverdienen
pluriempleo
副業

Moore's law
摩尔法则
Loi de Moore
Mooresche Gesetz
principio según el cual cada 18
meses la densidad de los chips se
dobla sin que se incremente el
precio
モアーの法則

moral hazard
道德危险
risque moral
subjektives Risiko; Risiko
unehrlichen od. fahrlässigen
Verhaltens
riesgo moral
倫理の欠如

moratorium
延期偿付
moratorium ou moratoire
Moratorium
moratoria
支払い猶予

more bang for your buck
高收益率
tirer le maximum de profit de son
investissement
mehr Spaß fürs Geld
mejor rendimiento
より良い投資利益率

mortgage[1]
抵押
emprunt immobilier
Hypothek
hipoteca
不動産ローン

mortgage[2]
抵押
hypothèque
Pfandbeleihung
hipoteca
不動産担保付ローン

mortgage-backed security
抵押担保证券
titre garanti sur hypothèque
hypothekarisch gesichertes
Wertpapier
valor con respaldo hipotecario
モーゲージ(担保)証券

mortgage bond
抵押债券
obligation hypothécaire
hypothekarisch gesicherte

Schuldverschreibung
cédula hipotecaria
抵当付き債権

mortgage broker
抵押经纪商
courtier en prêts hypothécaires
Vermittlungshaus zw.
Hypothekarkreditnehmern u.
Hypothekarkreditgebern
corredor(a) hipotecario(-a)
モーゲージ・ブローカー,
不動産ローン(の借り手と貸
し手の)仲介業者

mortgagee
受入人; 承受抵押者; 押入者
créancier hypothécaire
Hypothekengläubiger(in);
Pfandgläubiger(in)
acreedor(a) hipotecario(-a)
抵当権者、抵当債権者

mortgage equity analysis
抵押资产分析
analyse de fonds propres sur
hypothèque
Hypothekskapitalanalyse
análisis de los rendimientos de las
hipotecas
モーゲージ・エクイティ分析,
借入金・自己資本収益還元分析

mortgage insurance
抵押保险
assurance hypothécaire
Hypothekentilgungsversicherung
seguro hipotecario
抵当保険

mortgage lien
抵押留置权
droit de rétention sur hypothèque
Grundpfandrecht
privilegio hipotecario
モーゲージ・リーエン,
担保付留置権

mortgage note
抵押票据
documentation hypothécaire
hypothekarisch gesicherter
Schuldschein od. Solawechsel
pagaré hipotecario
抵当約束手形、モーゲージ付手形

mortgage pool
抵押组合
pool hypothécaire
Hypotheksgruppe
agrupación de hipotecas
モーゲージ・プール,
不動産担保貸付債券
(を仲介業者が当初融資者から買
い取った)集合物

mortgage portfolio
抵押资产

portefeuille d'hypothèques
Hypothekenportefeuille
cartera hipotecaria
モーゲージ・ポートフォリオ
(不動産ローンを提供する銀行-
が保有する)

mortgage rate
抵押利率
taux d'emprunt hypothécaire
Hypothenkenzins
tasa hipotecaria
モーゲージ金利、住宅ローン金利

mortgage tax
抵押税
impôt sur les hypothèques
Hypothekensteuer
impuesto hipotecario
モーゲージ課税

mortgagor
抵押者; 押出者
débiteur hypothécaire
Hypothekenschuldner(in);
Pfandschuldner(in)
deudor(a) hipotecario(-a)
抵当権設定者

Mosaic
Mosaic 浏览程序
premier logiciel de navigation sur
le Web pour Macintosh et
Windows
erster Web-Browser für Macintosh
und Windows. Entwickelt durch
den Gründer von Netscape, Marc
Andreesen.
Mosaic
モザイック(ウェブブラウザー)

most distant futures contract
最远期货合同
contrat sur transaction au plus
long terme
Option mit dem spätesten
Erfüllungsdatum
contrato de futuros lejanos
最長期先物取引

motion study
动作研究
étude des cadences
Bewegungsstudie;
Bewegungsanalyse
estudio de tiempo y movimiento
動作研究分析

motivate
争取; 提议
motiver
versuchen etwas durchzubringen
defender, argumentar a favor de
申し立て

motivation¹
激励; 动机; 书面提议
motivation

Motivation
motivación
動議書, 動機

motivation²
动机
motivation
schriftlicher Vorschlag
propuesta formal por escrito
見積書

MOTOS
异性成员
membre du sexe opposé
Mitglied des anderen Geschlechts
persona del otro sexo
異性メンバー

MOTSS
同性成员
membre du même sexe
Mitglied des gleichen Geschlechts
persona del mismo sexo
同性メンバー

mouse milk
得不偿失
faire un travail demandant des
efforts disproportionnés pour un
projet qui donne peu de bénéfices
einen unverhältnismäßig hohen
Arbeitsaufwand für ein Projekt
einsetzen, das relativ wenig Ertrag
bringt
trabajar muchísimo para obtener
muy poco a cambio
報われない骨折れ仕事

mouse potato
鼠标迷; 痴迷于计算机的人
accro de la souris
Sofahocker(in)
persona que está colgada del
ordenador
マウスいじりで一日を費やす人

mover and shaker
领袖人物
rocker d'entreprise
bewegende Kraft
persona que mueve los hilos
影響力の大きい人

move time
搬运时间
temps de déplacement (d'un
produit)
Transportzeit
tiempo de maniobra; tiempo de
ciclo
製品移動時間

MRP II
制造资源计划系统
système informatique de
fabrication, planification et
contrôle d'inventaire
Fertigungsmittelplanung

Translations appear in the following order: Chinese, French, German, Spanish/Latin American Spanish, and Japanese

sistema de planificación de los
recursos para la fabricación
製造資源計画 II

multi-channel
多渠道发展
à canaux multiples
ein Mehrkanalsystem nutzen
multicanal
マルチチャネル

multicurrency
多元通货; 多种货币
multidevise
Möglichkeit eines Ausgleichs v.
Kontensalden in verschiedenen
Währungen
multidivisa
マルチカレンシー, 多通貨選択

multi-employer bargaining
多雇主讨价
négociations salariales du patronat
Tarifverhandlungen mit mehreren
Arbeitgebern
negociación colectiva
多数雇主交渉

multifunctional card
多功能卡
carte multifonctions
Mehrzweck-Karte
tarjeta multiusos
多機能カード

multimedia
多媒体
multimédia
Multimedien; multimedial
multimedia
マルチミディア

multimedia document
多媒体文件
document multimédia
Multimediendokument
documento multimedia
マルチメディア・ドキュメント

multinational business
跨国商务; 跨国公司; 多国公司
multinationale
multinationales Unternehmen
multinacional
多国籍企業

multiparty auction
网上多方拍卖
vente aux enchères à participants
multiples (sur Internet)
Mehrteilnehmer-Auktion
subasta electrónica
マルチパーティー・オークション

multiple application
多重申请
souscription multiple
Mehrfachzeichnung
especulación con nuevas

emisiones de acciones
多数株式申込み

multiple exchange rate
双重汇率
taux de change multiple
multipler Wechselkurs
tipos de cambio múltiples
複数為替レート

multiple sourcing
多方进货
approvisionnement à source
multiple
Einkauf bei mehreren Zulieferern;
Bezug aus mehrfachen Quellen
adquisición de varios proveedores
マルチプル・ソーシング

multiple time series
多重时间系列
séries chronologiques multiples
mehrstufige Zeitreihen
serie cronológica múltiple; serie
temporal múltiple
複数時系列

multiskilling
多技能培训
formation pluridisciplinaire
Mehrfachqualifizierung;
Multi-Skilling
polivalencia
マルチスキル

multitasking
多任务(处理)化
traitement multitâches
Multitasking
multitarea
複式作業制

multivariate analysis
多变量分析
analyse à plusieurs variables
Multivariatenanalyse
análisis multivariable
多重変数分析

multivariate data
多元数据
données à plusieurs variables
multivariate Daten
datos multivariantes; datos
multivariables
多変数データ

mum and dad investors
家庭投资者
personnes qui souhaitent investir
dans des titres et valeurs mais qui
ont peu d'expérience du marché
financier
Unerfahrene Kleinanleger
inversores novatos
素人投資家

municipal bond
地方政府债券, 市政债券
obligation municipale
Kommunalobligation
obligación municipal
地方債

mushroom job
无趣的工作
boulot à mycose
unerfreuliche oder leidige Aufgabe
trabajo desagradable
不快な仕事

mutual
互助组织
mutuelle
Versicherungsverein auf
Gegenseitigkeit
mutua
相互

mutual company
互助公司
mutuelle
Versicherungsverein auf
Gegenseitigkeit
sociedad mutua; mutua
相互会社

mutual insurance
互助保险
mutuelle d'assurances
Versicherung auf Gegenseitigkeit
seguro mutuo
相互保険

mutual savings bank
互助储蓄银行
caisse mutuelle d'épargne
gemeinnützige Sparkasse;
genossenschaftsähnliche
Sparkasse
banco mutualista de ahorro
相互貯蓄銀行, 相互預金銀行

Myers-Briggs type indicator
梅尔-布利格斯指标
indice de Myers-Briggs
Myers-Briggs-Index
indicador de comportamiento tipo
Myers-Briggs
マイヤーズ-ブリッグス・
タイプ指標

mystery shopping
秘访采购
shopping en incognito: utilisation
d'employés ou agents qui visitent
un; magasin ou utilisent un service
'en incognito' dans le but d'en
évaluer les qualités
anonymer Einkauf
compra de un producto o
utilización de un servicio de
manera anónima para comprobar
su calidad
客になりすまして店やサー
ビスの質を調査

Translations appear in the following order: Chinese, French, German, Spanish/Latin American
Spanish, and Japanese

naked option
无担保期权
option sans garantie
Nacktoption
opción descubierta
ネイキッドオプション,
裸のオプション

naked writer
无股交易者
vendeur d'options à découvert
ungedeckte(r) Verkäufer(in) einer
Option
vendedor(a) al descubierto
ネイキッド・ライター
(株を所有していない売り手)

name
劳埃德投资人，劳氏公司成员
nom: un particulier qui est
membre de Lloyd's de Londres
Mitglied von Lloyd's of London
nombre
ロイズのメンバー

Napsterise
(3 观 念)
napstériser: distribuer
gratuitement quelque chose qui
est la propriété de quelqu'un
d'autre. Le terme vient du modèle
commercial pair-à-pair dont
Napster fut le pionnier, soit un
progiciel de distribution de copies
de pièces musicales sous
copyrights
wenn einem gesetzlich untersagt
wird, Dinge zu verschenken, die
das Eigentum Dritter sind
distribuir grauitamente y sin
permiso algo que pertenece a otra
persona
ナップスター社の提供する共有サ
ービス,
ピアツーピアネットワークモデル

narrowcasting
窄播
câblodistribution (à un public
choisi)
Konzentration auf ein schmales
Nischensegment des Publikums
envío de información a una
audiencia selecta
ナローキャスティング

narrow market
不活跃市场
marché étroit
enger od. begrenzter Markt
mercado estrecho; mercado poco
activo
閑散な市場

NASDAQ
全国证券交易商自动化报价协会
indice des valeurs du marché hors
cote
automatisiertes
Kursnotierungssystem der
Vereinigung der
US-Wertpapierhändler(in)nen
NASDAQ
ナスダック, 全米証券業協会・
店頭銘柄気配自動通報システム

NASDAQ Composite Index
全国证券交易商自动报价协会综
合指数
indice groupé NASDAQ
Anzeige der Geld- und Briefkurse
für über 5000 Aktien in den USA
über ein zentrales
Computersystem
índice NASDAQ
ナスダック総合株価指数

**National Association of
Investors Corporation**
投资者俱乐部全国协会
Association Nationale des Clubs
d'Investissement (USA)
Organisation, die
Investment-Clubs fördert
Asociación Nacional de
Comisionados de Seguros
全国投资家协会

**National Association of
Securities Dealers**
全国证券交易商协会
N.A.S.D.: abbréviation pour
Association nationale des courtiers
en titres et valeurs
Vereinigung der
US-Wertpapierhändler(in)nen
NASD (Asociación Nacional de
Operadores de Bolsa)
全米证券业协会

national bank¹
国有银行
banque nationale (contrôlée par
l'état)
Nationalbank; amerikanische Bank
mit Bundeszulassung
banco nacional
国立银行

national bank²
国民银行
banque fédérale (Etats-Unis)
von der amerikanischen
Bundesregierung zugelassene
Bank, die Mitglied des Federal
Reserve System sein muss
banco nacional
国法银行, 連邦政府認可を受けた
商業銀行, 国立银行

national debt
国债; 公债
dette publique; dette nationale
Staatsschuld; Verschuldung des
Bundes; Staatsverschuldung
deuda nacional
中央政府債務残高, 国债, 政府债,
国家債務

national demand
国民需求
demande publique
Gesamtnachfrage
demanda nacional
国民需要

National Guarantee Fund
国家保证基金
caisse de garantie nationale
nationaler Investitionsschutzfonds
fondo de garantía de la bolsa
australiana
国民保证基金

national income
国民收入
revenu national
Volkseinkommen
renta nacional
国民所得, NI

national income accounts
国民收入帐
comptabilité du revenu national
(statistiques économiques)
volkswirtschaftliche
Gesamtrechnung
renta nacional
国民所得勘定

**National Insurance
contribution**
国民保险分担额
contributions de sécurité sociale
Sozialversicherungsbeitrag
cotización a la seguridad social
国民保険料

nationalisation
国有化
nationalisation
Verstaatlichung; Nationalisierung;
Vergesellschaftung
nacionalización
国营化

National Market System
全国市场体系
système des marchés financiers
nationaux (Etats-Unis)
amerikanisches Marktsystem zur
Förderung der Zusammenarbeit
zwischen den inländischen Börsen
Sistema Nacional de Mercado
(NMS)
全国市场制度

---

*Translations appear in the following order: Chinese, French, German, Spanish/Latin American
Spanish, and Japanese*

National Occupational Health and Safety Commission
国家职业卫生安全委员会
service national de l'inspection du travail et sanitaire
Berufgenossenschaft
comisión australiana responsable de la higiene y la seguridad en el trabajo
全国労働安全衛生委員会

National Savings
国民储备
épargne nationale au Royaume Uni
britische Regierungsstelle, untersteht dem Schatzamt und bietet direkt oder über die Post eine Reihe von Sparprodukten an
caja de ahorros estatal británica
国民貯蓄機関

National Savings Bank
国民储备银行
caisse d'épargne nationale au Royaume Uni
Postsparkasse
Corporación Bancaria del Estado (NSB)
国民貯蓄銀行

National Savings Certificate
国民储备券
bon d'épargne britannique (N.S.C.)
Volkssparzertifikat
Certificado de ahorro nacional (NSC)
国民貯蓄証書

National Vocational Qualification
国家职业证书
qualification professionnelle nationale ou NVQ: qualification britannique accordée suite à une formation professionnelle basée sur des normes nationales développées par des organismes leader des secteurs industriels et commerciaux
britische nationale Berufsqualifikation
título de formación profesional
全国職業資格

national wage agreement
国家工资协定
accord salarial national
Tarifvertrag
convenio salarial a nivel nacional
全国賃金協定

natural capitalism
自然資本主義
capitalisme naturel
Naturkapitalismus

capitalismo natural
自然資本主義

navigate
浏览; 漫遊
naviguer
navigieren
navegar
ナビゲート

nearby futures contract
近期期货合同
contrat sur transactions au plus proche terme
Terminkontrakt mit der kürzesten Fälligkeitsfrist
contrato de futuros próximos
期近先物

nearby month
近期月份
mois le plus proche
frühester Monat, für den es einen Terminkontrakt für eine bestimmte Ware gibt
mes más próximo
期近物

near money
准货币
quasi-monnaie
leicht liquidierbare Einlagen; geldähnliche Forderungen
cuasidinero
(直ぐに現金化できる資産)ニアマネー、準貨幣、近似通貨

negative amortisation
负分期偿还
amortissement négatif
negative Amortisation
amortización negativa
逆の割賦償還,
ネガティブ・アモーティゼーション, 未収利息による元本の増価

negative carry
负持有; 负融资性投资
port d'intérêt négatif
Netto-Bestandshaltekosten
traslado negativo
逆金利, 逆鞘

negative cash-flow
现金流出
trésorerie négative: rentrée de liquidités inférieures aux sorties
Einnahmenunterdeckung
flujo de caja negativo
マイナス資金繰り

negative equity
负资产
moins-valeur
negativer Marktwert
valor líquido negativo
マイナスのエクイティ,
担保物権時価下落等で負債額が
担保評価額を上回る状況

negative gearing
负债投资股市
ratio d'endettement négatif
negativer Verschuldungsgrad
apalancamiento negativo
ネガティブ・ギアリング

negative income tax
负所得税
impôt négatif
negative Einkommensteuer
impuesto sobre la renta negativo
負の所得税、逆所得税

negative pledge clause
反面保证条款; 禁止质押条款
clause de non sollicitation: clause de promesse de ne pas solliciter de nouveaux prêts qui privilégieraient les nouveaux créanciers
Nichtbesicherungsklausel
cláusula de pignoración negativa
ネガティブ担保化否定条項,
担保提供制限条項, プレッジ条項

negative yield curve
负收益率曲线
hiérarchie inversée des taux
negative Zinsstrukturkurve
curva de rendimiento negativo
ネガティブ・イールド・カーブ

negligence
玩忽职守; 疏忽; 过失
négligence
Fahrlässigkeit
negligencia
過失

negotiable certificate of deposit
可转让定期存款证;
可转让定期存单
negotiable certificate of deposit
begebbares od. übertragbares Einlagenzertifikat
certificado de depósito negociable
譲渡可能定期預金証書;(米の)
譲渡可能(定期)預金証書,
譲渡性預金

negotiable instrument
可流通票据，可转让票据
instrument négociable
begebbarer Titel; umlauffähiges Wertpapier; übertragbares Handelspapier
instrumento negociable
流通証券

negotiable order of withdrawal
可转让提款单
ordre de retrait négociable
NOW-Konto; übertragbare Zahlungsanweisung

Translations appear in the following order: Chinese, French, German, Spanish/Latin American Spanish, and Japanese

cuenta a la vista con interés
譲渡可能払戻指図書,
NOW勘定

negotiable security
可转让证券; 可流通证券
titre négociable
begebbares od. übertragbares
Wertpapier
título negociable
有価証券

negotiate
议付，转让，贴现
négocier
übertragen
negociar
裏書流通

negotiated budget
协议预算
budget négocié
ausgehandeltes Budget;
ausgehandelter Etat
presupuesto negociado
相対予算

negotiated commissions
商议佣金
commissions négociées
ausgehandelte Provisionen
comisiones negociadas
相対コミション

negotiated market
议价市场
marché négocié
ausgehandelter Markt
mercado de negociación
顧客市場、場外市場

negotiated offering
出售证券协议
offre publique négociée
ausgehandelte Emission
oferta ngociada
協議募集、競争入札でなく幹事が
発行会社との協議で
募集条件を決める方式

negotiated sale
议价销售
vente publique négociée
ausgehandelte Emission
venta negociada
協議発行

negotiation
谈判; 协商
négociation
Verhandlung
negociación
交渉

nest egg
存款
pécule

Notgroschen
ahorrillos
ネスト・エッグ

nester
传统型顾客; 保守型顾客
en pub ou marketing, un
consommateur aux habitudes
ancrées, qui ne se laisse pas
influencer
in der Werbung oder im
Marketing, Verbraucher, der sich
nicht von Werbung beeinflussen
lässt und preiswerte und
traditionelle Produkte bevorzugt
consumidor(a) que mira la calidad
relación-precio
広告宣伝に影響されにくい消
費者

net advantage of refunding
再投资净收益
bénéfice net de remboursement
Refinanzierungsbonus
valor neto de los ahorros de una
consolidación
債務借り換えによる正味利益

net advantage to leasing
租赁净利益收益
bénéfice net à bail
die Summe, um die ein
Leasinggeschäft günstiger ist als
die Darlehensaufnahme zum
Erwerb der gleichen Sache
valor neto de un acuerdo de
arrendamiento financiero
リーシング正味利益

net advantage to merging
合并净利益收益
bénéfice net à fusion
die Summe, um die der Wert
eines fusionierten Unternehmens
den Wert der früheren
eigenständigen Unternehmen
übersteigt, abzüglich der
Fusionskosten
valor neto descontado los gastos
de fusión
合併の正味利益

net assets
净资产
actif net
Nettovermögen
activo neto
正味財産, 純財産, 純資産

net asset value
净资产值
valeur liquidative
Inventarwert; Liquidationswert;
Nettovermögenswert
valor (de) activo neto
純資産価額、正味資産額

NetBill
网络帐单
Net-effet ou Net-Bill: système de
micropaiement sur Internet
NetBill: Zahlungssystem für den
Kauf digitaler Güter im Internet
sistema de micropagos NetBill
ネットビル

net book value
帐面净值减记
valeur comptable nette
Nettobuchwert; Restbuchwert
valor activo neto; valor neto en
libros
正味帳簿価格

net capital
净资本额
capital net
Nettokapital
capital neto
正味資本, 純資本

net cash balance
净现款结存
solde de caisse net
Netto-Kasse; Nettosaldo;
Reinüberschuss
balance en efectivo neto
ネットキャッシュ残高,
純キャッシュ残高

NetCheque
网上支票
Net-chèque
NetCheque: Warenzeichen für
elektronisches
Scheck-Zahlungssystem
sistema NetCheque de pago con
cheques electrónicos
ネット・チェック

net current assets
流动资产净额
actif de roulement net
Nettoumlaufvermögen;
Liquiditätsüberschuss
activo neto circulante
正味流動資産, 運転資本

net dividend
净股息
dividende net
Reindividende
dividendo neto
正味配当

net domestic product
国内净产值
produit intérieur net
Nettoinlandsprodukt
producto interior neto
国内純生産

net errors and omissions
净错漏
erreurs et omissions nettes

Translations appear in the following order: Chinese, French, German, Spanish/Latin American Spanish, and Japanese

Nettorestposten der
Zahlungsbilanz
errores y omisiones netos
純誤差脱漏項目

net fixed assets
固定资产净额
valeurs immobilisées nettes
Nettoanlagevermögen
activo fijo neto
純固定資産, 正味固定資産

net foreign factor income
净海外收入
facteur de bénéfice étranger net
Summe, um die das
Bruttosozialprodukt eines Landes
sein Bruttoinlandsprodukt
übersteigt
ingreso neto de los factores
extranjeros
純海外要素所得

nethead
网络迷
quelqu'un qui est obsédé par
Internet
Internetbesessener
pirado(-a) por Internet
ネットヘッド

Net imperative
网络时代
impératif Internet
Net-Imperativ
imperativo de la Red
ネット・インパラティブ
（インターネットビジネスが必
須とする考え）

net income¹
净收益
revenu net
Reingewinn
ingresos netos
純所得

net income²
税后收入
revenu brut après déduction
d'impôt
Nettogewinn
ingresos netos
税引き後の純利益

net income³
净收入
salaire ou paie après déduction
d'impôt ou autres déductions
statutaires
Nettoverdienst
ingresos netos
手取り所得

net interest
净利息
intérêt net
Nettozins

interés neto
純利息

netiquette
网络礼节
savoir-vivre sur Internet
Netikette
netiqueta
ネチケット

netizen
网民
utilisateur régulier d'Internet
jemand, der das Internet
regelmäßig nutzt
internauta
ネティズン（インター
ネットの常連）

net lease
净租赁
net à bail
Netto-Leasing
arrendamiento neto;
arrendamiento más gastos
諸経費賃借人負担型賃貸借

net liquid funds
净流动资金
fonds liquides nets
Nettofonds
disponibles líquidos netos
純流動資金

net margin
净利润; 净赚
marge nette
Reingewinn
margen neto
正味利益, 純益

net operating income
营业净收入
bénéfice d'exploitation net
Nettobetriebsgewinn; Reingewinn
vor Steuern
beneficios netos de explotación
正味営業利益

net operating margin
净经营利润
marge nette d'exploitation
Umsatzrendite
margen neto de explotación;
margen operativo neto
正味売上高営業利益率

net position
净头寸
position nette
Nettoposition
posición neta
差引建玉, 持ち高

net present value
净现值
valeur actuelle nette
Kapitalwert

valor actual neto
正味現在価値

net price
净价
prix net
Nettopreis
precio neto
正味価格

net proceeds
净收入
produit net (d'une transaction)
Nettoerlös
producto neto
純手取金、正味売上高、正味手取額

net profit
净利润; 利润净额
bénéfice net
Reingewinn
beneficio neto; ganancia neta
純利益、純益、当期利益

net profit ratio
销售净利率
rapport de bénéfice net
Verhältnis Reingewinn zu
Nettoerlös
coeficiente de beneficio neto
純益率

net realisable value
可变现净值
valeur nette réalisable
realisierbarer Verkaufserlös;
Netto-Realisationswert
valor realizable neto
正味実現可能価額、
正味実現可能価格

net residual value
净残余价值
valeur résiduelle nette
Nettorestwert
valor residual neto (VRN)
正味残存価値

net return
净收益
revenu net
Nettoertrag; Nettoverzinsung
rendimiento neto
純収益

net salvage value
净残值
valeur de sauvetage nette
Nettorestwert
valor de salvamento
neto
純転用価額

network¹
网络
établir des contacts
Netzwerk bauen
establecer contactos
ネットワーク

Translations appear in the following order: Chinese, French, German, Spanish/Latin American Spanish, and Japanese

network[2]
网络
réseau
Netzwerk
red
ネットワーク

network analysis
网络分析
technique de l'analyse par réseaux
Netzwerkanalyse
análisis de redes
ネットワーク分析

network culture
网络文化
culture des réseaux
Netzwerk-Kultur
cultura de la red
ネットワーク文化

network management
网络管理
gestion de réseaux
Netzverwaltung
gestión de redes
ネットワーク管理

network marketing
网络营销; 网状结构营销
marketing par réseau
Network-Marketing
marketing de red
ネットワーク・マーケィング

network organisation
网络组织
organisation en réseau
Organisationsnetz
organización en forma de red
ネットワーク組織

network revolution
网络革命
révolution des réseaux
Netzwerk-Revolution
revolución de la red
ネットワーク革命

network society
网络社会
société de réseaux
Netzwerk-Gesellschaft
sociedad de la red
ネットワーク社会

net worth
资本或资产净值
situation nette
Nettowert; Reinvermögen;
Eigenkapital
valor neto
純資産, 正味資産

net yield
净收益率
rendement net
Nettorendite

rendimiento neto
ネット利回り、税引き利回り

neural network
神经网络
réseau informatique de mimique
neurale
Neuronennetz
red neuronal
中性ネットワーク

neurolinguistic programming
神经语言学计划
programmation neurolinguistique
neurolinguistische
Programmierung
programación neurolingüística
神経言語学プログラム

newbie
因特网新用户
novice du Net
Internet-Neuling
novato(-a)
ネット新米

new economy
新经济体制
économie nouvelle: entreprises
dans le secteur du e-commerce
(électronique) et faisant partie de
l'économie numérique qui opèrent
souvent en ligne sur Internet plutôt
qu'à partir de locaux physiques
avec pignon sur rue
neuer Markt; neue Wirtschaft
nueva economía
ニュー・エコノミー、
インフレなき長期景気拡大

new entrants
市场新进入者
nouveaux venus
Neueinsteiger
recién llegados
新規参入

new issue[1]
新股发行
nouvelle émission: création et
distribution d'un nouveau titre, par
exemple un bon ou effet, une
obligation, ou une action
Neuemission
nueva emisión
新規発行

new issue[2]
新发行
nouvelle émission: émission de
droits de souscription ou émission
supplémentaire d'un titre ou d'une
valeur existante
Neuemission
nueva emisión
既存証券の追加発行

new issues market
新证券发行市场

marché des nouvelles émissions
Emissionsmarkt
mercado de emisiones
新株発行市場

**newly industrialised
economy**
近期工业化国家
pays nouvellement industrialisé
(PNI)
Schwellenland
economía de reciente
industrialización
新興工業国

new product development
新产品开发
développement de produit
nouveau
Produktentwicklung
desarrollo de nuevos productos
新製品開発

newsletter
新闻简报
bulletin (d'entreprise)
Mitteilungsblatt
hoja informativa
会報

newsreader
网上研讨程序
programme présentateur (de
messages pour forum de
discussion)
Nachrichtensprecher(in)
lector de noticias
ニュースリーダー

**New York Mercantile
Exchange**
纽约商品期货交易所
Marché à terme des produits
pétroliers, gaz divers et métaux
précieux de New York (NYMEX)
New Yorker Rohstoff- und
Warenterminbörse
Bolsa de Comercio de Nueva York
(NYMEX)
ニューヨーク商品取引所

New Zealand Stock Exchange
新西兰证券交易所
Bourse néo-zélandaise
Neuseeländische Börse
bolsa de Nueva Zelanda
ニュージーランド証券取引所

**New Zealand Trade
Development Board**
新西兰贸易发展局
conseil pour le développement
commercial néo-zélandais
Neuseeländische
Handelsentwicklungskammer
consejo neozelandés para el
fomento del comercio
ニュージーランド貿易振興公社

---

*Translations appear in the following order: Chinese, French, German, Spanish/Latin American
Spanish, and Japanese*

next futures contract
下月期货合同
contrat sur transactions à terme
futur (au mois suivant le mois le
plus proche)
Option für den nächsten Monat
contrato de futuros para el
próximo mes
ネクスト・フューチャー・
コントラクト, 準期近物

nice guys finish last
好人吃亏
axiome qui suggère, qu'en affaires,
il vaut mieux être égoïste
wer nett ist, hat das Nachsehen
los buenos siempre llegan los
últimos
己のことをまず考える

nice-to-haves
附加便利条件
petits bénéfs sympas
Elemente einer Stelle, wie etwa ein
Gratisparkplatz oder vergünstigte
Mahlzeiten, die man gerne hat, die
aber nicht absolut nötig sind
ventajas accesorias
付加給付

niche market
专门市场
marché créneau
Nischenmarkt
nicho de mercado
ニッチ・マーケット

niche player¹
特定投资银行家
acteur de secteur spécialisé
Nischenakteur
operador de nicho
特定分野担当バンカー

niche player²
特定行业经纪商
maison de courtage négociant
exclusivement les titres d'une seule
industrie
Nischenspieler(in)
operador de nicho
一分野ブローカー

nickel
五点浮动
cinq points de base
5 Basispunkte
cinco puntos base
5ベーシス・ポイント

nifty fifty
头50种最流行股票
sur Wall Street, les cinquante titres
les plus populaires parmi les
investisseurs professionnels
famose Fünfzig, die fünfzig bei
Kapitalsammelstellen beliebtesten
Werte an der New Yorker Börse

las 50 empresas principales de Wall
Street
機関投資家の間で最も人気の高
い50種の株式

night shift
夜班
poste de nuit
Nachtschicht
turno nocturno
夜勤

NIH syndrome
排外症状
syndrome du PII (Pas Inventé Ici)
ein Problem bei großen und
altmodischen Unternehmen, die
Ideen einfach aus dem Grunde
verwerfen, dass sie nicht aus dem
eigenen Stall kommen, da sie nicht
hier erfunden wurden
el síndrome de aceptar ideas
nuevas inventadas por otros
「部外のアイデア」だから受け
付けない症候群

Nikkei 225
日经225家平均指数
indice Nikkei 225
Nikkei-Index der 225 stärksten
Werte an der Börse von Tokio
índice Nikkei
日経25種平均

nil paid
零付款
nul payé
nichts bezahlt
pago nulo
無支払い

no-brainer
无须考虑的(俚语)
(une) sans-cervelle: une
transaction tellement favorable
qu'il ne faut aucune intelligence
(ou cervelle) pour se décider à la
faire (terme argotique)
idiotensicheres Geschäft
transacción tan favorable que no
se necesita tener inteligencia para
decidir si participar en ella o no
ノーブレイナー

node
网点; 节点
noeud
Knoten
nodo
ノード

noise
无用数据
données 'bruitage'
Verzerrung
ruido
有害情報

no-load fund
无负担基金
fonds de placement sans frais
d'acquisition
zuschlagfreier Investmentfonds;
veranschlagt keine
Abschlussgebühren
fondo de inversión que no cobra
comisión
ノーロード・ファンド

nominal account
名义帐户
compte de résultats
Erfolgskonto
cuenta nominal
名目勘定

nominal capital
名义资本
capital social
Nominalkapital; Grundkapital;
Stammkapital
capital nominal
名目資本, 公称资本

nominal cash-flow
名义现金流动
cash-flow nominal
nomineller Geldumlauf
flujo de caja nominal
名目キャッシュフロー

nominal exchange rate
名义汇率
taux de change nominal
Nominaler Wechselkurs
tipo de cambio nominal
名目為替レート

nominal interest rate
名义利率
taux d'intérêt nominal
Nominalzins
interés nominal
名目金利

nominal ledger
会计总帐
grand-livre général
Erfolgskonto; Hautbuch Aufwand
und Ertrag
libro mayor nominal
総勘定元帳

nominal price
虚价
prix fictif: prix d'un article étant
vendu quand la considération ne
reflète pas la valeur
Nominal-Notierung
precio nominal
名目価格

nominal value
面值
valeur nominale
Nennwert

Translations appear in the following order: Chinese, French, German, Spanish/Latin American Spanish, and Japanese

valor nominal
名目価値, 額面金額, 名目値

nominee holding
被委任人持股
actionnariat de personne désignée
anonymer Aktienbesitz;
Aktienbeteiligung eines
Strohmannes
tenedor nominativo de un título
cuyo dueño es otro; persona
interpuesta
受取名義人株

nominee name
被委任人
institution ou personne désignée
anonymer Aktienbesitz
depositario
受取名義人

nonacceptance
拒绝承兑，不承兑，不认付
non-acceptation
Nichtannahme
rechazo/falta de aceptación
引受拒絶

non-branded goods
非品牌产品
produits sans marque
(commerciale) spécifique
markenfreie Güter
productos sin marca
ノンブランド商品

nonbusiness days
非营业日，休假日
jours chômés
geschäftsfreie Tage
días inhábiles/no laborables
休日

nonconforming loan
不符合规定的贷款
prêt non conforme
nicht vertragsgemäßes Darlehen
préstamo no conforme
不良貸出, 不適合ローン

non-contributory pension scheme
非(分)摊缴(款)养老金计划
caisse de retraite sans versement
de la part des bénéficiaires
beitragsfreier Pensionsplan
régimen de pensiones no
contributivas
非分担年金制度

nondeductible
不可减免的; 非减免的
non déductible
nicht abzugsfähig
que no se puede deducir
非控除, 損金不参入

non-disclosure agreement
不公开协定; 保密协定
contrat de non divulgation
Vertraulichkeitsabkommen;
Geheimhaltungsvertrag
acuerdo para no relevar
información
非開示協定

non-disparagement agreement
不公开指责协定; 不公开贬损协定
contrat de non dénigrement
Antidiffamierungsabkommen
Abkommen über üble Nachrede
acuerdo prohibiendo las críticas
públicas a la empresa
非中傷協定

non-executive director
非常务董事; 非执行董事
consultant (de conseil
d'administration)
nicht geschäftsführende/r
Direktor(in); nicht an der
Geschäftsführung beteiligtes
Mitglied des Board of Directors
director(a) no ejecutivo
非常勤ディレクター

nonfinancial asset
非金融资产
actif non financier
Sachvermögen
activo no financiero
非貨幣的資産

non-financial performance measures
非财务性绩效考核手段
mesures de performance non
financières
nicht-finanzielle Leistungskriterien
medidas no financieras del
rendimiento
非金融業績測定

non-interest-bearing bond
无息债券; 不附息债券
obligation non productive d'intérêt
zinsfreies Darlehen
pagaré sin intereses
無利息手形債券

non-judicial foreclosure
非司法判决止赎权
saisie non judiciaire
nichtgerichtliche Verfallerklärung
od. Zwangsvollstreckung
ejecución sin necesidad de
autorización judicial
裁判によらない物の担保実行手
続き, 裁判手続きによらない競売

non-linear programming
非线性规划
programmation non linéaire
nichtlineare Programmierung

programación no lineal
ノンリニアプログラム

non-negotiable instrument
非转让票据; 非流通票据
instrument non négociable
Namenspapier; Rektapapier; nicht
begebbares Wertpapier
instrumento no negociable
非流通性金融証券, 譲渡不能手形

non-operational balances
非营运存款
soldes non opérationnels
non Banken bei der Bank of
England geführte Konten ohne
Abhebungsermächtnis
cuentas con el Banco de Inglaterra
sin poder de reintegro
(英)ノンオペレーショナル・バ
ランス,イングランド銀行に銀行
が維持する勘定

nonoptional
强制的
non optionnel
keiner Einwilligung durch die
Aktionäre unterliegend
no sujeto a la aprobación de los
accionistas; no opcional
ノンオプショナル

nonparticipating preference share
无分红权优先股
actions privilégiées sans
participation aux bénéfices
Vorzugsaktie ohne
Gewinnbeteiligung
acción preferente sin participación
en el beneficio
非参加優先株

non-performing asset
非运作资产
actif non performant
ertragslose Aktiva
activo improductivo
不良資産, 不稼動資産

non-profit organisation
非盈利组织
organisation à but non lucratif
Unternehmen mit primär
nicht-erwerblichen Zielsetzungen
organización sin ánimo de lucro
非営利団体

non-random sampling
非随机抽样
échantillonnage prédéfini
nichtzufällige Stichprobennahme
muestreo no aleatorio
故意抽出法

non-recourse debt
无追索权贷款
dette sans recours

Translations appear in the following order: Chinese, French, German, Spanish/Latin American Spanish, and Japanese

Verbindlichkeit ohne Rückgriffmöglichkeit
deuda sin posibilidad de recurso
無償還負債

non-recoverable
不可追回的; 不可恢复的
non recouvrable
uneinbringlich
a fondo perdido
回収不能

non-recurring charge
一次性收费
frais extraordinaire
einmalige Gebühr
cargo no recurrente
特別費用, 臨時費用,
非経常的費用

non-resident
非居民
non-résident(e)
beschränkt steuerpflichtige Person
no residente
非居住者

Non-Resident Withholding Tax
非居民预扣税
retenue à la source pour non résidents: taxe imposée par le gouvernement néo-zélandais sur les intérêts et dividendes touchés par un non résident sur des investissements
Kapitalertragssteuer für Nichtansässige
impuesto neozelandés sobre los ingresos procedentes de inversiones de ciudadanos no residentes
非居住者源泉徴収

nonstore retailing
无店面零售
commerce de détail sans magasin physique
Einzelhandel ohne Laden
venta exclusivamente por Internet
ノンストア・リテーリング,
無店舗販売

nontaxable
非课税的
non imposable
steuerfrei; nicht steuerpflichtig
libre de impuestos; no tributable
非課税

non-verbal communication
非言语交流
communication non verbale

nichtverbale od. nicht verbale Kommunikation
comunicación no verbal
非言語コミュニケーション

non-virtual hosting
非虚拟托管
option d'hôte non virtuel
nicht-virtuelles Hosting
alojamiento or hospedaje no virtual
ノンバーチャル(非仮想)
ホスティング

non-voting shares
无投票权股票
actions sans droit de vote
stimmrechtslose Wertpapiere
acciones sin derecho a voto
無議決権株

norm
范数
norme
Norm
norma
標準

normal capacity
正常生产能力
capacité normale
Normalkapazität; Kannkapazität
capacidad normal
正常操業度

normal distribution
正态分布
répartition normale
Normalverteilung
distribución normal
正規分布

normal loss
正常损失
perte normale
normale Schadenerwartung
pérdida normal
正常損失

normal profit
正常利润
profit normal
Normalgewinn; Unternehmerlohn
beneficio normal
正常利潤, 正常利益

normal yield curve
正常收益率曲线
courbe de rendement normal
Zinsstrukturkurve
curva de rendimiento normal
順イールド

no-strike agreement
无罢工协议
accord de non-grève: accord entre le patronat et les syndicats

garantissant que les syndicats n'inviteront pas leurs membres à faire grève
Streikverzichtsabkommen
acuerdo de no hacer huelga
ノーストライキ協定

notch
长工资; 薪级
point (sur l'échelle des salaires)
Gehaltserhöhung
grado
昇給一段階

notes to the accounts
帐目附注; 帐目款项注释附注
notes accompagnant les comptes
Anhang
notas a las cuentas
勘定書の脚注

notes to the financial statements
财务报表脚注; 财务报告款项注释
notes accompagnant les bilans financiers
Abschlusserläuterungen; Anhang zum Jahresabschluss
anexo a la memoria financiera
財務諸表の脚注

notice period
通知期
période de préavis
Kündigungsfrist
plazo de aviso de despido
離職告知期間

notional cost
名义成本
coût fictif
fiktive Kosten; theoretische Kosten
coste teórico; coste nocional
名目原価

notional principal amount
象征性本金
somme principale notionnelle
fiktiver Darlehendbetrag
importe del principal teórico
名目元本

not negotiable
不可转让的, 不流通的
(chèque) non négociable
nicht übertragbar
no negociable
流通禁止

NTB
非关税壁垒
type de réglementation économique d'un pays qui empêche les importations, souvent de pays en voie de développement
nicht tarifäres Handelshemmnis;
NTH

Translations appear in the following order: Chinese, French, German, Spanish/Latin American Spanish, and Japanese

barreras no arancelarias
非関税障壁

nuisance parameter
多余参量
paramètre de nuisance
unerwünschter Parameter
parámetro enojoso
ニューサンスパラメーター

numbered account
编号帐户
compte numéroté
Nummernkonto
cuenta numerada
番号のみ登録の銀行口座,
ナンバー・アカウント

numerical control
数字控制
commande numérique
numerische Steuerung
control numérico
数値制御

NYSE
纽约证券交易所
NYSE: abbréviation pour la Bourse
de New York
New Yorker Börse
Bolsa de Nueva York
ニューヨーク株式取引所

NZSE10 Index
新西兰证券交易所头10家公司指数
indice NZSE10: indice des valeurs
boursières basé sur les 10 plus
grosses compagnies cotées à la
Bourse néo-zélandaise
NZSE10 Aktienindex
índice 10 de la bolsa de Nueva
Zelanda
NZSE10指数

NZSE30 Selection Index
新西兰证券交易所头30家公司选
择指数
indice de sélection NZSE30: indice
des valeurs boursières basé sur les
30 plus grosses compagnies cotées
à la Bourse néo-zélandaise
NZSE30 Aktienindex
índice 30 de la bolsa de Nueva
Zelanda
NZSE30セレクション指数

NZSE40
新西兰证券交易所头40家公司选
择指数
NZSE40: indice des valeurs
boursières basé sur les 40 plus
grosses compagnies cotées à la
Bourse néo-zélandaise
NZSE40
índice 40 de la bolsa de Nueva
Zelanda
NZSE40指数

object and task technique
目标任务预算法
technique de budgétisation selon
les objectifs et tâches
Ziel-und-Aufgabe-Methode;
Methode zur Budgetierung nach
Zielvorgaben, Aufgaben und
Kosten
técnica de objetivos y tareas
目的と任務テクニック

objective
目标
objectif
Ziel; Zielvorgabe
objetivo
目的

obscuranto
模糊概念
obscuranto
Obskuranto
jerga incomprensible
ＥＣなどのわけの分からない用語

obsolescence
废弃，淘汰
obsolescence des produits
Produktveraltung
obsolescencia de los productos
製品老朽化, 陳腐化

occupational health
职业卫生
médecine du travail
betriebliche Gesundheit
salud ocupacional
職業医療

occupational illness
职业病
maladie du travail
Berufskrankheit
enfermedad profesional
職業病

occupational pension scheme
职业养老金计划
plan de retraite professionnel
betriebliche Pensionskasse
plan de pensión de empresa
職業年金制度

occupational psychology
职业心理学
psychologie du travail
Arbeitspsychologie;
Betriebspsychologie
psicología del trabajo
職業心理学

OECD
经济合作与发展组织
Organisation de Coopération et de
Développement Economiques
Organisation für wirtschaftliche
Zusammenarbeit und Entwicklung
OCDE
経済協力開発機構

off-balance-sheet financing
资产负债表以外的融资
financement hors bilan
nicht ausgewiesene od.
bilanzunwirksame
Finanzierungsgeschäfte
financiación fuera del balance
general
オフバランス(シート)金融,
簿外資金調達

offer
报价
offre
Briefkurs
oferta
売り値

offer by prospectus
根据招股说明书招股
offre par prospectus (d'émission)
Aktienangebot über einen
Prospekt
oferta de venta directa de acciones
目論見書募集

offer document
报价文件
document d'offre
Angebotsunterlageno
documento de oferta
(ローンの貸し手が提示する)
オファー・ドキュメント

offer for sale
提供销售，兜售证券
mise sur le marché
Verkaufsangebot; Angebot zum
Verkauf
oferta de venta de acciones
オファー・フォーセール

offering memorandum
发行新证券备忘录
note de mise sur le marché
Emissionsprospekt;
Verkaufsprospekt
memorándum de oferta
募集覚書, 目論見書

offeror
发盘者; 提出建议者
offrant/auteur de l'offre
Offerent(in); Anbietende/r;
Auslobende/r
ofertante
売り申込者, 申出人

offer price
售价; 卖价
prix d'offre
Angebotspreis; Zeichnungskurs;
Emissionskurs; Ausgabepreis
precio de oferta
売り出し価格, 販売価格

Translations appear in the following order: Chinese, French, German, Spanish/Latin American Spanish, and Japanese

office design
办公室设计
conception de l'espace bureau
Bürokonzeption; Bürogestaltung
diseño de oficinas
オフィス・デザイン

office-free
不坐班的
sans bureau
bürolos
sin tener que ir a una oficina
事務所外で働く人

office junior
初级职员; 小职员
employé de bureau
untere/r Büroangestellte/r
auxiliar administrativo(-a)
事務員

office politics
办公室政治
politique de bureau
Bürorangeleien
relaciones en la oficina
オフィス・ポリティックス
(人間間力学)

officer of a company
公司高级职员
membre du comité directeur d'une entreprise
Führungskraft
cargo directivo de una sociedad
企業経営役員

official banks
官方银行; 国家中心银行
banques officielles
amtliche Banken
bancos oficiales
公認銀行

official books of account
官方帐簿
livres de comptabilité officiels
offizielle Geschäftsbücher
libros contables oficiales
正式会計帳簿

official cash rate
官方利率
taux de trésorerie officiel: le taux d'intérêt actuel établi par une banque centrale
offizieller Zinssatz
tipo de interés oficial
公定歩合

official development assistance
官方发展援助
aide officielle au développement
staatliche Entwicklungshilfe
asistencia oficial para el desarrollo
政府開発援助

official list
正式牌价
cote officielle
Kursblatt der Londoner Börse
boletín de cotización oficial
株式相場表

official receiver
官方接收员; 破产接收官;
清算管理官员
administrateur judiciaire (en cas de faillite)
Konkursverwalter(in)
administrador(a) judicial de una quiebra
公式管財人

off-line transaction processing
离线交易
traitement de transaction hors-ligne
Offline-Transaktiosbetrieb
procesado de transacciones fuera de línea
オフライン・トランズアクション・プロセッシング,
実店舗取引処理

offset
抵消; 弥补; 胶印; 脱机借记卡
compensation
Verrechnung
compensación
差引勘定

offset clause
抵销条款
clause de compensation
Verrechnungsklausel
cláusula de compensación
相殺条項

offshore bank
离岸银行
banque offshore
Offshore-Bank
banco extraterritorial
オフショア金融

offshore company
境外公司
compagnie offshore: compagnie n'ayant pas, ou peu d'activités dans le pays de son siège social
Offshore-Gesellschaft
sociedad offshore; sociedad extraterritorial
域外(オフショア)会社

offshore finance subsidiary
境外财政附属公司;
海外财政附屬公司
filiale financière offshore
Offshore-Finanzniederlassung
filial financiera extraterritorial
オフショア金融子会社

offshore financial centre
境外金融中心
centre financier offshore
Offshore-Finanzplatz
centro financiero extraterritorial
域外金融センター

offshore holding company
海外持股公司; 境外控股公司
société de portefeuille offshore
Offshore-Holding;
Offshore-Holding-Gesellschaft
sociedad de cartera extraterritorial
オフショア持ち株会社

offshore production
境外产品
production d'outre-mer ou étrangère
Offshore-Produktion
producción en el extranjero
域外生産(オフショア・プロダクション)

offshore trading company
境外贸易公司; 海外贸易公司
compagnie commerciale offshore
Offshore-Handelsgesellschaft
sociedad mercantil extraterritorial or situada en un paraíso fiscal
海外取引会社

off-the-shelf company
空白公司，挂名公司
entreprise immédiatement disponible
Standardunternehmen
sociedad con respecto a la cual se han completado todas las formalidades legales, de modo que un comprador puede transformarla en una sociedad nueva con facilidad relativa y a bajo coste
直ぐ取得できる会社

off-topic
不相关; 走题
hors sujet
außerhalb des Themas
no relacionado(-a)
事務所外で働く人

ohnosecond
省悟时刻
seconde du 'oh zut'
Oh-nein-Sekunde
segundo ¡oh no!; momento que pasa antes de descubrir un grave error
「しまった！」と分かる瞬間

OINK
没有孩子的单收入家庭
un seul revenu, pas de gosse
Ein Gehalt, Keine Kinder
pareja con un ingreso y sin hijos
単独収入，子供なし

Translations appear in the following order: Chinese, French, German, Spanish/Latin American Spanish, and Japanese

older worker
老职工
travailleur plus âgé
ältere/r Mitarbeiter(in)·
trabajador(a) de edad avanzada
老労働者

Old Lady of Threadneedle Street
针线街老妇人，英格兰银行俗称
Banque nationale d'Angleterre
Bank von England
banco central del Reino Unido
スレッドニードル通りの老婦人
（英国銀行）

old old
老年段; 老年组
en marketing, les plus de 75 ans
die oberste Altersgruppe im
Marketing, Personen über 75
grupo de edad de más de 75 años
75歳以上の年寄り

oligarchy
寡头政治; 寡头统治
oligarchie
Oligarchie
oligarquía
少数独裁寡頭経営

oligopoly
寡头垄断; 寡头专卖; 寡占
oligopole
Oligopol
oligopolio
寡占、少数独占

ombudsman
申诉问题调查员，调查官，巡视官
médiateur
Ombudsman
defensor del pueblo; ombudsman
行政監察員

omitted dividend
遗漏股息
dividende omis
ausgefallene Dividende
dividendo omitido
未払い配当

omnibus account
综合帐户
compte de transactions multiples
Sammelkonto;
Gemeinschaftskonto
cuenta combinada
乗合勘定, 乗合口座

omnibus survey
综合调查
étude à sujets multiples
Mehrthemenbefragung
encuesta ómnibus
オムニバス検査

on account
记帐; 赊帐; 支付赊帐款; 暂付
à valoir
als Teilzahlung
en cuenta
掛売り, 内払い

on demand¹
即期
sur demande
bei Vorlage
a la vista
要求次第の

on demand²
立即偿还贷款
(prêt) à demande
auf Anfordern
a la vista
要求払いの

on demand³
见票即付
à vue
bei Vorlage
a la vista
呈示払いで

one-stop shopping
可提供全部金融服务的金融机构
institution 'tout-en-un': institution
financière unique qui offre une
gamme complète de services
financiers
Finanz-Supermarkt
ventanilla única; one-stop
shopping
ワン・ストップ・ショッピング

one-to-one marketing
一对一式营销
marketing en tête-à-tête
One-to-One Marketing
marketing cara a cara
ワン・トゥ・ワン・マー
ケティング

one-year money
一年期货币存款
argent placé pour un an
Einjahres-Geld
dinero que se coloca en un
mercado monetario durante un
período fijo de un año, con un
interés variable o fijo
ワン・イヤー・マネー

on-hold advertising
通话等候广告
pub sur attente téléphonique
Telefonwerbung, die auf
Verbraucher abzielt, die in einer
Warteschlaufe sind, während sie
auf ein Gespräch warten
publicidad telefónica en espera
電話で保留中の客への広告

online capture
在线支付
saisie en ligne
Online-Erfassung
transacción completada
オンライン・キャプチャー

online catalogue
联机目录
catalogue sur ligne
Online Katalog
catálogo en línea
オンライン・カタログ

online community
网络社区
communauté en ligne
Online-Gemeinschaft
comunidad online
オンライン・コミュニティー

on-pack offer
包装促销
promotion sur paquet
Dreingabe
oferta anunciada en el envase
オンパック・キャンペーン

on-target earnings
实现定额收入
rémunération correspondant aux
résultats atteints
ergebnisorientierter Verdienst
ingresos por objetivos
目標達成所得

on-the-job training
在职培训; 不脱产培训
formation sur le tas
Ausbildung; Arbeitsplatz
formación continua
実務教育職場研修

OPEC
石油输出国组织
Organisation des Pays
Exportateurs de Pétrole
Organisation Erdöl exportierender
Länder
Organización de Países
Exportadores de Petróleo
石油輸出国機構

open-book management
开放式管理
gestion à livre ouvert
offene Unternehmensführung
estilo de gestión abierto
オープン・ブック経営

open buying on the Internet
网上开放式购买
achat ouvert sur Internet
offener Kauf im Internet
sistema de micropago para
compras por Internet;
especificación OBI
インターネットでのオープン売買

Translations appear in the following order: Chinese, French, German, Spanish/Latin American Spanish, and Japanese

open cheque¹
普通支票，不划线支票
chèque non barré
Barscheck
cheque abierto
普通小切手

open cheque²
空白支票
chèque ouvert
Blankoscheck
cheque abierto
オープン小切手

open-collar worker
苏豪族; 在家工作族
employé qui travaille de chez lui
Heimarbeiter(in)
teletrabajador(a)
自宅で仕事する人

open communication
开发式交流
politique de communication transparente
offene Kommunikation
comunicación abierta
オープン・コミュニケーション

open-door policy
开放政策
politique d'ouverture
Politik der offenen Tür
política de puertas abiertas
解放政策

open economy
开发式经济体制
économie ouverte
offene Volkswirtschaft
economía abierta
開放経済

open-ended credit
无限制贷款; 开放式信贷
crédit flexible
Revolving Kredit; Blankokredit
crédito abierto
オープン・エンド型クレジット

open-ended fund
开放式基金
fonds de placement à capital-actions variable
offene Investmentgesellschaft
sociedad de inversión de capital variable, fondo común de inversión
オープン・エンド型ファンド

open-ended investment company
无限额投资公司
compagnie d'investissement à capital variable
offene Investmentgesellschaft
sociedad de inversión de capital variable

オープン・エンド型投資(信託)会社

open-ended management company
开放式管理公司
société de gestion de fonds de placement ou d'investissement
offene Verwaltungsgesellschaft
empresa de fondos de inversión
オープン・エンド管理会社

open-ended mortgage
开放式抵押
créance hypothécaire avec paiement anticipatif autorisé
offene Hypothek
hipoteca ampliable
開放式担保付き社債

opening balance
期初余额
solde d'ouverture
Eröffnungsbestand
balance de apertura
繰越し残高

opening balance sheet
期初余额平衡表; 期初资產負債表
bilan d'ouverture
Eröffnungsbilanz
balance de apertura
繰越し貸借対照表

opening bell
开盘
cloche d'ouverture
Börsenbeginn
campana de apertura
寄り付き

opening price
开盘价格
cours d'ouverture
erster Kurs; Eröffnungskurs;
Eröffnungsnotierung
precio de apertura
始値, 生まれ値

opening purchase
开盘买入
achat d'ouverture
Eröffnungskauf
compra inicial
初購買

opening stock
期初存货
stock reporté
Anfangsbestand
stock inicial; existencias iniciales
寄付株

open interest
开放权益; 未结清权益;
未平仓合约
intérêt non arrêté/ouvert
offenes Interesse

interés abierto
未決済契約残高, 未決済建玉総額

open learning
开放式教学
enseignement à la carte
offener Unterricht; Fernlernen;
flexibles Lernen; Fernunterricht
educación abierta; aprendizaje abierto
オープン・ラーニング

open loop system
开环系统
système en boucle ouverte
offene Steuereinrichtung
sistema de curva libre/abierta
開放ループ式

open-market operation
公开市场操作
opération sur marché libre
Offenmarktgeschäft
operación de mercado abierto
公開市場操作

open-market value
公开市场价值
valeur sur le marché monétaire libre
Normalwert
valor del mercado abierto
市中価格

open standard
兼容标准
norme ouverte
offener Standard
estándar abierto
オープン基準

open system
开放系统
système ouvert
offenes Kommunikationssystem;
offene Systeme
sistema abierto
オープンシステム

open systems thinking
开放系统思维
réflection sur les systèmes ouverts
systemunabhängiges Denken
pensamiento de sistemas abiertos
オープン・システム思考

open trading protocol
网上公开贸易规程
protocole de commerce ouvert
Protokoll für den offenen Handel
especificación OTP
オープン・トレーディング・プロトコル

operating budget
营业预算
budget d'exploitation
Betriebsbudget; operativer Rahmenplan

Translations appear in the following order: Chinese, French, German, Spanish/Latin American Spanish, and Japanese

presupuesto de explotación
営業予算

operating cash-flow
营运现金流量
cash-flow d'exploitation
Betriebsmittelfluss
caja operativa generada
営業キャッシュフロー

operating costing
经营成本; 营业成本
frais d'exploitation
Produktbündelrechnung
coste de explotación
costo de explotación
営業活動原価計算

operating cycle
营运周期
cycle d'exploitation
betriebliche Durchlaufzeit
ciclo operativo
取引周期

operating income
经营收入; 营业收入
revenu d'exploitation
Betriebsertrag
rendimiento de explotación
営業収入

operating lease
经营租赁
contrat de location-exploitation
Form des Leasings, die von
Steuerfachleuten eher als Miete als
Finanzierungsleasing erachtet
wird
arrendamiento de explotación
短期賃貸し

operating leverage
运营杠杆
ratio d'endettement d'exploitation
Umsatz-Leverage
apalancamiento operativo;
palanca de la operación financiera;
ventaja de operación
営業レバレッジ

operating risk
经营风险
risque d'exploitation
Betriebsrisiko
riesgo operativo
営業リスク

operating statement
营业费用报表，营业损益表
bilan d'exploitation
Betriebsergebnisrechnung
informe operativo, balance
operativo
営業計算書

operating system
操作系统
système d'exploitation
Betriebssystem

sistema operativo
基本ソフト(OS)

operational audit
操作审计
audit opérationnel
interne Revision
auditoría operativa
業務監査

operational control
运作控制
contrôle d'exploitation
Innenrevision; laufende
Überwachung
control operacional
業務管理

operational gearing
经营传动作用; 固定成本之比例
ratio d'endettement d'exploitation
kurzfristiger Verschuldungsgrad;
betriebliche Leverage: Verhältnis
der Festkosten zu den
Gesamtbetriebskosten einer
Betriebseinheit
apalancamiento operativo
営業ギャリング比率

operational research
运筹学; 作业研究
recherche opérationnelle
betriebswirtschaftliche Planung
investigación operacional
業務調査

operations management
操作管理; 作业管理; 运行管理
gestion opérationnelle
Betriebsführung
gestión de operaciones
業務管理

operations plans
作业计划
plans d'activités
Ablaufplanung;
Arbeitsvorbereitung
planes de operaciones
事業計画

operation time
商业周期
durée d'opération
Betriebszeit
tiempo de operación
稼動時間

opinion leader
观念领导者
meneurs d'opinion
Meinungsmacher
líderes de opinión
オピニオン・リーダー

opinion leader research
领导者意见研究
étude des leaders d'opinion
Meinungsführerforschung

encuesta sobre el líder de opinión
オピニオン・リーダー調査

opinion shopping
意见采购
recherche d'opinions
concordantes
Meinungsumfrage
búsqueda de un auditor afín a la
empresa
オピニオン・ショッピング

opinion survey
意见调查
étude d'opinion
Meinungserhebung
encuesta de opiniones
意見調査

opportunity cost
机会成本; 替代成本
valeur de renonciation
Opportunitätskosten
coste de oportunidad
costo de oportunidad
機会原価

optimal portfolio
最佳投资组合
portefeuille optimum
Optimalportefeuille
cartera óptima
最適ポートフォリオ

**optimal redemption
provision**
最优赎回条款
clause de remboursement
optimum
Vorgabe über die optimale Tilgung
einer Anleihe
provisión que permite amortizar
bonos antes de su vencimiento
最適償還条項

optimise
使最优化; 使最佳化;
使。。。发挥最大的效益
optimaliser
optimieren
optimizar
最適化

**optimised production
technology**
最优化生产技术
technique de production optimisée
optimierte Produktionstechnik
tecnología de producción
optimizada
適量化生産技術

optimum capacity
最佳生产能力
capacité optimale
Optimalkapazität
capacidad óptima
最適能力

Translations appear in the following order: Chinese, French, German, Spanish/Latin American Spanish, and Japanese

opt-in
让客户选择加入邮寄名单
choix de participer à
Abonnementprozess für Nutzer
einer Webseite
suscripción activa
オプトイン

option
期权
option
Option; Optionsgeschäft;
Bezugsrecht
opción
オプション, (証券, 通貨,
商品等の基礎資産を)売買する
権利, その契約

option account
期权帐户
compte d'options
Optionskonto
cuenta de opciones
オプション・アカウント

optionaire
股票期权百万富翁
millionnaire par l'acquisition
d'actions de participation dans des
entreprises
Options-Millionär(in)
millonario gracias a las opciones
sobre acciones
株式オプションの億万長者

option buyer
期权买方
acheteur d'option
Optionskäufer(in)
comprador(a) de opciones
オプションの買い手

option class
选择级别
catégorie d'option
Optionsklasse; Optionsgattung
clase de opción
オプション・クラス

option elasticity
期权弹性
élasticité de l'option
Optionselastizität
elasticidad de una opción
オプションの弾力性

option income fund
期权收入基金
fonds de placement à revenus sur
options
Options-Einkommensfonds
fondo de ingresos por opciones
オプション・インカム・ファンド

option premium
期权费; 期权酬金
prime d'option
Prämie; Optionspreis

prima de opción
オプション・プレミアム,
オプション料

option price
期权价格
prix d'option
Optionspreis
precio de opción
オプション価格

option pricing model
期权价格模式
modèle d'établissement de prix
d'option
Optionspreismodell
modelo de valoración de las
opciones
オプション価格設定モデル

options clearing corporation
期权清算公司 (OCC)
corporation de compensation
d'options/de primes
zentrale Verrechnungsstelle für
den US-Optionshandel
cámara de compensación de
opciones
オプション・クリアリング会社

option series
期权系列
série d'options
Optionsserie; Optionsreihe
serie de opciones
オプション・シリーズ

options market
期權市场
marché à options
Optionsmarkt
mercado de opciones
オプション市場

options on physicals
固定利率证券期权
options sur titres à taux fixes
Optionen auf physische Papiere
opciones sobre activos físicos
現物オプション

option writer
期权卖方
vendeur d'options
Optionsverkäufer(in)
vendedor(a) de una opción
オプションの売り手

order¹
定单
commande
Bestellung; Auftrag
pedido
注文

order²
指令
commande
Auftrag

orden
注文; 指図

order book
订货簿
carnet de commandes
Auftragsbestand
libro de pedidos
注文控帳

order confirmation
订货确认信息
confirmation de commande
Auftragsbestätigung
confirmación de pedido
発注の確認

order picking
挑选订货
sélection ou triage pour
commande
Bestückung
retirada bajo pedido
オーダー・ピッキング

order point
订购点; 订购日期
point de commande
Bestellpunkt
punto de pedido
発注点

order processing
定单处理
traitement de commande
Auftragsabwicklung
procesado de pedidos
注文処理

orders pending
未决的定单
ordres en souffrance
vorliegende Aufträge
órdenes pendientes
未決指図

ordinary interest
普通利息; 单利
intérêt ordinaire
gewöhnlicher Zins
interés ordinario
通常利息, 通常利子

ordinary shares
普通股
actions ordinaires
Stammaktien; Stämme
acciones ordinarias
普通株

organisation
机构; 组织
organisation
Organisation
organización
組織

organisational analysis
组织分析
analyse organisationnelle

Translations appear in the following order: Chinese, French, German, Spanish/Latin American Spanish, and Japanese

Organisationsanalyse
análisis organizativo
組織分析

organisational commitment¹
组织忠诚度; 雇员忠诚度
engagement organisationnel:
engagement d'une organisation
envers des buts et objectifs donnés
Zusagen einer Organisation zu
vorgegebenen Zielsetzungen;
äußert sich in verbindlichen
Aussagen zu Zielen,
firmenpolitischen Grundsätzen,
Maßnahmen und der Zuweisung
von Mitteln
compromiso de la organización
組織理念,

organisational commitment²
组织忠诚度; 雇员忠诚度
engagement organisationnel
Maß des Engagements der
Arbeitnehmer(in)nen in der
Belegschaft einer Organisation für
die Erfüllung der Zielsetzungen
dieser Organisation
compromiso con la organización
従業員姿勢

organisational development
组织发展
développement organisationnel
Anpassung eines Unternehmens
an die Umwelterfordernisse
desarrollo organizativo
組織発展

organisational learning
组织学习
apprentissage organisationnel
Lernen in der Organisation
aprendizaje organizativo
学習する組織

organisational planning
组织计划
planification structurelle
Organisationsplanung
planificación organizativa
組織構造計画

organisation behaviour
组织行为
comportement organisationnel
Organisationsverhalten
comportamiento de las
organizaciones
組織挙動

organisation chart
组织結構圖
organogramme
Organigramm; Organogramm;
Organisationsplan;
Organisationsschaubild
organigrama
組織図

organisation hierarchy
组织层级
hiérarchie organisationnelle
Unternehmenshierachie
jerarquía de la organización
組織ヒエラルキー

organisation man
组织人; 机构人; 机关人 机关人员
homme d'organisation: façon de
décrire toute personne qui accepte
entièrement, travaille et peut être
absorbée par les valeurs et
objectifs d'une organisation.
S'applique en particulier à
quelqu'un qui travaille dans une
grosse bureaucratie
treues Firmenmitglied
hombre de empresa
組織人組織志向社員

organisation structure
组织结构
structure organisationnelle
Organisationsstruktur
jerarquía de la organización
組織構成

organisation theory
组织理论
théorie organisationnelle
Organisationstheori
teoría de la organización
組織理論

**original equipment
manufacturer¹**
设备组装生产商; 组装生产商
constructeur OEM
OEM; Wiederverkäufer
fabricante de producto original
原機製造者

**original equipment
manufacturer²**
原始设备制造商
fabricant OEM
OEM-Lieferant
fabricante de producto original
OEM(相手先ブランドによる
供給)

original face value
原始面值
valeur nominale initiale
anfänglicher Marktwert
valor nominal original
当初額面価格

original issue discount
原始发行折价
escompte sur émission initiale
Erstausgabediskont
bono emitido con descuento
発行時割引, ＯＩＤ, 発行差金

original maturity
'原定满期日

échéance initiale
Fälligkeitstermin
vencimiento original
当初満期

origination fee
初始费
frais de constitution d'hypothèque
Gebühr für Bereitstellung von
Hypothekendarlehen
comisión por tramitación de
solicitud
取り組み手数料,
貸し付けて数量,
オリジネーション・フィー

orthogonal
互不相关的(统计数字)
orthogonal
orthogonal
ortogonal
統計上独立した変数

other capital
其它资本
capital autre
sonstige Anlagewerte
otro capital
その他の資本

other current assets
其它流动资产
autre actif réalisable
sonstige Posten des
Umlaufvermögens
otros activos circulantes
その他の流動資産

other long-term capital
其它长期资本
capital autre à long terme
sonstige langfristige Anlagewerte
otro capital a largo plazo
その他の長期資本

other prices
其它价格
prix autres
sonstige Preise
otros precios
その他の価格

other short-term capital
其它短期资本
capital autre à court terme
sonstige kurzfristige Anlagewerte
otro capital a corto plazo
その他の短期資本

OTOH
另一方面
d'autre part
andererseits
por otro lado
他方, 一方

outdoor advertising
室外广告
publicité en extérieur

Translations appear in the following order: Chinese, French, German, Spanish/Latin American Spanish, and Japanese

Außenwerbung
publicidad en exteriores
野外広告

outlier
远离本体的观测值，非正常值
point d'aberration
Ausreißer
observación extraña
アウトライアー(偏差の大
態きい状)

out-of-date cheque
过期支票
chèque périmé
abgelaufener Scheck
cheque caducado; cheque
obsoleto
失効小切手

out of the loop
信息隔离
exclu(e) de la communication au
sein d'un groupe
uninformiert
excluido(-a)
仲間はずれ

outplacement
安排新工作(服务)
outplacement: aide à la réinsertion
professionnelle après une perte
d'emploi
Herausplatzierung
recolocación
アウトプレースメント(再就職
援助業)

output
产出; 产值
rendement
Leistung; Produktion
producción
産出, 生産高

output gap
产出缺口
écart de production
Output-Lücke; Produktionsloch
brecha de producción
GDPギャップ

output method
产出法
comptabilité de rendement
Entstehungsrechnung
método de producción
産出高比例法、アウトプット法

output tax
产出税额
impôt ressortant: contributions à
payer après déduction des crédits
d'impôt sur dépenses
commerciales
Umsatzsteuer-Zahllast
cantidad del impuesto sobre
bienes y servicios una vez

efectuados los descuentos
売上税

outside director
外邀董事; 外界董事; 不任职董事
directeur extérieur
außenstehendes Mitglied des
Board of Directors
directivo(-a) externo(-a)
社外取締役

outsourcing
业务外部化
approvisionnement à l'extérieur
Outsourcing; Fremdbeschaffung;
Auslagerung; externe Beschaffung
subcontratación
tercerización
アウトソーシング

outstanding share
已发行股票
actions en circulation
ausstehende Aktie
acción en circulación
既発債

outstanding share capital
现有股票价值
capital actions en circulation
ausstehende Aktien
capital en acciones pendiente
発行済み株式資本

out tray
文件篮
casier de documents à traiter
Ablage für Ausgänge
bandeja de asuntos resueltos
未決書類入れ

outwork
外包工作; 外发工作
travail à domicile
Heimarbeit
teletrabajo
出張勤務仕事

outworker
外包工
employé qui travaille à domicile
Heimarbeiter(in)
teletrabajador(a)
出張勤務者, 請負業者

overall capitalisation rate
总资本化比率
taux de capitalisation global
Gesamtkapitalisierungsfaktor;
Gesamtkapitalisierungssatz
tasa de capitalización global
総合資本化率

overall market capacity
市场总吸收力
capacité de marché globale
Gesamtmarktkapazität
capacidad global del mercado
市場の総許容力

overall rate of return
总收益率
taux de rendement global
Gesamtertrag
tipo global de rendimiento
全体の収益率

overall return
全部收益
revenu global
Gesamtkapitalrentabilität
rendimiento global
総体の収益

overbid[1]
出价更高; 出价高于(某人);
出价过高
suroffre/surenchère
überbieten
sobrepostular
掛値, 高せり値

overbid[2]
过高的出价
sur-offre
unnötig hohes Gebot
sobrepostura
掛値, 高せり値

overbought market
买超市场
marché surévalué: marché dans
lequel les prix ont augmenté
au-delà de niveaux pouvant être
supportés par une analyse
fondamentale
Markt mit überdurchschnittlichen
Ankäufen; überkaufter Markt
mercado sobrevalorado
物価高騰市場

overcapacity
生产能力过剩
surcapacité
Überkapazität
exceso de capacidad
過剰設備能力

overcapitalised
投资过剩
(société) surcapitalisée
überkapitalisiert
sobrecapitalizado
資本過剰

overdraft
透支，透支的款项
découvert
Kontokorrent
descubierto; sobregiro
当座貸(借)越し

overdraft facility
透支安排; 透支协议
autorisation de découvert
Überziehungskredit
facilidad de sobregiro
当座借越し制度

Translations appear in the following order: Chinese, French, German, Spanish/Latin American Spanish, and Japanese

overdraft line
透支线; 透支额度
ligne de découvert
Kreditlinie
límite de descubierto
当座借越レベル

overdraft protection
透支保护
protection par avance bancaire
Schutz für Überziehungskredite
protección contra descubierto
貸越貸越保護; 当座借越し

overdraw
透支; 超支
tirer à découvert (compte)
überziehen (Kredit od. Konto)
sobregirar
当座借越しをする

overdrawn
透支
à découvert
überzogen
en descubierto
超過振り出しされた(当座預金)人

overdue
过期(未付的); 迟付的; 延误的;
迟到的
échu
überfällig; rückständig;
abgelaufen
vencido(-a)
期限を過ぎた

over-geared
资本结合过度
(compagnie) surendettée
überschuldet
sobreapalancado
超過負債比率

overhanging
悬货
excédent: se dit de l'élément d'une
nouvelle émission laissé dans les
mains des soumissionnaires
Überhang
sobresaliente
持ち越し品

overhead absorption rate
间接管理费率
taux de ventilation des frais
généraux
Gemeinkostenverrechnung
tasa de absorción de gastos
indirectos
経費吸収率

overhead cost
管理成本; 间接成本
frais généraux
Gemeinkosten; laufende Kosten
costos or costes generales
間接費, 経費

over-insuring
超额保险
surassurer
Überversicherung
sobreasegurar
超過保険

over-invested
过度投资
surinvesti
überinvestiert
sobreinvertido
過剰投資

overnight position
隔夜头寸
position du jour au lendemain
kurzfristiger Posten;
Tagesgeldposten
posición de cierre-apertura
オーバーナイト・ポジション

overprice
价格过高的; 标价过高的
demander trop cher
überhöhten Preis fordern;
überbewerten
marcar un precio excesivo
高過ぎる値段設定

overrated
估价过高的
surévalué
überbewertet
sobrevalorado
高く評価し過ぎた

overseas company
海外公司
compagnie d'outre-mer
Auslandsunternehmen
sociedad extranjera
海外法人

**Overseas Investment
Commission**
外国投资委员会
commission sur les investissements
étrangers
Überseeinvestitionskommission
comisión neozelandesa reguladora
de las inversiones extranjeras
外国投資委員会

oversold
卖超市场
(marché ou titre) sous-évalué
überdurchschnittlich viel verkauft
sobrevendido(-a)
売られ過ぎ市場

overstocked
存货过多的
approvisionné à l'excès
mit zu hoher Vorratshaltung
con exceso de existencias
在庫過剰

**over the counter (OTC)
market**
场外交易市场
marché des valeurs hors cote
dritter Markt
mercado extrabursátil
店頭取引市場

overtime
加班
heures supplémentaires
Überstunden
horas extras o extraordinarias
超過勤務残業時間

overtime pay
加班费; 加班工资
rémunération des heures
supplémentaires
Überstundenvergütung
paga por horas extras
超過勤務手当て

overtrading
交易过度
opérations financières excédant les
ressources d'une entreprise
Überspekulation; Spekulation
ohne Deckung
exceso de comercialización; exceso
de inversión; sobreinversión
資金超過取引

own brand
自家商标产品; 用自己品牌的;
自己商标的; 自定牌名的
propre marque
Hausmarke
marca blanca
独自ブランド

owner[1]
所有者; 业主; 物主; 拥有人
propriétaire
Eigentümer(in)
dueño(-a)
所有者

owner[2]
所有者
propriétaire
Eigentümer(in)
propietario(-a)
オーナー, 所有者

owners' equity
业主产权
capitaux propres
Eigenkapital
capital propio
所有主持分

ownership of companies
公司所有权
possession de parts dans des
entreprises
Unternehmensbeteiligung

---

*Translations appear in the following order: Chinese, French, German, Spanish/Latin American
Spanish, and Japanese*

propiedad de empresas
会社所有権

P2P
点对点，对等互联
pair-à-pair
Peer-to-Peer
comercio electrónico de terminal a terminal
ピア・ツー・ピア

paced line
生产线
chaîne de production à cadence constante
getaktete Produktionsstraße
cadena de montaje a ritmo constante
定速ライン

packaging[1]
包装
conditionnement
Verpackung
embalaje
パッケージ取引

packaging[2]
包装
conditionnement
Verpackung; Packungsgestaltung; Verpacken
embalaje
梱包材料; パッケージ取引

Pac Man defence
派克曼防卫
défense Pac Man
Abwehr durch Übernahmeangebot an ein Unternehmen, das den Anbieter schlucken will
defensa comecocos
パックマン・ディフェンス

page counter
网址访问计数器
compteur de page
Seitenzähler
contador de páginas
ページ・カウンター

page impressions
访问网址顾客数
impressions par page: nombre de clients qui accèdent à une page Web, comme dans nombre de visualisations de pub
Seitenkontakt
impresiones de páginas
ページ・インプレッションズ

paid cheque
付讫支票
chèque payé
bezahlter Scheck
cheque pagado
支払済小切手

paid circulation
报章杂志销售量
tirage acheté
verkaufte Auflage
tirada vendida
売り上げ部数

paid-up policy[1]
已缴费保险
police (d'assurance) payée
beitragsfreie Versicherung
póliza liberada
払込済保険証券

paid-up policy[2]
已缴费保险
police (d'assurance) entièrement payée
beitragsfreie Versicherung
póliza con las primas al día
払込済保険証券

paid-up share
缴足股票
action libérée
voll eingezahlte Aktie
acción cubierta; acción liberada
払込済株式

paid-up share capital
已缴股本
capital-actions libéré
eingezahltes Aktienkapital
capital desembolsado
払込済み株式資本

painting the tape
粉饰业绩
pratique boursière illégale selon laquelle les courtiers divisent les grosses commandes en petites unités pour donner l'illusion d'une grosse activité d'achat
illegale Praxis an der Börse, wobei Händler große Aufträge in kleinere Einheiten aufspalten, um die Illusion einer Kaufwelle zu vermitteln. Dadurch werden Anleger zum Kauf ermutigt und die Händler verkaufen bei steigendem Wertpapierkurs
compra ilegal fraccionada de un valor
大きい取引を小さく分けて市場を刺激し、利益を不法に得る方法

palmtop
掌上电脑; 掌中宝
ordinateur de poche
Palmtopcomputer
palmtop
パームトップ(手のひら)パソコン

pandas
熊猫金银币
série de lingots d'argent chinoises, sur lesquelles figurent un panda
Panda-Münzen

pandas
パンダ(中国の金・銀貨)

panel interview
小组面试
entretien devant jury
Panelinterview; Vorstellungsgespräch mit mehreren Gesprächspartnern
entrevista ante un grupo de personas
パネル・インタビュー

panel study
定组研究
étude d'un groupe sélectionné (dans le temps)
Panelerhebung
panel; técnica de panel
パネル調査

panic buying
恐慌抢购
achats de précaution
Angstkäufe; Panikkäufe
compra provocada por el pánico
恐慌買い

PANSE
政治活跃但不熱中工作
politiquement actif et ne recherche pas d'emploi
politisch tätig und nicht erwerbssuchend
persona activa políticamente que no está buscando empleo
政治運動家で雇用を求めていない

paper[1]
票据
titre fiduciaire
Geldmarktpapiere
valores
証券証書

paper[2]
指增发的股票或发行的债券(俚语)
papier d'émission (de droits de souscription ou d'obligations lancés par une compagnie pour lever un capital additionnel); terme familier
kurzfristig begebbare Wertpapiere
títulos a corto plazo
株主割当発行

paper[3]
票据
instruments (de dette)
Geldmarktpapier
deuda emitida
証券

paper architecture
纸上谈兵
architecture en carton
Luftschloss; Makulatur
proyecto que se queda en papel

Translations appear in the following order: Chinese, French, German, Spanish/Latin American Spanish, and Japanese

mojado
紙上に止まるプロジェクト

paper company
皮包公司
compagnie sur papier
Scheinfirma; Übungsgesellschaft;
Briefkastenfirma
papelera
ペーパー・カンパニー

paperless office
无纸办公室
bureau sans papier
papierloses Büro
oficina informatizada, sin papel
無書類オフィス

paper millionaire
帐面百万富翁
millionnaire sur papier
Papiermillionär(in)
persona que posee acciones por
valor de más de un millón en
divisas, pero cuyo valor puede
pagar
紙上億万長者

paper money[1]
纸币
papier-monnaie
Banknoten
papel moneda
紙幣

paper money[2]
支票汇票等可作为货币使用
的票据
argent écrit
Papiergeld
papel moneda
有価証券

paper profit
帐面利润，帐面盈余
plus-value non matérialisée
Buchgewinn
ganancias teóricas; ganancias
sobre el papel
紙上利益

paper trail
书面记录
traces écrites
die Gesamtheit der Unterlagen, die
zu einer Entscheidung geführt
haben
rastro de papel, rastro de
documentación
決定事項書類

PAR
平价，票面价值
(le) PAIR
Nennwert; Pari
par; paridad; equivalencia; valor
nominal; cambio a la par; valor a la
par; reserva agregada obligatoria
額面

paradigm shift
思维习惯的改变
évolution de paradigme
Paradigmenwechsel
cambio de paradigma
パラダイム・シフト(規範変更)

parallel pricing
平行定价
fixation de prix en parallèle
gleichgerichtete Preisgestaltung;
gleichgerichtete Kursbildung
fijación de precios en paralelo
平行価格設定

paralysis by analysis
分析的瘫痪
paralysie de la sur-analyse
Paralyse; durch Analyse
parálisis por análisis
分析し過ぎによるビジネスの
麻痺

parameter
参数，参量
paramètre
Parameter
parámetro
パラメーター

parameter design
参数(量)设计
conception de paramètre
Parameter
diseño de parámetros
パラメーターデザイン

parent company
母公司
maison mère
Muttergesellschaft
empresa matriz
親会社, 支配会社

Pareto's Law
帕累托定律
loi de Pareto
Pareto-Verteilung; Paretosche
Gesetzmäßigkeit; Paretosches
Gesetz
ley de Pareto
パレト法

pari passu
同步; 以相同比率; 以相同速度;
同级
pari passu
gleichrangig; gleichberechtigt;
gleichwertig
pari passu
パリ・パス(均等, 同順位)

Paris Inter Bank Offered Rate
巴黎银行同业拆借率
PIBOR: taux interbancaire des
devises européennes à Paris

Pariser Interbankenangebotssatz
Tipo de Interés Ofertado del
Mercado Intercambiario de París
(PIBOR)
パリ銀行間取引金利

parity
平价
parité
Parität
paridad
平価

parity bit
奇偶位; 同位; 奇偶检验位
bit de parité
binäre Prüfziffer; Prüfbit
bit de paridad
奇遇検査ビット

park
公园交易
garer
in Pension geben
aparcar
株の所有権を他人に託す

parking[1]
寄存
transfert d'actions
in Pension geben
aparcamiento de acciones
パーキング(株の不正譲渡)

parking[2]
寄存
garer son argent
Geld während der Entscheidung
über seine endgültige Investition
sicher anlegen
aparcar
暫定的投資

Parkinson's Law
帕金森法则
Loi de Parkinson
Parkinsonsches Gesetz
ley de Parkinson
パーキンソンの法則

Parquet
巴黎证券交易所
(le) Parquet
die Bourse von Paris
El Parquet
(仏)株式取引市場

participating bond
参与(分红)债券
bon avec participation
Gewinnobligation;
Gewinnschuldverschreibung
obligación participante or
preferente
利益配当付き社債

Translations appear in the following order: Chinese, French, German, Spanish/Latin American Spanish, and Japanese

participating insurance
共享保险; 互助保险; 分红保险;
参与保险
assurance à participation
Versicherung mit Ausschüttung v.
Dividenden
seguro con una mutua
利益配当付き保険, 参加保険

**participating preference
share**
参与分红优先股
action ou titre de priorité
participative
Vorzugsaktie
acción preferente participante
参加優先株

participative budgeting
参与式自下而上式预算
budgétisation de la base au
sommet/inclusive
partizipative Finanzplanung
presupuesto de participación
共同予算編成

partly-paid share
部分缴款股票
actions non entièrement libérées
teilweise eingezahlte Aktie
acción parcialmente liberada
一部支払済み株

partnership
合伙企业; 合伙关系
association en nom collectif
Teilhaberschaft;
Personengesellschaft; Sozietät
sociedad colectiva
パートナーシップ

partnership accounts
合伙帐户
comptes des associés
Partnerschaftsbücher
cuentas colectivas
組合勘定

partnership agreement
合伙协议书
contrat d'association
Gesellschaftsvertrag
contrato de sociedad
パートナーシップ契約

part-time work
非全日性工作
travail à temps partiel
Teilzeitarbeit
trabajo a tiempo parcial
パートタイム労働

party plan
晚会促销计划
vente par réunions
Erlebnis-Marketing

venta en reuniones de
demonstración
パーティー・プラン

passbook
存折; 存摺
livret de banque
Sparbuch
libreta de ahorro; cartilla de ahorro
銀行預金通帳

passing off
假冒产品; 冒充
faire passer
Ausgeben eigener Ware als
Fremde; Kennzeichenmissbrauch
disimulación
詐欺通用

**passive investment
management**
被动投资管理
gestion d'investissements passive
passive Anlage- od.
Vermögensverwaltung
gestión de inversiones pasivas
パッシブ運用, 消極的な投資管理

passive portfolio strategy
被动投资组合策略
stratégie de gestion de portefeuille
passive
passive Portfoliostrategie
estrategia pasiva de inversión
パッシブ・ポートフォリオ戦略

password
口令; 密码
mot de passe
Passwort
contraseña
パスワード

patent
专利; 专利权; 土地拥有权(美)
brevet
Patent; Marken;
Ernennungsurkunde;
Bestallungsurkunde
patente
特許

patent attorney
专利代理人; 专利授权人
conseil en propriété industrielle
Patentanwalt(in); Patentanwältin
abogado(-a) de patentes
特許弁理士

paternity leave
父亲假
congé de paternité
Vaterschaftsurlaub
permiso por paternidad
父親育児休暇

path analysis
关系路径分析
analyse de trajectoire de

corrélation
Pfadanalyse
análisis de rutas
方向分析

path diagram
关系路径图
diagramme de corrélation
Pfaddiagramm
diagrama de trayectoria
方向图表

pathfinder prospectus
试用募股说明书
prospectus de mesure (des
réactions des investisseurs aux
offres publiques initiales)
wegbereitender Emissionsprospekt
prospecto exploratorio
予備目論見書

pawnbroker
典当商
prêteur sur gages
Pfandleiher(in)
prestamista sobre prenda
質屋

pay
报酬; 工资
paie
Lohn; Gehalt; Bezahlung;
Besoldung
paga; sueldo
給料, 賃金

payable to order
按指定应付
payable à ordre
zahlbar an Order
pagadero a la orden
指図人払い

Pay As You Earn
按收入缴税制度
système salarial avec retenue
d'impôt sur le revenu à la source
Quellenabzug
retención en nómina del impuesto
sobre la renta
源泉課税

pay-as-you-go
现收现付
retenue à la source de l'impôt sur
le revenu (des salariés actuels pour
financement des retraites
actuelles)
Umlageverfahren
financiación sobre la marcha
現金支払主義

Pay-As-You-Go
商业投资所得税分期付款
système australien de paiement de
l'impôt sur le revenu par
versements échelonnés
Regelmäßige

---

*Translations appear in the following order: Chinese, French, German, Spanish/Latin American
Spanish, and Japanese*

Einkommenssteuerzahlungen für
Geschäfts- und Kapitaleinkünfte
retención automática del impuesto
sobre la renta
事業・投資収入に対する分割納
税

payback
(投資)回收期，还本期限
délai de récupération
Amortisation
período de recuperación; plazo de
recuperación; plazo de
amortización; recuperación de la
inversión
ペイバック

payback period
回收期
période d'amortissement
Amortisationszeit
período de devolución
回收期間

payee[1]
收款人，受款人
bénéficiaire (d'un chèque)
Remittent(in)
beneficiario
被支払人

payee[2]
收款人，受款人
bénéficiaire
Zahlungsempfänger(in)
beneficiario
受領者

payer
付款人
payeur
Zahler(in)
pagador
支払人

paying agent
付款代理人
agent payant
Zahlstelle
agente de pagos
支払い業者

paying banker
付款银行
banquier payant
zweitbeauftragte Bank
banco pagador
払出銀行

paying-in book
付款簿，缴款帐簿
carnet de bordereaux de
versement
Einzahlungsbuch
libreta de ahorros
入金帳

payload
輸船載重量
charge commerciale/payante
Nutzlast; Arbeitskosten
carga útil
有料荷重

paymaster
工薪出纳员
intendant
Zahlmeister; Schatzmeister
pagador
給料支払係

payment by results
成果薪给制
prime au rendement
Ergebnislohn
sueldo según resultados
能率給, 出来高賃金払い

payment gateway
付款闸道
portail de paiement
Zahlungs-Gateway
pago por visión
支払いゲートウエー

payment in advance
预先付款; 先後貨
paiement anticipé
Vorauszahlung
pago anticipado
前払い

payment in due course
届时付款，到期付款
paiement à échéance voulue
Zahlung bei Fälligkeit
fecha de vencimiento del pago
支払い期日

payment-in-kind
实物支付; 实物工资
paiement en nature
Sachleistung; Naturalleistung
pago en especie
品払賃金, 現物払い

payment-in-lieu
以薪酬代替
paie de remplacement: paiement
octroyé à la place de quelque
chose auquel on a droit, par
exemple des congés non pris
Ausgleichszahlung
pago a cambio de derecho
代替手当て

payment terms
付款条件，支付条款
termes de paiement
Zahlungsbedingungen
condiciones de pago
支払い条件

payout ratio
股息率
coefficient de récupération

Dividendendeckung;
Ausschüttungskennzahl
coeficiente de reparto
配当性向

Pay Pal
网上缴款
Pay-Pal
PayPal
servicio de pagos electrónicos Pay
Pal
ペイ・パル

pay-per-click
点击收费
paiement par cliquage/à chaque
cliquage
Zahlung per Mausklick
pago por clic
ペイ・パー・クリック

pay-per-play
收费游戏
payez comme vous jouez: site web
qui fait payer un micropaiement
pour jouer à un jeu interactif sur
Internet
Bezahl-Per-Spiel
pago por jugar
ペイ・パー・プレー

pay-per-view[1]
收费浏览
paiement par visualisation
Per-Sendung-Bezahl
pago por visión
ペイ・パー・ビュー(視聴毎に
支払い)

pay-per-view[2]
收费频道; 收费收视; 付费收视
paiement par visualisation
Per-Sendung-Bezahl
pago por visión
ペイ・パー・ビュー

payroll
工资单; 在职人员名单; 工薪总额;
雇员总数
registre des salaires; registre du
personnel
Lohnbuchhaltung; Lohn- und
Gehaltsliste; Löhne und Gehälter;
Lohnsumme
nómina
plantilla
給料支払名簿

payroll analysis
工资单分析
analyse du registre des salaires
Personalkostenanalyse
análisis de nómina de salaries o
sueldos
給料支払い分析

pay scale
薪级表

échelle de paie
Lohnskala
escala salarial
給与スケール

payslip
工资单
feuille de paie
Lohnstreifen
nómina (papel)
給料明細書

PDA
掌上个人电脑
agenda de poche électronique
avec accès à Internet
Taschencomputer
asistente personal, PDA
携帯情報端末

PDF
Adobe的可移植文档格式文件的扩
展名
format de document électronique
übertragbares Dokumentenformat
PDF
電子ドキュメント・フォーマット

peg[1]
钉住汇率; 掛鉤匯率
stabiliser (le cours du change)
stützen
vincular
為替安定

peg[2]
钉住，限定,掛鉤
indexer (les salaires)
fixieren
fijar
給与固定

penalty
违约金，罚款
pénalité
Vertragsstrafe
penalización
違約金

penalty rate
超時工作值
taux de pénalité
Überstundenlohn
tarifa extraordinaria
残業手当

pencil-whip
书面批评
sacquer par écrit
jdn. schriftlich kritisieren; verreißen
criticar por escrito a
文章で人を批判する

penetrated market
已渗入市场
marché pénétré
durchdrungener Markt
mercado penetrado
市場内の既存客

penetration pricing
渗透定价
fixation de prix afin de pénétrer
des marchés/intelligente
Penetrationspreispolitik;
Niedrigpreisstrategie
fijación de precios de penetración
浸透価格設定

penny shares
小额股票; 低价股; 廉价股;
便士股票
actions spéculatives valant moins
d'un dollar
Aktien mit sehr niedrigem Kurs
und Nennwert
acciones especulativas de menos
de un dólar
投機の低位株, ペニー株

pension
退休金
retraite
Altersversorgung; Pension; Rente
pensión
年金

pensionable earnings
应计养老金的收入
salaire sur lequel la retraite est
basée
pensionsfähiges Gehalt
ingresos sometidos a retención por
jubilación; ingresos para el cálculo
de la pensión
年金対象所得

people churner
流失人才的老板
balanceur de bon personnel
schlechter Arbeitgeber, der im Ruf
steht, dass ihm die talentierten
Mitarbeiter abwandern
quematalentos; jefe(-a)que pierde
empleados brillantes
優秀な人材をなくしてしまう上司

P/E ratio
市盈率，价格-收益比率
P/E ratio: abbréviation anglaise de
price-earnings ratio: coefficient de
capitalisation des résultats (C.C.R)
ou quotient cours-bénéfice
Kurs-Gewinn-Verhältnis
relación PERSONA/B
株価収益率

per capita income
人均收入
salaire individuel
Pro-Kopf-Einkommen;
Einkommen auf den Kopf der
Bevölkerung
renta per cápita
一人当り国民所得

percussive maintenance
碰撞维修
maintenance de matos par la
frappe
die Gewohnheit, Elektrogeräte zu
schlagen oder zu schütteln, um sie
zum Funktionieren zu bringen
solución de problemas a base de
golpes
電子機器などを叩いて直そうとす
る方法

per diem
按日; 每天
par jour
Tagegeld
dieta
一日当り

perfect capital market
完善的资本市场
marché financier idéal
vollkommener Kapitalmarkt
mercado perfecto de capital
完全資本市場

perfect competition
完全(自由)竞争
concurrence idéale
vollkommener od. vollständiger
Wettbewerb
competencia perfecta
完全競争

perfect hedge
完全套期
parfait arbitrage
vollkommenes Sicherungsgeschäft
cobertura perfecta
完全ヘッジ

performance appraisal
员工考绩; 绩效评定; 实绩评估
évaluation des performances
Leistungsbeurteilung;
Leistungsbewertung
evaluación del rendimiento
業績考査

performance bond
履约保证书，履约保单
garantie donnée par un tiers
Leistungsgarantie
garantía de pago
契約保証金

performance criteria
业绩标准; 考绩标准
critères de performance
Effizienzkriterien; Erfolgskriterien
criterios de rendimiento
業績基準

performance fund
运营基金，速利基金
fond d'investissement de bonne
performance
Investmentfonds, mit dem ein

Translations appear in the following order: Chinese, French, German, Spanish/Latin American Spanish, and Japanese

möglichst hoher Wertzuwachs
angestrebt wird
fondo de rendimiento
バランス投資

performance indicator
业绩指标
indice de performance
Leistungsindex; Leistungsindikator
indicador de rendimiento
達成度指針

performance management
绩效管理
gestion des performances
Performance-Management;
Leistungsmanagement
gestión del rendimiento
業績管理

performance measurement
绩效评估
mesure de performance
Leistungsmessung
medición de ejecución; medición
de realización; medición del
rendimiento
業績測定

performance-related pay
绩效工资
salaire au rendement
Leistungslohn
sueldo según el rendimiento
実力給

period bill
期票，定期汇票
traite ou lettre de change à délai
fixé
Terminwechsel
letra a plazo fijo
期日指定為替手形

period cost
期间成本
coût sur période définie
Periodenkosten
coste del período
costo del período
期間原価

**periodic inventory review
system**
定期盘存系统
système de révision de stock
régulière
periodische Bestandsaufnahme
sistema de revisión periódica del
inventario
定期的在庫調査システム

periodicity concept
周期概念
concept de la périodicité
Periodizitätskonzept;
Periodizitätshypothese
estados financieros en períodos

fijos obligatorios
期間概念

permalancer
长期自由撰稿人
travailleur indépendant bien
incrusté
freie/r Mitarbeiter(in) im
Dauerarbeitsverhältnis
freelancer veterano en una
empresa
半永久的に社内にいるフリーラ
ンス・スタッフ

**permanent interest-bearing
shares**
永久带息股份
actions avec intérêts postcomptés
permanents
langfristige Rentenwerte
acciones con interés permanente
永久利付き株

permission marketing
许可营销
marketing par permission
Marketing mit Einwilligung
marketing de permiso
パーミション・マーケティング

Perot
意外放弃
abandonner qc à la Ross Pérot
plötzlich aussteigen
marcharse; fracasar; abandonar
algo de repente
いきなり諦めること

perpetual bond
永久债券
titre/bon perpétuel
Annuitätenanleihe
bono perpetuo
無期限社債，無期債権

perpetual debenture
永久公司债券; 不兑换公司债券;
永久债券
obligation à intérêts perpétuels
untilgbare Schuldverschreibung
obligación perpetua
永久債券，永久債，永久社債

perpetual inventory
永续存盘
inventaire permanent
laufende Inventur; Buchinventur
inventario permanente
継続記録棚卸し

perpetuity
永久持续期
perpétuité
ewige Rente; lebenslängliche
Rente
perpetuidad
永久年金

per se
本身，本质上
en soi
an sich
en sí
それ自体で

personal account
个人帐户
compte personnel
Privatkonto
cuenta personal
人的勘定

personal allowances
个人免税额
déductions personnelles
persönliche Freibeträge
deducción/desgravación por
gastos personales
所得控除

personal contract
个人谈判合同
contrat personnalisé
individuell gestalteter
Arbeitsvertrag;
personengebundener Vertrag
selección en grupos
对人契约

personal development
个人发展; 自我发展
développement personnel
persönliche Entwicklung
desarrollo personal
自己開発

Personal Equity Plan
个人股份计划
plan d'investissement personnel
en actions ordinaires
staatliches Programm zur
Vermögensbildung mit Aktien
plan de ahorro en acciones; plan
personal de inversión en bolsa
incentivado fiscalmente
個人持分プランPEP

personal financial planning
个人财务计划
organisation financière
personnelle
persönliche Finanzplanung
planificación financiera personal
個人金融プラン

**Personal Investment
Authority**
个人投资局
autorité de supervision des
investissements personnels
Amt für persönliche Investitionen;
Selbstverwaltungskörperschaft zur
Überwachung der Aktivitäten
finanzieller Mittelsleute, die
Finanzprodukte an Privatpersonen
verkaufen

Translations appear in the following order: Chinese, French, German, Spanish/Latin American
Spanish, and Japanese

organismo autoregulador de la
inversión de particulares
個人投資機関

personalisation
个性化
personnalisation
Personalisierung
personalización
ウェブサイトの個人化

personality promotion
名人促销
promotion qui utilise une vedette
Prominenten-Werbung
promoción con famoso
有名人起用拡販

personal pension
个人养老金
plan d'épargne retraite
private Rentenversicherung
pensión personal
個人年金

personnel[1]
职工; 人事; 人事人员; 人事处
personnel: personnes employées
dans une organisation,
considérées collectivement
Personal; Belegschaft
personal
全職員,

personnel[2]
人事部门
service du personnel
Belegschaftsabteilung
personal
人事,

personnel management
人事管理
gestion du personnel
Personalwirtschaft;
Personalverwaltung;
Personalmanagement
gestión de personal
人事管理

personnel manager
人事主管
chef du personnel
Personalleiter(in); Personalchef(in)
jefe(-a) de personal
人事担当マネージャー

personnel policy
人事政策
politique relative au personnel
Personalpolitik
política de personal
職員規則

PEST analysis
商业环境分析框架
analyse de type PEST
PEST-Analyse

análisis político, económico, social
y tecnológico
PEST分析

PESTLE
影响市场六因素
politique, économique, sociale,
technologique, légale et
environnementale
Beschreibung der sechs
Einflussfaktoren, denen ein Markt
unterliegt: politische,
wirtschaftliche, soziale,
technologische, rechtliche und
umweltbezogene Faktoren
las influencias política, económica,
social, tecnológica, legal y
medioambiental
市場に影響を及ぼす要素の頭文字

Peter Principle
彼特原理
le principe de Peter
Peterprinzip
principio de Peter
ピーターの原理

**petites et moyennes
entreprises**
中小企业
petites et moyennes entreprises
kleinere und mittlere
Unternehmen
PYME
中小企業

petty cash
零用(现)金; 小额出纳金
petite caisse
kleine Kasse; Portokasse;
Handgeld; Bargeld
caja pequeña; caja para gastos
menores
小口現金, 小払資金

phantom bid
虚假投标
offre fantôme
Scheinangebot
oferta ficticia
幽霊入札, 架空競売

phantom income
虚假收入
revenu fantôme
Scheingewinn
ingresos ficticios
架空収益, ファントム・インカム

phased retirement
分阶段退休
prise de retraite progressive
schrittweise Pensionierung
jubilación progresiva
段階的定年

Phillips curve
菲利浦[斯]曲线
représentation graphique de la

relation entre le chômage et le
taux d'inflation
Phillips-Kurve
curva de Phillips
フィリップス曲線

phone lag
电话时差
fatigue due aux coups de fil passés
pour affaires dans d'autres fuseaux
horaires
Phone-Lag
desfase horario causado por
conversaciones telefónicas con
otros husos horarios
時差のある国との電話により出て
くる疲れ

physical asset
有形资产
valeurs/biens physiques
Sachvermögenswert; Sachanlage
activo físico
物理的財産

**physical distribution
management**
物流管理; 物资分配管理
gestion de distribution physique
Management; der physischen
Verteilung; Vertriebsleitung;
Verteilungsmanagement; durch
den Handel
gestión de la distribución física
物的流通管理

physical market
现货市场
marché au comptant
Kassamarkt
mercado físico
実物市場

physical price
立即送货价
prix matériel: prix des matières
premières disponibles, vendues et
achetées au comptant
Effektivpreis
precio físico
物理的納品価格

physical retail shopping
传统零售方式
shopping physique (par contraste
au shopping en ligne)
Einkauf in Ladengeschäften, nicht
Online
compras en tiendas
物理的に店舗に出向いて行う
ショッピング

physicals
现货
biens matériels
Effektivware
físicos
現物

Translations appear in the following order: Chinese, French, German, Spanish/Latin American Spanish, and Japanese

physical stocktaking
存货盘点
inventaire physique
effective Inventur; körperliche
Bestandsaufnahme
cotejo de los valores físicos con los
libros; recuento de existencias;
inventario
実地棚卸し

physical working conditions
实地工作条件
conditions de travail physiques
physische Arbeitsbedingungen;
Arbeitsumfeld
condiciones físicas de trabajo
物理的労働環境

pick and shovel work
烦琐工作
travail de scribouillard
akribische Kleinarbeit
trabajo minucioso y tedioso
面倒くさい仕事

picture
票象
(le) tableau (idée générale des prix
et quantité de transactions d'un
titre particulier sur Wall Street)
Kurs und Handelsumfang eines
bestimmten Wertpapiers an der
amerikanischen Wall Street
precio y cantidad de unas acciones
determinadas que son objeto de
especulación en Wall Street
市况

piece-rate system
计件工资系统
système du salaire à la pièce
Akkordsystem; Stücklohnsystem
sistema de pago por unidad
単位請負制, 出来高賃金制

pie chart
圆 [扇] 形图
camembert ou graphique à
secteurs
Torten- od. Kuchendiagramm
gráfico circular; gráfico de sectores
円グラフ

piggy-back advertising
搭配广告
publicité prise en charge
Huckepack-Kampagne
publicidad simultánea
便乗広告

piggyback loan
背负式负债
prêt pris en charge
Huckepackanleihe
préstamo concatenado
ビギーバック(相乗り)ローン

piggyback rights
随同行销认股权
droits de transaction qui en
entraîne une deuxième
Huckepackrechte
derechos concatenados
ビギーバック方式販売権,
抱き合わせ販売権

pig in a python
生育高峰
terme démographique décrivant
l'explosion du taux de natalité
entre 1946 et 1964
demographischer Begriff zur
Beschreibung des starken
Anschwellens der Geburtenrate
zwischen 1946 und 1964
boom demográfico entre 1946 y
1964
グラフでみた団塊の世代

pilot fish
追随者
poisson pilote
untere Führungskraft, die dicht an
einer vorgesetzten Führungskraft
bleibt
ejecutivo(-a) junior que acompaña
de cerca a otro más veterano
幹部に付きまとう後輩

pilot survey
试行调查
étude pilote
Probebefragung; Probeerhebung
encuesta piloto
試験調査

pin-drop syndrome
寂静压迫综合症
syndrome de l'épingle qui tombe
Bürostress, der durch extreme Stille
im Arbeitsumfeld verursacht wird
síndrome del silencio extremo
仕事場の静けさによるストレス

pink advertising
同性恋人群广告
publicité destinée à la
communauté homosexuelle
Randgruppen-Werbung
publicidad dirigida a
homosexuales y lesbianas
同性愛者向け広告

pink-collar job
粉领工作
terme sexiste pour un poste
habituellement occupé par une
femme
sexistischer Begriff für
normalerweise durch Frauen
ausgeführte Arbeiten,
insbesondere junge Frauen
trabajo para jovencita
ピンク・カラー(伝統的な女性向
き)職業

pink form
股票首次公开发行的优先申购表,
粉紅色表格
formulaire rose: au Royaume Uni
un formulaire de demande
préférentielle pour une offre
publique initiale qui est réservé aux
employés de la compagnie
émettant les actions
Vorzugsantragsformular bei
Erstausgaben, vorbehalten für
Mitarbeiter(in)nen der
Gesellschaft, die an die Börse
geht
impreso rosa
優遇株式申込書式

pink pound
桃色英镑
livre rose
Pink Pfund
poder adquisitivo de los
homosexuales
ピンク貨幣(同性愛者が使うお
金)

pink slipper
炒鱿鱼
personne ayant reçu son avis de
licenciement
Entlassene/r
trabajador(a) despedido(-a)
首になった人

Pink 'Un
金融时报
'Pink 'Un': argot anglais du
Financial Times désignant un
formulaire rose
die *Financial Times*
Pink 'Un
ファイナンシャル・タイムズ

piracy
盗版
piratage
Plagiat; Piraterie; Seeräuberei;
Raubdruck
piratería
海賊行為, 著作権侵害

pit
高台，特定交易场
corbeille: zone d'une Bourse où
les transactions ont lieu
Ring
corro
ピット(取引所の仕切りセリ売
買場)

pit broker
交易经纪人
agent de change à la corbeille
Börsensaalmakler(in)
corredor(a) del área de

Translations appear in the following order: Chinese, French, German, Spanish/Latin American Spanish, and Japanese

operaciones
ピット・ブローカー

pitch
推销活动
territoire (de vente)
Verkaufsgespräch
territorio
顧客獲得販売促進(ピッチ)

placement fee
股票经纪人售股费; 配售费用;
募集资金费用
frais de placement
Vermittlungsgebühr
honorarios de colocación
委託手数料

placing
安排出售，配售
placement
Platzierung; Platzieren
colocación; colocación de una
emisión de acciones
私募, プレースメント

plain text e-mail
纯文本电子邮件
message e-mail avec texte simple
E-Mail im Klartext
correo electrónico sin formato
プレーン・テキストeメール

plain vanilla
普通发行
(de la) vanille pure: instrument
financier dans sa forme la plus
simple, sans aucune fanfare (terme
argotique)
routinemäßig; ohne
Schnickschnack
corriente; clásico
基本金融商品

plan comptable
会计方案
plan comptable
einheitlich gestaltetes und
detailliertes Buchführungssystem,
dessen Befolgung für
Unternehmen in Frankreich
obligatorisch ist
plan de contabilidad francés
(仏)標準簿記システム

planned obsolescence
人为的商品废弃; 计划报废
obsolescence calculée
geplantes Veralten; geplante
Obsoleszenz
obsolencia planeada
計画的陳腐化

planning
规划，规划制定
planification
Planung
planificación
計画

planning horizon
计划期距
horizon de planification
Planungshorizont
horizonte de planificación
計画期限

planning period
规划期
période de planification
Planungszeitraum;
Planungsperiode
período de planificación, de
acuerdo con producto o proceso
del ciclo de vida
計画期間

plant
车间; 工厂; 成套设备; 厂房设备
usine
Anlage
planta
工場施設

plant layout
厂房设备布局
agencement d'usine
Auslegung; von Betriebsanlagen
distribución de planta
工場配置

plastic
塑料货币，信用卡
(argent en) plastique: voir argent
en plastique
Plastikgeld
tarjeta
クレジットカード支払い

plateauing
停滞状态; 高原期
atteindre un palier ou se stabiliser
Einpendeln; Gleichbleiben
estabilización
頭打ち伸び悩み

platform
载体产品
plate-forme
Plattform
plataforma
プラットフォーム

plentitude
产品充足经济
pleinitude
Fülle
plenitud
物品潤沢説

plough back
再投资
réinvestir
reinvestieren
reinvertir
再投資する

ploughed back profits
再投资利润
bénéfices réinvestis
thesaurierte Gewinne
beneficios reinvertidos
再投資利益

plug and play
即插即用; 即插即用的
nouveau membre du personnel qui
n'a pas besoin de formation pour
commencer dans son emploi
sofort einsatzbereite/r
Mitarbeiter(in)
empleado(-a) que no necesita
formación
トレーニングを必要としない新入
社員

plug-in
插件
plug-in
einsteckbar
conector
プラグイン

plum
意外分红，成功的投资
superdividende (terme argotique)
erfolgreiche Kapitalanlage
chollo
プラム(成功投資)

poaching
挖人; 挖取
braconnage
Abwerben; Wilderei; Abwerben
von Kunden od. Arbeitskräften
robo
人材の横取り

point
点
point
Punkt
punto
ポイント

point of presence
节点
point de présence
Anwesenheitsstelle
punto de presencia
ポイント・オブ・プレゼンス

point-of-purchase display
销售点展示
affichage PLV
Schauwerbung am Verkaufsort
expositor en el punto de venta
購買時点表示

point of sale
销售驱动程序; 销售点
point de vente
Kassenplatz
punto de venta
販売時点

points plan
计分工作评价法
système des points: méthode pour
évaluation d'un travail, parfois
appelée système points-facteurs,
qui utilise une échelle de points
pour noter des critères divers
Punktebewertungsverfahren;
Methode zur Arbeitsbewertung,
auch Punkt-Faktor-System
genannt, bei der eine Punkteskala
zur Wertung verschiedener
Kriterien zur Anwendung kommt
sistema de evaluación por puntos
ポイント評価制

poison pill
毒药丸政策
mesure prise par une compagnie
pour éviter un rachat hostile, par
exemple faire une transaction qui
rend l'acquisition peu attrayante
pour l'acheteur potentiel
Anti-Übernahme-Strategie
píldora venenosa o envenenada
敵対的買収を避けるための手段

policy
政策，方针
politique
Grundsatz; Strategie
política; norma
政策

policyholder
保户，投保人，保单持有人
titulaire d'une police d'assurance
Versicherungsnehmer(in)
asegurado
(被)証券保持者

political economy
政治经济学
économie politique
Volkswirtschaft
economía política
政治経済学、広義の経済学

political price
政策价; 政治代價
prix politique
politischer Preis
precio político
政治の価格

political risk
政治风险
risque politique
politisches Risiko
riesgo político
政治的リスク

politics
政治
politique
Politik; Staatskunst; politische
Grundsätze

política
政治, 政策, かけ引き

POP
存在点; 入网点
POP
POP
protocolo POP
POP(ポストオフィスプロ
トコール)

population
总体，人口
population
Population
población
母集団

population pyramid
种群锥体，人口金字塔
pyramide des populations
Populationspyramide
pirámide de edades
人口分布グラフ

pop-under ad
弹出式广告
publicité dans sous-fenêtre
distincte sur Internet
Internetwerbung, die in einem
separaten Fenster vom Rest der
Webseite geöffnet wird
banner flotante
ポップアンダー広告

portable pension
可移动养老金
retraite transférable
übertragbare Pension
pensión transferible
移動継続年金

portal
门户; 入口
portail
Portal
portal
ポータル・サイト

portfolio
有价证券清单;
有价证券组合(搭配)
portefeuille
Portefeuille; Wertpapierbestand
cartera (de valores)
ポートフォリオ

portfolio career
职业组合
carrière au portefeuille varié
Werdegang mit Risikostreuung,
basierend auf einer Reihe
unterschiedlicher kurzfristiger
Aufgaben
currículum con empleos de corta
duración
複数の企業に短期間ずつ勤めて
きた人

portfolio immunisation
有价证券组合免疫
vaccination de portefeuille
Maßnahmen, die Händler zum
Schutz ihres Wertpapierbestands
ergreifen
protección de carteras
ポートフォリオの保護手段

portfolio insurance
组合证券保险
assurance de portefeuille
Portfolio-Versicherung
seguro de cartera
ポートフォリオ保険

portfolio investment
证券投资; 间接投资; 组合投资
investissement en portefeuille
Portfolio-Investition
inversión de cartera
間接投資

portfolio manager
组合投资管理经理
portefeuilliste
Vermögensverwalter(in)
gestor(a) de carteras
ポートフォリオ・マネジャー

portfolio working
身兼多职工作方式
travail avec portefeuille d'activités:
modèle de travail selon lequel on
poursuit plusieurs carrières à la
fois. Le travail avec portefeuille
d'activités fut iventé par Charles
Handy pour décrire un style
possible de vie professionnelle
dans laquelle trav
Portfolio-Arbeit
seguimiento de varias carreras
profesionales al mismo tiempo
ポートフォリオ・ワーキング

POSDCORB
计划, 组织, 员工, 领导, 协调, 报告
和预算
POSDCORB: acronyme inventé par
Luther Gulick qui signifie
planification, organisation,
pourvoi de postes, direction,
coordination, présentation de
rapports et établissement des
budgets. POSDCORB fut inventé
en 1935, avec l'intention de
décrire les divers
Beschreibung der funktionellen
Elemente der Arbeit eines Chief
Executive geprägt
planificación, organización,
dotación de personal,
coordinación, redacción de
informes y elaboración de
presupuestos
POSDCORB

---

*Translations appear in the following order: Chinese, French, German, Spanish/Latin American
Spanish, and Japanese*

position
财务状况; 头寸
position
Wertpapierposition; Position
posición
持ち高, ポジション

position audit
现状审查
audit de situation
Bestandsaufnahme
auditoría de posición
ポジション監査

position limit
头寸限制; 成交量限制
limite de positions: quantité
maximum de positions ouvertes
autorisée à une seule personne ou
à un seul groupe
Positionslimit
límite de posición
持ち高枠, ポジション枠

positive discrimination
防止(纠正)歧视性雇佣做法的
优惠待遇
mesures antidiscriminatoires en
faveur des minorités
positive Diskriminierung;
Förderungsmaßnahmen; zu
Gunsten von Minderheiten
discriminación positiva
優遇政策

positive economics
实证经济学
économie positive
positive Wirtschaftswissenschaft
economía positiva
実証的の経済学

possessor in bad faith
非法所有者
possesseur de mauvaise foi
bösgläubige/r Besitzer(in)
poseedor(a) de mala fe
不誠実な占有者

possessor in good faith
合法所有者
possesseur de bonne foi
gutgläubige/r Besitzer(in)
poseedor(a) de buena fe
誠実な占有者

possessory action
财产留置; 扣货留置
action de possesseur
Besitz(schutz)klage
acción posesoria
所有権確定訴訟

post a credit
信贷过帐
passer écriture d'un crédit
Guthaben ausweisen; Guthaben
od. Gutschrift ausweisen od.

verbuchen
abonar
仕訳する, 仕訳帳から元帳に
転記する

postal survey
邮寄调查
enquête par correspondance
postalische Befragung
encuesta por correo
郵便調査

Post Big Bang
指伦敦股票交易所的交易规则
Post Big Bang: terme utilisé pour
décrire le mécanisme des
opérations boursières à la Bourse
de Londres, après le 26 octobre
1986
Handelsmechanismus an der
Londoner Börse nach dem 26.
Oktober 1986
post-big bang
ビッグバン以降

postdate
日期填迟; 注迟日期; 远期
postdater
vordatieren
extender con fecha posterior
当日以降の日付を記入する

post-industrial society
后工业社会
société post-industrielle
nachindustrielle Gesellschaft
sociedad postindustrial
脱工業化社会

post-purchase costs
购后成本
frais d'après-achat
Folgekosten; nach dem Kauf
anfallende Kosten
costes poscompra
購買後経費

potential GDP
潜在国内生产总值
PIB potentiel
Vollbeschäftigungs-Output
PIB potencial
潜在GDP, 潜在国内総生産

pot trust
证券转销信托
trust cagnotte: société de
placement créée de façon typique
dans un testament, pour un
groupe d'ayants droit
Trust für eine Gruppe von
Begünstigten
fondo para un grupo de
beneficiarios
(複数受益者への財産の)信託,
ポット・トラスト

pound cost averaging
英镑成本平均法
moyenne de coût régulier:
investissement d'une somme égale
dans un titre à intervalles réguliers
regelmäßiges Investieren der
gleichen Summe in ein Wertpapier,
unabhängig von dessen Kurs
inversión periódica de sumas fijas
ボンド・コスト・アベレージング,
英の定期的で均等の証券投資

poverty trap
贫困陷
piège de la pauvreté: situation où
se trouve les familles avec faibles
revenus, où une augmentation de
leurs ressources leur fait dépasser
le plafond autorisé pour recevoir
des prestations sociales, ou
entraîne une augmentation de
leurs impôts
Armutsfalle
trampa de la pobreza
貧困の泥沼の状況

power
权力
pouvoir
Macht
poder
権限

**power and influence theory
of leadership**
权力与影响理论
théorie du pouvoir et de l'influence
du leadership
Führungshypothese von Macht
und Einfluss
teoría del poder y la influencia en
el liderazgo
力と影響の理論

power centre
权力中心
centre de pouvoir
Machtzentrum
centro de poder
パワー・センター

power of attorney
授权书, 委托书
procuration légale
Vollmachtsurkunde
poder
代理委任状

power structure
权力结构
répartition des pouvoirs
Machtstruktur
estructura de poder
権力構造

pp
代表
per pro: abbréviation du latin per

---

*Translations appear in the following order: Chinese, French, German, Spanish/Latin American
Spanish, and Japanese*

procurationem: par procuration
pp.
p.a.
代理人として

PR
公共关系; 个人代表; 遗嘱代理人;
遗嘱执行人; 利润率
relations publiques
Public Relations
relaciones públicas
涉外, 广报, 宣传活动(PR)

prairie dogging
探头探脑
faire le chien de prairie
plötzliches Auftauchen von
Köpfen über den Trennwänden
eines Großraumbüros es etwas
Interessantes gibt oder wenn es
laut wird
las cabezas que se asoman por
encima de las particiones cuando
ocurre algo
区切られた事務所の中で何かが
あった時に頭がプレーリー
ドッグのように現れる現区切ら
れた事務所の中で何かがあった
時に頭がプレーリードッグのよ
うに現れる現象

pre-acquisition profits/losses
先得收益损失
bénéfices/pertes de pré-acquisition
Gewinne vor Übernahme
pérdidas o ganancias previas a la
adquisición
取得日以前の留保利益損益

**preauthorised electronic
debit**
预先授权资金电汇
débit électronique autorisé par
avance
vorbewilligte elektronische
Lastschrift
cargo electrónico autorizado de
antemano
事前承認電子振替,
自動引き落とし, 自動振替

prebilling
预先开票; 预先开发票
préfacturation
Vorfakturierung
prefacturación
プレビリング

precious metals
贵重金属
métaux précieux (or, argent,
platine et palladium)
Edelmetalle
metales preciosos
貴金属

predatory pricing
掠夺性定价
établissement de prix prédateur
Verdrängungswettbewerb;
rücksichtsloser Wettbewerb;
räuberische Preisfestsetzung
fijación de precios depredadores
狙い打ち価格設定

**predetermined motion-time
system**
预定动作时间系统
systèmes de cadences prédéfinies
Systeme vorbestimmter Zeiten;
Systeme vorbestimmter
Bewegungszeiten
sistemas predeterminados de
ritmo de producción
設定動作時間システム

predictive maintenance
预测性维修
maintenance selon prédiction
prognostische Wartung
mantenimiento preventivo
予想メンテナンス

pre-emptive right
优先认购权
droit de préemption
Vorkaufsrecht
derecho preferente
先買権

preference shares
优先股
actions privilégiées
Vorzugsaktien
acciones preferentes, acciones
privilegiadas
優先株

preferential creditor
优先债权人
créancier privilégié
bevorrechtigte/r
Konkursgläubiger(in)
acreedor(a) preferente
優先債権者

preferential issue
优先发行
émission privilégiée
Vorzugsemission;
Präferenzemission
emisión preferencial
特定バイヤー向け優先株式発行

preferential payment
优先债权人
paiement privilégié
bevorzugte Befriedigung
pago preferente
優先支払い

preferred position
优良的财务状况
position privilégiée
bevorzugte Position
posición preferida
希望広告形態

preferred risk
选择风险
risque préféré
Schadensfreiheit
riesgo preferente
優先的リスク

pre-financing
先期货款
préfinancement
Vorfinanzierung
prefinanciación
事前出資

prelaunch
预发行; 新产品推出前活动
prélancement
der Begebung vorangehend; der
Begebung od. Einführung
vorangehend
lanzamiento previo
発売前準備

preliminary prospectus
初步公开说明书; 初期说明书
prospectus préliminaire
vorläufiger Prospekt
prospecto de emisión preliminar
予備目論見書

premarket
市前交易
pré-placement: transactions entre
membres d'un marché effectuées
avant l'ouverture officielle de ce
marché
vorbörslich
mercado previo
立会い前取引

Premiers' Conference
州长会议
conférence des chefs des états et
territoires d'Australie et du
gouvernement fédéral
Premierminister-Konferenz
reunión anual de las autoridades
federales y territoriales australianas
州知事会議(豪)

premium[1]
优质的; 高价的; 高级的; 溢价;
加价; 优惠; 保险费; 赠品
prix majoré (pour produits ou
services rares)
Belohnung
prima
プレミアム商品

premium[2]
升水，涨价
prix fort (pour indiquer la haute
qualité)
Methode zur Preisfestlegung, bei

Translations appear in the following order: Chinese, French, German, Spanish/Latin American Spanish, and Japanese

der ein hoher Preis für hohe
Qualität steht
prima
プレミアム価格設定

premium³
保证金，期权费
prix convenu
Prämie
prima
プレミアム付き価格

premium⁴
溢价
différence entre le prix des options
à terme et le prix comptant d'un
actif sous-jacent
Agio
prima
割増金

premium⁵
保险费
prime (d'assurance)
Prämie
prima
保険料

Premium Bond
(抽签)有奖债券
obligation à prime (obligation
britannique rémunérée par tirage
au sort mensuel)
Prämienanleihe
obligación del Estado con prima
割増金付債権

premium income
保(险)费收入
revenu des primes
Prämienaufkommen
ingresos por primas
収入保険料

premium offer
有奖促销
offre de cadeau gratuit
gratis Angebot
oferta especial
景品贈呈による販促商法

premium pay plan
奖金支付计划
système d'échelons de salaire
supérieur
Prämienlohnsystem
plan de incentivos salariales
奨励金プラン

premium pricing
溢价定价方式; 溢价
fixation de prix à la hausse
Festlegung von Höchstpreisen
fijación más alta de precios
名声価格, 特別価格

prepackaged choice
预先包装产品(尤指计算机行业
中的软件等); 不可拆装型产品

choix informatique multimédia
prédéfini
fertig abgepackte Auswahl an
Computermaterial, nicht durch
den Anwender anpassbar
configuración predeterminada
汎用商品

prepaid interest
预付利息
intérêt prépayé
vorausbezahlte Zinsen;
Zinsvorauszahlung
interés anticipado
前払利息

prepayment
预付项目
paiement par anticipation
Zahlung vor Fälligkeit
pago previo or por adelantado
期限前弁済

prepayment penalty
预付金罚款
pénalité de paiement par
anticipation
Aufschlagfür vorzeitige
Darlehenstilgung
penalización por reembolso
anticipado
途中償還違約金

prepayment privilege
提前还款特权
privilège de paiement anticipé
Recht auf aufschlagsfreie
vorzeitige Tilgung
privilegio de pago previo or por
adelantado
期限前弁済権

prepayment risk
预付风险
risque de paiement anticipé
Risiko der vorzeitigen Tilgung
riesgo por pago previo or por
adelantado
期限前返済リスク

prequalification
资格预审
préqualification
Vorqualifikation; vorbereitende
Qualifikation
precalificación
事前選別

prescribed payments system
指令付费系统
système des paiements prescrits
vorgeschriebenes Zahlungssystem
sistema de retención de impuestos
en los pagos en efectivo
建設業などにおける分割納税制度

presentation
展示; 演示; 展示会

présentation
Präsentation; Vortrag; Vorlage;
Darbietung
presentación
プリゼンテーション, 発表

presenteeism
过于积极; 过分表现
présentéisme: opinion selon
laquelle les nombreuses heures
passées au travail sont plus
importantes que la productivité ou
les résultats. Le présentéisme est le
contraire de l'absentéisme
Präsentismus
presentismo
出勤主義

present value¹
现值
valeur actuelle
Zeitwert
valor actual
現在価値

present value²
现值
valeur actuelle
Gegenwartswert
valor actual
現在価値

preservation of capital
资本存储; 资本储备
préservation de capital
Kapitalerhaltung;
Substanzerhaltung
conservación del capital
資本の保全

press advertising
报刊广告
publicité de presse
Printmedienwerbung
publicidad en prensa
活字メディア広告

press communications
媒介交流
communications de presse
Pressestelle
comunicaciones de prensa
プレス・コミュニケーション

press conference
记者招待会
conférence de presse
Pressekonferenz
rueda de prensa; conferencia de
prensa
記者会見

press cutting
剪报
coupure de presse
Presseausschnitt,
Zeitungsausschnitt

Translations appear in the following order: Chinese, French, German, Spanish/Latin American Spanish, and Japanese

recorte de prensa
新聞の切り抜き

press date
发行日期
date d'impression
Erscheinungsdatum
fecha de publicación
発行日

press release
新闻发布
communiqué de presse
Pressemitteilung
comunicado de prensa
プレス・リリース

press the flesh
握手
serrer les pognes
Hände schütteln
apretar las manos
ビジネス・イベントで大勢の
人と握手する

pressure group
压力小组
groupe de pression
Interessengruppe; Pressuregroup
grupo de presión
压力团体

pre-syndicate bid
（新股上市）优先出价
offre pré-consortium
Angebot, das gemacht wird, bevor
ein Käufersyndikat in einem
Publikumsangebot Aktienpakete
anbieten kann
oferta realizada antes de la
colocación en el mercado
secundario
プレ・シンディケート・ビッド,
引受組合による公募前入札

pretax
税前的
avant impôt/brut
vor Steuern
antes de impuestos
税引き前の

pretax profit
税前利润
bénéfice brut
Gewinn vor Steuern
beneficio antes de impuestos
税引き前利益

pretax profit margin
税前利润率
marge de profit brute
Gewinnspanne vor Steuern
margen de beneficio antes de
impuestos
税引き純利益率

pretesting
试验; 试用
étude préliminaire sur petite

échelle
Minimarkttest
pruebas previas
プレテスト

prevalence
流行
prédominance
Prävalenz
prevalencia
普及率

preventive maintenance
预防性维修
maintenance préventive
vorbeugende Wartung
mantenimiento preventivo
予防メンテナンス

price
标价; 定价; 价格
prix
Preis; Kurs; Notierung
precio
価格, 相場

price ceiling
价格上限; 最高价
plafond de prix
oberste Preisgrenze; Höchstpreis
precio límite
価格上限

price competition
价格竞争
concurrence des prix
Preiswettbewerb
competencia de precios
価格競争

price control
价格管理; 物价控制
contrôle des prix
Preiskontrolle; Preisüberwachung
control de precios
価格統制、物価統制

price differentiation
价格差异
différentiation de prix
Preisdifferenzierung
diferenciación de precios
価格差別化

price discovery
价格形成
détermination du prix
Preisfindung
búsqueda del precio
価格発見

price discrimination
价格歧视; 差别取价;
价格上的差别待遇
discrimination par les prix
Preisdiskriminierung;
Preisdifferenzierung
discriminación de precios
価格差別、価格差別化

price-dividend ratio
价格-股息(红利)比率
rapport cours-dividende
Preis-Dividenden-Rate
coeficiente entre precio y
dividendo
株価配当率, 配当利回り

price-earnings ratio
价格-收益比率
rapport cours-bénéfices
Kurs-Gewinn-Verhältnis
coeficiente precio/beneficio
株価収益率, PER

price effect
价格作用
influence due au prix
Preiseffekt
efecto de los precios
価格効果

price elasticity of demand
需求价格弹性
élasticité du prix de demande
Preiselastizität der Nachfrage
elasticidad-precio de la demanda
需要の価格弾力性

price elasticity of supply
供应价格弹性
élasticité du prix de l'offre
Preiselastizität des Angebots
elasticidad-precio de la oferta
供給の価格弾力性

price escalation clause
价格调整条款
clause d'escalade des prix
Preisgleitklausel
cláusula de ajuste de precios
価格上昇条項

price fixing
固定价格; 限价; 非法固定价格;
非法价格垄断
fixation des prix
Preisfestsetzung; Preisabsprache;
vertikale Preisbindung
fijación de precios
価格の固定, ヤミ価格協定

price floor
价格下限; 最底限价
plancher de prix
Mindestpreis; niedrigster Preis
precio mínimo
価格の底

price index
物价指数; 价格指数
indice des prix
Preisindex
índice de precios
物価指数

price indicator
价格指标
indice des prix

Translations appear in the following order: Chinese, French, German, Spanish/Latin American Spanish, and Japanese

Preisindikatoren
indicador de precios
价格指標、物価指標

price instability
价格摇动; 价格摆动
instabilité des prix
Preisinstabilität; Unbeständigkeit
der Preise; Schwanken der Preise
inestabilidad de los precios
物価不安定性

price leadership
领头价格; 价格领导
dirigeants des prix
Preisführerschaft; Preisführung
liderazgo en precios
価格決定指導権, 価格指導

price list
价格表; 价目表
prix courant
Preisliste; Preisverzeichnis;
Kurszettel
lista de precios
価格表

price range
价格幅度; 物价幅度
gamme de prix
Preisspanne; Preislage; Kursspanne
escala de precios
値幅, 価格帯

price ring
价格垄断集团
monopole des prix
Kartellring
cártel de precios
価格操作人

prices and incomes policy
价格與收入政策
politique des prix et revenus
Preis- und Einkommenspolitik
política de precios e ingresos
物価と所得政策

price-sensitive
价格敏感的
pouvant être influencé par les prix
(marché)
preisempfindlich; preiselastisch;
kursempfindlich; börsensensibel
sensible al precio
価格敏感型

price-sensitive information
影响股市的信息
information risquant d'influencer
les prix
börsenempfindliche Informationen
información privilegiada
株価左右情報

price stability
价格稳定性; 价格稳定
stabilité des prix
Preisstabilität

estabilidad de los precios
価格安定

price support
价格补贴; 价格支持
soutien des prix
Preisstützung
mantenimiento de los precios
価格支持、価格維持

price tag[1]
价格标签; 价格卡片; 标价条
étiquette
Preisschild; Preis; Kostenpunkt
etiqueta del precio
値札

price tag[2]
价格标签
prix ou valeur (d'une personne ou
chose)
Wert einer Person oder Sache
etiqueta de precio
値札

price-to-book ratio
价格对帐面价值比例
rapport cours-livre de compte
Kurs-Buch-Verhältnis
coeficiente precio a valor en libros
株価純資産倍率

price-to-cash-flow ratio
价格对现金流动比例
rapport cours-cashflow
Verhältnis Preis zu Cashflow
coeficiente precio/flujo de capital
株価キャッシュフロー倍率,
P C F R

price-to-sales ratio
价销比
rapport cours-ventes
Preis-Absatz-Quote
coeficiente precio/ventas
株価売上高倍率

price war
价格战
guerre des prix
Preiskrieg
guerra de precios
価格競争

price-weighted index
价格加权指数; 價格比重指數
indice des prix mesurés
kursgewichteter Index
índice de precios ponderados
価格加重インデックス

pricing
定价
fixation du prix (de vente)
Preisgestaltung; Preisbildung
fijación del precio de venta
価格設定

pricing policy
定价政策
politique des prix
Preispolitik
política de precios
価格決定方針

primary account number
主要帐号; 初级帐号
numéro de compte primaire
primäre Kontonummer
número de cuenta primario
プライマリー・アカウント番号

primary data
原始数据; 一手数据
données primaires
Primärdaten
datos primarios
一次データ

primary liability
主要债务
responsabilité première
Hauptverbindlichkeit;
Primärverbindlichkeit
responsabilidad directa
第一次負債

primary market
初级市场; 第一市场
marché primaire
Primärmarkt; Emissionsmarkt
mercado primario
発行市場, 主要市場

primary sector
國家經濟的主要生產公司或企業
secteur primaire
primärer Sektor
sector primario
第一次産業部門

prime assets ratio
基本资产比率
ratio d'actif de premier ordre
Mindestreservesatz
coeficiente de pasivo total
優良資産率

prime cost
主要成本, 直接成本
prix coûtant
Anschaffungskosten;
Fertigungseinzelkosten
coste directo de producción
元値

prime rate
最优惠利率
taux de base
Prime Rate; Vorzugszins für erste
Adressen
interés preferencial; tipo de interés
preferencial
プライムレート, 最優遇貸出金利

---

*Translations appear in the following order: Chinese, French, German, Spanish/Latin American
Spanish, and Japanese*

principal budget factor
首要预算因素
facteur de budget principal
Engpassfaktor
factor principal de presupuestos
主予算要素

principal shareholders
主要股东们
actionnaires principaux
Hauptaktionäre
número de cuenta primario
主要株主

print farming
印刷管理
gestion des exigences d'impression
Druck-Management
gestión de preimpresión y
producción
印刷ニーズの総合管理

prior charge capital
优先偿付资本
capital avec droit prioritaire
(d'intérêt ou de dividende)
Sondervorzugsaktien
capital de cargo previo preferencial
優先債権資本

priority-based budgeting
优先权预算
budgétisation basée sur les
priorités (de changement)
prioritätenorientierte
Finanzplanung
cambios prioritarios de
presupuesto de base anticipada
優先順予算

priority percentage
优先权比率
pourcentage de priorité
Prozentsatz an bevorrechtigten
Forderungen
proporción de los beneficios netos
de un negocio que se paga en
interés a los accionistas
preferentes y a los tenedores de
capital ajeno
優先債権率

prior lien bond
优先留置权债券
obligation de privilège antérieur
Anleihe mit älterem Pfandrecht
bono de gravamen superior
旧債の担保権に優先する担保権
の付いた債券,
優先特権付き社債, 先取特権社債

privacy policy
保密协议，隐私条款
politique de protection de la vie
privée
Geheimhaltungsgrundsatz
política de privacidad
プライバシー防護策

private bank[1]
私营银行; 私人银行
banque privée
Privatbank
banco privado
個人銀行

private bank[2]
私人银行
banque privée
Privatbank
banco privado
個人銀行

private bank[3]
私营银行
banque privée
Privatbank
banco privado
民間銀行

private banking
私人银行服务业务
services bancaires privés
Bankdienstleistungen für
Privatkundschaft
banca privada
プライベート・バンキング

private company
私人公司
société privée
personenbezogene
Kapitalgesellschft;
Privatunternehmen
compañía de un solo propietario;
empresa sin cotización en bolsa;
compañía privada
私会社有限会社

private cost
企业成本
coût personnel
private Kosten; Privatausgaben
coste privado
costo privado
私的費用

private debt
私人债务
dette personnelle
Privatverschuldung; individuelle
Verschuldung
deuda privada
民間負債

private enterprise
私有企业
entreprise privée
freie Marktwirtschaft;
Privatwirtschaft
empresa privada
民間企業, 個人経営

Private Finance Initiative
私筹资金政策
initiative de financement privé
Initiative für freie Finanzierung

iniciativa de financiación privada
民間融資イニシャティブ

private placing
募集; 安排出售; 配售
placement de titres par voie privée
Privatplatzierung
colocación privada
私募発行

private sector
私营(经济)部门
secteur privé
Privatwirtschaft; privater Sektor
sector privado
民間部門

private sector investment
私人部门或私营经济投资
investissement du secteur privé
Investitionen der Privatwirtschaft
inversión del sector privado
民間部門投資

private treaty
私下(交易)协定
traité privé
freihändiger Verkauf
tratado privado
個人不動産取引

privatisation
私有化
privatisation
Privatisierung
privatización
民営化

probability
概率; 或然率
probabilité
Wahrscheinlichkeit
probabilidad
確率

probability distribution
概率分布
loi de probabilité
Wahrscheinlichkeitsverteilung
distribución de probabilidad
確率分布

probability plot
概率图
courbe graphique de probabilité
Wahrscheinlichkeitsdiagramm
gráfico de probabilidad
確率プロット

probability sample
概率样本
échantillon de probabiliste
Wahrscheinlichkeitsstichprobe
muestra probabilística; muestra de
probabilidad
確率サンプル

probability sampling
概率取样
sondage probabiliste

Translations appear in the following order: Chinese, French, German, Spanish/Latin American Spanish, and Japanese

Durchführung einer
Wahrscheinlichkeitsstichprobe
muestra probabilística; muestra de
probabilidad
確率サンプル

probation
试用期
période à l'essai
Probezeit; Einstellung auf Probe
período de prueba
見習期間

problem child¹
问题儿童; 问题子公司
caractériel/problème difficile
Problemkind
filial problemática
問題(要注意)子会社

problem child²
问题儿童，新兴产业
produit avec une faible part de
marché mais un gros potentiel de
croissance
Produkt mit geringem Marktanteil
aber hohem Wachstumspotenzial
producto con cuota de mercado
pequeña pero gran potencial de
crecimiento
潜在的成長商品だが
多額の投資が必要

problem-solving
解决问题
résolution de problèmes
Problemlösung
resolución de problemas
問題解決

procedure
程序; 步骤; 流程
procédure
Verfahren; Prozedur
procedimiento
手順

procedure manual
程序手册; 程序指南
manuel des procédures
Arbeitsablauf-Handbuch
manual de instrucciones; libro de
normas
作業手順書

proceeds
收入; 收益; 进款
recettes
Erlös; Gegenwert
ingresos
売上金額, 収益

process
程序; 流程; 处理
processus ou procédé
Verfahren; Fertigungsverfahren;
Prozess; Arbeitsgang; Arbeitsweise
proceso
プロセス工程

process chart
流程图
organigramme de processus
Ablaufdiagramm;
Programmablaufplan
diagrama de procedimientos
プロセス図表

process control
程序控制
gestion des processus industriels
Prozessteuerung
control de procesos
工程管理

process layout
流程布局
plan d'installation par procédés
Prozessauslegung;
verfahrenstechnische Auslegung
distribución de equipo por
procesos
工程レイアウト

process management
程序管理
gestion des procédés
Prozessteuerung;
Prozessverwaltung
gestión de procesos
工程管理

process production
程序式生产
production par processus
industriels
Prozessproduktion
producción en serie
一貫生産

process time
过程时间
durée de processus ou de procédé
Bearbeitungszeit
tiempo de procesado
プロセスタイム

procurement exchange
采购集團
échange d'approvisionnement/
approvisionnement réciproque
Beschaffungsaustausch
intercambio de adquisiciones
電子共同購買

producer price index
产品厂商价格指数;
生产者价格指数
indice des prix à la production
Erzeugerpreisindex
índice de precios a la producción
生産者物価指数

product
产品
produit
Produkt; Erzeugnis; Fabrikat

producto
製品

product abandonment
产品废弃
abandon de produit
Produktaufgabe
abandono de productos
製品廃止

product bundling
捆绑式销售
escompte pour produits groupés
Produktbündelung
descuento por agrupamiento de
producto
製品纏め売り

product churning
撒大网式产品营销
lancement en masse de produits
Masseneinführung von Produkten
inundación del mercado con
productos
製品の市場氾濫

product development
产品开发; 產品發展; 產品改良
développement de produit
Produktentwicklung
desarrollo de productos
製品開発

product differentiation
产品差异; 产品差别化
différenciation de produit
Produktdifferenzierung
diferenciación de productos
製品差別化

product family
产品家族
famille de produits
Produktfamilie
familia de productos
同種目製品

production
生产; 制造; 产量
production
Produktion; Fertigung;
Herstellung; Erzeugung
producción
生産

production control
生产控制; 生产管理
contrôle de production
Fertigungssteuerung;
Fertigungsplanung
control de la producción
生産管理

production cost
生产成本
coût de production
Herstellkosten; Produktionskosten
coste de producción
生産コスト

---

*Translations appear in the following order: Chinese, French, German, Spanish/Latin American
Spanish, and Japanese*

production management
生产管理
gestion de la production
Produktmanagement
gestión de la producción
生産管理

production planning
生产计划
planification de production
Fertigungsplanung;
Fertigungssteuerung
planificación de la producción
生産スケジュール

production smoothing
平稳生产; 均衡生产
nivellement de la production
Produktionsglättung
suavizado de la producción
生産スムーズ化

productive capacity
生产能力
capacité de production
Produktionskapazität;
Leistungsfähigkeit;
Ertragsfähigkeit
capacidad productiva
生産容量能力

productivity
生产率; 生产力
productivité
Produktivität
productividad
生産性

productivity bargaining
劳动生产率谈判
négociations sur la productivité
Produktivitätsverhandlungen
negociación colectiva basada en la
productividad
プロダクティビティ・バーゲニ
ング
(賃金上昇と引き換えに生産性
向上に協力)

product launch
产品推出; (新)产品投放市场;
新产品推出
lancement de produit
Produkteinführung
lanzamiento de un producto
製品発売

product layout
以产品为基础设定厂房
agencement optimal des postes de
fabrication de produit
produktorientierte Konzeption;
od. Auslegung
racionalización de la producción
製品レイアウト

product liability
产品责任

**responsabilité de produit/due au
produit**
Produkthaftung
responsabilidad civil sobre el
producto
商品損害責任

product life cycle
产品生命周期
cycle de vie de produit
Produktlebenszyklus
ciclo de vida de un producto
製品ライフ・サイクル

product line
产品系列; 产品(生产)线
ligne de produits
Produktlinie; Produktgruppe
línea de productos
製品種目

product management
产品管理
gestion de produit
Produktmanagement
dirección de producto
製品管理

product market
产品市场
marché des produits
Gütermarkt
mercado de productos
製品市場

product mix
产品结构; 产品组合; 产品搭配
mix de produits
Produktmix; Produktsortiment;
Sortiment
gama de productos
製品構成

product placement
一种通过电影电视展示产品的广
告方式
placement de produit de marque
Product Placement
publicidad consistente en la
aparición de un producto en una
película o programa televisivo
プロダクト・プレースメント

product portfolio
产品种类; 产品范围
portefeuille de produits
Produktpalette
cartera de productos
製品ポートフォリオ

product range
产品范围; 产品种类
gamme de produits
Sortiment; Produktangebot
gama de productos
製品群

product recall
产品回收
retrait d'un produit de la vente
Produktrückruf; Rückruf; eines
Produkts; aus dem Verkauf
retirada de un producto del
mercado
製品回収

product-sustaining activities
生产持续性活动
activités de support de produits
produktstützende Tätigkeiten
actividades de sostenimiento del
producto
製品維持活動

profession
专业; 职业
profession
Berufsstand
profesión
專門職

professional[1]
专业人员
professionnel: un membre d'une
profession spécifique
Mitglied eines Berufsstandes
profesional
專門家

professional[2]
专门人员
professionnel: une personne payée
pour faire un travail, à l'opposé
d'un bénévole ou d'une personne
dont l'activité représente un hobby
Berufstätige/r
profesional
プロ

professional[3]
专家
professionnel: une personne qui
montre un niveau élevé de
compétence
Profi
profesional
プロ

professionalism
专业人员技能; 专业能力和标准;
專業態度
professionalisme: le savoir-faire, la
compétence ou les normes
attendues d'un membre d'une
profession
Professionalität
profesionalismo
專門家気質

profile
简介; 概况; 形象; 传略; 分析
profil
Profil; Querschnitt;
Bekanntheitsgrad

Translations appear in the following order: Chinese, French, German, Spanish/Latin American Spanish, and Japanese

perfil
会社案内

profile method
档案法
méthode du profil de fonction
Profilmethode
método analítico de evaluación
プロフィール法

profitability index
获利能力指数
indice de rentabilité
Rentabilitätsindex
índice de rentabilidad
収益性指数

profitability threshold
赢利临界值
seuil de rentabilité
Rentabilitätsgrenze
umbral de rentabilidad
収益創出ライン

profitable
盈利的; 可获利的; 有利(可图)的
rentable
rentabel; einträglich;
gewinnbringend
rentable
利益の上がる

profit and loss
盈利和损失; 损益
pertes et profits
Gewinn und Verlust
pérdidas y ganancias
損益

profit and loss account
盈利及损失帐;
损益调整或分配帐户
compte de résultats
Gewinn- und Verlustrechnung;
Aufwands- und Ertragsrechnung
cuenta de pérdidas y ganancias
損益計算書

profit before tax
税前利润
bénéfice avant impôt
Gewinn vor Steuern
beneficio antes de impuestos
税込み利益

profit centre
利润中心; 利润单位
centre de profit
Profitcenter; Ergebniseinheit
centro de beneficios
プロフィット・センター

profit distribution
利润分配
distribution des bénéfices
Gewinnausschüttung;
Gewinnverteilung
distribución de beneficios
利益配分

profit from ordinary activities
正常营业利润
profit des activités ordinaires
Gewinn aus ordentlicher
Geschäfttätigkeit; ordentlicher
Gewinn
beneficios de actividades
ordinarias
通常営業活動利益

profit margin
利润边际; 利润率
marge bénéficiaire
Gewinnspanne; Gewinnmarge;
Umsatzrendite
margen de beneficios
利益幅

profit motive
正常营业利润; 利润动机
motif de profit
Gewinnmotiv; Profitmotiv
búsqueda de beneficio
利潤動機

profit per employee
人均毛利率
bénéfice par employé
Gewinn pro Arbeitnehmer
beneficio por empleado antes de
intereses e impuestos
従業員１人当り利益

profit-related pay
与利润搭钩的工资
système de majoration de salaire
liée aux bénéfices
Gewinnbeteiligung
paga vinculada a los beneficios
利潤分配制度

profit retained for the year
利润留存
bénéfice non distribué/réinvesti
pour l'année
thesaurierter Gewinn im
Geschäftsjahr; thesaurierter
Jahresgewinn
resultados pendientes de
aplicación; remanente; beneficios
del ejercicio no distribuidos
利益保持

profit sharing
利润分成; 利润分享; 职工分红;
分红利
(système de) participation aux
bénéfices
Gewinnbeteiligung;
Ergebnisbeteiligung
reparto de beneficios
利益配当

profit-sharing debenture
利润分成债券; 利润分红债券
obligation participante
Gewinnschuldverschreibung;

Schuldverschreibung mit
Gewinnbeteiligung
obligación participativa
利潤分配社債

profits tax
利润税，利得税
impôt sur les bénéfices
Ertragssteuer
impuesto sobre los beneficios
利得税

profit–volume/contribution graph
贡献图
courbe de contribution/
rentabilité-volume
Umsatz-Gewinn-Diagramm
volumen de ganancias /gráfico de
contribución y beneficio de
conjunto
限界利益図表

profit warning
利润警示
avertissement quant au profit
Gewinnwarnung
alerta sobre la caída de beneficios
プロフィット・ウォーニング,
利益下落警報

pro-forma
预开发票; 估价单; 草案
pro forma
pro forma; Schein-; nur des
Scheines wegen
proforma
見積りの, 仮の

pro-forma financial statement
财务预测报告
bilan provisoire
Probeabschluss
estado financiero proforma
見積財務諸表

pro-forma invoice
样本发票; 形式发票; 估价单
facture pro forma
Proformarechnung; fingierte
Rechnung
factura proforma
仮請求書, 試算送り状

program
程序
programme
Programm
programa
プログラム

programme trading
程序贸易
transactions par informatique
Programmhande
contratación electrónica
プログラム売買, プログラム取引

Translations appear in the following order: Chinese, French, German, Spanish/Latin American Spanish, and Japanese

progressive tax
累积税
impôt progressif
progressive Steuer
impuesto progresivo
累進税

project
项目,计划
projet
Vorhaben; Projekt
proyecto
プロジェクト

project finance
项目资金
financement de projet (en général
des projets de construction ou de
développement)
Projektfinanzierung
financiación de proyectos
資源開発融資

projection
价格预测,预测
prévision
Projektion; Hochrechnung;
Prognose
proyección
計画

project management
项目管理
gestion de projet
Projektleitung;
Projektmanagement
gestión de proyectos
プロジェクト管理

promissory note
期票; 本票
billet à ordre
Schuldschein; Eigenwechsel;
Solawechsel
pagaré
約束手形

promotion
提升
promotion
Beförderung
ascenso
昇進

proof-of-purchase
购物凭证
preuve d'achat
Kaufnachweis
justificante de compra
購入証明

property
财产; 产权; 所有权
propriété
Eigentum; Besitz; Vermögenswert;
Grundstück; Liegenschaft;
Immobilie

propiedad
資産, 財産, 不動産

property bond
财产债券
obligation foncière
Immobilienanleihe
bono de propiedad
不動産債券, プロパティ・ボンド

property damage insurance
财产损失保险
assurance habitation
Sachschadenversicherung
seguro de daños materiales
財物損壊保険(自動車などで
他人の財産に与えた損害の)

proportional tax
比例税
impôt proportionnel
Proportionalsteuer
impuesto proporcional
比例税, 定率税

proprietary ordering system
业主订货系统
système de commande breveté
herstellereigenes Bestellsystem
sistema para pedidos
proporcionado por el distribuidor
専売的発注システム

ProShare
(伦敦) 一个股东团体
ProShare
Interessengruppe für
Privatanleger(in)nen an der
Londoner Börse
grupo que representa a los
inversores privados en valores en la
bolsa londinense
プロシェアー

prospect
潜在用户; 准用户; 可能的客户
client potentiel prometteur
Interessent
cliente potencial
見込客

prospecting
潜在用户预测
prospection
Zielgruppen-Scanning
identificación de clientes
potenciales
見込客探し

prospectus
招股书
prospectus
Prospekt; Emissionsprospekt
prospecto
目論見書

prosuming
自给自足
producteur-conso
produzieren + konsumieren, etwa

bei einem interaktiven
Computerspiel
producción-consumo
生産・消費の両方をする

protected class
抢手人才
employé dont les compétences
sont très demandées parce que
rares
Arbeitnehmer mit Qualifikationen,
die derzeit gefragt sind
trabajador(a) en demanda
必要とされるスキルの持ち主

protectionism
保护(贸易)制; 保护(贸易)主义
protectionnisme
Portektionismus
proteccionismo
保護貿易主義、保護政策、保護貿
易論、保護主義

protective put buying
保护性看跌买进
achat protecteur d'options de
vente
Schutzkauf von Verkaufsoptionen
für Aktien, die man bereits besitzt
compra protectiva de opciones de
venta
プロテクティブ・プット(オプ
ションの原資産保有状態の)購入

protective tariff
保护关税
tarif protecteur
Schutzzoll
arancel proteccionista
保護関税

protocol
协议; 规程; 协定
protocole
Protokoll;
Verhandlungsniederschrift
protocolo
プロトコール

prototype
样机; 试制型式
prototype
Prototyp
prototipo
試作品

provision
备付金额
provision ou réserve
Rückstellung
reserva
引当金

provisional tax
临时预付税
impôt provisionnel
Steuervorauszahlung

---

*Translations appear in the following order: Chinese, French, German, Spanish/Latin American
Spanish, and Japanese*

coeficiente de pasivo total
予定納税

proxy
代理委托书; 代理人; 代表
procuration
Vertreter(in); Bevollmächtigte/r;
Stimmrechtsvollmacht;
Vollmacht(surkunde)
variable representativa
代理人

proxy fight
代表票争夺战
conflit par personnes interposées
Stimmrechtskampf;
Proxy-Auseinandersetzung
lucha por la obtención de votos
委任状争奪戦

proxy server
代理服务器
serveur proxy
Proxy-Server
servidor proxy
プロクシー・サーバー

proxy statement
委托书
déclaration par procuration
Vollmachtsformular;
Stimmrechtsvollmacht
informe dado a los accionistas que
van a votar algo
委任勧誘状

psychic income
精神收入
rendement psychique
seelisches Einkommen: das Maß
an Zufriedenheit, das einem die
Arbeit bringt, nicht das verdiente
Geld
satisfacción con el trabajo
自分の満足度からみた仕事の価値

psychological contract
劳资心理合同
contrat psychologique ou contrat
mental
psychologischer Vertrag
contrato psicológico
心理契約

psychometric test
心理测验
test psychométrique
psychometrischer Test
prueba psicométrica
計量心理学テスト

Pty
私人有限公司
société privée à responsabilité
limitée
bezeichnet als Teil des
Firmennamens eine Gesellschaft
mit beschränkter Haftung
sociedad de responsabilidad

limitada
(保)証券保持者

public corporation
国营公司
société à participation étatique
öffentliche Körperschaft
entidad pública
公共企業

public debt
公债; 国债; 政府债务
dette publique
Staatsschuld; Staatsverschuldung;
öffentliche Schuld; Verschuldung
der öffentlichen Hand
deuda pública
公共負債

public deposits
政府存款, 国库存款
dépôts (de fonds) publics
Staatseinlagen
depósitos públicos
公金預金

public expenditure
政府开支; 公共支出
dépense publique
Ausgaben der öffentlichen Hand;
Staatsausgaben
gasto público
公共支出、財政支出

public finance law
公共财政法
droit des finances publiques
Gesetz über das öffentliche
Finanzwesen
derecho financiero
財政法

public issue
公开发行，公开募股
émission publique (d'actions)
öffentliche Emission
emisión pública
株式の公募

public-liability insurance
公众责任保险; 公众责任保险单
assurance responsabilité civile
allgemeine
Haftpflichtversicherung
seguro de responsabilidad civil
一般損害賠償責任保険,
対人対物賠償責任保険

public limited company
公共有限公司
société anonyme
Aktiengesellschaft
sociedad anónima
株式会社

public monopoly
公共垄断
monopole public
Staatsmonopol; staatliches

Monopol
monopolio público
公共国営事業独占

public offering
公开发行; 公开买卖
offre publique
öffentliche Auflegung; öffentliches
Zeichnungsangebot
oferta pública de venta
公開, 公募

public placing
公开配售
placement dans une société
anonyme
öffentliche Platzierung
colocación pública
プレーシング

public relations consultancy
公共关系咨询公司
cabinet expert en relations
publiques
Public Relations Agentur
asesor(a) de relaciones públicas
ＰＲコンサルタント事務所

public sector
公共部门; 政府部门;
国营(经济)部门
secteur public
öffentliche Hand; öffentlicher
Sektor; Staatswirtschaft
sector público
公共部門

**public sector cash
requirement**
公共部门现金需求
besoins de trésorerie du secteur
public
Kapitalbedarf der öffentlichen
Hand
necesidades de endeudamiento
del sector público
公共部門借入需要

public servant
公务员
fonctionnaire
Beamter
funcionario(-a) (público(-a))
公務員

public service
公共服务
service public
öffentlicher Dienst
funcionariado (público)
公益事業

public spending
公共费用; 国营(经济)部门支出
dépenses publiques
Staatsausgaben; Ausgaben der
öffentlichen Hand

---

*Translations appear in the following order: Chinese, French, German, Spanish/Latin American
Spanish, and Japanese*

gasto público
公共支出

published accounts
公开帐目
comptes publiés
veröffentlichter Abschluss
situación contable publicada
公表会計

puff
鼓吹
gonfler ou faire du battage autour
d'un produit
superlative Werbung für ein
Produkt betreiben
exagerar las ventajas de
誇大評価する

puffery
过分夸张; 吹嘘
gonflage de produit
Superlativ-Werbung
exageraciones
大袈裟な宣伝や主張

puff piece
宣传文章
article qui gonfle
Artikel in einer Zeitung/Zeitschrift,
mit dem für ein Produkt, eine
Person oder eine Dienstleistung
Reklame gemacht wird
artículo con publicidad
宣伝記事

pull system
前拉系统
système de gestion de contrôle et
planification de production
Zugsystem; Pull-System
sistema de control de la
producción vinculado al pedido
プル·システム

pull technology
拉技术
technologie d'extraction
Pull-Technologie
tecnología informativa en la que el
usuario va a buscar la información
プル· テクノロジー

pull the plug on something
停办; 停止
couper le jus
einem Vorhaben das Wasser
abgraben, finanzielle
Unterstützung abschneiden
acabar con
打ち切る【(財源を)切る,
中止する】

pump priming
刺激经济的政府投资
injection d'investissements
supplémentaires
Ankurbelung

reactivación económica
呼び水政策

punt
放弃
arrêter de ramer (boursicoter)
ein Ziel aufgeben und einfach
versuchen, keine weiteren Mittel
zu verlieren
dejar de gastar recursos
intentando algo
損なことから手を引く

purchase contract
进货合同; 购货合同
contrat d'achat
Kaufvertrag
contrato de compra
買入契約

purchase history
购物记录
historique (de transactions)
d'achat
Umsatzdaten
historial de adquisiciones
パーチェイス· ヒストリー

purchase ledger
购货分类帐; 进货分类帐;
应付帐款分类帐
grand livre des achats
Kreditorenbuch
libro mayor de compras
仕入先元帳

purchase money mortgage
购买抵押
hypothèque au prix d'achat
Restkaufpreishypothek
hipoteca de dinero de compra
購入代金抵当,

purchase order
定购单; 购货订单; 购买财产担保;
订购单
ordre d'achat
Kaufauftrag; Bestellung; Auftrag
orden de compra
買い注文

purchase price
购进价格; 买价
prix d'achat
Kaufpreis; Anschaffungspreis;
Einkaufspreis; Erwerbskurs
precio de compra
購入価格, 買値

purchase requisition
请购单
requête d'achat
Bedarfsmeldung;
Bestellanforderung;
Materialanforderung
solicitud interna de orden de
compra; pedido interno
材料購入請求

purchasing
购买; 购置; 采购
achat
Einkauf; Beschaffungswesen
adquisiciones
購買

purchasing manager
采购经理
directeur du service achats
Beschaffungsleiter(in);
Einkaufsleiter(in)
jefe(-a) de compras
購買マネージャー

purchasing power
购买力
pouvoir d'achat
Kaufkraft
poder adquisitivo
購買力

purchasing power parity
购买力平价理论
parité du pouvoir d'achat
Kaufkraftparität
paridad del poder adquisitivo
購買力平価

purchasing versus production
自制或采购; 自制或外购
achat contre production
Fremdbezug oder Eigenfertigung;
Einkauf oder Eigenfertigung
comprar o producir
購買対生産

pure competition
纯粹竞争
concurrence pure
Wettbewerb; reiner Wettbewerb;
vollkommen homogener
Wettbewerb
competencia perfecta
純粋競争

pure endowment
纯养老保险单
assurance en cas de vie
reine Erlebnisversicherung
seguro de ahorro
使途指定寄付

pure play
单纯网上商务; 单一网上业务
entreprise qui effectue ses affaires
uniquement sur Internet, fournit
uniquement des services Internet
et vend uniquement à d'autres
entreprises sur Internet
Unternehmen, das nur über das
Internet handelt; ausschließlich
Internet-Dienstleistungen anbieten
oder ausschließlich an andere
Internetfirmen verkauft
empresa que opera
exclusivamente en Internet
ピュア· プレー

---

*Translations appear in the following order: Chinese, French, German, Spanish/Latin American
Spanish, and Japanese*

purpose credit
专用贷款
crédit d'utilité
Zweckdarlehen
seguro de ahorro
目的貸付

push and pull strategies
后推前拉战略
stratégies de poussée et
d'attirance
Push-und-Pull-Strategie
estrategias de marketing directo y
marketing a través de un canal de
distribución
押込み引き寄せ戦略

push system
后推系统
push-system: système de gestion
de production selon lequel les
prévisions de demande sont
centralisées et où chaque poste de
travail pousse la production sans
tenir compte si le poste suivant est
prêt à la recevoir ou non.
Push-System; Drucksystem
sistema de control de la
producción centralizado
プッシュ・システム

push the envelope
大胆创新
repousser les limites
den Rahmen sprengen, über das
normal Geläufige hinausgehen
sobrepasar los límites
限界に挑戦する

put
卖出选择权; 敲出; 空仓期权;
看跌期权; 约期出售选择权
option de vente
Verkaufsoption
opción de venta
プット, (オプションの)売付選
択権

pyramid selling
金字塔式推销; 传销
vente pyramidale
Vertrieb nach dem
Schneeballprinzip; Absatz per
Verkauf gestaffelter
Verkaufsrechte an einem Produkt
venta piramidal
ねずみ講式販売方法

qualification payment
资力证书附加工资
prime de qualification
(Nouvelle-Zélande)
Qualifikationszulage
complemento salarial por
obtención de título
資格手当

qualified lead
预期销售前景
initiation mitigée
potentielle(r) Kunde(-in)
cliente potencial
適格潜在的顧客

qualified listed security
上市证券
titre coté en bourse avec réserve
qualifiziertes börsennotiertes
Wertpapier
valor mobiliario cotizado en bolsa
限定上場証券

qualitative analysis
定性分析
analyse qualitative
qualitative Analyse
análisis cualitativo
定性分析

qualitative factors
质量因素
facteurs qualitatifs
Qualitätsattribute; Gütefaktoren
factores pertinentes de decisión no
numéricos
質的要素

qualitative lending guideline
定性贷款指南
directive qualitative pour prêt
qualitative Kreditvergaberichtlinie
criterios cualitativos para la
concesión de créditos
質的信用規制,
信用の質的ガイドライン

qualitative research
质量研究
étude qualitative; recherche
qualitative
qualitative Forschung
investigación cualitativa
質的調査法

quality
质量
qualité
Qualität
calidad
品質

quality assurance
质量保证
assurance de qualité
Qualitätssicherung
garantía de calidad
品質保証

quality audit
质量审计
audit de la qualité
Qualitätsprüfung
auditoría de calidad
品質監査

quality award
质量奖
prix de la qualité
Qualitätsauszeichnung
premio a la calidad
品質賞

quality bond
优质债券
obligation de qualité
hochwertige Anleihe
bono de calidad
優秀債券

quality circle
质量管理小组
groupe pour la qualité
Qualitätszirkel
círculo de calidad
品質サークル

quality control
质量控制; 质量管理
contrôle de qualité
Qualitätskontrolle
control de calidad
品質管理

quality control plan
质量控制计划
plan de contrôle qualité
Qualitätskontrollplan
plan de control de la calidad
品値管理計画

quality costs
质量成本
frais de qualité
Qualitätskosten
costes de la calidad
costos de la calidad
品質原価

quality equity
优质股权
actions ou fonds propres de qualité
hochwertige Aktie
acciones de calidad
優秀持ち株

quality function deployment
质量功能设计
déploiement de la fonction qualité
Einsatz der Qualitätsfunktion
despliegue de la función de calidad
品質機能展開

quality management
质量管理
gestion de qualité
Qualitätssicherung; Gütesicherung
gestión de la calidad
品質管理

quality manual
质量管理手册
manuel de qualité
Gütesicherungshandbuch

Translations appear in the following order: Chinese, French, German, Spanish/Latin American Spanish, and Japanese

manual de calidad
品質マニュアル

quality of design
设计品质
qualité de la conception
Konstruktionsqualität
calidad del diseño
デザインの質

quality of life¹
生活质素
qualité de la vie
Lebensqualität
calidad de vida
生活の質

quality of life²
生活质素
qualité de la vie
Lebensqualität
calidad de vida
生活の質

quality of working life
工作生活质素
qualité de la vie professionnelle
Lebensqualität am Arbeitsplatz
calidad de vida en el trabajo
労働の質

quality standard
质量标准
norme de qualité
Qualitätsnorm
norma de calidad
品質標準

quality time
质量时间
moments privilégiés
Quality Time
tiempo reservado para disfrutar de
actividades importantes
充実した時間

quango
半自立性非官方组织，准自治管理
机构，半官方机构，
quango: acronyme anglais de
quasi-autonomous
non-governmental organization:
organisme non-gouvernemental
quasi-autonome
quasi-autonome nichtstaatliche
Organisation
organismo para-estatal
独立政府機関

quantitative analysis
定量分析
analyse quantitative
quantitative Analyse
análisis cuantitativo
定量分析

quantitative factors
数量因素
facteurs quantitatifs

Mengenattribute;
Mengenfaktoren
factores pertinentes de decisión
numéricos
量的要素

quantitative research
数量研究
étude quantitative; recherche
quantitative
quantitative Forschung
investigación cuantitativa
量的調査法

quantum meruit
尽所能去挣
quantum meruit: expression latine
signifiant autant qu'a été gagné
(en revenu)
leistungsgerechtes Entgelt
quantum meruit
労働価値に対する分け前

quarterback
指导
déterminer la stratégie pour un
projet
Anweisungen zu einem Projekt
geben
dar órdenes
プロジェクトの指揮を取る

quartile
四分位数
quartile
Quartil
cuartila
四分位数

quasi-contract
准合同
quasi-contrat
Quasikontrakt
cuasicontrato
準契約

quasi-loan
准贷款
quasi-loan
Quasdarlehen
cuasipréstamo
準ローン

quasi-public corporation
准公共公司; 半国有企业
corporation quasi-publique
Quasikörperschaft des öffentlichen
Rechts
sociedad privada con intervención
pública
準公益会社

quasi-rent
准租金
quasi-paiement
Quasirente
cuasi-renta
準地代

questionnaire
问卷; 调查表
questionnaire
Fragebogen
cuestionario
質問状アンケート

queuing theory
排队理论
techniques développées pour
déterminer le niveau optimal de
fourniture de service
Warteschlangentheorie
teoría de las colas
待ち時間理論

queuing time
排队时间
temps d'attente
Wartezeit
tiempo de cola
待ち時間

quick ratio¹
速动比率
coefficient rapide
Liquidität zweiten Grades
test ácido
当座比率

quick ratio²
速动比率
coefficient de liquidité
Liquidität zweiten Grades
test ácido
当座比率

quid pro quo
交换物，补偿物
quid pro quo: expression latine
signifiant en contrepartie de
Gegenleistung
contrapartida
代償

quorum
法定决议票数，法定人数
quorum
Quorum
quórum
定足数

quota¹
配额
quote-part
Anteil
contingente
分担額

quota²
限额
quota
Höchstquote
contingente
割当投資額

quota³
限额，配额
contingent

Translations appear in the following order: Chinese, French, German, Spanish/Latin American Spanish, and Japanese

Kontingent
contingente
輸入額等の割当制度

quote
报价; 开盘
cotation
Preisangebot
cotización
見積り額を言う, 相場を付ける

quoted company
上市公司; 挂牌公司
société cotée en Bourse
börsennotierte Gesellschaft
empresa que cotiza en bolsa
上場会社

quote driven
报价驱动
(système) dirigé par la cotation
notierungsbestimmt
dirigido por precios
相場率先型

quoted securities
上市证券; 挂牌证券
titres cotés en Bourse
börsennotierte Aktien
valores cotizados
上場債券

R150 Bond
R150债券
obligation de référence du
gouvernement sud-africain avec
un taux d'intérêt fixe
R150 festverzinsliches Wertpapier
bono R150 del gobierno
sudafricano
R150国債

racial discrimination
种族歧视
discrimination raciale
Rassendiskriminierung
discriminación racial
人種差別

radio button
选项钮
bouton de radio
Wahlknopf
botón de tipo radio
ラジオ・ボタン

raid
扰乱市场
raid boursier (illégal)
(illegaler) Versuch den Kurs einer
Aktie zu drücken
ataque; incursión
相場を下落の目的で一斉に売る
こと, 売り崩し

raider
蓄谋投资者; 企图收购者;
公司袭击者
raider

Übernahmegeier; räuberischer
Übernahmeinteressent
tiburón
敵対的企業買収

rainmaker
造雨者
faiseur de pluie
jemand, insbesondere ein Anwalt,
der Kunden anzieht, die viel Geld
für die Geschäfte ihrer Firma
ausgeben
persona que atrae clientes muy
rentables
(弁護士が)見入りの良い顧客
を確保する

rake it in
发财
remuer le fric à la pelle
das Geld nur so scheffeln
forrarse
多額のお金を儲ける
(熊手で掻き集める)

rake-off
佣金
pourcentage
Provision
comisión
分け前

rally
跌停回升; 反弹
reprise
Erholung; Versammlung;
Kurserholung; Auftrieb; sich
recuperación
回復, 反発, 持直し

ramp
买股抬价
acheter des actions pour
augmenter les prix
Aktien kaufen, um den Preis zu
erhöhen
comprar para subir el precio
価格吊り上げのため株購入

rand
兰特
rand
Währungseinheit
rand
ランド(南アフリカの通貨単位)

Randlord
兰特大亨
roi ou magnat des mines basé à
Joannesbourg (fin XIXe, début XXe
siècle)
reicher oder einflussreicher
Johannesburger Geschäftsmann
rico ejecutivo de Johanesburgo
ヨハネスブルグの大立物

random
随机
fortuit ou par hasard
zufällig
aleatorio
任意の

random sampling
随机抽样
échantillonnage au hasard
Zufallsstichprobenverfahren;
Zufallsstichprobenverfahren
muestreo aleatorio
ランダム・サンプリング
(任意抽出法)

range
值域
variation ou écart
Spannweite
gama; recorrido; rango; campo de
variación
分布範囲

range pricing
幅度定价
fixation des prix par gamme (de
produits)
Sortimentpreisgestaltung
gama de precios
範囲価格設定

ranking
秩评定, 等级评定
classement
Rangfolge
clasificación; ranking;
ordenamiento
整列

ratable value
可估价值; 可评定值
valeur matricielle
Einheitswert; Steuerwert
valor imponible
課税評価額, 課税見積価格

ratchet effect
齿轮效应
effet de cliquet
Sperrklinkeneffekt
efecto de trinquete
ラチェット効果, 歯止め効果

rate of interest
利率
taux d'intérêt
Zinssatz
tipo de interés
利率, 金利

rate of return
收益率
taux de rendement
Rentabilitätsziffer
tasa de rentabilidad
収益率

Translations appear in the following order: Chinese, French, German, Spanish/Latin American Spanish, and Japanese

ratings
收视率; 收听率
indice d'écoute
erreichte Zielgruppe
índices de audiencia
視聴率

ratio analysis
比率分析
analyse des ratios ou coefficients
Kennziffernanalyse
análisis de coeficientes
比率分析

rationalisation
合理化
rationalisation
Rationalisierung
racionalización
合理化

ratio pyramid
比率金字塔
pyramide des coefficients
Kennzahlenhierarchie
pirámide de razones; pirámide de
ratios vinculados
比率ピラミッド

raw materials
原料; 原材料
matières premières
Rohstoffe; Rohmaterialien
materias primas
原材料

RDO
串休日
RDO (rostered day off): journée de
congé accordée selon certains
accords de travail à la place d'une
accumulation des heures
supplémentaires
arbeitsfreier Tag, der nach
manchen Arbeitsverträgen an
Stelle von angelaufenen
Überstunden vorgesehen ist
día libre a cambio de horas extras
acumuladas
代替休日

RDP
重建和发展计划
programme de reconstruction et
développement
Rekonstruktions- und
Entwicklungsprogramm
plan de reconstrucción y desarrollo
del gobierno sudafricano
再建開発プログラム

reactive maintenance
反应性维修
maintenance réactive
reaktive Wartung
mantenimiento reactivo
事後メンテナンス

readership
读者群
nombre de lecteurs
Leserschaft
perfil de los lectores
読者属性

Reaganomics
里根经济政策
économie reaganienne: politique
du président américain Reagan
dans les années 1980 qui réduisit
les impôts et le soutien à la sécurité
sociale et augmenta le déficit
budgétaire national à un niveau
sans précédent
angebotsorientierte
Wirtschaftspolitik des
amerikanischen Präsidenten
Reagan in den 80iger Jahren,
geprägt von Steuersenkungen,
Kürzung der Sozialleistungen,
sowie von einem Anstieg des
Haushaltsdefizits auf nie vorher
dagewesenes Niveaus
política económica de Reagan
レーガノミックス

real
实际的
réel
effektiv
real
実質

real asset
真实资产; 不动产; 房地产
biens immobiliers
Immobiliarvermögen;
Realvermögen
bienes inmuebles
不動産

real balance effect
真实余额效应
effet d'équilibre réel
realer Kassenhaltungseffekt;
Pigou-Effekt
efecto de saldos reales
実質残高効果

real capital
实际资本
capital réel
Sachkapital; Realkapital;
Kapitalsubstanz
capital real
現実資本, 実物資本, 実体資本

real estate
房地产; 物业; 不动产
propriété immobilière
Grundeigentum; Immobilien
propiedad inmobiliaria
土地建物(不動産)

real estate developer
房地产开发商; 物业开发商
promoteur (de construction
immobilière)
Immobilienunternehmer(in)
promotor(a) inmobiliario(-a)
不動産開発業者

real exchange rate
实际汇率
taux de change réel
effektiver Wechselkurs
tasa de cambio real
真の為替相場

real GDP
实际国内生产总值
PIB réel
Real-BIP; effektives BIP
PIB real
実質GDP

real growth
实际增长
croissance réelle
reales Wachstum
crecimiento real
実質成長(率)

real interest rate
实际利率
taux d'intérêt réel
Realzins
tasa de interés real; tipo real/
efectivo de interés
実物利率

real investment
实物投资
investissement immobilier
Investition in Immobilien
inversión en bienes muebles
実物投資

realisation concept
实现概念
concept de la réalisation (de l'actif)
Realisationsprinzip
concepto de realización al alcance
de la mano
現金化概念

reality check
现实性检验
contrôle de réalité
Betrachtung begrenzender
Faktoren wie Kosten bei der
Diskussion oder Erwägung eines
ehrgeizigen Vorhabens
realismo
現実との直面

real purchasing power
实际购买力
pouvoir d'achat réel
reale Kaufkraft; effektive Kaufkraft
poder adquisitivo real
実質購買力

---

*Translations appear in the following order: Chinese, French, German, Spanish/Latin American
Spanish, and Japanese*

real time company
实时公司
compagnie répondant en temps
réel (sur Internet)
Echtzeit-Unternehmen
empresa en tiempo real
リアル・タイム会社

**real time credit card
processing**
实时信用卡交易
traitement de carte de crédit en
temps réel
Echtzeit-Kreditkartenabwicklung
procesamiento de tarjetas de
crédito en tiempo real
リアルタイム・クレジットカー
ド・プロセッシング

real time data
实时数据
données en temps réel
Echtzeitdaten
datos en tiempo real
リアルタイムデータ

real time EDI
即时商业数据处理
échange de données électroniques
en temps réel
elektronischer Datenaustausch in
Echtzeit
intercambio electrónico de datos
en tiempo real
リアルタイムEDI、
実時間電子データ交換

real time manager
实时业务主管
manager ou directeur en temps
réel
Echtzeit-Geschäftsleiter(in)
gerente que atiende a los clientes
en tiempo real
リアル・タイム・マネジャー

real time transaction
即时转帐
transaction en temps réel
Echtzeit-Transaktion
transacción en tiempo real
リアルタイム・トランザクショ
ン、実時間取引

rebadge
重新包装
assigner un nouvel insigne
mit neuem Logo od.
Firmenkennzeichen versehen
renombrar
リバッジ(メーカー名のみ変更し
て再販)

rebate¹
退款
remboursement ou dégrèvement
Rückvergütung

devolución
割戻し

rebate²
折扣
remise
Rabatt
bonificación
割引

rebate³
打折扣
escompte
Rabatt
descuento
リベート、払込みの割戻し

rebating
折扣; 打折
ristourne pour grand volume
d'achat
Volumenrabatte
descuento por compra en grandes
cantidades
リベート・プログラム

receipt
收据，收条
reçu
Quittung
recibo
領収書

**receipts and payments
account**
收支帐户，现金收支帐
compte des rentrées et sorties
Einnahmen-Ausgaben-Rechnung
cuenta de transacciones en dinero
收支勘定

receiver
接管人; 清算管理人
receveur/syndic de faillite
Zwangsverwalter(in);
Empfänger(in); Telefonhörer;
Vermögensverwalter(in);
Liquidator(in);
Konkursverwalter(in)
administrador(a) judicial
管財人

Receiver of Revenue¹
税收办公室; 收税者
bureau de la perception en Afrique
du Sud
örtliches Finanzamt
oficina de la Hacienda sudafricana
歳入地方局

Receiver of Revenue²
南非税务局
le fisc sud-africain (terme informel)
örtliches Finanzamt
Hacienda sudafricana
歳入局

receivership
破产管理
(sous) règlement judiciaire

Konkursverwaltung
administración judicial
管財人業務

recession
衰退
récession
Rezession; Konjunkturabschwung;
Konjunkturrückgang
recesión
景気後退、不景気、リセッション、
不況

recessionary gap
经济衰退缺口
écart de récession
Rezessionslücke; Rezessionsloch
brecha recesionista
リセッション・ギャップ、景気
後退ギャップ

reciprocal cost allocation
互惠成本分配法
imputation réciproque des coûts
reziproke Kostenaufteilung od.
Kostenumlage
administración judicial
相互原価配分

reconciliation
调整; 对帐
ajustement (des écritures)
Abstimmung
conciliación
勘定尻の調整

record date
登记日; 记录日期
date de rapport
Dividendenstichtag; Stopptag
fecha de registro
記録日

recourse
追索权
recours
Regress; Rückgriff
recurso (judicial)
遡求

recourse agreement
收回协定
accord de recours de saisie (dans
un contrat de vente à crédit)
Regressvereinbarung
acuerdo de recuperación
償還請求協定

recovery
回升; 复苏
redressement
Aufschwung;
Konjunkturbelebung; Erholung
recuperación (absorción de gastos
indirectos)
回復、景気回復

---

*Translations appear in the following order: Chinese, French, German, Spanish/Latin American
Spanish, and Japanese*

recovery fund
复苏基金
fonds de placement de reprise
Fonds, der in Aktien investiert,
deren Kurs gefallen ist, die sich
jedoch erwartungsgemäß in
absehbarer Zeit erholen werden
fondo de recuperación
回収債権投資基金

recovery stock
复苏股票
titre de reprise
Aktie, deren Kurs wegen
ungenügender
Geschäftsleistungen gefallen ist,
die jetzt jedoch erwartungsgemäß
wegen verbesserter Aussichten
des Unternehmens wieder steigen
wird
acción en proceso de recuperación
回復株

recruitment
招聘; 招收
recrutement
Einstellung od. Anwerbung von
Arbeitskräften;
Personalbeschaffung
contratación
社員の募集, 採用

recurring billing transaction
循环自动转帐
transaction de facturation
périodique
laufende Rechnungserstellung
transacción de pagos recurrentes
定期的請求システム

recurring payments
重复付款
paiements périodiques
laufende Zahlungen
pagos recurrentes
電子決済システム

red
借方余额; 负债,透支
rouge
rot
rojo
赤字記入

Red Book
红皮书
copie du discours du ministre des
finances britannique publié le jour
du Budget de la nation
in Großbritannien, ein Exemplar
der Haushaltsrede des
Schatzkanzlers, am Budgettag
veröffentlicht
texto conteniendo el discurso del
Ministro de Hacienda británico con
la presentación de los
presupuestos generales del Estado

レッド·ブック(英国政府予算に
付随する年次報告書)

redeemable shares
可赎回股
actions amortissables
rückzahlbare Aktien
acciones rescatables
償還可能株式

redemption¹
(股票回购)
rachat
Rücknahme von Anteilsscheinen
rescate
買戻し

redemption²
偿还
remboursement ou amortissement
Tilgung
amortización
償還

redemption yield
偿还收益率
rendement à échéance ou
rendement actuariel brut
Effektivverzinsung;
Fälligkeitsrendite
rendimiento de una acción en la
fecha de rescate
償還利回り

redeployment
人员调动; 人员调整
reconversion ou redéploiement
Umgruppierung od. Umsetzung
von Arbeitskräften
redistribución
配置替え

red eye
红眼
prospectus d'information
préliminaire
vorläufiger Emissionsprospekt
prospecto para sondear el
mercado ante la flotación de una
nueva empresa
予備目論見書

redistributive effect
再分配效应
effet de redistribution
Umverteilungseffekt;
Umverteilungswirkung
efecto redistributivo
再配分効果(税などの)

red screen market
红屏市场, 跌价市场
marché dans lequel les prix sont en
baisse et donc affichés en rouge
britische Bezeichnung f. einen
Markt, dessen Kurse gefallen sind.
Diese werden auf den
Händerbildschirmen in rot

angezeigt.
mercado en números rojos
レッド· スクリーン市場

red tape
官样文章
paperasserie ou bureaucratie
tatillonne
Bürokratismus; Papierkrieg;
Amtsschimmel
burocracia
役所流形式主義

redundancy
裁员
licenciement (économique)
Entlassung
despido
余剰人員整理

redundancy package
裁员补贴
prime de licenciement
Entlassungsabfindung;
Abfindungspaket
indemnización por despido
余剰人員補償金パッケージ

redundancy payment
裁员补贴
indemnité de licenciement
Abfindung; Entlassungsabfindung
indemnización por despido
余剰労働者補償金

reference
推荐信
référence
Referenz; Führungszeugnis
referencia; informe
信用照会身元保証

reference population
参考人口
population de référence
Vergleichspopulation
población de referencia
基準母集団

reference rate
参考利率
taux de référence
Referenzzins
tasa de referencia
基準レート

reference site
参考网页
site de référence
Bezugsseite
sitio de referencia
成功している企業現場

referred share
无分红股
action référée ou ex dividende
Aktie ohne Dividende
acción sin derecho a dividendo
配当落ち株

Translations appear in the following order: Chinese, French, German, Spanish/Latin American Spanish, and Japanese

refer to drawer
洽询出票人; 请与出票人接洽;
暂停止付
retour au tireur
keine Deckung, an den Aussteller
zurück
devuélvase al librador
(銀行で不渡り手形等に記入する)
振出人回し, RD

refer to drawer please represent
出票人请补款
refus d'honorer un chèque,
veuillez le représenter
keine Deckung, an den Aussteller
zurück
frase escrita en un cheque por el
banco indicando que no hay
suficientes fondos en la cuenta
pero que probablemente estarán
disponibles pronto
差出人へ回し, 再度提出すること

refinance
再融资; 重新筹集资金
refinancer
umschulden; umfinanzieren;
refinanzieren
refinanciar
財政の立て直し, 証券類の新たな
発行, 借り換え

refinancing
再融资; 重新筹集资金
refinancement
Umschuldung; Refinanzierung
refinanciación
借り換え, 債務再編成

reflation
通货恢复
relance
Reflation
reflación
通貨再膨張、リフレーション

refugee capital
逃亡资本
capital réfugié
vagabundierende Gelder; heißes
Geld
capital errante
避難資本

refund
退钱; 退款
remboursement
Rückvergütung; Rückerstattung
reembolso; reintegro
返金

regeneration
再生; 回收; 革新; 改造; 复兴; 复兴
régénération
Regenerierung; Mitkoppelung
regeneración
地域再建, 復興

regional fund
区域性基金
fonds de placements régionaux
Regionalfonds
fondo regional
リージョナル·ファンド,
地方ファンド

registered bond
记名债券; 已登记债券; 登记债券
obligation nominative
Namensschuldverschreibung
bono nominativo
登録社債, 記名公債

registered broker
注册经纪人
courtier agréé
registrierte/r Makler(in)
corredor(a) colegiado(-a)
登録ブローカー

registered company
注册公司
société inscrite au tribunal de
commerce
im Gesellschaftsregister
eingetragene Handelsgesellschaft
empresa inscrita en el Registro
Mercantil
法人会社

registered name
注册名称
nom déposé
eingetragener Handelsname
nombre registrado
登記名義

registered number
注册号码
numéro d'inscription au registre du
commerce
Registrierungsnummer
número de registro
登記番号

registered office
注册办事处
siège social
(eingetragener) Hauptsitz einer
Gesellschaft
domicilio social
会社の登記住所

registered security
登记证券
valeur nominative
Namensaktie
título nominativo
登録証券

registered share
登记股; 记名股
action nominative
Namensaktie
acción nominativa
記名株

register of companies
公司名单
registre du commerce
Gesellschaftsregister
registro mercantil
会社登録登記(簿)

register of directors and secretaries
公司董事和书记记录
registre des administrateurs et
secrétaires de compagnie
Register der
Geschäftsführer(in)nen und
Verwaltungsleiter(in)nen
registro con los nombres y las
direcciones de los directores y
secretarios
役員及び会社秘書の登録原簿

register of directors' interests
董事利益记录
registre des intérêts détenus par les
administrateurs
Register über die Beteiligungen der
Direktoren od. Direktorinnen
registro de acciones y otros valores
en manos de los directores
役員の所有株原簿

Registrar of Companies
公司注册官
conservateur du registre des
compagnies
Führer des Gesellschaftsregisters
encargado(a) del Registro
Mercantil
会社登記係

registration statement
注册说明书
document d'immatriculation
Registrierungsangaben
registro de emisión
有価証券届出書

regression analysis
回归分析
analyse de régression
Regressionsanalyse
análisis de regresión
回帰分析

regressive tax
累退税; 递减税
impôt dégressif
regressive Steuer
impuesto regresivo
逆進税

regulated price
管制价格
prix réglementé
regulierter Preis
precio regulado
統制価格

Translations appear in the following order: Chinese, French, German, Spanish/Latin American Spanish, and Japanese

regulated superannuation fund
合乎规定的养老基金
caisse de retraite réglementée
gesetzlich geregelter Pensionsfonds; Pensionsfonds mit Steuervergünstigung
fondo de pensiones regulado
適格退職年金基金

regulation
规章
réglementations
Regulierung
reglamento
規則, 法規

regulator
监督管理员
régulateur
Regulierungsbehörde
organismo regulador
取り締まり組織

regulatory body
法定代理; 管理机构;
条例制定机构
organisme régisseur
Aufsichtsbehörde;
Regulierungsstelle; Aufsichtsstelle
organismo regulador
(企業の管理,
監督する)管理機関

regulatory framework
规章制度
structure de réglementations
rechtliche Rahmenbedingungen od. Rahmenvorschriften
marco o ámbito regulador
管理フレームワーク

regulatory pricing risk
价格管制风险
risque de fixation des prix réglementée
Risiko der regulativen Preisfestsetzung
riesgo de regulación de precios
(保険の)規制的価格リスク

reinsurance
再保险; 分保; 转保
réassurance
Rückversicherung; Reassekuranz
reaseguro
再保険

reintermediation
重新通过中间媒介; 使用中介;
使用中间人
introduction d'intermédiaires, par exemple des services qui accumulent des données de plusieurs institutions financières électroniques indépendantes
Einsatz von Mittelspersonen, die bei einem Geschäftsvorgang

Mehrwert erbringen
introducción de intermediarios; utilización de intermediarios para añadir valor a una transacción
仲介業者再導入

reinvestment rate
再投资率
taux de réinvestissement
Reinvestitionsrate
coeficiente de reinversión
再投資率

reinvestment risk
再投资风险
risque de nouvel investissement
Wiederanlagerisiko;
Reinvestitionsrisiko
riesgo de reinversión
再投資リスク

reinvestment unit trust
再投资单位信托
société de réinvestissement de type SICAV
Investmentgesellschaft mit Reinvestition von Dividenden
fondo de inversión que reinvierte con ventajas fiscales en la compañía que emite las acciones
再投資ユニット信託

rejects
不合格品
(produits) de rebut/défectueux
Ausschuss
productos rechazados por ser defectuosos
不良品

relational database
相关数据库
base de données relationnelle
relationale Datenbank
base de datos relacional
リレーショナル・データベース

relationship management
关系管理
gestion des relations
Relationship Management
gestión de relaciones
リレーションシップ・
マネジメント

relative income hypothesis
相对收入假设
hypothèse de la relativité des revenus
relative Einkommenshypothese
hipótesis de la renta relativa
相対所得仮説

release
发布; 发行
décharge
Erlass; Veröffentlichung; Freigabe;
Entbindung; Freistellung;

Entlassung
lanzamiento
リリース

relevancy concept
相关性概念
concept de la pertinence
Sachdienlichkeitsprinzip;
Erheblichkeitskonzept
concepto de relevancia
関連性理論

relevant costs/revenues
相关成本收入
coûts/revenus pertinents
relevante Kosten und Einnahmen
gastos /ingresos relevantes y apropiados para decisiones específicas
関連コスト収入

relevant interest
股东利益
intérêt pertinent: position légale d'investisseurs en actions qui peuvent légalement vendre ou influencer la vente d'actions
rechtserhebliches Interesse
derecho a la venta de acciones
関係権利者

relevant range
相关范围
gamme (d'activités) pertinente
fixkostenrelevante Tätigkeit
ámbito de validez pertinente
関連範囲

reliability
可靠性
fiabilité
Zuverlässigkeit
fiabilidad
信頼性

reliability-centred maintenance
功能可靠性维护
maintenance centrée sur la fiabilité
zuverlässigkeitsorientierte Wartung
mantenimiento centrado en torno a la fiabilidad
信頼性中心メンテナンス

reliability concept
可靠性概念
concept de la fiabilité
Zuverlässigkeitsprinzip
concepto de fiabilidad e integridad
信頼性理論

relocation
重新安置; 重新布局; 公司搬迁
réimplantation (d'entreprise)
Verlagerung; Standortänderung
traslado
移転再配置

remuneration package
薪酬支出; 报酬; 工资待遇
contrat de rémunération
Gehaltspaket; Vergütungspaket
paquete de remuneración
報酬パッケージ

renounceable document
所有权证明
document indiquant la possibilité
future de l'abandon d'un droit de
souscription
kündbares Schriftstück
documento de propiedad por un
período limitado
所有権放棄確認書

reorder level
再订货水平
niveau ou seuil de
réapprovisionnement
Meldebestand; kritischer
Lagerbestand; Sicherheitsbestand
nivel de reaprovisionamiento
追加注文レベル

reorganisation bond
组织债券
obligation (titre) de restructuration
Gewinnschuldverschreibung
bono concedido a los acreedores
de una empresa que está
reorganizándose
更生債券

repayment mortgage
偿还抵押
emprunt-logement sans capital
différé
Tilgungshypothek
hipoteca de pago
償還モーゲージ

repeat business
重复订购
commande répétitive
Wiederholungsgeschäft;
Nachbestellung
pedidos repetidos
再注文

repertory grid
矩阵信息存储
grille répertoire
Konstruktgitter-Verfahren
técnica de análisis de percepciones
レパートリー・グリッド

repetitive strain injury
重复性肌肉拉伤
microtraumatisme permanent
Wiederholungsüberbeanspruchung
lesión por movimiento repetitivo
反復動作筋肉痛

replacement cost
更换成本; 重置成本
coût de remplacement

Wiederbeschaffungskosten
coste de reposición
costo de reposición
取替原価, 再取得価格

replacement cost accounting
更换成本会计
comptabilité des coûts de
remplacement
Rechnungslegung zu
Wiederbeschaffungskosten
coste de reposición
costo de reposición
再取得原価勘定

replacement price
更换成本
prix de remplacement
Wiederbeschaffungspreis
precio de sustitución
取替価格

replacement ratio
补偿比率
rapport de remplacement
Einkommensersatzrate
tasa de reposición
置換え率、欠員補充率

replenishment system
补充系统
système de réapprovisionnement
Auffüllsystem
sistema de reposición
在庫品補充システム

repo¹
回购协议
accord de rachat
Pensionsgeschäft
acuerdo de recompra
買い戻し条件付き取引

repo²
回购
mise en pension (de titres)
Rückkaufvereinbarung
operación de compra de valores
レポ取引

report
报告
rapport
Bericht
informe
報告

repositioning
重新定位
repositionnement
Neupositionierung
reposicionamiento
再位置付け

repossession
收回
reprise de possession ou saisie
Wiederinbesitznahme
recuperación

支払い不履行で引き取る,
再所有する

repudiation
拒付债务
refus d'honorer une dette
Nichtanerkennung
negativa a reconocer
債務履行の拒否

repurchase
买回，赎回
rachat
Rücknahme
recompra
買戻す

repurchase agreement
回购协议
accord de réméré
Pensionsgeschäft
acuerdo de recompra
買戻し契約

request form
申请表
formulaire de requête
Abfrageformular
formulario de solicitud
リクエスト用紙

required rate of return
必要报酬率
taux de rendement minimum
erforderliche Mindestverzinsung
tasa de rentabilidad requerida
必要最低限収益率

required reserves
必要储备
réserves obligatoires
Mindestreserven
reservas obligatorias
法定準備金

requisition
征用令; 征用; 订购单; 请购单;
领料单
demande
Aufforderung; Verlangen;
Materialanforderung
requisición
注文書, 要求書

resale price maintenance
统一再售价; 转售价格控制;
转卖价格维持; 维持转售价格
prix de vente imposé
vertikale Preisbindung
fijación de los precios de venta al
público
再販売価格維持

research
研究
recherche(s)
Forschung
investigación
調査

Translations appear in the following order: Chinese, French, German, Spanish/Latin American Spanish, and Japanese

research and development
研究与发展; 研究与开发
recherche et développement
Forschung und Entwicklung
investigación y desarrollo
研究開発

reserve bank
储备银行
banque de réserve
Reservebank
banco de reserva
準備銀行

Reserve Bank of Australia
澳大利亚储备银行
Banque de Réserve d'Australie
australische Zentralbank
Banco de la Reserva de Australia
オーストラリア準備銀行

Reserve Bank of New Zealand
新西兰储备银行
Banque de Réserve de
Nouvelle-Zélande
neuseeländische Zentralbank
Banco de la Reserva de Nueva
Zelanda
ニュージーランド準備銀行

reserve currency
储备货币
monnaie de réserve
Reservewährung
divisa de reserva
準備通貨(ドル等)

reserve for fluctuations
波动储备
réserve pour fluctuations
Rückstellung für
Währungsschwankungen
fondo de fluctuación
(価格)変動準備金

reserve price
保留价格，最低价格
prix minimal
Mindespreis
precio de reserva
最低競売価格

reserve ratio
储备率
ratio de réserve obligatoire
Mindestreservesatz
coeficiente de caja, coeficiente de
encaje legal
準備率

reserve requirements
储备要求; 储备需求
exigences de réserve
Mindestreserven
encajes legales; reserva obligatoria
準備必要額, 支払準備率,
預金準備率

reserves
储备; 储备金
réserves
Rücklagen
reservas
準備金, 積立金, 引当金

residual income
剩余收益
bénéfice résiduel
residualbestimmtes Einkommen
ingresos residuales
残余収入

residuary legatee
剩余遗产受赠人
légataire universel(le)
Testamenterbe
legatario(-a) residual
残余遺産受領者

resignation
辞职
démission
Kündigung
dimisión
辞職

resolution
提案，决议案
résolution
Beschluss
resolución
決議

resource allocation
资源分配; 资源配置
allocation des ressources
Ressourcen-Allokation
asignación de recursos
人的物的資源配分プログラム

resource productivity
资源生产率; 资源生产力
productivité des ressources
Ressourcenproduktivität
productividad de los recursos
資源生産性方式

resources
资源
ressources
Ressourcen; Vermögenswerte;
(finanzielle) Mittel; Einsatzmittel
recursos
資産, 資源, 財源,

response bias
反应偏差
distorsion de réponse
Antwortverzerrung
sesgo en las respuestas
返答バイアス

response level
反映水平
degré de réponse
Reaktionsquote

nivel de respuesta
レスポンス率

response marketing
响应行销
marketing réactif
Reaktionsmarketing
marketing de respuesta
レスポンス管理

response mechanism
反映机制
véhicule de réponse
Antwortsystem
mecanismo de respuesta
レスポンス・メカニズム

response rate
回应率
taux de réponse
Antwortrate
índice de respuesta
応答率

**response surface
methodology**
回应表面方法学
méthodologie de surface
d'efficacité
Antwortflächenmethodik
metodología de superficie de
respuesta
応答表面法

responsibility
责任; 职责
responsabilité
Verantwortung
responsabilidad
責任

responsibility accounting
社会责任会计
comptabilité de responsabilité
Kostenrechnung nach
Zuständigkeiten
contabilidad de responsabilidad
責任会計

responsibility centre
责任中心
centre de responsabilité
Verantwortungszentrum
centro de responsabilidad
責任センター, 収入センター

restated balance sheet
重报平衡表; 调整后平衡表
bilan énoncé de nouveau
berichtigte Bilanz
balance regularizado
改訂貸借対照表

rest break
间休
pause-repos
Arbeitspause
descanso
休憩時間

Translations appear in the following order: Chinese, French, German, Spanish/Latin American Spanish, and Japanese

rest period
休息时间; 间休时间
période de repos
Pausenzeit
período de descanso
日毎週毎月毎の休息時間

restraint of trade
贸易限制
obligation de non-currence
wettbewerbsbeschränkendes
Verhalten
limitación al libre comercio
営業制限

restricted tender
限制性投标
soumission restreinte
eingeschränkte Ausschreibung
licitación restringida
制限入札引受

result-driven
成果导向
dirigé par les résultats
ergebnisorientiert
centrado(-a) en los resultados
結果重視

retail banking
零售银行业务
opérations bancaires portant sur
des comptes personnels
Privatkundengeschäft
banca minorista
小口金融

retail co-operative
零售合作社
coopérative de commerce au détail
Einzelhandelsgenossenschaft;
Konsumgenossenschaft;
Ladengenossenschaft
cooperativa de minoristas
共同小売システム

retailer
零售商
détaillant(e)
Einzelhändler(in)
minorista
小売業者

retail investor
零售投资商
investisseur de détail
Privatinvestor(in)
inversor(a) detallista
小口取引家

retail management
零售管理
gestion de vente au détail
Einzelhandelsmanagement
gestión de la venta al por menor
小売マネジメント

retail price
零售价格; 零售价
prix de détail
Einzelhandelspreis; Endpreis;
Ladenpreis
precio al por menor
小売価格

retail price index
零售价指数
indice des prix de détail
Index der Einzelhandelspreise
índice de precios al consumo
小売物価指数

retained profits
保留利润; 留存利润
profits non distribués
Gewinnvortrag; nicht
ausgeschüttete Gewinne;
einbehaltene Gewinne
beneficios no distribuidos
利益積立金, 内部留保金

retention money or payments withheld
保留款项或延迟付款
retenue de garantie ou paiements
différés
Sicherheitssumme; einbehaltene
Garantiesumme
retención de dinero o pagos
retenidos como colateral o
prenda
保留額

retirement
退休
(prise de) retraite
Ruhestand; Pensionierung;
Ausscheiden; Verrentung
jubilación; retiro
退職

retraining
再培训
recyclage
Umschulung
reciclaje profesional
再教育訓練

retrenchment
削减(开支); 紧缩(开支)
réduction (des dépenses)
Kürzung; Personalabbau;
Senkung; Betriebsverkleinerung
reducción de gastos
経費削減

retrospective study
回顾性调研[分析]
étude rétrospective
rückblickende Untersuchung
estudio retrospectivo
回顧調査

return
收益

recette
Ertrag
rendimiento
収入, 収益

return on assets
资产利润率
recettes sur actif
Geamtkapitalrentabilität
rendimiento del activo
返却, 還付

return on capital
资本收益率; 资本利润率
rapport ou rendement de
capital
Kapitalrendite
rendimiento del capital
資本収益

return on capital employed
动用资本收益
taux de rendement ou rentabilité
du capital employé
Rendite aus investiertem Kapital
rendimiento del capital invertido
資本収益

return on equity
资本利润
revenu sur fonds propres
Eigenkapitalrendite
rendimiento de los activos or de los
recursos propios
自己資本収益率,
株主持分収益率, ROE

return on investment
投资收益率
rentabilité des investissements
Ertrag aus Kapitalanlage
beneficios antes de intereses e
impuestos
投資利益(ROI)

return on net assets
净资产收益率
rentabilité de l'actif net
Eigenkapitalrendite
rendimiento de los activos
netos
純資産収益

return on sales
销售收益率
rentabilité des ventes; recettes
provenant des ventes
Umsatzrendite
rendimiento de las ventas
販売営業収益率

returns to scale
随生产规模扩大而增长的收益;
与生产规模成正比例收益;
规模报酬
rentrées à échelle
Skalenerträge;

Translations appear in the following order: Chinese, French, German, Spanish/Latin American Spanish, and Japanese

Niveaugrenzerträge
rendimiento a escala
規模に関する収穫、規模に関する収益

revaluation
货币重估; 重新定值
réévaluation
Aufwertung
revalorización
平価切上げ, 価格復旧

revaluation of currency
货币重新定值
réévaluation de devise
Aufwertung
revalorización de moneda
平価切上げ

revaluation reserve
重估资产储备
réserve de réévaluation
Rücklage aus Neubewertung;
Neubewertungsrücklage
reserva de revaluación
再評価積立金

revalue
重新估价
réévaluer
neu bewerten; aufwerten;
deflationieren
revaluar
貨幣価値の再評価

revenue
收入; 税收; 国内税收; 收益
revenu
Einnahmen; Einkünfte; Erträge;
Umsatzerlöse; Staatseinkünfte;
Steueraufkommen
ingresos
収入, 財源

revenue anticipation note
预期收入本票
note d'anticipation de revenu
Einkommensgutschein
pagaré a corto plazo en espera de
ingresos no tributarios
歳入見越し証書

revenue bond
收入债券
bon du Trésor
kurzfristige Anleihe der
öffentlichen Hand
bono a largo plazo pagadero con
los ingresos
特定財源債, 収入担保債,
レベニュー・ボンド

revenue centre
收入中心
centre de génération de revenus
Ertragszentrum
centro de generación de ingresos
収入センター

revenue ledger
收益分类帐
grand livre des revenus
Einkommensbuch
libro mayor de ingresos
収入元帳

revenue sharing[1]
分享收益
répartition de revenu
kurzfristige Anleihe der
öffentlichen Hand
participación en los ingresos
fiscales
(米連邦政府による)地方交付金,
歳入分与レベニュー・シェアリング,

revenue sharing[2]
收入分成
redistribution des revenus
vertikaler Finanzausgleich;
Gewinnbeteiligung
participación en los ingresos
収入分配

revenue stamp
印花; 印花税票
timbre fiscal
Steuerstempel; Steuermarke;
Steuerzeichen; Steuerbanderole
timbre fiscal
収入印紙

revenue tariff
收入关税; 财政岁入关税
impôt douanier
Finanzzoll
arancel fiscal
収入関税, 財政関税

reversal stop
反转点
point de revirement: prix auquel un
contrepartiste arrête d'acheter et
commence à vendre un titre, ou
vice-versa
Umkehrpunkt
cambio de la compra a la venta de
un valor, y viceversa
リバーサル・ストップ

reverse commuter
反方向通勤
banlieusard à contre-courant
Gegenpendler(in), fährt in die
entgegengesetzte Richtung
persona que se desplaza al trabajo
en sentido contrario al de la
mayoría
逆方向の通勤者

reverse engineering
反向工程
ingénierie inverse
Rückproduktion; Reverse
Engineering
retroingeniería; ingeniería

retroactiva
分解工学リバース・
エンジニアリング

reverse leverage
反向杠杆融资
ratio d'endettement inversé
umgekehrter Verschuldungsgrad
apalancamiento inverso
負の梃子効果, ネガティブ・
レバレッジ

reverse mortgage
反向抵押
contre-hypothèque
Hypothek, durch die eine private
Altersversicherung unterstützt
wird
hipoteca inversa
逆年金抵当, RAM

reverse split
反向分割
fractionnement d'actions inversé
Aktienzusammenlegung
reagrupamiento de las acciones
株式合併, 逆株式分割

reverse takeover
反向接管; 反向收购; 逆收购
contre-OPA
gegenläufige Übernahme od.
Fusion; Übernahme einer größeren
durch eine kleinere Gesellschaft
adquisición inversa
逆買収

revolving charge account
周转赊购帐户
compte-crédit d'achat
renouvelable
revolvierende
Teilzahlungsvereinbarung
cuenta de crédito rotatorio
回転売掛金勘定

revolving credit
循环信贷
crédit sur acceptation renouvelée
revolvierender Kredit
crédito rotativo; crédito renovable
回転信用勘定

revolving fund
周转基金; 周转金; 运转基金
fonds renouvelable
revolvierender Fonds
fondo rotatorio
回転資金, RF,
米連邦政府回転資金

revolving loan
循环贷款
prêt renouvelable
Revolving-Kredit
préstamo rotatorio renovable
回転ローン

---

*Translations appear in the following order: Chinese, French, German, Spanish/Latin American
Spanish, and Japanese*

reward management
激励管理制度
gestion de récompense
Verwaltung; des
Vergütungswesens
gestión de las recompensas
報償制度管理

rich media
多媒体
médias riches
Rich Media
tecnología enriquecida
リッチ・メディア

ride the curve
顺势而为
tirer profit de la croissance rapide
dans la demande pour une
nouvelle technologie
das schnelle Anwachsen der
Nachfrage für eine neue
Technologie nutzen
aprovecharse de la demanda de
una nueva tecnología
ビジネスの流れに便乗

rigged market
受非法操纵的市场
marché (financier) manipulé
manipulierter Markt
mercado manipulado
買煽り, 市場の人為的操作

right first time
无次品概念
'bien du premier coup': concept
selon lequel on s'engage envers les
clients à ne commettre aucune
erreur
beim erstem Mal fehlerfrei
acertar a la primera
ライト・ファースト・タイム
(総合的品質経営)

rights issue
权力股; 认股权发行
droit préférentiel de souscription
Bezugsrechtsemission
emisión de acciones con derecho
preferencial de suscripción
株主割当増資, 株主割当発行

rightsizing
机构调整; 缩减机构
rationalisation d'effectif
Umstruktuierung oder
Rationalisierung mit dem Ziel der
Kostensenkung und der
Verbesserung der
Wirtschaftlichkeit und Effektivität.
reajuste
適正規模化

rights offering
附权发行
offre de droits de souscription

Bezugsrechtsangebot
emisión de acciones con derecho
preferencial de suscripción
株主割当増資の売り値

ring¹
交易场地
Parquet
Börsenstand
corro
商品取引所の取引場.

ring²
歌舞表演会
clique ou coterie
Konsortium
acuerdo para manipular el precio
de una acción
共同投資行為

ring³
伦敦金属交易所交易会
séance de la Bourse des métaux de
Londres
Auktionsverkauf an der Londoner
Metallbörse
sesión en el Mercado de Metales
de Londres
ロンドン金属取引所での取引

ring-fence¹
围钱
allouer (une somme)
bestimmen
proteger, apartar
資金取り置き

ring-fence²
围钱
aider à sortir du ring
bestimmen
permitir que una compañía de un
grupo vaya a la quiebra sin afectar
al resto
リングフェンス
(グループ内の1社を清算)

ring member
伦敦金属交易所会员
membre du Parquet de la Bourse
des métaux de Londres
Mitglied der Londoner Metallbörse
miembro del Mercado de Metales
de Londres
リング・メンバー(ロンドン金
属取引所の公認会員)

ring trading
大厅交易
transactions sur le parquet d'une
Bourse
Handel an einem Börsenstand
transacciones en el corro
リングでの取引

rising bottoms
底部上升
configuration de creux ascendants

Grafik, die den Preis eines
Wertpapiers oder Wirtschaftsgutes
im Zeitverlauf anzeigt, und die
nach einer Periode niedriger Preise
eine Aufwärtstendenz aufweist.
gráfico que muestra una tendencia
alcista para un valor con precio
bajo
反発後下落

risk
风险
risque
Risiko; Gefahr; Wagnis
riesgo
リスク

**risk-adjusted return on
capital**
按风险定的资本收益
rapport de capital ajusté pour le
risque
risikoangepasster Kapitalertrag
rentabilidad del capital ajustada a
riesgos
リスク調整資本収益

risk analysis
风险分析
analyse du risque
Risikoanalyse
análisis de riesgos
リスク分析

risk arbitrage
风险套利; 风险套汇
arbitrage à risque
Risikoarbitrage
arbitraje con riesgo
危険裁定危険を伴った裁定取引,
リスク・アービトラージ

risk assessment
风险评估
évaluation de risque
Risikobewertung
evaluación del riesgo
リスク査定

risk-bearing economy of scale
带有风险的规模经济;
风险规模经济
économie d'échelle comportant
un risque
risikotragende Skalenerträge od.
Kostendegression
economía de escala de riesgo
危険分散型規模の経済

risk factor
风险因素
facteur de risque
Risikofaktor
factor de riesgo
リスク要素

risk-free return
无风险利润; 无风险收益

retour libre de risque
risikofreie Rendite; risikoloser
Ertrag
ingreso exento de riesgo
安全利益率

risk management
风险管理
gestion du risque
Risikomanagement; Absicherung;
von Risiken
gestión de riesgos
リスク・マネジメント(危機管理)

risk profile[1]
风险档案; 風險定格
résumé des risques auxquels une
organisation est exposée
Risikoprofil
perfil de riesgo
リスク・プロフィール

risk profile[2]
风险档案; 風險定格
analyse du degré auquel les
personnes ou organisations sont
prêtes à prendre des risques
Risikobereitschaftsprofil
perfil de riesgo
リスク・プロフィール

robot
机器人
robot (chercheur)
Roboter; Robby
robot
産業ロボット

robotics
机器人学; 机器人技术
robotique
Robotik
robótica
産業ロボット工学

rocket scientist
财务工程学家，又被称为火箭科
学家
employé d'une institution
financière qui crée des titres
innovateurs
Mitarbeiter(in) eines
Finanzinstituts, der innovative
Wertpapiere entwickelt
creador(a) de valores innovadores
ロケットサイエンティスト(金融
商品創造社員)

rodo kinko
小企业信贷金融机构
au Japon, une institution
financière spécialisée dans la
fourniture de crédit aux petites
entreprises
spezialisiert auf die Vergabe von
Darlehen an kleine Unternehmen
institución japonesa de crédito
para pequeñas empresas
労働金庫

rogue trader
流氓交易商
contrepartiste malhonnête solitaire
unehrlicher Händler
intermediario(-a) financiero(-a) sin
escrúpulos
不正ディーラー

role ambiguity
职责不明确
ambiguïté de rôles
Rollenmehrdeutigkeit
ambigüedad en el reparto de
responsabilidades
役割不透明性

role conflict
职责冲突
conflit de rôles
Rollenkonflikt
conflicto de roles
役割衝突

role culture
职责文化
culture des rôles
Rollenkultur
cultura empresarial de roles
企業役割文化

role playing
角色扮演
jeu de rôle
Rollenspiel
juego de roles
役割演技法

rolling budget
滚动预算
budget renouvelable
rollendes Budget
presupuesto de rotación,
renovación o continuo,
permanentemente actualizado
転がし継続予算

rolling forecast
滚动预测
prévision renouvelable
rollende Prognose
pronóstico sucesivo de
actualización permanente
連続予想

roll-out
全面展开; 全面开展
implémentation de grande
envergure
Rollout
puesta en marcha
ロール・アウト

roll up
复利
ajout d'intérêts au capital dans des
remboursements de prêt
Hinzurechnen von Zinsen zur
Darlehenssumme bei

Darlehenstilgungen
sistema roll up de liquidacion de
un préstamo
ロール・アップ(利子加算)

root cause analysis
根源分析
analyse de cause première
Ursachenanalyse
análisis de las causas
fundamentales
根本原因分析

rootless capitalism
无根资本主义经济;
全球化资本主义经济
capitalisme sans racine
Form des Kapitalismus, die nicht
an ein bestimmtes Land oder an
eine bestimmte Volkswirtschaft
gebunden ist
capitalismo sin raíces
根無し資本主義

rort
舞弊
entôlage
illegale Strategie
tejemanaje
不法, 内密取引

RosettaNet
电子商务发展共同体
consortium RosettaNet
RosettaNet
consorcio Rosetta Net
ロゼッタ・ネット

ROTFL
笑得在地板上打滚
à se tordre de rire
vor Lachen auf dem Boden
herumkugeln
partiéndose de risa
笑って床を転げまわる

round figures
约数; 大概数
chiffres ronds
runde Zahlen
números redondos
端数のない数字

rounding
舍入，四舍五入
arrondissement (des chiffres)
Auf- oder Abrunden
redondeo
概数で表す

router
路由器
routeur
Überleiteinrichtung
direccionador
代替通信網

Translations appear in the following order: Chinese, French, German, Spanish/Latin American
Spanish, and Japanese

royalties
版权使用费; 专利使用费; 版税;
稿酬
droits d'auteur
Ertragsanteil; Förderabgabe;
Tantieme; Autorenhonorar
derechos de autor
権利使用料

RPIX
扣除抵押贷款利息的零售物价指数
indice basé sur l'indice des prix de
l'INSEE, mais qui exclut les
paiements des intérêts sur
hypothèque
auf dem Einzelhandelspreisindex
basierender Index, der die Tilgung
von Hypothekenzinsen mit
beinhaltet, auch als
Grundinflationsrate,
Inflationssockel bezeichnet
IPC que no incluye el pago de
préstamos hipotecarios
住宅ローンを除いた小売物価指数

RPIY
扣除抵押贷款利息和间接税的零
售物价指数
indice basé sur l'indice des prix de
l'INSEE, mais qui exclut les
paiements des intérêts sur
hypothèque et les impôts indirects
auf dem Einzelhandelspreisindex
basierender Index, der die Tilgung
von Hypothekenzinsen sowie
indirekte Besteuerung nicht mit
beinhaltet
IPC que no incluye ni el pago de
préstamos hipotecarios ni los
impuestos indirectos
住宅ローンと間接税を除いた小
売物価指数

RUBBY
富有的城市骑车人
riche motard urbain
reicher Stadt-Biker'
motero(-a) rico(-a) de ciudad
裕福な都会のバイカー

Rucker plan
亚克利润分配计划
Plan Rucker: un type de
programme de répartition des
bénéfices
Rucker-Plan
plan Rucker de participación en los
beneficios
(安定賃金の)ラッカー方式

rule of 78
78规则
règle de 78: méthode utilisée pour
calculer la remise sur un emprunt
avec intérêt initial remboursé de
bonne heure

Berechnungsmethode für den
Abzug von einem Darlehen, das zu
Beginn der Laufzeit hochverzinst
ist, und dessen Anfangszinsen
vorzeitig getilgt wurden
método de la regla del 78 para
calcular la prima no devengada
78の法則

rumortrage
并购证券投机
spéculation sur rumeurs
Spekulation mit Wertpapieren, die
nach Gerüchten Ziel eines
bevorstehenden
Übernahmeversuchs sind
movimientos motivados por la
rumurología
買収の噂に伴う投機的証券取引

run[1]
同值连续序列
séquence tendancielle
Lauf
secuencia
統計の続き数字

run[2]
挤兑; 银行挤提
ruée
Bankrun
retirada masiva de depósitos de un
banco
銀行の取付け

run[3]
抛售货币
ruée
gleichzeitiger Massenverkauf einer
Währung wegen mangelnden
Vertrauens in ihre Stabilität
venta en masa
通貨の大量売却

running account credit
往来账户信贷
crédit de compte courant
Dispositionskredit; Dispokredit
cuenta con facilidad de
descubierto
当座借(貸)越しクレジット

run with something
坚持不懈; 追求
poursuivre une idée ou un projet
ein Vorhaben, eine Idee verfolgen
ir detrás de algo
プロジェクトを推進する

rust belt
锈带 (指重工业衰退的地区)
ceinture de rouille
Gebiete der verarbeitenden
Industrie im Mittleren Westen, die
durch die Abkehr von der
Fertigung hin zur Serviceindustrie
einen schweren Abschwung
erlitten

la industria pesada en declive del
Medio Oeste de Estados Unidos
以前盛んだった米国中西部の製造
地帯

sabbatical
学习假; 进修假; 研究期; 公休假
(année) sabbatique
Sabbatjahr; akademischer Urlaub;
Forschungsjahr
año sabático
有給休暇(サバティカル)

sabotage
怠工; 破坏
sabotage
Sabotage
sabotaje
妨害行為

SADC
非洲南部发展共同体
comité pour l'harmonisation du
développement économique des
pays du sud de l'Afrique
südafrikanische
Entwicklungsgesellschaft
SADCC
南部アフリカ開発共同体

safe hands[1]
安全投资者，中长期投资者
investisseurs qui achètent des titres
qu'il est peu probable qu'ils
vendent à court ou moyen terme
Käufer(in)nen von Wertpapieren,
die aller Wahrscheinlickeit nach
kurz- und mittelfristig nicht wieder
verkaufen werden
manos seguras
長期債務所持者

safe hands[2]
友好投资者
titres détenus par des investisseurs
amis
Aktien, die sich im Besitz
freundlicher Anleger(in)nen
befinden
manos seguras
親切な投資家の所持する債券

safe keeping
代保管业务
dépôt de valeurs en coffre-fort
Verwahrung; Aufbewahrung
custodia de valores
貴重証券類の金庫保管

safety stock
安全库存
stock de sécurité
Sicherheitsbestand
existencias de seguridad; acción
segura
安全在庫

Translations appear in the following order: Chinese, French, German, Spanish/Latin American Spanish, and Japanese

salaried partner
领薪金的合伙人
partenaire salarié
besoldete/r Gesellschafter(in)
socio(-a) asalariado(-a)
定額給パートナー

salary
薪金，工资
salaire
Gehalt
salario; sueldo
給与

salary ceiling[1]
工资最高限额
plafond salarial
Höchstgehalt
techo salarial
給与上限

salary ceiling[2]
工资最高限额
plafond salarial
Höchstgehalt
techo salarial
給与の上限

salary review
工资重估
révision des salaires
Gehaltsprüfung
revisión salarial
給与見直し

sale and leaseback
信用租回，售后租回
vente avec cession-bail
Verkauf eines Leasingobjekts mit
anschließender Rückvermietung
venta y arrendamiento
不動産リース契約付き売買

sale by tender
招标出售
appel d'offres
Verkauf durch Submission
venta por oferta
入札販売

sales
销售额; 营业额; 销售; 销售部
vente(s)
Absatz; Vertrieb; Umsatz;
Verkäufe; Abschlüsse
ventas
販売, 営業

sales channel
销售渠道
canal de distribution
Verkaufsweg
canal de venta
販売経路

sales conference
销售会议
conférence de vente
Verkaufskonferenz

conferencia de ventas
営業会議

sales contest
销售竞赛
compétition de performance de
vente
Verkaufswettbewerb
competición de ventas
販売コンテスト

salesforce
销售力量; 销售人员
force de vente
Außendienstmitarbeiter(in)nen;
Vertreterorganisation;
Außendienst; Verkaufspersonal
personal de ventas
販売陣

salesforce communications
推销队伍交流
communications pour la force de
vente
Verkaufsförderungsprogramm
comunicaciones con el personal de
ventas
営業チーム向けコミュニケー
ション

sales forecast
销售预测
prévisions de vente
Absatzprognose
previsión de ventas
売上高予測

sales manager
销售经理; 营业经理
directeur commercial
Verkaufsleiter(in)
jefe(-a) de ventas
セールス・マネジャー

sales network
销售网络
réseau de distribution (des ventes)
Verkaufsnetz
red de ventas
販売網

sales office
销售部; 销售部门
bureau de vente
Verkaufsbüro
oficina de ventas
営業所, 営業部

sales order
销售订单
commande de vente
Verkaufsauftrag; Bestellung
acuse de recibo de un pedido
販売注文

sales outlet
销售渠道; 销路; 销售分部
point de vente
Vertriebsstelle

punto de venta
販売支店

sales per employee
职工人均销售量
ventes par employé
Absatz pro Arbeitnehmer
venta media por empleado
従業員1人当り売上

sales plan
销售计划
stratégie commerciale (de vente)
Absatzplan
plan de ventas
販売計画

sales presentation
推销展示
présentation de produits
Sonderverkaufsaktion
promoción de ventas
営業プレゼン

sales promotion
促销; 销售促进(活动)
promotion des ventes
Verkaufsförderung;
Absatzförderung
promoción de ventas
販売促進活動

sales promotion agency
促销代理商
agence de promotion des ventes
agencia de promoción de ventas
Verkaufsförderungagentur
販売促進代理店

sales quota
销售定额
quota de vente
Absatzquote
cupo de ventas
販売割当

sales representative
销售代表; 业务代表
représentant(e) de commerce
Verkaufsvertreter(in)
representante comercial
販売人セールスマン

sales resistance
销售抵制; 拒(绝购)买; 推销阻力
résistance de l'acheteur
Kaufunlust
resistencia a la venta
需要鈍化傾向

sales statistics
销售统计
statistiques de vente
Verkaufsstatistik
estadísticas de ventas
販売統計

sales territory
销售区域
territoire de vente

Translations appear in the following order: Chinese, French, German, Spanish/Latin American Spanish, and Japanese

Aufsatzgebiet
territorio de ventas
販売地域

sales turnover
销售总额
chiffre d'affaires
Absatz
cifras de ventas
営業売上

salmon day
徒劳日
pêche au saumon
Ein Tag, an dem man trotz
ungeheurer Anstrengungen
nichts erreicht. Man
kann,,Lachstage' und
,,Lachswochen' haben
día agotador tirado por la borda
たくさん働いても何も達成でき
ない日

sample
样本
échantillon
Stichprobe
muestra
サンプル

sample size
试样量，样本大小
taille d'échantillon
Stichprobenumfang
tamaño de la muestra
サンプルサイズ

sample survey
样本调查
étude par échantillon (de
population)
Stichprobenerhebung
reconocimiento por muestreo;
inventario por muestreo
サンプル調査

sampling[1]
样品赠送
échantillonnage
Sampling
muestreo
製品サンプルの配布

sampling[2]
取样
échantillonnage
Stichprobennahme
muestreo
サンプリング

sampling design
取样设计
conception d'échantillonnage
Stichprobenaufbau
diseño muestral
サンプリングデザイン

sampling error
取样错误
erreur d'échantillonnage
Stichprobenfehler
error muestral; error en el sondeo
サンプリング誤差

sampling units
取样单位
unités d'échantillonnage
Stichprobeneinheiten
unidades de muestra; elementos
de la muestra
サンプリング単位

sampling variation
取样变化
variation des échantillons
Stichprobenvariation
variación de muestreo
サンプリング変動

samurai bond
武士债券
obligation libellée en yens émise
au Japon par une institution
étrangère
Yen-Auslandsanleihe
bono samurai
サムライ債

sandbag
沙袋式反收购
faire retarder le plus possible un
rachat par la partie prenante en cas
de situation hostile
abschotten
en una situación de opa hostil,
entrar en negociaciones con el
responsable de ella para ganar
tiempo hasta la llegada de un
caballero blanco
防波堤(敵対的な企業買収を長引
かせ時間を稼ぐための)

sanity check
错误检查
contrôle de bon sens
Test, um zu prüfen, dass keine
offensichtlichen Fehler begangen
wurden
comprobación de errores
見落としなどの最終チェック

Santa Claus rally
过年行情，圣诞行情
hausse des cours dans la dernière
semaine de l'année
Kurserholung in der letzten Woche
des Jahres
subida de la Bolsa en la última
semana del año
サンタクロース効果による株価
の持続的上昇

sarakin
(日本語)高利的个人消费信贷公司
terme japonais pour une

compagnie financière qui fait
payer des taux d'intérêt élevés à
ses clients personnels
Finanzierungsunternehmen, das
Privatkunden hohe Zinsen
berechnet
institución financiera que cobra
intereses altos
サラ金

SARS
南非税收服务
SARS: le fisc sud-africain
südafrikanisches Finanzamt
Hacienda sudafricana
歳入局

satellite centre
卫星中心
télécentre (pour employés
satellites)
Satellitenzentrum; augelagerte
Datenstation
centro de teletrabajo (de una
empresa)
サテライト・センター

save as you earn
工资扣存储蓄计划;
边挣边储蓄(计划);
小额或定期储蓄计划
'save as you earn': plan d'épargne
par prélèvements mensuels aux
intérêts exonérés d'impôts
Sparprogramm für
Arbeitnehmer(in)nen; durch die
britische Regierung; über
Steuervergünstigungen; gefördert
plan de ahorro en el que las
contribuciones se descuentan del
sueldo
源泉徴収定期積立制度

savings
储蓄
économies (argent épargné)
Ersparnisse
ahorros
貯金

savings account
储蓄账户
compte (de caisse) d'épargne
Sparkonto
cuenta de ahorros
普通預金口座

savings and loan association
储蓄贷款协会; 信用合作社;
储蓄贷款社
société de crédit foncier
Bausparkasse;
bausparkassenähnliches Institut
sociedad mutua de ahorro y
préstamo
貯蓄金融機関, S&L, 貯蓄貸付組合

Translations appear in the following order: Chinese, French, German, Spanish/Latin American Spanish, and Japanese

savings bank
储蓄银行
caisse d'épargne
Sparkasse
banco de ahorros; caja de ahorros
貯蓄銀行

savings bond
储蓄债券
bon d'épargne (USA)
Sparbrief;
Sparschuldverschreibung
bono de ahorro
(米)合衆国貯蓄債券, 貯蓄国債

savings function
储蓄函数
fonction épargne
Sparfunktion
función de ahorro
貯蓄関数

savings ratio
储蓄比率
proportion de l'épargne
Sparquote
índice de ahorro
貯蓄率

scaleability
规模能力
potentiel d'agrandissement
d'échelle
Skalierbarkeit
capacidad de ampliación or
crecimiento
拡張性, スケーラビリティ

Scanlon plan
斯勘龙计划
Plan Scanlon: système de
distribution de bénéfices
Scanlon-Plan
plan de Scanlon
スカンロン計画

scatter
散布(量)
diffusion
Streuung
dispersión
散在量

scatter chart
散布图
diagramme de diffusion
Streudiagramm
diagrama de dispersión
点点表; 点点图

scenario
方案; 远景; 設想情況
scénario
Szenarium; Szenario
situación hipotética
シナリオ

scenario planning
远景计划
technique des scénarios
stratégiques
Szenarioplanung
planificación de situaciones
シナリオ・プランニング

schmooze
讨好; 献媚
faire du screugneugneu
bei einer Veranstaltung all denen
schmeicheln, die der eigenen
Karriere förderlich sein könnten
adular interesadamente a
自らの出世のためにお世辞を使う

science park
科学园区
parc scientifique
Forschungspark
parque científico
サイエンス・パーク(先端科学
集中地域)

scientific management
科学化管理
gestion scientifique
wissenschaftliche
Unternehmensführung
gestión científica
科学的経営

scorched earth policy
焦土政策
politique de la terre brûlée
Politik der verbrannten Erde
política de tierra quemada
焦土政策

scrap
(有少許剩餘價值的)廢料
rebut
Ausschuss; Rest
material descartado
スクラップ, 再製用廃物

screen-based activity
需要使用电脑的工作
activité basée sur écran
(d'ordinateur)
bildschirmorientierte Tätigkeit
actividad en pantalla
PCスクリーンに基づいた仕事

screening study
筛析
étude de dépistage (médical)
medizinische Vorsorgestudie zur
statistischen Erhebung einer
Grundgesamtheit zur
Untersuchung des
Krankheitsaufkommens
estudio selectivo; estudio de
detección
疾病選別調査

screensaver
屏幕保护
écran d'attente
Bildschirmschoner
salvapantallas
スクリーンセーバー

scrip dividend
临时凭证股息; 用期票支付股利;
日后兑现的股票红利证书;
股利票; 股息凭证
certificat de dividende provisoire
Dividende in Form von
Zwischenscheinen
dividendo en acciones
証書配当

scrip issue
红股发行; 权力股发行
attribution d'actions gratuites
Ausgabe von Gratisaktien
dividendo en acciones
株式配当, 無償交付

scripophily
收集旧股票或债券
scripophilie
Sammeln wertloser Aktien- oder
Anleihezertifikate
coleccionismo de acciones y
certificados de bonos sin valor
無価値証券証書の束

scroll bar
滚动条; 展示條
barre de défilement
Bildlaufleiste
barra de desplazamiento
画面上下左右送りバー

SCUM
以自我为中心的男市民
mâle urbain égocentrique
egozentrischer Stadt-Mann'
hombre egoísta de ciudad
利己的都会人男性

seagull manager
海鷗经理
manager style pie qui chante
Geschäftsleiter, der ein Projekt
übernehmen soll, viel Aufhebens
macht, nichts erreicht, und wieder
geht
administrador(a) tipo mucho ruido
y pocas nueces
うるさいばかりで何の役にも立た
ずに帰っていく外部からのマネー
ジャー

SEAQ
证券交易所自动报价系统
base de données informatique des
titres britanniques de la Bourse de
Londres
elektronisches
Börseninformationssystem an der
Londoner Börse für britische

Translations appear in the following order: Chinese, French, German, Spanish/Latin American Spanish, and Japanese

Wertpapiere
sistema informático de la Bolsa de
Londres con información sobre el
mercado de valores
SEAQシステム(ロンドン証券
取引所の株式売買システム)

SEAQ International
国际证券交易所自动报价系统
base de données informatique de
la Bourse de Londres pour les titres
étrangers
elektronisches
Börseninformationssystem für
internationale Wertpapiere
sistema informático de la Bolsa de
Londres con información sobre los
valores del extranjero
SEAQインターナショナル(ロ
ンドン証券取引所の外国債売
買システム)

search
搜索; 搜尋
recherche
Suche
búsqueda
検索

search engine
搜索引擎
moteur de recherche
Suchmaschine
motor de búsqueda
サーチエンジン

search engine registration
搜索引擎注册
inscription d'un moteur de
recherche
Suchmaschinen-Registrierung
registro con un motor de
búsqueda
サーチエンジン登録

seasonal adjustment
季节调整
ajustement saisonnier
Saisonbereinigung
ajuste estacional
季節調整

seasonal business
季节性营业
commerce saisonnier
Saisongeschäft
negocio de temporada
季節的営業, 販売

seasonal products
季节性产品
produits saisonniers
Saisonprodukte
productos de temporada
季節商品

seasonal variation
季节变化; 季節性差異

variation saisonnière
saisonale Schwankung;
jahreszeitbedingte Schwankung;
Saisonschwankung
variación estacional
季節的変動

seasoned equity
优质股权
actions matures (dont la valeur est
bien établie)
Standardwert
acciones consolidadas
安全株

seasoned issue
适时发行
émission de bonne renommée
(gut) eingeführte Emission
emisión consolidada
堅実銘柄, 安定銘柄, 既発銘柄

SEATS
证券交易所自动贸易系统
système d'opérations boursières
électroniques automatisées
automatisches Handelssystem der
Börse
sistema de contratación
electrónica de la bolsa australiana
オーストラリア証券取引所自動
取引システム

secondary issue
再次发行股
émission secondaire
Sekundäremission
emisión secundaria
株の再売り出し

secondary market
二级市场
second marché
Sekundärmarkt; Zirkulationsmarkt
mercado secundario
流通市場、二次市場;
(米)証券取引委員会

secondary offering
出售新股(但该種新股與市場所有
者同類)
offre d'achat secondaire
Angebot von Wertpapieren im
Sekundärmarkt
colocación en el mercado
secundario
第二次分売, 再売出し

secondary sector
第二部门; 二级部门; 後備勞動力
(包括主婦,半退休人仕和青少年)
secteur secondaire
sekundärer Sektor
sector secundario
第二次部門

secondment
借调; 借用

détachement ou affectation
provisoire
Abstellung
traslado temporal
出向

second mortgage
第二抵押
deuxième hypothèque
Sekundärhypothek
hipoteca de segundo grado
二番抵当

second-tier market
二板市场
marché de deuxième niveau
nachgeschalteter Markt
mercado de segunda línea
二次市場

Section 21 Company
非盈利公司
compagnie établie en tant
qu'organisation à but non lucratif
gemeinnütziges Unternehmen
organización sin ánimo de lucro
セクション21会社(非営利団体)

sector index
部门指数
indice de secteur
Branchenindex
índice sectorial
業種別株価指数

secular trend
长期趋势
tendance séculaire
säkularer Trend; Langzeittrend
tendencia secular
永続する傾向

secured[1]
安全的，有担保的
(emprunt) garanti
gesichert
con garantía
(担保·抵当で借金の)支払いを
保証する

secured[2]
安全的，有担保的
(créancier) privilégié
bevorrechtigt
con garantía
(担保·抵当を取って)貸出金を
保証する

secured bond
保证债券
obligation garantie
gesicherte Obligation
bono con garantía
担保付社債

secured creditors
有担保的债权人
créanciers privilégiés
bevorrechtigte Kreditoren

*Translations appear in the following order: Chinese, French, German, Spanish/Latin American
Spanish, and Japanese*

acreedor(a) asegurado
被保証債権者

secure server
安全服务器
serveur protégé; serveur
haute-sécurité
sicherer Server
servidor seguro
セキュアー・サーバー

securities account
(有价)证券帐户
compte de titres
Wertpapierkonto; Depotkonto;
Depot
cuenta de valores
有価証券勘定

securities analyst
证券分析师
analyste de portefeuille
Wertpapieranalyst(in)
analista de valores
証券アナリスト

**Securities and Exchange
Commission**
证券交易(管理)委员会
Commission des opérations de
Bourse (USA)
amerikanische
Börsenaufsichtsbehörde
comisión estadounidense de
control del mercado de valores
米証券取引委員会, SEC

**Securities and Futures
Authority**
证券期货局
commission de supervision des
opérations de titres et
d'instruments à terme
Behörde für Wertpapier- und
Termingeschäfte
autoridad en materia de valores y
futuros
証券先物協会

**Securities and Investment
Board**
证券投资委员会
Société de réglementation des
transactions de titres et
investissements
Aufsichtsbehörde für den
britischen Finanz- und
Wertpapierhandel
consejo de inversiones de
acciones, bonos y valores;
Comisión Nacional del Mercado de
Valores
証券投資委員会

Securities Commission
证券委员会
commission néo-zélandaise des
titres et valeurs

Börsenaufsichtsbehörde
comisión neozelandesa reguladora
del mercado de valores
ニュージーランド証券委員会

securities deposit account
证券存款帐户
compte de dépôt de titres
Depotkonto; Depot;
Wertpapierkonto
cuenta de depósito de valores
差入有価証券勘定

**Securities Institute of
Australia**
澳大利亚证券学院
Institut australien des titres et
valeurs
australische Wertpapierinstitut
organismo australiano
representativo del sector de valores
y de servicios financieros
オーストラリア証券協会

**Securities Investor Protection
Corporation**
证券投资人保护公司
corporation d'assurance pour la
protection des investisseurs en
titres (Etats-Unis)
amerikanische Schutzkörperschaft
für Investoren in Wertpapiere
sociedad estadounidense que
actúa como fondo de seguro
mutuo para proteger a los clientes
de empresas de valores
証券投資家保護組合

securities lending
证券借贷
prêt de titres
Gewähren von Effektendarlehen
préstamo de valores
債券ローン

securitised paper
证券化票据
document titrisé
handelbares Wertpapier zur
Verbriefung von Krediten
papel negociable
証券化証書

security[1]
证券
titre ou valeur
Wertpapier
valor
有価証券

security[2]
担保，担保品
caution ou nantissement
Sicherheit; Garantie; Bürgschaft
garantía
担保

security deposit
证券寄托; 证券预付金;
证券抵押金
dépôt avec garantie
Kaution; Sicherheitsleistung
depósito de garantía
担保預り金

security investment company
证券投资公司
compagnie d'investissements
cautionnés
Wertpapier-Investment-
Gesellschaft
sociedad de inversión mobiliaria
証券投資会社

seed capital
原始资本; 种子资金; 创办基金
capital de départ
Startkapital; Gründungskapital
capital simiente o generador
元手, 資金金

segmentation
分割
segmentation
Segmentierung
segmentación
細分化政策

selection bias
选择偏差
distorsion de sélection
Auswahlverzerrung
sesgo de selección
選択バイアス

self-actualisation
自我实行
auto-réalisation (de ses
compétences et talents)
Selbstverwirklichung
autoactualización
自己現実化

self-appraisal
自我鉴定
auto-évaluation
Eigenbeurteilung;
Selbstbeurteilung
autoevaluación
自己査定

self-assessment[1]
自我评估
auto-évaluation
Selbstbeurteilung
autoliquidación tributaria
組織自主評価

self-assessment[2]
自我评估
déclaration de revenus avec
auto-évaluation des impôts à payer
Selbstveranlagung
autoliquidación tributaria
(英)税金自主評価

---

*Translations appear in the following order: Chinese, French, German, Spanish/Latin American
Spanish, and Japanese*

self-certification
自我签名病假条
système selon lequel un employé
remplit personellement un
certificat médical pour les sept
premières journées d'absence pour
raisons de santé
Krankmeldung von seiten des
Arbeitnehmers
justificación de baja por
enfermedad por parte del
empleado
自己証明

self-employment
自由职业者; 个体经营者
travail à son compte
selbständig
autoempleo
自営業

self-insurance
自动保险; 自保; 自办保险;
自行保险
auto-assurance
Selbstversicherung;
Eigenversicherung
autoseguro
自家保険

self-liquidating
自偿性; 自偿的; 自动清偿的;
自行生息还本
auto-amortissable
sich liquidierend
autoliquidable
自己流動性、自己弁済的な,
借入金弁済可能な

self-liquidating premium
保本廉价奖品
prime auto-amortissable
sich automatisch liquidierende
Prämie
prima autoliquidable
自己清算型プレミアム商品購入

self-liquidating promotion
自负型促销
promotion auto-amortissable
sich selbst tragende Werbung
promoción autoliquidable
自己充足的なプロモーション

self-regulatory organisation
自治组织
organisme autorégulateur
Selbstverwaltungskörperschaft
organización autorregulada
自主規制機関,
(業界の)自主管理機関,
自己規制組織

self-tender
自我收购
offre de rachat par une compagnie
de ses propres titres (Etats-Unis)
Rückkauf der eigenen Aktien am

Markt per Tender
autooferta
入札による再購入

sell and build
先订货后制造
technique de la construction d'un
produit une fois qu'il est vendu et
payé
Fertigungsmethode, bei der ein
Hersteller erst dann in die
Fertigung geht, wenn ein Kunde
eine Bestellung aufgegeben und
bezahlt hat
fabricación sobre pedido
注文生産

seller's market
卖方市场; 求过于供市场
marché favorable au vendeur
Verkäufermarkt
mercado de vendedores
売り手市場

selling cost
销售成本, 推销成本
frais commerciaux
Vertriebskosten;
Vertriebsgemeinkosten
gastos comerciales; gastos de
comercialización; gastos de venta
販売費

selling season
销售旺季
saison de vente
Verkaufssaison
temporada de ventas
売出し期

sell short
卖空
vendre à découvert
leerverkaufen; fixen
vender al descubierto, especular a
la baja
空売り, 見越し売り

seminar
研讨会; 研究班
séminaire
Seminar; Kolloquium
seminario
セミナー

semi-variable cost/semi-fixed cost/mixed cost
半固定成本
coût semi-variable/coût semi-fixe/
coût mixte
teilvariable Kosten; Mischkosten
coste mixto; coste semifijo; coste
semivariable
準固定費

Sendirian
有限(公司)
terme malais pour des sociétés à

responsabilité limitée
beschränkte Haftung
S.A.
有限

senior debt
优先债务
dette supérieure
vorrangige Verbindlichkeiten
deuda prioritaria or privilegiada
優先弁済債務, 上位債務、上位債

senior management
高级领导层
haute direction ou cadres
supérieurs
obere Geschäftsleitung; oberes
Management
dirección de alto rango
管理職

senior mortgage
优先抵押债务
hypothèque de premier rang
erststellige od. im Rang
vorgehende Hypothek
hipoteca privilegiada
先順位譲渡抵当

sensitivity analysis
灵敏度分析
analyse de sensibilité
Sensitivitätsanalyse;
Empfindlichkeitsanalyse
análisis de sensibilidad
感応度分析

sensitivity training
敏感性培训
formation de sensibilisation aux
compétences interpersonnelles
Sensitivitäts-Training
formación sobre sensibilidad
感応訓練
(人間関係トレーニング)

separation
停业; 停止
séparation: terme américain pour
désigner le renvoi ou la démission
Trennung; Abgang
finalización del empleo
辞職

serial entrepreneur
系列企业家
créateur des nouvelles entreprises
en série
Serienunternehmer(in)
empresario(-a) emprendedor(a) de
proyectos
連続起業家

seriation
顺序排列, 系列化
sériation
Gruppieren von Gegenständen
aufgrund von Ähnlichkeiten oder

Translations appear in the following order: Chinese, French, German, Spanish/Latin American Spanish, and Japanese

Unterschieden
creación de series
連続的に起こる

SERPS
收入关联养老金计划
système de retraite calculée sur le
salaire (Royaume Uni)
lohngekoppelter staatlicher
Pensionsplan
pensión británica adicional a la
pensión del estado
(英)国の賃金比例年金制度

server
服务器
serveur
Server
servidor
サーバー

server farm
服务器农场
centre de serveurs
Server-Farm
centro de servidores
サーバー・ファーム

service
服务
service
Dienstleistung; Service
servicio
サービス

service charge¹
服务费
service
Bearbeitungsgebühr
servicio
サービス・チャージ

service charge²
服务费
service ou frais d'administration
Bearbeitungsgebühr
tarifa por servicio
サービス・チャージ

service contract
服务契约; 服务合同
contrat de service
Arbeitsvertrag
contrato de servicios
サービス契約

service cost centre
服务成本中心
centre de coût et services
sekundäre Kostenstelle
centro de costos
サービス・コスト・センター

service/function costing
服务功能成本计算
comptabilité analytique de service/
fonction
Dienstleistungskalkulation
cálculo de costos de servicios y

funciones
サービス機能原価計算

service level agreement
服务标准协议
accord sur le niveau de service
Dienstvertrag
acuerdo sobre la cobertura de un
servicio
サービス・レベル協定

servicing borrowing
偿还贷款利息
assurance du service d'un emprunt
Schulden bedienen
pago del interés de un préstamo
ローンの利子支払い

SET
安全电子交易
SET: TES: protocole de transaction
électronique sécurisée
verschlüsselte elektronische
Geldtransaktion
protocolo SET
セキュア・エレクトロニック・
トランザクション・プロトコル,
公開鍵暗号方式

set-off
扣除; 抵消
balance (d'une dette)
Aufrechnung
compensar
相殺

set the bar
设定高目标
motiver son personnel en
établissant des cibles à la barre
haute
Mitarbeiter(in)nen durch
Zielsetzungen motivieren, die
höher gesteckt sind als ihr
derzeitiger Leistungsstand
subir el listón
高い目標を掲げ動機付けする

settlement¹
协议; 解决; 清偿; 结清; 付清; 结帐;
清算
règlement
Verrechnung; Regelung;
Erledigung; Bezahlung;
Abrechnung; Liquidation;
Schlichtung; Vergleich; Beilegung;
Abfindung
pago
决济

settlement²
结算
règlement
Begleichung
liquidación
清算

settlement date
结帐日; 交割日
date de liquidation
Abrechnungstermin
fecha de liquidación
决算日

set-up costs
设立费用
frais de montage
Aufstellungskosten;
Installationskosten; Einrichtkosten;
Rüstkosten
gastos de montaje
設立費

setup-fees
商业帐户开户费
frais de montage
Einstellungsgebühren
tarifa de alta
(マーチャント・アカウント)
開設手数料,
セットアップ・フィー

set-up time
准备时间; 建立时间
temps de montage
Aufstellungszeit; Installationszeit;
Einrichtzeit; Rüstzeit
tiempo de montaje
設立時間

seven-day money
七日存款
dépôts à sept jours
Mittel, die für eine Laufzeit von
sieben Tagen im Geldmarkt
platziert wurden
dinero invertido durante siete días
7日払い資金

sexual discrimination
性别歧视
discrimination sexuelle
Sexualdiskriminierung;
Geschlechtsdiskriminierung
discriminación sexual
性差別

sexual harassment
性骚扰
harcèlement sexuel
sexuelle Belästigung am
Arbeitsplatz
acoso sexual
セクシュアル・ハラスメント
(性的いやがらせ)

shadow price
影子价格
prix virtuel
Schattenpreis
coste de oportunidad; precios
contables; precios fantasmas
潜在価格

---

*Translations appear in the following order: Chinese, French, German, Spanish/Latin American
Spanish, and Japanese*

shakeout
清除弱小投资者
remaniement des investisseurs
Ausschalten schwacher oder
vorsichtiger Anleger während
einer Krise am Finanzmarkt
reestructuración eliminando
inversores cautos
危機での弱気投資家の排除

shamrock organisation
三叶草型组织
organisation à structure en trèfle
Kleeblatt-Organisation
organización en trébol
シャムロック組織

shape up or ship out
改善绩效否则被辞退
fais mieux ou casse-toi
reiss dich am Riemen oder geh'
o mejoras o te largas
業績を上げないと首だ

share
股票; 股份
action
Aktie; Anteil; Beteiligung;
Wertpapier; Quote
acción
株式, 持ち株

share account[1]
股份账户
compte d'actions
Beteiligungskonto
cuenta de participación
株式口座

share account[2]
股份账户
compte d'actions
Beteiligungskonto
cuenta que paga dividendos
株式勘定

share capital
股(份资)本
capital actions
Aktienkapital; Stammkapital
capital accionario
株式資本

share certificate
股份证书; 股票
certificat d'action(s)
Aktienzertifikat; Globalaktie;
Anteilsschein
título de acción
株券

shared drop
直接促销共享
livraison promotionnelle groupée
simultane Angebotsvergabe
promociones entregadas a mano
simultáneamente
共同配布

shared services
分享服务
services partagés
gemeinsame Dienste
servicios compartidos
共同サービス

share exchange
股票交易
service d'échange d'actionnariat
Aktienaustausch
intercambio de acciones
株式交換

share-for-share offer
现股转换收购
offre de rachat action-pour-action
Übernahmeangebot, bei dem der
Interessent seine eigenen Aktien
oder eine Verbindung von liquiden
Mitteln und Aktien für das
Zielunternehmen anbietet
oferta de acción por acción
企業買収時の相手株に対する
自社株オファー

shareholder
股东; 股票持有人
actionnaire
Aktionär(in); Anteilseigner(in);
Aktieninhaber(in)
accionista
株主

shareholders' equity
股东权益
(l')avoir des actionnaires ou fonds
propres
Eigenkapital
patrimonio neto
自己資本

shareholders' perks
股东额外收入或好處
avantages annexes des
actionnaires
Vergünstigungen für Aktionäre
ventajas para los accionistas
株主優待

shareholder value
股东价值
valeur pour les actionnaires
Aktionärsnutzen;
Unternehmenswert; Nutzen für
die Aktionäre
valor del accionista (dividendos,
plusvalía, etc.)
株主価値

shareholder value analysis
股东价值分析
analyse de la valeur pour les
actionnaires
Analyse des Aktionärswertes
análisis del valor para los
accionistas
株主価値分析

shareholding
持股
actionnariat
Aktienbestand; Aktienbesitz;
Beteiligung
participación accionarial
株式所有

share incentive scheme
股票鼓励计划
programme d'acquisitions
d'actions par les employés
Anreizprogramm mit
Aktienerwerbsmöglichkeit für
Angestellte
plan de incentivos con acciones
持株奨励システム

share issue
股票发行
émission d'actions
Aktienemission
emisión de acciones
株式発行

share of voice
广告费用份额
part des voix
Stimmesanteil
audiencia potencial
セクター毎の広告料比率内訳

share option
认股选择权; 优先购股权
option de prise de participation
des employés dans leur entreprise
Aktienoption; Aktienbezugsrecht
opción sobre acciones
株式オプション

shareowner
股东
propriétaire d'actions
Aktionär(in); Anteilseigner(in)
accionista
株主

share premium[1]
股票溢价
prime d'émission
Aktienagio; Emissionsagio
prima de emisión
株式発行差金, 株式払込剰余金

share premium[2]
股票溢价
prime d'émission
Aktienagio
prima de emisión
株式プレミアム

share premium account
股票溢价账户
compte de prime d'émission
Agio
reserva para prima de emisión
株式プレミアム勘定

---

*Translations appear in the following order: Chinese, French, German, Spanish/Latin American
Spanish, and Japanese*

share register
股票登记簿; 股东名册
registre des actions
Aktienregister; Aktienbuch
registro de acciones
株式名簿

share shop
股票交易部
bureau des actions (pour vente et
achat au public)
Aktienladen
oficina de acciones
株式ショップ

shareware
共享软件
partagiciel
Shareware
shareware
シェアウェア

shark repellent
反收购条款; 反恶意收购; 驱鲨术
clauses anti-requin
Übernahmeabwehr-Klausel
medidas contra OPAs hostiles o
cambios de estatus; medida
anti-OPA
敵対的買収を避けるための手段

shark watcher
鲨鱼观察者
spécialiste de surveillance de
Bourse pour détection de squales
Firma, deren Spezialgebiet die
Beobachtung des Marktes auf
Übernahmeaktiviäten hin ist
empresa especializada en detectar
intentos de OPAs hostiles
シャーク・ウォッチャー(企業買収
動向を監視する)

shelf registration
暂搁注册
inscription avant émission ou vente
Vorausregistrierung;
Globalregistrierung
registro de una corporación
発行登録

shelfspace
陈列空间
rayonnage
Regalplatz
espacio en enstante
棚スペース

shell company
空壳公司
société-écran
Firmenmantel
sociedad ficticia
ペーパー・カンパニー

shibosai
私募
terme japonais pour le placement

privé
Privatplatzierung
colocación privada
私募債

shibosai bond
私募债券
obligation samurai vendue
directement aux investisseurs par
la société émettrice
vom emittierenden Unternehmen
direkt an die Anleger verkaufte
Yen-Auslandsanleihe, ohne die
Vermittlung einer Finanzinstitution
bono samurai vendido por la
empresa que lo emite
私募発行債

shift¹
道班; 轮班
poste
Schicht
turno
交替時間

shift²
轮班
équipe (de relais)
Schichtarbeiter(in)nen
turno
交替労働者

shift differential
道班补贴; 轮班补贴
différentiel de salaire pour travail
posté
Schichtzuschlag
complemento salarial por trabajo
por turnos
番方差別賃金

shiftwork
道班工; 轮班工
travail posté ou par roulement
Schichtarbeit
trabajo por turnos
交替制

shinyo kinku
小业信贷机构
au Japon, une institution
financière qui offre des services de
financement aux petites
entreprises
Finanzinstitut, die spezialisiert auf
Finanzierung für kleine
Unternehmen
institución japonesa de crédito
para pequeñas empresas
信用金庫

shinyo kumiai
小企业信用合作社
au Japon, un syndicat de crédit qui
offre des services de financement
aux petites entreprises
Kreditgenossenschaft, die
spezialisiert auf Finanzierung für

kleine Unternehmen
cooperativa japonesa de crédito
para pequeños empresarios
信用組合

shipping confirmation
发货确认信息
confirmation d'expédition
Auslieferungsbestätigung
confirmación de envío
出荷確認書，シッピング・
コンファーメーション

shogun bond
将军债券
obligation libellée dans une devise
autre que le yen qui est vendue sur
le marché japonais par une
institution financière non
japonaise
Anleihe, die nicht in Yen gestückelt
ist und auf dem japanischen Markt
von ausländischen
Finanzinstituten verkauft wird.
bono shogun
ショウグン債

shopbot
搜索服务器
robot acheteur
automatisiertes System zur Suche
nach bestimmten Produkten oder
Dienstleistungen im Internet
robot de compras
ショップボット

shopping cart
电子购物车
chariot: progiciel qui collecte et
enregistre les articles sélectionnés
pour achat
Einkaufswagen
cesta or carrito de la compra
ショッピング・カート

shopping experience
电子购物过程
expérience de shopping
électronique
Einkaufserlebnis
preparación del pedido
バーチャルな購入経験

shop steward
工会代表; 工厂或车间的工会代表
délégué(e) syndical(e)
betriebliche Vertrauensperson;
Personalvertreter(in)
delegado(-a) sindical
ショップ・スチュワード,
職場委員

shop window website
橱窗网站
site Web vitrine
Schaufenster-Webseite
sitio escaparate

---

*Translations appear in the following order: Chinese, French, German, Spanish/Latin American
Spanish, and Japanese*

ショップウィンドウ(オンライン会社案内)

short[1]
短期的
obligations d'Etat à court terme
Kurzläufer
bono del Tesoro a corto plazo
短期国債

short[2]
短头寸，空头
actif ou valeur pour laquelle un marchand de titres a une position à découvert
Baisseposition
activo a corto plazo
空売り総高

short covering
空头回补，补仓，平仓
rachat à découvert (de titres ou produits étrangers)
Deckung zum Ausgleich eines Leerverkaufs
compra de activos para cubrir posiciones vendidas
手仕舞い買い，空売りの買戻し

shorthand
速记
sténographie
Stenografie; Kurzschrift; stenografisch
taquigrafía
速記

shorting
买空
vendre à découvert
Leerverkauf
venta al descubierto
空売りをする

short-interval scheduling
短间隔进度
programmation de travail à intervalle déterminé
Kurzintervall-Zeitplanung
planificación en plazos de tiempo cortos
ショート・インターバル・スケジュール

short-run production
短期生产线
production de petite série
Kleinserienfertigung; Kleinserienproduktion; Einzelproduktion
producción a corto plazo
短期生産

short-term bond
短期债券
obligation à courte échéance
kurzfristige Schuldverschreibung
bono a corto plazo
短期公債

short-term capital
短期资本
capital à courte échéance
kurzfristiges Kapital
capital a corto plazo
短期資本

short-term debt
短期债务
dette à court terme
kurzfristige Verbindlichkeiten
deuda a corto plazo
短期国債，短期負債

short-term economic policy
短期经济政策
politique économique à court terme
kurzfristige Konjunkturpolitik
política económica a corto plazo
短期経済政策

short-termism
短期主义
court-termisme
Kurzsichtigkeit
soluciones a corto plazo
短期主義

shovelware
将传统媒介(如公司简介现有的资料内容等照搬到新媒介上(如互联网))
torchiciel: terme péjoratif signifiant que le logiciel produit pour convertir, par ex, un catalogue existant est bâclé et ne tire pas avantage des possibilités audiovisuelles et de liaison du véhicule numérique
Schaufelware: abschätziger Begriff für Material, das durch die Umwandlung bestehender Medien, etwa eines Katalogs, erstellt wurde, ohne dass die audio-visuellen oder Verknüpfungsmöglichkeiten des digitalen Mediums berücksichtigt wurden
producto electrónico acartonado
シャベルウエア

show stopper
暗藏的缺陷
clou du spectacle: une autre forme de pilule empoisonnée
andere Form der Anti-Übernahmestrategie
píldora venenosa
毒薬条項

shutdown of production
停产
arrêt total de production
Produktionsstillstand
paralización de la producción
生産休止

sickie
装病假
journée de congé maladie quand on n'est pas malade
Blaumachen
día de baja por enfermedad (simulada)
(偽の)病欠

sick leave
病假
congé maladie
krankheitsbedingtes Fehlen; krankgeschrieben sein
baja por enfermedad
病欠

sickness and accident insurance
疾病意外保险
assurance maladie et accident
Kranken- und Unfallversicherung
seguro de accidente y enfermedad
疾病事故保険

sickout
装病怠工
absentéisme protestataire
Krankheitsausfall
protesta laboral consistente en simular enfermedad
集団病欠

sight bill
见票即付汇票; 即期汇票
effet à vue
Sichtwechsel
letra a la vista
一覧払い為替手形, 要求払い手形, SD

sight deposit
即期存款; 活期存款
dépôt à vue
Sichteinlage; Giroeinlage
depósito a la vista
一覧払預金

sight draft
即期汇票
traite à vue
Sichttratte
letra a la vista
一覧払為替手形

signature
签名; 标记
signature
Signatur
firma
eメール署名

signature guarantee
签字担保
garantie de signature
Unterschriftsbeglaubigung
garantía de la firma
印鑑証明

Translations appear in the following order: Chinese, French, German, Spanish/Latin American Spanish, and Japanese

silversurfer
银色冲浪者，中老年上网者
utilisateur du net âgé de 45 à 65
ans
Internetanwender(in) im Alter
zwischen 45 und 65
internauta de entre 45 y 65 años
シルバーサーファー(45–65歳の
インターネットユーザー)

silvertail
有钱人
personne riche de haut standing
reiche Person hohen Standes
persona rica y de alta posición
social
上流階級のお金持ち

simple interest
单利
intérêt simple
einfache Zinsen; Kapitalzinsen
interés simple
单利

simple moving average
简单平均选移
moyenne mobile simple
einfacher gleitender Mittelwert
media móvil simple
単純移動平均

simulation
模拟
simulation
Simulation; Nachbildung
simulación
シミュレーション

simulation game
模拟活动
exercice de simulation
Simulationsspiel
juego de simulación
シミュレーション・ゲーム

simulation model
模拟模式
modèle de simulation
Simulationsmodell
modelo de simulación
シミュレーション・モデル

simultaneous management
同步协调管理
gestion simultanée
Simultanmanagement; parallel
integrierte Unternehmensführung
gestión simultánea
同時管理

SINBAD
辛巴达
seul revenu, pas de petit copain et
absolument désespérée
ein Gehalt, kein Freund und
verzweifelt auf der Suche

soltera, sin novio y completamente
desesperada
单一收入，ボーイフレンドなし，
欲しくてたまらない

Singapore dollar
新加坡元
dollar singapourien
Singapur-Dollar
dólar singapurense
シンガポールドル

Singapore Exchange
新加坡证券交易所
Bourse de Singapour:
Börse von Singapur: entstanden
durch die Fusion von zwei früheren
Börsen 1999.
Bolsa de Singapur
シンガポール株式金融市場

**Singapore Immigration and
Registration**
新加坡移民登记局
service de l'immigration
singapourien
Einwanderungsbehörde
Departamento de Inmigración de
Singapur
シンガポール移民登録局

single currency
单一货币
devise unique
einheitliche Währung;
Einheitswährung
moneda única
单一通货

single customs document
单一海关收据; 标准海关申报单
document de douane simple
einheitliches Zollpapier
documento aduanero único
单一通関書類

single entry
单式分录; 单式记录
inscription en partie simple
einfache Buchführung; einfacher
Eintrag
partida simple
単式記入

**single minute exchange of
dies**
快速换模法
changement de matrice à la
minute
Werkzeugaustausch in nur einer
Minute
técnica para la optimización del
tiempo de instalación de
equipamiento
短時間金型交換

single-payment bond
一次付清债券
obligation à remboursement

unique
mit Einmalzahlung ablösbare
Anleihe
bono de pago único
一括払い債券，一回払い債券

single premium assurance
延缴保费保险
assurance à prime unique
Einmalprämien-Versicherung
seguro de prima única
保険料一時払い保険

**single premium deferred
annuity**
一次付清保险费延期年金
annuité différée à prime unique
aufgeschobene Rente mit
Einmalprämie
anualidad diferida de prima única
一時払い据え置き年金、
一時払い据置年金契約

single sourcing
单一供应渠道; 单方进货
approvisionnement à source
unique
Einkauf bei nur einem Zulieferer;
Einzelquellenbezug
utilización de un solo proveedor
シングル・ソーシング

single tax
单一税制
impôt unique
Alleinsteue; Einsteuer
impuesto único
单一税，一物件税

site analysis
网站分析
analyse de site
Seitenanalyse
análisis de un sitio
サイト分析

six-month money
六个月货币
dépôt à six mois
Halbjahresgeld
dinero invertido durante seis
meses
6ヶ月払い資金

Six Sigma
6个标准差技术
Six Sigmas: méthode basée sur les
données visant à arriver à une
qualité quasi parfaite
Six Sigma
plan Six Sigma de mejora de la
productividad
シックスシグマ

size of firm
企业规模
taille d'entreprise
Unternehmensgröße

---

*Translations appear in the following order: Chinese, French, German, Spanish/Latin American
Spanish, and Japanese*

tamaño de la empresa
企業規模

skeleton staff
骨干人员; 基干工作人员
personnel réduit
Rumpfbelegschaft;
Stammpersonal
plantilla reducida
少数の当番社員

skewness
偏斜
dissymétrie
Schiefe
asimetría
非対称性

skill
技巧; 技能
compétence
fachliche Fertigkeit; od. Fähigkeit;
Qualifikation; Fachkenntnis
habilidad; destreza
技能

skills analysis
技能分析
analyse des compétences
Befähigungsanalyse;
Kompetenzanalyse;
Qualifikationsabbildung
análisis competencial or de
habilidades
技能分析

skills shortage
技术工人短缺
pénurie de compétences
Fachkräftemangel; Mangel an
Fachpersonal
falta de mano de obra cualificada
技能者不足

skunkworks
革新促进小组
mouffettes: groupe d'action
rapide qui travaille en périphérie
de la structure d'une organisation
et dont le but est d'accélérer le
processus d'innovation
Gruppe, die kann ohne
Einschränkungen durch
Unternehmenspolitik und
-verfahren arbeiten
grupo paralelo de fomento de la
innovación
スカンクワーク

slack variables
松弛变量
variables de stagnation des
ressources
Schlupfvariable; Leerlaufvariable
variables flojos por desuso
可変的資源

sleeping partner
隐名合伙人
associé commanditaire; bailleur de
fonds
heimlicher Gesellschafter; stiller
Gesellschafter
socio(-a) sin derecho a voto
休眠パートナー

slowdown
放慢; 减缓
ralentissement
Verlangsamung;
Konjunkturabschwächung
ralentización
スローダウン、鈍化, 減速,
景気沈滞

slump
萧条; 衰退; 暴跌; 狂跌
effondrement ou baisse soudaine
starker Konjunkturrückgang;
Geschäftsflaute
recesión
スランプ, 暴落, 景気沈滞

slumpflation
萧条膨胀; 衰退膨胀; 滞胀
slumpflation: crise économique
avec effondrement total comme
en 1929 et avec inflation des prix
et salaires
Konjunktureinbruch mit Lohn- und
Preisinflation; Slumpflation
recesión con inflación
スランプフレーション,
不況下のインフレ

slush fund
行贿基金
caisse servant à payer les
pots-de-vin
Bestechungsfonds;
Schmiergelderfonds;
Geheimfonds; Kasse für
Schmiergelder
fondo para corrupción
裏金

**small and medium-sized
enterprises**
中小型企业; 中小企业
petites et moyennes entreprises
kleine und mittlere Unternehmen
pequeña y mediana empresa,
PYME
中小企業

small business
小型企业; 小企业
petite entreprise
Kleinunternehmen
pequeña empresa
小企業

small change
小面值硬币
petite monnaie

Wechselgeld
cambio, suelto
小銭

**Small Order Execution
System**
小额委托交易系统
système d'exécution de petit ordre
(sur le NASDAQ)
Ausführungssystem für
Kleinaufträge
sistema automatizado del
NASDAQ para pedidos pequeños
小額注文行使システム

small print
附属细则
clauses non évidentes
Kleingedrucktes
letra pequeña
小文字印刷

smart card
智能卡
carte à puce
Chip-Karte
tarjeta inteligente
スマート・カード

smart market
电子化市场
marché intelligent
elektronischer Markt mit
Netzkommunikation
mercado inteligente
スマート市場

smartsizing
精简裁员
réduction d'effectif intelligente,
par élimination des incompétents
Entlassung von Mitarbeitern nach
Kompetenzkriterien
reajuste inteligente de plantilla
効率の悪い社員から人員整理する

smoking memo
证据信件
mémo qui pue
Memorandum, Brief oder E-Mail
Nachricht mit Hinweisen auf ein
Firmenvergehen
mensaje incriminador
企業犯罪の証拠となるような手
紙など

smoko
间休
pause cigarette
Zigarettenpause
descanso (para fumar, tomar café)
(一服用の)休憩

smoothing methods
平整法
méthodes de lissage
Glättungsmethoden
métodos de suavizamiento
スムーズ法

---

*Translations appear in the following order: Chinese, French, German, Spanish/Latin American
Spanish, and Japanese*

SMS
短邮件传递服务
système pour envoi de messages
textuels par téléphone portable
System zum Versenden von
Textnachrichten über
Mobilfunknetze
SMS
携帯電話網での送信システム

SMTP
简单邮件传送协议
protocole pour courrier
électronique
einfaches
Postübertragungsprotokoll
SMTP
SMTPプロトコール

snail mail
蜗牛信件，由邮递员分发传递的
传统信件
courrier escargot
Schneckenpost
correo caracol
カタツムリ郵便

snowball sampling
滚雪球取样
échantillonnage par (effet) boule
de neige
Schneeballauswahl
muestreo de tipo 'bola de nieve'
ネズミ算式サンプリング

snowflake
雪花(圖表)
graphique en flocon de neige
Diagramm, das multivariate Daten
aufweist
diagrama que muestra datos
multivariantes o multivariables
スノーフレーク

SO
其他值得注意的
partenaire
Bezugsperson
media naranja
重要な他人

social audit
社会审计
audit social
Sozialaudit Betriebsprüfung auf
soziale Gesichtspunkte hin
auditoría social
社会的監査

social capital
社会资本
capital social
Sozialkapital; Sozialfonds
capita; de la sociabilidad de los
empleados
社会資本

social cost
社会成本; 社会代價
coût social
volkswirtschaftliche Kosten
coste social
社会的費用

socialism
社会主义
socialisme
Sozialismus
socialismo
社会主義

social marginal cost
社会边际成本
coût de marge social
soziale Grenzkosten
coste social marginal
costo social marginal
社会的限界費用

social responsibility
社会责任
responsabilité sociale
soziale Verantwortung
responsabilidad social
社会的責任

**social responsibility
accounting**
社会责任会计
comptabilité des responsabilités
sociales
Sozialkostenrechnung
contabilidad de responsabilidad
social
社会的責任計算

Sociedad Anónima
私人有限公司
équivalent espagnol de société
anonyme
span. Gesellschaft mit
beschränkter Haftung
Sociedad Anónima
(西)非公開有限会社

Sociedade Anónima
私人有限公司
équivalent portugais de société
anonyme
port. Gesellschaft mit
beschränkter Haftung
Sociedad Anónima
(ポルトガル)非公開有限会社

**società a responsabilità
limitata**
未上市有限责任公司
société italienne à responsabilité
limitée non cotée en Bourse
it. Gesellschaft mit beschränkter
Haftung, die nicht börsennotiert ist
sociedad de responsabilidad
limitada
(伊)非上場有限会社

società per azioni
公共有限公司
société italienne à responsabilité
limitée cotée en Bourse
it. Aktiengesellschaft
sociedad anónima
(伊)株式会社

Société Anonyme
私人有限公司
Société Anonyme
frz. Gesellschaft mit beschränkter
Haftung
Sociedad Anónima
(仏)非公開有限会社

**Société à responsabilité
limitée**
未上市有限责任公司
Société à responsabilité limitée
frz. Gesellschaft mit beschränkter
Haftung, die nicht börsennotiert ist
Sociedad de responsabilidad
limitada
(仏)非上場有限会社

**Société d'investissement à
capital variable**
共同投资
Société d'investissement à capital
variable (SICAV)
frz. Begriff f. kollektives
Investitionsunternehmen
sociedad de inversión en capital
variable
集団投資

socio-cultural research
社会文化研究
recherche socioculturelle
soziokulturelle Marktforschung
investigación sociocultural
社会文化調査

socio-economic
社会经济的
socioéconomique
sozio-ökonomisch;
sozialwirtschaftlich
socioeconómico
社会経済の

socio-economic environment
社会经济环境
environnement socioéconomique
sozialwirtschaftliches Umfeld
entorno socioeconómico
社会経済環境

**socio-economic
segmentation**
社会经济部门; 社会经济分割;
社会经济划分
segmentation socioéconomique
sozialwirtschaftliche
Segmentierung
segmentación socioeconómica
社会経済的細分化

---

*Translations appear in the following order: Chinese, French, German, Spanish/Latin American
Spanish, and Japanese*

Sod's Law
草地法则
principe selon lequel si quelque chose peut aller de travers, c'est ce qui va se passer
Prinzip, nach dem eine Sache, die schief gehen kann, auch garantiert schief gehen wird.
la ley de Murphy
悪いことが起これば最悪の状態になる(ソッドの法則)

soft benefits
软福利
petits bénéfs en nature
weiche, qualitative Nebenleistungen
contrapartidas no monetarias
社員に対する非金銭的給付

soft commissions
经纪人佣金
commissions discrètes
weiche Maklerprovisionen
comisiones con descuento
ソフト・コミション

soft commodities
软性商品
biens non durables
Weichwaren
productos básicos agrícolas
非耐久財

soft-core radicalism
道德促销术
technique marketing qui joue sur le souci qu'ont les gens des questions éthiques et écologiques
Vermarktungsmethode, die Sorgen der Menschen im Hinblick auf Umwelt und Ethik ausnutzt, um ihnen ein Produkt zu verkaufen
marketing que utiliza la sensibilidad medioambiental y ética
環境・人権派の社会意識を利用した商法

soft currency
软通货
devise faible
weiche Währung
divisa débil
軟貨

soft landing
软着陆
atterrissage en douceur
weiche Landung
aterrizaje suave
ソフトランディング, 軟着陸

soft loan
软贷款
prêt à des conditions favorables
zinsgünstiger Kredit
crédito blando

ソフト・ローン,
条件の緩やかな貸出

soft market
疲软的市场
marché en baisse
rückläufiger Markt
mercado a la baja
小緩み市況

sole practitioner
独资商人
praticien(ne) à son compte
Einzelfirma; Einzelunternehmung; Einzelkauffrau; Einzelkaufmann
propietario único de un consultorio profesional
個人自営業

sole proprietor
独资商人
propriétaire unique
Einzelfirma; Einzelunternehmung; Einzelkauffrau; Einzelkaufmann
propietario único
個人事業主

sole trader
个体商人
propriétaire unique/personne à son compte
Einzelunternehmer(in)
autónomo; empresario individual
個人商人

solus position
单独位置
position isolée
alleinstehende Anzeige
cláusula de exclusividad en una página
広告の独占的位置

solution brand
方案型商标
offre de solution totale (pour produits et services)
Gesamtlösungsmarke
solución de marca
ソリューション・ブランド商品

solvency margin¹
偿付准备金
marge de solvabilité
Liquiditätsmarge
margen de solvencia
会社の支払い能力

solvency margin²
边际清偿能力
marge de solvabilité
Liquiditätsmarge
margen de solvencia
保険会社の支払い能力

solvency ratio¹
偿债能力比率
rapport de solvabilité
Solvenzkennzahl; Liquiditätsquote

coeficiente or índice de solvencia
会社の支払い能力比率

solvency ratio²
偿债能力比率
coefficient de solvabilité
Liquiditätsgrad
coeficiente de solvencia
保険会社の支払い能力比率

solvent
有清偿能力者
solvable
zahlungsfähig; liquide
solvente
支払能力のある

sort code
分类码; (英國)银行分行代码
code guichet
Bankleitzahl; BLZ
número de sucursal bancaria
ソートコード(支店番号)

sort field
分類排列域
champ de tri
Sortierfeld
campo de clasificación
ソートフィールド

source document
原始凭证, 原始单据
document source
Originalbeleg
documento fuente; documento original
入力伝票

sovereign loan
主权贷款
prêt souverain
Anleihe staatlicher Kreditnehmer
préstamo soberano
ソブリン・ローン(貸手負担の債務償還ローン)

sovereign risk
主权风险
risque souverain
Länderrisiko
riesgo soberano
ソブリン・リスク(貸手負担の債務償還危険)

spam
兜售信息
bloc de e-mail non sollicité
Spam
correo basura
スパムメール

spamkiller software
垃圾邮件消除软件
logiciel tueur de spam
Software, die unerwünschte Werbung per E-Mail blockieren kann

---

Translations appear in the following order: Chinese, French, German, Spanish/Latin American Spanish, and Japanese

software anti-correo basura
耐スパムメールソフト

span of control
管理面(广度和幅度); 管制幅度;
管理跨度
envergure du contrôle (sur les
employés)
Kontrollspanne;
Subordinationsquote;
Leitungsspanne
ámbito de control
管理範囲

spare parts
备用零件
pièces de rechange
Ersatzteile
repuestos
スペアパーツ

spatial data
空间数据
données spatiales
Raumdaten
datos espaciales
空間的広がりデータ

speako
讲述错误
erreur d'ordinateur durant
l'utilisation d'un programme avec
reconnaissance vocale
Sprechfehler: Fehler, den ein
Rechner während der
Verwendung eines
Spracherkennungsprogramms
macht
error de reconocimiento del habla
スピーコ(音声認識プログラム
によるエラー)

spear carrier
中层领导
hallebardier d'entreprise
Person, die in einer Organisation
an zweiter Stelle steht und für die
Durchführung der Befehle und
Kommunikationen der obersten
Führungsriege zuständig ist
jefe(-a) que ejecuta las órdenes de
los ejecutivos
幹部の命令を実行する一ランク
下の人

special deposit
特种存款; 专用存款
dépôt spécial
Festgeldkonto; hinterlegte
Geldsumme für die Sanierung
eines mit einer Hypothek
belasteten Hauses
depósito especial
別段預金, 別口預金

special leave
特假; 特许假
congé exceptionnel
Sonderurlaub

permiso especial
特別休暇

special presentation
特别兑付
présentation spéciale (d'un
chèque)
Sondereinreichung
presentación al banco sin pasar
por el sistema de compensación
小切手等の銀行への直接提出

special purpose bond
专用债券
obligation à but particulier
Spezialanleihe
bono garantizado con impuestos
特定目的債券

specie
硬币
espèces (monnayées)
Münzgeld
monedas
硬貨

specification
详细说明; 规格说明; 产品说明;
说明书
spécification
Spezifikation; Beschreibung;
Patentschrift; Ausfuhrerklärung;
Packliste
especificación
仕様書

specific charge
固定费用
charge ou frais spécifique
feste Gebühr
tarifa fija
固定料金

specific order costing
特别订单成本计算方法,
分批成本法
évaluation de coût de commande
spécifique
Auftragskalkulation
cálculo de costos por trabajos
específicos
個別原価計算

speculation
投机行为; 买空卖空; 高风险交易;
期货投机; 期货买卖
spéculation
Spekulation
especulación
投機

speech
讲话; 演講; 演說
discours
Rede
discurso
スピーチ

spider food
诱饵
mots imbriqués dans une page
Web pour attirer des moteurs de
recherche
in eine Webseite eingebettete
Worte, die Suchmaschinen
anziehen sollen
palabras incrustadas en una
página para atraer motores de
búsqueda
スパイダー・フード

spiffs
推销佣金
petits cadeaux
Angebot von Geschenken oder
Geld als Gegenleistung für
Werbung für ein bestimmtes
Produkt
incentivos irregulares a los
encargados de tiendas
ある製品を推してもらうために
店頭マネージャーに与える金銭
やギフト

spin-off
分立子公司; 分离出去
nouvelle entreprise dérivée d'une
autre
von der Muttergesellschaft
gebildetes Unternehmen
empresa formada a partir de
otra
派生企業

splash page
醒目页面
page manchette
erste oder einführende Seite mit
Werbung, die Besuchern einer
Webseite gezeigt wird, bevor sie
zur Startseite gelangen
página introductoria
スプラッシュページ

split
分割
split: distribution gratuite de
plusieurs actions par action
détenue
Aktiensplit
fraccionamiento
株式分割

split-capital investment trust
分类投资信托投资公司
société de placement à capital
fractionné
Investmentfonds mit
Kapitalaufteilung
fondo de inversión en capital
dividido
資本分割投資信託

Translations appear in the following order: Chinese, French, German, Spanish/Latin American Spanish, and Japanese

split commission
分享手续费;
经纪人之间分享的佣金
commission partagée
geteilte Provision; gespaltenes
Gremium; in zwei Lager
comisión dividida
コミッション分割

sponsorship
主办; 赞助; 发起
parrainage
Sponsoring
patrocinio
スポンサーシップ

Spoornet
南非交通局铁路分局
division ferroviaire de la
compagnie de transport
sud-africaine nationalisée,
Transnet Ltd
Eisenbahn
compañía de ferrocarril estatal
sudafricana
スポーネット(南アフリカ国営
運輸会社鉄道部門)

spot
广播电视广告
spot
Werbespot
espacio publicitario
C M

spot colour
套印色彩
touche de couleur
Farbe für kleine Flächen
color plano
スポット・カラー

spot exchange rate
现汇汇率; 现货市场汇率
taux de change au comptant
Devisenkassakurs; Bardevisenkurs
tipo de cambio al contado
現物為替相場

spot goods
现货
biens ou produits au comptant
Lokowaren
mercancías al contado
現物市場商品

spot interest rate
即期利率
taux d'intérêt du disponible
Kassazins; Spotzins
tipo or tasa de interés al contado
スポット・レート

spot market
现货市场; 直接市场
marché du comptant
Warenbörse für reine
Kassageschäfte; Spot Market

mercado al contado
現物市場

spot price
现货价格
prix du comptant
Kassakurs; Sport-Kurs
precio al contado
現物値段

spot transaction
现货生意
transaction au comptant
Kassageschäft
operación al contado
現物為替取引, 実地取引

spread¹
差额; 差价; 毛利; 分散; 扩散
écart
Marge; Spanne
margen; diferencial
価格差, サヤ, スプレッド

spread²
范围
gamme (d'investissements dans un
portefeuille)
Stellage
margen; diferencial
投資商品の種類

spreadsheet
展开式分列分析表; 总分析表;
电子表格; 攤析表
tableur
Arbeitsblatt; Abschlussblatt;
Kalkulationstabelle
hoja de cálculo
スプレッド・シート

sprinkling trust
散分信托
fonds de placement à distribution
discrétionnaire
Privatvermögensverwaltung
fideicomiso cuyo administrador
decide su reparto
スプリンクリング・トラスト

spruik
叫卖推销
promouvoir des biens ou services
en haranguant les passants à
l'entrée d'un magasin à l'aide d'un
micro
werben
hacer publicidad en la puerta de
una tienda con un micrófono
街頭宣伝をする

squatter
牧场主; 大地主
gros propriétaire terrien
reicher Landbesitzer
terrateniente rico(-a)
お金持ちの地主

squattocracy
大地主
ensemble des gros propriétaires
terriens
Landadel
clase terrateniente
羊産貴族

squeaky wheel
吱吱叫的轮子，自信的人
personne qui obtient des bons
résultats en étant extrêmement
sûre d'elle lors de ses transactions
avec les autres
jemand, der mit extrem
bestimmtem Verhalten gegenüber
anderen gute Ergebnisse erzielt
persona muy enérgica y decidida
自身のやり方を通す人

squeeze
紧缩
restriction
Verdrängung; Restriktionen;
Verknappung; Druck
restricción oficial crediticia o
económica
(金融)引締め

squirt the bird
卫星信号传播
transmettre un signal jusqu'à un
satellite
ein Signal an einen Satelliten
übertragen
transmitir una señal a un satélite
信号を人工衛星に送る

SSL
安全套接层
système de raccordement
haute-sécurité
SSL
protocolo SSL
SSL(セキュアー・ソケット・レイ
ヤー)

stabilisation fund
稳定基金; 平准基金
fonds de stabilisation
Währungsausgleichsfonds
fondo de estabilización
為替安定資金, 安定基金

staff costs
员工成本
coûts salariaux et de personnel
Personalaufwand
costes de personal
スタッフ経費

staffing level
员工配备水平
niveau de dotation en personnel
Personalbestand
dotación de personal
スタッフ数

Translations appear in the following order: Chinese, French, German, Spanish/Latin American Spanish, and Japanese

stagflation
停滞性通货膨胀; (停)滞(膨)胀
stagflation: situation économique
avec chômage et inflation
simultanés
Stagflation
estanflación
スタグフレーション, 不況下の
インフレ, 不況下の物価上昇

stakeholder
利益相关者
détenteur d'enjeux
Teilhaber(in)
persona con interés en una
empresa
ステークホルダー

stakeholder pension
利益相关者养老金
retraite de type 'stakeholder' ou
détenteurs d'enjeux: en
Angleterre, retraite achetée chez
une compagnie privée
Beteiligungspension
plan de pensiones privado
complementario de la pensión de
empleo
(英)ステークホルダー年金

stakeholder theory
利益相关者理论
théorie du détenteur d'enjeux: elle
maintient qu'une organisation
peut mettre en valeur les intérêts
de ses actionnaires, sans porter
préjudice aux intérêts de ses
détenteurs d'enjeux au sens plus
large
Hypothese von Interessengruppen
teoría que sostiene que se pueden
mejorar los intereses de los
accionistas sin dañar los de los
interesados en una empresa
ステークホルダー価値分析

stakeholder value analysis
利益相关者价值观分析
analyse de la valeur du détenteur
d'enjeux
Analyse des Teilhaberwertes
medición de las opiniones de las
personas interesadas en una
empresa
ステークホルダー価値分析

stamp duty
印花税
droit de timbre
Stempelsteuer;
Börsenumsatzsteuer
sellado fiscal; timbre
印紙税

standard
标准 , 规范
norme

Norm; Standard;
Qualitätsanforderung; Maßstab
norma; estándar; patrón

Standard 8
电子商务标准8
Standard 8: norme utilisée dans le
commerce sur Internet
Standard 8; ein im Internethandel
genutzter Standard
Standard 8
スタンダード・エイト

Standard & Poor's 500
标准普尔氏500家公司
indice des 500 'Standard & Poor'
S&P 500
índice bursátil de Standard & Poor
S & P500種株価指数

Standard & Poor's rating
标准普尔氏公司排序
classification des 'Standard & Poor'
S & P – Klassifizierung od.
Einstufung
clasificación de Standard & Poor
S & P信用格付け

**standard business
transaction**
标准交易处理
transaction commerciale standard
geschäftliche Standardtransaktion
transacción comercial estándar
標準ビジネス取引

standard cost
标准成本
coût standard
Plankosten; Richtkosten
coste normalizado; coste estándar
標準原価

standard cost card
标准成本卡标准产品说明
fiche de coût standard
Standardkostenkarte;
Standard-Lastenheft;
Standard-Leistungsverzeichnis
ficha de coste normalizado;
especificación del producto
normalizado
標準原価票標準製品仕様書

standard costing
标准成本计算
évaluation des coûts et revenus
standard
Plankalkulation;
Standardkalkulation
cálculo de costos estándar
標準原価計算

standard deviation
标准差
écart standard
Standardabweichung

desviación típica or estándar
標準偏差

standard direct labour cost
标准直接劳动成本
coût standard de main d'œuvre
directe
Standard-Lohneinzelkosten;
Standard-Fertigungslohn
coste normal de la mano de obra
directa
標準直接人件費

standard of living
生活水准; 生活水平
niveau de vie
Lebensstandard
nivel de vida
生活水準

**standard
performance–labour**
标准劳动绩效
niveau de performance-travail
standard
Standardleistung-Personal
nivel de desempeño de los
trabajadores
標準労働実績

standard time[1]
标准时间
durée standard: temps passé par
un travailleur pour compléter un
mouvement spécifique
Normalzeit; Standardzeit
tiempo estandar
動作標準時間, 基準時間

standard time[2]
标准时间
durée standard: temps total requis
pour compléter une tâche
spécifique
Vorgabezeit; Sollzeit; Richtzeit
hora legal
動作標準時間

standby credit
备用信贷
crédit de soutien
Standby-Kredit; Beistandskredit;
Stützungskredit
crédito contingente
(IMFの)スタンドバイ・クレジット

standby loan
备用贷款
prêt conditionnel
Bereitstellungsdarlehen;
Bereitschaftsdarlehen
préstamo contingente
スタンドバイ・ローン

stand down
停薪挂职
renvoyer quelqu'un sans salaire
jemanden ohne Lohnzahlung
entlassen

---

*Translations appear in the following order: Chinese, French, German, Spanish/Latin American
Spanish, and Japanese*

suspender sin sueldo
一時帰休

standing instructions
临时指示
instructions permanentes (qui
peuvent être révoquées à tout
moment)
Dienstanweisung
instrucciones
常設命令, 服務規定

standing order
长期(有效)委托书
ordre de transfert permanent
Dauerauftrag
domiciliación bancaria
常設命令

standing room only
等候室销售策略
technique du 'pas de places assises
dans la salle'
,,nur Stehplätze',
Verkaufsmethode, bei der dem
Kunden der Eindruck vermittelt
wird, dass viele andere Kunden das
Produkt zu eben dem Zeitpunkt
auch erwerben wollen
impresión artificial de que hay
mucha demanda de un producto
大勢の人々が購入チャンスを待っ
ていると見込客に伝える商法

staple commodities
主要商品
denrées principales
Stapelwaren
producto básico
主要商品

star
优质投资
star: investissement avec une
excellente performance
Investition, die extrem rentabel ist
inversión estrella
スター商品

start-up
开业; 创业;
风险投资中的启动基金
start-up
Start-up
puntocom nueva; empresa
incipiente
新規小企業, スタートアップ
(新規インターネット取引会社)

start-up costs
启动成本
frais de démarrage
Startkosten
gastos de puesta en marcha
初期立ち上げ費用

start-up model
风险投资中的快速启动模式

modèle de jeune entreprise
innovante à succès
Anlauf-Modell
modelo de crecimiento rápido
短期ビジネス成功モデル

state bank
州立银行
banque d'Etat
Staatsbank; konzessioniert durch
einen Staat der USA
banco estatal
(米州法により設立認可された)
州法銀行, 国立銀行

state capitalism
国家资本主义
capitalisme d'état
Staatskapitalismus
capitalismo de Estado
国家資本主義

state enterprise
国有企业
organisation étatisée
staatliches Unternehmen
empresa estatal
国営企業

statement of account
帐单, 财务收支表
relevé de compte
Kontoauszug; Abrechnung;
Rechnungsauszug
estado de cuenta
勘定書

statement of affairs
财务状况说明书
bilan de liquidation
Konkursbilanz;
Vermögensaufstellung
balance de liquidación
財政状態計算書

**Statement of Auditing
Standards**
审计标准说明
déclaration des normes pour
audits
Grundsätze des
ordnungsgemäßen Prüfwesens
declaración sobre las normas de
práctica de auditoría
監査基準書

statement of cash flows
现金流动表
relevé de marge brute
d'autofinancement
Kapitalflussrechnung
estado de flujo de fondos
現金収支表

**statement-of-cash-flows
method**
现金流动表法
méthode du relevé de cashflows

Kapitalflussrechnungsmethode
metódo de estado de flujo de
fondos
現金収支表会計

**statement of changes in
financial position**
财务状况变动表;
财务状况变动报告
rapport de changements de
position financière
Bilanz; Finanzbericht
estado de origen y aplicación de
fondos
財政状態変動表

**Statement of Financial
Accounting Standards**
财会标准说明
déclaration des normes
comptables financières applicables
(Etats-Unis)
Grundsätze ordnungsgemäßer
Rechnungslegung
estado de los estándares de
contabilidad financiera
財務会計基準書

**Statement of Standard
Accounting Practice**
标准会计实务说明
déclaration des normes de
pratiques comptables
Allgemein anerkannte Grundsätze
der Rechnungslegung; Grundsätze
ordnungsgemäßer Buchführung;
Abk. GoB
declaración sobre las normas de
práctica contable
標準会計実務書

state of balance
平衡状态
état d'équilibre (type de
capitalisme)
Zustand der Ausgewogenheit
equilibrio entre la ecología y la
economía
バランス状態

state planning
国家计划
planification d'état
staatliche Planung
planificación estatal
国家計画

statistic
统计数; 统计值
statistique
statistische Maßzahl
estadística
統計量

statistical expert system
统计专家系统
système (informatique) d'expertise
statistique

statistisches Expertensystem
sistema experto en estadística
統計エキスパートシステム

statistical model
统计模式
modèle statistique
statistisches Modell
modelo estadístico
統計モデル

statistical process control
统计过程控制
contrôle statistique des procédés
statistische Prozesskontrolle
control de procesos estadísticos
統計プロセスコントロール

statistical quality control
统计质量控制
contrôle de qualité statistique
statistische Güteprüfung
control estadístico de la calidad
統計的品質管理

statistical significance
统计意义
importance statistique
statistische Signifikanz
importancia estadística
統計学的重要度

statistics
统计学; 统计数字
la statistique
Statistik
estadística
統計学

statute-barred debt
受法律限制的债务
dette caduque
verjährte Forderung
deuda prescrita
時効債務

statutory auditor
法定审计师
vérificateur de comptes imposé par la loi
gesetzliche/r Rechnungsprüfer(in)
auditor(a), censor(a) de cuentas
監査役

statutory body
法定团体
organisme officiel
Körperschaft des öffentlichen Rechts
organismo legal
法定組織

STC
公司二级税
type de taxe secondaire levée sur les dividendes d'entreprise
Kapitalertragssteuer

impuesto secundario sobre dividendos
第二次税

stickiness
(吸引并留住客户的能力)粘性;
招徕回头客
capacité d'attirer et de retenir les clients
Fähigkeit, Kunden anzuziehen und beizubehalten
capacidad de enganche
スティックネス(顧客獲得保持性)

stick to the knitting
保障重点; 集中重点;
坚持主业策略
'cantonne-toi à ce que tu sais faire': exhortation à une organisation de se concentrer sur son activité principale
bleib bei deinem Leisten; bei seinem Leisten bleiben
estrategia de no diversificación
コア・ビジネスに絞る

sticky site
有吸引力的网址
site qui colle
klebrige Seite
sitio Web atractivo
スティッキー・サイト

stipend
定期生活津贴; 薪俸
traitement
Gehalt
estipendio
俸給

stock¹
库存; 储存; 家畜; 证券; 股票; 债券
stock
Aktien; Wertpapiere
acción
株式

stock²
股票
stock
Grundkapital
capital en acciones
資本金

stockbroker
证券经纪人
courtier en Bourse
Wertpapiermakler(in)
agente de cambio y bolsa;
corredor(a) de bolsa
株式仲買人, 株式ブローカー

stockcount
点货; 盘点库存
comptage de stock

Lagerinventur
beneficios de una acción
ストックカウント(株式利益)

stock exchange
证券交易所; 股票交易所
Bourse
Wertpapierbörse; Effektenbörse
bolsa (de valores)
株式取引所, 証券取引所

stock market
证券市场
marché financier
Aktienmarkt; Börse; Effektenbörse
bolsa (de valores)
株式市場, 株式取引所、株式売買

stockout
存货售完; 缺货
rupture de stock
Fehlbestand
falta de existencias
棚卸し

stock symbol
股票名称
version abrégée du nom d'une compagnie
Organisationssymbol
símbolo de la acción
ストック・シンボル(銘柄)

stocktaking
清点存货; 盘点; 盘存
(faire) l'inventaire
Bestandsaufnahme
inventario
棚卸し

stokvel
循环储蓄计划
programme informel de plan d'épargne coopératif qui fournit des prêts de petite envergure
Spar- und Dahrlehensystem
cooperativa de ahorros
小規模ローンスキーム

stop-go
停停走走; 收放
situation de 'stop-go': situation économique en dents de scie
Ankurbelung und Bremsung der Wirtschaftspolitik
expansión y contracción
ストップ・ゴー政策

stop limit order
撤销限制命令
ordre limite
Stop-Limit-Order
orden stop con límite
ストップ・ロス注文

stop loss
限定亏损; 扭亏; 停止损失
ordre stop
Stop-Loss-Order

Translations appear in the following order: Chinese, French, German, Spanish/Latin American Spanish, and Japanese

orden stop con límite
ストップ・ロス(設定価格を下回
った時の指値注文)

stop order
停止损失指令;
停止损失指示(股票)
ordre stop à la hausse/à la baisse
Stop-Order
orden de stop
ストップ・オーダー(現行価格
を上下した時の指値注文)

stop-work meeting
工作时间会议
réunion organisée par les
employés pendant les heures de
travail
Gewerkschaftssitzung
reunión de trabajadores durante el
horario laboral
労働時間内労使会議

story stock
内情股票
titre à histoire
Aktie, um die in der Presse oder in
der Finanzwelt viel Aufhebens
gemacht wird, was sich auf ihren
Kurs auswirken könnte
acciones a punto de cambiar de
cotización
うわさ株, 会社について魅力的
噂で買われる株

straight-line depreciation
直线折旧
dépréciation linéaire
lineare Abschreibung
amortización lineal
定額償却

Straits Times Industrial Index
海峡时报指数
indice de 30 titres singapouriens le
plus communément utilisé comme
indicateur d'activité à la Bourse de
Singapour
Straits Times Industrieaktienindex
índice de la Bolsa de Singapur
ストレイツタイムズ工業指標

strata title
小业主登记制
titre de strate immobilière
Wohn- oder
Büroraumbesitzanmeldung
título de propiedad de un
apartamento y la parte
proporcional del espacio
comunitario
多層階ビルの区分所有権

strata unit
单元
unité de strate immobilière
Wohnung oder Büro
apartamento dado de alta junto

con el espacio comunitario
correspondiente
多層階ビルの区分

STRATE
电子股票交易
système de transactions d'actions
entièrement électronique
voll elektronisches
Aktienhandelsystem
sistema de contratación
electrónica de la Bolsa de
Johanesburgo
株取引完全電子化システム

strategic alliance
战略同盟; 战略联盟
alliance stratégique
strategische Allianz; strategische
Verbindung
alianza estratégica
戦略的協定, 提携

strategic analysis
战略分析
analyse stratégique
strategische Analyse
análisis estratégico
戦略分析

strategic business unit
策略性经营单位
unité d'activité stratégique
strategische Geschäftseinheit;
strategischer
Unternehmensbereich
unidad de negocio estratégico;
unidad estratégica de negocio;
unidad de estrategia comercial
戦略営業ユニット

**strategic financial
management**
策略性财政管理
gestion financière stratégique
strategische Finanzverwaltung od.
Finanzbuchhaltung
gestión financiera estrategia
戦略財務管理

strategic fit
战略适应度
degré de bon ajustement
stratégique
strategische Übereinstimmung od.
Eignung
complementariedad estratégica
戦略適合性

strategic goal
策略目标
objectif stratégique
strategisches Ziel; langfristiges Ziel
objetivo estratégico
戦略的ゴール

strategic inflection point
战略转变点

point de modification stratégique
strategischer Wendepunkt
punto de inflexión estratégico
戦略変更ポイント

**strategic information
systems**
战略信息系统
systèmes d'informations
stratégiques
strategisches Informationssystem
sistemas de información
estratégica
戦略情報システム

**strategic investment
appraisal**
策略性投资评估
évaluation stratégique des
investissements
strategische Investitionsrechnung
evaluación de la inversión
estragética
戦略的投資評価

strategic management
战略管理
gestion stratégique
strategisches Management
gestión estratégica
戦略管理

**strategic management
accounting**
策略性管理会计
comptabilité de gestion
stratégique
strategisches
entscheidungsorientiertes
Rechnungswesen
contabilidad de gestión
estratégica
戦略管理会計

strategic marketing
战略性营销
marketing stratégique
strategische Direktmarketing
marketing estratégico
戦略的マーケティング

strategic partnering
战略伙伴
partenariat stratégique
Bildung strategischer
Partnerschaften
asociación estratégica
戦略同盟

strategic plan
战略计划
plan stratégique
strategischer Plan
plan estratégico
戦略的計画

strategy
战略; 策略

Translations appear in the following order: Chinese, French, German, Spanish/Latin American Spanish, and Japanese

stratégie
Strategie
estrategia
戦略

straw man
稻草人，不成熟的建议
homme de paille
Strohmann
propuesta de partida
ストロー・マン(暫定策)

streaming
多线程
streaming ou transmission sur
plusieurs niveaux
Streaming
reproducción en tiempo real
ストリーミング

street
行家
branché
schlauer Kopf
persona bien informada sobre la
Bolsa
ストリート(市場情報豊富な人
物)

street name
街名经纪人
courtier qui détient les titres d'un
client au nom de l'intermédiaire au
lieu de celui du client propriétaire
Scheinfirma
operador a cuyo nombre están
depositados valores de un cliente
仲買人名簿

stress
精神压力
stress
Stress
estrés
ストレス

stress puppy
压力爱好者
toutou qui aime le stress
jd., der sich häufig beschwert und
augenscheinlich gerne gestresst ist
quejica que parece disfrutar del
estrés
ストレスを糧にしているように
見える，愚痴の多い人

strike
罢工
grève
Streik
huelga
ストライキ

strike pay
罢工期间津贴
salaire de gréviste (payé par un
syndicat)
Streikgeld

subsidio de huelga
罷業手当て

strike price
价格协定; 敲定价格; 执行价
prix d'émission d'une action
Basispreis; Ausübungskurs;
Abrechnungskurs; Emissionskurs
precio de ejercicio
行使価格

stripped bond
不付息票债券
obligation dépouillée
Stripped Bond; Anleihe, wo der
Zinsschein von der Schuldurkunde
getrennt ist
bono sin cupón
ストリップ債、ストリップボンド

stripped stock
剥离式股票
stock dépouillé
leeres Wertpapier
acciones sin cupón
ストリップ株

strips
息票
fonds talons
Strips
valores procedentes de la
segregación de un bono
ストリップ債

structural change
经济结构变化
changement structurel
Strukturwandel; strukturelle
Änderung
cambio estructural
構造変化

structural inflation
结构性通货膨胀
inflation structurelle
strukturelle Inflation
inflación estructural
構造的インフレーション

structural unemployment
结构性失业
chômage structurel
strukturelle Arbeitslosigkeit
desempleo estructural
構造的失業

**structured systems analysis
and design method**
结构化系统分析与设计法
analyse structurée des systèmes et
méthodologie de conception
Methode der strukturierten
Systemanalyse und
Entwurfsplanung
método de diseño y análisis de
sistemas estructurados

构造化システム分析及び
デザイン方法

stub equity
烟蒂资产
fonds propres souches
Restkapitallaufzeit
capital obtenido de la venta de
bonos de alto riesgo
スタブ株式

subcontract
分包合约; 转包合约; 外判合约
contrat de sous-traitance
Unterauftrag;
Subunternehmervertrag;
Zulieferervertrag
subcontrato
下請け契約

subcontracting
分包合约; 转包合约; 外判合约
sous-traitance
Untervergabe
subcontratación
下請け

subject line
主题行; 题目
ligne du sujet
Betreff
línea de asunto
eメールの宛先・件名ライン

subject to collection
有待领取
sujet à perception
Eingang vorbehalten
sujeto(-a) a cobro
債務回収を条件に

subliminal advertising
速闪广告; 潜在广告
publicité insidieuse
unterschwellige Werbung
publicidad subliminal
潜在意識広告

subordinated loan
附属贷款，后偿贷款
prêt subordonné
nachrangiges Darlehen
préstamo subordinado
劣後ローン

subscriber¹
认购者
souscripteur (acheteur d'actions)
Zeichner(in)
suscriptor(a)
株式申込者

subscriber²
签名人
souscripteur (signataire de statuts
d'une société)
Unterzeichner(in)
firmante de la escritura de
constitución
株式引受人

---

*Translations appear in the following order: Chinese, French, German, Spanish/Latin American
Spanish, and Japanese*

subscription-based publishing
订阅式发行
publication sur abonnement
Abonnement-Veröffentlichung
publicaciones por suscripción
定期購読者向け刊行配布

subscription process
注册程序
moyen d'abonnement
Abbonieren
proceso de suscripción
予約購読プロセス

subscription share
认购股份
action de souscription
Zeichungsaktie
acción suscrita
出資者引き受け株

subsidiary account
辅助帐目
compte affilié
Unterkonto
cuenta subsidiaria; subcuenta
補助元帳勘定

subsidiary company
子公司; 附属公司
filiale
Tochtergesellschaft
empresa filial
子会社

subsistence allowance
生活津贴
indemnité de subsistance
Tagesgeld
dietas
生活費手当て

subtreasury
金库分部; 国库分部
sous-Trésorerie
Staatskasse
subsecretaría del Tesoro
(国庫などの)支金庫, 財務省分局

succession planning
继任安排
planification de succession
Nachfolgeplanung
planificación de la sucesión
引継ぎ計画

suggestion scheme
点子计划; 建议计划
système de boîte à idées
betriebliches Vorschlagswesen
plan de sugerencias
提案箱システム

suit
西装工作者
mec en costard
jd., der für eine große Firma
arbeitet und im Anzug zur Arbeit

erscheinen muss
empleado(-a) trajeado(-a)
大企業で背広の着用を義務づ
けられるサラリーマン

sum
总数; 总额
total/montant
Summe; Betrag;
Vereinigungsmenge
suma
総計, 合計, 総額

sum at risk
风险保险额
montant à risque
Risikosumme; Risikobetrag
suma arriesgada
損失リスク総額

sum insured
投保总额
somme assurée
Deckungssumme
suma asegurada
保険金額

sum-of-the-year's-digits depreciation
年限总和折旧
dépréciation des chiffres du total
de l'année
Abschreibung nach der
Jahressumme; digitale
Abschreibungsmethode;
arithmetisch-degressive
Abschreibung
amortización por el método de la
suma de los dígitos del año
級数減価償却

Sunday night syndrome
周日晚间抑郁症
syndrome du dimanche soir
Sonntagabend-Syndrom
la depresión del domingo por la
noche pensando en la vuelta al
trabajo
日曜の夜症候群

sunshine law
阳光法
loi imposant la divulgation
publique des débats pour une
décision ou action
gouvernementale
Gesetz, das die Öffentlichkeit von
Behördensitzungen vorschreibt
ley que requiere que las decisiones
regulatorias estén al alcance del
público
情報公開法

super
养老退休金
retraite
Rente

pensión
年金(省略形)

superannuation plan
养老退休金计划
plan de retraite
Rentensystem
plan de pensiones
年金プラン(オーストラリアで
の呼び方)

superannuation scheme
养老退休资金计划
programme de retraite
Rentensystem
plan de pensiones
年金プラン(ニュージーランド
での呼び方)

superindustrial society
超工业化社会
société superindustrielle
Superindustriegesellschaft
sociedad superindustrial
超工業化社会

superstitial
在上網下載期間加插的廣告
supersticiel
extrem großflächiges Pop-up
Fenster
anuncio entre páginas
スパースティシャル

supervisor
监察员; 督导员
responsable (de groupe ou
d'équipe)
Aufsichtsperson; Aufseher(in);
Vorgesetzte/r
supervisor(a)
現場監督

supervisory management
督导管理
gestion de première ligne
leitende(r) Angestellte(r)
gestión de primera línea
監督管理

supplier
供应商
fournisseur
Zulieferer
suministrador(a)
サプライヤー

supplier development
供应商发展
développement des relations avec
les fournisseurs
Entwicklung; der Beziehungen;
mit Lieferanten
desarrollo de las relaciones con los
proveedores
サプライヤー開発

supplier evaluation
供应商评估
évaluation des fournisseurs

Translations appear in the following order: Chinese, French, German, Spanish/Latin American Spanish, and Japanese

Lieferantenbeurteilung
evaluación de proveedores
potenciales
サプライヤー評価

supply and demand
供与求
offre et demande
Angebot und Nachfrage
oferta y demanda
需要と供給

supply chain
供应链
chaîne d'approvisionnement
Lieferkette; Zuliefererkette
cadena de suministro
サプライ・チェーン

supply chain management
供应链管理
gestion du réseau
d'approvisionnement
Lieferketten-Management
gestión de la cadena de suministro
サプライ・チェーン管理

supply-side economics
供应学派经济学; 供给经济学(派)
économie de l'offre
angebotsorientierte
Wirtschaftspolitik
economía de la oferta or basada
en la oferta
サプライサイドの経済学,
サプライサイド・エコノミック
ス

support
购买意愿; 支持; 维持; 售后服务
soutien/subvention
Unterstützung; Betreuung;
stützen; Beistand; Hilfe; Stützung;
betreuen; unterstützen
apoyo
サポート

support price
支持价格; 扶助价格
prix de soutien
Stützungspreis
precio de soporte o garantía
支持价格

surety[1]
担保人; 保证人; 担保额; 押金
garant(e)
Garant(in); Bürgin; Bürge;
Interzedent(in);
Schuldmitübernehmer(in);
Sicherung; Bürgschaft; Garantie
fianza; garantía
保证人

surety[2]
担保人，担保品
caution
Bürgschaft

fianza
抵当

surplus capacity
生产能力过剩
capacité excédentaire
Überkapazität
capacidad excedentaria
余剩生产能力

surrender value
退保金额; 保险退还金
valeur de rachat
Rückkaufwert
valor de rescate
解约払戻金

surtax
附加税
surtaxe
Zusatzsteuer
sobretasa
付加税, (英)所得税特别付加

survey
调查
étude; enquête
Umfrage
encuesta
調査

survivalist enterprise
勉强维持生存的小企业(活命主义
企业)
entreprise qui n'a pas de salariés et
génère un revenu en dessous du
seuil de pauvreté
Kleinstunternehmen
microempresa de sobrevivencia
微小企業

sushi bond
寿司债券
obligation non libellée en yen et
émise sur un marché quelconque
par une institution financière
japonaise
nicht in Yen gestückelte Anleihe,
die an einem beliebigen Markt von
einem japanischen Finanzinstitut
begeben wird
bono sushi
スシ・ボンド

sustainable advantage
可持续性优势
avantage (concurrentiel) durable
nachhaltiger Vorteil
ventaja sostenible
持続的利点

sustainable development
可持续发展
taux de croissance envisageable
nachhaltige Entwicklung
desarrollo sostenible
持続的開発

swap
交换; 互换
crédit croisé
Swap; Swapgeschäft; Tausch
permuta; swap
スワップ、スワップ取引、交換

swap book
互换记录
livre d'échanges
Swapbuch
libro de permutas financieras
スワップ・ブック

swaption
互换期权
swaption: contrat d'option sur un
swap ou crédit croisé
Options-Swap; Option aus
Ausübung eines Swap
contrato de permuta; opción de
intercambio
スワップション,
スワップとオプション
の組み合わせ

sweat equity
人力资本
investissement dans le travail
intensif de la main d'oeuvre (plutôt
que dans les liquidités d'une
entreprise)
Investition von Arbeit in ein
Unternehmen, im Gegensatz zur
Investition von Geld.
inversión en forma de mano de
obra
労働提供型投資

sweep facility
转账便利
système de mouvement rapide:
transfert automatique de sommes
d'un compte chèque courant à un
compte de dépôt
Giro-Fazilität
transferencia automática de
cuenta corriente a cuenta de
depósito
自動一掃振替システム

sweetener[1]
行贿物; 贿赂; 刺激
carotte ou pot-de-vin
zusätzlicher Anreiz
propina; soborno
スィートナー(奨励するもの)

sweetener[2]
优惠
caractéristique ajoutée à un titre
pour le rendre plus attrayant
ein Zusatz zu einem Wertpapier,
der dieses für Anleger(in)nen
attraktiver machen soll
incentivo

Translations appear in the following order: Chinese, French, German, Spanish/Latin American Spanish, and Japanese

投資勧誘のため有価証券に
組込まれる権利

sweetener[3]
甜头
titre à gros rendement qui a été
ajouté à un portefeuille pour en
améliorer le rendement global
ertragsstarkes Wertpapier, das
einem Portfolio zugefügt wurde,
um dessen Gesamtertrag zu
verbessern
valor de alto rendimiento
incorporado a una cartera
高利回り付加金融商品

sweetheart agreement
私下劳资合同
accord à l'amiable
außergerichtliche Einigung
acuerdo amistoso
事業者・社員間のスイートハー
ト協約

SWIFT
环球银行间财务电讯协会
organisation coopérative à but non
lucratif avec pour mission de créer
un réseau mondial partagé pour
les communications et traitement
de données
nicht auf Erwerb ausgerichtete
Genossenschaft
SWIFT
スイフト(国際的資金移動の標
準的ネットワーク運営機関)

swing trading
过渡贸易
transactions sur fluctuations
rapides
Swing-Handel
contratación fluctuante
スイング・トレーディング

swipe box
读卡机
fente électronique (pour carte de
crédit)
Magnetkartenlesegerät
lectora magnética de tarjetas
スワイプ・ボックス

switch[1]
转换投资
arbitrage
einwechseln, austauschen
intercambiar
スイッチ(証券の乗換え)

switch[2]
互换汇率
opération croisée d'échanges sur
devises
Wechselkurs für Swap-Geschäfte
tipo de cambio swap
為替レートの交換

switch[3]
借记卡; 過數咭
type de carte de débit britannique
britische Guthabenkarte
tarjeta de débito Switch
(英)デビット・カード

switch[2]
转移商品
permuter (des biens ou
marchandises)
umschichten
cambiar de lugar
商品移動

switching
互换
report de position d'une échéance
à une autre plus éloignée
Umschichtung
compraventa simultánea de
contratos de futuros con
diferentes fechas de caducidad
スイッチング(先物の同時売買)

switching discount
转换折扣
escompte pour arbitrage
Umschichtungsagio
descuento por cambio
スイッチング(投資先変更手数
料)割引

SWOT analysis
现状与前景分析; 公司前途分析;
(一个组织的)优势与劣势;
机会与挑战分析
analyse SWOT: évaluation des
forces, faiblesses, opportunités et
menaces
Analyse von Stärken, Schwächen,
Chancen und Risiken;
SWOT-Analyse [strengths,
opportunities, weaknesses and
threats]
análisis de fortalezas, debilidades,
oportunidades y amenazas;
análisis SWOT
SWOT(長短所, 好機, 脅威評価)
分析

Sydney Futures Exchange
悉尼期货交易所
marché à terme de Sydney
Sydney Termingeschäftsbörse
mercado de futuros de Sidney
シドニー先物取引所

symmetrical distribution
对称分布
répartition symétrique
symmetrische Verteilung
distribución simétrica
对称分布

syndicated research
联合研究
données d'étude provenant

d'agences de recherche
gemeinsame Marktforschung
datos de mercado suministrados
por agencias de investigación
シンジケート調査

sysop
系统操作员，站长
opérateur de systèmes
Systembetreiber(in)
operador(a) del sistema
シソップ(システムオペレー
ター)

system attack
系统攻击
attaque sur un système e-mail
Systemangriff
ataque al sistema
システム・アタック

systems administrator
系统管理员
administrateur de systèmes
Systemverwalter(in)
administrador(a) del sistema
システム管理者

systems analysis
系统分析
analyse des systèmes
Systemanalyse
análisis de sistemas
システム分析

systems approach
系统方式
technique des systèmes
Systemansatz
planteamiento de sistemas
システム的接近

systems audit
系统审计
audit des systèmes
Systemmethode
auditoría de sistemas
システム監査

systems design
系统设计
conception de systèmes
Systementwicklung
diseño de sistemas
システム・デザイン

systems dynamics
系统动态学
dynamique des systèmes
Systemdynamik
dinámica de sistemas
システム・ダイナミックス

systems engineering
系统工程
ingénierie des systèmes
System-Engineering
ingeniería de sistemas
システム監査

---

*Translations appear in the following order: Chinese, French, German, Spanish/Latin American
Spanish, and Japanese*

systems method
系统方法
méthodologie des systèmes
Systemmethode
método de sistemas
システム論

T+
交易期限表达式
indique le nombre de jours
autorisés pour le règlement d'une
transaction
bezeichnet die Anzahl an Tagen bis
zum Glattstellungstermin für ein
Geschäft
número de días para el cierre de
una transacción
取引完了までの猶予期日

tactical campaign
战术运动
campagne de tactique
strategische Direktmarketing
campaña táctica
戦術的キャンペーン

tactical plan
战术计划战术
plan tactique/tactiques
taktischer Plan; Taktik
plan táctico; tácticas
戦術的計画戦術

Taguchi methods
TAGUCHI 方法
méthodes Taguchi: méthodes de
contrôle qualité
Taguchi-Methoden
métodos de control de calidad de
Taguchi
タグチ方式

tailgating
尾随购买
pratique d'achat ou de vente d'un
titre par un courtier,
immédiatement après la
transaction d'un client, afin de tirer
profit de l'impact de la transaction
du client
dicht auffahren
compra o venta de un valor por
parte de un corredor
inmediatamente después de
haberse efectuado la transacción
de un cliente, a fin de
aprovecharse del impacto de la
transacción del cliente
テールゲート

tailormade promotion
特制推广; 特制推销
promotion spécialement conçue
pour un client
kundenfokussierte Werbung
promoción a medida
オーダーメード・プロモーション

take a flyer
投机，乘快车
spéculer en prenant des risques
spekulieren
especular
思惑買い

take a hit
投资损失
se prendre une claque: faire une
perte sur un investissement
getroffen werden
ser vapuleado
投機損をする

takeaway
顾客印象
impressions qui restent
Eindruck, den ein(e)
Verbraucher(in) von einem Produkt
oder einer Dienstleistung gewinnt
impresión
テイクアウェイ(商品等の印象)

take-home pay
实得工资
salaire après déductions
Nettoverdienst
salario neto
手取り額

takeout financing
用来替换过渡融资的融资
financement par souscription à un
emprunt
langfristige Finanzierung über
Darlehen anstelle von
Überbrückungskrediten
financiación una vez completada la
construcción
テークアウト・ファイナンス

takeover
收购
prise de contrôle
Übernahme
absorción; toma de control; toma
de mayoría
企業買収

takeover approach
股票收购价格
prix offert pour prise de contrôle
Übernahmeangebot
oferta de compra
企業買収提示価格

takeover battle
收购战
bataille pour prise de contrôle
Übernahmeschlacht
batalla de adquisición
公開買取戦争

takeover bid
收购发盘; 收购出价; 接管价;
合并出价
offre publique d'achat (OPA)

Übernahmeangebot
OPA; oferta pública de adquisición
de acciones
株式公開買付(TOB)

takeover ratio
收购比率
coefficient de prise de contrôle
Übernahmenquotient
índice de adquisición
公開買取価格

taker[1]
期权接受者
acheteur
Optionsgeber(in)
adquiriente
購買者

taker[2]
购买者
emprunteur(-euse)
Kreditnehmer(in)
prestatario(-a)
借用者

takings
进款
recette (nette d'un détaillant)
Einnahmen; Bareinnahmen
recaudación; caja
小売業者売上高, 所得

talent
天才
talent
Talente, besonders befähigte
Mitarbeiter(in)nen
talento
有能社員

talk offline[1]
离线谈话; 私下讨论
continuer une ligne de discussion
spécifique en dehors du contexte
de départ
eine Besprechung am Rande
haben
pasar a hablar de un asunto
diferente; hablar informalmente
オフラインで話す

talk offline[2]
發表與公司政策不同的言論
exprimer une opinion opposée à la
position officielle de l'organisation
qui vous emploie
eine Meinung äußern, die der
offiziellen Position des
Arbeitgebers entgegenläuft
expresar una opinión en
desacuerdo con la postura oficial
オフラインで話す

tall organisation
多层管理结构
organisation avec des niveaux
multiples de gestion

Translations appear in the following order: Chinese, French, German, Spanish/Latin American Spanish, and Japanese

vielstufige Organisation
organización muy jerarquizada
縦長組織

tall poppy
杰出人物
personne prominente
Promi
personaje público destacado
成功を収めた人

tall poppy syndrome
贬低杰出人物现象
tendance des médias et du grand
public à déprécier les
accomplissements des personnes
prominentes
Trend in der Presse, Leistungen
prominenter Leute herabzusetzen
tendencia a restar importancia a
los logros de la gente renombrada
成功を収めた人を妬むこと

talon
股息调换券(债券，股票等)附单
talon
Erneuerungsschein
talón; talón de renovación
タロン(公社債権に付属する
利札の最終回分)

tangible assets
有形资产
actif matériel
Sachvermögen
activos tangibles
有形資産

tangible book value
有形资产帐面价值
valeur comptable tangible
Substanzbuchwert
valor contable tangible
有形簿価

tangible fixed asset statement
有形固定资产表
déclaration des immobilisations
corporelles et valeurs immobilisées
Aufstellung der Sachanlagen
estado de activos fijos tangibles;
resumen de inmovilizado material;
inmovilizaciones materiales
有形固定資産報告書,
有形固定資産表

tank
股价暴跌
chuter à toute allure (prix de titres)
abstürzen
hundirse
急落

tap CD
零售定存单
(émission de) bons de caisse de gré
à gré

laufend emittiertes
Depositenzertifikat
certificado de depósito sin límite
譲渡性預り証書

target audience
目标客户
cible
Zielgruppe
audencia objetivo
対象者

target cash balance
目标现金余额
solde de caisse cible
Kassenziel
balance de caja óptimo
ターゲット・キャッシュ・バラ
ンス,目標手許現金残高

target company
目标公司
compagnie cible
Zielgesellschaft
sociedad blanca; empresa asesiada
標的会社

target cost
目标成本
coût cible
Sollkosten; Budgetkosten;
vorkalkulierte Kosten;
Vorgabekosten
coste indicativo; objetivo de costes
目標原価

targeted repurchase
目标性回购
rachat ciblé
gezielter Aktienrückkauf
recompra dirigida
自社株再取得, ターゲッテッド・
リパーチェーシング

target population
对象总体，全域
population cible
Zielpopulation
población objetivo
標的母集団

target savings motive
目标储蓄动机
raison d'épargne ciblée
Zielsparmotiv
motivo para los ahorros de cara a
una pensión
目標貯蓄動機, ターゲット・
セービングス・モーティブ

target stock level
目标库存水平
niveau de stock cible
Richtvorratshöhe; Zielvorratshöhe
nivel ideal de existencias
目標在庫水準

tariff¹
关税; 税则
tarif douanier
Tarif; Zoll
arancel
関税(率), 料金表

tariff²
价目单
tableau des prix
Tarif
lista de precios
価格票

Tariff Concession Scheme
关税减免计划
programme de concession sur
tarifs douaniers
Zollermäßigungssystem
plan australiano de reducción
arancelaria para importaciones de
productos que no se producen en
el país
関税譲許制度

tariff office
关税部门; 关税办公室
bureau des tarifs douaniers
Tarifversicherungsgesellschaft
aseguradora cuyas primas son
determinadas por una escala
acordada por varias compañías
関税事務所、協定加入会社

task analysis
任务分析
analyse des tâches
Tätigkeitsanalyse
análisis de tareas
タスク分析

task culture
任务文化
culture des activités
(professionnelles)
aufgabenorientierte Firmenkultur
cultura empresarial basada en
proyectos individuales
タスク・カルチャー

task group
工作组
groupe de détachement spécial
Arbeitsgruppe
grupo de trabajo
タスク・グループ

taste space
同一类顾客群
consommateurs de même
espace-goûts
Verbrauchergruppe für die
festgestellt wurde, dass sie einen
ähnlicher Geschmack oder
ähnliche Interessen haben, etwa
bei Musik oder Büchern, sodass
Firmen Kaufempfehlungen
machen können oder ihre

Translations appear in the following order: Chinese, French, German, Spanish/Latin American Spanish, and Japanese

Werbung auf sie ausrichten
können
consumidores con gustos similares
同じし好の消費者集団

tax
税収; 税款
impôt
Steuer; Abgabe; besteuern;
Steuern erheben; taxieren;
schätzen
impuesto
租税, 税金

taxability
应纳税额
assujettissement à l'impôt
Steuerpflicht; steuerliche
Belastung
imponibilidad
課税対象

taxable
应征税的; 有税的
imposable
steuerpflichtig
imponible
課税できる、当然請求できる

taxable base
税基; 计税依据; 课税基础
base imposable
Steuerbemessungsgrundlage
base imponible
課税対象額

taxable income
应纳税收入
revenu imposable
steuerpflichtiges Einkommen
líquido imponible
課税標準, 課税所得

taxable matters
税项
affaires imposables
Besteuerungsangelegenheiten;
Besteuerungsgegenstände
hechos imponibles
課税品, 有税品

tax and price index
税收和物价指数
indice des prix et impôts
Steuer- und Preisindex
índice de precios e impuestos
税と物価指数

tax avoidance
(合法)避税; 税收避免; 逃避纳税
évasion fiscale
Steuervermeidung;
Steuerumgehung;
Steuerausweichung
evasión legal de impuestos
租税回避行為, 節税,

tax bracket
税级
tranche d'imposition
Steuerstufe
tramo impositivo
税率等級

tax break
税率降低，减税
allègement fiscal
steuerliche Förderung
desgravación fiscal
租税優遇措置

tax consultant
税务顾问
conseiller fiscal
Steuerberater(in)
asesor fiscal
税務相談

tax-deductible
可减税的
déductible de l'impôt
steuerlich abzugsfähig
desgravable
所得税計算過程で控除できる，
税控除の

tax-deductible public debt
可减免课税的公债
dette publique déductible de
l'impôt
steuerlich abzugsfähige
Staatsverschuldung
deuda pública desgravable
課税控除公共負債

tax-deferred
延期付税
à imposition reportée
steuergestundet
de impuestos aplazados
課税猶予の、課税繰り延べの

tax domicile
征税居住地
domicile fiscal
steuerlicher Wohnsitz
domicilio fiscal
税住居

tax-efficient
节税
efficace fiscalement
steuerergiebig; steuerwirksam;
steuerminimierend
que genera beneficios fiscales
租税効率的

tax evasion
逃税; 漏税; 偷税
fraude fiscale
Steuerhinterziehung
evasión fiscal
(不正申告による)脱税

tax evasion amnesty
逃税特赦
amnistie de fraude fiscale
Amnestie für illegale
Steuerhinterziehung od.
Steuervermeidung
amnistía fiscal
脱税特赦

tax-exempt
免税; 税收豁免
exempt d'impôts
steuerfrei
exento(-a) de impuestos
免税の

**Tax Exempt Special Savings
Account**
免税特别储蓄账户
compte d'épargne spécial avec
somme de plafond pour
exemption d'impôt
steuerfreies Sparkonto
cuenta que permite ahorrar hasta
£9.000 anuales durante cinco años
libres de impuestos si no se realiza
ninguna retirada en ese período de
tiempo
(英)TESSA預金口座

tax exile
為避税而離境的人
exil fiscal (visant à fuir le fisc pour
éviter de payer des impôts)
Steuerexil
exilio fiscal
(納税回避の)国外移住者

tax-favoured asset
有纳税优势的资产
actif à avantage fiscal
steuerbegünstigter
Vermögenswert
activo con tratamiento fiscal
preferente
税制上優遇措置対象資産,
税優遇資産

tax file number
税收档案编号
numéro fiscal (Australie)
Steuernummer; allen
Steuerzahlern in Australien
zugewiesene Kennziffer
número de identificación fiscal
オーストラリア納税者番号

tax-free
免税的
net d'impôt
steuerfrei
libre de impuestos
非課税の, 免税の

tax harmonization
税收协调
harmonisation fiscale
Steuerharmonisierung

---

*Translations appear in the following order: Chinese, French, German, Spanish/Latin American
Spanish, and Japanese*

armonización fiscal
税調和策

tax haven
避税港
paradis fiscale
Steueroase
paraíso fiscal
タックス・ヘイブン

tax holiday
非课税期; 免税期
période d'exemption d'impôts
Steuerfreijahr
tregua tributaria
一時的免税,
納税減免期間、タックスホリ
デー

taxi industry
出租汽车公司
industrie des taxis (en Afrique du Sud)
Taxiindustrie
sector del taxi
タクシー・サービス

tax incentive
賦税刺激
remise sur impôt
steuerlicher Anreiz; Steueranreiz
incentivo fiscal
税制上的優遇措置

tax inspector
税务稽查员
inspecteur des impôts
Finanzamtsleiter(in) in GB
inspector(a) de Hacienda
税調査員

tax invoice
税收清单
facture pour fiscalité
Mehrwertsteuerrechnung
impreso detallando los impuestos pagados
消費税も記載した請求書・領収書

tax law
税法
droit fiscal
Steuergesetz; Steuerrecht
derecho fiscal
税法

tax loophole
税法漏洞
possibilité légale d'échapper à l'impôt
Steuerschlupfloch
vacío legal tributario
租税の抜け穴

tax loss
税收损失; 税损
déficit fiscal reportable
Steuerverlust

pérdida fiscal
税務上の欠損金

tax loss carry-back
纳税时亏损转回 (以本年虧損去减低往年的計税收入)
report rétrospectif de déficit fiscal reportable
steuerlicher Verlustrücktrag
compensación fiscal retroactiva
課税金の繰戻し

tax loss carry-forward
纳税时亏损结转 (以本年虧損去减低來年的計税收入)
report prospectif de déficit fiscal reportable
steuerlicher Verlustvortrag
compensación fiscal retardada
課税金の繰越し

tax obligation
纳税义务
obligation fiscale
Steuerpflicht; Steuerverpflichtung
obligación tributaria
納税義務

tax on capital income
资本所得税
impôt sur les recettes de capital
Steuer auf Kapitalerträge
impuesto sobre rendimientos del capital mobiliario
資本利潤税

tax payable
应付税款
impôt exigible
ausstehende Steuern; zu entrichtende Steuern
deuda tributaria
未払い税金

taxpayer
纳税人
contribuable
Steuerzahler(in)
contribuyente
納税者、納税義務者

tax rate
税率
taux d'imposition
Steuersatz
tipo impositivo
課税率

tax refund
退税
bonification de trop-perçu
Steuerrückzahlung;
Steuerrückerstattung;
Steuerrückvergütung
devolución fiscal
還付された租税

tax relief[1]
减免税; 税款减免; 税项宽免
allègement d'impôt
Steuervergünstigung;
Steuerbefreiung
desgravación fiscal
租税負担の軽減

tax relief[2]
税收减免
dégrèvement d'impôt
Steuererleichterung
desgravación fiscal
租税負担の軽減

tax return
(纳)税(申报)单; 报税单
déclaration d'impôts
Steuererklärung
declaración de impuestos
(納税の)所得申告(書)税務申告書

tax revenue
税收收入
recettes fiscales
staatliche Steuereinnahmen;
Steueraufkommen
ingresos fiscales
租税収入, 税収

tax sale
欠税财产拍卖
vente fiscale
Zwangsversteigerung zur Eintreibung von Steuerschulden
venta de bienes embargados
公売(滞納処分に基づく)

tax shelter
税收隐蔽所;
為减税而作的财务安排
avantage fiscal
Steuerbegünstigung
refugio tributario
税金逃れの隠れ蓑,
タックスシェルター

tax subsidy
税收补贴
subvention fiscale
Steuersubvention
subvención tributaria
租税補助金

tax system
税收系统
système fiscal
Steuersystem
régimen fiscal
租税制度, 税制

tax treaty
税收协定
traité fiscal
Steuerabkommen
acuerdo fiscal
租税条約

Translations appear in the following order: Chinese, French, German, Spanish/Latin American Spanish, and Japanese

tax year
税收年度
année fiscale
Steuerjahr; Haushaltsjahr
año fiscal
課税年度, 事業年度

T-commerce
电视商务
commerce effectué aux moyens de
TV interactive
Geschäftstätigkeit, die über
interaktives Fernsehen
abgewickelt wird
comercio a través de la TV
interactiva
インターラクティブ・テレビ
経由で行う商業

TCP/IP
传输控制协议和互连网协议; TCP
IP协议
protocole de commande de
transmission/protocole Internet
TCP/IP
Netzwerkprotokoll(in)ternet-
protokoll
TCP/IP (protocolo de control de
transmisiones/protocolo de
Internet)
TCPIP(インターネット利用の
標準プロトコール)

team briefing
小组简报会
briefing d'équipe
Gruppenbesprechung
reunión informativa de equipo
チーム・ブリーフィング

team building
组建
développement d'équipe
Gruppenbildung
construcción de equipo
チーム・ビルディング

Team Management Wheel™
小组管理轮
outil visuel en forme de roue
servant à la coordination efficace
du travail d'équipe
Team-Management-Rad
herramienta visual para la
coordinación del trabajo en equipo
チーム・マネジメント・ホイール

team player
善于合作者; 富有团队精神的人
joueur d'équipe
Teamspieler(in)
buen(a) trabajador(a) en equipo
チームの一員としてうまく機能
する人

teamwork
小组工作
travail d'équipe

Teamarbeit; Gruppenarbeit
trabajo en equipo
チームワーク

teaser rate
新顾客优惠利率
taux d'intérêt de faveur temporaire
offerts sur des hypothèques, cartes
de crédit, ou comptes épargne afin
d'attirer des nouveaux clients
Anreizrate
tipo de interés preferente temporal
que se ofrece en hipotecas,
tarjetas de crédito o cuentas de
ahorro a fin de atraer a nuevos
clientes
特別金利

technical analysis
技术分析
analyse technique
technische Analyse
análisis técnico
テクニカル分析

technical rally
技术性反弹
reprise technique
markttechnische Erholung
recuperación momentánea del
mercado
相場のアヤ戻し

technical reserves
技术性储备
réserves techniques
versicherungstechnische
Rücklagen
reservas técnicas
内的保留金

technocracy
专家管理
technocratie
Technokratie
tecnocracia
テクノクラシー, 技術主義

techno-determinist
坚信技术进步者
techno-déterministe
Person, die dem technischen
Fortschritt gegenüber
deterministisch eingestellt ist, ihn
für unabwendbar hält
tecnodeterminista
技術革新至上主義

technographics
技术统计学
technographie
Technografie
tecnografía
テクノグラフィックス

technological risk
技术性风险
risque technologique

technisches Risiko
riesgo tecnológico
技術的リスク

technology adoption life cycle
技术采用生命周期
cycle de vie de l'adoption des
nouvelles technolologies
Lebenszyklus der Annahme neuer
Technologien
modelo de adopción de nuevas
tecnologías
新技術採用
ライフサイクルモデル

technology laggard
保守派
organisation à la traîne en ce qui
concerne l'adoption des nouvelles
technologies
technischer Nachzügler
rezagado tecnológicamente
技術革新の波に乗り遅れた会社

technology stock
高科技股
titre de haute technologie
Technologiewerte
acciones en empresas de
tecnología
ハイテク株

teeming and lading
截留移用, 挪用现金
fourmillière frauduleuse
technische Analyse; die durch
Belegfälschung vertuscht wird
ciclo de fraude ingente constante
連続横領穴埋め

telcos
电信公司
compagnies de
télécommunications
Telekommunikationsunternehmen
telecos
電気通信会社(省略形)

telebanking
银行电信业务
opérations bancaires à distance
Tele-Banking
telebanca
テレバンキング,
テレホン・バンキング

telecentre
远程办公中心
télécentre ou centre de télétravail
Datenstation
telecentro
テレセンター

telecommute
在家里远距离工作
télétravailler
Telearbeit verrichten

Translations appear in the following order: Chinese, French, German, Spanish/Latin American Spanish, and Japanese

teletrabajar
(テレコミュート)在宅勤務者

teleconferencing
电视会议
téléconférence
Telekonferenz
teleconferencias
テレコンファレンス(遠隔地
会議)

telegraphic transfer
电汇
virement télégraphique
telegrafische Auszahlung
transferencia telegráfica
電信為替

telephone banking
电话银行服务
opérations bancaires par
téléphone
Bankgeschäfte
banca por teléfono
テレフォン・バンキング

telephone interview survey
电话采访调查
enquête par téléphone
Telefonbefragung
encuesta telefónica
電話インタビュー調査

telephone number salary
高薪; 六位七位数字工薪
salaire à rallonge
sechs-, bzw. siebenstelliges Gehalt
sueldo astronómico
ドル・ポンドで6～7桁の年収

telephone selling
电话销售
télévente
Telefonverkauf
telemarketing
電話勧誘

telephone survey
电话调查
étude téléphonique
Telefonumfrage
encuesta por teléfono
電話調査

telephone switching
电话交换; 電話接駁
connexion téléphonique
Fernsprechvermittlung
conmutación telefónica
電話交換

telephone tag
电话迷藏
cache-cache téléphonique
gegenseitiges Anrufen und
Hinterlassen von Nachrichten von
zwei Personen, die sich sprechen
wollen, aber nie telefonisch
verfügbar sind, wenn die jeweils

andere Person anruft
llamadas entre dos personas que
se dejan recados porque nunca
consiguen hablar entre ellos
テレフォン・タッグ(相互通話
伝言システム)

teleshopping
电话购物
téléshopping
Tele-Einkauf
telecompra
テレショッピング

**television audience
measurement**
电视观众测量
audimat (des téléspectateurs)
hochgerechnete Zuschauerquote
medición de los hábitos de los
telespectadores
テレビ視聴率記録

teleworker
远程工作者
télétravailleur
Telearbeiter(in)
teletrabajador(a)
テレワーカー(在宅勤務社員)

teleworking
居家就业
télétravail
Telearbeit
teletrabajo
テレワーキング

teller
出纳员
caissier de banque
Bankkassierer(in)
cajero
銀行の金銭出納係

tender¹
投标; 出价; 清偿手段
faire une soumission
anbieten; andienen; einreichen;
vorlegen
ofertar
入札

tender²
投标，出价
faire une soumission
anbieten
suscribir
入札引受

tenor
票期，期头
échéance d'une lettre de change
Laufzeit
período de tiempo que ha de
transcurrir antes de que sea
pagadera una letra de cambio
支払い猶予期間

term
时期，期限
terme
Laufzeit
plazo
満期日

term assurance
定期保险单，定期人寿保险契约
assurance à terme
Risikolebensversicherung;
verkürzte Todesfallversicherung
seguro (de vida) temporal
定期保険

term deposit
定期存款
dépôt à terme
Termineinlage; Festgeld;
Termingeld
depósito a plazo
定期預金

terminal date
终止日期
date du terme
Terminierungsdatum
fecha final
契約満期日

terminal market
期货市场
marché à terme
Terminmarkt
mercado final
先物現物商品取引所

termination interview
解职面谈
entretien de licenciement
Kündigungsgespräch
entrevista para la notificación de
despido
終了インタビュー

termination of service
解职; 雇佣合同终止
résiliation de contrat de travail
Beendigung des
Beschäftigungsverhältnisses
finalización de contrato
雇用終結

term insurance
定期(人寿)保险
assurance vie temporaire
Risikoversicherung; abgekürzte
Todelfallversicherung
seguro de vida temporal
定期保険, 掛け捨て保険

term loan
定期贷款
emprunt à terme
mittelfristiger Kredit
préstamo a medio y largo plazo
期限付貸出

---

*Translations appear in the following order: Chinese, French, German, Spanish/Latin American
Spanish, and Japanese*

term shares
定期股票
actions à terme
Wertpapiere mit fester Laufzeit
cuenta de acciones en una
sociedad de crédito a la vivienda
para un período fijo de tiempo
定期株式口座

terms of trade
贸易条件; 进出口(商品)比价
conditions commerciales
Austauschverhältnis; Terms of
Trade
términos de intercambio
交易条件

terotechnology
维修工艺学
construction et installation
d'exploitations technologiques
Anlagenwesen; Anlagenwirtschaft
terotecnología
テロテクノロジー

tertiary sector
第三部门; 三级部门; 第三重經濟
(指非牟利團體如消費者協會,
自助社團)
secteur tertiaire
tertiärer Sektor;
Dienstleistungssektor
sector terciario
第三次部門

testacy
留有遺囑的人
fait de mourir en laissant un
testament valide
Rechtszustand einer Erblasserin
oder eines Erblassers mit gültigem
Testament
sucesión testamentaria
有効な遺言書のあること

testate
(形容)留有遺囑的(死者)
laissant un testament valide
ein gültiges Testament
hinterlassend
testado
有効な遺言書を残した人物

testator
立遺囑者 , 遺囑人
testateur
Testator; Erblasser
testador(a)
(男性)遺言者

testatrix
女遺囑人
testatrice
Testatrix
testadora
(女性)遺言者

testimonial advertising
推荐式广告
publicité avec recommandation
Testemonialwerbung
publicidad con famosos
証言広告

test marketing
试销; 营销活动试用
marketing d'essai
Testmarktforschung
marketing de prueba
テスト・マーケティング

TFN Withholding Tax
纳税号预扣税
retenue fiscale sur TFN: retenue
imposée sur les transactions
financières concernant un individu
qui n'a pas donné son numéro
fiscal individuel
Strafe, bei Nichtangabe der
Steuernummer
tasa cobrada en transacciones sin
el número de identificación fiscal
オーストラリア国税庁
番号源泉徴収

Theory E
E 理论;
自上而下的集权式管理理论
théorie E: théorie dont le seul but
est de satisfaire les marchés
financiers
Theorie E
teoría E (del cambio en las
organizaciones)
理論E

Theory J
J理论
Théorie J: elle décrit la gestion à la
japonaise.
Theorie J; beschreibt die
Unternehmensführung nach
japanischer Art.
teoría J
理論 J

Theory O
O 理论;
自下而上的参与式管理理论
Théorie O: cette théorie décrit un
mécanisme de changement
organisationnel basé sur une
culture d'entreprise en évolution
Theorie O
teoría O (de cambio en las
organizaciones)
理論O

theory of constraints
约束理论
théorie des contraintes
Restriktionstheorie
teoría de contención optima
制約理論

theory of the horizontal fast track
横向高速线路理论
théorie de la filière rapide
horizontale
Hypothese von der horizontalen
Überholspur
teoría del desarrollo de personas
con talento trabajando en
diferentes tareas
水平ファースト・トラック理論

Theory W
W理论
théorie W: la théorie que non
seulement il faut forcer les
employés à agir, mais que la force
est souvent nécessaire pour arriver
à ce but
Theorie W
Teoría W
理論W(鞭打ち理論)

Theory X
X理论
théorie X: gestion basée sur
l'hypothèse que, de nature, la
plupart des gens n'ont pas envie
de travailler
Theorie X
Teoría X
理論X

Theory Y
Y理论
théorie Y: gestion basée sur
l'hypothèse que les employés
veulent travailler
Theorie Y
Teoría Y
理論Y

Theory Z
Z理论
théorie Z: gestion basée sur
l'hypothèse qu'une participation
plus importante des employés
entraîne une productivité accrue
Theorie Z
Teoría Z
理論Z

think tank
智囊团
cellule de réflexion
Expertenkommission; Denkfabrik
grupo de expertos
シンク・タンク

thin market
呆滞的市场 , 交易呆滞(不旺)的
市场
marché étroit
flauer Markt; enger Markt
mercado estrecho; mercado
escaso o con poco movimiento
閑散な市況

Translations appear in the following order: Chinese, French, German, Spanish/Latin American Spanish, and Japanese

third market
第三(证券)市场
troisième marché
Dritter Markt
tercer mercado
第三市場

three-dimensional management
三维管理; 三度管理
gestion en trois dimensions
dreidimensionale Geschäftsführung
gestión tridimensional
３次元マネジメント

three generic strategies
三类策略(波特)
(les) trois stratégies génériques
drei generische Strategien
tres estrategias genéricas
３つの総括戦略

three martini lunch
马提尼酒午餐会
déjeuner bien arrosé
Geschäftsessen, bei dem viel Alkohol fließt, um den Kunden zu entspannen
comida de trabajo con alcohol para relajar al cliente
顧客がリラックスするように酒をたくさん飲ませるビジネス・ランチ

three Ps
3P模型
'purpose' (avoir un but), 'process' (procédé ou processus) et 'people' (personnes)
,,purpose'' (Zielbewusstsein), ,,process'' (Verfahren, Prozess) et ,,people''
propósito, proceso y gente
スリーP(目的, 工程, 人材)

360 degree appraisal
360度评估
évaluation sur 360 degrés
360-Grad-Beurteilung
evaluación de 360°
360度評価

360 degree branding
360度品牌塑造
commercialisation de marque sur 360 degrés
360-Degree Branding
exposición de marca permanente
総合的ブランド付け

three Ss
3S要素
les trois S: classification de la prise de décision se rapportant à la stratégie, à la structure et aux systèmes
Die drei S; Klassifizierung der Entscheidungsfindung nach Strategie, Struktur, Systemen.
estrategia, estructura y sistemas
スリーS(戦略, 構造, システム)

three steps and a stumble
三窜一跌 (股市常见规律)
règle de la bourse américaine selon laquelle si la Réserve Fédérale augmente les taux d'intérêt trois fois de suite, les prix boursiers baissent
drei Schritte vorwärts, dann ein Stolperer: eine Faustregel an der Börse, nach der die Aktienkurse sinken, wenn die amerikanischen Federal Reserve Zentralbanken die Zinssätze dreimal in Folge erhöhen
regla según la cual a cada tres subidas de los tipos de interés por la Reserva Federal le corresponde una bajada de la bolsa
連邦準備制度理事会が利率を連続で三回上げると株式市場が下がるという経験則

threshold company
入门企业
entreprise sur le seuil d'être bien établie
Aufsteiger
empresa a punto de consolidarse
今にも成功,
業績を収めそうな会社

thrift institution
储蓄机构
caisse d'épargne
Bausparkasse; Sparkasse
institución de ahorro
(米)貯蓄機関

THRIP
工业技术及人力资源计划
programme pour les ressources humaines et technologiques pour l'industrie
Technologie- und Personal-Programm für Industrie
programa sudafricano para el fomento de la investigación y desarrollo en tecnología, ciencia e ingeniería
官民産学共同技術
人材開発プログラム

throughput accounting
产量会计
comptabilité de la production maximale
Durchsatzrechnung
contabilidad de contribución marginal bruta
一貫会計

throw somebody a curve ball
打弧线球; 出乎意料
envoyer une balle à effet
etwas Unerwartetes tun oder sagen, etwa bei einer Tagung oder in einem Projekt. Die Metapher rührt aus dem Baseball her
poner a alguien en un aprieto
予想外の行動をとる,
または発言をする

tick
价格变动的最小单位
écart maximum des cours du marché
Mindestkursschwankung
fluctuación mínima
ティック(金融商品価格が変化する際の最小単位)

tied loan
限制性贷款
emprunt à emploi spécifique
gebundener Kredit
préstamo condicionado; préstamo vinculado
ひも付き融資

tie-in
搭配在一起出售的(货品) 关系; 联系; 联合广告; 搭配出售
campagne publicitaire dans laquelle deux compagnies ou plus partagent les frais de la campagne en combinant produits ou services
Kopplung; Kopplungsbindung
campaña publicitaria conjunta; relación
タイ・イン広告

tigers
特指太平洋地区除日本之外的重要市场
tigres: les plus importants marchés de la région de bassin du Pacifique, à l'exclusion du Japon, et incluant Hong Kong, la Corée du Sud, Singapoure et Taiwan
Tiger-Volkswirtschaften
tigres
タイガーズ

tight money
银根(抽)紧
argent rare
Geldknappheit
dinero escaso
金融逼迫, 金詰まり

time and material pricing
时间和材料定价法
évaluation de prix basé sur le coût de la main d'oeuvre et des matériaux
Preisermittlung unter Berücksichtigung von Arbeitszeit und Material

---

Translations appear in the following order: Chinese, French, German, Spanish/Latin American Spanish, and Japanese

cálculo del precio en función del
tiempo y el material empleados
時間プラス材料価格設定

time and motion study
时间和动作研究
étude des cadences (et temps)
Zeit- und Bewegungsstudie;
Arbeitsanalyse
estudio de tiempo y movimientos;
estudio del aprovechamiento del
tiempo
作業研究

time bargain
定期交易，定期买卖
bonne affaire à terme
Fixgeschäft
venta al descubierto
投機的契約

time deposit
定期存款，通知存款
dépôt à terme
Festgeld
depósito a plazo
譲渡性定期預金

time draft
远期汇票，定期(承兑)汇票
traite à échéance
Nachsichtwechsel
letra a plazo fijo
一覧後定期払い手形

time keeping
时间记录
respect des horaires
Arbeitszeitkontrolle
control de la puntualidad
作業時間記録

time management
时间管理
gestion du temps
Zeitwirtschaft
administración del tiempo
時間管理

time off in lieu
补假作偿
congé de remplacement: congé
octroyé pour compenser un
employé des heures de travail
supplémentaires
arbeitsfreie Zeit als
Überstundenausgleich
vacaciones a cambio de horas
extras
賃金の代わりに休暇提供

timeous
及时; 迅速
opportun
rechzeitig
oportuno
事前の

time series
时间序列
série de mesures à intervalles
donnés
Zeitreihe
serie cronológica
時系列

time sovereignty
时间主权
souveraineté temporelle: avoir le
contrôle sur la façon dont on passe
son temps
Verfügungsgewalt über die eigene
Zeit
control de la administración del
tiempo
時間統治

time span of discretion
可自由安排工作的时间长度
(用于衡量
企业内个人的责任高低)
période de liberté d'agir: la période
de temps entre le commencement
et l'achèvement de la plus longue
tâche dans un travail
Entscheidungshorziont
plazo de finalización de la tarea
más larga
自己裁量業務の長さ

time spread
时间分布
transaction avec échéances étalées
Kauf und Verkauf von Optionen
für die gleiche Ware oder das
gleiche Wertpapier zum selben
Kurs und mit unterschiedlichen
Fälligkeiten
diferencial horizontal
満期の開き

time study
时间研究
étude des cadences (du temps
passé à effectuer une tâche)
Zeitstudie
estudio de tiempos
時間研究

time value
时间价值
valeur à terme
Aufgeld
valor tiempo
時間価値

timing difference
时间性差异
différence de calendrier
Periodenverschiebung
diferencia de períodos; diferencia
de sincronización
損益の計上期間の不一致

TIN
转帐密码
numéro d'identification fournie
par une banque pour identifier de
façon unique le commerçant pour
les transactions point de vente
Transaktions-Kennziffer
número de identificación de
terminal
(銀行がPOS取引業者に発行する)
ＩＤ番号, トランザクション・
アイデンティフィケーション・
ナンバー

tip
内部信息，小道信息
tuyau (de Bourse)
Tipp
información bursátil confidencial
投機相場の情報

tip-off
警告; 提示
avertissement basé sur une
information confidentielle
gezielter Hinweis
aviso; consejo; soplo
内報

title
所有权
titre de propriété
Eigentumsrecht
título de propiedad
所有権

title inflation
职衔膨胀; 职称膨胀
gonflement d'intitulé (de poste)
künstliches Aufblähen von
Berufsbezeichnungen
cambio pomposo del nombre de
un puesto
役職名インフレーション

TLS
加密付款程序
protocole de paiement, basé sur le
système SSL, qui offre une sécurité
accrue pour les transactions par
carte de crédit
Sicherheit der Transaktionsebenen
protocolo TLS
トランザクション・レイヤー・
セキュリティ

toasted
丢钱
qui a perdu de l'argent
geröstet
término utilizado para referirse a
alguien o algo que ha perdido
dinero
お金を失った人物

toehold
持有限度
intérêts détenus dans une

Translations appear in the following order: Chinese, French, German, Spanish/Latin American Spanish, and Japanese

corporation accumulés par
l'enchérisseur potentiel qui
représentent moins de
5% des titres de la
corporation
Beteiligung unter 5%
participación en una empresa
acumulada por un postor potencial
que es menos del 5 por ciento de
las acciones de dicha empresa
足がかり5%以下の投資資金)

Tokyo Inter Bank Offered Rate
东京银行业拆借率
TIBOR: taux interbancaire des
devises à Tokyo
Tokioter Interbankenangebotssatz
tipo de interés ofertado del
mercado interbancario de Tokio
(TIBOR)
東京銀行間取引金利

tombstone
'墓碑', 证券发行公告
notification dans la presse
financière donnant des détails sur
des moyens de prêt importants à
une entreprise
Finanzanzeige, die Schuldner und
Details vollzogener Emissionen od.
Anleihen od. Fusionen/
Übernahmen bekannt gibt
anuncio de emisión sindicada;
anuncio de emisión efectuada
証券の発行広告

top-down approach
自上而下的专制作风
leadership autocratique du
sommet à la base
hierarchischer Ansatz
enfoque descendente
上からのアプローチ

top level domain
高级域
domaine haut niveau
Top-Level-Domain
dominio de alto nivel
トップレベルドメイン

top management
高级领导层
haute direction
oberste Führungsspitze
alta dirección
管理職

top slicing[1]
削顶
vendre la part de gâteau d'un
actionnariat
Verkauf eines Teils eines
Wertpapierbestands, der
insgesamt eine Summe erbringen
wird, die größer ist als die
Ursprungsinvestition. Der

Restbestand ist daher potenziell
reiner Gewinn.
parte de venta de unas acciones
que convertirán en efectivo una
cantidad igual al coste original de
inversión
トップ·スライス

top slicing[2]
顶部切割
méthode de la tranche supérieure
komplexe Methode der britischen
Steuerbehörde zur steuerlichen
Bewertung bestimmter
festverzinslicher Anlagepapiere
oder gemischer
Versicherungspolicen bei Fälligkeit
oder vorzeitiger Einlösung
en el Reino Unido, método
complejo utilizado por Hacienda a
fin de evaluar qué impuestos, si los
hay, se pagan al vencer
determinados bonos de iversión o
pólizas mixtas, o al canjearse los
mismos antes de su vencimiento
トップ· スライス制

total absorption costing
全面归纳成本法，全面吸收成本
计算
ventilation des coûts d'absorption
totaux
Vollkostenrechnung
absorción total de costes
全部原価吸収計算

total assets
总资产
total de l'actif
Gesamtvermögen; Gesamtaktiva;
Bilanzsumme
activos totales; activos contables
資産総計

total cost of ownership
总所有权成本
coût total de propriété ou de
possession
Opportunitätskosten des Anlage-
und Umlaufvermögens
coste total de la propriedad
costo total de la propriedad
所有維持全費用

total-debt-to-total-assets
总负债对总资产
montant total de la dette en
pourcentage de l'actif
Verhältnis Gesamtverschuldung zu
Gesamtvermögen
coeficiente de deuda total por
activos totales
総資産対総負債比率

total loss control
全损控制
contrôle de perte totale

Gesamtschadenkontrolle
control de las pérdidas totales
総合損失管理

total productive maintenance
总生产性维护
maintenance de productivité totale
totale Produktivwartung
mantenimiento total de la
productividad
全社的生産力維持管理

total quality management
全面质量管理
gestion de qualité totale
Gesamtqualitätsleitung;
Gesamtqualitätssicherung; Total
Quality Management
gestión de calidad total
総合的品質経営

total return
总收益
rendement total
Gesamtgewinn
rendimiento total
総収益率

touch
最佳出价和报价的差异
différence entre la meilleure offre
et le meilleur prix d'offre cité par
tous les marchands qui 'font' le
marché pour un titre particulier,
l'écart le plus étroit
knappster Spread
diferencia entre el mejor precio de
compra y el de venta dado por
todos los mercados con respecto a
un título determinado; la
diferencia más pequeña
タッチ(最小売買価格差)

touchdown centre
商务中心
centre terrestre avec services de
bureautique
Kontaktstelle, wo Geschäftsleute
auf Reisen telefonieren, Computer
und Internet nutzen können
centro de negocios
旅行中にインターネットなどが
使えるビジネス· センター

touch price
最佳的出价和报价
prix de touche: la meilleure offre et
le meilleur prix disponible
bester Geldkurs und Briefkurs
precio alcanzado
タッチ価格

tourist
游客; 以受训名义逃脱工作的人
stagiaire tire-au-flanc
Tourist(in), Person die eine
Schulung macht, um vom
Arbeitsplatz weg zu kommen

Translations appear in the following order: Chinese, French, German, Spanish/Latin American Spanish, and Japanese

trabajador(a) que acude a un curso de formación para no estar en la oficina
仕事場を離れるためにトレーニング・コースに申し込む社員

toxic employee
恶意散布者
employé vénimeux
aufgebrachter oder grollender Mitarbeiter, der in einer Firma oder Abteilung Missstimmung sät
empleado(a) resentido(a) y perjudicial
社内で不満を広げる社員

Toyota production system
东芝生产系统
système de production Toyota
Toyota Produktionssystem
sistema de producción de Toyota
トヨタ生産システム

tracking
跟踪研究
tracking
Werbetracking
seguimiento
トラッキング

tracking error
循迹误差
erreur de traçabilité
Verfolgungsfehler
error con respecto a la cartera de referencia
トラッキング・エラー

tracking stock
跟踪股票
titre à dividende lié à performance
Tracker-Aktie
acción vinculada a los resultados de la filial que es propietaria de ella
トラッキング株

trade barrier
贸易障碍
barrière commerciale
Handelshemmnis;
Handelsrestriktion;
Handelsschranke
barrera al comercio
貿易障壁

trade bill
贸易汇票，商业汇票
effet de commerce
Warenwechsel; Handelswechsel
efecto comercial; efecto mercantil;
letra comercial
貿易手形, 商業手形

trade credit
贸易信用，贸易信贷，信用交易
crédit fournisseur
Warenkredit

crédito comercial
貿易信用

trade creditors
贸易债权人
créances aux fournisseurs
Zulieferer
acreedores comerciales
買掛金

trade debt
贸易债务
dette commerciale
Handelsschuld
deuda comercial
取引負債

trade delegation
贸易代表团; 贸易访问团
délégation commerciale
Handelsdelegation
delegación comercial
貿易派遣団

Trade Development Board
贸易发展委员会
Agence gouvernementale pour le développement du commerce
Handelentwicklungskammer
organismo del gobierno de Singapur para el fomento del comercio exterior
商業開発委員会

traded option
可买卖期权，贸易期权
option négociée
handelbare Option
opción negociable
取引オプション

tradefair
商(业)展(览会); 贸易展销会;
商品交易会
foire (exposition) commerciale
Handelsmesse
feria de muestras
メッセ

trade gap
贸易逆差
déficit commercial
Handelsbilanzdefizit;
Außenhandelsdefizit;
Handelslücke
déficit comercial; déficit de la balanza de pago
貿易収支の赤字

trade investment
商业投资，业务性投资
investissement commercial
Vermögensanlage im Interesse des Geschäftsbetriebs
participación de una sociedad en otra
営業関係投資

trademark
商标
marque commerciale; marque (de fabrique)
Warenzeichen; Handelsmarke
marca comercial; marca de fábrica
トレードマーク, 商標

trade mission
商务代表团, 贸易使团
mission commerciale
Handelsmission
misión comercial
通商使節団

trade name
商标; 商标名称
nom de marque
Warenbezeichung; Handelsname
marca comercial
商品名

Tradenet
贸易网
Tradenet
elektronisches System für Im- und Exportlizenzanträge
sistema electrónico para la concesión de licencias de importación y exportación
トレードネット

trade point
交易点
centre d'opérations boursières: une Bourse qui est moins formelle que les Bourses majeures
Handelsplatz
bolsa pequeña
トレード・ポイント

trade press
贸易出版
presse professionnelle
Brancheninformationen
prensa sectorial
業界誌

trades and labour council
贸易及劳动力委员会
comité des ouvriers et professionnels
Gewerkschaftsrat
confederación sindical
労働組合地方協議会

trade union
工会
syndicat
Gewerkschaft
sindicato
労働組合

trade union recognition
工会认可
reconnaissance d'un syndicat
offizielle Anerkennung einer Gewerkschaft durch Arbeitgebe

Translations appear in the following order: Chinese, French, German, Spanish/Latin American Spanish, and Japanese

reconocimiento de los sindicatos
労働組合承認

trade war
贸易战
guerre commerciale
Handelskrieg
guerra comercial
貿易戦争

trade-weighted index
按贸易额加权的指数
indice commercial pondéré
Index des Außenwertes
valor relativo de la divisa en
comparación con la de los socios
comerciales
貿易加重指数

**trading, profit and loss
account**
营业和益损帐户; 贸易盈虧表
compte d'exploitation, de pertes et
profits
Erfolgs-, Gewinn- und
Verlustrechnung
cuenta de beneficios brutos,
pérdidas y ganancias
売買損益勘定

trading halt
交易暂停
arrêt de transaction
Handelsunterbrechung
suspensión de la contratación
トレード・ホールト,
売買の一時停止

trading partner
交易伙伴; 贸易合伙人
partenaire commercial
Handelspartner(in)
socio(-a) comercial
取引先,
トレーディング・パートナー

traffic
流量
traffic
Verkehr
tráfico
トラフィック

traffic builder
销售创造
générateur de commerce
Ankurbler: Werbeaktion, die mehr
Kunden anziehen soll
promoción de marketing para
generar clientes
トラフィック・ビルダー(顧客増
大策)

training
培训
formation
Schulung; Ausbildung
formación

capacitación
トレーニング

training needs
培训需求
besoins de formation
Ausbildungsbedarf
necesidades de formación
トレーニング・ニーズ

training needs analysis
培训需求分析
analyse des besoins de formation
Ausbildungsbedarfsanalyse
análisis de las necesidades de
formación
トレーニング・ニーズ分析

trait theory
特性理论
théorie des traits de caractères
Charaktertheorie
teoría de los rasgos
リーダーシップ人材理論

tranche CD
定期存款单
certificat de dépôt par tranche
Tranchen-Depositenzertifikat
certificado de depósito de tramo
トランシュCD(割り当て,
割賦預金証明)

transaction¹
交易
transaction
Transaktion
transacción
トランザクション

transaction²
交易; 处理
transaction
Transaktion
transacción
証券取引, トランザクション

transactional analysis
交互作用分析
analyse transactionnelle
Transaktionsanalyse
análisis transaccional
処理能力分析

**transactional theory of
leadership**
领导者交互作用分析
théorie transactionnelle sur le
leadearship
Transaktionstheorie der
Unternehmensführung
teoría transacional del liderazgo
リーダーシップの駆引き理論

transaction e-commerce
电子交易
e-commerce de transaction
Transaktions-E-Commerce
comercio electrónico

トランザクションeコマース,
電子商取引

transaction exposure
交易风险
Risque ou mise à nu de transaction
Anschlussrisiko;
Umrechnungsrisiko;
Transaktionsrisiko
compromisos netos de
transacciones; exposición de
transacciones; extensión del riesgo
de transacciones
取引危険度

transaction history
交易历史
historique de transaction
Geschäftsdatei
historial de transacciones
取引経歴

transaction message
转帐信息
message de transaction
Transaktions-Nachricht
mensaje de transacción
トランザクション・メッセージ

transactions motive
交易动机
raison pour transactions
Transaktionsmotiv
motivo para las transacciones
取引動機

transfer¹
转账, 过户
transfert
Überweisung
transferencia
振替

transfer²
(资金)转移
transfert
Überweisung
transferencia
為替

transfer³
(产权)转移，转让
transmission de propriété
Übertragung
traspaso
譲渡

transferable skill
可转换技术
compétence transférable
übertragbare Fähigkeit
destreza transferible
振替可能技能

transfer of training
训练转移
transfert de formation
Ausbildungsübertragung

---

*Translations appear in the following order: Chinese, French, German, Spanish/Latin American
Spanish, and Japanese*

transferencia del aprendizaje
トレーニング内容の移行

transferor
转让人
cédant ou personne cédante
Zedent(in)
cesionista
讓渡人

transfer-out fee
转帐费
frais de clôture de compte
Schlussgebühr
comisión que ha de pagarse para
cerrar una cuenta con un
intermediario; gastos de cierre de
cuenta con un broker
口座閉鎖料

transfer price
内部转让价格
prix de transfert
Verrechnungspreis
traspaso de costes internos; precio
de cesión interna; precio de
transferencia

transfer pricing
转让定价; 调配定价
prix de cession interne
Verrechnungspreismethode
fijación de los precios de
transferencia
移转价格操作

transfer stamp
转让印花，过户印花，过户戳记
sceau sur acte translatif de
propriété
Transfer-Marke
sello del impuesto de transmisión
讓渡証印

transfer value
转移价值
valeur au transfert
Übertragungswert
valor de transferencia
(英)年金の振替価値

**transformational theory of
leadership**
变革式领导理论
théorie transformationnelle sur le
leadership
Transformationstheorie der
Unternehmensführung
teoría transformacional del
liderazgo
リーダーシップの感化理論

transformative potential
改革潜力; 改造潜力
potentiel de transformation
Wandlungspotenzial
potencial de transformación
変革させる潜在的力

transit time
传送时间
temps de transit
Durchgangszeit
tiempo de tránsito
作業終了から材料入手までの
待ち時間

translation exposure
外汇折算风险
risque de transposition
Währungsrisiko; Verlustrisiko aus
Währungsumrechnungen
compromisos netos por diferencia
de conversión; extensión del riesgo
de diferencias en moneda
extranjera; diferencias de cambio
換算危険度

transmission
数据转移; 转帐
transmission
Übertragung
transmisión
トランスミッション，伝送

**transmission control
standards**
数据转移控制标准
normes de contrôle des
transactions
Übertragungssteuerungsnorm
estándares de control de las
transmisiones
トランスミッション・コントロー
ル・スタンダード，伝送管理基準

Transnet
南非交通局
Transnet
staatliche Holdinggesellschaft des
Transportwesens
empresa estatal sudafricana de
transportes
トランスネット(南アフリカ国
営運輸会社)

transparency
透明度
transparence
Transparenz
transparencia
透明性

travel accident insurance
旅行意外人身险
assurance (contre les) accidents de
voyage
Reiseunfallversicherung
seguro de accidentes durante viaje
旅行傷害保険

travel insurance
旅行保险
assurance voyages ou assurance
tourisme
Reiseversicherung

seguro de viaje
旅行保険

treasurer
财务员
trésorier
Finanzleiter(in); Schatzmeister;
Kassenführer(in)
tesorero(-a)
財務担当者，出納係

Treasurer
财务经理; 司库; 财务主任
ministre des finances
Finanzminister
Ministro(-a) de Economía
(連邦政府，州政府，
準州政府の)財務大臣

treasuries
国库券
bons du Trésor
langfristige Staatspapiere
títulos del Tesoro
流通債務証券

treasury[1]
财政部
ministère des finances
Schatzamt; Finanzministerium
Tesoro público; erario; Hacienda
Pública
財務省

treasury[2]
财务部门
trésorerie
zentrale Finanzabteilung
tesorería; tesoro; fisco
財務部，出納部

Treasury bill
短期无息国库券; 财政部短期库券
effet de Trésorerie (américain)
Schatzwechsel
letra del Tesoro a corto plazo
(米)財務省短期証券,
(英)大蔵省証券

Treasury bill rate
国库券利率
taux (d'intérêt) de bon du Trésor
Zins auf Schatzwechsel
tasa de la letra del Tesoro a corto
plazo
短期国債レート

Treasury bond
(长期)国库券; 财政长期债券
bon du Trésor (américain)
Schatzobligation
bono del Tesoro
(米)財務省長期証券

treasury management
财政管理
gestion de trésorerie
Finanzmitteldisposition
gestión de liquidez
財政管理

---

*Translations appear in the following order: Chinese, French, German, Spanish/Latin American
Spanish, and Japanese*

Treasury note¹
国库中期债券; 财政中期债券;
中期国库券
(bordereau de) bon du Trésor
américain
Schatzanweisung
letra del Tesoro a medio plazo
(米)財務省中期証券

Treasury note²
中期国库券
bon du Trésor (Australie)
kurzdatierte Bundesanleihen
pagaré del Tesoro australiano
短期国債

treaty¹
条约，协定
accord écrit entre nations
Staatsvertrag
tratado
条約

treaty²
协议，协定
traité d'assurance
Rückversicherungsvertrag
tratado de excedente
保険特約協定

trend
趋势
tendance
Trend
tendencia
傾向

trendline
趋势线
ligne de tendance
Trendkurve
línea de tendencia
トレンドライン

trial balance
试算平衡表
balance de vérification
Saldenbilanz; Rohbilanz
balance de comprobación
簿記の試算表

trickle-down theory
滴入论
théorie du goutte-à-goutte:
théorie économique américaine
selon laquelle la richesse finit par
toucher les plus pauvres
Theorie des Sickereffekts
teoría de la filtración
浸透効果

triple I organisation
三艾机构; 3i机构; 三艾组织
organisation triple I
Drei-I-Organisation
cultura empresarial centrada en la
información, la inteligencia y las
ideas
トリプル・アイ(I)組織

triple tax exempt
三重税收豁免
triplement exonéré d'impôts
dreifach steuerbefreit
exento(-a) de los tres tipos de
impuesto
三重の免税措置

Trojan horse
特洛伊木马(一种计算机病毒)
cheval de Troie
trojanisches Pferd
caballo de Troya
トロイの木馬型(コンピューター
ウイルス)

troll
钓鱼
annotation sur un site Web conçu
pour provoquer un grand nombre
de réponses, surtout de la part des
internautes novices
Plakatierung auf einer Webseite,
die sehr viele Antworten
provozieren soll, insbesondere von
unerfahrenen Internet-Anwendern
mensaje provocador
たくさんの反応を起こすように書
かれたウェブサイト上のメッセ
ージ

trolling
兜售
appeler à froid
ungezielte Kundenwerbung
machen, um Aufträge
hereinzuholen
hacer llamadas sin previo aviso
新規顧客を取得するためにコー
ルド・コール(セールス電話)
をする

trophy wife
年长主管的少妻
épouse (souvent plus jeune) que le
mari exhibe comme signe extérieur
de réussite
Vorzeigefrau
esposa joven de un ejecutivo de
cierta edad
トロフィー・ワイフ(年配役員
の若い妻)

troy ounce
金衡制盎司
once de Troy: unité de poids
traditionnelle utilisée pour la pesée
des métaux précieux tels que l'or
et l'argent
Edelmetallgewicht
onza troy
トロイ・オンス

true interest cost
纯利息成本
coût d'intérêt réel

effektive Zinskosten
coste real de intereses
costo real de intereses
純粋利子コスト, 総利子費用

trump
王牌
mettre dans le mille ou tomber à
pic (avec son produit, par rapport à
la concurrence)
übertrumpfen
ridiculizar
切り札, 奥の手の商品

trust¹
信任; 投资信托公司信托; 托拉斯;
托拉斯组织
société holding
Treuhandgesellschaft
fideicomiso
信託財産

trust²
垄断公司
trust
Trust
trust
信託財産

trust account
信托帐户
compte en fidéicommis
Treuhandkonto
cuenta fiduciaria
信託勘定, 受託者勘定

trust bank
信托银行
banque de fidéicommis
Treuhandbank
banco fiduciario
信託銀行

trust company
信托公司
société fiduciaire
Treuhandgesellschaft;
Treuhandbank;
Investmentgesellschaft
compañía fiduciaria
信託会社

trust corporation
信托公司
corporation fiduciaire
staatlich zugelassene Institution
institución fiduciaria
信託会社(ノンバンク)

trustee
受托人; 受托管理人;
信托资产管理人; 被信托人
fidéicommissaire; syndic de faillite
Treuhänder(in); Fiduziar(in);
Vermögensverwalter(in);
Beauftragte/r;
Verwaltungsgesellschaft eines
Fonds

Translations appear in the following order: Chinese, French, German, Spanish/Latin American Spanish, and Japanese

administrador(a) fiduciario(-a)
被信託人, 受託人

trustee in bankruptcy
破产信托人; 破产(财产)管理人
syndic de faillite
Konkursverwalter(in)
síndico(-a) de quiebra
破産管財人

trustee investment
信托投资; 受托人投资
investissement de fidéicommissaire
mündelsichere Kapitalanlage
inversión en fideicomiso
信託投資

trusteeship
托管; 受托人的职责(地位)
fidéis curatelle /poste
d'administration
Vermögensverwaltung;
Nachlassverwaltung
administración fiduciaria
受託人の職, 受託統治

trust fund
信托基金
fonds de placement en
fidéicommis
Treuhandfonds
fondo fiduciario or de fideicomiso
信託資金, トラストファンド

trust officer
信托官员; 信托公司高级职员
administrateur mandataire
Mitglied der Treuhandabteilung
einer Bank
responsable de fondos
信託管理者, 受託者

Truth in Lending Act
借款真实法
loi sur l'authenticité des prêts et
emprunts: équivalent américain de
la loi britannique sur le crédit à la
consommation
Gesetz ber die wahrheitsgemäße
Angabe von Kreditkosten
ley sobre veracidad en los
préstamos
(米)消費者信用法

tshayile time
下班时间
fin de la journée de travail
Feierabend
final del día
業務終了時間

TTFN
回头见
salut pour l'instant
Tschüss einstweilen
hasta la vista
(俗)さようなら

TTP
可信第三方
organisme indépendant et de
toute confiance qui vérifie
individus, compagnies et
organisations sur Internet
unabhängige vertrauenswürdige
Organisation, die Personen,
Unternehmen und Organsiationen
über das Internet verifiziert
organización de verificación por
Internet
TTP(インターネットの独立承
認機関)

turbulence
激流
turbulence
Turbulenzen
turbulencia
社会的不穏

turkey
赔钱的投资; 差劲的投资，火鸡
investissement ou entreprise de
performance médiocre
Pleite
negocio o inversión que no está
rindiendo bien
七面鳥(実績不振)

turkey trot
將问题雇员调往別部門
faire trotter le dindon
das Versetzen schwieriger,
unkompetenter oder unnötiger
Mitarbeiter von einer Abteilung in
die nächste; aufs Abstellgleis
schieben
deshacerse de un trabajador
molesto pasándolo a otro
departamento
難しい社員を部門間で異動す
る習慣

turn
买卖价差
marge (entre le prix d'achat et le
prix de vente) d'un contrepartiste
Provision von Wertpapierhändlern
ganancia
売買価格差, サヤ

turnaround management
扭亏为盈管理
gestion de renversement (de
situation)
Sanierungsmanagement;
Turnaround-Management
salvación de empresas en crisis
リストラクチャリング政策

turnkey contract
全承包合同
contrat clés en main
Bauvertrag, der die schlüsselfertige
Übergabe des Objekts vorsieht

contrato llave en mano
ターンキー契約

turnover ratio¹
周转率
vitesse de rotation des stocks
Umschlaghäufigkeit
velocidad de circulación;
coeficiente de facturación
棚卸し資産回転率

turnover ratio²
固定资产周转率
rapport de chiffre d'affaires
Umsatzquote für Sachanlagen
coeficiente de facturación
固定資産回転率

turnover ratio³
总资产周转率
rapport de chiffre d'affaires total
Umsatzquote für das
Gesamtvermögen
coeficiente de facturación
総資産回転率

twenty-four hour trading
24小时全天候贸易
transactions jour et nuit
Handel rund um die Uhr
compraventa 24 horas al día
24 時間証券取引

24
美国国家标准协会承认的商业交-
易电子交换协定
24 (vingt-quatre)
24, Amerikanischer EDI Standard
protocolo 24
米国規格協会の
電子データ交換プロトコル

24/7
全周全天候服务
24 (vingt-quatre) heures sur 24, 7
(sept) jours sur 7
24/7
apertura permanente
24 時間週 7 日, 年中無休, 24 7

2L8
太迟
trop tard
zu spät
demasiado tarde
遅すぎる(ツーレイト)

two-tier tender offer
双重股权收购
offre de prise de contrôle à deux
étages
zweistufiges Übernahemangebot
OPA de dos niveles
二重公開買付け

type I error
第一型差误
erreur de type I (première)
Fehler vom Typ I

---

*Translations appear in the following order: Chinese, French, German, Spanish/Latin American
Spanish, and Japanese*

error tipo I
タイプIエラー

type II error
第二型差误
erreur de type II (seconde)
Fehler vom Typ II
error tipo II
タイプIIエラー

tyrekicker
踢轮胎的人
client potentiel qui demande
beaucoup de temps et d'attention
mais qui n'achète rien
Zeitverschwender(in)
cliente que demanda mucha
atención y no compra nada
ひやかし客

UCE
未经要求的商业邮件
junk-mail électronique
unerwünschte E-Mail-Nachrichten
od. Spam
correo basura; spam
スパムメール(招かざるコマーシ
ャル電子メール)

UIF
失业保险基金
système administré par le biais de
déductions sur salaires qui assure
les employés contre les pertes de
revenus en cas de perte d'emploi
pour raisons de réduction des
dépenses, maladie, maternité
Arbeitslosenversicherung
fondo de seguro contra el
desempleo financiado con
deducciones del salario
失業保険基金

ultra vires activity
超越法定期限活动; 越权活动
activité au-delà des pouvoirs
Tätigkeit einer Gesellschaft, die
über ihren satzungsmäßigen
Geschäftszweck hinausgeht
actividad ultra vires
越權行為, 權能外活動

unbalanced growth
不平衡增长
croissance déséquilibrée
ungleichgewichtiges Wachstum
crecimiento desequilibrado
不均衡成長, 不均整成長

unbundling
分类计价;
把被收購的公司分割出售
dégrouper
Zerlegung eines Unternehmens in
separate Einzelfirmen
disgregación, segmentación
会社分離

uncalled share capital
未缴股股本
capital-actions non appelé
nicht eingefordertes Kapital
capital en acciones no
desembolsado
未払込株式資本

uncertainty
不确定性
incertitude
Ungewissheit; Unsicherheit;
Unbestimmtheit
incertidumbre; duda
不確実性

uncertainty analysis
不定性分析
analyse d'incertitude
Ungewissheitsanalyse
análisis de incertidumbre
不確定性分析

uncollected funds
未收取资金
fonds non perçus
nicht eingezogene Gelder
fondos no cobrados
未資金化資金

uncollected trade bill
未收贸易汇票
effet de commerce non réclamé/
non perçu
ausstehender Handelswechsel
efecto impagado
未徴収の商業手形

unconditional bid
无条件报价
offre sans réserve
uneingeschränktes od.
bedingungsloses Angebot
oferta incondicional
無条件株式公開買い付け

unconsolidated
独立核算的; 不合并计算的
non consolidé
nicht konsolidiert; unfundiert
sin consolidar
非連結

uncontested bid
非竞争性报价
offre non contestée
unangefochtenes Angebot; Gebot
ohne Gegenbieter
puja no disputada
独占入札

UNCTAD
联合国贸易与发展会议
comité de focalisation au sein de
l'ONU pour le traitement intégré
des questions de développement
et questions qui y sont liées
Handels- und

Entwicklungskonferenz der
Vereinten Nationen
UNCTAD
国連貿易開発会議

underbanked
组建银团受挫
sous-négocié
ohne eine ausreichende Anzahl
von Maklern zum Verkauf einer
Neuemission
sin apoyo para asegurar una
emisión
新発行引受不足の

underlying asset
基础资产
actif active sous-jacente
Basisobjekt; Bezugsobjekt
activo subyacente
原資産

underlying inflation
潜在通货膨胀
inflation sous-jacente
Grundinflation
inflación subyacente
基調インフレ

underlying security
承保附属公司债券;
(期权)基层证券
nantissement/caution sous-jacente
Basiswert; Basisprodukt;
zugrundeliegendes Wertpapier
título subyacente
原証券

undermargined account
保证金不足账户
compte en sous-marge
Effektenkonto, das nicht
ausreichend Deckung für seinen
Margenforderungen hat
cuenta submarginal
基準委託保証金を下回る証拠
金勘定

undervalued
售价过低的; 估值偏低的; 便宜的;
价值偏低的
sous-évalué
unterbewertet
infravalorado(-a)
割安

undervalued currency
定值偏低的货币; 价值偏低通货
devise sous-évaluée
unterbewertete Währung
moneda infravalorada
過小評価通貨

underwrite
承担风险; 包销证券或股票
garantir une souscription
übernehmen; versichern
asegurar
アンダーライト, 引き受ける

Translations appear in the following order: Chinese, French, German, Spanish/Latin American Spanish, and Japanese

underwriter
保险商; 经营保险业者;
证券包销商
assureur /syndicataire
Garant; Syndikatsmitglied bei
Lloyd's; Bürge; Emissionsbank;
Konsortialmitglied; Versicherer
compañía de seguros; aseguradora
保険業者

underwriters' syndicate
保险商协会
syndicat des agents souscripteurs/
assureurs
Emissionskonsortium
consorcio garante
保険シンジケート

underwriting
同意负担(成本; 费用);
承担风险或商业损失; 保险
garantie d'émission
Risikoübernahme; Versicherung;
Garantie einer Emission
aseguramiento
(保険, 債券等)引受業務

underwriting income
承担风险收入
revenu de souscription
Zeichnungseinkommen
diferencia entre primas y pagos
保険業者の営業利益

underwriting spread
承购差价
répartition de garantie d'émission/
souscription
Konsortialspanne
margen de suscripción
引受業務取引価格差

undistributable reserves
不可分配储备
réserves non distribuables
unverteilbare Rückstellungen
reservas no distribuibles
(英)未配分準備金

UNDP
联合国开发计划署
programme pour le
développement de l'ONU; la
source la plus importante au
monde pour les subventions pour
un développement humain viable
et durable
Entwicklungsprogramm der
Vereinten Nationen
PNUD
国連開発計画

unearned income
非营业收入; 非劳动收入; 利润
revenu non professionnel
provenant d'un capital

Besitzeinkommen; Einkommen
aus Vermögen; transitorische
Passiva
ingresos no salariales
不労所得

unearned increment
自然增值; 不劳增值
plus-value foncière
unverdienter Wertzuwachs von
Grundbesitz
plusvalía; incremento no ganado
自然増価(分), 不労増価分

unearned premium
未满期保险费; 不应得保险费
primes non gagnées
nicht verdiente Prämie
prima no cobrada
未経過保険料

uneconomic
不经济
peu économique
unwirtschaftlich
antieconómico
不経済な, 不採算の

UN/EDIFACT
UNEDIFACT 标 准
UN/EDIFACT: norme pour EDE
utilisée en Europe occidentale et
très similaire à la norme ANSI X. 12
in Westeuropa gebräuchlicher
Standard zum elektronischen
Austausch von Informationen,
ähnelt weitgehend dem Standard
ANSI X.12
estándar UN/EDIFACT
ＵＮ電子データ交換FACT

unemployment
失业
chômage
Arbeitslosikgeit
desempleo
desocupación
失業, 失職

uneven playing field
不公平竞争市场
terrain de jeux inégal
ungleiche Grundvoraussetzungen
desigualdad de condiciones
不平等な競争市場

unfair dismissal
不公正解雇
licenciement abusif
grundlose Entlassung
despido improcedente
不当解雇

**unfranked investment
income**
未付税投资收入
crédits d'impôt non attachés aux
dividendes reçus

nicht besteuerte Kapitalerträge
ingresos derivados de inversiones
no liberadas
税引き前投資利益

unfunded debt
短期债务
dette non consolidée
schwebende Schuld
deuda flotante
短期無担保借入金

ungluing
业务关系终止
faire craquer (décomposer des
chaînes ou groupes
d'approvisionnement
traditionnels)
Auseinanderlösen
separación, despegue
アングルーイング(サプライ
チェーンの解体)

unhappy camper
不满僱主的僱員
personne qui a des récriminations
contre son employeur
jemand, der an seinem oder ihrem
Arbeitgeber etwas auszusetzen
hat
trabajador(a) instatisfecho(-a)
アンハッピー・キャンパー
(上司に不満のある人)

uniform accounting
统一会计
comptabilité uniforme
einheitliche Buchführung;
einheitliches Rechnungswesen
contabilidad uniforme de sector
统一会计

uniform costing
统一定价
évaluation de coût uniforme
einheitliche Kalkulation
cálculo uniforme de costos
統一原価見積り

unimodal
单峰的
unimodal
eingipflig
unimodal
(統計)頻度などの曲線が)
单峰型

uninstalled
被解雇; 被炒鱿鱼
versionnage
de-installiert; entlassen
despedido(-a)
首になった

uninsurable
非可保的
inassurable
nicht versicherungsfähig

no asegurable
(危険が多くて)保険の付けられ
ない

unique selling point
独特的销售特点
avantage unique
einmaliges Verkaufsargument
proposición única de venta
USP(商品の差別特性)

unique visitor
唯一访问者
visiteur unique
jemand, der eine Webseite
innerhalb eines bestimmten
Zeitraums mehrfach besucht.
visitante único
ユニーク・ビジター，
ユニーク・ユーザー

unissued share capital
未发行的股票资本
capital-actions non émis
genehmigte, aber noch nicht
emittierte Aktien
acciones no emitidas
未発行株式資本

unit
单位
unité
Einheit; Abteilung; Betrieb;
Fondsanteil; Börsenschluss; Stück;
Teil; Gerät; Aggregat; Gruppe;
Einerstelle
unidad
ユニット(証券取引の単位)

unit cost
单位成本
prix de revient unitaire
Stückpreis; Stückkosten
coste unitario
costo unitario
単価

unit of account
记帐单位
unité de compte
Rechnungseinheit
unidad de cuenta
(欧州の)計算単位

unit of trade
交易单位
unité commerciale
Mindestmenge; Kontrakteinheit;
Schluss
unidad de negociación
売買単位、取引単位

unit trust
单位信托; 互惠投资公司
société d'investissement à capital
variable (SICAV)
Investmentfonds
fondo de inversión

ミューチュアル・ファンド，
ユニット投資信託

universe
大市场
univers
Universum
universo
全市場

unlimited liability
无限责任; 无限赔偿责任
responsabilité illimitée
unbegrenzte Haftung
responsabilidad ilimitada
無限責任

unlisted
非上市; 非挂牌
non coté en Bourse
ungeregelt; nicht amtlich notiert
que no cotiza
非上場

unlisted securities market
非上市证券市场; 非挂牌证券市场;
无牌价证券市场
marché hors cote
Zweiter Markt; Freiverkehr;
geregelter Markt; Markt für nicht
notierte Wertpapiere
mercado de valores no cotizados
非上場証券市場

unofficial strike
非正式罢工; 野貓式罷工
grève sauvage
wilder Streik
huelga no oficial
無承諾ストライキ(山猫ストラ
イキ)

unquoted
未报价; 未挂牌; 未上市;
沒有上市的(股票)
non coté
ungeregelt; nicht amtlich notier
sin cotización
未上場証券、非上場証券

unrealised capital gain
未实现资本收益
plus-value non réalisée
nicht realisierter Kursgewinn od.
Kapitalertrag
ganancias de capital no realizadas
未実現資本売却利益

unrealised profit/loss
未实现的利润损失
perte/profit non réalisé
nicht realisierter Gewinn/ Verlust
beneficios no realizados/pérdidas
no realizadas
未実現利益損失

unreason
非理智阶段; 非逻辑阶段;
神來之筆; 誤打誤撞;

盲拳打死老師傅
agir de façon improbable
Unvernunft
pensar lo impensable
理に適わず、非現実的思考だが，
成功につながる

unremittable gain
不可转移的收入
au Royaume Uni, plus-value sur
capital qui ne peut pas être
importée dans le pays du
contribuable
nicht überweisbarer Kapitalertrag
ganancia de capital no importable
送金不能利得

unseasoned issue
不适时发行
émission sans précédent
unerfahrene Emission
emisión no consolidada
不確実銘柄、不安定銘柄

unsecured
无担保的
non garanti
ungesichert
sin garantía; no garantizado(-a)
抵当のない、無担保の

unsecured debt
无担保债务
dette chirographaire/ sans garantie
unbesicherte Forderung; nicht
bevorrechtigte Konkursforderung
deuda sin garantía
無担保負債

unsecured loan
无抵押贷款; 无担保贷款
prêt non garanti
ungesicherter Kredit;
unbesichertes Darlehen
préstamo sin garantía
無担保貸付、信用貸付

unsocial hours
非常规工时; 加班时间
travail en dehors des heures
normales
unsoziale Stunden
horas fuera del horario laboral
normal
非社会的就労時間

unstable equilibrium
不稳定均衡
équilibre instable
unbeständiges od. schwankendes
Gleichgewicht
equilibrio inestable
不安定均衡

upsell
上层销售
vendre à prix fort
Kunden eine teurere Version eines

Translations appear in the following order: Chinese, French, German, Spanish/Latin American Spanish, and Japanese

bereits früher von ihnen gekauften Produkts verkaufen
vender una versión más cara
以前購入した商品よりアップグレードの品を売る

upstairs market
上层市场; 所外市场
marché de la haute: endroit de la Bourse où les contrepartistes des grosses institutions et maisons de courtage opèrent
feste Börse
transacciones al margen de la bolsa
アップステアズ(ディーラー)マーケット,
大手証券業者の取引する市場

upstream progress
在逆境中前进(或取得进展)
progrès à contre-courant
Aufstieg; gegen den Strom
avance contra corriente
上流へ向かう進歩

Urgent Issues Task Force
紧急问题工作组
groupe de travail de gestion des questions urgentes
Arbeitsgruppe für dringliche Fragen zu einem Grundsatz der Rechnungslegung
equipo de trabajo sobre cuestiones urgentes; fuerza de choque para cuestiones urgentes
緊急問題機動班

URL
網址全式寫法
adresse de ressources constante
einheitliche Adressierung im World Wide Web
URL (localizador uniforme de recursos)
URS(ユニフォーム・リソース・ロケーター)

usability
可用性
utilité
Brauchbarkeit
facilidad de uso
ユーザビリティ(ウェブサイトの使い勝手の良さ)

usenet
(世界性的)新闻组网络系统
immense espace d'information englobé dans les forums de discussion
Usenet
Usenet
ユーズネット

utopian socialism
空想社会主义
socialisme utopique

utopischer Sozialismus
socialismo utópico
ユートピア社会主義

value added¹
售价与成本差
valeur ajoutée
Wertschöpfung
valor añadido
付加価値

value added²
附加价值
valeur ajoutée
Wertschöpfung
valor añadido
付加価値

value-added network
增值网络
réseau à valeur ajoutée
Value-Added Network; Mehrwertdienstnetz
red de valor añadido
付加価値通信網サービス

value-added reseller
增值销售商
revendeur de plus-value (VAR)
Wiederverkäufer(in)
vendedor(a) de valor añadido
付加価値転売者

value-added services
增值服务
services à valeur ajoutée
Zusatzleistungen
servicios de valor añadido
付加価値サービス

value-adding intermediary
增值环节
revendeur ajoutant de la valeur
Zwischenhändler(in)
intermediario de valor añadido
価値付加仲介業者

value analysis
价值分析
analyse de la valeur
Wertanayse
análisis del valor
価値分析

value-based management
价值管理
gestion basée sur la valeur
auf Werten beruhende Unternehmensführung
gestión con estímulo al valor
価値基準管理

value chain¹
价值链
chaîne de valeur
Wertkette
cadena de valor
価値チェーン(出世コースのアプローチ)

value chain²
价值链
chaîne de valeur
Wertkette
cadena de valor
価値チェーン

value engineering
价值工程
ingénierie de valeur
Wertanalyse
ingeniería del valor
価値エンジニアリング

value for customs purposes only
海关专用价值
valeur en douane uniquement
ausschließlich zur Zollwertermittlung
valoración aduanera
顧客の目的に適った価値のみ

value for money audit
现金价值审计
audit de rapport coût-performance
Wirtschaftlichkeitsprüfung
auditoría del buen uso de los recursos
価値監査

value innovation
价值创新
innnovation de valeur
Werte-Innovation
valor en la innovación
価値革新

value map
价值增值图示
carte de la valeur
Wertschlüssel
mapa de valor
価値マップ(市場での価値レベル)

value mesh
价值罗网
grille de valeur
Wertnetz
reevaluación de un trabajo en el mercado laboral global
バリュー・メッシュ(仕事の再位置付け)

value proposition¹
价值主张; 销售价值提议; 市场价位
proposition de valeur: déclaration par une organisation des moyens par lesquels elle peut offrir une bonne valeur au client potentiel
Wertangebot; Wertbeitrag; Wertvorschlag
declaración de valor
価値提案

Translations appear in the following order: Chinese, French, German, Spanish/Latin American Spanish, and Japanese

value proposition[2]
价值建议
proposition de valeur
Vorhaben, mit dem man Gewinn
machen will
plan para obtener beneficios
利益創出提案

value share
价值股
action ou titre de bonne valeur
preiswerte Aktie
acción de valor
価値のある株(実際の価格よりも)

variable
变量
variable
Variable
variable
変数

variable annuity
可变动年金
annuité variable
Rente mit veränderlichen
Auszahlungsbeträgen
anualidad variable
変動年金

variable cost of sales
销售的可变成本
coûts de vente variables
variable Selbstkosten
costes variables de ventas
変動売上原価

variable interest rate
可变汇率; 变动汇率
taux d'intérêt variable
variabler Zinssatz
interés variable
変動金利

variable rate note
可变利率票据
billet à taux variable
variabel verzinslicher Wechsel
pagaré de interés variable
変動利付き手形

variance
差异;
(预算成本与实际成本的)不符
écart: mesure de la différence
entre la performance réelle et la
prévision la performance normale
Abweichung
desviación
差異

variance accounting
差异会计学
comptabilité des écarts ou de
variance
Verrechnungsbuchung
contabilidad comparativa de
variación
原価差額勘定

variance analysis
差异分析
analyse des écarts
Varianzanalyse
análisis de la varianza
差異分析

variance components
方差分量
composantes de variance
Varianzkomponenten
componentes de varianza
可变性要素

variety reduction
种类减少策略
standardisation des types
Abbau der Warenvielfalt
reducción de tipos
種類減少

VAT
增值税
TVA
MwSt.; Value Added Tax =
Mehrwertsteuer
IVA
付加価値税

VAT collected
收纳的增值税
TVA perçue
eingezogene MwSt.
IVA cobrado
徴収済みVAT

VAT paid
已付增值税
TVA payée
abgeführte MwSt.
IVA pagado
支払済みVAT

VAT receivable
应收增值税
TVA à recevoir
ausstehende MwSt.
IVA por cobrar
支払われるべきVAT

VAT registration
增值税注册
enregistrement pour TVA
Anmeldung für Mehrwertsteuer
registro del IVA
VAT登録

**velocity of circulation of
money**
货币流速; 流通周转率; 流通速度
vélocité de circulation d'argent/de
devises
Umlaufgeschwindigkeit des
Geldes
velocidad de circulación del dinero
貨幣の流通速度

vendor placing
买主出盘
actions de fondation
Verkäuferplatzierung
colocación directa
売り手による私募

vendor rating
厂商评比
évaluation des vendeurs
Lieferantenbeurteilung
calificación de proveedores
売主評価

Venn diagram
维恩图，文氏图
diagramme de Venn
Venn-Diagramm
diagrama de Venn
ベン図形

venture capital[1]
风险资本; 冒险资本; 投机资本
capital risque
Risikokapital; Wagniskapital;
Spekulationskapital
capital de riesgo
ベンチャー·キャピタル、
危険負担資本、冒険資本

venture capital[2]
风险资本
capital risque
Risikokapital; Wagniskapital
capital de riesgo
ベンチャービジネス資本

Venture Capital Market
风险资本市场
marché des capitaux à risque
Risikokapitalmarkt
sección para pequeñas empresas
en desarrollo del mercado de
valores de la Bolsa de
Johanesburgo
ベンチャーキャピタル市場

venture funding
风险投资
financement des sociétés à
capitaux risqués
Wagnisfinanzierung
financiación de capital de riesgo
投機の事業資金調達

venture management
风险管理
gestion d'innovation
Wagnis-Management
administración del riesgo
ベンチャー管理

venturer
合资方
participant dans une co-entreprise
ou opération en commun
Joint-Venture-Partner(in)
socio(-a) en una joint venture
合弁企業相手先

---

*Translations appear in the following order: Chinese, French, German, Spanish/Latin American
Spanish, and Japanese*

verbal contract
口头合同
contrat verbal
mündliche Vereinbarung
contrato verbal
口頭契約

verification
查证
vérification
Verifizierung
verificación
監査での検証, 実証

versioning
量体裁衣; 用不同的资料提供法
去迁就不同的顾客
versionnage
Variantenwerbung für
unterschiedliche Kundengruppen
manipular la información para
adaptarla a los diferentes clientes
顧客属性にあった情報のバー
ジョン作り

vertical equity
纵向公平
équité verticale
vertikale Steuergerechtigkeit
equidad vertical
垂直公平性(支払い能力に応じ
た税)

vertical form
纵向表
format vertical
vertikale Darstellung eines
Abschlusses, in der Guthaben und
Salden in einer Ziffernspalte
ausgewiesen werden
formato vertical
垂直コラム形式

vertical integration
纵向合并; 纵向一体化; 纵向整合;
垂直一体化
intégration verticale
vertikale Verflechtung
integración vertical
垂直合并

vertical linkage analysis
纵向联系分析
analyse des relations verticales
Vertikalverbunds-Analyse
análisis vertical del ligamiento
垂直連係分析

vertical market
纵向市场
marché vertical
vertikaler Markt
mercado vertical
垂直(特定一産業)市場

vested employee benefits
既有雇员利益
bénéfices de salariés acquis
gesicherte Arbeitnehmerrechte
derechos a prestaciones adquiridos
por el trabajador
社員受給権確定給付

vested rights
既得权利
droits acquis
wohlerworbene Rechte;
Besitzstand
valor de la contribución ya
efectuada
既得権、確定的権利

v-form
V形表格
représentation graphique de
quelque chose dont la valeur avait
chuté et qui est maintenant en
hausse
V-Form
gráfico en forma de valle
V形

videoconferencing
电话会议; 影音會議
vidéoconférence
Videokonferenz
videoconferencias
ビデオ会議

viewing figures
收视人数
nombre de téléspectateurs
Zuschauer
cifras de audiencia
視聴者数

viewtime
展示时间
temps de visualisation
Sichtzeit
tiempo de visualización
ビュータイム, 閲覧時間

viral marketing
电子式口碑营销
marketing viral
virales Marketing
marketing viral; marketing de boca
en boca
ウィルス・マーケティング

virement
转账
virement
Mittelübertragung
translación
予算転用操作

virtual hosting
虚拟托管
(option d') hôte virtuel
virtuelles Hosting
alojamiento virtual, hospedaje

virtual
仮想ホスティング

virtualisation
虚拟化; 虚拟产品; 虚拟组织
virtualisation
Virtualisierung
virtualización
仮想化

virtual office
虚拟办公室; 虚拟办公
bureau virtuel
virtuelles Büro
oficina virtual
仮想事務所

virtual organisation
虚拟组织
organisation virtuelle
virtuelle Organisation
organización virtual
バーチャル組織体

virtual team
虚拟团队
équipe virtuelle
virtuelles Team
equipo virtual
バーチャル・チーム

virus
病毒
virus
Virus
virus
コンピュータ・ウィルス

visible trade
有形贸易
commerce visible
Warenhandel
comercio visible
貿易取引, 商品貿易, 有形品貿易

vision statement
宗旨说明
formulation de vision future
Zukunftsvision eines
Unternehmens
declaración de objetivos
未来声明

visit
访问
visite
Besuch
visita
ビジット, 訪問, 閲覧

vocational qualification
职业证书; 职业资格
qualification professionnelle
berufsbezogene Qualifizierung
título de formación profesional
職業資格

vocational training
职业培训
formation professionnelle

Translations appear in the following order: Chinese, French, German, Spanish/Latin American Spanish, and Japanese

Berufsausbildung
formación profesional
職業訓練

voetstoots
买主自担风险的
acheté au risque de l'acheteur ou
sans garantie
'der Käufer trägt alle Risiken'
bajo responsabilidad del
comprador
危険買手持ち

volume of retail sales
有形贸易
volume des ventes au détail
Einzelhandelsabsätze;
Einzelhandelsvolumen
volumen de ventas al por menor
小売販売量, 小売売上高

volume variances
数量差异
variations de volumes
Beschäftigungsabweichungen
diferencias de volumen
操業度差異

voluntary arrangement
自愿的安排; 自愿偿债安排
accord volontaire
freiwilliger Vergleich
acuerdo voluntario
自主協定

voluntary liquidation
自动清理
liquidation volontaire
freiwillige Liquidation
liquidación voluntaria
任意破産, 任意清算

voluntary registration
自愿登记
inscription volontaire
freiwillige
Mehrwertsteuer-Anmeldung
inscripción voluntaria
任意登録

vortal
垂直门户
vortal
Vortal
portal vertical
ポータル(一産業に限ったポー
タルウェブサイト)

vostro account
来帐户头
compte vostro
Vostrokonto
cuenta vostro
ボストロ口座

votes on account
临时拨款
votes pour acompte
parlamentarische

Vorausbewilligung von Mitteln vor
endgültiger Genehmigung der
Gesamtbudgets für das Jahr
dinero adicional concedido por el
parlamento antes de la autorización
de los totales para ese año
(英)議決勘定

voting shares
有表决权股份
actions avec droit de vote
stimmberechtigte Aktien
acciones con derecho a voto
議決権株式

voting trust
投票信托; 投票托付
trust avec droits de vote
auf das Stimmrecht beschränkter
Trust
grupo con acciones con derecho a
voto
議決権行使信託

voucher
凭单
pièce comptable
Beleg; Buchungsbeleg
comprobante de pago;
comprobante; vale; bono; boleta;
recibo; resguardo; justificante
証憑

vouching
担保; 翻查單據審計法;
翻查單據核數法
garantie de validité et d'exactitude
Belegvergleich
verificación de la documentación
立証する

Vredeling Directive
宛达林建议
directive Vredeling
Vredeling-Richtlinie
Directiva Vredeling
ヴレデリング指令書

Vulcan nerve pinch
三指礼; 按某些電腦指令鍵時
手部的不適
contorsion de mains sur clavier
die unbequeme Handstellung, die
nötig ist, wenn man für bestimmte
Rechnerbefehle alle Tasten
erreichen will
posición incómoda de los dedos
para ejecutar ciertos comandos
パソコンのコマンドを入力する
ために必要な不快な指の位置

vulture capitalist
秃鹰资本家
capitaliste rapace
Finanz-Geier
capitalista de riesgo que beneficia
a los inversores más que al
empresario

投資家に利益を与えるように企
業家の契約をつくるベンチャー・
キャピタリスト

wage earner
雇佣劳动者
salarié(e)
Lohnempfänger(in)
asalariado(-a)
賃金労働者

wage freeze
工资冻结
blocage des salaires
Lohnstopp
congelación salarial
賃金凍結策

wage incentive
鼓励工资
prime de rendement
Lohnanreiz
incentivo salarial
奨励給

wages
工资
paye
Lohn
salario; sueldo
賃金

waiting time
等待时间
temps d'attente
Wartezeit
tiempo de espera
労働の待機時間

waiver of premium
免交保费
abandon de paiement de prime
Beitragsbefreiung
clásula de exensión del pago de la
prima
保険料払込免除

walk
辞职走人
démissionner
kündigen
largarse
辞任する

walled garden
固定电子商务园
jardin clos: environnement sur le
Net dans lequel les clients peuvent
uniquement accéder aux
e-commerçants sélectionnés par le
propriétaire de l'environnement
ummauerter Garten
entorno comercial cerrado
ウオールド・ガーデン

wallet technology
电子钱包技术

---

*Translations appear in the following order: Chinese, French, German, Spanish/Latin American
Spanish, and Japanese*

technologie de porte-monnaie
électronique
Geldbörsen-Technologie
entorno comercial cerrado
ウオレット・テクノロジー

Wall Street
华尔街
Wall Street: le quartier de la Bourse
à New-York
Beitragsbefreiung
Wall Street
ウオールストリート

WAP
无线应用协议
WAP
WAP
WAP
WAP(ワイヤレス・アプリケー
ション・プロトコール)

warehousing
仓储; 货仓业; 仓储业务; 储藏费用;
缓慢收购
entreposage
Lagerhaltung; Lagerung;
Lagergeschäft
almacenamiento
倉庫保管

war for talent
人才之争
guerre des talents
Kampf um besonders fähige
Mitarbeiter(innen)
guerra cazatalentos
有能人材確保競争

warrants risk warning notice
担保风险警告通知
notice d'avertissement de risques
liés aux opérations à option ou
prime
Warnhinweis britischer Makler an
Kunden, der diese auf die Risiken
des Optionshandels aufmerksam
machen soll
notificación sobre los riesgos de la
contratación de acciones
リスク警告証書

waste
废物
déchet
Abfall; Müll
desperdicio; no útil
廃物

waste management
废物管理
gestion des déchets
Abfallwirtschaft
gestión de residuos
塵芥処理

wasting asset
递耗资产
actif qui se détériore
Wirtschaftsgut mit begrenzter
Nutzungsdauer
activo con vida útil limitada
空资产

wealth
财富
richesse
Vermögen; Reichtum
riqueza
富, 财, 资产、富裕

wealth tax
财产税; 财富税
impôt sur les grandes fortunes
Vermögenssteuer
impuesto sobre el patrimonio
富裕税

wear a hat
负责
porter un chapeau
einen Hut aufhaben, eine
bestimmte Rolle erfüllen
desempeñar un papel
ある役目を負う

wear and tear
磨损
dépréciation ou détérioration
Abnutzung
desgaste
摩損(自然消耗)

web bug
在线跟踪工具
bogue du Web
Netz-Wanze
tipo de cookie
ウェブバグ(WWWサーバーの
ユーザー管理システム)

webcast
多媒体网广播
diffusion d'information sur le Web
Webcasting
emisión por la web
ウェブキャスト

web form
表单
formulaire Web
Webformular
formulario en la web
ウェブフォーム

web log
网页访问日志
journal d'activité du Web
Weblog
registro de actividad de un sitio
web
ウェブログ

web marketing
网络市场开发
marketing web
Marketing im Internet
marketing en la Web
ウエッブ・マーケティング

web marketplace
网上商城
marché sur Web
elektronischer Marktplatz
mercado electrónico
ウェブマーケットプレース

webmaster
网页主管人
maître du Web
für eine Webseite verantwortliche
Person
webmaster; administrador(a) de
páginas web
ウェブマスター

web server¹
网络服务器
serveur Web
Webserver
servidor web
ウェブサーバー

web server²
网页服务器
serveur Web
Webserver
servidor web
ウェブサーバー

website classification
站点分类
classification sur site Web
Webseiten-Klassifierung
clasificación de un sitio web
ウェブサイト分類

weighted average
加权平均值
moyenne pondérée
gewogener Mittelwert
media ponderada
加重平均值

**weighted average number of
ordinary shares**
普通股加权平均数
moyenne pondérée du nombre
d'actions ordinaires
gewogene Durchschnittsanzahl an
Stammaktien
media ponderada
加重平均普通株数

weighting
加权，权重; 比重
pondération
Gewichten
ponderación
重要性を加える

---

*Translations appear in the following order: Chinese, French, German, Spanish/Latin American
Spanish, and Japanese*

weightlessness
无形经济模式
apesanteur
Schwerelosigkeit
dependencia de una economía en
bienes inmateriales o el
conocimiento más que en activos
físicos
無重量経済状態(知識や無形物
に基づいた)

welfare
福利
bien-être (professionnel et social)
Wohlfahrt
bienestar
福利厚生

wellness program
生活健康计划
programme de bonne forme
Wellness-Programm
programa de mantenimiento de la
forma física
ウエルネス・プログラム

wet signature
亲笔签字
signature stylo-encre
Unterschrift in Tinte
firma en papel
実在の紙の上での署名

wharfie
码头工人
docker
Docker
estibador(a)
港湾労働者

Wheat Report
维特报告
rapport Wheat (Etats-Unis)
Wheat-Bericht
informe de 1972 que examinaba la
situación de la contabilidad en
Estados Unidos
ウィート報告書

whisper stock
小道消息股
titre à rumeur
Wertpapier, über das Dinge
gemunkelt werden, die auf eine
Wertveränderung hindeuten,
normalerweise nach oben
acciones sobre las que corren
rumores
ウィスパー株

whistleblowing
揭发; 披露; 揭露
vendre la mèche; tirer la sonnette
d'alarme
über etwas auspacken
denuncia desde dentro de
prácticas irregulares de una
empresa
内部告発

white coat rule
白衣规章(禁止演员等身份的人
化妆成像真正医生做广告)
réglementation américaine
interdisant aux acteurs d'être
habillés en médecin pour la
promotion d'un produit dans une
pub TV
Regel der Federal Trade
Commission in den USA, nach der
Schauspieler nicht als Ärzte in der
Fernsehwerbung für Produkte
erscheinen dürfen
norma que prohíbe la aparición en
los anuncios de actores disfrazados
de doctores
CMで俳優が医師を演じてはなら
ないというルール

white-collar crime
白领犯罪
crime en col blanc
Wirschaftskriminalität
delito de oficinista
ホワイトカラー犯罪, 知能犯罪

white-collar job
白领工作
emploi de bureau (qui ne demande
aucun travail physique)
Bürotätigkeit
trabajo de oficinista
ホワイトカラー仕事

white-collar worker
白领
employé de bureau ou col blanc
Angestellte/r
oficinista
ホワイト・カラー

white goods
大型家用电器; 白色家用电器
appareils ménagers
elektronische Haushaltsgeräte
línea blanca
白物家電

white squire
白色护卫
écuyer blanc: actionnaire qui
achète un nombre important
d'actions, cependant non suffisant
pour obtenir le contrôle d'une
entreprise, afin d'empêcher
qu'une OPA ne réussisse
weißer Knappe: Anleger, der eine
beträchtliche, aber nicht
mehrheitliche Anzahl an Aktien
erwirbt, um ein
Übernahmeangebot zu vereiteln
escudero blanco
白い騎士の従者

whizz kid
神童
jeune personne douée
Senkrechtstarter(in)
joven prodigio
ウィズ・キッド(証券取引で巨
額の富を築く若者)

wholesale price
批发价格
prix de gros
Großhandelspreis; Kurs im
Freiverkehr
precio al por mayor
卸値

wholesale price index
批发价格指数
indice des prix de gros
Großhandelspreisindex
índice de precios al por mayor
卸売り物価指数

wholesaler
批发商
grossiste
Großhandelsunternehmen
mayorista
卸売業

wholesale trade
批发贸易; 批发业
commerce de gros
Großhandel
comercio al por mayor
卸売業

wholly-owned subsidiary
独资子公司
filiale à cent pour cent %
Tochtergesellschaft
filial totalmente propia
完全所有子会社

widow-and-orphan stock
寡妇孤儿股票(特别安全)
titres de la veuve et de l'orphelin
mündelsichere Wertpapiere hoher
Sicherheit; Wertpapiere mit hoher
Sicherheit
acciones muy seguras
ウィドー&オーファンストック
(超安全株)

wiggle room
斡旋余地
place pour remuer (une certaine
flexibilité)
Spielraum in Vertrags- oder
Terminangelegenheiten
flexibilidad
柔軟性のあること

Willie Sutton rule
威利萨顿法则
maxime selon laquelle il est
logique de se concentrer sur les
domaines les plus lucratifs

Translations appear in the following order: Chinese, French, German, Spanish/Latin American Spanish, and Japanese

Maxime, nach der es am
logischsten ist, sich auf die Gebiete
zu konzentrieren, wo am meisten
Profit herausspringt
principio según el cual es más
lógico concentrarse en lo que
produce más beneficio
ウィリー・サットンの法則

windfall gains and losses
意外收入和损失
profits et pertes exceptionnels
Zufallsgewinne und -verluste
beneficios y pérdidas inesperados
偶発損益

windfall profit
意外利润
bénéfices exceptionnels
Zufallsgewinn
beneficios inesperados
望外の利益, 偶発利益

windfall tax
意外收入所得税
impôt exceptionnel
Spekulationssteuer
impuesto sobre beneficios
extraordinarios
法外な利益に課する税

winding-up
破产; 结业
liquidation (d'une société)
Liquidation
cierre
企業閉鎖, 解散

winding-up petition
破产申请; 结业申請
requête de liquidation d'une
société
Liquidationsantrag
solicitud de liquidación obligatoria
強制解散の嘆願

window dressing
粉饰, 弄虚作假
truquage ou habillage de bilan
Bilanzkosmetik
alteración falaz de un balance;
falseamiento; manipulación de la
contabilidad mediante
operaciones
粉飾

win win situation
双赢
situation gagnant-gagnant
Geschäftssituation, die für alle
Beteiligten vorteilhaft ist
situación en la que todos ganan
皆が得するはずの取引

wired company
计算机化公司
entreprise bien chébran
verdrahtetes Unternehmen

empresa que aprovecha al máximo
las tecnologías de la información
ＩＴをフルに活用している企業

witching hour
魅力时刻
l'heure fatale
Zeitpunkt der Fälligkeit eines
derivaten Instruments wie einer
Verkaufs- oder Kaufoption oder
eines Vorverkaufsvertrags
petición de cierre
先物取引行使期限

withdrawal
提款
retrait ou transfert de solde
Abhebung; Entnahme
retirada, retiro
払い戻し

withholding tax[1]
预扣税; 预提(所得)税金
retenue fiscale
Quellensteuer
impuesto retenido en origen
源泉徴収税、源泉課税

withholding tax[2]
代扣所得税
retenue à la source
Quellensteuer
impuesto retenido en la fuente
源泉課税

word of mouse
鼠标口碑
word of mouse: le bouche à souris:
utilisation de la souris d'un
ordinateur comme outil de
marketing viral
Mauspropaganda
marketing de internauta en
internauta
ワード・オブ・マウス

work
工作
travail
Arbeit
trabajo
仕事

workaholic
工作狂
accro du boulot; drogué du travail
Arbeitstier
persona obsesionada con el
trabajo
仕事依存症

work cell
工作组
cellule de travail
Arbeitszelle
celda de trabajo
セル方式

worker control
工人管理
contrôle par les travailleurs
Lenkung durch Arbeitnehmer
control de los trabajadores
労働者による生産管理

worker director
工人董事
travailleur-directeur
Arbeitnehmer(in) der/die
gleichzeitig dem
Unternehmensvorstand angehört
empleado(-a) en la directiva
社員重役

work ethic
樂业精神
éthique du travail
Arbeitsethik
ética del trabajo
倫理感としての勤勉性

work experience
实习经验, 工作经验
placement en entreprise
Praktikum
prácticas
勤労経験

workforce
劳动力
personnel; main d'œuvre
Personalbestand
trabajadores
労働力

working capital
周转资本; 运营资本
capital d'exploitation ou fonds de
roulement
Betriebskapital;
Nettoumlaufvermögen
capital circulante; capital de
explotación; fondo de maniobra
運転資本金

working capital cycle
营运资本周期
cycle du capital d'exploitation
Betriebskapitalzyklus;
Betriebsmittelkreislauf
ciclo del capital circulante
運転資本サイクル

working lunch
工作午餐
déjeuner de travail
Arbeitsessen
almuerzo de trabajo
ビジネス昼食

work in progress
半成品
produit en cours de fabrication
unfertige Erzeugnisse
trabajo en progreso
仕掛品

Translations appear in the following order: Chinese, French, German, Spanish/Latin American Spanish, and Japanese

work-life balance
工作与生活间的平衡
équilibre entre vie active et vie
personnelle
Vereinbarkeit von Privatleben und
Berufsleben
equilibro entre el trabajo y la vida
privada
公的·私的生活のバランス

work measurement
工作测定
mesure de temps de performance
Zeitmessung; Arbeitsmessung
medición del trabajo
作業測定

work permit
工作许可证
permis de travail
Arbeitserlaubnis
permiso de trabajo
労働許可書

workplace bullying
工作场所凌辱行为
persécution ou intimidation sur le
lieu de travail
Mobbing am Arbeitsplatz;
Schikane
intimidación en el lugar de trabajo
職場でのいじめ

work rage
工作狂怒
fureur du boulot
irrationale Wut eines verärgerten
Arbeitnehmers am Arbeitsplatz
cólera laboral
仕事が原因で起こる激怒

works council
劳资联合委员会
comité d'entreprise
Betriebsrat
comité de empresa
労使協議会

work shadow
见习生; 工作见习; 实习生
ombre d'un travailleur: personne
qui observe un travailleur en
action, avec pour objectif
d'apprendre la façon dont il agit
dans son rôle
Arbeitsschatten
persona que observa el trabajo que
hace otra como forma de
aprendizaje
ワーク·シャドウ(仕事見習)

work simplification
工作简单化; 流程简化
simplification des tâches
Arbeitsvereinfachung
simplificación del trabajo
業務簡素化

works manager
生产经理
directeur ou directrice d'usine
Werksleiter(in); Fertigungsleiter(in)
director(a) de fábrica
工場長

workstation¹
高级電腦
poste de travail
Arbeitsplatzrechner; Datenstation;
Workstation
estación de trabajo
ワークステーション

workstation²
工作站
poste de travail
Arbeitsplatz; Arbeitsstation
estación de trabajo
ワークステーション

work structuring
工作结构安排; 工作过程设计;
工作岗位设计
structuration des tâches
Arbeitsgestaltung
estructuración del trabajo
作業編成

work study
工作研究
étude des activités professionnelles
Arbeitsstudium
estudio de trabajo
労働研究

work-to-rule
怠工; 按章工作
grève du zèle
Dienst nach Vorschrift;
Bummelstreik
huelga de celo
契約書通りの作業のみ行う

world class manufacturing
世界级生产
fabrication de classe internationale
Produktion; od. Fertigung der
Weltklasse
manufactura de clase mundial
ワールドクラス製造業

world economy
世界经济
économie mondiale
Weltwirtschaft
economía global
世界経済

wrap fund
包裹基金(专用于投资其它
基层单位基金,;
但本身并非单位基金〕
fonds de placement 'dissimulé'
zertifizierter Investmentfonds
fondo similar a una cartera de
valores que invierte en fondos de

inversiones
ラップ·ファンド

WRF
网络调查表
WRF
WRF
formulario web
ウェブ·レスポンス·フォーム

write-down
减记的折扣
provision pour créance douteuse;
réduction de la valeur inscrite d'un
actif
Wertberichtigung
depreciación de un activo;
amortización de activos
帳簿価格切下げ

write off
注销
perte sèche
Abschreibung
reducción del valor de un activo
帳消し, 償却

writing down allowances
折旧备抵
déductions fiscales pour actif
défectible
Teilabschreibung von Freibeträgen
depreciación de los activos fijos
減価償却控除

wrongful trading
不正当贸易
commerce injustifié
unrechtmäßiger Handel
negociación ilegal
不当取引

WYSIWYG
所见即所得
WYSIWYG
WYSIWYG
WYSIWYG
ウィジーウィグ(ワット·ユー
·シー·イズ·ワット·ユー·
ゲット)

XBRL
可扩展商业报告语言
language informatique
Computersprache für die
Finanzberichterstattung
XRBL
XBRL(財務報告用コンピュー
ター言語)

XML
可扩展标示语言
XML
XML
XML
XML(インターネットに対応し
た構造化文書の
データ記述言語)

---

*Translations appear in the following order: Chinese, French, German, Spanish/Latin American
Spanish, and Japanese*

yakka
干活; 工 作
boulot
Arbeit
curro
chamba; laburo
仕事

Yankee bond
杨基债券
obligation Yankee
Yankee Bond
bono yanqui
ヤンキー債

year-end
年终
fin d'exercice
Jahresende
fin de año
会計年度末

year-end closing
年终结帐
fermeture de fin d'exercice
Jahresabschluss
cierre del ejercicio
会計年度末決算報告書

Yellow Book
黄页
Livre jaune des admissions des
titres à la cote officielle de la
Bourse de Londres
enthält die Vorschriften zur
Zulassung und weiteren
Mitgliedschaft an der Londonder
Börse sowie das offizielle
Verzeichnis der dort notierten
Gesellschaften
libro con las reglas de admisión al
listado de empresas de la Bolsa de
Londres
イエロー・ブック

yield
收益率
rendement
Nominalverzinsung;
Effektivverzinsung; Rendite; Ertrag
rendimiento; rentabilidad
利回り、利益

yield curve
收益率曲线
courbe de rendement
Zinsertragskurve
curva de rendimiento
利回り曲線、イールドカーブ

yield gap
收益率差额
écart de rendement
Ertragslücke

margen de rendimiento
利回りギャップ

yield to call
至通知赎券收益率; 通知收益率
rendement à date d'appel
Rendite einer kündbaren Anleihe
rendimiento a la redención
繰上げ償還利回り、初期利回り

young old
中老年
en marketing, le groupe des 55 à
75 ans
im Marketing die Altersgruppe
zwischen 55 und 75
grupo de edad entre los 55 y los 75
años
若い年寄り,
即ち５５～７５歳の消費者

yugen kaisha
(日本)私人有限责任公司
yugen kaisha: au Japon, une
société anonyme.
Gesellschaft mit beschränkter
Haftung
sociedad de responsabilidad
limitada japonesa
有限会社

zaibatsu
纵向一体化财阀
zaibatsu: conglomérats japonais
de type extraction-à-production
datant d'avant la deuxième guerre
mondiale
japanische Bergbau- und
Fertigungskonglomerate aus der
Zeit vor dem Zweiten Weltkrieg
zaibatsu
財閥

Z bond
末位债券
obligation Z
Z-Bond
bono cero cupón
Ｚボンド, アクルーアル

zero-balance account
零余额账户
compte à solde zéro
Nullsaldokonto
cuenta con balance cero
ゼロ・バランス・アカウント

zero-based budgeting
零基预算
budget à base zéro
Nullbasis-Budgetierung
presupuesto base cero
ゼロベース予算

zero coupon bond
无息票债券
obligation àcoupon zéro
Nullkoupon-Anleihe; Zero Bond;
Nullprozenter
bono con cupón cero
ゼロクーポン債, 無利子債券

zero defects
零缺陷
taux de défauts zéro
Nullfehler
calidad total; cero defectos
ゼロ・ディフェクツ(無欠陥運
動)

zero fund
零投资
ne pas financier
nicht finanzieren
no asignar fondos a
ゼロ資金

zero growth
零增长
croissance zéro
Nullwachstum
crecimiento cero
ゼロ成長

zero out
拨零找接线员
composer le zéro
bei der Nutzung eines
automatisierten Anrufsystems die
Null wählen, in der Hoffnung, dass
eine Person aus Fleisch und Blut
antworten könnte
marcar el cero para hablar con
alguien en un sistema automático
de llamada
ゼロをダイアルする(自動コール
システムで
人物が応答することを
期待して)

zero-rated supplies
零增值税供应品或服务
fournitures exemptes de TVA
mehrwertsteuerbefreite
Betriebsstoffe von der
Mehrwertsteuer befreite Güter
und Dienstleistungen
productos y servicios con IVA del
cero por ciento
非VAT課税商品, サービス

Z score
Z-比率
chiffre Z
Z-Punkt
Juego de pérdidas más ganancias
igual a cero; empate a cero
Ｚスコア

Translations appear in the following order: Chinese, French, German, Spanish/Latin American Spanish, and Japanese

FACTS AND FIGURES

Currencies and Capitals of the World's Top Business Centres

COUNTRY	CAPITAL	CURRENCY
Algeria	Algiers	Algerian dinar
American Samoa	Pago Pago	US dollar
Andorra	Andorra la Vella	euro
Angola	Luanda	kwanza
Antigua and Barbuda	St John's	East Caribbean dollar
Argentina	Buenos Aires	Argentine peso
Aruba	Oranjestad	Aruba florin
Australia	Canberra	Australian dollar
Austria	Vienna	euro
Bahamas	Nassau	Bahamas dollar
Bahrain	Manama	Bahraini dinar
Bangladesh	Dhaka	taka
Barbados	Bridgetown	Barbados dollar
Belarus	Minsk	Belorusian rouble
Belgium	Brussels	euro
Belize	Belmopan	Belize dollar
Bermuda	Hamilton	Bermuda dollar
Bolivia	La Paz (administrative) Sucre (judicial)	boliviano
Botswana	Gaborone	pula
Brazil	Brasilia	real
British Virgin Islands	Road Town	US dollar
Brunei	Bandar Seri Begawan	Brunei dollar
Bulgaria	sofia	lev
Cameroon	Yaoundé	CFA franc
Canada	Ottawa	Canadian dollar
Cayman Islands	George Town	Cayman Islands dollar
Channel Islands	St Helier (Jersey) St Peter Port (Guernsey)	UK pound
Chile	Santiago	Chilean peso
China	Beijing	yuan
Colombia	Bogotá	Colombian peso
Costa Rica	San José	Costa Rican colón
Côte d'Ivoire	Yamoussoukro (official) Abidjan (commercial)	CFA franc
Croatia	Zagreb	kuna
Cuba	Havana	Cuban peso
Cyprus	Nicosia	Cyprus pound Turkish lira
Czech Republic	Prague	Czech koruna
Denmark	Copenhagen	Danish krone
Dominica	Roseau	East Caribbean dollar
Dominican Republic	Santo Domingo	Dominican Republic peso
Ecuador	Quito	US dollar

COUNTRY	CAPITAL	CURRENCY
Egypt	Cairo	Egyptian pound
El Salvador	San Salvador	US dollar
Estonia	Tallinn	kroon
Ethiopia	Addis Ababa	birr
Faeroe Islands	Tórshavn	Danish krone
Finland	Helsinki	euro
France	Paris	euro
French Guiana	Cayenne	euro
French Polynesia	Papeete	CFP Franc
Gabon	Libreville	CFA franc
Georgia	Tbilisi	lari
Germany	Berlin	euro
Ghana	Accra	cedi
Gibraltar	Gibraltar	Gibraltar pound
Greece	Athens	euro
Greenland	Nuuk	Danish krone
Grenada	St George's	East Caribbean dollar
Guadeloupe	Basse-Terre	euro
Guam	Hagåtña	US dollar
Guatemala	Guatemala City	quetzal
Hong Kong	Victoria	Hong Kong dollar yuan
Hungary	Budapest	forint
Iceland	Reykjavík	Icelandic króna
India	New Delhi	Indian rupee
Indonesia	Jakarta	rupiah
Iran	Tehran	rial
Iraq	Baghdad	Iraqi dinar
Ireland	Dublin	euro
Isle of Man	Douglas	UK pound
Israel	Jerusalem	shekel
Italy	Rome	euro
Jamaica	Kingston	Jamaican dollar
Japan	Tokyo	yen
Jordan	Amman	Jordanian dinar
Kazakhstan	Astana	tenge
Kenya	Nairobi	Kenya shilling
Kuwait	Kuwait city	Kuwaiti dinar
Latvia	Riga	lat
Lebanon	Beirut	Lebanese pound
Libya	Tripoli	Libyan dinar
Liechtenstein	Vaduz	Swiss franc
Lithuania	Vilnius	litas
Luxembourg	Luxembourg	euro

COUNTRY	CAPITAL	CURRENCY
Macao	Macao	pataca
Malaysia	Kuala Lumpur	ringgit
Malta	Valletta	Maltese lira
Martinique	Fort-de-France	euro
Mauritius	Port Louis	Mauritius rupee
Mexico	Mexico City	Mexican peso
Monaco	Monaco-Ville	euro
Morocco	Rabat	Moroccan dirham
Mozambique	Maputo	metical
Namibia	Windhoek	Namibian dollar
Netherlands	Amsterdam	euro
Netherlands Antilles	Willemstad	Netherlands Antilles guilder
New Caledonia	Nouméa	CFP franc
New Zealand	Wellington	New Zealand dollar
Nigeria	Abuja	naira
North Korea	Pyongyang	won
Northern Mariana Islands	Saipan	US dollar
Norway	Oslo	Norwegian krone
Oman	Muscat	Omani rial
Pakistan	Islamabad	Pakistan rupee
Palau	Koror	US dollar
Panama	Panama City	balboa
Papua New Guinea	Port Moresby	kina
Paraguay	Asunción	guaraní
Peru	Lima	new sol
Philippines	Manila	Philippine peso
Poland	Warsaw	zloty
Portugal	Lisbon	euro
Puerto Rico	San Juan	US dollar
Qatar	Doha	Qatar riyal
Réunion	Saint-Denis	euro
Romania	Bucharest	leu
Russia	Moscow	rouble
Saudi Arabia	Riyadh	Saudi riyal

COUNTRY	CAPITAL	CURRENCY
Seychelles	Victoria	Seychelles rupee
Singapore	Singapore	Singapore dollar
Slovakia	Bratislava	Slovak koruna
Slovenia	Ljubljana	tolar
South Africa	Pretoria	rand
South Korea	Seoul	won
Spain	Madrid	euro
Sri Lanka	Colombo	Sri Lankan rupee
St Kitts and Nevis	Basseterre	East Caribbean dollar
St Lucia	Castries	East Caribbean dollar
Sudan	Khartoum	Sudanese dinar
Sweden	Stockholm	Swedish krona
Switzerland	Bern	Swiss franc
Syria	Damascus	Syrian pound
Taiwan	Taipei	New Taiwan dollar
Tanzania	Dodoma	Tanzanian shilling
Thailand	Bangkok	baht
Trinidad and Tobago	Port of Spain	Trinidad and Tobago dollar
Tunisia	Tunis	Tunisian dinar
Turkey	Ankara	Turkish lira
Turks and Caicos Islands	Cockburn Town	US dollar
Uganda	Kampala	new Uganda shilling
Ukraine	Kiev	hryvnia
United Arab Emirates	Abu Dhabi	UAE dirham
United Kingdom	London	UK pound
United States	Washington DC	US dollar
Uruguay	Montevideo	Uruguayan peso
US Virgin Islands	Charlotte Amalie	US dollar
Uzbekistan	Toshkent	som
Venezuela	Caracas	bolívar
Vietnam	Hanoi	dòng
Yugoslavia	Belgrade	new dinar
Zambia	Lusaka	kwacha
Zimbabwe	Harare	Zimbabwe dollar

Note: The countries referred to in this and the following tables have been selected as top business centres on the criteria of their GNI per capita and their GNI.

Stock Exchanges

COUNTRY	CITY/CITIES	STOCK EXCHANGE
Algeria	Algiers	Algiers Stock Exchange
Argentina	Buenos Aires	Bolsa de Comercio de Buenos Aires
Australia	Sydney Brisbane Perth Melbourne Adelaide Hobart	Australian Stock Exchange (ASX)
Austria	Vienna	Vienna Stock Exchange
Bahamas	Nassau	Bahamas Stock Exchange
Bahrain	Manama	Bahrain Stock Exchange
Bangladesh	Dhaka	Dhaka Stock Exchange (DSE)
Barbados	St Michael	Barbados Stock Exchange
Belarus	Minsk	Belarus Stock Exchange
Belgium	Brussels	Euronext Brussels
Bermuda	Hamilton	Bermuda Stock Exchange (BSX)
Bolivia	La Paz	Bolivian Stock Exchange
Botswana	Gabarone	Botswana Stock Exchange
Brazil	Rio de Janeiro	Rio de Janeiro Stock Exchange
Brazil	Sao Paolo	Sao Paulo Stock Exchange
Brunei	see Singapore	
Bulgaria	Sofia	Bulgarian Stock Exchange
Canada	Montreal	Montreal Stock Exchange (Mx)
Canada	Toronto	Toronto Stock Exchange (TSE)
Canada	Winnipeg	Winnpeg Stock Exchange (WSE)
Cayman Islands	Grand Cayman	Cayman Islands Stock Exchange
Channel Islands	Guernsey	Channel Islands Stock Exchange
Chile	Santiago	Santiago Stock Exchange
China	Shanghai	Chinese Stock Exchange
Colombia	Bogota	Columbian Stock Exchange
Costa Rica	San José	Costa Rican Stock Exchange
Cote d'Ivoire	Abidjan	Abidjan Stock Exchange
Croatia	Zagreb	Zagreb Stock Exchange
Cyprus	Nicosia	Cyprus Stock Exchange (CSE)
Czech Republic	Prague	Prague Stock Exchange
Denmark	Copenhagen	Copenhagen Stock Exchange (KFX)
Ecuador	Guayaquil	Guayaquil Stock Exchange
Ecuador	Quito	Quito Stock Exchange
Egypt	Cairo	Cairo and Alexandria Stock Exchange

COUNTRY	CITY/CITIES	STOCK EXCHANGE
El Salvador	San Salvador	San Salvador Stock Exchange
Estonia	Tallin	Tallinn Stock Exchange (TSE)
Faeroe Islands		see Denmark
Finland	Helsinki	(Helsinki Stock Exchange) HEX
France	Paris	Euronext Paris
Georgia	Tblisi	Georgian Stock Exchange
Germany	Frankfurt am Main	Deutsche Börse
Ghana	Accra	Ghana Stock Exchange
Greece	Athens	Athens Stock Exchange
Greenland		see Denmarki
Guadeloupe		see France
Guam		see USA (Pacific Exchange)
Hong Kong	Hong Kong	Stock Exchange of Hong Kong (HKEx)
Hungary	Budapest	Budapest Stock Exchange (Fornax)
Iceland	Reykjavik	Iceland Stock Exchange (ISE)
India	Mumbai	National Stock Exchange (NSE India)
Indonesia	Jakarta	Jakarta Stock Exchange (JSX)
Iran	Tehran	Tehran Stock Exchange (TSE)
Iraq	Baghdad	Baghdad Stock Exchange
Ireland	Dublin	Irish Stock Exchange
Israel	Tel-Aviv	Tel-Aviv Stock Exchange (TASE)
Italy	Milan	Borsa Italiana
Jamaica	Kingston	Jamaica Stock Exchange (JSE)
Japan	Tokyo	Tokyo Stock Exchange (TSE)
Jordan	Amman	Amman Stock Exchange
Kazakhstan	Astana	Kazakhstan Stock Exchange
Kenya	Nairobi	Nairobi Stock Exchange
Kuwait	Kuwait City	Kuwait Stock Exchange
Latvia	Riga	Riga Stock Exchange
Lebanon	Beirut	Beirut Stock Exchange (BSE)
Lithuania	Vilnius	National Stock Exchange of Lithuania (NSEL)
Luxembourg	Luxembourg City	Luxembourg Stock Exchange
Malaysia	Kuala Lumpur	Kuala Lumpur Stock Exchange (KLSE)
Malta	Valletta	Malta Stock Exchange
Mauritius	Port Louis	Mauritius Stock Exchange
Mexico	Mexico City	Bolsa Mexicano de Valores (BMV)

COUNTRY	CITY/CITIES CAPITAL	STOCK EXCHANGE	CURRENCY	COUNTRY	CITY/CITIES	STOCK EXCHANGE
Morocco	Casablanca	Casablanca Stock Exchange		Taiwan	Taipei	Taiwan Stock Exchange
Mozambique	Maputo	Bolsa de Valores de Mozambique		Tanzania	Dar es Salaam	Tanzanian Stock Exchange
Namibia	Windhoek	Namibian Stock Exchange (NSE)		Thailand	Bangkok	Stock Exchange of Thailand (SET)
New Zealand	Wellington	New Zealand Stock Exchange (NZSE)		The Netherlands	Amsterdam	Euronext Amsterdam
Nicaragua	Managua	Bolsa de Valores de Nicaragua (BVDN)		Trinidad Tobago	Port of Spain	Trinidad and Tobago Stock and Exchange
Nigeria	Lagos	Nigerian Stock Exchange (NSE)		Tunisia	Tunis	Tunis Stock Exchange (BVMT)
				Turkey	Istanbul	Istanbul Stock Exchange (ISE)
Norway	Oslo	Oslo Stock Exchange		Uganda	Kampala	Ugandan Stock Exchange
Pakistan	Karachi	Karachi Stock Exchange (KSE)		Ukraine	Kiev	Ukrainian Stock Exchange
Papua New Guinea	Port Moresby	Papua New Guinea Stock Exchange		United Arab Emirates	Abu Dhabi	Abu Dhabi Securities Market
Peru	Lima	Bolsa de Valores de Lima (BVL)		United Kingdom	London	Euronext LIFFE
Philippines	Manila	Philippines Stock Exchange		United Kingdom	London	London Stock Exchange (LSE)
Poland	Warsaw	Warsaw Stock Exchange (GPW)		United Kingdom	London	FTSE International
Portugal	Lisbon	Euronext Lisbon		United Kingdom	London	London Metal Exchange (LME)
Qatar	Doha	Qatar Stock Exchange		Uruguay	Montevideo	Bolsa de Valores Uruguay
Romania	Bucharest	Bucharest Stock Exchange		USA	Chicago	Chicago Board Options Exchange (CBOE)
Russia	Moscow	Russian Stock Exchange (INDX)		USA	New York	New York Stock Exchange (NYSE)
Saudi Arabia	Riyadh	Saudi Arabian Stock Market		USA	Rockville, Trumbull, Washington DC	NASDAQ
Singapore	Singapore	Singapore Stock Exchange (SGX)		USA	San Francisco	Pacific Exchange PCX
Slovakia	Bratislava	Bratislava Stock Exchange		USA	New York	American Stock Exchange (AMEX)
Slovenia	Ljubljana	Ljbliana Stock Exchange (LjSE)		Uzebekistan	Taskent	Uzbekistan Stock Exchange
South Africa	Johannesburg	JSE Securities Exchange		Venezuela	Caracas	Caracas Stock Exchange
South Korea	Seoul	Korea Stock Exchange		Vietnam	Ho Chi Minh City	Vietnam Stock Exchange
Spain	Barcelona	Bolsa de Barcelona (BCN)		Yugoslavia	Belgrade	Belgrade Stock Exchange
Spain	Madrid	Bolsa de Madrid		Zambia	Lusaka	Lusaka Stock Exchange
Spain	Madrid	Bolsa de Madrid		Zimbabwe	Harare	Zimbabwe Stock Exchange
Sri Lanka	Colombo	Colombo Stock Exchange (CSE)				
Sudan	Khartoum	Sudan Stock Exchange				
Sweden	Stockholm	Stockholm Stock Exchange				
Switzerland	Geneva	Geneva Stock Exchange (SWX)				

National Income and Growth

	GNI ($ MILLION) 2000	GNI PER CAPITA ($) 2000	GDP GROWTH (% p.a.) 1990–2000		GNI ($ MILLION) 2000	GNI PER CAPITA ($) 2000	GDP GROWTH (% p.a.) 1990–2000
United States	9,601,505	34,100	3.5	Tunisia	20,057	2,100	4.7
Japan	4,519,067	35,620	1.3	Uruguay	20,010	6,000	3.4
Germany	2,063,734	25,120	1.5	Slovenia	19,979	10,050	2.7
United Kingdom	1,459,500	24,430	2.5	Slovakia	19,969	3,700	2.1
France	1,438,293	24,090	1.7	Guatemala	19,164	1,680	4.1
Italy	1,163,211	20,160	1.6	Kazakhstan	18,773	1,260	−4.1
China	1,062,919	840	10.3	Luxembourg	18,439	42,060	–
Canada	649,829	21,130	2.9	Dominican Republic	17,847	2,130	6.0
Brazil	610,058	3,580	2.9	Lebanon	17,355	4,010	6.0
Spain	595,255	15,080	2.5	Sri Lanka	16,408	850	5.3
Mexico	497,025	5,070	3.1	Ecuador	15,256	1,210	1.8
India	454,800	450	6.0	Syria	15,146	940	5.8
South Korea	421,069	8,910	5.7	Costa Rica	14,510	3,810	5.3
Netherlands	397,544	24,970	2.8	El Salvador	12,569	2,000	4.7
Australia	388,252	20,240	4.1	Bulgaria	12,391	1,520	−2.1
Argentina	276,228	7,460	4.3	Lithuania	10,809	2,930	−3.1
Switzerland	273,829	38,140	0.8	Kenya	10,610	350	2.1
Belgium	251,583	24,540	2.0	Yugoslavia	10,028	940	0.6
Russia	241,027	1,660	−4.8	Sudan	9,599	310	8.1
Sweden	240,707	27,140	1.9	Côte d'Ivoire	9,591	600	3.5
Austria	204,525	25,220	2.1	Cyprus	9,361	12,370	–
Turkey	202,131	3,100	3.7	Panama	9,308	3,260	4.1
Hong Kong	176,157	25,920	4.0	Tanzania	9,013	270	2.9
Denmark	172,238	32,280	2.5	Uzbekistan	8,843	360	−0.5
Poland	161,832	4,190	4.6	Cameroon	8,644	580	1.7
Norway	155,064	34,530	3.6	Iceland	8,540	30,390	–
Saudi Arabia	149,932	7,230	1.5	Jordan	8,360	1,710	5.0
Finland	130,106	25,130	2.8	Bolivia	8,206	990	4.0
South Africa	129,171	3,020	2.0	Paraguay	7,933	1,440	2.2
Greece	126,269	11,960	2.1	Latvia	6,925	2,920	−3.4
Thailand	121,602	2,000	4.2	Jamaica	6,883	2,610	0.5
Indonesia	119,871	570	4.2	Ethiopia	6,737	100	4.7
Portugal	111,291	11,120	2.7	Uganda	6,699	300	7.0
Iran	106,707	1,680	3.5	Ghana	6,594	340	4.3
Israel	104,128	16,710	5.1	Trinidad and Tobago	6,415	4,930	3.0
Venezuela	104,065	4,310	1.6	Macao	6,385	14,580	–
Singapore	99,404	24,740	7.8	Zimbabwe	5,851	460	2.5
Egypt	95,380	1,490	4.6	Botswana	5,280	3,300	4.7
Ireland	85,979	22,660	7.3	Estonia	4,894	3,580	−0.5
Colombia	85,279	2,020	3.0	Bahamas	4,533	14,960	–
Philippines	78,778	1,040	3.3	Mauritius	4,449	3,750	5.3
Malaysia	78,727	3,380	7.0	French Polynesia	4,064	17,290	–
Chile	69,850	4,590	6.8	Gabon	3,928	3,190	2.8
Pakistan	61,022	440	3.7	Angola	3,847	290	1.3
Czech Republic	53,925	5,250	0.9	Mozambique	3,746	210	6.4
Peru	53,392	2,080	4.7	Papua New Guinea	3,607	700	4.0
New Zealand	49,750	12,990	3.0	Namibia	3,569	2,030	4.1
Algeria	47,897	1,580	1.9	Malta	3,559	9,120	–
Bangladesh	47,864	370	4.8	New Caledonia	3,203	15,060	–
Hungary	47,249	4,710	1.5	Georgia	3,183	630	−13.0
Romania	37,380	1,670	−0.7	Zambia	3,026	300	0.5
Kuwait	35,771	18,030	3.2	Barbados	2,469	9,250	–
Ukraine	34,565	700	−9.3	Belize	746	3,110	–
Morocco	33,940	1,180	2.3	Antigua and Barbuda	642	9,440	–
Nigeria	32,705	260	2.4	St Lucia	642	4,120	–
Vietnam	30,439	390	7.9	Seychelles	573	7,050	–
Belarus	28,735	2,870	−1.6	Grenada	370	3,770	–
Croatia	20,240	4,620	0.6	St Kitts and Nevis	269	6,570	–

Highest GNI Per Capita

	GNI PER CAPITA ($) 2000		GNI PER CAPITA ($) 2000
Luxembourg	42,060	Malaysia	3,380
Switzerland	38,140	Botswana	3,300
Japan	35,620	Panama	3,260
Norway	34,530	Gabon	3,190
United States	34,100	Belize	3,110
Denmark	32,280	Turkey	3,100
Iceland	30,390	South Africa	3,020
Sweden	27,140	Lithuania	2,930
Hong Kong	25,920	Latvia	2,920
Austria	25,220	Belarus	2,870
Finland	25,130	Jamaica	2,610
Germany	25,120	Dominican Republic	2,130
Netherlands	24,970	Tunisia	2,100
Singapore	24,740	Peru	2,080
Belgium	24,540	Namibia	2,030
United Kingdom	24,430	Colombia	2,020
France	24,090	El Salvador	2,000
Ireland	22,660	Thailand	2,000
Canada	21,130	Jordan	1,710
Australia	20,240	Guatemala	1,680
Italy	20,160	Iran	1,680
Kuwait	18,030	Romania	1,670
French Polynesia	17,290	Russia	1,660
Israel	16,710	Algeria	1,580
Spain	15,080	Bulgaria	1,520
New Caledonia	15,060	Egypt	1,490
Bahamas	14,960	Paraguay	1,440
Macao	14,580	Kazakhstan	1,260
New Zealand	12,990	Ecuador	1,210
Cyprus	12,370	Morocco	1,180
Greece	11,960	Philippines	1,040
Portugal	11,120	Bolivia	990
Slovenia	10,050	Syria	940
Antigua and Barbuda	9,440	Yugoslavia	940
Barbados	9,250	Sri Lanka	850
Malta	9,120	China	840
South Korea	8,910	Papua New Guinea	700
Argentina	7,460	Ukraine	700
Saudi Arabia	7,230	Georgia	630
Seychelles	7,050	Côte d'Ivoire	600
St Kitts and Nevis	6,570	Cameroon	580
Uruguay	6,000	Indonesia	570
Czech Republic	5,250	Zimbabwe	460
Mexico	5,070	India	450
Trinidad and Tobago	4,930	Pakistan	440
Hungary	4,710	Vietnam	390
Croatia	4,620	Bangladesh	370
Chile	4,590	Uzbekistan	360
Venezuela	4,310	Kenya	350
Poland	4,190	Ghana	340
St Lucia	4,120	Sudan	310
Lebanon	4,010	Uganda	300
Costa Rica	3,810	Zambia	300
Grenada	3,770	Angola	290
Mauritius	3,750	Tanzania	270
Slovakia	3,700	Nigeria	260
Brazil	3,580	Mozambique	210
Estonia	3,580	Ethiopia	100

Lowest GNI Per Capita

	GNI PER CAPITA ($) 2000		GNI PER CAPITA ($) 2000
Ethiopia	100	Brazil	3,580
Mozambique	210	Estonia	3,580
Nigeria	260	Slovakia	3,700
Tanzania	270	Mauritius	3,750
Angola	290	Grenada	3,770
Uganda	300	Costa Rica	3,810
Zambia	300	Lebanon	4,010
Sudan	310	St Lucia	4,120
Ghana	340	Poland	4,190
Kenya	350	Venezuela	4,310
Uzbekistan	360	Chile	4,590
Bangladesh	370	Croatia	4,620
Vietnam	390	Hungary	4,710
Pakistan	440	Trinidad and Tobago	4,930
India	450	Mexico	5,070
Zimbabwe	460	Czech Republic	5,250
Indonesia	570	Uruguay	6,000
Cameroon	580	St Kitts and Nevis	6,570
Côte d'Ivoire	600	Seychelles	7,050
Georgia	630	Saudi Arabia	7,230
Papua New Guinea	700	Argentina	7,460
Ukraine	700	South Korea	8,910
China	840	Malta	9,120
Sri Lanka	850	Barbados	9,250
Syria	940	Antigua and Barbuda	9,440
Yugoslavia	940	Slovenia	10,050
Bolivia	990	Portugal	11,120
Philippines	1,040	Greece	11,960
Morocco	1,180	Cyprus	12,370
Ecuador	1,210	New Zealand	12,990
Kazakhstan	1,260	Macao	14,580
Paraguay	1,440	Bahamas	14,960
Egypt	1,490	New Caledonia	15,060
Bulgaria	1,520	Spain	15,080
Algeria	1,580	Israel	16,710
Russia	1,660	French Polynesia	17,290
Romania	1,670	Kuwait	18,030
Guatemala	1,680	Italy	20,160
Iran	1,680	Australia	20,240
Jordan	1,710	Canada	21,130
El Salvador	2,000	Ireland	22,660
Thailand	2,000	France	24,090
Colombia	2,020	United Kingdom	24,430
Namibia	2,030	Belgium	24,540
Peru	2,080	Singapore	24,740
Tunisia	2,100	Netherlands	24,970
Dominican Republic	2,130	Germany	25,120
Jamaica	2,610	Finland	25,130
Belarus	2,870	Austria	25,220
Latvia	2,920	Hong Kong	25,920
Lithuania	2,930	Sweden	27,140
South Africa	3,020	Iceland	30,390
Turkey	3,100	Denmark	32,280
Belize	3,110	United States	34,100
Gabon	3,190	Norway	34,530
Panama	3,260	Japan	35,620
Botswana	3,300	Switzerland	38,140
Malaysia	3,380	Luxembourg	42,060

Highest GDP Growth 1990–2000

	GDP GROWTH (% p.a.) 1990–2000		GDP GROWTH (% p.a.) 1990–2000
China	10.3	Finland	2.8
Sudan	8.1	Gabon	2.8
Vietnam	7.9	Netherlands	2.8
Singapore	7.8	Portugal	2.7
Ireland	7.3	Slovenia	2.7
Malaysia	7.0	Denmark	2.5
Uganda	7.0	Spain	2.5
Chile	6.8	United Kingdom	2.5
Mozambique	6.4	Zimbabwe	2.5
Dominican Republic	6.0	Nigeria	2.4
India	6.0	Morocco	2.3
Lebanon	6.0	Paraguay	2.2
Oman	5.9	Austria	2.1
Syria	5.8	Greece	2.1
South Korea	5.7	Kenya	2.1
Costa Rica	5.3	Slovakia	2.1
Mauritius	5.3	Belgium	2.0
Sri Lanka	5.3	South Africa	2.0
Israel	5.1	Algeria	1.9
Jordan	5.0	Sweden	1.9
Bangladesh	4.8	Ecuador	1.8
Botswana	4.7	Cameroon	1.7
El Salvador	4.7	France	1.7
Ethiopia	4.7	Italy	1.6
Peru	4.7	Venezuela	1.6
Tunisia	4.7	Germany	1.5
Egypt	4.6	Hungary	1.5
Poland	4.6	Saudi Arabia	1.5
Argentina	4.3	Angola	1.3
Ghana	4.3	Japan	1.3
Cuba	4.2	Czech Republic	0.9
Indonesia	4.2	Switzerland	0.8
Thailand	4.2	Croatia	0.6
Australia	4.1	Yugoslavia	0.6
Guatemala	4.1	Jamaica	0.5
Namibia	4.1	Zambia	0.5
Panama	4.1	Estonia	-0.5
Bolivia	4.0	Uzbekistan	-0.5
Hong Kong	4.0	Romania	-0.7
Papua New Guinea	4.0	Belarus	-1.6
Pakistan	3.7	Bulgaria	-2.1
Turkey	3.7	Lithuania	-3.1
Norway	3.6	Latvia	-3.4
Côte d'Ivoire	3.5	Kazakhstan	-4.1
Iran	3.5	Russia	-4.8
United States	3.5	Ukraine	-9.3
Uruguay	3.4	Georgia	-13.0
Philippines	3.3		
Kuwait	3.2		
Mexico	3.1		
Puerto Rico	3.1		
Colombia	3.0		
New Zealand	3.0		
Trinidad and Tobago	3.0		
Brazil	2.9		
Canada	2.9		
Tanzania	2.9		
United Arab Emirates	2.9		

Lowest GDP Growth 1990–2000

	GDP GROWTH (% p.a.) 1990–2000		GDP GROWTH (% p.a.) 1990–2000
Georgia	-13.0	Uruguay	3.4
Ukraine	-9.3	Côte d'Ivoire	3.5
Russia	-4.8	Iran	3.5
Kazakhstan	-4.1	United States	3.5
Latvia	-3.4	Norway	3.6
Lithuania	-3.1	Pakistan	3.7
Bulgaria	-2.1	Turkey	3.7
Belarus	-1.6	Bolivia	4.0
Romania	-0.7	Hong Kong	4.0
Estonia	-0.5	Papua New Guinea	4.0
Uzbekistan	-0.5	Australia	4.1
Jamaica	0.5	Guatemala	4.1
Zambia	0.5	Namibia	4.1
Croatia	0.6	Panama	4.1
Yugoslavia	0.6	Cuba	4.2
Switzerland	0.8	Indonesia	4.2
Czech Republic	0.9	Thailand	4.2
Angola	1.3	Argentina	4.3
Japan	1.3	Ghana	4.3
Germany	1.5	Egypt	4.6
Hungary	1.5	Poland	4.6
Saudi Arabia	1.5	Botswana	4.7
Italy	1.6	El Salvador	4.7
Venezuela	1.6	Ethiopia	4.7
Cameroon	1.7	Peru	4.7
France	1.7	Tunisia	4.7
Ecuador	1.8	Bangladesh	4.8
Algeria	1.9	Jordan	5.0
Sweden	1.9	Israel	5.1
Belgium	2.0	Costa Rica	5.3
South Africa	2.0	Mauritius	5.3
Austria	2.1	Sri Lanka	5.3
Greece	2.1	South Korea	5.7
Kenya	2.1	Syria	5.8
Slovakia	2.1	Oman	5.9
Paraguay	2.2	Dominican Republic	6.0
Morocco	2.3	India	6.0
Nigeria	2.4	Lebanon	6.0
Denmark	2.5	Mozambique	6.4
Spain	2.5	Chile	6.8
United Kingdom	2.5	Malaysia	7.0
Zimbabwe	2.5	Uganda	7.0
Portugal	2.7	Ireland	7.3
Slovenia	2.7	Singapore	7.8
Finland	2.8	Vietnam	7.9
Gabon	2.8	Sudan	8.1
Netherlands	2.8	China	10.3
Brazil	2.9		
Canada	2.9		
Tanzania	2.9		
United Arab Emirates	2.9		
Colombia	3.0		
New Zealand	3.0		
Trinidad and Tobago	3.0		
Mexico	3.1		
Puerto Rico	3.1		
Kuwait	3.2		
Philippines	3.3		

Growth of Output 1990-2000

	AGRICULTURE (% p.a.) 1990-2000	INDUSTRY (% p.a.) 1990-2000	MANUFACTURING (% p.a.) 1990-2000	SERVICES (% p.a.) 1990-2000		AGRICULTURE (% p.a.) 1990-2000	INDUSTRY (% p.a.) 1990-2000	MANUFACTURING (% p.a.) 1990-2000	SERVICES (% p.a.) 1990-2000
Algeria	3.6	1.8	-2.1	1.9	Lebanon	1.8	-1.6	-4.3	4.1
Angola	-1.5	3.7	-0.4	-2.0	Lithuania	-1.1	-7.0	-8.5	-0.3
Argentina	3.4	3.8	2.8	4.5	Malaysia	0.3	8.6	9.8	7.2
Australia	3.1	3.2	2.4	4.5	Mauritius	-0.9	5.5	5.6	6.4
Austria	4.4	2.5	2.3	1.8	Mexico	1.8	3.8	4.4	2.9
Bangladesh	2.9	7.3	7.2	4.5	Morocco	-0.9	3.2	2.7	2.8
Belarus	-4.1	-1.9	-0.8	-0.5	Mozambique	5.5	14.0	17.6	1.7
Belgium	3.7	1.8	–	1.8	Namibia	4.1	2.3	2.7	4.6
Bolivia	3.3	4.0	–	4.3	Netherlands	1.6	1.6	–	3.1
Botswana	0.8	2.9	4.1	6.9	New Zealand	2.7	2.4	–	3.7
Brazil	3.2	2.6	2.1	3.0	Nigeria	3.5	1.0	1.2	2.9
Bulgaria	0.4	-3.7	–	-1.3	Norway	2.4	3.9	2.3	3.4
Cameroon	5.6	-0.8	1.4	0.2	Pakistan	4.4	3.9	3.5	4.4
Canada	1.1	2.6	3.8	2.6	Panama	2.0	5.4	2.8	4.0
Chile	1.5	6.0	4.6	5.6	Papua New Guinea	3.7	5.5	5.6	3.0
China	4.1	13.7	13.4	9.0	Paraguay	2.5	3.2	0.7	1.6
Colombia	-2.2	1.7	-2.3	4.3	Peru	5.8	5.4	3.8	4.0
Costa Rica	4.1	6.2	6.7	4.7	Philippines	1.6	3.3	3.0	4.1
Côte d'Ivoire	3.6	5.1	3.8	2.6	Poland	-0.2	4.2	–	4.1
Croatia	-2.0	-2.5	-3.3	0.9	Portugal	-0.3	3.2	–	2.3
Cuba	5.2	6.6	6.3	2.5	Romania	-0.6	-0.8	-2.8	-0.5
Czech Republic	3.3	-0.8	–	1.8	Russia	-6.0	-7.6	–	-1.0
Denmark	2.9	2.0	2.1	2.6	Saudi Arabia	0.7	1.5	2.7	2.0
Dominican Republic	3.7	7.1	4.9	5.9	Singapore	-1.6	7.9	7.1	7.8
Ecuador	1.7	2.7	2.1	1.3	Slovakia	1.2	-2.7	4.1	6.5
Egypt	3.1	4.9	6.3	4.5	Slovenia	-0.1	2.9	4.0	3.9
El Salvador	1.3	5.3	5.3	5.4	South Africa	0.6	1.0	1.2	2.6
Estonia	-3.1	-3.2	2.5	1.8	South Korea	2.0	6.3	7.5	5.7
Ethiopia	2.1	6.1	6.6	7.1	Spain	-0.6	2.5	–	2.7
Finland	1.2	4.8	5.8	2.3	Sri Lanka	1.9	7.0	8.1	6.0
France	2.0	1.2	2.1	1.9	Sudan	11.3	7.7	4.0	6.3
Gabon	-1.4	2.5	0.6	3.9	Sweden	0.0	3.4	–	1.7
Georgia	1.7	5.1	3.2	15.6	Syria	5.3	9.9	10.8	4.6
Germany	1.7	-0.1	-0.4	2.4	Tanzania	3.2	3.1	2.7	2.7
Ghana	3.4	2.6	-3.3	5.7	Thailand	2.1	5.3	6.4	3.7
Greece	0.5	1.1	–	2.4	Trinidad and Tobago	1.9	3.4	5.9	2.7
Guatemala	2.8	4.3	2.8	4.7	Tunisia	2.4	4.6	5.5	5.3
Hungary	-2.2	3.8	7.9	1.4	Turkey	1.4	4.1	4.8	3.7
India	3.0	6.4	7.0	8.0	Uganda	3.7	12.3	13.6	7.9
Indonesia	2.1	5.2	6.7	4.0	Ukraine	-5.8	-11.4	-11.2	-1.1
Iran	3.8	-3.8	4.7	9.2	United Kingdom	-0.2	1.3	–	3.2
Italy	1.6	1.2	1.5	1.7	Uruguay	2.8	1.1	-0.1	4.6
Jamaica	1.9	-0.5	-1.9	1.1	Uzbekistan	0.1	-3.2	–	0.3
Japan	-3.2	-0.4	0.5	2.5	Venezuela	1.4	2.9	0.9	0.4
Jordan	-2.0	4.7	5.4	5.0	Vietnam	4.8	12.1	–	7.7
Kazakhstan	-7.9	-9.0	–	2.8	Zambia	3.9	-4.0	1.2	2.6
Kenya	1.3	1.7	2.1	3.3	Zimbabwe	4.3	0.4	0.4	3.1
Latvia	-7.0	-8.4	-7.8	2.5					

Total External Debt

	TOTAL EXTERNAL DEBT (% OF GDP) 2000	TOTAL EXTERNAL DEBT ($ MILLION) 2000	DEBT PER CAPITA ($) 2000		TOTAL EXTERNAL DEBT (% OF GDP) 2000	TOTAL EXTERNAL DEBT ($ MILLION) 2000	DEBT PER CAPITA ($) 2000
Zambia	197	5,730	550	Pakistan	52	32,091	227
Mozambique	190	7,135	390	Argentina	51	146,172	3,947
Yugoslavia	142	11,960	1,133	Grenada	50	207	2,202
Sudan	137	15,741	506	Slovakia	49	9,462	1,753
Côte d'Ivoire	130	12,138	758	Latvia	47	3,379	1,396
Ghana	128	6,657	345	Algeria	47	25,002	825
Syria	128	21,657	1,338	Malaysia	47	41,797	1,881
Angola	115	10,146	772	Lithuania	43	4,855	1,314
Cameroon	104	9,241	621	St Kitts and Nevis	43	140	3,684
Jordan	99	8,226	1,674	Czech Republic	42	21,299	2,074
Ecuador	98	13,281	1,050	Colombia	42	34,081	809
Indonesia	93	141,803	669	Oman	42	6,267	2,469
Ethiopia	86	5,481	87	Uruguay	42	8,196	2,456
Bulgaria	84	10,026	1,261	Paraguay	41	3,091	562
Nigeria	83	34,134	300	Vietnam	41	12,787	164
Tanzania	82	7,445	212	Dominica	40	108	1,521
Gabon	81	3,995	3,248	Poland	40	63,561	1,646
Panama	71	7,056	2,471	Brazil	40	237,953	1,396
Bolivia	70	5,762	692	Ukraine	38	12,166	245
Papua New Guinea	68	2,604	541	Kazakhstan	37	6,664	412
Philippines	67	50,063	662	Trinidad and Tobago	34	2,467	1,906
Belize	66	499	2,208	St Lucia	34	237	1,601
Estonia	66	3,280	2,355	Bangladesh	33	15,609	114
Thailand	65	79,675	1,269	Venezuela	32	38,196	1,580
Hungary	64	29,415	2,951	El Salvador	30	4,023	641
Russia	64	160,300	1,102	South Korea	29	134,417	2,876
Croatia	64	12,120	2,604	Egypt	29	28,957	427
Lebanon	63	10,311	2,949	Costa Rica	28	4,466	1,110
Kenya	61	6,295	205	Romania	28	10,224	456
Turkey	58	116,209	1,743	Seychelles	27	163	2,038
Jamaica	58	4,287	1,664	Mexico	26	150,288	1,520
Uzbekistan	57	4,340	174	Guatemala	24	4,622	406
Sri Lanka	56	9,066	479	Dominican Republic	23	4,598	549
Uganda	55	3,409	146	India	22	99,062	98
Tunisia	55	10,610	1,122	South Africa	20	24,861	574
Mauritius	54	2,374	2,045	China	14	149,800	117
Zimbabwe	54	4,002	317	Taiwan	13	40,000	1,796
Georgia	54	1,633	310	Botswana	8	413	268
Morocco	54	17,944	601	Iran	8	7,953	113
Peru	53	28,560	1,113	Belarus	3	851	84
Chile	52	36,978	2,431				

Largest Debtors

	TOTAL EXTERNAL DEBT ($ BILLION) 2000
Brazil	238.0
Russia	160.3
Mexico	150.3
China	149.8
Argentina	146.2
Indonesia	141.8
South Korea	134.4
Turkey	116.2
India	99.1
Thailand	79.7
Poland	63.6
Philippines	50.1
Malaysia	41.8
Taiwan	40.0
Venezuela	38.2
Chile	37.0
Nigeria	34.1
Colombia	34.1
Pakistan	32.1
Hungary	29.4
Egypt	29.0
Peru	28.6
Algeria	25.0
South Africa	24.9
Syria	21.7
Czech Republic	21.3
Morocco	17.9
Sudan	15.7
Bangladesh	15.6
Ecuador	13.3
Vietnam	12.8
Ukraine	12.2
Côte d'Ivoire	12.1
Croatia	12.1
Yugoslavia	12.0
Tunisia	10.6
Lebanon	10.3
Romania	10.2
Angola	10.1
Bulgaria	10.0
Slovakia	9.5
Cameroon	9.2
Sri Lanka	9.1
Jordan	8.2
Uruguay	8.2
Iran	8.0
Tanzania	7.4
Mozambique	7.1
Panama	7.1
Kazakhstan	6.7
Ghana	6.7
Kenya	6.3
Oman	6.3
Bolivia	5.8
Zambia	5.7
Ethiopia	5.5
Lithuania	4.9

	TOTAL EXTERNAL DEBT ($ BILLION) 2000
Guatemala	4.6
Dominican Republic	4.6
Costa Rica	4.5
Uzbekistan	4.3
Jamaica	4.3
El Salvador	4.0
Zimbabwe	4.0
Gabon	4.0
Uganda	3.4
Latvia	3.4
Estonia	3.3
Paraguay	3.1
Papua New Guinea	2.6
Trinidad and Tobago	2.5
Mauritius	2.4
Georgia	1.6
Belarus	0.9
Belize	0.5
Botswana	0.4
St Lucia	0.2
Grenada	0.2
Seychelles	0.2
St Kitts and Nevis	0.1
Dominica	0.1

Largest Per Capita External Debt

	DEBT PER CAPITA ($) 2000
Argentina	3,947
St Kitts and Nevis	3,684
Gabon	3,248
Hungary	2,951
Lebanon	2,949
South Korea	2,876
Croatia	2,604
Panama	2,471
Oman	2,469
Uruguay	2,456
Chile	2,431
Estonia	2,355
Belize	2,208
Grenada	2,202
Czech Republic	2,074
Mauritius	2,045
Seychelles	2,038
Trinidad and Tobago	1,906
Malaysia	1,881
Taiwan	1,796
Slovakia	1,753
Turkey	1,743
Jordan	1,674
Jamaica	1,664
Poland	1,646
St Lucia	1,601
Venezuela	1,580
Dominica	1,521
Mexico	1,520
Brazil	1,396
Latvia	1,396
Syria	1,338
Lithuania	1,314
Thailand	1,269
Bulgaria	1,261
Yugoslavia	1,133
Tunisia	1,122
Peru	1,113
Costa Rica	1,110
Russia	1,102
Ecuador	1,050
Algeria	825
Colombia	809
Angola	772
Côte d'Ivoire	758
Bolivia	692
Indonesia	669
Philippines	662
El Salvador	641
Cameroon	621
Morocco	601
South Africa	574
Paraguay	562
Zambia	550
Dominican Republic	549
Papua New Guinea	541
Sudan	506

	DEBT PER CAPITA ($) 2000
Sri Lanka	479
Romania	456
Egypt	427
Kazakhstan	412
Guatemala	406
Mozambique	390
Ghana	345
Zimbabwe	317
Georgia	310
Nigeria	300
Botswana	268
Ukraine	245
Pakistan	227
Tanzania	212
Kenya	205
Uzbekistan	174
Vietnam	164
Uganda	146
China	117
Bangladesh	114
Iran	113
India	98
Ethiopia	87
Belarus	84

Manufacturing Output and New Patent Applications

	MANUFACTURING OUTPUT (% OF GDP) 2000	GROWTH OF OUTPUT (% p.a.) 1990–2000	NEW PATENT APPLICATIONS 1999		MANUFACTURING OUTPUT (% OF GDP) 2000	GROWTH OF OUTPUT (% p.a.) 1990–2000	NEW PATENT APPLICATIONS 1999
Cuba	37	6.3	111	Netherlands	17	–	6,395
Yugoslavia	36	–	340	Sri Lanka	17	8.1	0
China	35	13.4	146	Uruguay	17	–0.1	27
Ukraine	34	–11.2	5,415	Chile	16	4.6	–
Malaysia	33	9.8	179	Estonia	16	2.5	14
Thailand	32	6.4	477	India	16	7.0	14
Belarus	31	–0.8	1,002	Iran	16	4.7	366
South Korea	31	7.5	56,214	Jordan	16	5.4	0
Ireland	28	–	1,226	New Zealand	16	–	1,650
Slovenia	28	4.0	292	United States	16	–	156,393
Romania	27	–2.8	1,069	Zimbabwe	16	0.4	1
Syria	27	10.8	–	Bangladesh	15	7.2	32
Indonesia	26	6.7	0	Pakistan	15	3.5	–
Singapore	26	7.1	374	Turkey	15	4.8	325
Taiwan	26	–	–	Colombia	14	–2.3	68
Finland	25	5.8	2,644	Latvia	14	–7.8	94
Hungary	25	7.9	787	Paraguay	14	0.7	–
Brazil	24	2.1	1,957	Peru	14	3.8	48
Costa Rica	24	6.7	0	Venezuela	14	0.9	201
Mauritius	24	5.6	3	Australia	13	2.4	9,537
Croatia	23	–3.3	267	Bolivia	13	–	–
El Salvador	23	5.3	–	Guatemala	13	2.8	7
Germany	23	–0.4	74,232	Jamaica	13	–1.9	–
Malta	23	–	–	Kenya	13	2.1	28
Philippines	23	3.0	144	Mozambique	13	17.6	–
Canada	22	3.8	5,197	United Arab Emirates	13	–	0
Japan	22	0.5	361,094	Zambia	13	1.2	5
Slovakia	22	4.1	222	Greece	12	–	72
Austria	21	2.3	3,075	Iceland	12	–	–
Italy	21	1.5	9,613	Norway	12	2.3	1,731
Lithuania	21	–8.5	86	Cameroon	11	1.4	–
Mexico	21	4.4	468	Cyprus	11	–	–
Poland	21	–	2,286	Namibia	11	2.7	–
Belgium	20	–	1,786	Lebanon	10	–4.3	–
Spain	20	–	3,394	Saudi Arabia	10	2.7	72
Côte d'Ivoire	19	3.8	–	Uzbekistan	10	–	769
Egypt	19	6.3	536	Ghana	9	–3.3	0
France	19	2.1	20,998	Papua New Guinea	9	5.6	–
Portugal	19	–	133	Sudan	9	4.0	2
South Africa	19	1.2	116	Uganda	9	13.6	0
Argentina	18	2.8	899	Algeria	8	–2.1	34
Kazakhstan	18	–	1,358	Panama	8	2.8	–
Morocco	18	2.7	0	Trinidad and Tobago	8	5.9	0
North Korea	18	–	0	Ethiopia	7	6.6	0
Tunisia	18	5.5	–	Georgia	7	3.2	273
United Kingdom	18	–	31,326	Tanzania	7	2.7	0
Vietnam	18	–	37	Hong Kong	6	–	42
Bulgaria	17	–	302	Botswana	5	4.1	0
Denmark	17	2.1	3,339	Gabon	4	0.6	–
Dominican Republic	17	4.9	–	Nigeria	4	1.2	–
Ecuador	17	2.1	15	Angola	3	–0.4	–

Fastest Growth of Manufacturing Output 1990–2000

	GROWTH OF OUTPUT (% p.a.) 1990–2000		GROWTH OF OUTPUT (% p.a.) 1990–2000
Mozambique	17.6	Nigeria	1.2
Uganda	13.6	South Africa	1.2
China	13.4	Zambia	1.2
Syria	10.8	Venezuela	0.9
Malaysia	9.8	Paraguay	0.7
Sri Lanka	8.1	Gabon	0.6
Hungary	7.9	Japan	0.5
South Korea	7.5	Zimbabwe	0.4
Bangladesh	7.2	Uruguay	-0.1
Singapore	7.1	Angola	-0.4
India	7.0	Germany	-0.4
Costa Rica	6.7	Belarus	-0.8
Indonesia	6.7	Jamaica	-1.9
Ethiopia	6.6	Algeria	-2.1
Thailand	6.4	Colombia	-2.3
Cuba	6.3	Romania	-2.8
Egypt	6.3	Croatia	-3.3
Trinidad and Tobago	5.9	Ghana	-3.3
Finland	5.8	Lebanon	-4.3
Mauritius	5.6	Latvia	-7.8
Papua New Guinea	5.6	Lithuania	-8.5
Tunisia	5.5	Ukraine	-11.2
Jordan	5.4		
El Salvador	5.3		
Dominican Republic	4.9		
Turkey	4.8		
Iran	4.7		
Chile	4.6		
Mexico	4.4		
Botswana	4.1		
Slovakia	4.1		
Slovenia	4.0		
Sudan	4.0		
Canada	3.8		
Côte d'Ivoire	3.8		
Peru	3.8		
Pakistan	3.5		
Georgia	3.2		
Philippines	3.0		
Argentina	2.8		
Guatemala	2.8		
Panama	2.8		
Morocco	2.7		
Namibia	2.7		
Saudi Arabia	2.7		
Tanzania	2.7		
Estonia	2.5		
Australia	2.4		
Austria	2.3		
Norway	2.3		
Brazil	2.1		
Denmark	2.1		
Ecuador	2.1		
France	2.1		
Kenya	2.1		
Italy	1.5		
Cameroon	1.4		

Most New Patent Applications Filed by Residents

	NEW PATENT APPLICATIONS 1999		NEW PATENT APPLICATIONS 1999
Japan	361,094	Hong Kong	42
United States	156,393	Vietnam	37
Germany	74,232	Algeria	34
South Korea	56,214	Bangladesh	32
United Kingdom	31,326	Kenya	28
France	20,998	Uruguay	27
Russia	20,131	Ecuador	15
Italy	9,613	Estonia	14
Australia	9,537	India	14
Sweden	9,122	Guatemala	7
Switzerland	6,412	Zambia	5
Netherlands	6,395	Mauritius	3
Ukraine	5,415	Sudan	2
Canada	5,197	Zimbabwe	1
Spain	3,394	Botswana	0
Denmark	3,339	Costa Rica	0
Austria	3,075	Ethiopia	0
Israel	2,728	Ghana	0
Finland	2,644	Indonesia	0
Poland	2,286	Jordan	0
Brazil	1,957	Morocco	0
Belgium	1,786	North Korea	0
Norway	1,731	Sri Lanka	0
New Zealand	1,650	Tanzania	0
Kazakhstan	1,358	Trinidad and Tobago	0
Ireland	1,226	Uganda	0
Romania	1,069	United Arab Emirates	0
Belarus	1,002		
Argentina	899	Source: World Intellectual
Hungary	787	Property Organisation
Uzbekistan	769		
Czech Republic	618		
Egypt	536		
Thailand	477		
Mexico	468		
Singapore	374		
Iran	366		
Yugoslavia	340		
Turkey	325		
Bulgaria	302		
Slovenia	292		
Georgia	273		
Croatia	267		
Slovakia	222		
Venezuela	201		
Malaysia	179		
China	146		
Philippines	144		
Portugal	133		
South Africa	116		
Cuba	111		
Latvia	94		
Lithuania	86		
Greece	72		
Saudi Arabia	72		
Colombia	68		
Peru	48		

Highest Passenger Car Ownership

Country	Passenger cars per 100 people, 2000*	Country	Passenger cars per 100 people, 2000*
Italy	54	Turkey	6
Germany	51	Hong Kong	6
Austria	50	Guatemala	5
Switzerland	49	Georgia	5
Australia	49	Jordan	5
New Zealand	48	Namibia	5
United States	48	Colombia	4
France	47	Ecuador	4
Canada	46	Jamaica	4
Belgium	45	Morocco	4
Sweden	44	Iraq	4
Slovenia	42	Botswana	3
Norway	41	El Salvador	3
Finland	40	Iran	3
Japan	40	Tunisia	3
Spain	39	Bolivia	3
Netherlands	38	Zimbabwe	3
United Kingdom	37	Dominican Republic	3
Denmark	35	Thailand	3
Czech Republic	34	Peru	3
Lithuania	33	Algeria	3
Estonia	33	Egypt	2
Kuwait	32	Gabon	2
Lebanon	31	Côte d'Ivoire	2
Portugal	31	Angola	2
Ireland	27	Zambia	2
Greece	25	Cuba	2
Poland	24	Sri Lanka	2
Hungary	24	Indonesia	1
Bulgaria	23	Paraguay	1
Puerto Rico	23	Kenya	1
Slovakia	23	Philippines	1
Israel	22	Sudan	1
Latvia	22	Syria	1
Yugoslavia	18	Nigeria	1
Malaysia	17	Cameroon	1
South Korea	17	Papua New Guinea	1
Libya	16	Ghana	1
Uruguay	16	India	1
Argentina	14	Pakistan	1
Belarus	14	China**	0
Romania	13	Uganda**	0
Russia	12	Ethiopia**	0
Ukraine	10	Tanzania**	0
Mexico	10	Bangladesh**	0
Oman	10	Mozambique**	0
Singapore	10		
Trinidad and Tobago	10		
South Africa	9		
Saudi Arabia	9		
Chile	9		
Costa Rica	9		
Panama	8		
United Arab Emirates	8		
Mauritius	7		
Venezuela	7		
Kazakhstan	7		

* data is for the most recent year available
** less than 0.5 passenger cars per 100 people

Source: International Road Federation

Highest TV Ownership

Country	TV sets per 100 people, 2000*	Country	TV sets per 100 people, 2000*
United States	85	Sudan	27
Denmark	81	Mauritius	27
Latvia	79	Saudi Arabia	26
Australia	74	Cuba	25
Japan	73	Chile	24
Canada	72	Kazakhstan	24
Finland	69	Costa Rica	23
Norway	67	Ecuador	22
United Kingdom	65	Paraguay	22
Portugal	63	El Salvador	20
France	63	Tunisia	20
Estonia	59	Jamaica	19
Spain	59	Panama	19
Germany	59	Egypt	19
Sweden	57	Venezuela	19
Oman	56	Vietnam	19
Switzerland	55	Malaysia	17
Belgium	54	Morocco	17
Netherlands	54	Iran	16
Austria	54	Indonesia	15
Uruguay	53	Peru	15
New Zealand	52	Philippines	14
Czech Republic	51	Libya	14
Italy	49	Zambia	13
Hong Kong	49	Pakistan	13
Greece	49	South Africa	13
Kuwait	49	Bolivia	12
Georgia	47	Ghana	12
Ukraine	46	Sri Lanka	11
Bulgaria	45	Algeria	11
Turkey	45	Dominican Republic	10
Hungary	44	Jordan	8
Lithuania	42	Iraq	8
Russia	42	India	8
Slovakia	41	Nigeria	7
Poland	40	Syria	7
Ireland	40	Guatemala	6
Romania	38	Côte d'Ivoire	6
Slovenia	37	North Korea	5
South Korea	36	Namibia	4
Brazil	34	Cameroon	3
Belarus	34	Zimbabwe	3
Trinidad and Tobago	34	Uganda	3
Israel	34	Botswana	3
Lebanon	34	Kenya	3
Puerto Rico	33	Tanzania	2
Gabon	33	Angola	2
Singapore	30	Papua New Guinea	2
Argentina	29	Bangladesh	1
China	29	Ethiopia	1
Croatia	29	Mozambique	1
United Arab Emirates	29		
Thailand	28		
Mexico	28		
Colombia	28		
Yugoslavia	28		
Uzbekistan	28		

Source: International Telecommunication Union

Total Credit with MasterCard and Visa

	CREDIT CARD TRANSACTIONS ($ BILLION) 2001	% OF WORLD TOTAL 2001
United States	1,081.89	52.6
United Kingdom	209.86	10.2
France	135.20	6.6
Canada	81.78	4.0
Japan	79.17	3.9
South Korea	67.31	3.3
Australia	44.88	2.2
Spain	32.08	1.6
Germany	22.73	1.1
Italy	21.95	1.1
Brazil	21.89	1.1
Taiwan	21.56	1.0
Israel	18.52	0.9
Hong Kong	16.98	0.8
Sweden	16.62	0.8
Norway	16.19	0.8
Mexico	14.76	0.7
Argentina	12.00	0.6
Denmark	11.35	0.6
China	11.32	0.6
Portugal	10.31	0.5
Switzerland	9.78	0.5
Turkey	9.58	0.5
South Africa	6.10	0.3
Netherlands	5.39	0.3
Rest of world (82 countries)	76.55	3.7
World total (107 countries)	2,055.76	100.0

Source: *The Nilson Report* (www.nilsonreport.com)

Retail Sales Growth for OECD Countries 1995–2001

	INDICES AT Q1 2002 (1995=100)		INDICES AT Q1 2002 (1995=100)
Ireland	152.0	Belgium	118.6
United States	148.0	Spain	118.5
Portugal	146.1	Czech Republic	115.5
Poland	144.9	Netherlands	115.0
South Korea	135.7	Austria	113.0
United Kingdom	131.7	Iceland	112.4
Greece	131.0	Denmark	109.0
Mexico	130.6	France	107.0
Canada	130.0	Italy	106.0
Finland	129.0	Switzerland	103.0
Sweden	128.0	Germany	98.0
Hungary	126.7	Japan	87.0
Australia	123.0		
Norway	121.0	Source: OECD	
New Zealand	119.0		

Billion-dollar Brands

BRAND	PRODUCT DESCRIPTION/SECTOR	GLOBAL SALES FOR 12 MONTHS ENDING Q1 2001 ($ BILLION)
Coca-Cola	Carbonated drink	15+
Marlboro	Tobacco	15+
Pepsi	Carbonated drink	5–15
Budweiser	Beer	3–5
Campbell's	Soups	3–6
Kellogg's	Cereals	3–7
Pampers	Diapers/nappies	3–8
Benson & Hedges	Tobacco	2–3
Camel	Tobacco	2–3
Danone	Yogurt	2–3
Fanta	Carbonated drinks	2–3
Friskies	Petfood	2–3
Gillette	Blades and razors	2–3
Huggies	Diapers/nappies	2–3
Nescafe	Coffee	2–3
Sprite	Carbonated drink	2–3
Tide	Detergent	2–3
Tropicana	Still drinks	2–3
Wrigley's	Chewing gum	2–3
Colgate	Toothpaste	1.5–2.0
Duracell	Batteries	1.5–2.0
Heineken	Beer	1.5–2.0
Kodak	Photography	1.5–2.0
L&M	Tobacco	1.5–2.0
Lay's	Snacks	1.5–2.0
Pedigree	Pet food	1.5–2.0
Always	Sanitary protection	1.0–1.5
Doritos	Snacks	1.0–1.5
Energizer	Batteries	1.0–1.5
Gatorade	Sports drinks	1.0–1.5
Guinness	Beer	1.0–1.5
Kinder	Chocolate	1.0–1.5
Kleenex	Tissues	1.0–1.5
L'Oréal	Beauty	1.0–1.5
Maxwell House	Coffee	1.0–1.5
Minute Maid	Still drinks	1.0–1.5
Nivea	Beauty	1.0–1.5
Pantene	Shampoo	1.0–1.5
Philadelphia	Cheese	1.0–1.5
Pringles	Snacks	1.0–1.5
Seven-Up	Carbonated drink	1.0–1.5
Tylenol	Pain remedies	1.0–1.5
Whiskas	Petfood	1.0–1.5

Source: ACNielsen

Distribution of Billionaires

	NO. OF BILLIONAIRES IN 2002	NO. OF BILLIONAIRES PER 10 MILLION PEOPLE IN 2002	TOTAL WORTH OF BILLIONAIRES ($ BILLION) 2002
Argentina	1	0.3	1.0
Australia	3	1.6	5.6
Austria	6	7.4	9.5
Belgium	4	3.9	7.6
Brazil	6	0.4	13.7
Canada	14	4.6	42.6
Chile	2	1.3	2.9
China	1	0.008	1.0
Colombia	1	0.2	1.1
Denmark	2	3.8	4.2
France	31	5.2	98.5
Germany	57	6.9	189.9
Greece	5	4.7	13.0
Hong Kong	11	16.5	39.4
Hungary	1	1.0	2.2
India	5	0.05	14.0
Indonesia	1	0.05	1.8
Ireland	1	2.6	1.3
Israel	3	5.0	6.3
Italy	19	3.3	40.7
Japan	25	2.0	59.2
Kuwait	1	5.2	5.7
Lebanon	1	2.9	4.0
Liechtenstein	2	606.1	5.7
Luxembourg	1	22.9	3.4
Malaysia	5	2.3	10.1
Mexico	12	1.2	31.6
Monaco	1	303.0	4.3
Netherlands	4	2.5	11.5
Norway	2	4.5	2.6
Philippines	4	0.5	5.3
Poland	1	0.3	2.9
Portugal	1	1.0	2.0
Russia	8	0.5	12.3
Saudi Arabia	8	3.9	41.3
Singapore	4	10.0	10.7
South Africa	2	0.5	4.4
South Korea	2	0.4	4.4
Spain	8	2.0	19.3
Sweden	8	9.0	30.2
Switzerland	19	26.5	57.3
Taiwan	5	2.2	14.1
Thailand	2	0.3	2.3
Turkey	6	0.9	14.4
United Arab Emirates	1	3.8	1.8
United Kingdom	29	4.9	59.4
United States	227	8.0	777.7
Venezuela	2	0.8	9.4
World	565	–	1,703.6

Sources: www.forbes.com (February 2002), *EuroBusiness magazine* (February 2002)

Most Billionaires

	NO. OF BILLIONAIRES IN 2002
United States	227
Germany	57
France	31
United Kingdom	29
Japan	25
Italy	19
Switzerland	19
Canada	14
Mexico	12
Hong Kong	11
Russia	8
Saudi Arabia	8
Spain	8
Sweden	8
Austria	6
Brazil	6
Turkey	6
Greece	5
India	5
Malaysia	5
Taiwan	5
Belgium	4
Netherlands	4
Philippines	4
Singapore	4
Australia	3
Israel	3
Chile	2
Denmark	2
Liechtenstein	2
Norway	2
South Africa	2
South Korea	2
Thailand	2
Venezuela	2
Argentina	1
China	1
Colombia	1
Hungary	1
Indonesia	1
Ireland	1
Kuwait	1
Lebanon	1
Luxembourg	1
Monaco	1
Poland	1
Portugal	1
United Arab Emirates	1
World	**565**

Highest Density of Billionaires

	NO. OF BILLIONAIRES PER 10 MILLION PEOPLE IN 2002
Liechtenstein	606.1
Monaco	303.0
Switzerland	26.5
Luxembourg	22.9
Hong Kong	16.5
Singapore	10.0
Sweden	9.0
United States	8.0
Austria	7.4
Germany	6.9
France	5.2
Kuwait	5.2
Israel	5.0
United Kingdom	4.9
Greece	4.7
Canada	4.6
Norway	4.5
Belgium	3.9
Saudi Arabia	3.9
United Arab Emirates	3.8
Denmark	3.8
Italy	3.3
Lebanon	2.9
Ireland	2.6
Netherlands	2.5
Malaysia	2.3
Taiwan	2.2
Spain	2.0
Japan	2.0
Australia	1.6
Chile	1.3
Mexico	1.2
Hungary	1.0
Portugal	1.0
Turkey	0.9
Venezuela	0.8
Russia	0.5
Philippines	0.5
South Africa	0.5
South Korea	0.4
Brazil	0.4
Thailand	0.3
Argentina	0.3
Poland	0.3
Colombia	0.2
India	0.05
Indonesia	0.05
China	0.008

Total Worth of Billionaires Per Country

	TOTAL WORTH OF BILLIONAIRES ($ BILLION) 2002
United States	777.7
Germany	189.9
France	98.5
United Kingdom	59.4
Japan	59.2
Switzerland	57.3
Canada	42.6
Saudi Arabia	41.3
Italy	40.7
Hong Kong	39.4
Mexico	31.6
Sweden	30.2
Spain	19.3
Turkey	14.4
Taiwan	14.1
India	14.0
Brazil	13.7
Greece	13.0
Russia	12.3
Netherlands	11.5
Singapore	10.7
Malaysia	10.1
Austria	9.5
Venezuela	9.4
Belgium	7.6
Israel	6.3
Kuwait	5.7
Liechtenstein	5.7
Australia	5.6
Philippines	5.3
South Africa	4.4
South Korea	4.4
Monaco	4.3
Denmark	4.2
Lebanon	4.0
Luxembourg	3.4
Chile	2.9
Poland	2.9
Norway	2.6
Thailand	2.3
Hungary	2.2
Portugal	2.0
Indonesia	1.8
United Arab Emirates	1.8
Ireland	1.3
Colombia	1.1
Argentina	1.0
China	1.0
World	**1,703.6**

Sources: www.forbes.com (February 2002), *EuroBusiness* magazine (February 2002)

Richest Person/Family Per Country

	RICHEST PERSON/FAMILY, AGE IN 2002	WORTH ($ BILLION)	SOURCE OF WEALTH
Argentina	Gregorio Perez Companc, 67	1.0	oil and gas
Australia	Kerry Packer, 64	2.5	media
Austria	Ferdinand A. Porsche, 66	2.2	automotive
Belgium	Baron Albert Frere, 76	2.7	scrap metal, investments
Brazil	Joseph and Moise Safra	4.0	banking and telecoms
Canada	Kenneth Thomson and family, 78	14.9	media
Chile	Eliodoro Matte and family, 56	1.5	paper
China	Liu Yongxing and Liu Yonghao, both 53	1.0	animal feeds, diversified
Colombia	Luis Carlos Sarmiento Angulo, 69	1.1	banking
Denmark	Maersk Mc-Kinney Møller, 88	2.3	shipping (A.P. Møller)
France	Liliane Bettencourt, 79	18.2	cosmetics (L'Oréal)
Germany	Theo Albrecht, 78	12.5	food retailing (Aldi Group)
Greece	Spiro Latsis, 55	4.8	shipping, banking (EFG Bank Group)
Hong Kong	Li Ka-shing, 73	10.0	diversified
Hungary	George Soros, 71	2.2	finance (Soros Fund Management)
India	Azim Premji, 56	6.4	IT/software (Wipro)
Indonesia	Rachman Halim and family, 54	1.8	tobacco
Ireland	Anthony O'Reilly, 65	1.3	media, diversified
Israel	Shari Arison Dorsman, 44	3.3	cruiseships, diversified
Italy	Silvio Berlusconi, 65	7.7	media (Fininvest)
Japan	Nobutada Saji and family, 56	8.6	beverages, diversified
Kuwait	Nasser al-Kharafi and family, 58	5.7	construction, diversified
Lebanon	Rafik al-Hariri and family, 58	4.0	construction, diversified
Liechtenstein	Prince Hans-Adam II, 56	4.4	investments (Liechtenstein Royal Family)
Luxembourg	Grand Duke Jean of Luxembourg, 80	3.3	investments (Luxembourg Royal Family)
Malaysia	Robert Kuok, 79	4.1	agriculture, diversified
Mexico	Carlos Slim Helú, 62	11.5	investments
Monaco	Lily Safra, 66	4.3	banking (Republic Bank)
Netherlands	Charlene de Carvalho, 47	3.8	beverages (Heineken)
Norway	Stein-Erik Hagen, 45	1.4	food retailing, diversified
Philippines	Lucio Tan, 67	1.7	tobacco, diversified
Poland	Jan Kulczyk, 52	2.9	diversified (Kulczyk Holdings)
Portugal	Antonio Champalimaud, 83	2.0	banking and insurance, diversified
Russia	Mikhail Khodorkovsky, 38	2.4	banking, commodities, energy (Yukos)
Saudi Arabia	Prince Alwaleed bin Talal al-Saud, 45	20.0	investments
Singapore	Ng Teng Fong, 73	3.1	real estate
South Africa	Nicky Oppenheimer and family, 56	3.3	mining (De Beers)
South Korea	Lee Kun, 60	2.5	electronics (Samsung)
Spain	Amancio Ortega, 66	7.8	fashion (Inditex), diversified
Sweden	Ingavar Kamprad, 75	7.2	retailing (Ikea)
Switzerland	Ernesto Bertarelli, 36	6.2	pharmaceuticals (Serono)
Taiwan	Tsai Wan-lin, 77	4.6	insurance
Thailand	Dhanin Chearavanont and family, 62	1.3	agriculture
Turkey	Mehmet Karamehmet and family, 48	4.0	telecoms (Turkcell)
United Arab Emirates	Abdul Aziz al-Ghurair, 48	1.8	banking (Mashreqbank), investments
United Kingdom	Duke of Westminster, 50	5.2	real estate (Grosvenor Estates)
United States	William Gates, 46	52.8	IT/software (Microsoft)
Venezuela	Gustavo Cisneros and family, 56	5.0	media

Chronological CV Example

MS. JOSEPHINE CATTERALL
5a, Hanton Street, London, SE13 1DF
Tel: (020) 8868 9854   Mobile: (07914) 248553   E-mail: jfcatterall@hotmail.com

OBJECTIVE:
To become a professional HR generalist manager with a leadership team role within a Blue-chip environment. Future positions to involve managing resourcing, development, and employee relations issues on pan-UK or global basis.

WORK HISTORY:

Jan 1999 – present GP International Trading and Shipping Company Ltd., Latin America
HR Organisational Development Advisor Latin America

To provide advice and support throughout Global Petroleum Products Latin America to identify, diagnose, and solve organisational effectiveness problems, and to establish a close working relationship with a disperse network of clients and change experts in order to provide advice that will increase the effectiveness of the clients organisation and at the same time produce alignment with the main elements of the LA Cultural Change Plan.

Achievements:
- Contributed to the formulation and implementation of the LA Cultural Change Plan, especially in areas related to: organisation design, development of leadership and change capabilities, engagement design and facilitation and measurement of organisational effectiveness.

- Designed and implemented change intervention for both large organisational units and small work groups by using internal and external resources.

- Co-ordinated and facilitated LA wide engagement events such as the LA Leadership Workshops and provide support to the CoBs in the design and implementation of their major engagement activities.

- Co-ordinated learning activities with a strong link to changing culture or related to collective & organisational development, such as: Change Management Programme, Coaching for Performance, and Creating Winning Teams. Provided change management support to cross business teams implementing new business process and to major cross LA change initiatives.

Dec 1996 – Oct 1998 GP International Trading and Shipping Company Ltd., London

Human Resources Policy Adviser
To provide professional advice on all HR policy matters including reward and recognition, employee relations, development, and resourcing, and to develop UK policy and implement policy changes within the business.

Achievements:
- Developed an Equal Opportunities policy and good practice guidance framework for GP Companies in the UK, which has enhanced its legislative compliance and understanding amongst staff and management. Revised the Career Break policy in conjunction with the policy committee

- Part of a Change Agent network responsible for implementing a new SAP HR system into the GP Group.

- Have advised the Line and HR colleagues on several employee relations issues including providing employment law advice on disciplinaries, grievances, and poor performance issues.

- Data Protection Focal Point for GP Trading (London) and GP Energy Trading Ltd, ensuring these companies' compliance with Data Protection legislation and handling all Subject Access Requests. Provide regular guidance to HR department on data handling.

May 1995 – Dec 1996 GP International Trading and Shipping Company Ltd., London

Human Resources Adviser: Marine, Shipping, and Aviation
To provide front-line, operational advice to 3 distinct entities of the Global Businesses group: Marine Products, Shipping, and Aviation.

Achievements:
- Coached the Line on how to managed disciplinaries, flexible working arrangements, Career Breaks and Poor performance processes.

- HR consultant to an external charitable body – the International Tanker Owners Pollution Federation (ITOPF) providing advice on the development of a fit-for-purpose remuneration strategy.

- Ran several internal and external recruitment processes through all stages from advert design and placement to candidate selection.

- Introduced competency-based interviewing skills for Line Managers.

- Designed and delivered Data Protection Act workshop for the HR department.

- GP Trading's London-based Policy adviser and representative on the UK Employment Policy Committee.

Sept 1993 – May 1995 GP U.K. Exploration and Production, Southampton

Human Resources Business Partner: Well Engineering, Merton Gas Terminal and Kirk C platform.
To provide business-focused advice on a range of issues, including the four main areas of HR (reward, development, employee relations, and resourcing) and specifically to help to manage a large-scale redundancy exercise.

Achievements:
- Part of an HR team responsible for delivering approximately 100 position reductions as part of a cost-reduction exercise.

- Staff Consultative Committee HR Representative and Secretary – delivered negotiating skills training and team-building workshops to Staff Reps to improve the quality of their participation.

- Led offshore consultation/awareness raising process on the Employment Relations Bill and the impact a successful union recognition claim would have on the employee relations environment.

EDUCATION/QUALIFICATIONS:
1999-2001   MSc in Employee Relations, University of Westminster, London
1996-1998   Graduate of the Chartered Institute of Personnel and Development
1994   Postgraduate Diploma in French, McGill University, Montreal, Canada
1990 – 1993   BA (Hons) Experimental Psychology. (Class IIi), University of Bristol
1982 – 1990   A' Levels: Biology (A), French (A), German (B), St Stephen's School, Ely, Cambs

Cover Letter Example

Ms. Jane Stevenson
Senior Personnel Officer
DataTech Ltd
Botley Road
Oxford
OX2 1ZZ

Adrianne Griffiths
20 Shakespeare Road
London
SE18 2PB

25 March 2003

Dear Ms Stevenson

I am very interested in the position of sales manager at DataTech Ltd as described in your advertisement of 20 March in the Guardian newspaper.

In my current position of deputy sales manager for Parker Smith Plc I have helped to increase our market share by 15% in the past year. I see from your website and annual report that DataTech have also increased their market share this year and are aiming to do the same in the next financial year, and I feel my track record and qualifications would fit in well with these plans for growth.

As requested in the advertisement, I enclose a copy of my CV which gives full details of my qualifications and work history. I would be very pleased to be considered for this position and I look forward to hearing from you.

Yours sincerely

Adrianne Griffiths